Estate
Planning
And Taxation

1996 ANNUAL EDITION

Estate Planning And Taxation

1996 ANNUAL EDITION

CHRIS J. PRESTOPINO

JOHN C. BOST, J.D., M.S.(Tax)

Associate Professor of Finance
San Diego State University

Formerly entitled *Introduction to Estate Planning*.

Copyright © 1987, 1989 by Richard D. Irwin, Inc.

Copyright © 1992, 1993, 1994, 1995, 1996 by Kendall/Hunt Publishing Company

Library of Congress Catalog Card Number: 95-78419

ISBN 0-7872-1383-7

Printed in the United States of America

10 9 8 7 6 5 4 3 2 1

To Chris' students, who were his ongoing inspiration, and to his wife Nancy, and their two children, Matt and Julie, whose patience and understanding were lovingly appreciated by the late Professor Chris J. Prestopino.

To students of estate planning, past, present and future, for whom this text was created and for whom it continues, and to my wife, Jennifer, and our two children, Heather and Laura, my personal reason for learning about estate planning. JCB

Chris J. Prestopino
1943 - 1994

This text is dedicated to Chris J. Prestopino, an outstanding leader in the field of estate planning and estate planning education. He was well loved by his students and colleagues at California State University, Chico, where, in over 20 years of teaching estate planning courses, he won numerous teaching awards.

This textbook, first published in 1987, became the leader in the growing field of estate planning education, as the only book truly aimed at university level academic programs. Its success is a testament to Professor Prestopino foresight and hard work. He believed in examples, examples, and more examples, a tradition that will be continued in this and future editions of the book.

Professor Prestopino received his A.B. in Economics from Cornell University, an M.B.A. and a Ph.D. in Finance from the University of Pennsylvania's Wharton School of Business; an M.B.A. in taxation from Golden Gate University in San Francisco. He served as an associate editor for tax and estate planning for the Financial Services Review (the journal of the Academy of Financial Services); he served on exam question audit committees for the CFP Board of Standards; and was the Program Director for the CFP education program at Chico State.

Perhaps, those of us who work and study in the area of estate planning think about death and dying more than most, nevertheless, when someone as young as Chris dies just as he is reaching the pinnacle of his profession, just as his children are entering young adulthood, we too deeply feel the loss. He will be missed. It is to Chris and students everywhere that this promise is made: to continue his tradition of excellence in our teaching and in this textbook.

Preface

Professor Prestopino's *Estate Planning and Taxation* really began in 1974, after his first unsuccessful search for a textbook. For the next eight years, each time he taught estate planning in the undergraduate or graduate business curriculum, he had to settle on a book not designed primarily for students. The options were limited to three types of publications: simple primers and paperbacks intended for the lay reader; technical references suited for the informed professional; and treatises written for the third-year law student. In 1987 Professor Prestopino published the first edition of this book.

Estate Planning and Taxation offers an alternative, one having a different format. It is a textbook, designed to be used in an academic program. Its concepts are introduced logically rather than encyclopedically; and as the reader's knowledge grows, more advanced principles are covered.

Estate Planning and Taxation is for the professional or student pursuing a career in financial services, taxation, or law in which estate planning and estate and gift taxation is but one of several principal areas of practice. Applicable careers include law, tax accounting, financial planning, insurance sales, paralegal work, banking, trust management, investment brokerage and management, and real estate. Since much of the subject matter is Internal Revenue Code driven the textbook draws heavily on primary sources of the law, both Code and case law. The textbook is adaptable to law school courses in estate planning and taxation, giving the law student a strongly quantitative slant that is often overlooked in traditional law books, even those dealing with taxes.

The book is divided into three parts. The first two present the basic language and constraints found in estate planning, including the underlying tax and nontax law that serve as the basis for planning. The third, and largest, part surveys the major estate planning strategies used currently by practitioners. Tax analysis is emphasized. This sequential approach aids learning because estate planning techniques presuppose a familiarity with many fundamental legal concepts, including tax principles.

The organization of *Estate Planning and Taxation* seeks to present a concise, integrated overview, highlighting the essence of concepts without confusing the reader with every technical qualification and reference, a problem which has impaired the readability of many books in the field. For example, the text expects the student to learn only those case names and code section numbers that have attained the status of common industry jargon (footnotes cite many others). Nonetheless, the book's content is comprehensive. For example, with its quantitative orientation, it demonstrates numerically, wherever possible, the consequences of planning, and of the failure to plan, on family wealth.

Many pedagogical devices are used to aid comprehension. Each chapter contains an outline, end-of-chapter questions and problems, and an extensive list of recommended readings. Numerous examples are included in each chapter to clarify concepts. Appendixes include a glossary, sample tax returns, tax and valuation tables, as well as those sections of the Internal Revenue Code most relevant to estate planning. To stress the typical reader's perspective as consultant in the estate planning process, the text uses the terms 'client' and 'planner' frequently. A manual containing both answers to end of chapter questions and a test bank is available to instructors who adopt the book.

Estate Planning and Taxation can be used in a two-hour or three-hour quarter or semester introductory college undergraduate course, or graduate or law school course. At the graduate level it should be supplemented with outside readings of cases and articles. It can be read in conjunction with a correspondence, certificate-type course offered to the financial services industry; and it can be read independently by anyone seeking a moderately technical overview, including the practitioner in accounting or financial services, the law student, the attorney in general practice, and the very determined lay reader.

Changes In The 1996 Edition

Writing an annual edition reflects the author's commitment to offer the most up-to-date material available. Sources of information include attendance at the country's leading estate planning institutes, review of legal and tax periodical reporters and new articles appearing in the most theoretical and trade journals. The 1996 edition incorporates new material through mid-May, 1995. A serious start has been to incorporate information found in footnotes into the text, leaving footnotes to cite primary and secondary sources of authority.

Other additions and revisions worth noting include:

Chapter 4: Clarified that the funding mechanism for testamentary trusts is the probate process. Added the term pretermitted heir as an alternative for omitted heir.

Chapter 5: An explanation of when the credit for gift taxes payable is not the same amount as the gift taxes actually paid. Corrected the extended example, and the answers for problem 12, to take into account, that because of pre-1977 gifts, the gift tax payable credit must be recalculated for estate tax purposes.

Chapter 6: Moved discussion of 5 & 5 powers to Chapter 7 since it is not an exception to the rule that general powers are included in the holder estate. Even a general power limited to 5% of a trust will cause 5% of its value to be included in the holders estate if unexercised at the holders death. The relief provision found at §2041(b)(2) applies only to lapse during the holders life time. Added a box exhibit that summarizes the connection between gifts and the donor's estate since students seem determined to apply a three year rule to every transfer, even those where it does not apply. Corrected the treatment of bargain sales between related parties. Expanded the discussion of the special marital deduction rules for transfers to non-U.S. citizen spouses.

Chapter 7: Extended the discussion of the 5 & 5 powers to clarify that the problem is not with the gift that would occur when one of these powers lapse but with the fact that the holder usually has a retained interest in the trust, hence, exceeding the 5 & 5 limit causes §2036 retained interest problems. Clarified that when a retained interest causes an earlier gift to come into the gross estate it is *not* an adjusted taxable gift for estate tax purposes. Problems 10 and 11 are new, covering powers to invade and the 5 &5 power, respectively.

Chapter 8: Up dated the various income tax tables and the various inflation adjusted figures. Extended the treatment of how basis is determined for gifts where gift tax is paid, and the rules for changing basis at death for the various means of holding title, i.e., whether as joint tenant, community property, or tenants in common. Added a corporate rate schedule. With help from Professor Karen H. Molloy, University of Illinois, revised the extensive Example NDNI-2 concerning the calculation of distributable net income.

Chapter 11: Corrections made to Figure 11-2.

Chapter 13: Corrections made to Figure 13-3. Clarified that both Crummey trusts and trusts that require immediate and continuous distribution of income use §2503(b), therefor the more descriptive term Mandatory Income Trust (MIT) is used for the latter.

Chapter 14: Corrected the discussion of bargain sales, the allocation of basis between the gift portion and the sale portion applies only to bargain sales where the buyer is a charity. Correction to example 14-12, retained interest results in the trust being included in the gross estate but the adjusted taxable gift falls to zero. Added an extended discussion of the qualified personal residence trust, including how to calculate the gift value. Removed the discussion of "lazy GRAT" as being confusing and of questionable utility, left in the citation for those that want to pursue it.

Chapter 15: Clarified the paragraph on "modified endowment contracts." Reduced the discussion of flower bonds, given their diminishing utility to estate planners. Added a discussion on how the purpose of an irrevocable life insurance trust will determine for the trustee the appropriate type of life insurance to purchase. With help from San Diego attorney Paul M. Cheverton, added an extended discussion of family limited partnerships; and with help from attorney and SDSU Associate Professor Russell L. Block, added a discussion of limited liability companies.

Suggestions for Simplifying Student Reading Assignments

Writing an estate planning text that can satisfy the needs of all instructors is a very challenging task; estate planning and estate taxation courses vary greatly in both depth and breadth. Over the years, some instructors have requested greater detail, particularly in the planning and taxation areas. Having accomplished this, others might be concerned about the presence of *too much* material; but with care, the instructor can significantly cut down the reading assignments without impairing student ability to learn the basics. Here's a list of topics you might delete from your assignments (* indicates topics likely to be tested on CFP examinations.):

Chapter 2: Section on Mathematics of Remainders, Reversions and Income Interests.

Chapter 6: Possibly the material on §2035-2038,* which is arguably the most difficult to understand in the entire book (or, omitting only §2035). Also, brief section on excess retirement accumulations.

Chapter 7: Two major sections: the GSTT, and the special valuation rules of §2701-04.

Chapter 8: Fiduciary income taxation, or just omitting the brief section on "exact method of calculating DNI and taxable income." Section on the alternative minimum tax.

Chapter 9: Perhaps the entire chapter, because it could be considered optional background material. Or omitting just the section on "the meaning of unification."

Chapter 10: Quantitative model for comparison of costs of probate versus living trust, particularly for students without preparation in the time value of money.

Chapter 12: Planning option #4. Contingent liabilities and QTIP planning. The QDT trust. Entire final section on GSTT planning.

Chapter 14: Section on grantor retained trust,* and possibly sections on private annuity, intentionally defective irrevocable trust, and gifts of split interest to charity.

Chapter 15: Flower bonds. Section on liquidity planning devices unique to business owners.* Section on valuation discounts and control premiums.

Chapter 16: Section on freezing the value of the business interest.

Chapter 17: Section on lapse problem and survival clauses.

Chapter 18: Perhaps the entire chapter, or omitting just the section on planning devices primarily designed to save income taxes.

Chapter 19: Entire chapter.

Suggestions For Making Assignments More Challenging

Some other instructors may wish to engage in just the opposite task: making the assignments even more challenging. Consider assigning articles from the trade journals, particularly from *Trusts and Estates* and *Estate Planning* magazines. For complex topics footnotes refer the reader to relevant articles that cover the topic in more detail, with the full cited found in the end-of-chapter Recommended Readings section.

Other suggestions for adding depth to certain chapters include:

Chapter 3: Require reading a more complex living trust instrument or trust-will, obtained from a local attorney.

Chapters 5-8: Require reading the code sections, found in Appendix B. Require preparation of tax returns.

Individuals thanked by Chris J. Prestopino whose contributions continue to be reflected in the text: Michael Ahearn, Martin Anderson, Robert Barnhill, Karen Booth, John C. Bost, J. Buckhold, Neil Cohen, Larry Cox, Mariel Damaskin, Jeffrey Dennis-Strathmeyer, Mark Dorfman, W.W. Dotterweich, Jon Gallo, Keith Fevurly, Mark Greene, Benjamin Henszey, Carole Hill, Jerry Kasner, Fred Keydel, Shekhar Misra, Burton Nissing, Phelder St. Germain, John Schooling, Jack Stephens, and Richard Wellman.

For their suggestions and help I thank the following: Chris' wife Nancy Prestopino and his nephew, Albuquerque attorney Donald A. DeCandia; Saint Louis University Associate Professor, Burton J. Nissing; Director of Academic Programs for the National Endowment for Financial Education (NEFE) Keith Fevurly, and Academic Assistant at NEFE, Gregg A. Parish; San Diego attorney Paul M. Cheverton; San Diego attorney and San Diego State University Associate Professor, Russell L. Block; University of Illinois at Urbana-Champaign Associate Professor, Karen Molloy; SDSU graduate students Russell May and William Majewski; undergraduate students D. J. Devin and Mary Reese; manuscript help from Fiona Becker and Georgina D. Knowles; editorial help from Kendall/Hunt Association/Business Editor Mariel Damaskin, Associate Editor Janice Samuells.

John C. Bost

(Postscript: It is our intention to have all future editions available in early April of the preceding school year.)

Contents

Illustrations

Overview and Conceptual Background

— 1

Introduction

WHAT ESTATE PLANNING IS ABOUT

Estate planning is the study of the principles of planning for the use, conservation, and efficient transfer of an individual's wealth. Its concepts are based on the premise that people do not live forever; sooner or later, death will bring about a fundamental shift in the possession and ownership of family wealth. Estate planning seeks to arrange future wealth transfers to maximize financial well being, both for the client and the client's survivors. Other definitions of estate planning include, as an additional estate planning activity, the accumulation of wealth. That would unrealistically broaden the subject's scope to include the field of investment management. Investment management is another specialty of great scope, one usually left to be covered in textbooks devoted to investment analysis. Practitioners specializing in estate planning might give little or no advice on investment management. The focus of this text will be estate planning as the study of financial planning in anticipation of death.

Planning for future wealth transfers usually requires the preparation of contracts, such as life insurance policies, and other documents, including wills, trusts, deeds, and powers of attorney. These documents implement the plan by arranging, in writing, the future financial affairs of the individual.

Learning how to plan wealth transfers with these documents requires an understanding of many legally related subjects, including the law of property, wills, trusts, future interests, estate administration, intestacy, insurance, income taxation, gift taxation, and death taxation.

How can the reader benefit from a knowledge of such an extensive subject? Foremost, as a planner, the reader can help avoid the adverse consequences of inadequate planning. Here are a few common examples of what can happen without proper planning.

EXAMPLE 1-1 Joanne died last week. She is survived by her husband and their two young daughters. Because Joanne did not write a will, the intestate laws of her state requires that two-thirds of her $300,000 estate must *pass to her daughters*, who will each receive the property outright from their guardian-father on their 18th birthdays. The other one-third passes to Joanne's husband, who is rather shocked that he is not inheriting it all and that as guardian of the daughters estate he will have to file annual accountings with the court.

In addition to the problem of inefficient distribution illustrated in the above example, in some states a greater state death tax will be paid. Larger estates may also pay a greater federal death tax.

EXAMPLE 1-2 Marge and Henry, parents of five-year-old twins, were killed in an auto accident last month. Who will be chosen by the court to be the twin's *guardians* remains uncertain, since the parents left no written evidence of any preference.

EXAMPLE 1-3 Maggie died last month at age 80. Six weeks prior to her death, she gave 1,600 shares of ABC common stock to her children, who sold it last week, incurring an *income tax* of over $22,000. No one told Maggie that had she instead given the stock to the children at her death, they could have sold it at little or no income tax cost.

EXAMPLE 1-4 Before Christine's death two years ago, her family lawyer drafted a *simple will*, leaving all of the family wealth to her husband Evan. Today, as outright owner of all of the family wealth, Evan realizes that, at his death, his estate will incur sizable *transfer costs*, much of which could have been eliminated had Christine's will incorporated a more sophisticated estate planning device known as a bypass trust.

EXAMPLE 1-5 Facts similar to Example 1-4, above, except that instead of receiving the property by will, Evan received it as survivoring *joint tenant.* Today, Evan anticipates the same transfer cost problem at his death.

EXAMPLE 1-6 Leslie was the founder of a highly successful real estate sales company. She died last year, having done no estate planning. Her children are struggling with several problems, including how to generate sufficient *liquidity* to pay the death taxes, and whether or not to sell the business. Further, they worry that no one will buy the business for an amount anywhere near its pre-death *value*.

EXAMPLE 1-7 Elmer had a *stroke* three months ago; since then he has been unable to communicate with anyone. He has a fairly large estate, and his family now realizes that they should have encouraged Elmer to consult an estate planner years ago, at a time when Elmer's knowledge and personal objectives could have been incorporated into an effective estate plan.

EXAMPLE 1-8 At the advice of a friend, Marty executed a revocable living trust by simply filling in the blanks on a *form document*, photocopied from a page from his friend's copy of a popular "how to" book. Marty did not realize that because most of his property was held in joint tenancy the trust was worthless.

EXAMPLE 1-9 At his death, Coldwell owned real estate in six states, including his state of residence.   In addition to the probate in his state of domicile, there were five ancillary probates and Coldwell's family was forced to hire attorneys all six states. Coldwell was not aware that using a living trust might have avoided these expensive procedures.

These and many other problems occur every day because of the failure to engage in effective estate planning. Estate planning is a technical, rapidly changing subject about which lay people have numerous misconceptions. And because it anticipates death, many who need it would prefer not to focus on it. Thus, estate planning requires the helpful encouragement of professionals.
How these professionals develop an estate plan is described next.

DEVELOPING AN ESTATE PLAN

Developing an estate plan culminates in the creation of a set of documents and related recommendations which skillfully allow for the best use, conservation, and transfer of the client's wealth. It requires several steps: acquiring client facts and objectives, reviewing the facts and preparing the plan, implementing the plan, and following up.

Acquiring Client Facts And Objectives

To be able to make good recommendations, the planner must first acquire sufficient information about the client and the client's family. Necessary information includes the client's financial and personal situation and the client's objectives.

The client's financial situation and objectives. To understand the client's financial situation, the planner will require several types of statements. First, he or she will need a current *balance sheet*, showing the fair market value of all assets and liabilities. Regarding each asset, information will be needed about the form in which title is held, date of acquisition, and current adjusted tax basis.

> EXAMPLE 1-10   Relying on the client's oral comment that she owned a parcel of investment property as an individual, an inexperienced planner didn't take the trouble to *examine the actual deed.* Two years after executing a will which left all property to her husband, the client died, at which time the planner discovered that the parcel was held in joint tenancy with the client's niece, who became the sole, outright owner of the parcel.

In addition to a description of assets and liabilities, the planner will need a *cash flow statement*, describing sources of income and major categories of expenses.

The planner will also need other facts, such as information about significant gifts or inheritances received or expected to be received, and a listing of all of the client's financial and other advisers, including accountant, lawyer, investment broker, life underwriter, realtor, physician and religious advisor. Further, the planner will need a description of the client's and the spouse's financial objectives, a self-appraisal of their ability to manage their finances, and the location of any wills.

The client's personal situation and objectives. The planner must also acquire personal nonfinancial information, including the names of all of the members of the family, their ages, their health, and their station in life (occupations, etc.).

The planner will also need an understanding of the client's personal objectives, especially with regard to dispositive preferences for the spouse and the children before and at the client's death, and any interests in donating to charities.

Many planners, often with the help of financial institutions, develop customized questionnaires and checklists to help them acquire this information as efficiently as possible. An example of a questionnaire can be found in Appendix 1A at the end of this chapter.

In addition to acquiring the checklist, the planner should routinely examine existing documents, such as the will and evidence of title to property. Too often, checklist information is inaccurate. Example 1-10, given earlier, illustrates this problem.

Reviewing The Facts And Preparing The Plan

After acquiring the necessary facts, the planner will review the facts and prepare a plan which incorporates preliminary recommendations. The most common recommendations fall in two areas: financial planning for property transfers, and personal planning for the client's incapacity and death.

Financial planning for property transfers. The major purpose of the plan is to efficiently distribute the client's wealth to the proper persons in the proper amount at the proper time. To do this, the planner will need to keep in mind the following considerations, which relate to more specific estate planning goals:

- Deciding whether or not to *avoid probate* as a means of transferring property at the death of the client;
- Examining alternatives to reduce and possibly eliminate *transfer taxes* at the death of the client and the client's spouse;
- Considering *lifetime transfers*, partly to reduce transfer costs and partly to shift taxable income to a lower tax bracket;
- Arranging to provide the *liquidity* needed at the client's disability or death;
- Devising a strategy to unwind the client's *business affairs* in a manner which can maintain the greatest income and value for the survivors.

Personal planning for incapacity and death. The major areas in personal planning for client incapacity and death include arranging for someone to care for the client and the client's property at the onset of incompetence, and arranging for someone to care for the client's children if both parents die before they reach adulthood.

Since this text is primarily devoted to an explanation of these and other objectives and techniques, further discussion will not be undertaken here.

Implementing The Plan

After the planner and the client meet to discuss and agree on specifics, the planner can implement the plan. Transfer documents will be drafted by the attorney and executed by the client. A life underwriter may be needed to secure the appropriate insurance contracts. If a trust managed by a corporate trustee is included in the plan, a bank trust officer will usually be contacted for authorization and advice.

Clients "execute" a document by completing it; that is, doing what is necessary to render it valid. For example, execution of a will normally requires, among other things, the client's signing the will in the presence of witnesses, who also sign, attesting to the authenticity of the client's signature.

Following Up

An indispensable part of the estate planning process is following up. Laws change. The client's personal situation and objectives change. By keeping-up-to-date, the planner can periodically recommend any necessary revisions to the plan. Events which may require plan revision include marriage, divorce, birth of a child, new legislation, and new court decisions.

> EXAMPLE ERTA-1 In 1981, Congress made many significant changes in the law of federal transfer taxation. One major change involved the taxation of property passing at death to a surviving spouse. Up to then, many planners used a provision in their client's wills and trusts that had the effect of passing to the spouse the maximum amount possible without resulting in a tax. Prior to the new law, this amount usually turned out to be about *one-half* of the client's estate. However, under the new law, the maximum amount would usually turn out to be the client's *entire* estate. Concerned that many clients with such a provision currently in their estate plans might not want to leave their entire estate to their spouse, Congress included a transition rule which continued to apply the *old* tax law to any client who died without revising the plan. Thus, to take advantage of the new, more beneficial tax provisions, transfer documents had to be revised, and most planners contacted all of their affected clients.

For a discussion of the use of disclaimers and the QTIP election as post-mortem tax planning techniques to remedy this problem for a client who died without revising the will, see Chapter 18.

For these and many other reasons, periodic follow-up has become a way of life for estate planners.

THE ESTATE PLANNING TEAM

Generally, estate planning is not conducted by just one professional; the job requires the diverse knowledge and skills of a number of practitioners, including attorneys, accountants, life underwriters, trust officers, and financial planners. Some in the industry call these individuals the *estate planning team*. How each member of the team uniquely contributes to the overall plan is described next.

Attorney

As the only professional legally permitted to draft documents and render legal advice, the attorney is the indispensable team member in the estate planning process. Document preparation requires the ability to make fine legal distinctions. Years later, these documents will usually become the final authority, and will usually be taken literally. Thus, by putting an estate plan in print, the attorney places his or her professional reputation on the line, for many to see, criticize, and, sometimes, second guess.

Most attorneys accept the responsibility of *coordinating* the actions of the other members of the estate planning team. This is especially common among lawyers specializing in estate planning and taxation.

Often, the attorney's role will not end at the client's death. He or she may be hired to advise the executor of the deceased client's estate or the trustee; that is, to complete the process involving the legal transfer of the client's assets to surviving beneficiaries. In addition, the attorney may engage in postmortem tax planning, a job which, as we shall see in Chapter 18, entails choosing certain tax options available after the client's death.

Accountant

By preparing the client's financial statements and tax returns, the accountant is often the professional having the earliest and most frequent contact with the client. Typically, these forms are so financially revealing to accountants that financial planners have described them as the client's "personal annual business report."

The accountant is often able to spot specific financial problems requiring attention, especially with regard to the client's business interests. And after the client's death, the accountant may be called on to complete any necessary income tax and death tax returns.

Life Underwriter

The life underwriter's crucial role is to provide insurance contracts to meet liquidity requirements expected to arise at the client's disability or death. The efficient use of life insurance requires an understanding of estate planning partly because proper planning can minimize both transfer costs and personal strain.

As an active solicitor, the life underwriter is often the first professional to recommend estate planning to the client, and may have the opportunity to select the other members of the client's estate planning team.

Trust Officer

As a skilled professional executor and trustee, the trust officer performs fiduciary services for clients and estates. A *fiduciary* is a person having a legal duty to act for the benefit of another. See Chapter 2 for a further discussion.

As *executor* of the client's estate, the trust officer is responsible for managing those assets which are being transferred through the probate process.

Similarly, as *trustee* of a trust created by a client, the trust officer is responsible for managing those assets placed in the trust. Thus, the trust officer can be particularly helpful in the planning stage by offering advice in the area of management and distribution of assets.

Financial Planner

As the newest member of the estate planning team, the financial planner is a professional potentially capable of recommending a complete integrated financial plan, one which includes recommendations concerning insurance, investments, retirement planning, and income tax planning, as well as estate planning. The financial planner does not, however, draft the legal documents. Customarily, only the attorney is legally permitted to do that.

THE NEED TO ENCOURAGE PLANNING

Many individuals need estate planning and fail to seek it. Many simply chose not to deal with issues involving their own death, refusing to face the fact that they could die soon, and must die someday. Others are so busily involved in pursuing their careers they do not feel they have time for planning. Still others feel their lives are too unsettled to undertake long-range planning. Finally, some fear the family conflicts and expenses that may arise at death as a result of their planning, unaware that good planning generally minimizes these problems. For these reasons, members of the estate planning team should actively encourage individuals to plan their estates. As implied or mentioned earlier, good planning can help dispose of assets fairly, minimize taxes and expenses at death, provide for care of disabled family members, generate sufficient liquidity, provide for continued income for dependent survivors, and arrange for efficient business succession.

Next, we turn to a description of the organization of this text.

ORGANIZATION OF THE BOOK

This book is divided into three parts. Part 1 includes this introductory chapter and Chapter 2, which introduces the major concepts that will be used throughout the text.

Chapter 2 describes the basic concepts of estate planning and defines many estate planning terms such as *fee simple, life estate, remainder, probate, trust, irrevocable*, and *insured*.

Part 2 provides the more detailed background knowledge needed to understand the techniques of estate planning. It introduces the constraints in planning, that is, the basic principles of tax and property law on which all planning rests.

Part 2 begins with Chapter 3, which explores the rudimentary contents of wills and trusts, the two major documents of property transfer. Sample forms illustrating the simple will, living trust, and trust-will are examined to give the reader an early concrete awareness of the focus of planning. An appendix introduces the rule against perpetuities.

Chapter 4 explains how property is actually transferred. The probate process is featured, and includes a discussion of supervised probate, probate alternatives in states adopting the Uniform Probate Code, and some examples of summary probate.

Chapter 5 introduces federal wealth transfer taxation by describing the computation of both the gift tax and the estate tax, and compares and contrasts their methodology.

Continuing the material on wealth transfer taxation, Chapter 6 contains a robust examination of the federal estate tax, exploring three major topics: components of the gross estate, estate tax deductions, and estate tax credits. In the same spirit, Chapter 7 covers the major principles of the federal gift tax and the generation-skipping transfer tax. It also introduces the special valuation rules under Internal Revenue Code §2701-§2704.

Chapter 8 concludes Part 2 with an introduction to the federal income tax, emphasizing the sale, gift, and exchange of property and the income taxation of estates, trusts, and their beneficiaries.

Part 3 utilizes the material in Parts 1 and 2 to survey the actual techniques used in planning. It begins with Chapter 9 by surveying the principal goals of estate planning. Examples include minimizing the costs of the property transfer process, shifting taxable income to a lower bracket taxpayer, and reducing and freezing the taxable estate.

Chapter 10 examines the controversial decision to avoid probate. We will contrast probate with its alternatives, including the very popular revocable living trust.

Chapters 11 and 12 focus on planning for those transfers at death that can defer or completely eliminate the client's death taxes. We will see that the two major transfer strategies incorporate the estate tax marital deduction and the bypass. We will also explore current techniques used to avoid the generation-skipping transfer tax.

Chapters 13 and 14 explore various aspects of planning for lifetime transfers. Chapter 13 surveys gift planning and shows that although gifting can save both income and transfer taxes, its harsh requirement of a complete relinquishment of control over the gifted assets forces many clients to consider instead property transfers which are not so total. Chapter 14 surveys incomplete lifetime transfers, ones in which the client retains some control over the gift property. It also highlights lifetime transfers that are less than total because the client will receive some consideration in exchange. The chapter also covers charitable transfers. An appendix summarizes several once popular lifetime transfers such as the short-term trust that have lost their appeal due to recent tax reform.

The death of a client owning significant wealth can trigger sizable cash outlays, such as for death taxes. Chapter 15 surveys common methods of providing the client's estate with adequate liquidity to fund these outlays. Topics include sale of assets before death, life insurance, flower bonds, liquidity planning devices unique to business owners, and valuation discounts.

Chapter 16 explores the principles of planning for closely held business interests. Frequently, their owners have special estate planning problems, including maintaining sufficient income after withdrawing from the business and transferring to their chosen beneficiaries the maximum value attributable to that business. In addition to an extended discussion of these problems, the chapter covers several specific techniques, including sale of the business during lifetime, the business buyout, and the business estate freeze.

Chapter 17 surveys other miscellaneous techniques that estate planners routinely employ, including providing for minor children, selecting a trustee, planning for nontraditional relationships, and planning for the client's incapacity through the use of durable powers of attorney.

Chapter 18 examines the principles of post-mortem tax planning, a topic which illustrates that income tax and death tax planning are still possible even after a client's death. Major topics include expense elections, disclaimers, and QTIP planning.

Finally, Chapter 19 presents two hypothetical estate planning case studies, with questions, for review. The first case actually appeared in at least one Certified Financial Planner (CFP) comprehensive examination. The chapter also includes the complete CFP outline of CFP estate planning topics. The next chapter surveys many of the basic estate planning concepts that will be used throughout the text.

QUESTIONS AND PROBLEMS

1. At a dinner party, the wife of one of your clients asks you what estate planning entails. Define it, and name the legally related subjects that it embraces.

2. A man comes into your office to inquire about your services. You find out that he owns a closely held business and has a wife and two young children. He has never written a will. Explain briefly how failure to help him plan could lead to adverse consequences.

3. Fill in the questionnaire in Appendix 1A with information about yourself, a client, or a friend. Which items would you expect would usually be most difficult to acquire?

4. Outline the steps required in developing an estate plan.

5. Explain the unique contribution made by each member of the estate planning team.

RECOMMENDED READING

Astrachan, John M. "Why People Don't Make Wills." *Trusts & Estates* 118 (1979), p. 45.

Barr, Katherine. "General Practitioners Beware: The Duty to Refer an Estate Planning Client to a Specialist." *Cumberland Law Review* 14 (1984), pp. 103-34.

Burns, W. Peter, "Avoiding and Handling Malpractice Claims Against Estate Planners." *Estate Planning*, September, 1989, pp. 264-68.

Crumbley, D. Larry, and Edward E. Milam, "Personalizing the Estate Planning Process." *Trusts and Estates* 116 (1977), p.8.

Eber, Victor. "The Personal Audit: The First Step in Lifetime Financial and Estate Planning." *Estate Planning* 1 (1973), p. 30.

Hakala, Thomas J. "The CPA Performs Varied but Vital Roles as a Member of the Estate Planning Team", *Estate Planning*, Nov. 1988, pp. 352-56.

Herting, Claireen L. "How to Build and Maintain a Successful Personal Financial Planning Practice." *Estate Planning*, Nov. 1986, pp. 254-56.

Johnston, Gerald. "An Ethical Analysis of Common Estate Planning Practices- Is Good Business Bad Ethics?" *Ohio State Law Journal* 45 (1984), pp. 57-141.

_____. "Estate Planners' Accountability in the Representation of Agricultural Clients" *Kansas law Review* 34 (1986), pp. 611-50.

Langbein, John H. "The Twentieth-Century Revolution in Family Wealth Transmission", *Michigan Law Review*, 86 (1988), pp. 722-51.

Luton, James. "Accountant's Role in Estate Planning." *Estate Planning* 5 (1978), p. 40.

McCarter, Charles. "Cost-Efficient Estate Planning." *Journal of the Kansas Bar Association*, Spring 1984, pp. 51-57.

McDermott, Michael J. "Baby-Boom Generation Stands To Inherit $8 Trillion," *Financial Planning*, January, 1982, pp 22-24.

*Moore, Malcolm A. & Jeffrey N. Pennell. "Practicing What We Preach: Esoteric or Essential." *1993 University of Miami Estate Planning Institute*.

Obegi, Joseph C. "Handling Conflict of Interest Problems in Estate Planning." *Community Property Journal* 13 (1987), pp. 47-72.

Pedrick, Willard H. "When Does the Estate Planning Team Huddle?" *1971 University of Miami Institute on Estate Planning*, p. 1900.

Prestopino, Chris J. "What Strategies Are Experienced Estate Planning Attorneys Recommending"? *Financial Services Review*, Vol. 2, 1993, pp. 111-30.

_____. "Strategies Recommended by Experienced Estate Planners." *Trusts & Estates*, January, 1994, pp. 47-54.

Tate, Mercer D. "Handling conflicts of Interest That May Occur in an Estate Planning Practice." *Estate Planning*, January 1989, pp. 32-37.

_____. "Strategies for Establishing a Fair Rate of Compensation for Planning a Client's Estate." *Estate Planning*, July 1986, pp. 194-97.

Wohl, Steven J. "Guidelines for Avoiding Estate Litigation." *Estate Planning*, March, 1992, pp. 67-74.

Sample Client Fact-Finding Questionnaire*

Date:_____

CONFIDENTIAL ESTATE PLANNING QUESTIONNAIRE

Family and Financial Information

The following questionnaire is designed to expedite our efforts to plan your estate. Whether you are a new or an established client, we have found this questionnaire extremely helpful and therefore ask your indulgence in completing it fully. Those questions that are irrelevant to your family or financial situation may simply be ignored. Please feel free to attach additional pages where space is insufficient or to provide other information you feel is relevant.

A. Husband

    1. Name_____

    2. Other names used_____

    3. Address_____County_____

    4. Telephone (Home)_____(Business)_____

    5. Employer_____

    6. Birthdate_____

    7. Citizenship_____

---

*   Reprinted with permission of its author, Robert N. Grant.

APPENDIX 1A *(continued)*

B. Wife

   1. Name_____

   2. Other or former names_____

   3. Date and place of marriage_____

   4. Telephone (Business)_____

   5. Employer_____

   6. Birthdate_____

   7. Citizenship_____

   8. Beginning dates and states (or countries) of residence since current marriage, and approximate net worth at each time.

Beginning Date	State	Approximate Net Worth
_____	_____	_____
_____	_____	_____
_____	_____	_____

   9. Have either you or your spouse been married before?_____(If yes, give for each prior marriage: *(a)* the prior spouse's name; *(b)*whether marriage was terminated by death or divorce; and *(c)* the date and place of termination.)

_____

_____

_____

C. Children and Grandchildren

   1. Children of present marriage (living and deceased).

Name	Current Residence	Birth Date	Check if Adopted
_____	_____	_____	_____
_____	_____	_____	_____
_____	_____	_____	_____
_____	_____	_____	_____
_____	_____	_____	_____
_____	_____	_____	_____

APPENDIX 1A *(continued)*

2. Children of Husband's prior marriage to_____

Name	Current Residence	Birth Date	Check if Adopted

3. Children of Wife's prior marriage to_____

Name	Current Residence	Birth Date	Check if Adopted

4. Grandchildren

Name	Current Residence	Birth Date	Check if Adopted

D. Gifts

Have you or your spouse filed federal or state gift tax returns?_____If yes, please provide a copy of the most recent returns.

E. Will

Do you or your spouse currently have a will? Husband_____Wife_____
If yes, please provide a copy.

Assets Owned by Husband and/or Wife - in General

1. Jewelry, Clothing, Household Furniture and Furnishings, Personal Automobiles, Boats, Paintings, Books and Other Tangible Articles of a Personal Nature and Special Collections

How Title is Held

Estimated Fair Market Value (Where appropriate, indicate whether husband's separate property [HSP], wife's separate property [WSP], or community property [CP].)

————— ————— —————
————— ————— —————
————— ————— —————
————— ————— —————
————— ————— —————
————— ————— —————
————— ————— —————

2. Cash or Equivalents (Checking and savings accounts, money market accounts or funds)

————— ————— —————
————— ————— —————
————— ————— —————
————— ————— —————
————— ————— —————

APPENDIX 1A *(continued)*

3. Real Estate - Principal Residence, Vacation, and Investments	How Title is Held	Estimated Fair Market Value (Where appropriate, indicate whether husband's separate property [HSP], wife's separate property [WSP], or community property [CP].)

_____ _____ _____

_____ _____ _____

_____ _____ _____

4. Publicly Traded Stocks and Bonds

_____ _____ _____

_____ _____ _____

_____ _____ _____

_____ _____ _____

_____ _____ _____

5. Interest in Closely Held Corporations, Proprietorships, and Limited or General Partnerships

_____ _____ _____

_____ _____ _____

6. Promissory Notes Receivable

_____ _____ _____

_____ _____ _____

_____ _____ _____

_____ _____ _____

APPENDIX 1A *(continued)*

7. Other Assets (annuities, patents, and copyrights, etc.)

How Title is Held

Estimated Fair Market Value (Where appropriate, indicate whether husband's separate property [HSP], wife's separate property [WSP], or community property [CP].)

_____ _____ _____

_____ _____ _____

_____ _____ _____

_____ _____ _____

Liabilities of Husband and/or Wife

Amount of Present Liability (Where appropriate, indicate whether husband's separate liability [HSL], wife's separate liability [WSL], or community liability [CL].)

1. Mortgages on Real Property

_____ _____

_____ _____

_____ _____

_____ _____

2. Notes, Loans, Support Obligations, and Other Liabilities

_____ _____

_____ _____

_____ _____

_____ _____

APPENDIX 1A *(continued)*

Life Insurance

Company/ Policy Number	Face Amount	Cash Surrender Value	Insured	Owner	Beneficiary

Employee Benefit Plans

Employment Benefit--Describe type of plan (Pension, profit sharing, IRA, Keogh) and company	Employee	Approximate Value	Beneficiary

APPENDIX 1A *(concluded)*

Interest in Estates or Trusts

Do you or your spouse have an interest in an estate or trust as a beneficiary, trustee, holder of a power of appointment or trustor? If yes, please provide a copy of each trust and an estimate of the current fair market value of the asset thereof. Yes_____ No_____

Name of Estate or Trust	Fiduciary	Value of Interest

Expectancies

Do you or your spouse expect to receive anything from another person's will?_____

From Whom	Value of Interest

— 2

Survey of the Basic Concepts of Estate Planning

OVERVIEW

This chapter will introduce many of the basic concepts commonly employed in estate planning. They will be referred to throughout the text, and the reader is advised to study them carefully. Some of these concepts are so straightforward that mere use of them in a sentence will make their meaning clear. Other more involved terms must be defined and illustrated. Along with others introduced in later chapters, most of these terms are included in the Glossary at the back of this book.

The terminology can be subdivided into several classes, including those dealing with estates, transfers of property, beneficiaries, wills, trusts and probate, disclaimers, life insurance, taxation, and types of property interests.

CONCEPTS DEALING WITH ESTATES

An *estate* is a quantity of wealth or property. *Property* represents things or objects over which one may lawfully exercise the right to use, control and dispose. More simply, property is anything that can be owned.

Ordinarily, for a person or for a family, an estate represents the total amount of property owned. However, the word *estate* is often used in several other contexts in estate planning to mean some type of smaller amount. First, in certain situations, estate means the *net* value of property owned, calculated by subtracting the amount of the estate owner's liabilities from the value of the property. Second, estate can be limited to the *probate estate*, which constitutes all of the property that passes to others by means of the probate process on the death of the owner. Third, estate could be limited to the *gross estate* and *taxable estate*, two concepts used only in connection to taxation at death. Later it will be shown that the probate estate and the tax-related estate may be very different in size and composition.

CONCEPTS DEALING WITH TRANSFERS OF PROPERTY

The main emphasis of estate planning is on property transfers. This section will cover the commonly used basic terminology in the property transfer area.

Transfers of Legal, Beneficial, or Legal and Beneficial Interests

A *transfer* or *assignment* of property can mean any type of passing of property in which the *transferor* gives up an *interest* to the *transferee*. The interest transferred can be purely legal, purely beneficial, or a combination of legal and beneficial. Where only title is passes, the interest given up can be purely *legal*. As explained later, this is all that the typical trustee receives. Title alone gives trustees the ability to manage property but not enjoy it. Another example of the holder of a purely legal interest is a stockbroker holding customer shares in street name. The customer, of course, owns beneficial interest.

On the other hand, where the transferee receives something that carries an economic benefit, but not title, the interest transferred can be purely *beneficial*. Examples of beneficial interest in property include the temporary or permanent right to possess, consume, pledge or otherwise benefit from the property. As we shall see, the rights of a trust beneficiary are entirely beneficial.

Finally, an interest given up by the transferor can be both legal and beneficial, whereby the transferee receives both title and economic benefit. An *outright* transfer is said to occur when one transferee receives both legal and beneficial interests, without restrictions or conditions.

Complete Versus Incomplete; Property In General Versus A Specific Property Interest

Complete versus incomplete: overview. Speaking generally, a transfer of property is said to be *complete* and *irrevocable* when it is no longer rescindable or amendable, i.e., when the transferor has totally relinquished all dominion and control over that property. For example, after purchasing this book, at the expiration of the returns period, you made a completed transfer of money. On the other hand, a transfer is said to be *incomplete* and *revocable* while it is still rescindable or amendable, i.e., made without total relinquishment of dominion and control over that property.

Property in general versus an interest in property. More specifically, however, to be able to fully distinguish between complete and incomplete transfers, one must grasp the difference between property in general and a specific interest in property. *Property in general*, such as 100 shares of ABC stock, means the entire asset, whether physical or intangible. In contrast, an *interest in property* means one or more rights to property, such as the right to the first five years of dividends from 100 shares of stock.

In estate planning, more than one interest in a given item of property in general is often transferred in a single transaction. For example, in one transaction, T may transfer 100 shares of stock in trust, giving A the right to receive the first five years of dividends, B the right to receive the next ten years of dividends, and C the right to the entire stock in year 15. Each has received an "interest" in the stock. Trusts will be described in greater detail later in the chapter.

Complete, incomplete, and partially complete transfers. A transfer of each specific interest in property can only be either complete or incomplete, while the transfer of more than one interest can be either totally complete, partially complete, or totally incomplete. Continuing with the same facts as above, if T retained the right in general to revoke or amend the trust, T's transfers of A, B and C's specific interests would each be incomplete, and T's transfer of the stock in general would be totally incomplete. On the other hand, if T retained the right to revoke or amend only A's interest, the transfer of A's interest would be incomplete, the transfer of B and C's interests would be complete, and T's overall transfer of the stock would be said to be *partially complete*. Finally, if T retained no rights whatsoever over the stock, the transfers of A, B, and C's interests would all be complete, as would be the transfer of stock in general. As we shall see in Chapter 7, this issue is important because gift tax law treats as gifts subject to gift taxation transfers of specific interests, but only those that are complete.

Sale Versus Gift

Most commonly, completed transfers of property interests are undertaken by sale, by gift, or by a combination of both sale and gift. A *sale* is a transfer of property under which each transferor receives an amount of *consideration* that is regarded as equivalent in value. By contrast, a gift is commonly but loosely regarded as a transfer of property for which a transferor receives nothing in exchange. (The precise definition of a gift is developed in the next paragraph). The two most common methods of making gift transfers are outright and in trust.

Bargain sale is a gift. Technically speaking, when a person transfers property in exchange for other property whose value is less than the amount transferred, but greater than zero, a *bargain sale* has occurred. A bargain sale, therefore, involves a transfer that is part sale, part gift. The notion of the bargain sale causes most estate planning practitioners to define a gift somewhat more broadly than above. While the above definition of a gift is for the most part correct, estate planners (and the IRS) also consider a bargain sale to be a type of gift, even though some property is received in exchange. Federal tax law treats the actual amount of the gift as the difference between the respective values of the consideration exchanged. Thus, in this text, a transfer will be considered either a gift or a sale, with a *gift* defined to include a bargain sale: a completed transfer in exchange for any amount that is *less than* full consideration.

Inter Vivos Transfer Versus Transfer At Death

A transfer of property can be *inter vivos*, made while the transferor is alive, or it can be made at death. Inter vivos is Latin for "between the living." Transfers at death are made pursuant a valid document, also called an *instrument*, prepared by the owner before death (e.g., will, trust, title by joint tenancy, or insurance beneficiary designation) or pursuant to state law (intestate succession), in the event that no such document exists.

Fair Market Value Of Transfer

The value of a transfer is measured by its *fair market value* at the time of the transfer. Determining fair market value is the subject of several sections in the text. For the present, we will use the IRS' often quoted definition of *value*: "the price at which the property would change hands between a willing buyer and a willing seller, neither being under any compulsion to buy or to sell and both having reasonable knowledge of the relevant facts."[1]

BENEFICIARIES

A *beneficiary*, or *donee*, is a person who is receiving or will receive a gift of a beneficial interest in property from a transferor, who is also known as a *donor*. Although in the most general sense, donee and beneficiary are synonymous, in certain contexts one or the other term is used more commonly. For example, the recipient of an outright inter vivos gift from the donor is usually called a donee. On the other hand, the recipient of a gift under a will or a trust, whether inter vivos or at death (see following section) is usually called a beneficiary.

WILLS, TRUSTS, AND PROBATE

In estate planning, a person who has died is called a *decedent*. When a person dies, property owned by the decedent must be transferred. Each state takes special interest in ensuring that each piece of property owned by the decedent will be transferred to the proper parties. They do this in two basic ways. First, state law looks to any valid documents prepared by the decedent (wills, trusts, joint tenancy arrangements, life insurance policies, etc.) to determine proper disposition. A *will* is a written document disposing of a person's probate property at death. The will is said to make *testamentary* transfers. It is *executed* at the time it is properly signed by the *testator*. A *trust* is a legal arrangement between trustor and trustee that divides legal and beneficial interests among two or more people. A more precise but less intuitive definition of a trust is "a fiduciary relationship in which one person is the holder of the title to property subject to an equitable obligation to keep or use the property for the benefit of another." Trusts will be described in greater detail later in the chapter.

Intestate, testate, and partially intestate. Second, if no such documents are found which dispose of one or more items of the decedent's property, the decedent is said to have died *intestate* with regard to that property. More common, though less consistent, usage holds that a person dying without any valid will has died intestate. However, if all of the

---

1. IRS Reg. 20.2031-1(b).

decedent's property is disposed of by alternative means, (e.g., trusts), a will may not be necessary and the absence of a will may not actually result in a probate "intestacy."

If a valid will is found, the decedent is said to have died *testate* with regard to the property disposed of by the will. If the document(s) found do not dispose of all of the decedent's property, the decedent is said to have died *partially intestate*.

In some cases, the moment that death occurs can be the subject of disagreement. Its determination is important because it often influences the rights of beneficiaries and the liabilities of the estate. The Uniform Determination of Death Act, adopted in at least 15 states, addresses this issue by defining death to include brain death, as well as "cessation of circulatory and respiratory functions."[2]

Probate and the personal representative. *Probate* is the legal process of administering the estate of a decedent. It focuses upon the will and the probate estate, that is, property which will be disposed of by, and *only* by, either the will or by the state laws of intestate succession. Typical *probate assets* fall into one of three groups: property owned by the decedent as an individual, interests of the decedent held "in common" with others, and, in community property states, the decedent's one half interest in community property. *Nonprobate assets* include property held in trusts and in joint tenancy, most insurance policies on the life of the decedent (unless payable to his or her estate), and most retirement plan assets. Many of these terms will be described later in the chapter. An extended discussion of probate versus non probate assets will be found in Chapter 4.

Essentially, in probate administration, the governmental unit, often the county court, determines the validity of the will, if any, and authorizes distribution of the probate estate to creditors and beneficiaries. The court appoints a *personal representative* to act as fiduciary, to represent and manage the probate estate. If the court appoints the person nominated in the will to be personal representative, that person is called the *executor*. Otherwise, the personal representative appointed by the court is called the *administrator*. In some states, a female personal representative is called an *executrix*. Other states have eliminated this word from their probate vocabulary. This text will use the term executor to refer to either gender.

The word fiduciary derives from the Latin word for "trust." A *fiduciary* is a person in a position of trust and confidence who has the legal duty to act for the benefit of another. Besides personal representatives, fiduciaries include trustees, guardians and agents.

---

2. For a discussion, see the Moses article cited at the end of the chapter.

Recipients of probate property. Beneficiaries of a decedent's probate property are called heirs, devisees, or legatees. An *heir* is a beneficiary who will receive property that passes by intestacy. Attorneys in most states employ this more narrow use of the terms "heir" and "inherit" then does the general public, which thinks of heirs as also receiving property by will. This text will conform to the expert's usage. A *devisee* is a beneficiary, under a will, of a gift of real property. A devisee is said to receive a *devise*. A *legatee* is a beneficiary, under a will, of a gift of personal property. A legatee is said to receive a *legacy*, more commonly known as a *bequest*. For simplicity, this text will conform to common trade usage and usually refer to a testamentary gift of any property, real or personal, as a bequest. Interestingly, the Uniform Probate Code uses only the term "devise," both as a noun and a verb. The Uniform Probate Code is introduced in the next chapter.

The term *issue* refers to a persons's direct descendants, or offspring, including, children, grandchildren, great-grandchildren and the like. Degrees of blood relationship will be further examined in Chapter 4. The modern trend is to use the term *descendants* rather than issue to avoid biological connotation, thereby more clearly extending its application to adopted children.

Types of bequests. Most bequests are either specific, general, or residuary. Other types are called pecuniary bequests and class gifts. A *specific bequest* is a gift of a particular item of property which is capable of being identified and distinguished from all other property in the testator's estate. For example, the bequest: "I leave all my household furnishings to...", and "I leave my high school ring to..." are specific bequests because they specify particular, identifiable property. If the property subject to a specific bequest is sold, given away or lost before the testator's death, in many states the bequest fails under the common law doctrine of *ademption*. The statutes of many states have exceptions that do not result in ademption. A common example is if an asset is acquired as a replacement for specifically devised real or tangible property.[3]

A *general bequest* is a gift payable out of the general assets of the estate, but not one that specifies one or more particular items. For example, the bequest: "I leave ten percent of my estate to..." is a general bequest because it can be paid from more than one asset.

A *pecuniary bequest* is a bequest of a specific dollar amount, that maybe payable in specific assets or in cash. It is commonly found in more complicated estate plans that attempt to minimize death taxes. The bequest

---

3. For the Uniform Probate Code's six exceptions, see UPC §2-606.

is usually expressed in terms of a *formula*, such as: "I leave to my spouse the least amount needed to reduce my death taxes to zero." A pecuniary bequest is distinguished from a *fractional share bequest*, which leaves to the spouse (and others) a fractional interest in each and every asset of the estate.

A *residuary bequest* is a gift of that part of the testator's estate not otherwise disposed of by the will. For example, the bequest "I leave the rest of my estate to..." is a residuary bequest. The *residue* is the remainder of an estate.

A *class gift* is a gift to a group of individuals that may not be completely defined at the time the gift is made. Thus, the gift in a will "...to my grandchildren living at the time of my death..." is a class gift, and the exact make-up of this group may not be known until the testator's death.

Occasionally a testator dies leaving insufficient assets to satisfy all bequests and pay all creditors. Under the procedure called *abatement*, bequests are eliminated or reduced so that all debts (and administration expenses) are paid in full. In those states that follow the Uniform Probate Code, shares of the beneficiaries abate in the following order: (1) property not disposed of in the will, (2) residuary bequests, (3) general bequests, and (4) specific bequests.

> EXAMPLE ABAT-1 Lehman's will leaves his car to A, $20,000 cash to B and the residue of his estate to C. If at his death Lehman owned only the car and $10,000 cash, and he owed $6,000 in debts, in many states abatement would require paying the $6,000 debt in full, with nothing to C, $4,000 cash to B and the car to A.

Disclaimer

Very few beneficiaries would refuse a sizable bequest. After all, such gifts should make them financially more secure. Yet there are times when an estate planner will suggest that the beneficiary disclaim a gift. Why? Because sometimes disclaiming will be financially preferable, such as when it can prevent or delay a large tax bill. And the planner will usually recommend disclaiming only in situations where the property will passing to a person acceptable to the original beneficiary.

A *disclaimer* is an unqualified refusal to accept a gift. To be effective it must meet the requirements of both state property law and federal tax law. Under property law, a disclaimant is treated as having *predeceased* the decedent-donor. Consequently, the disclaimed property will pass under one of two possible sets of legal guidelines. Either it will pass to the "alternate taker" in accordance with the terms of the decedent's transfer document, usually the will or trust, if any. Or, if no document, or if the document does not name an alternate taker, the property will pass under laws of intestacy.

EXAMPLE 2-1 Barry died recently, and his twenty year old will left Barry's valuable super bowl ring to his football loving father-in-law, Bob, and the residue of his estate to his grandson. Bob, age 87 and in poor health, validly disclaims the ring, which will instead pass under the will to Barry's grandson.

EXAMPLE 2-2 Changing the facts in Example 2-1 a bit, assume Barry's will did not have a residuary clause, that is, the residue of his property was not disposed of in the will. The ring will pass under the state's laws of intestacy.

Chapter 7 will describe the federal tax requirements for a valid disclaimer, and Chapter 18 will illustrate other ways in which disclaimers can uniquely rectify some inefficient or obsolete estate plans.

LIFE INSURANCE

A *life insurance* policy is a contract in which the insurance company agrees to pay a cash lump-sum amount (called the *face value* or *policy proceeds*) to the person named in the policy to receive it (the *beneficiary*) upon the death of the subject of the insurance (the *insured*). One other important party in the life insurance contract is the *owner*, who typically possesses both legal and present beneficial interests in the policy. As legal owner, the policy owner has title to the policy. As present beneficial owner, the policy owner has the right to benefit from the policy. Beneficial rights usually include the right to receive policy dividends, the right to designate and to change the beneficiary, and the right to surrender the policy. These rights can have economic value, even before the death of the insured. Whether or not a life insurance policy has economic value prior to the insured's death depends upon the type of policy. For a more detailed introductory explanation, see the "Types of Insurance" section in Chapter 15.

A *term life insurance* policy has no value prior to the death of the in-sured because the premium charged, which increases over time along with increasing risk of death, simply buys pure protection: If the insured dies during the policy term, the company will pay the face value; otherwise, it will pay nothing.

In contrast to a term policy, a *cash value* policy accumulates economic value because the insurer charges a constant premium that is considerably higher than mortality costs require during the earlier years. Part of this overpayment accumulates as a *cash surrender value*, which, prior to the death of the insured, can be enjoyed by the owner, basically in one of two ways. First, at any time the owner can surrender the policy and receive this value, in cash. Second, the owner can request a policy loan and borrow up to the amount of this value.

Because life insurance policies can have value prior to the insured's death, and because the insured's death usually triggers the obligations to pay a substantial amount of cash, life insurance can make a significant contribution to estate planning. For example, life insurance proceeds can be used to provide needed cash to pay the death taxes on the death of a closely held business owner. However, to use life insurance properly, the planner must be aware of the impact of taxes, a subject to be introduced briefly next, and explained in considerable detail in chapters 5 through 8.

TAXATION

In estate planning, the two principal types of taxing authority are the individual states and the federal government. The four major types of taxes are gift tax, death tax, generation-skipping transfer tax, and income tax.

A *gift tax* is a tax on a lifetime gift; that is, a lifetime transfer of property for less than full consideration.

A *death tax* is essentially a tax levied on certain property owned or transferred by the decedent at death. Death taxes have two forms, an estate tax and an inheritance tax. An *estate tax* is considered to be a tax on the decedent's right to transfer property, while an *inheritance tax* is considered to be a tax on the right of a beneficiary to receive property from a decedent. Either way, their net effect is essentially the same: they are both death taxes because each is based on a certain amount of property owned by the decedent at death. The federal death tax is an estate tax and is appropriately called the federal estate tax. At the state level, some states impose an estate tax and others have an inheritance tax. About one half of the states including California, Florida and Nevada impose a type of death tax, but one that results in no additional cost to the estate. Called a "pickup tax," although it must actually be paid to the state, it will reduce the federal death tax by an equivalent amount. The upshot is that in planning in such states, planners ignore their state death tax. For details, see chapter 6.

A *generation-skipping transfer tax* is a tax on certain property transfers to a skip person, that is, for the benefit of someone who is two generations or more younger than the donor. Without this tax, wealth could skip several generations and escape one level of transfer tax. For example, without it, a lifetime or deathtime gift to a grandchild may be subject once to a gift tax or death tax, but it would probably not be taxed twice, as it would have if the property first passed from the client to the child, and then from the child to the grandchild. We'll see in Chapter 7 that the federal generation-skipping transfer tax has a fairly large exemption, making careful planning necessary only for clients with large estates.

An *income tax* is essentially a tax levied on income earned by a taxpayer during a given year. Income tax laws usually distinguish four different taxpayers: individuals, corporations, estates and trusts. Principles of taxation can differ substantially for each, as we shall see. Each is required to annually submit an income tax return that reports certain items, including income, deductions, credits, and the tax due, calculated by using tax tables applicable to that entity. Married individuals may file a *joint income tax return*, in which they report their combined income, deductions, and other information on one return. Since income tax rates are *progressive*, that is, they increase as taxable income increases, the joint return often results in lower total taxes than if the spouses file individually.

PROPERTY INTERESTS

Estate planning seeks to preserve and efficiently transfer an individual's wealth or property. This section will describe the legal forms in which property can be owned. Essentially, ownership can be classified in the following ways: extent of interests in property (e.g., fee simple); physical characteristic of property (e.g., real versus personal); number of owners and type of ownership (e.g., individual versus tenants in common); legal versus beneficial interests (e.g., property held in the name of the trustee versus a trust beneficial interest); present versus future interests (e.g., an income interest in a trust versus a remainder interest); and vested versus contingent interests (e.g., the right to the income from a trust versus a remainderman's interest which requires the remainderman being alive at the trust termination otherwise the property reverts back to the trustor's estate).

Basic Interests In Property

The three basic interests in property are fee simple, life estate, and estate for years.

Fee simple. A fee simple interest, often called simply a *fee*, represents the greatest interest that a person can have over property, and corresponds to our usual notion of full ownership. Common rights include the right to possess, use, pledge, transfer, or destroy the property. You probably own this textbook in fee. Under traditional property law, fee simple interests are associated only with land, but in this text the concept fee simple will be used to describe either type of property, real or personal, because over the years common usage has come to regard fee simple as the nearly absolute dominion and control enjoyable over most property, whether real or personal. A fee simple interest is, therefore, subject to the highest dollar valuation of any interest in property.

Life estate. A life estate interest in property, like a fee simple, is a powerful form of ownership, but is different in that the interest ceases upon someone's death. Ordinarily, the *measuring life* is that of the owner of the interest. However, it could be any other person.

> EXAMPLE 2-3 Doctor Bud assigns his interest in a house to his widowed mother for her to use and enjoy until her death. Mother has received a life estate in the house. Her own life is the measuring life.

A life estate for the life of someone other than the owner of the interest is simply called an estate *for the life of another*.

> EXAMPLE 2-4 Facts are similar to Example 2-3, except that Mother's interest will cease upon the death of Bud. Mother still has a life estate in the house but now Bud's life rather than her life is the measuring life. She has an estate for the life of another.

Ordinarily, the owner of a life estate enjoys, for the length of a measuring life, a complete ownership, one that is nearly equivalent to a fee. However, life estates are sometimes created so that the recipient enjoys only a partial present interest in the property.

> EXAMPLE 2-5 Aunt Jane, owner of dividend-paying common stock, gives to her niece Barbie the right to receive those dividends for as long as Barbie lives. Barbie is said to have received a life estate in the income of the stock. Under the customary arrangements, Barbie does not have many rights in the stock itself. For example, she does not have the right to possess or sell the stock, or to use it as collateral against a loan. The stock will be held by someone else, either the original owner or, more commonly, a trustee under a trust arrangement.

Trusts will be used in many contexts in almost every chapter of this text and will be described further within the next few pages.

Interest for years. Often a person transfers property to another person, giving the transferee the right to possess it for a fixed period. This is called an estate for years even if the fixed period is something other than a certain number of years.

> EXAMPLE 2-6 Professor Jackson lets his student Byron, a graduating senior, use one of his bicycles for three months. Byron has received an interest in the bicycle "for years."

> EXAMPLE 2-7 Mary is presently enjoying a life estate, for her life, in the income from certain common stock. Today Mary transfers to Mark her interest for the next two years. If Mary does not survive the full two years, Mark's interest will be cut off upon Mary's death; Mary cannot transfer any greater interest than she actually owns, and Mark's interest is limited to that which Mary can legally give. Thus, Mark has an income interest in the stock, ending at the earlier of two years or Mary's death.

A common example of an interest for years is a *leasehold*, which entitles the lessee to possess and use the property (e.g., a house or computer) for a specified time, usually in exchange for a fixed series of payments. Leasehold interests can amount to a valuable part of a lessee's wealth if the fixed payments are below current market rates, and if the lessee is permitted to "sublet" the property.

> EXAMPLE 2-8 For the past two years, Freda has owned a ten year leasehold interest in a commercial building, and is obligated to pay $15,000 per year for the entire period. If the rent for comparable buildings is expected to be $25,000 per year for the next eight years, and assuming a discount rate of 10 percent, the value of Freda's leasehold is the present value of $10,000 for eight years, discounted at 10 percent, or $53,349. Freda could possibly sell her interest for that amount.

Classification of Property by Physical Characteristics

Property may also be classified as real or personal. *Real property* includes fee simple or life estate interests in land and any improvements. Hence, a fee or a life estate in a house would constitute real property. Curiously, an interest for years (a leasehold) in real estate is considered personal property. Accordingly, *personal property* is defined as all property except fees and life estates in land and its improvements.

Personal property may be classified as tangible or intangible. In some cases, this distinction is not entirely clear. Tangible property has several common definitions. Some say it is capable of being "apprehended by the senses, which is accessible, identifiable". For our purposes, however, we shall use the U.S. Supreme Court's definition, in a tax case, that *tangible personal property* is personal property which has value of its own. Conversely, *intangible personal property* is not in itself valuable, but derives its value from that which it represents. For example, a computer is tangible personal property. The common stock of a corporation is intangible personal property. Intangible personal property includes a *chose in action*, which is a claim or debt recoverable in a lawsuit. A chose in action, pronounced "shows," can constitute a part of an individual's wealth for two reasons. First, it represents money owed to the holder of the chose. Second, the owner is usually permitted by law to transfer this claim to another, who can then act on it in his or her own name. The buyer would be entitled to keep any recovery.

> EXAMPLE 2-9 Another driver negligently wrecks George's new car. Since he can potentially recover money damages in a court of law, George has a chose in action, which can be assigned. For example, if George decides to ask for reimbursement from his own insurance company, the company will pay only if George assigns his right to sue (subrogates) to the insurer, who will probably pursue the claim in its name.

Concurrent Ownership

Property may be owned individually, in which case one person owns and uses it, or it may be owned concurrently, by two or more persons. Common forms of *concurrent ownership* are joint interests, interests by the entirety, interests in common, and community property interests.

A common characteristic of all types of concurrent ownership is the *undivided* right to use the entire property, not just a physically identifiable portion. In addition, the co-owners usually each have the right to have the property physically divided, at which time concurrent ownership ends.

Joint interests. When two or more persons own an equal undivided interest in and right to possess property that, upon death of one owner, automatically passes to the surviving owner(s), they are said to hold title in *joint tenancy* or that they are *joint tenants*.

> EXAMPLE 2-10 John and Mary owned a house as joint tenants. At John's earlier death, Mary automatically became sole owner of the house.

Under joint tenancy, ownership passes to the surviving co-tenants automatically at a cotenant's death by what is called *operation of law* and does not legally depend upon physical transfer of title. However, some authorities, such as banks, require formal document revision in order to transact further business.

Joint interests can only be created by a writing. In many states, one cotenant can unilaterally "sever" a joint interest without knowledge or consent of the other tenant(s).

The automatic right of survivorship inherent in joint tenancy prevails over other means of transfer at death, including the will and the trust instrument.

> EXAMPLE 2-11 Continuing Example 2-10, if, prior to his death, John had executed a will that left his one half interest in the house to his son, Mary would still receive it by right of survivorship. The joint tenancy designation supersedes the will.

However, in certain jurisdictions, agreements can be executed between joint owners to nullify a joint tenancy designation.

> EXAMPLE 2-12 Continuing Examples 2-10 and 2-11 above, if John and Mary were to execute a written *agreement* stating that it is their intention that the house, presently in joint tenancy, is in fact to be held by them as community property, or as tenants in common (see description below), many jurisdictions will honor the agreement, and the house may not pass to Mary by automatic right of survivorship.

Whether or not such documents will be recognized will hinge, in part, upon whether all joint owners are included in the agreement.

Joint tenancy's are most commonly created among family members, who often wish to transfer property, at their death, to co-owning relatives.

Interests by the entirety. An *interest by the entirety* is much like a joint tenancy; however, it can be created only between husband and wife. And unlike joint tenancy, neither spouse may transfer the property without the consent of the other. About fifteen states do not recognize interests by the entirety.

Interests in common. Like joint tenancy, *interests in common* are held by two or more persons, each having an equal undivided right to possess property. Unlike joint interests, however, interests in common may be owned in unequal percentages, and when one owner dies the remaining owners do not automatically succeed in ownership. Instead, the decedent's interest passes through his or her estate, by will, by some other document, or by the laws of intestate distribution.

> EXAMPLE 2-13 Jack owns a 16 percent real estate interest in common with two other individuals who, combined, own the other 84 percent. Upon Jack's death, his interest will not pass to the other co-tenants, but to his wife, who was named to receive it in his will.

In contrast with joint interests, interests in common are more frequently created between nonrelated parties, as a means of enjoying common ownership without losing the right of disposition at death.

Community property interests. In the eight states recognizing it, *community property* includes all property acquired by the efforts of either spouse during marriage while living in a community property state, except property acquired by only one of the spouses by gift, devise, bequest or inheritance, or by the income therefrom. The traditional community property states are Arizona, California, Idaho, Louisiana, Nevada, New Mexico, Texas, and Washington. In addition, Wisconsin recently adopted a form of community property known as "marital property", based on the Uniform Marital Property Act (UMPA).[4] Three community property states, Texas, Idaho, and Louisiana, treat income earned from separate property during the marriage as community property. Community property is considered to be owned equally by both spouses, and those ownership interests are created at the moment the property is acquired. Generally, both spouses must consent to a gift of community property. Community property states allow couples to convert community property to separate property, and vice versa, although some states require a written agreement wherein the spouse whose interest is reduced acknowledges that fact.

In contrast, all property in community property states that is not community property (that is, all property acquired by a person not during marriage, and property acquired by one spouse during a marriage by gift, devise, bequest or inheritance, or, often, income earned on property so acquired) is called *separate property*. Separate property is considered entirely owned by the acquiring spouse. In states without community-property provisions, of course, separate property is the only recognized type of property, in this context. In those states, it would simply be called "property owned by an individual."

> EXAMPLE 2-14 Pat and Mary live in a community property state. When they married two years ago, Pat owned a sports car, which Mary also uses. Pat works as a shoe salesman and Mary is a bank teller. Last year Mary's father gave her 100 shares of XYZ stock, which pays a quarterly dividend. Mary used the last dividend check to buy a bicycle. Pat bought a rowboat from money saved from his July paycheck. The stock and bicycle are Mary's separate property, except in Texas, Idaho, and Louisiana, where the bicycle would be community property. The car is Pat's separate property. All of the other assets, including both salaries, are community property, since their source is the effort of one or the other spouse while domiciled in a community property state.

---

4. For a UMPA bibliography, see the Wenig article cited at the end of the Chapter.

Community property laws represent certain state government's attempt to impose greater fairness in property ownership between married couples. According to old common law, in the absence of community property, the husband became the owner of all property that he acquired. Typically earning all or most of the outside income while the wife performed the non income-producing household chores, husbands usually acquired virtually all of the family wealth. By common law, a wife was entitled to own none of this property until her husband's death, at which time she received only a life estate in one-third of her husband's real property. Called a "dower" interest, it has been modified by many states, but nowhere as radically as in those states incorporating community property laws, which implicitly assume that during their lives the husband and wife should immediately share the property acquired by their joint efforts during their marriage.

Summarizing, the major distinction between community property states and "common law states," as they are called, hinges on when the nonacquiring spouse attains beneficial interest in the property. In common law states the non-acquiring spouse is technically not entitled to ownership, dominion or control over any of the property acquired by the other spouse during the latter's lifetime; such rights will eventually arise in different degrees, but usually only upon divorce or at death of the acquiring spouse. In contrast, the nonacquiring spouse in community property states attains fifty percent legal and beneficial interest in any community property at the moment of acquisition.

Idaho, Washington and California also have a concept called *quasi-community property*, which is defined as property acquired by residents of non-community property states that would be considered community property if acquired in a community property state. For example, common stock acquired with salary income by New York residents during their marriage would be considered quasi-community property if they moved to California. Essentially, California quasi-community property is treated as separate property of the acquiring spouse until divorce or death. If the parties divorce, the property is divided in a manner similar to community property. Treatment at death depends on which spouse dies first. If the acquiring spouse dies first, the surviving spouse is entitled to one half of the property. On the other hand, the nonacquiring spouse's rights to the property cease at his or her earlier death.

As different types of co-ownership of property, joint tenancy (JT) and community property (CP) have several major similarities and differences, which are summarized in the outline below.

1. *Major Similarities:*
   a. Ownership by more than one person.
   b. The owners have equal ownership rights and equal rights to use the entire property. Their interests are undivided.
   c. Any owner may demand a division of the property into separate, equal shares.
2. *Major Differences:*
   a. CP exists only between spouses. JT can exist between any two or more persons.
   b. CP rights arise automatically, by operation of law, under state statute. Hence, they are created immediately upon acquisition of the property. JT rights usually arise at the time of the agreement between the parties and are not governmentally imposed.
   c. JT includes automatic right of succession to ownership (right of survivorship) by surviving joint owners. This right takes priority over any will. In contrast, CP includes no automatic succession to ownership of the decedent's share by the surviving spouse. Therefore, at death, a spouse can transfer his or her share of CP, by will, to someone other than the spouse. However, intestacy will ordinarily result in succession by the surviving spouse under most state laws of intestate succession.
   d. Property held in JT will not be subject to the probate process. In contrast, the decedent's share of CP will be subject to probate, or possibly to a form of summary probate, as described in Appendix 4-A.

Two observations regarding item 2c: First, some states, such as New York, recognize an agreement between the spouses declaring that specified property is held in joint tenancy "for convenience only." Second, Idaho, Nevada and Washington statutes sanction the designation, "community property with right of survivorship," which, upon the death of the first spouse, results in the passing of the property to the surviving spouse, free of probate administration.

Legal Versus Beneficial Interests: Introduction To The Trust

Ordinarily, the owner of an interest in property has some right to possess and enjoy the property. Sometimes these interests are divided so that one party has only "bare legal title," responsible solely for preserving and managing property for the benefit of another, who is entitled to enjoy the property in specified ways. The former holds *legal interest* while the latter holds *beneficial interest*, also called equitable interest, in the property. The trust is the most common legal arrangement employing this division.

There are three major parties to the trust: trustor, trustee and beneficiary. The *trustor*, also called *grantor*, *creator*, or *settlor*, is the person who creates the trust, and whose property usually winds up in it. The property in a trust is called the *principal* or the *corpus*. The *trustee* is the person, persons or firm named by the trustor in the trust instrument to administer the trust. The trustee holds legal interest to the trust property. The trust *beneficiary* is the person or persons who are named to enjoy beneficial interest in the trust. Placing property in a trust is called *funding* the trust. It is done by transferring title of the property into the name of the trustee. Figure 2-1 illustrates the relationship between the parties to the trust.

A trust can be *living* or *inter vivos*, to take effect during the life of the trustor, or it can be *testamentary*, to take effect at the trustor's death. A testamentary trust is created in a will. An example of the provisions of a testamentary trust can be found in Chapter 3, Exhibit 3-3.

EXAMPLE 2-15 Trustor Stuart transfers 1,000 shares of ABC stock in trust to Uncle Jay as trustee, with the dividend income payable to Stuart's son Chet for 11 years. Jay receives only legal title and is responsible for managing the property during this period. He may not use it for his own benefit, and he is required to pay all dividend income received to Chet, the beneficiary. Chet has a beneficial interest, that is, an estate for years in the income of the trust.

FIGURE 2-1 The Parties To a Trust

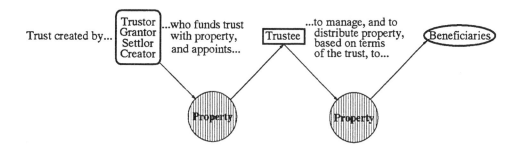

Reasons for creating trusts. Clients may wish to include trusts in their estate plans for four principal reasons: to provide for multiple beneficiaries, to manage their property if they become incapacitated, to protect beneficiaries from themselves and others, to avoid probate, and to avoid or reduce taxes. Since these factors are discussed in detail in numerous sections of the text, the following exposition will be brief.

First, clients may wish to leave their property to *more than one person*, either at the same time or successively, over a period of time, and may need an arrangement that will fairly protect each beneficiaries' individual property rights.

EXAMPLE 2-16 After his death, Constantine wants to let his second wife enjoy the use of his property for the rest of her life. After her death, Constantine wants the income from his property to be payable to the children of his first marriage until they reach age 30, at which time he wants them to receive the principal, outright. By executing a trust, Constantine can appoint a responsible trustee to manage the property for what may turn out to be a very long time. And the trustee can be charged with preserving a proper balance between the differing interests of the beneficiaries.

A transfer into a trust is sometimes called a *split interest* transfer, because it divides rights to the corpus into two or more interests, usually an income interest for a specified period of years or for the beneficiary's life, and a "remainder" interest in the principal. Remainder interests will be described shortly. Discussions of income versus principal interests will be found in numerous later sections.

Second, clients may create trusts to *manage their property if they become incapacitated*.

EXAMPLE 2-17 Several years ago, Linda Smith created a *revocable living trust*, changing the title of all her property to read "Linda Smith, trustee of the Linda Smith Revocable Living Trust dated March 19, 1992." The terms of the trust provide that if Linda becomes incapacitated during her lifetime, her brother Tom will become successor trustee. Linda has taken steps to prevent the need for expensive court procedures to determine who should be appointed guardian or conservator of her property if she became incapacitated before death.

Third, clients may wish to create trusts to *protect beneficiaries from themselves and others.*[5] As we shall see in the next chapter, trust documents typically contain provisions restricting use of the property by beneficiaries. For example, trust instruments often provide that the trustee's discretion will determine the amount and timing of distributions to beneficiaries. In addition, they often prohibit any beneficiary from pledging his or her interest in the trust property as collateral for a loan. Many other restrictions can be included.

Fourth, clients may wish to use trusts to *avoid or reduce taxes*. This text will have a great deal to say about tax planning with trusts after examining the principles of taxation of individuals and trusts in Chapters 5 through 8.

Power of Appointment

In arranging property transfers into trust or otherwise, clients can add considerable flexibility to their estate plans by granting a power of appointment. A power of appointment is a power to name someone to receive a beneficial interest in property. The grantor of the power is called the *donor*. The person receiving the power is called the *holder* or donee. The parties whom the holder may appoint by *exercising* the power are called the *permissible appointees*, and the parties whom the holder actually appoints are called the *appointees*. In addition, the persons who receive the property if the holder permits the power to *lapse* (i.e., does not exercise the power within the permitted period) are called the *takers in default*. The holder of a power of appointment can *release* the power by formally relinquishing the right to exercise the power.

A power of appointment can be exercisable either during lifetime or at death, or both during lifetime and at death. If exercisable during lifetime, it is exercisable either sometime during the holder's entire lifetime, or only for a stated period. If it is exercisable at this very moment, it is said to be "presently exercisable." A *testamentary* power is only exercisable at death, by a provision in the holder's will. The broadest powers allow the holder to exercise both during lifetime and at death.

Summarizing in an example, if A transfers to B a power of appointment over A's 100 shares of IBM stock, permitting B to appoint C, D, or E, and B eventually appoints D to receive the stock, then A is the donor, B is the holder (of the power): C, D, and E are the permissible appointees, and D is

---

5. Somewhat humorously, Edward Schlesinger has described the trust as capable of protecting assets from "inability, disability, creditors and predators."

the appointee (of the stock). There are no takers in default because the holder did not permit the power to lapse. Figure 2-2 illustrates the relationship between the parties involved in the power of appointment.

FIGURE 2-2   The Parties to a Power of Appointment

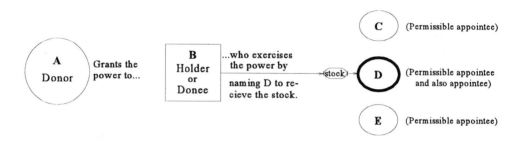

Powers of appointment are most often established within the framework of a trust. Relating the parties to a power of appointment with the parties to a trust, the donor of the power is usually the trustor. The holder is commonly the trustee but may also be one or more beneficiaries or a trusted friend of the trustor. The permissible appointees are usually the trust's beneficiaries. Trustee powers of appointment may be over trust income, or principal, or both income and principal. Trustees may also be granted the power to "sprinkle" distributions of income or "spray" principal, or both, in different amounts among permissible beneficiaries "...as the trustee in his or her absolute discretion may deem proper..." Trust powers of appointment are extremely important estate planning tools, and will be discussed frequently in this book.

In Chapter 6, we shall see that death taxes play an important role in the use of powers of appointment, so much so that we commonly classify two types of powers as they are classified in the Internal Revenue Code. Under the Code, a power of appointment is either a general power of appointment or a nongeneral power of appointment, also called a limited or special power of appointment. Defining these terms will be deferred until Chapter 6. The next example shows a common use of the power of appointment.[6]

---

6. *"A power of appointment is also a power of disappointment."* Edward C. Halbach Jr.

EXAMPLE 2-18 Charles, a single parent, died recently, and his will places some of his property in trust for the benefit of his children. A bank is named trustee and is given a nongeneral power of appointment over the corpus. The bank has, among other things, discretion to distribute corpus to the children in accordance with their needs "for their proper support, health, and education." This year, the trustee has distributed $6,000 to one son and $4,000 to a daughter to pay their college tuition.

Thus, powers of appointment add great flexibility to a client's estate plan by enabling someone to direct trust dispositions after taking into account changes in circumstances that occur long after the trustor's death. This flexibility is enhanced by a widely accepted rule of local property law that the property subject to a power of appointment is not considered legally owned by the holder, who is simply treated as an agent for the donor. As we shall see in Chapter 6, however, federal tax law is not nearly as liberal if the power is a general one.

Present Versus Future Interests and Vested Versus Contingent Interests

A beneficial interest in property may be classified as a present interest or a future interest, depending upon whether or not the owner has the immediate right to possess or enjoy the property. We shall see later that this distinction is of great importance in connection with the $10,000 annual gift tax exclusion.

An owner of a *present interest* has an immediate right to possess or enjoy the property while an owner of a *future interest* does not, because the latter's right to possess or enjoy the property is delayed, either by a specific period of time, or until the happening of a future event.

The most common types of future interests are reversions and remainders. A *reversion* is a future interest in property that is retained by the transferor after the transferor transfers to another some interest in the property. The reversion will become a present interest of the transferor, or the transferor's estate, at the termination of all of the interests that were transferred.

EXAMPLE 2-19 Jerry transfers property to Eve for her life. Jerry has implicitly retained a reversion, also called reversionary interest. It will become Jerry's (or his estate's) present interest at Eve's death.

Technically, in the law of future interests, a *remainder* is the right to use, possess and enjoy property after a prior owner's interest ends, in a situation where both interests were created at the same time and in the same document. It is a type of future interest held by someone other than the transferor, and will become a present interest when all other interests have ended. The preceding definition of remainder is unnecessarily technical for our purposes because most remainders in estate planning are quite simple. In estate planning, remainders usually arise in the context of trusts, where the remainderman is entitled to the remaining trust assets at the termination of the trust. In many, if not most trust situations, the remaindermen are the clients' children or grandchildren, who will receive the remainder at the death of both client-spouses, who are likely to have had joint life estates in a revocable trust. In some of these estate plans, the trust changes at the death of one spouse into several trust, including one or more irrevocable trusts. Where multiple trusts are formed at the death of one spouse, the survivor probably will be the income beneficiary, and the children wait as remaindermen until the surviving spouse dies..

EXAMPLE 2-20 George irrevocably transfers property to Sally for her life, then to John or his estate. John's future interest in the property is a remainder. It is not a reversion because John was not the transferor.

A *vested remainder* is a remainder that is nonforfeitable; i.e., it is a remainder whose possession and enjoyment are delayed *only by time*, and are not dependent upon the happening of any future event.

EXAMPLE 2-21 With regard to the transfer by George in Example 2-20, John's remainder is vested: Nothing prevents him or his estate from receiving possession, except the passage of time. Morbidly but accurately speaking, Sally will die; it's only a matter of time.

A *contingent remainder* is a remainder that is not vested; that is, it is a remainder whose possession and enjoyment are dependent upon the happening of a future event, not on just the passage of time.

EXAMPLE 2-22 Catherine transfers property to Flo for her life, then outright in fee simple to Jason, if alive, otherwise to Chris, if alive. Jason and Chris each have a contingent remainder interest in the property. Both interests are dependent on each of them living long enough. From today's perspective, each may or may not survive the required period; either Jason's or Chris's or both of their interests will be cut off by the happening of an event: their own prior death.

A vested remainder is usually enforceable in court, while a contingent remainder is usually not. Both, however, may be subject to transfer taxation.

A few more examples, presented in the context of common transfer devices, should help to clarify these distinctions.

> EXAMPLE 2-23 When Gary died his will created a trust, funded with his entire estate. The terms of the trust give income to his wife, Joan, for her life. At Joan's death, the trust will terminate and the property will pass outright in fee to Gary's son Max, if still alive, otherwise to the Salvation Army. At Gary's death, Joan received a present interest called a life estate in the income, and Max and the Salvation Army each received a future interest, called a contingent remainder. Max and the Salvation Army share something in common: Only one of the interests can ever become a present interest since an event will occur which will defeat one or the others interest. Max's interest will cease if he predeceases Joan. The Salvation Army's interest will cease if Max survives Joan. Therefore, both have contingent remainder interests because possession is dependent upon the happening of a future event, not on just the mere passage of time.

> EXAMPLE 2-24 Sam's left property in trust, giving his wife, June, income for life, with the remainder going to Sam's son, Kurt, or his estate. Kurt has a vested remainder in the property. Although initially a future interest, it is certain that it will become a present interest someday; it cannot be defeated. Only the passage of time keeps Kurt's interest from being a present interest. Of course, Kurt may not be alive to enjoy the property, but the beneficiaries of his estate will.

We have seen that the transfer of property in trust results in a division into two interests, with the trustee receiving the legal interest and the beneficiaries receiving the beneficial interests. In addition, transfers into trust typically result in a second type of division of interests when the beneficial interests are split among two or more beneficiaries. Ordinarily, one group of beneficiaries, called the *income beneficiaries* receive a life estate or estate for years in the trust income, while the other group, called the *remaindermen*, receive the remainder at the termination of the income interests. There are many reasons for splitting beneficial interests into a life estate, or into an estate for years, and a remainder, and there will be much written about them in later chapters. At present, the reader should simply be aware of the interest-splitting nature of the trust, and should recognize that at the time of the transfer into the trust the life estate and estate for years are usually, but not always, present vested interests, while the remainder is a future interest, which may be vested or contingent.

Mathematics of Remainders, Reversions and Income Interests

The previous section described the nature of remainders, reversions, life estates, and interests for years. These concepts will be important to understanding later chapters; many common estate planning techniques require their creation.

Up to now, the description of these interests has been qualitative rather than quantitative. But most of the chapters to come emphasize numerical analysis. Estate planning is inherently "numbers oriented," for two principal reasons. First, estate planning decisions often have a sizable impact on *family wealth*, and clients will want to discuss that influence with the planner. Second, property transfer decisions often have *tax consequences*, which must be projected and evaluated.

Thus, it is important to understand the quantitative nature of remainders, reversions, life estates and interests for years. This section will demonstrate how they are calculated.

Overview of IRS valuation tables. The calculations can be most easily performed with the help of tables published by the Internal Revenue Service. The Service's complete "Alpha" volume runs 795 pages and costs about $32.[7] It includes six different tables and lists tens of thousands of values, most of which are derived from discount rates ranging from 2.2 percent to 26 percent, at two tenths of one percentage point intervals. This conforms precisely with Internal Revenue Code valuation rules, often requiring the use of a current monthly discount rate that is equal to 120 percent of what is called the "applicable federal mid-term rate" (AFMR), which, in turn, is derived from the average market yield on U.S. Treasury obligations of maturities of three to nine years.[8] The rate, often referred to as the §7520 rate, has been rounded to the nearest two tenths of a

---

7. The Alpha volume, Publication 1457, can be purchased by phone from the U.S. Government Printing office at (202) 783-3238. These tables are also available in the form of easy-to-use computer software. For example, *Tiger Tables*, available from Lawrence P. Katzenstein at 314-231-2800, computes all Alpha values plus many other factors, including unitrust remainder factors for from one to ten lives, probabilities of survival, annuity adjustment factors for annuities due, the value of an income beneficiary's interest in a trust with a 5 and 5 power, and commutation tables.

8. See Internal Revenue Code §7520 (see App. A) and §1274(d)(1). Current AFMR rates are released regularly by popular income tax report publishers, such as Prentice Hall and Commerce Clearing House (CCH). CCH reports the monthly changes in Volume 13 ("New Developments") of it's *Standard Federal Tax Reports*. In that volume, see "New Matters....Cumulative index to 199_ developments," under §7872, under "Applicable Federal Rates Established for (Month), 199_ Rulings" section. CCH also reports these rates in the "Cumulative Index" of its *Federal Estate and Gift Tax Reports*, again under Code §7872. Look for "Applicable Federal Rates..." Monthly news releases are usually issued by the IRS one to two weeks prior to the beginning of the current month, and are published in the report of the first week of that month.

percentage. Since these rates are published monthly by the Treasury Department you do not have to figure out the rate. If a rate is given in an example or in problems at the end of the chapters use that rate for determining the appropriate table to use.

For obvious practical reasons, this text can not include all pages from the IRS volume. But it does reproduce many of the most useful ones. Tables 9, 10 and 11 of Appendix A include part of IRS Tables "S," "B," and "80CNSMT," respectively, the three most commonly used tables in estate planning. Text Tables 9 and 10 list present values derived from discount rates ranging from three percent to fourteen percent, at one percentage point intervals. They offer a clear idea of the magnitude the values can take, and can be especially helpful in the *planning* stage, when estimates are useful and for practice in calculating the values of life estates, remainders, and the like. Table 11 is a one page mortality table, useful for valuing interests that are contingent upon survival.

The following series of examples will illustrate the use of these three tables for the valuation of four basic property interests: remainders, reversions, annuities for life and annuities for a term certain. The discussion will make it clear that the choice of table for a particular problem will depend in part upon whether the interest to be valued is predicated on the fact that someone will be paid either all income or a fixed annuity 1) for a fixed number of years, or 2) for life. All examples will assume a rate of 10.0 percent unless another rate is specified..

Valuations predicated on income for term certain: IRS Table B. Each of the next four examples will calculate the value of an interest which is (directly or indirectly) dependent upon the fact that someone will be paid income for a *fixed number of years*, also called a term certain. In each case, the proper table to use is IRS Table B, found, as mentioned earlier, in Table 10 of Appendix A of this text.

Valuation of income for term certain. IRS Table B indicates what percentage of a given quantity of property reflects the value of a beneficiary's income for a term certain.

EXAMPLE 2-25 Today Drapinski creates an irrevocable trust, transferring $200,000 in property to the trustee. The trustee is required to distribute annually all income earned from the property to Harms (or his heirs) for a period of twelve years. Then, the trust will terminate, and all trust principal will be distributed to Shadwell (or his heirs).

The current value of Harms' twelve year annuity for a term certain is calculated as follows: Using IRS Table B, found in Table 10 of Appendix A ("eighth of 12 pages"), for 10%, the "income interest" value corresponding to 12 years is .681369. Thus, the current value of Harms' income interest is

$136,274 (= $200,000 x .681369).[9]

Valuation of vested remainder after income for term certain. Similarly, IRS Table B can indicate what percentage of a given quantity of
property reflects the value of a beneficiary's vested remainder interest at the
termination of income for a term certain.

> EXAMPLE 2-26 Continuing Example 2-25, the current value of Shadwell's
> vested remainder interest after income for a term certain can be calculated
> starting with the same table. For 10%, the "remainder" value in Table 10
> corresponding to 12 years is .318631. Thus the current value of Shadwell's
> vested remainder interest is $63,726 (= $200,000 x .318631).

In the previous two examples, since Harms' and Shadwell's interests
represent the only two interests in the trust assets, it is logical that the sum
of their current values should total $200,000, the current total value of the
trust principal. And for the same reason, is also logical that the sum of the
two table values should add up to one. Consequently, each table value can
be determined in a slightly different way, if one value is know the other can
be determine by simply subtracting the known value from 1.0. Thus the
table value for Shadwell's interest, .318631, could have been calculated by
subtracting the table value for Harms' interest, .681369, from the number
1.0, or the remainder value could have been determined by subtracting the
value of the income interest from the value of the whole trust ($200,000 -
$136,274 = $63,726).

Valuation of reversion. Reversions are calculated the same way as
remainders.

> EXAMPLE 2-27 Revising the terms of the trust in the above ongoing example,
> assume that at the end of 12 years, the trust will terminate and trust principal
> will be distributed back to trustor Drapinski (or his heirs). The initial value of
> Drapinski's *reversion*, $63,726, is exactly equal to the value of Shadwell's
> remainder, calculated using Table B.

---

9. The number .681369 can be derived using simple financial mathematics: "Annuitizing"
a hypothetical $200,000 investment at ten percent produces an annuity of $20,000 per year
forever ($20,000 = $200,000 x .10). To answer the question, "What percentage of the
$200,000 total value does *the first 12 years of payments* represent?" calculate the present value
of $20,000 a year for 12 years at a discount rate of 10%. That present value, $136,274, is
68.1369 percent of $200,000. The advantage of the IRS tables is that they avoid the need to
calculate a hypothetical annuitized income amount.

Valuation of remainder (after term certain) contingent upon survival. A remainder after a term certain that is contingent on the remainderman's survival of the term is calculated by multiplying the value of the vested remainder by the probability of the remainderman being alive at the end of the trust. IRS mortality Table 80CNSMT, reprinted in Table 11 of Appendix A, shows the number of people expected to be living at each age based upon statistics for the 1980 census. For example, out of 100,000 people born alive (age 0 = birth) only 94,926 of them are expected to be alive at age 40. Calculating the probability of a person age x surviving to age y involves simply dividing the number of people alive at age y by the number alive at age x. Thus, the probability of a newborn reaching age 40 alive is .94926 (= 94,926 ÷ 100,000).

> EXAMPLE 2-28 Revising the facts of Example 2-25 a bit, assume that Shadwell is currently age 40, that his remainder is contingent upon his surviving the twelve year period, and that if he fails to survive, the trust principal will pass to someone else. The probability of Shadwell surviving to age 52 is calculated using Table 11 by dividing 90,402 (# alive at age 52) by 94,926 (# alive at age 40). This quotient equals .9523418. Thus, the value of Shadwell's *contingent remainder* is $60,689 (= .9523418 x $63,726).

Valuation of annuity for term certain. Now consider a new example in which the annual annuity payment for a term certain is known.

> EXAMPLE 2-29 A trust provides for an annual distribution to Barlow of $4,000 per year for 15 years, with the first payment to be made exactly one year after the trust is established.
>
> The current value of Barlow's 15 year annuity interest can be calculated in the following manner: Using IRS Table B, for 10%, the annuity value corresponding to 15 years is 7.6061. Thus, the current value of Barlow's annuity interest is $30,424 (= $4,000 x 7.6061). The values in the annuity column are simply the present value factors for an annuity of $1.

All of the calculations in the above examples have in some way involved an income interest or an annuity for a fixed number of years. The next section deals with examples involving a different inherent property interest: an income interest or an annuity for life.

Valuations predicated on income interest for life: IRS Table S. Each of the next three examples will calculate the value of an interest which is (directly or indirectly) dependent upon the fact that someone will be paid an income or an annuity for life. In each case, the proper table to use is IRS Table S, found in Table 9 of Appendix A of this text.

Valuation of life estate. IRS Table S indicates what portion of a given quantity of property reflects the value of a beneficiary's income or annuity interest for life.

> EXAMPLE 2-30 A trust containing $100,000 in principal provides for payment of a life estate in the trust income to Cordano, age 50, and, at Cordano's death, distribution of the remainder to Shmilinsky (or his heirs). The current value of Cordano's life estate in the income of the trust can be calculated in the following manner: Using IRS Table S, found in Table 9 of Appendix A for 10%, the "life estate" value corresponding to age 50 is .86818. Thus, the current value of Cordano's life estate interest is $86,818 (= $100,000 x .86818).

Valuation of vested remainder after life estate. Similarly, IRS Table S indicates what percentage of a given quantity of property reflects the value of a beneficiary's vested remainder after the termination of an annuity for life.

> EXAMPLE 2-31 Continuing Example 2-30, the current value of Shmilinsky's remainder interest after Cordano's life estate can be calculated starting with the same table. For 10%, the "remainder" value corresponding to age 50 is .13182. Thus the current value of Shmilinsky's vested remainder interest is $13,182 (= $100,000 x .13182).

Similar to the earlier discussion, since Cordano's and Shmilinsky's interests represent the only two interests in the trust assets, it is logical that the sum of their current values should total $100,000, the current total value of the trust principal. And, again, for the same reason, the sum of the two table values add up to 1.0. Finally, each of the table values can be determined by subtracting the a known table value from the number 1.0.

Valuation of reversion after life estate. As with reversions after and income interest or an annuity interest for a term certain, reversions after a life estate are calculated in exactly the same manner as are remainders.

Valuation of annuity for life. Now consider a different example in which the *actual* annuity payment is known.

> EXAMPLE 2-32 Muhammad, age 40, is the beneficiary of a testamentary trust which is required to pay him the amount $10,000 per year for life, with the first payment to be made in exactly one year. Again, using IRS Table S, found in Table 9 of Appendix A, for 10%, the "annuity" value corresponding to age 40 is 9.2945.[10] Thus the current value of this life estate is $92,945, the product of

---

10. Students of finance may notice that traditional financial mathematics can *not* derive this number. It is based not only on the time value of money, but also on a life expectancy.

that number and $10,000.

These IRS tables will be used to value property interests in several sections of the text, covering such estate planning techniques as annual exclusion gifts (Chapter 7), minor's income trusts (Chapter 13), private annuities (Chapter 14), and charitable remainder trusts (Chapter 14).

OVERVIEW OF GOALS OF ESTATE PLANNING

Finally, this introductory chapter will list in outline form the major goals of estate planning. These goals are described in detail in Chapter 9 as an overview of the specific techniques detailed in Chapters 10 through 18.

A. Nonfinancial Goals
  1. Caring for future dependents.
  2. Accomplishing fair and proper distribution of property.
  3. Attaining privacy in the property transfer process.
  4. Attaining speed in the property transfer process.
  5. Maintaining control over assets.
B. Financial Goals
  1. Non-tax financial goals
    a. Minimizing nontax estate transfer costs.
    b. Maintaining a satisfactory standard of living.
    c. Ensuring proper disposition by careful drafting.
    d. Preserving business value.
    e. Attaining pre- and postmortem flexibility.
    f. Maximizing benefits for the surviving spouse.
  2. Tax saving goals
    a. Income tax saving goals
      1) Obtaining a stepped-up basis.
      2) Shifting income to a lower bracket taxpayer.
      3) Deferring recognition of income.
    b. Transfer tax saving goals and planning
      1) Reducing the estate tax value.
      2) Freezing the estate tax value.
      3) Leveraging the use of exclusions, exemptions, and the unified credit.
      4) Delaying payment of the transfer tax.
      5) Minimizing the generation-skipping transfer tax.

The next chapter will apply many of the concepts introduced in this chapter to describe the provisions of the major documents utilized in the property transfer process.

IMPORTANT CONCEPTS COVERED IN THIS CHAPTER

Estate
Property
Probate estate
Gross estate
Taxable estate
Transfer
Assignment
Transferor
Transferee
Legal interest
Beneficial interest
Transfer
Outright
Complete (transfer)
Irrevocable (transfer)
Incomplete (transfer)
Revocable (transfer)
Interest in property
Partially complete (transfer)
Sale
Consideration
Gift
Bargain sale
Inter vivos
Instrument
Beneficiary
Donee
Donor
Decedent
Will
Testamentary
Executed
Testator
Trust
Intestate
Testate
Partially intestate
Probate

Personal representative
Fiduciary
Executor
Administrator
Heir
Devisee
Legatee
Legacy
Issue
Descendant
Specific bequest
Ademption
General bequest
Pecuniary bequest
Residuary bequest
Residue
Class gift
Abatement
Disclaimer
Life insurance
Insured
Term life insurance
Cash surrender value
Cash value life insurance
Gift tax
Death tax
Inheritance tax
Estate tax
Generation-skipping
    transfer tax
Fee simple
Life estate
Measuring life
Interest for years
Leasehold
Real property
Personal property
Tangible personal property

Intangible personal property
Chose in action
Concurrent ownership
Joint interest
Interest by the entirety
Interest in common
Community property
Separate property
Trust
Trustor, grantor, creator
    or settlor
Trust principal or corpus
Trustee
Trust beneficiary
Living trust
Testamentary trust
Power of appointment
Holder or donee (of a
power)
Permissible appointee
Appointee
Exercise (a power)
Release (a power)
Lapse (of a power)
Taker in default
Release (of a power)
Present interest
Future interest
Reversion
Remainder
Vested remainder
Contingent remainder
Income beneficiary
Remainderman

QUESTIONS AND PROBLEMS

1. Describe four different meanings of the concept "estate".

2. (a) Contrast a legal interest from a beneficial interest. (b) Why might a person want to transfer such interests in the same property to different individuals, rather than outright to one person?

3. Kasner "sells" a $10,000 car to his son for $4,000. Technically speaking, is this more of a sale or a gift? Why?

4. One of your clients shows you the following clipping from a trade journal:

   "John Smith, the prominent local celebrity, died on Thursday. His generosity was legend. Last year, he made a large *outright inter vivos gifts* to his alma mater and to another charitable *donee*. In addition, in a lengthy handwritten *will executed* last year, the *decedent* made several large *general bequests* and *specific devises* to the local orphans' fund, including a *transfer* into a *testamentary trust*. Finally, as *holder* of a *power of appointment* over several parcels of land on the outskirts of town, Smith *exercised* the power in favor of several *permissible appointees*, one of whom is a grandson of the *donor*. To the surprise of almost everyone in the family, two *appointees* refused some gifts by exercising valid *disclaimers*. And interestingly, no *residuary bequest* was included in the will, which means that the *testator* died *intestate* with regard to a considerable portion of his *estate*. Smith nominated as *executor* of his *probate* estate several of his surviving *issue*..."

   Explain to your client the meaning of each highlighted word.

5. (a) What is probate? (b) What types of assets are subject to probate administration? (c) What types of assets are not subject to probate? (d) Does having a will avoid probate?

6. Contrast the insured, the owner, and the beneficiary of a life insurance policy.

7. At the moment of Lou's death, a life insurance policy was in force in the amount of $250,000 and had a cash surrender value of $60,000. Lou had the power under the policy to change the beneficiary. After Lou's death, Mary, his wife received a check from the insurance company.
   a. Explain who were the likely parties to this policy:
      1. Insured
      2. Beneficiary
      3. Owner
   b. Did Lou's wife probably receive $60,000, $190,000, $250,000, or $310,000? Why?
   c. Why will this policy likely help in estate planning for Lou's family?

8. (a) Why is a fee simple interest greater than a life estate or an interest for years? (b) Can you think of any sense in which all three interests can be considered nearly equal?

9. Compare and contrast joint interests with interests in common.

10. Beth tells you that she has an interest in property having all of the following characteristics: concurrent ownership; automatic right of succession to ownership; owners own unequal percentages. What valid form of property ownership, if any, is she describing? Explain.

11. A client asks you to define community property and separate property.

12. Compare community property with joint interests.

13. Cindy and Dennis were married in 1980. They have resided in a community property state. At that time, they each owned a car and some furnishings. Since then Dennis has been working full-time and Cindy worked as the mother and homemaker. In 1982, Dennis was given 100 shares of IBM stock. In 1983, Cindy inherited her father's computer. This year, Dennis put one half of a year's salary as down-payment on a house for his family. Making your own assumptions when necessary, identify the community property and the separate property.

14. Continuing the problem immediately above, suppose Dennis paid the down payment on the house with dividend income from the IBM stock, but the house payments were made from Dennis' salary. Is the house community property, separate property or part community and part separate property?

15. One day client Parrish asks you "Why do you recommend trusts"? Briefly answer his question.

16. If you are the holder of a power of appointment, how might you be assisting in the donor's estate plan?

17. Contrast a present interest with a future interest.

18. (a) If Walsh named Paul today to be the sole beneficiary under her will, does Paul today have a present or future interest? (b) If future, is it vested or contingent? (c) If contingent, when will it vest, if ever? Explain each answer carefully.

19. Today Edwards transfers $300,000 to an irrevocable trust, whose terms provide that all income will be payable annually to son Dale (or his heirs) for a period of eighteen years. At the end of that period, the trust will terminate and all corpus will be distributed to grandson Kevin, age 14 (or his estate). (*a*) At a rate of eight percent, calculate the current value of Dale's and Kevin's property interests. (*b*) Recalculate Kevin's remainder interest if it were contingent upon his surviving the income period.

20. Rogers died recently, leaving $500,000 in trust. Roger's husband Mo, age 64, will receive a life estate in all of the income, payable annually. At his death, all principal will pass outright to Roger's daughter Sherie (or her estate). (*a*) At a rate of six percent, calculate the current value of Mo's and Sherie's property interests. (*b*) Also, calculate the values at 14 percent. (c) Comment on the influence of a higher discount rate.

21. Recalculate the answers to part *a* of the question immediately above instead using the rate in effect exactly two weeks before the day this assignment is due.

22. Thomas Smith, age 29, is beneficiary of a trust which will pay him $3,500 a year for life. At 12%, calculate the current value of this life estate.

RECOMMENDED READING

Abney, David L. "Impact of California Community Property Presumptions on Joint Tenancy." *Community Property Journal* 13 (January 1987), pp. 40-45.

Bergin, Thomas F., and Paul G. Haskell. *Preface to Estates in Land and Future Interests.* 2nd ed. New York: Foundation Press, 1984.

Doyle, Robert J. And Stephan R. Leimberg. "New IRS Valuation Rules: Impact On the Tools and Techniques Of Estate and Financial Planning," *Taxes--The Tax Magazine*, May, 1990, pp. 376-96.

Hilker, Anne K. "Planning for the Married Couple Moving Into Or Out Of Community Property States." *Estate Planning*, July 1987, pp. 212-16.

*Kwall, Roberta R, and Aiello, Anthony J. "The Superwill Debate: Opening the Pandora's Box"? *Temple Law Review* Vol. 62, Spring, 1989, pp. 277-315.

McCoy, Jerry J. "Keeping Up With The New 'Rate Of The Month' Tables," *Trusts & Estates*, February, 1990, pp. 35-39.

*Moses, A.L., "Uniform Determination of Death Act Adds Certainty to the Definition of Death." *Estate Planning*, September, 1989, pp., 276-279.

Raabe, William A., and Rick J. Taylor. "Wisconsin's Uniform Marital Property Act: Community Property Moves East." *Community Property Journal* 12 (Spring 1985), pp. 83-117.

Stephenson, Gilbert T., and Norman A. Wiggins. *Trusts and Estates.* 5th ed. New York: Appleton-Century-Crofts, 1973.

*Wenig, Mary M. "UMPA Bibliography." *Community Property Journal*, July 1986, pp. 92-97.

PART 2

The Constraints in Planning

– 3

Introduction to Property Transfers I: The Documents of Transfer

OVERVIEW

Estate planning seeks to facilitate the transfer of the client's wealth as efficiently as possible. Efficiency in estate transfer usually requires the preparation of one or more formal documents, ones which will be accepted by those authorities that ultimately authorize and make the transfers. For example, the proper preparation and execution of a will is essential to the efficient disposal of any probate property. The will must be drafted correctly to ensure proper disposition, and it must be signed and witnessed according to law so that officials, such as the probate judge, the court clerk, the county recorder, and the bank officer will accept it as the guide for the title transfer process.

This chapter is the first of two introducing the principles of property transfer. It will explore the *documents* used in the process of transferring wealth. Specifically, it will examine the creation of four common property transfer mechanisms: joint tenancy, property disposition by contract, the will, and the trust instrument. Appendix 3A at the end of the chapter will introduce the rule against perpetuities, a legal doctrine that acts to prevent a transferor from controlling the disposition of property for an unreasonably long time after making the transfer. The next chapter will examine the actual *process* of transfer of the property disposed of by these documents, with emphasis on the probate process. And, because probate also administers the decedent's intestate property, the next chapter will also survey the law of intestate succession.

Property transfers are regulated by state, not federal, law. State laws in this area vary greatly, making generalization difficult. However, a sizable minority of the states have many property distribution laws in common because they have adopted all or a significant part of the Uniform Probate Code (UPC). The UPC was introduced in 1966, partly in answer to the criticism that probate procedures in the United States were too costly, too time-consuming, and too complicated. In 1972, Idaho was the first state to adopt it, and since then, a total of 28 states have adopted the UPC in whole or in large part.[1] In presenting the material in this and the next chapter, we will often refer to the laws of those states which have adopted the UPC, especially in three major areas: will execution, intestate succession, and probate administration.

JOINT TENANCY ARRANGEMENTS

The acquisition of title in joint tenancy is ordinarily a simple matter, requiring the completion of one or two preprinted forms. Ordinarily, an attorney is not needed. Title to real property is usually completed in the realtor's or title company's office. Similarly, written title in joint ownership of personal property, when it can easily be created, is completed in the office of the professional who helps to acquire it. Examples include title to securities by the investment broker, to a car by the motor vehicle bureau, and to a bank account by the bank.

Later in the text, particularly in Chapter 10, the reader will learn several significant disadvantages to taking title in joint tenancy. The decision as to whether to do so or not can be far from clear, and may require the advice of an expert. However, the focus of the present material is on how title in joint tenancy is taken, not whether it should be taken.

---

1. Alabama, Alaska*, Arizona*, California, Colorado*, District of Colombia, Florida, Hawaii, Idaho*, Indiana, Kentucky, Maine, Maryland, Michigan, Minnesota*, Missouri*, Montana*, Nebraska*, New Mexico*, New Jersey*, North Dakota*, Pennsylvania*, South Carolina, Tennessee*, Texas*, Wisconsin, Wyoming and Utah*. (States marked with * have adopted the UPC entirely or nearly entirely.

PROPERTY DISPOSAL BY CONTRACT

There are a number of significant ways in which property can be transferred pursuant to a contract. Life insurance and pension and profit sharing plans are common examples.

Life Insurance

Wealth derived from life insurance comes in two forms, the policy death proceeds and the policy itself. Different means are undertaken in arranging the transfer of each.

Planning the transfer of the *proceeds* of a life insurance policy is arranged prior to the policy inception during the application process, when the chosen beneficiary is designated in the written application. The beneficiary's name will then be designated in the policy when it is issued. Anytime thereafter, the beneficiary designation can easily be changed by the owner by giving written notice to the company using the company's beneficiary designation form.

Arranging the transfer, by sale or gift, of title to the life insurance *policy itself* is also simple, requiring the completion of a short assignment form provided by the insurance company.

Pension and Profit Sharing Plans

Pension and profit sharing plans are contracts between the employee-client and the employer. Ordinarily, the employer requests that the employee fill out a written form designating the beneficiary, the party who will be entitled to any benefits paid after the employee's death. Thus, the actual process of beneficiary designation for most retirement plans is simple and straightforward.

In contrast with the above transfer arrangements, the document preparation process for the will and the trust are not simple, for two reasons. First, unlike joint tenancy and written contracts, the will and the trust are capable of disposing of *nearly all* of the client's estate, as well as providing for the care of the client's minor children. Thus, the will and the trust will inevitably be more complicated. Second, unlike insurance and retirement contracts, which are drafted by the insurer or the employer, the *responsibility for drafting* the will and the trust falls on the individual client.

The following material presents an overview of will and trust construction. Major topics include the legal requirements for a valid will, common will provisions, essential characteristics of trusts, and common provisions of the living trust and the trust-will.

THE WILL

Many people die leaving no formal directions as to how to dispose of their probate property or as to who should care for their minor children. In such cases, the state seeks to make these decisions equitably and sensibly, using statutory rules tailored according to the surviving family situation. However, state law may conflict with the wishes of a decedent, whether unstated or even as recollected by the survivors. Compared to a properly planned estate, intestacy can result unsuitable property disposition and higher taxes. Individuals can avoid an undesirable outcome by expressing their wishes while still alive, in a legally acceptable document that serves, as a direction and guide for those who will survive. The will is the most common formal document for this purpose.

A will is a written document disposing of a person's probate property at death.

In most states, wills can be *oral*, but laws usually greatly restrict the scope of their ability to dispose of wealth. Most oral will statutes apply only to personal property. And often, a limit is placed on the value that can be disposed of, such as $2,000. In addition, the testator, on execution, is often required to be a member of the armed forces or in peril of death. Practically speaking, all wills prepared in the estate planning process are written.

Who May Execute a Will

In most states, any individual 18 or older who is of sound mind may dispose of his or her property by will. The implications of this are twofold. First, individuals under the age of 18 cannot transfer property by will unless they are emancipated minors. Their probate property will pass, at death, in accordance with the laws of intestate succession. This usually means that their parents will inherit it. Second, a will can be denied probate if it can be established that the testator, at date of execution of the will, lacked testamentary capacity, was subject to undue influence or to fraud, or acted mistakenly.[2] These four concepts are discussed next.

---

2. For a discussion of the psychiatrist's role in determining incapacity and undue influence in connection with assessing competency to make a will or trust, see the Spar/Garb article cited at the end of the chapter.

Testamentary capacity. Testamentary capacity concerns the testator's mental ability to validly execute a will. A testator has testamentary capacity if he or she possesses each of the following three attributes:

1. Sufficient mental capacity to understand the *nature of the act* being undertaken (executing a will).
2. Sufficient mental capacity to understand and recollect the general nature of his or her *property*.
3. Sufficient mental capacity to remember and understand his or her relationship to the *persons* who have natural claims on his or her bounty and whose interests are affected by the provisions of the will.

Essentially, then, testators must know that they are executing a will, they must be aware of what they own, and they must be cognizant of their heirs. On its face, this test is quite severe; strictly construed, it would prevent many older testators from executing a valid will. However, because the law holds that mere age and physical disability will not negate testamentary capacity, probate courts have not usually been nearly so strict, and at various times they have admitted to probate wills executed by individuals who have been forgetful, absent minded, behaving peculiarly, alcoholic, even persons declared mentally incompetent, under conservatorship, insane, or have committed suicide shortly after executing a will. Nonetheless, failure to meet one or more of these three requirements will result in a finding of insufficient testamentary capacity. Examples of sufficient evidence of incompetence include senility, ongoing hallucinations and irrational beliefs combined, and irrational, totally groundless beliefs about the testator's spouse, children or siblings.[3] Generally, the outcome hinges on whether or not, at or about the specific time the will was executed, the three-prong test was met. It should be kept in mind, however, that appellate courts do not like "setting a will aside," and have reversed many jury set-aside decisions. As a consequence, affirmed findings of testamentary incapacity are infrequent.

Anticipating the possibility of a will contest based on lack of testamentary capacity, some attorneys *videotape* the will execution of a testator who may have questionable capacity, believing that the taping will make capacity more credible. Others believe that videotaping can enhance the success of a contest, reasoning that testators may look terrible on the screen (especially if they are shown lying in a hospital bed), and that the

---

3. For a listing of cases discussing these issues, see the Calleton/Rose paper cited at the end of the chapter.

taping constitutes additional evidence that even the attorney lacked confident in the testator's capacity.[4]

Undue influence. A will executed by a testator who was subject to undue influence by someone who stands to benefit may also be denied probate. Undue influence is influence by a confidante which has the effect of impeding the testator's free will. Examples include threats, the use of force (duress), and the use of over persuasion and psychological domination, as when "Snake Oil Sam," the smooth-talking newcomer, makes a romantic play for the 92-year-old widow, "encouraging" her to disinherit her children and leave her entire estate to him.

Winning an undue influence case can be difficult. In her article cited at the end of the chapter, Jenkins cites a California court which notes that undue influence "...cases typically involve a weak, unsound or impaired mind or a will procured by one who occupied a fiduciary relationship to the decedent who was not the natural object of the decedent's bounty and who benefited substantially under the will. An element of fraud or deceit was also found to be a common thread..." Jenkins adds that juries frequently ignore the court's instructions that state that testators have a fundamental right to dispose of property as they see fit, and too often seek to rewrite a will that reflect what the jurors think is fair. Appellate courts usually reverse such jury verdicts.

Fraud. Fraud involves deception through false information, as, for example, when niece tells her great uncle that she is penniless when, in fact, she is wealthy, or when a daughter incorrectly tells her mother that only her sister instigated a conservatorship proceeding, when actually they both did.

Mistake. A will can also be contested on the basis of a mistake. Examples include: (*a*) the testator leaves her estate to only one son, mistakenly believing that the other is wealthy; (*b*) the testator mistakenly leaves out an intended clause; or (c) the will mistakenly includes an unintended clause.

Ordinarily, a finding of lack of testamentary capacity will invalidate the entire will, while a finding of undue influence, fraud or mistake might invalidate only those provisions that relate to the specific problem.

---

4. For an in depth article advocating use of videotape in the probate process, see the Beyer/Buckley paper cited at the end of the chapter.

Statutory Format Requirements for Wills

Most states, including those that have adopted the Uniform Probate Code, recognize at least two types of wills, the *witnessed will* and the *holographic will*.

Witnessed will. Although state laws vary, a witnessed or "attested" will must usually meet the following three requirements:

1. Must be *in writing* (handwritten, typed, etc.)
2. In the presence of *two witnesses* (three in a few states), the *testator must sign* the will.
3. The *witnesses must sign* their names to the will, understanding that the instrument they sign is the testator's will. The main purpose of requiring witnesses is to prevent forgery and coercion of the testator.

Beneficiaries should not be witnesses to a will because that could imperil their right to receive some or all of their bequest. In most states, a bequest to a witness is void, unless the witness is an heir. And in that case, the witness can take no more than his or her intestate share. In some other states, if challenged, an "interested witness" may take more than the intestate share only if he or she is able to rebut a statutory presumption that the devise was procured by duress, menace, fraud, or undue influence. Although inability to rebut this presumption will not totally invalidate the will, it will invalidate some or all of the bequest to that witness.

Holographic will. If a written will does not meet all of the requirements for a witnessed will, in many states, including those adopting the UPC, it can still be admitted to probate if it meets the requirements for a holographic will. Typical state requirements for a holographic will are:

1. Signature is in the testator's handwriting.
2. All of the "material provisions" of the will are in the testator's handwriting.

Years ago, the courts of most states applied will format and formality requirements more strictly than they do today. Two examples will be cited.

First, courts often refused to admit to probate holographic documents written on printed stationery, such as letterhead. This restriction is less common today. In determining what parts of the will must be in the testator's handwriting, some states currently use the following test: if the non-testator's portion is excluded, will the remaining handwritten portion make sense? Reflecting the position of perhaps a minority of states, an Arizona court recently concluded "no" in a situation where the testator completed a preprinted will purchased at a retail store.[5] However, the modern trend is to admit documents that reflect "substantial compliance." The "material provisions" requirement of some state holographic will requirements described above reflect this trend. UPC §2-503 was recently added to recognize imperfect documents intended by the decedent to be his or her will, implicitly accepting the premise that a "harmless error" will be disregarded.

Second, most states have required the testator's signature to be placed at the end of the will. But one state in a recent case approved a will in which the testator had simply written her name at the beginning.[6]

Holographic wills are recognized in about two fifths of the states.

Contrasting witnessed and holographic wills. The differences between the two sets of formal requirements are twofold: First, the witnessed will requires the performance of certain activities in connection with two witnesses. In contrast, the holographic will may, but need not, be witnessed. Second, the holographic will requires that all material provisions of the will be in the testator's handwriting. In contrast, the witnessed will requires that only the testator's signature be handwritten, and even this may be unnecessary when a proper authorization is arranged.

No Contest Clause

In the last few pages, we have seen a number of technical requirements for a valid will including testamentary capacity, absence of undue influence, fraud, mistake, and certain specific execution requirements such as signatures by witnesses and the testator. Anticipating that dissatisfied persons may cite one or more violations of these requirements in a *will contest* as a pretext for obtaining more of their estate, testators may insert a "no contest" clause in their will. Here's an example of a typical one:

> *I have purposely made no provisions herein for any other person or persons...and if any person...shall contest this will.. I give such person...one dollar..in lieu of the provisions which I have made...*

---

5. *Estate of Muder*, 751 p. 2d 986 (Ariz. 1988).

6. *Estate of McEod* 206 Cal. App.3d 1325 (1988).

Of course, its purpose is to discourage will contests. It usually succeeds, but not always, for several reasons. First, it will discourage only beneficiaries named in the will, not disinherited persons who stand to lose nothing by contesting. Second, beneficiaries may still wish to contest if they expect to gain considerably more than they'll lose. Finally, courts in most jurisdictions tend to narrowly construe no contest clauses, and will not enforce them if the contestant acted in good faith or with probable cause. Perhaps most testators would desire this result, anyway.

What situations tend to invite will contests? Where the testator chooses to disinherit family members in favor of a friend, a charity, or a spouse married shortly before death; or where a testator treats children unequally. And a contest is even more likely in these situations if the testator is very old, or is ailing, either physically or mentally.

Will contests are infrequent, and *successful* contests are very uncommon. It is believed that fewer than one percent of wills offered for probate are challenged, and over two-thirds of these challenges are unsuccessful. However, will contests have probably become relatively more common recently for at least three reasons. First, during recessionary periods, more claimants will look to estates as a source of funds. Second, as the general population continues to age, more elderly people of means will acquire 'friends' who offer to assist them in their finances. And third, a higher divorce rate has increased the number of children of former marriages, a group that is less likely to get along with the client's surviving spouse. When any of these situations or factors apply to a particular client, attorneys will want to take special precautions in drafting and executing the will.[7]

The Simple Will

Wills can be quite lengthy and complex, but this section focuses on a relatively simple will. In fact, that's just what the profession calls its most common uncomplicated will. A *simple will* is a will prepared for a family having a small estate, one for whom death tax planning is not a significant concern. For tax reasons that will become clear later, a small estate is considered less than about $600,000. A medium-size estate ranges between $600,000 and $1,200,000, while a larger estate is considered to exceed $1,200,000.

---

7. Numerous precautions are described in the articles by Buckley, Beyer, Crown, and Nash, all cited at the end of the chapter.

The simple will contains few or no tax provisions but it usually does include all of the following: nominating both an executor and a guardian for minor children, waiving the probate bond, and, in most cases, disposing of most or all of the testator's property to the spouse, if alive, otherwise to the children. Estate planning strategies for the small family estate will be discussed in the chapters in Part 3.

A three page example of a simple will is presented in Exhibit 3-1 to demonstrate, by example, the essential nature of that probate property transfer document. The reader is encouraged to study it carefully, so that the analysis that follows be more readily understood.

EXHIBIT 3-1 Simple Will

WILL OF WILLARD THOMAS SMITH

I, Willard Thomas Smith, declare this to be my will. I revoke all prior wills and codicils.

First: Family and Guardian

My immediate family consists of my wife, Sue ("my wife"), and our three children, Kristi, Heather, and Todd. We all reside at 8887 Custer St., Mytown, Anystate. This will shall apply to all my children, including all children who may hereafter be born to or adopted by me, and to their issue.

If my wife does not survive me, and it is necessary to appoint a guardian, I appoint Curtis J. Quint guardian of the person and estate of each such minor child. If for any reason Curtis J. Quint does not act as guardian, I appoint Maria S. Cruise as guardian of the person and estate.

Second: Executor

A. *Designation* I appoint my wife as my executor. If for any reason she does not so act, I appoint James A. Reliable to be my executor. If for any reason neither my wife nor James A. Reliable acts as executor, I appoint Third National Bank of Mytown to be my executor.

B. *Bond waiver* No bond, surety, or other security shall be required of my executor.

C. *Taxes from residue* All death taxes imposed because of my death and interest and penalties on those taxes, whether on property passing under this will or otherwise, shall be paid by my executor from the residue of my estate.

EXHIBIT 3-1 *(continued)*

Third: Disposition of Property

A. *Tangible personal property* If my wife survives me by 30 days, I give her all of my interest in our tangible personal property.

If my wife does not survive me by 30 days, I give my tangible personal property (except vehicles and boats) in equal shares to those of my children who survive me by 30 days. My executor shall consider their personal preferences in making that division. My executor has my permission to sell any of that property and distribute the proceeds to equalize the shares. My executor shall be discharged for all tangible personal property so given to any minor child if the child or adult having the child's custody gives a written receipt to my executor.

B. *Residue* If my wife survives me by 120 days, I give her the residue of my estate. If my wife does not survive me by 120 days, I give the residue in equal shares: one to each of my children who survives me by 120 days and one to the descendants per stirpes who survive me by 120 days of each of my children who does not so survive me.

If neither my wife nor any of my descendants survives me by 120 days, I give the residue of my estate according to Mystate's laws of descent and distribution, one half as if I had died with no will on the last day of that 120 day period and one half as if it were my wife's estate and she had died with no will on that last day.

Fourth: Powers of Executor

My executor shall have unrestricted powers, without court order, to settle my estate as this will provides. In addition, my executor shall have all powers my executor thinks necessary or desirable to administer my estate, including the following:

1. To make interim distributions of principal and income on a interim basis to those entitled to it.
2. To sell, exchange, mortgage, pledge, lease or assign any property belonging to my estate.
3. To continue operation of any business belonging to my estate.
4. To invest and reinvest any surplus money.

EXHIBIT 3-1 *(concluded)*

    I have signed my name to this instrument on March 19, 1999, at Mytown, Anystate.

_____ (Signature) _____

Statement of Witnesses

The undersigned witnesses declare under penalty of perjury under Anystate law, on March 19, 1999, that we are over 21, that the testator declared to us that this instrument is his will, that he signed this will, and that he requested us to act as witnesses to it. We believe that the testator is of sound mind and did not act under fraud, duress or undue influence.

_____ (Signature) _____

_____ (Address) _____

_____ (Signature) _____

_____ (Address) _____

    Analysis Of The Simple Will. Let's analyze the major provisions of this will, section by section.

    "Will of Willard Thomas Smith." In this introductory paragraph, the testator explicitly "declares" it to be his will, primarily to satisfy the law's requirement that a testator have an intent to make a will.

    A *codicil* is a separate written document that amends or revokes a prior will. It is executed if the testator wishes to make one or more brief changes or additions to the will. As a separate document, it also must meet all of the legal requirements of a witnessed will, including subscription by witnesses.

    The most common method of *revoking* a prior will is by executing a later will that explicitly declares such revocation. Our simple will does just that. Revocation by "cancellation" with a "subsequent instrument," as it is termed, can also be undertaken in any other signed, witnessed statement. A will can also be revoked by a physical act, such as by burning, tearing, canceling, obliterating or destroying it, combined with an intent to revoke.[8]

    Revoking all prior wills and codicils eliminates the danger that provi-

---

8. Uniform Probate Code §2-507.

sions in prior wills which are not inconsistent with the present will may have to be construed together with the current will. Without a revocation clause, needless litigation can arise over whether or not the provisions in two or more wills are inconsistent. For example, in one state supreme court case, a decedent-testator had written two "last" wills within three weeks. The first simply left "a tract of land" to a friend. The second contained no revocation clause and left "all my effects" to siblings Y and Z. The court permitted a trial to determine whether the first will should be construed along with the second, reasoning that they were not necessarily inconsistent because the testator could have used the word "effects" to mean only personal property.[9] If the testator's intent was to leave everything to Y and Z, inclusion of a revocation clause would have assured this result.

"First: Family and Guardian." Naming all members of the immediate family can assist a personal representative in finding relatives and locating assets.

Including *afterborn children* in the will can prevent a child born after the execution of the will and not provided for in it from being left to inherit under the laws of intestate succession, a consequence which might conflict with the testator's intent.

As we shall see in Chapter 17, a minor child who out-lives both parents is required by law to have a *guardian* of the person and of the estate appointed. The guardian of the person is responsible for a minor child's care, custody, control and education, while a guardian of the child's estate is responsible for managing the minor child's property. A testator's nominations carry great weight and will usually be respected, but the probate judge has the power to appoint other persons as guardians. Nominating an alternate guardian increases the likelihood that the testator's preferences will be followed.

"Second: Executor." Similar to nomination of a guardian, nomination of an executor and an alternate executor can be helpful to the probate court in its selection process.

Often, the executor is required to give a *bond*, which commercially insures the estate assets against a breach of trust by the executor. However, the will can waive this requirement, one which the testator may consider unnecessary for two reasons: first, because it results in additional expense to the estate, and second, because it may be largely unnecessary if a highly trusted party, such as the spouse, is being nominated.

Declaring that all *death taxes* be paid from the residue of the estate may be the fairest plan, and one that can minimize administrative delay. On the

---

9. *Wolfe's will* 185 NC 563, (1923).

one hand, it relieves recipients of nonresidue property from having to share in this burden. On the other, it relieves the executor from the responsibility of *seeking reimbursement* from individuals who may have received only specific benefits of relatively illiquid assets, such as a painting or a piano. And reimbursement for death taxes can be difficult to obtain from individuals not at all connected with the probate process, such as those succeeding to ownership as former joint tenants with the decedent, and beneficiaries of a life insurance policy on the life of the decedent. In some circumstances, however, fairness would dictate apportioning the taxes among all beneficiaries. See Chapter 17 for a further analysis.

"Third: Disposition of property." This simple will essentially leaves all property to the testator's spouse, if surviving, otherwise to the children in what is sometimes called an alternative "gift-over." The will distinguishes the residence and tangible personal property from the residue, which consists of all other probate assets. Thus, the spouse must survive by 30 days to take the residence and tangible personal property. If the spouse doesn't, the tangible personal property passes to the children who survive by 30 days.

Inclusion of a survival requirement, such as 30 days or 120 days, reduces the likelihood that the death of both spouses in a common accident will result in subjecting some of the family property to two successive probates. This *survival clause*, as it is called, helps in situations not covered by the Uniform Simultaneous Death Act (USDA).

Enacted by *every* state, the USDA provides that when transfer of title to property depends on the order of deaths and when no sufficient evidence exists that two people died other than simultaneously, the property of each is disposed of as if each had survived the other. Thus, in the case of a married couple, the husband's estate would likely pass to his blood relatives and the wife's estate would likely pass to her blood relatives. This statute is of limited value, however, because it will not avoid double probate when the order of deaths can in fact be established. In some states, if it *can* be established that one spouse survived the other, even only by seconds, then the USDA will not apply and, absent a survival clause, there will be a *double probate* of the property owned by the first spouse to die. Perhaps worse, *all* of the property may ultimately pass to that spouse's in-laws, rather than the surviving relatives. Some states, including California, have legislated safeguards against inheritance by in-laws by requiring the portion of the decedent's estate attributable to the predeceased spouse pass, in some circumstances, to the predeceased spouse's children, parents, or other kin.[10] The Uniform Probate Code's version of the USDA, in Section 2-104,

---

10. Cal. Probate Code §6402.5.

provides that the property of each is disposed of as if each had survived the other when it cannot be established that the other person survived by *120 hours*.

With regard to *insurance* on the life of a decedent, the USDA states that in the event of an apparent simultaneous death of the insured and the beneficiary, the policy proceeds are to be distributed as if the insured survived the beneficiary. Thus, the proceeds will be paid to the contingent beneficiary, and if none, then to the owner's probate estate. For a further discussion of survival clauses, see Chapters 4 and 17.

Section B covering the "residue" is called the *residuary clause*. Failure to include it in a will can result in *partial intestacy*. In a recent case, the attorney who had drafted the decedent's will admitted that he mistakenly omitted the residuary clause, but indicated that the decedent wanted the residue to go to a friend. The court would not allow admission of this evidence, ruling that extrinsic evidence is admissible to explain what is *in* the will, not to *add* to the will.[11]

Disposing of estate property by differentiating the tangible personal property from the residue can speed up probate distribution and can often save income taxes. In Chapter 8, we'll learn about the concept distributable net income, or DNI. A *specific bequest* (rather than a general bequest) of property such as the personal property can prevent estate distribution of property from being labeled DNI. This will generate less taxable income to the distributee (often the spouse) and correspondingly more taxable income to the estate, which is (hopefully) in a lower rate bracket.

Instead of "tangible personal property," some wills ill-advisedly use the term "personal effects," which means "tangible personal property, worn or carried about the person or having some intimate relation with the person." Since automobiles and some other property are not considered "personal effects," the broader term *tangible personal property* is usually preferred.

Distribution by *per stirpes*, or by right of representation, is a method of allocating a gift of the decedent's property to the descendants of a predeceased heir of a person named in the will and is covered in detail in Chapter 4.

The   of intestate succession also know as "laws of descent and distribution," are also described in Chapter 4. They vary somewhat from state to state. They spell out the priority of succession rights of the decedent's spouse and kin, in the event of intestacy. In this will, the testator has in effect generously chosen to divide his property in half, with one half going by intestate succession to his relatives and the other half going by

---

11. Knupp v. District of Columbia 578 A. 2d 702 (D.C. Ct. App., 1990).

intestate succession to his wife's relatives, in the event that his wife and descendants all fail to survive him by 120 days.

"Fourth: Powers of Executor." Explicitly granting powers to the executor can eliminate the need to secure permission of the probate court to undertake certain administrative actions. Ordinarily, testators would like their executors to act without such unnecessary delay.

"Statement of Witnesses." Every state imposes formal requirements regarding the role of witnesses in the execution of a will. The sentences included in this section of the will offer additional evidence of the testator's capacity to execute a will. They also maximize the likelihood of compliance with these formal requirements by explicitly stating them, which the witnesses acknowledge by signing.

Other aspects of the simple will. Simple wills are most commonly drafted by attorneys for clients with smaller estates. If two such clients are married, a simple will is usually prepared for each spouse. In most cases, the dispositive clauses are identical. Thus, husband's will leaves all to wife, if she survives, otherwise to the children. And wife's will leaves all to husband, if he survives, otherwise to the children. Such simple wills are commonly called *reciprocal wills*, *mirror wills*, or *mutual wills*.

Occasionally clients will want *contractual wills*, ones which cannot be revised once one of the parties (usually spouses) dies. Sometimes, these are done in the form of a single will for two people, called a *joint will*, although a joint will need not be contractual. Contractual wills are rare because most clients want the flexibility of changing their estate plan after one spouse dies. Joint wills should be avoided unless the clients really want a contractual will, because even if the clients did not intend the joint will to irrevocable once one of the testator dies a court may rule that was the intent since there can be little other reason to create one document for two people.

Wills that are more complex are hardly ever found to be reciprocal in content because they are usually prepared by attorneys specializing in estate planning to reflect the inherently different preferences and different financial and tax circumstances of the spouses. This text will highlight many of these differences in later chapters.

Where should the original copy of the will be kept? The client's safe deposit box makes good sense only in those states (e.g., California) that do not *seal* boxes at the owner's death to more ensure payment of state death taxes. Some attorneys recommend their own safe, but this might be viewed as self-serving. Others simply recommend a secure, handy place in the client's home.

Next, we'll examine the trust, the other major planning document of transfer.

THE TRUST

The principal parties to a trust are the trustor, the trustee, and the beneficiary. As a legal arrangement, a trust is created by the trustor and divides and transfers interests in property between two or more people. Any interests or control over the trust that are not given to the beneficiaries are either retained by the trustor, granted to the trustee, or exercised by both.

A trust can take effect during the lifetime of the trustor, or it can take effect at the trustor's death. As we have seen, the former is called a *living* (or inter vivos) *trust*, while the latter is called a *testamentary trust*, that is, a trust created in a complex will that professionals call a "trust-will." The trust-will document is covered later in the chapter.

At any given moment, a trust is either revocable and amendable, in which case the trustor is capable of voiding or amending it, or it is irrevocable, that is, not voidable or amendable. A living trust usually contains specific language stating whether it is revocable or irrevocable. A revocable living trust is usually, but not always, specified to become irrevocable at the death of the trustor(s). Like the contents of most wills, the provisions of a testamentary trust can be amended or revoked before the testator's death by codicil, revocation or destruction of the trust-will. At the testator's death, a testamentary trust takes effect and becomes by nature irrevocable, since the only person capable of amending or voiding it, the testator, will, of course, be permanently unavailable.

A trust usually contains two different legal types of property, principal and income. The *principal* of a trust is its invested wealth, and its size will fluctuate as additions are made to it and as charges are made against it. Additions to principal accrue from such things as asset appreciation and stock share dividends. Charges against principal are made for such things as costs of investing the principal (commissions, legal fees, etc.), and transfer taxes.

In contrast with trust principal, the *income* of a trust is the return in money or property derived from use of the trust principal. In Chapter 8, we shall call this income "fiduciary accounting income," or FAI. Examples of income include cash dividends, rent, and interest. Trust income also has charges against it, most of which usually reflect expenses incurred in managing the trust property, such as insurance premiums, and some or all of the trustee's fee. Any trust income not distributed to beneficiaries is said to be *accumulated* in the trust and is generally accounted for as retained income, not principal.

The accounting distinction between principal and income is particularly important because, most trusts contain provisions that will bestow rights to principal and income to different beneficiaries. In Chapter 8, we'll see that the distinction between principal and income will influence trust income taxation.

The beneficiaries of an irrevocable trust are usually either *income beneficiaries* (i.e., those having an interest in the income) or they are *principal beneficiaries* (for example, a remainderman, one who stands to receive principal outright when the trust terminates). These two types of beneficiaries may have conflicting or "adverse" interests, since the distributions to one of them may influence the amount of future distributions to the other.

There are other ways of classifying trusts, especially in connection with tax planning. The chapters in Part 3 of this text, will introduce several tax-saving trusts, including the bypass trust, the Crummey trust, and the QTIP trust. First, however, the reader will explore the law of estate, gift, and income taxation to understand how taxes can be saved. The purpose of focusing on trusts in the present chapter is, more basic: to enable the reader to learn the essential structure of the two principal documents creating the trust. To do this as plainly as possible, the following material will highlight an uncomplicated living trust and a testamentary trust, the latter also known as a trust-will.

Living Trust Instrument

A living trust is created by a document of agreement between trustor and trustee. Before we examine the actual instrument, let's compare and contrast the characteristics of that document with its common legal alternative, the will.

Similarities. The will and the living trust instrument are similar in three important ways. First, both are capable of disposing of property at the client's death. Second, both have a fiduciary (executor or trustee) who is responsible for managing property for a period of time. Third, both the will and the living trust instrument can be made amendable and revocable. The will can nearly always be amended by a codicil, or revoked by its destruction or by execution of a later will that explicitly revokes it. One exception , of course is the *contractual will*, which becomes irrevocable after the death of the first cotestator. The living trust instrument can either be made revocable or irrevocable. In most states, a trust must provide in its instrument that it is revocable, otherwise it becomes irrevocable upon execution. In the other states, a trust is revocable unless otherwise specified.

Differences. The will and the living trust instrument are also different in three important ways. First they dispose of a totally different set of property. A living trust instrument disposes of property owned by the trustee, while a will disposes of (probate) property owned by the decedent at death. Thus, with regard to property transfers, the living trust instrument and the will are mutually exclusive; property owned by the trustee is not probate property, while probate property is owned by the decedent, not the trustee. Of course the decedent's will can transfer property, by way of the probate process, to the trustee of his or her living trust. Wills that do this are called *pour-over wills* because they take property left out of trust corpus and pour that property into the trust.

Second, with regard to choosing a fiduciary, a living trust instrument always *appoints* a trustee while a will always *nominates* an executor. However, as we shall see, a trust-will also nominates a trustee. Since the trustor of a living trust is alive when the trustee is appointed, the trustor has control over the appointment. In fact, a trust instrument is a legal *contract* executed by trustor and trustee. On the other hand, the probate judge appoints the executor of a will after the testator's death. The judge may appoint someone else for any number of reasons, including the nominee's inability to serve due to death, disability, or incompetence.

Third, while the formal execution requirements for writing a will are quite strict, the requirements for properly executing a trust instrument are simple to meet. In most cases, the trust document is simply dated and signed by the trustor and the trustee. Witnesses are not required, however some attorney have the trustor's signature notarized to assure others who might have to rely on the document at a time when the trustor is incapacitated or dead.

Exhibit 3-2 presents an instrument creating an uncomplicated living trust.

EXHIBIT 3-2 Living Trust Instrument

JOHN C. JONES

Revocable Living Trust

Dated March 19,1999

TRUST AGREEMENT made March 19,1999, between John C. Jones, as trustor, resident of Common County, Mystate, and John C. Jones, resident of Common County, Mystate, as trustee.

    1. Trust property. The trustor hereby transfers to the trustee the property described on Schedule A attached hereto and made a part hereof. The trustee agrees to hold such property and any other property which it may receive during the trustor's lifetime or thereafter, in trust, under the terms and conditions provided therein.

EXHIBIT 3-2 *(continued)*

2. Successor trustee. If John C. Jones for any reason ceases to act as trustee, First National Bank of Anytown shall become trustee.

3. Power to amend or revoke. The trustor reserves the right at any time to amend or revoke this trust, in whole or in part, by an instrument in writing signed by him and delivered during his lifetime to the trustee.

4. Operation of trust during trustor's lifetime. During the trustor's lifetime, the trustee shall administer and distribute the trust as follows:

a. Trust income. The trustee shall pay the net income of this trust to the trustor at convenient intervals but at least quarteranually.

b. Trust principal. The trustee shall pay to the trustor from time to time such amounts of the principal of this trust as the trustor shall direct in writing or as the trustee deems necessary or advisable for the trustor's support and comfort.

5. Operation of trust after trustor's death. Upon the death of the trustor, the trust estate shall be held, administered, and distributed as follows:

a. Wife survives by four months. If the trustor's wife survives trustor by four months, the trustee shall distribute the entire trust estate to her and the trust shall terminate.

b. Wife does not survive by four months. If the trustor's wife does not survive the trustor by four months and if no then-living child of the trustor is under age 21, then the trustee shall divide the trust into as many equal shares as there are children of the trustor's then living and children of the trustor's then deceased with descendants then living. Each share set aside for a child then deceased with descendants then living shall be further divided into shares for such descendants, by right of representation. The trust estate shall be held, administered, and distributed in the manner described in sub-sections 5(b)(2)(a) and (b), below.

If neither the trustor's wife nor any of the trustor's descendants survive the trustor by four months, the trustee shall distribute the entire trust estate according to Mystate's laws of descent and distribution, one half as if the trustor had died with no will on the last day of the four-month period and one half as if it were the trustor's wife's estate and she had died with no will on the last day.

If the trustor's wife does not survive the trustor by four months and if any then-living child of the trustor is under age 21, then the trust estate shall be held, administered, and distributed as follows:

EXHIBIT 3-2 *(continued)*

(1) *Any child under age 21.* So long as any of the trustor's children are living who are under twenty-one (21), the trustee shall pay to or apply for the benefit of all of the trustor's children as much of the net income and principal as the trustee in the trustee's discretion deems necessary for their proper support, health, and education, after taking into consideration, to the extent that the trustee considers advisable, the value of the trust assets, the relative needs, both present and future, of each of the beneficiaries, and their other income and resources made known to the trustee and reasonably available to meet beneficiary needs. The trustee may make distributions under this provision that benefit one or more beneficiaries to the absolute exclusion of others. Any net income not distributed shall be accumulated and added to principal.

(2) *Youngest child reaches age 21.* When the youngest of the trustor's then-living children reaches the age of 21, the trustee shall divide the trust into as many equal shares as there are children of the trustor's then living and children of the trustor's then deceased with descendants then living. Each share set aside for a child then deceased with descendants then living shall be further divided into shares for such descendants, by right of representation. Each such share shall be distributed, or retained in trust, as hereafter provided.

(*a*) Each share set aside for a descendant shall be distributed to that descendant free of trust if that descendant has then reached age twenty-one (21).

(*b*) Each share set aside for a descendant who had not then reached age twenty-one (21) shall be retained in trust. The trustee shall pay to or for the benefit of that descendant as much of the income and principal of the trust as the trustee, in the trustee's discretion, considers appropriate for that descendant's support, health, and education. When that descendant reaches age 21, that descendant's share shall be distributed to that descendant, free of trust. If that descendant dies before receiving distribution of that descendant's entire share, the undistributed balance of that descendant's share shall be distributed, free of trust, to that descendant's then-living descendants, by right of representation, or if there are none, to the trustor's then-living descendants, by right of representation.

6. Restriction against assignment, etc. No interest in the principal or income of this trust shall be anticipated, assigned, encumbered, or subject to any creditor's claim or to legal process before its actual receipt by the beneficiary.

EXHIBIT 3-2 *(continued)*

7. Perpetuities saving. Any trust created by this will that has not terminated sooner shall terminate twenty-one (21) years after the death of the last survivor of the class composed of my wife and those of my descendants living at my death.

8. Powers of trustee. To carry out the purposes of this trust the trustee is vested with the following powers with respect to the trust estate and any part of it, in addition to those powers now or hereafter conferred by law:

a. To continue to hold any property, including shares of the trustee's own stock, and to operate at the risk of the trust estate any business that the trustee receives or acquires under the trust as long as the trustee deems advisable.

b. To manage, control, grant options on, sell (for cash or on deferred payments), convey, exchange, partition, divide, improve, and repair trust property.

c. To lease trust property for terms within or beyond the term of the trust and for any purpose, including exploration for and removal of gas, oil, and other minerals and to enter into community oil leases, pooling, and unitization agreements.

d. To borrow money, and to encumber or hypothecate trust property by mortgage, deed of trust, pledge, or otherwise.

e. To invest and reinvest the trust estate in every kind of property, real, personal, or mixed, and every kind of investment, specifically including, but not by way of limitation, corporate obligations of every kind, stocks, preferred or common, shares of investment trusts, investment companies and mutual funds, and mortgage participations, which men of prudence, discretion, and intelligence acquire for their own account, and any common trust fund administered by the trustee.

f. In any case in which the trustee is required, pursuant to the provisions of the trust, to divide any trust property into parts or shares for the purpose of distribution, or otherwise, the trustee is authorized, in the trustee's absolute discretion, to make the division and distribution partly in kind and partly in money, and for this purpose to make such sales of the trust property as the trustee may deem necessary on such terms and conditions as the trustee shall see fit.

EXHIBIT 3-2 *(concluded)*

IN WITNESS THEREOF this instrument has been executed as of the date set forth on the first page of this instrument.

<u> (Signature of Trustor) </u>

<u> (Signature of Trustee) </u>

Analysis of the living trust instrument. Let's examine the major provisions of this living trust instrument, section by section.

Trust Agreement. A trust is, in effect, a contract or agreement between two parties, the trustor and the trustee. Both sides agree to perform certain tasks: among other things, the trustor agrees to deliver property described in Schedule A (not shown) to the trustee, and the trustee agrees to hold, administer, and distribute the trust property in the manner prescribed.

In this living trust instrument, the trustor names himself to be trustee, and names a successor trustee to take over if and when he is incapable of performing, usually at his death, or sometimes earlier, at the onset of incompetence.

1. "Trust property." The instrument specifies that additional assets may be put in trust in the future, even after the trustor's death. For example, a decedent's will can be directed to "pour over" probate property into a trust after the trustor-testator's death. For a further discussion of the *pour over will*, see Chapter 10.

2. "Successor trustee." Since the trust instrument states the trustee's name in the opening paragraph, this section need only name a successor trustee. Naming a bank or other corporate trustee virtually ensures that a competent trustee will be available to serve for the life of the trust.

3. "Power to amend or revoke." This trust can be amended or revoked by a written document, signed by the trustor and delivered to the trustee. An amendment is similar to a codicil to a will, without the strict formal execution requirements.

4. "Operation of trust during trustor's lifetime." During the trustor's lifetime, the trustee is required to pay to the trustor all income at least quarterly, and any principal as requested. The reader will notice that the wording assumes that the trustor and the trustee are *different parties*. However, as mentioned above, many, perhaps most living trust agreements name the trustor to be trustee. Then, as in Exhibit 3-2, this paragraph would still be used, but would be meaningful only if the client became incompetent, thus requiring the appointment of a different, successor trustee.

5. "Operation of trust after trustor's death." This section is substantially longer than the Disposition of Property section in the simple will. It provides for several alternative outcomes depending upon who survives. First, the trust terminates if the trustor's *spouse survives* the trustor by four months, and all trust property passes outright to her.

Second, if the trustor's spouse does not survive by four months but one or more of the trustor's living children is *under 21*, the trust does not terminate and the trust corpus is not yet divided into the descendant's respective shares. Instead, the trustee is instructed to collectively use trust principal and income to provide for all the children's support, education, and other legitimate needs. Thus, the trustee has a power of appointment over the entire trust income and principal, with all living descendants named as permissible appointees. Then, when the youngest child reaches 21, the trust is divided into equal shares, one for each child then living, and one for each child not living but having living descendants. These descendants, an example of which is any living child of the decedent's deceased children, will share equally in the share of the child-ancestor. The wording implicitly directs a distribution by right of representation, also called "traditional per stirpes," a concept fully explained in Chapter 4. Each share is then distributed outright to each descendant when he or she reaches age 21. Thus, at the time of the splitting of the corpus, each child and any other descendant beneficiary at least age 21 will immediately receive one share.

Third, if the trustor's spouse fails to survive the trustor by four months and if no living child is under age 21, the trust may or may not terminate, depending upon whether there are underage descendants of deceased children. In any event, however, the trust estate is immediately divided into shares, and each child immediately receives one share. The balance of the trust corpus (held for these underage descendants of deceased children) will be administered in a manner (described below) quite similar to the way it is administered for a living child when under 21. As each of these descendants reaches age 21, he or she will receive an outright distribution of his or her share. Accordingly, the trust will terminate when the youngest living descendant of deceased children reaches age 21.

Finally, if the trustor is survived neither by a spouse nor any descendants, the trust terminates and the trust property passes by *intestate succession*, with one half to the trustor's relatives and the other half to the trustor's spouse's relatives. The laws of intestate succession are covered in Chapter 4.

The above disposition, via trustee, has much to recommend it over the will's provisions making outright gifts to the minor children, via a property guardian. A description of these advantages, however, will be deferred to the material in Part 3 of the text.

    6."Restriction against assignment." This is an example of a *spendthrift clause*. Without it, the laws of many states would allow trust beneficiaries to transfer and encumber their interests in the trust property and would enable the beneficiaries' creditors to seize trust assets to satisfy their litigated claims. For example, beneficiaries could mortgage their share of trust property, sell a future interest in it, and devise it. A spendthrift clause restricts such transfers. However, it only protects trust property while held by the trustee, not after it has been transferred outright to the beneficiary. For more information on the spendthrift clause, refer to Chapter 17.

    7."Perpetuities saving." This clause is included to prevent a contingent gift from being ruled invalid under current law because it vests too long after the death of the decedent. A further description of the common-law rule against perpetuities and statutory modifications to that rule will be found in Appendix 3-A.

    8."Powers of trustee." Since the trustee may manage estate property for a considerably longer period than the executor, powers explicitly granted to the trustee are usually more detailed than those explicitly granted to the executor. In addition to these powers, both the executor and trustee automatically have other implicit powers, ones derived from statutory law and from case law. For example, trustees have the power to defend against claims brought against the trust property, whether or not that power is explicitly granted in the document.

    This completes the analysis of an uncomplicated living trust instrument. This living trust is considered uncomplicated primarily because it terminates if the other spouse survives the trustor spouse. At that time, all corpus will pass outright to the surviving spouse. Like the simple will, it is created for clients with a small family estate, one for whom death tax planning is not usually a significant concern. A more complicated tax-saving living trust, one that continues at least through the lifetime of the surviving spouse, will be introduced in Chapters 11 and 12, which focus on tax planning for transfers at death.

    The third and final document, covered next, combines the disposition characteristics of a will with the many benefits of a delayed trust, one that takes effect at the client's death.

THE TRUST-WILL

At this point we discuss the trust-will, the third principal document of property disposition commonly prepared by attorneys in the estate planning process. In essence, a trust-will is actually one type of *will*: it serves to distribute the testator-trustor's probate property at death. But instead of transferring all the probate property to individuals, it disposes of some or all of it to the trustee of a trust which is newly created by the document. Usually, this trust is directed to take effect at the testator's death.

As a will, the trust-will must conform to all of the formal legal requirements for the execution of wills. And, as a will, it will contain all of those essential provisions found in any will-- such as the one that nominates a guardian of the person and estate of the testator's minor children, the one that nominates one or more executors, and the provisions that make outright gifts of certain property. Finally, as a will, the trust-will includes the entire section dealing with witnesses.

In addition to containing all of the provisions customarily found in the nontrust-will, the trust-will, like the living trust, must include *other unique clauses* that relate to the trust itself. Thus, it will include provisions for distributing probate property into the trust, for naming one or more trustees, for indicating who will be the trust beneficiaries, for specifying how much income and principal they will receive and when they will receive it, and for describing the trustee's duties and powers in connection with managing the trust property. All but the first clause just mentioned are also included in the living trust.

It should be noted that as a will, the trust-will is not an "agreement" between testator and future trustee. In fact, the potential trustee may not even be aware that he or she may be performing this task, and may not even be born at execution date of the trust-will.

Exhibit 3-3 presents a relatively uncomplicated trust-will.

EXHIBIT 3-3 Trust-Will

WILL OF WILLARD THOMAS SMITH

I, Willard Thomas Smith, declare this to be my will. I revoke all prior wills and codicils.

First: Family and Guardian

My immediate family consists of my wife, Sue ("my wife"), and our three children, Kristi, Heather, and Todd. We all reside at 8887 Custer St., Mytown, Anystate. This will shall apply to all my children, including all children who may hereafter be born to or adopted by me, and to their descendants.

If my wife does not survive me, and it is necessary to appoint a guardian, I appoint Curtis J. Quint guardian of the person and estate of each such minor child. If for any reason Curtis J. Quint does not act as guardian, I appoint Maria S. Cruise as guardian of the person and estate.

EXHIBIT 3-3 *(continued)*

Second: Executor and Trustee

A. Designation of executor I appoint my wife as my executor. If for any reason she does not so act, I appoint James A. Reliable to be my executor. If for any reason neither my wife nor James A. Reliable acts as executor, I appoint Third National Bank of Mytown to be my executor.

B. *Designation of trustee* I appoint James A. Reliable as the trustee of all trusts provided for under this will. If for any reason he does not act as trustee, I appoint Third National Bank of Mytown as trustee.

C. *Bond waiver* No bond, surety, or other security shall be required of my executor or my trustee.

D. *Taxes from residue* All death taxes imposed because of my death and interest and penalties on those taxes, whether on property passing under this will or otherwise, shall be paid by my executor from the residue of my estate.

Third: Disposition of Property

A. *Home and tangible personal property* If my wife survives me by 30 days, I give her all of my interest in our residence and all tangible personal property.

If my wife does not survive me by 30 days, I give my tangible personal property (except vehicles and boats) in equal shares to those of my children who survive me by 30 days. My executor shall consider their personal preferences in making that division. My executor has my permission to sell any of that property and distribute the proceeds to equalize the shares. My executor shall be discharged for all tangible personal property so given to any minor child if the child or adult having the child's custody gives a written receipt to my executor.

B. *Residue* If my wife survives me by four months, I give her the residue of my estate. If my wife does not survive me by four months, I give the residue in equal shares: one to each of my children who survives me by four months and one to the descendants per stirpes who survive me by four months of each of my children who does not so survive me.

If neither my wife nor any of my descendants survives me by four months, I give the residue of my estate according to Mystate's laws of descent and distribution, one half as if I had died with no will on the last day of that four-month period and one half as if it were my wife's estate and she had died with no will on that last day.

If my wife does not survive me and if any then-living child of mine is under age 21, then the residue of my estate shall not vest in my descendants as provided above; rather, such property shall be distributed to my trustee, to be held, administered, and distributed as follows:

EXHIBIT 3-3 *(continued)*

---

1. *Any child under age 21* So long as any of my children is living who is under age twenty-one (21) the trustee shall pay to or apply for the benefit of all of my children, as much of the net income and principal as the trustee in the trustee's discretion deems necessary for their proper support, health, and education, after taking into consideration, to the extent that the trustee considers advisable, the value of the trust assets, the relative needs, both present and future, of each of the beneficiaries, and their other income and resources made known to the trustee and reasonably available to meet beneficiary needs. The trustee may make distributions under this provision that benefit one or more beneficiaries to the absolute exclusion of the others. Any net income not distributed shall be accumulated and added to principal.

2. *Youngest child reaches age 21* When the youngest of my then-living children reach the age of 21, the trustee shall divide the trust into as many equal shares as there are children of mine then living and children of mine then deceased with descendants then living. Each share set aside for a child of mine then deceased with descendants then living shall be further divided into shares for such descendants, by right of representation. Each such share shall be distributed, or retained in trust, as hereafter provided.

a. Each share set aside for a descendant shall be distributed to that descendant free of trust if that descendant has then reached age twenty-one (21).

b. Each share set aside for a descendant who has not then reached age twenty-one (21) shall be retained in trust. The trustee shall pay to or for the benefit of that descendant as much of the income and principal of the trust as the trustee, in the trustee's discretion, considers appropriate for that descendant's support, health, and education. When the descendant reaches age 21, that descendant's entire share shall be distributed to that descendant, free of trust. If that descendant dies before receiving distribution of that descendant's entire share, the undistributed balance of that descendant's entire share shall be distributed, free of trust, to that descendant's then-living descendants, by right of representation, or if there are none, to my then-living descendants, by right of representation.

C. *Restriction against assignment, etc.* No interest in the principal or income of this trust shall be anticipated, assigned, encumbered, or subject to any creditor's claim or to legal process before its actual receipt by the beneficiary.

EXHIBIT 3-3 *(continued)*

D. *Perpetuities saving* Any trust created by this will that has not terminated sooner shall terminate twenty-one (21) years after the death of the last survivor of the class composed of my wife and those of my issue living at my death.

Fourth: Powers of Executor

My executor shall have unrestricted powers, without court order, to settle my estate as this will provides. In addition, my executor shall have all powers my executor thinks necessary or desirable to administer my estate, including the following:

1. To make distributions of principal and income on a interim basis to those entitled to it.

2. To sell, exchange, mortgage, pledge, lease or assign any property belonging to my estate.

3. To continue operation of any business belonging to my estate.

4. To invest and reinvest any surplus money.

Fifth: Powers of Trustee

To carry out the purposes of any trust created under this paragraph third, and subject to any limitations stated elsewhere in this will, the trustee is vested with the following powers with respect to the trust estate and any part of it, in addition to those powers now or hereafter conferred by law:

1. To continue to hold any property, including shares of the trustee's own stock, and to operate at the risk of the trust estate any business that the trustee receives or acquires under the trust as long as the trustee deems advisable.

2. To manage, control, grant options on, sell (for cash or on deferred payments), convey, exchange, partition, divide, improve, and repair trust property.

3. To lease trust property for terms within or beyond the term of the trust and for any purpose, including exploration for and removal of gas, oil, and other minerals and to enter into community oil leases, pooling, and unitization agreements.

4. To borrow money, and to encumber or hypothecate trust property by mortgage, deed of trust, pledge, or otherwise.

EXHIBIT 3-3 *(concluded)*

5. To invest and reinvest the trust estate in every kind of property, real, personal, or mixed, and every kind of investment, specifically including, but not by way of limitation, corporate obligations of every kind, stocks, preferred or common, shares of investment trusts, investment companies and mutual funds, and mortgage participations, which men of prudence, discretion, and intelligence acquire for their own account, and any common trust fund administered by the trustee.

6. In any case in which the trustee is required, pursuant to the provisions of the trust, to divide any trust property into parts or shares for the purpose of distribution, or otherwise, the trustee is authorized, in the trustee's absolute discretion, to make the division and distribution in kind, including undivided interests in any property, or partly in kind and partly in money, and for this purpose to make such sales of the trust property as the trustee may deem necessary on such terms and conditions as the trustee shall see fit.

I have signed my name to this instrument on March 19, 1999, at Mytown, Anystate.

_____(Signature)_____

Statement of Witnesses

The undersigned witnesses declare under penalty of perjury under Anystate law, on March 19, 1999, that we are over 21, that the testator declared to us that this instrument is his will, that he signed this will, and that he requested us to act as witnesses to it. We believe that the testator is of sound mind and did not act under fraud, duress or undue influence.

_____(Signature)_____

_____(Address)_____

_____(Signature)_____

_____(Address)_____

Notice that unlike the living trust established in Exhibit 3-2, the trust-will provides for only a *contingent trust*, i.e., a trust coming into effect only if both the testator's wife fails to survive and one or more living children are under age 21.

Further comparison of these documents will be deferred to the material in Part 3 of the text, with particular emphasis in Chapters 10, 11 and 12.

This chapter has introduced the documents used in the transfer of an estate, with particular emphasis on the simple will, the living trust, and the trust-will. The next chapter focuses on the actual process of transfer of the property disposed of by these documents, with particular emphasis on the probate process and its handling of intestate succession.

QUESTIONS AND PROBLEMS

1. (*a*) Name the major documents used in the estate planning process to transfer wealth. (*b*) Do they all require the same effort in their preparation? Why or why not?

2. Describe the five major reasons why a will might not be admitted to probate.

3. Name and describe the two different types of wills recognized by many states.

4. Can a valid will meet the typical statutory requirements for both the witnessed will and the holographic will? Why or why not?

5. (*a*) What is a simple will? (*b*) List its major sections.

6. (*a*) What is a codicil? (*b*) Why is it mentioned in the typical will?

7. (*a*) Why does the will nominate two types of guardians? (*b*) Must the probate judge follow the testator's nominations?

8. The lawyer for one of your clients advises against waiving the executor's bond. Can you think of any reason why? (Hint: consider whom a court might appoint as executor.)

9. What is the purpose of the clause directing that all death taxes be paid from the residue?

10. Why does the disposition section in a will often contain a survival clause?

11. Describe the contents of the "statement of witnesses" section of a will.

12. (*a*) Distinguish between a living trust and a testamentary trust. (*b*) Are all testamentary trusts established in wills?

13. (*a*) Of the three documents highlighted in this chapter, how many are wills? (*b*) How many create trusts?

14. Contrast the living trust in Exhibit 3-2 with the trust-will in Exhibit 3-3 in terms of:
   a. When the trust takes effect.
   b. Who is the appointed trustee.
   c. Whether the trust principal is subject to probate administration at the trustor's death.
   d. Who are the income beneficiaries.
   e. Who are the remaindermen.

15. (a) Describe in general how the living trust included in Exhibit 3-2 disposes of income and principal. (b) Which parties stand to receive a contingent future interest? (c) When, if ever, will each future interest become vested?

16. List the sections of a trust-will that are common to all witnessed wills and the sections that are found only in trust wills.

17. Finnegan, a widower, died last week. He is survived by the following family members (current ages in parentheses): Two children, Joe (26) and Gary (17). Joe has four children, Jackie (5), John (3), Carol (2), and Bob (1). Finnegan is also survived by three other grandchildren: Floyd (4), Fred (3) (who are the sons of Finnegan's deceased daughter, Kerri), and Kitty (9) (who is the daughter of Finnegan's deceased daughter, Shirley). Kerri's and Shirley's husbands, Kurt (23), and Rolf (26), are still alive. Joe has come to your office requesting some information. Assuming that Finnegan's large estate will be distributed in accordance with the trust-will contained in Exhibit 3-3, *who* will receive the property (i.e., principal), and *when* will they receive it? Assume that none of the living persons named above die prematurely. (Note: Determining *how much* property each person will receive requires further study of the principle 'per stirpes' in the next chapter. Question 5 in that chapter will ask you for some numerical answers.)

18. Write your own holographic will, tailoring the provisions learned in this chapter to your personal situation.

RECOMMENDED READING

*Buckley, William R. "Videotaped Wills: More than a Testator's Curtain Call." *Trusts & Estates*, October 1987, pp. 48-49.

*Beyer, Gerry and William R. Buckley, "Videotape and the Probate Process: The Nexus Grows" *Oklahoma Law Review* Vol. 42, 1989, pp 43-77.

Bruce, Jackson M. "Multistate Uniformity in Trust and Estate Substantive Law and Some New Wrinkles and Concepts: Revised Articles II and VI of the Uniform Probate Code." *1992 University of Miami Estate Planning Institute.*

*Calleton, Theodore E., and Bruce S. Rose. "Estate and Trust Litigation," *1990 UCLA/CEB Estate Planning Institute.* Discusses the will contest and its grounds.

Charrow, Veda R. "Write a Will that Can be Understood," *California Lawyer*, November 1981, pp. 45-62.

*Crown, Jeffrey L. "Battle Stations! Evasive, Defensive and Attack Maneuvers for Will Contests." *1989 University of Miami Estate Planning Institute.*

Dubovich, Debra L. "The Blockbuster Will: Effectuating the Testator's Intent to Change Will Substitute Beneficiaries." *Valparaiso University Law Review* 21 (1987), pp. 719-40. The type of will discussed would override joint tenancy and life insurance beneficiary designations.

Early, Charles E., and Robert L. Freedman. "Some Boiler Plate Pitfalls," *Probate Notes* 9 (1983), pp. 111-128.

Effland, Richard W. "Will Construction under the Uniform Probate Code," *Oregon Law Review* 63, no.3 (1984), pp. 337-380.

Fieldman, Leon. "'Simple Will' Can Be Simplified Further to Produce a More Concise but Effective Document," *Estate Planning*, September 1983, pp. 290-293.

Freedman, Robert L. "Use of a Super Will Can Reduce the Risk of a Haphazard Estate Plan", *Estate Planning*, March 1990, pp.92-3

Haskell, Paul G. *Preface to Wills, Trusts and Administration.* New York: Foundation Press, 1987.

Heaton, J. Andrew. "The Intestate Claims of Heirs Excluded by Will: Should 'Negative Wills' Be Enforced?" *University of Chicago Law Review* 52 (1985), pp. 177-93.

*Jenkins, Patricia H, "Undue Influence-The Missing Element" *Estate Planning, Trust and Probate News*, California State Bar, Fall, 1987, pp. 27-29.

Langbein, John H., and Lawrence W. Waggoner "Reformation of Wills on the Ground of Mistake: Change of Direction in American Law?," *University of Pennsylvania Law Review* 130 (January 1982), pp. 521-590.

Levin, Leonard. "Legal Ramifications of Unethical Estate Planning Practices." *Trusts & Estates*, October 1985, pp. 47-56.

Mucklestone, Robert S., and Lynn B. Squires, "Drafting a Truly 'Simple Will' that Can Effectively Communicate to Both Client and Court," *Estate Planning*, March 1983, pp. 80-84.

*Nash, Jodi G. "A Videowill: Safe and Sure," *Estate Planning* 70 (October 1984), pp. 87-89.

*Spar, James E. & Andrew S. Garb, "Assessing Competency To Make A Will" *American Journal of Psychiatry*, February, 1992, pp 169-74.

Walsh, Karen J. "The Statute of Frauds' Lifetime and Testamentary Provisions: Safeguarding Decedents Estates," *Fordham Law Review* 50 (1981), pp. 239-270.

Whitman, Robert, and David Hoopes. "The Confidential Relationship in Will Contests," *Trusts and Estates*, February 1985, pp. 53-55.

Wong, William. "Iron Curtain Statutes, Communist China, and the Right to Devise." *UCLA Law Review* 32 (1985). pp. 643-89.

The Rule against Perpetuities

The rule against perpetuities (the Rule) originated in English common law. The statutes of all states except Idaho, Wisconsin, North Dakota, and South Dakota contain some variation of this rule.[1] Charitable trusts are exempt from the Rule, making them potentially infinite in duration.

The Rule acts to prevent a transferor from controlling the disposition of property for an unreasonably long period after making the transfer. The classic, concise statement of the Rule, with this author's emphasis added, is:

No *interest* is good unless it must *vest*, if at all, not later than 21 years after some *life in being* at the creation of the interest.

In simpler though a bit less exact language, the Rule has the effect of invalidating a future contingent interest which does not vest within 21 years after the death of certain people alive at the time the interest took effect. This will require some explanation.

In estate planning, an interest in property can take effect during the transferor's lifetime, or it can take effect at the transferor's death. A transfer into an irrevocable living trust is an example of the creation of a property interest that will take effect during the transferor's lifetime, while a transfer into the typical revocable living trust and a transfer by will are examples of transfers creating interests that take effect at the transferor's death.

1. For a proposal to exploit this freedom by creating a generation-skipping transfer tax-free "dynasty trust," one that is "truly perpetual," see the McDowell article cited at the end of Chapter 12.

Thus, to satisfy the requirements of the Rule, the interest must *vest*, if at all, within 21 years after the death of someone alive at the moment of transfer into an irrevocable trust, or at the moment of the transferor's death, for interests created by will or by revocable living trust.

Interests that vest immediately when they take effect will automatically meet the requirements of the Rule. Thus, a transfer in a will "to John, for his life, then to Mary or her estate" creates vested interests for both John and Mary at the testator's death. Nothing (except perhaps the passage of time) will prevent them from receiving possession of the property. Therefore, the Rule need only be used to determine the validity of contingent future interests, that is, interests that are *not vested* when created.

The requirement that the interest must vest "if at all" means that a contingent future interest will not violate the Rule merely because it failed to vest because the happening of the contingency did not work favorably for the named party. Thus, the transfer "to Jane if she survives Margo" gives Jane a contingent future interest that must vest or fail to vest within the permitted time. Failure to vest will not violate the Rule, so long as that failure (along with vesting) must occur within the required period. Thus, Jane will or will not survive Margo. What is required is that the interest must either vest or fail to vest within the required period. If we can't be sure that either of these will happen, then the interest violates the Rule.

To qualify under the Rule, an interest must vest or fail to vest "not later than 21 years after some life in being at the creation of the interest". The "life in being" concept is difficult to explain precisely. For our purposes, however, we can say that the persons permitted to be lives in being are usually those mentioned or implied in the transfer document itself. Thus, for the transfer "to Carrie for her life, then to Carrie's living children," Carrie would be the sole measuring life. She is alive at the creation of the children's interest, and the length of her lifespan will determine the devolution of the property. Taking a second example, the provision that a trust will terminate no later than "21 years after the death of the last survivor of the class composed of my wife and those of my issue living at my death" explicitly creates the measuring lives to be used in the test. This "perpetuities saving clause," included in the trust-will in Exhibit 3-3, is a clause that can further protect an interest from vesting too remotely. It will be discussed further, shortly.

The requirement of vesting within "21 years" after the death of a life in being was originally included to enable the transferor to control the disposition of property for his or her life, for the lives of the children, and for the period of the grandchildren's minority, but no longer. For those individuals, all interests created which are contingent solely upon *parent survival* will usually vest within the required period. The children's interest will vest by the time of the death of the transferor, and the grandchildren's interest will vest within 21 years of the death of the last surviving child. All of their interests will vest within the required period. On the other hand, a great-grandchild's interest will typically (but not always) vest *after* the 21 year period, and thus will usually fail.

A violation of the Rule will cause that particular interest to be void. The interest will then revert to the transferor or the transferor's successors.

Let's consider some examples. In each case, assume that T has died leaving a will containing the following disposition of property:

EXAMPLE 3A-1 "To my wife, Mary, for her life, then to Bill or his estate." Both Mary's and Bill's interests vested immediately when the will took effect (at T's death) because at that point nothing except the passage of time will delay their possession or enjoyment. Therefore, neither interest is at any time contingent, that is, dependent upon the happening of a future event, other than the passage of time. Applying the Rule, their interests "must vest...not later than....". Thus, both interests are valid under the Rule.

EXAMPLE 3A-2 "To my husband, Bert, for his life, then to my son James, if still living, otherwise to Ron or his estate." Bert's vested interest is valid under the rule, for the same reason that Mary's was, in the preceding example. Both James and Ron have contingent interests in the property. Thus, we must ask whether they must vest within the specified time. Bert is a "life in being" at the time of T's death. Both James's and Ron's interests will vest, if at all (either one or the other will never vest, depending upon whether or not James survives Bert) within "21 years after some life in being". Bert is a life in being, and both interests will vest or will fail to vest at his death, obviously well within 21 years after his death. Therefore, both James's and Ron's interests are valid under the Rule.

EXAMPLE 3A-3 "To my wife Sarah, for her life, then to my son Greg, for his life, then equally to Greg's living children when the youngest child reaches age 25." Are Greg's children's interest valid under the Rule? Sarah, Greg and any children alive when the trust became irrevocable at T's death are "lifes in being" at the creation of the interest. But more children could be born to Greg, and they would not be lives in being at the time the trust became irrevocable, yet they would (by the terms of the trust) each have an interest that could vest, more than 21 years after the deaths of Sarah, Greg and any of the children that were born when the trust became irrevocable. However a later born child is not have been a life in being and that child's interest could vest later than 21 years after all the measuring lives are gone. Therefore, all of the grandchildren's interests are void, and T or his successors would receive a reversionary interest in them, which would probably mean the interests vest in fee in Greg. Note that had the trust called for the interests to vest when Greg's oldest living child reaches age 21, then all the children's interests would vest within a life in being plus 21 years, even if none of the children were born when the trust became irrevocable, since all children would be born within Greg's life time. The law tacks on the period of gestation to the 21 years.

EXAMPLE 3A-4 "...then to my great, great, great-grandchildren..." Assuming that T is survived only by children and grandchildren, it is possible that the great, great, great-grandchildren's contingent interest will vest after 21 years after the death of all children and grandchildren, who are the only apparent lives in being at T's death. Thus, their interests are void.

Here are two general *rules of thumb* when applying the Rule to transfers of interests to surviving issue:

1. Transferors usually can create valid contingent interests for their *grandchildren*, as long as the interests must vest by the time their grandchildren reach age 21.
2. Transferors usually can create valid interests for the *great-grand-children* only if they outlive all of their children.

Today, not all dispositions in violation of the Rule are invalid. Two types of *safeguards* designed to overcome the Rule are available to transferors. First, most states have enacted *statutes* that limit application of the Rule, or even invalidate it entirely. For example, many states have enacted a "wait and see" statute which, in effect, will find an interest void only if the interest turns out *in fact* not to vest within the required period. In addition, some states have a type of wait-and-see statute which states that any interest which actually vests within a certain period of time (e.g., 60 years) after its creation cannot be declared void, even if it violates the Rule. In 1986 the National Conference of Commissioners on Uniform State Laws approved the Uniform Statutory Rule Against Perpetuities, recommending that it be enacted in all states. It includes a wait-and-see period of 90 years after creation.[2]

Another statutory safeguard is the application of the "*cy pres*" rule to enable the courts to correct violations of the rule, if at all possible, so that the transferor's intentions can be respected. Cy pres, French for "as near as possible", is a principle used primarily in the context of charitable bequests, which permits the substitution of one beneficiary for another when the original charitable purpose is impossible, illegal or impracticable to carry out. For example, over a century ago, one testator left property in trust to fight for the cause of abolition. After the 13th Amendment freed the slaves, a court applied *cy pres* to permit the trust to continue by assisting freed slaves.

---

2. For a discussion of the proposal, see the Young article cited at the end of this Appendix.

A second type of safeguard against a perpetuities violation involves the lawyer's insertion in the document of the earlier mentioned *perpetuities saving clause*, similar to the one in the *trust-will* in Exhibit 3-3. Such a provision, however, may act to prevent the client from making an otherwise valid transfer, perhaps simply because the attorney chose not to test the interest against the Rule. In fact, none of the above safeguards is as effective as the thoughtful analysis and planning of an expert.

Yet, one must have some sympathy for the lawyers who use the clause. The Rule often requires complex analysis to test a given interest, and it can even puzzle experts. One state supreme court called it "a dangerous instrumentality in the hands of most members of the bar." It held that even though an attorney sued by a client for malpractice did in fact violate the Rule, he was innocent because he did not fail to use ordinary skill commonly exercised by lawyers![3]

The purpose of this appendix has been to present an overview of the rule against perpetuities, without exploring the complexities occasionally encountered by attorneys. This author believes that all members of the estate planning team should acquire a general understanding of the Rule, primarily because it constitutes a material constraint on the temporal boundaries of intelligent planning.

---

3. *Lucas v. Hamm*, 56 Cal. 2d 583. For a discussion of this case and a general analysis of attorney malpractice suits in estate planning, see the Burns article cited in the recommended reading at the end of Chapter 1.

QUESTIONS

1. What is the purpose of the Rule Against Perpetuities?

2. Helen's will leaves one half of her wealth outright to Vinnie and the other half in trust for Johnny, with all income payable annually to Johnny and, at the earlier of Johnny's death or his reaching age 21, corpus to Johnny or his estate. Does this will violate the Rule? Why or why not?

3. Holly's will leaves all of her property in trust, with income to her living children for life, then income to her then-living grandchildren for their lives, and then remainder over to her then living great-grandchildren. Who will get Holly's property?

4. How is the Rule frequently avoided today?

5. ("Off the wall" question.) How did our subject matter arise in the 1981 movie, "Body Heat," starring William Hurt and Kathleen Turner? Did the movie make any pertinent legal mistakes?

RECOMMENDED READING

Becker, David M. "Understanding the Rule against Perpetuities in Relation to the Lawyer's Role-To Construe or Construct." *San Diego Law Review* 20 (1983), pp.733-761.

Dukeminier, Jesse. "A Modern Guide to Perpetuities." *California Law Review* 74 (December 1986), pp. 1867-1913.

_____. "Perpetuities: The Measuring Lives." *Columbia Law Review* 85 (1985), pp. 1648-1713.

Jacobs, Frank D. "The Thrills and Chills of Simple Wills." *The Practical Tax Lawyer,* Winter, 1992, pp. 63-73.

Leach, W. W. Barton. "Perpetuities in a Nutshell." *Harvard Law Review* 51 (1938), p.638.

_____. "Perpetuities: The Nutshell Revisited." *Harvard Law Review* 78 (1965), pp. 973-92.

Waggoner, Lawrence W. "Perpetuities: A Perspective on Wait-and-See." *Columbia Law Review* 85 (December 1985).

Sisson, Roger G., "Relaxing the Dead Hand's Grip: Charitable Efficiency and the Doctrine of Cy Pres." Virginia Law Review, 74 (1988), pp. 635-54.

*Young, Raymond H. "Uniform Statutory Rule Against Perpetuities." *Probate Notes* 12 (1987), pp. 244-46.

— 4

Introduction to Property Transfers II: The Transfer Process

OVERVIEW

This is the second of two chapters that introduce the principles of property transfer. Chapter 3 examined the documents employed in the planning of property transfers. Documents covered included joint tenancy arrangements, property dispositions by contract, the will and the trust instrument. This chapter will look at the actual *process* of transfer of the property disposed of by these documents, emphasizing transfers taking effect at death.

The most common planning document disposing of property *during lifetime* is the living trust instrument. It directs the trustee to make the distributions, if any. The procedure is uncomplicated and usually unsupervised by the state. Thus, our study of the property transfer process will focus mainly on probate.

RATIONALE FOR PROBATE DISTRIBUTION

When a person dies, steps must be taken to transfer ownership of his or her property interests to the proper beneficiaries. Authorized agents try to undertake these transfers as well as possible, hopefully in accordance with the deceased's prior wishes. The documents covered in Chapter 3 are the legal embodiments of those wishes and are used as the basis for transferring the property.

Historically, each of the 50 states and the District of Columbia has assumed a significant role in the estate distribution process. Each has chosen to protect the decedent's property in two basic ways. First, each state has enacted succession or intestacy laws that specify *who is to receive* property in the event that the decedent died owning property not disposed of by formal transfer documents. Succession laws are designed to reflect the probable disposition preferences of decedents.

The second way in which the states have sought to protect the decedent's property is by developing probate administration procedures designed to ensure that the beneficiaries, the creditors, and the taxing authorities, *receive* their rightful share of the estate property with a clear title.

Transfers at death are subject to far greater state supervision for property that is held in title in a manner which does not itself indicate a method of transfer. Where title to property itself provides for transfer it will not ordinarily be subject to state supervision. Examples of the latter are *tenancy by the entirety* and title in *joint tenancy* with right of survivorship. The automatic ownership by the surviving co-tenants without the any right held by the decedent-owner's estate is said to be by *operation of law*. The state does not "oversee" this title transfer. It occurs automatically and instantly. An additional step may be necessary to clear title to joint tenancy property: The decedent's name will need to be removed from the actual document. But this is usually processed quickly by those authorities (banks, motor vehicle bureau, etc.,) keeping record of the title when a surviving cotenant appears before them with a certified copy of the death certificate.

In contrast with title held in joint tenancy, title that had been held by a decedent either as an *individual*, as a *tenant in common*, or as a spouse owning an interest in *community property*, in themselves indicate no procedure for title transfer, so the states have established a process to transfer title by reference to an independent, acceptably drafted document. The state-administered process of transferring such title is called *probate*. The transfer document to which the probate process refers is called, of course, the will.

NONPROBATE VERSUS PROBATE ASSETS

At this point, the reader might be asking where *trusts* fit into this transfer scheme. The answer is that it depends on the type of document creating the trust. Property that at the decedent's death is held in a revocable or irrevocable *living trust* is not held in the decedent's name. Legal title is in the name of the trustee. Since probate administration is concerned with transfer of property held in the decedent's name (individually or concurrently), property held by a trustee is not subject to probate administration. If, in accordance with the underlying trust document, the trustor's death triggers a transfer, out of trust, to the remainderman, the transfer process is uncomplicated and not supervised by the court. The trustee simply makes the distribution by deed or assignment, depending on the nature of the assets.

Suppose the decedent created a living trust naming herself as sole trustee during her lifetime and naming a successor trustee to take over at her incapacity or death. Will probate administration be required at her death so that a court can ensure that the proper successor trustee is in fact appointed? In most states, the answer is no; the trustee change is considered a private matter, not one requiring court supervision.

Property owned by the decedent to be transferred *at death* into, rather than out of, a trust will be subject to probate administration. In such instances the probate process is the funding mechanism for the trust. This will occur for all testamentary trusts because no separate trust exists prior to the death of the testator. Near the conclusion of the probate, the court order for distribution to the trustee has a dual purpose: (1) it serves as the trust funding mechanism and (2) it serves as the trust document since the terms of the trust, taken from the will are repeated as part of the order. Generally, when a living trust is used a probate is unnecessary, nevertheless, the trustor will have created a pour-over will, so called because it scoops up assets left out of the trust and "pours" them into it. This "pouring" is done through the probate process which concludes with an order for distribution to the trustee of the living trust. In this case, the order for distribution to the trustee of the living trust. In this case the order does not include the language of the trust because the trust is already in existence as a separate document.

Property disposed of by contract, including *life insurance proceeds* on the life of the decedent, and *retirement benefits*, are not subject to probate administration because title to those assets is not actually held by the decedent. Instead, title is held by the insurance company or the pension fund, respectively, and each has agreed to transfer title directly to the named beneficiary at the death of the decedent; the insurance company or pension fund makes payment to the named beneficiary in accordance with the payout option selected by the decedent or the beneficiary.

One study found that 40 percent of adults die intestate. In such circumstances, the state's intestate succession law will determine proper distribution. Intestate distribution is carried out by the probate process. In fact, probating an intestate decedent's estate might be even more important than for a testate decedent, to ensure correct identification of heirs, as well as to ensure distribution to them.

Figure 4-1 diagrams the probate and nonprobate interests of a decedent at the moment of death. The right side contains the nonprobate property, including interests in living trusts that are revocable by the decedent, jointly owned property, life insurance policies on the decedent's life other than those payable to the decedent's estate, and certain other nonprobate interests. Life insurance proceeds payable to the decedent's (probate) estate must, by definition, be a probate asset, since the probate estate will collect the proceeds and hold them pending an order for distribution.

FIGURE 4-1 Pictorial Representation of Probate and Nonprobate Interests of a Decedent at Moment of Death

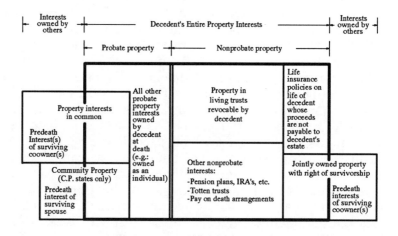

The left side contains probate assets, including the decedent's one-half interest in community property, the decedent's interests in probate held in common with others, and the catchall-- all other probate property owned individually by the decedent. Of course, the portion of interests held *by others* whether as tenants-in-common, joint tenants, or as community property are not part of the decedent's probate or nonprobate estate. One should also note that some community property states , such as California, no longer require a probate for property going to a surviving spouse whether by virtue of the decedent's will or by intestate succession. Those states may require a simple filing of a request for confirmation by the court of the survivors right to take the property, followed by notice to interested parties, a hearing and a court order granting the confirmation.

The logic of Figure 4-1 suggests a relatively straightforward *procedure* to determine the assets of a decedent that will be subject to probate administration. First, list all of the decedent's property interests held immediately prior to death, including all insurance policies. Then delete from the list all assets for which there is a nonprobate mechanism of transfer, such as property in living trusts, joint tenancy property, and interests payable to a designated beneficiary, such as life insurance, pensions, and finally miscellaneous nonprobate interests such as Totten trusts. What is left should be the decedent's property interests subject to probate administration, mostly property in the decedent's name alone or held with others as tenants-in-common, and for states that still require probate for community property even when it goes to the surviving spouse, the decedent's half of the community property .

So far, we have seen how the decedent's probate property is determined. The next logical step is to decide who will receive this property. To do this, one first looks to the will. If there is no will, the state laws of intestate succession are applied. Details of these succession laws are covered next.

STATE LAWS ON INTESTATE SUCCESSION

We have seen that a decedent who dies leaving probate property not disposed of by a valid will is said to die intestate, and that property will pass under the state's laws of intestate succession. Further, a person receiving property under these laws is called an heir and is said to inherit the property.

In determining who should inherit, state laws are designed primarily to dispose of a decedent's estate in a manner similar to the probable intent of the typical decedent. Thus, they usually give priority to the decedent's spouse, next to the decedent's issue, and, if there is no spouse nor issue, then to the decedent's other blood relatives, with higher priority given to closer relatives. A more detailed description of the Uniform Probate Code's intestate succession priority arrangement will be examined shortly, but first, let's explore two important underlying concepts in the area of inheritance.

Degrees of Consanguinity

Let's examine a family tree. Figure 4-2 depicts *degrees of consanguinity*, or blood relationship, between a decedent and the decedent's relatives. As we have said, descendants (issue) of the decedent include children, grand-children, great-grandchildren, and so on. Ascendants (ancestors) include parents, grandparents, and the like. Descendants and ascendants of a person are said to be in the person's *lineal*, or vertical, line. The other relationships shown are *collateral*, meaning that they share with the person a common ancestor, but they are neither ascendants nor descendants of the person, and thus are not in the person's lineal or vertical line. For example, a nephew of a person is not his or her issue, but shares a common ascendant with the person, namely the person's parent. Since a relative's share of a person's intestate estate is determined by the closeness of the relationship, the person at the "center" of Figure 4-2 is shown as the "decedent."

FIGURE 4-2 Degrees of Consanguinity

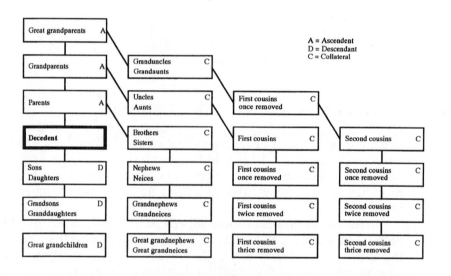

The most common method of measuring degree of affinity to the decedent is the civil law procedure of counting blocks along degree lines. For example, the decedent's uncle is three steps from the decedent, because we first count upward to the common ancestor and then laterally, or diagonally down to the box where the uncle is located. Figure 4-2 can be helpful in determining relative nearness to the decedent of distant surviving relatives, especially useful in those states that have not adopted the more restrictive succession rules of the Uniform Probate Code.

Per Stirpes versus Per Capita

If an intestate decedent's only heirs are one living son and two grandchildren, who are the daughters of the decedent's predeceased daughter, how much will each one inherit? Will they each inherit one-third of the estate, or will the son be entitled to a larger proportion because he is a closer descendant? To answer questions like this, we must distinguish between a per capita and a per stirpes distribution. A *per capita* distribution requires that all descendants receive an equal share of the property, or "share and share alike." On the other hand, a *per stirpes* distribution, also known by the more descriptive term *by right of representation,* may result in an unequal distribution, with larger distributions to descendants of a closer degree of affinity to the decedent than to those of a further degree. In the examples below, we'll contrast two different types of per stirpes rules, called 'traditional' per stirpes and 'per capita at each generation' per stirpes. Per capita is Latin for "by the head" and per stirpes comes from the Latin for "by the roots."

For a better understanding of the difference between per stirpes and per capita, consider the following description of the family tree illustrated in Figure 4-3. Cross-marks in the diagram indicate descendants who have predeceased the decedent. The decedent had the following descendants: Two daughters, D1 and D2, and four sons, S1, S2, S3 and S4. Only D1, S1 and S3 survived the decedent. D1 has three children, D1A, D1B and D1C, all alive. D2 is survived by three children, D2A, D2B, D2C, all alive, but the fourth child, D2D, predeceased the decedent, leaving no issue. S1 had only one child, S1A, who is deceased, but is survived by two children, S1A1 and S1A2. S2 had two children, S2A and S2B. S2A is deceased, but is survived by two children, S2A1 and S2A2. S2B is alive. S2 has no other descendants. S3 and his son S3A both survived the decedent. S4 and his daughter D4A predeceased the decedent, leaving a spouse but no descendants.

FIGURE 4-3   Example Illustrating Distribution by Per Stirpes and Per Capita

---

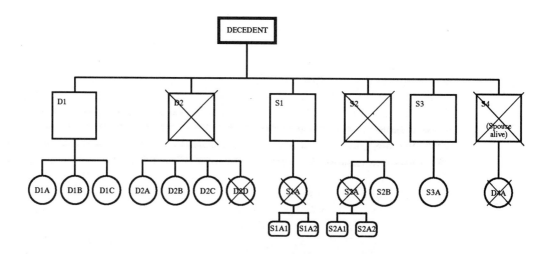

All three rules of distribution, described next, share one basic characteristic: the same people receive a share of the estate only the various portions change depending on which rule is applicable. Under all three rules, as one goes down the line of descent, only the surviving members of the *closest generation level* receive a share. In other words, if an ancestor is alive those in line below do not receive a share.

Thus, in our illustration, only the following nine descendants will receive property under any of the three rules: D1, D2A, D2B, D2C, S1, S2A1, S2A2, S2B and S3. Why won't the others receive anything? Either because they did not survive the decedent (D2D, S1A, S2, S2A, and S4), or because one of their ancestors (who were descendants of the decedent) survived the decedent (applies to D1A, D1B, D1C, S1A1, S1A2, and S3A).

It follows then also that no property will be allocated to any family line if all descendants in that line have predeceased the decedent. For example, S4's blood line, including D4A, and S4's spouse, receive nothing.

The three distribution rules differ, however, with regard to *how much* property each descendant will receive. The discussion below will analyze each rule separately.

Per capita. A per capita distribution simply requires that all eligible descendants receive an *equal amount* of the property. Thus, in the example, D1, D2A, D2B, D2C, S1, S2A1, S2A2, S2B and S3 would each receive a one ninth share.

Per stirpes. A per stirpes distribution would produce a larger distribution to those descendants who are closer to the decedent than to those who are further removed. Historically, two different forms of per stirpes have evolved: traditional per stirpes and per capita at each generation per stirpes. *Traditional per stirpes,* also referred to as by *right of representation,* has been used for hundreds of years. Under it, surviving descendants of predeceased children may take unequally depending upon how many in their family survive. *Per capita at each generation per stirpes,* which treats all members of each generational level equally, has become more common since it replaced traditional per stirpes in the 1990 revision of the Uniform Probate Code.[1]

Determining heirs' interests under either form of per stirpes requires a two step process. First, as in a per capita distribution, the property is divided into shares, one share for each of the decedent's predeceased children having living issue (two in our example-- D2 and S2) and one share for each surviving child (three in our example-- D1, S1 and S3). How these five shares are distributed for each per stirpital rule under the second step is described next.

Traditional per stirpes. Traditional per stirpes would pass each child's share of property to the closest surviving descendant(s) of the decedent. Thus, in our illustration, each living child, D1, S1 and S3, will receive a one fifth share and their descendants receive nothing. The surviving descendants of a deceased child share equally in their deceased parent's share. Thus, D2's living children, D2A, D2B, and D2C, will share equally in D2's one fifth share. They are said to "represent" their mother. Further, with regard to the one fifth share of the estate that goes to S2's descendants, S2A1 and S2A2 will share equally in what S2A would have received had S2A been alive at decedent's death. Thus, S2B will receive one tenth (one half of the S2 one fifth share) and S2A1 and S2A2, representing their father, each will receive one twentieth.

Summarizing, a traditional per stirpes distribution of the decedent's estate will be divided as follows: D1: 1/5; D2A, D2B, and D2C: 1/15 each (= 1/5 x 1/3); S1: 1/5; S2A1 and S2A2: 1/20 each (= 1/5 x ½ x ½); S2B: 1/10 (= 1/5 x ½); S3: 1/5.

Per capita at each generation per stirpes. Application of per capita at each generation per stirpes would distribute property similar to traditional per stirpes, except that when there are an unequal number of eligible children of two or more of the decedent's children, the shares of these children are combined and divided equally, and then distributed as if all surviving

---

1. UPC §2-106.

children and their descendants had predeceased the decedent. Thus, in the illustration, similar to traditional per stirpes, first, each living child, D1, S1, and S3 would receive a one fifth share. Next, unlike traditional per stirpes, because there are an unequal number of eligible children of two of the decedent's children (three from D2 and two from S2), the distribution to the grandchildren and great grandchildren will be different. The two one fifth shares meant for the grandchildren D2A, D2B, D2C, S2A (for representation purposes) and S2B are combined and distributed equally to D2A, D2B, D2C and S2B, and S2A1 and S2A2 will split equally S2As share, by representation. Thus each of the four eligible grandchildren will receive two twenty-fifths ($= 2/5 \times 1/5$), and each of the two eligible great grandchildren will receive one half of their parent S2A's two twenty-fifths share, or one twenty-fifth ($= \frac{1}{2} \times 2/25$).

Summarizing, a per capita at each generation distribution of the decedent's estate will be divided as follows: D1: 1/5; D2A, D2B and D2C: 2/25 each; S1: 1/5; S2A1 and S2A2: 1/25 each; S2B: 2/25; S3: 1/5. Notice that each eligible grandchild inherits the *same amount* (2/25s), rather than different amounts (i.e., not 1/15 each to D2A, D2B and D2C, and 1/10 to S2B, as in the case of traditional per stirpes). Whew!

Comparison of the three rules. One advantage of the per capita at each generation form of per stirpes rule is that it gives equal shares to those who are equally related. One advantage of the traditional per stirpes rule is that it passes the same share that the descendants would receive had their ancestors survived, and then died bequeathing the property to the next generation. One advantage of the per capita rule is that it treats everyone equally. This issue is important in planning because clients may strongly prefer one of these schemes over the others, and their will or trust document should reflect that preference. One survey revealed that most *clients* prefer the per capita at each generation per stirpes method. In contrast, most client's *attorneys* believe that their clients prefer the traditional per stirpes distribution rule. The Moore-Pennell survey, cited at the end of Chapter 1, found that 81 percent of experienced estate planning attorneys "often" use traditional per stirpes and 16 percent "always" use it. Only one percent use ordinary per capita at least "often" and only 8 percent use per capita at each generation at least that frequently. Most state intestate succession laws, including those that have adopted the UPC, do not use per capita, choosing instead for intestate succession one or the other types of per stirpes distribution.

As mentioned, all three distribution rules are similar in that they dispose of an intestate estate to the same descendants. For each, all descendants who are more remotely related to the decedent will not inherit if an ascendant in a generation closer to the decedent is alive. Preventing inheritance by more remote descendants has the advantages of reducing the number of heirs, thereby making inheritable property more marketable, and minimizing the likelihood of inheritance by minors and the need for court-appointed guardians to care for their inherited property.

Finally, answering the question posed at the beginning of this section, under either per stirpes distribution rule, the son would inherit one half and the granddaughters would each inherit one quarter of the estate. Under per capita distribution, each would inherit one third.

Intestacy in UPC States

We are now ready to look at the rules of intestate succession used by those states which have adopted the Uniform Probate Code. Note that the UPC uses the term descendant rather than issue, reflecting a modern trend to avoid a biological connotation and extend inheritance rights to adopted children.

The Code's principal intestate sections, revised in 1990, are reproduced in Exhibit 4-1. In general, Section 2-101 prefaces the next four sections, which specify actual succession. The intestate share of the surviving spouse is determined by referring to §2-102 for common law states, or to §2-102A for community property states. The intestate share of heirs other than the surviving spouse is determined by referring to §2-103. §2-104 covers survival situations. Finally, if there are no "takers" under the above sections, §2-105 requires a procedure called "escheat" whereby the property ends up going to the state of domicile. A more specific analysis follows the code.[2]

EXHIBIT 4-1 Intestate Succession under the Uniform Probate Code

---

2-101 Intestate Estate

(a) Any part of a decedent's estate not effectively disposed of by will passes by intestate succession to the decedent's heirs as prescribed in this Code, except as modified by the decedent's will.

(b) A decedent by will may expressly exclude or limit the right of an individual or class to succeed to property of the decedent passing by intestate succession. If that individual or a member of that class

---

2. For a critical commentary on several of these sections, see the Mora article cited at the end of the chapter.

EXHIBIT 4-1 *(continued)*

---

survives the decedent, the share of the decedent's intestate estate to which that individual or class would have succeeded passes as if that individual or each member of that class had disclaimed his (or her) intestate share.

2-102 Share of Spouse (Common Law States)

The intestate share of a decedent's surviving spouse is:
(1) the entire intestate estate if:
  (i) no descendant or parent of the decedent survives the decedent; or
  (ii) all of the decedent's surviving descendants are also descendants of the surviving spouse and there is no other descendant of the surviving spouse who survives the decedent;
(2) the first ($200,000), plus three fourths of any balance of the intestate estate, if no descendant of the decedent survives the decedent, but a parent of the decedent survives the decedent;
(3) the first ($150,000), plus one half of any balance of the intestate estate, if all of the decedent's surviving descendants are also descendants of the surviving spouse and the surviving spouse has one or more surviving descendants who are not descendants of the decedent;
(4) the first ($100,000), plus one half of any balance of the intestate estate, if one or more of the decedent's surviving descendants are not descendants of the surviving spouse.

2-102A Share of the Spouse (Community Property States)

(a) The intestate share of a surviving spouse in separate property is:
  (1) the entire intestate estate if:
    (i) no descendant or parent of the decedent survives the decedent; or
    (ii) all of the decedent's surviving descendants are also descendants of the surviving spouse and there is no other descendant of the surviving spouse who survives the decedent;
  (2) the first ($200,000), plus three fourths of any balance of the intestate estate, if no descendant of the decedent survives the decedent, but a parent of the decedent survives the decedent;
  (3) the first ($150,000), plus one half of any balance of the intestate estate, if all of the decedent's surviving descendants are also descendants of the surviving spouse and the surviving spouse has one or more surviving descendants who are not descendants of the decedent;

EXHIBIT 4-1 *(continued)*

    (4) the first ($100,000), plus one half of any balance of the intestate estate, if one or more of the decedent's surviving descendants are not descendants of the surviving spouse.
(b) The one half of community property belonging to the decedent passes to the surviving spouse as the intestate share.

2-103 Shares of Heirs Other than Surviving Spouse

Any part of the intestate estate not passing to the decedent's surviving spouse under Section 2-102, or the entire intestate estate if there is no surviving spouse, passes in the following order to the individuals designated below who survive the decedent:
    (1) to the decedent's descendants by representation;
    (2) if there is no surviving descendant, to the decedent's parents equally if both survive, or to the surviving parent;
    (3) if there is no surviving descendant or parent, to the descendant of the decedent's parents or either of them by representation;
    (4) if there is no surviving descendant, parent, or descendant of a parent, but the decedent is survived by one or more grandparents or descendants of grand-parents, half of the estate passes to the decedent's paternal grandparents equally if both survive, or to the surviving paternal grandparent, or to the descendants of the paternal grandparents or either of them if both are deceased, the descendants taking by representation; and the other half passes to the decedent's maternal relatives in the same manner; but if there be no surviving grandparent or descendant of a grandparent on either the paternal or the maternal side, the entire estate passes to the decedent's relatives on the other side in the same manner as the half.

2-104 Requirement that Heir Survive Decedent for 120 Hours

An individual who fails to survive the decedent by 120 hours is deemed to have predeceased the decedent for purposes of...intestate succession...

EXHIBIT 4-1 *(concluded)*

2-105 No Taker

If there is no taker under the provisions of this Article, the intestate estate passes to the state.

Intestate share to surviving spouse. In *common law states*, under §2-102, the surviving spouse is entitled to all of the decedent's intestate estate if the decedent leaves no parent or descendant, or if the decedent does leave descendants, but neither the decedent nor the surviving spouse have other descendants (e.g., child of a former marriage). Alternatively, the spouse takes the first $100,000 to $200,000, plus a fraction of the rest ranging from one half to three fourths depending upon whether parents or descendants of the decedent and/or spouse survive. An example of §2-102(3) is where the decedent and surviving spouse leave a child and the surviving spouse has a child from a former marriage. An example of §2-102(4) is where the decedent leaves a child from a former marriage.

Under §2-102A, the surviving spouse's intestate share in *community property states* is identical to that for common law states, except for an additional provision for the distribution of the community property. Thus, that spouse takes the same share of the decedent's separate property as he or she would take in a common law state. In addition, the surviving spouse is entitled to the decedent's entire half of the community property.

Intestate share to others. According to §2-103, other relatives of the decedent are divided into a hierarchical list of classes, corresponding to the degree of blood relationship to the decedent. Thus, to determine which class is entitled to succession of an intestate decedent's property, one would move down the list, stopping at the first class containing at least one living member. Distribution would be made only to members within that class. A summary of this prioritized list follows:

1. Surviving descendants, per stirpes.
2. Parents
3. Descendants of parents, per stirpes.
4. Paternal and maternal grandparents, and their descendants, one-half to each side, per stirpes.

UPC §2-106, not quoted above, requires a 'per capita at each generation' form of per stirpes whenever descendants inherit by right of representation.

Under §2-104, any heir must survive the decedent by 120 hours to take by intestate succession. This state-imposed survival requirement has the effect of avoiding double probate in some common accident situations.

Finally, under §2-105, if none of the above relatives survive, then the decedent's intestate property passes to the state, under the doctrine of *escheat*. In English feudal law, escheat meant that the feudal lord received a reversion in the property, either because the tenant died without issue or because the tenant committed a felony. In American law, escheat has come to mean a reversion of the decedent's property to the state because no individual is "competent" to inherit. In most states, including California, there will be no escheat unless the decedent is not survived by *any* kin, no matter how remote the relationship. The UPC, on the other hand, limits inheritance to the closer relatives, under the arguable premise that more remote "laughing heirs" would be receiving a windfall not ever intended by the decedent. One wonders whether the typical decedent really would have preferred leaving property to the state rather than to distant relatives. Because many people die leaving no close relatives, "heir hunting" firms use probate court files to help locate missing heirs, in exchange for a sizable contingent fee, usually based on a percentage of the inherited property.

The examples listed next should help to illustrate these principles. In each case, assume that D is a decedent who died a resident of a common law UPC state, and owned $300,000 in property. Relevant UPC sections are cited parenthetically.

> EXAMPLE 4-1 D is survived only by spouse and a cousin. Spouse will inherit all. [§2-102(1)(i)]

> EXAMPLE 4-2 D is survived by spouse and their five children, one of whom has a daughter. Spouse will inherit all. [§2-102(1)(ii)]

> EXAMPLE 4-3 Facts similar to Example 4-2, above, except that spouse also has a child of a former marriage. Spouse inherits $150,000 plus one half of the rest, or a total of $225,000. Each of the five children inherits an equal share of the rest, or $15,000. D's granddaughter inherits nothing. [§2-102(3) and §2-103(1)]

> EXAMPLE 4-4 Facts similar to Example 4-2, above, except that decedent also has a child of a former marriage. Spouse inherits $100,000, plus one half of the rest, or a total of $200,000. Each of the children inherits an equal share of the rest, or $16,667 ($100,000 / 6). D's granddaughter inherits nothing. [§2-102(4) and §2-103(1)]

EXAMPLE 4-5 Facts similar to Example 4-2, above, except that spouse survived decedent by only 5 hours. Spouse will not inherit. Each of the five children will inherit one-fifth of the total, or $60,000. D's granddaughter still inherits nothing. [§2-104 and §2-103(1)].

EXAMPLE 4-6 D is survived by parents and two children. The children take all. [§2-103(1)]

EXAMPLE 4-7 D is survived by spouse, a parent, and a sister. Spouse inherits $275,000 and parents inherit $25,000. Sister receives nothing. [§2-102(2) and §2-103(2)]

EXAMPLE 4-8 D is survived by a sister, and two nephews, the sons of D's deceased brother. Based on the required per stirpes distribution, sister inherits $150,000, and each of the nephews takes $75,000. [§2-103(3)]

EXAMPLE 4-9 D's closest surviving relative is a second cousin. All property will escheat to the state. [§2-105]

Each of the above dispositions of the decedent's individually owned property would still be correct if the decedent had been a resident of a community property state, and, in addition, the decedent's half of the community property would pass to the surviving spouse, with the result that the surviving spouse would end up owning with all of their community property.

Intestacy in Non-UPC States

The intestate succession laws in non-UPC states vary considerably, but all have a common thread: they are all more or less determined by degrees of affinity. For example, if an intestate decedent is survived by children but no spouse, the children usually take all. If the decedent leaves a spouse and children, the spouse and the children will usually share the property, with the spouse receiving from one third to one half. If the decedent is survived by a spouse but no children, the spouse usually receives all. If, in addition to the spouse, the decedent's parents are still alive, then in some states the spouse gets all, and in others the spouse shares with the parents.

Since state intestate succession laws do vary, the reader is urged to make an independent investigation of the succession laws in his or her own state.

Advancements

Sometimes an advancement will reduce an heir's intestate share. An *advancement* is a lifetime gift to an heir intended by the donor to represent all or a part of that heir's intestate share.

> EXAMPLE ADV-1 Mom died intestate, survived by her three children, A, B, and C. Her estate consists of $120,000 in property, not including her $30,000 cash gift to A three months before she died. If Mom's gift is treated as an advancement, the children will inherit the following amounts: $20,000 to A and $50,000 each to B and C. If Mom's gift is not treated as an advancement, each of the children will inherit $40,000. In either outcome, A will keep the $30,000 gift.

Whether or not a gift is treated as an advancement depends primarily upon evidence of the donor's intent. Nearly all states have statutes spelling out what is needed to prove this intent. Some, like those adopting the UPC, require that the donor's intent be in writing.[3] Some presume that gifts are not advancements, and others presume that gifts are advancements. These presumptions are rebuttable by contrary evidence. The rules apply only to intestate succession, since the law assumes that a testator wishing to reduce a beneficiaries' share will do so in the will itself.

LEGAL RIGHTS OF OMITTED AND ADOPTED CHILDREN

After-born, Omitted Child

Occasionally, a parent will die leaving a will that was executed prior to the birth of a child. Will that after-born child receive anything? Most often, yes, although the amount can range between nothing and a significant portion of the estate. In most states, including UPC states,[4] an after-born child is entitled to take the share he or she would receive had the decedent died without a will, unless any one of the following is true: (a) the omission was intentional; (b) the will left substantially all of the estate to the other parent; or (c) the testator made some other provision for the child.

The child's intestate portion can be the entire estate where the child has

---

3. UPC §2-110.

4. UPC §2-302.

no brothers or sisters and the decedent-parent was unmarried or it might be nothing as in community property states where the surviving spouse inherits all the community property. Of course, in a community property state the omitted child might have a claim to a share of the decedent's separate property.

An Omitted Child

An after-born child is one of two common examples of an omitted child, which is defined as any living child (or living issue of any deceased child) who was not provided for in the will. The second common example of an omitted child is one not named in the will, although alive at the time the will was executed. While some states still permit this latter type of omitted child to take an intestate share, others, including UPC states, do not. An omitted child or omitted spouse is referred to as a *pretermitted* heir.

The most common planning strategy to avoid an excessive inheritance by after-born children is to treat them similar to other children by using class gift terminology. For example, by using the terms "descendants" or "issue" in the will or trust to designate the persons who will inherit, rather than specifically naming children, will probably avoid the pretermitted child situations and thus keep property left to someone other than the children from being reduced by an omitted heir's claim.

Adopted Children

With regard to *adopted children*, many states, including those that have incorporated the UPC,[5] treat adopted children similar to natural children, so that an adopted child can inherit from the *adoptive parents* (and their blood relatives), and the adoptive parents (and their blood relatives) can inherit from the adopted child. Conversely, most states give the *natural parents* of a child adopted by another no rights to inherit by intestate succession from their natural child. Similarly, adopted children usually have no succession right to the interests of their natural parents. Called the "fresh start" policy, this rule breaking inheritance rights between adopted children and their natural parents reflects public policy belief that implementing a complete substitution of the adoptive family for the natural family is in the child's best interest.

---

5. UPC §2-114(b).

EXAMPLE 4-10 Sam and Sue placed their infant child, Gloria, up for adoption. Sometime later, Gloria was adopted by Kevin and Kay. If Sam later dies intestate, in many states, Gloria cannot inherit any of Sam's property. If Kay then dies intestate, Gloria will inherit equally with Kay's natural children. If Gloria subsequently dies intestate, Kevin and Kay's issue can inherit, but neither Sue, her issue, nor Sam's issue will inherit. Of course, any of these individuals may receive property if they are named in a given decedent's will.

The rule does not usually apply in the case of a "stepparent adoption," where an adult child is adopted by a stepparent, usually after divorce, or after death of a natural parent. An exception is made, allowing inheritance by these adopted children from both their natural parents and their stepparent, reflecting public policy belief that such children will be better off maintaining contact with their biological relatives.

EXAMPLE 4-11 Mike was six years old when his natural parents, Edith and Frank divorced. Edith subsequently married Archie, who adopted Mike. In many states, Mike will be able to inherit from both Edith and Frank, and from Archie, his stepparent.

Stepparent adoptions appear to be growing in popularity, concomitant with the rising rates of divorce and remarriage. Although direct data is not available, one study determined that 48 percent of all adoptions in 1984 were of children at least five years old. Many of these were likely to have been stepparent adoptions.

Omitted heir situations have a peculiar consequence: They result in the limited application of the intestacy laws to a decedent who actually died testate, I. e., with a valid will. Another example of the need for intestacy proceedings when a valid will exists is the situation called *partial intestacy*, in which a will does not dispose of all the decedent's probate property, as when it fails to contain a residuary clause. The latter is more likely to occur when a layperson does a holographic will than when one has an attorney draft the will.

LEGAL RIGHTS OF OMITTED, DIVORCED, AND DISINHERITED SPOUSES

Omitted Spouse

An omitted, "after acquired" spouse whom the testator marries *after* executing a will is usually treated in the same manner as an omitted child. In most states, the spouse takes an intestate share, unless the omission was intentional or unless the spouse was otherwise provided for. And, as in the case of omitted children alive at the execution of the will, an omitted spouse whom the testator married *before* executing the will may or may not take an intestate share, depending upon the state. In UPC states, that spouse would not take an intestate share.

> EXAMPLE 4-12 Prior to Claude and Betty's engagement, Claude prepared his only will. Then the couple married, and Claude subsequently died. Assuming no other relevant contract exists, if Claude's premarital will *does not provide* for Betty and the omission appears unintentional, the will can be admitted to probate and in many states Betty will receive her intestate share of Claude's property. In some of those states, if, on the other hand, the will *has provided* for Betty, she will receive just the amount devised to her, which could range between nothing and the entire estate. In others, Betty will still receive an intestate's share where the will has provided her with less.

Effect Of Divorce

In most states, a *dissolution of marriage* will ordinarily revoke a will executed before the dissolution with regard to the surviving ex-spouse's share. In effect, the surviving ex-spouse is treated as having predeceased the testator. Thus, in most situations, the property will pass to a named alternate taker, or, if none, to the residuary beneficiary.

In some states, divorce revokes the entire will. In contrast, for life insurance policies and retirement contracts, a divorce in itself will not usually have the effect of invalidating an existing provision designating the ex-spouse as a beneficiary. Nor will it invalidate a bequest to relatives or friends of the ex-spouse (unless the bequest is conditional on continued marriage).

Protection Against Disinheritance Of Spouse

Can one spouse totally "disinherit" the other? Most states have laws designed to prevent this. States handle the potential problem of a penniless widow (or widower) by enforcing one or more of the following concepts: community property, dower and curtesy, the spousal right of election, family allowance, and homestead property.

Community property. As we have seen, *community property states* protect spouses by attributing to each spouse ownership of one half of property acquired by their efforts during the marriage while domiciled in a community property state. Thus many, perhaps most, spouses in community property states own a nearly equal amount of property. Recently married spouses, however, will own little community property and the laws of the community property states do not require the decedent to leave the survivor any of the decedent's half of the community property. Nevertheless, some protection may be available under the Retirement Equity Act of 1984, which provides that after a person is married for one year to an employee who is a participant in a retirement plan the only payment option is a joint annuity unless the nonparticipant spouse consents in writing to some other option.

Dower and curtesy. Originating in English common law, a *dower* represents a surviving wife's life estate interest in a portion of the real property owned by her deceased husband. A *curtesy* represents a surviving husband's life interest in a portion of the real property owned by his deceased wife. In the few states still recognizing dower and curtesy rights, the surviving spouse would be able to exercise that right against the deceased spouse's property.

Spousal right of election. All common law states except Georgia have enacted legislation replacing dower and curtesy with a spousal right of election, which essentially gives a surviving spouse the right to a choice. Either the spouse can "take under the will," that is, accept the provisions of the deceased spouse's will, if any, or the spouse can "take against the will," that is, elect instead to receive a statutorily specified minimum "elective share," which in most states is that share the spouse would have inherited had the decedent died intestate.

The elective share statues are not foolproof, however, for at least two reasons. First, spouses may be encouraged to execute premarital and postmarital agreements *waving* their elective share rights. Such agreements are recognized in most states, provided that they are entered into freely, fully disclose both spouses finances, are not misrepresentational, and clearly spell out those elective rights to be waived. Second, lifetime giving strategies, either outright or in trust, may be successful in circumventing forced share litigation. While the courts in many states have tried to overcome these transfers, success has been spotty.[6]

The elective share provisions of the Uniform Probate Code were revised in 1990 in an attempt to overcome these deficiencies by being more equitable and less arbitrary than elective share statutes predicated solely on intestacy. They allow the surviving spouse a sliding scale elective share amount equal to a "percentage of the augmented estate," which includes the

---

6. For more detail, see the Zaritsky, Johnstone, and Kwestel/Seplowitz articles cited at the end of the chapter.

probate estate plus the decedent's interest in property characterized by right of survivorship (joint tenancy, etc.) held with a nonspouse, proceeds on certain life insurance on the decedent's life payable to a nonspouse, and many transfers of property by the decedent during the two year period preceding death if the decedent retained certain interests in the property transferred, such as assets transferred to a revocable trust. The percentage allowed ranges from 3 percent if the spouses were married less than one year to 50 percent for marriages of 15 years or more, with a minimum share of $50,000. These provisions tend to reduce the significance of the manner in which the decedent held title on the share the pretermitted surviving spouse is allowed to claim.

Family allowance. All states give the probate court legal authority to grant a family allowance, funds awarded by the court to support the decedent's spouse and minor children during the period of estate administration. This special award is needed because the court will ordinarily delay property distributions until it can determine that all debts can be paid. In fact, the family allowance takes precedence over claims by taxing authorities and unsecured creditors. Even a disinherited spouse or child might be given a family allowance. The size of the family allowance, which is usually paid in installments, will vary, depending on the survivor's needs and the size of the estate.

Homestead and other exempt property. Finally, most states protect surviving family members from being dispossessed of certain property by the decedent's unsecured creditors or by the terms of the decedent's will. The *homestead*, as it is called, usually includes the family home and adjacent property, subject to maximum acreage limitations. Some state statutes may also exempt other property, such as household furnishings, a vehicle, wearing apparel and the like. Depending on the state, such assets are offered the following protection: Exemption from forced sale while the surviving spouse and the decedent's descendants are minors, restriction from inter vivos alienation, testamentary disposition and intestate descent, and exemption from certain taxation. These statutes vary greatly from state to state. The UPC also grants a monetary homestead allowance of $15,000 for the spouse and $15,000 divided among all dependent minor children.[7]

Thus, most states have laws which prevent the death of one spouse from impoverishing the surviving spouse, however, surviving children are generally not afforded the same protection. In some other countries, such as France and Switzerland, most of a parent's estate must be left to the spouse and children. It may seem unfair that children in the USA are not

---

7. UPC §2-402.

similarly protected since spouses have the ability to protect themselves when they marry but children have no choice when they enter the parent-child relationship. In addition, young children generally cannot support themselves. However, our society's refusal to protect children likely stems from a policy interest in discouraging expensive guardianships on the assumption that the protected spouse will support the minor children. Nonetheless, this is not an ideal solution in a world filled with second and third marriages, where the surviving spouse and the decedent's children may not be related.

Next, we direct our study to the final major subject in this chapter: probate administration process.

PRINCIPLES OF PROBATE ADMINISTRATION

The principles underlying probate administration of an American decedent's estate originated in Old England, where public officials and the Church of England commonly took control of a decedent's property, or at least supervised those individuals taking control, and then distributed it to the heirs and devisees. The word *probate* stems from the Latin word *to prove*, meaning to certify the validity of a will. When a will is "approved," it is admitted to probate. Today, attorneys seldom use probate in this restrictive sense. In modern usage, probate refers to the entire process in the administration of a decedent's estate, including those estates of people who die intestate, and thus have no will to prove.

Probate has been said to have three main *purposes*. First, it *protects creditors* by mandating that valid debts of the decedent be paid. Second, it implements the dispositive wishes of the testator by *supervising the distribution* of estate assets to beneficiaries. And third, probate serves to *transfer clear title* to property, that is, it enables survivors to receive property in a form which is marketable.

Presenting a comprehensive overview of the principles of probate administration in the United States requires generalization since each state has its own set of laws, however, there are many similarities. Nearly all have at least one set of *formal probate* procedures characterized by the following four attributes:

1. Appearance in *court* before a judge.
2. Presentation of at least two *petitions*, and at least two court *hearings*, for which written *notice* has been given to all interested parties. (Interested parties are those who could be influenced by the probate process. They include beneficiaries, creditors, and

fiduciaries nominated in the will, including executors, guardians, and trustees.) Notice to creditors is usually done through newspaper publication.

3. Issuance, by the court, of signed *orders* as a precondition to the performance by the personal representative of certain major steps, such as the sale of real property.

4. Review and approval, by the court, of one or more financial *accountings* and *reports* on significant matters of concern to the interested parties.

These commonly found requirements reflect the strong interest each state has in protecting creditors and beneficiaries from mistakes in estate administration.

In addition to providing these elaborate procedures, about half of the states offer the option of other, *less formal* settlement procedures. These states have adopted all or most of the provisions of the Uniform Probate Code. Flexibility under the UPC enables the estate's interested parties to choose whether to be extensively supervised by the court in the usual manner, to be supervised only with regard to certain specific acts, or to be almost totally unsupervised. While the states that do not allow for less formal administration might still allow for some degree of informality, most of their estates must follow the traditional formal procedures.

This section will examine the traditional approach and the flexible approach to estate administration, partly to show that their underlying philosophies are very different, and partly to give the reader an indication of the current trend in probate reform. Actually, this reform has influenced all states to some degree, including those offering much less flexibility. The traditionalist states are deregulating, but in a more fragmentary manner, as we shall see.

Substantial Formal Supervision: The Non-UPC Model

A somewhat detailed study of the formal probate procedures imposed by a typical non-UPC state such as California can give the reader a reasonable grasp of the major requirements of a *formal* probate found in all states, although the details will vary from state to state. In UPC states the executor has the option of using the formal or nonformal unless another interested party objects, in which case the formal process is mandatory. Sections of the California Probate Code are cited parenthetically.

The formal probate process. After a person has died, the executor is expected to start the formal probate process as soon as is reasonably possible.

Petition for probate. The executor nominated in the will is required to petition the court for probate of the will within 30 days from the date of knowledge of the nomination (§8001). During that time, the will is also taken to the clerk of the superior court of the county where the decedent resided. California law currently recognizes a cause of action in tort for fraudulent destruction, concealment, or "spoilation" of a will.[8]

In addition, any person "interested" in the estate may make a similar petition (§8000). Where there is no will, hence no executor, the interested person is likely to be a close relative. Rarely is more than one petition filed. Upon filing the petition, the county clerk must schedule a hearing on the petition within 45 days (§8003). Ordinarily, the person nominated in the will to be executor files the petition, requesting (1) probate of the will, (2) letters testamentary, and (3) authorization to administer under the Independent Administration of Estates Act. Each request will be described briefly.

1. *Probate of the will:* If, after the hearing, the will is "admitted to probate," that will is thereby considered to be the only valid will and, except in the most unusual circumstances, it will serve as the blue print for distribution.

2. *Letters testamentary* or *letters of administration:* Also known as "Letters," this document, usually just one page long, contains the court's formal authorization of the person selected as the personal representative of the estate. A court certified copy of the letters testamentary, or letters of administration in cases where the selected personal representative was not named in the testator's will, empowers the personal representative to deal with third parties on behalf of the estate.

3. *Independent Administration of Estates Act*: The California Probate Code allows a somewhat simplified formal probate administration. Essentially, it eliminates the requirement of obtaining court approval for many of the common transactions undertaken by the personal representative. However, some actions are not exempt and require either express court approval or written notice to all beneficiaries of a proposed course of action, with a period in which to lodge an objection before the action is taken. (§10,400-10,600)

In addition to making these requests, the petition also makes several representations, including facts about the bond and the heirs and beneficiaries. A *probate bond* is required unless the will waives it or unless all potential beneficiaries agree to waive it (§8481). The bond protects the estate

---

8. *Estate of Legas* 208 CA 3d 1516 (1989).

from a financial loss in the event of wrongful conduct by the personal representative. If the personal representative misappropriates estate property, or loses it due to negligence, the bonding company must make the estate whole and then has the right to pursue the personal representative. This right of the bonding company to seek to recover the money it had to pay the estate from the personal representative is call a *right of subrogation.* Some planners do not consider a bond to be worth the cost. Ordinarily, the bond amount will be set equal to the total value of the personal probate property plus one year's estimated income from all of the probate property, the idea being the personal representative cannot run off with the real property (§8482). The bond premium, typically one-half to one percent of the amount of the bond, is charged to the estate. The petition for probate must state either that the will waived bond or that the requirements for a bond will be met. Where a bond is required, evidence that it has been issued is required before the court will issue letters. As a second representation, the petition for probate is required to identify all beneficiaries named in the will and any heirs at law even though not named as beneficiaries.

Two other forms are ordinarily filed with the county clerk at the time of filing the petition for probate. First, a *Proof of Subscribing Witness* is submitted, in which at least one witness to the will declares that he or she signed the original document, that the decedent appeared to be of sound mind and over age 18 at the time of the signing, and that the witness knows of no evidence that the will was signed under duress, menace, fraud or undue influence. If a witness cannot be found, or if all witnesses have died, proof can be offered by handwriting analysis. To make this task unnecessary, in the spirit of probate simplification, most states now recognize a *self-proved* will, also called a *self executing* will, that is, a will containing a formal affidavit as part of the original attestation portion of the will, wherein the witnesses state that all formalities were followed. This statement will stand unless an interested party challenges the validity of the will. At a minimum, this generally eliminates the need to locate witnesses to attest to the will's validity many years after the execution of the will, and in some states, such the affidavit creates a presumption that all formalities were complied with, putting the burden on the challenger to prove that such was not the case. The "statement of witnesses" sections in the wills in Exhibits 3-1 and 3-3 are self-proving.

The second form ordinarily filed along with the probate petition is the *Notice of Petition to Administer Estate*. This form contains essentially the same information as the announcement notice that must be published (three times prior to the hearing) in a newspaper of general circulation in the city in which the decedent resided. A replica of the published notice is shown in Exhibit 4-2.

EXHIBIT 4-2 Replica of Published Newspaper Notice of Petition to Administer Estate

NOTICE OF PETITION TO ADMINISTER ESTATE OF
JOHN PAUL JONES, aka J. P. JONES
CASE NUMBER: 111111

To all heirs, beneficiaries, creditors, contingent creditors, and persons who may otherwise be interested in the will or estate, or both, of JOHN PAUL JONES, aka J. P. JONES. A PETITION has been filed by Mary Jones in the Superior Court of Anystate, County of Anycounty.

THE PETITION requests that Mary Jones be appointed as personal representative to administer the estate of the decedent.

THE PETITION requests the decedent's WILL and codicils, if any, be admitted to probate. The will and any codicils are available for examination in the file kept by the court.

A HEARING on the petition will be held on 03-19-99 at 8:30 a.m. in Department 1 located at Superior Court of Anystate, County of Anycounty, 25 County Center Drive, Anycity, Anystate 99999.

IF YOU OBJECT to the granting of the petition, you should appear at the hearing and state your objections or file written objections with the court before the hearing. Your appearance may be in person or by your attorney.

IF YOU ARE A CREDITOR or a contingent creditor of the deceased, you must file your claim with the court and mail a copy to the personal representative appointed by the court within four months from the date of first issuance of letters as provided in section 9100 of the Anystate Probate Code. The time for filing claims will not expire before four months from the hearing date noticed above.

YOU MAY EXAMINE the file kept by the court. If you are a person interested in the estate, you may file with the court a formal Request for Special Notice of the filing of an inventory and appraisal of estate assets or of any petition or account as provided in section 1250 of the Anystate Probate Code. A Request for Special Notice form is available from the court clerk.

Attorney for petitioner: Gordon C. Brown, BROWN, AND BROWN, P.O. Box 0000, Anycity, Anystate, 99999-1111.
PUBLISH: February 19, 22, and 26, 1999.

The filed notice and the published notice are intended to announce the following to the public:

1. That a petition for probate has been filed.
2. That a hearing will be held.
3. That interested parties may attend the hearing to object to the granting of the petition.
4. That creditors must file claims against the estate within four months after the issuance of Letters.
5. That anyone may examine the probate file kept by the county clerk.
6. That the petitioner is requesting authority to administer the estate under the Independent Administration of Estates Act.

Copies of the filed notice must be mailed to all heirs and potential beneficiaries at least 10 days prior to the date of the hearing.

The hearing. The "hearing" for any particular probate estate may last only a few seconds. The judge gives anyone in the court the opportunity to object, but objections are rarely raised. Grounds for objection include the allegation that there exists a more recently executed will, or that even though the will in question is the only one or the most recent one, it is invalid due to a serious mistake in drafting, or that it was not properly executed due to the testator's lack of capacity, or to undue influence, or fraud, or mistake. If there are objections, the judge will set the matter for further proceedings to settle the dispute, which, if not resolved, can turn into a *will contest* in civil court. If the petition for probate is granted, the judge signs an *Order for Probate* that first states the court's findings, specifically:

1. All notices have been filed.
2. The decedent died on the specified date.
3. The will in question should be admitted to probate.

Then, the Order usually mandates that:

1. The will is admitted to probate.
2. The named personal representative is appointed.
3. Letters will be issued.
4. The personal representative is given authority to administer the estate under the Independent Administration of Estates Act.
5. A bond is or is not required.

Upon issuance of the Order for Probate, the executor secures his or her Letters from the probate clerk. As we have noted, letters testamentary is the formal court document, usually just one page long, that identifies the person appointed as the personal representative of the estate.

This completes the first stage of formal dealings between the personal representative and the court.

After the hearing. After letters are issued, the personal representative, usually in conjunction with the executor's attorney, undertakes the marshaling of estate assets and expected claims. Within three months of appointment, the personal representative must file with the probate court a formal document called *Inventory and Appraisement.* This form lists all probate assets showing their fair market value. The personal representative is permitted to determine the value of cash items (bank deposits, etc.) but other assets must be appraised by a "probate referee," who is a court appointed person located in that county.

The Inventory and Appraisement performs several important functions. First, it delineates those assets for which the personal representative is responsible. Second, as a public document available for public inspection at the court house, it describes the contents of the probate estate to all interested parties, including potential heirs, legatees, devisees, and creditors. Third, it provides information to the court to determine, among other things, the proper bond amount, the amount of the family allowance, and, if property is sold, the minimum bid that the court will approve. Finally, it may influence the taxing authorities with regard to valuation of assets included on the estate tax returns.

During the *creditors' claim period*, which lasts for four months after the date Letters are issued, each creditor is expected to file with the court or personal representative a document called a *creditor's claim form.* Failure to file within the claim period will bar later collection, unless an exception is allowed (§9100). Exceptions include:

1. Certain creditors who did not have actual knowledge of the proceedings (§9103).
2. Taxes owed (taxing authorities are not subject to the creditor's period (§9201)).

Availability of a shortened creditor's period is said to be a major advantage to the probate process for estates that anticipate potential problems with creditors. Additional details are found in Chapter 10.

During estate administration, the personal representative is responsible for handling the financial affairs of the estate, such as:

1. Paying bills (rent, utilities, property insurance premiums).
2. Accumulating liquid assets so that large bills can eventually be paid (e.g., taxes and legal fees).
3. Protecting estate assets from exposure to loss by insuring and safeguarding them.

Distribution of estate assets. The net estate will be distributed to the beneficiaries only after all matured debts and taxes, except the federal estate tax, have been paid. However, a partial distribution to beneficiaries may be made upon court approval of a *Petition for Preliminary Distribution*. Ordinarily, this petition is filed only after the end of the creditor's period. Further, the court must be satisfied that the distribution can be made "without loss to creditors or injury to the estate or any interested person." No more than 50 percent of the estate can be distributed in a preliminary distribution (§11,620-24).

"Final Distribution" is made upon approval of a petition, at a hearing, after the court determines that all current debts and taxes have been paid (§11,640). At the same time, the judge normally approves a final estate accounting, attorney's fees, and executor's commissions (§12,200-252). The accounting may be avoided by waiver of all of the beneficiaries (§933). After distribution and the payment of fees, the executor requests and receives a final discharge (§12,200-252).

The entire formal probate administration procedure takes from 6 to 24 months, in most cases.

Attorneys fees for California probate administration work are determined by statute, in the absence of a different agreement by the parties. Statutory probate fees are summarized in Table 4-1.

TABLE 4-1 California Statutory Probate Administration Fees

Probate Estate	Rate
First $15,000	4%
Next $85,000	3
Next $900,000	2
Next $9,000,000	1
Next $15 million	0.5
Over $25 million	Reasonable amount to be determined by the court.

California Probate Code §901,910.

These fees are based on the *gross* probate estate, not net of liabilities. California executors are entitled to the same amount (§901 & §910). California is one of many states that have statutory fees but for most states probate administration fees simply must be "reasonable;" specific amounts or percentages are not mandated.[9] In other states, probate fees must be "reasonable," but not in excess of a certain percentage, i.e., Iowa sets an upper limit of 2 percent times the value of the probate estate. One attorney in that state has indicated that local courts in Iowa typically and automatically grant the 2 percent ceiling, if the executor signs a "waiver of attorney's fee" (routinely done), without making any effort to determine reasonableness, resulting in a universal 2% rate regardless of time spent.

> EXAMPLE FEE-1 The attorney's fee on a $500,000 California probate estate is $11,150 [= ($15,000)(0.04) + ($85,000)(0.03) + ($400,000)(0.02)]. Additional fees will be allowed for "extraordinary services," such as sale of real property, estate litigation, and preparation of tax returns. The executor's commission will also be $11,150, resulting in a combined charge of 4.5 percent of the probate estate.

Sometimes, attorneys are asked by survivors to act as both estate attorney and executor. Whether they will receive a full double fee will depend upon several factors, including state law and the attitude of the specific probate judge. Some states, including California and New York, have made this 'double dipping' illegal, in the absence of prior court approval. In other states, probate judges frequently reduce the fee in such situations. A possible solution is for clients to negotiate probate fees

---

9. For a general comparison of probate fees, see the Miller article cited at the end of Chapter 10.

before death makes them unavailable to stand up for the grieving survivors.

Summarizing the essential components of formal supervision: Formal probate in most non-UPC states requires at least four document filings (petition for probate, notice of death, inventory and appraisement, and final distribution). It also requires at least two formal court hearings (prior to admission of will to probate and appointment of Letters, and prior to final distribution), one newspaper publication of notice, and at least one and possibly two accountings (inventory and appraisement, and final accounting). With these detailed legal formalities in mind, it is not surprising that many states have acted to simplify probate administration, a major example of which is outlined next.

We turn to the second major type of state probate supervision, the flexible approach under the Uniform Probate Code. A discussion of one non-UPC state's less comprehensive attempt at simplifying probate procedures can be found in Appendix 4A.

Estate Administration in UPC States: A Study in Flexibility

Except for their ability to utilize summary probate procedures for smaller estates and for property passing outright to the surviving spouse, personal representatives in California and other states, usually must use formal probate. In contrast, probate procedures in a UPC state are much more liberal, allowing interested parties to largely select the degree of supervision they desire. The basic choices are three: completely court supervised administration, totally unsupervised (informal) administration, or a combination of unsupervised and supervised administration. The UPC also provides a simple summary procedure for estates worth less than $5,000. It is basically similar to that of California's affidavit-of-right procedure, described in Appendix 4A. Thus, very small estates will often be able to be settled without any administration.

Complete court supervised administration. Some estates in UPC states will be subject to supervised administration essentially the same as California's formal continuing court supervision model, such is available in nearly all states. UPC supervised administration is a bit less regulated, however, because the personal representative is given greater freedom to act independently. Usually, there is no court involvement between the time letters are issued and the time that the personal representative petitions the court for closing of the estate. In contrast, probate administration in non-UPC states, as we have seen, requires court approval of all major transactions.

Most personal representatives of estates in UPC jurisdictions choose not to be subject to supervised administration. Occasionally, another interested party will request it because he or she does not fully trust the estate's personal representative and believes that supervision is necessary to ensure notice as to what the personal representative is doing.

Informal and formal administration. In addition to supervised administration, which is pretty much a court-supervised process, UPC jurisdictions allow two other types of procedures, called informal and formal administration.

Informal administration procedures usually require no court appearances and very little notice. The application for informal appointment is the simplest way for a personal representative to be appointed. The prospective personal representative files an application with a court registrar, whose role is administrative rather than judicial. Once appointed, the personal representative has the powers needed to perform the job, including the power to deal with creditors and distributees. The personal representative is required to give notice of the appointment to all heirs and devisees by ordinary mail within 30 days of appointment. Within three months, the personal representative must prepare an inventory of the estate and mail it to all parties requesting it. The entire inventory can be valued by the personal representative unless an interested party objects.

Even with informal administration, the personal representative must give formal newspaper notice, similar to the procedure for a formal probate, in order to limit the creditor's claim period to four months from date of first publication. Without published notice to creditors, the limitations period usually runs to three years after the date of the decedent's death.

Six months after appointment, the personal representative can apply to the registrar to close the estate, then after another six months, assuming no one has lodged an objection, the personal representative is discharged from all liability, except due to fraud and other major offenses. Distributees of estate property will continue to be liable for estate debts, unless the newspaper notice was given, until the **later of** three years after date of the decedent's death or one year after the date of the distribution.

Formal administration procedures under the UPC include the petition for *formal testacy* (proving the will), petition for formal appointment of the personal representative, and petition for formal closing. Each is undertaken in a manner similar to that for supervised administration and requires giving proper notice to interested parties, filing a petition with the court, and appearing at a court hearing.

The UPC's unique method of settling disputes has been described as an "in and out" method. During informal proceedings, a dissatisfied interested party can petition the court for a formal resolution of a controversy, whereupon the matter will be taken up "in" court. Once the dispute is settled, administration can resume in informal proceedings "out" of court.

In addition to the right to petition the court, interested parties have other protective remedies, including the right to request that the personal representative obtain a bond even though it was waived in the will, the right to request a restraining order to keep the personal representative from doing some act (such as selling a family heir-loom), and the right to demand notice; that is, to receive a copy of any filings or orders in connection with the estate. With the exception of the right to notice, the requests are subject to the court's discretion.

We can now see the relationship between informal and formal proceedings under the UPC. At each significant step in the probate process, the interested parties can elect a different degree of supervision. For example, the probate process may begin with an application for informal appointment of the personal representative. Then a controversy may arise that requires court resolution. Finally, the personal representative may feel compelled to file a formal petition for closing. Only in the unusual case will an interested party early-on petition for complete supervised administration, making the informal process unavailable. The underlying premise throughout is the desire on the part of all beneficiaries of the estate to minimize judicial supervision because it tends to delay distribution.

The movement toward reduced court involvement in estate administration has spread to many non-UPC states is due in part to the influence of the UPC. As illustrated in Appendix 4A, traditional states have moved to reduce court supervision by adopting summary procedures, set-asides, and procedures to reduce the personal representative's court reporting requirements. The overall effect of all state deregulation has been to reduce court congestion considerably.

The next chapter will require a change of focus, from the qualitative to the quantitative. It will be the first of four to introduce the principles of taxation.

QUESTIONS AND PROBLEMS

1. True or false: A decedent's intestate property does not go through the probate administration process. Explain.

2. Harry, who is single, has an interest in a house, some furniture, a car, some common stock, and a life insurance policy on his life, with Joe the named beneficiary. The *car* is in joint tenancy with his mother. The *house* is in trust, and the trust instrument says "for Harry's use for life, then to cousin Joe." Harry owns the *furniture* and the *policy* as an individual. With regard to the *stock*, Harry is an equal tenant in common with Sam. Harry's (valid) will says: "I leave my car, my stock, my life insurance proceeds and my house to Betty." It has no other dispositive provisions.
   a. Assuming that Mother and Joe are Harry's only living relatives, who will receive what if Harry dies?
   b. What will be included in Harry's probate estate? His non-probate estate? His testate estate? His intestate estate?
   c. Who will be an heir? A legatee? A devisee?
   d. In your state (or under the UPI, if state law is unavailable), will your answers to the above questions change if Harry was also survived by a son? Why or why not?

3. Describe your state's laws covering inheritance by intestate succession. They are usually found in a chapter of that state's probate or estates and trusts code. If unavailable, describe the UPC rules.

4. Mary and John are married residents of your state, and own the following property: As joint tenants, they own their home and a car. They own 1000 shares of ABC Corporation stock, worth $28,000, as equal tenants in common (assume community property if you are in a community property state). As individuals, Mary owns $350,000 in a money market fund and a life insurance policy on her business partner's life, having a current (terminal) value of $22,000. John owns an apartment house. How will this property be distributed, in accordance with your state's laws on intestate succession (if unavailable, use UPC rules), if Mary dies without a will, leaving only the following surviving relatives (unless otherwise specified, assume that all surviving children are descendants of both John and Mary):
   a. Only John
   b. John and one child

    c.   John and one child, who is the child of Mary and her first husband, Kirk. (Query: does it matter whether the child had been adopted, either by Kirk's second wife or by John, and does it matter when this adoption occurred?)

    d.   John and three children

    e.   John, Mary's mother and three children

    f.   John and Mary's mother

    g.   John and Mary's sister

    h.   John, Mary's mother and Mary's fifth cousin

    i.   John and Mary's fifth cousin

    j.   Mary's fifth cousin (Note: What happens to the home, the car, and the stock?)

    k.   There are no surviving relatives.

How would your answers to the above questions change if Mary died with a valid will containing a residuary clause?

5. (*a*) Based on the facts in question 17 of Chapter 3, for a $1 million estate, how much of the residue will each beneficiary receive, assuming that the trust-will in Exhibit 3-3 required the following alternative distribution rules:

    1.   Traditional per stirpes

    2.   Per capita at each generation per stirpes

    3.   Per capita

(*b*) Describe the advantages of each of the above three rules.

6. Assume that Mary and John own the property stated in question 4 above, that Mary and John are childless, and that Mary's and John's sole surviving relatives are their parents. In your state, or under the UPC, who will inherit Mary's money market fund account if John and Mary both die intestate and, alternatively,

    a.   John predeceased Mary by one year

    b.   John, in fact, survived Mary by 10 minutes, but there is no evidence of this

    c.   John survived Mary by six hours

    d.   John survived Mary by six days

7. Frank and Joan, husband and wife, had two living children, C1 and C2, four years ago when Frank executed his only will. The will leaves half of his property each to C1 and Joan. A year later, C3 was born. Today Frank tells you that he would like to leave all his property (owned as an individual and worth $180,000) to Joan when he dies. Advise Frank, being sure to tell him who would get how much of his property if he died now. Apply your state law or, if unavailable, the UPC.

8. Ten years ago George, who was single, executed his first and only will, leaving everything to his mother. Two years later, George married Karla. Today, George is in your office telling you that he would still like his mother to receive all his property at death. Based on your state law, or the UPC if unavailable, advise George.

9. Who is closer to you, your first cousin or your niece? Why?

10. Imagine that a close friend has died, and that you believe she named you executor in her will. Based on the laws of your state, or the UPC if necessary, what steps would you need to undertake, before and during probate?

11. List the purposes of the form "petition for probate."

12. Find, cut out, and bring to class a newspaper published "notice of petition." It need not be current. What is its purpose?

13. You have been asked to attend a hearing for probate. What is its purpose?

14. A client of yours shows you an "inventory and appraisement". What are its uses?

15. What is the purpose of the creditor's claim? Who files it?

16. Ordinarily, what must the personal representative accomplish before a judge will permit final distribution under supervised probate?

17. Summarize the minimum legal procedures which are involved in supervised probate in most states.

18. Why is probate in UPC states considered so flexible?

19. Describe the informal probate administration procedures under the UPC.

20. Fifteen years ago, your client's uncle wrote a will leaving his entire estate to your client. Five years ago, he wrote a second will leaving his entire estate to your client's brother. In each case, he asked you to safeguard the original. You believe that he made no copies. Uncle died last week. What do your ethics tell you to do?

21. *a.* To what extent do you think the laws of intestate succession in your state (or the UPC, if unavailable) are inefficient for parents of minor children?
   b. To what extent does a will leaving everything outright to the surviving parent solve the problem? To what extent do you think such a will fails to solve it?
   c. Can you recommend a better disposition?

22. Denise died recently, having many different ownership interests in property. Determine how much, if any, of each property below will be a probate asset in Denise's estate.
   a. An automobile, held jointly with Jake.
   b. A money fund account, owned by Denise as an individual.
   c. A life insurance policy (L1) on Denise's life, owned by Denise. Herb is beneficiary.
   d. A life insurance policy (L2) on Denise's life, owned by her. James, the sole beneficiary, died three years ago.
   e. A life insurance policy (L3) on Herb's life, owned by Denise, who is also beneficiary.
   f. Common stock, owned by the trustee of a living trust. At the moment of her death, Denise was trustor, trustee, and one of the beneficiaries.
   g. Commercial real estate owned in common by Denise (40%) and Herb (60%).
   h. Defined benefit pension plan. Denise was participant, and Bob is named surviving beneficiary.
   i. (Community property states only) Residence, owned by Denise and Herb as community property.

RECOMMENDED READING

(Anonymous.) "Inheritance Problems of Frozen Embryos (The Child *En Ventre Sa Frigidaire*)". *Probate Law Journal* 7 (1986), pp. 119-43.

(Anonymous.) "Social Changes Outpace the Laws of Inheritance." *Trusts and Estates,* April 1986, p. 22ff. (Interview with a New York County surrogate court law assistant discussing the impact of unwed couples and multiple marriages on succession laws.)

Berger, Michael J. "How Title to Assets is Held Can Determine Whether Probate is Avoided." *Estate Planning*, March, 1991, pp. 98-101.

Cicero, Jill M. "How to Handle Efficiently the Myriad Details Required to Settle an Estate." *Estate Planning*, July 1987, pp. 208-11.

Cohen, Donald G. "Adoption Can Have Unexpected Effects on Inheritance and Overall Estate Plan." *Estate Planning*, January, 1991, pp. 8-13.

Decker, Andrew. "The Billion-Dollar Picasso Estate." *ARTnews*, December 1986, pp. 81-99.

Dunham, Allison. "The Method, Process and Frequency of Wealth Transmission at Death." *University of Chicago Law Review* 30 (1963), pp. 241-85.

Falsey, Marie. "Spousal Disinheritance: The New York Solution--A Critique of Forced Share Legislation." *Western New England Law Review* 7 (1985), pp. 881-908.

Fellow, Mary L. "The Slayer Rule: Not Solely a Matter of Equity." *Iowa Law Review,* 71 (1986), pp. 489-555.

Friedman, Lawrence M. "The Law of the Living, the Law of the Dead: Property, Succession, and Society." *Wisconsin Law Review,* Spring 1966, pp.340-78.

Harris, Marlys. "The War of the Wills." *Money*, July 1985, pp. 150-63. (Regarding the controversy over the estate of Darryl F. Zanuck.)

Haskell, Paul G. *Preface to Wills, Trusts and Administration.* New York: *Foundation Press,* 1987.

*Johnstone, William S., and Susan S. Westerman. "Estate Planning for Spouses and Prospective Spouses-Drafting and Enforcing Pre and Post Marital Agreements." *Estate Planning 1986*, California Continuing Education of the Bar, 1986.

*Kwestel, Sidney & Rena C. Seplowitz. "Testamentary Substitutes--A Time for Statutory Clarification." *Real Property, Probate and Trust Journal*, Fall, 1988, pp. 467-534.

Mason, Peter I,. and Mark W. Weisbard. "The Pitfalls of Will Contest Litigation." *John Marshall Law Review* 16 (1983), pp.499-522.

*Mora, Abraham M. "Uniform Probate Code Revises Spouse's Rights."*Estate Planning*, May, 1992, pp. 143-49.

Nommay, Tina. "One Way to Insure Inheritance Is Murder, or Is It?" *Vallparaiso University Law Review* 21 (1987) pp. 763-96. (Review of state statutes prohibiting a killer from inheriting or receiving a legacy, etc., from the victim, and a proposal for change.)

Pennfield, Edward B. "Fiduciaries Administrative Duties Cover a Wide Range of Responsibilities." *Estate Planning*, March, 1991, pp. 74-79.

Stein, Robert A. "Probate Administration Study: Some Emerging Conclusions." *Real Property, Probate and Trust Journal* 9 (Winter 1974), pp.596-610.

Stein, Robert A. and Ian G. Fierstein. "The Demography of Probate Administration." *Baltimore Law Review* 15 (1985), pp. 54-107. (A detailed survey of probate administration practices in the states of California, Florida, Maryland, Massachusetts, and Texas, based on data gathered in 1976.)

Sugayan, Catalina. "Abandoning Ad Valorem Estate Administration Charges." *Probate Law Journal* 7 (1985), pp. 33-60.

Tucker, James B. "If a Will Is Contested." *California State Bar Journal,* September/October 1975, pp.382-412.

Wellman, Richard V. "The New Uniform Probate Code." *American Bar Association Journal* 56 (July 1970), pp. 636-40.

_____.*Palmer's Trusts and Succession.* 4th Ed. St. Paul Minn.: West Publishing, 1983, chap.1.

_____."Recent Developments in the Struggle for Probate Reform." *Michigan Law Review* 79 (January 1981), pp. 501-49.

_____."Solving the Probate Mess." *Graduate Woman*, January/February 1980, pp. 15-17.

*Zaritsky, Howard M. "Attack of the Surviving Spouse: The Evolving Problems of the Elective Share." University of Miami Institute on Estate Planning, 1989.

Summary Probate Proceedings in California: One Non-UPC State's Alternatives to Formal Probate

As we have seen, formal probate typically requires at least four document filings, two formal court hearings, one newspaper publication of notice, and at least one and possibly two accountings. Although these procedures were allegedly designed to protect estate assets and ensure their proper distribution, many are considered unnecessary in rather simple estate situations. Over the years, non-UPC states have also simplified probate procedures for less complicated estates.

This appendix will summarize the progress of probate simplification in California. Presently, California has two major types of "summary probate", as it is called, neither of which require newspaper notice, and both of which require not more than one petition and hearing. The two types, discussed next, are the affidavit of right and the summary distribution to the surviving spouse. As you read this, keep in mind that many UPC states, perhaps your own, have procedures similar to these.

AFFIDAVIT OF RIGHT [1]

The affidavit of right is a procedure that acknowledges a valid will (or the application of the laws of intestacy) and permits a settlement of the decedent's affairs more rapidly than formal probate. This action speeds up the transfer of property to the named heir. Essentially, an affidavit, signed by the heir, is presented to the person or institution holding the property or title to it. That party is then required to turn ownership of the property over to the heir, who becomes liable on the assets for any liens, etc. The affidavit of right for *personal property* can only be used if the decedent's total estate does not exceed $60,000, an amount that does not include joint tenancy property, life estate interests, a motor vehicle or mobile home, $5,000 in salary, and any property subject to a summary distribution which is described below. The affidavit of right for *real property* can only be used if the decedent owned no more than $10,000 in California real property. A court-certified affidavit is issued by the county clerk to the county recorder.

SUMMARY DISTRIBUTION TO SURVIVING SPOUSE [2]

Married spouses in California frequently own separate and community property which at death will wind up passing outright to the surviving spouse, either because the spouse was named in the will or by the operation of the laws of intestate succession. In two important ways, California probate law has simplified the administration requirements of such property.

Spousal Set-Aside

First, the surviving spouse may elect to have separate or community property "set aside," that is, pass to him or her without formal probate administration.

---

1. California Probate Code §13,100-209.

2. California Probate Code §13,500-660.

Summary Distribution Petition

Second, the surviving spouse can also elect, under a summary distribution, one court hearing for the purpose of obtaining written confirmation by the court that such property has in fact passed to him or her. This may be helpful to clear title and to distinctly isolate that property which is not subject to formal probate administration. Essentially, at the hearing the judge confirms that the property is, in fact, either community or separate property, and that it should, in fact, pass to the surviving spouse. The judge will sign an order confirming these findings. A summary distribution petition may be filed regardless of the amount or type of other property owned by the decedent at death, and therefore formal probate may be required for other assets. Further, an affidavit of right and a summary distribution petition may both be used in the same estate, provided that all of the requirements are met.

Attorney fees for summary distribution legal work are not set by statute, but in practice these fees are substantially less than those for formal probate. One third of the statutory fee is an amount commonly charged and many attorneys will do this for an hourly fee that is substantially cheaper for large estates. Even less is charged for a spousal set-aside without the petition for summary distribution.

Introduction To Federal Unified Wealth Transfer Taxation

OVERVIEW

This chapter is the first of four covering federal taxation, and the first of three surveying the federal taxation of wealth transfers. Since individual wealth can be transferred during lifetime and at death, we must examine the tax effects on both types of transfers. And since individuals may be able to save taxes by transferring wealth directly for the benefit of grandchildren, we must study the constraints imposed by the federal generation-skipping transfer tax, introduced at the end of Chapter 7. This first chapter will emphasize the quantitative nature of gift and estate taxes, and will show how these systems are similar (or "unified") and how they differ.

BRIEF HISTORY

Congress first created a wealth transfer tax during the Civil War, with the enactment of an inheritance tax. It was repealed shortly after the war. In 1916, Congress passed an estate tax, with rates ranging between 1 and 10 percent. As a tax only on transfers at death, it was relatively easy to circumvent through the use of lifetime gifts which, at death, had the effect of reducing the size of a person's taxable estate. In 1924, Congress plugged this loophole somewhat by enacting a gift tax, which was repealed in 1926 and reenacted in 1932, applicable to gifts made after June 5 of that year.

To gauge more clearly the extent to which the adoption of the gift tax discouraged planning, we must distinguish tax rate planning from planning in general. First, with regard to tax *rate* planning, lifetime gift strategies were worth pursuing up to 1977, because up to then gift tax *rates* were twenty-five percent lower than estate tax rates. With the passage of the Tax Reform Act of 1976, a single "unified" rate schedule was adopted taxing lifetime gifts and death transfers at the same rate.

Second, with regard to gift *planning in general*, we shall see in detail later in the text that there remain several excellent tax reasons for making lifetime gifts. They include exploiting the annual exclusion, avoiding grossing up, and freezing the estate tax value.

UNIFIED TRANSFER TAX FRAMEWORK

An overview model for federal *gift* taxation is presented in Table 5-1. The general scheme for calculating the gift tax can be described as follows: Annual exclusions and deductions are subtracted from the current year's gross gifts to arrive at current taxable gifts. Adding taxable gifts in prior years determines total taxable gifts. Then from the tentative tax on total taxable gifts is subtracted the tentative tax on prior taxable gifts, leaving the tentative tax on current taxable gifts. Finally, the unused unified credit is subtracted to arrive at the gift tax that must be paid.

The scheme is simpler for a one-gift, individual donor who has made no prior taxable gifts, and can be summarized by the following steps: Subtract the annual exclusion ($10,000) from the amount of the gift and calculate a tentative tax on that amount. The net tax is equal to the tentative tax reduced by the unified credit.

Appendix D at the end of the text includes a copy of the Federal Gift Tax Return, Form 709, which should help to illustrate the gift tax scheme. The *donor* is responsible for filing the return and paying the tax. However, if the donor fails to do so, the donee is secondarily liable for payment of the tax.

TABLE 5-1 Federal Gift Tax (Form 709) Overview Model

Total current year's gross gifts	$xxx,xxx.		
Less: Annual exclusion(s) and deductions	xxx,xxx.		
Equals: Current taxable gifts		xxx,xxx.	
Plus: Total prior taxable gifts		xx,xxx.	
Equals: Total (current and prior) taxable gifts			xxx,xxx.
Calculate: Tentative tax on total taxable gifts			xx,xxx.
Less: Tentative tax on total prior taxable gifts			x,xxx.
Leaves: Tentative tax on current taxable gifts			x,xxx.
Less: Unused unified credit			xx,xxx.
Equals: Current gift tax			$xx,xxx.

An overview model for federal *estate* (death) taxation is presented in Table 5-2.

TABLE 5-2 Federal Estate Tax (Form 706) Overview Model

Gross estate	$xxx,xxx.		
Less: Total deductions	xxx,xxx.		
Leaves: Taxable estate	xxx,xxx.		
Plus: Adjusted taxable gifts (post-76)	xx,xxx.		
Equals: Estate tax base			xxx,xxx.
Calculate: Tentative estate tax			xxx,xxx.
Less: Gift taxes payable on adjusted taxable gifts			xxx,xxx.
Less: Unified credit			xxx,xxx.
Less: State death tax credit			xx,xxx.
Less: Other credits			xx,xxx.
Equals: Net estate tax			$xxx,xxx.

The scheme for calculating the net federal *estate* tax can be described as follows: Deductions are subtracted from the gross estate to arrive at the taxable estate. Then lifetime ("adjusted") taxable gifts are added to determine the estate tax base, on which a tentative tax is calculated, using the unified rates found in the tax table. Technically, line 5 on the Form 706 has no title. It simply says "add lines 3 and 4." We'll call it the *estate tax base* because that title describes its content: the sum of the net estate transfered at death (line 3) and lifetime (line 4) taxable gifts that constitute the base from which the tentative tax is calculated.

Finally, various credits are subtracted, including the full unified credit, to arrive at the net estate tax. Appendix C at the end of the text includes a copy of the multi-paged Federal Estate Tax Return, Form 706, which illustrates the estate tax structure and the actual form used for tax compliance. The *executor* of the decedent's estate is responsible for filing the estate tax return and paying the tax. According to the IRS, about 50,000 estate tax returns were filed in 1990, of which about 45 percent owed a tax.

Obviously, gift and estate taxation is somewhat complicated and will need careful explanation. These tax models have been presented at the outset not to overwhelm, but simply to provide the reader with the overall scheme as reference while reading this and the next two chapters. Each of the major components will be introduced sequentially, with illustrations.

For the moment, the reader should simply be aware of five computational steps that federal gift taxation and estate taxation share in common. First, one starts with the fair market value of the *property transferred*. Second, *deductions* are subtracted before arriving at the taxable amount. Third, certain *prior lifetime gifts* are added to the current taxable amount. Fourth, the *tentative tax* on the total taxable amount is calculated for both the gift tax and the estate tax from the same unified transfer tax rate schedule. Fifth, because certain prior gifts are included in the tax base, a credit is allowed for the gift tax *on prior gifts* to prevent double taxation. These are represented by "tentative tax on total prior taxable gifts" in Table 5-1 and by "gift taxes payable on adjusted taxable gifts" in Table 5-2. Finally, one or more *credits*, including a "unified credit," are subtracted from the tentative tax to arrive at the net tax that must actually be paid..

UNIFIED RATE SCHEDULE

Table 5-3 depicts the Federal Unified Tax Rate Schedule presently in effect. A more complete table showing the changes in maximum rates since 1977 appears as Table 4 in Appendix A at the end of the book.

TABLE 5-3 Federal Unified Transfer-Tax Rates - Since 1/1/84

If the Amount is:		Tentative Tax		
Over	But Not Over	Base Amount +	Percent	On Excess Over
$ 0.	$ 10,000.	$ 0.	18.0%	$ 0.
10,000.	20,000.	1,800.	20.0	10,000.
20,000.	40,000.	3,800.	22.0	20,000.
40,000.	60,000.	8,200.	24.0	40,000.
60,000.	80,000.	13,000.	26.0	60,000.
80,000.	100,000.	18,200.	28.0	80,000.
100,000.	150,000.	23,800.	30.0	100,000.
150,000.	250,000.	38,800.	32.0	150,000.
250,000.	500,000.	70,800.	34.0	250,000.
500,000.	750,000.	155,800.	37.0	500,000.
750,000.	1,000,000.	248,300.	39.0	750,000.
1,000,000.	1,250,000.	345,800.	41.0	1,000,000.
1,250,000.	1,500,000.	448,300.	43.0	1,250,000.
1,500,000.	2,000,000.	555,800.	45.0	1,500,000.
2,000,000.	2,500,000.	780,800.	49.0	2,000,000.
2,500,000.	3,000,000.	1,025,800.	53.0	2,500,000.
3,000,000.	10,000,000.	1,290,800.	55.0	3,000,000.
10,000,000.	21,040,000.	5,140,800.	60.0*	10,000,000.
21,040,000.	-	11,764,800.	55.0	21,040,000.

(Post-87, between $10 million and $21,040,000 the rate jumps to 60% due to a 5% surcharge)

As a result of the Economic Recovery Act of 1981 (ERTA), revised by the Tax Reform Act of 1984 and the Revenue Act of 1987, rates on amounts over $2.5 million have been decreasing periodically. Hence, the schedule shown as Table 4 at the end of the book is divided into five parts. The first part shows rates for *all* transfer years after 1976 for taxable amounts up to $2.5 million. The next four parts represent transition rates on amounts over $2.5 million, which apply for transfers during 1977-81, 1982, 1983, and 1984 and thereafter.

The Revenue Act of 1987 phased out the transfer tax benefits of the lower rates and the unified credit (described below) for amounts exceeding $10 million for transfers after December 31, 1987. The net effect is a "recapturing" of the taxes saved by the lower rates and the unified credit. This recapture is implemented with the imposition of an additional 5 percent tax ("bubble") on amounts between $10 million and $21,040,000.[1] Thus, the effective marginal FET rate for all transfers of between $10 million and $21,040,000 is 60 percent.

A few examples will demonstrate the application of the unified rates. The facts in these examples are intended to be sufficiently general to apply to both lifetime gifts and transfers at death.

EXAMPLE 5-1 The *tentative tax* on the taxable amount $600,000 is $192,800. This represents the sum of $155,800 plus $37,000, which is 37 percent of $100,000, the excess of $600,000 over $500,000. Since the same rate table applies to all years for amounts up to $2.5 million, $192,800 would be the tentative tax on the amount $600,000 for all years after 1976.

EXAMPLE 5-2 The *tentative tax* on the taxable amount $3,250,000 in any year after 1983 is $1,428,300. This represents the sum of $1,290,800 plus $137,500, which is 55 percent of $250,000, the excess of $3,250,000 over $3,000,000.

EXAMPLE 5-2A The *tentative tax* on the taxable amount $21,040,000 in 1995 is $11,764,800. This amount represents the sum of *a*) $5,140,800 [the tentative tax on $10,000,000] and b) $6,624,000 [which is 60 percent of $11,040,000, the excess of $21,040,000 over $10,000,000]. $11,764,800 - $192,800 = $11,572,000 which is exactly 55% of $21,040,000.

Thus, federal unified transfer tax rates are progressive, with marginal rates ranging from 18 percent, to as high as 60 percent for certain amounts in excess of $10 million. The *marginal rate* is the rate levied on the next dollar of taxable amount. The *average rate*, on the other hand, is the result obtained by dividing the tax by the total taxable amount. For estates over $21,040,000 the marginal and the average rate are the same, 55 percent.

UNIFIED CREDIT

In federal estate and gift tax law, a *credit* is a dollar-for-dollar reduction in the *tentative tax*. It is to be distinguished from a *deduction*, which is a dollar-for-dollar reduction in the *amount taxable* and provides only a fractional reduction in the tentative tax, with the fraction determined by the particular

---

1. §2001(c)(2). For noncitizen nonresidents, the additional five percent tax is applied only to the extent necessary to phase out the graduated rates and unified credit actually allowed ($13,000), by statute or treaty. §2101(b)

estate's marginal tax rate. In the next two chapters, we will study several credits, but the most significant one, the unified credit, will be introduced now.

Prior to 1977, the first year of the unified credit, estate and gift tax law permitted a deduction of $30,000 (in addition to the $3,000 per donee annual exclusions) on the gift tax return for total lifetime gifts, and a deduction of $60,000 on the estate tax return for decedent's estates. These had the effect of eliminating taxation of small amounts of lifetime gifts and small estates. These two deductions were called the $30,000 lifetime gift exemption and the $60,000 estate exemption. Using the gift exemption did not reduce the estate exemption. Thus, for example, in the estate tax area prior to 1977, the first $60,000 of taxable estate was tax free regardless of the amount of life time taxable gifts by the decedent. The Tax Reform Act of 1976 (TRA 76) eliminated the two exemptions and substituted a single *unified credit*, applicable to both taxable gifts and taxable estates after 1976. The unified credit has increased over the years, as shown in Table 5-4 (also reproduced in Table 5 of Appendix A).[2] The third column in that table shows the *unified credit equivalent* estate, or the *credit shelter* amount, for that year's unified credit, representing the amount by which the taxable amount can exceed zero and still have the tentative tax be completely sheltered (offset) by the unified credit.

---

2. In 1992, H.R.4848, sponsored by Congressmen Waxman and Gephart, and S.2571 sponsored by Senators Mitchell, Rockefeller and others (both bills relating to long-term health care), proposed to reduce the tax free estate to $200,000, but the proposal generated so much opposition it was deleted when the House bill was reintroduced as H.R. 6076.

TABLE 5-4 Federal Unified Credit Amounts Effective Beginning In 1977

Year	Amount of Credit	Credit Shelter Amount
1977	$ 30,000.	$120,667.
1978	34,000.	134,000.
1979	38,000.	147,333.
1980	42,500.	161,563.
1981	47,000.	175,625.
1982	62,800.	225,000.
1983	79,300.	275,000.
1984	96,300.	325,000.
1985	121,800.	400,000.
1986	155,800.	500,000.
1987 and thereafter	192,800.	600,000.

EXAMPLE 5-3 After the unified credit is subtracted, the *net tax* on the amount $600,000 in 1983 is $113,500, which is the tentative tax of $192,800, reduced by the 1983 unified credit of $79,300.

EXAMPLE 5-4 Facts similar to Example 5-3 above, except the applicable years include any year after 1986. After the unified credit is subtracted, the net tax on the amount $600,000 is zero, which is the tentative tax of $192,800, reduced by the post-1986 unified credit of $192,800. Thus, since the starting of 1987, the first $600,000 in taxable transfer is totally sheltered by the unified credit.

Warning: *do not deduct the credit shelter amount instead of subtracting the unified credit in any tax calculations. Doing so will produce an incorrect tax result! The major use of the credit shelter equivalent is in giving general advice to clients, such as "the first $600,000 in transfers will be tax free."*

In many situations, the allowable unified credit will be less than the amount in Table 5-4. The actual amount of the allowable unified credit is the *lesser of either* the full or unused unified credit in the year of the transfer, *or* the amount of the tentative tax. For example, the allowable unified credit for a 1990 taxable amount of $250,000 (assuming no prior taxable gifts) is $70,800, which is the lesser of $192,800, the full or unused unified credit, and $70,800, the actual amount of the tentative tax.

UNLIMITED MARITAL DEDUCTION

Since 1982, virtually all transfers to a *spouse*, whether made during lifetime or at death, have been tax free; the amount of the transfer is treated as a "marital" deduction from the total gross estate or gross gifts. A brief history of the gift tax and estate tax marital deductions is described next.

The *gift tax marital deduction* was first enacted in 1948 to equalize tax treatment for married taxpayers in common law and community property states. It allowed a deduction for up to 50 percent of the value of noncommunity property gifts made to a spouse. TRA 76 changed this limit to 100 percent of the first $100,000, no deduction for the next $100,000, and 50 percent for all amounts exceeding $200,000.

The *estate tax marital deduction* was also first enacted in 1948, also to equalize tax treatment across the states. Its amount was limited to one half of the adjusted gross estate. TRA 76 changed this limit to the greater of $250,000 or one half of the adjusted gross estate, subject to further adjustments for any gift tax marital deduction taken and for property held as community property. The *adjusted gross estate* was defined essentially as the decedent's separate property, reduced by deductions for funeral and administration expenses, claims against the estate, and losses during administration.

The *present* 100 percent, "unlimited" gift and estate tax marital deductions became effective in 1982.[3]

> EXAMPLE 5-5 Last year, Wildcard gave $10 million in property to his wife Bimba, a U.S. citizen. Although Wildcard's "gross gift" was $10 million, his taxable gift will be reduced to zero by an (unlimited) marital deduction of $10 million. Thus, there will be no tentative tax.

> EXAMPLE 5-6 Based on the facts in Example 5-5, above, assume instead that Wildcard died last year leaving his entire $10 million estate to his wife. His taxable estate and tentative tax will also be zero, as a result of subtracting the $10 million marital deduction from the $10 million gross estate.

The current unlimited marital deduction will be examined in greater detail in the next two chapters. Wealth transfer taxes incorporate other significant deductions, but their examination will also be deferred.

---

3. The marital deduction for lifetime gifts to a noncitizen spouse is limited to $100,000. For details, see Chapter 7.

$10,000 ANNUAL EXCLUSION FOR LIFETIME GIFTS

The first $10,000 of total post-1981 lifetime gifts by any donor to each donee in a given year is treated as a deduction. Technically, it is called the annual exclusion.

> EXAMPLE 5-7 In 1982, Dad gave $21,000 cash to both son Bob and Uncle Bill. Assuming no other deductions and that Dad made no other gifts in that year, he would file only one gift tax return, and his current taxable gifts for 1982 would equal $22,000. The first portion of Dad's gift tax return would look as follows:
>
> | | |
> |---|---:|
> | Total current year's gross gifts | $42,000. |
> | Less: Annual exclusions and deductions | 20,000. |
> | Equals: Current taxable gifts | $22,000. |

> EXAMPLE 5-8 Mary gave husband Karl $200,000 in 1983. Assuming that it was her only gift in 1983, Mary's "total taxable gifts" for 1983 equals zero, which is $200,000, the amount of the gross gift, reduced by $200,000, the amount of the marital deduction. For intraspousal gifts, the annual exclusion is not really needed to reduce the tax to zero.

Prior to 1982 the annual exclusion amount was $3,000. To qualify for the annual exclusion, the gift must be one of a present interest, meaning that the donee has immediate access to the gift for use and enjoyment. Thus a gift to an irrevocable trust giving one person a life estate and another the remainder creates two gifts, the value of the life estate qualifies for the annual exclusion because it is a gift of a present interest but the remainder does not qualify because it is a future interest.

WEALTH TRANSFERS ARE UNIFIED AND TAXED CUMULATIVELY

In wealth transfer taxation, succeeding transfers are unified, in part because they are taxed cumulatively. Under the *cumulative gift doctrine*, all past and present gifts are accumulated; that is, prior taxable gifts are added to current taxable transfers (whether lifetime or death time) to determine the transfer tax base. Generally, this causes current gifts to be pushed into higher marginal rates. In the example below, for simplicity, assume no annual exclusion for gifts.

EXAMPLE 5-9 If Carla gives Katie $500,000 cash all at once, Carla's tentative gift tax will be $155,800. Instead, if Carla gives Katie $250,000 each year for two years, her total tentative tax will still be $155,800, calculated as follows:

	First Gift	Second Gift
Total current taxable gifts	$250,000.	$250,000.
Plus: Total prior taxable gifts	0.	250,000.
Equals: Total taxable gifts	250,000.	500,000.
Tentative tax on total gifts	70,800.	155,800.
Less: Tentative tax on prior gifts	0.	$70,800.
Equals: Tentative tax on current gifts	70,800.	85,000.
Total cumulative tentative tax	$70,800.	$155,800.

Thus, in the second gift year, the tentative tax on the same size gift was larger, due to accumulation and taxation at a higher rate bracket (up to a maximum of 34 percent rather than 32 percent). Prior taxable gifts are similarly accumulated on the estate tax return, as we shall see later, in Example 5-12.

As we have seen, TRA 76 created the *unified transfer tax*, combining gift and estate taxation into a single tax structure having one rate schedule. Thus, the transfer at death is treated as just the last in a series of transfers. However, TRA 76 did not achieve complete unification, for instance the annual exclusion is available only for lifetime gifts. Unification did not produce a tax system that makes planners indifferent as to the timing of transfers, that is whether one would recommend gifts over holding property until death or vice versa depends on the circumstances. For instance, life time gifts use up less unified credit because of the annual exclusion but appreciated property transferred at death receives a step-up in basis. We shall see in later chapters, particularly Chapters 9 and 13, how our current transfer tax system is still quite imperfect and how the planner can employ various strategies to capitalize on these imperfections.

Before considering an example of the complete unified transfer tax scheme, consider four important technical points:

First, regarding taxable gifts, in calculating the gift tax one includes in the item called "total prior taxable gifts" all taxable gifts made *since 1932*, the year of enactment of the gift tax. On the other hand, as we have said, in calculating the (FET) estate tax base one includes in the item called "adjusted taxable gifts" only the taxable gifts made since 1977, the year of unification.

Second, in the *gift tax* model, the "unused unified credit" is the amount of the current unified credit reduced by the unified credit amount already used up to offset tentative gift taxes on gifts in prior years. It is based on the premise that once the amount of the (lifetime) unified credit is fully used up, each additional dollar of taxable gift is fully taxable. By way of contrast, in the *estate tax* model, the entire unified credit is subtracted from the tentative tax, because the FET reduction for prior gift taxes is limited to the amount of gift taxes that would have been paid on the post-1976 gifts using the rates in effect at the date of death. This means that the gift taxes payable credit might be less than what was actually paid. This occurs where there were pre-1977 taxable gifts that pushed the post-1976 taxable gifts into higher marginal rates, or where very larger post-1976 gifts were given at a time when the top marginal rates were higher than those in effect when the donor died. For instance, a $7,000,000 gift made in 1981 (when the top marginal rate was 70%) would have resulted in gift tax of $3,903,800. Using post-1984 rates the gift tax would be $3,443,800. Since the purpose of using adjusted taxable gifts as part of the estate tax calculation is solely to move the taxable estate into its proper (taking into account cumulative transfers) marginal rate the gift tax payable credit would be $3,443,800 even though $3,903,800 was paid.

Fortunately for most estates, the gift taxes payable credit will equal the gift taxes paid because most decedents did not make taxable gifts both before and after the change in the law (1/1/77) nor are there many that made gifts so large (above $3,000,000) between 12/31/76 and 12/31/83 that the marginal rate for the gift was higher than the rate in effect at the donor's death. Notice that the tentative tax has remained the same since 12/31/76 on transfers up to $3,000,000.

Third, the top marginal rates have decreased over the years until they reached their current level in 1984, while the unified credit increased every year after its introduction in 1977 until it reached its present $192,800 level in 1987.

Fourth, gifts are valued as of the day given and estates are valued as of the day of the decedent's death. However, some estates are allowed to elect alternate valuation, which means valuing the estate property as of six months after the date of death. An estate is not allowed to make this election unless doing so will decrease (1) the gross estate, and (2) the estate tax and, if applicable, the generation skipping transfer tax. If the alternate valuation election is made, in addition to the six month rule for valuing assets that remain in the estate, assets transferred during the six months are valued transferor estate tax purposes as of their date transfer, thus assets sold, distributed, or otherwise disposed of, are valued as of the date transferred.

COMPLETE UNIFIED TAX FRAMEWORK: SOME EXAMPLES

We are ready to apply the overall scheme of the gift and estate tax to a series of connected examples.

> EXAMPLE 5-10 In 1973, Dan, a widower, gave his son Tom $260,000 cash. In 1978, Joe, a widower, gave his son Tom an apartment house worth $260,000. In 1982, Pete, a widower, gave his son Tom a parcel of land worth $260,000. Assuming that each donor had not made prior taxable gifts, Dan's, Joe's, and Pete's net gift-tax liabilities are calculated on gift tax returns in the following manner:

	Dan 1973	Joe 1978	Pete 1982
Current gross gifts	$260,000.	$260,000.	$260,000.
Less: Annual exclusion	3,000.	3,000.	10,000.
Less: Lifetime exemption	30,000.	n.a.	n.a.
Current taxable gifts	227,000.	257,000.	250,000.
Plus: Total prior taxable gifts	-0-	-0-	-0-
Total taxable gifts	227,000.	257,000.	250,000.
Tentative tax on total taxable gifts	44,100.	73,180.	70,800.
Less: Tentative tax on prior taxable gifts	-0-	-0-	-0-
Tentative tax on current taxable gifts	44,100.	73,180.	70,800.
Less: Unused unified credit	n.a.	34,000.	62,800.
Net gift tax	$44,100.	$39,180.	$8,000.

n.a.= not applicable

Note several points: First, for each taxpayer, since there were no prior gifts, there is no tentative tax on prior gifts. Second, two different rate tables and two different annual exclusion amounts were used for calculating the tentative tax, depending on the year of the gift. Third, the lifetime exemption applies only to pre-1977 gifts, and the unified credit applies only to gifts made after 1976. Finally, the actual gift tax returns for each taxpayer would have been due, on April 15 of the year following each (calendar) gift year.

Now let's change the facts a bit to illustrate the impact of the cumulative gift doctrine.

EXAMPLE 5-11 Continuing Example 5-10, suppose that Dan, Joe, and Pete are really just one person, named Steve, who has a net worth of $1,940,240 be for making the three gifts to his son, Tom. Steve's gift tax liabilities for the three years indicated are calculated on gift tax returns in the following manner:

	1973 Gift	1978 Gift	1982 Gift
Current gross gifts	$260,000.	$260,000.	$260,000.
Less: Annual exclusion	3,000.	3,000.	10,000.
Less: Lifetime exemption	30,000.	n.a.	n.a.
Current taxable gifts	227,000.	257,000.	250,000.
Plus: Total prior taxable gifts	0.	227,000.	484,000.
Total taxable gifts	227,000.	484,000.	734,000.
Tentative tax on total taxable gifts	44,100.	150,360.	242,380.
Less: Tentative tax on prior taxable gifts	0.	63,440.	150,360.
Tentative tax on current taxable gifts	44,100.	86,920.	92,020.
Less: Unused unified credit	n.a.	34,000.	28,800.
Net gift tax	**$44,100.**	**$52,920.**	**$63,220.**

n.a.= not applicable

Please be sure to carefully trace each of the three sets of calculations, and then note several points: First, for the 1978 gift tax return the tentative tax of $63,440 on prior gifts (referring to the 1973 gift) is not equal to the actual tentative tax of $44,100 for that gift, the reason being that for each gift tax return all tentative tax calculations use the *current* year's tax rates, i.e., the tax rates in effect for the year for which the tax return is being filed. Remember the purpose of using these prior gifts in the calculation is simply to move the current gifts into the appropriate marginal rates given the cumulative nature of the transfer tax system. Second, as mentioned above, the unused unified credit is equal to the amount of the full unified credit in the year of the gift, less the amount of the unified credit used in prior years. Therefore, the 1982 unused unified credit equals $62,800 minus $34,000, or $28,800.

EXAMPLE 5-12 Continuing Example 5-11, assume that Steve dies this year. Let's calculate Steve's estate tax. Assume that after making the three gifts and paying the gift taxes, Steve's gross estate is $1,200,000 and the total debts and expenses allowable as deductions are $200,000, leaving a taxable estate of $1,000,000. The following summarizes Steve's estate tax return:

Gross estate	$1,200,000.
Less: Deductions	200,000.
Taxable estate	1,000,000.
Plus: Adjusted taxable gifts (post-1976)	507,000.
Estate tax base	1,507,000.
Tentative estate tax	558,950.
Less: Gift taxes *payable* on adj. taxable gifts (post-1976)	95,590.
Less: Unified credit	192,800.
Less: Other credits	0.
Net estate tax	**270,560.**
Total transfer taxes (estate tax plus gift tax)	$430,800.

Referring to the example, notice that the line "adjusted taxable gifts" does not include the 1973 taxable gift of $227,000 since it a pre-1977 gift, and that the gift tax payable does not include the gift tax of $44,100 on the 1973 gift. Note that a recalculation of the 1978 and 1982 gifts without taking into account the 1973 gift results in a $95,590 gift taxes payable credit even though $116,140 was actually paid on the post-1976 gifts. Again, this is appropriate when you consider that the sole purpose of the adjusted taxable gifts entering the calculation is to move the taxable estate into its appropriate marginal rates.

Students often ask, "If only the unused unified credit is subtracted from the tentative tax on the gift tax return, why is the *full* unified credit subtracted on the estate tax return?" *The reason is that the tentative estate tax is reduced not by the entire tentative gift tax on lifetime gifts, but only by the gift tax payable, which (for most gifts) is lower than the tentative tax on the gifts by the amount of the unified credit taken during lifetime.* For a more extensive explanation, with a numerical example, see Appendix 5A.

As mentioned earlier, the actual amount of the unified credit taken on the tax return is always limited by the amount of the tentative tax. This means that the allowable unified credit is the *lesser* of the Table 5-4 credit amount for the year or the amount of the tentative tax. Thus, in Example 5-11, if the tentative tax on current (1982) gifts had been less than $28,800, then the unified credit would have been limited to that smaller amount, to allow otherwise would result in a negative number for the tax, indicating a refund. Most tax credits work similarly, an exception is the earned income credit for low income working families with children, in the income tax area.

> EXAMPLE 5-13 Continuing Example 5-12, if Steve's will reads: "...all to Tom...," Tom will receive a bequest of $729,440 at Steve's death. In total, Tom will have received $1,509,440 of Steve's $1,940,240 original estate, with the IRS collecting a total of $430,800.

Figure 5-1 illustrates the chronological disposition of Steve's estate, reflecting the lifetime gifts to Tom, gift taxes paid, estate tax paid, and, finally, the net bequest to Tom.

The numbers in these examples simplify reality by assuming, no other credits, and no asset appreciation. The discussion in Chapter 11 will relax the assumptions; it will introduce the influence of the marital deduction, and it will take account of the time value of money by allowing for asset appreciation in the context of a numerical example.

This chapter has introduced federal wealth transfer taxation, emphasizing the tax calculations. The next two chapters cover the estate tax, the gift tax, and the generation-skipping transfer tax, with regard to other important characteristics, mostly nonquantitative in nature.

FIGURE 5-1 Illustration of Examples 5-11, 12, and 13: The Chronological Disposition Of Steve's Estate

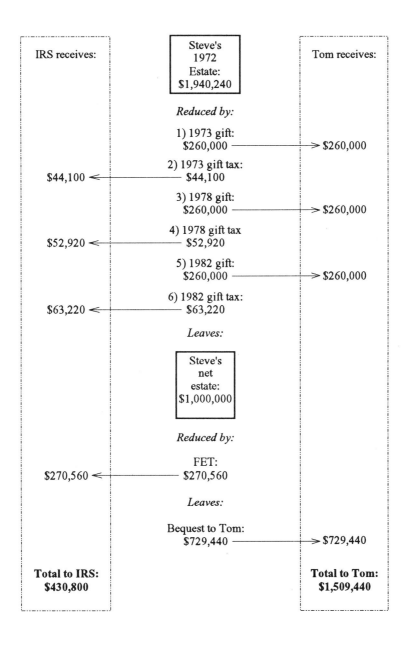

QUESTIONS AND PROBLEMS

1. Outline the history of federal wealth transfer taxation.

2. Why would the imposition of a transfer tax at death without an accompanying gift tax be largely ineffective?

3. Outline the basic computational scheme of the federal gift tax and the federal estate tax.

4. Describe the five computational steps that the gift tax and estate tax calculations have in common.

5. Calculate the tentative tax, the net tax, the marginal tax rate, and the average tax rate on the taxable amount $600,000 for the current year. Assume the transfers are made by different parties and that there are no other taxable gifts and no credits, except the unified credit.

6. Redo Question 5 for the taxable amount $3,250,000.

7. Redo question 5 assuming the (gross) amount $3,250,000 for the current year, and that instead of a unified credit, our system has a 1) deduction (exemption) of $600,000, and, alternatively, 2) neither a deduction nor a unified credit.
   a. Why are your results different from those of question 6?
   b. Is there any estate size for which your calculated tax using a deduction versus using a credit would be the same?
   c. Which taxpayers would prefer a $600,000 deduction? A $192,800 credit? Why? Is a choice available under federal transfer taxation?
   d. Other things the same, which would you prefer, a $1 deduction or a $1 credit?

8. (*a*)Describe the chronological progression of the amounts of the unified credit. (*b*)What is the meaning of the term `exemption equivalent'?

9. Describe the unlimited marital deduction.

10. During his lifetime, Dad gave his wife and his daughter $42,000 cash each outright in both 1981 and 1982. Calculate Dad's "total current taxable

gifts" for each year. Assume no prior taxable gifts and no gift splitting.

11. (*a*) Years ago, Robert was interested in giving his wife outright his entire estate, which consisted of $350,000 in property owned by him as an individual. Calculate the amount of Robert's marital deduction if he wound up giving her all of this property:
    1. During his lifetime in 1981.
    2. During his lifetime in 1982.
    3. At his death if he died in 1981.
    4. At his death if he died in 1982.
    (*b*) Review Example ERTA-1 in Chapter 1. Do you think most wealthier clients with wills drafted prior to 1982 would want to revise them to reflect new law? Explain why or why not.

12. This is a comprehensive transfer tax problem in which you will calculate each gift tax and an estate tax. In 1975, Mary, a widow, owned $1.2 million in wealth (assume for simplicity that it is all cash in her mattress). In that year, she gave $36,000 to each of her two sons. In 1983, Mary gave $400,000 to one son. Assume that Mary died this year. Hints: Be sure that your 1975 calculations reflect pre-1977 law, including different tax tables, the lifetime exemption, a lower annual exclusion for gifts prior to 1982, and no unified credit. (Answers: gift taxes of $3,060 and $44,020; state death tax credit of $17,237 and federal estate tax of $125,740. Remember to re-calculate the gift tax payable credit. Author's suggestion: The answers to this question constitute the foundation for several aspects of gift planning and are referred to in Chapter 9, Problem 12. You may care to save your notes.)

13. The following depicts the total amounts Joe has given to his son Tom and his daughter Mary:
    1978: $1,000 to Tom and $1,000 to Mary
    1980: $1,000 to Tom and $2,000 to Mary
    1983: $1,000 to Tom and $3,000 to Mary
    1985: $6,000 to Tom and $4,000 to Mary
    1986: $6,000 to Tom and $8,000 to Mary
    1987: $11,000 to Tom and $7,000 to Mary
    Current Year: $15,000 to Tom and $27,000 to Mary

In the past, Joe has given property to many other people, but never more than $100 in value to anyone in a given year. In what year, if any, did Joe incur his first amount of "taxable gifts"? Assume no gift splitting.

RECOMMENDED READING

Armstrong, Arthur A., and Ronald R. St. John. "Estate Planning Overview: Federal Estate and Gift Taxes, Past, Present and Future." *Taxes*, (October 1986), pp. 634-53.

Dodge, Joseph M. "The Taxation of Wealth and Wealth Transfers: Where do We Go after ERTA?" *Rutger's Law Review* 34 (1982), pp. 739-75.

Estate and Gift Tax Reporter. Chicago: Commerce Clearing House.

Federal Tax Estate and Gift Taxes. Englewood Cliffs, N.J.: Prentice-Hall.

Taggart, John Y. "The New Estate and Gift Tax Regime." *Buffalo Law Review* 31 (1982), pp. 797-882.

Answer to Question: "Why not Subtract only the *Unused* Unified Credit in Calculating the Federal Estate Tax"?

This Appendix has been written to explain why the full unified credit, rather than just the remaining unused unified credit, is subtracted on the federal estate tax return.

Consider a highly abstract example, which, for ease of comprehension, makes the following assumptions:

- the tax rate on all transfers is a flat 50 percent;
- the unified credit is $30;
- there is no annual exclusion;
- there are no deductions.

Assume Marie's total wealth consists of $200 in cash. If our basic federal unified transfer tax scheme is working properly and consistently, this wealth should incur a total tax of $70, regardless when she makes her transfers, during lifetime or at death. Proof:

Total transfer taxes = $200 times .50, less $30 = $70

Now suppose Marie makes post-1976 lifetime gifts of $40 and $20 in two different years. Her gift tax returns are shown thus:

	First Gift	Second Gift
Current taxable gifts	$40.	$20.
Plus: Total prior taxable gifts	0.	40.
Equals: Total taxable gifts	40.	60.
Tentative tax on total taxable gifts	20.	30.
Less: Tentative tax on prior taxable gifts	0.	20.*
Equals: Tentative tax on current taxable gifts	20.	10.
Less: Unused unified credit	20.	10.
Leaves: Net gift tax	$0.	$0.

Next, assume that Marie dies. Her gross estate will be $140, which is the amount of her original wealth, $200, reduced by $60, the amount of the lifetime gifts. Marie's FET, assuming that the full unified credit is taken, will be $70, as shown below:

Gross estate	$140.
Plus: Adjusted taxable gifts	60.
Equals: Estate tax base	200.
Tentative estate tax	100.
Less: Gift taxes payable on adjusted taxable gifts	0.*
Less: Unified credit	30.
Leaves: FET	$70.

Thus, total lifetime plus death time transfer taxes are $70, as they should be. The average tax rate is 35% (=$70/$200). Had we mistakenly subtracted only the "unused" unified credit on the FET return (which, because of the gifts, would have been reduced to $0 at death), total transfer taxes would have been $100, resulting in an average tax rate of 50%. The upshot would have been the total failure to utilize the unified credit.

The critical reason that the full unified credit is subtracted on the estate tax return is that the tentative estate tax is reduced not by the entire tentative gift tax on lifetime gifts, (as we did for the second gift, above), but only by the net gift tax on lifetime gifts which is lower than the tentative tax on lifetime gifts by the amount of the unified credit taken during lifetime. (These items are marked with asterisks above). Since we have not yet received the benefit of the already used portion of the unified credit, we must take it now, by subtracting the entire unified credit.

The estate tax return subtracts the gift taxes paid on lifetime gifts from the tentative estate tax only because it reflects a *prepayment of the transfer tax*; not to do so would result in a double tax payment for the gifts. The gift tax return, on the other hand, subtracts the tentative gift tax on prior gifts for a totally different reason: it subtracts it to consistently implement the law's intent to push current gifts into a (potentially) *higher tax bracket*. And since the gift tax return subtracts the full tentative gift tax on prior gifts, it must deduct only the unused unified credit; to subtract the full unified credit on the gift tax return would double count the benefit of the unified credit.

It would have been simpler to understand the unified scheme if the gift tax were calculated like the estate tax: by figuring a tentative tax on *all* taxable gifts--current and prior--and then subtracting from it the entire unified credit, as well as any gift tax paid on prior gifts. Such a scheme would truly make the two transfer taxes appear more similar. But although the gift tax and the estate tax schemes appear to produce inconsistent results, their effect on net transfer taxes, as we have seen from the above, is the same.

6

The Federal Estate Tax

OVERVIEW

A comprehensive outline of the Federal Estate Tax (FET) is shown in Table 6.1.

Basically, as outlined in the previous chapter, the unified transfer tax rate schedule forms the basis to calculate a tentative tax. The rate schedule may be found in Table 5-1 of Chapter 5, and in Table 4 of Appendix A at the end of the book. This tentative tax is on the sum of the decedent's property interests (gross estate), reduced by allowable deductions, and increased by certain gifts (post-1976 taxable gifts). Credits are subtracted from the tentative tax to arrive at the net tax liability.

In general, a federal estate tax return must be filed for all decedents who are *citizens or residents* of the United States dying with a total gross estate (regardless of where the property is situated[1]) plus adjusted taxable gifts equaling or exceeding the amount of the unified credit equivalent for the

---

1. §2031(a).

year of death.[2] For example, the estate of a decedent-citizen who died after 1987 having a gross estate of $550,000 and adjusted taxable gifts of $100,000 must file a return because the sum of the two transfers exceeds $600,000. Filing is required even though no FET will be due, as in the case where the entire estate is left to a surviving spouse or where the gross estate exceeds $600,000 but debts reduce it below that level.

In addition, a federal estate tax return must be filed for *noncitizen, non residents* having property situated in the United States exceeding $60,000.[3] Only such U.S. property will be subject to tax.[4] Regarding calculation of the tax, while the estates of these nonresident aliens can qualify for the unlimited marital deduction, they are entitled to a maximum unified credit of only $13,000.[5] Exceptions apply for residents of both U.S. possessions and countries having special treaties with the U.S.[6]

The executor is responsible for paying the FET.[7] If there is no executor, all persons in actual or constructive possession of any of the decedent's property are liable for the tax to the extent of the value of that property.[8] That includes surviving joint tenants[9] and trustees of the decedent's revocable living trust.[10]

This chapter is divided into three major parts. Each part will examine one of the three principal items found on the estate tax return: components of the gross estate, allowable deductions, and allowable credits. All Code

---

2. §6018(a)(1).

3. §6018(a)(2).

4. §2103.

5. §2102(c)(1).

6. For a discussion of the advantages and disadvantages of expatriation to avoid U.S. taxes, see the Guiterrez paper cited at the end of the chapter. For tax planning for nonresident aliens, see the Mirabello paper cited at the end of Chapter 17.

7. §2002; *Fleming v. Commissioner*, No. 90-2576, 7th Cir. 1992.

8. §2002, §2203.

9. Estate of Guide v. Commissioner 69 T.C. 811 (1978).

10. LR 8335033.

sections (e.g., §2033) included in this chapter refer to those found in the Internal Revenue Code. Many of these sections are included in Appendix B at the end of the book. The actual section numbers will be mentioned frequently, partly for economy in exposition and partly because estate planners regard them as common industry jargon.

While studying this chapter, the reader is urged to look over Form 706, Federal Estate Tax Return, shown in Appendix C, and those pertinent sections of the Internal Revenue Code, to strengthen comprehension in this complex area.

TABLE 6-1 Federal Estate Tax (Form 706) Comprehensive Outline

Gross estate		$xxx,xxx.
Less: deductions:		
Expenses and indebtedness	$xxx.	
Losses during administration	xxx.	
Charitable bequests	xxx.	
Marital deduction	<u>xxx.</u>	<u>xx,xxx</u>
Leaves: Taxable estate		xxx,xxx.
Plus: Adjusted taxable gifts (post-1976)		<u>xx,xxx.</u>
Equals: Estate tax base		xxx,xxx.
Calculate: Tentative tax on tax base		xxx,xxx.
Less credits, etc.:		
Gift tax payable on adjusted taxable gifts	xxx.	
Unified credit	xxx.	
Credit for state death tax paid	xxx.	
Credit for estate tax on prior transfers	xxx.	
Credit for foreign death taxes	xxx.	
Credit for gift taxes on pre-1977 gifts included in the gross estate	xxx.	<u>xx,xxx.</u>
Leaves: Net estate tax (FET)		$xxx,xxx.

ONE: COMPONENTS OF THE GROSS ESTATE

There is no short definition of the term *gross estate*. One might think that it would consist solely of property in which the decedent had a clear beneficial interest at death. However, in developing the rules, Congress has added other items which, in its judgment, must be included in the gross estate to prevent substantial FET avoidance through planning. For example, as we shall see below, included in a decedent's gross estate will be all gift taxes paid on gifts made within three years of death.

Another example involves retained interests. In the past, property owners attempted to reduce FET by making lifetime gifts with "strings attached," retaining some power to control beneficial enjoyment. For example, a Mom and Dad might have wanted to transfer title to the family residence to their adult son with the agreement that the parents could continue to live there. Recognizing that such strings attached transfers of ownership meant that the property owner had retained a substantial beneficial interest, Congress enacted Code Sections 2036, 2037, and 2038, thereby including such property in Mom and Dad's gross estates at their death.

Analysis of the components of the gross estate will be divided into three parts. First, we'll examine those sections covering basic interests owned at death (§2033-4, 2039-42). Second, we will focus on those sections which include in the gross estate certain transfers made with retained interests or with control over beneficial enjoyment (§2036, §2037, and §2038). And third, we'll cover certain other transfers within three years of death (§2035), including transfers of life insurance policies and relinquishments of retained interests. Again, in studying the components of the gross estate, it would be well to remember that many peculiar items have been included over the years solely to prevent what Congress has perceived to be substantial FET avoidance.

An important and simple rule regarding valuation should be kept in mind while reading this major section. All items includable in the gross estate must be valued at fair market value as of the decedent's date of death.[11] This is important because property values are usually higher then, rather than earlier, when good planning can seek to reduce them, or freeze them at a lower, pre-death amount.

Basic Interests Owned At Death

§2033: Property owned by the decedent. Section 2033 broadly includes in the gross estate all property in which the decedent had a beneficial interest at death. Common examples are fee simple interests, such as ownership interests typically held in assets such as a house, furniture, personal effects, business interests, investments, and even intangible property such as patent rights. However, many less obvious interests, including those less encompassing than fee simple interests, are also included. In principle, if the property had some value and the decedent had some beneficial interest in it at death, it is probably includable. A few not-so-obvious examples follow:

EXAMPLE 2033-1 Decedent died on June 18 owning 100 shares of XYZ

---

11. §2031(a).

stock, worth $10,000. On May 26, a *dividend* of $1.50 per share was declared, payable to stockholders of record on June 14, with payment on June 22. Included in the gross estate will be $10,150, representing the value of the stock plus the dividends declared. At death, decedent was entitled by right to receive the dividend.

EXAMPLE 2033-2 Same facts as Example 2033-1, except that the holder-of-record date was June 24. The value of the dividends is not included in the decedent's gross estate because at date of death, decedent was not legally entitled to the dividend.

EXAMPLE 2033-3 Prior to his death this year, decedent had the right to receive his parents' new Cadillac automobile when his Dad retired in three years. This was an arm's length agreement, negotiated for valuable consideration. (Decedent, in exchange, gave Dad 10 shares of XYZ stock). The gross estate will include the value of the *remainder interest* in the car. Its value is the present discounted value of the car's estimated worth in three years.

EXAMPLE 2033-4 At her death, decedent owned local *municipal water district bonds*. Although income from such bonds is exempt from federal income tax, the value of the bonds, plus the accrued interest on them, is includable in her gross estate.

EXAMPLE 2033-5 At his death, decedent shared with his wife an ownership in $100,000 of *community property*. His gross estate will include $50,000, representing his one-half interest in the property.

EXAMPLE 2033-6 The present value of a *joint and survivor annuity*, one which continues to be payable in whole or in part to another after the decedent's death, is includable in the decedent's gross estate if the deceit purchased the annuity. Its value would be the present discounted value of the survivor's expected income payments.

Code Section 2039, which includes survivorship annuities in the decedent's gross estate, more directly deals with this last fact situation. §2039 will be covered shortly. This is the first of many examples of an interest includable both in the broadly written section 2033 and a more narrowly written, more detailed code section.

EXAMPLE 2033-7 The present value of a decedent's *life estate for the life of another* is includable in the decedent's gross estate. Prior to his death, decedent had a vested right to receive an annual income of $60,000 for as long as his disabled daughter was alive. She was 64 years old when he died. His gross estate will include the present actuarial value of the remaining income, based upon daughter's life expectancy. At 7 percent, that value is $536,442.[12]

---

12. Use the tables at the end of the book to see if you come up with the same value.

EXAMPLE 2033-8 Same facts as Example 2033-7, except that his daughter predeceased decedent. Decedent's gross estate will not include any amount in connection with the annuity, other than any unspent income, since *decedent's annuity interest terminated* prior to his death.

EXAMPLE 2033-9 When she died, Carol ("or her estate") was a named beneficiary in her dad's revocable trust. Dad is still alive. Carol's gross estate will not include the value of this remainder. Although her estate may one day receive some of Dad's property, at her death her right to it was contingent upon her father's not changing the terms of his trust. *Discretionary contingent future interests* normally are not includable in a decedent's gross estate.

However, a contingent future interest that is not discretionary, i.e., not subject to someone's control, may be includable, particularly if the contingency is related to survival. The next two examples illustrate this.

EXAMPLE 2033-10 In Example 2033-9, above, if Carol ("or her estate") had been named in Dad's irrevocable trust to receive principal if Dad outlived Carols sister, Carol's *contingent remainder* can be actuarially valued and will be includable.

EXAMPLE 2033-11 Jenny died in an accident that was probably caused by the negligence of her employer. The date of death expected value of Jenny's estate's *chose in action*, although contingent, must be included in her gross estate. Based on evidence that was "reasonably foreseeable" on that date, the value of this interest can be quite speculative, and a low value may be disputed on audit by the IRS.[13]

EXAMPLE 2033-12 Prior to his death, Jim created an irrevocable trust, with income to his daughter Jodi for her life; then corpus reverts to Jim or his estate. Jim's gross estate will include the value of his *vested reversionary interest*, which will depend upon Jodi's age at Jim's death. For example, if Jodi had been age 40, based on Appendix A, Table 9, at 10 percent, the value of Jim's interest would equal 7.055 percent of the total value of the trust corpus.

---

13. For a recent case discussing such valuation, see *Davis*, T.C. Memo 1993-155.

Finally, consider the harsh consequences of current transfer tax laws on the estates of people who were engaged in illegal activities.

EXAMPLE 2033-13 Decedent died while piloting a plane load of marijuana and cash. His gross estate must include the street value of the drugs and the cash because he had "exclusive possession and control" over it when the plane crashed. Further, his estate was not entitled to deduct that value of cash and marijuana forfeited under state drug enforcement laws either as a claim against the estate or a loss during administration. The IRS rationale was that such deductions would "frustrate the sharply defined state and federal public policy against drug trafficking." Thus, decedent's other assets must be used to pay any FET due.[14]

The above examples are illustrative of the broad scope of §2033. As implied earlier, the gross estate embraces other interests defined in Code sections described below many of which overlap with §2033. That is, you might quite correctly think that §2033, which covers all beneficial interests owned at death, is so all-encompassing as to make some of the other sections superfluous. Congress created these additional sections to provide more specific detail in its requirements for overall includability in the gross estate. Sometimes the seemingly redundant section is there to avoid taxpayer suits claiming that a tenuous interest is not part of the decedent's estate.

§2034: Dower and curtesy interests. As mentioned in Chapter 4, a dower represents a surviving wife's life interest in a portion of the real property owned by her deceased husband, and a curtesy represents a surviving husband's life interest in a portion of the real property owned by his deceased wife. The extent of these statutory interests varies from state to state. Some states grant surviving spouses dower and curtesy interests in a percentage of the deceased spouse's real and personal property. As we have seen, one purpose of these laws is to prevent a decedent from entirely disinheriting the surviving spouse, especially when the decedent, as breadwinner, acquired and owned most or all of the family estate. §2034 includes the surviving spouse's dower or curtesy interest in the gross estate of the first spouse to die.

From an FET point of view, dower and curtesy interests and community property interests of the surviving spouse have the same effect. Dower and curtesy interests are includable in the gross estate but are fully deductible, under the marital deduction, as interests passing to the surviving spouse. In community property states, the surviving spouse's interest in community property is excludable from the decedent's gross estate. Whether deductible

---

14. TAM 9207004.

or excludable, these interests are not taxed at the first spouse's death.

§2039: Survivorship Annuities. An annuity is a series of two or more periodic payments, usually received by the annuitant monthly, quarterly or annually. Annuities are commonly used in retirement planning, often in conjunction with pension and insurance contracts. Ordinarily, an employee-"participant," upon retirement, will begin receiving a monthly annuity, possibly for as long as the retiree lives or, perhaps more commonly, for as long as the retiree and the retiree's spouse live. §2039 includes in the decedent's gross estate the date of death value of an annuity "receivable by any beneficiary by reason of surviving the decedent."

From the above description and from earlier examples, it should be clear that a single life annuity for the decedent's life will not affect the decedent's gross estate under §2039, since nothing will be receivable by any beneficiary by reason of surviving the decedent. And such an annuity won't be considered property owned at death under §2033 because the date of death value of an annuity that terminates at the death of a decedent is zero.

Because the gross estate can include the value of a survivorship annuity at the date of death of either the participant or the participant's spouse, whoever dies first, this section will discuss the taxation for each.

Inclusion in participant's gross estate. The value of a survivorship annuity includable in the decedent-participant's gross estate will basically depend upon when the decedent retired, whether or not the pension plan is "qualified" under §401(a), and whether the annuity is to be paid in periodic installments or in a lump sum. §401(a) is quite long and complex, detailing the requirements necessary for plan qualification. The major tax advantages of qualified plans are that employer contributions are tax deductible to the employer but are not reportable as taxable income to the employee until distributed, usually after retirement. In addition, periodic earnings on contributions are tax-deferred. Nonqualified plans do not enjoy all these advantages.

The following summarizes a rather complex set of FET rules for survivorship annuities. As will be seen, the rule is quite simple for decedents who retired after mid-1984.

1. *Fully includable annuities.* With regard to *any* annuity whose payments began *after July 17, 1984*, or for which prior to that date the decedent had not made an irrevocable election to designate the beneficiaries, the *entire value* of the annuity will be includable in the gross estate. It will not matter how the survivor elected to receive payment, in a lump-sum or in installments.

2. *Partially or totally excludable annuities.* With regard to certain annuities for retirees who separated from service before Jan 1, 1985, and made the above irrevocable election before July 18, 1984, up to at least

$100,000 of the combined value of certain survivorship annuities can be made excludable from the gross estate. The $100,000 grandfathering exclusion applies to participants retiring or making the irrevocable election from January 1, 1983 to July 17, 1984. And for retirees separating from service prior January 1, 1983, an *unlimited* estate tax exclusion is available. Both exclusions are available only if the proceeds are not payable to the estate, and if the decedent did not change the form of benefit before death. These exclusions are important because such clients need not rely on the marital deduction to avoid FET at their death. Thus, for these retirees, some or all pension assets can be transferred for the benefit of someone other than the surviving spouse free of estate taxation.

Annuities qualifying for this exclusion include the following:

a. Tax-sheltered annuities or tax deferred annuities (TSAs or TDAs).
b. Individual retirement arrangements (IRAs).
c. A portion of the value of the periodic payments under pension plans that have been "qualified" under §401. The amount qualifying for the exclusion is that portion attributable to the employer's contributions.
d. A lump-sum payment to a surviving beneficiary if that beneficiary elects to forego "5-year averaging." Five-year averaging is a method of reducing the beneficiary's tax burden by enabling the lump sum to be taxed at favorable tax rates in the year of receipt. In effect, the lump sum is divided by 5. Then, using income tax rates and assuming no other income, the calculated tax is multiplied by 5. The possible result is avoidance of a higher rate bracket.[15]

EXAMPLE 2039-1 Decedent died this year, after retiring from work in 1985. At death, decedent was receiving joint and survivor annuities from the former employer's qualified retirement plan, a tax-sheltered annuity, and an individual retirement account, all of which began paying amounts after retirement. The value of the gross estate will include the entire value of all three annuities.

EXAMPLE 2039-2 During his employment, Stan contributed $25,000 to his qualified pension plan, and his employer contributed $75,000. The plan provides that Stan will receive a joint and survivor annuity upon retirement. Several years after his retirement in 1983, Stan died and the value of his spouse's survivorship annuity was $300,000. Since Stan's pension payments began during 1983, his gross estate will include $200,000. The amount excluded is the less of $100,000 or the value of the portion of the annuity attributable to the employer's contributions. That value is: ($75,000 / ($25,000+$75,000)) x $300,000), or $225,000. Thus the amount excluded is $100,000.

---

15. See §402(a).

EXAMPLE 2039-3 In example 2039-2 immediately above, had Stan retired before 1983, his estate would be able to exclude $300,000, the entire annuity value, and had he retired after July 17,1984 the entire value would have been included.

Summarizing this complex subject, a simple rule applies to decedents who retired after July 17, 1984: The *full* value of all retirement annuities are includable in the gross estate. For decedents retiring between January 1, 1983 and July 17, 1984, all but as much as $100,000 is includable. Finally, for those retiring prior to 1983, the *entire* value of all qualifying retirement annuities is excludable.

Inclusion in gross estate of retiree's spouse. The above survivorship annuity examples all assumed that the first spouse to die was the participant-retiree, rather than the participant-retiree's spouse. When the *participant-retiree's spouse dies first*, inclusion of a portion of the value of the participant's annuity in that nonparticipant spouse's gross estate will depend upon local property law. In community property states, the nonparticipant spouse's community interest in the annuity will be includable in his or her own gross estate. That value could be as much as one half of the total annuity value. On the other hand, in common law states, nothing will usually be includable. Regarding property rights to the remaining benefits, case law has held that at the nonparticipant spouse's earlier death, any community interest passes 100% to the participant; the Retirement Equity Act precludes that person from making any disposition of it.[16]

FET on excess retirement accumulations. Designed to recoup part of the benefit of income tax-free accumulation of earnings during the decedent's lifetime, tax law imposes an additional 15 percent excise tax on an individual's "excess retirement accumulation," which is the excess of the value of the decedent's interests in qualified plans and IRAs over the present value of an annuity of ordinarily $150,000 (or $112,500 indexed since 1986) payable for the life expectancy of persons decedent's age at the time of death. While the additional tax constitutes an FET deduction, it cannot be offset by the unified credit, and the excess accumulation cannot be reduced by the marital deduction, however, if the surviving spouse is the sole beneficiary of the pension interests, her or she can make a special election to have the interest avoid or more probably delay the tax by having the interest treated as though it was the surviving spouse's pension. Thus the tax may be levied when she draws the funds out or upon her death if measured by her age at death there is still an excess accumulation base upon

---

16. *Ablamis v. Roper* 937 F2d 1450 (9th Cir. 1991).

her age at time of death. The accumulation is also subject to income tax (as "income in respect of a decedent") and, unless a marital deduction applies, to the regular estate tax. The amount of the excess accumulation as of August 1, 1986 could have been "grandfathered" (i.e., exempt from later tax), if elected by 1989.[17]

The net effect of these taxes can be devastating. One commentator has cited a "worst case" example of a 65 year old widow who made life time gifts that used up her GSTT $1,000,000 exemption and placed her estate in a 50% marginal tax bracket when she died. Her estate left an accumulated $2 million pension fund to a trust held exclusively for the benefit of her grandchildren. The net amount passing to this trust will be $2,000,000, the gross amount, reduced by the following: excise tax on excess retirement accumulation of $143,735; FET of $928,132; generation-skipping transfer tax of $309,378; and income taxes of $327,654,[18] Thus, the trust will receive $291,101, or about only *14.5 percent* of the original pension amount.[19]

§2040: Joint interests. Includability of joint interests in the gross estate of a deceased joint owner depends upon whether or not a surviving spouse is the sole co-owner and, if not, the source of the consideration used to acquire the property.

In general, for decedents dying after 1981, the gross estate will include the *entire* value of property held jointly with others, subject to two very important exceptions. First, for joint tenancies created after 1976,[20] if the only surviving joint owner is the decedent's *spouse*, the property is called a "qualified joint interest," and *one half* of the total value will be includable, *regardless* of that spouse's original contribution.

Second, for spouse-only joint tenancies created before 1977, or for jointly owned property created anytime that is held by the decedent and at least one person who is *not* the surviving spouse, the gross estate will include that portion of the DOD FMV value of the property attributable to that portion of the consideration (money or money's worth) contributed by the decedent. This is called the *consideration furnished test*. It sounds complex, but in most cases its application is fairly simple. However, any

---

17. For details, see the Hastings and Silfen articles cited at the end of the chapter.

18. Only spouses of decedent-participants may roll over a decedent's plan benefits. §402(c)(9).

19. See pages 7-36to 7-39 of the 1993 Mezzullo paper, cited at the end of the chapter.

20. *Gallenstein* 975 F. 2d 286 (CA6, 1992) affg. 68 AFTR 2d 91-5721.

gift by the decedent to a co-owner who uses the gift as consideration for purchase of the property, is considered as having come from the donor-decedent and not from the donee.

> EXAMPLE 2040-1 At his death, Joel owned a house in joint tenancy with his wife, Susan. She bought the house in 1977 with her separate property. Joel's gross estate will include one half of the value of the house since it is a *qualified joint interest*. The result does not depend upon who originally acquired it or the source of the funds, the result would be the same if the house had been purchased with Joel's separate property or with as combination of their funds.

> EXAMPLE 2040-2 Based on the facts in Example 2040-1 immediately above, had Joel and Susan acquired the house in joint tenancy *in 1976*, the amount includable in Joel's gross estate will depend upon whether contribution can be (and is) proved. If Joel's wife does not prove any contribution, the entire date of death value of the house will be includable. If she can and does prove full contribution, nothing attributable to the house will be includable.

In situation 2040-2, Susan might not wish to prove any contribution at all since, for reasons explained later in this chapter (regarding the marital deduction) and in Chapter 8 (basis step-up rules), full inclusion in the gross estate should result in no additional FET but would give her an income tax basis equal to the property's FMV on Joel's date of death.

> EXAMPLE 2040-3 At her death, Rose owned a farm worth $100,000 jointly with her brother Tom. The farm was originally acquired for $50,000, with Rose paying $10,000 and Tom paying $40,000. Assuming the contribution of the survivor can be proved, under the consideration-furnished test, her estate will include only one fifth the farm's value, or $20,000, [($10,000/$50,000)*$100,000]. Tom's basis in the farm will be his contribution plus the amount included in Rose's estate, I. e., $60,000 [$40,000 he contributed and $20,000 included in Rose's estate].

> EXAMPLE 2040-4 At her death, Dottie owned $90,000 ABC common stock jointly with her husband and her son. The survivors know that Dottie actually contributed only $10,000 to the original $50,000 purchase price, (and the two of them paid $20,000 each) but they are not sure they can prove it. If they cannot, Dottie's gross estate will include the full $90,000. If they can, her gross estate will include only her proportional share, or $18,000, which is $90,000 reduced by the survivor's proportional share, or $72,000. This is not a qualified joint interest because a non-spouse was also a surviving co-owner.

For purposes of §2040, "joint interests" encompass only two forms of concurrent ownership: joint interests, as the book defined them in Chapter 2, and interests by the entirety. In contrast, the two other major forms of co-ownership, tenancies in common and community property, is included in the decedent's gross estate based upon the decedent's interest.[21]

§2041: Power of appointment. As we saw in Chapter 2, a power of appointment is a power to name someone to receive a beneficial interest in property. The grantor of the power is called the donor. The person receiving the power is called the holder or donee. The parties whom the holder may appoint are called the permissible appointees. The parties whom the holder actually appoints are called the appointees.

For federal estate tax purposes, a power of appointment is either a general power or it is not a general power. A *general* power of appointment is a power in the holder to designate beneficial enjoyment to a class of people including any one of the following: the holder, the holder's estate, the holder's creditors or the creditor's of the holder's estate. A *nongeneral* power of appointment, often called a "special" or "limited" power of appointment, is a power to designate beneficial enjoyment to a class of people, none of whom consist of any of those four named above.

Subject to several exceptions, a decedent's gross estate will include the value of any property subject to a *general* power of appointment held by the decedent-holder at death. General powers are includable in the gross estate regardless whether the decedent-holder *exercised* the power at death, or, alternatively, permitted the power to *lapse* at death, unexercised. The key fact is that at the moment of death, the decedent was the holder of the power.

> EXAMPLE 2041-1 At her death, decedent was trustee of an irrevocable trust possessing the right to invade the corpus of the trust for the benefit of anyone. In her will, she appointed her son to receive the entire corpus. Her gross estate will include the entire value of the trust corpus, since it was subject to a general power which she *exercised* at her death.

> EXAMPLE 2041-2 Facts similar to Example 2041-1, above, except that decedent did not exercise the power at her death. The entire trust corpus is still includable in her gross estate. Her power *lapsed* at her death. A lapse of a power of appointment is treated similar to an exercise.

> EXAMPLE 2041-3 Facts similar to Example 2041-1, above, except that the power to invade was on behalf of *anyone except* herself, her creditors, her estate, or the creditors of her estate. This is a "special" or "limited" power, not a general power, and thus the property subject to the power is not includable under §2041.

---

21. §2033. For community property, see Example 2033-5.

The reader should note carefully that §2041 focuses on a decedent who is a *holder* of a general power, not on the donor or the appointee of a general power.

Exceptions. There are two major exceptions to the basic rule that property subject to a general power is included in the decedent-holder's gross estate. Each exception has the effect of restricting the scope of the appointment power to something significantly less than a full control by the holder.

Under the first exception, if the decedent's right to exercise a general power is limited by an *ascertainable standard*, that is, limited for reasons of "health, education, support or maintenance," it will not constitute a general power.

Second, if the decedent's right to exercise the power depends on the *approval* of either the creator of the power or an *adverse party*, it will not constitute a general power. According to the Code, an adverse party "is a person having a substantial interest in the property, subject to the power, which is adverse to exercise of the power in favor of the decedent."[22]

> EXAMPLE 2041-4 During his lifetime, decedent was the income beneficiary of a trust created by his father. The trust gave him the right to invade corpus on his for reasons of his "health, education, support, or maintenance." Since the power is limited by an *ascertainable standard*, this right to invade is not a general power and the trust is not includable in the decedent's gross estate even if decedent was the trustee.

> EXAMPLE 2041-5 Same facts as Example 2041-4, except decedent could invade corpus for reasons of his "health, education, support, maintenance, *or happiness*". The power is not limited by an ascertainable standard, and therefore the invasion right constitutes a general power of appointment and the entire value of the trust will be included in the decedent's estate even though he never exercised the right to invade.

> EXAMPLE 2041-6 During her lifetime, decedent had been an income beneficiary under a trust, which provides that upon her death, corpus was to be distributed to her son. Decedent could invade corpus for any reason provided she could get the written approval of her son. Since her son was an *adverse party*, i.e., his interest (i.e., the remainder interest) would have been adversely affected had decedent exercised the power in her own favor, her right to invade is not treated as a general power of appointment and the trust is not part of her estate..

Why should a general power of appointment over property subject the property to inclusion in the holder's gross estate? Because the rights

---

22. §2041(b)(1)(C)(ii).

underlying a general power are considered to be tantamount to ownership of that property. If a person has the right to appoint property to either herself, her creditors, her estate, or the creditors of her estate, tax law considers her the equivalent of an owner of that property, even if she died not having exercised that right. This tax rule contrasts makes sense even though under *property law* the holder is not the legal owner of the property regardless of whether the power is general or limited. Given that the holder does not have legal title, even if the property subject to the power is included in the holder's gross estate, it is not includable in the holder's probate estate unless the holder transfers it there which is not likely to happen.

§2042: Insurance on decedent's life The value of the decedent's gross estate will include the face value of a life insurance policy on the decedent's life under *either* of two circumstances: first, if the policy proceeds were receivable by the decedent's executor, or second, if the decedent, at his or her death, possessed "incidents of ownership" in the policy.

Receivable by executor. Ordinarily, life insurance proceeds will be receivable by the decedent's executor if (*a*) the decedent-insured's estate is the primary beneficiary, (*b*) if the decedent-insured's estate is contingent beneficiary and the primary beneficiary predeceased the decedent, or (c) if at the insured's death no named beneficiaries are living and the proceeds are payable to the estate by default, if the decedent was the policy owner. In life insurance planning for FET avoidance, advisors find it easier to prevent these outcomes than the one described next.

Decedent possesses incidents of ownership. Commonly, ownership of a policy gives the owner numerous rights, including the right to assign and to terminate the policy, the right to borrow the cash surrender value, if any, the right to receive dividends, and the right to change beneficiaries. Possession by the decedent of *any one* of the rights to the economic benefits of the policy, called "incidents of ownership," will subject the proceeds to inclusion in the gross estate.

Payment of part or all of the policy premiums is not, however, an incident of ownership for purposes of §2042. Nonetheless, if the decedent has incidents of ownership, source of premiums can indicate a shared ownership with another person, which could reduce the amount includable in the gross estate to the amount of the decedent's share. For example, a policy purchased by the decedent but paid for entirely with community property would subject only one half of the proceeds to inclusion in the decedent's gross estate. Example 2042-2, below, illustrates this point.

§2042 versus §2033. It is important to distinguish between policies on the decedent's life and policies on the lives of others. §2042 embraces only policies on the *decedent's life*. If the decedent died owning a policy on someone else's life, only the terminal value (see below), if any, of that

policy (which, of course, remained in force after decedent's death) would be includable in the decedent's gross estate under §2033 (beneficial interests in property owned at death.) The true taxable value of a policy in force is called its "interpolated terminal reserve," which is usually nearly equal to its cash surrender value. For simplicity, in this text we shall call it the policy's *terminal value*.

One way to distinguish §2042 and §2033 is to ask whether the insurance company is paying the proceeds as a result of the decedent's death, or whether the policy has not yet "ballooned" into something worth such a large amount, because at the time of the decedent's death the insured is still alive. If the proceeds are payable because the decedent has died, the decedent is the insured, and the applicable code section to check is §2042 (or, possibly, §2035, as you'll learn in a few pages). Otherwise, look only to §2033 for possible inclusion of the policy's terminal value.

> EXAMPLE 2042-1 At decedent's death, decedent's wife owned a policy on *his life*, with the proceeds payable to his estate. Decedent's gross estate will include the value of the proceeds, under §2042. (Policy on decedent's life receivable by decedent's executor).

> EXAMPLE 2042-2 At the moment of his death, decedent *owned* a $100,000 life insurance policy *on his own life*. Under §2042 (incidents of ownership), $100,000 will be includable in his gross estate. However, if all premiums had been paid for with community property, or with 50-50 tenancy in common spousal property, only $50,000 would be includable.

After one spouse dies, if the surviving spouse continues to own a policy on his or her own life, the entire proceeds will be included in the surviving insured's estate when he or she dies, then, regardless of whether community property funds had been the source of most of the premiums.[23]

> EXAMPLE 2042-3 Decedent died owning a $60,000 life insurance policy on his mother's life. The policy is still in force and had a terminal value of $14,000 at decedent's death. §2042 does not apply because the insurance is not on decedent's life, however, the gross estate will include the $14,000 *terminal value* under §2033.

The material above indicated that payment of premiums on a policy on the life of the decedent does not constitute an "incident of ownership" for purposes of *§2042*. The rule is different for policies on the life of someone other than the decedent covered under *§2033*. Under this latter section,

---

23. *Estate of Cavenaugh* 100 TC, CCH ¶12,927 (1993).

premiums paid by the decedent can very well indicate ownership, unless they are shown to have been gifts made to someone else.

> EXAMPLE 2042-4 At decedent's death a life insurance policy on his wife's life was in force, with wife the named owner and decedent the primary beneficiary. All premiums were paid from a bank account owned by decedent and his wife as equal tenants in common (or as community property-- the result will be the same). Unless it can be shown that the payment of decedent's one half of the premiums constituted gifts to spouse, decedent's gross estate will include one half of the terminal value.

So far, we have studied Code sections 2033, 2034, 2039, 2040, 2041 and 2042, all of which cover interests owned by the decedent at death and includable in the gross estate. The next section examines a second group of Code sections that are similar to those above in that they make certain interests includable in the gross estate even though the property was no longer owned by the decedent at the time of death. The property is included because the decedent transferred property but kept some control, sometimes just a *little string* attached, such that Congress thought the string justified including the property in the gross estate as if no transfer had taken place.

Transfers with Retained Interest or Control

A second general type of property interest includable in the gross estate is an interest that the decedent transferred before death but, in the process, retained the right to control or enjoy. Such strings attached transfers are treated by the Code as if the decedent never made the transfer and, instead, continued to own the property until death, thus if the rule applies, the property is valued in the gross estate at the DOD FMV and will not be treated for estate tax purposes as an adjusted taxable gift even though it had been treated as a taxable gift when the transfer occurred. The latter sounds bad but it is actually good, it keeps the transfer from being twice taxed, since any gift tax payable on the earlier transfer is allowed as a credit even though the adjusted taxable gift goes to zero. These transfers are the subject of §2036, Transfers with Retained Life Estate; §2037, Transfers Taking Effect at Death, and §2038, Revocable Transfers.

Characteristics common to all three sections. These three "string" sections have at least six characteristics in common: First, to fall under these provisions, the transfer must have been made by the *decedent*.

Second, the transfer must have involved a gift, that is, a transfer "for less than full and adequate consideration in money or money's worth." This phrase even includes situations where the consideration received was only slightly less than the full amount. The FET consequences can be severe, particularly for such transfers as the private annuity (see Chapter 14) where the annuity amount is miscalculated such that it is less than the value of the property transferred. To minimize this problem, estate planning would suggest an accurate property appraisal, especially in the case of assets whose value is difficult to judge.

Third, similar to other components of the gross estate, if property is includable in the gross estate under §2036, §2037, or §2038, its includable value will be the value as of the *date of death* (or alternate valuation date), rather than the value at date of transfer. This is important because inflation and good fortune can result in date of death values far exceeding date of transfer values.

Fourth, the amount includable will be only that *portion* of the transferred property over which the decedent retained control. For example, if the retained control was only over one third of the property, then only one third of its value will be includable in the gross estate.

Fifth, transfers with retained controls usually, but not always, arise in the context of a *transfer into trust.*

Sixth, §2036, §2037, and §2038 often overlap. Not infrequently, a single transfer will be includable in the decedent's gross estate under more than one of these sections. If more than one section applies and different amounts are includable under each, the actual amount includable is the one of greatest value.

An examination of each section covering transfers with retained interest or control follows.

§2036: Transfer with retained life estate. A transfer with retained life estate arises when a decedent has made a transfer, by trust or otherwise, for less than full and adequate consideration, under which he or she has both (*a*) retained one or more specified *controls* over assets *and* (*b*) has retained this control for a certain *period of time.* Each aspect will be examined in some detail below.

Retained controls. Essentially, for §2036 to apply, the decedent-transferor must have retained either (1) the possession or enjoyment of, or the right to *income* from, the property transferred, or (2) the right, either alone or in conjunction with any person, to *designate* who will enjoy or possess the property or its income. Included is the retention of the right to vote shares of stock in a corporation over which decedent, alone or with anyone else, has at least 20 percent of the voting power.[24]

Period of retention. In addition to the above retained control, §2036 applies only if the decedent-transferor retained that control for any one of three periods: (1) for life, (2) for any period that does not in fact end before

---

24. §2036(b).

the decedent's death, or (3) for any period not ascertainable without reference to the decedent's death.

In the following §2036 examples, assume that decedent D, before death, made a transfer for less than full consideration. The reader is urged to independently test the facts for each example against the two requirements described above.

EXAMPLE 2036-1 At a time when D's vacation home was worth $11,000, D says: "Son, here's title to my vacation home. It's yours now, but I will need to use it occasionally." When D died the home was worth $20,000. The date-of-death value of the home will be includable in D's gross estate because at the time of D's death D still retained the *right to enjoy* the property.

EXAMPLE 2036-2 D transfers property into an irrevocable trust, with income to D for D's life and with remainder to C. The property's value at date of death will be includable in D's gross estate for the same reason as in Example 2036-1; D retained the right to the income, for life. Although the remainder value was treated as a taxable gift when the trust was established, it will not be an adjusted taxable gift for estate tax purposes since the entire trust has been included in D's gross estate.

EXAMPLE 2036-3 D transfers property into an irrevocable trust, with income to D for 20 years, then remainder to C. D dies before the trust terminated. The property's value will be includable because the *period of retention* did not in fact end before D's death. The adjusted taxable gift would be zero insofar as this trust goes. However, had D lived beyond the 20 year term, D's gross estate would not include the trust property but then the remainder value (as of date of the gift, the establishment of the trust) would be an adjusted taxable gift, boosting the rest of D's taxable estate into higher marginal rates.

EXAMPLE 2036-4 D transfers property into an irrevocable trust, with income to D for up to one month before D's death, then remainder to C. This is includable because the retained period is *not ascertainable without reference* to D's death.

EXAMPLE 2036-5 D transfers property into an irrevocable trust, with income to S or C as D chooses, then remainder to C. This is includable, because D retained the *right to designate*, who will enjoy the income from the property.

EXAMPLE 2036-6 Same facts as Example 2036-5, except that the choice between S or C is made by D and C together. The property's value is still includable, partly because D has the right to designate the recipient "alone or *in conjunction with* any other person." §2036 does not contain an "adverse party" exception, such as the one found under §2041.

EXAMPLE 2036-7 Facts similar to any one of the above examples, except that the transfer was of either *community property*, 50-50 tenancy in common spousal property, or jointly owned spousal property. Only one half of the value of the property will be includable, because only half of the property is traceable to a transfer by D.

EXAMPLE 2036-8 D transfers property into an irrevocable trust, with one quarter of the income to D, the other three quarters to C; then, upon D's death, remainder to C. Only *one quarter* of the property's entire value will be includable, since D retained an interest over only that portion.

EXAMPLE 2036-9 D transfers property into an irrevocable trust, authorizing trustee F, a bank, in its sole discretion, to distribute or accumulate trust income. D retains the power to replace F with another corporate trustee. The value of the property is not includable in D's gross estate under §2036 because D's right to replace trustees does not amount to the right by D to designate enjoyment of the property.[25] However, the property would be includable if D reserved the right to appoint herself as successor trustee.

In the following example, let's alter a basic assumption:

EXAMPLE 2036-10 E transfers property into an irrevocable trust, with income to D for life, remainder to C. The value of the property is not includable in D's gross estate under §2036, because D was *not the transferor*. This arrangement is referred to as a bypass trust because the trust assets "bypass" the income beneficiary's estate.

The *reciprocal trusts doctrine*, illustrated in the next example, was established by the courts to apply §2036 to family planning situations which in form avoid the literal terms of that section, but in substance do not. In essence, the transferor has made a transfer of property, and at about the same moment has received the right to enjoyment of other property arising from a separate but related transaction.

EXAMPLE 2036-11 Husband transfers $100,000 in property into an irrevocable trust H, with income payable to his wife for her life and remainder to their children. At about the same time, wife transfers $100,000 into trust W, with income payable to her husband for his life and remainder to their children. Under §2036, the corpus of trust H will be includable in husband's gross estate and the corpus of trust W will be included in wife's gross estate. These interrelated trusts leave the spouses in essentially the same economic position that they would have been had they created trusts naming themselves life beneficiaries.[26]

---

25. *Estate of Helen S. Wall*, 101 TC No. 21 (1993). This court rejected the IRS' long standing position in RR 79-353, applying §2036(a). IRS is expected to continue to litigate this issue.

26. *Estate of Grace* 395 US 316 (1969).

Aggressive minded clients may be tempted to engage in transfers which are intended to appear complete but which actually involve an implied, unwritten *understanding* of a retained life interest. They should be informed that the IRS may successfully attack such schemes. Consider the following situation, in which a court found §2036 to apply to facts which appear, on their face, inapplicable.

EXAMPLE 2036-12 Mom, age 82 and in poor health, transferred title to her home to her son and his wife in exchange for $270,000, which was the home's fair market value. The terms of this "sale-leaseback" called for a $20,000 down payment and a five year mortgage loan of $250,000. Mom immediately forgave the down payment of $10,000 by each of the spouses. In the next two years, in payment of rent, Mom gave son and his wife $10,000 each, and they promptly returned these amounts in payment of the mortgage interest. Two days after the sale, Mom executed her last will, which contained a provision forgiving any of the remaining debt at the time of her death. The date of death value of the home is includable in her gross estate under §2036. In spite of a total lack of direct evidence, circumstances strongly suggest an (expressed or implied) understanding that decedent was permitted to live in the house until death (which she did), and that none of the consideration offered in exchange was ever really to be paid. Thus, all consideration is disregarded. The following circumstantial factors, all taken together, indicate a strings attached transfer: decedents' age and health concerns; her forgiveness of the mortgage both during her life and by her will, the fact that the rent payments approximated the interest payments on the note, and the fact that the son was the decedent's only heir and natural object of her bounty. As a result, Mom was treated as having made a transfer of property for less than full and adequate consideration in which she retained, for a period which did not in fact end before her death, the right to possess or enjoy the property.[27]

§2037: Transfers taking effect at death.[28] A "transfer taking effect at death" will arise when (1) possession or enjoyment of the property through ownership can be obtained only by surviving the decedent and (2) the decedent, at the time of the transfer, retained a reversionary interest, which, at the decedent's death, exceeded 5 percent of the value of the property. Such reversionary interest is defined as the possibility that the property may return to the decedent or may be subject to a power of

---

27. *Maxwell* 3 F. 3d. 591, affirming 98 T.C. 594 (1992).

28. This section can be skipped without significant comprehension loss. §2037 is of much more narrow application than §2036 or §2038, and arises much less frequently in planning an estate.

disposition by him.

> EXAMPLE 2037-1 D transfers property into trust, with income to S for D's life, reversion to D if he survives S, otherwise remainder to C. Assume that D dies, predeceasing S, and that on the date of D's death the value of the trust property was $1 million. Assume further that, based on actuarial tables, at D's death there was a 12 percent chance that D would survive S. The value of D's gross estate will include $120,000 (or .12 times $1 million), the value of the reversionary interest, despite the fact that the property can no longer revert to D. Possession and enjoyment through ownership could only be obtained by surviving D, and the value of D's reversionary interest at death was greater than 5 percent of the value of the property.

In the preceding example, D had a 12 percent chance of surviving S at D's death. The reader might find this strange, since D *in fact* did predecease S. However, as in certain other valuation situations, this calculation must be made without regard to that fact. Thus, the calculation assumes that at the moment before D's death, D was in normal health for his or her age.

§2038: Revocable transfers. A §2038 revocable transfer will have been made if a decedent-transferor retained, at death, the *power to alter, amend, revoke or terminate* the right to enjoy the property transferred.

> EXAMPLE 2038-1 D transfers property into a *revocable living trust*, retaining the power to revoke the trust at any time. D's gross estate will include the value of this property under §2038.

> EXAMPLE 2038-2 D transfers property into an irrevocable trust, with income to S and C, remainder to R. D retained the right to have corpus distributed to S, C, or R. The trust property will be includable in D's gross estate because D retained the power to "alter" the right to enjoy the property.

In the example immediately above, §2036 would also apply. Can you see why?

> EXAMPLE 2038-3 D transfers five bonds to C under the state's *Uniform Gift to Minors Act* and appoints herself custodian. If D dies before C reaches majority, the value of the bonds will be includable in D's gross estate because, under the Uniform Act, D had the power to terminate the arrangement (i.e., until C reaches majority), and distribute the proceeds to the minor.

> EXAMPLE 2038-4 D transfers cash to the local savings and loan association for an account for C, naming herself (D) as trustee of the account. This is a revocable trust. During her lifetime, D has sole control over the account. At her death, C, as beneficiary, will receive the proceeds. In the states recognizing it, the deposit account in this *Totten trust* arrangement is includable in D's gross estate under §2038, because D had the right to withdraw it or change the beneficiary at any time.

Application of §2036, 2037 and 2038 to certain gifts. All three "strings attached" sections can apply to incomplete annual exclusion "gifts." An *annual exclusion gift* is a gift of property worth no more than the annual gift tax exclusion. Such gifts will produce very different estate tax results, depending upon whether or not the gift is completed.

As we have seen, a *completed* annual exclusion gift is not a "taxable" gift because its taxable value is zero.[29] Thus it is not subject to gift taxation. And in most cases it is not subject to estate taxation. Except for completed §2035 transfers, to be discussed in the next section, it is not includable in the gross estate because it is a completed gift. And is it not an "adjusted taxable gift," again because its taxable value is zero.

On the other hand, an *incomplete* annual exclusion "gift" is treated, for both gift tax and estate tax purposes, as if it had never been made, and is fully includable in the gross estate at its date of death value.

> EXAMPLE A D makes §2036, 2037, and 2038 (incomplete) transfers of real property, with each of the three worth $2,000 at date of transfer and $50,000 at date of death. These are not transfers subject to gift taxation. At D's death, the gross estate will include $150,000. Incomplete annual exclusion transfers are not exempt from the *strings attached* provisions.

> EXAMPLE B Same facts as example A, above, except that the three transfers were *completed gifts*, not subject to §2036, 2037, or 2038. These transfers are subject to gift taxation but are sheltered by the annual exclusion. And nothing attributable to the gifts will be includable in the gross estate, unless they fall under §2035.

To complicate matters a bit, a single, split interest transfer, usually to a trust, may involve two or more separate transfers (we'll call them "subtransfers" here), each of which may or may not be complete. Gift tax law may require that each subtransfer be examined in isolation to determine its completeness, independent of the other components of the transaction.

> EXAMPLE C Atchison transfers property into an irrevocable trust, with all income payable annually to Jones for ten years. Then, the trust will terminate and the remainder will pass to Smith. Atchison has retained no interest whatsoever in the trust property, and the entire transfer is complete. Neither subtransfer is incomplete.

> EXAMPLE D Facts similar to Example C above, except Atchison, as trustee,

---

29. Recall that the value of a taxable gift is the value of the gross gift reduced by the amount of the annual exclusion.

retains the discretionary power to distribute the first ten years income to himself or Jones. While the subtransfer of the remainder interest is still complete, the subtransfer of the income interest is incomplete. Thus, only the current value of the remainder interest will be subject to gift tax, in a manner described in Chapter 7. Further, if Atchison dies within 10 years, the full value of the trust property will be includable in his gross estate under §2036. However, to avoid double counting, the taxable gift value of the remainder will not be added to adjusted taxable gifts.[30]

EXAMPLE E Facts similar to Example C above, except the transfer is to a *revocable trust*. Since Atchison has retained the right to revoke both interests, neither subtransfer is complete.

Sections 2036, 2037, and 2038 all involve transfers in which the decedent had retained the *string* up to the time of the transferor's death. The next section will examine the *three year rule,* which covers very few transfers, but when it is applicable the transferred property will be included in the gross estate at DOD value, even though the decedent had retained no interest whatsoever at the time of death.

§2035(d)(2): Certain Transfers Within Three Years of Death

Under §2035(d)(2), a property interest includable in the gross estate arises if the decedent made one of two fairly uncommon types of completed transfers (i.e., no strings attached), within three years of death. First, gratuitous relinquishments or transfers of a property interest, which, had the relinquishment or transfer not been made, would have been includable in the decedent's gross estate under Sections 2036, 2037, 2038, or 2042, are includable in the gross estate under §2035(d)(2). Second, §2035(c) also includes in the gross estate the gift tax paid for *any gift* made within three years of death. The following material on the three-year bringback rule is subdivided into these two parts: relinquishment or transfer of certain interests, and gift tax in the gross estate.

Relinquishment or transfer of certain interests. A decedent's gross estate includes the value of property under which a relinquishment or transfer had been made within three years of death and which would have been included in the decedent's gross estate under Sections 2036, 2037, 2038, or 2042, had the relinquishment or transfer not been made. This sounds tricky, but it is not, provided you do not try to apply the rule to every transfer made within three years of death. Keep in mind it applies *only to two* types of

---

30. §2001(b)(2).

transfers, a gift of *life insurance* or the *severance* of a *retained* interest.

> EXAMPLE 2035-1 D transfers property into trust, with income to S or C for S's life, as D chooses, then remainder to B. If D died possessing this right to "sprinkle" the trust income, the value of the trust property would be includable in D's gross estate, as we have seen, under both §2036 and §2038. Anticipating this estate tax consequence, if D later irrevocably gave away (relinquished) this right before death, neither §2036 nor §2038 will apply. However, §2035 might apply, depending on how long D lived. If D died within three years of the relinquishment, the property would be includable under §2035. On the other hand, if D lived more than three years after the relinquishment, not even §2035 will apply.

> EXAMPLE 2035-2 Within three years of death, D assigned his ownership interest in a *life insurance* policy on his life. At D's death, the value of the proceeds will be includable in his gross estate because (*a*) the transfer occurred within three years of death, and (*b*) the proceeds would have been includable in D's gross estate under §2042 had the assignment (transfer) not been made.

Until recently, the IRS adamantly and persistently took the position that §2035 would apply even if the decedent-insured never owned a life insurance policy, if he or she nonetheless either paid the premiums directly or provided the funds with which to pay the premiums. In 1991, to the relief of many estate planners, the I.R.S. announced that it would no longer litigate this issue.[31] To avoid the three year rule planners often every effort to see that wealthy client never possesses any incidents of ownership in a policy. Thus, for example, while the insured will usually have to sign the policy application *as insured*, he or she should never sign *as owner*. If the policy is owned by the trustee of an irrevocable trust, the insured should not be granted any power to change beneficial ownership of the policy or its proceeds. Particular care must be taken if the policy is to be held by a corporation that is owned by the insured.[32]

Finally, the three year rule of §2035 does not apply to *premiums* paid by the insured-transferor even if within three years of death nor will such payments cause the insurance to be included in the insured estate. Of course if the policy itself was transferred within three years then §2035(d)(2) will bring the policy into the gross estate. Thus, although all or a portion of the *premiums* may be treated as an adjusted taxable gift, no portion of the *proceeds* are includable in the gross estate just because

---

31. However, it would like to amend §2035(d)(2) to include in the gross estate the face value of *all* policies on the decedent's life issued within three years of death.

32. For further analysis, see the Beehler article cited at the end of Chapter 15.

premiums were paid by the decedent-insured.[33] The premiums will be adjusted taxable gifts if they exceed the annual exclusion amount or are transferred in such a manner that no one has a present interest in them, i.e., to an irrevocable life insurance trust which does not contain a crummey power. More on life insurance trusts later in the book.

Most common transfers will not be subject to §2035(d)(2). Thus transfers of stocks, bonds, cash, gold, jewelry, land and other *garden variety* transfers, even if within three years of the transferor's death, are not brought into the gross estate, they are, and remain, adjusted taxable gifts. Had the gift not been made, the property, if still owned by the decedent at death, would only be includable in the gross estate under §2033, not one of those four sections specified in §2035. *Thus, except in the case of life insurance, single transaction gifts, even those made within three years of death, are* not *includable in the gross estate.* Accordingly, to understand this material fully, the reader must be able to distinguish a single transaction gift from a multiple transaction strings attached transfers followed by the transferor later relinquishing the retained interest and dying within three years of the relinquishment.

> EXAMPLE 2035-3 On her death bed, Leslie gave outright to her son $18,000 in common stock. She died one year later when the stock was worth $200,000. Hey, it was a good investment. Assuming she made no other gifts to him during that year, *nothing* related to this gift will be includable in Leslie's gross estate and it will be an adjusted taxable gift of $8,000. It is not a §2035(d)(2) gift because it would not have been includable under §2036, 2037, 2038, or 2042 had the gift not been made.

The facts in the example immediately above demonstrates that just because a lifetime gift is not includable in the gross estate does not necessarily mean that it will not be includable in the estate tax base since adjusted taxable gifts do boost the taxable estate into higher marginal rates. Recall that the *taxable* portion of any post-1976 gift is includable in adjusted taxable gifts. The distinction between inclusion in the *gross estate* versus inclusion in *adjusted taxable gifts* can be quite important for valuation reasons. All items in the gross estate are includable at date-of-death (or alternate valuation date) value, while adjusted taxable gifts are includable in the tax base (not the gross estate) at date-of-gift value and are reduced by the annual exclusion.

> EXAMPLE 2035-4 Continuing earlier Example 2035-2, assume that at the time of the transfer the policy's terminal value was $18,000 and its face value

---

33. *Estate of Morris R. Silverman* 61TC338 (1973), acq., 1978-1 C.B.2.

was $200,000. If D died more than three years after the transfer, the gross estate would be unaffected, and adjusted taxable gifts would include $8,000 (the $18,000 terminal value reduced by the $10,000 annual exclusion). On the other hand, if D died within three years of the transfer, the gross estate would include the entire $200,000 *face value*, but adjusted taxable gifts would be zero.

Congress singled out life insurance because of its unique characteristic of suddenly and radically increasing in value when the insured dies, a trait that strongly motivates taxpayers to avoid subjecting that increase to transfer taxes. In the absence of §2035, a deathbed gift of a policy on the life of the donor could cause a quick, relatively large avoidance of FET at little or no gift tax cost. For example, without §2035, a deathbed gift of a $1 million term policy could avoid FET on the entire face value with no gift tax consequences. For additional details, see the discussion of postgift appreciation in Chapter 13.

The impact of §2035(d)(2) can be further illustrated by the timeline in Figure 6-1, depicting when transfers will and will not be includable in the transferor's gross estate. The central frame of reference is year 0, when the decedent, if still alive, will be assumed to have either relinquished all retained §2036, §2037, or §2038 interests or controls, or transferred all incidents of ownership in an insurance policy on his or her life. Sometime earlier (year -1, -2, etc.) the decedent is assumed to have either made the initial §2036, §2037, or §2038 transfer with retained interest or control, or initially acquired §2042 incidents of ownership in the policy. If the decedent dies prior to year 0, the date of death value of the property will be includable in the gross estate under §2036, §2037, §2038, or §2042, as the case may be. If the decedent dies after year 0 but before year +3, the property will be includable under §2035 but will *not* be an adjusted taxable gift. Finally, if the decedent dies after year +3, nothing related to the property will be includable in the gross estate but the adjusted taxable gift value will boost the decedent's estate into higher marginal rates.

FIGURE 6-1 Timeline Illustration of Impact of Section 2035

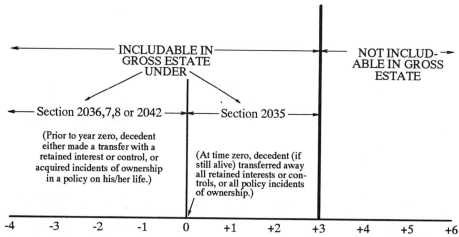

Timeline in years: when death occurs relative to the Section 2035 "transfer"

Gift tax in gross estate: "Grossing up." §2035(c) subjects a second important item to inclusion in the gross estate: gift taxes paid on *any* gifts made within three years of death.

EXAMPLE 2035-5 (The table after this narrative outlines the numbers described next.) X and Y, widowers each owning $10 million in property, are planning their estates. X does no planning. Making simple single assumptions, if X dies owning the entire $10 million, X's estate tax is $4,948,000, and thus X's children receive $5,052,000. By contrast, Y gives his children $5 million in property before death, paying a gift tax of $2,192,500. Assuming that Y dies within the year owning $2,807,500 ($10 million reduced by the gift and the gift tax paid), Y's estate tax base will be $7,797,500 (property owned at death plus adjusted taxable gifts), and his net estate tax will be $1,544,125. Therefore, in addition to the $5 million gift, at Y's death Y's children will receive $1,263,375, which is the difference between the amount of property owned at death ($2,807,500) and the net estate tax ($1,544,125). In total, Y's children will have received $6,263,375, which is greater than the $5,052,000 received by X's children. The $1,211,375 difference is explained partly by the $10,000 gift tax exclusion but mostly by the exclusion from the gross estate of the gift tax paid at the marginal rate of 55%.

	X	Y
Gross gifts	N/A	$5,000,000.
Less: Annual exclusion	N/A	10,000.
Taxable gifts	N/A	4,990,000.
Tentative gift tax	N/A	2,385,300.
Less: Unified credit	N/A	192,800.
Net gift tax	N/A	$2,192,500.
Gross estate	$10,000,000.	$2,807,500.
Plus: Adjusted taxable gifts	0.	4,990,000.
Estate tax base	10,000,000.	7,797,500.
Tentative estate tax	5,140,800.	1,736,925.
Less: Gift taxes payable		
on adjusted (post-1976) taxable gifts	0.	2,192,500.
Less: Unified credit	192,800.	192,800.
Net estate tax	$4,948,000.	$1,544,125.
Total transfer taxes (estate tax		
plus gift tax)	4,948,000.	3,736,625.
Total net to children	**$5,052,000.**	**$6,263,375.**

Compare the preceding example to Example 2035-6 that follows where Y's dies within three years of making the gift. §2035(c) requires inclusion in the gross estate of any gift tax paid on gifts made within three years of death.

EXAMPLE 2035-6 (The table at the end of this example outlines the numbers described next.) Same facts as before except Y dies two years after making the gift. Inclusion of the gift tax in Y's gross estate will give Y's estate a gross estate of $5,000,000 (= $2,807,500 + $2,192,500), an estate tax base of $9,990,000, a tentative tax of $5,135,300, and, allowing for a credit on the gift tax paid, an FET of $2,750,000. Thus, Y's children will receive a total of $5,057,500 ($10 million minus $2,192,500 minus $2,750,000), which exceeds the total $5,052,000 received by X's children by only $5,500, the amount of the tax advantage of the $10,000 gift tax exclusion.

	X	Y
Gross gifts	N/A	$5,000,000.
Less: Annual exclusion	N/A	10,000.
Taxable gifts	N/A	4,990,000.
Tentative gift tax	N/A	2,385,300.
Less: Unified credit	N/A	192,800.
Net gift tax	N/A	$2,192,500.
Gross estate	$10,000,000.	**$5,000,000.**
Plus: Adjusted taxable gifts	0.	4,990,000.
Estate tax base	10,000,000.	9,990,000.
Tentative estate tax	5,140,800.	5,135,300.
Less: Gift taxes payable on adjusted (post-1976) taxable gifts	0.	2,192,500.
Less: Unified credit	192,800.	192,800.
Net estate tax	$4,948,000.	$2,750,000.
Total transfer taxes (estate tax plus gift tax)	4,948,000.	4,942,500.
Total net to children	**$5,052,000.**	**$5,057,500.**

The doctrine that requires inclusion in the gross estate of gift taxes paid on lifetime gifts is called *grossing up*, and it prevents wealth used to pay gift taxes from escaping estate taxation. Current law, as we have said, however, requires grossing up only for taxes on gifts made within three years of death. Thus, the gift tax paid on a gift made *more than three years before death* still escapes transfer taxation, and continues to be the basis for significant FET savings.

Tax exclusive versus tax inclusive calculations. Based on the language of the trade, a different way of describing the grossing up rule is that the gift tax is calculated on a tax exclusive basis, i.e., the amount of the gift tax is not included in the quantity `taxable gifts.' On the other hand, the FET is calculated on a tax inclusive basis, i.e., the amount of the FET paid is implicitly included in the gross estate. Grossing up in effect converts a tax exclusive gift into a tax inclusive one. As we shall see in Chapters 7 and 12, an exception to the generation-skipping transfer tax subjects certain transfers ("direct skips") to tax on a tax exclusive basis, thereby reducing the effective tax rate.

RULES

THE CONNECTION BETWEEN GIFTS & THE DONOR'S ESTATE

The following rules should help you understand how post 76 gifts relate to the donor's estate:

One: Generally, gifts given are simply "adjusted taxable gifts" to the extent such exceed the annual exclusion.

Two: Gift taxes paid (or payable) are generally allowed as a credit against the tentative tax to offset the fact that the adjusted taxable gifts are used to boost the estate into its appropriate marginal rate.

Three: Gift taxes paid on <u>any</u> gift within three years of death are added to the gross estate.

Four: Retained interests in transfers (usually transfers in trust) will cause the property transferred to be included in the transferor's estate as though the transfer never took place. Sec 2036 - 2038.

Five: There are only two exceptions to rule number one

   a. transfers of an interest in **life insurance** within three years of death will result in the date of death value being included in the transferor's estate.

   b. **release** of a **retained** interest within three years of death will result in the date of death value of the trust assets being included in the settlor's estate as though no release occurred.

Notes to rules four & five: if a transferred property ends up in the gross estate, it will not also be an adjusted taxable gift for <u>estate</u> tax purposes. If transferred property is in the gross estate, it must be valued as of the date of death not the date of the gift.

§2043: Part-Sale, Part-Gift Transfers

Many clients believe that a transfer will not be treated as a gift if they receive some amount of consideration in exchange. They think that a small receipt from the donee will entirely exclude the transfer from gift taxation. That is not correct. As we have learned in Chapter 2, the amount of a gift is measured by the *difference* between the respective values of the consideration exchanged.

However, when the property is the subject of a §2035-§2038, or §2041 transfer, the consequence of subtracting only the *date-of-gift* value of the consideration received (i.e., given by the donee) can be far more disturbing, because the law requires including the property given by the donor in the estate at the *date-of-death value*. IRC §2043 provides that the amount of any property included in the gross estate under §2035 through §2038 (and §2041) will be the date-of-death value of the property, reduced only by a "consideration offset," that is, the original value of the consideration received.

> EXAMPLE 2043-1 Continuing Example 2036-1, shown earlier, had D "sold" the vacation home for $1,000 in speculative stock that is worth $17,000 at the gross estate will include the date-of-death value of the home ($20,000), less only $1,000, the date of gift value of the consideration received. The postgift appreciation on both the stock received (because D owns it) and the vacation home (because of the retain interest) will be in D's estate.

> EXAMPLE 2043-2 Continuing Example 2035-4, shown earlier, had D "sold" the policy for $1, the gross estate would include $199,999, the face value of $200,000 less $1, the amount of consideration received.

The two examples immediately above illustrate relatively uncommon incomplete estate planning transfers. Most bargain sale-type *completed* gift transfers are treated differently. They will not be subject to §2043, since they are not includable in the gross estate under any of the five Code sections, §2035 through §2038 or §2041. However, they will be included in the *estate tax base* at their adjusted taxable gift value, which equals the original gross gift value, less the annual exclusions and the original consideration received.

> EXAMPLE 2001-1 In 1984, Jessie "sold" her son Charles a parcel of land worth $18,000 for $200. As a completed transfer, it is not a strings attached gift. And it is not a transfer involving a general power of appointment or a gift of life insurance. Thus, this sale is not subject to §2035 through §2038, or §2041. Therefore, §2043 does not apply. Jessie will be treated as having made a gross gift of $17,800 and a taxable gift of $7,800. The latter amount will be

added to Jessie's adjusted taxable gifts when she dies, even though the land may have appreciated since the transfer.

It should be kept in mind that §2043 applies only to transfers includable in the gross estate under §2035, §2036-2038, *and §2041*. §2043 does not specifically mention §2042. Thus, transfers of life insurance in exchange for consideration will be subject to §2043 only if the transfer is also subject to §2035(d)(2).

> EXAMPLE 2043-3 Four years ago, Nissing sold for $500 to Rita a $100,000 face value policy on Nissing's life having a terminal value of $1,800. Nissing died last month, and his gross estate will not include anything in connection with this policy. (However, the transfer for value rule will render the proceeds in excess of the purchase price taxable as income to Rita).

> EXAMPLE 2043-4 Based on the facts in Example 2043-3, if Nissing died two years ago, $99,500 would be includable in Nissing's gross estate, based on §2043 (a $500 offset) with reference to §2035(d)(2) which in turn makes reference to §2042 (life insurance).

TWO: ESTATE TAX DEDUCTIONS

Estate tax deductions include funeral expenses, expenses in administering the estate, claims against the estate, debts of the decedent, certain taxes including any estate tax on excess retirement accumulations[34], losses incurred during estate administration[35], charitable bequests[36], and the marital deduction.[37] In this section we will introduce the marital deduction and develop it in detail in later chapters. The other deductions will be explored somewhat in the context of deduction planning in Part 3 of the text.

---

34. §2053. Covers expenses, debts and taxes.

35. §2054.

36. §2055.

37. §2056.

§2056: Marital Deduction

In calculating the taxable estate, the gross estate may be reduced by the value of any qualifying interest in property passing from the decedent to the surviving spouse. Thus, essentially an "unlimited" amount of property passing to the surviving spouse can avoid estate taxation, provided that certain requirements are met.

Requirements for the unlimited marital deduction. Subject to several exceptions, a property transfer to a spouse will qualify for the unlimited marital deduction if it meets the following three requirements:

1. *Includable in decedent's gross estate.* First, the property must be *includable* in the decedent's gross estate.

2. *Must "pass" to surviving spouse.* Second, the property must actually *pass* to the surviving spouse.

> EXAMPLE MD-1 Ordorica died recently, leaving a $1 million cash bequest to her husband in her will, which specified that any federal estate tax will be paid out of this particular bequest. The amount deductible under the marital deduction in Ordorica's estate will equal the $1 million reduced by the net tax payable that is not "passing" to him.

Thus, to qualify for the full marital deduction, most planners will plan for taxes and other expenses to be paid from property *not* qualifying for the marital deduction. An additional problem of paying estate taxes out of the marital share is the need to make interrelated computations: In order to calculate the amount of the marital deduction, one needs to know the amount of the net tax. However, in order to calculate the net tax, the amount of the marital deduction must be calculated. A solution is determinable, but it requires an iterative sequence of calculations.

Special rules for transfers to non-U.S. citizen spouse. Property passing at death to a *surviving spouse* who is not a U.S. citizen will qualify for the marital deduction only if it passes to a "qualified domestic trust," commonly called a QDT created for the benefit of that spouse or if the surviving spouse becomes a U.S. Citizen.[38] The rationale for requiring the creation of this trust is to ensure collection of the estate tax on the death of a surviving spouse who might otherwise remove the wealth from the United States. This is covered in greater detail in Chapter 12.

3. *Not a terminable interest.* Third, to qualify for the unlimited marital deduction, the interest passing to the surviving spouse cannot be a

---

38. §2056A(a), some authorities refer to the QDT as a QDOT.

terminable interest. A *terminable interest*, defined in §2056, is
> *(an interest) which will terminate or fail...on the lapse of time, on the occurrence of an event or contingency, or on the failure of an event or contingency to occur.*

The terminable interest rule was created to ensure that property will be subject to estate taxation in at least one of the two spouse's estates. Without it, property could qualify for the marital deduction in the estate of the first spouse and not even show up in the gross estate of the surviving spouse.

> EXAMPLE 2056-1 In his will, decedent transfers property into a trust, with income to his wife for her life, then remainder to his child. The value of the life interest to the wife will not qualify for the marital deduction because it will "terminate ... on the occurrence of an event or contingency." Her interest will terminate at her death. In general, a *life estate interest* passing to a surviving spouse does not qualify for the marital deduction and it is not included in the surviving spouse's estate, unless a special election is made..

Four exceptions to the terminable interest rule. One exception to the rule arises when no other person will possess or enjoy any part of the property after the termination of the interest passing to the surviving spouse.

> EXAMPLE 2056-2 At her death, decedent was receiving an annuity that is payable until her husband's subsequent death. This is a joint and survivor annuity. If the value of the survivor's annuity is includable in decedent's gross estate under Code §2039, a marital deduction would be allowed because *no other person* will enjoy any part of the property after the husband's later death.

There are three other important exceptions to the terminable interest rule written into §2056:

First, the rule will not be violated if decedent-testator conditions a spousal bequest upon surviving no more than *six months* after the decedent's death.[39] Thus, the survival clauses lasting "thirty days" and "four months" included in the wills in Chapter 3 create terminable interests that still qualify for the marital deduction. Some states such as California have enacted *marital deduction saving* statutes for will and trusts intended to qualify for the marital deduction but which ill-advisedly include long a survivorship period in excess of six months. The statutes reduce the survivorship period to 6 months. Unfortunately, judicial reaction to these

---

39. §2056(b)(3)(A).

statutes has been less than enthusiastically supportive.[40]

Second, a transfer in which the surviving spouse receives a life estate in all of the income, payable at least annually, plus a *general power of appointment*, exercisable during life or by will, does not violate the terminable interest rule.[41] This arrangement is used in what is called a *power of appointment trust*, an example of one type of marital trust explained in Chapter 12.

Third, if the decedent's executor elects to treat certain property as "qualified terminable interest property," or "QTIP," it will qualify for the marital deduction despite the fact that the surviving spouse will not receive the property and might have at most a limited no power over the property.[42] A further discussion of the important estate planning uses of these exceptions will be postponed until Chapter 12, which explores marital deduction and bypass planning.

THREE: ESTATE TAX CREDITS

There are five basic estate tax credits: the unified credit, credit for state death taxes, credit for gift tax, credit for tax on prior transfers, and the credit for foreign death taxes. Since the unified credit was explained in the last chapter, the following material discusses only the four others. All four of them have the effect of preventing the imposition of some form of multiple transfer taxation from being imposed on any one particular estate.

Credit for State Death Taxes

§2011 allows a credit for *state* inheritance or estate taxes actually paid, up to a maximum credit calculated from Table 6 of Appendix A. Use of the table requires calculation of the "adjusted taxable estate," which is defined as the taxable estate reduced by $60,000.

---

40. See CA Probate Code §21,525. For a discussion of these statutes, see the Durham Jr. article cited at the end of the chapter.

41. §2056(b)(5).

42. §2056(b)(7).

EXAMPLE 2011-1 D died last year, having a gross estate of $755,000 and total deductions amounting to $46,000. The estate paid a state death tax of $15,000. The federal credit for state death tax is limited to $15,000, which is the lesser of $15,000 or $18,432, the table amount. To arrive at this latter figure, we obtain the adjusted taxable estate, which equals $649,000 (i.e., $755,000 less $46,000 less $60,000), upon which the rates are calculated. $18,432 equals the sum of $18,000 plus 4.8 percent of $9,000 (i.e., $649,000 less $640,000). Therefore, the lesser amount is $15,000, which is the proper federal credit for state death taxes.

In the above example, the state could have imposed a death tax of $18,432, or $3,432 more, at no extra cost to the estate. This is shown in the next example.

EXAMPLE 2011-2 Assuming no credits except the unified credit and the credit for state death taxes, the total federal and state death taxes in Example 2011-1 are $40,330. (Tax base: $709,000; tentative tax: $233,130; total credits: $207,800, which is $192,800 plus $15,000; FET: $25,330. Total state and federal death taxes of $40,330 represents the sum of $15,000 plus $25,330). Alternatively, had the state imposed a tax of $18,432, total state and federal death taxes would still equal $40,330. Proof: Tentative tax: $233,130 less unified credit of $192,800 less state death tax credit of $18,432 (lesser of $18,432 or $18,432) leaves an FET of $21,898. State tax was $18,432 and therefore total taxes are still $40,330.

Thus, any state can impose a death tax as high as the federal maximum table credit at no extra cost to the estate, since up to that point a higher federal credit will offset, dollar for dollar, a higher state tax. We can conclude from this that to maximize their own fiscal self-interest, the states ought to ensure that each estate pay a state death tax in an amount at least equal to the maximum federal credit. As a matter of fact, all states do this, and practitioners call this provision a "pickup," "soakup" or "sponge" tax.

In those one half of the states imposing *only* a pickup tax, no state death tax will be owed by estates that owe no FET. The following states (and District of Columbia) impose only a pickup tax: Alabama, Alaska, Arizona, Arkansas, California, Colorado, Florida, Georgia, Hawaii, Idaho, Illinois, Maine, Missouri, Minnesota, North Dakota, New Mexico, Nevada, Oregon, Texas, Utah, Virginia, Vermont, Washington, West Virginia, Wyoming. Among the states that actually have their own death tax rates, several impose a rate high enough to result in a state tax on larger estates that is *higher* than the maximum federal credit. Nonetheless, the estate is permitted to report only the maximum federally table-determined amount on Form 706. The upshot will be a state tax partially unprotected by the credit. For example, the New York state inheritance tax on $600,000 is approximately $25,000. For additional information on actual state death taxes, see the case study section in Chapter 12.

Credit/Offset for Gift Taxes

To help prevent double taxation, the unified transfer tax system allows some level of offset for gift taxes on all gifts includable in the decedent's estate tax base. Without this offset, the FET would be calculated on all accumulated deathtime and lifetime gifts, unfairly disregarding the fact that a transfer tax had already been paid on some of them.

The law allows offsets for two different categories of gift taxes: those paid on pre-1977 gifts, and those paid on post-1976 gifts.

Credit for gift taxes (pre-1977 gifts). The credit for gift tax, line 17 on page 1 of the federal estate tax return, technically includes only gift taxes paid on pre-1977 gifts which are required to be included in the decedent's gross estate.[43] More exactly, the amount of the credit is limited to the lesser of the gift tax attributable to that property subject to the gift tax, or the estate tax attributable to that property. Thus, if in the year of the gift decedent paid a total combined gift tax of $30,000 for gift A, worth $100,000 and gift B, worth $200,000 and only gift B was later includable in the gross estate, the gift tax attributable to B is $20,000 [= $30,000 x ($200,000/$300,000)]. The reader might be wondering what pre-1977 gifts could possibly show up in the gross estate. At death, if decedent's total FET was $300,000, based on a total gross estate)reduced by marital and charitable deductions) of $5 million, of which gift B was includable at a value of $500,000, the FET attributable to gift B is $30,000 [=$300,000 x ($500,000/$5,000,000)]. Thus, the allowable credit for gift taxes paid for gift B is $20,000 (lesser of $20,000 or $30,000). Ordinarily, pre-1977 gifts will not in any way affect the estate tax return of post-1981 decedents, since §2035 includes in the gross estate only certain transfers made within *three years* of death, and §2001 includes in "adjusted taxable gifts" (not the gross estate) only *post-1976* taxable gifts. However, a pre-1977 gift can wind up in the gross estate under §2036, §2037, §2038, or §2035 if the donor-decedent had made a pre-1977 (partially complete) transfer with a retained interest or retained control, or relinquished such an interest within three years of death.

> EXAMPLE 2012-1 In 1962, decedent, then age 50, created an irrevocable trust, funding it with $2 million in property. Under the terms of the trust, income was payable to the decedent for life, with remainder to his descendants.

---

43. §2012.

Decedent paid a gift tax of $235,118 on the completed gift of the *remainder* interest. If decedent dies today, his gross estate will include today's value of the entire trust corpus, under §2036. A credit for gift tax paid will be allowed, based on the gift tax the decedent would have paid *this year* on the 1962 gift Rationale: Pre-1977 gifts were subject to lower gift tax rates and this credit only avoids double taxation, it is not intended as a refund.

Offset for gift taxes (post-1976 gifts). Based upon material covered earlier, it should be clear that two categories of post-1976 gifts will be includable in the decedent's estate tax base. First, similar to the pre-1977 gifts described in the previous section, post-1976 gifts also subject to §2036, §2037, §2038, or §2035 will be includable in the gross estate. Second, the taxable portion of other completed post-1977 gifts ("adjusted taxable gifts") will be added to the estate tax base. Again, to prevent double taxation, the law allows an offset to the tentative tax for gift taxes paid on these gifts.[44] Although the return does not call this offset a "credit," and includes it on line 9, it has the effect of reducing the tentative tax to an amount called the "gross estate tax," and it clearly is a credit.

Thus, *any* gift tax paid on *any* gift that is included in the estate tax base will be allowed as a credit or the equivalent of a credit. Either way, it will be subtracted from the tentative tax.

Credit for Tax on Prior Transfers

Occasionally, a person will die shortly after receiving a bequest of property. To reduce double FET taxation, a credit is allowed for certain federal estate taxes previously paid on property *received* by a decedent. It applies only to deathtime transfers, and arises most commonly in situations where the transferor and the decedent-transferee were not married, thus unable to enjoy the shelter of the marital deduction. Common examples include transfers from parent to child and transfers between unmarried partners in nontraditional relationships.

> EXAMPLE 2013-1 Harold died intestate three years ago, and his entire net estate passed to his mother, Gladys. A federal estate tax was paid on the estate. Gladys died yesterday. Gladys's estate will be allowed a credit for a portion of

---

44. §2001(b)(2). This offset is calculated by determining the amount that would have been "payable" had the tax rates in effect at the decedent's death been applicable at the time of the gift. Since rates for taxable amounts up to $3 million have been the same for all years after 1976, the tax *payable* may be different from the actual gift tax *paid* only for very large total taxable gifts, i.e, whose level exceeded this amount.

the federal estate tax paid at Harold's death.

The purpose of the credit for tax on prior transfers (TPT), also called the previously taxed property (PTP) credit, is to prevent multiple federal transfer taxation of property that passes by death to successive estates within a fairly brief period. Calculation of the credit is complex; only the two major steps will be summarized:

Step 1: Calculate the amount of the maximum credit before the percentage limitation (Step 2), by determining the *lesser* of (*a*) the amount of the federal estate tax attributable to the transferred property in the *transferor's* (e.g., Harold's) estate, or (*b*) the amount of the federal estate tax attributable to the transferred property in the *present decedent's* (Gladys's) estate.

Step 2: Multiply the amount obtained in Step 1 by the following percentage limitation, which depends upon how long the decedent-transferee survived the deceased transferor:

Decedent Survived by	Percent Allowed
0 to 2 years	100.%
Over 2 to 4 years	80.
Over 4 to 6 years	60.
Over 6 to 8 years	40.
Over 8 to 10 years	20.
Over 10 years	0.

Thus, if the decedent-transferee survives the deceased transferor by more than 10 years, no credit for previously taxed transfers is allowed.

Credit for Foreign Death Taxes

A credit is allowed for foreign death taxes (of many, but not all nations) paid on property which is (*a*) includable in the U.S. gross estate, and (*b*) situated in that foreign country.

This chapter has examined the principal items found on the estate tax return, including components of the gross estate, FET deductions, and FET credits. The next chapter examines the components of the gift tax return, covers certain special tax valuation rules, and introduces the federal generation-skipping transfer tax.

QUESTIONS AND PROBLEMS

1. Explain in general the meaning of the gross estate.

2. (*a*)Identify several "not so obvious" examples of property interests falling and not falling under §2033. (*b*) What common tax principal applies to all of them?

3. (*a*) What is a dower interest? (*b*) How is it taxed?

4. During his lifetime, decedent contributed $30,000 to his pension plan, and his employer contributed $70,000. He retired in 1986. At his death, his wife is entitled to receive a survivor's pension of $1,800 per month for life. The present actuarial value of the pension at decedent's death is $122,000. How much is includable in decedent's gross estate if the pension is (*a*) "nonqualified"; (*b*) "qualified"? (Hint: There is a simple answer to both parts.)

5. Assume Decedent D owned a building worth $200,000 at D's death in joint tenancy with the alternative persons named below. In each case, assume the surviving cotenant(s) paid four fifths of the $50,000 purchase price and D paid one fifth. For each, calculate the amounts included in D's gross estate if the surviving co-tenant(s) are:

   a. D's spouse, and contribution can be proved.
   b. D's spouse, and contribution cannot be proved.
   c. D's spouse and D's son, and contribution cannot be proved.
   d. D's spouse and D's son, and contribution can be proved.
   e. D's son, and contribution cannot be proved.
   f. D's son, and contribution can be proved.

6. At his death, decedent-trustee was the holder of a power of appointment. Determine whether any portion of the trust principal is includable in decedent's gross estate under §2041, if decedent had each of the following alternative trustee powers.

   a. The unrestricted power to appoint property to his surviving descendants. In his will, decedent appointed a grandson to receive the entire corpus.
   b. Same as part a, except decedent did not appoint anyone during his lifetime or at his death.

     c. The unrestricted power to appoint property to himself or his descendants. In his will, he appointed a grandson.

     d. Same as part c, except decedent did not appoint anyone during his lifetime or at his death.

     e. The power to appoint property to himself for "health" reasons.

     f. The power to appoint property to himself for his "comfort."

     g. The power to appoint property to himself upon the approval of his son, who is remainderman.

     h. The power to appoint to himself or his children annually no more than the greater of $5,000 or 5 percent of the trust property. In his will, decedent exercised the power, naming his son to receive $60,000 of the $1 million trust corpus.

7. Can you think of any estate planning reason for creating a power of appointment?

8. (*a*) State the general principles of transfer taxation of powers of appointment. (*b*) What are the three exceptions?

9. Consider the following ten alternative hypothetical situations. For each, assume that at the moment of D's death, an insurance policy having a $150,000 face value and a $70,000 terminal value was in force. In the table below, determine for each situation the amount includable in D's gross estate and fill in the reason and the controlling code section. (Note: Uncle and wife are D's surviving uncle and wife. Community property states: Assume property held as tenancy in common (TIC) is, instead, community property. IOP is individually owned or separate property.

Owner Named on		Beneficiary	Premiums Paid with	How Much Includable in Gross Estate?	Reason
Insured	Policy				
a. D	D	D's estate	D's IOP	____	_____
b. D	D	D's estate	D and wife's TIC	____	_____
c. D	D	Wife	D and wife's TIC	____	_____

Owner Named on		Beneficiary	Premiums Paid with	How Much Includable in Gross Estate?	Reason
Insured	Policy				
d. D	Wife	D's estate	D's IOP	_____	_____
e. D	Wife	Wife	Wife's IOP	_____	_____
f. Uncle	D	Uncle	D's IOP	_____	_____
g. Uncle	D	Uncle	D and wife's TIC	_____	_____
h. Uncle	Wife	Wife	D and wife's TIC	_____	_____
I. Uncle	Uncle	D's estate	Uncle's property	_____	_____
j. Uncle	Uncle	Uncle	Uncle	_____	_____

10. What do Sections 2033, 2034, 2039, 2040, 2041, and 2042 all have in common?

11. What do Sections 2036, 2037, and 2038 all have in common?

12. Under §2036 what, technically, is included in the notion "strings attached"?

13. Give three common examples of transfers includable in the gross estate under §2038.

14. Explain the impact of §2035, and give specific examples of:

    a. a single transaction lifetime gift not includable under §2035.
    b. a single transaction lifetime gift includable under §2035.
    c. a relinquishment of a "string" not includable under §2035.
    d. a relinquishment of a "string" includable under §2035.

15. Redo part e of Question 9 assuming that the policy was purchased two years ago by decedent and given to wife, who then started paying all premiums with her own property. Assume, alternatively that the purchase was from (*a*) decedent's property and (*b*) an equal amount of both spouse's property.

16. How would your answers to the question immediately above change, if at all, if the policy was purchased two years ago by wife, but the source of the first year's premiums was the decedent's funds. Why?

17. (*a*) Two years before his death, decedent directed the trustee of his revocable living trust to give his daughter a block of common stock, then worth $10,000. At his death, the stock was worth $100,000. Assuming no other lifetime gifts, will there be any estate tax consequences? (Hint: Consider §2035 and §2038). (*b*) Would your answer be different if the decedent had lived two more years?

18. (*a*) Terrill owns an estate of $6 million. This year, he gave $3 million to his daughter. Assuming for simplicity no other lifetime gifts, no annual exclusion or deductions, a flat transfer tax rate of 50 percent, a unified credit of $200,000, and no asset appreciation, calculate Terrill's FET if (1) he lives four years; (2) he dies in two years; (*b*) Is grossing up an advantage or a disadvantage?

19. D died yesterday. While alive, he made one outright gift of cash in the alternative amounts listed below. In each assumed set of facts, indicate how much, if any, would be added to D's (1) gross estate and (2) adjusted taxable gifts.

    a. Gift of any size made in any year prior to 1977.
    b. Gift of $2,500 made in 1977.
    c. Gift of $3,500 made in 1981 (gift tax paid was $90)
    d. Gift of $3,500 made last year.
    e. Gift of $12,000 made last year (gift tax paid was $360).

20. (a) Would any of your answers to the problem immediately above change if the gifts were all of real property that have since doubled in value? (b) How would your answer to Parts *c* and *d* change if the gift property was a life insurance policy (face value of $100,000) on the decedent's life?

21. In 1973, Mom "sold" $100,000 worth of IBM stock to her son Jim for $10,000, under the condition that if she ever wanted it she could have it back. (*a*) If Mom dies this year when the stock is worth $420,000, how much, if anything, is includable in her gross estate? *b*) Would your answer change if last year Mom gave up all right to impose the condition stated above? If she gave it up four years ago?

22. Frank died with a gross estate of $800,000. During administration, the following checks were written: Partial distribution to Frank's son: $100,000; executor's commission: $16,500; attorney's fee: $20,000; funeral expenses: $4,200; accountant's fee: $4,600. Frank owed $62,000 at his death. During administration a $6,000 auto was stolen, and insurance paid $4,100. Frank's will left $8,000 to the Second Unified Creditable Church (assume a legitimate charity), $200,000 to his wife, and the rest to his mother. He had made no lifetime gifts. Calculate Frank's taxable estate. (Answer: $482,800).

23. At his death, Steve was a man of great wealth. The following are facts about his and his wife Mary's property interests:

    - He owned a $2 million hotel in joint tenancy with Mary.
    - He was the grantor of a revocable trust (T1), with the principal ($750,000) payable to Mary at his death, if Mary survived him by six months.
    - He owned a $3 million life insurance policy (L1) on his life, payable to Mary. Steve paid all premiums.
    - Mary owned a $1.2 million life insurance policy (L2) on Steve's life (purchased by her eight years ago), payable to her.
    - A second trust (T2) gave Steve a general power of appointment over $900,000, and in his will Steve appointed Mary.
    - In a third "bypass" trust (T3), Steve left $600,000 in common stock at his death, with income to Mary for her life, then remainder to their son. Mary had a general power of appointment over the trust corpus, limited by the ascertainable standard of health and maintenance.
    - A successful wholesale distributor, Steve died owning $400,000 in customer account receivables, and he had arranged with his firm to pay these receivables over a 10 year period to his wife, or his children, who were the contingent beneficiaries.
    - Mary validly disclaimed the residue of Steve's estate, which amounted to $60,000 cash.

    Calculate Steve's (*a*) total gross estate and (*b*) marital deduction.

Be sure to determine whether each transfer either meets the requirements for the marital deduction, and/or falls within an exception. (Answers: (a) $6.710 million; (b) $5.650 million.)

24. (*a*) In the question immediately above, explain how your answer would change, if at all, if Trust T1 provided that certain taxes, amounting to $385,000, will be payable out of corpus? (Hint: How much will pass to Mary?) (*b*) How could this result have been avoided?

25. You are engaged in estate distribution planning for client Cowell, who owns $1,200,000 in property. Alternative dispositions include:

    1. All property outright to Cowell's spouse, if surviving.
    2. All property outright to Cowell's descendants.
    3. $600,000 outright to spouse, if surviving, and $600,000 outright to Cowell's descendants.

    a. If Cowell dies today and is survived by his spouse and some descendants, calculate Cowell's FET under each of these three dispositions. Assume no prior taxable gifts, no debts, and no credits except the unified credit. (Answers: 1. $0, 2. $235,000, 3. $0.)
    b. Continuing the events depicted in part *a*, above, if Cowell's spouse dies ten years later, not having remarried and simply owning only the exact value of any property she received at Cowell's death (she owned no property of her own while he was alive), calculate that spouses's FET under each of the three dispositions, assuming she leaves everything outright to her descendants. (Answers: 1. $235,000, 2. $235,000, 3. $0.)
    c. Calculate the combined FET for both spouses for each disposition.
    d. In Chapter 11, you will learn that disposition #1 has the effect of "overqualifying" for the marital deduction, needlessly increasing the total family FET. Can you see why?

26. Name the three page numbers of Form 706 (appendix C) where you will find the total amount of the marital deduction required to be included.

27. (a) Calculate the decedent's "table credit" and maximum federal credit for state death taxes for the following three taxable estates:

	Taxable Estate	Total State Death Taxes	Table Credit	Maximum Credit
1.	$100,000.	$1,000.	_____	_____
2.	1,100,000.	20,000.	_____	_____
3.	1,100,000.	40,000.	_____	_____

(b) If the decedent resided in a state such as Florida, which imposes only a pickup tax, for each part of the preceding table, how much will be the amount of this state tax?

28. (a) What is the purpose of the credit for tax on prior transfers? (b) Why does its amount depend upon how recently the transfer occurred?

29. (Note: Instructors will want to choose which of these three parts their students should answer.) Barrett died yesterday, owning all of the property interests and making all of the spousal dispositions described for Steve in question 23, above. In addition, all but two of the facts about Frank in question 22, above, apply to Barrett. (Not applicable: comments referring to the gross estate of $800,000, and to the $200,000 left to the wife.) Further, Barrett gave his son $80,000 cash (no gift splitting) five years ago, his only lifetime taxable gift. Assuming that Barrett resided in a pickup tax-only state (or, in your state, if different) and making any other simplifying assumptions where necessary, calculate Barrett's FET:
a. On a blank sheet of paper
b. On form 706, entering numbers only on *first three pages only* (photocopy or write on pages from Appendix C)
c. On form 706, entering numbers on *all pertinent pages* (you may photocopy or write on pages from Appendix C)

30. How much attributable to the assets of each of the following trusts, each worth $1 million, will be includable in D's gross estate? Assume an AFR of 11 percent.

    a. Trust created by D's father, with income payable to D for life and remainder to D's son.

    b. Trust created by D's mother, with income payable to D for life and remainder to D or his estate.

    c. Trust created by D's aunt, with income payable to D's father for life and then remainder to D or his estate. At D's death, D's 79 year old father was alive.

31. In 1964, Franco created a trust, with income payable to his daughter for life, then remainder to his daughter's descendants. Franco reserved the right to change the remainder beneficiaries at any time. If Franco dies this year when his daughter is age 50, calculate the amount includable in Franco's gross estate attributable to the trust, whose corpus is now worth $2 million. Assume an AFR of 9 percent.

32. Based on the facts in the question immediately above, how would your answer change if Franco (*a*) also retained the right to change the income beneficiary, or (*b*) retained only the right to change the income beneficiary?

33. True or false? A decedent's gross estate will never include the value of any single transaction completed gift of anything other than life insurance made within three years of death.

34. Americus died recently owning $800,000 in property. In 1974 he gave his nephew a taxable gift of $16,000, paying a gift tax of $3,200. How would these 1974 amounts influence Americus' federal estate tax return?

35. Referring to Question 2 at the end of Chapter 4, indicate whether each asset in which Harry had an interest will or will not be includable in his gross estate. Also, for each, give your appraisal as to how confident you can be about your answer.

36. In many, if not most situations, do you think the size of client's probate estate will be smaller than, larger than, or about equal to the gross estate?

RECOMMENDED READING

Abbin, Byrle M. "The Politics of Estate and Graft Taxation, Or Watching The Sausage Being Made-Is Anyone in Charge." *1991 University of Miami Estate Planning Institute.*

Abrams, Howard E. "A Reevaluation of the Terminable Interest Rule." *Tax Law Review* 39 (1983), pp.1-29.

Ashby, Robert S. "Successful Handling of Retirement Benefits: An Estate Planning Overview." *Trusts & Estates*, July 1984, pp.13-19.

Bittker, Boris I. "Transfers Subject to Retained Right to Receive the Income or Designate the Income Beneficiary." *Rutgers Law Review* 34 (1982), pp.668-699.

Blake, John F. "'Control' and the Estate Tax Implications of Retained Voting Rights under Section 2036(b)." *Estate Planning*, January, 1988, pp. 22-26.

Cairns, J. Donald, and Stephen W. Jones. "Appraisals, Audits, and Appeals-The Practical Side of Tax Practice." *Probate Notes* 12 (1987), pp. 210-43.

Cooper, George. "A Voluntary Tax? New Perspectives on Sophisticated Estate Tax Avoidance." *Columbia Law Review* 77 (March 1977), pp.161-247.

Curzan, Robert L. "Federal Gift and Estate Tax Aspects of Marital Dissolutions." *Gonzaga Law Review* 16 (1981), pp. 923-945.

Durham Jr., Robert J. "Protective Legislation: Does it Work? Does it Need Revision? Can It Be Effective?" *1992 University of Miami Estate Planning Institute.*

Estate and Gift Tax Reporter. Chicago: Commerce Clearing House.

Federal Estate and Gift Taxes. Englewood Cliffs, N.J.: Prentice-Hall.

Feldman, Charles F. "Estate Planning For Executives: Retirement and Death Benefits." *22nd Annual Estate Planning Institute, 1991*, Practising Law Institute.

*Gutierrez Jr., Max. "Expatriation-- Worth the Trip?" *1993 University of Miami Estate Planning Institute.*

Harrison, Louis S. & John M. Jamiga. "Maximizing the Use of the State Death Tax Credit." *Estate Planning*, March, 1992, pp. 104-10.

*Hastings, Dan T. "Death and 'Supplemental Taxes: Coping With I.R.C. Section 4980A." *1989 University of Miami Institute on Estate Planning.*

Helle, Steven. "The Impact of Estate Taxes on Independent Daily Newspapers: An Illinois Case Study." *DePaul Law Review* 33 (1984), pp.323-55.

Hoffman, Paul G, "Estate Planning For Non-Qualified Plan Benefits: Wednesday the Rabbi Retired." *1990 University of Miami Estate Planning Institute.*

Kinskern, Douglas. "When Will Transferees and Executors Be Personally Liable For Estate and Gift Taxes?" *Estate Planning*, March 1987, pp. 106-11.

Kisling, Stephen C. "The Life Estate and The Availability of The Section 2013 Credit." *Taxes - The Tax Magazine*, February 1982, pp. 146-53.

Lawrence III, Robert C. "U.S. Estate and Gift Taxation for the Nonresident Alien with Property in the United States." *1990 University of Miami Estate Planning Institute.*

Lowe, Henry T. "Transfer Taxes on Survivor Annuity Benefits." *Missouri Law Review* 50 (1985), pp.737-58

Mezzullo, Louis A. "TAMRA Bars Marital Deduction for Alien Spouses; Makes Other Changes As Well." *Estate Planning* May, 1989, pp. 130-34.

*_____. " Planning for Distribution From Qualified Plans and IRAS." *1993 University of Miami Estate Planning Institute*, Chapter 7.

Moore, Charles K., Jr., and James W. Childs. "Econometric Model Useful in Calculating State Death Tax Effect on Marital Deduction." *Journal of Taxation*, October 1985, pp. 252-53.

*Moore, Malcolm A. "Recognition and Uses of Federal Estate Tax Credits in Estate Planning and Administration." *1987 University of Miami Estate Planning Institute.*

Newlin, Charles F. & Cynthia D. Glenn. "The Estate Tax Audit: How to Prepare and Succeed." *Estate Planning*, January, 1992, pp. 37-37-43.

Newman, Joel S. "Incompetency and Federal Wealth Transfer Taxation." *Tax Law Journal* 2, no. 1 (1984), pp.77-87.

Newman, Stephen M. "Recent Changes Make It Easier to Keep Nonqualified Plan Benefits Out Of Estate." *Taxation For Accountants*, April 1986, pp. 234-39.

Newton, William M. III. "Estate, Gift, and Generation-Skipping Transfer Tax Treaties." *Southwestern Law Journal* 37 (1983), pp. 563-599.

Oliver, Harry G. "Estate and Gift Tax Planning for Nonresidents." *International Tax Journal* 12:4 (Fall 1986), pp. 299-317.

Pennfield, Edward B., and Charle J. Seidler, Jr. "Adverse Estate Consequences of Ownership of Reversionary Interests can be Avoided." *Estate Planning*, May 1983, pp.144-147.

Redd, Charles A. "When and How to Take Maximum Advantage of the Credit for Tax on Prior Transfers." *Estate Planning*, May 1985, pp.162-167.

Ridley, James I. "Estate Tax Credits, Other than the Unified Credit, Offer Planning Possibilities." *Estate Planning*, Nov., 1988, pp. 358-62.

Ruane, Thomas P. "Federal Estate and Gift Tax Changes Under the Economic Recovery Tax Act: An Ideological Retreat." *Loyola Law Review* 28 (1982), pp.13-33.

*Silfen, Martin. "Timing of Distributions Is Vital When a Client Has Large Retirement Plan Assets." *Estate Planning*, May, 1990, pp. 130-37.

Stephens, Richard B., Guy B. Maxfield, and Stephen A. Lind, *Federal Estate and Gift Taxation*. Boston: Warren, Gorham and Lamont. Numerous editions.

Surrey, Stanley S., William C. Warren, Paul R. McDaniel and Harry L. Gutman. *Federal Wealth Transfer Taxation* 2nd ed. New York: Foundation Press, 1982.

— 7

The Federal Gift Tax;
§2701-04 Special Valuation Rules;
The Federal Generation-Skipping Transfer Tax

OVERVIEW

Chapter 5 introduced the gift tax by outlining how it is calculated and how it is unified with the estate tax. This chapter will examine more qualitative factors, such as the requirements for a valid gift, types of taxable gifts, how gifts qualify for the annual exclusion, and how certain specific transfers are subject to gift tax. The chapter will also introduce the so-called Chapter 14 transfer tax valuation rules of §2701-2704, and the generation-skipping transfer tax. While reading the chapter, the reader is urged to review both the overview of the gift tax scheme in Table 5-1 and the copy of Form 709, United States Gift Tax Return, which is included in Appendix D.

FEDERAL GIFT TAX

We begin by resolving a semantics problem, stemming from the fact that planners use the word "gift" in two different ways. Chapter 2 defined a gift as a completed transfer of an interest in property by an individual in exchange for any amount that is less than full and adequate consideration. This definition is accurate, but possibly misleading. It implies (correctly) that the word gift includes transfers at *death*. Thus, planners will (correctly) say, "...in his will he *gave*..." However, the subject of this chapter is traditionally called the federal gift tax, and here planners mean only *lifetime* gifts. Consequently, to avoid the necessity of always using the modifier "lifetime," as in "lifetime gift," whenever the word gift is mentioned *in this chapter*, a lifetime gift will be assumed.

Requirements for a Valid Gift: Influence of Local and Federal Law

Whether or not a transfer is treated as a gift is important for two reasons in estate planning. First, it will influence the respective property rights of the parties. Second, it will determine whether a federally taxable event has occurred. In deciding these issues, two different sets of rules must be examined: local property law and federal gift tax law.

Local property law. To be valid under local property law, a gift must ordinarily meet four requirements.

1. The donor must be capable of transferring property.
2. The donee must be capable of receiving and possessing the property.
3. There must be delivery to, and some form of acceptance by, the donee or the donee's agent. A gift of money by check is not complete until the funds are *paid* by the donor's bank; until then the donor has not totally relinquished dominion and control. Thus, certain last minute deathbed gifts may not work. An example of an agent would be an escrow agent who is holding the property on behalf of the donee.
4. Finally, under local law, a valid gift ordinarily requires donative intent on the part of the donor.

Federal gift tax law. To be subject to taxation under federal gift tax law, a gift must meet all of the above local property law requirements, subject to two major federal modifications.

a. Federal tax regulations explicitly state that *donative intent is not required* for a transfer to be subject to gift tax. The first series of examples depicted shortly will illustrate this point.[1] Although not required for a gift, the existence of donative intent would be strong evidence that a gift had actually been made.
b. Under the unique language of federal law, the gift tax applies only to a *completed* gift, which arises when "...the donor has so parted with dominion and control as to leave him no power to change its disposition, whether for his own benefit or for the benefit of another..."[2]

---

1. Examples 2512-1 and -2.

2. Reg. §25.2511-2(b).

Ordinarily, completed gifts are made either outright or in trust. *Outright transfers* made beyond the donor's dominion and control are virtually always complete for gift tax purposes. Transfers in trust, on the other hand, may be totally complete, totally incomplete, or partially incomplete.[3] An example of a *totally complete transfer in trust* is a transfer to an irrevocable trust with no retained interests or controls; the entire transfer is subject to gift taxation. An example of a *totally incomplete transfer in trust* is a transfer to a typical revocable trust; it is not at all subject to gift taxation because the trustor has retained the power to demand return of the trust property. An example of a *partially incomplete transfer in trust* is one to an irrevocable trust over which the trustor has simply retained interest in or control over the income (or remainder) but not the remainder (income). The trustor will be treated as having made a completed gift of just the remainder (income) interest. Thus, for transfers in trust in which more than one property interest is created, gift tax law requires that each interest be examined independently to determine whether a completed gift of that interest has been made.

Thus, federal tax law and local property law both influence gift taxation. Summarizing, the relationship between federal law and local law in regard to the requirements for a valid gift may be stated as follows: Local law dictates whether a transfer of *property rights* has in fact been made, irrespective of taxability. On the other hand, federal tax law, in conjunction with local law, specifies whether a gift subject to taxation has been made. Federal law also spells out rules relating to the taxation of specific types of gifts, such as those in connection with powers of appointment, life insurance, joint ownership, and disclaimers. Gift tax aspects of each of these dealings is discussed later in this chapter. Issues related to who is subject to gift tax and what is the value of the gift are described next.

Who Is Subject To Gift Tax

Under federal law, a gift subject to gift taxation applies to *individual U.S. citizens or residents*, regardless of where the property is located, whether the transfer is direct or indirect, real or personal, intangible or tangible. U.S. gift tax law also applies to *nonresident aliens* but only with regard to transfers of real property and tangible personal property situated within the U.S.[4]

---

3. For an additional discussion and review, see Examples A, B, C, D and E at the end of the section covering §2036 in Chapter 6.

4. §2501(a)(2), §2511(a).

Aspects Of Taxable Gifts.

Valuation of gift. The value of the gift for tax purposes is its fair market value at the date of the gift. Any consideration received in exchange is subtracted in determining the gross value of the gift.

EXAMPLE 2512-1 If Mom "sells" to son a $25,000 automobile for $1, Mom has made a gross gift in the amount of $24,999 and a taxable gift of $14,999.

Measuring the consideration received in exchange. To be recognized, consideration received in exchange must be measurable in money or money's worth. If it is not reducible to money or money's worth, it will be disregarded.

EXAMPLE 2512-2 In Example 2512-1, consideration received by Mom is still only $1, even though son gave her incredible amounts of love and affection before and after the gift, and even though son had graduated college and quit smoking, achievements Mom required as conditions for the gift.

The above example illustrates a situation where a gift is subject to gift taxation despite the fact that local law may view the exchange of consideration to be equal, and donative intent, therefore, to be nonexistent.

Some gifts are difficult to value. Gifts themselves, though potentially reducible to money or money's worth, may be extremely difficult to value.

EXAMPLE 2512-3 Last year, Dad guaranteed a bank loan made to Son. The IRS takes the position that by transferring a valuable economic benefit on behalf of Son, Dad made a completed gift, measured by the value of the guarantee, an amount that clearly would be difficult to value.[5] Moreover, if Son defaults on the loan, any amounts which Dad pays on the obligation will *also* be gifts subject to gift tax, without any offset for the earlier gift. Thus, the total of taxable gifts could exceed the amount of the guarantee.[6]

Fortunately, in the case of property settlements between divorcing spouses, federal law no longer requires a determination of the total value of the consideration exchanged by each spouse. Such transfers of property

---

5. At Dad's death, none of this contingent claim is likely to be deductible against his gross estate, if Son has not defaulted. Reg 20.2053-4.

6. LR 9113009; Rev. Rul. 84-25 1984-1 C.B. 191. For a discussion, see the August paper cited at the end of the chapter. In mid-1992, the IRS announced it will (eventually) revise this ruling.

subject to a written agreement are deemed to be made for full and adequate consideration even when it is clear that the "exchange" is not for money or money's worth.[7]

Gifts versus sales. Practically speaking, larger sales between *related parties* are frequently treated with suspicion by the Internal Revenue Service, which may contend that a gift rather than a sale has been made. On the other hand, larger sales made in the ordinary course of business between unrelated parties are presumed not to be gifts.

EXAMPLE 2512-4 Herb, owner of a retail drugstore, sells his aging delivery pickup truck to Karl, a *stranger*, who read about the truck in the classified section of the newspaper. Karl paid Herb $4,200 and promptly took out a similar ad and sold the truck three days later for $6,700. Herb has made a bad bargain, but not a gift, because the truck was sold in an *at arms-length* transaction.

EXAMPLE 2512-5 Same facts as Example 2512-4, except that Herb, who had already made gifts in excess of $10,000 to his son, Jerry, sold him the car for $4,200. Jerry then advertised and sold the car for $6,700. Herb may have great difficulty establishing to the satisfaction of the IRS that the deal was at arm's length, inasmuch as it was transacted between relatives.

Below-market dividend yield results in gift. Gifts can arise in the context of family oriented closely held business settings. Consider this fairly involved situation.

EXAMPLE 2512-6 Two years ago MacKay created the MCK Corporation, transferring assets to it in exchange for 300 shares of voting common stock, and 6,000 shares of voting preferred stock that pays a $3 dividend on a per share market value of $900. Dividing $3 by $900 produces a preferred dividend yield of only one third of one percent. Dividend yields for preferred shares of comparable corporations have been yielding much higher levels. Two weeks later, MacKay gave all of the common stock to his children. From that time to the present, MacKay has continued to hold majority voting control of MCK. MacKay is considered to have made annual gifts to his children of the difference between the actual dividend paid and the amount MCK was capable of paying (up to a rate commensurate with the prevailing market rate). The children are considered to have acquiesced in the receipt of low dividends. By holding voting control, MacKay could have prevented this gift, either by increasing the preferred dividend yield or by converting his preferred shares into common shares.[8] In the first full year, the market rate for comparable pre-

---

7. §2516.

8. TAM 9301001.

ferred stock was 12 percent, and MCK was capable of paying this rate. Thus, in that year, the value of MacKay's gift to his children was $630,000 (= 6,000 x [(.12 x $900) - $3]).[9]

Filing And Payment Requirements

When a return must be filed. In general, a gift tax return must be filed by any individual donor who, in any calendar year, gave:

- more than $10,000 to *any* nonspouse donee, or
- a gift of a *future interest* in any amount, or
- total gifts exceeding $100,000 to a *non U.S. citizen spouse*, or
- a gift for which spouses want to elect *gift splitting*.

The terms *future interest* gift and *gift splitting* will be described shortly.

Who files. Only *people* file gift tax returns. For example, if a partnership or a corporation makes a gift, the individual partners or stockholders are ordinarily considered the donors, liable for filing the return and paying the tax. In the case of a gift subject to gift taxation of property from an irrevocable trust or an estate, the donor would ordinarily be the person acting as trustee or executor, but only in exercising a general power of appointment. On the other hand, in the case of a revocable living trust that makes a gift subject to taxation, the grantor would be treated as the donor. If a donor dies before filing a return, the donor's executor must file. The return is due April 15 of the year following the calendar year in which the gift occurred.

---

9. For a discussion of this and other types of shareholder "passive gifts," including consenting to recapitulations, allowing the business to use the shareholders' property, consenting to a bargain sale of stock, waiving the bargain available under a stock option or buyout agreement, lending money to the business or guaranteeing a business loan, see the Newlin article cited at the end of the chapter.

Who pays. The donor is responsible for paying the gift tax[10]; the *donee* is not subject to either gift tax or income tax[11] on the gift. However there is transferee liability if the donor fails to pay the tax. This means that any donee can be forced to pay the gift tax up to the value of the gift received.

Net gift. Some clients, however, might wish to make a *net gift*, that is, to arrange in advance for the *donee* to be responsible for paying the gift tax. The Supreme Court has ruled such a transaction to be part sale, part gift, causing the donor to realize taxable income to the extent that the gift tax paid by the donee exceeds the donor's adjusted basis.[12] However, other advantages may still make the net gift attractive.

Deductible Gifts

Four types of gifts are fully deductible, thereby reducing the taxable gift amount to zero.

Charitable gifts. First, gifts to qualified charities are fully deductible from gross gifts for donors who are U.S. citizens or residents.[13] We'll see in Chapter 14 that gifts to charity in any one year are also deductible from *income tax*, but only up to certain percentages of adjusted gross income. Chapter 14 will discuss strategies for charitable gifting in detail.

Interspousal gifts. Second, under the unlimited marital deduction, gifts to a *U.S. citizen spouse* are fully deductible, provided that they are not terminable interests.[14] However, even terminal interest gifts might qualify for the marital deduction by using a gift QTIP election.[15] For an analysis of terminable interests, see the discussion on the estate tax marital deduction in Chapter 6, and the material on marital trusts in Chapter 12. Lifetime gifting between spouses is analyzed in Chapter 13.

Since 1988, only the first $100,000 per year in gifts to a *non U.S. citizen*

10. §2502(c)

11. §102(a)

12. *Dietrich* 457 U.S. 191 (1982).

13. §2522(a).

14. §2523.

15. §2056(b)(7)

spouse escape gift taxation.[16] In addition, all amounts of future interest gifts (see below) to a noncitizen spouse are subject to tax. Thus there is no marital deduction for gifts above $100,000 per year to a non U.S. citizen spouse. The annual exclusion and the concept of present and future interest gifts are discussed in the next section.

Gifts for tuition and medical care. Third and fourth, qualified payments in any amount made directly to an educational institution for tuition and payments in any amount made directly to a provider of medical care on behalf of any individual are fully deductible. Two things to emphasis here: the transfers must be *directly* to the providers, and not to the individuals themselves, and the person benefiting by the payments does *not* have to be related to the donor.[17]

Gift Tax Annual Exclusion And The Present Interest Requirement

The first $10,000 of the total annual value of gifts of a *present interest* to each donee is excluded from the donor's taxable gifts.[18] Note that the donor and donee do not have to be related. Present interests are those were "enjoyment" can start immediately whereas future interests by the terms of the transfer have possession or enjoyment delayed.

EXAMPLE 2503-1 This year, Mom gave Daughter a corporate bond valued at $24,300. Even though Daughter may not collect the par value until maturity, and even though the periodic interest income is payable in the future, the gift is of a present interest and qualifies for the annual exclusion. Daughter has a *present right to enjoy* the bond, for example, by selling it. Assuming that Mom, a widow, made no other gifts to Daughter during the year, the taxable value of the gift is $14,300, i.e., $24,000 - $10,000.

EXAMPLE 2503-2 Changing the facts of Example 2503-1, if Mom transferred the bond to an irrevocable trust whereby the trustee was to deliver the bond to Daughter in one year, the gift, which is reportable this year, is of a future interest and will not qualify for the annual exclusion because by the terms of the transfer the enjoyment is delayed for a period of time. The taxable gift is $24,300, assuming that Daughter will also get any income that accrues during the year.

---

16. §2523(i).

17. §2503(e).

18. §2503(b).

Congress in 1932 chose to deny the annual exclusion for gifts of future interests for three reasons: (1) future interests are often difficult to value; (2) the number of donees of a future interest is often indeterminable at date of gift; and (3) future interests are often created to avoid taxes.

Gifts into trust. Most problems regarding future interest gifts arise in the context of trusts.

> EXAMPLE 2503-3 T creates an irrevocable living trust, funding it with dividend-paying common stock worth $8,000. Under the terms of the trust, the trustee may *accumulate or distribute the income* to B for 10 years. No principal may be distributed during that time. At the expiration of 10 years, the trust terminates and all principal and accumulated income is payable to B, or if B is dead, to B's estate. Assuming B is currently an adult, T has currently made a gift of a future interest of $8,000, for which no annual exclusion will be available because beneficiary B's possession and enjoyment is delayed.

No annual exclusion means, of course, that absent any deductions, the gift will be entirely taxable, such that part or all of the donor's unified credit will have to be used. Further, at the donor's death, the value of the taxable gift is added to the estate tax base, which will raise the donor's marginal FET rate. Thus, the client may prefer a disposition that, as in the next example, is at least partly sheltered by the annual exclusion.

> EXAMPLE 2503-4 Altering the facts a bit in Example 2503-3, assume that instead of accumulating the income, the trustee is required to *pay all income* to B, an adult, at least annually, and the remainder goes to R at the end of the 10 year term. The result is that a portion of the value of the stock will represent a gift of a present interest and will qualify for the annual exclusion. Upon creation of the trust, two interests arose: a *present interest in the income* for 10 years and a remainder interest. At ten percent, the present value of an income interest for a 10 year period equals .614457 times the value of the stock. The product of .614457 * $8,000 is $4,916, which represents the portion of the gift that is considered a present interest qualifying for the annual exclusion up to a maximum for any one donee of $10,000. Hence, the total taxable gift equals $3,084 [$8,000-$4,916], the value of the future (remainder) interest which does not qualify for the annual exclusion.

2503(c) Trusts. There is an exception to the present interest requirement for gifts in trust of future interests on behalf of minors found in IRC §2503(c). This code section allows the annual exclusion even though there is no present interest provided the trust follows all the requirements of the section. In the absence of §2503(c), grantors might be encouraged to make outright gifts to minors, a practice which many argue would run contrary to public policy. A further discussion of gifting to minors will be found in Chapter 13. These trusts are referred to as *2503(c) trusts*, to qualify for §2503(c), the provisions of the trust must be specific that (1) the income and principal may be spent for the benefit of the minor before age 21, and (2) any amount not so spent will either pass to the minor when he or she reaches age 21, and (3) if the minor dies before age 21, the corpus and accrued income must either be payable to the minor's estate or be subject to the minor's general power to appoint.

> EXAMPLE 2503-5 Stephanie transfers $10,000 in property into an irrevocable trust whose trustee is permitted to expend principal and income for the benefit of her minor son. When son reaches age 21, the trust terminates and all principal and accumulated income will be distributed to him. If he dies before the trust terminates the principal and accumulated income is subject to his general power to appoint it, but if he fails to appoint it then the corpus will go to his sister Sue's trust if it has not then terminated, and if it has then directly to Sue. Although Stephanie has actually made a gift of a future interest, under the exception of §2503(c), the entire value of the property will qualify for the annual exclusion.

Gift Splitting

Gift splitting treats a gift of the property owned by one spouse as if it were made one half by each spouse. It is conceptually similar to federal spousal income splitting on a joint income tax return. For example, if husband earns $48,000 taxable *income*, and wife earns $2,000, higher income taxes would be paid if each spouse filed a separate return than if both filed a joint return, reporting the single amount $50,000. In effect, a joint income tax return will result in a tax which approximates applying the rate schedule to one-half, or $25,000, and then multiplying the tax by two. Total income taxes are lower for several reasons, including the fact that progressively higher marginal rates may be avoided and, that more importantly, wife might not otherwise be able to enjoy the full benefits of the standard deduction and the personal exemption. These two terms will be explained in the next chapter.

Under federal gift tax law, spouses may also split a *gift*. Thus, a gift by one spouse of his or her *individually owned property*, with the consent of the other spouse, will be treated as if made one-half by each spouse.[19] Thus one spouse can enjoy the benefit of two annual exclusions (and two unified

---

19. §2513.

credits, if needed) in a given year.

EXAMPLE 2513-1 Wife wishes to give $18,000 of her own cash assets to a nephew. Assuming no other gifts and no gift splitting, wife's taxable gift, after the annual exclusion, will be $8,000. Thus, she may either have to pay a gift tax, or at least use up a portion of her unified credit. Alternatively, wife can *split* this gift with husband, so that each spouse will be considered to have made a gross gift of $9,000. After each donor's annual exclusion, there will be no taxable gift by either spouse.

To make the split gift election the consent of the other spouse is required and gift tax returns must be filed by both spouses if the split values exceed the annual exclusion, but only by the donee spouse if the split brings the gifts below the annual exclusion.

EXAMPLE 2513-2 Billy and Millie are married parents. This year Millie gave $20,000 of her individually owned property to their son. Assuming no other gifts, even if the couple agrees to gift splitting, only Millie will be required to file a gift tax return; Billy's consent appears on Millie's return.

Gift splitting is appropriate only for individually owned property since co-owned property is by its nature already "split," making the election unnecessary.

EXAMPLE 2513-3 In Example 2513-1, above, had the $18,000 been community property, jointly held property, or an in-common interest in property (here assume 50%-50%), gift splitting would not be permitted. However, the gift would be considered made one half by each spouse of his or her one half interest in the gift. Since the value of each spouse's gift is $9,000, neither will have to file a gift tax return.

EXAMPLE 2513-4 Continuing Example 2513-3 above, if the couple gave $28,000 in 50%-50% concurrently held property to their nephew in the following year, each will have made a gross gift of $14,000 and a taxable gift of $4,000. Again, gift splitting is not permitted, but each spouse will now be required to file a gift tax return.

Somewhat oddly, if a split gift results in the payment of a gift tax and the donor-spouse dies within three years of the gift, the *entire* gift t tax paid, not just the one-half, is grossed up in the donor's gross estate.[20]

---

20. TAM 9128009; §2035(c).

EXAMPLE 2513-5 This year, Husband makes two $150,000 gifts of his individually owned property each to the couples son and daughter, and wife gives $9,000 of her individually owned property to their son. The effects on reportable gross gifts, annual exclusions and taxable gifts of the choice to gift split or not to gift split is outlined numerically below. Without gift splitting, wife will not have to file a Form 709, since her gift is covered by the annual exclusion for her gift. If gift splitting is elected, both spouses' gift tax returns will be identical.

	Without Gift Splitting		------Gift Splitting------	
	Husband's	Wife's	Husband's	Wife's
	Form 709	"Form 709" (Not filed)	Form 709	Form 709
Current gross gifts:				
To son	$150,000.	$9,000.	$79,500.	$79,500.
To daughter	$150,000.	$0.	$75,000.	$75,000.
Total per return	$300,000.	$9,000.	$154,500.	$154,500.
Total per family	$309,000.		$309,000.	
Less annual exclusions:				
For son	$10,000.	$9,000.	$10,000.	$10,000.
For daughter	$10,000.	$0.	$10,000.	$10,000.
Total per return	$20,000.	$9,000.	$20,000.	$20,000.
Total per family	$29,000.		$40,000.	
Equals current taxable gifts:				
Total per return	$280,000.	$0.	$134,500.	$134,500.
Total per family	$280,000.		$269,000.	

Electing gift splitting will reduce total family taxable gifts by $11,000 (= $280,000 - $269,000). This reduction is entirely explained by the additional $11,000 in total family annual exclusions that may be taken, since wife will be allowed $20,000, rather than just $9,000. Therefore, while gift splitting can mean lower gift taxes, it usually just results in using up less of the family's unified credits.

Completing the analogy with income splitting, gift splitting of individually owned property can lower gift taxes because it can permit the deduction of two full annual exclusions each year, in situations where only one spouse wishes to give away sufficient individually owned property to make that possible.

Powers of Appointment

General power holders and taxable events. Gift taxation of powers of appointment substantially parallels estate tax treatment. Hence, only *general powers* will be subject to gift tax, and only the *donee-holder* of the power will usually be taxed.[21] However, the *donor* of a general power will often be considered to have made a gift subject to gift tax when the power is created, such as when the donor/trustor creates and funds an irrevocable living trust.

Three events during lifetime can trigger gift tax to the holder of a general power of appointment: exercise by the holder, release by the holder, or lapse of the holder's right to exercise or release the power.

> EXAMPLE 2514-1 Dad transfers property into an irrevocable trust, with income to Mom for her life, then remainder to anyone Mom chooses during her lifetime or in her will. The trust provides that their three children will share the remainder if Mon does not exercise her power to appoint. Although Dad, as donor, created a general power of appointment in Mom, the holder, he did not make a §2514 transfer because he did not exercise, release, or let lapse, a power. Only the holder of a power can exercise, release, or let a power lapse.

In the above example, Dad would be treated as having made a gift (completed transfer for less than full consideration) because his transfer was into an irrevocable trust.

Exercise and release by holder. Exercise of a general power in favor of someone other than the holder, or the release by the holder of a general power, will be treated as a transfer subject to taxation.

> EXAMPLE 2514-2 Continuing Example 2514-1, Mom died recently. Since Mom held a general power at the time of her death the value of the trust is included as part of her estate whether she exercised the power by appointing it to a friend or failed to exercise it and allowed the remainder to go to the children as the takers by default.

Lapse and 5 & 5 powers. The general rule is that the lapse of a general power is treated as a transfer from the holder to whomever is the taker by default. However, §2041(b)(2) creates an exception that allows the lapse of certain general powers *during the life* of the holder to occur without the lapse being deemed a taxable gift. The exception applies to the lapse of a power but only to the extent that what could have been transferred (but for the lapse) does not exceed the greater of $5,000 or 5% of the value of the

---

21. §2514(b).

property out of which the exercise of the power could have been satisfied. Powers which are drafted to make use of this exception by permitting to withdraw property from a trust up to the greater of $5,000 or 5% of the value of the trust corpus are referred to as "5 & 5" powers. Usually the right is given such that it can be exercised annually but failure to exercise the right in one year will not increase the dollar amount or the percentage for the next year, in other words it is a noncumulative annually lapsing right.

Lapsing powers are often placed in irrevocable trusts created for the benefit of minors in order to obtain the annual exclusion for the parent-donor. The power of withdrawal creates a present interest for the child-donee even though the power to withdraw lapses after a short time, as set forth in the trust, and even though there is a strong expectation that the child will not exercise the right to with draw. This demand right is referred to as a "Crummey demand right" or as a "Crummey power." Trusts for minors with this type provision are called either *Crummey Trusts* or *Minors' Demand Trusts*.

EXAMPLE 2514-3: Grantor has set up a minors' demand trust for three grandchildren. Each grandchild can claim up to the lesser of one third of the amount transferred into the trust that year or the annual exclusion amount. If a grandchild does not demand out his or her share, the right to claim the gift lapses at the close of the year (with demand rights for gifts made late in the year extended to a minimum of thirty days). If no demand is made during the demand period, the transfer is locked into corpus and by other trust terms stays there until the youngest of the three grandchildren reaches age thirty. If a grandchild dies before termination of the trust, his or her share goes to the other grandchildren who do survive. If initially the trust is funded with less than $15,000 and none of the beneficiaries demand their share, no gift from the beneficiaries is deemed to have been made by the lapse because of the §2041(b)(2) exception.

EXAMPLE 2514-4: If the initial transfer was $24,000, then each child would be deemed to have made a transfer to the extent his or her share lapsed and exceeded the "5 & 5" limits. Thus, each grandchild will be deemed to have transferred $3,000 to the trust. Since there are the two other grandchildren who will be the remaindermen if a grandchild dies, each grandchild will be deemed to have made a gift of a contingent future interest that vests when the youngest child reaches age thirty. The value of the gift from each grandchild can be determined actuarially. For each child, it would be based upon the probably of that grandchild dying before the termination of the trust. Obviously the gift is very small in value considering the unlikelihood of the event which would cause the gift to vest in the other children (the death of a child before the youngest turns thirty) and the fact that the gift is one of a future interest since enjoyment upon lapse is postponed until the termination of the trust. Because the gift is one of a future interest, no annual exclusion is available and a gift tax return would have to be filed for each grandchild.

The real estate planning significance of creating lapsing powers of appointment which exceed the "5 & 5" limit is not the gift tax implications, since the gift value is usually extremely small, but rather the retained life estate implications. If a beneficiary has a retained life estate in any property previously transferred, whether into trust or otherwise, §2036 causes it to be included in his or her estate at death. The Regulations make it clear that the lapsing of powers which exceed the 5% limit are simply cumulated,[22] there is no attempt to apply sophisticated mathematics to take into account the fact that each subsequent release of a power includes a release of a portion of the trust previously released. Thus the mathematics are kept simple but this works against the taxpayer (the holder who lets the power lapse) in that it causes greater inclusion in the estate of a beneficiary-holder who dies before the trust terminates.

One other comment before an example to further clarify, the "5 & 5" exception does not apply to lapses which take place at the death of the holder. Hence, a noncumulative power, which was not exercised during the holder's last year of life, to annually claim up to 5% of the corpus of a trust would cause 5% of the DOD value of said trust to be included in the holder's estate.

> EXAMPLE 2514-5: Upon his death in 1984, Benny's father established a trust which gave Benny income for life, and a noncumulative annually lapsing general power of appointment over a portion of the trust. At Benny's death, the trust terminates and the remaining corpus goes to Benny's sister, Rachael. At all times relevant to this example the value of the trust remained constant at $1,000,000. Benny died in 1988, never having exercised the power. If the power was exercisable over 5% of the trust, then 5% ($50,000) of the trust value would be included in Benny's estate, even though none of the lifetime lapses of the power were deemed to be transfers.

> EXAMPLE 2514-6 If the power had been over 8% of the trust (instead of 5%), then for the years 1984, 1985, 1986 and 1987 each lapse is treated as though 3% (that which exceeded 5%) was transferred by Benny to the trust with Benny retaining a life estate in the transfers. §2036 would cause 12% of the trust to be included in Benny's estate and, since Benny died with an unexercised general power over 8% of the trust, §2041 causes another 8%

---

22. Reg. 20.2041-3(d)(5), see also Reg. 20.2041-3(d)(4).

to be included. Thus, a total of 20% of the value of the trust is included in Benny's estate. Query #1. How much would be included if Benny had been given a 15% annually lapsing power? Answer at the end of the chapter.

Ascertainable standard, adverse party exceptions. Similar to estate tax law, a power of appointment to name oneself, one's creditors, one's estate or the creditors of one's estate are not treated as a general powers if the power is subject to an ascertainable standard of health, education, maintenance or support, or if it is exercisable only in conjunction with either the creator of the power or an adverse party. Ascertainable standard language is commonly used in trust instruments to give flexibility but to keep a trust out of the holder's estate. More about this in Chapter 11.

Life Insurance

A taxable gift of life insurance can arise either during the insured's lifetime or at the insured's death.

Assignment. During the insured's *lifetime*, an assignment of ownership rights in the policy may constitute a taxable gift equal to the value of the rights assigned. Ordinarily, a donor will assign all rights to a policy, and their total value is considered to be the policy's terminal value.

> EXAMPLE L1: Joe presently assigns to his son his life insurance policy having a face value of $600,000 and a terminal value of $87,000. Joe has made a present interest gross gift of $87,000 and a taxable gift of $77,000.

In contrast to the assignment of ownership interests, the simple *naming of a beneficiary* by the owner does not constitute a taxable gift since no property rights are transferred; the beneficiary receives a "mere expectancy," contingent upon the owner's keeping the policy in force and not changing the beneficiary designation. The creation of such a discretionary contingent future interest does not constitute a taxable gift.

At insured's death: the unholy trinity. Second, a taxable gift of life insurance can arise at an insured's *death*. This will occur when the insured, owner, and beneficiary are all different parties. Sometimes this arrangement is referred to as the unholy trinity.

> EXAMPLE L2 Wife purchases with separate property a $100,000 life insurance policy on husband's life, naming son beneficiary. Upon husband's death, wife will be held to have made a $100,000 gift to son. Solution, wife should have given the policy to son prior to the husband's death.

EXAMPLE L3 Changing the facts a bit in the preceding example, assume that husband purchased and owned the policy until his death, paying the premiums entirely with jointly owned funds (or with community property). At husband's death, wife will be held to have made a $50,000 gift to son, reflecting her one-half interest in the proceeds. Under typical state law, wife can legally require that half of the proceeds be payable to her.

In the above example, the other $50,000 will be includable in husband's gross estate under §2042. Can you see why?[23] We will see in Chapter 15 that estate planners typically avoid this tax trap by selecting the same person to be both owner and beneficiary on a life insurance policy held on the life of another.

Gifts of Property in Joint Tenancy Ownership

Ordinarily, gifts are made when a fee simple owner of property transfers his or her entire interest to the donee. Sometimes, however, a donor transfers only a fraction of the total interest owned. For example, a donor can transfer his or her property into joint tenancy ownership with others.

General rule. The actual moment that a gift into joint tenancy occurs for gift tax purposes depends upon the nature of the property. In general, ownership and possession of most types of property are considered transferred when documents evidencing a transfer of title are *executed* and *delivered* or *recorded*. Where there are co-owners the donee need not physically take possession of the document of title but need only acknowledge acceptance of the gift. Thus, acquisition of a joint interest by the donee usually arises when the donor simultaneously acquires the asset and names the donee co-owner, or when the donor adds the donee's name as a co-owner of property already owned by the donor. Either way, a gift will occur at that time, and the value of the gift will be the net value of the property interest transferred at the time of the gift. In the examples that follow assume that the donee accepts the gift.

---

23. Because husband/decedent/insured had a $50,000 incident of ownership in the policy at his death.

EXAMPLE JT-1 Uncle Charlie buys an automobile for $30,000 cash, *taking title* in joint tenancy with his nephew Brad. Charlie has made a gift of $15,000 to Brad in the year of purchase.

EXAMPLE JT-2 Changing the facts in Example JT-1 a bit, assume that Charlie bought the car two years ago for $48,000, taking title as an individual. This year, when the car is worth $30,000, Charlie instructs the motor vehicle bureau to *change the title* to read: "Charlie Jones and Brad Smith, as joint tenants". This year, Charlie has made a gift to Brad of $15,000.

EXAMPLE JT-3 This year, Dad purchased a building for $120,000, taking title in joint tenancy with his five adult sons. This year, Dad has made a gift of $20,000 to each son.

Two exceptions. There are two principal exceptions to the rule that the inclusion of others as cotenants for less than full consideration results in an immediate gift. First, in the case of a *joint tenancy bank account*, in most states a gift arises upon withdrawal of the funds by the donee, not upon creation of the donee's interest. The statutes of a few states, such as New York, however, presume that a gift into a savings account arises at time of deposit, thereby giving rise to immediate federal gift taxation. Second, for a joint tenancy *U.S. government savings bond*, a gift, if any, arises when the bond is redeemed. Thus, if the initial purchaser redeems the entire bond, no gift has occurred.

EXAMPLE JT-4 On June 1, last year, Mom deposited $40,000 in a savings account held jointly with Son, who withdrew $6,800 on February 1, this year. In most states, Mom will be considered to have made a gift to Son, but not until February 1, this year. The gross gift amount is $6,800.

EXAMPLE JT-5 Dad purchased a $10,000 EE savings bond years ago, taking title with his son as joint tenants. At the bond's maturity next month, if Dad redeems the entire bond, there will be no gift. If son redeems the entire bond, Dad will have made a gift this year to son of $10,000. If both redeem $5,000 each, Dad will have made a gift this year to son of $5,000.

Disclaimers

Suppose, for some reason, that the intended donee does not want to accept a sizable gift made under a will, trust instrument, or other document. Inasmuch as the unified transfer tax system will often include in the donee's transfer tax base any gift property received by the donee and later transferred to another during lifetime or at death, a donee might wish to refuse the gift, to minimize his or her own future transfer taxes. Section 2518 allows the donee, in some situations, to "disclaim" a gift. In effect, a valid disclaimer treats the gift as never having been made, and in the case of a death time transfer, treats the disclaimant as having predeceased the decedent-donor.

In order to properly disclaim, the following requirements must be met:

1. The disclaimer must be "an irrevocable and unqualified refusal...to accept" the interest,
2. The refusal must be in writing,
3. The refusal must be received within nine months after the later of:
   a) the date on which the transfer creating the interest was made, or
   b) the day on which the person disclaiming reaches age 21,[24]
4. The intended donee cannot have accepted any interest in the benefits; and
5. As a result of the refusal, the interest will pass, without the disclaiming person's direction, to someone else.

With regard to requirement 4, examples of acts indicating "acceptance" include using the property, accepting dividends, interest or rents from the property, and directing others to act with regard to the property. However, acceptance will not be found in cases where the disclaimant merely accepted title to property, or merely because title vested immediately in the disclaimant on death of the decedent, as in the case of survivorship under joint tenancy. Also, requirement 4 is not applicable to benefits received by a minor.

Meeting all of these requirements is particularly important because failure to meet any one could result in two completed gifts subject to taxation.

EXAMPLE 2518-1 Dad gives his adult Son his vacation bungalow, completing the necessary transfer of title. After spending a weekend there, Son retransfers title to Dad, refusing the gift. Dad resumes vacationing there. Son's act is not a valid disclaimer because he *had already accepted* a benefit. Therefore, two successive completed gifts were actually made, first by Dad and then by Son.

EXAMPLE 2518-2 During their lifetimes, husband and wife owned their home in joint tenancy with right of survivorship. Within nine months of husband's

---

24. The statutes of some states such as New York do not provide for this delay for underage disclaimants.

death, wife acts to disclaim her survivorship interest. Her disclaimer will not be invalid merely because her survivorship interest vested immediately at his death and she continued to live in the house and pay all expenses and related taxes prior to making the disclaimer, provided that while husband was alive the tenancy could be unilaterally partitioned.[25]

EXAMPLE 2518-3 Mom died, disposing of her entire $1.8 million estate by will. It read, "to Dad if living, and if not then to our children." Within nine months of Mom's death, Dad, before receiving any interest or benefit in the property, presented a written refusal of $600,000 of the gift to the executor of Mom's estate. Dad has made a valid disclaimer, and he will not be considered to have ever owned that portion of the property, which will pass by the terms of the will to the children. This will utilize Mon's unified credit and reduce Dan's taxable estate.

Chapters 12 and 18 will demonstrate several other ways that disclaimers can be used in estate planing.

Some commentators have maintained that a disclaimer should be taxed as a completed gift for the same reason that the lapse of a power of appointment by the holder is treated as a taxable gift. They contend that by disclaiming, the disclaimant in effect relinquished a vested right to receive property, which passed instead to someone else. Others support the disclaimer's favorable tax treatment on policy grounds, saying that it is a sufficiently valuable method for correcting inefficient transfers in wills and trust instruments to justify special tax treatment. Fortunately, current law is on the side of the latter group.[26]

Miscellaneous Gift Tax Applications

Reciprocal trusts revisited. In Chapter 6, in the section on §2036, we saw that *reciprocal trusts* were subject to FET. They may also be subject to gift taxation.

EXAMPLE RECIP-1 Mr. Garbanzo gives $10,000 to his son and $10,000 to Mrs. Ceci's daughter, and at the same time Mrs. Ceci gives $10,000 to her daughter and $10,000 to Mr. Garbanzo's son. The IRS will treat the cross-family transfers as "mirror images," as if they were made to each donor's own child instead. Thus, each parent will be treated as having made a $20,000 gross

---

25. Reg. §25.2518-2 (d)(1); LR 9135043; LR 9135044; TAM 9208003.

26. Reg. §25.2518-1(b).

gift to their own child.[27]

Multiple taxation of transfers. Certain transfers may be subject to both gift tax and estate tax.

> EXAMPLE GTET-1 Today Pope, age 55, transfers $100,000 in property into an irrevocable trust, retaining a life estate in the income. Pope's son is remainderman. Assuming no other retained interests, at 8 percent, Pope has made a completed gross gift this year of $22,601, the current value of the remainder (based on Table 9 of Appendix A, $22,601 = .22601 x $100,000). As a gift of a future interest it will not qualify for the annual exclusion. At Pope's death the date of death value of the entire trust corpus will be includable in his gross estate under §2036(a). The adjusted taxable gift is reduced to zero and a credit for any gift tax payable is allowed to prevent double taxation.

Where transferred property comes back into the gross estate because of a string being attached or because of the transfer falls under one of the §2035(d)(2) exceptions (transfer of life insurance or the severing of a string), the earlier gift will not be considered an adjusted taxable gift for purpose of calculation of the donee's estate tax. The last sentence of §2001(b) defines "adjusted taxable gifts" as being post-1976 taxable gifts "other than gifts which are includable in the gross estate of the decedent." The gift tax payable credit (§2001(b)(2)) is still available because the gift taxes would indeed have been paid on such gifts (if the tentative tax exceeded the available unified credit) and the property subject to the prior gift does enter into the estate tax calculation by being included in the gross estate as if no gift had ever taken place. The credit is the amount of gift taxes payable, not the gift taxes actually paid, see subparagraph (2) of §2001 for the wording which limits the credit to the amount of taxes which would have been paid if the rate schedule at the time of the gift had been the same as the rate at the time of death.

---

27. T.A.M. 88717003.

SPECIAL VALUATION RULES: §2701-§2704[28]

Historical Background

Pre- §2036(c) transactions. Based on the material in Chapters 5, 6, and 7, the reader will probably assume that any gift-type transfer of property in which the client retains a valuable interest is not recommended by planners attempting to save FET. After all, it may constitute a gift subject to immediate gift taxation, and will eventually subject the date of death value of the property to FET at the client's death.

> EXAMPLE SV-1 Twenty-five years ago, Gustavson transferred $100,000 in stock in a closely held business into an irrevocable trust, with all income payable to Gustavson for life, and then remainder to Gustavson's son. Based on Gustavson's age, $38,000, the value of the gifted remainder, was subject to gift taxation, with no annual exclusion available for this gift of a future interest. At Gustavson's death this year, his gross estate will include $388,000, the date of death value of the stock, under §2036(a). The estate will be allowed a credit for any gift tax actually paid on the original gift and it will not be treated as an adjusted taxable gift.

Clearly, Gustavson gained no FET savings from this particular transaction. However, prior to 1987, certain *other types* of transfers with retained interests were known to be less vulnerable to transfer taxation, and until then, estate planners were able to fashion strategies that succeeded in both avoiding any gift taxation and substantially lessening the FET. The most common transfers have been in the corporate recapitalization and grantor retained trust areas.

> EXAMPLE SV-2 Twenty years ago Weiner, sole shareholder of the common stock of his $1 million closely held corporation, redeemed all shares in a transaction in which the corporation issued three new classes of stock: 1) 100 shares of nonvoting, noncumulative preferred stock, all to Weiner. Based on the sizable amount of the estimated annual dividend, this stock was appraised at a total value of $1 million; 2) 20 shares of voting common stock, all also to Weiner; and 3) 480 shares of nonvoting common stock, all to Weiner's son Ted. Since the value of the preferred stock equaled the total value of the firm, the value of all common shares was determined to be zero. Each year for the

---

28. This section may be omitted to simplify the reading assignment. However, reading at least the first part can help better understand the future extended discussions of corporate recapitalizations (Chapter 16) and grantor retained trusts (Chapter 14).

succeeding 20 years, Weiner gave Ted one share of his voting common. At Weiner's death this year, the corporation was worth a total of $6 million. Because of a decline in prevailing interest rates the value of the preferred stock had risen to $1,200,000. Weiner's gross estate will include only $1,200,000, the current value of the preferred stock owned at death. This transaction generated no gift tax whatsoever, and saved about $2.64 million in FET (= ($6,000,000 - $1,200,000) x .55).

EXAMPLE SV-3 Eighteen years ago, Warshauer transferred $200,000 in property into an irrevocable trust, retaining the right to all trust income for fifteen years. According to the terms of the trust instrument, had Warshauer died during this period, the trust would have terminated and all principal would have reverted to his estate. If he survived the period, the trust would continue until his death, with all principal passing to his daughter. Based on market rates eighteen years ago, the initial value of the income interest was exactly $200,000, which meant that the value of the gifted remainder was zero. Thus, Warshauer did not even need to file a gift tax return. Warshauer did in fact survive the fifteen year period, and his gross estate will now include nothing in connection with this property, which is worth $600,000. At his death, Warshauer had no interest in it. Warshauer's estate has saved $330,000 in FET (= $600,000 x .55).

Advent of §2036(c) and Chapter 14. The last two examples illustrate two of several types of popularly discussed "estate freezing" transactions involving gift tax-free completed transfers producing outstanding FET savings in which a client had retained a significant interest in property. As one might imagine, their predominant success in the courts over the years was immensely frustrating to both the IRS and certain members of Congress, who saw such schemes as tax abusive. Attempting to restrict them, Congress in 1987 first enacted §2036(c), which took an *estate tax approach.* Using very general language, §2036(c)required inclusion in the decedent's gross estate of the *entire* date of death value of virtually all property in which the transferor retained significant interests. Incredibly confusing and sweeping, §2036(c) created such taxpayer opposition that it was repealed retroactively in 1990 and replaced by the more limited special valuation rules of §2701-04, also called "Chapter 14," for their location in the Internal Revenue Code.

Chapter 14: §2701-§2704[29]

In adopting Chapter 14, Congress abandoned the estate tax approach, and instead focused on *gift taxation*, which means subjecting the date of gift value of certain transfers to gift taxation when the initial transfer is made, rather than later taxing the date of death value of all of the property at the transferor's death.[30] In essence, the Chapter 14 rules require for gift tax purposes that certain transfers of property incorporating retained interests must be valued in their entirety, reduced only by the value of "qualified" retained interests. Thus, any retained interests that do not qualify under the Code are disregarded, with the result that the entire value of the transferred property may be subject to immediate gift taxation. Thus, for gift tax purposes, Chapter 14 treats the nonqualifying retained interests as if they had, in fact, not been retained.

> EXAMPLE SV-5 In Example SV-2, had Weiner undertaken his corporate recapitalization today, under Chapter 14 he would be required to report a gift subject to taxation of $990,000 (= $1 million less one $10,000 annual exclusion). Thus, Weiner would be forced to use up all of his unified credit and pay some gift tax, and all future gifts of the voting common would be sheltered only by the annual exclusion. Later, at his death this year, Weiner's gross estate would include the date of death value of the preferred stock, but adjusted taxable gifts would not include the $990,000. A credit for gift taxes would be available. From a transfer tax point of view, the result under the Chapter 14 rules is no different than had Weiner made a simple outright gift of the original common stock.

> EXAMPLE SV-6 In Example SV-3, had Warschauer made his transfer today, he would probably be required to report a gift subject to taxation of $200,000, the entire value of the property transferred into the trust. The value of the (non-qualifying) retained income interest would probably be set equal to zero.

---

29. The full text of §2701-04 will be found in Appendix B at the end of the book.

30. For an excellent overview of §2701-04, see the (1990) McCaffrey paper cited at the end of the chapter.

Now let's examine each of the sections within Chapter 14 individually, in some greater detail.[31] Please keep in mind this analysis constitutes only a brief survey of a very technical area.

§2701: Transfers of corporate or partnership interests. In essence, under §2701, the value of a gift of an interest in a corporation or partnership to a family member will not be reduced by any interests retained by the donor unless certain specific conditions are met.

Stated in the broadest terms, the §2701 valuation rules apply to:

a post-October 8, 1990 transfer by an individual of certain junior equity interests in a corporation or partnership to a member of the transferor's family, if the transferor or an applicable family member retains an applicable retained interest in the corporation or partnership immediately after the transfer.

Since this is a complicated rule with many technical terms having very specific meaning, each of the terms will be defined or described, although briefly. After that, the rule will be summarized with an example.

"Transfer." A transfer of a business interest can be direct or indirect. Examples of an indirect transfer include a contribution to capital, a redemption and a recapitalization or other change in capital structure.[32]

"Junior equity interest." A junior equity interest includes common stock, or, in the case of a partnership, any interest in which the rights to income and capital are junior to the rights of all other equity interests.

"Member of the transferor's family." Family members of the transferor include the transferor's spouse, descendants of the transferor and the transferor's spouse, and any spouse of such descendants.[33]

"Applicable family member." An applicable family member of the transferor includes the transferor's spouse, *ancestors* of the transferor or the transferor's spouse, and any spouse of such ancestor.[34]

---

31. Omission of the remaining parts of this section should not significantly impede a general understanding of the estate freezing material, particularly the grantor retained trust (Chapter 14) and the corporate recapitalization (Chapter 16).

32. §2701(e)(5).

33. §2701(e)(1).

34. §2701(e)(2).

"Applicable retained interest." An applicable retained interest is any interest (except publicly traded stock) having either (*a*) a *distribution right*, but only if the transferor and applicable family members hold control (50 percent or more) of the business immediately before the transfer, or (*b*) a liquidation, put, call or conversion right, irrespective of the degree of control held by the parties.[35] A distribution right is a right to a distribution from either a corporation with respect to its stock, or from a partnership with respect to the partner's interest. Two distribution rights are excepted from this definition: (*a*) a right to a distribution with respect to a junior equity interest (e.g., transferor gives preferred stock and retains common stock), and (*b*) a right to receive a "guaranteed payment" (as described in §707(c)) of a "fixed amount." A liquidation, put, call or conversion (LPCC) right is any LPCC right, the exercise or nonexercise of which affects the value of the transferred interest.[36] The code lists certain exceptions.

> EXAMPLE 2701-1 If undertaken today, the Weiner corporate recapitalization in Example SV-2 would fall within the valuation rules of §2701. Rationale: Weiner, an individual (indirectly) transferred a junior equity interest (common stock) in a corporation to a member of his family (his son), and retained an applicable retained interest (a nonmarketable distribution right with respect to preferred stock, which is not a junior equity interest or a right to receive guaranteed payments of a fixed amount), with respect to a business over which Weiner had control immediately before the transfer.

Section 2701 does not apply when the transferred interest is of the same class as the retained interest, or if market quotations are "readily available" for retained interest, or if the retained interest is proportionally the same as the transferred interest.[37]

> EXAMPLE 2701-2 Up to now, Rocky has been the sole owner of RR Corporation, which has issued only one class of stock. Today, Rocky gives 10 percent of his common stock to his daughter, retaining the remaining 90 percent. §2701 does not apply, and the traditional rules would be used to value the transferred shares.

---

35. §2701(b).

36. §2701(c)(2).

37. §2701(a)(2).

Effect of valuation treatment under §2701. When §2701 applies, three specific valuation rules must be observed:

1. The junior equity must be assigned a value of at least ten percent of the value of the business,[38]
2. The transferred interest must be valued by the "subtraction method," and
3. Retained rights other than "qualified payments" must be assigned a value of zero.[39] This is the so-called "zero valuation rule."

The second and third rules need some explanation.

Regarding the second rule, the U.S. Treasury has interpreted §2701 to require use of the subtraction method to determine the amount of the gift.[40] A simplified application of the subtraction method would start with the value of all family held equity interests in the entity immediately after the transfer. Then, the value of all family held senior equity interests (with nonqualifying retained interest set at zero) are subtracted, which leaves an amount that is then allocated among the transferred interests, pro rata, to family members.

> EXAMPLE 2701-3 Based on the Weiner recapitalization in the preceding examples, the value of Weiner's gift equals $1 million, which is $1 million, the value of all family held equity interests after the transfer, reduced by zero, the value of Weiner's nonqualifying retained interest. Since Weiner's son receives all transferred interests, the entire $1 million is allocated to him. Thus, Weiner will have incurred a $1 million gross gift to son subject to gift taxation.

Regarding the third rule, retained rights to *qualified payments* do not fall within the zero valuation rule. A qualified payment is a cumulative preferred dividend payable on a periodic basis determined at a specific rate.[41]

> EXAMPLE 2701-4 Had Weiner in the above examples retained a right to 12 percent *cumulative* preferred stock, the payment might be treated as a *qualified payment* if publicly traded stock of a similar quality had a dividend rate of 12

---

38. §2701(a)(4).

39. §2701(a)(3)(A).

40. Reg. §25.2701-3(b).

41. §2701(a)(3)(A).

percent. The upshot would be that the value of the retained preferred stock could be subtracted from the value of all family held senior equity interests in determining the value of Weiner's gift. Thus, if the value of the qualifying preferred stock was $700,000, Weiner would have made a gross gift of $300,000. If the preferred was worth $950,000, Weiner's gift would be $100,000, because the "junior equity interest" would be assigned a minimum value of 10 percent of the entire business.

This discussion has merely highlighted the valuation rules under §2701. Additional analysis will be undertaken in Chapter 16, in planning for corporate recapitalizations.

§2702: Transfers of interests in trusts. While §2701 deals specifically with transfers of corporate or partnership interests to family members, §2072 addresses certain types of transfers of *any* kind of property to *trusts*. The sections are similar, however in that both treat nonqualifying retained interests as having a value of zero. They also both use the subtraction method of valuation to determine the tax value of the gift. In general terms, under §2702, the special valuation rules apply when:

> *a transfer is made in trust for the benefit of a member of the transferor's family and an interest is retained by the transferor or an applicable family member.*

Again, the key terms will first be defined or described.

"Member of transferor's family." A member of the transferor's family, more inclusive than under §2701, includes the transferor's ancestors, descendants, spouse and siblings, ancestors and descendants of the transferor's spouse, and spouses of the transferor's ancestors, descendants and siblings.[42]

"Applicable family member." An applicable family member includes the same members included under §2701.[43] These are the transferor's spouse, ancestors of the transferor or the transferor's spouse, and any spouse of such ancestor.[44]

Exceptions to §2702. §2702 does not apply (a) to retained interests in a personal residence in which the term holder resides, and b) possibly for certain tangible property, such as undeveloped real estate or art. In

---

42. §2702(e).

43. §2702(a)(1).

44. §2701(e)(2).

addition, the zero valuation rule under §2702 does not apply to two types of qualified retained income interests, called a "qualified annuity interest" and a "qualified unitrust interest." Among other requirements, the income must be payable at least annually, and must be stated as a fixed dollar amount (annuity interest) or a fixed percentage of the fair market value of the trust property, determined annually (unitrust interest).

> EXAMPLE 2702-1 In example RT-3, had Warschauer made his transfer this year, and had his fifteen year income interest been structured to qualify as either an annuity interest or a unitrust interest, the full value of that interest could be deducted from the value of the transfer in calculating the value of Warschauer's immediate taxable gift resulting in a taxable gift of far less value.

Additional discussion of the valuation rules of §2702 will be found in Chapter 14 of the text, which also describes the specific techniques planners have developed to exploit these exceptions. We shall see that the trusts incorporating these techniques have come to be called grantor retained trusts, or GRITs, for short.

§2703: Valuation of property subject to rights and restrictions. §2703 requires that the value of any property subject to rights and restrictions on that property held by anyone shall be valued for transfer tax purposes without regard to the reduced valuation effect of those rights or restrictions.

> EXAMPLE 2703-1 Shortly before his death this year, Hansen, sole shareholder of the common stock of his $1 million closely held corporation, executed a contract with his daughter, who is obligated to purchase all of Hansen's stock at Hansen's death for $600,000. Under §2703, Hansen's gross estate will include the stock at a value of $1 million; the reduction in actual value attributable to the obligation to sell the stock must be disregarded.

More specifically, the rights and restrictions that must be disregarded under §2703 include:

1. Any option, agreement, or other right to acquire or use the property as a price less than the fair market value of the property (without regard to such option, agreement, or right), or
2. Any restriction on the right to sell or use the property.[45]

Section 2703 does not apply to any agreement, option, right, or restriction,

---

45. §2703(a).

which meet all of the following requirements:

- It is a bona fide business arrangement,
- It is not a device to transfer such property to members of the decedent's family for less than full and adequate consideration in money or money's worth, and
- Its terms are comparable to similar arrangements entered into by persons in an arm's length transaction.[46]

> EXAMPLE 2703-2 Shortly before his death this year, Trafalgar, sole owner of the common stock of his $1 million closely held corporation, executed a contract with a nonrelated business associate, who is obligated to purchase all of Trafalgar's stock at Trafalgar's death for $960,000. The valuation rules under §2703 are not likely to prevent the inclusion of Trafalgar's stock in his gross estate at a value of $960,000.

Planning under §2703 for business buyout agreements, as they are called, will be discussed further in Chapter 16.

§2704: Taxation of lapse of voting and liquidation rights and restrictions in a corporation or partnership. §2704, of relatively limited application, will only be briefly summarized here. It addresses the influence on federal transfer taxation of the lapse of a voting or liquidation right in a corporation or partnership.

In general, if there has been a lapse and the person holding the right before the lapse and the members of that person's family hold control of the entity both before and after the lapse, then the lapse is treated as gift or a transfer at death, as the case may be, subject to tax. The value of the transfer subject to taxation is equal to the excess of the value of all interests held by that person before the lapse (determined as if the rights were nonlapsing) over the value of such interests immediately after the lapse.

Clearly, properly applying the Chapter 14 valuation rules to client situations requires considerable expertise and careful thought, and should be undertaken only with the direct help of a tax expert. However, all planners should have a general understanding of this commonly discussed topic.

---

46. §2703(b).

FEDERAL GENERATION-SKIPPING TRANSFER TAX

One fundamental policy objective of federal wealth transfer taxation is to tax all individual wealth in excess of a certain amount each time it passes to the next generation. Can the unified estate and gift tax laws completely achieve that goal? They can not. It is true that they can ensure that property is subject to tax once when it is transferred. But since they both fail to distinguish between transfers made to the next generation and transfers made to more distant generations, they can not possibly meet that goal.

> EXAMPLE GSTT-1 Grandpa died last year leaving most of his large estate to his *granddaughter*. An estate tax will be imposed on this amount now, but not at the death of any of his children.

Only a tax that explicitly addresses the generational relationship between transferor and transferee can consistently tax wealth as it passes to succeeding generations. The generation-skipping transfer tax is designed to meet that objective.

The first generation-skipping transfer tax was enacted in 1976. Although planners found it quite complicated, they quickly learned that the tax was easy to circumvent. In fact, there is widespread belief among planners that no one ever filed a return under the 1976 Generation-Skipping Transfer Tax. As a result, in 1986, Congress acknowledged its error by repealing it retroactively, and at the same time, enacting the new, more comprehensive law described below. Trusts that became irrevocable prior to September 25, 1985 are grand fathered, that is, not subject any generation-skipping transfer tax.

While reading this material, keep in mind that this tax is not appreciably "unified" with gift and estate taxes; it is a separate tax having its own unique rules.

The tax is reported on Form 706 (for transfers at death) and Form 709 (for gifts), shown in Appendices C and D, respectively.[47]

Nature of the Tax

Three types of transfers to skip persons. The current federal Generation Skipping Transfer Tax (GSTT), effective September 1985, imposes a tax on

---

47. The GSTT applies to nonresident aliens to the extent that the transferred property is situated in the United States for purposes of the estate tax or the gift tax.

three types of generation-skipping transfers that would otherwise escape both the estate tax and the gift tax. These transfers are called direct skips, taxable terminations, and taxable distributions.[48] Under each, a transfer or its equivalent is made by a transferor to or for the benefit of a *skip person*; that is, a beneficiary who is at least two generations younger than the transferor.[49] A skip person can also be a *trust*, if all interests in the trust are held by skip persons, or if there is no person holding an interest in the trust and at no time after the transfer may a trust distribution be made to a nonskip person.

Contrasting the three transfers: While a taxable termination and a taxable distribution always involve a trust, a direct skip may involve a trust, but it usually does not.

Direct skip. A direct skip is a transfer to a skip person that is subject to the gift tax or the estate tax.[50] The GSTT is imposed at the time of the direct skip. The *transferor* (or the transferor's estate) is liable for the GSTT on direct skips.[51]

> EXAMPLE GSTT-2 In his will, T, who recently died, left outright $60,000 cash each to a grandnephew and a granddaughter. Since both legatees are skip persons and the cash is subject to the estate tax, both transfers are direct skips, subject also to immediate GSTT taxation. T's estate is liable for the GSTT.

It should be clear from this example that direct skips will be simultaneously and immediately subject to both estate or gift taxation *and* to the GSTT. In effect, a double tax will result, under the rationale that the property (a) immediately passes to an individual who is at least two generations younger than the transferor, and (b) would not otherwise be taxed to the generation that was skipped. Observe that in the context of direct skips, since the current GSTT makes no distinction between a transfer across two generations and one across more than two, it can not fully implement the

---

48. §2611(a).

49. §2613(a).

50. §2612(c).

51. §2603(a)(3).

policy objective stated at the beginning of this section. Thus, a direct skip to a great grandchild will still result in two taxes, not three, resulting in the skipping of a generation of transfer tax

Taxable termination. The Code's definition of a taxable termination is complex. In the formal language of §2612(a), a taxable termination is:

> *the termination (by death, lapse of time, release of power, or otherwise) of an interest of property held in a trust unless (a) immediately after such termination, a nonskip person has an interest in such property, or (b) at no time after such termination may a distribution (including distributions on termination) be made from such trust to a skip person.*

Paraphrasing at the risk of some slight inaccuracy: A taxable termination is a termination of a nonskip person's interest in income or principal of a *trust* with the result that skip persons become the only remaining trust beneficiaries. The GSTT is imposed at the time of the taxable termination. The *trustee* is liable for the GSTT on taxable terminations.[52]

EXAMPLE GSTT-3 T places property in trust, with income to T's daughter D for life, then remainder to T's grandchildren, per stirpes. A taxable termination will occur at D's death, because at that time, T's grandchildren and great grandchildren, etc., all skip persons, become the only remaining trust beneficiaries. Thus, at D's death, the trustee will pay a GSTT out of trust property.

Taxable distribution. A taxable distribution is any distribution of property (other than a taxable termination or a direct skip) out of a *trust* to a skip person.[53] The GSTT is imposed at the time of the distribution. The *transferee* is liable for the GSTT on taxable distributions.[54] This differs from the gift tax rule, which makes the donor responsible for filing the gift tax return and paying the tax.

EXAMPLE GSTT-4 H, trustee of a trust established by T, is holder of a power of appointment in which GD, T's granddaughter, and H, T's husband, are permissible appointees. This year, H distributed $19,000 to GD. This is a taxable distribution, and GD will pay a GSTT this year.

---

52. §2603(a)(2).

53. §2612(b).

54. §2603(a)(1).

GSTT rates. All transfers subject to the GSTT are taxed at the highest marginal unified transfer tax in existence that year. Thus, all taxable generation-skipping transfers will be subject to a 55 percent rate. As will be mentioned in Chapter 12, direct skips will experience a lower effective tax rate because they are taxed similar to a gift, on a "tax exclusive" basis, that is, the amount of the tax is excluded from the taxable amount. At a top rate of 55 percent, the upshot will be an effective rate of 35 percent on the entire transfer.[55]

Exceptions to GSTT Taxation

The impact of the GSTT is considerably softened by three exceptions: the GSTT annual exclusion; the predeceased parent direct skip rule; and, perhaps most importantly, the $1 million lifetime exemption for all skips.

GSTT annual exclusion. Similar to the gift tax, a $10,000 annual exclusion per donor per donee is available under the GSTT for *lifetime* generation-skipping *direct skip* transfers. And a spouse can consent to *splitting* gifts of up to $20,000 made by the other spouse.[56]

> EXAMPLE GSTT-5 In 1987, Grandpa plans to give granddaughter $10,000 each year for the rest of his life. These generation-skipping transfers will be entirely excluded from computation of the GSTT, as well as the gift tax.

The annual exclusion will qualify for gifts into trust for a minor, as long as the minor either has a present interest in the property or the trust qualifies as a §2503(c) Trust.[57] The Code does not state that GSTs qualify for the annual exclusion, but the wording in §2642(c)(1) recognizes the one: "In the case of a direct skip which is a nontaxable gift, the inclusion ratio shall be zero," and §2642(c)(3) includes as a "taxable gift" a §2503(b) annual exclusion gift.

Similar to the gift tax, qualified transfers of any amount to an educational institution for tuition and transfers of any amount to a provider of

---

55. $.35 = .55 \div 1.55$.

56. For a discussion of certain restrictions on the use of the GSTT annual exclusion as well as planning techniques, see the Blattmachr article cited at the end of the chapter.

57. Discussed earlier and in more detail in Chapter 13.

medical care on behalf of a skip person are excluded from GSTT.[58]

Predeceased parent direct skip rule. Ordinarily, a grandparent and a grandchild are considered two generations apart, and a transfer from the former to the latter will trigger the GSTT. However, if the parent who is a lineal descendent of the transferor predeceases both of them, for purposes of *direct skips only*, the grandparent-transferor and the grandchild are treated as if they are only one generation apart. The grandchild is considered to have "moved up" one generation.[59]

The Code definitions of parent and grandchild are generous. For the rule to apply, the *parent* of the transferee may be a lineal descendant of either the transferor or the transferor's spouse, but not collateral descendants such as grandnephews and grandnieces do not qualify.[60] Usually the transferee is a *grandchild* of the transferor, the transferor's spouse, or the transferor's former spouse. The rule also applies to an adopted grandchild; death of a natural parent of the grandchild can trigger the rule, despite the presence of a state statute terminating the parent-child relationship and all inheritance rights.[61]

> EXAMPLE GSTT-6 Sonny lost his dad in an auto accident last year. This year, Sonny's *paternal grandmother* died, and left him outright the bulk of her sizable estate. The property will be subject to the estate tax but not to the GSTT.

> EXAMPLE GSTT-7 Same facts as Example GSTT-6 above, except that the decedent-transferor was Sonny's *grandaunt*. At her death, the property will be subject to both the estate tax and the GSTT.

> EXAMPLE GSTT-8 Gamble died, leaving assets in a trust. Under its terms, income was to be payable to surviving wife Karlin for life. At her death, the trust was to terminate and principal would be distributed to their surviving children, or, if none, to other issue. At Karlin's death no children were surviving and all trust principal was distributed to the grandchildren. The trust property will be subject to the estate tax, and to the GSTT. This is a *taxable termination*, not a direct skip, therefore precluding application of the predeceased parent direct skip rule.

---

58. §2642(c)(3)(B).

59. §2612(c)(2).

60. TAM 9246009.

61. LR 9310005.

We'll see in Chapter 12 how careful planning can ensure that a direct skip will occur so as to be in a position to take advantage of this exception.

$1 million lifetime exemption for all skips. For each individual donor, the first $1 million in property being "transferred" by direct or indirect lifetime or death time skips to all skip persons combined can be declared exempt from the GSTT.[62] Again, with spousal consent, up to $2 million transferred by one spouse may be split by the spouses.

> EXAMPLE GSTT-9 In each of the last three years, Beulah, a widow, made lifetime gifts of $600,000 in property into a trust for her grandniece. In the first year, Beulah allocated $590,000 in transfers to her lifetime GSTT exemption, paying no GSTT. In the second year, Beulah allocated an additional $410,000 to her lifetime exemption, thus leaving $180,000 subject to the GSTT. At this point, she had fully allocated her $1 million exemption. Consequently, in the third year, Beulah could only shelter $10,000 of her last gift, with the result that $590,000 not only was subject to gift tax, but to the GSTT as well.

> EXAMPLE GSTT-10 Assume the facts in Example GSTT-9, and that the trust corpus appreciates to $2 million at Beulah's death five years from now. No additional GSTT will be due. In allocating the exemption, the value of the property is determined at the time the tax is imposed.

We will further examine planning for use of the $1 million lifetime exemption in Chapter 12, in connection with death time marital deduction and bypass planning.

Credit for state GSTT. A federal credit of up to five percent of the federal GSTT will be allowed for payment of any state GSTT on nondirect skip transfers arising from the death of an individual.[63]

This chapter has focused on certain qualitative aspects of the federal gift tax and the federal generation-skipping transfer tax. The next chapter will present an overview of the federal income tax.

Queries Answered:

1. Total of 55%, i.e. $550,000.

---

62. §2631(a).

63. §2604.

QUESTIONS AND PROBLEMS

1. List the customary local law requirements for a valid gift.

2. Addie sells her empty lot, fair market value $22,000, to a stranger for $19,500. Is there a gift? Why or why not?

3. Would your answer to Question 2 change if the donee was, in fact, Addie's son? One of her employees?

4. (*a*) If Jones gives Smith 200 shares of a nondividend-paying stock, is this a gift of a present or a future interest? Why? (*b*) Why might it matter?

5. Today Lois transfers $10,000 to an irrevocable trust that is required to distribute all income annually to her son, age 55, for his life. Then, remainder outright to his issue. Assuming 10 percent, calculate the amount of Lois' taxable gift.

6. Explain the public policy reason for the exception under §2503(c).

7. Two years ago, John gave his daughter $300,000, consisting of 300 shares of the closely held corporation that he owned as an individual. Last year, John gave his daughter $400,000 more of this stock.
  a. Assuming neither John nor his wife Jenny had ever made any other taxable gifts, calculate the total amount of gift taxes from these gifts, and also calculate John's and Jenny's remaining unused unified credits, available for this year, if
    1. No gift splitting was employed.
    2. John and Jenny split both year's gifts.
  b. Explain the advantages and disadvantages of gift splitting in this situation.

8. Wayne and his wife Sharon own a parcel of land worth $20,000 as equal tenants in common. This year they gave the land to their daughter Christina. Can this gift be split?

9. Assume that one of your wealthier clients is the reluctant holder of a general power of appointment and is not charitably inclined. What action on her part, if any, might minimize total unified transfer taxes?

10. Ralph established a trust in 1985 which gave Linda income for life, remainder to Linda's three children by right of representation. What would be the effect on Linda's estate at her death of each clause (considered independently) if such is part of the trust: (Explain your answer).

   a. The Trustee is given absolute discretion to transfer the principal of the trust to Linda, if doing so would be in her best interest.
   b. I give Linda the power to appoint, by direct reference to this power in her Will, the remainder of the trust amongst her children in such portion as she deems appropriate.
   c. I give Linda the right to invade the corpus up to a maximum of 3% of the trust in any one year. This right shall be noncumulative.
   d. I give Linda the power to invade the corpus of the trust, up to the whole amount, if such be necessary for her health, education, maintenance or support.

11. Rachel establishes a trust (worth exactly $1,000,000 at all times relevant here) for the benefit of Arthur during his lifetime, with remainder to Sarah upon Arthur's death. Arthur was 50 years old when the trust was established. The terms of the trust give Arthur the right to demand up to the greater of 5% or $5,000 from the trust in any year, but the right is noncumulative. In years 1, 2, 3, 5, and 6, he did not exercise the right. In year 4, he took out the maximum allowed. With appreciation in the remaining assets, the trust quickly returned to $1,000,000, which was its value in the 6th year when Arthur died.

   a. In the first year the power lapsed, what was the gift to Sarah?
   b. How much of this trust would be included in Arthur's estate?
   c. If the demand right had been the greater of 7% or $7,000, what would be the gift to Sarah in the first year? Would a gift tax return have to be filed?
   d. If the demand right had been the greater of 7% or $7,000, how much would be included in Arthur's estate?

12. Five years ago, Frank purchased a $280,000 face value life insurance policy on his own life. A year later he assigned (gave) the policy to his son, when it had a terminal value of $110,000. Four months after making this gift, Frank died. Frank's wife had always been beneficiary. Explain all gift and estate tax consequences. (Hint: there are at least three. Query: would the marital deduction apply at all?)

13. A client asks you to explain when the acquisition by gift of joint tenancy property is taxed.

14. Today, Karen and Sal buy 100 shares of ABC Corp. stock for $21,000, writing a check on their joint (or community) checking account and taking title in joint tenancy. Has a gift occurred? Why or why not?

15. Give an example of a way in which a qualified disclaimer can be a valuable estate planning tool.

16. Explain three reasons why gift splitting can be a valuable estate planning tool.

17. This year, Joe gave $1 million cash to his daughter Mary, who gave it to her son Sal, who gave it to his sister Sue. (*a*) How many gifts subject to taxation have been made? (*b*) Can §2518 (disclaimers) help? (*c*) How about §2013 (FET credit for tax on prior transfers)?

18. Congratulations! You have just won the state lottery, entitling you to $2 million cash a year for the next 20 years. You direct that your winnings be shared equally with your spouse and your 28-year-old daughter.
  a. Are there any tax consequences?
  b. Could there have been any way to avoid them?[64]

19. Five years ago, Francisco and Dagny executed a "joint and mutual will", which is a single will, revocable only by mutual consent. Essentially, it provided that the first to die leaves his or her property to the survivor, who then leaves everything to their children at his or her death. Francisco died today. (*a*) Can you think of any possible immediate tax consequences to Dagny? (*b*) If Francisco and Dagny wrote two different wills leaving everything to each other, and also executed an enforceable contract not to change these wills, would the result be any different from the result in part *a*? (Answer: No).

20. (*a*) Describe the GSTT. (*b*) What are its exceptions?

---

64. For considerable detail, see the Lowell article cited in the recommended reading.

21. Grandpa Gus, a widower, wishes his grandchildren Debra and Phil to receive a substantial amount of his $5 million estate. Determine the amount subject to the GSTT, if any, and the date that the tax will be incurred, for the following alternative dispositions.

    a. Outright lifetime gift this year of $1 million to each grandchild.
    b. A transfer now of $1 million into each of two revocable trusts, with income to Gus for his life, then income to Gus' daughter for her life (expected to span 10 years after Gus' death), then principal outright to the grandchildren. After Gus' death, daughter will have a general power of appointment over the trust property, subject to an ascertainable standard. Assume that at daughter's death, the aggregate value of the trust assets have not changed.
    c. Same as part b, above, except that outright distribution to the grandchildren may be delayed after daughter's death, since distribution will not be made until the youngest grandchild reaches age 30.

22. Last year, Finney, an American citizen, gave his son some land located in Bogota, Columbia. Will there be any U.S. gift tax consequences?

23. One of your clients is a citizen and resident of Mexico, but owns an apartment house in Phoenix. (a) If she gives this building to her son, a resident of Panama, is she subject to U.S. gift taxation? (b) Would her estate be subject to U.S. estate taxation if she instead devised the building to her son?

24. During the last ten years of her life, Queenie, a widow, undertook each of the following independent transactions. Explain whether or not each constituted a gift subject to taxation.

    a. Purchased a life insurance policy on her life, naming her son beneficiary.
    b. Transferred title to her personal residence to her daughter and continued to live there, rent-free, for two years, at which time she moved out and formally relinquished all rights to the property.
    c. Funded a revocable living trust.
    d. Funded an irrevocable living trust, under which her daughter was the sole beneficiary.
    e. Purchased some land, taking title in the names of herself and her son as joint tenants. Queenie paid $90,000 of the $100,000 purchase price, and son paid $10,000.

f. Purchased common stock, taking title in the names of herself and her husband as joint tenants.

g. Purchased life insurance on the life of her uncle, naming her daughter beneficiary. Two years later, uncle died and daughter was paid the proceeds.

h. Paid $21,000 in tuition and $8,000 in room, board, and other fees each year for five years for her son's college education.

i. Opened a joint checking account with her daughter, depositing $26,000 of her own funds.

RECOMMENDED READING

(Anonymous,) "Additional Thoughts on the Impact of the New Generation-Skipping Tax Provision, "*Estate Planning*, July 1987, pp.234-6. Commentary on Mulligan/Boulton articles.

August, Jerald D. "Planning Around Contingent Liabilities," *1992 University of Miami Estate Planning Institute.*

*Blattmachr, Jonathan. "Some New Opportunities in Transfers to Grandchildren," *Trusts and Estates*, August, 1990, pp. 49-54. Planning with the GSTT annual exclusion.

Doyle, Robert J., & Leimberg, Stephan R., "New IRS Valuation Rules: Impact on the Tools and Techniques of Estate and Financial Planning", *Taxes-The Tax Magazine*, May, 1990, pp. 376-96.

Gans, Mitchell M, "Gift Tax: Valuation Difficulties and Gift Completion." *The Notre Dame Law Review* 58 (February 1983), pp. 493-536.

Halbach, Edward C. Jr. "Generation-Skipping: Planning Opportunities and Drafting Problems," *1988 University of Miami Estate Planning Institute.*

Hellige, James R., and William C. Weinsheimer. "A New set of Complexities." *Trusts & Estates*, March 1987, pp. 8-26, and April 1987, pp. 10-26. Two-part article on the new GSTT.

Katzenstein, Andrew M. "The New Generation-Skipping Tax: A Road Map." *Taxes*, April 1987, pp. 259-66.

Lowell, Cym H. "Estate Planning For the Instantly Wealthy-Athletes, Executives, Heirs, Business Owners or Resident Aliens", *1989 University of Miami Estate Planning Institute.*

McCaffrey, Carlyn S., and Mildred Kalik. "Using Valuation Clauses to Avoid Gift Taxes." *Trusts & Estates*, October 1986, pp. 47-58.

*_____. "Asset Freezes - The New Valuation Rules," *1990 university of Miami Estate Planning Institute.*

McCoy, Jerry J., "Keeping Up With the new `Rate of the Month' Tables", *Trusts & Estates*, Feb., 1990 pp 35-39.

Mulligan, Michael D., and Scot W. Boulton. "New Generation-Skipping Tax: Higher Rates, Broadened Scope." *Estate Planning*, January 1987.

_____."Planning Opportunities that Take Advantage of the New Generation-Skipping Transfer Tax." *Estate Planning*, March 1987, pp. 66-71.

Murhta, John M & T. Ashley Edwards, "Many Aspects of the GST Tax Interpreted by Prop. Regs." *Estate Planning*, May, 1993, pp 131-39.

*Newlin, Charles F. "How To Avoid Tax Problems In Family Business Transactions," *Estate Planning*, September, 1993, pp 276-82.

Peithmann, William A. "A Look At The Principles And Uses of Powers of Appointment," *Trusts & Estates*, August, 1993, pp 38-47.

Rosenberg, Stanley. "Expensive Transfers." (Discusses the new GSTT.) *Financial Planning*, October 1987, pp. 224-29.

Schindel, Donald M. "Various Methods Exist for Establishing a Sustainable Value for Estate Assets," *Estate Planning*, September, 1990, pp. 258-64.

Sherman, Jeffrey G. "'Tis a Gift to Be Simple: The Need for a New Definition of 'Future Interest' for Gift Tax Purposes." *Cincinnati Law Review* 55, No. 3, pp. 585-675. Describes how the terms *present interest* and *future interest* have inconsistently evolved through the years, and proposes new definitions.

Siminerio, Andrew C. "With Strings Attached: Federal Income Tax Consequences to Donors of Conditional Gifts." *Duquesne Law Review* 20 (1982), pp. 463-483.

— 8

The Federal Income Tax

OVERVIEW

Albert Einstein is believed to have said that of all things in this universe, the most difficult to understand is the income tax. One can only wonder what Einstein thought of the estate tax. He was probably not a devoted student of either tax. Had he been, he would certainly have concluded, as you should, that the income tax, while not simple, is not nuclear physics.

In contrast to the federal estate tax, which is basically a tax on property owned at one moment in time, the federal income tax is a tax on income earned during a period of time, usually one year. The income tax was first introduced during the Civil War, and was repealed in 1871. It was reenacted in 1913, with the adoption of the 16th Amendment to the Constitution.

Today's income tax law distinguishes four basically different taxpayers: individuals, and three entities: estates, trusts, and corporations. This chapter will examine principles of taxation of each, with the greatest emphasis on the taxation of individuals.

INCOME TAXATION OF INDIVIDUALS

U.S. citizens and residents are subject to U.S. federal income tax on world-wide income. Nonresident aliens are subject to the tax only on income having a U.S. source, or income effectively connected with a U.S. trade or business.[1]

A general overview model for the federal income taxation of individuals is presented in Table 8-1. Summarizing the table, certain deductions are subtracted from gross income to arrive at adjusted gross income. Then the standard deduction (or total itemized deductions) and personal exemptions are subtracted, leaving taxable income. The tax is then calculated, from which credits are subtracted to arrive at the net tax.

TABLE 8-1 Federal Income Taxation of Individuals (Form 1040) Overview Model

Gross Income		$xxx,xxx.
Less: Deductions from gross income		xx,xxx.
Equals: Adjusted gross income		xxx,xxx.
Less: Standard deduction or total itemized deductions	$xx,xxx.	
Personal exemptions	x,xxx.	xx,xxx.
Leaves: Taxable income		xxx,xxx.
Calculate the tax		xx,xxx.
Less Credits		x,xxx.
Leaves: Net tax		$xx,xxx.

Let's now examine each item in some detail. While reading this section, you are urged to refer to the copy of Form 1040, U.S. Individual Income Tax Return, included in Appendix E at the end of the book.

---

1. §871, §872

Gross Income

Code §61 reads, "Except as otherwise provided... gross income means all income from whatever source derived." Thus, an item of income will be includable as gross income unless it is expressly excluded by another section of the Code. The most common types of income *includable* in gross income are compensation for services rendered (wages, salaries, commissions, etc.), business income, gains from dealings in property, interest, rent, dividends, alimony, annuities, and insurance and pension income. Examples of items *excludable* from gross income are most lump-sum life insurance death proceeds,[2] income from investments that represent a return of invested principal, gifts, devises, bequests, inheritances,[3] qualified moving expense reimbursements,[4] and interest on most state and local government obligations.[5]

An example of an unusual bequest includable in the beneficiaries' gross income is one representing compensation in connection for care for a testator. In one case, an invalid contracted with two others to move into her home to manage her affairs. In exchange, she agreed to leave her house to them in her will. The value of the house was treated as taxable income to the two care-takers rather than as a tax-free bequest.[6]

Deductions From Gross Income

The first group of deductions, called deductions from gross income (also called "above the line" deductions, or deductions "for" adjusted gross income), includes trade or business expenses, certain nonreimbursed employee expenses (travel, etc.), certain losses from the sale of property, alimony payments, certain work-influenced moving expenses, and certain retirement contributions. These deductions, subtracted before arriving at adjusted gross income (AGI), may be taken whether or not the taxpayer chooses to "itemize" other deductions.

---

2. §101.

3. §102.

4. §132(a)(6).

5. §103.

6. *Miller* T.C. Memo 1987-271.

Standard Deduction or Total Itemized Deductions

The second group of deductions is called deductions "from" adjusted gross income, or "below the line" deductions.

Individuals are allowed a choice of deducting from adjusted gross income a fixed lump sum, called the *standard deduction*, or the actual sum of personal itemized deductions. Of course, taxpayers will want to deduct the larger amount.

Standard deduction. The amount of the standard deduction in 1995 is $3,900 for single taxpayers and $6,550 for married individuals filing jointly. Each year, these amounts are indexed (increased) for inflation, as measured by the consumer price index. New indexed values for the coming year for most items discussed in this chapter are made public by the IRS in a news release in late December, and may be found reprinted in commercial tax reporters. For example, Commerce Clearing House's Standard Federal Tax Reports includes this information in the "New Matters" volume.

If an unmarried tax payer is blind or 65 or older, he or she is allowed to increase the standard deduction by $950, or $1,900 if both blind and 65 or older. On a joint return the increase is only $750 for each condition (assuming being over 64 is a condition) for a maximum possible increase of $3,000.

Itemized deductions. Itemized deductions are subdivided into two types. The first type, called *nonmiscellaneous itemized deductions*, includes certain personal expenses, such as certain interest on residential loans, taxes, gambling losses, unreimbursed casualty losses, charitable contributions, and medical expenses.

Interest expenses may or may not be deductible, depending upon the use of the loan. Interest expense incurred in connection with a trade or business is generally deductible. Interest in the amount of debt secured by the taxpayer's principal residence or second residence (called "qualified residence interest") is deductible up to the amount of the taxpayer's basis plus the cost of any improvements.[7] Interest in connection with "passive" activities may be used only to offset passive income. All other interest is considered "personal interest," the deductibility of which was totally phased out by 1991. The details, spelled out in §163, are quite complex.

The second type of itemized deductions, called *miscellaneous itemized deductions*, includes fees paid for tax return preparation, tax planning, investment planning, and certain employee expenses not deductible from gross income, such as job-hunting expenses, union dues, expenses for a home office, and transportation expenses. Miscellaneous itemized

---

7. For a detailed discussion, see the Kantor/Sparks article cited at the end of the chapter.

deductions are allowed only to the extent that they collectively exceed 2 percent of adjusted gross income.

From the above we can see that deductions from gross income are always usable, while itemized deductions are sometimes wasted: The first dollar of deductions from gross income will reduce taxable income, while only those itemized deductions in excess of the standard deduction will reduce taxable income. Therefore, individuals with modest amounts of total itemized deductions (e.g., less than $6,550 for a married couple filing jointly in 1995) will find that these deductions are entirely wasted, and tax planning would suggest that taxpayers incur such outlays only for tax reasons.

Cutdown of itemized deductions for wealthier taxpayers. Certain higher income individuals are required to reduce their itemized deductions. The reduction amount for 1995 is the lessor of either three percent of the excess of their adjusted gross income (AGI) over $114,700, or 80% of their itemized deductions. The 1995 threshold amount is $57,350 for married individuals filing separately.[8] These amounts are indexed annually. These limitations do not apply to medical deductions. The net effect of this cutdown is to raise the marginal tax rate for certain higher income taxpayers by approximately two to 4 percentage points.

EXAMPLE 8-1 Flo and Barney are married taxpayers filing jointly. In 1995, they have AGI of $200,000 and itemized deductions of $9,000. Flo and Barney may deduct only $6,441, which is $9,000 reduced by the lesser of either $2,559 [=.03*($200,000-$114,700)], or $7,200 [=80% of $9,000].

EXAMPLE 8-2 Assuming all of the facts in Example 8-1, above, except that Flo and Barney's AGI is $350,000, they will be permitted to deduct only $1,800, which is $9,000 reduced by the lesser of either $7,059 [=.03*($350,000-$114,700)], or $7,200, as calculated above.

Personal Exemptions

In 1995, additional amounts of $2,500 per person are deductible on behalf of the taxpayer, the spouse, and each dependent, as personal exemptions, in calculating taxable income. The personal exemption is also indexed for inflation.

Persons claimed as dependents on another individual's tax return will not be allowed a personal exemption and the amount of their standard

---

8. §68(b).

deduction is further limited to the greater of $650 or the amount of their earned income, up to the maximum allowable that year.[9] Thus, to be able to take a larger standard deduction, dependents must receive earned income. Examples of *earned income* are wages, salaries, tips, and self-employment income. Examples of *unearned income* are interest, dividends, rent, royalties, and capital gains.

Cutdown of personal exemptions for higher income taxpayers. Somewhat similar to itemized deductions, the deduction for personal exemptions is reduced for certain higher income taxpayers. The reduction amount is two percent for each $2,500 (or fraction thereof) by which adjusted gross income exceeds a threshold amount. Threshold amounts for 1995 (indexed annually even though the $2,500 amount is not indexed) are $172,050 for joint returns and $114,700 for single taxpayers.[10]

> EXAMPLE 8-3 Russ and Patty are married taxpayers filing jointly and claiming one personal exemption each. In 1995, they have AGI of $215,000. The amount of their total allowable personal exemptions is $3,282. The excess amount subject to the two percent reduction is $42,950, or $215,000 minus $172,050. This excess, divided by $2,500, equals 17.18, which is rounded up to 18. Thus, the two personal exemptions totaling $5,000 (=2 x $2,500) are reduced by 36%, or 2% times 18. Summarizing, $3,200 = $5,000 - (.36 x $5,000).

Taxable Income

The amount left after subtracting from gross income the total of deductions and exemptions is called taxable income. A tax is then calculated, using the proper tax table.

Individual income tax rates are shown in Tables 8-2 and 8-3, and also in Tables 1 and 2 of Appendix A at the end of the text. Table 8-2 depicts rates for married couples filing joint returns; Table 8-3 shows rates for unmarried individuals (other than surviving spouses and heads of households). Other rate tables not included in this text are for unmarried heads of households, and married individuals filing separately.

---

9. §63(c)(5).

10. §151(d)(3)

TABLE 8-2 Federal Individual Income Tax Rates: Married Individuals Filing Joint Returns and Surviving Spouses

Taxable Income				
Over	But Not Over	Base Amount +	Percent	On Excess Over
		1995		
$0.	$39,000.	$0.00	15.0%	$0.
39,000.	94,250.	5,850.00	28.0	39,000.
94,250.	143,600.	21,320.00	31.0	94,250.
143,600.	256,500.	36,618.50	36.0	143,600.
256,500.	-	77,262.50	39.6	256,500.

TABLE 8-3 Federal Individual Income Tax Rates: Unmarried Individuals (other than surviving spouses and heads of households)

Taxable Income				
Over	But Not Over	Base Amount +	Percent	On Excess Over
		1995		
$0.	$23,350.	$0.00	15.0%	$0.
23,350.	56,550.	3,502.50	28.0	23,350.
56,550.	117,950.	12,798.50	31.0	56,550.
117,950.	256,500.	31,832.50	36.0	117,950.
256,500.	-	81,710.50	39.6	256,500.

Married individuals will usually benefit from filing a joint return rather than filing separately, since tax rates are progressive. However, separate returns may reduce the tax liability in at least two situations. First, if a high joint income triggers the new cutbacks on itemized deductions or personal exemptions (described later), a spouse with relatively low income might be able to salvage some of them by filing separately. Second, if one spouse incurs sizable medical or miscellaneous deductions (both of which are subject to floors of 7.5% and 2% of AGI respectively), filing separately might secure some of these deductions.

Alternative minimum tax. Certain higher-income taxpayers may be subject to an additional tax, called the alternative minimum tax (AMT), which has a rate of 26 or 28 percent, depending upon taxable amount. In essence, the taxpayer will apply the tax rate to the excess of "alternative minimum taxable income" over $33,750 ($45,000 for married individuals filing jointly) to arrive at the tentative AMT. The excess, if any, of tentative AMT over the taxpayer's regular tax is the net AMT due. Alternative minimum taxable income is defined as regular taxable income, *plus or minus* "adjustments" (such as excess accelerated depreciation, passive activity losses (both added) and certain itemized deductions (subtracted), *plus* certain "preference items" (such as certain incentive stock option income, and tax-exempt interest on newly issued private activity bonds). The Congressional purpose of the AMT is to ensure that high income taxpayers who normally pay little or no tax due to tax preferences and other deductions will pay at least some reasonable amount of federal income tax. Similar AMT provisions apply to corporations and to fiduciaries.[11]

Importance of marginal rate in planning. How can one calculate the effective marginal income tax rate for a client? Expressed differently, what rate will a given taxpayer pay on one additional dollar of taxable income? From the above discussion, it should be clear that a taxpayer's *federal* marginal rate will be either 15%, 28%, 31%, 36%, or 39.6%, depending upon the amount of taxable income. But when factoring in *state and local* income taxes, the combined marginal rate may be eleven percentage points or more higher, such as for high income residents of Philadelphia, Pittsburgh, Seattle and New York City. In addition, several percentage points can be added for the effect of cutdowns of itemized deductions and personal exemptions for wealthier taxpayers. Thus, it would appear that certain estate planning clients will have an effective marginal income tax rate of over 55%!

---

11. §55.

Thus, effective combined marginal income tax rates will vary considerably from client to client depending upon income level, residence state, and several other factors. Generalizations are difficult to make, but most illustrations made in this book will assume that lower income taxpayers have an effective combined rate of 15%; middle income taxpayers, 35%; and high income taxpayers a combined rate of 50%.

As the next example demonstrates, marginal income tax rates are an important analytical tool in estate planning, especially when examining the impact of incremental income changes on the overall plan.

EXAMPLE 8-4 Pinkston expects to earn $280,000 in taxable income next year. Her 15-year-old daughter Cheryl will have only a very modest amount of taxable income. Ignoring deductions, Pinkston will save $350 for every $1,000 in taxable income that she can "shift" from her state and federal tax returns (at a total of 50 percent) to Cheryl's (at 15 percent). For every $1,000 shifted, Pinkston's income tax will fall by $500 (=$1,000 x .50), while Cheryl's income tax will only rise by $150 (=$1,000 x .15).

EXAMPLE 8-4A Changing the facts a bit in the example immediately above, if Pinkston's effective marginal rate is only 28 percent, she will save only $130 for every $1000 in income shifted to Cheryl.

Chapters 9 and 13 will discuss income shifting in greater detail. For the present it should suffice to observe two basic income shifting principles: First, under the assignment of income doctrine (discussed in the next chapter), individuals cannot shift earned income. Second, they can shift unearned income only by making a complete transfer of the *property* that generates the income, not just by transferring the income itself.

Credits

Credits are subtracted from the calculated tax, resulting in a "total tax," which is the net tax liability. Allowable credits include the child and dependent care credit, and the residential energy credit. There are several others.

At this point it can be useful to compare the tax rates for the income tax with those for unified transfer taxes. If we look at the 1995 income tax rates for an individual with no dependents, we see that the marginal rates effectively start at 15 percent and rise to 39.6 percent at $256,500. In some states, including the cutdown of itemized deductions and personal exemptions and the impact of state income taxes can push the combined marginal rate to above 50 percent for wealthier clients. In contrast, the unified transfer tax rate remains at zero percent, due to the unified credit, until the tax base exceeds $600,000, at which point the rate rises from 37 percent to 55 percent for amounts in excess of $3 million. Perhaps the single most outstanding difference is the amount excluded from the tax, for income taxes the first $6,400 ($3,900 standard deduction and $2,500 personal exemption), versus the first $600,000 transferred for gifts and estates. This point is important in estate planning because certain expenses associated with death, such as final medical expenses, are deductible either on the estate's estate tax return or on the decedent's income tax return, and a major consideration, of course, will be the alternative tax savings generated by the deduction, an amount that depends on the marginal tax rates for each tax entity. For a further discussion, see Chapter 18.

Form 1040 Summary: An Example

EXAMPLE 8-5 Let's calculate the net income tax liability for Rob and Paula Farrell, who file a joint return for 1994. Income: Rob's salary is $54,000; Paula's salary, $36,000; cash dividends, $4,200; interest received, $3,800; deductions from gross income, $1,000. itemized deductions: "qualified residential interest," $8,000; property tax on residence, $5,000; charitable contributions, $1,220. Assume four personal exemptions but no credits.

Gross Income			$98,000
Less: Deductions from gross income			1,000
Equals: Adjusted gross income			97,000
Less: Itemized deductions:			
Qualified residential interest	$8,000		
Property tax	5,000		
Charitable contributions	1,220	14,220	
Less personal exemptions		10,000	24,220
Leaves: Taxable income			72,780
Calculate the tax			15,308
Less: Credits			0
Equals: net income tax			$15,308

The Kiddie Tax

For 1995, all unearned income of children under age 14 in excess of $1,300 is taxed at the parent's marginal rate. The first $650 is sheltered by the standard deduction, which is the maximum standard deduction allowable on unearned income for persons claimed as dependents on another tax return. The next $650 is ordinarily taxed at the child's base rate of 15 percent.[12]

The amounts $650 and $1,300 (indexed, but not necessarily annually) are reported on a separate return, using IRS Form 8615. For convenience, the parent's return may include the income of a child under 14 having only dividend and interest income less than $5,000. "Piggyback" reporting on the parent's return (attaching Form 8614) has some drawbacks. First, instead of the above $650 and $1,300 amounts, a lower unindexed $500 and $1,000 must be used. Second, the child can't take advantage of certain other deductions, such as charitable donations and the additional standard deduction for being blind. Finally, using the parent's return increases their adjusted gross income, which in effect raises the threshold amount used to determine cutbacks in itemized deductions and personal exemptions, as discussed earlier.

The source of the child's unearned income is immaterial; excess unearned income is taxed at the parent's rate even though they were not the original source of the property producing that income.

> EXAMPLE 8-6 Dale and Josette's joint taxable income in the current year is $60,000, putting them in the 28 percent marginal rate bracket. Their 12-year-old daughter Lara has $2,100 in unearned income, including $1,300 in dividends from stock received as a gift from Dale's parents, and $800 in interest from a bank savings account, the deposits of which originated from earned income (compensation) to Lara when she was a newspaper delivery girl. Dale and Josette elect to report Lara's income on a separate return. Of the first $1,300 of unearned income, $650 will be tax-free, and $650 will be taxed at 15%. The amount $800, which is the excess of $2,100 over $1,300, will be taxed at the parents' marginal rate of 28%. Lara's total tax will be $321.50.

> EXAMPLE 8-7 Based on the facts of the example immediately above, if Dale and Josette report Lara's income on their own return, Lara's total tax will be $383. The first $500 will be tax-free, and $500 will be taxed at 15 percent, the remainder, $1,100, will be taxed at 28 percent, for a total tax of $383. Therefore, using reporting Lara's income on the parents' return increases the tax by $61.50.

This tax has come to be called the "kiddie tax," and has the effect of moving the federal government a step closer toward taxing the family as a single economic unit. And it restricts income shifting, as we will see in Chapter 9.

_____

12. §63(c)(5), §1(g)(7)(B)(i).

EXAMPLE 8-8 Continuing Example 8-6 above, if Lara turns age 14 the following year during which time she has exactly the same income, her total tax will drop to $217.50, since the $800 will also be taxed at her own rate of 15%.

Sale Or Exchange Of Property

In the preceding discussion of gross income, the reader may have sensed that one type of gross income listed appears to be quite different from the others. The item "gains from dealings in property" has many unique features, and must be examined in greater detail.

Gain and Loss Gain and loss realized from the sale of property are both calculated by subtracting an asset's "adjusted basis" from the "amount realized:"

Gain or Loss = Amount Realized - Adjusted Basis

EXAMPLE realized gain on sale of 100 shares of common stock having an adjusted basis of $13,000 and sold for $16,000, net of selling commissions, equals $3,000. Had the stock been sold for $11,000, a loss in the amount of $2,000 would be realized.

Amount realized is defined as the fair market value of all money or property received.

EXAMPLE 1001-2 In Example 1001-1, the $16,000 and $11,000 sales proceeds could have been in the form of cash or in kind. Alternatively, the buyer could have canceled an existing debt owed by the seller. Hence, if the buyer actually paid $6,000 cash and assigned to the seller title to his $8,000 automobile and also tore up a $2,000 IOU held on the buyer-debtor, the total amount realized would still have been $16,000.

Adjusted basis is nondescriptively defined in the Code as the "basis" that is "adjusted." The initial basis for an asset that is *purchased* is usually its cost. On the other hand, the initial basis for assets acquired by *gift or inheritance* is determined by different rules, which will be examined shortly. Adjustments to basis include items that reduce basis, such as allowance for depreciation, depletion, and obsolescence. Adjustment items that increase basis include capital expenditures for improvement.

EXAMPLE 1001-3 In Example 1001-1, the adjusted basis of $13,000 was probably simply the original purchase price of the stock, net of the trading commission. However, had the asset been a machine used in the taxpayer's business, adjusted basis would likely reflect its current book (depreciated) value, including all capital improvements made subsequent to its acquisition.

Hence, the $13,000 adjusted basis for the machine could, for example, be the net result of a $27,000 original purchase price, less $17,000 in accumulated depreciation, plus $3,000 in capital improvements.

Recapture of depreciation, which arises when a depreciable business asset is sold for greater than its adjusted basis, is beyond the scope of this text.

In many cases, no significant adjustments to basis will have been made, so that gain or loss will often simply equal the amount realized less the initial unadjusted basis. Dealings in publicly traded securities are perhaps the most common example.

Holding period. A gain or a loss can be either short term or long term, depending upon the length of the holding period, that is, how long the asset was held by the seller (and perhaps by prior owners, too). A gain or a loss is *short-term* if the holding period is not more than one year; it is *long-term* if the property is held more than one year.

By repealing the 60 percent deduction for long-term capital gains, TRA 86 made the short-term versus long-term distinction far less significant. As we shall see a little later in the chapter, short-term and long-term capital gains will almost always be taxed similarly. In drafting TRA 86, Congress chose not to eliminate the distinction from numerous sections in the code partly to allow for future legislation which might resurrect differential treatment.

Realized versus recognized gains and losses. A gain or loss is *realized* when the basic transaction, typically a sale, has occurred. On the other hand, a gain or loss is *recognized* when the taxpayer reports the gain or loss on a tax return. Recognition will commonly occur either because tax law requires recognition in that year or because the taxpayer elects a Code-permitted option to report it that year. Common examples of gains or losses which may be recognized in tax years *after* the year of realization include installment sales,[13] tax-deferred exchanges of like kind property,[14] rollover of gain on sale of a principal residence,[15] involuntary conversion[16] (e.g., destruction of a house by fire with insurance proceeds used to purchase a replacement home), and certain capital transactions between a corporation and its shareholders.

---

13. §453.

14. §1031.

15. §1034.

16. §1033.

Property acquired by gift. As described above, the initial basis for property acquired by *purchase* is its cost, which is later adjusted by such items as depreciation and capital improvements, if any. In this section we will cover the somewhat more complex rule for determining the basis of property which has been acquired by *gift*, rather than by purchase. In the next section we will examine the rule for the basis of property acquired by transfer at *death*.

Date of gift value equaling or exceeding donor's basis. A simple rule applies for gift property whose date of gift value is equal to or greater than the donor's adjusted basis at the date of gift: the donee's basis will equal the amount of the donor's adjusted basis[17] at the date of the gift. This is called the donee's *carryover basis*.

EXAMPLE 1015-1 Ten years ago, donor purchased common stock for $10,000. Two years ago, donor gave donee the stock when it was worth $11,500. At that date, donor's basis was still $10,000. This year, donee sold the stock for $14,500. Since date-of-gift value was greater than donor's basis, donee has realized a gain of $4,500, the difference between the amount realized ($14,500) and donee's basis ($10,000), which is donor's basis at date of gift.

EXAMPLE 1015-2 Same facts as Example 1015-1, except that donee sold the stock for $7,000. Since date-of-gift value is greater than donor's basis, donee's basis is still $10,000, the donor's basis at date of gift. Therefore, donee has realized a loss of $3,000, the difference between the amount realized and donee's basis.

Date of gift value less than donor's basis. However, if a donee sells gift property which had a date-of-gift value that is less than the donor's basis at the date of gift, for purposes of calculating a *loss* only, donee's basis will be date-of-gift value. For purposes of calculating a gain, though, the simple rule still applies; donee's basis will be the donor's basis at the date of the gift.

EXAMPLE 1015-3 Donor acquired property several years ago for $6,000. Last year, when it was worth $4,200, donor gave it to donee, who this year sold it for $3,600. Since date-of-gift value is less than donor's old basis, donee's *basis for loss* is the $4,200 date-of-gift value, and hence donee has realized a loss of only $600.

---

17. From now on, the word *basis* will be assumed to mean adjusted basis.

In effect, donee is not permitted to recognize the portion of the loss resulting from the property's decline in value while owned by the donor.

> EXAMPLE 1015-4 Same facts as Example 1015-3, except that donee sold the property for $7,100. Although date-of-gift value is less than donor's basis, donee's *basis for gain* is, as always, the donor's basis at the date of the gift. In this case, donee's basis is $6,000, and donee has therefore realized a gain of $1,100.

Occasionally gift property having a date-of-gift value that is less than the donor's basis will be sold for an amount that is less than donor's basis but more than date-of-gift value. In such case, the donee will realize neither gain nor loss.

> EXAMPLE 1015-5 Several years ago, donor acquired an asset for $2,000 and later gave it to donee when it was worth $1,450. If donee sells the asset for $1,800, no gain or loss will be realized. Since date of gift value ($1,450) is less than donor's basis at the date of the gift ($2,000), for purposes of calculating a *loss*, donee's basis will be date-of-gift value. There is no loss because the amount realized is greater than donor's basis (i.e., $1,800 minus 1,450 is not negative). On the other hand, for purposes of calculating a *gain*, donor's basis will be donor's basis at the date of the gift ($2,000). There is no gain because the amount realized is less than donor's basis (i.e. $1,800 minus $2,000 is not positive).

Summary. Summarizing in a bit different way, with regard to sale of property acquired by gift, donee's basis for calculating a potential gain is donor's old basis, while basis for calculating a potential loss is the lesser of (*a*) donor's old basis, or (*b*) date-of-gift value. Thus, in situations where date of gift value exceeds donor's old basis, basis for both gain and loss will be the same; both will be derived from donor's old basis.

For comparison purposes, Table 8-4 summarizes the results of the above five examples.

TABLE 8-4 Summary of Examples 1015-1 to 1015-5

Example	Donor's Old Basis	Date of Gift Value	Amount Realized	Basis for Gain	Basis for Loss	Taxable Gain	Deductible Loss
1	$10,000.	$11,500.	$14,500.	$10,000.	$10,000.	$4,500.	-
2	10,000.	11,500.	7,000.	10,000.	10,000.	-	($3,000.)
3	6,000.	4,200.	3,600.	6,000.	4,200.	-	(600.)
4	6,000.	4,200.	7,100.	6,000.	4,200.	1,100.	-
5	2,000.	1,450.	1,800.	2,000.	1,450.	-	-

Two additional refinements. Two additional points should be made with regard to the sale of gift property.

First, in determining whether the donee's gain or loss is short term or long term, the length of the donor's *holding period* is added or "tacked on" to the length of the donee's holding period. Regardless of how long the decedent had held property it is automatically long term for the estate or the beneficiaries.

Second, if the donor paid a gift tax on the gift, a portion of that tax is added to the donor's adjusted basis at the date of the gift. The amount added is that portion attributable to the appreciation while in donor's hands. Hence:

*New Basis = Old Basis + ((FMV Gift - Old Basis)/ FMV Gift)) * Gift Tax*

EXAMPLE 1015-6 Donor gave stock purchased for $400,000 twenty years ago to Donee when the stock was worth $1,010,000. Donor paid $153,000. Donee's new basis equals:

$400,000 + (($1,010,000 - $400,000) / $1,010,000) * $153,000 = $492,406.

The following example incorporates many of the basis principles we have been considering.

EXAMPLE 1015-7 Fourteen months ago, donor paid $22,000 for a personal computer for use in her business. After spending $1,000 in capital improvements and after depreciating it by $9,000, donor gave it to donee. It was then worth $21,300. Donor paid no gift tax. Today, donee sold it for $12,400. Donee's basis is $14,000, which is donor's old basis ($14,000 = $22,000 - $9,000 + $1,000). A loss of $1,600 is realized since this is the amount by which donee's basis for loss exceeds the amount realized (-$1,600 = $12,400 - $14,000). The $1,600 loss is long-term because donee's holding period is the length of time the computer was held by both the donee and the donor, a period exceeding one year. Since no gift tax was paid, no basis adjustment was made.

Inherited property. When a person inherits (i.e., bequest, devise or inheritance, or surviving joint tenant) property from a decedent , all or a portion of the property's basis for both gain and loss is the value of the property included in the decedent's gross estate.[18] There are several exceptions to this rule that we will discuss as we go.

---

18. §1014(a).

Notice that the change in the basis of property acquired by another's death can be "step-up" or "step-down" in the basis depending on whether the decedent's predeath basis was lower or higher than the value at death. However, to simplify expression when making general statements, we will follow common usage and refer to a change in either direction as a *step-up* in basis. Furthermore, if the alternate valuation date is elected, it is the alternate value that determines the basis, however to simply discussion we will use the term date of death (abbreviated DOD) value to include the alternate valuation when considering basis.

If an U.S. Estate Tax return (Form 706) is filed states there is a rebuttable presumption that the Form 706 values are correct.[19] However, the change in basis occurs even though no tax is due (perhaps because of the 100% marital deduction) and even for small estates that do not have to file an estate tax return.

How much of the basis of the property acquired by death is stepped-up will depend upon whether or not the property was individually owned at date of death, and, if not, how the property was co-owned.

Individually owned property. Individually owned property acquired by death is entitled to a full step-up in basis. Thus, seller's entire basis for both gain and loss is the entire value of the property at date of the donor's death.

> EXAMPLE 1014-1 Frank recently sold a vacant parcel of land for $75,000. The land had been purchased by Frank's dad for $500 in 1930 and was worth $40,000 in 1990 when it passed to Frank by inheritance. Dad's total estate was about $200,000, so no estate tax was owed and no return was filed. Frank has a realized gain of $35,000, the difference between the sale price and the basis established at date of death.

Concurrently owned property. If, at death, the decedent was sharing ownership in property, usually only the decedent's share will be stepped-up. The factor that determines whether any *surviving* co-owner can also enjoy a step-up in basis for his or her share depends upon the legal form of concurrent ownership. In general, no surviving co-owner's share will enjoy a step-up in basis unless the asset is either owned as community property or is includable in the predeceased co-owner's gross estate.

The rules for co-owner basis change at death are as follows:

Community property: The new basis is the FMV at date of death for both halves of the community property even though only half is included in the decedent spouse's estate. This is referred to as a full step-up in basis.

---

19. Revenue Ruling 54-97, 1954-1 C.B. 113

Joint tenancy: What is included in the decedent estate and the surviving co-owners new basis will follow one of two rules which depend on the relationship between the decedent and the surviving co-owner's.

Husband and wife rule: Where the only joint tenants (or tenants by the entire) are husband and wife then half of the FMV at date of death is included in the decedent's estate and the surviving spouse's new basis will equal half the total pre-death basis and half the FMV at date of death.

$$New\ Basis = (DOD\ FMV + Old\ Basis) / 2$$

Nonspouses rule: Where the joint tenants include nonspouses the rule is that the decedent's gross estate includes that portion of the property as the decedent's share of the consideration (price paid for the property) bears to the total consideration. Decedent's consideration includes any gifts given to other joint tenants and any share acquired by another person's death.

$$Include = (Decedent's\ Consideration\ /\ Total\ Consideration)\ *\ FMV\ DOD$$

The new basis for each surviving co-owner's interest is his or her old basis plus an increase for his proportional share of the amount included in the decedent's estate. The examples that follow demonstrate both rules.

EXAMPLE 1014-2JT: At Ricky's death, he and his wife Victoria owned common stock as *joint tenants*. Ricky had paid $5,000 and Victoria paid $11,000 of the original $16,000 purchase price. When Ricky died, the stock was worth $22,000, and Victoria acquired Ricky's interest by right of survivorship. Four months later, she sold the stock for $29,000. Victoria will realize a gain of $10,000. Victoria's basis is $19,000, the sum of $8,000 (half of the original basis) plus $11,000 (Ricky's one-half interest included in his estate).

Consider the very different outcome for *community property*.

EXAMPLE 1014-2CP: Same facts as in the prior example, except at Ricky's death, he and his wife Victoria owned the common stock as *community property*. Once again half would be included in Ricky's estate but Victoria's basis would be the FMV DOD amount, $22,000.

Thus, ordinary community property states have a decided advantage over common law states with regard to basis adjustments at death, and estate planners often recommend that clients residing in community property states hold appreciated, or appreciating, property in community property form, if possible. On the other hand, estate planners anticipating a *step-down* in basis will advise clients to convert community property to some other form of ownership to avoid a double step-down.

The IRS takes the position that states recognizing the concept "community property with right of survivorship" (e.g., Nevada and Wisconsin) will not have the advantage of a double step-up in basis, but will be treaded as husband and wife joint tenants.

> EXAMPLE 1014-3: Years ago, brothers Steve and Stan purchased stock for $10,000, taking title as joint tenants. Steve paid $6,000 and Stan paid $4,000 towards the purchase. At Steve's death the stock was worth $20,000. Included in Steve's gross estate is 60% of the stock's value because that corresponds to his share of the consideration paid for the stock, even though property law recognized that he 50% of the stock immediately before death. Stan's new basis would be $16,000 which is $12,000 (the amount included in Steve's estate) plus Steve's $4,000 basis in his pre-death interest in the property.

> EXAMPLE 1014-4: Three friends purchased a vacation cabin in 1980. Abe paid $20,000, Betty paid $30,000, and Cathy paid $50,000 of the $100,000 purchase price. In 1985, when the cabin was worth $160,000, Abe died. His estate included 20% of the DOD FMV, i.e. 20% * $160,000 = $32,000. Betty's new basis in her 50% interest in the cabin became $46,000 (1/2 * $32,000 + her original consideration of $30,000) and Cathy's new basis is $66,000 (1/2 * $32,000 + her $50,000).

> EXAMPLE 1014-5: Continuing from the last example, in 1990, Cathy died leaving Betty as the sole surviving joint tenant. The cabin was then worth $224,000. The amount included in Cathy's gross estate is based on her portion ($66,000) of the combined (hers and Betty's) predeath bases of $112,000. Therefor, included is $132,000 (($66,000 / $112,000) * $224,000), and Betty's new basis would be $178,000 (the $132,000 included in Cathy's estate plus Betty's old basis of $46,000).

It should be noted that a gift from one prospective cotenant to another is treaded as consideration from the donor not the donee.

> EXAMPLE 1014-6: Martin gave hs son, Andy, $50,000 shortly before they purchased a vacation condo for $150,000. Martin paid $100,000 on the purchase and Andy paid $50,000. When Martin died the condo was valued at $200,000, all of which had to be included in his estate because Andy's contribution was traceable to Martin's gift.

Tenants in Common Rule: Tenancy in common is the preferred form of ownership for nonrelatives. It does not have the survivorship feature found in joint tenancy, thus the co-owners control the disposition of their respective shares. Unlike joint tenancy, tenants in common can have unequal undivided shares, meaning that you could have one owner owning 20%, another owning 30%, and the third owning 50%. When a tenant in common owner dies his or her share of the total FMV DOD of the property is included in the gross estate. The disposition of a deceased tenant in common's interest depends on the decedent's will or, if there is no will, interstate succession laws.

> EXAMPLE 1014-7: Friends Arthur, Tony and Maria purchased property as tenants in common. They took title in equal shares even though Arthur generously paid $40,000, and Tony and Maria each paid only $30,000 of the $100,000 purchase price. Years later when Tony died the property was worth $240,000, and his estate included $80,000 since he owned a one-third interest. If Tony left his one-third interest to his wife, her basis would be $80,000. If he instead left his interest to co-owner Maria, her total basis in the two-thirds interest she would then own would be $110,000 ($80,000 + her $30,000 contribution).

Note, in the preceding example, because the interests were held as tenants in common property law recognizes unequal shares. Therefore, had the three agreed to hold percentage interests in proportion to each person's consideration, then Tony's share would have been 30% and only $72,000 would have been included in his estate.

Holding period. The holding period for property acquired from a decedent will be considered to have been *long term*, no matter how long the decedent and the devisee have held it. Thus, a decedent could have purchased the asset shortly before death and the devisee could have sold it shortly after death, and any gain or loss will be long term.

Character of the gain - capital versus ordinary gains and losses. In general, for tax purposes, property falls into *three* classifications: capital assets, depreciable and real property used in a trade or business, and all other assets. Thus, the Code defines capital assets as all types of property except items such as (*a*) depreciable and real property used in a trade or business, (*b*) inventory (*c*) copyrights, and (*d*) accounts receivables. Taxation of each of the three classifications will be examined briefly in reverse order, in the discussion that follows.

First, gains from the sale of noncapital asset items *b*, *c* and *d* are taxed at ordinary rates; that is, the entire gain is included in gross income. Losses from the sale of these items are subtracted from gross income.

Second, taxation of gains from the sale of noncapital asset item *a*, depreciable and real property used in a trade or business, depends upon the holding period. For property held not more than one year, (or six months, depending on the acquisition date), taxation is similar to that for other noncapital assets. For property held more than one year, (six months for certain property), taxation is similar to taxation of long-term capital gains, subject, however, to depreciation recapture. Principles of taxation of losses from the sale of depreciable business property is similar to the taxation of short-term capital losses, except for the absence of the $3,000 limitation, to be described shortly.

Third, taxation of capital assets may depend on the holding period. Assuming that a taxpayer incurs only one capital transaction during the year, the following summarizes the tax consequences:

1. A *short-term gain* is added to gross income and is therefore taxed at ordinary rates.
2. A *long-term gain* is also added to gross income but in no event will be taxed at greater than 28 percent.
3. Both a *short-term loss* and a *long-term loss* can be deducted against gross income up to a maximum of $3,000 per year, with the excess "carried over" to future years.

With regard to #3 above, all undeducted carryover losses become unusable after the taxpayer's death. Only $3,000 in losses are deductible in the year of death, and none may be carried over by succeeding taxpayers, such as the decedent's estate or the decedents heirs, legatees or devisees. Thus, planning advice should be: Use it during your lifetime, or lose it.

Personal capital losses are not deductible. Examples include losses on the sale of a personal residence and a personal automobile.

Multiple transactions in one year: the netting process. Taxation of capital gains and losses for a taxpayer involved in *more than one transaction* in a given year can be complex. An oversimplified summary follows: First, short-term gains are netted against short-term losses, resulting in either a net short-term gain (NSG) or a net short-term loss (NSL). Similarly, the "longs" are netted, resulting in a net long-term gain (NLG) or a net long-term loss (NLL). The two resulting net amounts are then compared, with the following possible consequences:

1. Net long-term gain and net short-term loss:
   a. If NLG exceeds NSL, then the excess is includable in gross income but in no event will be taxed at greater than 28 percent.
   b. If NSL exceeds NSG, then the excess up to a maximum of $3,000 is deductible against current gross income; the rest is carried over.
2. Net long-term loss and net short-term gain:
   a. If NLL exceeds NSG, then up to $3,000 of the excess is used to reduce income; the rest is carried over.
   b. If NSG exceeds NLL, then that excess is included in gross income.
3. Net long-term gain and net short-term gain:
   a. NLG is treated like a long-term gain from a single transaction.
   b. NSG is treated like a short-term gain from a single transaction.

4. Net short-term loss and net long-term loss:
    a. NSL is treated like a short-term loss from a single transaction.
    b. NLL is treated like a long-term loss from a single transaction.

Perhaps the most significant general conclusion to draw from these rules is that long-term capital gains are taxed relatively favorably. While the maximum rate for ordinary income is currently 39.6 percent, the maximum federal rate on long-term capital gains is just 28 percent. Planning opportunities which rely on this rate differential are discussed in later chapters.

We turn next to the second and third of the four types of taxpayers discussed in this chapter on income taxation: estates and trusts.

FEDERAL INCOME TAXATION OF ESTATES AND TRUSTS

Overview

The practice of estate planning focuses on one type of estate: the probate estate, and three different types of trusts: the simple trust, complex trust and grantor trust. This section describes the taxation of all four of these important fiduciary arrangements.

A decedent's estate, simple trust, and complex trust are all taxed as independent entities, subject to the same tax rate schedule. Their taxation is described first, under the heading: *fiduciary income taxation.*

On the other hand, a grantor trust, while an independent legal entity, is not an independent *taxable* entity. Because its "grantor" (trustor) has retained what tax law treats as at least one significant interest in the trust, all income will be taxed to that grantor, as an individual. Grantor trusts will be described second, near the end of the chapter.

Fiduciary Income Taxation: An Introduction

Overview and calculation of the tax. Generally speaking, taxable income for estates, simple trusts and complex trusts is computed in very much the same manner as for an individual. As shown in the overview model of Table 8-5, deductions are subtracted from gross income to arrive at taxable income, on which a tax is calculated. Credits are then subtracted to arrive at the net tax. The tax rate schedule for estates and nongrantor trusts is detailed in Table 8-6, and in Table 3 of Appendix A at the end of the book. Fiduciaries for estates and all nongrantor trusts report their income on Form 1041, Fiduciary Income Tax Return, which is illustrated in Appendix F.

Compared with the rate bracket for individuals, those for estates and trusts accelerate far more sharply. Thus the maximum marginal income tax rate of 39.6 percent applies to all estate or trust income in excess of $7,500, versus $256,500 for individuals.[20]

One specific similarity between fiduciary income taxation and individual income taxation should be mentioned now: Gross income for both includes all sources of income subject to federal taxation, including all forms of taxable interest, cash dividends, net rental income, and capital gains.

Although fiduciary income taxation appears entirely similar to the taxation of individuals, it has a major difference. As shown in Table 8-5, it includes a deduction called the *distribution deduction*, which serves to implement what is known as the *conduit principal*. To understand the meaning of and rationale for these two concepts, it is necessary to explore the unique philosophy underlying fiduciary income taxation.

The conduit principle and its influence on fiduciary income taxation. In general, trusts and estates may be viewed as repositories of principal and income, managed and held by executors and trustees as fiduciaries, for eventual distribution to their beneficiaries. Under tax law, if a trustee (or executor) receives interest or dividend income from invested trust (estate) principal and does not distribute it to beneficiaries in that year, tax policy seeks to tax this income to the trustee (executor) in the year received.

TABLE 8-5 Federal Income Taxation of Estates and Trusts (Form 1041) Overview Model

Gross Income		$xxx,xxx.
Less: Deductions, including:		
Charitable deduction	$xxx.	
Administration fees	x,xxx.	
Distribution deduction	x,xxx.	
Personal exemption	xxx.	x,xxx.
Equals: Taxable income		xx,xxx.
Calculate the tax		xx,xxx.
Less: Credits		xxx.
Leaves: Net tax		$xx,xxx.

20. Riddle: "When is a high-income taxpayer not a high-income taxpayer? When it is an estate or trust." *Bernard Barnett.*

TABLE 8-6 Federal Income Tax Rates: Estates and Trusts

Taxable Income

Over	But Not Over	Base Amount	+	Percent	On Excess Over
		1995			
$ 0.	$1,550.	$ 0.00		15.0%	$ 0.
1,550.	3,700.	232.50		28.0	1,550.
3,700.	5,600.	834.50		31.0	3,700.
5,650.	7,650.	1,423.50		36.0	5,650.
7,650.	-	2,161.50		39.6	7,650.

On the other hand, if the fiduciary does distribute the income to beneficiaries during the year, tax policy in general aims to tax this income to the beneficiaries instead. Expressed differently, the Internal Revenue Code often treats an estate or trust as a nontaxable *conduit*, to the extent that it merely passes through income from the source of that income to the beneficiaries. If the beneficiaries receive the income in the same year the fiduciary receives it, they will be taxed. The estate or trust will wind up not being taxed on this income because it will take a special deduction; it will offset its gross income by the amount of that income it distributes with an item called the distribution deduction.

Distribution deduction implements the conduit. Thus, the distribution deduction is an estate or trust deduction for certain income actually distributed to beneficiaries. Without it, that income could be subject to double taxation, first to the fiduciary, and then to the beneficiary. By taking the distribution deduction, the fiduciary will not be taxed on that income. The beneficiaries will be, because they are required to include in gross income their pro rata share of the amount that of that deduction. Income not taxable to the fiduciary because it is distributed to beneficiaries is said to be "passed through" to those beneficiaries.

Exception for capital gains; introduction to DNI and FAI. Complicating the picture a bit, not all income subject to taxation can be passed through to the beneficiaries; not all distributed income can be deducted.

Except in the estate or trust's final taxable year,[21] *capital gains*, even when distributed to beneficiaries, will still be taxable to the fiduciary. The way that tax law limits the distribution deduction to noncapital gains income is by limiting it to the *lesser* of the amount actually distributed to beneficiaries (up to 65 days after the close of the taxable year), or the amount of *distributable net income* (DNI). Calculation of DNI is somewhat complex and beyond the scope of this section. At the risk of overgeneralizing, in this section we will assume for simplicity that DNI always equals an amount called *fiduciary accounting income*, or FAI. In a later section, we'll drop that assumption and describe the exact method of calculating DNI.

FAI includes most sources of federal gross income, including cash dividends, interest, and net rental income (rent reduced by certain expenses). FAI also includes municipal bond interest. In contrast, FAI does not include stock share dividends, and capital gains, which are considered gains from sale of corpus.

> EXAMPLE FAI-1 A trust has a corpus of $600,000 invested in stocks, federal government bonds, municipal bonds and real estate. During the past year, its trustee received $4,000 in cash dividends, 200 shares of stock dividends (market value $800), $22,000 in federal interest, $6,000 in municipal bond interest, $3,000 in net rental income, and $5,000 in capital gains from the sale of securities. Its total FAI is $35,000 (= $4,000 + $22,000 + $6,000 + $3,000). Its DNI, based on our simplifying assumption, also equals $35,000.

Summarizing the terminology:

- Fiduciary *gross income* includes all sources of income subject to federal taxation, including all forms of taxable interest, cash dividends, net rental income, and capital gains.

- *FAI* includes cash dividends, taxable interest and net rental income, but not stock share dividends or capital gains.

- *DNI*, for purposes of this section, is considered equal to FAI.

- The *distribution deduction* is the lessor of DNI or the amount actually distributed to beneficiaries.

---

21. For a discussion of tax benefits related to unused net operating loss carryovers, capital loss carryovers, and excess deductions which pass through to beneficiaries upon termination of an estate or trust, see the King article cited at the end of the chapter.

- The *taxable income to any particular beneficiary* will be his or her pro rata share of the total amount of the fiduciary's distribution deduction.

Summarizing in a more comprehensive manner, DNI is a fiduciary tax return concept which acts as the measuring rod for estate and trust taxation. It implements the conduit principle since the lesser of it or the amount actually distributed to beneficiaries is 1) deductible to the fiduciary as the distribution deduction, and 2) reportable to the beneficiaries as gross income. The distribution deduction "conduit" distributes income from the estate or trust, which is not taxed on this income, to the beneficiaries, who are.

Some additional examples should help clarify these new terms. In each, assume the entity is either an estate or a nongrantor trust, reporting for a tax year sometime prior to its final year. Finally, assume no fiduciary personal exemptions. Later in this section, we'll include the influence of fiduciary personal exemptions, which range from $100 for certain complex trusts to $600 for estates.

> EXAMPLE DNI-1. During the year, the executor of an estate receives $2,000 in treasury bond interest, $4,000 in cash dividends, and realizes $7,000 in gains from the sale of stock. The executor made *no distributions* to beneficiaries during the year. Total estate gross income equals $13,000. DNI equals FAI, which is $6,000, the sum of the interest and dividends. The distribution deduction is $0, which is the lesser of DNI ($6,000) or the amount actually distributed to beneficiaries ($0). Thus, the fiduciary will be taxed on the entire $13,000 income received (= $13,000 - $0), and the beneficiaries will be taxed on none of this income.

> EXAMPLE DNI-2. Facts similar to Example DNI-1 above, except that the executor *distributed $3,000* cash to beneficiaries. While gross income still equals $13,000 and DNI is still $6,000, the distribution deduction will now equal $3,000 (lesser of $6,000 or $3,000). Thus, the fiduciary will be taxed on $10,000 (= $13,000 - $3,000), which is all but $3,000 of the $13,000 gross income received, and the beneficiaries will be taxed on the $3,000 distribution deduction, which is not taxed to the estate.

> EXAMPLE DNI-3. Facts similar to Example DNI-1 above, except that the fiduciary *distributed $8,000* cash to beneficiaries. The distribution deduction is now $6,000 (lesser of $6,000 or $8,000). Thus, the executor will be taxed on $7,000 (= $13,000 - $6,000), which is only the amount of the capital gain. The executor will not be taxed on the $6,000 of FAI, but the beneficiaries will be.

In each of the above examples, the fiduciary was required to report, as income, at minimum, the amount of the capital gain, which could not be passed through. However, the fiduciary was able to deduct any distributions to beneficiaries of FAI, which could be passed through.

With this overview of the influence of DNI and the distribution deduction on fiduciary income taxation, we are nearly ready to examine how simple trusts, complex trusts and estates are taxed differently. First however, we must make a distinction between fiduciary income and principal.

Accounting income versus principal. For *accounting* purposes, fiduciary income is simply the amount of the FAI. On the other hand, fiduciary principal includes the assets themselves, plus the current year's capital gains and stock share dividends.

The distinction between FAI and principal derives from state law. Most states have adopted the *Revised Uniform Principal And Income Act*, which details these distinctions. A deduction that reduces FAI is a trustee fee that is chargeable to income rather than corpus. The Act permits trust instruments to mandate trustee fees be charged to income, to principal, or a portion to both.

Taxation of Simple Trusts, Complex Trusts, and Estates

Simple trusts, complex trusts and estates are each taxed somewhat differently due to the size of the personal exemption each is allowed.

Simple trust. For any given taxable year, a simple trust is a nongrantor trust which distributes to beneficiaries all FAI but no principal, and takes no charitable deduction.

As the example below illustrates, the simple trust most clearly demonstrates the conduit aspect of DNI. Simple trusts as well as complex trusts that are required to distribute all FAI currently are allowed a $300 personal exemption, which, as shown in Table 8-5, is subtracted from gross income.

EXAMPLE 643-1 The terms of a nongrantor trust require that all fiduciary accounting income be distributed currently to its sole beneficiary. In the current year, this simple trust receives $6,000 in dividends, and $4,000 in net rental income, for a total of $10,000 in FAI and DNI. The trust also realizes a $9,000 short-term capital gain and a $1,000 short-term capital loss on the sale of stock. Assuming no deductions except the distribution deduction and the personal exemption, the trust's taxable income is $7,700, calculated as follows:

Trust gross income		$18,000.
Less: Distribution deduction (DNI)	$10,000.	
Less: Exemption	300.	10,300.
Leaves: Taxable income		$7,700.

The distribution deduction of $10,000 equals the lesser of DNI ($10,000), or the amount actually distributed ($10,000). The beneficiary will include this amount in his or her gross income.

Notice that the trust in the above example is effectively taxed only on the $8,000 net capital gain, reduced by the amount of the exemption.

Complex trust, estate. The second type of trust, called the complex trust, is defined as a nongrantor trust which, in a given year, either (*a*) accumulates some FAI (i.e., does not pay out all FAI it has received, to the beneficiaries), (*b*) distributes principal, or (*c*) takes a charitable deduction. Essentially, the complex trust will, similar to the simple trust, receive a distribution deduction for the amount of its DNI that it actually distributes (from income or principal) to the beneficiaries, who will include that same amount, pro rata, in gross income on their individual tax returns. But unlike the simple trust, the complex trust may have undistributed DNI, which will be taxable to the trust. And unlike the simple trust, total distributions from a complex trust may exceed FAI, and this excess will wind up untaxed, as a return of capital. Finally, like the simple trust, the complex trust will be taxed on any amounts included in gross income originating from principal transactions, such as capital gains.

Complex trust versus estate. With minor exceptions, *estates* are taxed similarly to complex trusts. Complex trusts that do not require all FAI to be distributed currently are allowed a $100 personal exemption. Estates, on the other hand, receive a $600 exemption.

Applying the conduit principle to complex trusts and estates. Applying the above rules for complex trusts and estates, let's examine the tax effects when an estate or trust accumulates FAI and, alternatively, distributes principal.

A trust or estate that *accumulates FAI* or, in more exact terms, distributes *less* than its total DNI in a given year will receive a distribution deduction equal only to the amount of the distribution, and will therefore have to report the amount accumulated as taxable income. The beneficiaries will still report as taxable income the amount received, which in the aggregate is equal to the limited amount deducted by the trust. Therefore, a full conduit in the amount paid to the beneficiaries still results, as in the case of a simple trust. The amount passed through however, is less than the amount for a simple trust with the same FAI. This is illustrated in the next two examples.

EXAMPLE 661-1 During the second year of its three-year existence, the *estate* of decedent Barnhill earned $52,000 in dividends, $18,000 in interest, and $21,000 in short-term capital gains. Thus, the estate's FAI and DNI both equal $70,000. During the year, the personal representative distributed $6,000 to the sole beneficiary. Assuming no deductions except the distribution deduction and the personal exemption, the estate's taxable income is $84,400, calculated as follows:

Estate gross income		$91,000.
Less: Distribution deduction (DNI)	$6,000.	
Less: Exemption	600.	6,600.
Leaves: Taxable income		$84,400.

The distribution deduction of $6,000 equals the lesser of DNI ($70,000) or the amount actually distributed ($6,000). The beneficiary will include that amount in her gross income.

EXAMPLE 661-2 Facts similar to Example 661-1, except that the entity is a *trust*, not an estate, which permits the trustee to accumulate fiduciary accounting income. All calculations will be the same, except since a complex trust is entitled to a personal exemption of only $100, trust taxable income will be $84,900, or $500 greater than that for the estate.

Alternatively, an estate or trust that distributes in a given year *more* than its DNI will be allowed a deduction only equal to the full amount of the DNI, which we assume equals only the total of its FAI. Therefore, taxable income for such an estate or trust will include only items of gross income that do not constitute FAI (e.g., capital gains). The beneficiaries will be required to include in gross income only their pro rata share of the DNI; all amounts received in excess of DNI constitute a nontaxable receipt of capital (principal). Again, a full conduit results, in the amount of FAI actually distributed.

EXAMPLE 661-3 Facts similar to Example 661-1, except that the personal representative distributed $115,000 to the beneficiary. The estate's taxable income is $20,400, calculated as follows:

Estate gross income		$91,000.
Less: Distribution deduction (DNI)	$70,000.	
Less: Exemption	600.	70,600.
Leaves: Taxable income		$20,400.

The beneficiary will include in her gross income the amount $70,000; this is equal to the amount of the estate's distribution deduction, which again equals the lesser of DNI ($70,000) or the amount actually distributed ($115,000). Inasmuch as she received a total of $115,000, the amount $45,000 represents a nontaxable distribution of principal, or a distribution of previously taxed accumulated income (which might now be subject to the throwback rules-- to be described shortly). The net effect is that the estate pays the tax on the capital gain and the beneficiary pays the tax on the fiduciary accounting income.

Trusts can change status from year to year. A given trust can be a simple trust in some years and a complex trust in others. For example, a trust's terms could provide that all income shall be accumulated until the sole beneficiary reaches age 21, at which time all income will thereafter be required to be paid to her annually. The trust will be a complex trust during the first period and a simple trust during the second.

Throwback rules. A certain type of tax planning is eliminated by tax provisions embodied in the so-called throwback rules. Suppose a trustee had discretion to distribute or accumulate income, and she chose to accumulate some income in year one when the beneficiary had a high personal marginal income tax rate, and to distribute more than one year of income in year two when the beneficiary had a lower tax rate. If allowed, some modest tax savings could result because each year trustees could direct income to that taxpaying entity having a lower marginal tax rate. The throwback rules thwart this opportunity by requiring excess distributions to a beneficiary to be taxed to the beneficiary as if they had been received in the years in which the trust actually *received* and accumulated them. However, the steep rate ladder for trusts probably discourages such planning more than do the throwback rules. The throwback rules do not apply, however, to estates or to any accumulations during which a trust beneficiary was under the age of 21.

Filing of estate income tax returns. Ordinarily, one return a year will be filed for a simple or complex trust. In contrast, the filing of returns on behalf of a decedent and the decedent's estate is more complicated, and will be described next.

First, the *decedent's final income tax return* (Form 1040) is filed, covering the period of the decedent's last calendar year of life, from January 1 to date of death. Or, a joint return may be filed with the surviving spouse for the entire year.

Second, when probate administration is involved, the first *estate income tax return* (Form 1041) will be filed covering the part of the year of death from one day after date of death until December 31. This assumes a *calendar tax year* (January 1-December 31). Estates (and nongrantor trusts) are permitted to choose instead a *fiscal* tax year (i.e., a year ending on the last day of some month other than December). Planning opportunities derived from the choice of tax year are discussed in Chapter 18.

Third, *estate income tax returns* (Form 1041) are then filed for probate estate income each succeeding year that the estate is in existence, with the last return covering the period January 1 to date of final distribution of the estate assets. Again, this assumes a calendar tax year.

Income in respect of a decedent. At the moment of death, many decedents are owed property that tax law considers income. This "income in respect of a decedent" (IRD) technically consists of income to which the decedent was entitled at death but which had not been actually received prior to death. Examples of IRD can include receipts from promissory notes, distributions from qualified retirement plans, dividends and business accounts receivables. IRD is subject to both FET and income tax, and is reportable by the actual recipient of the income (executor, trustee or beneficiary). And because an estate tax is paid on such amounts which later had to be used to pay income taxes, the recipient of IRD is allowed an income tax deduction for FET attributable to the IRD.[22]

Exact method of calculating DNI and taxable income. Up to now, we have made the simplifying assumption that DNI equals FAI. In this section we will drop that assumption and demonstrate the exact method of calculating DNI and taxable income for an estate or trust. Under this method, the distribution deduction is equal to the lesser of the amount actually distributed to beneficiaries (reduced by tax exempt income) *or* the amount of "net taxable DNI," which equals DNI reduced by certain trustee fees. Before calculating the distribution deduction, however, we must discuss two additional complexities, relating to trustee fees and tax exempt income.

Trustee fees. Trustee fees are ordinarily deducted in arriving at "net FAI" and net taxable DNI. However, the amount deductible for each will differ. In calculating net FAI, the amount of the total trustee fee that is deducted is that portion allocable to income, rather than principal.

On the other hand, in calculating net taxable DNI, the amount of the trustee fee deductible is a fraction of the entire fee based on the portion of gross fiduciary accounting income that is taxable.

EXAMPLE NDNI-1 A trust received $15,000 in taxable interest, $15,000 in dividends and $10,000 in tax-exempt interest. If total trustee fees are $8,000, of which one half is allocable to income, the amount of the trustee fee deductible in calculating net FAI is $4,000 (= $8,000 x .5). The amount of the trustee fee deductible in calculating net taxable DNI is $6,000 [= $8,000 x ($30,000/$40,000)].

---

22. §691(c)(3). For discussion, see the Ferguson book and the Thorne/Crowell article, both cited at the end of the chapter.

Tax-exempt income. In calculating net FAI, the entire amount of tax exempt income is included. In calculating net taxable DNI, the entire tax-exempt income is excluded, and that portion of the trustees fees allocated to tax-exempt income cannot be deducted.[23] The formula for determining the amount disallowed as a deduction is:

Disallowed = (Gross tax-exempt interest/gross fiduciary income) * Trustee's fees.

EXAMPLE NDNI-2 In addition to the facts in Example NDNI-1, assume that the trust has a capital gain of $8,000 and distributes $22,000 to beneficiaries in the current year. Its net FAI is calculated as follows:

Taxable Interest	$15,000.	
Dividends	15,000.	
Tax-exempt Interest	10,000.	
Gross FAI		$40,000.
Less Trustee Fee (allocated to income)		4,000.
Net FAI		$36,000.

The trust's DNI is computed as follows:

FAI	$36,000
Less Corpus Expenses	4,000
DNI	$32,000

The trust's net taxable DNI is calculated as follows:

Taxable Interest	$15,000.	
Dividends	15,000.	
		$30,000.
Less Trustee Fee		6,000.
Net Taxable DNI		$24,000.

The trust's taxable income is calculated as follows:

Trust gross income		$38,000.
Less trustee fee	$6,000.	
Less distribution ded'n	16,500.	
Less personal exemption	100.	
		22,600.
Trust taxable income		$15,400.

---

23. Regs. 1.652(b)-39b and 1.652(c)-4.

The beneficiaries will report $16,500, the amount of the distribution deduction. Note that the trust distributed only $22,000. Since total DNI is $24,000, only 24/32 of the $22,000 distribution (i.e., $16,500) is taxable. The remaining $5,500 of the distribution is tax-exempt. In this case, $2,000 of the trustee's fees are disallowed in arriving at net taxable DNI, i.e., ($10,000/$40,000) * $8,000. Checking the result: The trust reports $15,400 as taxable income, which represents $8,000 in capital gain and $7,400 of undistributed taxable income. The $7,500 represents the undistributed taxable income (24/32 multiplied by $10,000) reduced by the $100 exemption.

The fiduciary income tax material introduced in the preceding discussion presents a simple overview of a complex subject. As with all tax issues, detailed client questions should be referred to a competent accountant or tax attorney.

We turn now to the third type of trust, the one that is not a separate taxable entity; its income is taxable to its grantor.

Grantor Trust

A grantor trust is a living trust in which the trustor, also called the grantor, has *retained sufficient interest* in the trust to make the income received by the trust taxable *to the grantor*, not the trust or its beneficiaries. The income is includable in the grantor's Form 1040 for that year; hence, from an income tax point of view, the trust is treated as if it does not exist. In fact, a separate Form 1041 trust tax return is often not required to be filed. Regulations require filing of a Form 1041 *information return* by a grantor trust whose grantor is not a trustee. Of course, no tax would be payable.

Grantor trusts are therefore not income tax planning devices, and, in fact, in drafting irrevocable trusts, the estate planning attorney usually attempts carefully to avoid grantor trust status. As we shall see, a common example of a grantor trust is the revocable living trust.

Grantor trust rules. Generally speaking, the most common categories of interests retained by the grantor (any one of which will subject all income from the property to be taxed to the grantor) are: reversionary interests, the power to control beneficial enjoyment, certain administrative powers, the power to revoke, and the right to receive trust income. Since the grantor trust rules will become important later when we study trust planning, we must examine each in some detail. Sections 671-678 included in Appendix B at the end of the book, cover these rules.

First, if the grantor of a trust created after March 1, 1986 retains a *reversionary interest* in the trust income or principal that, at the trust's inception exceeds five percent of the value of the property, it is a grantor trust. An exception to the reversionary interest rule is that a trust is not a grantor trust if a reversion can occur upon the death before reaching age 21 of an income beneficiary who is a lineal descendant or the grantor and who holds all present interests in any portion of the trust.

Prior to TRA 86, a grantor could retain any size reversionary interest without risking grantor trust status, provided that interest did not take effect until more than 10 years after the date of transfer of the property into the trust. Up to then, planners widely advocated the use of the "short-term" or "Clifford" trust as an income-shifting device. TRA 86 killed it. For greater detail, see Example 676-2, and Appendix 14A.

Second, a trust will be a grantor trust if the grantor retains the *power to control beneficial enjoyment* of corpus or income during the first 10 years. Code §674, which covers this rule, has many exceptions. The major exceptions include: (*a*) situations where the grantor can only distribute corpus under a power limited by a "reasonably definite standard" (similar to the "ascertainable standard" under §2041, Powers of Appointment); and (*b*) situations where an independent, unrelated trustee is used.[24]

Third, a trust will be a grantor trust if the grantor retains certain *administrative powers*, including the power to deal with the trust property for less than full consideration, the power to borrow from it without adequate interest or security, the failure to repay a trust loan before the beginning of the taxable year, and certain voting powers over stock held in the trust corpus.

Fourth, a trust will be a grantor trust if the grantor retains the *power to revoke* the trust.

Fifth, a trust will be a grantor trust if, income from the trust is payable (or accumulated) for the *benefit of the grantor* or the grantor's spouse or if income may be used to pay premiums on a life insurance policy on the life of either the grantor or the grantor's spouse.

Sixth, a trust will be a grantor trust if income is actually used to support someone the grantor is *legally obligated to support*, such as purchasing food for a grantor's minor child.

Seventh, trust income may be required to be taxed to a person other than the grantor who has the power to invade income or principal for the benefit of him or herself.

Eighth, §679 treats certain trusts located *outside the United States* as grantor trusts. A "United States person" who either directly or indirectly

---

24. For a detailed discussion of the exceptions to §674 which allow a grantor numerous powers over a trust, see the Fink article cited at the end of the chapter.

transfers property to a foreign trust will be taxed currently on all of the income received by the trust if any portion of the assets of the trust may be held for a United States beneficiary. This rule will apply even though the trust is irrevocable, or the donor has retained no interests or powers in the trust. Thus, there are no income tax advantages to establishing a foreign trust. Nontax advantages include providing for family members living in other countries, the desire to avoid U.S. securities laws, and the greater ease of privately holding title to foreign property.[25]

Finally, the law treats a U.S. person as the grantor of a grantor trust if he/she 1) is a beneficiary; and 2) made direct or indirect gifts to a foreign person of property that was contributed to the trust, if the foreign person would otherwise be treated as a grantor. This plugs a loophole enjoyed by foreigners moving to the U. S.[26]

The following examples demonstrate several important grantor trust rules.

> EXAMPLE 676-1 Grantor creates a *revocable living trust* which is primarily designed to avoid probate and reduce estate taxes upon death of the surviving spouse. The trust is not an income tax saving device during the grantor's lifetime because the income will be taxed to the grantor, who possesses the right to revoke the trust at any time.

> EXAMPLE 676-2 Grantor creates a *short-term trust*, also called a Clifford trust, which is irrevocable for 10 years, with income payable to grantor's mother for the shorter of her life or 10 years, and then reversion to grantor. Created after March 1, 1986, this trust violates the grantor trust rules. The value of grantor's reversion exceeds 5 percent of the value of the trust property. Hence, the income will be taxable to the grantor.[27]

> EXAMPLE 677-1 Grantor establishes an irrevocable trust for her 16-year-old son, and the trust is required to use the income to purchase, among other things, clothing for the son. This trust violates the grantor trust rules because the income is required to be used to meet the grantor's *obligation of support*. The income is treated as for the benefit of the grantor, and thus will be taxable to the grantor.

---

25. For details, see the Christensen paper cited at the end of the chapter.

26. §672(f).

27. The short-term trust is discussed further in the Appendix to Chapter 14, which deals with defective incomplete transfers.

EXAMPLE 677-2 If the son in Example 677-1 had been 18 years old, the grantor trust rules would probably not be violated because parents usually are not legally obligated to support adult children.

Ordinarily, planners will try to avoid grantor trust status, particularly when attempting income shifting, which is described in the next chapter. However, in some situations it may be helpful to structure a trust as a grantor trust. For example, planners will recommend a revocable living trust when the client's primary motive is simply to avoid probate administration. Another example is a client who wishes to make gifts into trust to avoid future FET, (described in Chapter 13), but may want to be subject to taxation on the trust income. This will arise if, for example, the grantor wants trust passive activity income (loss) to be netted against his or her own individual passive activity loss (income), or may want trust income to offset his or her own net operating loss or capital loss, or when the grantor wishes to be the taxpayer, in order to reduce his or her future gross estate by the amount of the tax payments.[28] This is one objective of the intentionally defective irrevocable trust, to be described in Chapter 14.

THE CORPORATE INCOME TAX

Table 8-7 shows the basic scheme of corporate income taxation.

TABLE 8-7 Federal Corporate Income Tax (Form 1120) Overview Model

Gross Income		$xxx,xxx.
Less: Deductions	$xx,xxx.	
Losses	xxx.	xx,xxx.
Equals: Taxable income		xxx,xxx.
Calculate total tax		xx,xxx.
Less: Credits		x,xxx.
Leaves: Net tax		$xx,xxx.

---

28. For a general discussion of planning to render a trust "income tax defective" and "estate tax effective", see the Roth and Fink articles cited at the end of the chapter.

Corporate Income Taxes

TABLE 8-8 Federal Income Tax Rates: Corporation after 12/31/92

Taxable Income

Over	But Not Over	Base Amount	+	Percent	On Excess Over
		1995			
$ 0	$50,000.	$ 0		15.%	$ 0.
50,000	75,000	7,500		25	50,000.
75,000	100,000	13,750		34	75,000.
100,000	335,000	22,250		39	100,000.
335,000	10,000,000	113,900		34	335,000.
10,000,000	15,000,000	3,400,000		35	10,000,000.
15,000,000	18,333,333	5,150,000		38	15,000,000.
18,333,333	-	6,416,666		35	18,333,333.

The rate schedule has two "bubbles," that is, two bracket amounts subject to higher rates only to be followed by a lower rate bracket. Both are intended to eliminate the benefit derived by subjecting the earlier bracket amounts to the lower rates, in a manner similar to the "bubble" that existed for individual tax rates until 1990. There is actually still a small bubble for wealthier *individuals*, in the form of the 3 percent and 2 percent reductions in miscellaneous itemized deductions and personal exemptions, respectively. This was discussed earlier in the chapter. The first corporate tax bubble, at 39 percent, reflects a surcharge of 5 percentage points, and has the effect of eliminating the tax benefit of the lower 15 percent and 25 percent tax rates.

EXAMPLE 1120-1 If a corporation has a taxable income of $400,000 in 1995, its income tax liability before credits will be $136,000, computed as follows:

15% of first $50,000	$7,500
25% of next $25,000	6,250
34% of next $25,000	8,500
39% of next $235,000	91,650
34% of last $65,000	22,100
Total tax liability	$136,000

Notice that in the above example the tax of $136,000 is exactly 34 percent of the $400,000 taxable income. The second corporate tax bubble, at 38 percent, reflects a surcharge of 3 additional percentage points, and, similar to the first, eliminates the tax saving derived from the lower 34 percent tax rate. Thus the tax for a corporation with a taxable amount in excess of $18,333,333.33 is simply equal to the taxable amount multiplied by 35 percent.

Many deductions and credits for corporations are similar to those for individuals. For deductions, similarities include trade or business expenses, interest, taxes, losses, bad debts, depreciation, charitable contributions, net operating losses, and research expenditures. Differences between individuals and corporations include the dividends-received deduction (explained below), the unavailability of the personal exemption and the nonexistence of the concepts adjusted gross income and itemized deductions.

Capital Gains and Losses

Corporations receive no special treatment for long-term capital gains; like short-term capital gains, they are added to all other corporate income and taxed at the ordinary rate. Capital losses may be used to offset capital gains, similar to the procedure used for individuals, to arrive at a possible net capital loss. However, net corporate capital losses may not be deducted against ordinary income; they may only be carried back, then forward, to offset other years' capital gains.

Dividend Income

Corporations are permitted a dividend received deduction. The amount depends on how much of the other corporation's shares are owned by the corporate shareholder. If less than 20 percent is owned the corporate shareholder can deduct 70 percent of the amount of dividends received from the other corporation. If the percentage owned is between 20 percent and 80 percent, the deduction is 80 percent of the dividends received. Finally, if the ownership is equal to 80 percent or more, then 100 percent of the dividends are deductible..

Congratulations! You've just completed the last chapter in Part 2 of the text, which has dealt with the *underlying constraints* in estate planning. The next chapter introduces Part 3, the *techniques* of estate planning, by surveying the client goals underlying those techniques.

QUESTIONS AND PROBLEMS

1. Outline the general scheme for the income taxation of individuals.

2. Contrast the two types of deductions for individuals.

3. Calculate the net income tax for the Briggs, a married couple filing jointly, using the following information. Three personal exemptions; $62,000 salary income; $5,000 interest and dividend income; $3,500 net loss from sale of stock; $3,600 itemized deductions; no credits.

4. Based on the facts in question 3 above, if the Briggs' twelve year old daughter Marcia received $1,900 in interest income during the year from a bank savings account, how much minimum additional tax will the Briggs family owe?

5. Forty years ago, Curtis, now 82 years old, bought 10 acres of raw land for $10,000. Last year, when the land was worth $400,000, Curtis gave it to his son, Wright, who sold it three months later for $450,000.
   a. Assuming no gift tax, calculate any gains or losses from these transfers. Are they short-term or long-term? Explain.
   b. How would your answer to part a be different if instead of giving the land to Wright last year, Curtis died at that time and devised it to Wright? Explain.
   c. How would your answer to part a be different if instead of giving the land to Wright, Curtis sold it at that time for $400,000 to a stranger and gave (or devised) the cash proceeds to Wright, who in turn immediately repurchased the land for $400,000, and then sold it for $450,000? Explain.
   d. Based on your answers to a, b, and c, what would you recommend that elderly planning-oriented clients in Curtis' position consider doing?

6. Rework all of Question 5, assuming instead that Curtis originally purchased the land for $500,000.

7. (a) Terry and Chris owned nonbusiness property as joint tenants. They purchased it for $10,000, with each paying one half, and at Chris' death it was worth $18,000. If Terry later sells it for $24,000, calculate the taxable gain. (b) Will your answer depend on: 1) whether or not Terry and Chris were married; or 2) how much each initially contributed to the purchase?

8. Would your result in Question 7 differ if the property was held as a tenancy in common? As community property?

9. *a.* Can a person die owning or having an interest in a large amount of income producing property but not leaving an estate subject to income taxation as an independent entity? Why or why not?

   b. If your answer to part *a* is "yes," how would you define an "estate" for income tax purposes?

10. Explain the conduit principle as applied to the taxation of estates and trusts.

11. Contrast a simple trust with a complex trust.

12. An *estate* earned $80,000 in dividends, $6,000 in short-term capital gains, and $14,000 in interest during the second of its four-year existence. Assuming no deductions except the distribution deduction and the personal exemption, calculate the estate's taxable income and the beneficiary's gross income related to the estate activity if the beneficiary received a distribution of

    a. $90,000.
    b. $96,000.
    c. $110,000.
    d. Would your answer to parts *a*, *b* and *c* change if the facts stated that the actual property distributed in excess of FAI came from corpus or, alternatively, accumulated income?

13. (*a*) How would your answers to Question 12 change if the entity was a *trust* rather than an estate? (*b*) Would it matter how old the beneficiary was?

14. Is a grantor trust an estate planning device?

15. Outline the basic scheme of the corporate income tax.

16. (Note: This is a comprehensive problem requiring an understanding of all of the chapters covered so far.) Brett and Robin are a happily married couple in their late 60's who have two children, Neil, age 36: and Connie, age 34. Brett retired last year. Presently, Brett and Robin have the following property interests. In community property

states, assume that all tenancies in common (TIC) held by the spouses are actually held as community property.

$210,000   Home: Joint tenancy; cost: $50,000

$500,000   Money Market Fund: spousal TIC

$21,000   Autos: Brett's property

$160,000   Face value life insurance policy (L1) on Brett's life: cash value $31,000. Robin is owner and beneficiary. Premiums paid with her separate property.

$90,000   Face value life insurance policy (L2) on Robin's life: cash value $17,000. Brett is owner and beneficiary. Premiums are paid with spousal TIC property.

$130,000   (Replacement value) qualified pension, with income payable to Brett for his life, then to Robin for her life. Brett's contributions (his property) totaled 30 percent of the total contributions made. The employer contributed the rest.

$490,000   Revocable trust (Trust A) was set up in 1982, funded with land, owned by Brett, then worth $180,000. Presently it is worth $490,000. On Brett's death, the trust terminates and all property passes to Robin.

960,000   Apartment house: Brett's property

Brett and Robin are planning to have their first wills drafted next month. The wills will basically say "All to surviving spouse".
Last year, Brett made the following additional gifts: (1) $26,000 cash outright to Neil; (2) $14,500 cash outright to Connie; (3) $700,000 in stock into an irrevocable trust (Trust B) with all income accumulated until Neil reaches age 41; At that time, the trust terminates, and all income and principal will be paid to Neil and Connie equally. Brett has never made any other gifts.

a. Calculate Brett's total taxable gifts for the gift year, assuming gift splitting. This will be a single amount.

b. Calculate Brett's total gift tax liability. Assume no prior gifts.

c. Assuming that Brett died today, calculate the amount of Brett's probate estate.

d. Assuming that Brett died today, calculate the amount of Brett's gross estate. If applicable, be sure to gross up.

e. Assuming that Brett died today, calculate the amount, if any, of Brett's net estate tax. Assume no debts or expenses. Be sure to consider the marital deduction. Assume intestacy in a UPC state.

 f. Assuming that Brett died today, could any of Brett's assets be administered under your state's "summary" probate proceedings? (If unavailable, assume that you are in a UPC state.) Why or why not? Be sure to consider each type.

 g. In the fact description, two trusts are mentioned. In the gift year, *each* trust earned $1,000 in fiduciary accounting income and $2,000 in capital gains.

  (1) For each trust, who will be taxed on the fiduciary accounting income?

  (2) For each trust, who will be taxed on any gain?

 h. If Brett died today, calculate the gain or loss if the home is sold by Robin next year for:

  (1) $400,000

  (2) $40,000

(Numerical Answers: (*a*) $703,000; (*b*) $38,110; (*c*) $1,239,500; (*d*) $2,002,610; (*e*) $14,100.70; (*h*1) $270,000 long-term gain; (*h*2) $90,000 long-term loss.)

17. How would your answer to question 7 change if Terry and Chris owned the property as 60%-40% tenants in common, respectively, and, alternatively (a) Terry paid 60 percent of the purchase price and Chris paid 40 percent; (b) Each paid 50 percent of the purchase price?

RECOMMENDED READING

*Adams, Roy M., "Tax Consequences of Powers of Withdrawal Held Individually or as a Fiduciary: A Pandora's Box of Tax Consequences". *1990 University of Miami Institute on Estate Planning.*

Ascher, Mark L. "When to Ignore Grantor Trusts: Precedents, a Proposal, and a Prediction." *Tax Law Review* 41 (1986), pp.253-307.

Baetz, W. Timothy. "The Indefensible Kiddie Tax." *Trusts & Estates*, April 1987, pp.27-31, 60.

Barnett, Bernard. "The Taxation and Timing of Trusts and Estate Distributions." *The Tax Adviser*, January 1984, pp. 8-24.

_____, "How To Cope With And Plan For The Unfair Income Tax Discrimination Against Estates And Trusts," *1994 University of Miami Estate Planning Institute.*

*Christensen III, Henry, "Survivalist Planning: Trying to Preserve Wealth in the International Age", *1990 University of Miami Estate Planning Institute.*

Erdman, Joseph, & Diane E. Lederman, "Effective Drafting and Administration Under the Revised uniform Principal and Income Act." *Estate Planning,* March, 1991, pp. 92-95.

*Ferguson, M. Carr, Freeland, James J., & Stephens, Richard B., *Federal Income Taxation of Estates and Beneficiaries.* Boston:on: Little, Brown & Co., 1970

*Fink, Philip R. "Grantor May Have Powers Over Trust, Yet Not Be Subject to (Income) Tax." *Estate Planning*, July, 1992, pp. 232-36.

Harris, Philip E. "Allocating Basis for Jointly Owned Property Still Presents Unresolved Questions." *The Journal of Taxation*, April 1983, pp. 234-237.

*Kantor, Edwin L. & W. Donald Sparks. "Income Tax Planning Opportunities for Residential Realty." *Estate Planning*, July, 1992, pp. 216-22.

*King, Hamlin C. "Many Tax Benefits Exist When An Estate Or Trust Terminates," *Estate Planning*, September, 1993, pp 296-303.

Randall, Gary C. "Basis Considerations in Estate Planning: An Increasingly Important Approach," *Taxes - The Tax Magazine*, July 1983, pp. 459-467.

Rhine, David S. "Planning Tips to Lessen the Adverse Impact of the Throwback Rules on Accumulation Trusts," *Estate Planning*, March 1981, pp. 88-90.

*Roth, Randall W., "The Intentional Use of Tax-Defective Trusts," *1992 University of Miami Estate Planning Institute.*

Schnee, Edward J. "Recent Decisions Restrict the Planning Opportunities of Grantor Trusts." *Taxes*, June 1986, pp. 394-7.

Stewart, Dave N., Boyd C. Randall, & Robert L. Gardner, "Property Acquired From A Decedent: Establishing Basis," *Estate Planning*, November, 1993, pp. 355-61.

Thompson Mark S., and Jeb Brooks, "The Step-Up in Basis: Its Benefits for Estates," *Trusts and Estates*, September 1983, pp. 16-17.

*Thorne, Jack F. & Crowell, Steven J. "Income in Respect of a Decedent Affects both Income and Estate Taxes," *Estate Planning*, Sept., 1989 pp. 288-93.

Wenig, Mary M. "Estate Planning: The Name of the Game Is--Basis?" *The Review of Taxation of Individuals,* 1986, pp. 203-27

West Federal Taxation: Corporations, Partnerships, Estates and Trusts. St. Paul, Minn.: West Publishing Co, current year.

West Federal Taxation: Individuals. St. Paul, Minn.: West Publishing Co, current year.

Westfall, David. "Grantors, Trusts, and Beneficiaries under the Income Tax Provisions of the Internal Revenue Code of 1986." *Tax Lawyer* 40, no. 3 (1987), pp. 713-32.

PART 3

The Techniques of Planning

— 9

Introduction to Part 3:
The Goals of Estate Planning

OVERVIEW AND CAUTION

This chapter is an introduction to the many specific estate planning techniques to be covered in the remainder of the text. It will isolate the general goals that these techniques have in common. The goals can be categorized into two broad groups, nonfinancial and financial. Within the financial group, they can be further subdivided into tax and nontax goals.

In reading this chapter, it would be well to keep in mind that the client invariably has a very fundamental goal, one far more general than saving taxes or attaining any other specific goal. The client's primary goal is *happiness and peace of mind*, and specific estate planning strategies may conflict with it. For example, gift giving reduces client wealth, and may jeopardize happiness by imperiling financial security and comfort. The planner should be especially attuned to the client's emotional and psychological preferences, and be sure not to persist in recommending techniques that appear inconsistent with them. Planning strategies are not ends in themselves; they are means to an end: greater happiness.

NONFINANCIAL GOALS

Some specific objectives in estate planning are not strictly financial in nature; they can't be measured in dollars and cents. These nonfinancial goals will be examined first. They include caring for future dependents, attaining privacy and speed in the property transfer process, and maintaining control over assets.

Caring For Future Dependents

One of the client's objectives should be to provide care for family members affected by client's disability or death. For example, *disability* of the client may trigger the need to select others to care for the client and the client's property. In addition, *death* of a client who was the single parent of a minor child will require court selection of one or more persons to care for that child. In either case, prior planning can permit the eventual selection process to more likely reflect the current wishes of the client, the individual who is currently in the best position to arrange for future care. Methods of planning for care at death and disability are examined in Chapter 17, covering miscellaneous lifetime planning.

Accomplishing Fair and Proper Distribution of Property

Good estate planning seeks to dispose of the client's property to the proper parties in the proper amounts at the proper time. Many factors will influence the choice of the best succession and distribution techniques, and every ensuing chapter will discuss them.

Attaining Privacy In The Property Transfer Process

Other things equal, clients would prefer that their wealth be transferred as privately as possible. They realize that their intended beneficiaries will experience less stress by avoiding public scrutiny. We have seen in Chapter 4 that the methods of property transfer are characterized by different degrees of privacy, with the probate process considerably more public than the process of transferring property by trust. Of course, if privacy were the only criterion, no one would consciously prefer the probate alternative. Probate may, however, offer unique advantages, and the client should weigh them against its disadvantages. The decision whether or not to avoid probate is the main focus of Chapter 10.

Attaining Speed In The Property Transfer Process

Similar to privacy, speed in property transfer is desired by most clients and is often less attainable with the probate alternative. The decision to avoid probate requires a weighing of the benefits against the drawbacks, as outlined in Chapter 10.

Maintaining Control Over Assets

As we shall see in later chapters, many lifetime estate planning strategies require that the client relinquish beneficial interests in property by making actual transfers. Few clients relish this; other things the same, they would rather hold on to their property. They usually seek to protect their economic interests, and wish to prevent their children from gaining unrestricted control over their wealth. But other goals may change their mind. Their desire to accomplish other estate planning goals, such as saving FET, can motivate them to make lifetime transfers.

Further, different lifetime transfer strategies require different degrees of transfer. Usually, the more complete the transfer, the more likely other goals can be accomplished. As you cover the remainder of the text, you should contemplate the degree of transfer involved in the various strategies covered, and ask what kind of clients would be most willing to undertake them.

FINANCIAL GOALS

Financial goals include nontax and tax considerations and will be covered in that order.

Nontax Financial Goals

Financial goals that are not tax-related include acquiring adequate liquidity, minimizing nontax estate transfer costs, maintaining a satisfactory standard of living, ensuring proper disposition by careful drafting, preserving business value, and attaining pre- and postmortem flexibility.

Acquiring adequate liquidity. Death usually triggers the need for liquidity to pay taxes, administration expenses, claims, and the needs of the surviving family. Many if not most wealthier estate planning clients inherently lack sufficient liquidity, probably because the source of most of their wealth originated from investment in two types of illiquid assets: real estate and closely held business interests. Chapter 15 is devoted entirely to liquidity planning, and will describe in detail the major methods of increasing liquidity, including sale of assets during lifetime, acquiring life insurance and flower bonds, anticipating valuation discounts, and undertaking several tax-related elections available only to business owners.

Minimizing nontax estate transfer costs. Nontax estate transfer costs include attorney and trustee fees, executor commissions, court costs, and several other probate fees, such as the bond premium. Chapter 10 will examine these costs while exploring the decision to avoid probate.

Maintaining a satisfactory standard of living. We shall see that many tax objectives can be achieved with lifetime transfers. The planner should ensure, however, that clients will retain sufficient assets and income to maintain a satisfactory standard of living. This may require foregoing certain tax-saving transfers, such as outright gifts, in favor of retaining property. Or it may call for making other less complete or less costly transfers, such as an installment sale, which, in return, can generate valuable consideration. These alternatives will be explored in detail in Chapters 13 and 14, covering lifetime transfers.

Ensuring proper disposition by careful drafting. In the planning process, clients normally assume that no matter what happens, their intended beneficiaries will in fact receive their accumulated wealth. Clients trust the attorney to draft transfer documents properly. However, attorney drafting skill varies greatly, and poor drafting can frustrate a client's dispositive preferences in many ways. The examples below are merely illustrative.

> EXAMPLE 9-1 A simple will fails to include a survival clause, creating the risk that a client's property will be inherited by her *in-laws* rather than by her parents.

> EXAMPLE 9-2 Unaware of QTIP trust planning, an attorney drafts a simple will for Francis which leaves all of his property outright to his second wife, running the risk that she may neglect to adequately provide for her *stepchildren* (Francis' children of the former marriage), who are living with Francis' first wife.

> EXAMPLE 9-3 A trust-will is drafted for a client, in which estate property will be held in trust until the youngest of the client's grandchildren reaches age 25. The disposition may be ruled invalid for violation of the *rule against perpetuities*.

> EXAMPLE 9-4 Donald's attorney drafts a tax-saving testamentary trust into which nearly all of Donald's estate is intended to pass. However, because much of Donald's property is still held in *joint tenancy* with his wife, that property

will not pass to the trust at his death but will go outright to his wife by automatic right of survivorship. At that point, the only way for her to move the property into the trust will be by making a taxable gift. And, a §2036 problem can arise if the gift is made into a trust *for her benefit*. An example is the bypass trust, to be introduced in Chapter 11.

In each of these situations, more careful planning and drafting could have eliminated the risk of these unintended dispositions without significantly altering the client's objectives. Careful planning and drafting is an essential prerequisite to the achievement of dispositive goals. The client should be assisted in locating an attorney experienced in drafting estate planning documents.

Preserving business value. Death of an active closely held business-owning client can precipitate a serious decline in the amount of wealth receivable by the client's survivors. In Chapter 16, we shall see that *pre-arrangements by the client* can minimize this decline and increase the survivor's likelihood of receiving the full material fruits of the client's productive career.

Attaining pre- and postmortem flexibility. Flexibility in estate planning means that as circumstances change, the client or the client's surrogates can intelligently alter arrangements to accomplish desired goals. While the client is still alive and mentally competent, flexibility can fairly easily be maintained by the client periodically reviewing the estate plan and revising it when necessary. After the client either loses mental capacity or dies, flexibility, although not entirely impossible, is more difficult to sustain. Yet, as we shall see next, considerable flexibility can be maintained if the client anticipates the problem by providing in advance for *surrogate decision makers*.

The critical need for flexibility by naming surrogate decision makers emerges often in the context of providing for young adult children in the event that both parents die prematurely. For example, without planning, the parent's property is usually required by law to be held by a legal guardian, and transferred outright to the children when they reach legal adulthood at age 18. But most parents would prefer to delay outright distribution until the children are older and more mature. We shall see that they can accomplish this by designating responsible parties, such as trustees and attorneys-in-fact, to act on their behalf, parties who can make such an important decision after the parents are gone. Examples of written directives providing for extended flexibility through the use of surrogate decision makers include the trust power of appointment (Chapters 11 and 12), the durable power of attorney (Chapter 17), and the disclaimer (Chapter 18).

Maximizing benefits for the surviving spouse. Tax factors may impel a client to arrange future transfers to minimize the transfer tax bite to the surviving spouse. Different transfer devices accomplish this goal with different degrees of success. As the next example demonstrates, poor planning can result in an inefficient transfer, one that risks foregoing other benefits which could otherwise be enjoyed by the surviving spouse.

> EXAMPLE 9-5 Realizing that any property owned by Mom at her later death will be subject to transfer taxation, Dad *writes his own will*, one that will transfer a substantial amount of property outright to their middle-aged children in the event that he predeceases Mom. Dad has succeeded in arranging for some property to bypass Mom's taxable estate, but in so doing, he has unnecessarily denied to her all legal rights to the property.

> EXAMPLE 9-6 Continuing Example 9-5, an estate planner might instead recommend that Dad leave the property in *trust* for the benefit of Mom and the children. The trust would give Mom the following rights, without precipitating any greater transfer tax: (1) the right to income from the property for her life; (2) the right to invade the trust corpus for reasons of health, education, support or maintenance; and (3) the right to determine how much of the property to distribute outright to the children, and when to distribute it, at her death or sooner.

As we'll see in Chapters 11 and 12, careful planning for the spouse's welfare can often maximize tax saving without sacrificing other important objectives.

Tax Saving Goals

Income taxes and transfer taxes represent the largest cause of estate shrinkage to medium and larger sized estates. Most of the specific planning strategies covered in this text will seek to reduce these taxes. Next, let's isolate the general tax goals they share in common.

Income tax saving goals. The goals of those planning strategies designed to save income taxes include obtaining a stepped-up basis, shifting income to a lower bracket taxpayer, and deferring recognition of income.

Obtaining a stepped-up basis. Achieving a step-up in income tax basis on transferred property can be especially important to a transferee who wishes to sell a rapidly appreciating asset. As we have seen in Chapter 8, a step-up is the normal tax consequence when a transferee makes an ordinary *purchase* for full consideration. However, much of estate planning favors lifetime *gifts*, that is, lifetime transfers for less than full consideration, and, as we have seen, the basis rule for them is quite different: The donee-transferee receives not a step-up, but a carryover basis. On the other hand, a step-up is normally available for gifts received at death. Thus, other things the same, planners are sometimes inclined to recommend deferring the transfer of an appreciating asset until death.   This is just one of many basis considerations involved in making lifetime transfers, a subject that will be more thoroughly explored in Chapters 13 and 14.

Shifting income to a lower bracket taxpayer. Estate planning clients are often in the highest income tax bracket, while other family members, such as parents and children, are in lower brackets. As we have seen, under our progressive income tax rate structure, marginal and average rates of tax generally increase with increasing taxable income. Although somewhat reversed by the '93 tax act, tax reform since 1986 has to some degree lessened the significance of this as well as other factors that once strongly encouraged income shifting. Figure 9-1 illustrates the progression of maximum marginal federal income tax rates since 1952.

FIGURE 9-1 Maximum Marginal Federal Income Tax Rates, 1952-Present

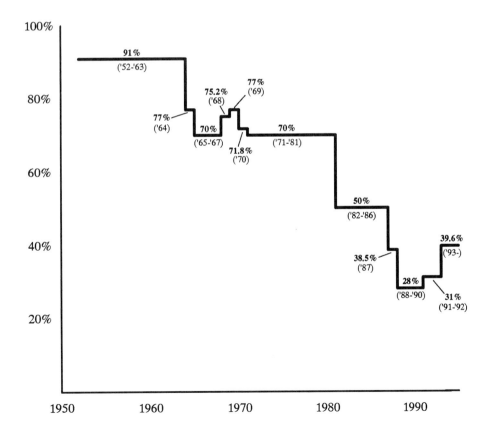

Congressional tax reform directed a three-pronged attack on the popular methods of shifting of income to a lower-bracket family member. First, it adopted the *kiddie tax*, described in Chapter 8. The kiddie tax virtually eliminates any successful shifting of income to children who haven't reached age 14 by the end of the calendar year. Second, by lowering the maximum marginal income tax *rate* from 50 percent to 39.6 percent, tax reform has made income shifting relatively less attractive. And third, as will be described in Appendix 14A, two major lifetime *incomplete* transfer devices, the short-term trust and the spousal remainder trust, have been all but destroyed by two brief but sweeping revisions to the *grantor trust rules*. However, *completed* transfers (gifts) can still shift some income effectively, subject to the first two factors mentioned above.

Many of the examples in the remainder of this book will assume a 50 percent "combined" marginal income tax rate (MTR) for wealthier clients, based on the premise that state and local taxes are commonly in the low double digit range. Thus, for each $1 more (or less) in taxable income, these taxpayers will incur (save) 50 cents in tax, based on the following simple formula:

Higher (lower) tax = Higher (lower) taxable income times MTR

= $1 times .50

= 50 cents

The following material answers several commonly asked questions related to income shifting.

What *transferors* are currently most suited to making income shifting transfers? Of course, taxpayers in the highest tax bracket. Based on Table 1 of Appendix A at the end of the text, a married couple with joint taxable income in excess of $250,000 are taxed at the top (39.6 percent) federal marginal rate.

Which *transferees* will be most able to benefit taxwise from income shifting? Those whose additional unearned income will be taxed at the zero or 15 percent marginal tax bracket. They include minor children over age 13, young adults in college, and, perhaps, the client's parents.

How much income can be shifted to another (dependent) *person* over age 13 and still be taxed at no more than the 15 percent marginal rate? For 1994, up to $22,750 (rate bracket) plus $600 (maximum standard deduction for a dependent), assuming that the donee has no other taxable income. On the other hand, any taxable income earned by a *trust* in excess of $1,500 plus its personal exemption will be subject to the higher 28, 31, 36 and 39.6 percent rates.

EXAMPLE 9-7 Dad, a surgeon, projects before-tax earnings from two sources next year: $120,000 from his surgical practice, and $64,000 from dividends on common stock. He wishes to use some of this income to help support a daughter in college. Assuming that Dad will have a combined marginal income tax rate of 50 percent, and that daughter's rate is 15 percent, each dollar of Dad's income up to $22,100 (plus $600) that can instead be taxed to daughter will save (at least) 35 cents in tax per year.

Can all income potentially receivable by one person be taxed to another? The answer is no, because tax law distinguishes two types of income: personal service income and other income. Under the *assignment of income doctrine*, earnings from services performed will always be taxable to the person performing those services.[1] However, income from nonservices, such as property, can be taxed to another if the underlying property is satisfactorily transferred for their benefit before the income is realized.

EXAMPLE 9-8 Continuing Example 9-7, Dad will not be able to tax shift his surgical services income to anyone. However, by properly transferring beneficial interest in some of the common stock to daughter, the stock's dividend income can be shifted to her, making it taxable at her lower rate.

Can a client gain by shifting income to a *spouse*? Not ordinarily, because most spouses file a joint income tax return, which subjects both of their income to taxation at the same marginal rate. Filing separately will usually result in a higher combined income tax. Thus, spousal income shifting will not usually save income taxes.

Must a transfer of property be complete and outright, such as by gift or sale, to effect a valid tax shift? Usually, but with some techniques, not entirely. Examples of partially incomplete or nonoutright transfer devices covered in later chapters which can successfully shift income include the custodial gift and the irrevocable trust.

We shall also see in Chapter 18 that income shifting can be arranged between nonindividuals. Transfers can be made in connection with estates and trusts to save income taxes. And occasionally multiple taxpaying entities can be created to spread income around, thereby possibly subjecting some or all taxable income for each entity to lower marginal rates.

---

1. For a discussion of the application of the assignment of income doctrine by courts and the IRS to futile and expensive attempts to transfer personal service income to family beneficiaries of a living trust, see the analysis of the so-called family estate trust in Appendix 14A.

EXAMPLE 9-9 Andy's will created three *trusts*, one for each of his three children, who are all over 13, transferring a total amount of property worth $450,000 ($150,000 in each trust) and generating approximately $30,000 ($10,000 per trust) in taxable income a year. For 1994, assuming that each trust is taxed as a separate entity and that all of the first year's income is *accumulated*, each trust will pay an income tax of $3,072.40, for a combined total tax of $9,217.20. If, instead, only one trust had been created, and if that trust was taxed as a single taxpaying entity, its income tax would total $10,992.40, which is $1,775.20.50 higher than the combined tax on the three trusts.

Estate planners describe this rate splitting technique as taking "three trips up the rate ladder," rather than one.

EXAMPLE 9-10 Continuing the three trust situation in Example 9-9, instead of accumulating all income, let's consider two alternatives. First, assume that each trust *distributes all income* to the children, who are also in relatively low brackets. Rates and income will still be split among the children, with similar tax savings.

As a second alternative to complete accumulation, assume that each trust *accumulates one half* of the income and distributes the other half to the children. Rate splitting will be further enhanced, since the income will be divided among six rather than three taxpayers. However, because of the throwback rule, discussed briefly in Chapter 8, this bonus will work only in special circumstances, such as when the income is being accumulated for beneficiaries under age 21, or when the distributing entity is an estate. However, multiple taxpaying *estates* for one decedent are not possible.

Tax reform since 1986 has particularly restricted the benefits of shifting income to trusts and estates. In addition to radically lowering its maximum marginal tax rate, Congress greatly reduced the tax bracket amounts that are subject to the lower rates. Thus, incremental income taxed to estates and trusts get pushed up the rate ladder far more quickly than for income taxed to individuals.

Deferring recognition of income. When a property transaction results in the realization of a gain, that gain will usually be subject to immediate recognition, that is, includable in that year's taxable income. However, careful planning can defer the gain to later years. By exploiting the time value of money, deferral of the tax enables the taxpayer to temporarily earn greater income. Examples of transfers that defer taxable gain are the installment sale and the private annuity, covered in Chapter 14. And in Chapter 18 we will see that an estate can defer income by carefully choosing its fiscal year end.

Transfer tax saving goals and planning. As with income tax saving techniques, devices designed to reduce transfer taxes all seek to accomplish just a few general goals. They include reducing and freezing the estate tax base, leveraging the use of exclusions, exemptions and the unified credit, delaying the payment of the transfer tax, and minimizing the GSTT. This section will first briefly describe those goals, each with a specific example. Then it will explore, with an ongoing example, the aspects of transfer tax theory underlying transfer tax saving goals by examining the meaning of transfer tax unification and how current imperfections in our unified transfer tax system give rise to tax planning.

To better understand the next two sections, it would be well to remember that we have defined the estate tax base as the sum of the taxable estate (gross estate minus deductions) plus adjusted taxable gifts. These techniques will therefore accomplish one of the following objectives: reduce or freeze the gross estate or adjusted taxable gift values, or, less commonly, freeze or increase deductions.

Reducing the estate tax base. Certain planning arrangements can actually reduce the estate tax base. Estate reduction subjects less of the client's wealth to transfer taxation. Dollar for dollar, it offers the greatest FET payoff.

EXAMPLE 9-11 Sharon, a widow, gave her son James $10,000 cash outright last year. Due to the annual exclusion, the gift was not taxable and no gift tax was owed. Sharon's gross estate is now $1 million rather than $1,010,000, which means that if she were to die today, her FET will be lower by $4,100, which is the product of 41 percent, her marginal FET rate, times the value of the gift.

Other techniques of estate reduction to be examined in later chapters include gifts into trust (Chapter 13), use of the unlimited marital deduction (Chapters 11 and 12), bypass planning (Chapters 11 and 12), establishment of a grantor retained trust (Chapter 14), election of the alternate valuation date (Chapters 15 and 18), and special-use valuation of farm or closely held business property (Chapter 15).

Freezing the estate tax base. In contrast with techniques that can reduce the estate tax base, certain property arrangements can *limit the future increase* in the estate tax base by freezing the taxable value of a portion of the client's wealth at its *current value*. Thus, all future appreciation in this portion is excluded from transfer taxation.

EXAMPLE 9-12 Nicky, a single parent, makes a *gift* of one of his vacation homes, worth $128,000, to his son Donny. Assuming Nicky has made no other taxable gifts this year, he will file a gift tax return and report a taxable gift of $118,000. Assuming no prior taxable gifts, no gift tax will be due because of the shelter of the unified credit. If Nicky dies 20 years later when the value of the vacation home is $500,000 (or, for that matter, any amount), Nicky's estate tax base will include the home at its (historical) taxable gift value, $118,000. With regard to that particular asset, Nicky's estate tax base has been frozen at its taxable date-of-gift value.

TABLE 9-1 Illustration of FET Savings from Estate Freeze on One Half of Total of Four Hypothetical Estates

---

ASSUMING NO ESTATE FREEZE

Assumed Present Estate Size	Estate Tax Base in 10 Years, 8 Percent Growth per Year on Entire Present Estate (=Estate Tax Base)	FET in 10 Years	FET As Percent of Original Estate Tax Base in 10 Years
$1,000,000.	$2,158,925.	$665,873.	30.8%
2,500,000.	5,397,312.	2,416,522.	44.8
5,000,000.	10,794,625.	5,424,775.	50.3
10,000,000.	21,589,250.	11,874,088.	55.0

ASSUMING ESTATE FREEZE OF ONE HALF OF PRESENT ESTATE

Assumed Present Estate Size	(Reduced) Estate Tax Base in 10 Years, 8 Percent Growth per Year on Only One Half of Present Estate	FET in 10 Years	FET As Percent of Estate Tax Base	FET Saved Due to Freeze
$1,000,000.	$1,579,460.	$398,758.	18.5%	$267,115.
2,500,000.	3,948,650.	1,619,758.	30.0	796,764.
5,000,000.	7,897,300.	3,791,515.	35.1	1,633,260.
10,000,000.	15,794,600.	8,424,760.	39.0	3,449,328.

The FET benefit of freezing is further illustrated in Table 9-1. The lower half calculates the effect of an estate freeze of one half of each of four hypothetical estate sizes, assuming an annual growth rate in all estate assets of 8 percent over a period of 10 years. The upper half calculates the FET for these appreciated estates assuming no freeze. Both halves calculate total FET as a percent of the ("inheritable") appreciated estate tax base values, if no freeze is undertaken. For example, at 8 percent, a present estate of $1 million will grow to about $2.16 million in 10 years. Assuming no estate freezing technique is used, the FET on $2.16 million will be $665,873, or 30.8 percent of the total estate tax base. Instead, assume a present estate freeze on one half of that $1 million, or $500,000. Although the total inheritable estate in 10 years will still be $2.16 million, the estate tax base will be only $1.579 million, or the sum of $500,000, the frozen half, plus $1,079,460, the appreciated date-of-death value of the other unfrozen half. Thus, FET will be only $398,758, which is only 18.5 percent of the total inheritable estate. Estate freezing saved over $267,000. As Table 9-1 indicates, larger estate sizes will save correspondingly larger amounts of FET. The reader might keep in mind that estates between $10 million and $21,040,000 are subject to an additional 5 percent estate tax.

FIGURE 9-2 Graphical Portrayal of Estate Freeze Illustration

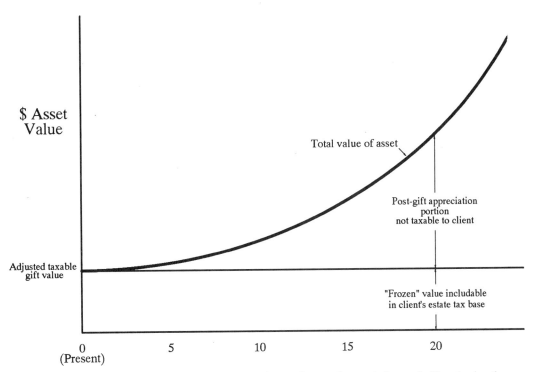

Number of years between date of transfer and date of client's death

The effect of an estate freeze can also be illustrated graphically. In Figure 9-2, the curved line represents the total appreciating value of a gifted asset subject to the freeze, from the present until the clients death, hopefully many years from now. It also represents the amount includable in the client's gross estate if no freeze is undertaken and the asset is owned at death. The slope of this curve is a direct function of the asset's rate of appreciation. The unchanging, frozen value of the asset includable in the client's future estate tax base is represented by the horizontal line, depicting the asset's future adjusted taxable gift value. The section above this line represents the increasing, (unfrozen) postgift appreciation portion of the asset's value, i.e., the amount not includable in the client's future estate tax base. The longer the client lives, the larger will be this portion, assuming ongoing appreciation.

Gifting is not the only available estate freezing technique. As we'll see later, some wealthier clients will prefer, instead of an outright gift, some type of incomplete estate-freezing asset transfer, i.e., one that either involves the client's receiving *consideration* in return, or enables the client to retain some rights or control over the transferred property. Such techniques include the private annuity, installment sale, grantor retained trust (all in Chapter 14), and the corporate recapitalization (Chapter 16).

As mentioned in Chapter 7, Congress, using two very different approaches since 1986, has attempted to impose greater limits on those estate freezing techniques that involve certain retained interests. First, Congress enacted Section 2036(c) in 1987, taking an *estate tax* approach. Very sweeping in nature, it required inclusion in the decedent's gross estate of the fair market value of all property in which the decedent had made a lifetime transfer of appreciating assets under which the transferor retained many significant interests not falling within the scope of §2036(a). But because the rules of §2036(c) were so complex and all-encompassing, and generated so much negative reaction from taxpayers, Congress in 1990 retroactively repealed this subsection. In its place, it enacted Sections 2701-2704.

In contrast to the estate tax approach of §2036(c), the provisions of §2701-04 take a *gift tax* approach. As described in Chapter 7, the new rules attempt to treat certain incomplete transfers as completed gifts, and in the process seek to impose a more conservative gift tax valuation of any retained interests, many of which are mandated under the rules to have no value at all. Thus, in many cases, the gift tax value of an estate freezing transfer (with retained rights) will wind up representing the entire value of the property transferred, reduced only by the value of legislatively permitted "qualifying" retained interests. As a result, estate planners, in attempting to keep gift taxes low, will structure these transfer techniques to specify only retained interests that "qualify" under the new law. Chapters 14 and 16 will briefly explore more how that can be done. In addition, Chapter 12 will discuss estate freezing techniques undertaken at the client's death that are not the subject of Sections 2701-2704.

Leveraging the use of exclusions, exemptions, and the unified credit. In business academics, to leverage means to magnify a benefit by engaging in one of a few special business transactions. Thus, one can *borrow* to magnify profitability (and loss) potential. Similarly, in estate planning, one can *gift appreciating assets* to magnify the tax saving benefit of the gift tax annual exclusion, the $1 million GSTT exemption, and the unified credit. Gifting appreciating assets can leverage these tax breaks by sheltering a larger future amount from estate taxation. And carefully done, it winds up eliminating an asset's entire value from the future taxable estate.

EXAMPLE 9-13 Jacob makes a lifetime gift of a $100,000 face value insurance policy on his life having a current terminal value of $10,000. If its current gift tax value is $10,000, Jacob has *leveraged the annual exclusion* with a leverage factor of ten: Each $1 in annual exclusion has potentially sheltered $10 from FET.

EXAMPLE 9-14 Ainge makes a lifetime gift of $50,000 of appreciating property into an irrevocable trust for the benefit of his granddaughter. Ainge allocates $50,000 of his $1 million lifetime GSTT exemption to this transfer. If this property appreciates in value to $300,000 at his death, Ainge has *leveraged the GSTT exemption* with a leverage factor of six: Each $1 of exemption has sheltered $6 from GSTT.

EXAMPLE 9-15 Five years ago, Julie, a successful entrepreneur, gave her son $610,000 of her corporation's closely held stock. No gift tax was due because the gift was totally sheltered by the annual exclusion and the unified credit. This year, Julie died when the value of that stock was $3,000,000. Julie's estate tax base will include only $600,000, the adjusted taxable gift value of the stock. It will now be totally sheltered by the FET unified credit. Had Julie died owning the stock, her estate tax base would have included $3,000,000. By making the gift, Julie was able to *leverage the gift tax unified credit* fivefold.

Which types of appreciating assets lend themselves to the highest rates of leveraging? Perhaps the best example is life insurance, which often starts with little or no value when leveraging is undertaken, but attains a relatively huge value (i.e., face value) at the time the asset finally escapes taxation, after the insured dies.[2]

Reducing, freezing, and leveraging contrasted. It may be helpful to contrast these three very important concepts. *Reducing* takes advantage of exclusions and deductions to actually drive down the future estate tax base

---

2. For an example illustrating leveraging of the GST exemption with insurance, see Example GST-1 in chapter 15.

below what it would have been had the client done nothing and died today. Reducing would lower the horizontal line in Figure 9-2. In contrast, *freezing* itself will not reduce the future estate tax base; although some estate freezing transactions incorporate the use of exclusions and deductions to reduce the tax base, others do not. The unique contribution of `freezing' is to keep the amount includable in the future estate tax base *equal or nearly equal to* its current level, even though assets may continue to appreciate. In Figure 9-2, freezing is represented by the vertical distance between the horizontal line and the curved line. Finally, by focusing on the potential magnification of the tax savings, *leveraging* connotes a `multiplier' effect. It compares the amount of the exclusion, deduction or credit exemption equivalent that has been taken to reduce or freeze the estate with the future magnitude of the appreciated transferred assets that would have been includable in the estate tax base had the transfer not been made, and consequently, the exclusion, deduction or credit had not been taken.

> EXAMPLE 9-15A The situation in previous example 9-15 actually incorporates all three of the goals under discussion. Here's why. It involves reducing, because the transfer has driven down the future estate tax base $10,000 below what it would have been had Julie made the gift and died today. It involves freezing because gifting the stock ensured that the amount includable in Julie's future estate tax base will be exactly $600,000, even though the stock may continue to appreciate. And it involves leveraging because the amount that will avoid taxation is a multiple of the transferred amount. When comparing $600,000, the amount of the credit exemption equivalent used to freeze the estate with $3,000,000, the magnitude of the value of the appreciated transferred stock that would have been includable in Julie's estate tax base had she not made the transfer, the upshot is a fivefold leveraging of the unified credit.

Delaying payment of the transfer tax. In certain situations, transfer taxes can be deferred, even though a completed taxable transfer has taken place.

> EXAMPLE 9-16 Danny is contemplating several transfers of property from his large estate. His wife, Barbara, has an equally large estate, and can live very comfortably off her own wealth. If Danny gives his wealth to Barbara at his death, there will be no immediate FET on that property, since the transfer will be totally sheltered by the unlimited estate tax marital deduction. But the FET will only be deferred, not eliminated, since the property will probably be taxed at Barbara's later death. In fact, the gift to her will probably increase the overall FET on that property (compared to the amount of tax that Danny's estate would pay if he left the property outright or in trust to the children) since the gift (*a*) foregoes the use of the unified credit at Danny's death; and (*b*) will increase the size of Barbara's gross estate, possibly subjecting it to a higher tax rate. Thus, Danny faces the alternative of either deferring a potentially larger tax or, more immediately, incurring a (smaller) estate tax on his wealth.

Factors to consider in answering the question whether or not to defer the FET by means of the unlimited marital deduction are examined in Chapters 11 and 12. Those chapters also discuss the interrelationship of the marital deduction and the unified credit. Other transfer tax deferral devices covered in later chapters include the application of §6166, dealing with the payment of the FET in future installments for a decedent-owner of a closely held business (Chapter 16), and the simple practice of delaying property transfers (Chapter 13).

Minimizing the generation-skipping transfer tax. Chapter 7 described the nature of the GSTT, including its 55 percent tax rate and its exemptions. Failure to plan for this tax could prove costly.

> EXAMPLE 9-17 Vaguely aware that federal GSTT law includes a $1 million GSTT exemption for each spouse, a general practicing attorney feels safe in drafting wills for most of his married clients that do not explicitly refer to the exemption. This attorney may never realize that more careful drafting to properly allocate these exemptions to certain of his client's property could have saved considerable GSTT.

Efficient allocation of the GSTT exemption, a complex subject, is surveyed in Chapter 12.

Now, let's examine in some detail the theory underlying these basic transfer tax saving goals.

The meaning of unification. Many transfer tax saving techniques take advantage of the fact that our "unified" transfer tax system is imperfect, that is, not completely unified. To appreciate fully how these strategies work, the reader must clearly understand both how perfect unification might function, and how the planner can exploit the imperfections inherent in our unified system. The following material will first portray what a tax world of perfect unification could be like, and then describe our present, imperfectly unified system. An ongoing example will illustrate the major points.

Perfect unification. According to this author, perfect unification of gift and estate taxes would imply a situation in which an individual would be *indifferent*, from a total transfer tax planning point of view, between making lifetime and deathtime gifts. Under perfect unification, total transfer taxes would be the same whether an individual owned property at death, or whether that person gifted the property away during lifetime. This view of perfect unification would require all of the following conditions:

1. A uniform system of *deductions and credits* for all lifetime and death-time transfers. Otherwise, individuals would prefer to make that transfer which enjoyed the shelter of higher deductions or credits.
2. A *tax on all completed transfers*, whether made during lifetime or at death, no matter the size of the transfer and no matter how long ago the

transfer was made. Otherwise, individuals would seek to make that transfer which would be tax-free. This would require complete imposition of the *cumulative gift doctrine*, described in Chapter 5, and would entail the following specific procedures:

a. *All prior gifts* made by the transferor would be added to the transferor's current transfer tax base. No gifts would be excluded, including gifts of very small value, and gifts made many years ago.

b. All prior gifts would be included in the estate tax base at their *current market value*, not date-of-gift value.

c. All *gift taxes* paid would be grossed up; that is, added to the estate tax base.

Failure to completely accumulate prior transfers and taxes in each of these ways would enable an individual to save taxes by timing transfers so as to make them subject to less transfer taxation. Continuing, the last two conditions required for perfect unification are:

3. A world in which the *time value of money* is negligible. Otherwise, individuals would prefer to pay the same (or even greater) transfer tax later rather than sooner.

4. Finally, only *one tax rate schedule* applicable to all lifetime and death-time transfers. Otherwise, individuals would seek to make transfers that would be subject to the lower tax rates.

To see the operation of perfect unification, consider the following numeric example, which incorporates all of the above assumptions. While reading it, please keep in mind that the present tax system does not reflect all of these assumptions; these calculations are made for illustration purposes only. All transfers will be assumed to be made after 1987.

EXAMPLE 9-18 Howard, a widower, died owning $2 million in property, consisting of $1 million in land and $1 million in cash. Ignoring all deductions and credits except the unified credit, Howard's FET is $588,000, calculated as follows:

Gross estate	$2,000,000.
Less: Deductions	-0-
Taxable estate	2,000,000.
Tentative tax	780,800.
Less: Unified credit	192,800.
Net estate tax	588,000.

Continuing the example, assume that instead of dying owning all of his wealth, Howard *gave* the land to his son four years before his death. At that time the land was worth $800,000. Under perfect unification, Howard's total combined transfer taxes would still be $588,000. First, Howard would have paid a gift tax of $75,000, calculated as follows:

Current gross gift	$800,000.
Less: Exclusions and deductions	-0-
Taxable gift	800,000.
Tentative tax	267,800.
Less: Unified credit	192,800.
Net gift tax	$75,000.

Howard's FET and total transfer taxes would be $513,000 and $588,000, respectively, calculated as follows:

Gross estate (date-of-death value of property plus gift tax paid)*	$1,000,000.
Less: Deductions	-0-
Taxable estate	1,000,000.
Plus: Prior gifts (date of death value)	1,000,000.
Estate tax base	2,000,000.
Tentative estate tax	780,800.
Less: Gift tax paid	75,000.
Less: Unified credit	192,800.
Net estate tax	513,000.
Total transfer taxes	*$588,000.*

*The gross estate of $1 million is the sum of property owned at death plus the gift tax paid. At death, Howard owned $925,000 in cash, which is the difference between the $1 million cash initially owned and the $75,000 gift tax paid. Grossing up then increases the gross estate back to $1 million.

Summarizing, under perfect unification, total transfer taxes would be the same whether an individual retained all property until death or whether he or she had made lifetime gifts. In Example 9-18, the gift tax plus estate tax in the case of a lifetime gift equals $588,000, which is the tax in the case of no lifetime gift.

Our present imperfectly unified system. Comparing our present transfer tax world with the list of conditions required for perfect unification, we see one similarity and several differences. They are similar with regard to item 4 (the existence of one transfer tax rate schedule applied to both lifetime and deathtime transfers). However, the two "worlds" are different with regard to all other conditions; our present transfer tax scheme does not fully reflect any of them. The dissimilarities are described in the following outline which, for ease of comparison, is numerically structured to parallel the previous list.[3]

1. Some *deductions and credits* are not uniformly applied to all transfers. For example, the $10,000 annual exclusion applies only to lifetime gifts. And the estate tax credit for tax on prior deathtime transfers (TPT Credit) is not allowable for prior lifetime transfers. (The advantage of the annual exclusion is discussed further under item 2 a. (2) of the cumulative gift doctrine, immediately below).

2. The *cumulative gift doctrine* has not been completely incorporated into our transfer tax system. Major omissions include the following:

   a. Not all prior gifts made by the transferor are added to the transfer-or's current transfer tax base. In fact, some gifts are not included at all.

      (1) Except in unusual situations, only *post-1976* gifts are added to the estate tax base. (Recall that Internal Revenue Code §2001 defines "adjusted taxable gifts" as only the total of all *post-1976* taxable gifts.) Pre-1977 gifts are usually totally excluded from the estate tax base. (The major exception applies to §2035 (d)(2) relinquishments within three years of death of pre-1977 transfers subject to retained interests and control under Code sections 2036, 2037, and 2038.)

      (2) Ordinarily, only the *taxable* gift value, not the value of the entire gift, is added to the gift tax or estate tax base. Taxable gift value is the net gift value after subtracting deductions and exclusions, including the $10,000 annual exclusion. In contrast, property owned and transferred at death is entirely includable in the estate tax base; there is no deathtime annual exclusion. Hence, the estate tax base will be lower by the amount of any annual exclusions taken, creating an advantage to making lifetime transfers.

   b. Prior gifts that are includable in the estate tax base reflect the *value of the transfer at the date of the gift*, not the current, date of death value. In many, perhaps most, circumstances, date-of-gift value will be lower than current value, thereby enabling individuals, as shown in Example 9-12, to make gifts of appreciating assets and thereby freeze the taxable value by eliminating estate taxation on their subsequent appreciation.

---

3. For a description of an additional imperfection based on the ability to obtain certain valuation discounts for lifetime gifts (but not gifts at death) of minority business interests by controlling owners, see Chapter 15.

    c. Not all *prior gift taxes* paid are grossed up, that is, added to the estate tax base. Only gift taxes paid on gifts made within three years of death are so included. Thus, certain gifts will be taxed on a tax-exclusive basis. We have seen in Chapter 6 examples illustrating the resulting tax advantage created by noninclusion of gift taxes in the gross estate.[4]

3.   Finally, our transfer tax structure can not ever be perfectly unified because we live in a world having a significant *time value of money*. Thus, other things the same, individuals will prefer to delay the payment of transfer taxes.

To see how real-world imperfections 2*a*(2), 2*b* and 2*c* affect the unified transfer tax, let's rework the numbers in Example 9-18. First, assuming no lifetime gifts, Howard's net estate tax will still be $588,000, calculated in exactly the same manner as shown in the original example. However, the lifetime gift alternative under today's imperfect unification has markedly different results. Howard's gift tax, at the time of the gift, will be $71,100, rather that $75,000, calculated as follows:

Current gross gift	$800,000.
Less: Exclusions and	
deductions	10,000.
Taxable gift	790,000.
Tentative tax	263,900.
Less: Unified credit	192,800.
Net gift tax	$71,100.

Assuming simply that Howard dies owning $928,900 cash ($1 million less gift tax paid of $71,100), Howard's net estate tax will be $390,405, rather than $513,000, calculated as follows:

Gross estate (date-of-death value of	
cash owned at death-- excludes the	
gift tax paid)	$928,900.
Less: Deductions	-0-
Taxable estate	928,900.
Plus: Adjusted taxable gifts (from	
gift tax return)	790,000.
Estate tax base	1,718,900.
Tentative estate tax	654,305.

---

4. Examples 2035-5 and 2035-7.

Less: Gift tax paid	71,100.
Less: Unified credit	192,800.
Net estate tax	$390,405.
Total transfer taxes	*$461,505.*

Howard's total transfer taxes will be $461,505, the sum of $71,100 (gift tax) and $390,405 (estate tax). Hence the use of the lifetime gift has saved $126,495 in transfer taxes. Imperfect unification has enabled Howard to *freeze* the tax value of the land at its taxable gift value and to *reduce* his taxable estate by the amount of the annual exclusion and the gift tax paid. Thus, a total of $281,100 escaped transfer taxation. This represents the sum of three amounts: the $10,000 annual exclusion, the $71,100 gift tax paid, and the $200,000 in postgift appreciation in the land. We can check our result, since the total tax saved will be the product of 0.45, the marginal estate tax rate, and $281,100. That product does in fact equal the tax saving of $126,495.

The effect of not grossing up can be interpreted in a different way: As mentioned in Chapter 6, the federal gift tax is calculated on what is called a *tax exclusive basis* (assuming no grossing up), since it is levied on the amount of the net gift not including the tax. On the other hand, the FET is calculated on a *tax inclusive basis*, since it is levied on the entire estate, including the amount that will be used to pay the FET. The requirement of grossing up in effect converts part of the federal gift tax from a tax exclusive calculation to a tax inclusive one. In contrast, not grossing up keeps the entire gift tax computation on a tax exclusive basis, enabling gifts to lower overall transfer tax costs.

Thus, careful exploitation of the present system's failure to completely unify estate and gift taxes can yield substantial transfer tax savings for clients owning medium to larger amounts of wealth. Further discussion of these issues will be deferred to the chapters on planning for lifetime transfers.[5]

This chapter has introduced the specific techniques of estate planning by presenting the main goals underlying them. The next chapter begins our detailed study of these techniques with an examination of the decision to avoid probate.

---

5. Chapters 13 and 14.

QUESTIONS AND PROBLEMS

1. (*a*) What is probably the typical client's principal goal in estate planning? (*b*) Give your own example of how a more specific goal described in this chapter can conflict with it.

2. List and briefly describe a client's nonfinancial estate planning goals.

3. List and briefly describe a client's nontax financial estate planning goals.

4. Describe the advantage of selecting a surrogate decision maker in the estate planning process.

5. List and briefly describe a client's income tax saving goals.

6. Mom and Dad are in the combined 50 percent marginal income tax bracket. Based on actual tax rates, how much income tax can the family save each year if they can shift $20,000 in taxable income to the following alternate taxpayers which, we will assume, have no current gross income? Also, for each taxpayer, state the maximum potential total income not taxable at all, and taxable at 15 percent.

   a. Shift to their 12-year-old daughter.
   b. Shift to their 18-year-old son.
   c. Shift to an irrevocable trust that distributes all the income annually to their 12-year-old daughter.
   d. Shift to an irrevocable trust that accumulates all income annually for the benefit of their 18-year-old son.
   e. Shift to an irrevocable trust that accumulates $1,600 and distributes the balance annually to their 18-year-old son.
   f. Shift to a new corporation owned by their 18-year-old son. No dividend is paid.

7. List and briefly describe a client's transfer tax saving goals.

8. (*a*)What is the meaning of perfect unification? (*b*) Why is our present unified transfer tax system imperfect?

9. Compare the *gift* tax calculations for Howard in Example 9-18 in the text, contrasting perfect unification with our present tax system.
   (*a*) On a piece of paper, list the major numerical gift tax calculations, in side-by-side columns.
   (*b*) Which lines are different in amount? Why?

10. Now let's compare the *estate* tax calculations for Howard's estate in Example 9-18 of the text, contrasting perfect unification with our present tax system, under both the no-gift and the gift alternatives.
   a. On a piece of paper, list the major numerical calculations, in side-by-side columns.
   b. Which lines are different in amount? Why?

11. Revise the numerical answers in Example 5-9 in the text of Chapter 5 to include the influence of the $10,000 annual gift tax exclusion. In addition, calculate the net tax on a single gift of $500,000. What conclusions can be drawn? (Answer: Total gift taxes for both gifts combined = $149,000; tax for the single gift = $152,400.)

12. Without doing any further calculations, explain what effect you think the following alternative *additional gifts* would have on your calculation of total taxes in Problem 12 at the end of Chapter 5:
   a. A deathbed gift of $10,000 cash to a different person.
   b. Instead, 48 equal lifetime gift amounts of $9,810.83, totaling $470,920. Assume that these gifts were made to eight children and grandchildren over a six-year period beginning in 1982. (Why the amount $470,920? To help answer this, refer to the amounts in your answer to Problem 12 in Chapter 5 for the gross estate and adjusted taxable gifts.)
   c. Instead, $470,920 all to one son in one year.
   d. What planning conclusions can be drawn?

13. Diana and her husband Bill have an estate worth $4 million. Each would like to give their only grandson a 40.0 percent interest in the stock of their wholly and equally owned closely held business, which is currently worth a total of $3,050,000. Assuming no prior taxable gifts by either spouse, if the business triples in value by the time of their deaths, would these gifts
   a. Reduce their estate tax base?
   b. Freeze their estate tax base?
   c. Leverage anything?
   Explain your answers.

RECOMMENDED READING

Eubank, J. Thomas. "Gifts and Other Bread and Butter Freezes," *Real Property, Probate and Trust Journal*, (1983), pp. 566-95.

Frazer, David R. "Five Myths of Estate Planning." *Trusts & Estates*, December 1985, pp. 16-18.

Rhine, David S. "Personal Financial Planning: A Map to the Minefield." *Trusts & Estates*, December 1985, pp. 20-22.

Stukenberg, M.W., and Douglas L. Giblen. "Techniques for Obtaining the Tax Benefits of More Than One Trust for the Same Beneficiary," *Taxation for Lawyers*, November-December 1983, pp. 162-165.

The Decision to Avoid Probate

OVERVIEW

As we have seen, the term probate has come to mean the entire court process by which the state supervises the orderly distribution of a decedent's probate property. Since probate has significant drawbacks, most clients prefer to avoid it by planning the disposition of property with one of its two major alternatives, joint tenancy or the living trust. These are referred to as *will substitutes* because they supersede any provisions that might be in the deceased co-owner or trustor's will. This chapter surveys the advantages and disadvantages of all three mechanisms of transfer. To some degree the choice is subjective, what is best depends on the client's personal assessment of the pros and cons in the light of his or her personal circumstances. Although generalization can be risky, we will conclude the chapter with a summary of various client circumstances which are apt to favor probate, joint tenancy, or the living trust.

Several other limited alternatives to probate will not be discussed. Contracts such as life insurance and retirement plans can avoid probate but have limited general application for two reasons. First, the decision whether or not to utilize these contracts is usually independent of the decision whether or not to avoid probate. For example, life insurance is purchased for reasons other than avoiding probate-- such as the need for cash at someone's death; acquiring it is not influenced by the method chosen to transfer property. Second, these limited alternatives to probate are "asset specific;" that is, they cannot be used to help other client assets avoid probate. For example, a Totten trust only avoids probating of that particular bank account. In contrast, the will (via probate) and the living trust each are means of transferring virtually any asset owned by the client. Joint tenancy also applies only to specific assets held in that form of title but almost any property can be held in this form. In this chapter, we'll use the term joint tenancy generically to include tenancy by the entirety keeping in mind that the latter is available only to married couples.

Another type of asset specific alternative to probate is the *pay-on-death* account, which is a bank or savings account controlled by the depositor so long as living but with a provision that the account is payable to another if it is still open when the depositor dies. Pay-on-death accounts may be used with checking and savings accounts, money market accounts, and certificates of deposit. Although such avoid probate, they are includable in the depositor's gross estate.[1] A few states require that they comply with the formal execution requirements of a valid will. If not, they become an intestate asset.

We begin our comparative study of probate and its two major alternatives by examining the pros and cons of probate.

THE BENEFITS AND DRAWBACKS OF PROBATE

Below, we describe probate's major benefits and drawbacks. For a more thorough understanding of the probate process, the reader is urged to first review the section called Principles of Probate Administration in Chapter 4.

The Benefits of Probate

The major benefits of probate include fairness promoted by court supervision, orderly administration of assets, greater protection from creditors, and income tax savings.

Court supervision promotes fairness. Formal probate requires substantial court supervision, a process which, at its best, promotes fairness. Through the use of petitions, accountings, hearings, and court orders, probate seeks to ensure that asset distribution is fair. No other estate transfer procedure is so controlled by public authorities.

---

1. §2036, §2038.

The public-forum nature of probate encourages *review and evaluation* by numerous observers. Judges and official clerks are called on to approve major estate activities. In addition, other interested, private parties such as beneficiaries and creditors have an opportunity to object to perceived inequities in estate administration. For example, they can object to many court rulings, including admission of a certain will to probate, appointment of a certain personal representative, payment of a certain creditor, and distribution of estate assets to a certain individual. They can raise these objections in the probate court itself; the parties need not seek a remedy elsewhere, and they can often do it without hiring a lawyer. In contrast, objections to disposition by joint tenancy and by the living trust require a different, procedurally more complicated legal action.

Critic's response. Critics of probate contend that the additional degree of equity fostered by probate administration is, at best, minimal. They argue that judges and other public officials too often give only superficial *rubber-stamp approval* of estate activities, and even occasionally dispense with certain onerous procedural requirements of their state's probate code. Supporters of probate respond to this criticism saying that judges implicitly and successfully rely on the interested parties, who are formally notified of the proceedings, to speak up in court if they feel they are being treated unfairly. Critics contend, however, that the average interested person would not be aware of the occurrence of many types of subtle or technical inequities.

The claim that probate encourages fairness is also subject to challenge because of the recent trend in the direction of *reduced supervision*. In Chapter 4, we learned that many states permit "informal" or "summary" probate procedures that can greatly reduce court surveillance. Also, we saw that UPC states permit the estate's interested parties to select the degree of supervision they desire. If they choose "informal probate," the estate will receive no direct supervision by the court. Thus, in many states, the risk of misadministration in probate is similar to that for trusts because of the opportunity to avoid the public forum. Of course, the ability in UPC states to request greater formal supervision later in probate reduces the risk of mismanagement.

In conclusion, through supervision, probate promotes fairness. However, the strength of this generalization has been weakened by the degree to which the courts only superficially oversee administrative activities, and by the recent movement of the states to reduce the degree of mandatory court supervision.

Orderly administration of assets. Probate offers an orderly administration of estate assets. Supervision by the court and by other public officials ensures further that property transfers and title clearance will be done correctly. Once again, however, this advantage is less pronounced to the extent that court approval is given only perfunctorily.

Greater protection from creditors. As we saw in Chapter 4, probate procedures typically require creditors to formally file their claims against probate assets within a certain period of time, such as four months from date of issuance of Letters Testamentary. Failure to timely file a creditor's claim can forever bar collection from those assets. Nonprobate assets, on the other hand, may only be protected by the state's general limitations period, which can be several years. Thus, asset disposition by probate can offer distributees greater protection from creditors much sooner, at least by the time of distribution.

Actual notice: the Tulsa decision. Recently, however, the U.S. Supreme court lessened this advantage, ruling in *Tulsa* that creditors who are "known or reasonably ascertainable" to the personal representative must be given "actual" notice of the limited creditor's period, rather than just "constructive" notice, by publication.[2] Notice by mail is considered acceptable actual notice.

The following is a partial listing of creditors who are usually known or reasonably ascertainable to the personal representative:

- Hospital where decedent died, all treating physicians, ambulance company and paramedics,
- Landlord or mortgage company,
- Poolman, gardener, maid, newspaper delivery service,
- Installment payment creditor,
- Creditors who have already sent decedent unpaid bills,
- Credit card issuers,
- Creditors receiving interest that was deducted on decedent's last four years local, state, and federal income tax returns,
- Creditors for whom decedent has prepared financial statements in the last four years,
- Ongoing creditors determined from decedent's correspondence and canceled checks,
- Persons given a guarantee by decedent as owner of a closely held business.

Under *Tulsa*, actual notice need not be given to potential creditors whose claims are a matter of "conjecture," i.e., deduced by surmise or guesswork.

---

2. Tulsa Professional Collection Services v. Estate of Pope 485 US 478, 108 S.Ct. 1340 (1988). For a discussion of this and other creditor's claims problems, see the Medlin and Wells articles cited at the end of the chapter.

An example of a conjectural claim would be a malpractice claim against a professional that has not yet resulted in a demand.

Clients who anticipate difficult to identify claims after their death may find the shorter limitations period a significant advantage. For example, professionals such as engineers and accountants are potentially vulnerable to malpractice claims which, if instituted after their death, stand a greater chance of succeeding, partly because the defense's best witness, the decedent, is not available to testify. The shorter creditors' period can sometimes minimize this undesired outcome.

However, some client's potential litigation claims will not be barred by the probate creditors period. Two examples will be cited. First, under the increasingly recognized theory of *delayed discovery*, the limitations period often starts when the negligence was or could have been discovered. The doctrine has been applied in situations of breach of trust, fraud and medical malpractice. Second, under the *injury or damage rule*, the limitations period does not begin to run until injury or damage actually occurs. This rule has been applied to legal malpractice situations, such as negligent will drafting, with the result that the limitations period begins to run at the testator's death, rather than at the execution date of the will. Thus, the shortened creditors period may be unavailable, in large part, for certain professionals, particularly physicians and attorneys.

Most nonprofessional clients, especially those not litigation prone, will usually find the benefit of the shorter creditors' period to be of little value. And, in view of the fact that probate publicly exposes a pot of assets for creditors to reach, some clients may prefer more private and more decentralized methods of asset distribution.[3]

In UPC states, clients' estates can have the same claims protection without supervised probate. For example, informal UPC probate offers the four-month creditors' period because its provisions allow for the filing of a legal notice to creditors. As mentioned in Chapter 4, if the notice is not issued, the UPC imposes a three-year creditors' limitations period, starting at date of death. Certain other forms of summary probate in non-UPC states do not offer this protection. For example, in California, the creditors' period is not available under summary distribution to the surviving spouse, described in Appendix 4A.

Income tax savings. As we saw in Chapter 8, the probate estate is considered a separate tax entity during its existence, taxable at its own

---

3. For a discussion of the protection from creditors of a deceased cotenant's property under joint tenancy agreements, see below in the section "advantages of joint tenancy"-- "reduced creditor's claims."

rates. Hence, some modest income shifting with an additional taxpaying entity is possible. For example, during estate administration, undistributed income (FAI) earned on estate property will be taxed to the estate rather than to the beneficiaries. This can reduce total income taxes if the estate is in a lower tax bracket than its beneficiaries. However, as mentioned in Chapter 9, the advantage has been somewhat undercut by tax reform since 1986, which generally lowered and compressed the income tax rate brackets.[4] Income tax planning for estates is described in Chapter 18.

The Drawbacks of Probate

Probate has several distinct disadvantages, including complexity, cost, lack of privacy, delay, and danger of unintended disposition.

Complexity. As we saw in Chapter 4, probate can be a complex process, requiring petitions, accountings, hearings, and other complicated legal procedures. Most laypersons understand neither their purpose nor their operation, and are forced to hire specialists to meet their requirements. Critics argue that supervised probate is usually an unnecessary, clumsy process offering considerable make-work for the legal profession, especially paralegals and legal secretaries. Others respond that the movement by many states toward less formal probate procedures has nearly made probate, in those states, no more complex than administration for a decedent whose assets had been placed in a living trust.

Cost. The cost of legal supervision under probate can be high. Studies have found that total probate administration expenses range between about 2 and 10 percent of gross estate assets, with larger estates and those subject to informal UPC administration experiencing the lowest rates.

The *personal representative's commission* usually constitutes the largest probate expense. Of course, a surviving beneficiary who acts as personal representative may wish to waive the commission. The statutes of most states either provide for "reasonable" compensation of the personal representative, or make no provision at all. Quite a few states have enacted statutory commissions based on a percentage of estate assets, such as the one included in Table 4-1, where the fee can reach as high as 4 percent. In general, personal representatives' commissions for formal probate range between 3 and 5 percent.

The next largest probate administration expense is usually the *attorney's fee*. Most states' statutes do not set attorneys' fees leaving it to the judge for

---

4. See Figure 9-1.

each case to decide and approve a *reasonable* fee. In general, attorneys' fees usually range between 2 and 4 percent of the value of the probate estate. Other administration expenses unique to probate include fiduciary bond fees, accountants' and appraisers' fees, and court costs, including filing fees.

Probate administration costs will be higher for estates containing real property located in other states. Under what is called *ancillary administration*, that property is probated in the state in which it is located. This usually required hiring an attorney who practices in the other state to handle the ancillary administration.

Other factors that will affect the level of probate administration costs include the nature of the estate property (e.g., closely held business interests, expensive artwork, etc., versus marketable securities), the complexity of the estate distribution plan, the risk of a will contest, and the general economic conditions prevailing during estate settlement.

Contrary to popular belief, probate does *not* increase a FET. Indeed, since probate costs are deductible, probate may actually reduce FET. However, increasing costs in order to decrease FET is not wise planning. As previously discussed in Chapters 4 and 6, the probate estate and the gross estate are independent (although not mutually exclusive) concepts.

Lack of privacy. Probate is a public process; all probate proceedings are subject to public scrutiny. For example, any person can inspect a decedent's probate file, which eventually includes the decedent's will, the estate inventory and appraisement, and the order for final distribution. Those particularly interested in inspecting a file would include survivors who are fighting and members of the press seeking a story about a newsworthy decedent. Commonly cited examples of celebrities receiving embarrassing publicity which arguably could have been avoided include the estates of Amanda Blake, Greta Garbo, Natalie Wood, John Wayne, Darryl Zanuck, and the controversy surrounding the conservatorship for Groucho Marx.

The probate files of most decedents are not seen by anyone other than court officials. Interested parties, such as the decedent's relatives and the executor can have the attorney for the estate send them copies of every document that is filed, and many probate attorneys do this as a matter of practice without any request that they do so, thus the most interested parties have no reason to review the court's file unless one harbors suspicion that not everything is being sent. Keep in mind, however, that clients receiving estate planning advice are typically the wealthier, more prominent citizens, who are likely to arouse greater than average curiosity.

In some situations, a client may actually prefer the lack of privacy inherent in probate. For example, the public aspects of probate might discourage or uncover fraudulent dealings undertaken by unscrupulous survivors.

Delay. Even for smaller estates, probate administration takes considerable time, ranging from nine months to several years before final distribution is made. In any particular case, the delay can be quite unpredictable. Delay can be especially hard on grieving survivors, partly because it can increase or prolong tension and conflict among them. As a specific example of delay in probate, payment of proceeds of life insurance on the decedent's life to the decedent's testamentary trust will be delayed until the trust takes effect, which usually can be no sooner than the expiration of the creditor's period, several months after date of death. Thus, complete, immediate liquidity cannot be provided to the decedent's survivors. However, preliminary distributions of significant amounts can usually be made earlier if the executor can make a good faith representation that doing so will not jeopardize creditors.

Danger of unintended disposition. The nature of probate may in some cases increase the risk of an undesired *will contest*, one which may be settled with a distribution of assets in a manner that conflicts with testator intent. For example, a person named only in a prior will might contest the decedent's last will on a technicality. The person might, for example, claim that the decedent failed, at the time of execution, to verbally request that the witnesses sign the will. In contrast with probate, other nonprobate documents of transfer are more difficult to contest, partly because execution requirements are less stringent; thus a mistake in execution formality that would invalidate the transfer is less likely occur.

With a better understanding of the pros and cons of probate, let us now consider the two principal alternatives to probate. We first turn to the simpler alternative, disposition by joint tenancy.

ONE ALTERNATIVE TO PROBATE: JOINT TENANCY

Disposition by right of survivorship under title held in joint tenancy is one major alternative to probate. It, too, has several advantages and disadvantages, which we consider next.

Advantages of Joint Tenancy

Joint tenancy has a number of distinct advantages, including low administrative cost; convenience, speed and privacy; clear, undisputed disposition; the ability to reduce creditors' claims; and income shifting.

Low administrative cost. Joint tenancy is inexpensive, both to create and to terminate. Both actions typically involve simply adding or deleting names on a certificate of ownership. Financial institutions and others holding record of title will usually aid the survivors in doing this, eliminating the need for an attorney. The removal of the deceased cotenant's name from title usually requires the presentation of a death certificate and the completion of a short, preprinted form signed by one or more of the surviving joint tenants.

Convenience, speed, and privacy. The simplicity inherent in creating and terminating joint tenancies makes them a convenient, easily understood, and speedy dispositive device. And since joint tenancy combines a method of disposition at death with a method of holding title, the property owner will not need to execute a relatively complex document, such as a will or a trust, to dispose of property held jointly. In fact, at time of disposition, any existing will or trust will be disregarded as irrelevant to the automatic survivorship inherent in joint tenancy. Finally, unlike probate property, which is a matter of public record, joint tenancy property will pass to the surviving cotenants in relative privacy. Joint tenancy documents are not made public.

Clear, undisputed disposition. Ordinarily, surviving joint tenants need not worry about not succeeding to ownership of the deceased cotenant's interest. Suits contesting joint tenancies are rare, partly because the legal formality requirements for taking title in joint tenancy are clear and minimal. There is little to challenge. In addition, the method of holding title in joint tenancy is usually clearly indicated. For example, some states require the words, "joint tenancy with right of survivorship and not as tenants in common," a title description that further minimizes confusion. In contrast, interested parties are more able to challenge the validity of a will, in part because its execution requirements and dispositive provisions are far more complex.

A few joint tenancies, however, have been successfully challenged. In some cases, courts have held that the decedent created a joint tenancy *for convenience only*, and did not intend to leave his or her interest to the surviving cotenants. For example, an elderly person may create a joint tenancy solely to seek assistance in property management. A younger individual may be named as a cotenant simply to help write checks on the elder's bank funds. As another example, consider the facts of an actual court case, in which a husband took title to his own stock in joint tenancy with his wife, in order to avoid probate. At their later divorce, the wife was required to release her interest in the stock. The court reasoned from the facts of this case that the husband had not created the joint tenancy with donative intent. To safeguard against any controversy over unintended gifts in these types of situations, the client might wish to write and keep a letter clearly stating actual intent.

Ability to reduce creditors' claims. Property held in joint tenancy is not subject to the claims of a *deceased cotenant's* unsecured creditors, because death results in an instantaneous and automatic transfer of ownership to the surviving cotenants. However, a creditor may be able to recover under the theory that the deceased cotenant made a transfer considered to be "fraudulent" as to creditors. In addition, the property will be subject to claims resulting from debts incurred by the *surviving cotenants*, whether or not incurred jointly with the decedent.

Thus, joint tenancy can be one method of insulating property from some creditors.

> EXAMPLE JT-1 Three years ago, Starfield financed the purchase of a car, which was used as collateral against the loan. Starfield died this year owning, among other things, the car (a probate asset), and some securities held in joint tenancy with his sister. If the bank loan goes into default, the bank will be able to recover the car. If proceeds from the sale of the car are not sufficient to pay off the loan, the bank may be able to reach other assets in Starfield's probate estate but it would not be able to seize the securities that now belong to the sister.

Income shifting. By placing property in joint tenancy with other family members, the client is able to shift income to lower-bracket taxpayers. Ownership interest of their share is usually immediately transferred to them (exceptions: bank accounts in some states and EE savings bonds), and, consequently, income generated by the transferred share belongs to them, too. If the cotenant is in a lower tax bracket than the creator, the combined tax on generated income may be reduced. However, we shall see shortly that the relinquishment of so much control can be a serious drawback to joint tenancy.

Disadvantages of Joint Tenancy

The disadvantages of joint tenancy as a dispositive device include nontax factors such as inflexible, uncontrolled and inefficient disposition, surrender of ownership and control, incomplete probate avoidance, as well as tax disadvantages, including the basis problem and the risk of higher transfer taxes. After studying them, the reader will probably conclude that joint tenancy is of limited use for most wealthy clients.

Inflexible, uncontrolled, and inefficient disposition. Joint tenancy is an inflexible, uncontrolled, and inefficient dispositive device. Disposition is clear but rigid: The surviving cotenants take outright, pro rata, the deceased cotenant's interest, and the last surviving cotenant winds up with an individual, fee simple interest in the property. In addition, all joint tenancies terminate at the death of the next-to-last surviving cotenant; thus right of survivorship cannot control disposition of property when the last cotenant dies. Several major disposition problems, discussed next, arise from these characteristics.

Danger of uncontrolled, undesired disposition. Joint tenancies can result in uncontrolled and undesired dispositions in three major ways.

First, by taking title in joint tenancy, clients risk distribution of their property to *unintended beneficiaries*, either as a result of chance, or by the intent of surviving cotenants. For example, consider a joint tenancy between a childless couple. If both were to die in fairly rapid succession, such as in a common accident, all of the property could wind up in the hands of the surviving cotenant's heirs or beneficiaries. If the survivor regained mental capacity, he or she would have the right to direct disposition of this property to anyone, by will, trust, or other document. As illustrated in Chapter 3, the risk to the unlucky cotenant of uncontrolled disposition can be avoided with a will or a trust, documents that can control asset disposition after the survivor's death with a survival clause and other provisions, such as giving the survivor only a life estate and leaving the remainder to someone else, but such planning will not apply to assets held in joint tenancy. By taking title in joint tenancy, spouses leave ultimate disposition to chance, empowering the survivor to disregard the other's dispositive wishes.

> EXAMPLE JT-2 Cheryl remarries after the death of her first husband, and wishing to have her estate avoid probate, names her new husband Donny as co-joint tenant of her residence. Although Cheryl's will leaves all of her property to her children, Donny will become the sole owner of the house if he survives Cheryl.

Second, disposition by joint tenancy, when not coordinated with other planning, can result in an unintended *disproportionate distribution* of the client's estate.

> EXAMPLE JT-3 Coco owned the following assets several months before her death: Common stock in her name as an individual worth $29,000; a bank account in joint tenancy with her sister worth $1,000; and the rest of her property in her name as an individual, worth $970,000. Her will leaves her entire estate to her children, and directs that all taxes be paid out of the probate estate. Shortly before her death, Coco sold the stock, depositing the proceeds in her bank account. Assuming that debts, expenses, and taxes amounted to $200,000 at her death, Coco's children will receive property worth $770,000 (= $970,000 - $200,000), which is 79% of the before-tax bequest, and her sister will receive

$30,000, which is 100 percent of the before-tax bequest. Although Coco intended to leave her sister a small sum, her inadvertent mistake wound up passing to her sister thirty times as much, free of all debts, expenses and taxes, which were paid entirely out of the children's share.

Third, joint ownership *prevents* the client from making other, less direct but *more desirable types* of transfers at death, such as giving an interest to a nonowner or splitting the interest by giving an income interest to one person and a remainder interest to another. Most planning arrangements to be discussed in the remaining chapters of this book require types of transfers not possible with joint tenancy.

Danger of inefficient disposition. Even if joint tenancies are expected to dispose of the client's assets to the right parties in the right amounts, they may do so inefficiently, generating delay and asset shrinkage. Three inefficiencies will be explored.

First, the property passing to the surviving cotenant will not be subject to those *protective provisions* often included in wills and trusts regarding responsible asset management. As a consequence, by selecting joint tenancy, clients often risk asset depletion by inexperienced cotenants who will enjoy complete discretion over care and management of the property.

EXAMPLE JT-4 In Example JT-2 above, if Cheryl had instead named her oldest child to be cotenant, disposition to Cheryl's husband could have been avoided, but that child would become the sole owner of all property, to the exclusion of the other children. If that lucky but generous child later splits the property with the siblings, he or she will have made one or more gifts subject to taxation. These two problems could have been avoided by naming all children as cotenants, but Cheryl may not have wished to make an immediate gift of all her property to the children.

Second, creating joint tenancies may expose those assets to the *claims of the creditors of the other cotenant* even though the client, merely seeking an inexpensive way to avoid property, did not really intend the cotenant to have an interest until the client died. For example, if son, who is named cotenant on property owned by Mom, incurs a court judgment due to an auto accident, the son's half interest in the joint tenancy asset may be subject to a judgment claim that could force partition and sale of the property.

Third, joint tenancies can result in *probate administration* and, possibly, intestacy. Joint tenancy does not in itself avoid probate administration at the death of the last surviving cotenant, nor in the case of simultaneous death situations.

EXAMPLE JT-5 While alive, Russ and his wife Patti were advised to avoid probate by creating joint tenancies. After Russ died, Patti survived only a few years, never realizing that at her death all of their property would be subject to probate administration. As the last surviving cotenant, Patti owned all of this property as an individual.

EXAMPLE JT-6 Based on the facts in Example JT-5, above, if Russ and Patti instead died in a common accident where there was no sufficient evidence as to who survived the other, under the Uniform Simultaneous Death Act each cotenant will be presumed to survive the other, resulting in each cotenant's half interest in the property being subject to probate administration.

The living trust, discussed in the next major section, does not have this drawback; it is designed to avoid probate administration at the death of both spouses.

Surrender of ownership and control. As discussed in Chapter 7, creating an interest in joint tenancy will usually constitute an immediate, completed *gift* to any cotenant who has not contributed an equal share of the consideration. Thus, each donee-cotenant will become the legal owner of an equal portion of the property. By receiving a (vested) present interest, each has the right to convert his or her share of the property into a tenancy-in-common interest, capable of being sold or devised to non-cotenants. This is not usually a problem for joint tenancies between people who contribute equal shares of property or between happily married spouses, furthermore, tenancy by the entire cannot be unilaterally changed, sold or encumbered. Between others, however, the probate avoidance of joint tenancy may not be worth the client's immediate surrender of significant property interests.

Creating an immediate vested present interest in the donee-cotenant can give rise to other problems. The donee may be unable to later disclaim the gift to save transfer taxes. If the donee becomes incompetent, a guardianship may have to be appointed. The donor may need the donee's permission to sell the asset. Finally, the asset may be subject to the claims of the donee's creditors.

In contrast with joint tenancy, other documents of transfer such as the will and the trust instrument can *delay* the making of an outright gift at least until the client's death. Instead of creating present interests, they provide for *future interests*, ones that are *contingent* upon future events, such as the client's not later revoking those interests. Most clients do not wish to make outright gifts at the time they are planning to avoid probate.

The basis problem. As we have seen in Chapter 8, the rule for basis adjustment for joint tenancy property at the death of one cotenant is clear and unalterable: Only the deceased cotenant's share of the property will receive a step-up in basis to date-of-death value. The surviving cotenant's basis will remain unchanged.

Avoiding joint tenancy may open up one or two of the opportunities described next to achieve a step-up in basis for the entire value of the property.

Gift-death-devise strategy. First, the property could be *given to a donee* who is expected to die before the donor. At the donee's death, the entire property, which is then devised back to the donor, will receive a full step-up in basis. This strategy will be certain to work satisfactorily only in situations where the donee can be trusted to actually devise the property to the donor, such as where the parties are happily married. It will also succeed only if the donee's death occurs at least one year after the initial gift. Under Internal Revenue Code §1014(e), failure of the donee to survive by at least a year will cause the gift to be treated, for purpose of basis adjustment, as if the original transfer never occurred.

Community property ownership. The second way in which avoiding joint tenancy can open up an opportunity for a step-up in basis for the entire value of property involves the ownership of community property between spouses. As we saw in Chapter 8, unlike joint tenancy property, both halves of community property receive a step-up in basis at the death of the first spouse. Thus, married clients in *community property* states (even those of modest wealth) may be especially interested in avoiding joint tenancy arrangements, choosing instead to dispose of community property by will or trust instrument.

When step-up not necessary. For some clients, however, a basis step-up may not be necessary. For example, their property may not have appreciated substantially. Or they do not expect survivors to sell the property. Or they may expect any gain from sale of the property to be sheltered by certain provisions of the Internal Revenue Code. Common methods of sheltering an otherwise taxable gain on a *principal residence* include the rollover (postponement) of the gain on sale,[5] and the one-time exclusion of $125,000 of gain by an individual who has attained age 55.[6]

Possible higher estate tax. Joint tenancies can increase FET for two reasons: because of the somewhat harsh provisions of §2040 and because of their effect on the size of the surviving cotenant's gross estate.

§2040 consequences. In Chapter 6 we learned that under §2040, the *entire value* of property held in joint tenancy by a decedent is includable in

---

5. §1034

6. §121.

the decedent's gross estate, except in two situations. First, if the joint tenancy was held solely with the surviving spouse, exactly one half will always be included. Second, if the joint tenancy was held by the decedent and at least one person who is not the decedent's spouse, the decedent's gross estate will include the entire value of the property, reduced only by an amount attributable to that portion of the consideration which can be shown to have been furnished by the survivors. Thus, a higher than necessary FET can result if a joint tenancy has a nonspouse cotenant and if the surviving cotenants are unable to fully prove contribution.

Larger survivor's gross estate. Joint tenancies between spouses and other cotenants can also result in a higher than necessary FET for the estates of *surviving cotenants* because their gross estates will be quite large, having been loaded up with the predeceased cotenant's property passing to them by automatic right of survivorship. We shall see in Chapter 11 that in the case of some spouses, total spousal FET can be reduced by rejecting such a "one hundred percent marital deduction" plan, and instead passing less property outright to the surviving spouse. This principal also applies to unmarried couples in nontraditional relationships, as detailed in Chapter 17. Such an FET saving "bypass" of the surviving partner's estate can only be arranged satisfactorily with a will or a living trust. And, as mentioned above, neither document can dispose of property held in joint tenancy.

Possible gift taxation. Creation of joint tenancies between nonspouses can result in a taxable gift if an unequal contributions are made and if the value of the gift exceeds the annual exclusion. In contrast, disposition by will or by the typical living trust instrument produces no immediate gift during the client's lifetime because, as we have said, the documents generally do not create vested interests.

Finally, the client may not be able to avoid joint tenancy with regard to certain property. For example, some bank lenders may require that spouses hold title in their home in joint tenancy rather that in trust as a condition to granting a loan secured by the property. As living trust become more popular as an estate planning device and lending institutions become more familiar with them, this requirement by lenders is less likely to occur, although the spouses may be asked to either personally guarantee the loan or give their written assurance that there is nothing in the trust document that would prevent them from using the property as collateral.

In view of the many significant drawbacks to joint tenancy, especially for clients with medium or large estates, planners generally recommend the other major alternative to probate, the living trust, discussed next.

THE OTHER ALTERNATIVE TO PROBATE: THE LIVING TRUST

The more popular alternative to probate for many estate planning clients is the living trust. As described in Chapter 3, it is a trust created during the trustor's lifetime and funded with some or all of the family wealth. While the trustor is alive, the living trust is usually revocable, which means that its terms are amendable and, if later desired, its assets can be retransferred to the trustor's name. Most trustors name themselves trustee of their living trust during their lifetime. However, under a doctrine called *merger*, a few states do not recognize trusts that name the same person to be trustor, trustee, and beneficiary.

At the trustor's death, the revocable trust becomes irrevocable and either terminates with the corpus distributed to the remaindermen, or continues in existence until a later date. In the case of a typical "joint" revocable living trust created by a husband and wife, all assets are placed in one trust, which is revocable by either of them during their lifetimes. At the first spouse's death, different things can happen, depending on the plan. A commonly used estate plan for smaller estates has the decedent's share of the trust property left in trust to the spouse, so that the trust becomes one large pot belonging entirely to the surviving spouse. Then, at his or her later death, the trust, which has avoided two probates, is either terminated or continued for the benefit of the children. Other distribution arrangements, particularly those designed to reduce FET at the surviving spouse's death, will be discussed in Chapter 11.

Taxation of a living trust depends on whether or not it is revocable. A *revocable* living trust usually has no additional transfer or income tax consequences during the trustor's lifetime. A transfer to it does not constitute a taxable gift since the transfer is not complete. And under the grantor trust rules, all income earned by a revocable trust is taxable to the grantor, that is, the trustor. In contrast, an *irrevocable* living trust is usually a separate income-taxpaying entity; all transfers into it usually constitute completed gifts, and, except when either the grantor trust rules or the kiddie tax apply, all undistributed FAI is taxed to the trust, while all distributed FAI is usually taxed to the beneficiaries.

Funded irrevocable living trusts also avoid probate. Not as commonly used as the revocable living trust because they involve gifting, they will be discussed at length in Chapters 13 and 15, in the context of gift giving and life insurance planning.

Advantages of the Living Trust[7]

The living trust has several distinct advantages over other transfer devices. They include greater organization, greater assurance of probate avoidance, lower total costs, greater privacy and speed, opportunity to test the future, ability to use the trust as an alternative to a conservatorship, and possible reduced litigation.

Greater organization. Establishing a living trust in effect requires the client to organize his or her property during lifetime, thereby enhancing efficient personal financial planning.

Greater assurance of complete probate avoidance. Compared with joint tenancies, the living trust offers greater certainty that probate will be avoided at the death of the surviving partner.

> EXAMPLE LT-1 Kim and Chris wish to provide for asset disposition in a manner similar to that directed in a simple will, but also wish to avoid probate on all property. Their planner makes it clear to them that joint tenancies will not achieve the latter goal because the surviving cotenant may wind up owning the property as an individual, making it subject to probate administration. Instead, they execute a living trust instrument, funding the trust with all of their property. The trust will continue to exist for both their lifetimes. At the survivor's death, the assets will pass from the trusts to their designated beneficiaries, free from probate.

The above example was intentionally unclear about both the clients' sex and marital status. In this context, neither is material; unmarried individuals, including members of the same sex, may legally take title in joint tenancy and may legally co-execute a single trust instrument.

Lower total cost than probate. Compared to will preparation and probate, the combined cost of preparation and administration of the living trust is usually significantly less. The following material discusses both preparation costs and total cost.

Preparation costs. Oddly, the cost of preparing the living trust instrument may be a bit higher than the cost of preparing a will for at least two reasons. First, the trust instrument is usually a more complicated document. Its provisions must arrange for the immediate receipt of property, for management of that property, and for the proper distribution of the property and its income for a period that might span several generations of

---

7. Throughout the rest of this chapter, we will often use the shorthand "living trust" to mean *revocable* living trust.

beneficiaries. However, if the probate alternative to a living trust is a *trust-will*, the difference in drafting costs may not be as large; the cost of the probate alternative of will drafting will be higher.

Second, the cost of preparing the living trust instrument is also higher than for planning for probate with a will because in addition to drafting a trust instrument, the attorney must *also* draft a type of will. Unfortunately, the establishment of the living trust does not totally eliminate the need for a will. Because clients often fail to continue to take the additional step necessary to completely fund the trust in a manner to be explained shortly, most clients will die owning some property in their own name, rather than in the name of the trustee. Planners provide for disposition of this probate property with what is called a *pour over will*, specifying that any of the testator's assets not in the trust shall be distributed or "poured over" into the trust at the client's death. Because it disposes of all property outright to only one party (the trustee), the pour-over will is usually a brief, simple document, adding little to the preparation cost of avoiding probate with the living trust. But, as a true will, it disposes of probate assets, hopefully few. Thus, some probate administration costs may be incurred on assets passing under the pour-over will.

Total cost. While the specific cost of preparing the living trust may be higher, the total cost of the living trust alternative is usually lower, due to the relatively high cost of formal probate *administration* at death. In contrast with formal probate, administration of a living trust at the client's death involves minimal or no legal work in court. The pour-over will may not need to be probated, depending upon the size of the probate estate and the scope of the state's informal or summary administration rules. However, some *other postmortem legal duties* that are required under the probate alternative may also have to be performed under the trust alternative. They include

- Obtaining appraisals
- Marshaling and safeguarding assets
- Preparing an informal inventory of the assets
- Preparing and filing death tax returns
- Paying creditors
- Instituting litigation to protect assets
- Changing title to assets
- Distributing assets to beneficiaries
- Obtaining receipts from beneficiaries

While the costs of these actions usually do not add up to anywhere near the total cost of formal probate administration, they are not insignificant.[8]

But the total cost of probate isn't always greater. The efficiency of *informal* probate administration in *UPC states* can make probate an attractive alternative to the living trust, measured by the criterion of cost.

Other factors influencing the relative costs of probate versus the living trust include whether someone other than the grantor or the grantor's spouse will serve as trustee or executor, the ability to deduct these costs as an income tax miscellaneous itemized deduction, and the schedule of local court costs.

At this point it should be reiterated that avoiding probate with the revocable living trust does not save additional transfer taxes. Chapter 12 will make it clear why the same amount of FET can be saved by disposing of property with a carefully drafted will.

As mentioned earlier, a detailed analytical model for comparing the costs of the living trust versus formal probate is presented later in the chapter.

Greater privacy. A trust instrument is usually very private, not subject to public inspection. Although property transfers into and out of a living trust may require *examination of the trust instrument* by financial and other institutions, the document usually need not be made publicly accessible. County recorders may require a filing of the trust in the public records, but usually only brief sections of the document need be submitted. In fact, many attorneys in the estate planning process draft a separate brief document called "memorandum of trust" or "confirmation of trust," available for examination by such institutions, in lieu of the trust instrument itself. At a minimum, it will contain sections describing the identity of trustee and successor trustee, and the trustee powers. It should be formally executed by trustor and trustee, and notarized. In this way critical parts of the trust, including dispositive provisions, may be kept completely secret.

However some states, such as New York which impose an inheritance tax on trust property, may require the public *filing of an inventory*, which can reveal the nature and value of the trust's assets and the names of its beneficiaries. In addition, in the litigation process, a determined contestant can gain access to the contents of a living trust through legal "discovery."

As mentioned earlier, privacy may be especially desired by particularly wealthy or prominent clients. They may wish to avoid any additional publicity and any inspection by disinherited or contentious survivors, who may be seeking the opportunity to initiate a will contest.

---

8. For a discussion of the postmortem duties of a trustee, see the Parks article cited at the end of the chapter.

Speed. Property can usually be transferred out of a trust somewhat more rapidly than out of a probate estate because the transfer process is not ordinarily subject to supervision and approval by the courts. However, failure to perform certain postmortem legal duties (detailed above) can subject the trustee to significant personal liability and can trigger costly and avoidable litigation for the beneficiaries. Thus, for example, in those states where creditors' claims can be made against trust assets, the trustee will want to delay distribution. And for larger trusts owing a sizable FET, the trustee may delay major distributions of trust assets until an estate tax "closing letter" from the IRS is received, about one to two years after date of death.

Speed of disposition of real property located in a *different state* can be more rapid if that property is held in a living trust rather than disposed of by will, because ancillary administration can often be avoided. Real property held in a living trust is considered by most states to be intangible personal property, not subject to ancillary administration. However, some states require reporting procedures quite similar to the probate administration process.

Opportunity to test the future. By placing assets into a revocable living trust, the client has the opportunity to test the future by making the estate plan largely operational during lifetime. The client can obtain a preview of how the assets will be *managed* after death and how the beneficiaries can be expected to react to the receipt of family property. By naming another party trustee, the client can observe firsthand how well the assets are being managed and can make needed adjustments in management provisions before death. In addition, the trustee can be given the opportunity to become *familiar* with the trust assets during the client's lifetime, thus increasing the likelihood of both more efficient future management and a more smooth transition period after the client's death. Finally, by initiating a predictable pattern of asset distributions to beneficiaries during lifetime, the client can help a family member *learn to use assets* more maturely. Of course, a program of gifting is possible without a living trust, but having the terms of distribution in writing further ensures a continuous and consistent transfer program. It is these reasons why a few commentators have loosely called the revocable living trust a form of "living will." But this should not be confused with the universally known "living will," discussed in Chapter 17, which is a popular document containing directions regarding health care decisions.

Alternative to guardianship or conservatorship. We shall see in Chapter 17 that a client who becomes physically or mentally incapable of managing assets will need someone to provide that management. Just as a guardianship may have to be established to manage a minor's estate, a guardianship or conservatorship may be necessary to manage the estate of an incapacitated adult. Like probate administration, guardianships and conservatorships are carefully supervised by the court, which usually requires periodic accountings and formal court approval for many acts of asset management.

Used in lieu of a guardianship or conservatorship, the living trust can thus be seen as a vehicle to also avoid the expense, delay and publicity of probate-type administration before the client's death. The typical living trust begins with the client acting as trustee. Subsequently, a successor trustee takes over when the client relinquishes the role, becomes incapacitated, or dies. Thus, the living trust instrument has an additional application not directly available with a will: It can be easily structured to provide for the client's incapacity. Some commentators consider this *the major advantage* of the living trust for older clients, making the will alternative seriously deficient by comparison.

Another less expensive alternative to the guardianship or conservatorship is the durable power of attorney for property, discussed in Chapter 17. It does not avoid probate.

Possible reduced litigation. As we have seen, the probate process can offer a relatively convenient opportunity for a dissatisfied survivor to initiate a will contest. Such disputes over disposition of the client's property may be minimized with a living trust for two reasons. First, the client, as trustor and beneficiary, is able to live with the trust, receiving and making distributions and transferring property to it. All of these acts can constitute additional evidence of a well thought out estate plan. In contrast, a will ordinarily is simply a document, one not perceived to have much impact on the testator's day-to-day life. Thus, disappointed parties may be more successful in showing that the testator's will does not reflect his or her actual intent.

Second, disputes over the client's estate plan may be minimized with a living trust to the extent that the actual litigation may be more difficult to accomplish. However, commentators are in disagreement over how difficult a trust is to contest. Some maintain that the living trust is quite difficult to contest since it requires a separate legal action in a different court, one often with more onerous legal requirements and perhaps the absence of a sympathetic jury. In addition, transfers from a trust do not require notice to the testator's heirs. In contrast, probating the will, as we have seen, does involve formal notice, and act which may in itself trigger a contest. Other commentators argue that a trust can be contested on substantially the same grounds that are used to contest a will. Common grounds, it will be recalled, include fraud, undue influence, lack of capacity and improper execution.

Other advantages of living trusts. Living trusts are normally simpler to revise than wills. While a *codicil* to a will requires certain execution formalities (described in Chapter 3), an *amendment* to a living trust needs no formalities or witnesses, and may be in the trustor's handwriting. However, if the trustee is someone other than the trustor, he or she should at least be notified of the revision, and most attorneys also have the trustee sign the amendment.

Use of a living trust eliminates any hiatus or time gap in the management of the decedent-client's assets immediately after death. While the trustee (or successor trustee) of a living trust is empowered to carry on immediately, no one is authorized to act with regard to probate property until the court appoints a personal representative, at least several days after the testator's death. Of course, most assets do not require immediate attention.

Disadvantages of the Living Trust

The living trust has several disadvantages, including the burden of funding, possibly greater legal uncertainty, and some minor tax factors.

Funding burden. Establishment of a joint tenancy is a one-step process. The very act of creation of the joint interest creates the appropriate title. On the other hand, establishment of a living trust to avoid probate is a two-step process. First, the trust document must be executed, somewhat like that of a two party contract. Second, the trust must be *funded*; that is, legal title to the property intended to avoid probate must be formally transferred from the trustor to the trustee. Some trustor-clients never do the latter, because they are unaware that the additional step of funding is necessary. Others are aware of it but simply never get around to it. Most find it downright inconvenient, because it requires trips to the bank and to other places where title is officially kept. And clients who actively trade their property, such as those involved in frequent real estate deals and securities transactions, may especially dislike the greater complexity inherent in continually keeping property in trust name. However, for securities held in street name and traded in the typical brokerage account under the trustee's name, proper title will automatically be taken with each purchase without further work by the trustee.

Failure to fund the trust will cause that property not to be subject to the trust's terms.[9] As a result, at the client's death the property will usually pass through probate, under the (pour over) will or by intestate succession. Some attorneys carefully avoid this undesired outcome by insisting on initially

---

9. *Heggstad v. Heggstad*, 20 Cal. Rptr. 2d 433 (1993).

funding the living trust themselves, rather than leaving the responsibility to the client. This may increase somewhat the legal cost of setting up the living trust. However, in at least one court decision, a trustor's written declaration stating the holding of certain specific property as trustee was held to be sufficient, even though the trustor had not made a legal *conveyance*, title change by deed.[10] In the specific facts of the case, the trustors listed a specific item of real property held as a tenant in common on "Schedule A," at the end of his living trust. The court ruled the property to be held in trust and not subject to probate. A footnote to the ruling said "We hasten to note, however, that to be effective as to strangers, the declaration of trust must be recorded."

On an ongoing basis, planners may be able to help the client spot non-trust assets by paying particular attention to the client's tax forms, such as 1099s and K1s, which are issued by partnerships, S corporations, banks and other asset account holders. Forms that do not indicate the trust as record owner of the account may imply that a title change is in order.

To eliminate the funding burden for married couples with joint tenancy property, one commentator has suggested executing a "joint declaration of trust ownership," designed to instantly convert all jointly owned property into trust owned property without having to change record title to any jointly held assets. Other suggested advantages of this largely untested "magic wand" type document include maximizing use of each spouse's unified credit and GSTT exemption,[11] greater privacy, possible additional protection from creditors, and no need to change title to all assets whenever there is a change in trustees.[12]

Greater legal uncertainty. Unlike the will, the living trust has not had the benefit of centuries of testing by the courts to resolve the inevitable conflicts that can arise. In the future, we can expect some continuing litigation in the area of the living trust, a prospect that raises a small degree of uncertainty over the outcome of any unresolved issues.

Longer creditor's period. As described in considerable detail earlier, probate can offer a shorter creditor's limitations period than can the living trust, which is often subject to the usual limitations period of from one to three years.

---

10. For an extended discussion of techniques in funding a revocable living trust, see the Schmidt article cited at the end of the chapter.

11. To be discussed in Chapter 12.

12. For details, see the Keydel (1989) article cited at the end of the chapter.

Living trust arrangements may be able to indirectly take advantage of the shorter creditor's period under probate. One commentator, an advocate of the living trust, includes in her trust forms a "pour-up" provision, giving the trustee discretion to distribute trust assets to the client's estate at the client's death. In this way, the living trust, with all of its advantages, may be used, unless a creditor's problem is anticipated later on. This arrangement is still considerably untested.[13]

A second way that living trusts can (arguably) take advantage of the shorter creditor's period involves simply probating a small but significant portion of the client's property, under the assumption that the probate notice to creditors will be effective in barring later claims against trust property, as well as probate property. Largely untested, this strategy rests on the premise that formal notice serves to inform creditors that they should seek recourse *in general*, because the debtor has died. Some critics, however, argue that a probate notice cannot be effective against a pot of property that is in no way identified in the notice. Others believe that such notice will be effective only if the claims are smaller than the value of the probate estate. At least one state statute makes revocable living trust assets subject to creditor's claims and probate administration expenses to the extent that the probate estate can not pay them.[14] This tie-in should lend support to the argument that the limited creditors period should also bar collection against living trust assets. In the future, as more and more trustors die, case law should decide this issue.

Tax factors. There are a number of minor tax disadvantages to the living trust.[15]

- Compared to the $600 available to an estate, a trust, after the grantor's death, has a smaller personal income tax *exemption*: either $100 or $300.
- 1A trust is subject to the income tax *throwback rules*, while an estate is not. However, the rapidly rising rate brackets for estates virtually destroy the benefit of avoiding the throwback rules. In addition,

---

13. Comment by Lynn P. Hart, at Practicing Law Institute's 1990 Estate Planning Institute.

14. CA Probate Code §18201.

15. For a discussion of several other minor tax disadvantages, as well as a general comparison of probate versus the living trust, see the Cornfeld paper cited at the end of the chapter.

most trust income beneficiaries will probably prefer receiving income sooner rather than later, making the application of the throwback rules to most trusts unlikely.

- For income tax purposes, the trustee of a nongrantor trust cannot select the close of the trust's *taxable year*, while the executor of an estate can. The advantage of selecting a fiscal tax year is illustrated in Chapter 18.
- As mentioned earlier, real property held in trust and located in states other than the client's residence state is usually considered by the client's residence state to be intangible personal property. Most states impose a death tax on such *distantly owned property*, which might otherwise escape taxation if it were disposed of by will, since "real property" located outside a state is not ordinarily subject to its tax. Of course no additional tax would be incurred in states imposing only a "pick-up" type death tax. And such real property may still escape death tax if it is owned by a corporation, rather than directly by a decedent-shareholder.
- Finally, the IRS has taken the position that property transferred by the trustee of a revocable trust within three years of the grantor's death will be included in his or her gross estate under *§2035*. The service argues that the property would have been included under §2038 had the "relinquishment" not been made.[16]

To avoid §2035 application under the last item, above, for *existing trusts*, planners recommend a two-step transfer: first the grantor should withdraw the amounts from the trust; second, he or she should directly make the gift. Rationale: when the grantor withdraws the property, there is no relinquishment since the grantor has control over it. To avoid §2035 application for *new trusts*, planners recommend that the instrument provide that during the trustor's lifetime, the trustor shall be the only permissible appointee, so that distributions to anyone else would have to be "characterized" as withdrawals by the trustor followed by later transfers to donees.[17]

Miscellaneous disadvantages. There are several other disadvantages to the living trust, all of which can be considered relatively minor for most clients.

---

16. In early 1993, a bill was introduced in the House of Representative that would treat a transfer from a revocable trust as having been made by the grantor. It did not pass.

17. TAM 9226007; TAM 9016002; TAM 9018004; TAM 9018004; TAM9117003; *Jalcut Estate* 96 TC 675 (1991). Acquiesced by IRS in AOD 1992-002.

Financing problems. In some states, property held in a living trust may not be secured as collateral against a loan by the trustor. In addition, if the trustor wishes to refinance property after it has been placed in trust, lenders may require that the trustor reassume title to it until the refinancing is completed. And some lenders may not finance trust property if they fear that the trust instrument may prohibit its sale.

Divorce. In some states, divorce may result in an improper distribution of assets from a living trust. As mentioned in Chapter 4, in most states, a dissolution of marriage will revoke a disposition to an ex-spouse in a *will* executed prior to the divorce. In contrast, these state statutes often do not apply to provisions in a living trust. However, in states adopting Uniform Probate Code §2-804(b), divorce revokes *any* revocable disposition or appointment of property for an ex-spouse or relative of an ex-spouse.

Other disadvantages. Living trusts may have disadvantages in certain special situations, two of which will be mentioned briefly without additional explanation. First, beneficiaries of a living trust may lose a defense against liability for *environmental clean-up* of real property held in the trust. In contrast, that defense is available to persons *acquiring* the property "by inheritance or bequest.[18] "Second, use of a living trust may reduce allowable *Medicaid benefits* for the beneficiary-spouse of a decedent who establishes a discretionary living trust. The problem will not arise for testamentary trusts.[19]

Not included among these disadvantages of a revocable living trust is any loss of a *basis step-up* at the grantor's death. Property held in a revocable living trust *will* receive a step-up because it is treated, from an income tax point of view, as owned by the grantor.

Living trusts require careful analysis, planning and preparation. Clearly, the decision whether or not to create a revocable living trust requires the planner's critical evaluation of many challenging issues, and drafting a living trust requires the knowledge of an experienced estate planning attorney. The tasks of evaluation and careful drafting require a skill level far above those of any practicing generalist, let alone someone lacking even rudimentary training in the issues. Nonetheless, recently, casual salespersons, sometimes traveling door-to-door, have been approaching the elderly in large numbers, offering to prepare living trusts. Tactics alleged by opponents include using high pressure sales pitches, imposing high prices, making misrepresentations and mistakes about the relative costs and

---

18. 42USC §9601(35)(A)(iii).

19. 42USC §1396a(k).

advantages of living trusts, naming themselves as trustees, carelessly failing to ensure that property is transferred to the trust, producing an ineffective document, and making false claims of endorsement by legitimate nonprofit organizations. At least two state's attorneys general have taken legal action against these organizations,[20] but these unprofessional practices will probably continue as long as some uninformed elderly, overly fearful of probate and guardianships and distrustful of lawyers, naively reach out for help from outwardly friendly "advisors."

QUANTITATIVE MODEL FOR COMPARISON OF COSTS OF PROBATE VERSUS LIVING TRUST

This section applies the principles of finance to develop a model for comparing the costs of probate with the costs of the living trust. The technique used will incorporate the *time value of money* concept known as present value.

> EXAMPLE QT-1 Patty is evaluating the decision whether to avoid probate of her assets, worth $1 million, by setting up a revocable living trust. With regard to costs, she has made the following estimates:
> Under the probate alternative: drafting her will, $600; probate administration, $25,000; other costs at death, including accountant's fees, $1,000.
> Under the trust alternative: drafting the trust and the pour-over will, $1,600; annual record-keeping until death,[21] $300 per year; nonprobate administration cost at death, $2,500; costs in higher income taxes due to inability to use a probate estate as a separate taxpayer, $1,100; other costs at death, including accountant's fees, $1,000.
> Her life expectancy is 10 years.

In calculating the total cost for each alternative, Patty could simply add up the expenses. That would result in a forecasted total cost under the probate alternative of $26,000, and a forecasted total cost under the trust of $11,100. Simple summation, however, does not take into account the time value of money. To correctly compare amounts incurred at different points

---

20. Maine and Florida, according to the Stiegel, et. al., article cited at the end of the chapter.

21. Fees incurred for the production of income, such as trustee fees of a living trust, income tax preparation fees and record keeping fees, are miscellaneous itemized deductions, subject to the 2 percent deduction floor.

in time, we must make adjustments to reflect the fact that money not payable today can be invested profitably until the time that it is payable. We can do this by calculating the sum of the *present values of the costs for each alternative*. The present value of a cost is the amount that would have to be invested today to accumulate the actual amount of that cost payable in the future.

To better understand the present value concept, consider an intuitively simple illustration. At an assumed annual rate of investment of 10 percent, one would need to invest $100 today to accumulate the amount $110 payable in one year. In other words, at 10 percent, the present value of $110 payable in one year is $100. Present values of any amount can be derived from present value tables such as Tables 12 and 13 of Appendix A at the end of the text. Table 12 depicts the present values of a single $1 amount to be paid in the future, assuming certain investment rates. Thus, the present value of $1 in one year at 10 percent is $0.909, or a bit less than 91 cents. Since we have been calculating the present value of the amount $110, not $1, our answer must be the product of $110 and 0.909, or $100. With regard to Patty's actual figures, at 10 percent, the present value of $1 to be paid in 10 years is $0.386. We will use this lump-sum discount factor in the calculations that follow.

How can we calculate the present value of the amount $300 payable each year for the next 10 years, with the first payment due in one year? Described in other words, we must calculate the total amount to be invested today which will enable us to fund this annuity, that is, to fund this entire progression of equal payments. To do this, we calculate the present value of the annuity. Table 13 in Appendix A shows the present values of a $1 annuity for specified periods, assuming certain investment rates. The "annuity factor," as it is called, corresponding to 10 years and 10 percent, can be seen to 6.145. Since we wish to determine the present value of an annuity of $300, not $1, the answer must be the product of $300 and 6.145, or $1,844.

We are now ready to calculate Patty's total costs for the two alternatives in a manner which adjusts for the time value of money. The figures are included in Table 10-1 and Table 10-2.

TABLE 10-1 Present Value of Costs of Probate

Item	Year	Amount	Discount Factor	Present Value
Drafting	Now	$600.00	1.0000	$600.00
Administration	10	25,000.00	.386	9,650.00
Other costs	10	1,000.00	.386	386.00
Total present value of probate costs				$10,636.00

TABLE 10-2 Present Value of Costs of Living Trust

Item	Year	Amount	Discount Factor	Present Value
Drafting	Now	$1,600.00	1.0000	$1,600.00
Record-keeping	1-10	300.00	6.145	1,844.00
Administration	10	2,500.00	0.386	965.00
Higher tax	10	1,100.00	0.386	425.00
Other costs	10	1,000.00	0.386	385.00
Total present value of living trust costs				$5,129.00

Thus the sum of the present values of the costs are $10,636 for probate and $5,129 for the trust. These represent the total amounts that Patty would have to invest today, at 10 percent, to properly accumulate and pay all of the individual forecasted costs when they are due.

The analysis could be refined slightly to include the tax deductibility of these expenses. For example, as we shall see in Chapter 18, administration costs may be deducted on the estate tax return. Thus, if T represents the marginal estate tax rate, the after-tax cost of an FET deductible expense is the product of that expense times the expression one minus T.

The estimates in Example 10-5 have been made for illustration purposes only and should not be used as a general indicator of costs. Actual costs will vary considerably, depending on specific factors, such as the laws of the decedent's particular residence state and the cost of professional services in the decedent's locale. However, at the risk of overgeneralizing, in this author's experience, the present-value cost of formal probate is usually higher than the present-value cost of the living trust by at least 20 percent.

WHICH ALTERNATIVE IS BEST?

From all of the material covered so far, the reader can gather that the decision whether or not to avoid probate is not always a simple one. It requires that the client examine and subjectively weigh the advantages and disadvantages of each, in the context of the laws and procedures of his or her state. It should be clear that there is no one absolutely correct answer for all situations. In fact, some clients owning larger estates may be advised to execute a will to probate certain assets and transfer the remaining assets by living trust, in order to obtain the unique benefits of both arrangements. Perhaps we can conclude with a description of a few of the circumstances in which clients are most likely to favor a particular alternative.

Probate

Clients who will be inclined to lean toward the probate alternative include:

1. *Professionals*, such as self-employed engineers and accountants, who stand to gain additional security from the short creditors' limitations period.
2. Those who have *large, complicated estates* or who expect family *disharmony* after their death may benefit from the extra protection potentially available through greater court supervision.
3. Wealthier residents of *UPC states* where the cost advantage to avoiding informal probate is minimal.
4. Young, healthy clients who expect to be acquiring numerous assets and would find onerous the constant *funding* requirement of the living trust.

Joint Tenancy

Since joint tenancy has some very significant disadvantages, clients are inclined to prefer it only if one, or perhaps all, of the following circumstances apply:

1. The client wants the property to pass *outright* to the surviving joint tenants. This implies that there is no need for trusts, to save income or transfer taxes, to avoid guardianships, to delay distributions to younger survivors, or to provide for multiple beneficiaries over time by creating life estate and remainder interests.
2. A complete *step-up* in income tax basis at the client's death is *not needed*, or is not available by other means.

3. The creation of the joint tenancy interest does *not* result in an immediate *gift*.

These circumstances usually apply only to smaller estates.

Living Trust

Clients who will tend to prefer a living trust typically include those who want to avoid probate but do not like joint tenancy because of its significant disadvantages. For example:

1. Those with *larger estates* who wish to avoid the FET consequences of joint tenancy.
2. Those who place high priority on *privacy and speed* in the property transfer process.
3. Clients for whom the *total cost* of the living trust is expected to be considerably lower than the cost of probate; reasons include the following:
   a. Probate administration expenses are expected to be high, perhaps because the client is a resident of a non-UPC state, or because an independent executor must be named.
   b. Nonprobate administration fees are low, perhaps because a private individual can be named as trustee, and that trustee will not need to pay for outside record keeping.
4. Clients who do *not* anticipate a trust *funding burden* associated with numerous acquisitions of property.
5. Finally, clients who wish to avoid the publicity and cost of court appointed *guardians or conservators* if and when they become incapacitated.

HOW FREQUENTLY ARE THEY USED?

Based on the results of a survey of experienced estate planning attorneys conducted by this author, the revocable living trust was the most popular dispositive document used, with 45.1 percent of clients using them as the principal method of asset disposition. Nonsimple wills were almost as popular (36.6%), followed by simple wills (13.8%) and joint tenancies (4.5%). Interestingly, while clients in general clearly chose to avoid joint tenancies, more than one half chose not to avoid probate.

The next chapter will explore marital deduction and bypass planning, two major methods of reducing the FET.

QUESTIONS AND PROBLEMS

1. Discuss the validity of the claim that probate promotes fairness.

2. (*a*) Why isn't probate private? (*b*) Is the living trust always private?

3. (*a*) How has the advantage of probate's limited creditor's period been undermined recently? (*b*) Will any clients still prefer probate to minimize creditor's problems?

4. (*a*) Who might wish to contest an invalidly executed will? (*b*) Why might it be easier to do than to challenge a living trust?

5. You wish to advise client Paxton about the income tax advantage to probate. Assuming that all of Paxton's survivors will be in the 28 percent marginal rate bracket, (*a*) how much income in the future Paxton estate could be subject to a lower rate? (*b*) what is the maximum amount of tax that could be saved by using the Paxton estate as a separate tax entity? (answer: $363) (*c*) answer parts (*a*) and (*b*) this time assuming a 39.6 percent marginal rate for all survivors (answer: $1,085.60).

6. One of your clients asks you to summarize the advantages and disadvantages of using joint tenancies to avoid probate.

7. Based on problems 7 and 8 in Chapter 8, how much lower will Terry and Chris' capital gain be if:
   a. They lived in a community property state and held title in community property form?
   b. They lived in any state and held the property as equal tenants in common?

8. (*a*) Why should the living trust cost less than the formal probate alternative? (*b*) Are all cost components lower?

9. Wes has just received his lawyer's bill for developing a plan that avoids probate with a living trust. Included is a charge for drafting a will. Did the law firm make a billing mistake?

10. Today Dennis executed a living trust, with his sister as the only remainder beneficiary. Upon driving home from the lawyer's office, Dennis is killed in an auto accident. All of his property is still held in joint tenancy and tenancy in common form with his brother, Elmer. Is there a problem? Why or why not?

11. Evaluate the cost factor in the decision whether or not to avoid *formal* probate with a living trust, under the following assumed set of facts. For the probate alternative: drafting the will, $1,300; formal probate administration, $60,000; other costs at death, including accountants' and appraiser's fees, $2,300.

   For the trust alternative: drafting costs, $2,200; record-keeping until death, $500 per year; nonprobate administration costs at death, $3,100; costs in higher income taxes due to the inability to use a probate estate as a separate taxpayer, $1,000 (assume a one year probate); other costs at death, including accountants' fees, $3,600.

   Also assume an investment rate of return of 10 percent, and that the client will live 12 years. (Answers: Present value of total costs: probate, $21,174; trust, $8,063.)

12. Now evaluate the cost of *informal* probate versus the living trust. Assume all facts given in the problem immediately above, except that informal probate administration will cost $25,000.

13. (*a*) What types of clients are most likely to prefer probate? (*b*) To avoid probate with joint tenancies? (*c*) To avoid probate with the living trust?

14. For each of the following individuals, explain which of the three major types of asset disposition would probably best suit them.

   a. A 19 year old single college student owning only personal effects totaling $6,000.
   b. A former stockbroker who spent two years in prison for securities fraud.
   c. Michael Jackson, the entertainer.
   d. A plumber and his wife who own only a house, two cars and some other personal property. They have two middle aged, financially responsible children.

15. For each of the individuals listed in the question immediately above, invent an additional hypothetical fact or circumstance that would move you to recommend a method of asset disposition *different* from your original choice.

RECOMMENDED READING

Blattmachr, Jonathan G. "The Master Trust," *1989 University of Miami Estate Planning Institute.*

Bostick, Charles D. "The Revocable Trust: A Means of Avoiding Probate in the Small Estate?" *University of Florida Law Review* 21(1968), pp. 44-58.

Brink, Rhonda H. "Planning Perspectives for Creditor-Conscious Clients." *1988 University of Miami Estate Planning Institute.*

*Cornfield, Dave L. "Loving Trusts or Hateful Wills?" *1993 University of Miami Estate Planning Institute.*

Daly, John K. "How Fiduciary Fees Are Determined." *Trusts & Estates*, May 1977, pp. 348-49.

Doussard, Joseph E. "The Effect of the Uniform Probate Code on Estate Administration and Tax Planning." *Estate Planning*, May 1981, pp. 142-44.

Ellwanger, Thomas J. "ERTA Gives New Impetus to the Use of Joint Tenancy in Planning for Gifts and Estates." *Estate Planning*, March 1982, pp. 84-89.

Elzer, Robert W. "Using a Revocable Trust to Minimize Probate Proceedings or Avoid Them Entirely." *Estate Planning*, September 1987, pp. 286-94.

Fetters, Samuel M. "An Invitation to Commit Fraud: Secret Destruction of Joint Tenant Survivorship Rights." *Fordham Law Review*, 1986, pp. 173-202.

Gibner, Allan J. "Effective Use of Probate Procedure Can Ease Administration, Saving Costs and Time." *Estate Planning*, July 1984, pp. 230-34.

Harrison, Louis S. "IRS Rulings Demand More Careful Use of Revocable Trusts to Make Gifts." *Estate Planning*, November, 1990, pp. 332-36.

Johnson, Michael L. "Survivorship Interests with Persons Other than a Spouse: The Costs of Probate Avoidance." *Real Property, Probate And Trust Journal*, 20 (1985), pp. 985-1007. (Discusses problems with joint and survivorship bank accounts.)

*Keydel, Frederick R. "The Revocable Trust Revisited." Fifth Annual Southern California Tax and Estate Planning Forum, 1985.

Kessler, Richard P., and Zoe M. Hicks. "Protecting a Professional Client's Assets from the Potential Claims of Creditors." *Estate Planning*, November 1986, pp. 340-44.

*Keydel, Frederick R. "The Magic Wand of Estate Planning: Converting Joint Property Into Revocable Trust Property." *Probate and Property*, January, 1989, pp. 12-17.

Langbein, John H. "The Nonprobate Revolution and the Future of the Law of Succession." *Harvard Law Review* 97 (1984), pp. 1108-41.

Lynn, Robert J. "Problems with Pour-Over Wills." *Ohio State Law Journal* 47, pp. 47-64.

*Medlin, S. Alan, "Creditors Claims: Traps and Problems." Probate Practice Reporter, Jan, 1989 pp. 1-4.

Mennell, Robert L. "Community Property with Right of Survivorship." *San Diego Law Review* 20(1983), pp. 779-800.

*Miller, Michael P. "Update on Whether to Consider Using a Funded Living Trust to Avoid Probate," *Estate Planning*, May 1989, pp. 140-46.

Moore, Malcolm A. "The Will Regenerate: From Whipping Boy to Workhorse." *The Probate Lawyer* 7 (Summer 1981), pp. 5-48.

*Parks, John Paul. "Varied Duties Face the Successor Trustee of a Revocable Trust." *Estate Planning*, July, 1992, pp. 203-07.

Ruebel, Richard J. "Planning for the Impact of Creditor's Claims against a Client's Non-probate Property." *Estate Planning*, January 1988, pp. 38-42.

*Schmidt, L. William. "How to Fund a Revocable Living Trust Correctly." *Estate Planning*, March, 1993, pp. 67-74.

*Stiegel, Lori A., Lee Norrgard, & Robin Talbert. "Scams in the Marketing and Sale of Living Trusts: A New Fraud for the 1990's." *Clearinghouse Review*, October, 1992, pp. 609-12.

Terrazzano, Jeann R. "Joint Tenancy Is Simple Way of Holding Property but May Not Produce the Best Tax Results." *Taxation for Accountants*, June 1983, pp. 348-51.

Thorne, Jack F. "Form of Joint Ownership Controls Results for Estate and Gift Tax and Income Tax Planning." *Taxation for Lawyers*, March-April 1985, pp. 308-13.

Topolnicki, Denise M. "Which Assets Should Be in Whose Name'?" *Money*, September 1984, pp. 105-10.

Wellman, Richard V. "The Uniform Probate Code: A Possible Answer to Probate Avoidance." *Indiana Law Journal* 44 (1969), pp. 189-205.

*Wells, H. Neal III, "The Check's in the Mail; Creditor's Claims after Tulsa," *Estate Planning, Trust and Probate News*, (publication of the California State Bar), Winter 1989, pp. 1, 14-16.

Winn, Edward B. "The Estate Lawyer: Relic of the Past or Firm Fixture of the Future'?" *Probate Lawyer* 9 (Summer 1983), pp. l-84.

Woodrum, V. L. "A Planner's Guide to Probate." *Financial Planning*, February 1985, pp. 203-7.

Yu, Diane C. "Revocable Trusts as an Alternative to Conservatorships." *California Lawyer* September 1983, pp. 23-26.

−11

Marital Deduction and Bypass Planning: I

OVERVIEW

As we have seen, estate planning embraces numerous goals. For medium size or larger estates, one of the most important goals is to minimize the impact of the federal estate tax at death. Several techniques seek to accomplish FET minimization, including planning with the marital deduction, bypass planning, using lifetime transfers, and freezing the estate. This chapter and Chapter 12 will focus on the first two, deathtime use of the marital deduction and bypass planning to defer or completely eliminate the federal estate tax.[1]

Since 1987, any decedent has been able to transfer as much as $600,000, FET free. Thus, in the family plan that incorporates a simple will, a husband *and* wife with a total estate as high as $600,000 are able to transfer their entire estate outright to their survivors, free of federal tax.

---

1. Lifetime transfers are the subject of Chapters 13 and 14. Freezing the taxable estate as a basic technique was described in Chapter 9. Specific examples of freezing will be found in Chapters 13-16.

EXAMPLE 11-1 Husband (H) owns $600,000 in property and wife (W) owns nothing. Each has a simple will. If their order of death is first H, then W, H will be able to leave his entire estate outright to W, estate tax free. Upon her later death, she can pass the entire amount to her children, tax free. In fact, the children will be able to receive the full $600,000 free of tax, no matter how ownership of the property is divided among the spouses and no matter which spouse dies first. No federal estate tax will be owed at either death because neither spouse will have died owning greater than $600,000, the amount of the exemption equivalent of the unified credit.

Thus, in general, planning to minimize the federal estate tax should be a concern only for families whose total estates are expected to exceed $600,000. However, because of the possibility of lifetime taxable gifts and the likelihood of certain FET deductions, especially administration expenses and debts, estates somewhat different than $600,000 will be transferable at death completely tax free. Thus, more accurately, we will be focusing on those estates having an expected *estate tax base* exceeding the exemption equivalent.

EXAMPLE 11-1A If H's estate in Example 11-1, above, incurred administration expenses of $50,000 and H had made a taxable gift of $40,000 prior to his death, his taxable estate would equal $550,000 and his estate tax base would be $590,000. Thus, there would still be no FET.

Since the material to follow is complex even without these refinements, the remainder of this chapter and all of the next will assume no lifetime gifting, and no deductions except the marital deduction.

EXAMPLE 11-2 Increasing the asset size in Example 11-1 a bit, assume H and W own a family estate of $800,000. Under a simple will arrangement, although the marital deduction will entirely shelter the estate of the first spouse to die from FET, the estate of the second spouse to die will have a gross estate of $800,000 and thus will pay an FET of $75,000, under simple assumptions.

This chapter will focus on planning for these wealthier individuals.

In the following material, we will often refer to the "first spouse to die," and "second spouse to die." To relieve the tedium of excessive wording, let's call these individuals S1 and S2, respectively. Further, let's continue to use FET as a shorthand for federal estate tax. Finally, in most of the discussion that follows, we won't make assumptions about whether the husband or wife dies first. From a tax point of view, the crucial factor is not the sex of the decedent, but wealth of the decedent. However, order of death has, of course, very significant nontax implications. And statistics indicate that there is a 75 percent probability that the wife will outlive the husband an average of 10 years.

Planning to minimize the FET through the use of the marital deduction and the bypass arrangement traditionally involves incorporating at least one of four different planning options, to be described in considerable detail next. They are called the *100 percent marital deduction, credit shelter bypass, bypass with estate equalization*, and the *100 percent marital deduction with disclaimer into bypass*. The reader should keep in mind that these options do not depict precise will or trust arrangements; instead they conceptually help trace the overall *flow of property values* to descendants, and represent the net financial consequences of most estate plans. Each of these four plans can be implemented with a will or a trust instrument, and most plans will incorporate the establishment of from one to three separate trusts after S1's death. Material at the end of Chapter 12 will detail the structure of some actual plans.

PLANNING OPTION 1: 100 PERCENT MARITAL DEDUCTION

One way to eliminate entirely the FET on all property owned by S1 at death is to leave all of it to S2. It will be sheltered by the unlimited marital deduction. Types of transfers by an S1 to an S2 that will qualify for the marital deduction include all outright transfers such as the transfer in Example 11-2, automatic right of survivorship when title is held in joint tenancy solely by the spouses, insurance on S1's life payable to S2, and, as we shall see in Chapter 12, several types of transfers in trust for the benefit of S2.

Advantages of the 100 Percent Marital Deduction

The 100 percent marital deduction is attractive to many clients who do not wish to burden an S2 with paying any avoidable *taxes at the first death*. And it can be a simple plan, easy to understand and inexpensive to establish. For example, the preparation of a *simple will* ordinarily will meet the objective of a zero FET for S1. And, as implied above, even *joint tenancy* ownership of property solely between husband and wife or *tenancy by the entirety* will produce a full marital deduction for S1's share.

Finally, the 100 percent marital deduction can confer on S2 *total dispositive control* over all of the family property. For example, the outright receipt of a *fee simple interest* will enable S2 to do anything with the property, including totally possess it, consume it, gift it, and exercise any other rights permitted such an owner.

Not all 100 percent marital deduction plans need to confer full dispositive control, however. We will see in Chapter 12 that certain nonoutright transfers for the benefit of S2 can restrict his or her control over the property and still qualify for the marital deduction. One commonly used technique is the transfer of qualified terminable interest property into a QTIP trust.

Disadvantages of the 100 Percent Marital Deduction

For medium to larger size estates, the 100 percent unlimited marital deduction has several significant drawbacks.

Higher total FET. First, and perhaps most important is a higher total FET. While the entire S1 estate will be sheltered by the S1 marital deduction, it will ordinarily pass outright to S2, and thus will be subject to inclusion in S2's gross estate, barring remarriage or a program of gifting or consumption.

> EXAMPLE 11-3 H and W own a family estate of $2 million with each owning one half. Assuming simple wills, upon S1's death there will be no FET, inasmuch as the entire $1 million passing to S2 will be sheltered by the marital deduction. However, assuming that S2 doesn't remarry and neither transfers nor consumes the property prior to death, S2's $2 million taxable estate will be subject to an FET of $588,000.

Under federal transfer tax law, even a *nonoutright transfer* by S1 that qualifies for the marital deduction will be includable in the S2 gross estate. An example is a transfer into a QTIP trust. The universal rule in this area is that, barring remarriage, gifting, or consumption, any property qualifying for the S1 marital deduction will inexorably be includable in the S2 gross estate.

In effect, complete use of the unlimited marital deduction will only *defer* the FET, not eliminate it. And because it fails to take advantage of the unified credit in the estate of S1, 100 percent marital deduction planning can have the effect of "over qualifying" or overusing the marital deduction, resulting in "loading up" of the taxable estate of S2, and later subjecting a greater amount to tax at the second death. And due to the progressive transfer tax rate structure, an even greater FET will result from subjecting the entire property to taxation at S2's death. Example 11-3 illustrated a situation that has both these effects.

May not avoid probate. Another disadvantage of the 100 percent marital deduction planning option is the possibility that more family assets will be subject to probate, and therefore to creditor's claims, while they reside in S2's probate estate. However, this will happen only if both S1 and S2 dispose of the property by will rather than by a will substitute.

Three Impractical Alternatives to a Bypass

For many wealthier individuals, the major deterrent to using the 100 percent marital deduction is the FET cost at S2's death. The second option, discussed shortly, called the credit shelter bypass, is the most common method used to reduce this cost. Before examining it, let's first touch on three simpler, though not usually practical, alternatives to a bypass that could work with the 100 percent marital deduction option to defer or reduce the FET for S2.

Remarriage. First, S2, having received all of S1's property outright, could anticipate remarrying and leaving the entire estate to the new spouse, S3, enabling the family to again secure the shelter of the marital deduction.

There are three problems with the anticipation of remarriage as a planning device. First, there is no assurance that it will occur. Demographically, the *odds are against it*. Second, an outright transfer from S2 to S3 may not be desirable, especially if the marriage occurred recently, because our former S2 would often have less than complete assurance that S3 would leave the property to *survivors* who are acceptable to S2, usually the children of the S1-S2 marriage. To solve this disposition problem, our S2 could create a more complex 100 percent marital deduction plan that would leave the estate in a QTIP trust (described in greater detail in Chapters 12 and 18), with income payable to the new spouse for life and the remainder to S2's chosen survivors. The property would become "qualified terminable interest property" (QTIP), resulting in a marital deduction for S2's estate. However, the tax laws covering qualified terminable interest property require that it must be taxed as if it were includable in the surviving spouse's (here, S3's) gross estate.

This last point brings up the third drawback to remarriage as a planning solution. Whether S2 leaves the property outright to S3 or in a QTIP trust, the property will still eventually be *taxed* once at the parent level (S3) before it is received by the younger-generation beneficiaries.

In conclusion, planning to take advantage of a possible remarriage may delay somewhat the FET on the parents' property until the new surviving spouse dies, but it will not reduce or eliminate it. And, of course, there is no assurance that a remarriage will occur. Finally, the assumption of remarriage creates a potential, though surmountable, problem of an undesirable disposition.

Consumption. A second simple yet often improbable method of deferring or reducing the S2 FET in the context of a 100 percent marital deduction is for S2 to plan to consume the property. Substantial consumption will in fact reduce the tax because it effectively depletes the estate. But expecting S2 to carry this out is usually unrealistic because old habits die hard. People grow accustomed to a standard of living and usually feel uncomfortable spending a great deal more. Also, clients usually want to pass on all or most of their wealth to their survivors, not deplete it. Moreover, they may need the extra feeling of security that accompanies the act of continued ownership of the bulk of their wealth until death. Finally, an older client might find it downright impossible to consume the estate, especially an illiquid one, in such a short period of time. For all of these reasons, substantial consumption is not usually a realistic expectation.

Lifetime gifting. As an alternative to remarriage or consumption, S2 could make lifetime gifts of the property, reducing the estate tax base to less than $600,000. For some clients, particularly those with larger estates, this is an ideal solution. Yet many clients will be reluctant, for the same reasons, to make the sizable lifetime transfers needed to substantially reduce a future FET. Lifetime gifting is the subject of Chapter 13, and for an extended discussion, with examples, of the use of interspousal gifts to reduce FET, see the section on 'gifts to the spouse' in that chapter. Thus, such gifts need not be discussed further here. As mentioned earlier, in this and the next chapter, we will assume that S2 will not make significant lifetime gifts.

We turn now to the most preferred method of reducing the S2 FET.

PLANNING OPTION 2: CREDIT SHELTER BYPASS

The credit shelter bypass is usually a more desirable method of reducing the FET for S2 than is a 100 percent marital deduction for S1, combined with S2 remarriage, consumption, or lifetime gifting. Unlike remarriage, it can truly reduce the FET, not just defer it. And unlike consumption and lifetime gifting, it does not require a significant disposition of the family estate before the death of S2.

A common version of the credit shelter bypass originates with a death-time transfer by S1, under which S2 is left, by formula, an amount equal to S1's entire estate, reduced by $600,000, the amount of the exemption equivalent of the federal unified credit.[2] The will or trust defines the marital and bypass amounts by a more complex formula designed to take account of the influence of other factors besides the unified credit, such as the deduction for debts and administration expenses and the credit for state death taxes. We will ignore these complications in the present section but will discuss them in general in the last section of this chapter. Since the $600,000 is not received by S2, it will not become part of S2's gross estate at death even if

---

2. For additional details, see the Covey book and the Bertels/Yudenfreund article cited at the end of Chapter 12.

it appreciates between the deaths of S1 and S2. The amount, even the amount in excess of $600,000, is said to *bypass* the S2 estate. This plan will reduce or, possibly, eliminate the S2 FET, without subjecting the S1 estate to any tax. S1's estate will incur no FET because the portion of S1's estate passing to S2 will be sheltered by the marital deduction, and the portion not passing to S2 will be sheltered by the unified credit.

> EXAMPLE 11-4 As in Example 11-3, H and W own a family estate of $2 million, with each owning one half. However, instead of a simple will in which S1 would have left all property to S2, assume that S1's will leaves only $400,000 (S1's estate reduced by $600,000) to the spouse. S1's estate will still incur no FET, since $400,000 will be sheltered by the marital deduction, and the other $600,000 will be sheltered by the unified credit. Yet the expected FET for S2's estate tax base (of $1.4 million) will be reduced from $588,000 to $320,000, a saving of $268,000.
> Here are the FET calculations for the S1 and S2 estates:

	S1	S2
Gross estate	$1,000,000.	$1,400,000.
Less deductions	400,000.	0.
Estate tax base	600,000.	1,400,000.
Tentative estate tax	192,800.	512,800.
Unified credit	192,800.	192,800.
FET	$0.	$320,000.

Thus, under the credit shelter bypass option, S2's estate will be loaded up less than it would have been had the 100 percent marital deduction option been chosen. This option enables the estate of *each spouse* to take advantage of the unified credit, rather than denying it to the S1 taxable estate. In the language of the trade, this option will more efficiently "zero out" or "reduce to zero" the S1 FET, and there will be "two trips up the rate ladder," rather than one.

In Example 11-4, S2 received $600,000 less of S1's estate. The reader may ask at this point, is it really worth saving $268,000 in FET if the transfer requires that S2 lose the right to receive $600,000, especially in view of the fact that the tax saving will not occur until both spouses have passed away? Surprisingly, the answer is usually yes, for reasons developed next.

Bypass Trust[3]

The bypass plan often works because the disposition to someone other than S2 can be arranged to conform to both S1's overall objectives and S2's desires. The bypass property could be transferred to those individuals who, besides S2, are also sometimes described as "the natural objects of (S2's) bounty." Usually, these individuals are the children of the S1-S2 marriage. As a potential S2, neither spouse will usually object to naming his or her children to be the bypass recipients since in all likelihood, these children would have been chosen to ultimately receive the entire family estate under a simple will plan.

Bypass share: outright or in trust. S1 and S2 might, however, have strong *reservations* about the bypass plan if, at S1's death, it gave rise to an immediate, *outright* transfer to the children. They may feel that the children may be too young to receive that amount of property. Or S2 may need either the income from the property, or the property itself, for support. Or S2 might prefer to retain control over the management of those assets ultimately intended for the children. These are common and legitimate objections to the use of an immediate, outright transfer to the children to effect a bypass. Happily, the bypass can be readily salvaged and these objections overcome by means of a transfer into *trust*.

What the trusts are called. Used in the context of bypass planning, a trust can take on at least two somewhat different names. In general, when incorporated in a plan to bypass S2's gross estate, it is called a *bypass trust*. More specifically, when the amount included in the bypass trust is set equal or nearly equal to $600,000, the amount of the exemption equivalent of the unified credit, it is called a *credit shelter bypass trust*, *credit shelter trust*, or simply a *credit trust*. In planning the will or trust instrument for division of the estate property into the bypass and the marital share, attorneys will usually choose one of two types of disposition clauses, providing for what are called pecuniary and fractional share bequests. As mentioned in Chapter 2, under a *pecuniary bequest*, complete interests in specific assets will pass to one or the other share. Under a *fractional share bequest*, both bypass and marital shares will receive a fractional interest in each and every asset in the estate. Factors in deciding which type of provision to use include expected estate and income taxes.[4]

---

3. For a summary comparison of the taxation of the bypass trust versus other popular trusts in estate planning, see Table 17-1 in Chapter 17.

4. The rules are complicated, for a discussion, see the Cornfeld paper and the Covey book cited at the end of Chapter 12.

A bypass trust is also known as a *nonmarital trust* to relate it to and distinguish it from the marital trust, to be described in Chapter 12. It is also sometimes called a *family trust*.

Bypass trust overcomes nontax problems only. Used in lieu of an outright transfer of the bypass share to the children, however, the trust does not save one additional cent of FET. The same saving could be achieved by an outright transfer of property to them. Instead, the bypass trust vehicle is employed to overcome some major *nontax* problems inherent in outright transfers to children, some of which were just mentioned. The trust arrangement attempts to solve those problems in a number of ways, described next.

Immaturity. First, if at S1's (or S2's) death the children are too young to properly handle an outright transfer, the trustee can be directed to manage the property until they are considered sufficiently mature. And the inclusion of a spendthrift provision can further protect against the consequences of beneficiary immaturity. However, younger beneficiaries often mature at rates different from those assumed by trust provisions. Thus, a trust providing for outright distribution of the remainder when a child attains age 30 could encourage dependence, and, not too subtly, convey to the child that mom and dad seriously believed that the child is not capable of managing his or her own affairs until then. The upshot is that these trust provisions only partly solve the problem of immaturity.

Income and principal for S2. Second, if S2 needs funding from the trust for support, the trust could be (and usually is) made to last at least until S2's death, for example, during which time S2 could enjoy a life estate in part or all of the *income* earned by the trust. Further, S2 could be granted a power of appointment to invade the *principal* of the trust for certain needs. Recall from Chapter 6 that a power to invade for the benefit of the holder, which is limited by an "ascertainable standard," will not be taxed as a general power of appointment. Hence, S2 could have the right to invade for his or her benefit for reasons of "health, education, support, or maintenance," without subjecting the property to inclusion in S2's gross estate.

A provision allowing the trustee to distribute principal on the basis of support to an individual whom the trustee is *obligated to support* (e.g., minor child and, in some states, the spouse) will cause the trust principal to be included in the trustee's gross estate under §2041, and if this power is actually exercised, a gift results.[5]

---

5. For details, see the Stout article cited at the end of Chapter 12 and Reg. §20.2041-1(c).

The words "health," "education," "support," and "maintenance" are carefully chosen from the code and the IRS Regulations under §2041. Careful draftsmen purposely avoid including other, non-"safe harbor" terms, such as "any other special need," "in any way she may deem proper," "comfort," "welfare," "convenience," "emergency,"[6] and "happiness." In one case, however, the clause "...required for the (decedent's) continued comfort..." was held to be subject to an ascertainable standard because it implied the level of the decedent's accustomed standard of living.[7] Unfortunately, mental or physical incapacity of the trustee, or resignation by S2 as trustee of a poorly worded trust will not solve the problem. S2 will be considered to have made a gift by releasing a general power of appointment over the property. And as a trust income beneficiary, S2, at death, will be considered to have made a §2036 transfer with a retained life estate. Happily, some states have added statutes limiting a trustee to conduct governed by the Code's ascertainable standard, unless the instrument clearly indicates a broader power. Such a statute might eliminate the threat of §2041.[8]

S2 as trustee. Third, the trust will often be preferable to an outright transfer if S2 wishes to *manage* the property during his or her lifetime. S2 could be named trustee of the bypass trust, without adverse FET consequences.

However, granting S2 other powers can be risky.[9] Alternatively, naming an "independent" party, such as a bank, to be trustee can enhance flexibility by giving the trustee greater freedom to distribute trust principal and income without adverse income, gift, and estate tax consequences. For example, an independent trustee could distribute corpus to S2 for his or her "happiness" without risking inclusion of the trust corpus in S2's gross estate.

S2 as surrogate decision maker. Fourth, besides having a limited power to invade and the power to act as trustee, S2 could also be given certain other powers over the bypass trust. S2 could be given a nongeneral power of appointment to dispose of the assets to certain *third parties* during lifetime

---

6. For a discussion of some other perils in using the word "emergency," see the Schlenger article cited at the end of Chapter 12.

7. *Vissering* 990 F. 2d 578 (CA-10, 1993).

8. See LR 9203047 for a favorable interpretation of Calif. Probate Code §16,081(b).

9. For a good general discussion of the tax risks in granting S2 too much trustee power, see the Stout article cited at the end of Chapter 12.

or at death. Thus, S2 may be given the power to appoint anyone except S2, S2's estate, S2's creditors, or the creditors of S2's estate. For example, S2 could be granted the power to determine the amount of property each child should receive, and when each should receive it, perhaps long after S1's death. Or S2 could be permitted to leave some or all of it to charity. In this way, S1 would be giving S2, as surrogate decision maker, the opportunity to respond, perhaps long after S1's death, to changed circumstances.

"Five and five" power for S2. Fifth, another power that S2 could be granted over the bypass trust is the right for any reason to withdraw the greater of $5,000 or 5 percent of the corpus each year. This "five and five" power adds some flexibility to bypass planning, without subjecting the value of the corpus to inclusion in S2's gross estate as property subject to a general power of appointment. However, S2's gross estate will include the value of the lapsed, unexercised right in the year of death. In addition, the IRS takes the position that §678(a)(2) of the Code makes an increasing amount of trust *income* taxable to the power holder, to the extent that the annual powers are continuously permitted to lapse.[10]

S2 discretion over income distribution. Sixth, in circumstances where S2 does not need the income from the bypass trust, S2 could also be given the power of discretion over distribution of the trust income. Called a *discretionary bypass trust*, it offers greater flexibility and can save income taxes if, for example, the children are in a lower tax bracket than S2. However, the discretionary trust has some significant tax traps and must be planned carefully.

Finally, in most situations, only the use of a trust can permit flexible generation skipping tax planning. An outright (nontrust) gift to a child will likely result in the imposition of an FET on the gift property when it passes to the grandchild, at the death of the child. Alternatively, with careful GSTT planning, a gift in trust naming the grandchildren as remaindermen will enable all or at least a significant amount of the gift assets to skip this second FET and the GSTT. And naming the child to be income beneficiary of the trust can help provide for the child's financial security. The last section in the next chapter will discuss generation skipping bypass planning in considerable detail.

For these and other nontax reasons, planners usually implement bypass planning with a trust.

---

10. For details, see the Adams article cited at the end of Chapter 8.

PLANNING OPTION 3: BYPASS WITH ESTATE EQUALIZATION

Although the credit shelter bypass can totally eliminate the S1 FET, and can reduce the S2 FET, it may not succeed in minimizing the combined FET for both deaths. To illustrate, consider the effect of reducing the marital deduction in Example 11-4 by $1. Notice that S1's estate has a marginal tax rate of 37 percent (taxable estate of $600,000) and S2 has a marginal tax rate of 43 percent (taxable estate of $ 1.4 million). Consequently, reducing the S1 marital deduction to $399,999 should, other things the same, increase the S1 FET by 37 cents and reduce the S2 FET by 43 cents, resulting in a net savings of 6 cents, or 6 percent of the reduction. Similarly, reducing the S1 marital deduction by a greater amount should continue to yield a net saving until the point is reached where the marginal tax rates are equal. At that point, the combined FET for both S1 and S2 will be lowest.

> EXAMPLE 11-5 As in Examples 11-3 and 11-4, H and W own a family estate of $2 million, with each owning one half. Instead of leaving all or some proper- ty to the spouse, as in the examples above, assume that S1 plans to leave noth- ing to S2. Instead, S1 bequeaths his or her entire $1 million estate, outright or in trust, to the children, via bypass. S1's FET will be $153,000, the net tax on a $1 million taxable estate with no marital deduction. S2's FET will also be $153,000, because S2's taxable estate will also be $1 million. S1 and S2's combined FET will be $306,000, which is $14,000 less than the amount calcu- lated in Example 11-4, using the credit shelter bypass option.

In the above example, reducing the S1 marital deduction to zero had the effect of *equalizing the taxable estates* of S1 and S2, consequently equaliz- ing the marginal tax rates and thereby minimizing the combined tax for both spouses.

Making several simplifying assumptions, the determination of the amount of the marital deduction needed to equalize the taxable estates for S1 and S2 can be arrived at with the following formula:

S1 taxable estate = S2 taxable estate

S1 gross estate - S1 marital deduction = Property presently owned by S2 + S1 marital deduction

Solving for Example 11-5,

$1 million - marital deduction = $1 million + marital deduction
2 x marital deduction = $0
marital deduction = $0

This formula is crude, however; it does not take into account many specific factors, such as the presence of other estate tax deductions and certain credits. Its value lies mostly in helping to develop a numerical sketch of the plan for clients. Yet, given most clients' limited ability to absorb excessive detail, it should be more than sufficient in most situations.

This third option, bypass with estate equalization, seeks to minimize total FET by means of a bypass which attempts to equalize both spouses' total taxable estates and marginal tax rates.

To summarize options 1, 2, and 3, consider the illustrations in Figure 11-1. For each option, circles represent property held in an estate. For example, in option 2, which illustrates the facts described in Example 11-4, S1 dies owning $1 million in property. S1's estate will incur no FET, and thus $400,000 will pass to S2 and $600,000 will pass to the bypass share. S2 will then die owning an estate of $1.4 million, which will incur an FET of $320,000. The children will receive $1,680,000, representing $1,080,000 from S2 and $600,000 from the bypass share.

The last two options described above, credit shelter bypass and bypass with estate equalization, demonstrate the trade-off the planner and client must face. The former seeks to *defer* the FET as much as possible, at the possible cost of a greater total tax, while the latter, by equalizing the taxable estates, seeks to *equalize* the two marginal tax rates and thereby minimize the total tax, at the cost of a greater S1 tax. Some commentators simply call this the trade-off between estate tax deferral and estate tax equalization.

Factors Influencing Deferral versus Equalization

In deciding between deferral and equalization, we must keep in mind the client's goals. If a major goal is simply to save as much S2 FET as possible while not incurring a single penny of S1 FET, then equalization is not possible and the plan must usually seek full deferral by means of the credit shelter bypass. On the other hand, if a primary goal is to minimize the combined effect of both estate taxes, then attempts at equalization may be practical. Finally, if a major goal is to maximize the amount passing to the next generation, equalization may or may not be more efficient, depending on the effect of the time value of money and rates of asset appreciation, discussed further shortly. Thus, the choice of a bypass planning strategy will depend partly on the client's specific FET reduction goal. Some of the factors that will influence these goals are explored next.

FIGURE 11-1 Illustration of Planning Options 1, 2 and 3 (no asset appreciation)

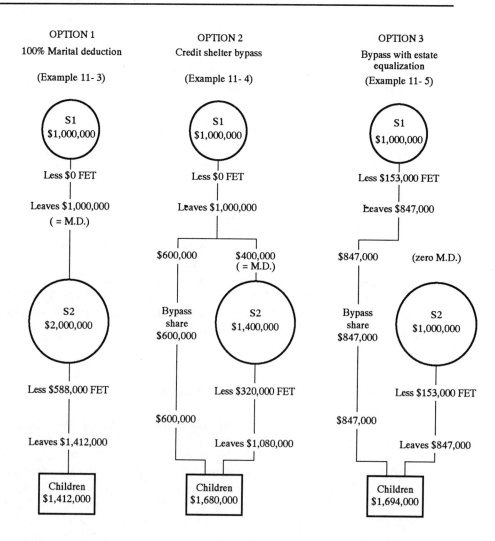

Avoidance of tax while spouses are alive. A factor that often motivates spouses to defer, i.e., to choose the goal of minimizing S2's FET subject to the requirement of a zero S1 FET, is a strong opposition to incurring any avoidable taxes during their lifetimes. Other reasons include the hope that the FET is eventually repealed or reduced, and the anticipation that S2, during lifetime, may consume or gift the estate assets. These factors favor deferral but do not rule out a bypass of the credit shelter amount.

Time value of money and asset appreciation. Some clients may be willing to incur an S1 FET, provided that significant offsetting benefits will result. Example 11-5 demonstrated how equalization can lower the combined S1-S2 FET. However, that arrangement may be financially inefficient, due to the effect of the time value of money. In that example, we saw that equalization by means of reducing S1's marital deduction to zero resulted in a total tax saving of $14,000. However, the cost of this result was to tax S1's estate by $153,000 more than the amount taxed to S1 by deferral. The opportunity income loss of $153,000 invested at even only five percent will be far greater than the $14,000 FET eventually saved. At a 5 percent after-tax rate of return, assuming that S2 survived S1 by 10 years, this represents a cumulative *opportunity income loss* in 10 years of $96,221. Stated differently, Option 2, credit shelter bypass, enabled the $153,000 FET not incurred at S1's death to accumulate $96,221 of income at the end of ten years. The analysis in Figure 11-2, presented shortly, illustrates this loss, allowing all family owned assets to appreciate by 5 percent per year. Surprisingly, the results actually favor paying the S1 FET (equalization) since the opportunity income loss is more than offset by the S2 FET saved by not subjecting a larger and growing bypass to S2 FET. This last point concerns the effect of *asset appreciation* on the S2 FET. It is reasonable to assume that family assets will grow in value after the death of S1 due to the combined influence of inflation and real capital appreciation. This growth will generate a larger S2 taxable estate, and greater deferral will make it even larger. Alternatively, increased equalization will result in a greater bypass and thereby reduce the S2 buildup. Hence, the expectation of greater asset appreciation justifies greater equalization by means of a larger bypass.

Yet actual client asset appreciation may not turn out to be as large as one might anticipate. Certain items may not appreciate significantly, particularly if they are high income-generating assets designed to be *distributed* on an ongoing basis to S2. Two examples would be bonds and public utility stocks. In such case, deferral may be favored over equalization, as the opportunity income loss from early payment of the FET may more than offset a modest additional bypass of modestly appreciating assets.

FIGURE 11-2 Illustration of Planning Options 1, 2 and 3 (5% asset appreciation)

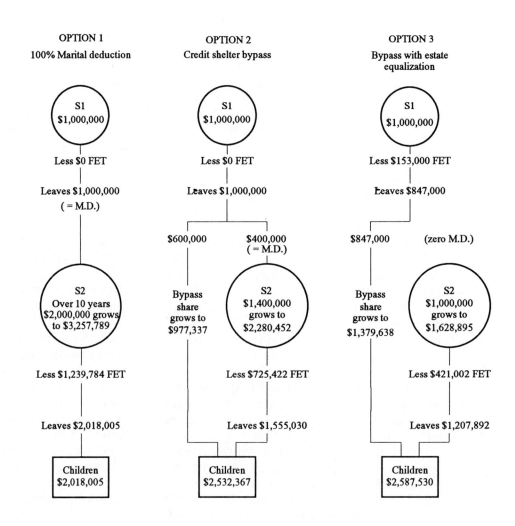

Thus, in conclusion, proper planning must consider the effect of the time value of money and rate of asset appreciation, since a substantial opportunity income loss from the early payment of the transfer tax may favor deferral, while greater asset appreciation may favor equalization. Which force should prevail will depend on factors such as rates of return and inflation, how long S2 survives S1, the composition of the client's assets, and whether income from the marital share must be distributed to S2.

Numerical illustration of effect of asset appreciation. To adequately reflect the influence of opportunity income loss and asset appreciation on the estate plan, clients must adopt the goal of maximizing the amount *passing to the next generation*, rather than minimizing the combined estate taxes. To see the effects of the time value of money on the amount that can pass to the next generation, refer to the illustrations in Figure 11-2, which assume that the family estate assets will appreciate an average of 5 percent a year during the assumed 10-year span between S1's and S2's death. Otherwise, the same initial estate sizes and plans incorporated in Examples 11-3, 11-4, and 11-5, and shown in Figure 11-1, are used.

Several conclusions can be drawn. First, appreciation will increase substantially the net amount passing to the children for all three plans. Second, compared to Option 1, Option 2, the credit shelter bypass, still results in a large FET saving for S2 and thus generates a much larger net transfer to the children. Third, Option 3, bypass with reduced marital deduction, still beats Option 2 in terms of the total amount passing to the children. Appreciation apparently increases Option 3's relative advantage from $14,000 to $55,163. In summary, the opportunity income loss on the S1 FET of $153,000 is more than offset by the gain from the S2 FET saving resulting from a complete bypass.

This illustration has assumed equal appreciation of all assets after S1's death. One page earlier, however, we saw one reason why certain assets may not, in fact, appreciate much. In general, assets such as cash and debt do not appreciate a great deal, while other, "hot" assets such as closely held business interests and life insurance policies can be expected to appreciate significantly. Planning to maximize the net amount passing to the children would suggest first funding the marital share with low growth assets and the bypass share with high growth assets, to avoid inclusion of this appreciation in S2's gross estate. Funding the bypass share with hot assets can greatly leverage the use of S1's unified credit.

Other factors. At least four other factors influence the choice of deferring or equalizing, in light of the client's goals.

Large estate size. First, truly large estates may gain little from equalization. FET rates peak at 55 percent for all amounts $3 million and higher. Thus, as long as the estate of the less wealthy spouse is expected to equal or exceed $3 million, both spouses' marginal tax rates will always be equal, no matter what their respective estate sizes.[11]

Liquidity. Second, liquidity can be a concern. The choice of greater deferral reduces the liquidity problem at S1's death. In the extreme case, complete elimination of S1's FET will eliminate what constitutes the typical medium- and larger-size estate's greatest cash need. Methods of meeting liquidity needs will be discussed in detail in Chapter 15.

Basis step-up. Third, in considering whether to defer or to equalize, the planner should consider the benefits of the step-up in basis received by all property included in the S2 estate. Complete use of the marital deduction under planning Option 1 will maximize the property subject to this adjustment. Use of the credit shelter bypass will result in a step-up, at S2's death, of *less* property (all of S2's assets owned at death, which include all but $600,000 of S1's assets). Equalization through the use of a substantially reduced marital deduction will further reduce the amount subject to an S2 step-up. Since bypass property will not be stepped-up at S2's death, income tax basis rules favor deferral, rather than equalization through bypass.

Unspent S2 income. Fourth, the prospect of unspent S2 income favors greater equalization. Up to now, we have assumed that S2 does not save any portion of the income earned on family assets. After S1's death, any income saved will, of course, likely increase the gross estate and FET of S2. This consideration is especially important for larger estates owned by relatively frugal clients.

Deferral versus equalization: one rule of thumb. In conclusion, when deciding whether to defer or to equalize, although generalization is difficult, practitioners have developed a rough rule of thumb essentially based on the time value of money considerations discussed above: Equalization should be seriously considered if either the assumed surviving spouse is not expected to live very long or if the estates contain relatively

---

11. For a discussion of bypass planning for the large estate, see the Parker article cited at the end of Chapter 12.

large amounts of highly appreciating property. Elderly clients with prosperous family businesses are prime candidates for consideration. In some cases, the size of the FET savings with equalization can be so large that one commentator, Owen Fiore, has described the marital deduction for them to be a "fraud," deferring payment of the tax to a time when asset values and the tax rate stand to be far higher. Otherwise, deferral will probably be more desirable.

How Frequently Are The Plans Being Used?

In our discussions of bypass planning so far, we have examined the various factors that influence the choice to defer with a larger marital deduction or to equalize with a larger bypass. At this point, the reader might wonder what plans clients are actually using. Based on the results of a survey of experienced estate planning attorneys conducted by this author, the credit shelter bypass plan is by far the most popular strategy of the three, with 88.1 percent of those clients having a potential estate tax liability electing that plan. Equalization with a larger bypass and a plan involving a 100 percent marital deduction accounts for the remaining 11.8 percent, divided fairly equally between the two. Thus, the overwhelming majority of clients seem to prefer a bypass, but only as long as the plan generates no S1 FET. Supporting the results of this survey is an informal poll taken in May, 1992, at a leading estate planning institute. One speaker determined from a show of hands that only about one percent of an audience of 400 experienced estate planners have had more than five clients who were willing to pay an FET at the first death. In addition to these three options, a few clients are selecting a fourth option, which will be described at the beginning of Chapter 12.

QUESTIONS AND PROBLEMS

1. What is the largest estate size that an *individual* can transfer, FET free, with a *simple will* to (*a*) a spouse; (*b*) all other individuals? Explain, and state any assumptions made.

2. (*a*) Under simple assumptions, what is the largest family estate size that a *husband and wife* can transfer, FET free, with *simple wills* to their children? (*b*) Does it make any difference how much is owned by each spouse? Explain.

3. (*a*) Under simple assumptions, what is the largest family estate size that a *husband and wife* can transfer to their children, FET free, with a *credit shelter bypass plan*? (*b*) Does it make any difference how much is owned by each spouse? Explain.

4. In this question, assume that H owns $1 million in property and W owns nothing to speak of, and at the moment we are planning for the possibility that H will survive W.
   a. Why won't the credit shelter bypass arrangement work?
   b. What is the minimum amount of property that either spouse as S1 must own to take full advantage of that bypass?
   c. Can you think of any device that will make the bypass work in this situation? Perhaps one with an income tax advantage, as well?
   d. Regarding the device in part *c*, how much should be involved?

5. A client asks you to describe the advantages of the 100 percent marital deduction.

6. How can each of the following defer or reduce the FET for S2: (*a*) remarriage; (*b*) consumption. Explain the drawbacks to each as an estate planning device.

7. How does the credit shelter bypass plan help overcome the limitations of the two strategies mentioned in Question 6?

8. (*a*) In selecting the amount of property to place into the bypass share, what factors should be considered? (*b*) Must this amount be precisely specified prior to S1's death?

9. H and W have come to you to help them do some FET planning. They own a family estate of $3 million in individually owned property, with H owning two thirds. Presently they have simple wills. Calculate the amount which, under simple assumptions, will pass to their children under the following plans: (*a*) the present arrangement with the 100 percent marital deduction; (*b*) a credit shelter bypass; (*c*) bypass with estate equalization. Be sure to do your calculations twice, reflecting a reversal in the order of deaths. Assume no appreciation, that the first death will occur this year and the second death ten years later, and that all FET will be paid out of the nonmarital share. (One answer: Under equalization, if H dies first: children will receive $2,274,000.) What conclusions can be drawn'?

10. Again regarding Question 9, could H and W wind up having very different plans? Why or why not?

11. (*a*) Rework parts *a*, *b* and *c* of Question 9, assuming that between the first and second deaths all property doubles in value. (*b*) What conclusions can be drawn?

12. (*a*) What factors help determine whether a bypass should entail an outright transfer or a transfer into trust? (*b*) Is FET savings a factor? Why or why not?

13. (*a*) Based on the facts in question 9 (part *a*), how much will pass to H's children and W's children with *no planning* if H and W die (H predeceases W by 10 years) with no will under the following alternative assumptions:
    1. H and W are survived by three minor children, all of whom are the natural children of both of them. (Note: if you have already done question 9*a*, obtaining this answer will be simple if you are in a UPC state).
    2. H and W are survived by three minor children: one child: A, who is the natural child of H and W, and also by two other children: B, who is H's child by a former marriage; and C, who is W's child by a former marriage. Assume no stepparent adoptions. Assume the intestate succession laws of your state, if available, or those of the UPC. A careful analysis of the sections may be necessary to determine inheritance shares. Be sure to indicate how much each child will inherit after payment of any FET. Assume that all FET will be paid, pro rata, only out of the shares actually subject to FET.
    (*b*)Why is this outcome not as satisfactory as that with a credit

shelter bypass trust?

14. Without making any additional calculations, estimate how your answers to and recommendations for question 9 would change under the following alternative assumptions:
  a. H and W own property worth ten times as much.
  b Both H and W are uninsurable.
  c. All major assets owned by H are rapidly appreciating, and H and W's children may wish to sell some of them immediately after W's later death.
  d. S2 does not want and will not need any income from the S1 estate assets.
  e. Same appreciation in asset values, but a greater time value of money (discount rates increase).

RECOMMENDED READING

(Please refer to the end of Chapter 12 for Recommended Readings.)

Marital Deduction and Bypass Planning: II

————————————————————

OVERVIEW

This chapter continues our discussion of marital deduction and bypass planning. We begin with a fourth popular planning option, one using a disclaimer. Next, we'll focus on the marital trust, and then we'll cover a brief case study in marital deduction and bypass planning. The chapter concludes with an examination of bypass plans involving nonimmediate family members, with emphasis on the impact of the generation-skipping transfer tax on marital deduction and bypass planning.

PLANNING OPTION 4: 100 PERCENT MARITAL DEDUCTION WITH DISCLAIMER INTO BYPASS

Clients often fail to properly revise wills and other planning documents when necessary. Too often, facts and circumstances change substantially between the date those documents are drafted and the date of the client's death. Yet the decedent's immediate, predeath, *verbal* desires or apparent wishes must be legally disregarded. The law requires that the terms of the documents themselves, however dated, be strictly observed to control asset transfer. For example, if Congress substantially reduced (increased) FET rates just after a potential S1 developed a plan that incorporated a credit shelter bypass, the bypass might become less (more) desirable. Under the changed circumstances, the clients might prefer to transfer, at death, more (less) property outright to S2 rather than to the bypass share. Yet unless the documents were revised prior to S1's death, this modification would not be possible. However, the provision in U.S. law for a disclaimer makes a constructive revision after death entirely possible.

Anticipating a disclaimer, instead of mandating a reduced marital deduction, the client could specify in the document that all property shall pass to the surviving spouse, except that amount which S2 validly disclaims, which will instead be directed to pass to the bypass share.[1] This would permit S2 to decide just how much equalization to arrange. The disclaimer would thus offer the estate plan an additional degree of flexibility, giving surrogate decision maker S2, just after S1's death, a second look at the entire family and legal situation.

Disadvantages

The use of Option 4, 100 percent marital deduction with disclaimer into bypass, has some drawbacks.

Emotional burden. First, the 100 percent marital deduction with disclaimer into bypass is a complex plan with which unsophisticated, grieving survivors may not be capable of dealing. During this difficult time, they might choose to do nothing. The wishes of an S1 who felt strongly about the benefits of the bypass could be completely frustrated by an S2 who elected to do nothing. S2 might be unable to understand the meaning of a bypass or, in a period of insecurity, might feel emotionally unwilling to "jeopardize my financial security." By default, failure to disclaim would result in a 100 percent marital deduction, which, as we have learned, invariably results in a larger S2 FET. Imposing on a grieving S2 this additional burden of having to decide whether or not to disclaim within nine months of the death of

---

1. In reality, since the effect of any valid disclaimer is to treat the disclaimant (here, S2) as having predeceased the decedent (here, S1), the document need only contain a standard survival clause [eg., *"If...(S2)... fails to survive me..., then I leave _____ to (the bypass share)...."*]. Directly referring to a disclaimer is not essential.

his/her spouse can also result in a hasty decision, additional pressure on S2, and conflicts between S2 and other survivors.

Loss of dispositive control by S1. Another drawback to Option 4 is that S1 must relinquish some or all ability to influence the manner of disposition of his or her property, particularly after the death of S2. For example, if S1 had created a bypass arrangement without a disclaimer provision, S1 would have had complete control over the ultimate disposition of the property channeled to the bypass. S1 could feel certain that the property would pass at a future date to chosen named survivors, such as S1's children, or even S1's children of a former marriage. On the other hand, use of the disclaimer enables S1's spouse to direct more property to him or herself outright, thereby enabling that spouse, as S2, to later transfer it to anyone S2 chooses. Of course, in practice, S1's and S2's distribution interests are usually similar, but they could be different, as is so often the case when there has been marital strife, when S1 has children of a former marriage, or when S1 anticipates the possibility that S2 could be "persuaded" after S1's death to make alternate dispositions.

As an alternative to Option 4, S1 could have incorporated a credit shelter bypass plan which gave S2 the right to disclaim *additional* property into the bypass share. This would ensure a minimum FET saving via bypass, enable S1 to retain dispositive control over that amount, yet still offer some flexibility to S2. This fifth option, *credit shelter bypass with disclaimer*, is becoming increasingly popular.

Reduced S2 control. Another drawback to use of the 100 percent marital deduction with disclaimer is that tax law will not allow S2 to retain the right to direct beneficial enjoyment of the disclaimed bypass property. For example, if the clients create a plan to permit S2 to disclaim property into a bypass trust, S2 cannot be given even a limited power of appointment over the trust corpus. However, S2 can be granted the power to invade principal under an ascertainable standard, and he or she can be named trustee of the trust. Thus, while the disclaimer adds some flexibility in the area of FET *saving*, it also removes some flexibility to the plan in the area of subsequent *S2 control.*

The 100 percent marital deduction with disclaimer into bypass is perhaps used most commonly in the medium size "borderline estate" (about $500,000 to $750,000) where the FET benefits of a bypass are not yet significant, but may become so in the future. Clients in this asset range who would otherwise specify a simple will plan may find Option 4 to offer added flexibility.

Disclaimer planning is further discussed in Chapter 18. A popular alternative method to the disclaimer which also uses a surrogate decision maker to select the degree of equalization and deferral is the QTIP election. It will be described in a few pages and also in Chapter 18.

PLANNING SOFTWARE

From the preceding discussion of the four planning options and the choice between FET deferral and FET equalization, it should be clear that selection of the proper estate plan will depend on many factors, both quantitative and qualitative. Recently, elaborate computer programs have been developed which attempt to take account of the quantitative factors. Developed primarily by independent software publishers, insurance companies, certified public accounting firms, and securities houses, the programs analyze the client's personal and financial position and, after making certain assumptions, suggest an optimal plan that usually incorporates a bypass. While a great many planners, especially attorneys, are reluctant to overwhelm their clients with complex computer printouts which often only confuse them all the more, others use these plans extensively, especially with knowledgeable clients.[2]

MARITAL TRUSTS[3]

So far we have assumed that all property that we wish to qualify for the marital deduction will pass *outright* to the surviving spouse. However, that property could still qualify for the marital deduction if, instead of being transferred outright, it was transferred into a *marital trust*.

A marital trust is simply defined as a trust structured to receive property that will qualify for the marital deduction. Several different types of marital trusts are commonly used, with the most popular being the power of appointment trust and the QTIP trust. Both will be described shortly. They differ in at least one important manner: how they qualify for one of the statutory exceptions to the *terminable interest rule*.

---

2. For reviews of some software, see the Shumaker, Leimberg and Mabley/VanLeuven Stewart articles cited at the end of the chapter.

3. For a summary comparison of the taxation of marital trusts versus other popular trusts in estate planning, see Table 17-1 in Chapter 17.

Rationale For Terminable Interest Rule And Its Exceptions

In Chapter 6, you learned that, in general, a transfer to a surviving spouse of property that is subject to a terminable interest will not qualify for the marital deduction. A common example is the transfer, at death, of a life estate. A deathtime transfer of property by S1 into a trust giving S2 only a life estate in the property's income would not qualify the property for the marital deduction in S1's estate because a life estate is a terminable interest.

By this point in the book, you should be able to see more clearly the rationale for the terminable interest rule. In creating the marital deduction, Congress intended that if the deduction was taken in a *donor*-spouse's estate, then the property qualifying for the deduction must stand a good chance of eventually being included in the *recipient* spouse's estate. The intent was to tax property owned by the spouses at *one* of the two deaths. Therefore, if an S1 leaves to S2 property that is subject to a terminable interest, an S1 marital deduction will be disallowed. Without the rule, property could be both deducted from S1's gross estate and excluded from S2's gross estate if S2's interest in it was set to terminate before or at S2's death. Thus, the property transferred would escape taxation at both spouse's deaths.

Without any exceptions, however, the terminable interest rule would be too sweeping and could deny the marital deduction for property that would in fact be destined for inclusion in the gross estate of the surviving spouse.

> EXAMPLE 12-1 S1's will provides for a transfer of property into a trust, with all income to S2 for life, then remainder to whomever S2 appoints. In the absence of the exceptions to the terminable interest rule, the property might not qualify for the marital deduction in S1's estate because S2 has been left property subject to a terminable interest. Nonetheless, the property would be includable in S2's gross estate because S2 possessed, at death, a general power of appointment over the property. Hence, without any exceptions to the terminable interest rule, the property would probably be includable in *both* S1's and S2's gross estate.

> EXAMPLE 12-2 S1's will provides for a transfer of property into trust, but only if S2 survives S1 by more than six months. If S2 does not live that long, then the property immediately passes outright to X. Without an exception to the terminable interest rule, the property would be rapidly subject to tax in both estates for reasons mentioned in the previous example.

To prevent these undesired results, Congress created several exceptions to the terminable interest rule, thereby saving the marital deduction for S1 in certain situations. These exceptions, introduced in Chapter 6, enable planners to use the three marital trusts to be discussed next as an alternative to an outright transfer to the surviving spouse.

Power of Appointment Trust

As mentioned earlier, planners today commonly use two different types of marital trusts. The power of appointment trust is one type. As in the facts in Example 12-1, it grants S2 the right to receive all income from the property for life, payable at least annually. It also gives S2 a general power of appointment over the principal, exercisable alone and in all events, at death or during life.

The exception to the terminable interest rule allowing for a power of appointment marital trust is found in §2056(b)(5), reproduced in Appendix B. For additional discussion, see Chapter 18.

QTIP Trust

The second and more frequently used marital trust is called the QTIP trust, a trust funded with "qualified terminable interest property," for which an FET election is made on Form 706. To qualify for the marital deduction, a "QTIPable" trust must provide that the surviving spouse is entitled to all of the income from the trust property, payable at least annually. In addition, the trust cannot give anyone a power to appoint any of the property to anyone other than the surviving spouse. In other words, S2 can be the only permissible appointee.[4]

QTIP election. Tax law grants the executor of S1's estate the right to make what is called the *QTIP election*.

QTIP election made. If the executor so elects, the QTIP property subject to the election will be part of the S1 marital deduction and will *automatically* be includable in the gross estate of S2.[5] Thus, Congress' rationale for imposing the above income and power of appointment requirements should now be more apparent: Requiring that S2 be entitled to all income from the QTIP trust and prohibiting anyone but S2 from being a permissible appointee of trust assets more ensures that all marital deduction property associated with the QTIP trust will be subject to S2 transfer taxation, at least by the time of S2's death. Thus, property the trust distributes to S2 will be subject to transfer taxation either as property owned by S2 at death, or as previously transferred property subject to gift taxation. Property retained by the QTIP

---

4. §2056(b)(7)(B)(ii)(II).

5. §2044

trust, as just mentioned, must be includable in S2's gross estate, by statute.

QTIP election not made. If the executor does not make the QTIP election, the property will not qualify for the marital deduction in S1's estate, but, with proper planning, can avoid inclusion in the S2 gross estate, via the bypass. Thus, as with a disclaimer, the QTIP election offers flexibility by enabling someone, at S1's death, to decide whether to defer or to equalize. For an additional discussion, see Chapter 18.

Power Of Appointment Trust And QTIP Trust Contrasted

Both types of marital trusts enable the property to qualify for the marital deduction at S1's death, and neither entail an outright transfer to the surviving spouse. They are employed to give S1 some post-death control over the disposition of the property, at least until the death of S2. The power of appointment trust can implement this S1 control by preventing S2 from hastily disposing of the property during life, because it can provide that S2's power may be exercisable *only* at death. The QTIP trust implements S1 control by letting S1, to the exclusion of S2, unilaterally designate who will receive the property at S2's death;[6] it is most useful if S1 wishes to be absolutely certain that S1's intended beneficiaries will actually receive the property.

Some clients will want their surviving spouse to determine who should receive their property after their death. They probably trust that spouse to make mature decisions. Allowing S2 to act as a *surrogate decision maker* can greatly enhance the flexibility of their estate plan. Maximum flexibility can be attained by creating a power of appointment trust, and by granting S2 both a lifetime and a testamentary general power to appoint property to other family members and loved ones. The QTIP trust lacks this flexibility because S2 may be the only permissible appointee during S2's lifetime.

In common law states, the QTIP trust may be viewed as potentially unfair, if it results in totally depriving the nonacquiring spouse of dispositive control over the family wealth. After all, assert some commentators, the accumulation of wealth is usually the product of both spouses, not just the one who legally earned it. Yet the QTIP trust is very commonly used, particularly in situations where there has been a remarriage, where the spouses are experiencing marital difficulties, where the client wishes to protect the estate from possible consequences of S2's immaturity or senility, or where

---

6. The reader should keep in mind that the bypass trust, like the QTIP trust, will also permit S1 to unilaterally control disposition of certain (i.e., bypass) property at S2's death.

the client strongly wishes that the property eventually passes to charity.[7]

The power of appointment trust is sometimes preferred because the death tax of some states excludes property from taxation in the estate of the holder of the power.

Estate Trust

A third type of marital trust called the estate trust is occasionally used. Under its terms the trust corpus is made payable to S2's estate. Its unique feature is that during S2's lifetime, S2 need not be required to receive any income. Consequently, trust income can be accumulated and taxed at trust rates. Or the income may be made immediately payable to *any* person. Thus the estate trust may be particularly useful when S1 wishes to provide temporary support to someone other than S2.

General Comparison of All Marital Trusts and Bypass Trust

Table 12-1 compares certain major characteristics of the three types of marital trusts and the bypass trust.

How Frequently Are They Used?

The reader may be wondering how frequently clients are using these alternative marital dispositions. Based on the results of a survey conducted by this author, the most popular marital disposition is the standard QTIP trust,[8] used by 43.5 percent of clients of experienced estate planning attorneys. Next, at 28.3 percent, is the outright marital transfer, which is inherent in simple wills. Less popular dispositions include the power of appointment trust (14.0%) and estate trust (2.9%). The relative popularity of the QTIP trust seems understandable, in view of the considerable and exclusive degree of dispositive control exercisable by the client, as a possible S1.

---

7. QTIP property ultimately passing to charity can qualify for both the marital deduction in the S1 estate and the §2055(a) charitable deduction in the S2 estate. LR 9242006.

8. A standard QTIP trust is meant to be contrasted with a 'reverse QTIP election' trust, described later in the chapter.

Table 12-1 Comparison of Trusts In Marital Deduction and Bypass Planning

CHARACTER-ISTICS	QTIP TRUST	POWER OF APPOINTMENT TRUST	ESTATE TRUST	BYPASS TRUST
Income required to be payable to S2 for life?	Yes (§2056(b)(7))	Yes (§2056(b)(5))	No	No
General power (GP) or special power (SP) exercisable by S2 during lifetime or at death?	SP not allowed during lifetime. GP allowed,* but trust terms usually do not grant (§2056(b)(7))	GP required, either during lifetime or at death (§2056(b)(5)) trust corpus payable	Not during S2's lifetime. Implicit GP at death, since and/or 5 and 5 power to S2's estate	Grants to S2 only a non-GP subject to ascertainable standard
Trust corpus formerly included in S1's estate tax base?	No, included in gross estate but qualified for MD	No; included in gross estate but qualified for MD	No; included in gross estate but qualified for MD	No, except for portion not sheltered by unified credit
Trust corpus includable in S2's gross estate?	Yes, required under §2044	Yes (§2041)	Yes (§2033)	No
Can S2 be trustee?	Yes	Yes	Yes	Yes
Ideal type of property to fund with?	Nonappreciating assets	Nonappreciating assets	Nonappreciating assets	Highly appreciating assets
Unique purpose	Qualify for MD without granting S2 any control over corpus	Grant S2 maximum control over corpus for greatest plan flexibility	Allow trust income to be payable to someone other than S2, or accumulated, with income taxation at trust rate.	Exclude property from S2's gross estate
Also called	Marital trust "C" Trust "Q" Trust	Marital trust "A" Trust	Marital trust "A" Trust	Nonmarital trust "B" Trust Family trust

* But S2 may be the only permissible appointee.

Contingent Liabilities and QTIP Trust Planning

The creation of *contingent liabilities* by clients can generate problems in QTIP trust planning.

EXAMPLE CL-1 Prior to his death, Matt *co-signed a loan* made by his daughter, guaranteeing repayment of the loan in the event of her default. The marital deduction for assets in Matt's QTIP trust has been jeopardized. The potential for invasion of the trust by the creditor for payment of the guarantee may violate the qualifying income requirement under §2056(b)(7).

EXAMPLE CL-2 Using the facts in Example CL-1, above, assume that Matt's estate plan also included a *marital estate trust*, funded with an amount equal to twice the present value of all payments which may have to be paid under the guarantee. The IRS takes the position that the QTIP assets still will not qualify for the marital deduction since the guarantee obligations could still be paid from QTIP assets because the estate trust may not be sufficient to pay the guarantee.[9]

Commentators believe that similar problems can arise for contingent liabilities created for nonfamily members, such as guarantees of business loans by the firm's owners. Prior to the recent IRS ruling, planners had little reason for concern, since such obligations were considered "not fixed and determinable" in terms of enforceability and value. The ruling has generated considerable concern and, as of this writing, the IRS is reexamining the issue. Commentators are anticipating considerable litigation, and are pressing for remedial legislation.

Retirement Plan Benefits

Who should be named beneficiary to receive the client-participant's retirement plan benefits at the client's death? Possible choices include the

---

9. LR 9113009. For a discussion of the problem and several possible solutions see the August paper cited at the end of Chapter 7. The IRS would like to add new §7872A to provide for the valuation of loan guarantees.

spouse, a marital trust,[10] a bypass trust, or charity.[11] Payment may be made in the form of an outright lump sum or in periodic payments. Experienced planners tend to prefer either an outright distribution to the spouse, or a distribution of periodic payments to a marital trust. Their two principal objectives are to keep the assets sheltered from income tax as long as possible under the qualified plan rules, and to qualify for the estate tax marital deduction. An outright transfer to the spouse can accomplish both; to delay income recognition until at least age 70 ½, the spouse can roll over the assets to his or her own Individual Retirement Account.[12] Alternatively, naming a marital trust to receive periodic payments ensures income tax sheltering by enabling the assets to be held in the plan as long as possible by exploiting the minimum distribution rules.[13] And, of course, it will qualify for the FET marital deduction.[14] Unfortunately, disposition of plan benefits to the marital share may result in underfunding the bypass share, to the extent that S1 does not own sufficient assets. This can be especially troubling in community property states.[15]

Multiple Trust Planning

From the analysis above, it should be clear that the marital trust (sometimes called the "A" trust) and the bypass trust (sometimes called the "B" trust) are the products of essentially different planning motives, and are legally two different trusts. Both trusts can be incorporated into one estate plan, and the combination has been called the "A-B" trust plan.

---

10. An IRA payable to a QTIP trust will qualify for the marital deduction. However, careful drafting may be necessary. LR 9245033.

11. For a numerical "worst case" example of the tragedy of naming a trust for the benefit of a *grandchild*, see the Chapter 6 discussion of §2039.

12. §402(c)(9). Rolling over the benefits defers recognition of gain until distributed.

13. For an analysis of marital trust planning for retirement benefits, see the Holding article cited at the end of the chapter.

14. For a discussion, see the Mezzullo (1993) paper cited at the end of Chapter 6.

15. Bilter, in his paper cited at the end of the chapter, offers possible solutions.

In the past few years, however, the A-B plan has become outmoded, as more and more plans are incorporating three or four trusts, the bypass trust and two or three marital trusts. Two types of plans will be mentioned briefly.

One type uses a bypass trust and two different types of marital trusts, primarily to extend to S2 *different degrees of control* over property qualifying for the marital deduction. First, it incorporates a power of appointment marital trust (the A trust) over which S2 is given virtually complete power to control disposition. And second, it uses a QTIP marital trust (the Q trust) to enable S1, to the total exclusion of S2, to dispose of other marital deduction property. This arrangement is sometimes called the "A-B-Q" or "A-B-C" trust plan.

The other, increasingly popular three or four trust plans use a bypass trust and two or three QTIP marital trusts, primarily to minimize transfer tax at the death of the children. These *generation-skipping* plans will be the subject of the last section of this chapter.

NonCitizen Surviving Spouses: The QDT Trust

All property passing outright to the surviving spouse will virtually always qualify for the marital deduction, unless that spouse is not a U.S. citizen. In that case, to qualify, the property must pass instead to a "qualified" domestic trust, called a "QDT" or "*QDOT trust*" by planners. The intent is to more ensure collection of the FET on marital deduction property intended for the benefit of a spouse who may have no legal or geographical ties with the U.S.

According to the requirements of IRC Section 2056A(a), at least one of the trustees of a QDT must be a U.S. citizen or domestic corporation. Trusts exceeding $2 million at S1's death must require either at least one trustee to be a bank, or that the trustee furnish a bond or security of at least 65 percent of the value of the corpus.

A deferred FET will be imposed both on any corpus distributed prior to the spouse's death, and on the value of the corpus remaining at the spouse's death (or sooner, if the trust ceases to qualify as a QDT).[16] However, distribution of income, and distribution of principal on account of "hardship," are exempt from the tax.[17] The tax is the amount that would have been

---

16. For details, see the Akers, Fijolek/Miller, Lawrence/Kaufman and Blase/Moul articles cited at the end of the chapter.

17. Reg. 20.2056A-2(d).

imposed, after all credits, had the property subject to the tax been included in S1's taxable estate.

The trust need not have been created by the decedent prior to death; either the executor or a surviving spouse may create the QDT prior to the due date of the S1 FET return. Also, by then the surviving spouse must irrevocably assign marital deduction property to the trust.

The surviving noncitizens spouse's choice of whether or not to transfer S1 property into a QDT trust may be based on the decision to defer or to equalize the FET, as discussed in Chapter 11. If S2 creates and funds a QDT trust, S1's estate will get a marital deduction for the property, but the property will be subject to FET at S2's death (or earlier, if S2 transfers trust property during lifetime). Alternatively, if S2 accepts the property without transferring it to a QDT, the property will be subject to S1 estate taxation immediately, but may avoid FET later to the extent S2 can convert the property into "non-U.S. situs" assets. Some noncitizen S2s may prefer to pay the tax up-front, then take the property, and disappear.

CASE STUDY IN MARITAL DEDUCTION AND BYPASS PLANNING

Let's now apply the principles of this chapter to a hypothetical fact situation.

> Jim and Mary Clark are both age 49 and have been happily married for 23 years. They have a son Joe, age 20, a junior at the local university, and a daughter, Donna, age 16. Jim is financial vice president of a Fortune 500 corporation and is currently earning an annual salary of $168,000. Mary, a research chemist for a fertilizer company, earns an annual salary of $32,000. From sizable inheritances and successful investing, the Clarks own a fair amount of property, with Jim's interests having a total fair market value of $1,660,000 and Mary's interests worth $980,000. Joe handles the management of all of the family assets. Most of the investment property is real estate, but some is common stock and other securities. The balance consists of the home, personal effects, and cash. The Clarks had a simple will prepared about 10 years ago, and now they would like to inquire about the possibility of reducing transfer taxes at the second death. Mary knows little about investing and would have difficulty managing the family estate by herself. The Clarks are not presently interested in initiating a lifetime program of gifting to their children.

Applying each of the four planning options introduced earlier to the Clarks' situation produces substantially different results, which are described next. The first three are illustrated in Figure 12-1. For each alternative, we shall assume that Jim will be the S1, dying this year, and Mary will live a normal life expectancy.

Option 1: 100 Percent Marital Deduction

The Clarks will, in effect, be choosing this option if they do not revise their wills. Jim's estate will incur no FET, but Mary's estate will be subject to an FET of $907,200, based on a taxable estate of $2,640,000 and a marginal tax rate (MTR) of 53 percent. The children will receive $ 1,732,800, representing the original family estate of $2,640,000, reduced by the total tax of $907,200.

Option 2: Credit Shelter Bypass

If Jim's will is revised so that instead of receiving his entire estate outright, Mary receives all but $600,000 (the amount that will pass to the bypass share), Jim's estate will still incur no FET since the entire gross estate will be sheltered by the combination of the marital deduction and the unified credit. However, Mary's estate, which will amount to $2,040,000, will incur an FET of $607,600, considerably less than the FET under Option 1. Joe and Donna will ultimately receive $2,032,400, representing the original family estate of $2,640,000, reduced by the tax of $607,600. Thus the children stand to receive $299,600 more if the credit shelter bypass option is implemented.

Option 3: Bypass with Estate Equalization

Instead of transferring the amount of the exemption equivalent of the unified credit to the bypass share, let's consider transferring a larger amount, one that will just equalize the marginal tax rates for the spouses. Accordingly, we'll have Jim transfer $410,000 at death to Mary, leaving the residue of his estate after payment of the tax to the bypass share. Jim's estate will incur an FET of $255,500, and Mary's estate, which will amount to $1,390,000, will pay an FET of $315,700, so that the children will later receive $2,068,000, an amount that exceeds Option 1 by $336,000 and Option 2 by $36,400.

The amount of the marital deduction necessary to equalize the S1 and S2 taxable estates calculated by the formula in Chapter 11 would be different from $410,000:

$$\$1,660,000 - \text{Marital deduction} = \$980,000 + \text{Marital deduction}$$

$$2 \times \text{Marital deduction} = \$680,000$$

$$\text{Marital deduction} = \$340,000$$

This amount is not as desirable as a $410,000 marital deduction, because the formula fails to take account of both the impact of the time value of money and the fact that the same marginal tax rate will apply over a range of taxable estates. Consider first the time value of money. In contrast with a marital deduction of $410,000, a marital deduction of $340,000 will generate a higher S1 FET (of $285,600 versus $255,500) and a lower S2 FET (of $285,600 versus $315,700), although it will still produce the same total combined S1-S2 FET of $571,200 and the same total amount received by the children ($2,068,800). The time value of money would suggest the larger S1 marital deduction in order to defer payment of the tax. To determine how much larger, we must examine the second issue, the influence of the tax rate brackets. The $410,000 marital deduction represents the greatest marital deduction possible that can still maintain equal spousal marginal tax rates. Examining Table 4 of Appendix A, the FET marginal tax rates for the $340,000 marital deduction alternative would be 43 percent for both spousal estates since the taxable estates would be the same ($1,320,000). Increasing the marital deduction by $1 will reduce S1's taxable estate by $1 and will increase S2's taxable estate by the same amount. In fact, since the marginal tax rate of 43 percent would apply to all taxable estates between $1.25 million and $1.5 million, S1's taxable estate could be reduced to $ 1.25 million (by a marital deduction of $410,000) before the marginal tax rate dropped. S2's taxable estate could be raised to $1.5 million (by a marital deduction of $520,000) before the S2 marginal tax rate rose. Thus, the maximum marital deduction that could be taken before either marginal tax rate changed is $410,000.

Option 4: 100 Percent Marital Deduction with Disclaimer into Bypass

Option 4, 100 percent marital deduction with disclaimer into bypass, is not shown in Figure 12-1 because it represents numerically a choice of one of many options, including the three outlined earlier. For example, if Mary elected to make no disclaimer, the numbers would be identical to Option 1.

FIGURE 12-1 Case Study: Effect of Planning Options 1, 2, and 3

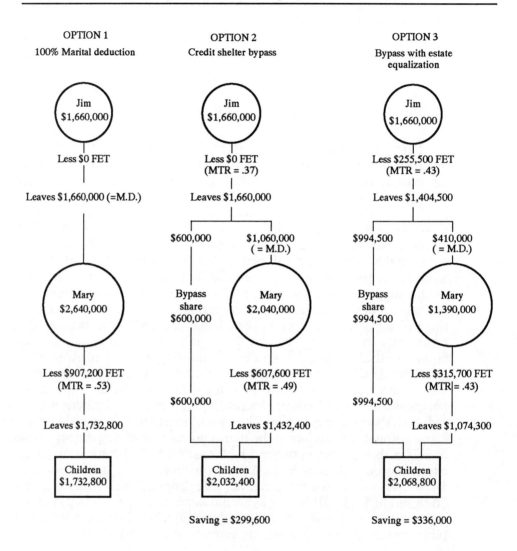

If Mary chose to disclaim the amount of the exemption equivalent, then the figures in Option 2 would apply. Instead, if Mary disclaimed all but $410,000, then Option 3 would apply. Of course, Mary could be permitted to disclaim other amounts.

Recommendations

Mary and Jim should be better able to weigh their choices after being presented with these figures. Of course, the order of deaths might be the reverse, so it is important to perform the same type of calculations assuming that Mary died first. This would probably also lead to a revision in Mary's will.

The analysis above suggests some possible recommendations for the Clarks. Based on the numbers, there is good reason for Jim to revise his current will.

Bypass planning. A bypass of at least $600,000 would save nearly $300,000 in federal estate taxes, which amounts to over 11 percent of the family estate.

But there are some *drawbacks* to this plan. The spouses will not live to enjoy this tax saving; it will be of benefit only to the children. Further, Mary and Jim must be willing to relinquish some control over the assets in the bypass. If Jim made an outright transfer to the children, they would, of course, become fee simple owners of the property and, in the extreme, could refuse to assist Mary in the event she became needy. If, instead, Jim made the transfer into trust, Mary could still have invasion rights over the corpus, but those rights would have to be limited to the standards of "health, education, support, or maintenance," factors Mary might consider too restrictive. Usually, though, spouses do not have difficulty living with these terms. However, since we have assumed that Mary is not an effective asset manager, even if Mary did object, Jim might prefer to have some of his assets protected from the potential peril of her mismanagement.

Option 3, bypass with estate equalization, may be attractive to Jim because it would place less property outright into Mary's hands and save a larger FET.

Finally, Option 4, the spousal disclaimer, is not likely to work very well in this situation, in view of Mary's limited financial management skills. Jim might well prefer to avoid the discretion inherent in a disclaimer to ensure that FET at S2's death will, in fact, be saved and that the children will be assured of receiving some portion of the family wealth. Summing up, Jim will probably wish to choose Option 2 or 3, alternatives both involving a substantial bypass.

Marital deduction planning. Regarding the marital deduction share, Jim might choose to direct that it be placed in a *marital trust* having an independent trustee in view of Mary's apparent lack of desire or inability to handle the management responsibilities. And assuming that Jim is confident that, at her death, Mary would leave the family property to the children, a power of appointment trust would probably be preferable to a QTIP trust because of its greater flexibility: at her death, Mary could act as *surrogate decision maker* for Jim, properly disposing of his property perhaps decades after he dies.

The facts in the case assumed no appreciation in asset values. If they were projected to increase between the deaths of the two spouses, the benefits of a bypass arrangement over the simple will would mount. Further, the benefits of the bypass with reduced marital deduction over the credit shelter bypass option would also be expected to increase. The Clarks would have even more reason to implement a bypass estate plan.

Other Factors

The Clarks' fact pattern oversimplifies reality in other ways besides assuming no property appreciation. The material below examines several other factors that, by altering the numerical results, can complicate bypass and marital deduction planning.[18]

State death tax. In this chapter we have ignored the influence of state death taxes. At worst, their effect will be relatively small, in view of the impact of the federal credit for state death taxes.

As mentioned in Chapter 7, twenty five states and the District of Columbia impose only a pickup tax, that is, an amount exactly equal to the federal (table) credit for state death taxes. Consequently, in these states, no additional cash flow will be incurred as a result of the state death tax. The remaining 25 states impose a death tax that is often larger than the pickup amount. Of these, in the case of a $1,200,000 estate, five states would levy no death tax on either the $600,000 bypass share or the $600,000 marital share. The other 20 states would impose a tax ranging from $5,850 (Nebraska) to $55,500 (Massachusetts) on the credit shelter bypass share and from $0 (14 states) to $35,880 (Pennsylvania) on the $600,000 marital

---

18. This section is not an exhaustive analysis. For example, for a technical discussion of the planning trade-off between the S1 marital deduction and a possible S2 credit for tax on prior transfers, see the Malcolm Moore article cited at the end of Chapter 6.

share.[19] The upshot is no additional state tax on a credit shelter bypass in all but twenty states, with the highest of these twenty, Massachusetts, imposing an effective average tax rate of 9.25 percent.[20] In conclusion, in most states, the state death tax will not influence the numbers. In the other states, the incorporation of a bypass plan will significantly reduce the net additional cash outflow required by the state tax, sometimes all the way to zero.

Revocable living trust.[21] To avoid probate, the spouses may wish to establish a revocable living trust, which can be coordinated with bypass planning, or even planning with a 100 percent marital deduction plan. Later, at S1's death, the single joint trust can be directed to transfer its contents into three new trusts, which we can call X, Y, and Z. Property belonging to S1 which is intended to qualify for the marital deduction will pass to trust X, the marital trust. Property belonging to S1 which is intended to bypass S2's estate will pass to trust Y, the bypass trust. And finally, property belonging to S2 will pass to trust Z, which can continue to be revocable until S2's death. All trust property will thus avoid probate at both S1's and S2's deaths and will also accomplish all of the FET savings described in this chapter.

With particular reference to S1's property, the evolution of a typical client-decedent's revocable trust estate plan is illustrated in Figure 12-2. This illustration assumes no generation-skipping transfer tax planning. At death, property in the decedent's own name passes to the probate estate, while the decedent's nonprobate property interests flow into the revocable trust, which then terminates. This trust property is then apportioned between the nonmarital (bypass) and marital trusts, based on principles covered in this chapter. At the surviving spouse's death, all trust property then passes outright to the children if they have reached the specified age, commonly 25, 30, or 35. On the other hand, if the children are younger, then the two trusts terminate and the property is merged into a single "pot" trust and then subdivided into equal shares, or into one trust for each child when the children reach their early 20s (here, age 23). Pot trusts are further discussed in Chapter 17.

---

19. In general, states imposing a death tax on the marital share include Connecticut, Delaware, District of Columbia, Kansas, Kentucky, Louisiana, Maryland, New Jersey, North Carolina, Pennsylvania and West Virginia.

20. Money magazine, January, 1992, p.75.

21. For a summary comparison of the taxation of the revocable living trust versus other popular trusts in estate planning, see Table 17-1 in Chapter 17.

FIGURE 12-2 A Typical Revocable Trust Estate Plan[*]

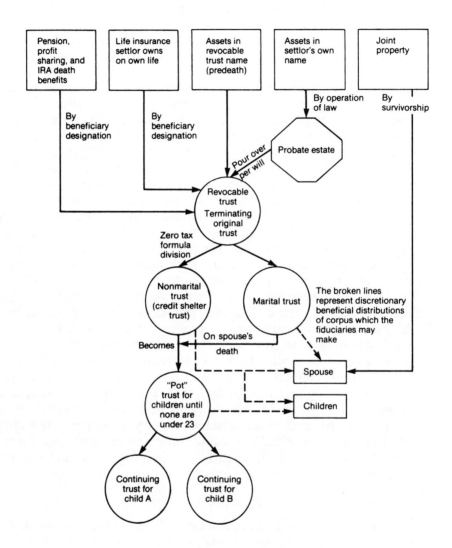

* Reprinted, with permission, from the Keydel paper cited at the end of Chapter 10.

One living trust. A one trust document plan for both spouses, called a *joint spousal grantor trust*, will work as long as the assets of each spouse are carefully identified and distinguished. It does not have the gift tax danger and dispositive restrictions of the joint and mutual will, which often becomes irrevocable over all probate assets at the first spouse's death. In contrast, the surviving spouse's assets in the joint trust remain subject to revocation.[22]

Two living trusts. If commingling of spousal assets (individually owned property) is a significant risk, each spouse could execute his or her *own* living trust document. Another reason for two trusts is that a poorly drafted joint spousal grantor trust document can give rise to estate and gift tax consequences for wealthier clients, particularly when the spouses fund the trust with different amounts of individually owned property. For example, the spouse contributing the greater amount may be deemed to have made a gift of a terminable life interest in a portion of the trust to the other spouse, one not qualifying for the marital deduction.[23]

A more complex illustration of deathtime trust planning for FET and the GSTT is included in the next major section of this chapter.

Debts and expenses. Of course, any estate will have deductible debts and expenses, which will alter the calculations. As we have seen in Chapter 10, expenses in administering a decedent's estate typically range between 5 and 10 percent of the total estate. Ordinarily, estate planners handle debts and expenses in the following manner: Regarding *debts*, in performing the calculations, planners use net worth as the value of the estate property; regarding *expenses*, planners either estimate the expenses or simply ignore them. Often, planners want to keep the calculations simple to avoid further confusing the client. The net effect of the existence of debts will be to increase the size of the gross family estate that can pass FET free. The net effect of expenses will be to reduce the amount passing to survivors, and frequently to increase the desirability of the revocable living trust as a probate avoidance device.

Uncertainty over date of death and order of deaths. The analyses in this and last chapter made two simplifying assumptions regarding the client's deaths. First they assumed that S1 will die today and S2 will die in ten years. In reality, the probability of that happening is less than five percent. Second, the discussion assumed either that the spouses owned an

---

22. A paper advocating the use of the joint trust approach was written by Esperti/Peterson and is cited at the end of the chapter.

23. For planning pointers, see the Flanagan article cited at the end of the chapter.

equal amount of property so that the order of their deaths was immaterial, or that one spouse (Mary) necessarily survived the other (Jim). In reality, one spouse is invariably wealthier, and the order of the spouse's deaths is uncertain. A more careful analysis, one requiring a computer, would treat the year of each spouse's death as a random variable. The program would be set to run hundreds of times, each time randomly selecting the year of death for each spouse, based on a mortality table and a random number generator. Each simulation run would calculate the amount passing to the children, and a mean of all runs could be used as the final measure.

BYPASS PLANS INVOLVING NONIMMEDIATE FAMILY MEMBERS, INCLUDING GENERATION-SKIPPING PLANS

Up to now, we have been focusing our discussion of FET saving on the family unit, including S1, S2, and the children. The same type of planning will often work as well with nonimmediate family members. For example, a childless S1 and S2 may develop a bypass plan for their nephews and nieces. In fact, such a plan will work as well for any survivors who belong to the next generation.

A problem can arise, however, when the purpose of a bypass is to skip not only the estate of a spouse but also the estates of the children. In Chapter 7, we learned that the Generation-Skipping Transfer Tax (GSTT) will be imposed on direct skips, taxable terminations, and taxable distributions to or for the benefit of a skip person. A skip person is a beneficiary who is at least two generations younger than the transferor. Thus, in the usual bypass situation, the GSTT will not be an immediate factor; it will be imposed only when the remainder beneficiaries are skip persons, not the client's children. However, since there may be contingent beneficiaries who are skip persons, careful planning is necessary.

> EXAMPLE GSTT-1 A client creates a bypass trust to take effect upon his death and directs that all income will be payable to his wife for her life, then remainder to his children, or their descendants, per stirpes. If all children survive their mother, the GSTT would not immediately apply because a child of the transferor is not a skip person. However, if one or more children do not survive and property passes for the benefit of the *descendants* of a deceased child, then the GSTT may apply. Yet under the *predeceased parent direct skip rule*, the assets may nevertheless be sheltered from GSTT, so long as the transfer is, in fact, a direct skip. This requires the creation of a separate trust, one for the benefit of anyone except nonskip persons, such as S2.

In addition to the predeceased parent direct skip rule, we learned in Chapter 7 of two other exceptions to the GSTT that considerably soften its impact: the $10,000 annual exclusion for lifetime gifts to a skip person and the $1 million lifetime exemption per donor for all skips. Chapter 13 will explore lifetime annual exclusion generation-skip gifting. The material immediately below discusses principles of efficient use of the $1 million exemption.

Allocating The $1 Million Exemption.

To appreciate how the $1 million GSTT exemption is efficiently utilized, the reader must first understand how to calculate the GSTT.
Calculating the GSTT. The GSTT is determined by multiplying the taxable amount by the product of the GSTT rate (the highest marginal FET rate currently in effect) and the so-called "inclusion ratio."[24] The taxable amount is essentially the amount involved in a particular direct skip, taxable termination, or taxable distribution. As indicated in Table 4 of Appendix A, the highest marginal FET rate is 55 percent.
Thus, the formula for calculating the GSTT is:

$$\textbf{GSTT = Taxable amount x .55 x Inclusion ratio}$$

The inclusion ratio is defined as the value one minus the "applicable fraction,"[25] or

---

24. §2602.

25. §2642(a).

$$1 \text{ Minus } \left(\frac{\text{Amount of GSTT exemption allocated to transfer}}{\text{Total value of property transferred minus certain taxes and deductions}} \right)$$

For simplicity, in the examples below we'll assume no deductible taxes and deductions, and that the highest marginal FET rate remains at 55 percent.

EXAMPLE GSTT-2 Eric allocates $500,000 of his $1 million GSTT exemption to a $1.5 million transfer into a newly created irrevocable trust. His inclusion ratio is .6666667 [= 1 minus ($500,000/$1,500,000)]. The trust assets will be subject to GSTT immediately if the transfer is a direct skip, as in the case where all trust beneficiaries are skip persons (eg., all grandchildren). Or they will be taxed later, whenever a taxable termination or a taxable distribution occurs.

Unlike a taxable distribution and a taxable termination, a direct skip is taxed similar to a gift, on a "tax exclusive" basis. That is, the amount of the tax is excluded from the taxable amount. Mathematically, the tax can be calculated from the following formula: Tax = [(amount of taxable termination) x (tax rate)]/(1 + tax rate). Thus, at a tax rate of 55 percent, the tax on a one dollar direct skip is 35 cents, calculated as follows: [($1) x (.55)]/(1 + .55) = $.35. The upshot is a lower, 35 percent rate, derived theoretically in the same manner that the rate is calculated when "grossing up" in the FET scheme can be avoided.

EXAMPLE GSTT-3 In Example GSTT-2, above, if the transfer were taxed immediately as a direct skip, the GSTT would be $354,839 [=($1,500,000 x .55 x .6666667)/(1.55)].

EXAMPLE GSTT-4 In Example GSTT-2, above, assume no direct skip was made earlier, that ten years have passed, and that the trust makes a taxable distribution of the entire corpus to a grandchild, when it is worth $3 million. The grandchild will pay a GSTT of $1,100,000 (= $3,000,000 x .55 x .6666667). Thus, the tax is calculated on a tax-inclusive basis, in a manner similar to the FET.

In the above examples, the client had allocated his GSTT exemption by an amount that generated an inclusion ratio falling between zero and one (i.e., .666667). The next section will explain why good planning will rarely do this.

Efficiently allocating the exemption. For transfers at death, the executor (or trustee, if there is no probate estate) allocates the deceased transferor's unused GST exemption on Form 706. In general, allocation of the exemption should be made effective at the moment the transfer becomes irrevocable, and no later, so as to maximize leverage by minimizing the actual earmarked exemption amount for assets that may be expected to appreciate.

Planners also recommend that the exemption be allocated so as to give each trust created an inclusion ratio of either exactly *zero or one*, but not an amount in between. Through a series of examples, we'll see why this is so, and how the exemption can be efficiently allocated, first for a single client, and then for married clients.

Single clients. GSTT exemption planning for single clients requires the use of two GSTT trusts.

EXAMPLE GSTT-5 At her death, Troughton, a widow, wishes to leave all of her property, expected to be $2 million after payment of FET, in trust for the benefit of her grandchildren. Her attorney (ill-advisedly) drafts a *one trust plan*, allocating Troughton's entire $1 million exemption to it. The trust's inclusion ratio is .5 [= 1 minus ($1 million / $2 million)]. The trust will contain just two types of assets: $1 million in bonds, and $1 million in stock of Troughton's successful closely held business.

EXAMPLE GSTT-6 Continuing the example immediately above, assume that the time is ten years after Troughton's death. The trust is now worth $3 million, consisting of $1 million in bonds and $2 million in the closely held stock. The entire corpus is distributed to the grandchildren as a taxable distribution, and the grandchildren pay a total GSTT of **$825,000** (= $3,000,000 x .55 x .5).

EXAMPLE GSTT-7 Based on the underlying facts in Example GSTT-5, assume that Troughton's attorney instead drafts a *two trust plan*. Trust N (nonexempt) will contain the bonds, and trust E (exempt) will contain the stock. The entire $1 million exemption is allocated to trust E, which will consequently have an inclusion ratio of zero [=1-($1,000,000/$1,000,000)]. In contrast, trust N's inclusion ratio will be 1.0 [=1-($0/$1,000,000)]. Ten years after Troughton's death, if, upon complete distribution, the trust assets again total $3 million, the grandchildren will pay a GSTT of only **$550,000** [= ($2,000,000 x .55 x 0) + ($1,000,000 x .55 x 1.0)]. By assuring that each trust has an inclusion ratio of exactly zero or one, but not an amount in between, the two trust plan has saved $275,000 in GSTT.[26]

To preserve the zero and 1.0 inclusion ratios, GSTT law requires that the property be kept in two separate trusts rather than just one, with each providing for separate shares.

Planners will not want to allocate any portion of the exemption to transfers either to a skip person for tuition or medical care, or to charity. Even unsheltered, these transfers will not be subject to GSTT.[27]

Leveraging the exemption. In addition to inclusion ratio strategies, planners try to leverage the GSTT exemption, that is, apply the exemption to appreciating assets so that each (present) dollar of exemption will be able to shield far greater than one (future) dollar from GSTT. In Example GSTT-6, above, every dollar in exemption was able to shelter two dollars from GSTT. Leveraging the GSTT will work best when the exemption is allocated to the client's most rapidly appreciating assets in a trust having an inclusion ratio of zero. Trust E in the example illustrates this situation.

Married clients. GSTT exemption planning for married clients involves similar strategies, except that a *three or four trust plan* is typically preferred.

EXAMPLE GSTT-8 Bob is married and owns $2 million in property. He wishes to create a generating-skipping credit shelter bypass plan, and to retain the assets in trust for the benefit of his wife, his children and his grandchildren. Bob's plan establishes *three trusts* at his death. First, trust B, the bypass trust, will contain approximately $600,000 of appreciating assets. $600,000 of Bob's $1 million exemption will be allocated to trust B. Thus, its inclusion ratio will be zero. Second, trust QN, a nonexempt QTIP trust, will contain the $1 million of Bob's property that is expected to appreciate least. None of Bob's exemption will be allocated to trust QN, which will therefore have an inclusion ratio of 1.0. Thus, the entire future value of all taxable terminations and taxable distributions from trust QN will be subject to GSTT. Third, trust QE, a second, exempt QTIP trust, will contain $400,000 in appreciating assets, and Bob will allocate his remaining $400,000 exemption to this trust, giving it an inclusion ratio of zero. Assuming that all of the appreciating assets double in value by the time they are distributed to the grandchildren, Bob's plan will have saved in excess of $125,000 in GSTT, compared with an arrangement incorporating a single QTIP trust containing $1,400,000. Part of this tax saving results because the transfer to trust QE can be arranged to be direct skip, which, as

---

26. One way to express the reason for the savings is that one hundred percent of $1 million is less than fifty percent of $3 million.

27. §2611(b)(1); A charity is treated as a nonskip person.

mentioned earlier, is subject to a lower effective rate of GSTT (35 percent) than is a taxable termination or taxable distribution because it is taxed on a tax exclusive basis.

As the above example illustrates, planners also try to allocate the GSTT exemption to those trusts (eg., bypass and certain QTIP trusts) that are most likely to retain and distribute the principal for skip persons, such as the grandchildren.

> EXAMPLE GSTT-9 Revising the facts in Example GSTT-8 a bit, assume that Bob owns more than $2 million in property. Bob's plan will include the three trusts already mentioned, plus a *fourth trust*, QN2, which contains all amounts in excess of $2 million, is not GSTT exempt, and would thus have an inclusion ratio of 1.0. If Bob's executor elected QTIP treatment for QN2, this property would qualify for Bob's marital deduction and would be includable in Bob's widow's gross estate. Alternatively, if Bob's executor chose not to so elect, the terms of the trust could enable the QN2 property to be taxed in Bob's estate, but bypass his widows's estate.

> EXAMPLE GSTT-10 Revising the facts in Example GSTT-9 above, Bob's plan could provide even greater postmortem flexibility by establishing *four QTIP trusts*, the three mentioned immediately above, and instead of trust B, the mandatory bypass trust, include a QTIP trust to hold the $600,000. As with trust QN2, above, Bob's executor would have additional flexibility over the amount to include in the bypass.

> EXAMPLE GSTT-11 In the three examples immediately above, if Bob's widow lacked sufficient property of her own to leave to skip persons, she could allocate her $1 million exemption to Bob's trusts QN and QN2, effectively rendering them totally or partially GST-exempt from that point on. For example, if she allocated at her death her entire $1 million exemption to trust QN, which has since appreciated from $1 million to $1.6 million. Trust QN's inclusion ratio will drop from 1.000 to .375 (= 1 - ($1.0 million/$1.6 million). This assumes no reverse election (described below) is made by Bob's executor for trust QN.

Reverse QTIP election. For the plans in the above four examples to work, a special election must be made. The law states that the GSTT exemption may be allocated at S1's death only to property with respect to which S1 is *transferor*, i.e., only to property subject to estate tax in S1's estate. While the bypass property is considered to be "subject to" S1 estate tax, property qualifying for the marital deduction is not. On its face, this would appear to preclude S1 from being able to allocate the exemption to any QTIP property. However, §2652(a)(3) provides that for any trust for which a standard QTIP election is made, a second, different election may be made to treat all property in that trust *as if* the standard QTIP election had *not* been made. Thus, under the so-called reverse QTIP election, for purposes only of allocating the GSTT exemption, S1 is treated as the transferor. For certain decedents having provided for only one QTIP trust, the IRS may allow the trust to be divided into two separate trusts so that the reverse election can be made on all of the assets on one trust. Thus, applying the facts in Example GSTT-8, had Bob provided for only one trust instead of QN and QE, at Bob's death this trust may be permitted to be split up into the two trusts described.[28]

As mentioned, a client's assets can be expected to appreciate at different rates, and to minimize the GSTT, low growth assets should be used to fund trusts for the benefit of nonskip persons while high growth, or "hot" assets should be used to fund trusts for skip persons.

> EXAMPLE GSTT-12 Continuing the facts in ongoing examples GSTT-8 through GSTT-11, Bob, owner of a closely held business, plans to allocate his firm's stock as follows: Trust QN will contain his firm's preferred stock, which is not expected to appreciate. Trusts B and QE, exempt trusts for the benefit of children and grandchildren, will contain the firm's common stock, a hot asset. Called a *postmortem funding freeze*, this strategy enables Bob to best leverage the million dollar GSTT exemption.

In addition, leveraging can be increased by accumulating all income from the exempt trusts, rather than distributing it to the children. This will prevent potentially exempt property from "leaking" into the hands of the nonskip generation. Accordingly, if distributions of income (or principal) are necessary, they should be made from nonexempt trusts first, where possible. Of course, while alive, S2 may be the only named permissible appointee of income or principal of all QTIP trusts.

Figure 12-3 illustrates the integration of FET and GSTT planning for both spouses, paralleling the plan for Bob in the series of examples immediately above. It originates with the client's revocable trust, but a trust-will will produce the same outcome. At S1's death, his assets are divided into three trusts, a credit (shelter bypass) trust (Trust B in Example GSTT-8) and two marital deduction trusts: a GSTT-exempt $400,000 trust (Trust QE) and a nonexempt trust containing all assets in excess of $1 million (in Example GSTT-8, this is trust QN, containing the excess over the sum of $600,000 and $400,000). S2's assets remain in the revocable trust (or owned outright by S2, in the case of will planning) until her death. Then, $1 million of her (exempt) assets join S1's exempt assets for future distribution to *grandchildren*, free of GSTT. The assets in this trust will also save FET by

---

28. LR 9133016; Prop Reg 26.2652-2; Prop Reg 26.2654-1(c)(2).

bypassing all children's estates. S2's non-GSTT exempt assets become part of the S1 nonexempt marital trust, for distribution to *children* (and the issue of deceased children), subject to GSTT at designated ages.

The following generation-skipping trusts are grandfathered, i.e., totally exempt from GSTT: those that were irrevocable on September 25, 1985; and trust-wills or trusts in existence on October 21, 1986 for decedents who died before January 1, 1987. To preserve their exempt status, no additions or modifications should be made to them.

Additional discussion of the flexibility of deathtime QTIP planning will be found in Chapter 18, covering postmortem death tax planning.

The Need For GSTT Planning

It should be evident by now that planning for the $1 million lifetime GSTT exemption requires careful thought and attentive drafting of complex will or trust clauses, and can add considerably to the expense of estate planning. It also forces the planner to openly discuss with the client an unpleasant fact: the eventual death of the client's children. These circumstances often make clients, even wealthier ones, resistant to discussing GSTT planning.

No GSTT planning necessary for some clients. Which wealthier clients most probably *do not need* GSTT planning? First, clients with estates not expected to exceed $1 million at their deaths need not ever worry about a GSTT. They may wish to do some trust planning to skip a generation by transferring some property for the eventual benefit of their grandchildren. In doing so, they can feel confident that GSTT law will automatically allocate the $1 million exemption, at their death, so that all trusts created will have an inclusion ratio of zero.

Second, those who do not wish to directly include grandchildren in their plan may not need GSTT planning. For example, clients preferring a one hundred percent marital deduction plan, as in a simple will, probably want their property to pass entirely to the surviving spouse and the children, all of whom are nonskip persons. Even clients anticipating a bypass may have no wish to provide for grandchildren. Of course, with either plan the property may wind up passing under the instrument to grandchildren (i.e., "descendants" or "issue") if a child predeceases a grandchild. However, as explained in Example GSTT-1, the property involved can usually be sheltered from the GSTT under the *predeceased parent direct skip rule*, with the help of some careful drafting, to ensure that a direct skip will in fact occur.

FIGURE 12-3 FET and GSTT Multiple Trust Planning

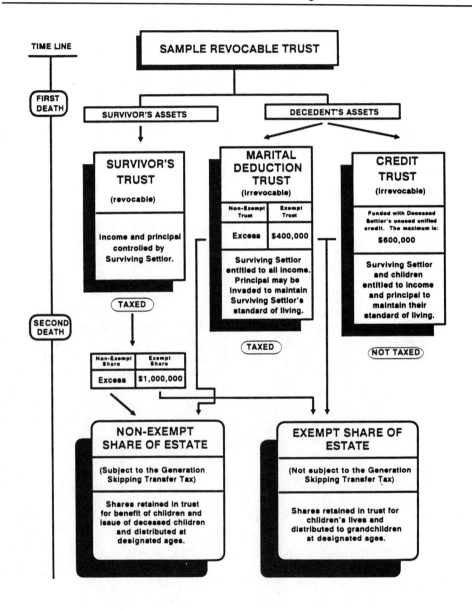

Reprinted with permission of Jon J. Gallo

Third, in some situations, GSTT trust planning should be avoided because it could result in more, not less, total transfer taxes. If the client is willing to leave the estate *outright to the children*, perhaps satisfied with only a hope that they will preserve the property for ultimate disposition to the grandchildren, a greater amount may wind up, GSTT-free, in the grandchildren's hands. The savings is based on two factors: 1) the unified credit can reduce the FET but not the GSTT, and 2) effective marginal FET rates begin at 37 percent (first $150,000 in excess of $600,000), while the GSTT rate is higher, at a flat 55 percent.

EXAMPLE GSTT-13 Based on the facts in Examples GSTT-5, 6, and 7, if Troughton instead left his entire $2 million estate (after FET) *outright* to his five *children*, the combined GSTT and FET incurred later would be zero, under simple assumptions, after the property finally passes to the grandchildren. Assuming a similar overall rate of appreciation on the property (50%), each child's $400,000 share would grow to $600,000, and, at each child's death, would be entirely sheltered from FET by the unified credit. No GSTT would result because there would be no transfer to a skip person. Thus, by using the children's five unified credits, Troughton's entire $3 million estate could pass to the grandchildren, transfer tax-free.

Clients needing GSTT planning. Which wealthier clients are most likely to need careful GSTT planning? Here are some common types:

- "dynastic"-oriented clients wishing to perpetuate themselves,
- clients with wealthy children,
- clients who believe that their children can not handle large amounts of money maturely, and
- clients who wish to give to their grandchildren things that their children can not or will not give, including an expensive education.

Summary. We have seen that there are several methods of at least partially circumventing the GSTT, particularly through the use of the $1 million GSTT exemption. The upshot is that in general, only family estates exceeding $2 million in total value at the first spouse's death will be prevented from arranging totally GSTT-free generation-skipping transfers.[29]

Generation-skipping planning is modestly popular to clients today. A 1992 survey found that only 15 percent of experienced estate planning

---

29. For a discussion of methods used to restructure trusts to qualify for additional GSTT saving, see the Harrington paper cited at the end of the chapter.

attorneys "often" find their clients choosing to make arrangements to hold property through the life of a child and distribute it to a more remote descendant (none of the attorneys replied "always" to the question). Of the clients who do frequently make these generation-skipping arrangements, the decision was "often" or "always" driven by tax reasons for 46 percent of the attorneys.[30] However, interest in generation-skipping estate planning should grow in the years to come, if only because clients will be living longer and will be more likely to know their great grandchildren. A recent U.S. Census Bureau report concluded that fifty years from now, the nation could have more people over 65 than under 21, and that the *four-generation family* will become common, as children will more often be able to know their great-grandparents, especially their great-grandmothers.

The next chapter focuses on gift planning; it is the first of two exploring lifetime transfer strategies.

---

30. See the Moore Pennell paper, cited at the end of Chapter 1.

QUESTIONS AND PROBLEMS

1. Describe the advantages and disadvantages of Option 4, 100 percent marital deduction with disclaimer into bypass.

2. *a.* What factors help determine whether marital deduction property should pass outright or in trust?
   b. Is FET savings for S1's estate a factor? Why or why not?
   c. Is FET savings for S2's estate a factor? (Hint: consider the outright bequest, and each marital trust separately.) Why or why not?

3. *a.* Explain the Congressional intent of the terminable interest rule.
   b. Describe the common marital trust plans used to take advantage of the exceptions to this rule.

4. True or false: A bypass trust and a marital trust cannot coexist in the same estate plan. Explain.

5. Your new client Saul shows you his latest will, executed in 1980. It provides that if Saul predeceases his wife Tilly, she will receive outright "... an amount equal to the maximum marital deduction.... (in effect in 1980)...." The residue of Saul's estate will bypass Tilly's estate. Assuming that Saul dies next month with an estate of $1,600,000 and that the maximum marital deduction in 1980 was one-half of the gross estate, compare the FET for Saul's and Tilly's estates based on the 1980 will with the FET based on a new will that incorporates a credit shelter bypass. Assume no prior gifts, and no deductions or credits except the marital deduction and the unified credit. What conclusions can be drawn? (One answer: Saul's FET under old will = $75,000).

6. The Drexlers own a total of $2 million in assets, with one half owned by each spouse. Their simple will passes all property outright to their *grandchildren*, rather than their children, at S2's death. Since there is a $1 million GSTT exemption per person, they tell you that this property will pass totally GSTT free. Advise them.

7. A bypass trust provides for income to the trustor's wife for her life, then remainder outright to his daughter, if she survives her mother; otherwise, to the daughter's *issue*.
   a. Could there be a potential GSTT problem?
   b. Is the size of the trust a factor?
   c. Can you suggest a solution to the problem?

8. (*a*) Burdick, a widower, wishes his grandchildren Diana and Chris to ultimately receive the bulk of his $1.6 million estate. Today he creates two revocable trusts, funding each with assets that are expected to be worth $1 million at his death. Diana's trust contains only fixed income securities and Chris' trust only common stock. At Burdick's death, each trust will begin distributing all income monthly to Burdick's daughter Heather for her life, and then each trust will terminate and all principle will pass to the respective grandchildren. Assuming that the corpus of Diana's trust remains unchanged while the corpus of Chris' trust triples between Burdick's death and Heather's death, calculate the GSTT due at Heather's death for Diana's trust, for Chris' trust, and for both trusts combined. Assume, alternatively, that at his death Burdick allocated his $1 million GSTT exemption in the following manner:
   1. Entirely to Diana's trust.
   2. One half to Diana's trust and one half to Chris' trust.
   3. Entirely to Chris' trust.
   (*b*) What conclusions can be drawn?

9. (*a*) Based on the facts in text Example GSTT-8 ("Bob is married..."), and assuming that all "appreciating assets" (i.e., all bypass assets, and $400,000 of QTIP assets) double in value between the date of Bob's death and the date that any GSTT is levied, while all other assets remain constant, calculate the total GSTT under the example's two alternative plans:
   1. Bob's GSTT plan simply creates one bypass trust, initially containing $600,000, and one QTIP trust, initially containing $1,400,000. He allocates $600,000 of his $1 million exemption to the bypass trust and $400,000 to the QTIP trust. Note: the QTIP trust will have an inclusion ratio of .714286. Can you see why?
   2. Bob's plan creates the three trusts described in the example.
   (*b*) Why has the three trust plan in alternative 2, above, saved GSTT?

10. Which types of clients probably do not need GSTT planning?

11. Which types of clients probably need GSTT planning?

RECOMMENDED READING

Acker, Alan S. "Added Dimensions: The Allocation of the GST." *Trusts & Estates*, February, 1991, pp. 61-67.

Akers, Stephen R. "Stirring The Alphabet Soup: ABCs Through XYZs of QTIPs and QDOTs," *1994 University of Miami Estate Planning Institute.*

(Anonymous) "Surviving the Surviving Spouse: Accommodating the Wives' Concerns." *Trusts & Estates*, April 1986, pp. 29-30.

Arnold, Richard S., and Peter S. Cremer. "The Unlimited Marital Deduction: Some Community Property/Common Law Disparities Still Remain." *Community Property Journal* 12 (Spring 1985), pp. 129-40.

*Bertles, James B. & Joel H. Yudenfreund. "Choosing a (Marital Deduction) Formula Clause Based on Funding Effects." *Estate Planning*, May, 1992, pp. 165-72.

*Bilter, D. Keith "Estate Planning for Community Property Retirement Plan Benefits" *1993 UCLA-CEB Estate Planning Institute.*

*Blase, James G., and Jane M. Moul, "New Rules Governing Qualified Domestic Trusts Among the Changes Made by New (1989) Law," *Estate Planning*, March, 1990, pp76-82.

Blattmachr, Jonathan C., and Ira H. Lustgarten. "Alexander v. Commissioner: The Ultimate Marital Deduction Freeze May Be Here." *Trusts and Estates*, March 1984, pp. 51-55.

*Cornfeld, Dave L. "A Tin Cup For QTIPS," *1992 University of Miami Estate Planning Institute.*

*Covey, Richard B. "Marital Deduction and Credit Shelter Dispositions and The Use of Formula Provisions," 1985, U.S. Trust Co.

Crabb, Ronald R. "Probabilistic Estate Planning." *Financial Services Review*, Vol. 1, No. 2, 1991/1992, pp. 143-57.

Dobris, Joel C. "Marital Deduction Estate Planning: Variations on a Classic Theme." *San Diego Law Review* 20 (1983), pp. 801-35.

Eck, E. Edwin. "Drafting Considerations in Appointing the Surviving Spouse as Trustee of the Nonmarital Trust." *Montana Law Review* 45(1984), pp. 215- 44.

Engel, Ralph M. "Surviving Spouse May Benefit From Revised Planning." *Estate Planning*, January, 1993, pp. 39-45.

Evans, Daniel B. "Administrative Powers and the Marital Deduction." *Real Property, Probate, and Trust Journal* 20(1985), pp. 1161-87.

*Esperti, Robert A. & Renno L. Patterson, "Joint Trusts Are A Good Planning Tool For A Married Couple" *Estate Planning*, May, 1993, pp 148-54.

*Fijolek, Richard M. & J. Mitchell Miller. "Marital Deduction Planning for Noncitizen Spouses." *Estate Planning*, January, 1993, pp. 20-26.

*_____, "Proposed Regulations Clarify QDOTs But Add New Requirements" *Estate Planning*, July 1993, pp 195-200.

*Flanagan, Timothy L. "Designing Trusts for Couples Owning a Substantial Amount of Jointly Held Assets." *Estate Planning*, March 1988, pp. 84-89.

Fruehwald, Kristin G. "Credit Shelter Trusts Should Not Be Limited to Just the Unified Credit." *Estate Planning*, July 1983, pp. 200-205.

Gallo, Jon J. "Drafting Strategies for Generation-Skipping Trusts," *1992 UCLA-CEB Estate Planning Institute.*

Geneva, Louis B. "Simplifying Qualified Terminable Interest Property Use Planning Considerations." *Review of Taxation of Individuals* 8 (1984), pp. 3-22.

Gutierrez, Max Jr. "Marital Deduction: An Update." (Covering the impact of the final disclaimer regulations on the marital deduction.) *1987 University of Miami's Estate Planning Institute.*

*_____. "The Five Trust Plan: Allocations and Clauses," *1990 UCLA/CEB Estate Planning Institute.*

*_____. "Godzilla Meets Rodan: Generation-Skipping Transfer Tax/Marital Deduction Planning," *1989 University of Miami Estate Planning Institute.*

Halbach, JR., Edward C. "Generation Skipping: Planning Opportunities and Drafting Problems." *1988 University of Miami Estate Planning Institute.*

_____. "Tax-Sensitive Trusteeships." *Oregon Law Review* 63(1984), pp. 381- 429.

*Harrington, Carol A. "Surgery for Generation-Skipping Trusts: A How-To-Fix-It Manual." *1993 University of Miami Estate Planning Institute.*

Hirschson, Linda B. "Marital Estate Planning," *1991 Institute on Estate Planning*, Practising Law Institute.

*Holding, Graham D., "Getting QTIP Treatment For IRAs And Qualified Retirement Plans," *Trusts & Estates*, February, 1992, pp 26-32.

Jones, John T. "Marital Deduction Planning with QTIP after the 1984 Tax Reform Act: The Flexibility, and Some Problems, Continue." *Boston University Journal of Tax Law* 4 (1986), pp . 139-56.

Kalik, Mildred, and Schneider, Pam H. "The New Generation-Skipping Transfer Tax." *Estate Planning 1987*, California Continuing Education of the Bar.

Ketchum, Robert S., and Kay I. Johnson. "Traditional Simultaneous Death Planning Must Be Reviewed in Light of ERTA, Social Changes." *Estate Planning*, March 1983, pp. 90-94.

Kurtz, Sheldon F. "Marital Deduction Estate Planning Under the Economic Recovery Tax Act of 1981: Opportunities Exist, but Watch the Pitfalls." *Rutgers Law Review* 34, No. 4 (Summer 1982), pp. 591-667.

Landroche, Marie. "The Qualified Terminable Interest Rule: An Overview." *University of Florida Law Review* 34 (1982), pp. 737-63.

Langstraat, Craig J. "Considerations in Valuation of Marital Deduction Assets." *Trust & Estates*, February 1986, pp. 18-19.

*Lawrence III, Robert C., and Nancy H. Kaufman, "Estate Plan of Nonresidents Requires Review," *Trusts and Estates*, February, 1989, pp 38-54.

*Leimberg, Stephan R. "Choosing Estate Planning Software for your Practice: Eight Programs Compared." *Estate Planning*, November 1987, pp. 322-31.

*Mabley, John D., and C. VanLeuven Stewart "Update on Estate Planning Software: A Wide Array of Programs For Varied Needs," *Estate Planning*, November, 1990, pp. 340-54.

Martin, Mary Jill Lockwood. "Multiple Options Provide Great Flexibility in Choosing the Proper Marital Deduction Form." *Taxation for Lawyers*, July-August 1984, pp. 30-36.

McCaffrey, Carlyn S. & Alan H. Hirschfield. "Restructuring Wills and Trusts to Reduce Generation-Skipping Taxes." *Trusts and Estates*, March, 1992, pp. 8-26.

McDowell III, Pierce H. "The Dynasty Trust: Protective Armor For Generations To Come," *Trusts & Estates,* October, 1993, pp. 47-54. Recommends the creation of a "truly perpetual" trust in South Dakota, one of several states having no rule against perpetuities.

Miller, Ralph G. "Using Computers to Present Estate Plans." *Trusts & Estates*, April 1986, pp. 50-56.

Moore, Malcolm A. "The New Marital Deduction Qualified Terminable Interest Trust: Planning and Drafting Considerations." *Probate Notes* 8 (1982), pp. 56-60.

Mulligan, Michael D. "Spouse's Use of Disclaimer on Outright Bequest Maximizes Credit and Adds Flexibility." *Estate Planning*, November 1984, pp. 328-34.

Mulligan, Michael D., and Scott W. Boulton. "New Generation-Skipping Tax: Higher Rates, Broadened Scope." *Estate Planning*, January 1987.

_____. "Planned Opportunities that Take Advantage of the New Generation Skipping Transfer Tax." *Estate Planning*, March 1987, pp. 66-71.

*Parker, James O. "Fine-Tuning the Use of the Bracket Run." *Trusts and Estates*, November, 1991, pp. 8-19.

Plaine, Lloyd L. "Generation-Skipping Transfer Tax Proposed Regulations Skip Into View." *1993 University of Miami Estate Planning Institute*.

Price, John R., "Powers to the Right People: Flexibility Without Taxability or Drafters Desiderata: Nontaxable Flexibility," *1991 University of Miami Estate Planning Institute*.

*Schlenger, Jacques T; Robert E. Madden; and William G. Murray. "Power to Invade a Trust Corpus for Emergency Purposes Is Not Limited by an Ascertainable Standard under Sections 2036 and 2038. Letter Ruling 8606002." *Estate Planning*, September 1986, pp. 300-04.

Schnee, Edward J., and Paula Wiehrs. "Using the Marital Deduction: A Simulation." *Tax Adviser*, February 1984, pp. 76-84.

*Shumaker, Roger L., Joseph G. Hodges, and C. VanLeuven Stewart "Selecting the best Estate Planning Software: An Updated Review of the Programs," *Estate Planning*, March, 1989, pp 66-81.

*Stout, Bruce L, "Should the Surviving Spouse Serve as Trustee of the Nonmarital Trust?" *Estate Planning*, May 1990, pp 168-78.

Westfall, David. "Lapsed Powers of Withdrawal and the Income Tax." *Tax Law Review* 39 (1983), pp. 63-76.

Wright, Earl L., and Marilyn K. Renninger. "Bringing Automation into the Estate Planning Process." *Trusts & Estates*, January 1986, pp. 26-29.

Zabel, William D., and Kim E. Baptiste. "Marital D Dissolution and the Lifetime QTIP Trust." *Trusts & Estates*, April 1984, pp. 19-22.

-13

Lifetime Transfers I: Overview and Survey of Gift Planning

OVERVIEW

The last two chapters focused on property transfers at death. This chapter will introduce lifetime transfers of property, examining the techniques utilized in *gifting*, the most popular type of intrafamily lifetime transfer. The techniques of planning for other lifetime transfers, including incomplete transfers, intrafamily sales, and charitable gifts will be described in Chapter 14.

Lifetime transfers take many forms and are made for many reasons. They are made to individuals and to charities. They are made outright or to a fiduciary such as a trustee or custodian. They can take the form of a completed transfer, such as a sale or a gift, or they can remain incomplete, as in the case of a transfer with a retained interest. They can be a transfer of a total interest in property or just a partial interest.

While you read this chapter and the next, you will want to keep in mind two important principles. First, different types of transfers are designed to accomplish different types of goals. Second, the less complete the transfer, the less likely the transfer will achieve desired *tax* goals. This latter point cannot be overemphasized because clients often prefer to retain some control over the transferred property. By definition, every lifetime transfer requires the relinquishment of some control. Gifts mean loss of access, control and flexibility, and clients who are especially reluctant to give this up are more likely to feel uncomfortable with their estate plan, no matter what the magnitude of the financial rewards. Planners should be sensitive to this issue.

To minimize loss of access, control and flexibility, some clients may contemplate gifts to family members who in turn secretly agree to always make the assets available to the donor. Besides not meeting the legal requirements for a completed gift and thereby risking inclusion in their own gross estate, prospective donors should consider two other risks. First, the donees may have a "change in attitude," later disposing of the gift asset or refusing to share it or return it. Second, the gift assets are subject to the claims of the donee's creditors.

We begin our discussion of lifetime transfers with an examination of completed lifetime gifts, hereafter simply called *gifts*. For present purposes, we shall define a gift as any transfer that gives rise to potential gift taxation. As explained in Chapter 7, a gift is *complete* for tax purposes when there is surrender of dominion and control and delivery of an interest in property by a donor capable of transferring that property to an accepting donee capable of receiving and possessing it.

Essentially, a gift may be made outright, or it may be made to another party, usually a fiduciary, for the benefit of the donee. An *outright* gift results in the receipt by the donee of a fee simple interest in the gift property, yielding to the donee all of the rights that accompany that interest. Thus, an outright gift extends to the donee the greatest flexibility of ownership and control. However, the donor may not wish to bestow that degree of flexibility. For example, a donor may wish to make a sizable gift to help his or her child finance *future* college expenses but is reluctant to make an outright gift.

The usual alternative to an outright gift is the transfer to a *fiduciary*, who is responsible for managing the property and distributing its income and principal in accordance with the legal conditions either contained in the underlying document or established by local law. Significant gifts for a minor are especially likely to be in the name of a fiduciary, such as a custodian, a trustee, or occasionally a guardian. Gifts to adult donees are usually outright but are sometimes made in trust.

The next two sections will describe the major nontax and tax considerations in making gifts larger gifts. For the most part, the discussion will assume that an outright gift is being made. Some unique aspects of nonoutright gifts to children will be examined in greater detail at the end of the chapter.

NONTAX MOTIVES FOR MAKING GIFTS

Consider the many nontax motivations that encourage clients to make gifts. Common examples include the desire by parents or grandparents to provide for an expensive education, to help children finance a home or an automobile, to help establish or expand a business, to encourage a child to work in the client's business, to help a child who has experienced a significant loss or who is unemployed, to care for elderly parents, and the simple desire to witness a donee's enjoyment over the benefits that a gift can bring. Clients will be most willing to make gifts for the *tax* advantages to be described next when they are also motivated by one or more of these *nontax* objectives.

TAX CONSIDERATIONS IN MAKING GIFTS

There are death tax and income tax advantages and disadvantages of making gifts that must be considered.

Tax Advantages of Gifting

Gifts are commonly made to save federal, state and local death taxes, GSTT, and federal, state and local income taxes. In the examples that follow, look for two common tax threads. First, many gifts can be made at no gift tax cost. Second, even if a gift tax is incurred, gifts may still be desirable because they often have the potential of reducing total transfer taxes and income taxes.

Death tax and GSTT advantages. Death tax and GSTT advantages include the ability to reduce or freeze the taxable estate in three ways: using the shelter of the annual exclusion and the unified credit, avoiding grossing up, and excluding postgift appreciation. Each will be discussed next.

1. Shelter of annual exclusion and unified credit. Most clients about to embark upon a program of gifting will be able to transfer a significant portion of their estate, free of gift tax, death tax and GSTT. The gift tax and GSTT annual exclusions enable a donor to gift, free of tax, $10,000 per donee per year. Spousal gift splitting doubles this amount to $20,000.

EXAMPLE 13-1 Mom wishes to gift maximum equal amounts of her own property to her three children and three grandchildren. Each of the six donees can receive $10,000 each year, gift tax and GSTT free, adding up to a current aggregate annual tax-free gift total of $60,000.

In the above example, because total gross gifts to any one donee during a given calendar year will amount to no more than the annual exclusion, the donor need not even file a gift tax return.

EXAMPLE 13-2 Altering the facts in Example 13-1 a bit, assume that Dad also wishes to make similar annual exclusion gifts of *his own* property interests. Each of the six donees can now receive $20,000 each year for a current annual gift total of $120,000. Neither Mom nor Dad need file a gift tax return.

EXAMPLE 13-3 In the $120,000 total gift example immediately above, if greater than $60,000 of the gift property belonged to one of the two donors, they would have to *split* the gifts and file two gift tax returns each year. However, the tax outcome would be unchanged; of the total of $120,000 in gifts per year, no gift tax or GSTT would be due because taxable gifts would still equal zero.

Generalizing from these examples, the total number of annual exclusions available over time equals the number of donors times the number of donees times the number of years of gifting. Thus, in the above examples, if the donors engaged in gifting each year for the next eight years, they could make 96 annual exclusion gifts totaling $960,000 [= (2 x 6 x 8) x $10,000].

Actually, a donor can gift a much larger amount, gift tax (and GSTT) free, but only at the if the donor is willing to use up some unified credits (and, if applicable, the GSTT exemptions).

EXAMPLE 13-4 In Example 13-2, if Mom and Dad gave $50,000 to each person, they will have made six taxable gifts of $30,000, or total taxable gifts for the year of $180,000. Assuming that the donors had made no prior taxable gifts, the tentative gift tax on their joint gift-tax return will be $48,400. Although the application of the unified credit would result in a zero gift tax, the amount of the spousal combined unused unified credit would be reduced by $48,400, from $385,600 (two times $192,800) to $337,200. Each donor would be able to gift an additional $510,000 in excess of all annual exclusions, without paying any gift tax since each has used up only $90,000 of the $600,000 unified credit equivalent.

Thus, spouses with five suitable donees can give away, tax free, a total of $2.2 million over a span of 10 years. Of course, the couple would totally use up their unified credits, making the lifetime or deathtime transfer of the next dollar in excess of the annual exclusion subject to tax at the marginal rate of 37 percent. Regarding *GSTT*, spouses can gift, GSTT free, a total of $2 million (two $1 million lifetime exemptions), plus $20,000 times the number of suitable beneficiaries per year.

EXAMPLE 13-5 Corey, a bachelor, has already made total lifetime taxable gifts of $600,000. This year, he makes a single gift of a painting Corey appraised at $20,000. His gift tax will be $3,700, determined as follows:

Gross gift	$20,000.
Less: Annual exclusion	10,000.
Equals: Current taxable gift	10,000.
Plus: Prior taxable gifts	600,000.
Equals: Total taxable gifts	610,000.
Tentative tax on total gifts	196,500.
Less: Tentative tax on prior gifts	192,800.
Equals: Tentative tax on current gifts	3,700.
Less: Unused unified credit	0.
Equals: Net gift tax payable	$3,700.

Since the annual exclusion applies only to lifetime transfers, a somewhat different tax result would occur if the most recent transfer was made at death.

EXAMPLE 13-6 Assume the same basic facts as in Example 13-5, except that Corey dies owning the $20,000 painting, and therefore transfers it at death. The FET due will be $7,400, calculated as follows:

Gross estate	$20,000.
Plus: Adjusted taxable gifts	600,000.
Equals: Estate tax base	620,000.
Tentative tax	200,200.
Less: Unified credit	192,800.
Equals: Net FET	$7,400.

The $3,700 difference in the tax for the two prior examples is due to the absence of a per donee exclusion in calculating the estate tax.

Summarizing, the making of annual exclusion gifts and gifts sheltered by the unified credit and the $1 million lifetime GSTT exemption represents a simple estate planning technique that enables clients to substantially reduce their gross estate prior to death without having to pay gift taxes or GST tax.

2. No grossing up. The second death tax and GSTT advantage of gifting derives from the ability to exclude from the gross estate the amount of any *gift tax* paid on gifts given more than three years before death. As mentioned, unlike the estate tax, the gift tax is calculated on a tax exclusive basis. At this point, please take a few minutes to review the three examples in the grossing up section of Chapter 6, which illustrate the estate tax advantage to paying a gift tax.[1]

One additional point might be mentioned. Grossing up can be avoided even for gift tax paid on gifts made within three years of death if the decedent and spouse elect gift splitting and the surviving spouse paid the entire gift tax.[2]

3. Postgift appreciation. The third death tax and GSTT advantage of gifting is the ability to exclude postgift appreciation of the gifted property from future FET and GSTT. It can accomplish this tax saving in two different ways. First, gifting will usually *freeze* FET values by limiting the estate tax value of the transferred asset to its adjusted gift value. Second, gifting can *leverage* the use of exclusions, exemptions and the unified credit by transferring assets whose present low value is totally sheltered by these tax breaks, thereby excluding from FET and GSTT the entire value of the asset, including all future appreciation. The unique effects of freezing and leveraging have been amply demonstrated with numerous examples in Chapter 9. The following illustrates the use of both techniques in a single fact situation.

> EXAMPLE 13-7 Eighty-two year old Jeanne's estate consists of $2 million in municipal bonds and $1 million in common stock. More than able to live well on the bond income, Jeanne gifts all of the stock to an irrevocable trust paying the income to her three children for their lives with the remainder going to her grandchildren. Jeanne allocates her $1 million GSTT exemption to this transfer. In this simple but effective estate freeze, Jeanne has virtually ensured that she will die with an estate tax base about $3 million, no matter how much the value of the stocks rise. And Jeanne has leveraged the use of her $1 million GSTT exemption. For example, if the stock is eventually worth $4 million when it passes to the grandchildren, each $1 in current GSTT exemption will have sheltered $4 from GSTT.

Comprehensive example. By way of a complete review of these three major tax advantages of making lifetime gifts, consider the following comprehensive example. Assume that all transfers occur after 1987. While the numbers focus solely on estate tax savings, please keep in mind that substantial GSTT savings could also have resulted had the gift been made

---

1. Chapter 6 Examples 2035-5, 6, and 7.

2. LR 9214027.

to a skip person.

EXAMPLE 13-8 Burt, a widower, owns $3 million in property. His estate planner predicts that the property will double in value to $6 million in 10 years, the length of Burt's expected life span. The adviser recommends a plan of periodic gifting. Let's assume, however, for simplicity, that Burt is advised to make only one gift before he dies: one half of his entire estate to his only child, this year. Burt's total transfer taxes will be $1,469,300 if the gift is made, rather than the $2,583,000 that will be due if the gift is not made.

Burt makes the gift. If Burt makes the gift, and assuming that he has made no prior taxable gifts, Burt will pay a gift tax of $358,700, calculated as follows:

Gross gift	$1,500,000.
Less: Annual exclusion	10,000.
Taxable gift	1,490,000.
Tentative tax	551,500.
Less: Unified credit	192,800.
Net gift tax	$358,700.

Assume Burt dies in 10 years, owning property worth $2,282,600, calculated in the following manner. First, at the time of the gift, Burt's estate is reduced by $1,500,000, the value of the gift, and by $358,700, the amount of the gift tax paid. The remainder $1,141,300, while in his hands, will double over the decade to $2,282,600. Burt's FET will be $1,164,230, calculated as follows:

Gross estate	$2,282,600.
Plus: Adjusted taxable gifts	1,490,000.
Equals: Estate tax base	3,772,600.
Tentative tax	1,715,730.
Less: Gift tax payable	358,700.
Less: Unified credit	192,800.
Equals: Net FET	$1,164,230.

Burt's child will receive a total of $4,118,370, which is the sum of $1,118,370, the value of Burt's after tax estate, plus $3 million, the date of death value of the gift property.

Burt does not make the gift. Alternatively, if Burt does not make the gift, his beneficiaries will receive only $3,252,000, which is the $6 million value of the estate, reduced by FET of $2,748,000, calculated as follows:

Gross estate	$6,000,000.
Plus: Adjusted taxable gifts	-0-
Equals: Estate tax base	6,000,000.
Tentative tax	2,940,000.
Less: Unified credit	192,800.
Equals: Net FET	$2,748,000.

Let's analyze the tax savings from this gift plan. As a result of Burt's gift, his donee and beneficiaries will receive $866,370 more in combined lifetime and deathtime gifts (= $4,118,370 - $3,252,000). This amount represents the mathematical difference between $1,225,070, the saving in total transfer taxes, and $358,700, the forgone appreciation in the property that will be used to pay the gift tax. The saving in total transfer taxes can be explained as follows: The FET tax base in the no-gift alternative exceeds the FET tax base under the gift scenario by $2,227,400. At a marginal tax rate of 55 percent, this means an FET reduction of $1,225,070.

Why will the gift alternative shelter $2,227,400 from estate taxes? The answer has four components. First, $10,000 is sheltered by the gift tax *annual exclusion*. Second, the $1.5 million postgift appreciation will escape taxation. Third, since Burt did not die within three years of the date of the gift, there is no *grossing up*, thus, the $358,700 gift taxes paid are not added to Burt's gross estate at death. Finally, since a gift tax is actually paid, Burt's gross estate will not include the $358,700 appreciation on the property used to pay the gift tax (this matches the gift tax only because we assumed everything doubled in value). The sum of these four components equals $2,227,400, the amount of the total reduction in the tax base resulting from Burt's $1.5 million gift.

This example assumed that Burt made only one lifetime gift to just one person, thereby reaping the benefit of only one annual exclusion. Substantially more transfer tax would be saved if Burt made many smaller gifts to several persons *each year* until his death, utilizing the shelter of multiple annual exclusions.

Must gifts be made more than three years before death to keep the assets out of the gross estate? No, except for gifts of life insurance or relinquishments of §2036, §2037 or §2038 transfers.[3] In fact, donors can make deathbed gifts to take advantage of the annual exclusion. Chapter 17 will describe the use of the durable power of attorney for property, that enables even an incapacitated client's agent to make gifts on the client's behalf. However, the IRS has ruled that the document creating the power must expressly authorize the attorney-in-fact to make gifts,[4] otherwise, any transfers will be treated as revocable, therefore incomplete.

In conclusion, a program of gifting can result in substantial estate tax and GSTT savings and, commonly, the ultimate transfer of a larger amount of wealth, tax free, to succeeding generations. The gifts can be tax sheltered by the annual exclusion as well as by the exclusion of both the gift tax and

---

3. See Chapter 6, under §2035 materials, for detailed explanations.

4. TAM 9231003.

postgift appreciation from the donor's taxable estate.

Income tax advantages. The making of gifts also offers some income tax advantages, including shifting income and obtaining a step-up in basis.

Shifting income. As we saw in Chapter 9, gifts can result in some income shifting. In general, since the donee (or trustee, for gifts into an irrevocable trust) becomes the owner of gifted property, any income earned on that property will be taxed to the donee (or trustee or trust beneficiary), who is usually subject to a lower marginal income tax rate. Further, the reduced taxable income to the donor might put her or him in a lower tax bracket.

As explained in Chapters 8 and 10, outright gifts to children under age 14 will not save much income tax due to the *kiddie tax*.

> EXAMPLE 13-9 The Gerards are in the 50 percent marginal income tax bracket, and wish to shift taxable income to a custodial account for their 13-year-old son, Wayne, who has no other income. They transfer $12,000 in 10 percent coupon bonds to Wayne, who will be taxed on the $1,200 interest received each year. After subtracting $600, the maximum standard deduction amount allowable against unearned income of a dependent, Wayne's income tax for the first year on the remaining $600 would be $90, which is $510 less than the $600 tax that would have been owed by the Gerards. The Gerards realize that it would not make any income tax sense at this time to shift additional income to Wayne by transferring a greater amount of securities since the additional income would be all taxed at their rate, not Wayne's.

Beginning in the taxable year that a child reaches age 14, the kiddie tax will not apply and all of the child's income will be taxable to the child.

> EXAMPLE 13-10 Continuing Example 13-9 above, in the following year Wayne turns 14, and the Gerards transfer an additional $48,000 in 10 percent coupon bonds for Wayne's benefit. Wayne's income tax on the total taxable $6,000 will be $810 (= ($6000 - $600) x .15), which is $2,190 less than the tax of $3,000 otherwise payable by the Gerards (i.e., .50 x $6,000 = $3,000).

The example immediately above involved the shifting of $6,000 in 15 percent taxable income. At the limit, as much as $23,350 in 1994 income could be shifted to a 15 percent tax bracket *individual* (age 14 or older) reporting no other income, assuming a standard deduction of $600.[5] On the other hand, a *trust's* 15 percent bracket ends at $1,500, reflecting Congress's strong interest in discouraging the use of trusts to shift income.

---

5. An indexed amount, increased to $650 for tax years beginning in 1995. Rev. Proc. 94-72, IRB 1994-50, 14.

As these examples suggest, parents anticipating paying their children's college expenses may wish to transfer assets to the children to reduce the income tax bite. However, tax law may help them to acquire certain investments to finance college expenses without transferring assets and at no tax cost. Interest on certain U.S. EE Saving Bonds purchased and owned by one or both parents themselves (or by the student, if at least 24 years old) after 1989 and redeemed to pay tuition and fees will not be subject to income tax. However, this interest exclusion is phased out for taxpayers having "modified" 1995 adjusted gross income (indexed) between $63,450 and $93,450 for joint returns, and between $42,300 and $57,300 for single and head of household returns.[6] According to §135, modified adjusted gross income is adjusted gross income without regard to §911, §931 or §933 (foreign income exclusions), and after application of §86 (taxable social security income), §219 (retirement contribution deductions), and §469 (limit on deductibility of passive losses).

Obtaining a step-up in basis. In Chapter 8 the reader learned that the income tax basis of any property owned by a decedent at death will be stepped-up to date of death value. This step-up is particularly valuable for people wishing to sell rapidly appreciating property. Unfortunately, the property owner must *die* to accomplish the step-up. Astute readers may wonder whether gifting may be able to accelerate the timing of this step-up. For example, could A, owner of a low basis asset and in excellent health, gift the asset to B, who dying, to achieve an earlier basis step-up in the asset, which A will later sell after having received the asset back by way of B's will or trust? As we'll see in two examples later in the chapter, the answer is yes, as long as B doesn't die within one year of the gift date.

Tax Disadvantages of Gifting

There are several tax dangers and disadvantages in making lifetime gifts, including prepaying the transfer tax, adverse §2035 consequences, the danger that the gift is later ruled incomplete, and loss of step-up in basis.

Prepaying the transfer tax. A *large gift* can result in a gift tax liability that must be paid by April 15 of the following year, thereby reducing the client-donor funds available for investment. Nonetheless, as we have seen, prepayment of the transfer tax is justifiable if it has the effect of substantially reducing the client's FET. This will happen if the gift property

---

6. Due to a mistake in drafting the 1993 tax law, post-1992 rather than post-1989 inflation adjustments are currently being used as the index, unless Congress corrects the error.

appreciates greatly before the client's death or if it appreciates modestly and the client can avoid grossing up by surviving at least three years after making the gift. On the other hand, gifting property and prepaying the transfer tax may turn out to have been a costly mistake, particularly in situations where the property actually *declines* in value and the client *dies within three years* of making the gift. Then no transfer taxes will have been saved, the client lost the use of the gift tax money, and the donee has a carry over basis on the property. Thus, to assess the likelihood of financial success resulting from a large gift, the planner should consider factors such as the life expectancy of the client-donor, the expected appreciation potential of the property, the different basis rules, and the utility of the property to the donor and to the donee.

Even if a large gift is totally sheltered by the unified credit, it will have the effect of reducing the amount that can be transferred at death free of tax since it will be included in the estate tax base as an adjusted taxable gift. Before recommending large gifts or a gift giving plan, one must determine whether the gifts will also be subjected to state gift taxes since there is no federal state gift taxes credit, whereas there is a federal state death tax credit.[7]

An additional adverse §2035 consequence: unsheltered postgift appreciation. We mentioned in the preceding discussion that if a gift is made within three years of death, §2035(c) requires the gift tax paid be included in the donor's gross estate under the grossing-up rule. In addition to this adverse consequence, recall the discussion in Chapter 6 that the entire *date-of-death value* of the gift property is included in the donor's gross estate if the retained interest rules of §§2036, 2037, 2038 apply, or an incident of ownership in life insurance was retained, §2042, at the date of death; and of course §2035(d)(2) causes inclusion if a transfer of a retained interest or of an incident of ownership in life insurance occurs within three years of death.

As mentioned in Chapter 10, another potentially common pitfall under §2035 can arise when a trustee of a revocable living trust makes a gift within three years of the trustor's death. The IRS has been very aggressively taking the position that the gift constitutes a relinquishment of revocability which under the combined influence of Sections 2035 and 2038 will subject the date-of-death value of the gift to inclusion in the trustor's gross estate. To avoid this result, either the gift should be made directly by the trustor, after withdrawal from the trust, or the trustee should be empowered to make distributions only to the trustor.

---

7. §2011.

In summary, §2035(c) and §2035(d)(2) can have the effect of taking back all three major advantages of gifting. These two sections require grossing up of gift taxes and, in the case of life insurance and transfers in which retained controls are relinquished within three years before death, including all postgift appreciation in the taxable estate. remember that if a transfer gets pulled back into the gross estate the benefit of the annual exclusion is lost. In essence, insofar as the death taxes are concerned, it is as though the gift never took place.

Gift later ruled incomplete. If it is later determined that a gift was not complete, the date-of-death value of the property will be included in the donor's gross estate in spite of the fact that the donor, in all good faith, paid a gift tax at the time of the gift. The estate will receive a credit for the gift tax paid, but from a transfer tax perspective the gift will be considered as not having been made. Common examples of defective gift schemes include giving stocks and bonds while retaining an interest, transferring title to the residence but continuing to live there rent-free, and transferring property to an irrevocable trust but retaining discretionary powers, or giving those powers to the trustee but reserving the right to serve as trustee. A different, timing problem is illustrated in the following example:

> EXAMPLE 13-11 On her deathbed, decedent made a gift by writing a check on her bank account. She died before the check was cashed. In her state, because she had the power to revoke by stopping payment, the gift was not complete, and therefore includable in her gross estate under §2038.[8]

Loss of step-up in basis. A major tax disadvantage of making lifetime gifts is the loss in the step-up in basis that would have been received on appreciated property had it been retained by the donor until death. This is a drawback for a donee who wishes to sell the appreciated property. On the other hand, if the donee has no plans to sell the property during his or her lifetime, or intends to trade the asset in a tax-deferred exchange, the problem might disappear since there will be a step-up in basis at the donee's death.

> EXAMPLE 13-12 Granny has always wanted to do something nice for her loving, adult grandson, and today she gives him some real property that she and her deceased husband acquired in the 1920s. When Granny dies, the gift property will not receive a step-up in basis, and grandson will own an asset with a sizable unrealized gain to be recognized if he sells it prior to his death. However, this potential taxable gain will vanish if grandson dies owning the

---

8. For details on the planning for check writing prior to death, see the Rubenstein article cited at the end of the chapter.

property.

Other disadvantages. Two other tax disadvantages to consider are noted briefly.

Net gifts. First, a particular income tax disadvantage applies to net gifts, discussed in Chapter 7, whereby the donee agrees to pay the gift tax thus reducing the value of the gift, which in turn reduces the gift tax. A net gift can result in a taxable gain to the donor if the gift tax paid by the donee exceeds the donor's basis in the property.

Valuation disputes with IRS. Second, a significant valuation problem can arise with gifting. The IRS will sometimes successfully challenge the value of a gift in both gift tax and estate tax audits, even many years after the gift was made because of the lack of an effective statute of limitations.

Estate and Gift Tax Statute of Limitations. The statute of limitations for both estate tax returns and for gift tax returns is three years after the return is filed, except for an early filed return the three years starts from the due date of the return.[9] There are exceptions to the three year rule; for instance, if the return under reports the value of the gross estate or the total gifts by more than 25% the statute of limitations is increased to six years after the return is filed, and there is no time limit if the return is filed with an intent to commit fraud or to willfully evade taxes. Finally, there is no time limit if no return is filed.[10]

Because Cory, in Example 13-5, had an appraisal of the painting he gave away, and he was not trying to evade gift taxes, the IRS is limited by the three year statute of limitations in challenging the value of the painting for gift tax purposes. However, the IRS may challenge the adjusted taxable gifts value of this gift on the estate tax return at Cory's death, even if his death occurs many years later. This later challenge would serve only to boost the taxable estate into higher marginal rates and would not result in any more gift tax being paid, in fact the gift tax payable credit would have to be recalculated based on the high value of the gift. Thus, the gift tax period of limitation is not increased but the estate tax would be higher if the revaluation of the gift moved the estate into a higher marginal rate.[11]

Another major consideration in giving is the selection of the best assets to gift.

---

9. §6501(a).

10. Exceptions to the three year rule, generally, see §6501(c), and the 25% under reporting, see §6501(e).

11. Estate of *Frederick R. Smith* (1990) 94 TC 872.

TYPES OF ASSETS TO GIVE

In giving, the client usually has a wide selection of assets from which to choose. From an estate planning perspective, some assets make better gifts than others. The following constitutes a basic set of guidelines for selecting gift property. As the examples will illustrate, the choice of the best asset will usually depend on the specific family situation.

Basis Considerations

An asset's basis will influence its potential gift appeal.

Gifting high basis assets to reduce taxable gain. Other things being the equal, a high-basis asset makes a better gift than a low-basis asset, if the donee is likely to sell the asset soon after receiving it. As we have seen, the general rule is that the donee retains the donor's basis. Sale by the donee at a price above this basis results in a taxable gain, thus, the higher the basis the lower the taxable gain.

> EXAMPLE 13-13 Donor wishes to give donee $100,000 in marketable securities and she owns stock A was purchased two years ago for $95,000 but now worth $100,000; and stock B was acquired 15 years ago for $20,000 but also worth $100,000. The donee plans to hold the stock until it reaches $110,000 in value and then to sell it. The donee would realize a gain of $15,000 on the sale of stock A and a gain of $90,000 on the sale of stock B, therefore, the donee would prefer to receive stock A.

Although a high-basis asset usually makes a good gift from an income tax point of view, it will make an unattractive gift if its basis is too high, i.e., higher than its date-of-gift value. Property in which the owner has an *unrealized loss* is not a good asset to give because the donee, upon selling it, will not be able to recognize that loss. Examples 1015-3 and 1015-5 in Chapter 8 demonstrate this effect, which prevents the donee from recognizing that portion of the loss resulting from the decline in value while the donor held the property. A better strategy would be for the donor to sell the property, realize the loss, and then give the cash to the donee.

Gifting low basis assets for other reasons. On the other hand, giving low-basis assets makes more sense in some circumstances. For example, if for liquidity or other reasons a donor *plans to sell* a retained asset at the time of giving another asset, he or she should consider gifting a lower-basis asset and selling the higher-basis asset in order to personally incur a lower tax outlay. This strategy will be especially productive if the donee either is in a lower tax bracket or has no immediate plans to sell the property received as a gift. Gain realized upon later sale by the donee will at least be deferred, and may be totally eliminated due to the step-up-at-death principle, if the donee dies before the asset is sold. Keep in mind the Code's one year rule for property that returns to the donor as a result of the donee's death. Code §1014(e) provides that when a person inherits appreciated property which he or she had gifted to a decedent within one year of decedent's death, the adjusted basis of the property to the donor will be decedent's adjusted basis immediately before the donee's date of death. Appreciated property means property worth more *at the time of the gift* than its basis.

> EXAMPLE 13-14 Husband gives his terminally ill wife his interest in land, purchased many years ago for $400, and currently worth $10,000. Wife, who dies two months later, devises the land back to husband, who then sells it for $11,000. Husband, because the property was appreciated at the time he gave it to his wife, must now realized a gain of $10,600, not $1,000. The wife's adjusted basis just before her death was a carry over basis of $400.

Hence, the advantage of gifting low-basis property works, in the case of a donor-devisee, only if the donee-decedent lives *at least one year* after the date of gift. This strategy will work even if the original donor is not the spouse of the decedent but the original gift might use up the donor's unified credit if the gift is not completely covered by the annual exclusion. §1014(e) does not apply if the donee-decedent leaves the property to someone other than the original donor or the donor's spouse. Thus, A give an appreciated asset to D, who can then transfer it at death to B; and B will obtain the step-up even if D's death occurred within one year of the transfer to D.

Assets having sentimental or utilitarian value are more likely to be kept by a donee. If a gifts is going to be kept by the donee basis considerations are unnecessary.

Postgift Appreciation

General considerations. If FET reduction is a major goal, the generous client should consider gifting *growth assets*, that is, assets expected to appreciate substantially, rather than assets whose value is likely to remain stable or to fall. Some assets have greater inherent appreciation potential than others, although in general this determination represents mere speculation. However, assets such as life insurance, or equity interests in either a closely held business or real estate may be likely growth prospects, while assets such as patent and royalty rights, whose value usually declines over time, would not make good gift assets in this context. Cash and cash equivalents are also less than highly desirable, because their value cannot be expected to rise. In general, from a transfer-tax point of view, assets having a combined low gift tax value and potentially high estate tax value make the best gifts.

Opportunity shifting. An excellent example of a type of gift of highly appreciating assets is called opportunity shifting. It involves the transfer of a wealth- or an income-producing opportunity before it is objectively ascertainable. For example, business clients may be able to recognize the prospect of a profitable commercial enterprise before it blossoms sufficiently into a verifiably valuable opportunity. By transferring ownership during its early stages, a value shift can occur without transfer-tax cost and before the income the venture generates is considered attributable to the client.

> EXAMPLE 13-15 Dad, owner of a successful computer component firm, has just established a new corporation to pursue the viability of a recently developed engineering idea. The new firm is capitalized at $50,000, and Dad gives an adult daughter 20 percent of the stock and places another 20 percent in an irrevocable trust for the benefit of his minor son.

This example demonstrates the creation of *additional taxpaying entities*, the new corporation and the trust, as well as the *splitting* income and wealth among more family members before the value of the enterprise has manifest itself. Similar techniques can be arranged for almost any asset that is expected to appreciate in value. Good hunches by savvy people are the major sources of intrafamily opportunity shifting.

Administration Problems

Assets that are likely to create problems in estate administration can make good gift assets. For example, *art works*, especially those currently worth less than the annual gift tax exclusion, may not need to be valued if transferred by lifetime gift, but could create valuation disputes, a potentially higher FET, and additional costs of valuation if transferred at death. Further, *illiquid assets* such as real estate may need to be sold to pay death taxes, if transferred at death. Alternatively, a lifetime gift of these assets may avoid a later problem.

Other Asset Choice Considerations

Transfer income earning assets to shift income. Where income shifting is a planning goal, high income earning assets make better gifts. As we have seen, income tax law in general requires an actual transfer of the "tree" (asset) in order to transfer the "fruit" (income) of that tree.

Avoid gifting assets with tax benefits to donor. The well-heeled donor should ordinarily consider gifting assets that do not have *built-in tax benefits* such as income exclusions, deductions, or credits which would be of less value to a lower bracket donee. The client should consider retaining assets such as tax shelters, municipal bonds, and income-producing real property in his or her own portfolio. However, when a tax-shelter property reaches the "crossover point" and begins to throw off "phantom income" to the investor, it may be a good time to gift the property, to shift the income to a lower bracket.

Gift nonbusiness assets to qualify for §303, §2032A and §6166. Giving nonbusiness property may offer death and income tax advantages by virtue of reducing the decedent's taxable estate, thereby increasing the portion that is considered business in the estate retained such that specific provisions of the Internal Revenue Code apply. These provisions allow the following tax saving opportunities:

a. To pay death taxes, funeral bills, and administrative expenses, cash from a closely held corporation can be used to buy back stock from the decedent's estate with the transaction being treated as a capital transaction instead of a dividend distribution. Since the stock held by the estate will have received a step-up in basis there should be very little, if any, capital gain.[12]

b. Special reduced valuation of the decedent's closely held business, in FET calculations,[13] and

c. Deferral of paying the FET attributable to the value of the decedent's closely held business.[14]

In each case, the Code requires that the value of the decedent's business must be *at least* a certain percentage of the total estate, commonly 35 percent. For nonqualifying clients, one way of increasing the likelihood of meeting this percentage requirement is to reduce the estate size by gifts of nonbusiness assets. For greater detail on the business liquidity boosting techniques available under the Code, see Chapter 15.

Miscellaneous tax factors. Some assets should not be gifted if they

---

12. §303.

13. §2032A.

14. §6166.

may generate adverse tax consequences. For example, consider an asset for which the donor had taken the *investment tax credit*, which was repealed by TRA 86. If the donor gifts the asset before the end of its useful life, he or she will be required to "recapture" part of the credit, that is, repay part of the taxes saved from the credit.

In at least one situation, gifts to children can generate a tax benefit otherwise unavailable to the parents.

> EXAMPLE 13-16 Because of their high income, the Piatts are not qualified to contribute before-tax dollars to an *Individual Retirement Account* (IRA). Their adult son, John, is qualified, he cannot afford to make the contributions. John enters in an informal agreement with his parents, who will give him $1,500 a year, to help contribute $2,000 to his own IRA. This annual arrangement is to continue indefinitely, so long as John adds $500 and does not make any premature withdrawals. Each year, John will save hundreds of dollars in income tax by taking the IRA deduction. The Piatts have the satisfaction of knowing that have increased the financial security of his later years.

As a result of the kiddie tax, generous parents may wish to transfer to their young children property that *does not generate taxable income*, at least not until the children reach age 14. Possible assets include U.S. government EE bonds, municipal bonds, interests in land, a closely held business, and growth stocks. In many situations, the parent can then determine the timing of the tax "hit" by choosing which year to liquidate the assets and, consequently, which year to realize the likely gain. It should be mentioned that the popular U.S. Government EE savings bonds are not transferable. An outright gift of them is considered a redemption. However, there is no restriction on an owner adding co-owners.

While the material up to now has centered on a discussion of the tax and nontax aspects of gifting to individuals in general, the next section discusses gifts to a spouse followed by a section on gifts to minor children. We choose to focus on these donees because several tax and nontax implications of gifts to them are unique and require further explanation. Gifts to spouses are different in part because of the additional tax saving available through the use of the marital deduction. Gifts to minors are unique in part because of the techniques by which the transfer is often arranged, usually with the assistance of a fiduciary

GIFTS TO THE SPOUSE: TECHNIQUES AND CONSIDERATIONS

This section will explore the tax characteristics of lifetime gifts between spouses. We shall see that the gift tax marital deduction offers unique planning opportunities to reduce taxes, in some cases by an even greater amount than for gifts to a nonspouse. The following material discusses interspousal gift considerations involved in saving death taxes and income taxes.[15]

Interspousal Gifts to Save Death Taxes

In the last two chapters, we examined in some detail several marital deduction techniques designed to minimize, or at least postpone, the estate tax for a married couple. We saw that four planning options are commonly used: the 100 percent marital deduction, credit shelter bypass, bypass with estate equalization, and the 100 percent marital deduction with disclaimer into bypass. We will now see that when one spouse is substantially wealthier than the other and there is a significant chance that the less wealthy spouse will die first, death taxes can sometimes be saved by means of bypass planning coupled with a program of interspousal gifts. However, this strategy will not work if the basic testamentary scheme involves the simple 100 percent marital deduction, as the following example shows.

> EXAMPLE 13-17 Husband has a $2 million estate and wife owns nothing. Their estate plan leaves everything to the survivor, who then leaves everything to their children. Without a change in their estate plan, restructuring the distribution of wealth between them by means of completed gifts will result in no FET saving. The first spouse to die, whether husband or wife, will leave an estate subject to no FET, either because there is no gross estate (wife dies first) or because the entire gross estate is sheltered by the 100 percent marital deduction (husband dies first or gifts were made to balance the estates). Thus, either spouse, as S2, will wind up owning the entire $2 million at death no matter how much each spouse owned prior to their deaths, and interspousal gifts will not change the total FET. See Figure 13-1.

---

15. For a description of the use of interspousal gifts designed to qualify a spouse under long-term medical care for Medicaid benefits, see the section in Chapter 17 entitled "Special Needs Trust and Other Asset `Spend-down Planning.'"

FIGURE 13-1 Illustration of Example 13-17: No Interspousal Gifts, 100 Percent Marital Deduction Plan

---

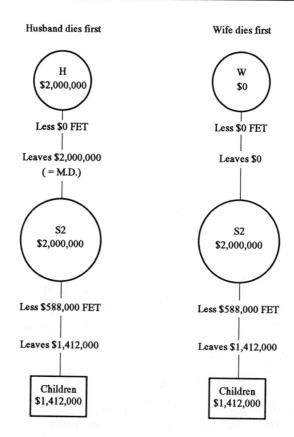

However, if the spouses use a bypass trust, FET may be saved by means of lifetime interspousal gifts, as the following two examples demonstrate. First we'll see the effect if no gift is made, and then we'll calculate the FET saving from an interspousal gift.

EXAMPLE 13-18 Let's assume that the couple in Example 13-17 create a *credit shelter bypass*, but the husband makes *no lifetime gifts*. The family wealth will devolve in the following manner: S1 will incur no FET no matter which spouse dies first, either because that spouse owns no property or because of the combined shelter of the marital deduction and the unified credit. If husband dies first, wife will receive $1.4 million and $600,000 will pass to the bypass share. Upon wife's later death, her estate will incur an FET of $320,000, leaving a net combined amount to the children of $ 1,680,000, which is the sum of $1,080,000 from her, plus 600,000 from the bypass share. Alternatively, *if wife dies first*, husband's $2 million estate at his later death will incur an FET of $588,000, leaving a total of only $1,412,000 to pass to the children. No bypass could be created if wife died first since wife had no assets to put into a bypass. See Figure 13-2.

FIGURE 13-2 Illustration of Example 13-18: No Interspousal Gifts, Credit Shelter Bypass Plan

---

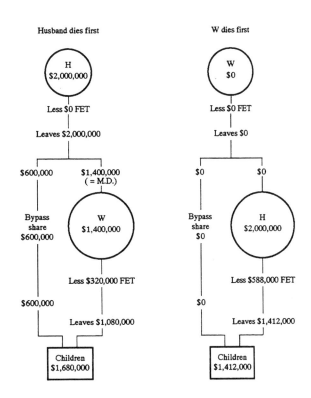

Now consider the effect of an *interspousal gift* upon this credit shelter bypass plan.

> EXAMPLE 13-19 Assume that husband in Example 13-18 *gives* his wife one half of his wealth. The effects on FET under a credit shelter bypass plan are as follows. Since the gift was made between the spouses no gift tax will be due. The gift will not even be listed on husband's estate tax return as an adjusted taxable gift because the transfer tax scheme subtracts the marital deduction amount in arriving at adjusted taxable gifts.
>
> If husband dies first, the results will be the same as in the 'no-gifts' Example 13-18: there will be no FET upon husband's death, and an FET of $320,000 upon wife's later death. However, if *wife dies first*, a markedly different result will occur as compared to when she had no estate. Wife's estate will still incur no FET, but on husband's later death there will be an FET of $320,000, an amount that is $268,000 less than the Example 13-17 result in which no gift had been made. Thus, the children will be able to receive a total of $1,680,000, rather than $1,412,000. Husband's gift of one half of his wealth to wife will, if wife predeceases husband, generate a transfer tax saving of $268,000. See Figure 13-3.

The interspousal gift saved FET because it enabled the less wealthy S1 to devise property into the bypass, thereby reducing S2's gross estate and FET. Similarly, other interspousal gifts can also generate large tax savings for other types of bypass arrangements.

Drawbacks. In spite of the large potential FET saving, the wealthier spouse may have some reservations about making a sizable gift to his or her spouse.

Relinquishment of control. First, for the transfer to be complete, the donor spouse must be willing to surrender complete dominion and control to his or her spouse. In this age of high rates of marital dissolution, planners should be mindful of the possibility of future marital strife and its effect on the overall plan: It could generate a bitter regret by the donor that the gift was ever made. Further, even if the spouses are happily married, the wealthier spouse may still be reluctant to relinquish control over so much wealth. As a possible solution, the donor spouse could instead transfer the property into a living QTIP trust, which could effectively prevent the donee spouse from exercising dispositive control over the corpus.[16] However, if the donee spouse does in fact die first, Section 2036 may require later inclusion of the corpus in the donor's (S2's) gross estate to the extent that the latter retained any benefits or controls (such as a life estate in the income).

---

16. For a description of the tax savings and asset protection derived from properly structured lifetime QTIPs, see the McNair article cited at the end of the chapter.

FIGURE 13-3 Illustration of Example 13-19: Gift of $1 Million To Wife, Credit Shelter Bypass Plan

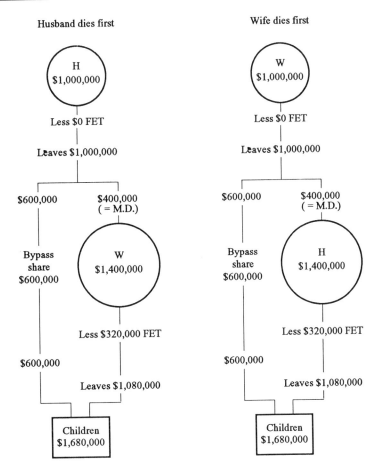

FET saving unlikely. Second, demographic statistics indicate two salient facts: many more wives survive their husbands than vice versa and husbands in noncommunity property states are likely to be wealthier than their wives. Thus, in the most common situations, where the wealthier spouse (husband) dies first, a prior lifetime gift to the less affluent spouse (wife) will have saved no FET, as Example 13-17 demonstrated. Thus, estate-leveling interspousal gifts designed to maximize FET saving through bypass plans will accomplish this goal in only a minority of family situations.

In conclusion, completed interspousal gifts, when added to an estate bypass plan, can occasionally result in FET savings. The strategy will work in situations where the less wealthy spouse is expected to die first and where the spouses are happily married, elderly, and reasonably confident in each other's ability to faithfully handle such an undertaking.

Interspousal Gifts to Save Income Taxes

Ordinarily, there is no *lifetime* income tax advantage to interspousal gifts. As we have seen, the joint income tax return, filed by the overwhelming majority of spouses, has the effect of combining spousal income and produces one tax, no matter which spouse earned the income. However, a completed gift from one spouse to the other can often save income taxes *after the donee's earlier death*, if the gift property is later sold at a gain. The tax-saving results from the opportunity to experience a step-up in basis before sale and was illustrated earlier in this chapter.

EXAMPLE 13-20 In Example 13-14 Husband was unable to obtain a step-up in basis upon the death of his wife on property he had given her two months before her death, due to the restriction in Code Section 1014(e). However, had wife *lived longer than one year*, husband's taxable gain upon later sale will be $1,000 rather than $10,600, because of the resulting step-up in basis.

EXAMPLE 13-21 In Example 13-20 above, had wife bequeathed the property to her *bypass trust* for the benefit of husband, §1014(e) would not apply because the property will pass to a different party (the trustee) and not back to the donor-spouse. Thus, a step-up would have been available even if the donee spouse had not lived one year after the gift had been made.

As a result, the gifting strategy used by couples such as those in the example illustrated in Figure 13-3 will save FET and income tax, regardless when the first spouse dies.

In community property states, of course, since the surviving spouse receives a step-up in basis at S1's death for all community property owned, this gifting strategy need only be considered for the client's separate property.

Next, we turn to considerations in making gifts to minor children.

GIFTS TO MINOR CHILDREN:
TECHNIQUES AND CONSIDERATIONS

Gifts to minor children are somewhat unique, not in their tax-saving potential so much as in the manner by which their transfer is usually arranged. As mentioned earlier in this chapter, gifts to minors are usually not made outright but are made instead through a *fiduciary* in the form of a guardianship, a custodianship, or a trust.

Outright gifts transfer the greatest amount of control to the donee, invite the least amount of challenge from the IRS, and are the least complicated to make. But an outright gift to a person, whether a minor or an adult, will only work satisfactorily when the donee has sufficient maturity to rationally possess, conserve, and enjoy the gift property. In other circumstances, the transfer should be made to a *fiduciary*. Many states have statutes that require gifts, above some set value, given to a minor be held for the minor by a fiduciary. The transfer to a fiduciary should be arranged to achieve the same tax advantages, use of the annual exclusion and shifting of income, available with an outright gift, yet protect the donee from the risks of his or her own immaturity, and, to conform to any restrictions state law places on the ownership and use of property by minors.

Before examining types of fiduciary gifts that meet these objectives, it will be helpful to review a tax issue that has bearing on the use of property given on for the benefit of a minor. If income from a gift is used to discharge the *obligation of support* of the donor-parent that income will be taxable to the parent.[17]

> EXAMPLE 677-1 Dad gives 14-year-old Junior $500 so that Junior can purchase lunch during his freshman year in high school. Junior deposits the money in his own savings account, subsequently withdrawing interest as well as principal to buy the lunches. The interest income will be taxable to Dad as income used in discharge of a support obligation.

This rule applies even if the source of the income is not from the parents (for example, income from a trust).

Thus, in order to enjoy the full tax advantages of a completed gift to a minor, income from the gift must not be used to discharge support obligations. Ordinarily, parents are not obligated to support their adult children, so the issue does not usually apply to adult donees. But there are exceptions. In about fifteen states including Illinois and New Jersey, judges in divorce cases have imposed the duty of support for *higher education* for adult children.

---

17. §677(b).

However, several factors limit the application of this exception. In 1992, Pennsylvania's supreme court ruled that divorcing parents will no longer be so obligated, reasoning that children become adults at age 18 and that the Legislature had not explicitly addressed the issue. Second, recall that this exception has arisen in the divorce, rather than the tax, arena. Finally, no state in the country has required parents of *intact families* to pay for an adult child's higher education.[18] Nonetheless, caution should be exercised in advising clients, and local law should be checked.[19]

Gifts under Guardianship

Individuals may make completed gifts to themselves or others as guardians for the benefit of minor children.

Drawbacks. Gifts under guardianships have some significant drawbacks. First, to be legally valid, the transfer must be made with local (probate) court supervision, which usually requires the expense of time and money in securing court approval, a bond, an annual accounting, and other legal necessities. State laws vary on specific requirements. Further, property held in a guardianship is difficult to manage efficiently because many actions, including the purchase and sale of property, often require court approval. Court supervision does afford the ward greater potential protection from misuse of the property by the adult fiduciary, but protection is rarely a major consideration. Finally, another disadvantage of guardianships is that the guardian must turn over the property outright to the ward at majority (age 18), an age donors usually consider too immature to receive a fee simple interest in most gift property.

Custodial Gifts

Uniform Gifts To Minors Act. The Uniform Gifts to Minors Act (UGMA), adopted in one form or other in all states, allows a relatively simple method of making fiduciary gifts to minors of certain property. No court supervision is required. The gift property is transferred in the name of someone, acting "as custodian for (minor's name) under the (state name) Uniform Gift to Minors Act." This type of titling serves to "incorporate by

---

18. Wall Street Journal, November 19, 1992, p. B1.

19. For more information, see the Blase article in this chapter's Recommended Reading section, and the Kline article cited at the end of Appendix 14A.

reference" all of the provisions of that Act, including broad investment powers under the "prudent person" standard, and the ability of the custodian to spend property on behalf of the minor without a court order. Further, a bond need not be given; and, unless the donor or donee request them, accountings are not necessary. Thus, custodial gifts have many advantages over guardianships.

Commonly permissible custodial gift property under UGMA includes securities, cash, life insurance, and annuities, but there is legislative movement by several states to greatly expand this list. In most UGMA states, real property cannot be held in custodial form.

Uniform Transfers To Minors Act. In 1983 the National Conference on Uniform Laws adopted the Uniform Transfers to Minors Act (UTMA) designed to replace the UGMA. Major changes include the following:

1. Allows *any property interests* to be transferred, including real estate, partnership interests, patents, royalty interests, and intellectual property,
2. Allows custodial gifts *at death* by permitting a fiduciary (executor or trustee) to establish a custodianship if authorized in a governing will or trust,
3. Authorizes transfers to a custodian from persons *other than* the transferor who are obligated to the minor (examples of situations include a personal injury recovery, life insurance proceeds payable to a minor beneficiary,[20] and a joint bank account of which the minor is a surviving cotenant), and
4. Allows a transferor to revocably nominate a custodian to receive property *in the future*.

The following states have adopted UTMA without significant alterations: Arkansas, California, Colorado, Connecticut, Florida, Hawaii, Idaho, Illinois, Missouri, Montana, Nevada, New Hampshire, North Carolina, North Dakota, Oregon, Rhode Island and West Virginia.[21]

Evaluation of custodial gifts. A custodial gift can save the time and expense involved in establishing a trust and custodianships are like trusts in many ways, but they are more restrictive for the following reasons:

---

20. For an exposition on transfers of life insurance proceeds to a family member as custodian under UTMA, see the McDonald article cited at the end of the chapter.

21. For further details, see the Ledwith-Robinson and Sciurba articles cited at the end of the chapter.

- A custodial gift may be *created for only one person*; a trust can provide for multiple beneficiaries, with unequal distributions among them.
- A custodianship is *not a separate legal entity*; all income is taxable to the minor. In contrast, an irrevocable trust is a separate taxpayer, enabling one additional "run up the rate ladder."
- Because the law gives the custodian the power to distribute income or principal to the minor, if the *donor is named custodian* and predeceases the minor, §2036/§2038 would include the custodial property in the custodian's gross estate.[22] In contrast, some irrevocable trusts can avoid this FET problem by denying the trustee this power.
- Donees usually must receive custodial property outright *by age 21*; trust beneficiaries' distributions of principal may be delayed to a later age.
- Finally, a custodianship *does not have spendthrift provisions*.

To preserve the income shifting advantage of custodial gifts, UTMA provides that custodial property may not be used to satisfy any obligation to support for the minor, such as an obligation in a divorce decree. Thus, custodial gifts if properly structured can achieve essentially all of the tax advantages of completed outright transfers.

Gifts to an Irrevocable Minor's Trust[23]

Although both gifts under guardianships and custodial gifts are usually an improvement over larger outright gifts to minors, they have some serious drawbacks, some of which have been mentioned above. They usually terminate at or shortly after the donee's age of majority, at which time the donee enjoys fee simple ownership of the property. And they may be restrictive, either in the red tape involved to create and continue them (gifts under guardianships) or in the type of property that usually may be given (custodial gifts) under the laws of many states. They are also inflexible in that the controlling state law usually is not or cannot be modified by private document. Thus, the donor under a guardianship arrangement usually cannot provide, by private document, that court supervision will not be required. The presence of these and other drawbacks lead many donors to use irrevocable trusts for gifts to minors.

---

22. See Example 2038-3 in Chapter 6.

23. For a summary comparison of the taxation of minor's trusts versus other popular trusts in estate planning, see Table 17.1 in Chapter 17.

In structuring gifts in trust for the benefit of minors, planners usually seek to obtain all of the tax benefits available to outright gifts. The four major tax objectives are:

1. Using the annual gift tax exclusion to avoid both gift taxes and the using up of the unified credit,
2. Excluding the gift from the donor's gross estate,
3. Excluding all postgift appreciation in the value of the gift property from the donor's estate tax base, and
4. Shifting the taxable income earned on the gift property to the trust or to the donee.

The irrevocable trust may also have the nontax advantage of insulating the gift property from the parents' creditors and, in some cases, from the child's creditors.

Drafting an irrevocable trust takes great care because the nature of such transfers seem to invite scrutiny by the IRS. For example, the donor may wish to act as trustee and to restrict the minor child's enjoyment of the trust principal and income for some period of time. These requirements reflect the donor's desire to retain a considerable degree of control over the gift property. The problem is that a very fine line exists between harmless controls and controls that are deemed to be retained interests by the donor. Earlier in this chapter we saw some outright gift situations in which the transferor was penalized by income and estate tax provisions for retaining too much control. To this list we must add certain ill-designed transfers into trusts for the benefit of minors. The following discusses particular tax hurdles facing the planners of irrevocable minors' trusts and several methods for dealing with these problems. The discussion will include qualifying transfers into minors' trusts for the annual exclusion, a word of estate tax caution, the mention of an income tax concern, and finally a GSTT caveat.

Qualifying for the annual exclusion. As mentioned in Chapter 7, to qualify for the gift tax annual exclusion, the donee must be given a *present interest*, that is, an unrestricted right to the immediate use, possession, or enjoyment of property or the income from property. The reader might ask how a gift into trust for the benefit of a minor can qualify for the annual exclusion when, in fact, the minor is not typically given the unrestricted right to the immediate use of either the principal *or* the income. The answer lies in an exception carved out by the Internal Revenue Code, and two planning devices sanctioned by the courts, even if not loved by the IRS, that form the basis for an added clauses in the trust documents. The three alternatives are called the 2503(c) Trust, the Crummey Trust, and the Mandatory Income Trust. The text of §2503 in included in Appendix B.

2503(c) Trust: Under §2503(c), a gift in trust is not considered a gift of a future interest (even though it really is one) if three conditions are met.

First, the trust must provide that the property and income may be expended by or for the benefit of the donee before the donee attains age 21.[24] This requirement creates the same potential §2036/§2038 problem for trustors wishing to be trustees as it does for custodial gifts.

Second, any portion of the property not so expended will pass to the donee at age 21. This is the most restrictive of the three conditions.

Third, if the donee dies before age 21, the property must either be payable to the donee's estate or the donee must hold a general power of appointment over the property. This is met even if the general power is exercisable only through the donee's will; and the trust contains a clause making siblings the takers by default. In many states, a minor may not legally execute a will. Thus, in the event of the death of the minor, the property would likely go to the.

As mentioned in Chapter 7, the 2503(c) exception was created to discourage the adoption of trusts which pay out income to presumably immature minors immediately upon the trustee's receipt, for the sole purpose of taking advantage of the annual exclusion. Thus, *2503(c) Trusts*, as they are called, normally terminate when the child reaches age 21. However, the §2503(c) trust need not terminate at this age, as long as the beneficiary can request a complete distribution at age 21.[25] In fact, a recent survey found that only eight percent of experienced estate planning attorneys "always" require in their trust documents mandatory distribution when a child-beneficiary reaches a specified age. Twenty-four percent "seldom" or "never" do.[26]

The Crummey Trusts and lapsing withdrawal powers. Crummey is the name of a taxpayer who succeeded in federal court in getting an annual exclusion for each year's transfer into a trust containing withdrawal rights for the benefit of minor children.[27] The typical *Crummey Trust* clause provides that the child has the right to withdraw, for a brief period (30 to 90 days) as set in the trust document, after each transfer of property into the trust, the *lesser* of the amount of the available annual exclusion or the value

---

24. Controls over the expenditures can disallow the annual exclusion. *Illinois National Bank of Springfield v. U.S.* 756 F.Supp. 1117 (1991).

25. LR 8507017

26. See the Moore/Pennell paper, cited at the end of Chapter 1.

27. *Crummey v. Commissioner*, 397 F.2d 82 (9Cir. 1968).

of the gift property transferred. Since the child has the right to withdraw that amount, the gift is considered a gift of a present interest satisfying the §2503(b) present interest requirement and the donor receives an annual exclusion for the gift. To be effective, the child must be given actual notice of the withdrawal right.

Use of a Crummey power can result in undesired gift tax and income tax consequences. For example, a beneficiary's failure to exercise a Crummey power in a given year may mean that the beneficiary has made a *taxable gift* by permitting a general power of appointment to lapse.[28] The gift tax value would be the amount that the value permitted to lapse exceeded the greater of $5,000 or 5 percent of the aggregate value of the assets out of which the exercise could be satisfied. For example, if $120,000 was contributed as an initial gift in trust, with a $20,000 demand right, $14,000 would be considered as transferred (the amount that $20,000 exceeds the greater of $5,000 or 5 percent of $120,000). As a gift of a future interest, it will not qualify for the annual exclusion, but the taxable gift value will be very small since only the amount that goes to someone other than the person who let the withdrawal right lapse is considered a gift; and even that must be discounted since it is a future interest. Furthermore, if the person who let the withdrawal right lapse eventually receives the corpus of the trust, the gift will not be an adjusted taxable gift since the transfer (a contingent remainder) has reverted to the beneficiary.[29] The latter situation is the usual case, since the beneficiary with the withdrawal right is usually the remainderman, especially for minors' trusts. Given the extremely small gift tax value and he likelihood that the transfer would not enter into the estate tax calculation most planners ignore this tax consequence. Some avoid the problem by limiting the annual withdrawal right to the 5 and 5 limits, i.e., the greater of *$5,000* (rather than $10,000) or 5 percent, or by giving the beneficiary a general testamentary power of appointment over the trust principal.[30]

Mandatory Income Trust (MIT): A trust that requires mandatory distribution of income annually to the minor, either outright or to the minor's custodial account, as the way of entitling the donor to the annual exclusion is called a *mandatory income trust*. The gift is considered as

---

28. §2514(e).

29. §2001(b)

30. For a detailed discussion, including possible solutions, see the Harris/Jacobson, Tarlow-Vacca and Harrison articles, as well as several others cited at the end of the chapter.

page 476 chapter 13

comprising two parts, the income interest and the remainder or reversion interest. Tax law considers the former to be a present interest qualifying for the annual exclusion and the latter to be a future interest that does not so qualify. The alternative fractions making up the gift are derived from Table 9 in Appendix A.

> EXAMPLE MIT-1 Gerry transferred $100,000 into an irrevocable trust established for his friend, Betty giving her income for life with the corpus to revert to Gerry or his issue after Betty's death. Betty just turned 86 years old and the rate for valuing split interest gifts was 8 percent The factor would be .31812, therefor $31,812 represents the value of the income interest and qualifies for the annual exclusion. Since the present value exceeds $10,000 the full annual exclusion is allowed. Query, how old would Betty have to have been before the annual exclusion would have been less than $10,000? How much would it have been? (The answer will be found right before the Questions and answers at the end of the chapter. Decide on your own answer before checking.)

Comparison of the three minor's trusts. By way of summary, Figure 13-4 highlights the differences between the three popular minor's trusts, tracing their evolution through the generations, with a focus on the rights of the beneficiaries and their taxation.

MITs and §2503(c) Trusts have become less attractive since the Crummey decision. Prior to Crummey, planners had to choose between an arrangement requiring annual distribution of all trust *income* to the minor [satisfying §2503(b)] or one effectively requiring distribution of the entire trust *corpus* at age 21 [satisfying §2503(c)]. Although some planners favored the MIT for larger gifts, the choice was not enthusiastically made, partly because the value of the income interest qualifying for the annual exclusion had to be discounted. The Crummey provision solved this dilemma by enabling the donor to give the child the *right to demand* a modest amount from the trust annually, without handing income or principal over to the child at age 21. Usually the child is made to realize that there is much to lose by exercising the demand right. For example, the child might lose a greater inheritance in the future, or the parent might simply refuse to make anymore gifts into the trust. However, the IRS takes the position that the child's power of withdrawal not be illusory, as it would be if there was an "understanding" or "agreement" not to exercise it.[31]

---

31. Rev. Rul. 81-7, 1981-1 CB 474.

FIGURE 13-4 Evolution of Irrevocable Mandatory Income Trusts (MIT), §2503(c), and *Crummey* Minor's Trusts: Beneficiaries and Taxation

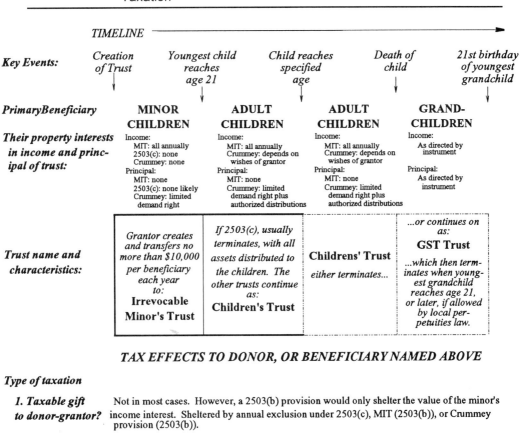

TIMELINE ──▶

	Creation of Trust	Youngest child reaches age 21	Child reaches specified age	Death of child	21st birthday of youngest grandchild
Key Events:	▼	▼	▼	▼	▼
PrimaryBeneficiary	**MINOR CHILDREN**	**ADULT CHILDREN**	**ADULT CHILDREN**		**GRAND-CHILDREN**
Their property interests in income and principal of trust:	Income: MIT: all annually 2503(c): none Crummey: none Principal: MIT: none 2503(c): none likely Crummey: limited demand right	Income: MIT: all annually Crummey: depends on wishes of grantor Principal: MIT: none Crummey: limited demand right plus authorized distributions	Income: MIT: all annually Crummey: depends on wishes of grantor Principal: MIT: none Crummey: limited demand right plus authorized distributions		Income: As directed by instrument Principal: As directed by instrument

Trust name and characteristics:	*Grantor creates and transfers no more than $10,000 per beneficiary each year to:* **Irrevocable Minor's Trust**	*If 2503(c), usually terminates, with all assets distributed to the children. The other trusts continue as:* **Children's Trust**	**Childrens' Trust** *either terminates...*	*...or continues on as:* **GST Trust** *...which then terminates when youngest grandchild reaches age 21, or later, if allowed by local perpetuities law.*

TAX EFFECTS TO DONOR, OR BENEFICIARY NAMED ABOVE

Type of taxation

1. Taxable gift to donor-grantor? Not in most cases. However, a 2503(b) provision would only shelter the value of the minor's income interest. Sheltered by annual exclusion under 2503(c), MIT (2503(b)), or Crummey provision (2503(b)).

2. Includable in beneficiaries' estate tax base at death?	No, except for 2503(c) trust, if a minor child dies	No, except for principal distributions that continue to be owned	No, except for principal distributions that continue to be owned	Yes, to extent of principal distributions that continue to be owned

3. Income taxable to grantor or beneficiaries? Not to grantor (no rights to income or principal retained).

Yes to minor children, to extent distributed or to extent it could be withdrawn.	Yes to children, to extent distributed.	Yes to children, to extent distributed.	Yes to grand-children, to extent distributed.

Undistributed FAI and all capital gains taxable to trust.

4. Any GSTT incurred? No, provided that grantor (and possibly grantor's children) allocated $1 million GSTT exemption(s) to the gift transfers. To extent not so sheltered, trust will have inclusion ratio, and a portion of any taxable termination or taxable distribution to a skip person will be subject to GSTT.

Income taxation has recently become a more important factor in choosing a minor's trust. The short tax rate "ladder" for trusts will encourage clients to seek to avoid trust taxation of income. A newly created Crummey-type trust may be able to avoid this result by subjecting the accumulated income to tax to the Crummey power holder by granting that individual a general power of appointment over trust income at the termination of the withdrawal period.

> EXAMPLE C-1 Eight years ago, Knute created routine irrevocable Crummey-type trusts for his two sons, then age 6 and 7. Each trust now contains approximately $140,000, generating about $9,000 in accumulated income which is taxable to the trust, some at its marginal rate of 39.6 percent.

A recent court decision made Crummey powers even more attractive by sanctioning annual exclusions for the trustor's *grandchildren*, who were given a 15 day $10,000 demand right, but who were only contingent beneficiaries of the trust principal, because they stood to receive principal distributions *only* if their parents predeceased the termination of the trust. In *Cristofani*, the IRS unsuccessfully argued that it was so unlikely that the grandchildren would receive the principal, there was "no imaginable reason" why the grandchildren would not exercise their withdrawal rights unless there was, in fact, a prior *understanding* that they would not do so, hence they really had no present interests in the transfers. The court rejected this implied agreement argument, ruling that the test of a Crummey power is the legal right of the beneficiary to demand the property be turned over by the trustee, not the likelihood of actually receiving the property. The IRS intends to continue litigating the court's broad interpretation of *Crummey* in situations similar to *Cristofani*, but only in cases arising outside the Federal 9th Circuit.[32] While this case supports the use of Crummey type gifts to contingent beneficiaries, commentators are increasingly concerned that Congress may restrict or eliminate the Crummey withdrawal power as a means of creating a present interest. If Congress chooses to do so, it might grandfather (allow the annual exclusion) for existing irrevocable trusts, or perhaps eliminate it even for them unless there is an assurance that the beneficiary will eventually receive the property or at least, as in the §2503(c) Trust, that it will be taxable in the beneficiary's estate if her or she does not get to enjoy it.

> EXAMPLE 2503-1 Christopher resides in the 9th Circuit. He creates an irrevocable trust to last for ten years. The trust provides for distribution of the

---

32. *Estate of Maria Cristofani* 97 TC 74 (1991).

remainder to his two children, if surviving, if a child predeceases termination of the trust that child's share shall go to his or her issue. One child has three children and the other has two, for a total of five grandchildren. All seven beneficiaries are given Crummey demand powers. Beginning this year, Christopher can fund the trust annually with $70,000 in property, entirely sheltered by annual exclusions even though the trust corpus will most likely go just to the two children.

Estate tax caution. In designing the irrevocable trust, the estate planner must be mindful of the dangers of letting the donor retain controls that would cause the property to be includable in the donor's gross estate. For example, as mentioned earlier in the chapter, naming the grantor to be trustee of a §2503(c) trust will cause estate tax inclusion of the trust assets at the grantor's death unless the trust has already terminated. The underlying Code provisions have been covered in Chapter 6, specifically: §2036, transfers with retained life estate, and §2038, revocable or amendable transfers. The reader is urged to review them at this point.

Income tax concern. The donor of a gift in trust for a minor child usually wishes to avoid being taxed on the income received by the trust, preferring instead to let the trust be taxed to the extent the income is accumulated, or to let the child be taxed to the extent that the income is paid to the child. However, the trust must be designed so as not to conflict with the numerous grantor trust rules, described in Chapter 8. For example, reservation by the donor of the unlimited right to make withdrawals from the trust will cause the income to be taxed to the donor. This will not apply if the grantor retains a reversion that can only occur on the death of a beneficiary (before age 21) who is a lineal descendant of the grantor and holds all present interests in any portion of the trust.[33]

GSTT Caveat. As implied above, Crummey trusts often provide for transfer to the beneficiaries' *issue or descendants* if the beneficiary fails to survive. As a taxable termination or taxable distribution, this transfer will *not* be sheltered from the GSTT as an annual exclusion gift because its origin was not a direct skip gift. Planners recommend avoiding this GSTT consequence either by having the client allocate a portion of the $1 million exemption to transfers to the Crummy trust, or enjoying a GSTT exemption by setting up a separate trust for each skip person, with each trust conforming to certain requirements under §2642(c)(2).

---

33. §673(b).

HOW POPULAR ARE COMPLETED GIFTS?

Based on the results of a survey of experienced estate planning attorneys conducted by Prestipino, the most popular larger gifts are outright annual exclusion gifts, with 29.2 percent of clients of experienced estate planning attorneys undertaking them. Next in order of popularity are gifts in trust (19.1%), custodial annual exclusion gifts (12.1%), outright gifts of an amount greater than the annual exclusion (5.5%), and, finally, custodial gifts exceeding the annual exclusion (1.3%). Of the clients using gifts in trust, 60 percent incorporated a Crummey demand provision, 6 percent a §2503(b) provision, and 12 percent an §2503(c) clause.

This chapter has introduced the planning for lifetime transfers, devoting considerable detail to gifts. Chapter 14 will explore another group of life-time transfers: ones different from gifts in that they are either incomplete, or are completed transfers to charity.

Query answered:

MIT-1 Betty at age 108 would have had a present interest determined by the factor .08319, this times $100,000 gives a present interest of $8,319; limiting the annual exclusion to that amount. Gerry's taxable gift would then be $91,681 instead of $90,000.

QUESTIONS AND PROBLEMS

1. Good planning requires that the client feel comfortable with a proposed lifetime transfer. How can lifetime transfers be a source of discomfort?

2. One of your clients explains to you that she'd like to make a lifetime transfer to her child, perhaps in the form of a gift. But she is not clear on how gifts differ from other lifetime transfers. Inform her.

3. Now that your client is aware of the unique nature of a gift, explain to her the difference between an outright and a nonoutright gift.

4. What is the approximate minimum net worth that (*a*) a single client and (*b*) married clients should own (or expect to own) before considering gifting amounts of $10,000 or more in order to save FET? Why?

5. Carrie, a rich elderly widow, expects to live 10 years. She would like to begin a program of lifetime gifting to her four children.
   a. What equal amount can Carrie give to each child, per year, without paying any gift tax, while fully using up her unified credit? In addition, calculate the combined value of all gifts *1*) each year, and *2*) over ten years. Assume no prior taxable gifts.
   b. How would your answers to part *a* change if Carrie created a trust naming her four children primary beneficiaries and her eight grandchildren contingent beneficiaries?
   c. Why might Carrie be willing to use up her unified credit?

6. In terms of FET saving, is a gift of $20,000 by an unmarried donor to one donee in one year necessarily twice as valuable as a gift of only $10,000? Why or why not? Discuss in terms of estate reduction and estate freezing.

7. Why is the ability to avoid grossing up a tax advantage to gifting?

8. Two years ago, Zack gave his daughter Luna a one-acre plot of desert land in Nevada, then worth $9,000. Subsequently, oil was found, making the plot worth $900,000. Assuming no prior taxable gifts,
   a. How much attributable to this land will be includable in Zack's estate tax base if he dies today? Explain.
   b. How much would be includable if, instead, Zack made the gift

four years ago and died today? Explain.

   c. How much would be includable if, instead, Zack made the gift in 1981 and dies today? Explain.

9. How would your answers to the question immediately above change, if at all, if at the time of the transfer Zack reserved the right to camp out on the land whenever he liked? (Assume further that Zack just died of a heart attack after discovering that shortly after receiving the land, Luna quickly sold it to a third party for $10,000.)

10. Describe the attributes of those clients who would be most willing to make sizable gifts.

11. Summarize the major tax disadvantages to gifting.

12. "Higher basis assets make better gifts." From an income tax point of view, is this statement true, false, or uncertain?

13. Discuss any significant reasons why each of the following assets have particularly attractive or unattractive gift potential.
    a. Stock: donor's basis, $60,000; fair market value, $20,000.
    b. Stock: donor's basis, $20,000; fair market value, $800,000. Does age of the donor matter at all?
    c. Life insurance on the donor's life.
    d. Rights to a patent.
    e. Raw land.
    f. A junk bond.
    g. A corporate dividend check that the donor endorses over to the donee.

14. (*a*) Under what circumstances can an interspousal gift save FET? (*b*) Under what circumstances can an interspousal gift save income tax?

15. Contrast the advantages and disadvantages of the alternative methods of making gifts to minors.

16. Paradiso, a client, asks you to review the recommendation of one of your competitors. That planner proposed transferring $10,000 per year for life into an irrevocable trust, whose terms provide that all income will be accumulated until Paradiso's son Max (age 4) reaches age 35. At that time all accumulated income will be distributed to Max, who will thereafter receive all income currently

until Paradiso's death, at which time the trust will terminate and all principal will be distributed outright to Max.

a. Will the periodic transfers be free of gift tax? Why or why not?

b. Will this arrangement reduce Paradiso's future FET or freeze any part of his estate? Why or why not?

c. If your answer to part *a* is no, suggest three alternative provisions in the trust that will change the result.

d. Which of the three provisions in part *c* probably most reduces the maximum life of the trust?

e. Which of the three provisions in part *c* will probably be most appealing to Paradiso, who is quite reluctant to allow distribution of either income or principal until Max reaches age 35?

f. How much income shifting per year, if any, will your answer in part *e* accomplish?

17. A client of yours needs some planning advice. She wants to start a college fund for her 8-year-old daughter. Her goal is to accumulate approximately $50,000 in 10 years, at which time equal monthly payments can be made to daughter over a period of the following 4 years.

a. If neither income shifting nor estate tax reduction are important, is a program of gifting really necessary? Why or why not?

b. If your client wishes to shift income to daughter (who for simplicity, we'll assume, has no taxable income of her own), recommend strategies for each of the following alternative sets of assumptions:

(1) Client wishes to accumulate a fund that can revert to the client if her daughter later decides not to attend college. (The answer to this part will not be found in this book. Hint: EE bonds)

(2) Client would like an arrangement under which she can continue funding after her daughter's graduation.

c. In part *b* above, recommend suitable investments to purchase. (Hint: is the daughter a "kiddie"?)

18. Under simple assumptions, what is the largest family estate size that a husband and wife can own and transfer, FET and gift tax free, assuming all of the following: a credit shelter bypass plan; that S1 is expected to live five years and S2 fifteen years; and both spouses wish to make annual exclusion gifts each year to each of their four children?

RECOMMENDED READING

Adams, Roy M., and Scott Bieber. "Making `5 and 5', Equal 20: Crummey Powers after ERTA." *Trusts & Estates*, September 1983, pp. 22-25.

Blake, John Freeman, and Lynn K. Pearle. "New Decision Expands Scope of Support a Parent May Be Required to Furnish." *Estate Planning*, November 1984, pp. 322-26.

*Blase, James G. "College Education and the Duty to Support." *Trusts & Estates*, March 1984, pp. 45-48.

Blattmachr, Jonathan, G. "Child's Income May Be Taxed at Parent's Tax Rate," *Journal of Taxation*, January 1987, pp. 487-52.

Buttita, John J. "Another Look at Income Shifting: The Qualified Subchapter S Trust," *Chicago Bar Record* 66 (January 1985), pp. 194-202.

Daniel, R. Michael, and William R. Nee. "Pre-death Planning Techniques for Clients without a Surviving Spouse." *Estate Planning*, May 1985, pp. 168-71.

Delorio, Maj. Dominik J. "Uniform Gifts to Minors Act." *Military Law Review* 112 (1986), pp. 159-73.

Devine, James D. "How Trusts for Minors Can Be Structured to Meet Grantors' Tax and Nontax Objectives." *Taxation for Accountants,* March 1984, pp. 140-46.

Dye, Douglas G. "Several Routes Exist to Avoid IRS' Income Tax Roadblock to Use of Crummey Trust Provisions." *Estate Planning*, July 1983, pp. 220-24.

*Eastland, Stacy, "Why my Algebra Teacher Rolls Over in her Grave: The Mathematics of Estate Planning," *1990 University of Miami Estate Planning Institute.*

Fiore, Owen G. and John F. Ramsbacker, "Crummey Powers For Contingent Beneficiaries OK'd," *Estate Planning*, January, 1992, pp. 10-15.

*Gilfix, Michael "Medicaid and Estate Planning: Asset Preservation and Long Term Care." *Estate Planning for the Aging or Incapacitated Client* 1986, Practising Law Institute.

Goggans, Travis P., and Candace J. Garcia. "Family Gifts of Real Estate: Avoiding Inclusion under Sec. 2036." *Tax Adviser* July 1984, pp. 394-02.

*Harris, Richard W., and Steven W. Jacobson. "Maximizing the Effectiveness of the Annual Gift Exclusion," *Taxes- The Tax Magazine*, March, 1992, pp. 204-14.

*Harrison, Louis S., "Lapse of Crummey Power need not result in Taxable Gift if Hanging Power is used," *Estate Planning*, May, 1990, pp. 140-43.

*Ledwith, James R., and Mary Ann Robinson. "Expanded Opportunities Avail-able under Uniform Transfers to Minors Act." *Estate Planning*, September 1986, pp. 258-62.

Lobenhofer, Louis F. "Who Do You Trust?-Planning Opportunities for Parents Making Gifts to Their Children with Themselves as Trustees." *Ohio Northern University Law Review 9*, no. 2 (1982), pp. 171-203.

McCue, Howard M. III, and Daniel. W. Luther. "New Rules Create New Problems." (Income and Value Shifting after TRA 86) *Trusts & Estates*, October 1987, pp. 10-18.

* McDonald, Elaine M. "Using The Uniform Transfers To Minor Act--A Primer For Life Insurance Companies And Professionals", *Journal of the American Society of CLU & ChFC*, July, 1993, pp 46-59.

*McNair, John R. "Lifetime QTIPs Can Achieve Tax And Asset Protection Goals" *Estate Planning*, September, 1993, pp 290-95.

Meade, Janet A. "Section 1014(e) and the Lock-In Problem: Basis Considerations in Trans-fers of Appreciated Property." *Taxes-The Tax Magazine* 64 (September 1986), pp. 588-94.

Metz, Leroy, and Wesley Yang. "Goal Tending Called on Net Gifts." *Taxes The Tax Magazine*, January 1983, pp. 13-19.

Mezzullo, Louis A. "New Regulations Make It Difficult, but Not Impossible, to Shift Income to Minors." *Estate Planning*, January 1988, pp. 2-5.

Moore, Malcolm A. "Tax Consequences and Uses of "Crummey" Withdrawal Powers: An Update," *University of 1988 Miami Estate Planning Institute*.

Morris, Malcolm L. "The Tax Posture of Gifts in Estate Planning: Dinosaur or Dynasty?" *Nebraska Law Review* 64 (1985), pp. 25-82.

Nechin Herbert B. "Gifts of Real Estate to Minors Can Shift Income While Satisfying Clients Other Needs." *Taxation for Lawyers*, March-April 1985, pp. 30-26.

Officer, Dennis T., and Warren E. Banks. "Estates vs. Gifts in a Period of Inflation." *Taxes-The Tax Magazine*, January 1980, pp. 68-72.

Rediess-Hoosein, Brenda J. "Methods of Transferring Assets to Minors Affected By Recent Tax Changes," *Estate Planning*, March, 1991, pp. 86-90.

Ross, Bonnie G, "Putting Crummey Powers In Perspective." <u>Estate Planning 1994</u>, Califor-nia Continuing Education of the Bar.

*Rubenstein, Joshua S. "Factors that Affect the Estate Tax Treatment of Checks Written Prior to Death," *Estate Planning*, November, 1988, pp. 338-43. Covers gift situations.

*Sciurba, Dennis V., "Custodial Gifts to Minors: Expanded Opportunities," *Journal of American Society of CLU & ChFC*, July, 1988, pp. 48-52.

Segal, Mark A. "Deductions and Exclusions Can Lower Education Cost," *Taxation For Accountants*, June, 1993, pp 340-45.

Spencer, Patti S. "Advantages Remain to Making Gifts in Trust to Minors that Qualify for Annual Exclusion." *Estate Planning*, September 1987, pp. 264-68. (Covers the 2503(c) trust.)

*Tarlow, Edward D., and Catherine M. Vacca. "Recent Developments Clarify Tax Effects of Lapse of Crummey Powers, but Problems Remain." *Estate Planning*, September 1986, pp. 272-75.

Vorsatz, Mark L. "Trust with Beneficiary's Power of Withdrawal Adaptable for Use in Many Family Situations." *Taxation for Accountants*, February 1986, pp. 98-103.

"What to Give Away." *Real Property, Probate and Trust Journal* 18(1983), pp. 678-707. (Report of the Committee on Estate Planning and Drafting: Inter Vivos Transfers and Property Ownership.)

Wicker, William H. "Spendthrift Trusts Are an Excellent Way to Leave Money to Someone Who Can't Handle It." *Estate Planning*, Summer 1975, pp. 202-5.

Wintriss, Lynn. "Gift-Splitting Can Increase Tax Effectiveness of Gift Program that Is Part of an Estate Plan." *Estate Planning*, November 1982, pp. 340-45.

Lifetime Transfers II: Other Intrafamily Transfers; Charitable Transfers

OVERVIEW

Gift planning, the subject of the previous chapter, is often rejected by clients for two reasons. First, by their very nature, gifts generally mean nothing in return. Giving reduces wealth which may make the donor feel less financially secure, a feeling many clients would rather not experience. Second, giving requires relinquishment of control over the property, a difficult step for many potential donors.

The client has other options and can select from alternative lifetime transfers. In this second chapter on lifetime transfers, we'll explore two more attractive intrafamily arrangements. The first, those involving the client receiving *consideration*, as in the installment sale and the private annuity. The second, the client retaining some control over the transferred property, such as the grantor retained interest trust. The chapter will also cover the popular types of lifetime charitable transfers, including outright charitable transfers and split interest charitable transfers, such as the annuity trust, the unitrust, and the pooled income fund where the client receives both income and an income tax benefit.

COMPLETED INTRAFAMILY TRANSFERS FOR CONSIDERATION

In this section, we'll study lifetime transfers that are different from the others in two important ways. First, they differ from gifts because they *generate consideration* to the transferor. Second, they differ from the second type of lifetime intrafamily transfer to be covered later in this chapter in that like gifts, they are *complete*, that is, they entail total transfer of (one or) all interests in the asset.

Intrafamily Loan

Lending money or other property to family members is a simple method of transferring assets in exchange for consideration. Often, the financial benefits of an intrafamily loan can be well worth the financial and emotional risks.

Financial benefits of intrafamily loans. Loans work best when borrowing rates and investing rates of return are far apart. In 1992, when short-term borrowing rates were 9 percent or higher and one-year certificates of deposit earned about 3.5 percent, a short-term loan of $10,000 at 6 percent could save the borrower at least $300 per year and generate additional annual pretax income to the lender of about $250. Long-term loans could save far less per year because rate differentials were not nearly as pronounced, but over a thirty year period, the accumulated amounts are still significant. Additional advantages of intrafamily home mortgages are the ability to both avoid or reduce up-front points and application fees charged by commercial lenders, reduce loan processing time, and parents are likely to make loans to children with credit histories that would not satisfy commercial lenders. In contrast, children wishing to make gifts to supplement their parent's income might borrow from them and pay an above-market rate.

Financial Risks of Intrafamily Loans. In addition to the risk of unexpected taxation (to be described shortly), intrafamily loans entail other financial risks. A child may not be a good credit risk, making the loan payments difficult to collect resulting in family friction. If the loan is secured, the lien must be properly filed to ensure the lien's priority over other creditors.

Nonfinancial risk of intrafamily loans. The risks of an intrafamily loan can also be partly emotional. Some parent-lenders later discover that their children have taken the immature attitude that since mom and dad have a lot of money they need not be repaid. Family loans can also engender jealousies and antagonisms between relatives and in-laws.

Taxation of nongift intrafamily loans. Taxation of intrafamily loans that contain no gift element is relatively straightforward.

Income taxation. Interest paid by the borrower is, of course, taxable income to the lender. Interest is not tax deductible to the borrower unless the loan is secured by a principal or secondary residence or incurred in connection with a trade or business.[1] If the loan is in default, the lender will not be able to deduct the loss unless a businesslike effort is made to collect it.

Gift taxation. No gift will result if the borrower's note reflects an arms-length transaction. Thus, there must be provision for repayment, and the interest rate charged must be reasonable.

The lender may elect to *forgive* loan payments under the shelter of the annual exclusion. However, if the IRS can establish that a prior agreement had been made to forgive all payments, it will contend that the entire loan constituted an immediate gift. To avoid this result, a lender intending to forgive payments might wish to accept each payment, and then sometime later gift a somewhat different amount.

Estate taxation. The value of the note is included in the lender-decedent's gross estate at death.[2]

Taxation of gift-type intrafamily loans. The income and gift tax effects discussed above assume a true loan, one that does not have a gift element; the borrower exchanges full consideration in the form of a note which is presently equal in value to the amount borrowed.

Other intrafamily loans entail additional tax risks. Clients may wish to charge no interest, or an interest rate that is below market rates. Tax law treats these "below market" loans between family members as "gift loans," subjecting the client-lender to income taxation and gift taxation.

Income taxation. In subjecting these loans to income tax, the law[3] assumes a fiction: The "forgone interest" is "treated as" if it had been transferred by the lender to the borrower, and then retransferred by the borrower to the lender, thereby subjecting the client to income taxation on this imputed interest income. Whether or not a loan is "below market" will essentially depend upon whether the lender charged a rate at least equal to the appro-

---

1. §163.

2. §2033.

3. §7872(a)(1).

priate applicable federal rate (AFR), as described in §1274(d) and announced by the U.S. Treasury each month.

There are two exceptions to the imputed interest rules. First, they do not apply to loans up to $10,000 used to purchase non income producing property, such as an automobile. Second, they do not apply to loans up to $100,000 if the borrower's net investment income is less than $1,000. This might work well for investment-poor students needing large amounts to fund educational expenses, such as for law school or medical school, or for a child needing the money for a down payment on a house. If net investment income exceeds the $1,000 limit, the imputed interest is limited to the actual amount of that income.

Gift taxation. If the loan rate is below market, the client will also be treated as having made a gift. If the loan is a term loan, one with a specified maturity, the value of the gift is the difference between the amount loaned and the discounted present value of the note. If the loan is a demand loan, one with no specified maturity date and lender has right at any time to demand full repayment, at the end of each year the lender will be treated as having made a gift of one year's imputed interest less the amount actually charged. A more detailed discussion of the tax effects of below market "interest free" loans is contained in Appendix 14A that immediately follows this chapter.

Properly structured, intrafamily loans can be beneficial to both lender and borrower, provided that both understand the terms, which should be reduced to writing.

Ordinary Sale

The client can sell property for cash to a family member at a fair market price. Under certain circumstances, an ordinary sale can be especially beneficial to both family members. The client may truly wish to sell at a fair price but would prefer to keep the asset in the family; the buyer will be spared the effort and expense of looking for similar property asset and commissions that might have been incurred are avoided. As a true sale, there may be income tax consequences to the seller. Careful records should be kept, since intrafamily sales might receive greater IRS scrutiny than a nonrelated party sale, especially if the transaction is sizable. The buyer, of course, has the burden of acquiring the cash or other acceptable property needed for the purchase. The seller is not allowed to deduct any loss incurred in the sale, due to the Code's prohibition against loss recognition on sales between related parties.[4]

Bargain Sale

If the client has mixed transfer motives, on the one hand wishing to gift a particular asset to a family member, and on the other hand not willing to completely forgo the receipt of all consideration in return, a bargain sale may be appropriate. As described in Chapter 2, under a bargain sale the client sells the asset for an amount less than what would be regarded full and adequate consideration. The difference between the consideration received by the client-donor and the value of the asset transferred is a gift, for tax purposes. Regarding income tax, the client would recognize a gain to the extent the consideration received exceeds the parent's basis.

> EXAMPLE 14-1 Mom owns property with a basis of $90,000 and a current value of $240,000, which she sells to her son for $110,000. Mom's taxable gain is $20,000, the difference between $110,000 and her $90,000 basis. Son's new basis is $110,000, his purchase price. Mom has also made a gift of $130,000, the difference between the property's FMV and the consideration paid.

A taxable bargain sale may not be the best outcome, however, if a true tax-free gift was intended. Occasionally, an intended gift is treated as a bargain sale.

> Example 14-2 La Croix borrows money from a bank to purchase a building. After claiming depreciation on the property for a number of years, he "gives" the land to his daughter, who assumes the debt. The transaction will be treated as a bargain sale, if his adjusted basis is less than the outstanding debt. La Croix will be considered to have received consideration in the amount of the debt assumed.[5]

As a compromise between a gift and a sale, the bargain sale can be arranged to closely reflect the client's degree of generosity.

The next transfers covered involve seller financed, deferred payment sales.

---

4. §267.

5. *Juden* 89-1 USTC 9142; 63 ¶ AFTR 2d 89-595 (CA-8, 1989)

Installment Sale

Instead of selling the asset to a family member for immediate cash, the client could sell it in exchange for an installment note, in which the buyer agrees to make periodic payments of principal and interest, based on a fair market rate of interest. This is referred to as seller financing; and the seller is said to *take back paper*, a reference to the seller receiving a note instead of cash. An installment sale can defer income tax on some or all capital gain while keeping post-sale appreciation out of the seller's gross estate.

Income taxation. Under income tax installment sales rules,[6] the seller may spread recognition of the gain over the collection period. Although it is presumed that the seller will use the installment method to recognize gain, the seller can make an election to recognize the entire gain in the year of sale, which would make good sense if the seller has offsetting capital loses for the year. The gain is recognized in proportion to the amount of each payment of principal. A percentage of each principal payment, measured by the gross profit (gain) divided by the selling price, is included as capital gain. There are restrictions on deferral of gain on an installment sale of certain trade or business property.[7] Losses are never reported on an installment basis.

> EXAMPLE 14-3 Mom, a widow, sells her rental house to her daughter for $80,000, payable with a down payment of $10,000. Interest is payable monthly, and principal will be payable in five equal annual $14,000 payments. Mom's current adjusted basis in the house is $20,000. Her gross profit is $60,000, and each year she will recognize a capital gain of $60,000/$80,000, or 75 percent of the principal amount received. Thus, in the year of sale, her reportable gain will be $7,500 of the total $10,000 received. In each of the succeeding five years she can expect to report a gain of $10,500 (=.75 x $14,000).

Any *interest* received on the balance due will also be taxable income. Interest paid will be fully deductible by the buyer if it is considered business interest, investment interest which is offset by investment income, interest on a debt secured by a primary or secondary residence, or some other type of qualified interest.

At least two different events will trigger to the seller an *immediate recognition* of part or all of the remaining gain. If the seller sells or "otherwise disposes" of the installment note, or if the seller cancels the note, then

---

6. §453

7. §453(C)(e)(l)(A)(i)(III).

he or she will have to report currently the remaining gain from the original transaction. Gain recognition will also be triggered if the buyer is a related party who resells the property within two years of the purchase.[8]

The buyer of the property, as in any valid sale, will enjoy a step-up in basis in the property to the amount of the purchase price. However, with regard to the seller's note, transfer of the note at the death of the seller *will not generate a step-up basis* in the note. The legatee-heir will continue to report installment gain in the same manner as the seller.

Gift taxation. If the installment transaction is a bona fide sale for full and adequate consideration, there will be *no gift tax* consequences to the lender. Lack of full consideration can arise when the interest rate specified in the note is considered inadequate.

> EXAMPLE 14-4 Continuing Example 14-3, above, assume the installment note specifies an interest rate of 10 percent, which is equal to the current applicable mid-term federal rate (AMFR). Since the rules for installment sales under §7520(a)(2) require a minimum rate of *120 percent* of the current mid-term AFR to avoid the inference of a gift, the present value of the sum of all principal and interest payments, discounted at 12%, will be less than $80,000, the current value of the house. Thus, Mom will be treated as having made a gift of the difference. For a small loan the annual exclusion will cover the gift.

A parent may wish to *forgive* one or more of the purchaser's future payments. In the usual case, only the amount forgiven constitutes a taxable gift in the year forgiven. The gift will qualify for the annual exclusion.

> EXAMPLE 14-5 Continuing the above series of examples, if daughter wants to use the money to buy a car so Mom forgives a $14,000 annual payment, Mom has made a gift of that amount. After the annual exclusion, Mom's taxable gift will be $4,000. If Mom is married and her husband agrees to split the gift, the taxable gift would be zero. However, from an income tax standpoint, Mom will be treated as though she received the payment and then returned it to daughter.

A serious tax problem can arise, however, when the seller is considerably more generous. The IRS maintains that if the seller, at the time of the sale, intended *not* collect on the note, the *entire value* of the property would then be taxable as a gift. However the IRS has rarely prevailed when challenging this type of transaction where the note has been correctly drafted and properly secured so as to be legally enforceable.

Estate taxation. Ordinarily, when the seller in an installment sale dies,

---

8. §453(e)(1).

only the present value of the installment note is included in his or her *gross estate*.

> EXAMPLE 14-6 Continuing Example 14-5, if Mom dies just before the fourth payment is due, her gross estate will include the discounted value of the note. Of course, Mom's gross estate will also include any proceeds from receipt of earlier payments from daughter, to the extent retained by Mom, or any assets she purchased with those proceeds. However, her gross estate will not include the value of the installment asset sold.

If the seller made a partial gift and took back paper secured by the property transferred, and dies before the note is paid off, the date-of-death value of the property sold to be included in the seller's gross estate, less only the actual consideration paid.[9] That would be considered a transfer for less than full and adequate money, or money's worth, with a retained income interest.

Since family transactions are often scrutinized more carefully by the IRS, the client should be strongly advised to determine the value of the asset by qualified appraisal, and to use an adequate rate of interest.

Self-canceling provision. The client may seek to avoid inclusion of the value of the note in his or her gross estate by incorporating a self-canceling provision, specifying that no further payments will be made after his or her death. Since the initial value of a *self-canceling installment note* (called a "SCIN") is less than one whose payments can not be prematurely canceled, the buyer will have to give additional consideration, usually in the form of a higher principal amount or a higher interest rate.[10] And, of course, the older the client, the greater the additional consideration. Otherwise, the IRS could assert the existence of a gift element in the transaction, again creating the risk of §2036(a) application.

> EXAMPLE SCIN-1 Marty, age 53, sells property currently worth $100,000 in exchange for a 20 year self-canceling installment note. Based on Table II in Appendix A (IRS table 80CNSMT) the likelihood of Marty dying before reaching age 73 is .3129964 [= 1.0 - (61673/89771)]. To reflect this additional consideration, Marty sets the face amount of the note at $131,299.64.

Case law has ruled that the value of the canceled notes under a SCIN are

---

9. §2043.

10. For an example of a successful SCIN involving a $12 million note, see *Wilson* TCM 1992-480.

not includable in the note holder's gross estate.[11] However, cancellation of payments will trigger recognition of entire remaining gain on the decedent-note holder's *estate income tax* return (Form 1041).[12] While the gain will be income in respect of a decedent, no income tax deduction for its proportionate share of the estate tax [13] is available because the note is not included in the decedent's gross estate. Because the tax on this gain is recognized by the estate it is not a debt at the time of death and therefore is not deductible from the gross estate. Planners may still wish to recommend the SCIN to wealthier clients whose potential FET rate exceeds their marginal income tax rate.

The SCIN represents aggressive planning and should be used only when the client is willing to be subject to potentially greater income tax exposure.

Increasing appeal of installment sales. Tax deferral through installment sales have become more attractive for two reasons. First, TRA 86's elimination of the preferential rate on capital gains has made tax rates for property transactions higher than in prior years. Second, rates on *ordinary income* are expected to be raised in future years, while capital gains rates are expected to be lowered.

On the other hand, recent tax reform placed restrictions on installment reporting of certain sales, thus, the sale of publicly traded property (e.g., stocks and bonds) will not qualify; and, a portion of the sale might not qualify (under the so-called "proportional disallowance rule") if the sales price exceeds $150,000. These exceptions leave the installment sale mainly for the occasional sale of real estate or tangible personal property.

Thus, the client has a number of ways to arrange the intrafamily sale of a highly appreciating asset. The sale will freeze a portion of the client's estate, since postsale appreciation will inure to the new owner, whose gross estate is probably far smaller than the client's and who will probably live considerably longer. Intrafamily sales, whether of the ordinary, bargain, or installment variety, are significant value-shifting devices.

---

11. *Estate of Moss* 74 TC 1239 (1980).

12. *Frane v. Commr.* 998 F. 2d 567 (8 Cir. 1993) in part reversing *Estate of Frane* 98 TC 26 (1992); §691(a)(5).

13. §691(c).

Private Annuity

Overview. A private annuity usually involves the sale of an asset by the client in exchange for the unsecured promise of a life annuity by another family member. It is distinguished from a commercial annuity, which is purchased from an insurance company or other financial institution.

> EXAMPLE 14-7 Schwab, age 65 and in poor health, agrees to transfer a $100,000 asset ($20,000 basis) to his son, under a private annuity arrangement. Based on Table 9 of Appendix A and assuming 10 percent, Schwab will receive $14,042.38 a year for life ($14,042.38 = $100,000/7.1213).

The private annuity can generate periodic income for the client and can completely exclude the transferred property from his or her gross estate.

Taxation of private annuity. Tax aspects of the private annuity are as follows.

Gift taxation. If the transaction is designed properly, there will be *no taxable gift* as long as the value of the property transferred equals the discounted present value of the annuity promised. If a gift element is present, there is the risk that it will be deemed a transfer for less than money's worth with a retained interest resulting in the date of death value of the asset being included in the annuitant's estate.[14]

Income taxation. *No gain* is immediately recognizable upon creation of a private annuity because the amount realized (i.e., the value of the unsecured promise to pay an annuity for someone's life) is not considered immediately ascertainable. Thus, as with the installment sale, gain is reported as the annuity payments are *received.* But unlike the installment sale, taxability of the payments is governed by the annuity rules of §72. A portion of each payment is treated as a tax-free return of the annuitant's basis, also called *investment in the contract.* The excluded fraction, called the *exclusion ratio,* is calculated by dividing the investment in the contract by the *expected return,* which is the total of all amounts the annuitant expects to receive under the annuity contract. In the typical case, the expected return equals the total of all expected payments over the annuitant's life expectancy obtained from the mortality table in IRS Reg. § 1.72-9.

> EXAMPLE 14-8 Based on the facts in Example 14-7, Schwab's tax-free portion of the payment is $1,000, which is the product of an annual payment, $14,042.38, and the exclusion ratio, of .07121. This ratio is calculated by dividing the investment in the contract, $20,000, by the expected return, $280,847.60, which is the product of $14,042.38 and 20.0, Schwab's life

---

14. §2036(a).

expectancy, derived from the regulations. Schwab will be required to report as gain $4,000, or one twentieth of his $80,000 total gain in each of the first twenty years. Thus, for the first twenty years, of the entire $14,042.38 payment, Schwab will report $4,000 as taxable gain and $9,042.38 as ordinary income. The remaining $1,000 will be an income tax-free return of capital. If Schwab outlives his 20 year life expectancy all subsequent payments constitute ordinary income. If he dies within 20 years, gain reporting stops and he will receive a loss deduction on his final income tax return for the unrecovered basis.

Estate taxation. Upon death of the client-annuitant, *nothing* connected with the transaction should be includable in the estate tax base, inasmuch as he or she no longer has an interest in the property transferred. As with any life estate on the life of its owner, the life annuity terminates, becoming valueless at the death of its owner.

> EXAMPLE 14-9 In Example 14-8 above, if Schwab lives for two years, his son will have paid less than $30,000 for an asset worth $100,000. In connection with this transaction, Schwab's gross estate will include nothing more than the portion of the two cash payments that Schwab received, and still retained at death.

However, as with the installment sale, if the original transaction were to be ruled a *gift* because the value of the annuity promised the client is less than the value of the property transferred, the client's gross estate will include the *entire* date-of-death value of that property as a §2036(a) transfer with retained life estate. Such effect would wipe away the major tax appeal of the transaction, a danger that can be minimized by securing a qualified professional appraisal. For some additional protection, several commentators have suggested incorporating as a provision in the transaction a "valuation readjustment" or "savings"-type clause. One such clause would require the purchaser to pay additional consideration if the IRS determines that a gift had been made. The IRS has attacked these clauses, arguing that (1), as completed gifts, the transactions can't be altered, and (2) they are contrary to public policy.[15]

Analysis of private annuity. Advantages and disadvantages of the private annuity are described next.

Two advantages. First, from an FET point of view, the private annuity is even better than the installment sale: It can result in *complete* exclusion of the asset value from the annuitant's estate tax base. Second, as illustrated in the most recent example, the total amount eventually paid by the payor

---

15. For a discussion, see the Buchanan-Moore paper cited at the end of the chapter.

can be expected to be *relatively small* in situations where nonterminal clients have shorter than average life expectancies. For example, one individual arranged a private annuity prior to open-heart surgery, which was successful. He died 17 months later. In court the IRS lost its argument that the value of the property transferred exceeded the present value of the annuity payments, which had been determined using the IRS table. Ordinarily, only in cases where death is "imminent" or "predictable, occurring within one year" will actual life expectancies be required.[16] However, the IRS is aggressively challenging situations in which the annuitant is terminal.[17]

Disadvantages. The private annuity has three significant drawbacks. First, while the seller in an installment sale can, and usually does, require security, the annuitant under a private annuity cannot use the transferred property as security because doing so will result in it being included in the annuitant's gross estate.[18] Thus, private annuity arrangements are always unsecured, a distinct disadvantage to the annuitant-client. Lack of security will increase the risk of not being repaid, a result that could be unsettling, especially to an annuitant who is more or less depending on the payments for support.[19] Second, while interest paid by the purchaser under an installment sale may be tax deductible, *no part* of the annuity payment under a private annuity is deductible.[20] Third, if the annuitant lives a very long life, the payor has made a *bad bargain.*

> EXAMPLE 14-10 Continuing Example 14-9, above, if, instead of dying, Schwab regains his health and lives 20 years, his son will have paid more than $280,000 for the $100,000 asset. Schwab's gross estate may have to include this amount (which is nearly three times the value of the asset transferred), plus its resulting income, if he doesn't consume or gift these receipts during his lifetime.

---

16. Estate of Fabric 83 TC 932, TAM 9133001. For a discussion of when the tables will and will not be used, see the Blattmachr-Cavalieri article cited at the end of the chapter.

17. For an example, see LR 9133091.

18. IRC Section 2036. See also *Bell Estate v. Commr.* 60 T.C. 469 (1973).

19. For a discussion of placing the transferred property in a trust managed by a trustee until the property is made available to the ultimate beneficiaries, see the Loftis article cited at the end of the chapter.

20. §453(b)(1); *Rye v. United States* 92-1 USTC ¶50,186.

Since the private annuity can accomplish significant estate freezing without gift tax consequences, it can be a very attractive transaction if the parties are willing to assume the inherent risks. As we have seen, it works best when the client wants to save FET, is not expected to live very long, anticipates a significant cash flow need for life, and has little or no worry that the payments won't be forthcoming. Unfortunately, all of these characteristics seem to apply to only a few clients. Private annuities are infrequently used, with less than one percent of clients of experienced estate planning attorneys adopting them.

INCOMPLETE INTRAFAMILY TRANSFERS

This section briefly covers three currently used incomplete intrafamily transfers, the intentionally defective irrevocable trust, gift-leaseback and grantor retained trust.

Intentionally Defective Irrevocable Trust

When a client wishes to make gifts to significantly reduce estate tax, has little interest in shifting income, and wishes to retain some control over the transferred assets, the planner may wish to consider recommending an intentionally defective irrevocable trust (IDIT).[21] Taking advantage of the differences in tax rules between §2036 - 2038 (estate tax) and §671-677 (grantor trust income tax rules) with regard to retained powers, transfers to an IDIT are made complete for federal estate and gift tax but incomplete for income tax. Thus, the trust corpus is not included in the grantor's gross estate, similar to the treatment of any other completed gift; but, because the trust provides for grantor retained powers uniquely proscribed by the grantor trust rules, all trust income is taxable to the grantor. This result offers an additional opportunity to save estate tax since income tax paid by the grantor rather than by the trust beneficiary will have the effect of additionally reducing the amount of assets held by the grantor at death, at no gift tax cost.

> Example IDIT-1   Maxwell transfers $610,000 to an IDIT for the benefit of his adult son, Kirk. Since Maxwell has made no prior taxable gifts, he can totally shelter the current gift from gift taxation with the annual exclusion and unified

---

21. For a summary comparison of the taxation of the intentionally defective irrevocable trust versus other popular trusts in estate planning, see Table 17-1 in Chapter 17.

credit. Required to distribute all income to Kirk annually, the trustee distributes $50,000 income in the first year. Maxwell is obligated to pay an additional $17,500 income tax, based on his 35 percent combined marginal rate. This year Maxwell has effectively transferred an additional $17,500 for the benefit of his son, free of gift tax.

Powers that the grantor may wish to retain over an IDIT include acting as trustee and having the grantor's spouse as one of the trust beneficiaries. As trustee, the grantor can have the following powers: to invest, to allocate receipts between income and principal, to vote shares of stock held in the trust, and to distribute income or principal to trust beneficiaries for such reasons as "sickness," "emergency" or "disability." Naming the spouse to be one of the beneficiaries enables the grantor to retain indirect access to the trust. Of course, any distributions to the spouse could increase his or her estate, which may run contrary to the FET goals of the trust.

The IRS may argue that payment of income taxes by the grantor constitutes a gift. At least one commentator believes the IRS will not succeed, provided the trust instrument is worded carefully.[22]

The advantages of the IDIT over a simple gift include retained control, and greater potential estate tax avoidance at little or no additional gift tax cost.

Gift-Leaseback

When a business-owning parent wishes to establish a program of gifting but is held back for lack of available assets, he or she might find the answer in a gift-leaseback arrangement. As its name suggests, the parent gives a business asset outright or in trust to a lower-bracket family member and leases the asset back for use in the business. The parent is able to continue using the asset, can take a deduction for the lease payment, and can still enjoy all the other advantages inherent in gifting.

The ability to *deduct* the lease payments under a gift-leaseback might depend in part on the location of the client's business, and in part on how carefully the arrangement is structured. In some circuits, the Federal appellate courts have disallowed the deduction, while other circuits have allowed it as a legitimate business expense. Even in circuits that allow the deduction, it will be denied if the transaction is poorly structured. Some

---

22. For a general discussion of the IDIT and some drafting suggestions, see the Mulligan and Belcher-Bridgeman articles cited at the end of the chapter.

requirements for success include having a legitimate business purpose, charging a reasonable lease payment, having a written and enforceable lease, and, if the gift is in trust, the trustee must be independent and not subservient to the donor.

Grantor Retained Interest Trust

With a grantor retained interest trust, the client transfers property into an irrevocable trust, retaining the right to income for a period of years. The acronym "GRIT" (pronounced "grit") is used in this text to refer in general to all varieties of grantor retained interest trusts, including common law types, GRATs, GRUTs and all others that fall under §2702. Who will eventually receive the corpus, and whether the corpus is includable in the client's gross estate usually depends upon the type of GRIT created and how long the client lives. With all GRITs, if the client *does not survive* the income period, §2036(a) will apply and the GRIT will have served no useful purpose. In fact, some GRITs (i.e., all those except GRATS and GRUTS--see below) provide that the corpus will revert to the client-grantor's estate, if he or she does not survive. This is accomplished by granting the client a contingent testamentary power of appointment over the trust corpus. Reversion is made contingent upon the grantor not surviving the period. If the client *does survive* the income period, the result is the same for all GRITs: the client's entire beneficial interest in the trust ceases, and the corpus vests in the remaindermen (usually the client's children).[23]

Tax consequences. A properly structured GRIT has the following tax consequences:

Gift Taxation. At the creation of the GRIT, the value of the gift equals the entire value of the property transferred into the trust reduced by the value of the retained interests. Whether the value of a retained interest is deemed to equal zero or some larger amount depends upon the facts of the GRIT and the provisions of §2702. As mentioned in the extended discussion in Chapter 7, in general, all *retained* interests are valued at zero (called the *zero valuation rule*) unless §2702 does not apply, or unless §2702 provides for an exception, such as where the retained interest is a qualified one or where the remaindermen are not related to the trustor. Types of §2702 GRITs for which retained interests can be valued at greater than zero, thereby reducing the gift tax valuation, include those for which

---

23. For a summary comparison of the taxation of the grantor retained interest trust versus other popular trusts in estate planning, see Table 17-1 in Chapter 17.

the transferor retained *qualified* annuity or unitrust interests (explained below), and GRITs funded with a personal residence or certain tangible personal property. Since the gift portion of a GRIT is one of a future (remainder) interest, it does not qualify for the annual exclusion. As a result, any resulting taxable gift must use some unified credit, if available, and will require payment of gift tax once all the donor's unified credit is used up.

Income taxation. As a grantor trust under, all trust income is taxable to the trustor until the end of the stated period, if he or she lives that long.[24]

Estate taxation. If the client *survives* the income period, none of the corpus will be includable in the gross estate. However, the taxable gift value will be included in the estate tax base as an adjusted taxable gift.

If the client *dies before* the expiration of the income period, as mentioned, §2036(a) will subject the date-of-death value of the corpus to inclusion in the client's gross estate, as a transfer with retained income or enjoyment which did not in fact end before the transferor's death. Thus, premature death of the client can not reduce FET. Fortunately, this type of estate planning has very little downside risk; if the client had not set up the GRIT the property would have been in the client's gross estate at date of death values anyway. Therefore, if the client outlives the term much is accomplished in the way of estate planning but dying during the term has as a cost only the cost of establishing the trust, mainly attorney's fees, and the cost of maintaining it, mainly accountant's fees. Remember, since the corpus comes back into the gross estate the earlier gift disappears as an adjusted taxable gift for estate tax purposes.[25]

GST taxation. The ability to leverage the $1 million GSTT exemption to a GRIT transfer is limited by statutory law. Under §2642(f),[26] the GSTT exemption can not be allocated to most GRIT's until the close of the "estate tax inclusion period" (called ETIP), which occurs when the property would no longer be includable in the grantor's gross estate in the event the grantor died. In most GRIT situations, this would be the *end of the specified income period*, at which point §2036(a) no longer applies. The value of the property against which the allocation may be made will equal the value that is included in the grantor's gross estate, or the GRIT's value at the end of the term. Ordinarily, an allocation of the GSTT exemption for most non-

---

24. §677(a)

25. §2001(b)

26. §2642 is included in Appendix B.

GRIT transfers is made *at the time the GSTT trust becomes irrevocable, which has the effect of attaining* maximum leverage for appreciating assets. In the case of a GRIT, the exemption allocation is delayed until the end of the income period. This means that more of the client's GSTT exemption will have to be used up for two reasons: First, the allocation will have to be made to the *entire value* of the property, rather than just the present value of the remainder, excluding the income interest. Second, in the case of assets *appreciating* during the income period of the GRIT, the allocation amount will necessarily be higher. However, even though the advantage of leveraging the exemption under a GRIT is restrained, it is not eliminated, since any appreciation *after the term* [i.e.,after the retained interest period] is sheltered from future GSTT. Thus, although allocating the GSTT exemption to a GRIT will not result in as much leveraging as with an ordinary lifetime gift, it generally will yield more leveraging than with a transfer at death because the leveraging period can also include a period during the grantor's lifetime.

Illustration of GRIT. Figure 14-1 illustrates the evolution of the GRIT, tracing the change in primary beneficiaries and their taxation where the grantor successfully outlives the retained income period. After the retained income period, the trust either terminates and the trustee distributes all assets to the children, or it continues, and can eventually become a GST trust.

FIGURE 14-1 Evolution of a GRIT: Beneficiaries and Taxation

TIMELINE ───►

Key Events:	Creation of Trust	Termination of income period	Death of Grantor	Death of last surviving child	21st birthday of youngest grandchild
	▼	▼	▼	▼	▼

PrimaryBeneficiary:	**GRANTOR**	**CHILDREN**	**CHILDREN**	**GRAND- CHILDREN**	
Their property interests in income and principal of trust:	Income: for a specified period	Principal: GRATs & GRUTs: none All other GRTs: reversion, but only if does not survive period	Income: (all, or as needed)	Principal: (as needed)	Income: (as needed)	Principal: (as needed)	Income: (as needed)	Principal: (as needed) all outright at age 21

Trust name and characteristics:	*Grantor creates and transfers assets to:* **Grantor Retained Trust**	*Grantor's interest terminates* **Grantor Retained/Bypass Trust** *Trust assets bypass G's estate* *Trust either terminates when youngest child reaches a specified age...*	**Children's Trust**	*...or continues on as:* **GST Trust** *...which then terminates when youngest grandchild reaches age 21, or later, if allowed by local perpetuities law.*

TAX EFFECTS TO DONOR, OR BENEFICIARY NAMED ABOVE

Type of taxation

1. Taxable gift to donor/grantor?	Yes, on future interest value of remainder	No: gifts are no longer made to this trust	No: gifts are no longer made to this trust
2. Includable in beneficiaries estate tax base at death?	Either #1 or #2: 1. Value of remainder as adjusted taxable if G survives. 2. Entire DOD value in gross estate if does not survive period certain.	Yes, to extent of principal distributions that continue to be owned	Yes, to extent of principal distributions that continue to be owned
3. Income taxable to beneficiary?	Yes, during the income period	Yes, to extent distributions to these beneficiaries. Undistributed FAI and all capital gains taxable to trust	
4. Any GSTT incurred?	To extent not sheltered, trust will have inclusion ratio of greater than zero, and a portion of any taxable termination or taxable distribution to a skip person will be subject to GSTT. Exemption allocation is made at termination of income period.		

GRIT planning. The following material explains how GRITs were structured before tax reform, and then describes planning opportunities currently available.

Pre-1986 'Classic' GRIT. Prior to the passage of §2036(c) and §2702, relatively uncomplicated GRITs were quite successful in freezing the value of appreciating property at little or no gift tax cost. The following example portrays what is now called a "traditional common law GRIT." The numbers reflect *current* IRS valuation tables, however, so that the reader can validate first hand the calculations with help from the tables in Appendix A. Keep in mind that since the appropriate but currently outdated 1985 tables were not used, the exact calculations will be somewhat different.

EXAMPLE 14-11 In 1985, Haney, when he was 58 years old, created a GRIT, funding it with $500,000 in common stock. The trust terms retain for Haney all income from the trust, payable at least annually, for the lesser of 10 years or for Haney's life. If Haney dies before the end of the 10-year period, the trust will terminate and the corpus will revert to his estate. If Haney survives the period, the trust will terminate at the end of 10 years and the corpus will then be distributed outright to Haney's son. When the trust was established, Haney made a *taxable gift* of the remainder interest in the stock, which, at 10 percent, is valued at $161,996 [= $500,000 x .385543 x (72082/85776). As a future interest, the remainder does not qualify for the annual exclusion. Haney owed no gift tax, he simply used up some of his unified credit.

EXAMPLE 14-12 Continuing the above example, if Haney *died four years later*, the date of death value of the corpus would be included in his gross estate, and the trust would have gained no FET advantage, but instead of there being an adjusted taxable gift of $161,996 it would be zero. Thus the only disadvantage was the fees paid to establish and maintain the trust for the four years.

EXAMPLE 14-13 Examining the consequences of the alternative outcome , if Haney instead *dies twelve years later* when the corpus is worth $1 million, his gross estate will include nothing in connection with this property, although adjusted taxable gift would be $161,996. By surviving the income period, Haney would have succeeded in freezing the transfer tax value of this stock at $161,996, the original gift tax value of the remainder interest, less than the value of the stock when transferred and far less that its value when Haney died. Described in other terms, Haney would have leveraged the gift tax unified credit many times over.

Review of §2702. As described in Chapter 7, §2702 applies in general when there is a transfer of an interest in a trust to or for the benefit of a member of the transferor's family where the transferor or an "applicable family member" has retained an interest in the trust. §2702 GRITs that fall under the zero valuation rule must treat the entire value of the transfer as a taxable gift.

> EXAMPLE 14-14 In the ongoing example above, had Haney instead created his GRIT today, the entire value of the transfer, $500,000, would be treated as a taxable gift. §2702 applies because the trust was for the benefit of a family member. The zero valuation rule applies because the arrangement does not fall under one of its exceptions. Thus, under the subtraction method of valuation, the gift tax value equals $500,000, the total value of the transfer, reduced by zero, the allowable value of the retained interest.

Careful GRIT planning will attempt one of two strategies: Either planners will structure a common law GRIT to avoid §2702 entirely. Or they will create a §2702 GRIT that is explicitly excepted from the zero valuation rule. A GRIT transfer to a nonfamily member (described next) is a common example of the former strategy. Examples of the latter approach will be explained shortly.

GRIT Transfers to nonfamily members. §2702 does not apply if the beneficiary of the transferred interest is not an *applicable family member*, which includes the transferor's spouse, an ancestor or descendant of the transferor or the transferor's spouse, a sibling of the transferor, or a spouse of such ancestor, descendant or sibling.

> EXAMPLE 14-15 In Example 14-14, above, had the beneficiary of today's transferred interest been Haney's *nephew* rather than his son, the entire actuarial value of the retained income interest could be subtracted in arriving at the gift tax value, with today's results similar to that generated by the traditional common law GRIT created before 1986, detailed in Examples 14-12 and 14-13.

Other examples of common non-'applicable family member' situations not falling within the grasp of §2702 are trusts for unmarried partners and close friends. It should be clear now that we call the GRIT in the above example a traditional common law GRIT because it does not fall under the restrictive requirements of §2702.

The five types of §2702 GRITs described in the next few pages avoid harsh zero valuation rule (for the retained interests) by falling within one or more exceptions found in the Code. They are the GRAT, GRUT, tangible personal property GRIT, and two types of personal residence GRITs.

GRAT and GRUT. The zero valuation rule of § 2702 does not apply to "qualified" retained income interests, i.e., one of the two types of income interests that meet §2702(b)'s detailed technical requirements. Trusts must have either a *qualified annuity interest* or a *qualified unitrust interest*, and the trusts prepared with these interest in mind are called the *grantor retained annuity trust*, GRAT, and the *grantor retained unitrust*, GRUT. Among other requirements, the payment must be made at least annually; and for a GRAT it must be stated as a *fixed dollar amount*, sometimes stated as a percentage of the initial value of the trust corpus, and for a CRUT the annual payment will be a *fixed percentage* of the fair market value of the trust property *determined each year*.

> EXAMPLE 14-16 Jake creates a GRAT, transferring $200,000 in trust and retaining the right an annual payment equal to 6% of the initial corpus, thus her will receive $12,000 each year.

> EXAMPLE 14-17 Pam creates a GRUT, transferring $200,000 in trust and retaining the right to six percent of the fair market value of the trust property, determined annually. The first year she will receive $12,000. If the trust is worth $210,000 on the valuation date of the second year she will receive $12,600 for that year. On the other hand, if the value has dropped to $190,000 the payment will be only $11,400. The annual valuation day is likely to be set in the trust agreement as January 1 of each year since most reporting and planning is done on a calendar year basis.

Clients choosing between a GRAT or a GRUT who would prefer to minimize their receipt of unneeded income that may someday augment their gross estate will probably prefer a GRAT, under which income payments are based on the *initial* value of the corpus. This is especially true if the corpus will be funded with assets expected to appreciate over the retained income period.

The detailed rules for GRATs and GRUTs are very similar to the rules for charitable remainder trusts (called CRATs and CRUTs), which are described later in this chapter.

"Zeroing out" a GRAT. Transfer tax reduction can be greater if relatively high discount rate tables can generate an artificially low remainder interest value for any qualifying GRIT. In fact, careful planning combined with a relatively high discount rate may be able to *zero out* a GRAT, that is, effect a transfer to a GRAT an asset with a large enough cash flow or growth to generate a retained term interest value equal to the *entire value* of the property. For example, at a discount rate of 10.4 percent, the remainder portion of a 15 year GRAT paying a fixed 15% annuity will have a value equal to 100 percent of the total value of the asset. When this value is subtracted from the total value of the asset, is there is no gift tax and the grantor does not use up any unified credit. Thus, the GRIT can result in a

large estate tax base *reduction*, as well as a freeze, at no gift tax cost. [27] The IRS has taken the position in several rulings that a GRAT can not be success fully zeroed out. First, it claims that for any GRAT whose annuity amount will exhaust the corpus precisely at the termination of the trust, the value of the retained interest can not equal the initial corpus because of the possibility that the grantor may die prior to the expiration of the trust term.[28] Scanlon, in his paper cited at the end of the chapter, indicates that planners can easily avoid this problem by providing for a remainder interest of at least 1 percent of the corpus. Second, the IRS has taken the position that an intended zeroed out GRAT may not be adequately funded to make all the payments if 1) the annual payment is set at a level that would exhaust the corpus before the end of the income period, or 2) the exercise of a trustee power to invest in highly speculative assets would substantially increase the chance of a loss.[29]

Tangible Personal Property Transfers. The zero valuation rule of §2702 does not apply to tangible personal property where: (*a*) the failure by a term interest holder to exercise his or her rights would not have a substantial effect on the value of the remainder interest, and (*b*) the property is of a type for which no depreciation deduction would be allowable. In such case, the value of the retained interest is set equal to the amount the interest could be sold for to an unrelated third party. One possible type of property is artwork, such as a painting.

> EXAMPLE 14-18 Drew, age 65, gives his daughter a remainder interest in a painting, worth $1 million, and retains a 13 year term certain interest. The gift tax value is the amount $1 million reduced by the amount Drew can show that an unrelated third party would pay for the right to possess the painting for 13 years.

In view of the fact that the IRS requires evidence of "...actual sales or rentals that are comparable..." to sustain the value of the term interest, few clients will be able to successfully employ this strategy.

Qualified Personal Residence Trust. Finally, the zero valuation rule of §2702 does not apply to a GRIT whose sole asset is a personal residence

---

27. For a detailed analysis, with numerical illustrations, of very aggressive estate planning using overlapping short term GRITs, see the Hollbrook/Murphy article cited at the end of the chapter.

28. LR 9239015.

29. LR 9248016, relying on RR 77-454.

of the term interest holder. The details and restrictions are quite complex, probably discouraging all but the most ambitious planners and clients.

> EXAMPLE 14-19 In Example 14-11, had Haney created his GRIT today, structuring it to contain only his personal residence, the result could be the same as that described in Examples 14-12 and 14-13.

Qualified personal residence trust. More planners will recommend a personal residence GRIT as a result of recent regulations which have outlined the conditions required for 'safe-harbor' residence trust called a qualified personal residence trust (QPRT).[30] Among the rules, the QPRT can hold an interest in only one residence. It can receive additions of cash to pay six months of mortgage payments, but any excess cash must be distributed to the term holder. The trustee may sell the residence, hold the proceeds, and buy another residence within two years from the sale. If the residence ceases to be a personal residence of the term holder, the trust corpus must be held for the balance of the term interest and must meet all of the requirements for functioning exclusively as a qualified annuity interest trust, similar to a GRAT. However, unlike a GRAT or a GRUT, a QPRT can provide for reversion of the corpus to the client's estate if he or she does not survive the term period. As with the traditional common-law GRIT, this contingent reversion will have the advantage of reducing the value of the remainder and thus the value of the taxable gift.

Calculating the gift for a QPRT. The remainder value is the gift. Its value when the grantor has contingent reversion is calculated as follows:

$$\text{Remainder value} = R_t * (\#Y / \#X) * \text{FMV of the property}$$

Where:
R_t = Term of years remainder factor[31] for given interest rate "t".
$\#X$ = Number alive[32] at starting age for grantor
$\#Y$ = Number alive at ending age for grantor

---

30. §25.2702-5

31. Table B, term of years remainder values. [Table 10]

32. 80 CNSMT, 1980 census survival values. [Table 11]

EXAMPLE 14-QPRT: The 7520 rate is 8.0% and the grantor is 75 at start of a 10 year QPRT. The house being used to fund the trust is worth $500,000.

R_t = .463193
Value for 75 (1980 census) = 56799
Value for 85 (1980 census) = 27960

Therefore, the remainder value for this QPRT is:

.463193*(27960/56799) = .20046*$500,000 = $100,230

Remember if the grantor dies during the term of the trust, its fair market value will be included in the grantor's estate but the adjusted taxable gift value drops back to zeros insofar as this gift goes because Section 2001(b) defines adjusted taxable gifts as being those post-1976 taxable gifts except for those "gifts that are includable in the gross estate...." Therefore, the QPRTs, like other qualified GRITs, carry very little downside risk, other than the attorney's fees in establishing them and accountant's fees in maintaining them.

Must a client who survives the term period of the QPRT vacate the residence? No, since he or she can repurchase the home, or rent it from the remainderman. However, the agreement must be arms length, with lease payments equal to fair rental value, in order to avoid the risk of §2036(a) application.[33] Clearly, some clients will not appreciate this aspect of the QPRT. Others, however, will welcome the ability to transfer property to their children at a greatly reduced transfer tax cost.

Summary FET example. Summarizing the FET savings available from GRITs, let's explore Haney's ongoing situation further and project the large tax savings possible from a taxable GRIT and a zeroed out GRAT, in comparison with either doing nothing or simply gifting the assets outright. In the next example, assume the following: Haney dies 12 years after he established the trust (1985 in Example 14-11); his top marginal FET rate is 55%; he has made no other gifts; all pertinent assets appreciate 10% annually; and Haney spends all income that he receives.

EXAMPLE 14-20 Based on the facts in the series of examples above, consider the net cash flow consequences of four alternative action plans:

Did nothing. If Haney did not create a GRIT and dies owning the assets (originally worth $500,000), his gross estate and estate tax base will include $1,569,214, the future appreciated value of the assets, accumulated at 10% per

---

33. LR 9249014.

year for 12 years. Haney's estate will pay an FET for these assets of $863,068 (= .55 x $1,569,214). Thus, the value of the assets, reduced by the FET attributable to them, will be $706,146 (= $1,569,214 - $863,068).

Made outright gift. If Haney made an outright gift of the $500,000 in assets without creating a GRIT, he would have paid no gift tax, but the frozen amount $490,000 will be included in adjusted taxable gifts at his death. His estate tax base will be reduced by $10,000 below the asset's original value of $500,000. Haney's estate will pay an FET on these assets of $269,500 (= $490,000 x .55). Thus the value of the assets, reduced by the FET attributable to them, will be $1,299,714 (= $1,569,214 - $269,500), a **savings of $593,568** (= 1,299,714 - $706,146) over doing nothing.

Created taxable GRIT. If Haney created a gift-taxable GRIT similar to the facts in Example 14-11, he would have made a taxable gift of $161,996, paying no gift tax. But the asset's contribution to Haney's estate tax base will be reduced from $500,000 to $161,996, the frozen value of the asset's adjusted taxable gifts. The additional FET for these assets is only $89,098 (= .55 x $161,996). Thus the value of the assets, after subtracting the FET attributable to them, will be $1,480,116 (= $1,569,214 - $89,098). This will reflect a **savings of $773,970** (= $1,480,116 - $706,146) over doing nothing.

Created zeroed out GRAT. If Haney created a zeroed out GRAT, he will have made no taxable gift, and the asset's contribution to Haney's estate tax base will be reduced from $500,000 to a frozen value of zero. Haney's estate will owe no FET on account of these assets. As a consequence, the value of the GRAT assets, after FET reduction, will be the entire $1,569,214, for a **savings of $863,068** (= $1,569,214 - $706,146) over doing nothing.

GRITs work best when the client is determined to save a large amount of FET, has substantial assets that can be transferred, does not want to lose current benefit from the property, has an above average life expectancy, and is willing to undertake a somewhat involved transaction, one with considerable risk of IRS challenge.

PLANNING FOR CHARITABLE TRANSFERS

We now shift gears and examine transfers designed to assist charitable institutions while providing significant benefits to the donor-client.

Introduction

Transfers to charity, whether lifetime or at death, are supported by several provisions of the Internal Revenue Code, which normally allows generous deductions on a contributor's income tax, gift tax, and estate tax returns. While charitable transfers can be made during lifetime or at death, lifetime transfers will be the primary focus of this section, partly for consistency with the chapter theme, partly because lifetime charitable transfers often are more complex and need greater elaboration, and partly because they have a significant income tax advantage over deathtime charitable transfers, as we shall see. Lifetime gifts to charity are of essentially two types (outright gift and split-interest gift), offering to clients considerable flexibility in the amount and type of interest in a given piece of property that can be donated.

At the outset, it should be noted that charitable gifts, unlike other lifetime transfers, will hardly ever result in no net decrease in wealth to the client's family unit as a whole. Thus, the client will usually need to possess a charitable motive to feel comfortable about making charitable transfers. The material presented below describes how to best minimize the decline in family wealth resulting from a charitable donation.

Tax Consequences of Charitable Transfers

Income tax consequences. To qualify for an itemized charitable income tax deduction, the donee charity must meet the requirements under the Code.[34] In addition, the Code contains rather complex *limitations* on the amount of charitable contributions deductible from income by individuals in any given tax year. As shown next, there are limitations on both the total amount deductible for all charitable gifts, and on the specific amount deductible for any particular gift.[35]

Limitations on total amount deductible. In general, total deductible charitable contributions may not exceed 50 percent of a taxpayer's "contribution base" (CB), the name for an amount that is approximately equal to

---

34. §170(c).

35. For a detailed discussion of the deductibility (and nondeductibility) of many types of 'strings attached' charitable gifts, including gifts benefiting the donor, restricted gifts, earmarked gifts, and gifts having redemption, resale of liquidation requirements, see the 1990 Teitell paper cited at the end of the chapter.

adjusted gross income.[36] However, there are some major exceptions with regard to this 50 percent limitation. Taxpayers are limited to 30 percent of CB for donations to public charities of certain "capital gain property" (see below), and to 20 percent for contributions to private foundations of cash or capital gain property.[37] Contributions in excess of these limits may be carried over, to be deducted during the next five years, except excess contributions to private foundations cannot be carried over.

> EXAMPLE CB-1 Fanny Superstar, prominent singer just donated her $15 million Malibu estate to charity. This year she has earned $20 million in income, enabling her to currently deduct $6 million (30 percent) from income and carry over the remaining $9 million to later years. At a combined marginal tax rate of 50 percent, by making the donation, Fanny saved $7,500,000 in total income taxes.

This summary of the annual limitations has been merely a capsule overview; individuals wishing to make contributions of this relative size should consult a tax adviser specializing in this area.

Amount deductible for a particular gift. The amount deductible from adjusted gross income for any particular charitable gift is usually its *fair market value*, subject to the total annual limitation outlined above. However, there are two important *exceptions for noncash gifts*. First, if sale of the property would have resulted in ordinary income or in short-term capital gain, the asset is called "ordinary income property," and the donor is limited to deducting the *adjusted basis* of the property, with a 50% CB limit.

Second, if sale of any tangible personal property except publicly traded stock would have resulted in a long-term capital gain, the asset is called "capital gain property," and one of two alternative tax consequences will occur. If the property is given to a public charity which can *properly use it* in its activities, then the entire *fair market value* is deductible (with a 30%

---

36. §170(b)(1)(F).

37. For informative discussions of the techniques and benefits of establishing a *private foundation* for wealthy clients, see the Rosen-Saper and McCoy papers cited at the end of the chapter. They state that the most common reasons for charitable giving by establishing a private foundation are to perpetuate the individual's strong desire to aid society in a unique manner through a controlled, formal, well-defined structure, and to serve as a family memorial by creating a sense of family legacy and tradition. These are very different reasons than the ones implied in Conrad Teitell's facetious definition of a foundation: a large body of money surrounded by people who want some.

CB limit). If, on the other hand, the charity is a private foundation, or if it is a public charity which *cannot* properly use the donated property in its activities, then the amount deductible is limited to the donor's *basis* (with a 50 percent CB limit). An example of a proper "related use" is the hanging of a donated painting on one of the walls of the donee art museum or university. An example of an improper unrelated use of such a gift would be its storage in the institution's basement, or its immediate sale by the donee.

> EXAMPLE 14-21 Charles, a real estate developer earning $380,000 in adjusted gross income this year, has four assets (each currently worth $100,000), one of which he is considering donating to a public charity. Besides *cash*, Charles has a parcel of *real estate* which his business purchased three years ago and which currently has an adjusted basis of $20,000. Charles also has two blocks of *common stock*, each of which cost $20,000. Stock A was purchased three years ago, and Stock B was acquired last month. The following describes the amount deductible if Charles contributes, alternatively, each asset to the charity which, for the moment we shall assume, can properly use any of the assets in its activities.
>
> 1. Cash: $100,000 deduction.
> 2. Business real estate: $20,000 deduction.
> 3. Stock A: $100,000 deduction. This stock could be the stock of Charles' real estate development corporation. The charity could be given the right to redeem the stock for cash.
> 4. Stock B: $20,000 deduction.

The charitable deduction for business real estate is limited to the developer's basis because the property represents his business inventory. A better alternative might be to sell the inventory and donate the after-tax cash proceeds. Assuming a 50% combined marginal tax rate, Charles could donate $60,000 cash (= $100,000-($100,000-$20,000)x.50), yielding a tax saving of $30,000 (=$60,000 x.50). In contrast, donating the property would save only $10,000 in tax (=.50 x $20,000). Of course, the charity would be receiving only $60,000 (cash) rather than $100,000 (real estate).

Any charitable contributions of $250 or more must be substantiated contemporaneously in writing by the donee charity, which states the amount of cash donated, a description (but not value) of the property, and a good faith estimate of the value of any property it provided in consideration for the donation.[38] In addition, a charitable donor of property exceeding $5,000 in value is required to obtain a "qualified appraisal" and supply additional

---

38. §170(f)(8).

information detailing the transaction.

Income tax planning for outright gifts to charity. Several planning strategies evolve from these and other income tax rules.

In many cases, contributing *capital gain property* to a public charity is more advantageous than contributing cash.

> EXAMPLE 14-22 Jeff, who is in the 35 percent combined income tax bracket, wishes to contribute $5,000 to his favorite public charity. Jeff could give an original oil painting, acquired for $1,000 and now worth $5,000, or he could sell the painting and donate the cash proceeds. If Jeff contributes the painting, his after-tax cost will be $3,250 which is the $5,000 value of the painting, less the $1,750 tax savings from the deduction. Alternatively, if Jeff sells the painting and still donates the full $5,000, his after-tax cost will be $4,370, which is the $5,000 donated cash, plus the $1,120 tax on the gain ($4,000 x .28), minus the $1,750 tax saving from the deduction.

From 1987 to 1992, the appreciation portion of the charitable deduction ($4,000 in the above example) was treated as a tax preference item, subject to the *alternative minimum tax*. The '93 tax act repealed this provision.

When a client is considering giving a large sum of money to a charity, his or her portfolio should be reviewed to see if there are highly appreciated assets which could easily be replace in the security markets. Using the money to replace the property increases the basis in the investment to the purchase price and the charitable deduction is the same as it would have been had cash been given.

> EXAMPLE 14-22A Anderson has been planning to gift $10,000 cash to charity. He also owns shares of publicly traded ABC corporation stock, currently worth $10,000 and having a basis of $1,000. Although Anderson likes the stock as an investment, if he donates it to charity and immediately purchases an equivalent amount of ABC stock on the market, the new shares will now have a basis of $10,000. Anderson's taxable gain will be $9,000 less, if he later sells the stock.

Owners of nonmarketable property that they wish to sell may consider making a *bargain sale* of the property to charity. The income tax consequences of a bargain sale to a private individual were described earlier in the chapter in Example 14-1. Bargain sales to charities are treated very differently. With the related party bargain sale no loss can be recognized and a gain is recognized only if the bargain price exceeds the seller-donor's basis. But for bargain sales to a charity the transaction is treated as though it is two transactions in one: a sale and a gift. The old basis is allocated to each part in direct proportion to the part's value when compared to the whole. Thus, where B_g represents basis allocated to the gift portion and

B_s represents the basis allocated to the sale porting, G stands for the value of the gift, which is the difference between the amount paid (S for sale) by the charity and the fair market value (FMV) of the property transferred to the charity at a bargain price.

$$B_g = (G/FMV)*B$$
$$B_s = (S/FMV)*B$$

The gain is: $G = S - B_s$.

EXAMPLE 14-22B. This year, Margaret transferred her vacant city lot to her church. She inherited the lot from her mother. It was valued in her mother's estate at $100,000, which of course established Margaret's basis. At the time of transfer, the lot was worth $500,000. Since Margaret is cash poor and wants to purchase a $500,000 life insurance policy, so her son won't be too disappointed about her transferring the lot, the church has agreed to pay Margaret $150,000 for the lot. Margaret's gain:

$$G = \$150,000 - (\$150,000/\$500,000)*\$100,000 = \$120,000$$

Of course Margaret will have a charitable deduction of $350,000, the difference between the FMV and the amount paid to Margaret. If Margaret has modest income, she and the church might wish to structure this as an installment sale whereby the church pays the price in five $30,000 annual installments, since Margaret's excess income tax charitable deduction can be carried forward, and the installment reporting will avoid bunching up the capital gain in the first year.

As in a private sale, an outright gift of *mortgaged property* to charity is treated as a bargain sale, resulting in taxable gain to the donor. However, the bargain sale may be a simpler way to sell difficult to market asset, such as an interest in a closely held business.

Gift tax consequences. Similar to the unlimited marital deduction, an unlimited gift tax deduction is allowed for the present value of gifts to qualifying charities.[39] The rules covering the charitable deduction require that a gift tax return must be filed if total gross gifts, including those to charity, exceed the amount of the annual exclusion.

---

39. §2522(a).

Estate tax consequences. Similar to lifetime outright interspousal gifts, *lifetime* gifts to charity are not included in the donor's estate tax base. They are not includable in the gross estate because they are not owned by the decedent at death. And they are not an adjusted taxable gift because they were deducted in arriving at that amount. The estate taxation of lifetime charitable gifts *in trust* will be described in the next major section, which details gifts of split interests.

Deathtime gifts to charity are totally deductible from the gross estate.[40] Thus, a multimillionaire could give all (or all but $600,000) of his or her entire estate to charity and ensure total avoidance of the FET. Of course, he or she could also accomplish this goal by making a series of lifetime charitable transfers. In fact, lifetime charitable transfers are preferable to donations at death, as the next example illustrates.

> EXAMPLE 14-23 Sampson wishes to make an outright gift of $100,000 to his church which has been a source of continuous spiritual support to him and his family for many years. Sampson's estate planner recommends a lifetime transfer over a similar transfer at death, reasoning as follows: If Sampson donates the property at his death, his gross estate will be reduced by the amount of the gift, but he will enjoy no income tax benefit.[41] Alternatively, if Sampson makes the gift during his lifetime (even a deathbed gift), not only will his gross estate and estate tax base be lower by the date-of-death value of the gift property, but Sampson will also be able to save income taxes by deducting some or all of the value of the gift from his income.

Other tax planning for outright gifts to charity. Several other strategies include interspousal transfers, redemption bailout of corporate stock, gifts of life insurance, and the gift annuity.

Interspousal transfers. If a particular client insists on making a deathtime gift to charity, the planner might urge the client to plan making an outright marital deduction gift to the surviving spouse, who could then donate the property to charity. While the FET consequences are the same, the income tax results will improve, since S2 will be able to enjoy a charitable income tax deduction. Of course, S2, as fee simple recipient of the property, could later refuse to make the donation. QTIPing the property will ensure receipt by the charity, but not until S2's death. Finally, the client may be encouraged to make a lifetime gift to the spouse of property destined for charity if more time is needed by that spouse to make full use

---

40. §2055(a).

41. U.S. Trust Co. v. U.S., 803 F. 2d 1363 (5 Cir., 1986).

of a charitable deduction carryover which arose as a result of the restrictive percentage limitations on total amounts deductible in a given tax year (discussed earlier).

Redemption bailout of corporate stock. A client owning stock in a closely held corporation may wish to gift some stock to a charity, which will later tender the stock for redemption by the corporation. Advantages include saving income tax, "bailing out" corporate earnings and profits without incurring dividend income, helping younger family shareholders concentrate their ownership, and enabling the charity to receive cash. This arrangement should be undertaken with great caution, however, and may be challenged if the IRS believes it can prove the existence of an "understanding" between donor and charity that the charity would surrender the shares for redemption. In that case, the donor would be forced to incur a taxable gain.[42]

Charitable gifts of life insurance. Lifetime gifts to charity of life insurance policies are popular. The client can transfer an existing policy to charity, or purchase a new policy naming the charity as beneficiary and then assigning to the charity all ownership rights in the policy. The client may agree to continue to pay the premiums. The client should be able to take income tax and gift tax charitable deductions for the policy's terminal value at date of gift (or adjusted basis, if less, in the case of income tax) and take additional income tax deductions for all premiums paid.

Gift annuity. As a way of increasing income during retirement, some clients arrange a gift annuity with a charity. A gift annuity involves the transferring of assets to charity, which agrees to pay a guaranteed annuity for life. If the starting payment date is delayed, such as until the client's retirement, the arrangement is called a *deferred payment gift annuity*. In states allowing it, the gift annuity may be funded with real property, such as the personal residence with the client gifting only a *remainder* interest, enabling the client to continue to live there.

Under the bargain sale rules, the client will report the proportional gain ratably over his or her life expectancy, upon commencement of the annuity payments. A portion of each annuity payment will be taxable income, under the annuity rules of §72. Besides augmenting retirement income with a guaranteed, partially income tax-free payment, advantages of the gift annuity include a sizable current income tax deduction, lower estate tax and probate costs, and reduced asset management worries.

---

42. For a discussion, see the Teitell paper cited at the end of the chapter.

Gifts of Split Interests

Despite the added income tax advantage of lifetime charitable gifts, clients with strong charitable motives are often reluctant to make outright, present interest gifts to charity because they are not willing to *relinquish total control* of an asset. For example, they may be relying on an asset as a source of income or enjoyment, or they may have been planning to pass the asset on to the children. Reluctant clients may be more willing, however, to make what could be called a compromise charitable gift; that is, a split-interest gift in which only part of an interest in property is given to charity. The client will often be able to accomplish *three objectives:* retain a much-desired portion of the interest, transfer the less-needed part, and still enjoy substantial income tax and death tax savings.

A split interest arrangement divides the asset into two separate property interests, the income interest and the remainder interest. The client has the ability either to retain the right to the income from the asset, and presently gift the remainder interest to charity, or to gift the income interest to charity and designate a private party to take the remainder.

Arrangements for donating remainder interests to charity. Three devices recognized by tax law are commonly used by clients to retain an income interest in an asset and to gift the remainder interest to charity. Two of them, broadly called *charitable remainder trusts*,[43] are the annuity trust and the unitrust. The third is called the *pooled income fund.* For each, the charity receives an irrevocable (vested) remainder interest in the asset. Ordinarily, any one of these 'strings-attached' arrangements will cause the date of death value of the remainder to be includable in the donor's gross estate.[44] Happily, an equivalent charitable deduction will reduce the taxable amount to zero.[45]

Charitable remainder annuity trust. Under the charitable remainder annuity trust (CRAT), the client receives a fixed annuity income of at least 5 percent of the *original value* of the assets transferred into trust, payable at least annually, usually for life. The value of the deductible interest is calculated from IRS valuation Table S, found in Table 9 of Appendix A.

---

43. For a summary comparison of the taxation of charitable remainder trusts versus other popular trusts in estate planning, see Table 17-1 in Chapter 17.

44. §2036(a).

45. §2055.

EXAMPLE 14-24 Carrie, age 74, creates a CRAT, funding the trust with $100,000 cash. The trust provides for a 5 percent annual payment to Carrie for her life. At an assumed rate of 10 percent, the value of Carrie's retained income interest, derived from Table 9 of Appendix A, is $28,905.50, the product of the table value (5.7805) and $5,000, the annual trust income. Therefore, Carrie's deductible remainder interest is $71,097.50, the difference between the total value of the property and the value of the retained income interest.

Charitable remainder unitrust. The charitable remainder unitrust (CRUT) is much like the CRAT, above, except that the annual income depends on a fixed percentage of the *current fair market value* of the assets in the trust, re-determined annually. Thus, the amount of the annual income paid to the client will vary (hopefully upward) from year to year.[46]

The CRUT can provide for the income to be the *lesser* of the unitrust amount or the amount actually earned on the trust property, with any deficiencies payable in later years when earnings are higher. Thus, the owner of a rapidly appreciating, low-dividend-paying corporation can contribute stock to a CRUT and enjoy a large stream of income years later, after retirement, when the stock starts paying dividends. This "net income with make-up" unitrust (NIMCRUT) represents risky planning; the IRS has challenged these arrangements.[47]

Calculation of the amount of the deductible remainder interest for a CRUT is complex and will not be derived in the examples that follow.

EXAMPLE 14-25 Bob and Jeanne Ferrell, both age 65, wish to establish a CRUT to supplement their income and to benefit their favorite charity. They fund the trust with $100,000 of rental real estate having a tax basis of $20,000. The rental property is appreciating at an average annual rate of 8% but has paid them only 2 percent a year in income ($2,000 this year). The trust provides that they will be paid an annual amount equal to six percent of the value of the trust corpus, determined annually. It will cost the Ferrells $4,000 in legal fees to establish the trust. If the trust corpus can grow by three percent annually (10 percent overall return less 6 percent to the Ferrells less one percent trustee fee),

---

46. Valuation of unitrust interests are calculated based on §7520 applicable federal rates released monthly by the IRS, along with unitrust valuation factors derived from the Treasury department's *Actuarial Values-- Beta Volume* (IRS Pub. 1458), available from the U.S. Government Printing Office ((202) 783-3238).

47. For a discussion, see the Teitell (1993) paper cited at the end of the chapter.

the Ferrells will receive the following pre-tax amounts during the first five years: $6,000, $6,180, $6,365, $6,556, and $6,753. Assuming that the surviving spouse dies in 20 years, the last annual income payout in that year will be $10,521. Based on the IRS valuation tables, at 10 percent, the Ferrells will be able to deduct a charitable remainder interest of approximately $36,000, which at their 50% combined tax rate will immediately save them $18,000 in income tax. The Ferrells have, of course, relinquished the right to transfer the remainder interest, which is projected to be $209,743 ($100,000 stock growing at 10% - 6% - 1% = 3% annually for 20 years, reduced by 55% FET at S2's death). This arrangement has significantly supplemented the Ferrell's income. However, the plan has modestly improved their wealth position. At 10 percent, the net present value of this strategy, compared with doing nothing, is +$9,853: Present value of benefits: tax savings from charitable deduction: $18,000; twenty years of new increasing after-tax income: $45,135. Present value of costs: preparation fees: $4,000; loss of old forfeited 2 percent rental income on appreciating asset: $18,105; after tax value of forfeited remainder: $31,177.

EXAMPLE 14-26 In the example immediately above, if the Ferrells like everything about the proposed CRUT except having to forfeit their disposition of the remainder interest, they may consider adopting what has been called a "wealth replacement plan," funding an *irrevocable life insurance trust* with a joint life (second death) insurance policy in the amount of approximately $210,000, naming their children as trust beneficiaries.

The facts in the two examples above make many favorable implicit assumptions about the clients, and probably represents the 'best case' scenario. At the other extreme, consider the following:

EXAMPLE 14-27 It is five years later, and the Ferrells have had some terrible luck. First, because of their poor health, Bob and Jeanne were able to acquire life insurance on their lives only at a *very high premium*. Second, market investment rates of return have declined significantly, generating far less income to the Ferrells than the amounts projected by the planner. In fact, the income generated has been far below the required trust distributions, and each year the Ferrells have had to report the amount of these deficiencies as a *taxable capital gain*. Third, lower market rates have caused the quarterly life insurance premiums to rise, and have delayed substantially how soon the "vanishing" premiums will actually end, which means the Ferrells can expect to pay far more in total for the policy than the planner's computer-forecasted "illustrations" initially projected. Fourth, due to sizable investments in junk bonds and unprofitable real estate, the life insurance company is in danger of *insolvency*, with its remaining assets being seized by the state Department of Insurance. Fifth, the Ferrells were unable to deduct the entire $36,000 in the first tax year, due to the *AGI limitations*. The nondeductible portion had to be carried over to the next tax year. Sixth, because the rental real property was subject to a mortgage, the transfer of it constituted a bargain sale, resulting in a *taxable capital gain* to the Ferrells,[48] and creating the risk of disqualification of the trust as a charitable remainder trust.[49] Seventh, the trust invested in a spaghetti factory, a trade or business considered not substantially related to the performance of its exempt purpose, causing the trust to *lose its tax exempt status* and making all undistributed trust income taxable.[50] Eighth, the land under the spaghetti factory was found contaminated with toxic waste, making the Ferrells potentially liable under federal law for clean-up costs. Finally, Bob and Jeanne have always been quite confused about this *complex* arrangement. For example, they are not able to fully understand why two trusts had to be created. They are now seeking another attorney to determine if they can recover damages from their once enthusiastic financial advisors.

Of course the above hypothetical depicts a "worst case" scenario, with certain trust assets encumbered, contaminated, and producing unrelated business income. Ordinarily, trustees will want to avoid acquiring such difficult assets, even when offered by the client. As a way of exploiting the use of client-owned assets in a charitable remainder trust framework while avoiding the potential problems, the Freeman, et. al. article, cited at the end of the chapter, has suggested that clients instead contribute to the trust an *option* to purchase the property. Largely untested, this technique represents aggressive planning.

A charitable remainder trust can be funded with the client's personal residence, provided that all trust beneficiaries vacate the premises before the transfer.

At their best, charitable remainder trusts offer to the client the advantages of higher cash flow during lifetime, lower investment risk and greater portfolio diversification. At their worst, they can be a confusing financial burden. Recent case law involves many planners battling with the IRS or attempting to reform their client's defective charitable trusts. In one recent case, a $25 million estate was not entitled to an $18 million deduction because its charitable trust was not in the form of an annuity trust, a unitrust

---

48. Reg. §1.1011-2(a)(3); LR 7908016.

49. In LR9015049, the IRS disqualified a proposed unitrust funded with mortgaged property.

50. §681(a). The rules on unrelated business taxable income are found in §511, et. seq. For a discussion of avoiding so-called "UBI" in the charitable remainder trust framework, see the Englebrecht, et.al., article and the Teitell (1993) article cited at the end of the chapter.

or a pooled income fund.[51]   Although the IRS Regulations are exceedingly complex, requiring the drafting of long and technical documents, the Treasury has issued safe harbor sample documents which may be suitable for most client's needs. However, this is an area where very experienced counsel is needed.

Disillusioned clients will become more prevalent if financial planners continue to aggressively promote these trusts primarily as a means of increasing retirement income and avoiding capital gains tax. In one quarter page advertisement in a local newspaper observed by this author, a planner's main pitch was "stop paying unnecessary taxes." The fact that a sizable charitable contribution would be required was not mentioned anywhere in the ad.

Charitable trusts is one area where clients need the advice of a truly rare breed: a highly skilled tax advisor and draftsman particularly adept at time value of money/cash flow analysis.[52]

Figure 14-3 reviews the above material by illustrating the evolution of charitable remainder trusts, depicting the successive beneficiaries (grantor, spouse and charity) over time, and their taxation.

Pooled income fund. Instead of a separate trust created by the client and advisors, a pooled income fund is an investment fund created and maintained by the *target charity*, which "pools" property from many similar contributors. Thus, the client is spared the expense of planning and drafting a trust, an arrangement which would be considered 'overkill' when the charitable donation is relatively small (eg., $10,000 to $100,000).

Many pooled income funds limit donations to cash and cash equivalents. The pooled income fund ordinarily provides that the charity will pay to the grantor an income for life and, if desired, for the life of the grantor's spouse, based on the rate of return actually earned by the fund as a whole. At their death, the property passes to the charity. Valuation of the charitable deduction is calculated using Treasury tables available from the IRS.

Comparison of the three techniques. All three techniques have the advantages of providing an income for life, reducing FET and obtaining a relatively immediate income tax deduction. The CRAT may appeal to clients who desire the certainty of a fixed income, even in a declining market. The CRUT may be preferred by those willing to risk fluctuating income for

---

51. *E. La Meres Estate*, TC CCH 12,880.

52. For a discussion of methods of salvaging the deduction by reforming defective documents, see the Baltz article cited at the end of the chapter.

the opportunity to realize higher income payments. Thus the CRUT can offer a hedge against inflation. Assets in a CRUT do require an annual valuation, a possible extra trust cost. The pooled income fund may be preferred by those who would like to avoid having to establish and maintain a trust. Pooled income funds, however, are not permitted to invest in tax-exempt securities. Not all qualifying charities have created pooled income funds. Most colleges, however, use them to encourage charitable contributions by well-heeled alumni.

FIGURE 14-2 Evolution of Charitable Remainder Trust: Beneficiaries and Taxation

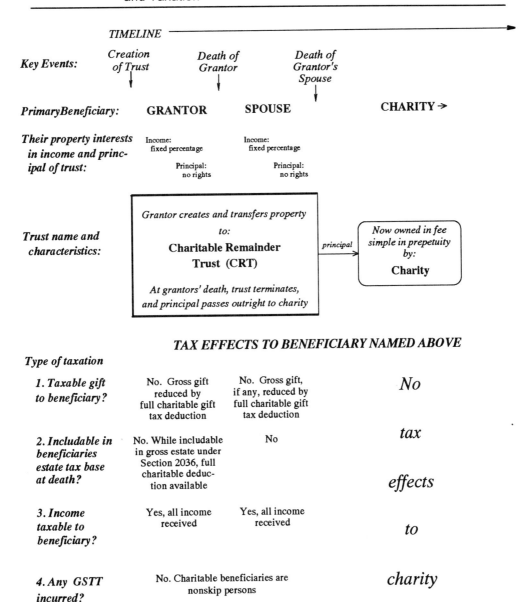

Arrangement for donating income interests to charity: The charitable lead trust. Instead of contributing a remainder interest, the client can donate an asset's income interest for a period of years to charity, with the remainder interest then passing to a private party (either reverting to the grantor or spouse, or passing to another person, such as a child or grandchild). The client or the client's estate will receive an income tax deduction for the value of the income interest, based on Treasury valuation tables. However, to get the charitable deduction, the trust must be set up as a grantor trust, making the income taxable to grantor.[53] This is not necessary if the trust is created in the client's will, and charitable lead trusts are therefore often designed to take effect after the client's death.

In a manner similar to a zeroed out GRAT, a charitable lead trust is often structured to generate an immediate charitable deduction equal to 100 percent of the current value of property transferred. If done successfully, so that the value of the charity's income interest equals the entire value of the property, the value of the private remainder interest will be determined to be zero, resulting in no taxable gift, and thus using no unified credit. Further, nothing is includable in the client's taxable estate because either the client will not own the property at death (lifetime charitable gift), or the estate will be entitled to a 100 percent charitable FET deduction (deathtime gift). As the examples below will show, success of the charitable lead trust will depend upon actual rates of future asset appreciation.

> EXAMPLE 14-28 Reed creates a lifetime charitable lead trust, funding it with $100,000 in stock of his closely held corporation. The trust is obligated to pay a "guaranteed annuity" of $11,750, or 11.75 percent of the initial value of the corpus annually to the charity for a period of 20 years. Then, the trust will terminate and the remaining corpus, if any, will be distributed outright to Reed's surviving children and grandchildren. Assuming a 10% discount rate, the IRS Table annuity factor is 8.5136. The value of the charity's 20 year income interest is $100,034.80, the product of $11,750 and 8.5136. Reed's deduction is limited to $100,000, the value of the property. Since the value of the present income interest is no less than the entire value of the property, the value of the remainder interest must be zero, which means that Reed has made no taxable gift.

---

53. Attaining grantor trust status without subjecting the corpus to estate taxation under §2036-2038 can be a challenge. For a discussion of two rulings allowing this attractive combination (LR 9224029 and LR 9247024), see the Painter paper cited at the end of the chapter.

EXAMPLE 14-29 Continuing the example immediately above, assume 20 years have passed. The closely held stock in the trust has performed so far in excess of 10 percent that its annual income has been more than ample to pay the annuity. And, as a result, the trust corpus and accumulated income is now worth $800,000. This amount will pass outright to Reed's descendants completely transfer tax free.[54]

EXAMPLE 14-30 Altering the projected outcome in the example above, assume again that 20 years have passed, but the closely held stock has earned only a 10 percent annual average rate of return, forcing the trustee to use trust corpus to satisfy in part the $11,750 annual distribution requirement. The corpus is now worth nothing (just as the IRS tables anticipated) and Reed's descendants, as remaindermen, will receive no trust distribution.

The outcomes in the preceding examples represent the two extremes of very good and very bad fortune; for most clients the likely result will be somewhere in between. Thus, the gift tax value of the remainder will not likely be zero, which means the grantor will have to partially use up his or her unified credit on a future interest gift that does not qualify for the annual exclusion. In addition, at eventual distribution date, the corpus will have appreciated somewhat, but not greatly.

Charitable lead annuity trusts are more attractive when interest rates are relatively low. A low (discount) rate results in a higher valuation of the deductible charitable interest donation, and therefore a lower valuation of the taxable remainder interest gift.

The charitable lead trust works best for wealthier, FET-avoiding clients who can afford to forego substantial income and own a significant amount of highly appreciating assets that also generate considerable income. Few clients can be expected to qualify.

This chapter has focused on viable nongift lifetime intrafamily transfers and charitable gifts. Appendix 14A that follows immediately after this chapter examines six defective incomplete transfers. The first five were once popular, but have been rendered ineffective by changing tax law. The sixth has always been defective. They are: the interest-free loan, short-term trust, spousal remainder trust, sale of a remainder interest, joint purchase, and family estate trust. You are urged to read this appendix, partly to gain a historical perspective, partly because some clients will still be involved in prior-consummated transfers of this kind, and partly to be aware of formerly popular devices about which clients will inquire for some time to come. The next chapter will survey the principles of liquidity planning.

---

54. For an in depth discussion of the use of a charitable lead trust to convey closely held business stock to grandchildren, see the Krasity article cited at the end of the chapter.

QUESTIONS AND PROBLEMS

1. Why are many planning-minded clients disinclined to make gifts?

2. How can a bargain sale add flexibility to gift planning?

3. (*a*) Describe the installment sale. (*b*) What tax advantage does it have over the ordinary sale?

4. Summarize the major advantages and disadvantages of the private annuity.

5. Crucible, a wealthy 60-year-old, asks you for advice on lifetime transfers. His daughter is interested in acquiring his antique car, which is worth $40,000 and has a basis of $10,000. In each of the following alternatives, calculate Crucible's taxable gain for each future year.
   a. Ordinary sale.
   b. Installment sale, over 10 years (no down payment), with equal annual payments on principal, plus interest at a rate of 10 percent on the outstanding balance. (Query - will there be any other taxable income?)
   c. Private annuity, assuming 10 percent. Additional information: 7.9882 percent of the payment is excluded from Crucible's taxable income for life (return on principal invested, based on annuity table in Treasury regulations 1.72-9). During the first 24 years, 4.1322 percent of the gross profit will be taxed as capital gain (thereafter, it is taxed as ordinary income). The balance of the annuity will be taxable as ordinary income.

6. The Platos are a husband and wife in their 70s, with an adult daughter age 45. They wish to make a lifetime transfer of a considerable amount of wealth to her, and you recommend four alternatives for consideration:
   Large outright gift.
   Installment sale.
   Private annuity.
   Grantor retained annuity trust.
   a. Which transfer would probably involve the greatest present value of expected total costs to daughter? Why?
   b. Which one will probably save the most FET? Why?
   c. Which is probably the safest, in terms of IRS challenge? Why?
   d. In which have the Platos retained the greatest interest? Why?

    e. Name several other factors that will influence which transfer, if any, the Platos will ultimately select.

7. Under what circumstances will a gift-leaseback work well?

8. Discuss the income-shifting and FET-reducing ability of the grantor retained interest trust.

9. In this question, please compare the advantages of the lifetime transfers you have studied. In each box on the next page, place the code number which you think describes how well that transfer accomplishes each goal. Use a range if the outcome is uncertain and be prepared to explain why you choose a number or a range. Code: 3 = excellent; 2 = good; 1 = fair; 0 = poor. (See Table 14-1.)

10. Explain the reason for the advantage of each of the following *charitable* transfers.
    a. Gift of appreciated property rather than cash derived from sale of the property.
    b. Lifetime gift rather than gift at death.
    c. Gift of a split interest rather than a whole interest.

11. Stover is 70 years old and is currently in the 35 percent combined state and federal marginal income tax bracket. He wishes to gift to charity his block of ABC Corp. stock, currently worth $20,000. His adjusted basis in the stock is $2,000.
    a. Calculate Stover's "after (income) tax cost" if he bequeaths the stock to the charity and dies shortly thereafter.
    b. Perform the same calculation as in part a, above, assuming that Stover sells the stock and gives the entire $20,000 cash to charity during his lifetime.
    c. Calculate Stover's after-tax cost, assuming instead that he makes a lifetime gift of the stock to charity.
    d. What should Stover plan to do?
    e. Would it matter at all in *a*, *b*, or *c*, above if Stover is president and controlling shareholder of ABC? Why or why not?

12. Compare the advantages of the CRAT, the CRUT, and the pooled income fund.

TABLE 14-1 Comparative Advantages of Lifetime Transfers

Types of Transfers	Goals									
	Ability to Retain:		Ability to Avoid Taxation:		Step-Up in Basis at Death of Client	Shift Income	Estate Tax Base		Avoid Probate	Absence of IRS Scrutiny - Low Risk
	Control	Income	Income Tax	Gift Tax			Reduce	Freeze		
Annual exclusion gift										
Large outright gift										
Ordinary sale										
Bargain sale										
Installment sale										
Private annuity										
Gift-leaseback										
Grantor retained trust (GRT)										

RECOMMENDED READING

Adams, Roy M., David A. Herpe, & Thomas W. Abendroth. "The Dollars an Sense of Value Shifting Techniques." *Trusts and Estates*, November, 1991, pp. 42-53.

Auster, Rolf. "Estate Planning Strategies after 1986." *Taxes-the Tax Magazine*, February 1987, pp. 11-23.

*Baetz, Timothy W. "Making Something Out of Nothing or How to Achieve Charitable Deduction by Repairing Defective Split Interest Trusts." *University of Miami 21st Annual Estate Planning Institute*, 1987.

Bailey, Lester D. "Tax Results of Many Transfers of Property Will Change When Made between Husband and Wife." *Taxation for Accountants*, July 1984, pp. 38-40.

Banoff, Sheldon I., and Michael O. Hartz. "It's No Sin to SCIN! A Reply to Professor Blum on Self-Canceling Installment Notes." *Taxes-The Tax Magazine*, March 1982, pp. 187-96.

_____ "Self-Canceling Installment Notes: New IRS Rulings Expand Opportunities." *Journal of Taxation*, September 1986, pp. 14-54.

Belcher, Dennis I. & James D. Bridgeman "Defective May Be More Effective: The Tax Advantages Of Intentional Grantor Trusts," *Probate and Property*, March, 1993, pp. 24-27.

Bilansky, Lawrence J. "Making the Most of Private Annuity Arrangements to Transfer Property and Reduce Estate Tax." *Estate Planning*, March 1981, pp. 102-7.

Blattmachr, Douglas J., and Jonathan G. Blattmachr. "Estate Planning for Individuals with Short Life Expectancies." *Trusts & Estates*, August 1985, pp. 22-28.

*Blattmachr, Jonathan G. and Vivian L. Cavalieri. To Apply or Not to Apply the Treasury Department Valuation Tables-That Is the Question." *New York University 45th Annual Institute on Federal Taxation*, 1986.

Blattmachr, Jonathan G. "Something Pretty Scary: Application of Private foundation and UBTI Rules in Estate Planning and Administration", *1992 University of Miami Estate Planning Institute*.

Blum, Walter J. "Self Canceling Installment Notes-The New SCIN Game." *Taxes-The Tax Magazine*, March 1982, pp. 183-96.

Brody, William J. "Taming GRITS, GRATS, QPRTS and Other Creatures Oozing From The Section 2702 Swamp," *1992 UCLA/CEB Estate Planning Institute*.

*Buchanan, Jeffrey D. and Malcolm A. Moore. "Valuation Readjustment Clauses: What's Possible?" *New York University 45th Annual Institute on Federal Taxation*, 1986.

Campisi, Dominic J. "Estate of Buck: Frustration of a Charitable Purpose." *Trusts & Estates*, January 1985, pp. 70-76.

Comstock, Paul L. "Planned Giving Issues and Techniques under Tax Reform." *CLU Journal*, January 1988, pp. 60-65.

*Englebrecht, Ted. D., Evelyn C. Hume, & Dana M. Le Fever, "How Charitable Trusts Can Avoid Unrelated Business Income" *Estate Planning*, July, 1993, pp 226-32.

Esterces, Howard M. "Residence GRITs Still Offer Estate Tax Savings," *Taxation For Accountants*, January, 1992, pp. 42-46.

Freeman, Douglas K, Fred J. Marcus and Stacey B. Fields "Funding the Charitable Remainder Trust With Tough Assets: The Use of an Option Arrangement" *Estate Planning, Probate & Trust News*, State Bar of California, Vol. 13 No. 1, Spring 1993, pp 9-.

Gelber Lawerence R. "Annuities: An Overview for the Estate Planner." *New York Law School Law Review* 26 (1981), pp. 1059-87.

Gleitman, Steven L. "Using Insurance Trusts to Increase Unified Credit, Avoid Kiddie Tax, and Fund Education." *Taxation for Accountants*, July 1987, pp. 37-7.

Goggans, Travis P., and John Tenbrunsel. "Trustee Independence in Trust Leaseback Arrangements." *Trust & Estates*, December 1984, pp. 29-32.

Grobe, Charles S. "The Tax Economics of a Qualified Personal Residence Trust." *Journal of the American Society of CLU & ChFC*, March, 1993, pp. 66-73.

Harrison, Melinda J., and Edward D. Tarlow. " How to Use Trusts and Estates to Maximize Deductions for Charitable Contributions." *Estate Planning*, March 1986, pp. 66-73.

Hartz, Michael O., and Sheldon I. Banoff. "Planning Opportunities Available Using a Private Annuity for a Term of Years." *Journal of Taxation*, November 1986, pp. 302-12.

Hass, Frederick W., and Joseph C. Skalcki. "The Charitable Lead Trust: New Appeal as an Executive Perk." *Trusts & Estates*, September 1986, pp. 4445.

Herbert, Marcel G., and Mary Sue Gately. "Gift-Leaseback Still Effective Income and Estate Tax Saver Despite IRS Opposition." *Taxation for Accountants*, April 1985, pp. 24044.

Hesch, Jerome M. & Elliott Manning. "Family Deferred Payment Sales: Installment Sales, SCINs, Private Annuities, OID and Other Enigmas," *1992 University of Miami Estate Planning Institute.* An excellent summary of the rules, and a proposal for taxing these strategies more consistently.

Hicks, Zoe M, "Charitable Remainder Trust May be more advantageous than a Qualified Plan" *Estate Planning*, May 1990, pp. 158-65.

*Holbrook, Dan W. & Daniel P. Murphy. "Two-Year, Overlapping GRATs Can Maximize the Benefits of Split-Interest Transfers." *Journal of Taxation*, March, 1993, pp. 154-58.

Jones, Alan B "Transfers of Remainders Can Be An Effective Technique, but Careful Planning Is Required" *Estate Planning* January, 1989 pp. 38-46.

*Krasity, Kenneth A. "Charitable Trust Can Be Used to Convey Stock in Close Corporation." *Estate Planning*, March, 1993, pp. 84-90.

Leimberg, Stephen R., and Jeff A. Schnepper. "SPLIT Interest Purchase of Property." *CLU Journal*, November 1987, pp. 44-55.

Lerner, Ralph E. "How to Coordinate Income and Estate Tax Savings of Donating a Collection to Charity." *Estate Planning*, May 1984, pp. 144-48.

Lichter, Jonathan M. "The Effects of the Proposed Regulations on Charitable Remainder Trusts." *Trusts & Estates*, June 1984, pp. 41-50.

*Loftis, Robert O., Jr. "When Can a Trust Be Used to Fund a Private Annuity without Creating a Retained Interest'?" *Estate Planning*, July 1987, pp. 218- 27.

McCoy, Jerry J. "Private Foundations and Related Entities in the Post Tax Reform Era." *1987 University of Miami Estate Planning Institute.*

_____, "Tax Planning: Beyond The Charitable Remainder Unitrust" *Trusts & Estates*, August, 1993, pp 24-29. Considers the bargain sale to charity as a possible alternative.

_____, "Family Foundations-- A User's Guide (Non-Tax Edition)," *1994 University of Miami Estate Planning Institute.*

Melfe, Thomas A. "When to Make Outright Gifts of Partial, Undivided Interests in Property." *Estate Planning*, July 1986, pp. 330-33.

Mering, Donald R. "Charitable Remainder Trusts: Comeback Player of the Year," *1992 University of Miami Estate Planning Institute.*

Monzo, Anthony P., and Robert N. Polans. "Interest-Free Loans and Other Planning Tools Can Still be Used to Shift Income." *Taxation for Accountants*, August 1987, pp. 82-8.

*Mulligan, Michael D. "Defective Grantor Trusts Offer Many Tax Advantages." *Estate Planning*, May, 1992, pp. 131-36.

*Painter, Andrew D. "Current Planning Developments With Charitable Lead Trusts," *Estate Planning, 1994*, California Continuing Education at the Bar.

_____, Andrew D. & Robert B. Caplan. "Charitable Lead Trusts Can Achieve Zero Transfer Tax if Properly Structured," *Estate Planning*, March, 1991, pp. 102-07.

Plaine, Lloyd Leva & Pam H. Schneider. "Proposed Valuation Regulations Provide Workable Exceptions for Transfers in Trust." *Journal of Taxation*, September, 1991, pp. 142-49.

Porcano, Thomas M. "Private Annuities and Estate Planning." *The Tax Adviser*, February 1983, pp. 72-82.

Rolfe, Robert J. "Trust-Annuity Plans Can Offer Substantial Income and Estate Tax Savings."

Rosen, David S & Michael S. Saper, "A Private Foundation Adds Flexibility to an Individual's Planned Charitable Giving" *Estate Planning*, January, 1989, pp 16-24.

Rothberg, Richard S, "Crummy Powers Enhance the Usefulness of Trusts for Minors and Life Insurance is Required" *Estate Planning*, Nov., 1988, P322-28. An excellent overview.

*Scanlan Jr., William. "GRITs, GRATs &GRUTs: A Phoenix Rises from the Ashes of Section 2036 (C)." *1993 University of Miami Estate Planning Institute*.

Schlesinger, Michael, and R. Arnold Handler. "Recent Developments May Expand the Use of Private Annuities, but Problems Still Exist." *Estate Planning*, March 1986, pp. 106-10.

Schnee, Edward J. "Partial Gifts to Charity: Estates Claim Larger Deductions." *Taxes-The Tax Magazine*, March 1983, pp. 219-24.

Schneider, Pam H. "GRIT, GRAT, GRUT, What Will Your Client Want"? *1992 University of Miami Estate Planning Institute*.

Shubert, Roy A., and Linda J. Reph. "How to Reduce the Tax Cost When an Individual Wants to Benefit Charity. *Taxation For Accountants*, September 1986, pp. 150-53.

Strizever, William J. "Self-Canceling Notes Increase Planning and.Risks of a Sale over Private Annuities." *Taxation for Accountants*, January 1984, pp.20-25.

Teitell, Conrad "Charitable Split Interest Trusts" 1989 UCLA-CEB Estate Planning Institute.

_____. "Charitable Gifts With Strings Attached" 1990 University of Miami Estate Planning Institute.

* _____. "Charitable Contributions, Windfalls, Pitfalls and Strategies." *1993 University of Miami Estate Planning Institute*.

Tidd, Jonathan G. "Using a Charitable Income Trust Provides More Flexibility than Lead Annuity or Unitrusts." *Estate Planning*, July 1986, pp. 214-18.

Veres, Joseph A. "Using Pooled Income Funds to Pass ITC and Depreciation through to Life-Income Donors." *Journal of Taxation*, July 1984, pp. 28-33.

Watenmaker, Alan S., "The Wealth Replacement Plan Using Life Insurance and a Charitable Remainder Trust- the A-B-Cs and W-H-Ys," 1991 UCLA/CEB Estate Planning Institute.

Defective Incomplete Transfers

OVERVIEW

This appendix will describe six defective transfer devices that, for one of two reasons, are presently not recommended by planners. The first five have been virtually legislated out of existence by Congress between 1984 and 1990. And the sixth has always been riddled with tax defects, making it inherently defective.

The evolution of income tax law in the last few years has resulted in depriving taxpayers of the major tax benefits earlier available through the use of the *interest free loan*, the *short-term trust*, the *spousal remainder trust*, the *sale of a remainder interest* and the *joint purchase*. The interest-free loan was first to go with the passage of TRA 84. The next two were killed by TRA 86. The last two were rendered ineffective by Case law and by the Revenue Reconciliation Act of 1990. They were all vulnerable to attack because, unlike the transfers covered in Chapter 13 and 14, each was able to accomplish, in a very large way, at least two of the following: shift large amounts of income; enable the transferor to retain a substantial interest in or control over the property; or freeze large estate tax values at little or no gift tax cost.

The *family estate trust* has never worked, since its operation clearly violates major holdings of case law and provisions of the Internal Revenue Code.

This appendix has been written for three reasons. First, it will give the reader a better historical perspective on lifetime transfers. Second, these strategies may have been employed by some clients in the past, and may still be in use. The reader should be aware of their operation since questions will be raised about their efficacy. Finally, the planner can expect even uninvolved clients to be curious about these formerly popular devices, for years to come.

INTEREST-FREE LOAN

Until 1984, the interest-free loan was considered to be an attractive, although somewhat tax-risky, device to shift income to a lower-tax-bracket family member. However, the Tax Reform Act of 1984 all but destroyed its appeal. The following material presents and overview of the major tax and nontax considerations in making IFLs and describes the few areas in which IFLs still might be put to use.

An arm's-length loan, in which the lender charges a fair market rate of interest, does not achieve many estate planning objectives. It does not shift income significantly, although it may provide for the borrower an otherwise unavailable loan opportunity. An interest-free loan (IFL) of cash, on the other hand, may be able to shift taxable income from the lender to the borrower. Since the borrower is free to use the loaned property to generate income without incurring a financing charge, the loan may put the borrower in a higher standard of living. Further, the income generated may be taxed at a significantly lower rate. Unfortunately, other tax consequences often render IFLs largely unattractive.[1] As the following material suggests, tax controversy has highlighted their brief history.

Gift Tax Consequences

In 1984, the U.S. Supreme Court settled a longstanding conflict between taxpayers and the IRS by ruling that an IFL constitutes a taxable gift of the reasonable value of the use of the money loaned.[2] In calculating the taxable

---

1. Actually, any loan made at a rate of interest below an acceptable market rate will be subject to taxation. However, we will continue to use the term *IFL* to refer to all below-market loans.

2. *Dickman v. Commissioner*, 104 S. Ct. 1086.

gift value, the taxpayer is required to use a federal rate of interest, which is published and revised semiannually by the IRS and set approximately equal to the rate that had been paid by the U.S. Treasury on securities of similar maturity several months earlier.

IFLs can be made for a fixed term, or they can have a demand provision. If the loan is made for a *fixed term*, the gift is considered as having been made as of the loan inception, with the gift amount equal to the difference between the amount loaned and the discounted present value of the note.

> EXAMPLE 14A-1 Dad and Mom lend $100,000 cash, interest-free, to Mary who has just graduated dental school and wishes to start a practice. Mary signs a 10-year note, with no principal payable until maturity. Assuming that the current federal long-term rate is 10 percent, the present discounted value of the note is approximately $38,500, and Mom and Dad are deemed to have made a gift of approximately $61,500, the difference between the amount transferred and the value received.

If, on the other hand, an interest-free loan incorporates a *demand loan*, with the loan callable by the lender at any time, then at the end of each year the lender will have made a gift of one year's imputed interest.

> EXAMPLE 14A-2 Assume the facts in Example 14A-1, except that the note is a demand loan, having no maturity. If the loan is still outstanding at the end of their first taxable year, Mom and Dad will have made a gift of one year's interest, imputed to be $10,000, calculated on the basis of the assumed 10 percent short-term federal rate. For every year that the loan remains outstanding, a similar gift computation will have to be made.

Thus, in order to minimize the gift tax, an IFL must have no maturity. And, to prevent the entire transfer from being treated as an outright gift, the nonmaturing loan must have a demand provision.

If an interest-free demand loan becomes unenforceable, a more significant taxable event will have occurred.

> EXAMPLE 14A-3 Assume the facts in Example 14A-2. Four years go by, and the state's statute of limitations on collection on the original note expires. In that year, a taxable gift of the entire loan principal is triggered.

Thus, IFLs must be redrafted periodically to prevent this unfortunate tax consequence.

Despite the court decision subjecting interest-free loans to gift taxation, many client-lenders will not owe any gift tax because of the combined shelter of the annual exclusion and the unified credit. Thus, the parents in the above examples will incur no gift tax liability, unless they have already made taxable gifts large enough to have fully used up their unified credits. In general, the gift tax issue should not discourage many from the use of interest-free loans as a method of shifting income to a lower tax bracket. However, the income tax issues, discussed next, usually will.

Income Tax Consequences

The IRS has argued, in a business context, that the interest forgone by a corporate lender constitutes taxable income to an employee-executive borrower. To date, the IRS has had little success in the courts, and unless it can influence Congress to act, imputed interest income on an interest-free loan will not likely be taxed to the *borrower*.

In 1984, Congress did act, however, to tax to the *lender* the amount of the interest forgone under an IFL.[3] This forgone interest is treated as if it had been received by the lender and paid by the borrower. Thus, the lender is deemed to have received taxable interest, which is includable in gross income. Similarly, the borrower is deemed to have paid interest, which, under TRA 86, ordinarily would not be tax deductible, unless it is considered business interest, investment interest which is offset by investment income, or interest on a debt secured by a primary or secondary residence. The upshot will usually be greater taxable income without the corresponding deduction. And the compression of tax rates under TRA 86 further reduced the income shifting attractiveness of the IFL.

> EXAMPLE 7872-1 Dad, in the 31 percent income tax bracket, makes a $20,000 interest-free demand loan to his son, who is in the 15 percent bracket and is able to invest the proceeds in a bank time deposit yielding an annual return of 8 percent. Assuming a federal rate of 10 percent, the tax consequences in the first full year are as follows:
> *Gift tax treatment*: At the end of each year, Dad will be deemed to have made a gross gift of $2,000, the amount of the calculated forgone interest. Because of the annual exclusion, there will be no taxable gift.
> *Income tax treatment in the absence of the 1984 Act*: Each year, son would earn $1,600 taxable income on the deposit, paying a tax of $240. Instead, had Dad invested the loan money, he would have paid a tax of $496. Thus, in the absence of the 1984 act, under TRA 86 tax rates the family would have saved $256 in income tax.
> *Income tax treatment under the 1984 Act*: Son will still pay a tax of $240. In addition, Dad will pay a tax of $620 on the $2,000 of imputed interest. The total tax paid by both will be $880, which is $384 *more* than Dad's tax on the bank income had the IFL not been made.

The 1984 Act incorporated four exceptions, which may provide the

---

3. §7872.

basis for a very modest degree of income shifting. First, where the proceeds of an IFL between individuals are invested by the borrower to yield less than $1,000 income in any given year, forgone interest will not be imputed. Thus, at an assumed 8 percent investment return, the client could lend $ 12,500 interest free, without being subject to income taxation.

The second exception to the 1984 Act applies to a loan balance of $10,000 or less to any individual, which is not subject to imputed interest unless it is used to purchase income-producing assets.

Third, the amount of the imputed interest is limited to the borrower's net investment income for the year in cases where the aggregate amount of outstanding loans between two individuals does not exceed $100,000, provided that one of the principal purposes of the loan is not federal tax avoidance.

The fourth exception to the 1984 Act applies to loans to employees and to corporate shareholders, who are permitted to owe up to $10,000 without imputing forgone interest, provided that one of the principal purposes of the loan is not federal tax avoidance.

Interest-free demand loans should be made in the form of cash, rather than other property. A transfer of noncash in exchange for a note might be treated as a taxable *sale* to the extent of the consideration received.

Estate Tax Consequences

At the lender's death, the gross estate will include the current value of the note. The market value of a *demand note* will equal the face amount of the note, since the decedent, just prior to death, could have demanded full repayment.[4] On the other hand, the market value of a *term note* will usually be different from the face amount and is calculated, as in Example 14A-1, by using a market rate of interest to discount the value of the future payments. In executing either kind of note, the lender has not really been able to reduce his or her gross estate significantly. The interest-free loan was never designed to reduce death taxes.

In conclusion, because of its serious tax consequences and the compression of income tax rates, the IFL will no longer be used much.

---

4. If the executor is not a family member, he or she (or it, in the case of a bank) may choose to call the note due and payable after the death of the lender in order to properly manage the estate.

SHORT-TERM TRUST

Prior to March 2, 1986, the short-term trust was a very popular device to shift income to a lower-bracket taxpayer. Also called the Clifford trust, after the taxpayer whose court case originally set the standards for satisfactory construction, it is arranged in the following manner.[5] The transferor creates and funds a living trust, irrevocable for at least 10 years, for the benefit of a lower-bracket beneficiary, who will receive all of the income earned on the trust property during that time. In this discussion, we'll assume 10 years. At the end of 10 years, the principal reverts to the transferor and the trust terminates.

Gift Tax Consequences

The transferor in a short-term trust is irrevocably parting with a 10-year income interest in the property, and the actuarial value of this income interest is taxable as a gift. Its calculation is derived by multiplying the total value of the property by a fraction representing the proportion of the total value of the property constituting that income interest. The fraction is obtained from U.S. Treasury Gift Tax Table B, found in Treasury Regulations 25.2512-5, which is similar to Table 10 of Appendix A. For a 10-year income interest, the fraction equals 0.614457. Thus, approximately 62 percent of the transfer represents the income interest, and about 38 percent represents the remainder interest. Since the remainder portion will revert to the trustor, it does not constitute a gift, for tax purposes.

> EXAMPLE 14A-4 Dr. Jones and his wife set up a short-term trust for the benefit of their daughter, who is 11 years old, to defray her future college expenses. They fund the trust with high-income stock, worth $32,000. The trust provides that all income will be accumulated until daughter reaches her 18th birthday. Then daughter will receive approximately equal amounts each year for the next four years, with all remaining accumulated income payable to her on her 21st birthday. At that time all principal will revert to the parents. Upon creation of the trust, the Joneses have made a gift of an income interest worth $19,662.62, which is $32,000, the total value of the stock, multiplied by 0.614457. However, no gift tax is owed, due to the annual exclusion of $20,000 available to spouses making a split gift.

---

5. Clifford lost the case, however. *Helvering v. Clifford* 309 U.S. 331 (1940). Subsequent to the Clifford decision, Congress added the 10-year requirement to the Code, under Section 673, et. seq.

The annual exclusion is available to the parents, above, despite the fact that technically the gift of the income to be accumulated is a future interest, because the short-term trust is structured to meet an exception under Section 2503(b) or 2503(c), mentioned in the discussion of trusts for minors in Chapter 13.

Income Tax Consequences

Grandfathered trusts. Income earned on the property placed in a 10-year short-term trust on or before March 1, 1986, will not be taxable to the transferor-grantor, except when the kiddie tax applies. Instead, the income will be taxed to the trust or to the beneficiary, depending on whether it is accumulated or distributed. And the accumulated income later distributed to the beneficiary could be subject to some additional tax, under the throwback rules, unless the beneficiary is under age 21.

The reader will recall from Chapter 8 that failure to avoid the grantor trust provisions of the Internal Revenue Code will cause income received by the trust to be taxable to the grantor. Thus, the short-term trust had to be carefully drafted to avoid running afoul of the grantor trust rules. For example, the trust had to be irrevocable for at least 10 years from the date the trust was *funded* with the property, not from the date the document was executed. For the other major grantor trust rules, refer to Chapter 8.

Nongrandfathered trusts. TRA 86 destroyed the income tax benefit of the short-term trust by deleting the 10-year exception under Internal Revenue Code (IRC) Section 673. Thus, for any transfers into trust after March 1, 1986, the grantor will be treated as the owner of any portion of a trust in which the grantor has any *reversionary interest which exceeds 5 percent* of the value of such portion. Based on the present values in Table 10 of Appendix A, the grantor of a 10-year short-term trust has a reversionary interest that is about 38.55 percent of the value of the trust. Thus, the typical new short-term trust will be treated as a grantor trust. Nonetheless, the new kiddie tax will apply even to these nongrandfathered trusts, subjecting most or all trust income for the benefit of a child under age 14 to taxation at the parent's marginal rate.

How long must a short-term trust created after March 1, 1986, last so that the present value of the remainder interest does not exceed 5 percent of the corpus? Table 10 indicates that the reversion can't occur for at least 32 years! Although several commentators are suggesting that there may be situations where this period is acceptable, in most cases, grantors will not wish to make an irrevocable transfer of property for such a long time. Most clients will no longer wish to shift income with the short-term trust. Thus, the short-term trust is no longer able to save significant income tax by shifting income.

Estate Tax Consequences to the Grantor

Several estate tax consequences may occur when the grantor dies. First, if creation of the trust resulted in a "taxable gift," that is, the transfer of an amount in excess of the annual exclusion and other deductions, then that taxable value will be added to the estate tax base, as an "adjusted taxable gift." Of course, a credit will be applied for any gift tax paid, but the taxation of adjusted taxable gifts along with the rest of a decedent's estate may subject the gift to a higher marginal rate of taxation than that incurred when the gift tax was calculated.

A second estate tax consequence at the grantor's death will be the addition to the gross estate of the actuarial value of the decedent-grantor's interest in the trust property. Determination of that amount will depend on when the decedent dies, as explained next.

If the grantor of a short-term trust dies *before the trust reverts*, the value of the gross estate will include the value of the grantor's reversionary interest at death. Derived from the U.S. Treasury estate tax valuation table found in Treasury Regulations 20.2031-7, included in Table 10 of Appendix A, the value depends on the assumed rate of interest and the number of years remaining to reversion. For example, assuming a 10 percent discount rate, if a grantor dies exactly four years prior to reversion, the gross estate will include 68.3013 percent of the decedent's share of the trust property.

If the grantor of a short-term dies *at or after reversion*, the value of the gross estate will include the deathtime market value of the property that had reverted, if still owned, or the value of any other assets acquired with the property.

From the above we can see that the value of the grantor's taxable estate may exceed the value of the trust principal, a decided estate tax disadvantage to the short-term trust. This will always happen when the grantor outlives the trust and the funding of the trust has created a taxable gift. It should be clear now why, the short-term trust was never designed to reduce death taxes.

As an income tax planning device, the short-term trust was often used for two common types of beneficiaries: children and elderly parents. Both are individuals whom many clients wish to assist, and who are often in a lower income tax bracket. Unfortunately, due to tax reform, the short-term trust will hardly ever be used in the future.

SPOUSAL REMAINDER TRUST

A popular income-shifting device prior to TRA 86 was the spousal remainder trust (SRT). As in the case of the short-term trust, the grantor, typically a high-income-tax-bracket parent, transferred income-earning property to an irrevocable trust, which for a specified period paid all income to a low-income-tax-bracket family member, typically a young adult child, and remainder to the grantor's spouse. Properly arranged, the value of the income interest, which is valued in a manner similar to the short-term trust, would qualify for the annual gift tax exclusion. However, unlike the short-term trust, whose property reverted to the grantor, the SRT corpus then passed to the grantor s spouse. Although the value of the remainder interest will not qualify for the annual exclusion, it will not be subject to gift tax, due to the unlimited gift tax marital deduction.

> EXAMPLE 14A-5 In 1985 Dad created an SRT, funding it with $30,000 in bonds. Income is required to be paid semiannually to daughter, a college freshman, for the next four years. At the end of the fourth year, the corpus will pass outright to Mom. Based on the valuation tables, the value of a gift of an income interest for a four-year term certain represents 31.6987 percent of the total value of the property transferred. Thus, Dad has made a gross gift to daughter of $9,510. There will be no taxable gift, since the gift of the income interest is sheltered entirely by the annual exclusion, and the gift of the remainder interest is sheltered entirely by the marital deduction.

Prior to TRA 86, the SRT had several advantages over the short-term trust. First, because the corpus does not revert to the grantor, the trust was not required, under the grantor trust rules, to remain in existence for at least 10 years. Thus, the trust could terminate at any time, and if it terminated sooner than 10 years, the relative value of the transferred income interest would be less than that for the short-term trust. This meant that a greater amount of property could be transferred to the SRT free of gift tax. Further, earlier termination might have encouraged grantors to make successive annual gift tax-free transfers into the trust, unimpeded by the requirement of waiting 10 years after date of the most recent transfer to terminate the trust.

The SRT often facilitated the client's estate tax planning objectives. It helped to equalize the spouses' estates in order to minimize the combined estate tax, and remainder interests were transferred to the less wealthy spouse by means of the SRT.

Compared with the short-term trust, the SRT had one potentially major disadvantage: At the termination of the trust, the property passes to the grantor's spouse, rather than the grantor. Thus, the SRT worked best in a harmonious family setting. And any SRT having an agreement in which the remainderman spouse agreed to immediately retransfer the remainder interest to the grantor was attacked by the IRS, which claimed that the grantor in fact retained a reversion, thereby destroying all income and transfer-tax benefits.

TRA 86 destroyed the usefulness of the spousal remainder trust by amending Section 672 to treat any power or interest held by a spouse (who lives with the grantor) as if that interest were held by the grantor. Thus, the traditional spousal remainder trust funded after March 1, 1986 will be treated as if it will revert to the grantor, making it a *grantor trust*, and thereby preventing the shifting of income to the lower-bracket-income beneficiary. Few clients will now choose this once appealing transfer strategy.

SALE OF A REMAINDER INTEREST AND JOINT PURCHASE

The ordinary sale, bargain sale, installment sale, and private annuity may all be unacceptable to some clients, who, during their lifetimes, do not want to surrender the present enjoyment of property. All of these sales techniques involve the immediate transfer of the right to possession and enjoyment. Prior to 1986, another type of sale, however, the *sale of a remainder interest*, did not have this drawback, and, although it was coming under increasing attack from the IRS, it was an attractive alternative. Like the other devices, it was able to freeze estate tax values, generate cash flow, and assist family members. But unlike the others, it also permitted the client to retain the right to possession and enjoyment of the property "sold" until death.

> EXAMPLE 14A-6 In 1982, 62-year-old parent had some valuable jewelry and had a physician-son who agreed to purchase the remainder interest in the gems. Assuming 10 percent, based on Table A in Treasury Regulation 25.2512-5(e), the son paid 27.998 percent of the current value of the jewelry for the right to receive it outright at the client's death. The client was able to own and enjoy the jewelry for life. And the FET value of the asset was still effectively frozen, since the client's gross estate would include only the amount of the sale proceeds that has been retained at death. Of course, the son would not receive possession of the jewelry until the client's death, but he probably would have received it no sooner anyway.

With an installment sale, the client could occasionally forgive a payment, which constituted a taxable gift, but one that qualified for the annual exclusion. Use of the installment sale also postponed recognition of the client's gain. In determining gain or loss, the client's tax basis is apportioned between the remainder interest and the retained life estate. Thus, in our example, the client's tax basis became 27.998 percent of the former basis.

Exclusion of the remainder interest from the seller's gross estate was not guaranteed, however, as the IRS may have contended that the only way to escape the trap of §2036 is for the purchaser to have paid the full value of the property, not just the value of the remainder interest. Of course, this would have made the transaction even less attractive to the buyer than an ordinary sale.

The passage of §2036(c) in the Revenue Act of 1987 (and a subsequent court decision) increased the likelihood of inclusion, due to the emphasis of that section on estate freezing transfers.[6] But the risk of §2036 could have been greatly minimized if, instead of making a transfer of property, the client and the family member joined in purchasing property from a *third party*, with the client purchasing a life interest and the family member acquiring the remainder interest. As a result, this "joint purchase","split purchase" or split agreement rapidly replaced the sale of a remainder interest as the preferred transfer after 1986.

Finally, the passage of §2702 in 1990 entirely killed both the sale of a remainder interest and the joint purchase. In either case, the client will be treated as having made a gift to the extent that the value of the underlying property exceeds the price paid by the other purchaser. Planners no longer recommend these two techniques to any of their clients.

THE FAMILY ESTATE TRUST: A TRAP FOR THE UNWARY

The reader should be cautioned against recommending one so-called estate planning device, the family estate trust. Also called a constitutional trust, an equity trust, and an ABC trust, the family estate trust is an arrangement fraught with tax danger. Many variations have been created, but they all have the following characteristics:

1. The same person acts in four different capacities: grantor, trustee, trust employee, and beneficiary.
2. The grantor transfers assets into the trust in exchange for "certificate units." The trustee leases the employees' services to others (typically

---

6. One court held that consideration for purposes of §2036 must equal the entire value of the property. *Gradow* 897 F.2d 516 (1990).

including the individual's current employer), who pay a salary directly to the trustee.

3. The certificate units entitle the grantor to share in the income "earned" by the trust.
4. Upon the grantor s death, the trust assets pass to others, not to the grantor's estate.

The family estate trust has been touted as a great tax saver. It is said to be able to reduce income tax by shifting income to a lower bracket (the trust and other family members), and to reduce the client's death taxes by shifting assets before death to other beneficiaries. In fact, just the opposite is true. The IRS has been aggressively and successfully challenging family estate trusts in the courts, which have regularly upheld the following tax consequences:

1. Under the *assignment-of-income doctrine*, explained in Chapter 9, wages assigned to the trust are still taxable to the client-wage earner, not to the trust.
2. Personal living expenses are not deductible.
3. Fees to set up the trust are not deductible.
4. The date of death value of the property owned by the trust is subject to inclusion in the *gross estate* of the client-trustor as an incomplete transfer.
5. At least two tax *penalties* will be imposed. First, if negligence is proven against the taxpayer, a negligence penalty of 5 percent of the additional tax due will be assessed. Second, tax preparers will be charged penalties of hundreds of dollars for each return found to exhibit negligent or willful attempts to understate the tax liability.

In view of the tax exposure, clients would do well to steer clear of the family estate trust.

APPENDIX 14A RECOMMENDED READING

Adams, Roy M. "Estate Planner's Guide to the Time Value of Money: Neither Borrower nor Lender Be." *Trusts & Estates*, June 1986, pp. 46-59.

Balk, Mark D. "Interest-Free No Longer." *Trusts & Estates*, September 1984, pp. 39-42.

*Kline, Terrance A. "Clifford Trusts and the Parental Duty to Provide a College Education: *Braun* v. *Commissioner*." *University of Pittsburgh Law Review* 46 (1985), pp. 537-54.

McCue, Howard M. and Patricia Brosterhous. "Interest-Free and Below-Market Loans after Dickman and the Tax Reform Act of 1984." *Taxes-The Tax Magazine*, December 1984, pp. 1010-21.

Orbach, Kenneth N.; Fireman, Harvey B,; and Howard A. Levinson. "Planning for Tax Advantages under Proposed Below-Market Loan Regs." *Journal of Taxation*, March 1986, pp. 144-50.

Plutchock, Jonathan. "Long Live Clifford!" *Financial Planning*, September 1987, pp. 130-34.

Weindruch, Linda, and Kim Smith. "Interest-Free Loans after the Deficit Reduction Act of 1984." *The Tax Adviser*, November 1984, pp. 642-52.

Weinbaum, Peter M. "Are Sales of Remainder Interests Still Available in Light of a New Decision?" *Estate Planning*, September 1987, pp. 258-63.

LIQUIDITY PLANNING

OVERVIEW

This chapter will explore the role of liquidity in estate planning. It will summarize the liquidity needs at death, examine the sources of liquidity available to the estate before and after death, and describe the planning techniques commonly undertaken with these sources. Planning devices covered include sale of assets during lifetime, life insurance, flower bonds, valuation discounts and control premiums, and several strategies unique to business owners, including sale of the business and three liquidity enhancing techniques arising from specific provisions of the Internal Revenue Code.

SUMMARY OF CASH NEEDS AT DEATH

Types of cash needs. Death will usually trigger the need for liquidity. Cash may be needed to pay a variety of obligations, which can be subdivided into three categories: last expenses, funds for the readjustment period, and liquidity needs for the dependency period.

With regard to last expenses, there may be *taxes*, including federal and state income and transfer taxes. There may be *expenses of (estate and trust) administration*, payable to lawyers, executors, accountants, appraisers, and trustees. There may be *debts and claims* against the decedent's estate, including last illness and funeral expenses. There may be immediate cash *needs* for the maintenance and welfare of the *surviving family*. And there may be *cash bequests* and other transfers that must be made to the decedent's heirs and beneficiaries.

Funds may be needed during the readjustment period as the surviving family members struggle to rearrange their lives.

Perhaps the largest amount will be needed to support the dependency period, determined by the number of surviving *dependents* and the length and nature of their needs, which will usually include *education*. Finally, there may be the need for funds to continue *running the family business*.

Cash needs for larger estates. Cash needs can be influenced by estate size and family situation. In general, cash needs rise with increasing estate size. For larger family estates, the FET usually constitutes the greatest cash need at the death of the surviving spouse. Most wealthier clients will probably choose an estate plan incorporating either a 100 percent marital deduction or a credit shelter bypass, both of which will result in a zero FET for S1. This delay in cash needs can influence the choice of the liquidity source, as we shall see.

Cash needs for smaller estates. In contrast with clients having larger estates, young families with smaller estates will often have *relatively* large cash needs at the death of *either* spouse.[1] Although transfer taxes may not be due, there will be the need to replace the economic value of the income or services that had been provided by the deceased spouse in the role of parent or breadwinner. As the children get older, the total present value of this cash need should decline.

Next, we turn our attention to the major sources of estate liquidity.

SALE OF ASSETS DURING LIFETIME

We will begin our discussion of the sources of estate liquidity with one of the simplest liquidity-generating devices. During lifetime, the client might be able to sell particularly illiquid assets. Relatively *high basis assets* are preferable, of course, because they result in little or no taxable gain. In fact, assets that have a built-in loss make the best assets for sale, because only the client can use the loss to offset other taxable gains or to reduce taxable

---

1. For a discussion of the cash needs of the two career family with minor children, see the Kinskern article cited at the end of the chapter.

income. Death eliminates this potential tax benefit by *stepping down* the basis to date-of-death value.

Relatively *low basis assets*, on the other hand, do not make the most desirable assets for sale because of the resulting tax on the sizable gain (a prospect which can be largely eliminated if the client dies owning the assets). However, the client might be able to offset the gain with losses, whether incurred during the present taxable year or carried over from previous years. Or a sale may be practical in situations where other factors justify paying a tax whose maximum marginal rate on long-term capital gains is 28 percent. For example, for reasons detailed in the next chapter, an interest in a *closely held business* will often command a substantially higher price if it is sold prior to the owner's death.

Thus, sale of assets during the client's lifetime can provide liquidity by converting an illiquid asset into cash in anticipation of the cash need.

LIFE INSURANCE

Next, we turn our attention to perhaps the most commonly used estate liquidity source, life insurance.

Introduction

Let's first review the basic terminology. In its simplest form, a life insurance policy is a contract owned by the person called the *owner*, which pays an amount called the *face value* to the person called the *beneficiary*, upon the death of the person called the *insured*. Life insurance has several uses, but in estate planning its major purpose is to provide funds to cover cash needs arising at the client's death.

We'll cover three major topics in this section. First, we'll survey the various types of insurance policies commonly used.[2] Next, we'll review the major concepts in the income, gift, and estate taxation of insurance. Finally, we'll examine the insurance planning techniques frequently used to provide needed liquidity.

---

2. In this chapter, the word *insurance* will be used as shorthand to mean life insurance.

Types Of Insurance

Hundreds of different insurance policies are sold in the United States today. However, most are simply minor variations of each other, and the number of really different types, for our purposes, are two. They are term insurance and cash value insurance. Each is briefly described next.

Term insurance. The simplest form of insurance is a one-year policy whose *increasing periodic premium* is based on the likelihood of death in that year. If the insured dies, the beneficiary is paid the face value. If the insured does not die, the company owes nothing and the contract terminates. This is the essence of term insurance; whether or not the company is financially obligated to pay depends solely on whether or not the insured dies during the contract period.

Most term insurance is *renewable*; that is, the company is obligated to sell another year's insurance at a previously agreed-upon price, at the option of the policy owner. Evidence of insurability, such as a physical exam, cannot now be required. Most term policies are renewable to ages 65 or 100. The premium, or cost of *annually renewable* term insurance policies rises annually with increasing age, reflecting the continuing increase in the likelihood of death. Other term insurance policies have premiums that remain constant for 5, 10, or 20 years, and then rise to a new plateau for another similar period, etc., until termination date. Most *illustrated* term insurance premiums are guaranteed for one, three, five, or ten years. Thereafter, premiums can be raised, up to a guaranteed maximum. Regardless of how often the premium rises, all term insurance is characterized by rising premiums and by the uncertainty as to whether the company will ever be legally obligated to pay the face value.

Cash value insurance. In contrast with term insurance, cash value insurance is characterized by a *constant* ("level") *periodic premium*. It is also characterized by certainty: When a cash value insurance contract ends, either because the insured dies or because the policy owner no longer wants coverage, the company will ordinarily be obligated to pay a significant amount of money. If the insured *dies*, the company will pay the face value, of course, as it does on its term insurance policies. If, on the other hand, the owner *surrenders* a cash value policy before the insured's death, the company will be obligated to pay an amount called the *cash surrender value*, described later. Actuarially, insurers can afford to do this because they charge a much higher premium for cash value insurance.

Cash value insurance, which is typically renewable to ages 65, 95 or 100, originated as a solution to a problem of early lapse perceived to be inherent in term insurance. Many years ago, when term insurance was just about the only policy sold, agents found that policy owners frequently terminated their insurance as it got more and more expensive with advancing age. To retain clients, companies started offering cash value insurance, charging a constant premium over time. Evidence has since shown that such policies are not as frequently surrendered by policyholders, despite advancing age. Essentially, the earlier year's premiums are more than the company actuarially needs to fund death and other claims, and the later years' premiums are less than the company needs. The overcharge in early years enables the company to accumulate a type of actuarial reserve, some of which is made contractually available as a cash value to the policyholder, either to borrow, to pledge, or in the event of surrender prior to the insured's death, to receive outright.

Today's cash value policy premiums typically range between three and five times the initial premium charged for annually renewable term insurance for a given policyholder. This is a substantial difference, and today all states have what are called *nonforfeiture laws*, which specify how to calculate the minimum cash surrender value that the company must legally make available to the policy owner at the end of each policy year. Competition usually compels carriers to offer more than the minimum statutory requirement. Guaranteed cash surrender values are listed, year by year, in the policy itself.

> EXAMPLE 15-1 Audrey, an insurance salesperson, offers Gerard, age 45, a choice of two policies, each having a face value of $100,000. First, she describes a cash value *whole life* policy, sold by the ABC Co., which has a level annual premium of $2,700. Its cash surrender value at the end of the fifth policy year will be $7,500. At the end of the 20th policy year, the cash value will be $43,500. Audrey then describes an annually renewable to age 100 term policy that is sold by the XYZ Co. The policy's first five years of premiums will be $500, $550, $610, $680, and $750. The premiums, which will be listed in the policy, rise annually until age 100. For example, Gerard's annual premiums will rise to $1,735, $4,620, $13,100, and $31,400 at ages 60, 70, 80, and 90 respectively.

Whole life policy. All cash value policies have a maturity date, that is, a date at which, if the insured reaches it alive, the face value will be paid. A whole life cash value policy, as its name implies, has a maturity date that extends beyond the "whole life" of most insured, typically the insured's 95th or 100th birthday.

> EXAMPLE 15-2 In Example 15-1, above, if Gerard purchases the whole life policy and keeps it in force, under simple assumptions ABC will send him a check for $100,000 if he reaches age 100 alive.

Universal life Policy. During periods of high inflation, traditional cash value policies such as whole life and endowment are not as attractive because the contractually guaranteed cash values are typically designed to appreciate at a relatively modest rate of growth in comparison with returns available on other short-term, interest-sensitive investments. Naturally, applicants are then more attracted to other products, including term insurance, where the cash saved from the significantly lower initial premiums can be separately invested with other financial institutions to earn higher yields.

In response, the insurance industry developed a product called universal life insurance, which is essentially a third type of cash value insurance that offers the policyholder greater flexibility and, sometimes, greater investment yield. It offers greater *flexibility* because the policyholder is permitted to vary the amount of the face value and the premium payments from time to time to meet changing financial conditions. It can sometimes offer greater investment *yield* because the insurer invests premium dollars in a portfolio of securities having a shorter average maturity. Thus, during periods of greater inflation (especially when yield curves are downward sloping), the insurer can often earn greater income, which it can pass on to the policyholder in the form of higher, nonguaranteed cash values. The typical universal life policy offers a guaranteed rate of appreciation of some low amount, commonly 4 percent, with the provision that a higher rate will be earned if the investments are more profitable. Thus, during periods of relatively high short-term rates, universal life insurance stands to gain in popularity. In contrast, in today's low rate-normal yield curve markets, universal life's popularity has not been as strong. For example, in 1990, the amount of universal life insurance purchased dropped 5 percent from the year earlier, and the number of universal life policies issued fell by 11%.[3]

Some commentators dislike universal life insurance because its complexity, flexibility, and uncertain future premium makes it virtually impossible to evaluate numerically and undertake cost comparisons with term policies and traditional cash value policies.

Split dollar cash value insurance arrangements. More a unique method of paying cash value insurance premiums than a different type of insurance, a split dollar arrangement is most commonly found as a nonqualified employee fringe benefit. In the typical plan, the employer pays to the insurer a portion of the premium equal to the lesser of the total premium or the increase in the cash value. The employee pays the balance of the premium. When the insured dies, or when the policy is surrendered, if earlier, the

---

3. 1991 *Life Insurance Fact Book Update,* American Council of Life Insurance.

employer ordinarily receives an amount equal to the premiums it paid and the remainder is paid to the policy owner (if surrendered) or the beneficiary (if the insured dies). Split dollar insurance enables the employee to purchase cash value insurance less expensively than if purchased alone.[4]

Taxation of Life Insurance

This section will survey the major concepts in the federal income, gift, and estate taxation of insurance. Many of these topics were covered in greater detail in Part 2 of the text, and the reader is referred there for elaboration and clarification.

Income taxation. Two major income tax aspects of life insurance are the taxation of the cash value accumulation and the taxation of the policy proceeds. To qualify for the two favored tax treatments described next, an insurance policy must meet the requirements under §7702, recently enacted to discourage the popularity of certain universal life and endowment type policies containing an unusually large investment element relative to the size of the death protection component.

Income taxation of cash value accumulation. Increases in cash value buildup will not ordinarily be subject to income taxation while the policy is in force, primarily because the taxpayer-policyholder is not considered able to actually or constructively receive these amounts without surrendering the policy.[5] When a cash value policy is surrendered, any excess of the cash surrender value (amount realized) over the total premiums paid (adjusted basis) will be includable in the owner's gross income. Usually this difference, if positive, will be quite small and not a significant tax burden.

An exception to the rule that loans from the cash build-up in a policy are not taxable unless what is withdrawn exceeds the amount paid into the policy occurs if the policy is "a modified endowment contract" as such is defined in IRC §7702(A). A modified endowment contract is a life insurance policy entered into on, or after, June 21, 1988, that fails the "seven pay test." Failure occurs anytime the cumulative premiums paid into the policy in the first seven years exceeds the total of net level premiums which would have been sufficient to provide a paid-up policy, based upon the initial death benefit, after seven annual payments. Congress set out to

---

4. For additional details, including the income and estate taxation of split dollar insurance, see the Low article cited at the end of the chapter.

5. *Theodore H. Cohen*, 39 TC 1055 (1963), acq. 1964-1 CB 4.

plug a loop-hole whereby insurance companies were selling single premium life insurance policies, with very little life insurance protection, as tax free investment vehicles rather than as life insurance. With a modified endowment contract withdrawals and distributions, even as loans, are treated as taxable income to the extent of any cash value accumulation. The portion of a withdrawal or distribution which is included in the policy owner's gross income (i.e., the amount equal to the accumulated cash build up at the time of withdrawal) is subject to an additional ten percent income tax unless the owner is over 59 ½, is disabled, or is receiving the payment as part of series of equal annuity payments for life.

Income taxation of policy proceeds. §101 generally excludes from gross income all proceeds received from a life insurance policy paid by reason of the insured's death.

The Code has carved out an exception to the proceeds exclusion rule for policies which have been transferred for valuable consideration. The amount includable in the transferee-owner's gross income in the year of the transfer will equal the policy proceeds, reduced by the amount of consideration paid and the total premiums paid by the new owner. This *transfer for value rule*, as it is called, does not apply to policy transfers to the following parties:

- The insured (or to a grantor trust[6] of the insured's)
- A partner of the insured.
- A partnership in which the insured is a partner.
- A corporation in which the insured is a shareholder or officer.
- A transferee whose basis will be determined by reference to the transferor's basis.[7]

EXAMPLE 101-1 For over 15 years, Terry had been owner of a $10,000 face value insurance policy on his life. Last year, he *gave* the policy to his beneficiary-son Ralph, who began to pay the premiums. Terry died last month. No portion of the proceeds will be includable in Ralph's gross income because Ralph did not give valuable consideration for the policy.

EXAMPLE 101-2 If, in Example 101-1, we assume instead that Terry *sold* the policy to Ralph for $100, and that the premiums paid by Ralph totaled $400, Ralph's gross income will include $9,500.

---

6. *Swanson*, 33 T.C.M. 296 (1974), aff'd. 518 F2d. 59 (8Cir., 1975); Rev. Rul. 85-13 1985-1 CB 184

7. §101(*a*)(2).

EXAMPLE 101-3 Ulysses and Zeno are *business partners*. For years, each had owned an insurance policy on his own life. Now, their attorney is drafting a "cross purchase business buyout" contract, and the partners have agreed to exchange policies, with some cash also included as part of the transaction. Thus, Ulysses will become owner and beneficiary of the policy on the life of Zeno, and Zeno will become owner and beneficiary of the policy on the life of Ulysses. Upon the death of either partner, no part of the proceeds will be includable in the other's gross income.

The last example illustrates the use of existing insurance policies to fund a business buyout agreement, which is discussed further in the next chapter.

In late 1992, the IRS issued regulations detailing how insurance companies may design policies to offer "living" or accelerated benefits for terminal insureds without subjecting the beneficiary to income taxation of a lump-sum benefit. Under the rules, the insured must be expected to die within twelve months, and the death benefit can be discounted by an amount consistent with a life expectancy of no more than one year. The discount rate must be based on a formula that takes into account the greater of the applicable mid-term federal rate or the policy loan rate.[8] Living benefits insurance can help clients whose liquidity needs begin before death, such as to pay final medical expenses and to replace lost income.[9]

Gift taxation As illustrated in Chapter 7, there are two common situations where insurance can be the subject of gift taxation. First, a taxable gift of the policy's replacement value will arise when the owner makes an *assignment* of one or more ownership rights to the policy. Ordinarily, the gift of an insurance policy will qualify for the annual exclusion, unless it is made to an irrevocable trust.

Second, a taxable gift of the policy proceeds will arise when the policy matures, at the *death* of a decedent-insured, if the insured, owner, and beneficiary are all different parties. The effect of this rule, as we shall see shortly, is to compel planners to recommend that the same (noninsured) party be both owner and beneficiary.

Estate taxation. Life insurance is most commonly included in a decedent's federal estate tax base under Code §§2033, 2042, 2001, and 2035. Since this material was covered and illustrated in detail in Chapter 6, each

---

8. Reg §1.7702-2(d).

9. For a technical discussion of the taxation of accelerated death benefits, see the Griffin article cited at the end of the chapter.

section will be reviewed only briefly here.

Under §2033 (property owned at death), the terminal value of a life insurance policy on the *life of someone other than the decedent* will be includable in the decedent's gross estate to the extent of the decedent's date of death ownership interest in the policy.

Under §2042, proceeds on the *life of the decedent* will be includable in the decedent's gross estate if, at the insured's death, either the proceeds were receivable by the decedent's executor, or the decedent possessed any incidents of ownership in the policy. Interestingly, the entire proceeds under split dollar arrangements will still be includable, even though part of the proceeds is payable to a third party, such as the employer.

Under §2035, the proceeds of a life insurance policy on the *life of the decedent* will be includable in the decedent's gross estate if, within three years of death, the non owning decedent made a completed transfer of incidents of ownership in the policy.

Finally, under §2001, the decedent's *adjusted taxable gifts* will include the date-of-gift taxable terminal value of *any* life insurance policy for which the decedent made a completed transfer more than three years before death.

With these tax rules in mind, let us turn to the techniques of insurance planning.

Life Insurance Planning

The fundamental goal in using life insurance in liquidity planning is to provide for cash needs while minimizing income, gift, and estate taxation, as well as other costs. This multifaceted criterion will be employed next to help determine who should be chosen to be the insured, the owner, and the beneficiary of a proposed life insurance policy. For simplicity, throughout this section we will assume an estate's need for cash will be met with insurance, rather than some other source of liquidity.

Selecting the insured. Proper family planning would provide for insurance on the life of that spouse whose death is expected to trigger a cash need. For *smaller estates*, this could occur at the death of either or both spouses, depending upon certain factors, such as the size of their economic contribution to the family.

For *larger estates*, we have seen that effective planning with the use of the marital deduction and the credit shelter bypass will usually eliminate cash FET needs at the death of the first spouse, but will create a relatively large need at the surviving spouse's death. Thus, ordinarily, little or no insurance will be required on S1's life to pay FET. The real insurance need will be on S2's life. However, some insurance may be needed to meet nontax "capital" needs, such as to cover certain last expenses, readjustment needs, and cash requirements during the dependency period. This will be particularly important for parents with a large amount of earned income who are supporting younger children.

Insurance arrangements for the second death. Since most clients do not know for certain whether the husband or the wife will be the surviving spouse, both may need to be insured. Several commonly used purchase arrangements are discussed next.

1. *Full coverage for both spouses.* One simple but costly plan would be to insure both spouses for the full amount of protection needed at the surviving spouse's death. Also duplicative, this plan is hardly ever recommended.

2. *Minimal coverage for both spouses.* An alternative method of insuring the spouses is to purchase immediately a small amount of insurance on both spouses which, upon either's first death, can be used to purchase a "fully paid up" larger policy on the life of the survivor. This can eliminate the cash flow drain on the surviving spouse's assets that would otherwise be used to pay the premium.

3. *Second to die insurance.* A third method of insuring both spouses for cash needs at the survivor's death is to purchase a joint life policy of second to die insurance, also called survivorship life insurance. It pays the proceeds only upon the death of the second spouse. This alternative should save premium dollars in two ways: First, only one policy need be purchased. Second, the contingency insured against is more remote in time than that insured against under a single-life policy; the policy proceeds are not payable until both of the insureds have died.

Second to die insurance may be particularly economical if one of the spouses is uninsurable. Medical underwriting standards are eased because the life expectancy of the healthier spouse becomes paramount. Unfortunately, many uncompetitive second to die policies can wind up costing nearly as much as a single-life policy, especially if the premiums have to be paid for a much longer period. Careful cost comparison is necessary.[10]

4. *Full coverage for wife only.* A final alternative is to insure only the wife, usually the probable survivor, for the required liquidity. If she survives her husband, the contract becomes, de facto, a second-death policy. If she predeceases him, the proceeds can be invested and then made available to pay the FET at his later death. The cost of insuring only the wife should be more expensive than the cost of a second to die policy; the

---

10. For a discussion of the uses and estate taxation of joint life policies, including first to die insurance, see the Zaritsky and Schlesinger/Ball papers cited at the end of the chapter.

latter will more likely pay the proceeds at a later date, since the wife may predecease the husband.

Selecting the owner and beneficiary. The amount of planning effort needed in choosing who will be owner and beneficiary will usually depend on the size of family estate, because transfer tax cost is the primary criterion. In the case of married clients, selecting the owner and beneficiary for a *smaller estate* is rather simple, since little or no transfer taxes will result from any selection alternative. The client and the client's spouse will be able to own policies on their own lives, making the proceeds payable to the other without generating any FET. The contingent beneficiary could be the client's children, if sufficiently mature, or it could be the trustee of a trust, perhaps the trustee of the couples probate avoidance living trust.

On the other hand, selecting the owner and beneficiary of insurance on the lives of the spouses of *larger estates* requires greater precautions, in order to minimize the effects of transfer tax costs. We consider next the effect of naming various parties as owners and beneficiaries.

Spouse as owner and beneficiary. Naming one or the other spouse as owner or beneficiary will not minimize transfer costs. It will usually subject the proceeds either to a transfer tax, or to probate administration, or to both, depending upon which spouse dies first. Consider the somewhat complicated tax and probate consequences for each of the possible outcomes.

First, if the *insured spouse dies first and is the owner,* the proceeds will be includable in his or her gross estate under §2042. If the proceeds qualify for the marital deduction, thereby avoiding S1 taxation, they will be included in *S2's gross estate*, barring consumption, gifting, or remarriage. If the *insured spouse dies second and is the owner* then the proceeds will be includable in his or her *gross estate*, again under §2042 and no marital deduction will be available.

Second, if the *insured spouse dies first and the noninsured spouse is the owner and beneficiary*, then the proceeds will likely be included in that *S2's gross estate*, barring gifting, remarriage or consumption. From the discussion of gift taxation of insurance earlier in the chapter, it should be clear that if the noninsured spouse is named *owner* and someone other than a spouse is named beneficiary, then that spouse will be deemed to have made a *taxable gift* to the beneficiary of the proceeds upon the death of the insured spouse. Thus, in the usual larger family estate, even the noninsured spouse should not be named either owner or beneficiary.

Conclusions. Two important conclusions can be drawn from the above. First, naming *either spouse* as owner or beneficiary of a policy on the life of a spouse will subject the proceeds to transfer taxation at least at the second death. Thus, to minimize transfer costs, *neither spouse of a larger estate should be designated as either owner or beneficiary* of an insurance policy on the life of either. Second, since a taxable gift will occur whenever the insured, owner and beneficiary are all different parties, *whoever is selected should be named both owner and beneficiary*, to avoid gift consequences. Designation of other possible parties, including a child and two types of trusts, is evaluated next.

Child as owner and beneficiary. Instead of a spouse, one of the client's children could be named owner and beneficiary. The child could be *requested* to use the proceeds to provide liquidity to the estate upon the death of the insured. This alternative will work best when the child is sufficiently *mature* to handle such a responsibility. Nonetheless, there will always be a risk that the child may permit the policy to lapse. Or the child, having received the policy proceeds upon the death of the insured parent, may be *unwilling* to provide the funding needed by the estate. Since the child will become the legal owner of the proceeds, any gratuitous transfer of the funds to the estate or to the surviving spouse will be treated as a *taxable gift*. However, as will be mentioned later, the child could purchase estate assets or lend money to the estate. Additionally, the proceeds, or at least their value, may inevitably wind up in the child's own gross estate.

Revocable trust as owner and beneficiary. To eliminate any doubts over whether a named beneficiary will cooperate to make the proceeds available to the estate and to remove the chance that the insurance proceeds will be subject to probate in a spouse's estate, the wealthy client could name a revocable trust to be the owner and beneficiary. However, a power to revoke the trust if held by the client or the client's spouse will cause the proceeds to be *includable in the insured's gross estate*. Thus, although avoiding probate of the proceeds, a revocable insurance trust offers no transfer tax advantage over the insured-owner arrangements considered so far.

Irrevocable trust as owner and beneficiary.[11] The irrevocable life insurance trust (ILIT) offers what most commentators consider to be the solution.

Organization and structure of an ILIT. The client-insured creates the ILIT and names the trustee to be owner and beneficiary of the policy. The grantor must not be named a trust *beneficiary*, because of possible §2036(a) problems; and since the noninsured spouse is usually one of the beneficiaries of an ILIT, he or she should not be a grantor. This will require greater care in preparation in community property states.

---

11. For a summary comparison of the income, estate, and gift taxation of the irrevocable life insurance trust versus other popular trusts in estate planning, see Table 17-1 in Chapter 17.

Upon the death of the insured, the trustee is authorized to lend the proceeds to the insured's estate or to purchase assets from the estate. If the insured is S1, then the trust corpus usually continues to provide benefits to S2 in the form of a bypass trust, similar to the one discussed in Chapters 11 and 12. At the death of S2, the trust is again authorized to lend cash to the S2 estate, or to purchase estate assets. Then, the trust is either terminated, with corpus payable to the children, or it is continued, distributing income to the children until either they reach a specified age or, in the case of a generation-skipping trust qualifying for the $1 million lifetime exemption, until the grandchildren reach a specified age, usually not later than 21.[12]

Ownership of insurance by an irrevocable trust requires that the clients be willing to surrender all interest in the policy. However, insurance having little or no cash value is usually one of the least distasteful assets to gift, for three principal reasons. First, the *gift tax value* is minimal. The typical policy will have little or no terminal value, either because it is a term policy or because it is a cash value policy that has been recently purchased or has a sizable outstanding loan. The gross gift value of a newly issued policy is simply the first year's premium. Second, in contrast with its gift tax value, its *estate tax value* will be very large, making it a desirable asset to exclude from the estate. Third, because it is merely a document that does not produce income, clients generally do *not experience loss* in the pleasure of ownership commonly felt when they gift tangible property or intangible income earning property.

A ILIT is likely to be used as a source of funds to pay estate taxes therefore it is important to choose a policy that the client knows will be there when it is needed. Since term insurance becomes increasingly expensive as the client gets older, it is a poor choice for a ILIT. For a single client a whole life policy makes sense. If another type of cash value insurance, such as universal life is considered, the client must make sure that there is a guaranteed proceeds amount sufficient to pay the taxes. A married couple has two choices, if the sole purpose is to create a fund to pay estate taxes at the second death, then a second to die policy would be least expensive for any given level of coverage. With a sophisticated estate plan incorporating bypass and marital trusts, the taxes are most likely to be postponed until the second death. But what about those rare situation where S2 is dying at the time of S1's death the executor will want to generate a tax at S1's death, will

---

12. For a discussion of the "private marital deduction annuity," see the Guiterrez article cited at the end of Chapter 12. At S1's death, the trustee of the QTIP trust is directed to purchase an annuity for the life of S2 from the life insurance trust. Its advantages include an S1 marital deduction, S2 estate reduction, and the use of the life insurance trust as a generation-skipping trust that is not subject to the GSTT.

use of a second to die policy cause hardship or force the executor to postpone the taxes to the second death even though it means more overall estate taxes? The answer is no. These situations anticipate the death of the second spouse shortly after the first death. §6161 allows the executor to postpone payment of the estate tax for reasonable cause, thus the executor of S1's estate would not be forced to sell assets, but would file the return, report the estate tax owed and request a one year extension with an explanation as to why cash is presently unavailable.

A second to die policy is not advisable if the primary purpose is to provide income to the surviving spouse. The income earners (one or both) should be separately insured taking into account the amount of insurance needed to replace the insured's earning capacity. For any given family wealth level (until we reach the very wealthy), a young couple with dependent children will need greater amounts of insurance than an older couple with grown children, therefore term insurance may be recommended so as to cover the years when children will be dependent. This will give the greatest coverage possible at the least cost. If the couple can afford additional insurance and are concerned about covering estate taxes in the event both die young, then they should consider another LIIT to purchase a significant whole life second to die policy.

Who should pay the premiums on the trust-owned policy? One alternative is to fund the trust with sufficient income-earning assets to enable the trust to pay them. Unfortunately, the grantor trust rules will make that income taxable to the client-grantor rather than the trust.[13] A preferred alternative has the client making annual gifts to the trust in amounts sufficient to pay the premiums. The insured-spouse in community property states should make the periodic gifts from his or her separate property to keep the proceeds out of the estate of the noninsured spouse, who is beneficiary of the trust. By having a Crummey demand right held by the insured's children, these gifts can qualify for the annual exclusion.

Impressive goals of ILIT. With regard to a *married client* owning an estate whose value exceeds $600,000, the exemption equivalent of the unified credit, only the designation of an irrevocable trust as owner and beneficiary can achieve all of the following goals:

1. Exclude the insurance proceeds from *income taxation* and from the *taxable estates* of both spouses and, perhaps, the children.
2. Exclude the insurance proceeds from the *probate estates* of both spouses.
3. Enjoy the shelter of the gift tax *annual exclusion* for transfers to the

---

13. §677(a)(3).

trust of both the policy and the funds needed to pay policy premiums.

4. Ensure that a *responsible party* will in fact provide the needed post-death liquidity

5. Make the *proceeds available* to the surviving spouse, for health or certain other reasons.

The following is an extended discussion of how a carefully structured ILIT can implement these goals.

1. Income tax, estate tax and GSTT issues. Regarding the first goal, an ILIT will not ordinarily fall within the grip of §2036(a). However, because they are not direct skips, annual exclusion transfers into the trust will not insulate the corpus from GSTT, and thus planners may elect to allocate the $1 million exemption to such transfers, anticipating that premature death of a child can give rise to a taxable distribution to, or a taxable termination for, the benefit of a skip person.

Excluding the insurance proceeds from the gross estate of a decedent can have an additional benefit: preventing the beneficiary's exposure to transferee liability for payment of the FET. In one case, the decedent died possessing incidents of ownership on a $50,000 policy. The IRS was unable to collect $62,378 in FET from the decedents' assets which were then owned by his nonresident alien widow, living in Venezuela. However, the policy beneficiary, a U.S. citizen, was held liable for the FET up to $50,000, the amount of the proceeds includable in the gross estate.[14]

The ILIT can also be effectively used by a *single person* to achieve similar tax and nontax goals.

Whether an existing policy is transferred to the trust, or whether a new policy is created and transferred when the trust is established, the client-trustor-insured must live *three years* after the policy is transferred to ensure the avoidance of inclusion of the proceeds in the gross estate under §2035(d)(2). Because of the drawbacks, and in spite of the life underwriter's frequent eagerness to sell the policy (perhaps in part because he or she thinks the attorney could kill the deal!), the policy should be purchased by the trustee, not the insured client, after creation of the trust, to completely avoid the three year rule. If the client transfers an existing policy, the annual exclusion will not be available unless the trust gives the beneficiaries a Crummey invasion power.

The trust can include a *contingent marital deduction clause*, so that if the three-year rule caused the proceeds to be includable in the insured's gross estate, then the proceeds would be paid outright to the spouse (or to

---

14. *Baptiste*, TCM 1992-198; §6324(a)(2).

a marital trust). This would save the marital deduction and avoid estate tax. On the other hand, if the insured lived longer than three years, causing the three-year rule not to apply, then the proceeds would be used to fund the ILIT; which then is called a bypass trust because the proceeds will be excluded (bypass) from the estates of both spouses.[15]

If each spouse is an insured, then two trusts will have to be established, with each trust owning one policy. These trusts must be drafted especially carefully to avoid §2036(a) problems and the reciprocal trust doctrine discussed in Chapter 6.

If the trust is *required* to use insurance proceeds to pay the decedent's estate debts, including taxes, the proceeds will be includable in the decedent's gross estate, under §2042. Thus, as we have said, the trustee should instead be simply *advised* that it may *lend* the proceeds to the estate or *purchase* estate assets to achieve funding.

Transfers into an ILIT can be structured to avoid the GSTT. To the extent that gift transfers for premium payments qualify for either the annual exclusion or the lifetime exemption, they and any appreciation resulting will avoid GSTT. Thus a life insurance trust can greatly leverage the transfers, creating a potentially large body of assets that are GSTT-free.

> EXAMPLE GST-1 Dorfman and his wife establish an irrevocable trust, funding it with $40,000 cash each year to pay the premium on a $4 million second-to-die policy. The first $20,000 is sheltered from gift tax by a Crummey provision, and the remaining $20,000 by the unused unified credit. In addition, Dorfman and his wife each allocate $10,000 of their $1 million GSTT exemptions to these transfers[16]. Thus, the entire $4 million proceeds will also be sheltered from any future GSTT, thus, a one hundredfold leveraging of the GSTT exemption is accomplished.

Although recent GSTT rules prevent annual exclusion gifts to a single trust for the benefit of both nonskip and skip persons from also being sheltered from the GSTT, planners achieve complete shelter from GSTT in one of two ways. Either they create one trust, and use the client's $1 million GSTT exemption to shelter these gifts, or they create two trusts, one for the benefit of only nonskip persons (e.g. spouse and children) and the other for

---

15. For a further discussion, see the Brand-LaPiana article cited at the end of the chapter.

16. Each must allocate the excess of their $20,000 share of the premium gift over their $10,000 annual exclusion amount.

the benefit of only skip persons (grandchildren, etc.).[17]

Figure 15-1 illustrates the single trust approach, depicting the evolution of an ILIT from its creation to its typical termination, when the youngest grandchild reaches age 21. As time passes and key events occur, the trust's descriptive name changes, from *ILIT* to *bypass trust* to *children's trust* to *GST trust*. Figure 15-1 also highlights the identity of primary beneficiary during each period, that beneficiaries typical property interests in trust income and principal, and the gift, estate, income and GST tax effects to that beneficiary.

2. Avoiding probate. Regarding the second goal for the ILIT, the policy proceeds will avoid probate at both spouses' deaths because neither S1, S2, or their estates, will ever own the proceeds.

3. Shelter of annual exclusion. With regard to the third goal of the ILIT, the gift of a policy to an irrevocable trust will not ordinarily qualify for the *annual exclusion* because it is not considered a gift of a present interest. However, both that transfer and the payments into a trust to fund the insurance premiums can be made to qualify with the use of a Crummey demand provision held by the children.

4. Selection of trustee as responsible party. An insured spouse who is also grantor should not be named trustee, since this could constitute an incident of ownership in the policy. The noninsured spouse could be named trustee, without this adverse result.

Most corporate trustees are extremely reluctant to become trustees of an insurance trust prior to the insured's death, if the trust is unfunded. And even if it is funded, the advent of higher risk, higher return life insurance policies and growing insurance company insolvency problems have made more and more trustees, particularly corporate trustees, increasingly concerned about possible *liability* if expected policy death benefits are not entirely paid or if the policy turns out to be relatively uncompetitive. In addition, an ILIT may not be profitable for a corporate trustee even after the proceeds are received, particularly if they must be allocated in one of two all too common ways: proceeds immediately distributed to trust beneficiaries, or used to acquire closely held business stock, an asset considered difficult to manage.[18]

---

17. For the complex details, see §2642(c)(2), and analyses in the papers written by Plaine, Bieck/Bauer and Chazan, cited at the end of the chapter.

18. For description of these and other issues, see the Maurer article cited at the end of the chapter.

FIGURE 15-1 Evolution of Irrevocable Life Insurance Trust: Beneficiaries and Taxation

TIMELINE

Key Events:	Creation of Trust	Death of Grantor/Insured	Death of Grantor's Spouse	Death of last surviving child	21st birthday of youngest grandchild

PrimaryBeneficiary:	**GRANTOR**	**SPOUSE**	**CHILDREN**	**GRAND-CHILDREN**

Their property interests in income and principal of trust:

Income and Principal: no rights	Income: (all, or as needed) Principal: Limited by-Ascertainable std. 5 and 5 Adverse party	Income: (as needed) Principal: (as needed)	Income: (as needed) Principal: (as needed) all outright at age 21

Trust name and characteristics:

Grantor creates and transfers: 1st year-- policy All years-- cash to pay premiums to: **Irrevocable Life Insurance Trust**	*LI Proceeds rec'd. by trustee; trust becomes:* **Bypass Trust**	**Children's Trust** *either terminates when youngest child reaches a specified age...*	*...or continues on as:* **GST Trust** *...which then terminates when youngest grandchild reaches age 21, or later, if allowed by local perpetuities law.*

TAX EFFECTS TO DONOR, OR BENEFICIARY NAMED ABOVE

Type of taxation

1. Taxable gift to donor-grantor?

No, except to extent not sheltered by annual exclusion	No new gift

2. Includable in beneficiaries estate tax base at death?

No, unless 2035(d)(2), if so, gross estate or taxable gift involved, if so, as adjusted taxable gift	No, except for principal distributions that continue to be owned

3. Income taxable to beneficiary?

No. All income is accumulated and taxed to trust	Yes, to extent distributed to spouse	Yes, to extent distributed to children	Yes, to extent distributed to grandchildren

Undistributed FAI and all capital gains taxable to trust

4. Any GSTT incurred?

No, provided that grantor (and possibly grantor's children) allocated $1 million GSTT exemption(s) to the gift transfers. To extent not so sheltered, trust will have inclusion ratio of greater than zero, and a portion of any taxable termination or taxable distribution to a skip person will be subject to GSTT

To overcome the liability concerns and encourage a fiduciary to act as trustee of a client's life insurance trust, the planner may have to take one or more of the following steps. First, the planner can include language in the trust instrument that *exculpates* the trustee from liability in connection with life insurance policy acquisition and ownership. Exculpatory clauses are enforced by the courts, but are strictly construed against the trustee, and offer no protection from acts of "bad faith," "reckless indifference," "gross negligence," and "willful misconduct."

Second, the beneficiaries may have to send a "letter of agreement," consenting to, and releasing the trustee from liability for, investments in life insurance. Obviously, investing in just one asset violates the prudent investor rule so the beneficiaries consent is needed.

Third, the grantor can agree to indemnify the trustee, i.e., reimburse the trustee for any related loss.

Finally, the planner can arrange a noncorporate fiduciary, such as a family friend, to act as initial trustee, with the corporate fiduciary succeeding as trustee only after the insured(s) have died and the proceeds have been paid.

Life insurance is an important liquidity source because it supplies cash exactly when it is needed: at death of the client. Planned carefully, it can also be structured to avoid all transfer taxes.

FLOWER BONDS

This topic could come under the heading: Sometimes Congress does the darnedest things. In the 1950s and early 1960s the federal government issued Treasury bonds with set maturity dates that could, nevertheless, be used at their par value to pay the federal estate tax provided the bonds were part of the decedent's estate. Since the bond yields, while reasonable when issued, were quite low (3% to 5%) compared to other safe investments in the 1970s and 1980s they began selling at deep discounts. This created some estate planning opportunities for persons with terminal illnesses to purchase bonds at as little as 85% of par shortly before death; and the decedent's executor could turn them in to the government at par to pay the estate tax, achieving a guaranteed 15% increase in value in a short time span. Of course, to the extent the bonds could be used to pay estate taxes their value in the estate was the par value, thus some of that 15% increase in value would be lost to increased estate taxes.

Discounts have decreased as the bonds still in circulation are reaching maturity, the last ones (yield of 3.5%) will come due November 15, 1998, thus the estate planning opportunities are generally very limited, especially when one weighs the opportunity cost of holding a low yielding bond for at least nine months.

LIQUIDITY PLANNING DEVICES UNIQUE TO BUSINESS OWNERS

Many owners of closely held businesses can anticipate a severe liquidity problem for their estates. Not infrequently, the largest portion of the estate consists of the interest in the business, that, almost by definition, is quite illiquid. The need to pay the FET in cash within nine months after date of death acts as a cloud that can force survivors to sell the business at distress prices, probably to outside parties. The business owner should plan in advance to minimize future liquidity problems. However, if certain conditions are met, the tax attributable to the business portion of the estate can be delayed four years, and then made payable in installments over the next ten years. See the discussion of §6166 in the next section. The following presents several liquidity generating or tax lowering devices that only apply to business-owning clients.

Sale Of the Business

First, consideration should be given to the predeath *sale* of the business to one or more individuals, or to a *merger* with a publicly held firm, as a means of converting a relatively illiquid asset into a liquid one. A pre-death sale will ordinarily trigger a capital gains tax, and a client who for that reason chooses not to sell or merge before death should consider executing a funded *buyout agreement* with the other owners, triggered at the client's death. The buyout contract, discussed in some detail in the next chapter, will obligate the other owner(s) to pay the client's estate a predetermined cash amount in exchange for the client's interest in the firm. Since the sale will occur after death, the resulting step up in basis of the decedent's interest will eliminate or substantially reduce any capital gains tax.

Three other liquidity generating devices created by Congress, and incorporated into the Internal Revenue Code, for business-owning clients are discussed next. Their sections numbers will be quoted frequently because that's how many in the industry identify the techniques.

§6166, §6161 and §6163: FET Deferral

§6166: Installment payment of the FET. To help reduce the risk of an immediate liquidity crisis at the business owner's death, Congress enacted §6166, which permits the estate of a decedent-owner of a closely held business to elect to defer payment of the FET attributable to the business, with interest owing at only 4 percent per year on the first $153,000 in deferred federal estate tax. The estate then can pay that FET in 10 installments starting in the fifth year.

The deferred taxes in excess of $153,000 is subject to whatever is the current applicable federal long-term rate, (AFLTR), which is approximately equal to the long-term rate at which the U.S. Treasury recently borrowed.[19] The executor has the option of deducting the interest paid on §6166 debt on either the FET return or the estate (fiduciary) income tax return. If deducted on the fiduciary return, deductibility is not subject to the personal interest limitations.[20] However, deducting the interest on the FET return may save more tax, because of the FET rate is likely to be higher. In order to take advantage of the interest as a deduction one must file a claim for refund (Form 843) and recalculate the estate tax with the interest as a deduction. Since the deduction can only be taken after the interest is paid,[21] most estates wait until after the seventh or eight principal payment (out of the ten scheduled) on a 6166 extension to do the recalculation as it will usually reduce the estate taxes so much that the last two payments do not have to be made, and if after the eight payment the estate might even be owed a small refund. Because the interest paid reduces the estate tax, less interest is owed and some of what was paid as interest becomes principal payment, which in turn reduces the interest deduction thereby increasing the tax, etc., which is obviously a complex interrelated calculation.[22]

Three conditions must be met for qualification under §6166. First, the value of the decedent's interest in the business must be at least *35 percent* of the value of the *adjusted gross estate*, which is the gross estate reduced by debts, expenses, and losses. Second, the decedent's interest must have been in a *closely held business*, which is defined as

---

19. §6601(j).

20. §163(h)(2)(E).

21. Rev. Rul. 80-250 1980-2 CB 278.

22. Cecil Cammack, Jr., at Cammack Computations Co., 1-800-594-5826, will do this computations for a very reasonable price.

1. A sole proprietorship; or
2. A partnership:
    a. In which at least 20 percent of the capital interest is included in the decedent's gross estate, or
    b. Which has 15 or fewer partners; or
3. A corporation:
    a. In which at least 20 percent of the voting stock is included in the decedent's gross estate, or
    b. Which has 15 or fewer shareholders.

Third, to qualify, the sole proprietorship, partnership, or corporation must have been actually engaged in carrying on a *trade or business* at the time of the decedent's death.

> EXAMPLE 6166-1 Decedent died owning 40 percent of the stock in a corporation, with the decedent's interest worth $600,000. Decedent had a gross estate of $1 million and an adjusted gross estate of $900,000. Assume that the FET is $120,000. Under the above rules, the estate will qualify under §6166, since the business qualifies as a closely held business, and decedent's interest is at least 35 percent of the adjusted gross estate. The amount of the tax that may be deferred is calculated to be $80,000, which is the amount of the FET ($120,000) times the ratio of the value of the business interest ($600,000) divided by the adjusted gross estate ($900,000).

Estate tax deferral under §6166 can be a source of estate liquidity by reducing the amount of the decedent's estate's immediate cash needs. However, it will offer only limited benefit to many clients because of three of the Section's restrictions. First, as shown in the example above, only a *portion* of the FET can be deferred, measured by the proportion of the estate consisting of the qualifying business. Second, while the tax can be deferred, the *interest* on the tax starts accruing nine months after death. Finally, the interest on the deferred FET in excess of $153,000 will be at *current market rates*, not 4 percent. Since this is a relief provision designed to avoid a force sale of the business it should not come as a surprise to learn that the sale, redemption, or other disposition of all, or a significant portion, of the business, or the failure to make timely interest or principal payments, will result in immediate *acceleration* of the deferred payments. However, §6161, discussed next, can be used to defer an installment, provide a timely request is made.

§6161: Extension to pay tax for reasonable cause. The IRS has discretion under §6161 to grant an extension to any estate of up to 10 years to pay the FET upon a showing of "reasonable cause." Examples of situations satisfying this requirement include:

- The estate has liquid assets but they are located in other states, not immediately available to the executor.
- A large part of the estate is in the form of assets which consist of rights to receive payments in the future (royalties, accounts receivables, etc.).
- The estate includes a claim to substantial assets which cannot be collected without litigation.
- The estate does not have sufficient funds to pay taxes and provide for a family allowance and claims, and
- The estate can not borrow except at rates that would constitute a hardship.

Ordinarily, reasonable cause will not be found merely because liquid assets (listed securities) must be sold at distress prices. However, in the last few years, the IRS, well aware of the difficulty of selling illiquid assets (land) in a recessionary market, has readily granted extensions for reasonable cause under §6161. Warning, a request must be made before the due date of the return; and subsequent requests must be made before the last extension has expired. Failure to timely file the request will result in it being denied regardless of how meritorious the reason.

Estates may use §6166 or §6161 installments to pay the *generation-skipping transfer tax* , but in the case of §6166, only if the tax results from a direct skip.[23]

§6163: Deferral of FET for reversion, remainder. §6163 allows FET deferral for tax attributable to a reversionary or remainder interest includable in a decedent's gross estate. The tax can be postponed until six months after the termination of the "precedent" interest, i.e., the interest immediately preceding the reversion or remainder. That termination could be many years after the decedent's death.

> EXAMPLE 6163-1 Exactly two years ago, Jake created an irrevocable living trust, with all income payable to Jake's son (or his estate) for five years. Then, remainder will be payable to Jake's daughter D (or her estate). If D dies today, the present value of her remainder interest in the trust will be includable in her gross estate. Under §6163, payment of the FET attributable to that interest may be delayed until three years and six months from today.

---

23. LR 9314050.

§303 Redemption

The Internal Revenue Code provides another method to lessen the impact of taxes on the estates of business-owning decedents. §303 permits the estate of a decedent-shareholder of a corporation to redeem the decedent's shares with favorable *income tax* treatment. Specifically, the transaction will be treated as a disposition of a capital asset rather than the receipt of a dividend.

> EXAMPLE 303-1 Decedent's estate redeemed decedent's 1000 shares of stock in a closely held corporation. Immediately before death, each share had an adjusted basis of $100. The date-of-death value of each share was $150. Upon redemption, the estate received $158,000 cash. If the redemption does not qualify for capital gains treatment, the estate will be deemed to have received a dividend of $158,000, that is treated as ordinary income. Alternatively, if the redemption qualifies under §303, the estate will have a taxable long-term gain of only $8,000, reflecting the step-up in basis at date of death.

Federal tax reform since 1986, by taxing most capital gains at not much less than ordinary income rates[24], reduced somewhat the tax advantage of the §303 redemption. But the ability to exclude the amount of the *adjusted basis* for taxation, as illustrated in the above example, continues to make the strategy very attractive.

There are two major requirements to qualify under §303. First, as with the §6166 deferral, the value of the decedent's interest in the stock must be at least *35 percent* of his or her adjusted gross estate. Second, the *amount paid* by the corporation in redemption of the shares *may not exceed* the sum of federal and state death taxes, generation skipping transfer taxes and funeral and administration expenses.

Regarding distributions, if a cash distribution exceeds the amount of the corporation's earnings and profits, the excess is considered a nontaxable return of capital. But if the firm distributes appreciated property instead of cash, the distribution will probably be considered a sale by the corporation, with the gain subject to immediate taxation.

Thus, a §303 redemption can provide liquidity to the estate by encouraging a postdeath cash-generating transaction which might otherwise produce

---

24. Currently, 28 percent for capital gains versus 31, 36, or 39.6 percent for ordinary income. For a long time prior to 1987, the maximum effective federal marginal rate on long-term capital gains was 20 percent, while maximum ordinary rates were either 70 percent (1971-81) or 50 percent (1982-86). See Figure 9-1.

very undesirable income tax consequences.[25]

By means of lifetime planning, §§6166 and 303 may be made available to a client who had anticipated not qualifying because he or she did not expect the estate to meet the 35 percent test. The client can be urged to acquire additional interest in the firm, or to reduce the size of the non-business estate by *gifting* in order to reduce the adjusted gross estate and thereby increase the proportion represented by the business.

§2032A: Special Use Valuation

One other liquidity source explicitly provided by the Code is available to the business owner's estate. Its purpose might be best explained with a hypothetical fact situation.

Suppose a client has owned a farm for many years, one that had originally been located well outside of the city limits. But with the progress of urban growth, the farm is presently in the heart of one of the high-rent districts. Although the general value of the land is considerably greater then the capitalized value of the farm as a business, the client has no interest in selling; she and her survivors are determined to remain working the farm in the indefinite future.

The reader might be wondering which value will be includable in the client-owner's gross estate at her death. Will it be the value of the farm in its *present use* or the value of the property in its *highest and best use*, available, for example, for construction of a high-rise building? Valuation at its highest and best use might force the survivors to sell the land to pay the large FET. On the other hand, valuation at its present use might enable the survivors to carry on the business.

§2032A permits qualifying estates to value at least a portion of real property in such situations at its *present, "qualified use" value*, as a farm or other trade or business.

Requirements. The five major requirements and conditions under §2032A are briefly described next.

1. The property must have been held for "qualified use" and actively managed by the decedent or the decedent's family for *five out of the eight years* prior to the decedent's death. For example, *passive leasing* for cash by the decedent of the property for farming by

---

25. For a quantitative comparison of borrowing from a closely held corporation versus employing a §303 redemption, see the Eastland paper cited at the end of Chapter 13.

others will later disqualify the estate from §2032A.[26] However, the surviving spouse may later rent the property to a family member.[27]

2. At least *50 percent* of the value of the gross estate, reduced by liens, must consist of real or personal property devoted to the qualifying use.[28]

3. The value of the real property portion must constitute at least *25 percent* of the adjusted gross estate.[29]

4. The qualifying property must pass to a qualifying heir and must continue to be used as a *qualified use* for at least *10 years* after the decedent's death. A qualified heir is a member of the decedent's family who acquired the property from the decedent.[30] A qualified use requires use of the property for farming or other trade or business.[31]

5. Perhaps most significant, the maximum amount by which the value of the special use *real estate* can be reduced by this election is $750,000.[32] Thus, assuming a 55% marginal FET rate, the greatest FET saving will be $412,500. While this is no small amount, very large disparities between highest and best use value and qualified use value may create too sizable a liquidity crisis for §2032A to solve, and may still force survivors to sell out involuntarily.

The §2032A election can reduce the need for liquidity by reducing the size of the gross estate and, therefore, the amount of the FET cash requirement. Since it applies only to real property and has some onerous requirements, it is not used very frequently. Whenever §2032A is available, the estate will also qualify for §6166 deferral since the threshold is higher for §2032(A) than it is for §6166.

---

26. *J. Fisher*, TC CCH 12,923 (1993).

27. §2032A(b)(5)(A).

28. §2032A(b)(1)(a).

29. §2032A(b)(1)(B).

30. §2032A(e)(1).

31. §2032A(b)(2).

32. §2032A(a)(2).

VALUATION DISCOUNTS AND CONTROL PREMIUMS

Over the years, the courts have offered taxpayers the ability to generate liquidity by significantly discounting the transfer tax value of closely held business interests, real property and securities subject to special market circumstances. The most common discounts are the minority discount, lack of marketability discount, and fractional interest discount.[33]

Minority Interest Discount For Business Interests

A *minority interest* is an interest in a business that, in terms of voting, is not a controlling interest. It lacks the power to effect changes in policy, structure, or strategy.

> EXAMPLE MD-1 Jack owns 50.1 percent of a corporation worth $1 million, and Jill owns 49.9 percent. Jill owns a minority interest. Alone, Jill cannot run or control the business, set compensation levels, sell or encumber business assets, elect herself an officer, or control corporate policy. Jill would most certainly have difficulty selling her interest to a third party for $499,000.

Ownership of a partnership interest may also qualify for a minority interest discount. Common law allows each partner one vote, regardless of his or her capital (investment), unless the partnership agreement provides to the contrary.

For transfer tax valuation, minority discounts of between 15 and 50 percent are obtainable for such interests. Factors influencing the size of the discount include overall quality of management, composition of other share holdings, size of the business and its history of profitability, existence of business opportunities not currently being exploited by management, and degree of the company's financial leverage.[34]

In some situations, minority interest discounts are not available. The IRS contends that a gross estate including two separate minority interests

---

33. For a discussion of other less common valuation discounts for real estate holding company assets, see the Korn/Hitchner article cited at the end of the chapter.

34. *John and Viola Moore v. Commissioner*, 62 TCM 1128 (1991) (35% discount on gift of partnership interest); *Estate of Winkler v. Commissioner*, 62 TCM 1514 (1991) (20% discount on nonvoting stock); *Estate of Catherine Campbell v. Commissioner*, 62 TCM 1514 (1991) (56% discount); *Estate of Lenheim v. Commissioner*, 60 TCM 356 (1990); *Nancy Moonyham v. Commissioner*, TC Memo 1991-178. See the Gibbs paper cited at the end of the chapter.

in the same property which add up to a majority interest should be denied the benefits of minority interest discounts.[35]

> EXAMPLE MD-2. Dad's estate plan will leave his 40 percent business interest at his death to a marital trust. At Mom's later death, her gross estate will include Dad's interest in the marital trust, as well as her own 40 percent business interest. The IRS will disallow a minority discount for either interest.

Planners should be able to circumvent this problem by either having S1 dispose of his or her interest to the bypass trust, which is not taxed to S2, rather than to the marital trust, or having one or both spouses make a lifetime transfer of the interest (by gift, installment sale, etc.).

Minority interest discounts are not available to stock subject to a §2032A special use valuation election.

A donor holding a majority stock position who gifts some of the shares can reduce both the retained shares and the gifted shares to a minority position.

Valuation discounts and imperfect unification. Chapter 9 described several factors explaining why our federal "unified" transfer tax system is not perfectly unified. Those factors included the allowance of an annual exclusion for lifetime gifts, failure to include postgift appreciation in the estate tax base, and ability to avoid grossing-up gift taxes on gifts made more than three years before death. To this group we may now include another factor, one whose tax saving potential rests on the ability to obtain valuation discounts for certain gifts made during lifetime but not at death.

> EXAMPLE VD-1 Fiore owns 100 percent of the stock in a closely held corporation worth $300,000. This year, he gave each of his three children one third of the stock. Taking a twenty five percent minority interest discount on each transfer, Fiore will report on Form 709 three gross gifts of $75,000 (= $100,000 - .25 x $100,000), totaling $225,000. Thus, in addition to saving taxes by taking three annual exclusions, Fiore has reduced his future gross estate by an extra $75,000 (= 3 x ($100,000 - $75,000)). Had Fiore planned instead to bequeath the stock to the children at his death, these minority discounts would not be available.

Revenue rulings have stated that a minority interest will not be disallowed solely because a transferred interest, if combined with interests held by family members, would be part of a controlling interest.[36]

---

35. TAM 9140002.

36. Rev. Rul. 93-12, 1993-7 IRB 13.

Valuation discounts for such gifts are allowed because the gift tax is computed on a *per gift* basis. They are not allowed for deathtime transfers of the same property because the estate tax is computed on *per estate* basis. Thus, valuation discounts create a fourth instance of imperfect unification.

Control premium. Fairly recently, case law has come to recognize that a fractional interest in property can actually be worth *more* than its proportional share.[37] For example, the value of a 51 percent interest in a particular closely held firm has been ruled to be worth greater than 51% of that firm, reflecting a premium in value for the benefit of majority controlling interest. In one case a decedent owned about 52 percent of voting stock in a corporation which gave him, among other things, the power to elect all directors. The court approved a 38 percent control premium, raising the value of the decedent's interest from $372,152 to $514,000.[38]

Thus, the control premium is essentially the `flip side' of the minority discount. While including property subject to a control premium in the gross estate will ordinarily increase FET, careful planning can actually reduce FET, to the extent that the majority interest is bequeathed to the surviving spouse.

> EXAMPLE CP-1 Anderson was the sole owner of a $1 million closely held corporation. At his death, he bequeathed 51% of the stock to his surviving widow and 49% to his son. In connection with this business interest, based on a control premium of 10%, Anderson's gross estate will include $1 million, and his marital deduction will include $561,000 (= 110% of 51% of $1 million). The control premium has reduced Anderson's taxable estate by $51,000.

In community property states, control premiums can not apply to community held stock since neither spouse can have majority control.

Lack of Marketability Discount for Business Interests

Due to lack of an established market, restricted stock, stock in a closely held business, and partnership interests are invariably more difficult to sell than business stock that is publicly traded.[39] Thus, discounts for lack of

---

37. *Estate of Chenowith v. Commissioner* 88 T.C. 1577 (1987).

38. *Estate of Salsbury v. Commissioner* 34 T.C. Memo (CCH) 1441 (1975).

39. For a discussion of two liquidity problems related to publicly held stock (blockage and restricted stock), see Chapter 16.

marketability ranging from 15 to as high as 50 percent for lack of marketability are obtainable, and apply to both minority and majority interests. Factors influencing the size of the discount include extent of resale restrictions and SEC restraints on marketability, size and dollar value of the stock, the firm's growth expectations, and size of the company's total assets and equity.

Use of minority interest and lack of marketability discounts can leverage the benefit of the gift tax annual exclusion.

> EXAMPLE LM-1 Crabb gives his daughter a $20,000, two percent interest in his $1 million closely held business. After applying minority interest and lack of marketability discounts, the value of Crabb's reportable gross gifts should be less than $10,000.

Some courts have allowed taxpayers both a minority discount and a lack of marketability discount, while others have collapsed the two into one discount. Whether collapsed or not, a combined discount of 30 to 40 percent is generally considered safe.

Fractional Interest Discount for Real Property

Undivided interests in real property can generate a fractional interest discount because they are neither easily partitioned nor readily marketable. In addition, they may be noncontrolling.

> EXAMPLE FI-1 Jones died owning a 58% interest in common in real property that was leased. His estate was allowed a 15% fractional interest discount.[40]

The fractional interest discount for real property, strongly opposed by the IRS, is analogous to the minority interest and lack of marketability discounts for stock. The IRS has taken the position that the only discount allowed should be the cost of a partition action.[41] It should be noted, however, that the problem of control premiums in real estate can not arise because all realty owners must agree about significant property decisions.

Other Valuation Discounts

Worth mentioning briefly are three other valuation discounts.

---

40. *Smythe v. U.S.* 86-1 U.S. Tax Cases (CCH)

41. See TAM 9336002.

- Securities, even those publicly traded, that are subject to special *securities laws restrictions* can be discounted. Restrictions include lack of registration, and the need to sell the stock by private placement.
- Large quantities of a stock listed on an exchange can receive a *blockage discount* if its sale all at one time could have a depressing effect on the market price. However, if the block represents a controlling interest in the corporation, possibly triggering an even higher price, a *premium* may be attached to its value. Blockage discounts may be available for other property, such as a large number of paintings left in the estate of a prominent artist.[42]
- A discount may be allowed for a business that lost a *key person* (e.g., the decedent) who was responsible for its good will.

Valuation discounts can generate liquidity by reducing the value of property subject to transfer tax, thereby saving transfer taxes.

FAMILY LIMITED PARTNERSHIPS

Family limited partnerships (FLPs) have been used by families in agricultural areas for decades as a means of getting children involved in running the ranch or farm, but only recently have they become a popular planning tool for any family run business. FLPs offer many attractive estate planning advantages over most other business forms and transfer devices. However, due to the costs of establishing them and appraisal costs associated with making multiple transfers of the limited partnership interests they usually are not recommended unless the parents owning the business have a net wealth in excess of two or three million dollars. For those that qualify, an FLP has numerous advantages: (1) the parents can give away wealth and still retain control; (2) transfers can be made at substantial discounts as compared to the value of underlying assets, thus saving unified credit and gift taxes; (3) restrictions can be placed on transfers by children; and (4) there is some protection from creditors.

Family partnerships are sanctioned by IRC with certain requirements set forth in §704(e). Among other things, the income and tax benefits must be distributed or allocated according to each owner's percentage in the partnership. The general partners may be paid for their personal services

---

42. *G.O'Keeffe Estate* TC ¶12,886(M) (50 percent blockage discount allowed).

to the partnership. Also, capital must be "a material income-producing factor." A family partnership cannot be used to redistribute income generated from personal services by the general partner.

Establishing a Family Limited Partnership. To establish a family limited partnership one must follow the requirements of the state's limited partnership act, which will probably require publication of the names of the general partner and the limited partners. The Uniform Limited Partnership Act requires that there be at least one general partner and one limited partner. With an FLP, one, or both parents, serve as the general partner. They may start by owning all but a very small portion of the limited partnership units. Over time the parents transfer by gift a significant portion of the limited partnership units to the children. Given the wealth of the parents, it is unlikely that this transfer can be accomplished utilizing gifts covered by annual exclusions alone; thus to make this work usually requires using up both parents' unified credit, and perhaps even incurring some gift taxes.

Under unusual circumstances, such as the death or bankruptcy of the general partner, most limited partnership agreements give the limited partners the right to elect a new general partner. As with most real estate limited partnerships a limited partner cannot take assets from the partnership or otherwise force liquidation of the partnership before its term is up. The term is likely to be set at 50 years, however once both general partners are dead, a vote by the limited partners could liquidate the partnership. Whether this would take a super majority depends upon the terms of the partnership agreement.

FLP Costs. The major cost are attorney's fees to establish the partnership, probably between $2,000 to $7,000 depending on the nature of the business assets, and appraisal fees to establish both the underlying value and the appropriate discounts, probably in the range of $5,000 to $15,000. In addition, when partnership shares are transferred as gifts, an appraisal will again have to be made. This is one reason that the parents should consider large initial gifts right after the partnership is established, however, subsequent appraisal fees by the same appraisal firm should be considerably lower than the first ones, since the company will be familiar with the business. There will also be annual accounting fees for preparation of the partnership returns and the K1s that must be distributed to all partners. The state may also charge an annual fee for the right to do business as a limited partnership in the state.

Discounts. The two types of valuation discounts discussed earlier in the chapter play a significant role, limited partnership units can be transferred at a huge discount because the units have limited marketability, being a business enterprise closely held by just a handful of owners, and the owners of limited partnership units have extremely limited control since the general partners manage the partnership assets.

> EXAMPLE FLP-1: The Jackson family wants to create a family limited partnership with Jack and Lilly Jackson as general partners. The net value of their combined estates is $17,600,000 which includes their ranch valued at $9,000,000. The limited partnership interests will represent 95% of the total value of the ranch, the other 5% being allocated to the general partnership interest. The limited partnership portion will be divided into 95 limited partnership units. This year the parents wish to transfer 20 units to each of their three children. If the lack of marketability discount is 30% and the minority interest discount is 25%, then the transfer of each 20 unit share to a child results in the following gift:

> Calculation: $9,000,000 *.70 *.75*.20 = $945,000
> [FMV ranch x (1 - .3) x (1 - .25) x .20 = discounted value of the share]

> Each gift is from both parents, therefore both unified credits are used and each is entitled to two annual exclusions, making the total taxable transfers from each parent $1,387,500 [3 * (945,000/2) - $10,000)]. The total gift tax for both parents is $629,250. The Jacksons have removed 60% [$5,400,000 at FMV] of the ranch to their children. Because of the size of their combined estate, assuming the plan calls for postponing all estate taxes until the second death, the estate of the last parent to die will be in the 60% marginal rate bracket. If that death occurs at least three years after the gifts so as to avoid grossing up, the discounted transfers and the reduction of the estate by the gift taxes paid will have saved total transfer taxes of $2,110,425.

Tax on $17,000,000 [S1's bypass holds $600,000]	$9,148,000
Tax on $11,570,750 [17,600,000 - 5,400,000 - 629,250]	$6,408,225
Plus gift taxes on the two gifts	$ 629,250
Total transfer taxes	$7,037,575
Taxes saved	$2,110,425

In addition, any postgift appreciation escapes estate taxes.

Appraisals. Despite numerous attempts by the IRS to disallow discounts in a family setting, it has lost numerous times in the tax court and finally conceded the existence of the discounts, provided the client can back them up by creditable professional appraisals using current market data for the discounts. These discount appraisals are in addition to the appraisal of the underlying assets owned by the partnership.

Ability to control gifted assets. In addition to the discounts, the most attractive feature of the FLP is the ability of the donor to retain control over the assets. While key rights of a limited partner must be recognized, the general partner maintains all the managerial control over the partnership assets, determining when and whether to make income distributions to all the partners or to reinvest the income into additional assets. For most wealthy clients, the biggest roadblocks to making substantial gifts are the donor's reluctance to lose control of his or her business, or other important valuable assets, and concern about how well the donee-children will use the gifts. The control offered to the parent-general partner makes this an acceptable vehicle to give assets now, especially when one can utilize the tax benefits of valuation discounts and low values on appreciating assets.

Getting the children involved. Once the children have a vested interest in the business they should take a greater interest in how it works. Annual reports must be given to all partners and formal partnership meetings with all the family partners present are a good time to discuss the family investments and why they performed well or poorly. To avoid having the children liable as though general partners, they cannot be involved in the actual management of the business and they must not appear to outsiders as general partners.

Using the children's lower tax brackets. One benefit of a family limited partnership is that it is possible to shift income into the lower tax brackets of the children. This applies to the percentage interest the child actually owns in the partnership. When a parent is in the 39.6% federal income tax bracket, this can make a significant difference if the child is only in the 15% tax bracket. For children under 14, however, they will be subject to the kiddie tax[43] for annual unearned income over $1,300 and thus subject to the parents' higher tax brackets.

Protection against failed marriages of children. One nice protection is the assets can be held as the separate property of each of the children. While the income distributed is usually commingled with the child's other assets, the partnership interest is usually clearly identified as the child's separate property. In community property states, only the community property is divided in a divorce proceeding, and while everything is presumed to be community property unless it can be traced to a gift, an inheritance, or to property owned prior to the marriage, it should be easy to establish the units as gifts, therefore, they can stay in the family. Of course, the child can change them into joint tenancy or into community property by written agreement with his or her spouse.

Loss of step-up in basis on gifted assets. One disadvantage in gifting

---

43. Discussed in Chapter 8.

assets is the donees (the children) lose the ability to get a step up in basis at the death of the parent of the part of the partnership that was given to the children. When the assets have a very low tax basis, this can reduce the tax benefits of the family limited partnership. Of course, if the children do not intend to sell the business, then the low basis is a price worth paying to avoid the transfer tax costs.

Limited asset protection. Often touted is the FLP's asset protection capabilities. It is true that limited partnership units given several years before the parents have financial difficulty should not be subject to levy by the parents' creditors. Most states have some form of fraudulent transfers act that allows creditors to attach property transferred by debtors for inadequate consideration when such transfer takes place in the face of mounting financial pressure, however, if sufficient time has passed, the parent is generally the only one liable to his or her personal creditors, and as general partner the only one liable to the creditors of the partnership.

In the past, creditors of limited partners collected by using a court issued *charging order* that allows creditors to collect the money distributed to a partner. Unfortunately for the creditor, the partnership income tax liability of the partner whose interest was seized was also passed on to the creditor. All limited partners must be treated the same insofar as distributions are concerned, and those distributions are controlled by the general partner. The idea in using the FLP as an asset protection device has been to starve out a creditor by not making distributions even though FLP profits force the limited partners and the creditor with the charging order to recognize taxable income. In theory the tax liabilities put the creditor in the mood to greatly discount the debt to avoid additional tax liability. Some recent state court decisions have held that if a charging order, because of the conduct of the general partner, does not allow a reasonable chance for the payment of the debt, the creditor can foreclose on the debtor's partnership interest, forcing the liquidation of some of the underlying assets sufficient to pay the creditor, provided the foreclosure does not unreasonably interfere with the partnership business. If other courts adopt this course, then a charging order can delay the creditors of a child-limited partner but it would eventually allow them to be fully paid by means of foreclosure if the income distributions were being withheld such that the creditors were not being paid timely. The partnership agreement should give the family a first right of refusal for any attempted sale by the limited partners.

If asset protection is crucial to family members involved in a business enterprise, they should consider the newest business organization to gain widespread acceptance, the limited liability company, discussed next.

THE LIMITED LIABILITY COMPANY

The limited liability company (LLC) is strictly a creature of the various state legislatures. Unlike the partnership it does not have common law roots but since the LLC first statute, Wyoming, 1977, almost every state has adopted one, bringing the total to 46 states and the District of Columbia. Legislation is pending in Hawaii, Massachusetts, Pennsylvania and Vermont. Why the sudden popularity? When done correctly, it offers business owners the chance to have the limited liability of a corporation but for the tax to pass through advantages of a partnership. Each owner-investor is called a *member* and his or her ownership share is called a *membership interest*.

Creating an LLC. Of course one must comply with the state statute. But one must also consider the IRS rules concerning taxation of business entities. Regardless of state law, for federal income tax purposes an entity will be taxed as a corporation if it has *more than four* of the six characteristics of a corporation. Those characteristics are:

1. Associates or co-owners
2. Intent to make a profit & divide income
3. Continuity of life
4. Centralized management
5. Entity alone liable for business debts
6. Ownership interests freely transferrable

Since the LLC is made up of co-owners intent on making a profit, and since the point of the LLC is to limit liability, three of the chacteristics are already in place. It is easy to avoid at least two of the other three by limiting the life of the LLC to a definite, even if long, term of years, restricting the sale of the membership interests by requiring they be offered first to the entity and next to the other members before a sale can take place to an outside third party, and requiring that all members agree on significant management decisions. The latter will work well for businesses with only two or three owners. If the owners intend to take on additional members it would be best to put a definite term into the agreement and restrict transferrability.

Advantages compared to corporations. Both LLCs and corporations enjoy limited liability for the owners. An owner is liable only for torts in which he or she is actually involved. If one drives the company car on business and causes an accident in which others are injured, only the business and the owner-driver are liable. Other co-owners are not. Furthermore, none of the co-owners are liable for contracts entered into in the company's name. Of course, for either of these business forms the owners may be asked to personally guarantee certain contracts, such as leases and loans, which will create personal liability but contractual liability is not characteristic of these two business forms. LLCs have the single level of taxation at the membership level. Of course, S corporations also have this characteristic, but LLCs do not have the restrictions on stock ownership that S corporations have. Trusts, foreign individuals, and other corporations can be members. Although LLCs are most likely to be closely held, there is no restriction on the number of owners, whereas federal law limits to 35 the number of S corporation shareholders. S corporations are limited to one class of stock whereas LLCs can have membership interests with different rights such as income, capital preferences, or voting.

Advantages compared to partnerships. Both share the advantage of single level taxation but partnerships have the disadvantage of all partners being fully liable for all contracts taken in the partnership name and any torts that arise out of the partnership business whether committed by other partners or by partnership employees. Both allow withdrawal of assets, subject to the partnership or LLC agreement, without such withdrawals being deemed income. Of course, withdrawals do affect the owners' capital accounts. Some states require LLCs to pay some minimal annual fee (less than $1,000) whereas general partnerships are not charged any fees.

Advantages compared to limited partnerships. The advantages and disadvantages are similar to those stated for the general partnership, except limited partners enjoy limited liability. Unlike LLCs the limited partnerhsip must have at least one person, the general partner, exposed to unlimited personal liabilty. Furthermore, limited partners must not be involved in the day to day management of the partnership or they will lose their limited liability insofar as third parties rely on their appearance as general partners in extending credit to the partnership.

Disadvantages. Not all states presently have LLC statutes, although that will probably cease to be a disadvantage within the next year or two as the last four states are considering adoption of LLC statutes. There is considerable variation among the LLC statutes already adopted.

OTHER LIQUIDITY SOURCES

Two other sources of liquidity to the estates of both nonbusiness and business owners also deserve brief mention.

Employee Retirement Benefits

As an employee, the client may have accumulated substantial retirement benefits on the job. If some of these benefits are payable after the client's death, the estate or the employee's spouse could be made beneficiary to provide a degree of needed liquidity.[44]

Postmortem Liquidity Planning Techniques

There are a host of techniques that can be undertaken after death over which the client has little or no control during lifetime. Postmortem devices, such as disclaimers and the alternate valuation date election, will be examined in Chapter 18, which surveys postmortem tax planning.

This chapter has examined the planning for liquidity. Chapter 16 will present the principles of planning for the closely held business.

---

44. For a discussion of FET planning for retirement benefits, see Chapter 12.

QUESTIONS AND PROBLEMS

1. How will the following factors influence liquidity needs at death?
   a. Size of the family estate.
   b. Whether the decedent is S1 or S2.
   c. Age of the family members.

2. "High-basis assets make desirable assets for a predeath sale designed to generate liquidity." True, false or uncertain? Explain.

3. (a)What traits distinguish cash value insurance from term insurance? (b) Universal life insurance from other types of cash value insurance?

4. Is life insurance ever subject to income taxation? Explain.

5. Explain the two primary ways in which life insurance can be subject to gift taxation.

6. Life insurance can be subject to estate taxation under §§2001, 2033, 2042, and 2035. Briefly explain the application of each.

7. Who, if anyone, should be the *insured* of a policy designed to provide liquidity to a family estate of $250,000, assuming the following alternative facts?
   a. Spouses in their 30s; husband working; wife at home with two young children.
   b. Spouses in their 30s; both working; no children.
   c. Spouses in their 50s; both working; children are self-supporting adults living elsewhere.
   d. Single adult; no children.
   e. Single parent of one six-year old child.
   f. Retired couple; self-supporting adult children living elsewhere.

8. Reanswer part a, d, and f of Question 7, assuming instead a $2 million family estate owned by spouses who wish to set up a credit shelter bypass plan. In each case, would it matter how liquid the family wealth was?

9. What factors influence the selection of the owner and primary and contingent beneficiary of an insurance policy on the life of a spouse in a small family estate situation?

10. (*a*) Describe the characteristics of the irrevocable life insurance trust. (*b*) What are its advantages?

11. A rich client of yours is about to acquire life insurance on his life and is thinking of naming his wife owner and beneficiary. They each own $1 million. Advise him.

12. Would any of your answers to Question 11 change if the family estate size was $800,000? Why or why not?

13. Five years ago, Mary assigned ownership of an insurance policy on the life of her husband, Bud, to the trustee of Bud's living trust. The trustee is beneficiary, and terms of the trust provide that at Bud's death Mary is entitled to a life estate in the trust income. If Mary survives Bud, could there be an estate tax problem?

14. April, age 40, is a recently divorced single mother of two young children. She is not on friendly terms with her ex-husband who, in her opinion, is a "selfish spendthrift." April owns few assets, and asks your estate planning advice to help achieve her goal of financial security for her children.

15. Great-Aunt Rachel is dying. She has a taxable estate of $2 million. Using the salient facts found in Example 6312-1 in the chapter, calculate the net benefit or cost to the estate of purchasing $100,000 in flower bonds. Assume the same 3% earnings differential. (Answer: Net benefit = $1,478.)

16. As an alternative method of solving the problem posed in Question 15 above, assume instead that the attorney-in-fact purchases 3 ½ percent Treasury bonds maturing on November 15, 1998, for the "asked" price listed in *The Wall Street Journal* (can be located using the index on the first page under "Treasury issues") published on the most recent Monday prior to the date this assignment is due. Assume the same 3% earnings differential.

17. How are the arrangements based on §§6166, 303, and 2032A each designed to provide estate liquidity?

18. At his death recently, Silva owned a successful farm, which, over the years, continued to be approached by an expanding metropolitan area. As a farm, the land is worth $350,000, but a real estate developer is now willing to pay Silva's estate $1,200,000 for it. If the rest of the estate amounts to $400,000, what should Silva's total gross estate be if the property (*a*) does not qualify, and (*b*) does qualify for special use valuation?

19. Minnie and Mark, both age 68, are married parents of two adult children, Betty and Bryan. They own a $500,000 interest in a closely held business and $100,00 in other assets. Betty pretty much runs the business and would like to continue to do so after her parents are gone. Bryan has no interest in owning or running the business. If Minnie and Mark wish to leave all their property equally to their children after their own deaths, is there a distribution problem? Can life insurance help solve it?

RECOMMENDED READING

Apfel, Kenneth S. & Brenda J. Rediess-Hoosein. "Special-Use Valuation Covers Business, as Well as Farm, Realty." *Estate Planning*, March, 1993, pp. 99-106.

Aucutt, Ronald D & Catherine V. Hughes. "Irrevocable Life Insurance Trusts Still Have Planning Possibilities After TAMRA", *Journal of Taxation*, Oct., 1989, pp 258-67.

*Beehler, John M. "IRS Action Makes it Easier to Keep Proceeds Out of an Insured's Gross Estate." *Journal of Taxation*, November, 1991, pp. 284-87.

Beiser, Scott L. "How To Make Estate Planning Less Taxing Under Chapter 14," *1992 UCLA/CEB Estate Planning Institute.*

Bieck, Erik E. & Bradford P. Bauer. "Life Insurance Trust Can Maximize the Generation-Skipping Tax Exemption," *Estate Planning*, January, 1991, pp. 36-41.

Billion, Michael M. "Saving Estate Taxes Through Special Use Valuation," *Taxation For Accountants*, September, 1993, pp 142-48.

Black Jr., Kenneth & Harold D. Skipper Jr. *Life Insurance*, 12 ed., Englewood Cliffs, NJ: Prentice-Hall, 1994.

Blake, John F. "Current Approaches to Avoiding Estate Tax Where Insured Dies within Three Years," *Estate Planning*, November 1986, pp. 246-48.

Blase, James. "Structuring Insurance Trusts to Avoid Estate Inclusion Under Section 2035," *Journal of Taxation*, March 1985, pp.154-159.

Blattmachr, Jonathan G., and Douglas J. Blattmachr. "Determining If Flower Bonds Are Warranted for a Client's Estate, and How Much to Buy." *Estate Planning*, September 1986, pp. 264-68.

Bloethe, Orville W. "Special Use Valuation: $$ Savings for the Family Farm - But for Others, Land Mines and Pot Holes," *1992 University of Miami Estate Planning Institute.*

*Brand, Ronald A., and William P. LaPiana. "Using Disclaimers Add More Flexibility to Escape Clauses for Taxable Insurance." *Estate Planning*, September 1986, pp.278-81.

Brody, Lawrence, "Putting A Premium on Generation-Skipping Transfer Tax Planning--The Use of Life Insurance" *University of Miami Institute on Estate Planning*, 1989.

*Caudill, William H. and James T. Budyak, "New IRS Position On Valuation May Result In Reduced Marital And Charitable Deductions," *Journal of Taxation*, September, 1993, pp 176-79.

Chandler, Darlene K. "The Irrevocable Life Insurance Trust and Section 2035: New Guideposts to Effective Planning," *C.L.U. Journal*, July 1987, pp.52-55.

Chandy, P.R., and Sharon Garrison. "Planning for Death with Flowers," *Journal of the Institute of Certified Financial Planners*, Fall 1986, pp. 187-91.

Chasman, Herbert. "Life Insurance As an Estate and Financial Planning Tool," University of Miami 22nd Annual Estate Planning Institute, 1988. An excellent summary of the characteristics of universal life, variable life, single premium life, and other insurance products.

*Chazan, Michael J. "Insurance Policy May be an Ideal Asset for a Gift by the Insured." *Estate Planning*, September, 1992, pp. 294-304.

Christensen, Burke A. "The Unfunded, Irrevocable Life Insurance Trust," *Trust and Estates*, March 1984, pp.72-73.

Davis, Herbert J., and Donald R. Dann, "Life Insurance in the '80s," *Trust and Estates*, July 1984, 23-28.

Dougherty, William M. "Basis of Inherited Property is Not Always Date of Death Value," *Taxation For Accountants*, January, 1992, pp. 17-22.

Gallo, Jon J. "Life Insurance Trusts Offer Tax Savings And Liquidity", *Taxation For Accountants*, June, 1993, pp 324-32

Gibbs, Larry W. "Do You Speak Tax, Mr. Appraiser? Evaluating the Appraiser and the Appraisal Report After 1990." *1993 University of Miami Estate Planning Institute*.

Gorfinkle, Robert A. "Many Choices Available to Owner Wishing to Transfer Business to Younger Family Members." *Estate Planning*, March 1986, pp. 98-103.

*Griffin, Mark E., "Taxation of Accelerated Benefits Under A Life Insurance Contract," *Journal Of The American Society Of CLU & ChFC*, July, 1993, pp 38-44.

Grudzinski, Chester W., and Steven E. Eisenberg, "Coordinating 303's Redemption Benefits with the Estate Tax Deferral Rules of 6166," *Taxation for Accountants*, July 1984, pp.32-36.

Holdmann, Lee F. "Income and Estate Planning Advantages of Life Insurance Enhanced by TRA 86 Changes," *Estate Planning*, May 1987, pp. 130-36.

Horn, Jerold I. "Proper Form of Life Insurance Gift Can Improve Tax Savings Significantly," *Estate Planning*, September 1981, pp. 258-266.

Jensen, David E., and Robert O. Smith. "How to Determine Whether Proposed Life Insurance Makes Economic and Tax Sense for a Client," *Taxation for Accountants*, December 1985, pp. 350-56.

*Kinskern, Douglas. "Two Career Families Causing Significant Changes in Estate Planning for Younger Couples." *Estate Planning*, March 1988, pp. 92-98.

Kiziah, Trent S. "Deferring Estate Tax is Not Always a Beneficial Move." *Estate Planning*, January, 1993, pp. 12-19.

Koenig, Rodney C. & Judith Williams. "Marital Deduction Loss for Noncitizens Provides Life Insurance Opportunities," *Journal of American Society of CLU & ChFC,* May, 1991, pp. 66-70.

*Korn, Terry H & James R. Hitchner, "Valuing Indirectly Held Real Estate Has Special Concerns" *Estate Planning*, July, 1993, pp 234-40.

*LeVan, Gerald. "Passing the Family Business to the Next Generation-Resolving Family Conflicts." University of Miami 22nd Annual Estate Planning Institute, 1988.

Lew, Harry J. "Buyer's Market" Financial planning, May 1988, pp.79-83. (Describes the evolution of term life insurance products since the early 1970s.)

"Life Insurance-How to Protect Your Family." *Consumer Reports*, June, July, and August 1986 issues. Three-part series.

Lowe, Henry T. "Combining Life Insurance Proceeds With Other Estate Assets," *Missouri Law Review*, Vol. 47 (1982), pp.661-692.

Low, Anthony, "Adverse Income and Estate Tax Consequences of Split Dollar Life Insurance can be Avoided," *Estate Planning*, May, 1990, pp. 150-55.

Lyons, Philip J. "Factors to Analyze in Selecting a Second-to-Die Life Insurance Policy." *Estate Planning* May, 1991, pp. 166-71.

*Maislin, Stephen D. "Liquidity Planning for Shareholders of Public Corporations." *Estate Planning*, March, 1993, pp. 91-98.

*Maurer, David V. "Irrevocable Life Insurance Trusts: Good Business For Banks?" *Trusts & Estates*, May, 1992, pp 24-32.

Meltzer, Alan L. "Implications of Survivorship Whole Life in Estate Planning," *Trust and Estates*, August 1984, pp.48-50.

Mering, Donald R. "Combination of Charitable Remainder and Insurance Trusts Can Increase Wealth," *Estate Planning*, November, 1990, pp. 350-62.

Millar, Sanford I. "Life Insurance for the Closely Held Business." In *The Closely Held Business: Financial Planning for the Owners*, 1986, Practising Law Institute, pp. 139-226.

Oliney, Dan. "Flower Bonds: Are the Flowers Wilting?" *Estate Planning & Probate News*, Winter 1985, p.9.

Paik, Soo Bong. "Estate Tax Deferral: An Assessment," *UCLA Law Review* 29 (1982), pp.642-660.

Paola, Suzanne. "New Policies: Many Insurance Agencies are Favorably Poised to Begin Offering Planning Services, but the Transition to this More Service-Oriented Outlook may Drastically Change the Way they Look and Feel," *Financial Planning*, February 1985, pp.110-114.

Petrie, Linda C. "Increasing the Liquidity of an Estate Involves Combination of Pre- and Death Planning," *Estate Planning*, March 1984, pp.98-103.

*Plaine, Lloyd Leva. "The Million Dollar Question Under the Generation-Skipping Transfer Tax." *1990 University of Miami Estate Planning Institute*.

Price, John R. "Life Insurance: New Products--Old Problems." *1986 Southern California Tax and Estate Planning Forum.*

Resnick, Joel. "Application of Incidents of Ownership Test to Life Insurance Trusts." *Wayne Law Review* 27 (Spring 1981), pp. 1151-99.

Sawyer, W. Whitney. "Irrevocable Life Insurance Trust Offers Tax Savings, Liquidity at Small Cost to Flexibility," *Estate Planning*, March 1981, pp.72-81.

Shechtman, Richard G. "New Concepts in Life Insurance Planning: Universal Life," *Cumberland Law Review*, Vol. 13 (1982), pp.219-237.

Schlesinger, Sanford J. "How to Get the Maximum Benefit Out of Life Insurance." *The Practical Accountant*, October 1986, pp.97-104.

*_____ & S. Timothy Ball. "Exploring Joint Lives Life Insurance Policies." *Trusts and Estates*, March, 1992, 34-37.

Shaw, Randall L. "Universal Life Insurance--How it Works." *American Bar Association Journal* 71 (February 1985),pp. 68-70.

Spewak, Steven B., and Bennett S. Keller. "Deferral Can Still Be Combined with Corporate Redemptions to Provide Liquidity, Tax Benefits," *Estate Planning*, September 1987, pp., 296-301.

*Staudt, Keith. "First-to-Die Life Insurance: An Analysis of Ownership Issues." *Journal of the American Society of CLU & ChFC*, September, 1992, pp. 56-62.

Switzer Jr., Ralph V., Marion W. Larson, & Marlaine Mitteldorf. "Recent Rulings, Regulations and Cases Affect Alternate Valuation," *Taxes - The Tax Magazine*, August, 1990, pp. 607-14.

Windsor, Jr, John R. "Split Dollar Insurance In S And Closely Held Corporations," *Trusts & Estates*, September, 1993, p 45.

*Zaritsky, Howard, "Life Insurance Trusts In The 90s-- Dealing With The Newest Types of Policies," *1994 University of Miami Estate Planning Institute.* Covers trust planning for second to die and first to die policies.

Planning for Closely Held Business Interests

OVERVIEW

A closely held business is a firm privately owned by one or a few individuals who actively participate in its management. Unique estate planning problems can arise for owners of a closely held business. Typically, the firm generates the major source of its owner's *income* and represents the single largest part of his or her *family wealth*. Too often, however, the firm can sustain or increase that level of income and value only if the owners continue to be actively involved in its management. For example, a nondividend-paying closely held corporation is rarely in a position to start paying a dividend after the client-owner dies.

This income and value can be jeopardized by two events, each of which is certain to occur. First, each owner's *involvement* with the firm is destined to end, and the enterprise will lose his or her economic contribution. Second, the ownership interest in the business must eventually be *transferred*, subjecting it to transfer costs, including taxes.

Estate planning seeks to minimize the adverse impact of these significant events by attempting to achieve four basic objectives:

1. To generate sufficient *income* for the owner and the owner's family after the owner's active involvement in the business ends.
2. To transfer to the owner's chosen beneficiaries the maximum *value* attributable to that business.
3. To minimize the *costs* of transferring the business interest to the owner's chosen beneficiaries.
4. To provide sufficient *liquidity* to pay the transfer costs.

This chapter will focus on how closely held business interests accomplish these goals.

*Publicly*held corporations require far less attention. Their owners can more easily accomplish these objectives, for two reasons. First, withdrawal of any one owner will usually have a far less depressing effect on business value and income, making continuity more assured. Publicly traded firms usually employ far more personnel, making business success much less dependent on the efforts of any one individual. In contrast, studies indicate that only 30-35 percent of successful closely held family businesses survive in the second generation, and only 10-20 percent in the third generation. In many cases, this is due primarily to unresolved family conflicts.[1] Second, the goal of liquidity is invariably easier to achieve for owners of publicly held firms because the client's survivors receive readily marketable securities.

However, liquidity problems can arise for wealthier clients owning publicly traded stock that is either a large block, or "restricted" under federal securities law. Large block holdings (i.e., tens of thousands of shares) may give rise to the problem of *blockage*, which is the temporarily depressing effect on the market price that results from selling a large block all at once. While federal tax law will allow some valuation discount for blockage effects, overall liquidity is nonetheless reduced. *Restricted stock* is usually acquired either from an affiliate of the issuing company, or in a private, unregistered transaction. Federal securities law prohibits restricted stock from being sold without either registering it under the Securities Act of 1933, or meeting an exemption from registration. The most common methods of disposing of such stock is by a secondary offering, a private

---

1. For an excellent overview of the unique sociological aspects of families in business, see the LeVan paper cited at the end of Chapter 15.

placement, or by "Rule 144 sales," none of which are simple transactions.[2] Although blockage and restricted stock can constitute significant liquidity problems, their consequences will be felt by a only a handful of estates, and their impact on overall liquidity is not nearly as great as the depressing effect of death or withdrawal of the owner on the value of a closely held business interest.

Thus, the many owners of closely held businesses have relatively unique problems, and this chapter will survey the major principles and techniques of estate planning devoted to assisting them. The chapter will first present an overview of general planning in this area, and then examine in greater detail the business buyout agreement, the corporate recapitalization and the partnership capital freeze.

PLANNING IN GENERAL FOR CLOSELY HELD BUSINESS INTERESTS

All estate planning for closely held business interests is premised on the fact that the client-owner cannot carry on forever. As mentioned, we are certain of the occurrence of two future events: that the client's active *involvement* in the management of the firm will terminate, and that the client's *ownership* interest will have to be transferred. Since these events have major economic implications for the four objectives mentioned earlier, we shall begin with a further discussion of them.

Withdrawal from the Firm: Minimizing Decline in Income and Value

Client-owners have the ability to choose when to terminate their active management of the firm. Some elect to remain active until disability or death. The rest withdraw sooner, for any number of reasons, including the desire to adopt a new lifestyle, to consume more of the wealth that time and hard work have created, and to step aside to provide a business opportunity for a son or daughter. No matter when the client plans to withdraw, if the departure is expected to reduce the value and income derived from the business, the client can take several steps to minimize the decline.

---

2. For an excellent description of these techniques, see the Maislin article cited at the end of the Chapter.

Delegate responsibility. First, the owner can plan early to "share the entrepreneurial spirit" by passing on knowledge of the business and by delegating greater and greater responsibility to those who one day may be able to replace his or her contribution. To provide an *incentive* to assume this responsibility, the business can contribute to certain tax-favored fringe benefit plans, including medical insurance contracts, group term life insurance, and retirement plans. In general, contributions to these plans are income tax deductible by the firm and are either tax free or tax deferred to the employee.

Execute contracts for future income. Second, the owner can use current business value to raise his or her own future *income* by executing certain *contracts*, such as a nonqualified deferred compensation plan, disability income insurance, and a qualified retirement plan. Nonqualified deferred compensation is a custom-tailored agreement under which the employer agrees to pay the employee in the future for services rendered presently. Tax law ordinarily permits the income tax to be similarly deferred. The professional athlete, a person with a brief but often lucrative career, is a frequent party to the deferred compensation contract.

Freeze the estate. Third, the firm may be able to undertake a corporate recapitalization or create a partnership capital freeze. These are intricate transfer devices which, in addition to sustaining value and income, can *reduce transfer taxes*. Each can offer additional employment incentives to family members, and each may be able to freeze the value of the client's interest in the business, and still continue to provide him or her with rights to substantial income and voting power in the business affairs. However, as we shall see later, recent tax legislation has severely restricted their potential value, and the client should be advised to seek expert tax counsel when exploring these techniques.

Maintain a list of instructions. Fourth, the client can place in a safe deposit box a list of business instructions for the surviving family. The list could include recommendations as to whether to sell the firm or continue running it, the name of the chosen successor, a list of business advisors, and the location of key company documents. These arrangements can reduce stress and risk of failure, particularly after the sudden death of the client-owner.

Execute a buyout contract. Finally, if no amount of planning can be expected to prevent substantial postwithdrawal depreciation in the value and income derived from the business, the client might consider, while still active, selling or negotiating a contract for future sale of the business prior to the onset of that depreciation. This latter alternative will be explored in some detail shortly.

In summary, by planning early, the client can usually take one or more significant steps to forestall a large decline in the future income from, and the value of, interests that will pass to his or her chosen beneficiaries.

Transferring the Business Interest

As well as minimizing the decline in business value resulting from withdrawal from the firm, the client will want to choose *when* and *to whom* to transfer the business interest. Planning for the transfer will depend in large part on whether the client wishes to transfer the equity interest itself to a family member, or whether the client intends to sell it to a nonrelated party and later transfer the sale proceeds to the chosen beneficiaries. The next two sections will probe these alternatives.

Transfer of an equity interest to a family member. Some clients will want to make a transfer of some or all of the business to a particular family member who is willing and able to take over its management. Many transfer devices are available, and the most common ones are discussed next.

Lifetime strategies. As mentioned earlier, to encourage the family member to adopt a long-term commitment and to prevent deterioration in business value and income, the client should consider starting a program to prepare a family member for eventual ownership and control. In addition to delegating increasing amounts of responsibility, the owner can offer incentives, such as *gifts* of ownership interests in the business, possibly in the form of stock or stock options. The transfers can be outright, or they can be in trust, with the client and family member acting as co-trustees. Transfers into trust can promote a more orderly transition by enabling the client to monitor and develop the family member's interest, abilities, and commitment.

Instead of making a completed gift, the client may wish to arrange a gift-leaseback, installment sale, sale-leaseback, or private annuity. In fact, an installment sale can be a simple, inexpensive, and relatively tax-safe estate freezing alternative to the corporate recapitalization or the partnership capital freeze. The latter two are discussed later in the chapter. In general, most aspects of gifts and other transfers of business interests can be analyzed in a manner similar to lifetime transfers of business interests that are not closely held. The reader is referred to Chapters 13 and 14 for greater detail.

Deathtime strategies. Instead of making a lifetime gift of the business interest to a family member, the client, to retain complete control, may prefer to delay and pass it on at death. However, there are several drawbacks to making deathtime transfers of closely held business interests.

Liquidity problems. First, estate liquidity problems may arise if a non-spouse survivor winds up owning a relatively illiquid asset having a substantial taxable value. For a discussion of several methods of handling liquidity problems, review the material on liquidity planning in Chapter 15.

> EXAMPLE D1 Keith, a widower, died two years ago, the very successful owner of a business whose going concern value was $6 million. The FET attributable to this value was $3,300,000 (= .55 x $6 million). Due to lack of succession planning, Keith's children were forced to sell the business last month to a competitor for the firm's $3 million liquidation value, with the unfortunate result that the IRS became a larger "beneficiary" than the children.

Unprepared survivors. Second, transfers at death of closely held business interests to unprepared survivors who subsequently decide to carry on the business can generate severe problems. The combined tasks of dealing with grief and assuming new business duties can cause panic, guilt, exhaustion, family squabbles, and finally, failure. Adverse parties such as customers, employees and creditors may be tempted to take advantage of the new owner's naivete. While careful planning can reduce this risk, it cannot entirely eliminate it, particularly if the successors are not very experienced in business. Realistically, only a minority of client-owners will actually plan for this outcome. A 1988 Laventhal & Horwath poll of family business owners found that only 45 percent had selected successors, and only one in three had developed a strategic plan.[3]

Uncertainty and friction. Third, transfers at death of closely held business interests to beneficiaries not involved in the business but who do not intend to sell may be ill-advised if the beneficiaries have no desire to manage the firm. By its nature, the closely held business requires active cooperation among its owners, cooperation which usually requires constant interaction. Unaware of the firm's precise manner of operation, uninvolved owners can precipitate uncertainty and friction among the manager-owners and other employees, especially if they disagree with how the business is being run.

Hard for survivors to sell. Fourth, transferring business interests at death can create problems for surviving transferees who do wish to sell out. In structuring the terms of the sale, survivors will not be able to take advantage of the client's knowledge and experience. The business may no longer be as productive, a fact that could substantially lower the bid price. The bidders may not be willing to pay the surviving beneficiaries a fair value for the client's interest, particularly if it is a minority interest. The

---

3. *Wall Street Journal*, May 7, 1990, p. B1.

survivors will have little bargaining power, in view of both their apparent need for cash and the illiquidity of the interest.

Legal and tax complexities. Fifth, legal and tax complexities may arise. If a client's interest in S corporation stock is to be distributed at death to a trust, such as a bypass or a marital trust, that trust must be designed to qualify as a "Qualified Subchapter S Trust" in order not to jeopardize the corporation's Subchapter S status. Requirements include the naming of only one income beneficiary.[4] Essentially, an S corporation is a corporation that is treated by federal income tax law as if it were a partnership; income is taxed to the individual shareholders rather than to the corporation.[5]

Valuation disputes with IRS. Finally, *disputes with the IRS* over the FET valuation of a closely held business are common and often result in litigation or settlement at higher than expected values. And the Code imposes an FET penalty of 20 percent of the tax underpayment for *valuation understatements* at less than 50 percent of the correct value. The penalty applies only if the additional tax owed exceeds $5,000.[6] A predeath sale can at least more ensure that the owner will be available to intelligently confront the IRS.

For these and many other practical reasons, the client would normally be well-advised not to delay until death the gifting of a business interest to a family member.

Sale to a nonrelated party. Instead of transferring an ownership interest to the surviving beneficiaries, the client could arrange the sale of the business interest to a nonrelated party. Potential buyers include the client's key employees, individual strangers, and other firms, including competitors. In addition to eliminating potential friction, this alternative can yield to the beneficiaries other far more liquid assets (cash or publicly traded stock), assets requiring less income generating effort. The following material explores several aspects of the sale option, including timing and tax effects.

Timing. The business could be sold before or after the client withdraws from active management. *While the client is still active*, the entire firm could be sold outright, or some of its assets could be sold and then leased back to the firm. Or prearrangements could be made to sell the firm when the client withdraws at retirement, disability, or death. Actual timing of the sale will often depend largely on the personal, noneconomic preferences of

---

4. §1361(d)(3).

5. For a discussion of planning with the S Corporation, see the Lang and the Gamble articles cited at the end of the chapter.

6. §6662(a) and (g).

the client. The material below discusses the economic and tax factors influencing that decision.

In general, the greater the expected decline in the value of the firm resulting from the client's withdrawal, the greater the economic motive to sell it while it is still being actively run by the client. Value will fall most for single-owners, especially those offering professional services, such as physicians, accountants, and attorneys. Often, the primary business assets of these firms are the personal customer relationships which, in may cases, are not transferable. Other closely held businesses, such as product-oriented firms and service firms with more than one owner, may be more able to retain their value after departure of the owner-client.

Sale of the business interest prior to the owner's withdrawal will often bring a *higher price* since potential buyers can currently observe that the business is operating successfully under the direction of an active owner-client. Further, the client's astute awareness of the firm's identity and its earnings potential will provide additional bargaining power during the negotiations. And if the sale is completed while the client is alive, the agreement may include an obligation of the new owner to retain the client as an "adviser" or "consultant," as a way of increasing the client's future income. Finally, sale of a closely held business prior to the client's death can minimize unsettling disputes with the IRS over the firm's actual FET fair market value.

In the alternative, the business interest could be sold at or after *the client's withdrawal* from the firm. If the sale is structured in advance to take effect at the client's disability or death, it is called a *business buyout agreement*, an arrangement to be discussed shortly.

Taxable gain. Selling the business for cash prior to the owner's death will give rise to the *immediate recognition* of a taxable gain, unless the transaction is an installment sale or other tax-deferred exchange. On the other hand, transferring the interest at death can eliminate most or all of the taxable gain because of the *step-up* in basis that the interest will receive at death. However, at a maximum tax rate of 28 percent, the tax impact of a predeath sale for cash may turn out to be a reasonable price to pay to achieve substantial estate liquidity, in view of the high costs of alternate liquidity sources, such as insurance on the life of an elderly client. In addition, many commentators expect the Congress to enact a lower maximum rate on capital gains, perhaps down as low as the 20 percent maximum capital gains rate in effect prior to TRA 86.

Form of the transaction. Sale of the business can take one of several forms. It can be for *immediate cash*, either to one or a few individuals, to many individuals, as in a public offering, or to a corporation. It can be in the form of an installment sale with any of these parties, with the client's recognition of the taxable gain spread over the collection period. Or the sale can be for *stock*, in a tax-deferred exchange with a publicly held firm. And the capital gains tax may be eliminated entirely by a step-up in basis if the transfer is after the owner's death.

A common planning device employed to sell a closely held business to one or a few individuals is the *business buyout agreement*, also called a buy-sell agreement, in which the firm, one or more owners, employees, or other parties contract in writing with the client in advance to purchase the client's interest in the business, usually at the client's death or disability. The buyout agreement offers many advantages, including future liquidity, a guaranteed market, and possibly greater certainty over the selling price. Often, the purchase is funded with life and disability insurance.

If a client whose business is not incorporated plans to retain it for an indefinite period, consideration should be given to *incorporating*.[7] Incorporating will generate divisible shares of ownership which may be easier to transfer or liquidate when the need arises. Incorporating will also enhance continuity, since a corporation has an indefinite existence, one that might be more able to survive the client's departure. One disadvantage of forming a typical C corporation is that almost any distribution of corporate property to the shareholders will be taxed to them as dividend income and thus subject to double taxation, once at the corporate level and again to the shareholder. Two exceptions are the §303 redemption to pay death taxes, covered in Chapter 15, and a complete redemption of the deceased shareholder's stock.

The Need for Early Planning

When should planning for closely held business interests begin? For many reasons, planning should begin early, when the client is still active and in good health. First, the client can more clearly express specific estate planning *objectives* at this point, and the client's knowledge and expertise can provide professional planners with greater help in reaching these objectives. Second, the client will be able to take advantage of planning concepts that are available only to *healthy* clients, including relatively inexpensive life

---

7. For a discussion of whether or not to elect "S Corporation" status, see the article by Russell cited at the end of the chapter.

and disability insurance. Third, as implied earlier, if the business will eventually have to be sold, *careful planning* can eliminate the need for a sudden forced sale at the client's incapacity or death, both times when the business, having lost the client's services, is clearly less valuable.

With these general principles in mind, let's examine the specific legal arrangements to which we have been referring.

BUSINESS BUYOUT AGREEMENT

Earlier we learned that placing upon one's survivors the burden of selling the business after the client's death can create problems. These problems can be eliminated or minimized by the client's careful preparation of a business buyout agreement. Executed by the client and one or more prospective purchasers, the buyout agreement obligates the other parties to purchase the interest of the client upon the occurrence of specific future events, such as the client's death and, often, the onset of his or her permanent disability.

Types Of Agreements: Cross Purchase, Entity-Redemption, or Mixed

The three most common types of buyout agreements are distinguished by the identity of the contracting parties. The first type, called the *cross-purchase* agreement, provides that the owners, usually all of them, purchase the interest of a particular owner. In many contracts between owners, a reciprocal type of cross purchase agreement is undertaken, in which each owner agrees to purchase a pro rata share of the interest of any owner that dies. The second type, called the *entity* or *redemption* agreement, has the business itself purchase the interest of one or more owners. The third type, called the *mixed* agreement, usually gives the business an option to purchase an owner's interest, and gives the other owners the option or obligation to purchase the balance. As a hybrid of the other two, the mixed agreement has the characteristics of both cross purchase and entity-redemption, and is often considered the most flexible arrangement.

Taxation of Buyout Agreements

As we shall see, the most critical issues in taxation of buyout agreements arise in the estate tax area.

Gift taxation. Generally, the execution of a buyout agreement does not result in a taxable gift. However, an agreement having a contract price below fair market value will, if it gives a purchaser an unqualified present purchase right.

Income taxation. Income tax effects of buyout agreements will depend on the type of the agreement.

Cross-purchase agreement. The *selling owner*, usually the estate of a decedent-business owner, will be selling a capital asset subject to capital gain treatment. However, in view of the *step-up* in basis at decedent's death, the only recognizable gain will be on any appreciation above FET value. The *buyer's* new basis will be the purchase price of the business interest acquired.

Entity-redemption agreement. The *acquiring business's* new basis will be its purchase price, which is not a tax deductible expense. If the business has been paying premiums on life insurance to fund the arrangement (see below) it will not be allowed a tax deduction for those premiums; they must be paid with after-tax dollars.[8] Further, any cash value buildup on a policy, and any receipt of proceeds, while not includable as ordinary income, may be subject to the alternative minimum tax.[9]

The *selling party*, again usually the decedent-owner's estate, will be taxed on the sale proceeds as a dividend, to the extent of the corporation's earnings and profits. Dividend treatment can be avoided if the sale can qualify for favorable redemption treatment under §302 or §303, both sections permit the redeeming party to treat the sale as a disposition of a capital asset rather than the receipt of a dividend. This means that there will be little or no taxable gain, due to the step up in basis at death. Without this favorable treatment, the entire receipt would be taxable at ordinary income rates.

Mixed agreement. Tax aspects for contracting parties under a mixed agreement follows the patterns mentioned above, to the extent that it takes on the characteristics of both of the other two types.

---

8. §264(a)(1).

9. §56(g)(4)(B). For details and planning suggestions, see the Wolf/Kupferberg article cited at the end of the chapter.

EXAMPLE BO-1 Stan and Oliver, equal owners of a corporation, are trying to decide whether to arrange a cross-purchase or an entity-redemption buyout plan. The adjusted basis of each of their stock in the business is $20,000. They project that the business will be worth $200,000 when the first owner dies. Thus, under either arrangement, the purchase price is expected to be $100,000, and the total value of the surviving owner's stock will equal $200,000, the total value of the business. However, the survivor's basis will be different, depending on which arrangement is selected. If a cross-purchase plan is chosen, the surviving shareholder's basis in his stock will increase to $120,000, which is $20,000, the basis of the preowned stock, plus $100,000, the purchase price of the decedent's stock. Alternatively, if an entity-redemption arrangement is chosen, the basis of the surviving shareholder's stock will remain $20,000, because he will not have purchased any additional shares.

Estate taxation. The deceased owner's gross estate will invariably include some value attributable to the decedent's ownership interest held at the moment of death. Ordinarily, the estate executor will prefer avoiding a dispute with the IRS over this value. One method of avoidance has been to establish a selling price in the buyout agreement that will, by law, *fix the value* for FET purposes. Only half jokingly, one commentator has said that in the absence of a price "set" by a buyout agreement, the "value" of the business can be said to be the amount agreed upon by "a willing IRS agent and a willing executor, neither of whom has ever owned a business."[10]

Agreements prior to §2703. Prior to October 9, 1990, the effective date of §2703, fixing the value of the business for FET purposes was far simpler because case law was quite generous in allowing fixed values that may have been substantially below fair market value. Three valuation methods are commonly included in buyout contracts:

First, a *specific dollar amount* has been specified, with a provision normally made for periodic review so the owners can agree to revise the amount as conditions change. Without provision for a review, if, for example, the value of the business subsequently increased, the purchasing owners would receive a windfall at the expense of the selling owner. Unfortunately, experience has shown that inertia reduces the likelihood of periodic reviews.

Second, the selling price can be determined by *appraisal*, the agreement specifying that a qualifying appraiser will determine the value of the business at the time of sale. The appraisal method has the advantage of ensuring that a current value will be used.

Third, business buyout agreements can use a *formula* method of valuing business interests, preferably with the appropriate formula determined by

---

10. For an excellent article on buyout agreements, see the Adams, et. al. (1993) paper cited at the end of the chapter.

an expert appraiser. Its terms ordinarily call for valuation to be a specified percentage of book value, or a multiple of current earnings. A formula is more flexible and often more accurate than a specific amount, since the derived selling price can vary with economic conditions. However, because a formula is more arbitrary than an appraisal, it may later turn out not to be reflective of current economic conditions.

Impact of §2703. Currently, to fix the FET value of the business equal to the buyout agreement amount, agreements (executed after October 8, 1990) must meet specific statutory requirements under §2703(b)[11] and its final regulations:

1. The agreement must be a *bona fide* business arrangement.
2. The agreement *can not be a device* to transfer property to members of the decedent's family for less than full and adequate consideration in money or money's worth.
3. The terms of the agreement must be *comparable* to similar arrangements entered into by persons in an arm's length transaction.

Some comments on these requirements: The thrust of these requirements is to ensure a value reasonably close to the value of the business interest at the moment of the transfer. Thus, an agreement under which the surviving owner, a son, is obligated to purchase the client's $1 million business interest (current value) for a fixed $300,000 (historical contract value) would be currently labeled a "disguised bequest," and not meet requirements 1 and 2. On the other hand, prices set between nonrelated owners are not usually subject to intense scrutiny by the IRS if the transaction otherwise appears to be made at arm's length. And IRS regulations provide that a buyout agreement will meet all three requirements if more than 50% of the value of the property subject to the agreement is owned by persons who are not "natural objects of the transferor's bounty."[12]

Planners feel that the comparability requirement of item 3 will create considerable uncertainty and additional expense for difficult appraisals, in particular because typical buyout agreements are not public documents. However, for businesses in some industries, agreements may be able to specify a formula, such as a multiple of sales or earnings, if that formula is known to be the predominant valuation method for the industry.

Even though valuation discounts may be available, if valuation is not set

---

11. §2703 is included in Appendix B.

12. Reg. §25.2703-1(b)(3).

for FET purposes, the estate could wind up owing more FET. Anticipating those possibilities, planners heed the §2703 valuation rules carefully, and also suggest that the agreement either require the buyer(s) to pay any additional state and federal death taxes resulting from this problem. Or they recommend including a "savings" clause increasing the selling price to estate tax values, however, such clauses have been ruled against public policy[13] if they are merely an attempt to pass the property to a family member at a below market price.

> EXAMPLE BO-2   Dad's will provided for a credit shelter bypass plan, leaving $600,000 to a bypass trust and the residue of his estate to a marital trust for Mom. Dad executed a business buyout agreement with his son, who was obligated to buy Dad's 1,000 shares of closely held business stock for $1 million. Dad died owning the stock and $800,000 in other property. Son paid Dad's estate $1,000,000 for the stock, and Dad's executor distributed $600,000 in property to the bypass trust and the residue of $1.2 million to the marital trust. After an IRS audit, Dad's executor was agreed that the stock's fair market value was $2 million. Thus, Dad's gross estate totaled $2,800,000. Since only $1.2 million went to Mom, only that amount qualified for the martial deduction, leaving a taxable estate of $1,600,000. This generates estate taxes of $408,000. The additional $1 million is considered as having been left to the son and, in the absence of a clause allocating taxes to the credit shelter trust, he must pay 10/16ths of the tax and the other 6/16ths would be charged to the credit shelter trust. This tax would have been avoided had the buyout agreement provided a more realistic selling price. The figures shown next detail the FET calculations for the two alternatives.

	Selling price of $1 million (actual)	Selling price of $2 million (preferred)
Gross estate$	2,800,000.*	$2,800,000.*
Less:Marital deduction	$1,200,000.**	$2,200,000.***
Gives:Taxable estate	$1,600,000.	$600,000.
Tentative estate tax	$600,800.	$192,800.
Less Unified Credit	$192,800.	$192,800.
Leaves FET	$408,000.	$0.

* $2 mil. [IRS valuation of stock] + 800,000 [other property].

**   "Passing" to Mom = $1 mil. [sale of stock] + $800,000 [other property] - $600,000 to bypass trust.

*** $2 mil. [sale of stock] + $800,000 [other property] - $600,000 to bypass trust.

---

13. In *Commissioner vs. Procter* 142 F.2d 824 (4th Cir. 1944).

Funding

A business buyout agreement can require that the survivors pay a cash lump sum at the triggering event, or it can require payment of cash in periodic installments. The choice sometimes depends upon the nature of the triggering event.

Cash lump-sum payment. Buyout agreements that require payment of a cash lump sum equal to the entire contracted price are most likely to be funded with life insurance and/or lump-sum disability insurance.

Life insurance. The principles of the acquisition of life insurance to fund a business buyout agreement will be influenced by the type of buyout chosen. Under an *entity* agreement, the firm purchases and acts as beneficiary of a policy on the life of each business owner, with each policy in the amount of money that that owner can expect to pay. In a (reciprocal type) *cross-purchase agreement*, each contracting party purchases and acts as beneficiary of a policy on the life of each of the other contracting owners.

> EXAMPLE BO-3 Sol and Harry are equal shareholders of a corporation that has a net worth of $300,000. The men have executed an *entity* buyout arrangement. The corporation will own and be the beneficiary of two $150,000 face value policies, one on Sol's life and one on Harry's life. The men plan to review and update this amount periodically, as the value of the business changes.

> EXAMPLE BO-4 Facts essentially similar to those in Example BO-3, except that a *reciprocal cross-purchase* plan is adopted. Sol will own and be beneficiary of a $150,000 policy on Harry's life, and Harry will own and be beneficiary of a $150,000 policy on Sol's life.

A reciprocal cross-purchase arrangement funded with life insurance becomes *unwieldy* when the agreement includes numerous owners, because each other contracting party will have to purchase a policy on the life of each other contracting owner. For example, although only 2 policies would have to be purchased for a firm with two contracting owners, 6 policies would have to be purchased for three owners, and 12 policies for four owners. In general, the number of policies purchased under a cross-purchase plan would be $n(n-1)$, where n equals the number of contracting owners. Under an entity plan, the business itself would simply purchase one policy on the life of each contracting owner. Thus, only n policies would have to be purchased.

The number of policies needed under a cross purchase arrangement can be reduced somewhat by using one of two specialized life insurance contracts. First, two contracting parties may be able to purchase a *first to die* joint lives policy, whose proceeds are payable only on the death of the first insured. The premium cost should be less than the total cost for two separate policies because only one life is insured. Second, some companies offer a policy covering more than two insured owners for different amounts based on the their respective ownership interests.[14]

Besides the problem of purchasing numerous policies under a cross purchase agreement, an income tax problem can arise from the *transfer for value rule*, if on the death of one corporate owner the surviving owners purchase the remaining decedent-owned policies. At their later deaths, part of the proceeds may be subject to income taxation.[15]

Compared with the cross purchase agreement, the entity agreement may raise the client's FET, if the infusion of policy proceeds into the corporation increase the stock's value. And an entity agreement funded with life insurance can trigger a corporate *alternative minimum tax*, to the extent that the "book income" of the corporation, which will include the insurance proceeds, exceeds taxable income, which will not.

For any buyout agreement, insurance premiums are not deductible from income, even if paid by the firm.[16] Thus all premiums must be paid with after-tax dollars.

With a cross purchase agreement between owners who are not close in age (or who have unequal interests), a larger premium will likely be paid by the younger (or smaller) owner(s), who are usually less affluent.

Using the firm's assets. A second method of funding a lump-sum payment under an entity arrangement is with the firm's own *cash or noncash assets*. This can also make life insurance unnecessary, but too often the business will not own sufficient distributable assets, particularly the amount of cash that may be needed to pay estate debts.

Lump-sum disability insurance. Finally, in an attempt to accommodate buyout agreements, more and more insurance companies are offering disability policies promising to pay a lump sum at the onset of disability, rather than the usual income stream.

---

14. For a discussion of the estate taxation and planning with these policy, see the Schlisinger/Ball and Staudt articles cited at the end of Chapter 15.

15. The transfer for value rule was described in Chapter 15. Tobisman, in a paper cited at the end of the chapter, suggests a solution to both problems: the creation of a trust to acquire only one policy on each owner's life. However, there may be a §2042 risk.

16. §264(a)(1).

Certain triggering events not conducive to lump-sum agreements. Other, usually uninsurable events triggering the buyout could be retirement, divorce, insolvency of an owner, criminal activity, and loss of a professional license. However, since none of these other events can be reasonably expected to generate a sizable cash flow, full-cash buyouts under such circumstances may be financially difficult to consummate.

Installment payments. In lieu of choosing a lump-sum payment, the parties can agree to an *installment sale* of the business interest. The installment sale can make the purchase of life insurance unnecessary and can be a source of periodic income to the client and the client's family. However, installment payments carry the risk that the purchasers will be unable to make the payments, a situation that can lead to disaster if the family again winds up owning a business that is now failing. Further, a decedent owner's family may dislike receiving deferred payments if the estate has the need for immediate liquidity to pay a large FET or other outlay incurred at death. Finally, an installment note creates a potentially stressful creditor-debtor relationship between the decedent's surviving family and the successor business owners.

In conclusion, the advantages of the business buyout agreement include business continuity, liquidity, a guaranteed market, and possibly greater certainty over the selling price. The preceding overview material merely highlights the general principles of this complex subject. A business buyout agreement should not be executed without the help of expert legal advice.

FREEZING THE VALUE OF THE BUSINESS INTEREST

Overview

The world contains more than a few outstandingly successful owners of closely held corporations. Some have amassed a degree of wealth that they themselves consider to be more than adequate to provide for their income and capital needs for the rest of their lives. To them, the prospect of acquiring more property may be relatively unimportant, perhaps in part because of the additional FET it will trigger. Few of them, however, look forward to relinquishing control of their business interests. They may be having too much fun, or they may have yet been unable to sufficiently groom a younger generation family member.

Prior to 1987, highly successful entrepreneurs had several relatively safe, although complicated methods of freezing the FET value of their business without losing effective control. The most common methods are called the corporate recapitalization and the partnership capital freeze. Through a reorganization of the firm's capital accounts, these techniques enabled the owner to retain complete voting control of the firm and continue to receive the same amount of income from the firm, yet freeze future transfer taxes by arranging for other family members to benefit from the future appreciation of the business.

As mentioned in Chapter 7, by enacting §2701 in 1990, the federal government has substantially restricted the use of business estate freezing. The material that follows first discusses the use of business estate freezing during its heyday, and then traces the influence of recent legislation. The reader might wish to review the material on §2701 in Chapter 7.

Corporate Recapitalization

Recapitalizations prior to §2036(c). Prior to §2036(c),[17] corporate recapitalizations (recaps) were structured in varying manners. A commonly used variation has the following characteristics: Prior to the recap, the client possessed controlling interest in the firm through ownership of the voting common stock. After the recap, the client owned a combination of some voting shares, usually common, and some nonvoting preferred shares, which were entitled to a substantial dividend. The younger generation family members, to whom the client wished to transfer future wealth, were issued nonvoting common shares and, if the client approved, some voting shares. In the following three examples, assume the date to be prior to December 18, 1987.

> EXAMPLE RECAP-1 Alfred is the owner of a highly successful computer software corporation, owning all 1000 shares of the common stock, valued at $2,000 per share. Presently, this is the only class of stock. This year, the company will earn a net income of $260,000. Within the next six months, the company expects to be releasing a revolutionary new software package, one that can triple the company's sales and net worth. Alfred is divorced and has two children, Kyle and Maude. Kyle, age 32, has worked for the firm for ten years and shows great promise to take over when Alfred departs. Maude, age 28, a tenured biology professor, has never been interested in working for the company. At his death, Alfred wishes to leave his entire estate in approximately equal shares to the children.
>
> A recapitalization of the firm is undertaken. In exchange for Alfred's 1,000 shares of common, the corporation issues three classes of new stock:

---

17. Revenue Act of 1987.

1. 20,000 shares of nonvoting, 13% *preferred stock*, all to Alfred. The stock is noncumulative, and has a par value of $100 per share.
2. 480 shares of nonvoting common stock, one half to Kyle and one-half to Maude.
3. 20 shares of voting common stock, all to Alfred.

Both types of common stock will share, pro rata, in any income available after payment of the preferred dividend.

EXAMPLE RECAP-2 Continuing the facts in Example RECAP-1, assume that Alfred will die in ten years, when the business is worth $6 million. The value of Alfred's business interest included in his gross estate is expected to be $2,160,000. This is the sum of $2 million, (the value of the preferred stock) plus $160,000 (the value of the 20 shares of voting common), derived in the following manner: Of the $6 million market value capitalization, since the preferred stock is still expected to be worth $2 million at Alfred's death, the total value of the common shares will be worth $4 million, or $8,000 per share. Thus, nearly all of Alfred's interest in the firm will be frozen at its value as of date of recapitalization, and nearly the entire postrecapitalization appreciation will inure to Kyle and Maude, free of transfer tax.

EXAMPLE RECAP-3 In Example RECAP-2, instead of passing the voting common shares at his death, Alfred could make periodic gifts of them to Kyle in amounts not exceeding the annual gift tax exclusion. In this way, Alfred would have both given additional incentive to Kyle to remain with the firm and, at the same time, reduced even further the value of the business interest taxable in his estate at his death.

The ideal recap was designed to have the following tax-related benefits:

1. No taxation to the corporation arising from the recap.
2. No taxable income to the client upon receipt of the new shares.
3. No taxable gift by the client.
4. At death, the amount included in the client's taxable estate attributable to the firm would approximately equal the value of the client's interest in the business at the date of the recap.

Even prior to the passage of §2036(c), one or more of these benefits could have been lost with an improperly structured recap. In fact, even a state-of-the-art recap may not have been able to achieve all of them, in view of the zeal with which the IRS was attacking them. For many years, the IRS took the position that the value of the common shares transferred could not possibly equal zero because the value of the preferred shares could not be made to equal the total value of the firm. Consequently, some positive value would have remained in the common stock, value which was therefore transferred as a taxable gift to the other family member. Referring to Example RECAP-2, if the preferred stock was actually determined to be worth $1,600,000, rather than $2 million, the 500 shares of common would have had a total fair market value of $400,000. Under the simple assumption that each share was worth $800, Alfred would have been deemed to have made a gift of $384,000.

Former impact of §2036(c). Until is was repealed, §2036(c) virtually eliminated the use of the estate freezing recapitalization after December, 1987. Using very sweeping language, it included in the decedent's gross estate the date of death value of the entire business that had been the subject to the estate freezing recap. The reader will be spared a discussion of the specific application of this subsection, since it was repealed retroactively by the 1990 Act.

Current impact of §2701. As more fully described in Chapter 7, §2701 has taken a very different approach to throttling business estate freezes. While the thrust of §2036(c) was to impose an *estate tax* at the transferor's later death, §2701 is directed at imposing a *gift tax*, at the time of the transfer. Thus, instead of including the date of death value of the business in the decedent-transferor's gross estate, it seeks to subject the date of gift value of the transfer to gift taxation.

The value of the gift, under the new law, will likely be considerably greater than zero. §2701 limits the value of retained interests that can be subtracted in arriving at that taxable gift value. Thus, in the ongoing example shown earlier, Alfred's retention of preferred stock would be valued at zero under the new law, partly because the dividends were specified to be noncumulative, i.e., the corporation did not have an ongoing obligation to pay Alfred previously unpaid dividends. On the other hand, in planning situations where the dividends are made cumulative, payable on a periodic basis, and determined at a fixed "market" rate, the present value of these dividends, considered a "qualified payment," can be subtracted from the total value of the business in determining the value of the gift of the common stock. However, the new law sets a minimum value in the transferred common equal to at least *ten percent* of the value of the entire business. Thus, the corporate recap will likely result in the reporting of a sizable taxable gift. And another transfer tax could arise later. In situations where the corporation fails to make one or more preferred dividend payments to the transferor within four years of the due date, the new law imposes an additional transfer tax, at death or sooner if the retained interest is transferred during lifetime, on the accumulated value of those unpaid dividends.

One final drawback to the recap is that a *decline* in business value can result in an *inflated*, rather than a frozen, client gross estate.[18]

When may recaps work? Estate freezing recaps of the type created prior to §2036(c) may still work for *nonfamily members*, such as nieces and nephews, since §2701 does not apply to recaps benefiting such transferees. The definition of "applicable family members" includes only the transferor's spouse, descendants, descendants of the spouse and all spouses of the above.[19]

Estate freezing recaps that are subject to §2701 may be attractive for smaller businesses, particularly those recaps giving rise to a gift that can be entirely sheltered by the spouses's unified credits. Preferred stock resulting from such a recap need not pay a dividend, and the taxable gift could be reduced by giving the preferred stock a valuable feature, such as voting rights or preemptive subscription rights. Risks abound, however, and expert tax counsel is needed.

In lieu of a recap, which is clearly a complex transaction, the client might consider a simple outright gift of the business. Gifting is simple, and control can be retained by transferring nonvoting stock.

Finally, there are available other types of business freeze techniques not affected by the antifreeze rules because no form of lifetime gifting is involved. They are discussed briefly next.

Testamentary freeze. This involves a bequest of common stock to younger generation beneficiaries and preferred stock to the spouse.

Postmortem recapitalization freeze. A recapitalization after the client's death, in which the marital trust receives the preferred stock and the bypass trust receives the common stock.

Postmortem funding freeze. The marital trust receives assets not likely to appreciate and the bypass trust receives appreciating assets.

Generation-skipping freeze. The children receive, by gift or bequest, the preferred stock and the grandchildren receive the common stock.

Notwithstanding these possible opportunities, the current limitations and restrictions are numerous, and commentators have been guarded about the extent to which corporate recapitalizations will be used in the future.

Partnership Capital Freeze

It may be possible to reorganize an unincorporated firm to achieve the same

---

18. For a discussion, see the Harl article cited at the end of the chapter.

19. §2701(e)(1).

results as the estate-freezing recap. Conceptually similar to the recap, under the partnership capital freeze, two classes of partnership interests are created, one for the client and one for the younger family members. The client's interest could similarly be frozen at its present value, with future appreciation in the business accruing to the other share.

As with the recap, the partnership capital freeze deals in a complex, rapidly changing area of tax law, subject to the provisions of §2701 and also to frequent IRS attack. Again, planning should be approached carefully, with the help of competent counsel.

VALUING THE BUSINESS

The subject of the *value* of a closely held business has arisen in several contexts in this chapter. How is business valuation determined? Often, as we have seen, correct valuation is necessary for tax purposes, and the IRS and the courts have written much on the subject. The following briefly outlines the major influences on business value by summarizing the eight general factors invariably requiring careful consideration. These items are taken from Revenue Ruling 59-60,[20] the IRS' classic exposition on valuation of the shares of closely held stock.

1. Nature and history of the business.
2. Economic outlook and conditions of the economy and industry.
3. Book value of the stock and financial condition of the company.
4. Company earning capacity.
5. Company dividend-paying capacity.
6. Extent of company goodwill and other intangibles.
7. Recent sales of the company's stock and the size of the block to be valued.
8. Market price of publicly traded stock in the same industry.

Extent of use of each factor will depend upon the underlying facts concerning the specific business interest.

This chapter has presented an overview of the objectives and techniques of estate planning for closely held business interests. The next chapter will examine miscellaneous planning techniques not covered in earlier chapters.

---

20. 959-1 C.B. 237.

QUESTIONS AND PROBLEMS

1. What could you say to client owning a closely held business who respects your advice but seems to be stubbornly refusing even to consider estate planning?

2. What unique estate planning problems are common to owners of closely held businesses?

3. Identify the objectives of estate planning for owners of closely held business interests.

4. One of your clients is worried about the possible future decline in the value of his firm upon his departure. Recommend ideas that can help minimize that decline.

5. (*a*) Describe the inter vivos methods of transferring business interests to a family member. (*b*) Under what conditions will such transfers be ill-advised?

6. (*a*) You are trying to encourage one of your clients to consider selling her business to a third party while she is still alive. Describe the benefits of this strategy. (*b*) Is planning for a sale after death always unwise? Why or why not?

7. Horne, a closely held business-owning client, requests your advice. He has a simple will, but has done no other planning. Neither his wife nor his children have any interest in continuing the business after his death. Horne does not wish to retire. Recommend a significant planning strategy for his consideration.

8. Describe the alternative methods for payment that can be arranged when a business is sold.

9. When should planning for closely held business interests begin? Why?

10. (*a*) Describe the essential characteristics of the typical business buyout agreement. (*b*) What are its advantages?

11. What is the tax advantage of including a method for determining the selling price in a properly drafted business buy-out agreement?

12. (*a*) Describe the three methods by which a business buyout agreement can be funded. (*b*) Why might types of funding influence the choice of whether a cross-purchase or an entity plan is adopted?

13. Why might income taxation influence the choice of whether a cross-purchase or an entity plan is adopted?

14. McQueen is the surviving shareholder of the M-C Corporation. Forty years ago, he and Cross acquired the business, and just prior to Cross's death two years ago each had a $46,000 basis in their stock. McQueen purchased Cross's shares from the Cross estate for $180,000, pursuant to a buyout agreement. Presently, McQueen is thinking of selling the firm. Analyze the overall economic desirability of each of the following alternatives. Be sure to consider all of the objectives of planning for closely held business interests, including income taxation. Assume a combined marginal tax rate of 50 percent for ordinary income, 35 percent for capital gains, and 55 percent for FET.

   a. McQueen presently sells his shares for $600,000 cash.
   b. McQueen presently exchanges his shares for 6,000 shares of the publicly traded XYZ Corporation, which is currently trading at $100 per share.
   c. McQueen continues to own the shares until death, which is actuarially expected to occur in five years. The shares, worth $600,000 at death, will be bequeathed to his wife, who we believe may be able to sell them for $400,000 cash.
   d. McQueen continues to own the shares until death (date of death value is still $600,000), at which time the KR Corporation, a competitor of M-C, purchases the shares from McQueen's estate for $700,000 cash, pursuant to a buyout agreement, executed presently.
   e. Can you recommend any alternative methods of disposition? (Hint: the M-C Corporation currently has an ESOP.)

RECOMMENDED READING

Abbin, Byrle M. "Mitigating the Chernobyl Syndrome of Asset Value Freeze Meltdown." *University of Miami 21st Annual Estate Planning Institute*, 1987.

*Adams, Roy M., David A. Herpe and James R. Carey, "Buy-Sell Agreements After Chapter 14." *Trusts & Estates*, May, 1993 pp 22-32.

_____, Allan J. Sweet; and Scott Bieber. "Recapitalizations Revisited." *Trust & Estates*, August 1984, pp. 21-25.

Akre, Steven H. "Buy-Sell Agreement Can Meet the Conflicting Needs of Parties When a Shareholder Departs." *Taxation for Accountants*, November 1985, pp. 308-15.

Aucutt, Ronald D. "Is Anybody Doing Corporate and Partnership Freezes Anymore?," *1992 University of Miami Estate Planning Institute.*

Bailin, Deborah M., "Using a Split-Off In Estate Planning For A Closely Held Business," *Estate Planning*, May, 1993, pp 156-62.

Blackburn, Joseph, and R. Thomas Blackburn. "Estate Planning with Recapitalizations: Realistic Expectations." *Cumberland Land Review* 12(1981), pp. 1-26.

*Buchanan, Jeffrey D. and Malcolm A. Moore. "Valuation Readjustment Clauses: What's Possible?" *New York University 45th Annual Institute on Federal Taxation*, 1986.

Buydens, Robert G & MacFarlane, J. Thomas, "Salary Continuation Agreements Provide a Valuable Alternative to Qualified Plans, "*Estate Planning*, Nov. 1988, pp. 330-36.

Cezer, Frederick. "Planning for Retirement, Disability or Death of the Owner of a Small Business Interest." *Estate Planning*, January 1984, pp. 32-37.

Checkoway, Allan B. "Insuring the Disability Hazard in the Small Closely Held Corporation." *Journal of American Society of CLU*, January 1985, pp. 44- 51.

Christensen, Burke A. "Funding a Buy-Sell Agreement." *Trusts & Estates*, July 1984, pp. 57-59.

Cornfeld, Dave L. "Non-Tax Considerations In Preparing Buy-Sell Agreements," *1994 University of Miami Estate Planning Institute.*

Draneas, John H. "S Corp. or Partnership: Which Meet Clients' Business and Estate Planning Objectives?" *Estate Planning*, January, 1986, pp. 30-36.

_____. "Departure of Owner of a Service Business Requires Special Estate Planning Strategies." *Estate Planning*, September, 1990, pp. 280-86.

Eastland, S. Stacy Use of Partnerships As an Alternative to Trusts in Estate Planning." *Ninth Annual UCLA/CEB Estate Planning Institute*, 1987, California Continuing Education of the Bar.

Edwards, Mark B. "Planning and Drafting To Avoid Sibling Rivalry: Can We Prevent What nature Hath Ordained?" *1994 University of Miami Estate Planning Institute.* Discussed sibling rivalry in the context of business succession planning.

Fowler, Anna C. "Planning for Recapitalizations in Light of Recent Administrative and Legislative Developments." *Taxes-The Tax Magazine*, March 1985, pp. 202-9.

*Gamble, E. James, "The Repeal of General Utilities and its Impact on Estate Planning" 1989 UCLA-CEB Estate Planning Institute. See Particularly the Appendix on "Corporations".

_____, "Will Chapter 14 Freeze Buy-Sell Agreements and Make Lapsing Rights Disappear?" *1992 University of Miami Estate Planning Institute.*

Gerson, David "How Family Partnerships Can Be Used to Shift Income and Capital Appreciation." *Estate Planning*, March 1983, pp. 86-9.

Goldstein, Arnold S. *Business Transfers-An Accountant's and Attorney's Guide.* New York: John Wiley and Sons, 1986.

Gorfinkle, Robert A. "Many Choices Available to Owner Wishing to Transfer Business to Younger Family Members." *Estate Planning*, March 1986, pp. 98-103.

*Harl, Neil E. Handling Risk and Debt Resolution in Farm Estates in an Era of Declining Asset Values." *1986 University of Miami Estate Planning Institute.*

Harmon, Michael R. "Should Partnership Interests Gifted in a Multi-Level Freeze Be Included in the Donor's Gross Estate under Section 2036?" *Taxes-The Tax Magazine*, November 1986, pp. 741-45.

Higgins, David M. "Installment Sales, Private Annuities, Recapitalizations, and Charitable Lead Trusts." In *The Closely Held Business: Financial Planning for the Owners*, Practicing Law Institute, 1986, pp. 507-43.

Kaplan, Steven P. & Egon Fromm. "The Impact of Taxes on the Value of Close Corporations." *Estate Planning*, May, 1992, pp. 137-42.

Klinger, Leslie S. "Compensation Planning Techniques in Estate Planning for Owners of Closely Held Businesses." In *The Closely Held Business: Financial Planning for the Owners*, Practicing Law Institute, 1986, pp. 227-440.

Kowalski, Lawrence W., and Brent B. Nicholson. "Buy-Sell Agreements Can Avoid Disputes As to the Value of a Minority Interest." *Taxation for Lawyers*, July-August 1984, pp. 56-60.

Landsman, Stephen A. "Divorce Planning in the Closely Held Business Context. *Trust & Estates*, May 1984, pp. 4l-46.

*Lang, Dudley M., "Subchapter S in Estate Planning," presented at the 10th Annual UCLA/CEB Estate Planning Institute. Article published in *Estate Planning, 1988*, California Continuing Education of the Bar.

LeVan, Gerald: "Keeping the Family in the Business: Estate Planning May Not be Enough" *Probate & Property*, November 1989 pp 28-31.

Levun, Charles R. "Partnerships The Preferred Form of Doing Business after the Tax Reform Act of 1986." *Taxes-The Tax Magazine*, September 1987, pp.600-603.

Mathias, Bruce R. "How Buy-Sell Agreements Can Produce The Best Tax Results for Both the Partners and Partnership." *Taxation for Accountants*, October 1986, pp. 24-52.

McMahan, Kent H. "What Me Worry? Limited liability For The Operation Of Family Businesses Without Extra Tax Costs-- A Comparison Of Limited Liability Companies, Family Partnerships, And Corporations," *1994 University of Miami Estate Planning Institute.*

Melgren, Eric. "No Mere Yeoman: Incorporating the Family Farm-Considerations and Consequences." (Pre-TRA 86 discussion.) *Washburn Law Journal* 24(1985), pp. 546-73.

Mulligan, Michael D. "Estate Freeze Rules Eased By New Tax Law but Other Restrictions Imposed," *Estate Planning*, January, 1991, pp. 2-7.

Petrie, Linda C. "Partnership Freezes: Determining When and How This Estate Planning Technique Should Be Used." *Taxation for Accountants*, April 1985, pp.22-3I.

Pudlin, David. "Maximizing the Income Shifting and Estate Planning Potentials of Family Partnerships." *Taxation for Accountants*, November 1985, pp. 28-31.

*Russell, Walter J. "The New Impetus to Elect S Status Requires Prompt Review of Shareholder's Planning." *Estate Planning*, March 1987, pp. 98-102.

Saper, Michael S. "Strategies for Managing a Closely Held Business during the Period of Administration." *Estate Planning*, September 1985, pp.266-73.

Schlenger, Jacques T.; Stephen L. Owen; and John B. Watkins V. "Freezing the Value of Closely Held Business Interests." *Taxes-The Tax Magazine*, November 1983, pp. 719-42.

Schmidt L. William. "How to Plan a Recapitalization that Will Meet a Client's Needs and Withstand IRS Scrutiny." *Estate Planning*, September 1982, pp. 274-79.

Sherwood, Arthur M "Family Businesses Breed Conflict" *Trusts & Estates* Feb. '89, pp 30-36.

Tarlow, Edward D., and Andrew M. Curtis. "How to Overcome Complications of Owner-ship Attribution for Closely Held Corporations." *Estate Planning*, September 1987, pp. 270-78.

Thater, William, C. "Buy-Sell Agreements: A New Funding Vehicle," *CLU Journal*, September 1986, pp. 82-84. Discusses life insurance product whose face value can vary as much as 25 percent per year.

Tobisman, Stuart P. "How to Deal With Situations Where Some Children are Active and Some are Inactive in the Business" 1989 UCLA/CEB Estate Planning Institute.

*_____. "Drafting Buy-Sell Agreements With Estate Planning Implications," *1992 UCLA/CEB Estate Planning Institute.*

*_____. "Corporate Buy-Sell Agreements." In The Closely Held Business: *Financial Planning for the Owners*, Practicing Law Institute, 1986, pp. 7-137.

*Wolf, Robert M & Kupferberg, Alan, "What is the Best Form for Structuring Corporate Buy-Out Agreements Now"? *Estate planning* Jan, 1989 pp 2-6.

Wood, Harleston R. "Estate Planning for the Professional Corporation Shareholder." *Journal of Taxation*, October 1987, pp. 222-26.

Zankel, Jeffrey A. "Choosing the best Method of Handling the Partnership of a Deceased Partner." *Estate Planning*, July 1986, pp. 198-202.

Zatt, Mark E. "Structuring Shareholder Buyout Agreements to Meet Business, Tax and Estate Planning Goals," *Taxation for Accountants*, September 1985, pp. 170-74.

Miscellaneous Lifetime Planning

OVERVIEW

In the past seven chapters, we have covered six major lifetime planning topics: avoiding probate, wise use of the marital deduction, bypass planning, lifetime transfers, liquidity planning and planning for closely held business interests. This chapter will cover other miscellaneous aspects of lifetime planning. First, it will explore a number of more narrow topics, many of which are interrelated only because they influence the preparation of a client's will or trust instrument. Examples include provisions for the care of minor children, that select the executor and trustee, and that deal with survival clauses and the allocation of death taxes. Next, the chapter will examine estate planning for unmarried couples in nontraditional relationships. Then, a final but in no way less important section focuses on documents and strategies used in planning for the client's own incapacity, and includes a discussion of two types of durable powers of attorney, and the living will.

WILL AND TRUST PLANNING

By now the reader should agree that the will and the trust instrument are the major documents used in estate planning. Both have been referred to in every chapter so far, especially those in Part 3 outlining the techniques of planning. The material below describes several other types of planning frequently undertaken in drafting the will and the trust instrument. In reading this material, the reader is urged to refer back frequently to the will and trust documents illustrated in Exhibits 3-1, 3-2 and 3-3.

Planning for the Care of Family Members: An Introduction

The occurrence of both disability and death of the client can require the making of important decisions as to how to care for affected family members who are unable to care for themselves. Disability of the client may require the selection of others to care for the *client* and the client's property, and death of the surviving client-parent of a minor child will require selection of one or more persons to care for that orphaned *child*. In either case, prior planning can enable the selection process to reflect the wishes of the client, whose direct input can better ensure that the proper care will be provided. Planning for care of minor orphaned children will be discussed in the next section. Planning for the disabled client's care will be surveyed at the end of the chapter. We begin, however, with a discussion of factors common to both.

Planning for the care of both the orphaned child and the incapacitated client have three factors in common. First, by not making prearrangements, clients force their local *court* to assume greater responsibility in arranging for this care. Without help from the client, the court, in its attempt to act in the dependent's best interest, must rely on *secondhand information* obtained from other family members and from friends. To best ensure that the court's decisions reflect his or her wishes, the client should plan to express those wishes in writing now, before it is too late.

Second, for both minors and incapacitated adults, the law distinguishes two types of care: care of the person and care of the property. An individual legally responsible for care of the *person* is charged with providing everyday physical and psychological needs. An individual legally responsible for care of the *property* of a minor or incapacitated person is charged with safeguarding, investing, and expending that person's income and wealth.

Third, because care of the person and care of the property entail such dissimilar responsibilities, *different parties* will often be nominated and appointed to perform each, as we shall see.

Planning for the Care of the Client's Minor Children

The material below explores the prearrangements that can be undertaken to provide care for the client's minor children in the event that both parents die prematurely.

Planning for the orphaned minor's personal care: The parental guardian. In the typical household, the married parents of a child are the *natural* and *legal guardians* of their children. Thus, upon the death of one parent, the surviving parent will continue as sole guardian. Only in the most unusual situations will the courts deny this right. On the other hand, when a minor child survives the death of *both* parents, the state must select a successor guardian. The selection process typically culminates in an order by a judge of the probate court after a noticed hearing. The court will usually appoint the person nominated in the parent's will, unless the nominee is unwilling, unable, or unsuitable to perform. If the will contains no nomination, or if there is no will, the court must examine the family situation more carefully, relying on other information, including a list of willing friends and relatives, as well as the expressed preferences of the child, if sufficiently mature to have and express an opinion. Since the court's main criterion is the best interests of the child, it seeks to appoint that person who is best capable of providing the minor with such basics as food, clothing, shelter, medical care, and schooling, as well as providing psychological well-being, love, and attention.

Since the court's eventual selection of a guardian may not reflect the deceased parent's unexpressed wishes, and to avoid guardianship "warfare," the client-parent should clearly assert that preference by nominating a personal guardian in the will. Considering the stakes, it can be the most important estate planning action made by young parents.

The ideal parental guardian. Whom should the client nominate? An ideal parental guardian will possess the following qualities:

1. The *integrity, maturity, physical stamina*, and *experience* needed to be a parent.
2. A strong *concern* for the minor's welfare.
3. The ability to provide a *stable personal environment* conducive to raising a child in a manner consistent with the client's particular moral, religious, social, and financial situation.

Of course, these attributes are ideals; the usual client will have difficulty identifying more than one or two capable and willing nominees, none of whom might be ideal. But however imperfect, a nomination greatly reduces the risk of an undesired appointment. Nominating more than one parental guardian will allow for an alternate/successor guardian who will serve in the event that the preferred person named is unwilling or unable to serve or continue to serve.

Once the choice is made, the client should be encouraged to review periodically the nomination in light of both the minor's changing needs and the nominee's changing personal and financial situation.

Planning for the orphaned minor's financial care: Three fiduciary choices. Anticipating the possibility that their spouse will not survive them, clients will usually want to provide for adequate financial care for their orphaned minor children. They will ordinarily want to transfer all or most of their probate and nonprobate property for the benefit of the children. Common nonprobate sources of property for the children include life insurance proceeds, survivorship under joint tenancy arrangements, trust property, and gifts from others.

While most states allow a minor to receive outright a modest amount of property, larger amounts will be required to be turned over to a *fiduciary* who is legally responsible for their care and custody. What legally acceptable fiduciary arrangements are available? While the law recognizes parental guardianships as the only legal arrangement for the minor's *personal* care, it recognizes several arrangements for the minor's *financial* care. The client may choose a financial guardianship, a trust, or a custodianship under one or the other Uniform Acts. Each is surveyed briefly.

Financial guardianship. A financial guardian, also called an estate guardian, is typically appointed by the court in a manner similar to the procedures used for appointment of a parental guardian. Usually required to file a formal accounting with the court every one or two years, the financial guardian must obtain written permission from the court to undertake nonroutine transactions, such as the sale of real property. Reflecting the general trend in probate reform, some states have enacted streamlined guardianship proceedings to minimize court involvement.

In general, the *criteria* for selecting a financial guardian are radically different from those used in selecting a parental guardian. As we have mentioned, while the primary consideration in selecting the parental guardian is parental ability, the primary focus in selecting the financial guardian is *skill in financial management*. Since skill in financial management is also the primary criterion used to select a trustee, we shall defer further discussion of its attributes to the sections on selecting the executor and the trustee.

Trust for the minor. Instead of a financial guardian, a trustee can be chosen to manage the client's property left for the benefit of a minor child. The trust can be created and funded during the client's life. Or it can be created by the client's will and funded with probate and nonprobate property.

The trust has sizable advantages over the financial guardianship. First, it is a *private* arrangement, not usually subject to court supervision and control. While a guardianship requires filing of a bond, periodic accountings and court approval for asset transfers, a trust can avoid these costly and time consuming activities. However, some states require ongoing probate court supervision of testamentary trusts after the trustor's death. But the trend has been to eliminate this requirement.

Second, the trust offers great *flexibility*; the client can tailor it to his or her personal wishes. For example, while guardianship property usually must be surrendered outright to the minor upon reaching age 18, the age of majority, trust property can be retained in trust until the age specified by the client. Further, while a separate guardianship must usually be established for each minor, a single trust can have multiple beneficiaries, as in the case of the family pot trust, described later in the chapter. And the trustee can be given discretion to distribute different amounts of trust assets to different beneficiaries at different times. For example, the trustee can be given the power to distribute principal to an income beneficiary, or to accumulate income and add it to principal, or to "spray" or "sprinkle" income among the beneficiaries. Finally, the trust is more flexible because it can include a spendthrift provision, a protective clause to be described later. Financial guardianships are not established with such refinements.

A third advantage of the trust over the financial guardianship rests on the fact that the *statutory and case law* of trusts is much more well defined. Thus, a trustee will often feel less uncertain than a guardian about the potential adverse consequences of a particular fiduciary act or decision.

A financial guardianship usually arises by default when the client dies having done no planning. Because it is expensive and cumbersome, it is rarely preferred over a trust.

Custodianship under the Uniform Acts. Finally, the client may wish to leave property to a custodian for the benefit of a minor child under the Uniform Gifts to Minors Act or the Uniform Transfers to Minors Act in the manner described in Chapter 13. Like trusts, custodianships offer far greater privacy than financial guardianships, since they are not subject to court supervision. However, like guardianships, custodianships are quite inflexible because they are usually controlled by statute. For example, in most states property held by the custodian must be turned over to the minor upon reaching age 21. Also, most states limit the kinds of property that can be transferred under the Uniform Gifts to Minor's Act, which is the only one of the two acts that has been adopted in many states.

Selection of Executor and Executor's Powers

As we have said, the executor is responsible for representing and managing a decedent's probate estate. Specific tasks of this multifaceted job include marshaling and valuing the decedent's assets, filing tax returns, paying taxes and debts, distributing assets, and accounting for the entire process. It also involves dealing with grieving family members, distributing personal effects, and resolving family conflicts, all of which can be emotionally taxing. Finally, the executor must keep assets invested, or sell them to pay taxes, and, possibly manage or liquidate the decedent's business. While most of these jobs can be performed by the estate attorney's office, total estate expenses may be higher due to a larger attorney fee, and the executor is still primarily responsible to the court for completing these acts.

Selection. Whom should the client consider nominating for the job of executor? An ideal nominee will possess the following qualities:

1. *Longevity*, that is, the likelihood of being able to serve after the death of the client, perhaps many years hence.
2. *Skill in managing* legal and financial affairs.
3. *Familiarity* with the testator's estate and the testator's wishes.
4. Strong *integrity*, coupled with *loyalty* to the testator and the testator's family.
5. *Impartiality*, and absence of conflicts of interest.

An ideal financial guardian will also possess these qualities.

Let us use these criteria to evaluate the types of potential candidates who are normally available to serve.

Family member, friend. Nominating a family member or friend to be executor can often reduce administration costs paid to nonbeneficiaries. Family members and friends usually possess a strong degree of familiarity and loyalty. However, they often have only modest legal and financial skills, which may compel them to incur expenses by hiring professional advice. While they can normally delegate some of their work to the estate attorney, they cannot delegate their legal responsibility, since the executor cannot avoid personal liability for certain types of mistakes that might occur in administration. Nonetheless, in small estates most mistakes are not costly, and, in general, nominating as executor the spouse, an adult child, or a good friend makes sense. Naming the spouse is probably the most popular choice.[1]

Corporate executor. The testator may prefer to select a corporate

---

1. See the Moore-Pennell paper cited at the end of Chapter 1.

executor such as a bank trust department. Reasons include inability to find and select a responsible family member or friend, conflict among family members, or a complex estate. Banks usually do a technically satisfactory job in managing estate assets. However, because they are usually unfamiliar with the decedent's family, they cannot offer much of a personal touch in the administration process. For example, they may have difficulty deciding to whom should be given minor personal effects of which the decedent made no specific mention. Finally, many banks will not agree to be executor if the estate is too small, if they dislike certain provisions of the will, or if they are not also nominated trustee under the estate plan's trust arrangements.

Attorney. Should an attorney, such as the testator's attorney, be considered for nomination as executor? Probate attorneys will usually do a satisfactory job in managing assets during the probate period, because they commonly possess a substantial degree of expertise acquired over the years by doing the work delegated by their many executor-clients. Nomination of the testator's attorney, however, may increase the risk of a *will contest*. Dissatisfied with the will provisions, an aspiring beneficiary might allege that the nomination is further evidence that the testator was subject to "undue influence" by over persuasion and intimidation, and might petition that the will not be admitted to probate. But it would be well to keep in mind that successful will contests are rare.

In addition, nominating an attorney might not reduce administration costs, since many attorney-executors hire other attorneys to represent the estate. Finally, and perhaps most significant, acting as an executor can create potential *conflicts of interest* for the attorney in the areas of drafting, confidentiality, and the duty to deal impartially with beneficiaries. For example, an attorney who anticipates becoming a fiduciary may be tempted to insert in the client's will an unconventional, self-serving exculpation (hold harmless) clause for all simple negligence acts.[2] In fact, these ethical issues may compel an attorney to refuse the nomination. Based on EC5-6 of the attorney's Code of Professional Responsibility:

---

2. For an example of a hold harmless clause in a trust exculpating the attorney-trustee for acts or omissions other than intentional breaches of trust, gross negligence, bad faith, or reckless indifference, etc., see the Alvarez UCLA paper cited at the end of the chapter. Interestingly, in her California Lawyer article (also cited), which was written to advise fellow attorneys who may be considering the role of trustee, executor or other fiduciary, the author recommends inserting just this type of exculpatory clause, as a "tip" to help "reduce the potential risks."

> *A lawyer should not consciously influence a client to name him as executor, trustee or lawyer in any instrument. In those cases where a client wishes to name his lawyer as such, care should be taken by the lawyer to avoid even the appearance of impropriety.*

However, not all attorneys so refuse. In a 1992 survey of 463 experienced estate planning attorneys practicing in 49 states, only 14 percent indicated they "never" accept fiduciary appointments when asked, while 38% "seldom" accept, 24% "sometimes" accept, 20% "often" accept, and 4% "always" accept.[3]

In general, caution should be exercised when considering the nomination of an attorney.

Other considerations. The testator should also nominate an *alternate* executor to serve in case the primary nominee is unwilling or unable to serve. Many clients nominate a bank as the alternate because they are confident that a corporate executor will always be available to serve. Regardless of the choice of executor, the testator should always consult with the nominees to get their consent, and should periodically review the choice in light of changing circumstances.

Executor's powers. What powers should be explicitly granted to an executor? Most simple wills either do not delineate the powers of the executor, or list just a few powers. The will in Exhibit 3-1 explicitly grants to the executor the powers to distribute principal and income; to sell, lease, mortgage, pledge, assign, invest, and reinvest estate property; and to operate a business.

When a will "is silent" regarding a specific proposed action of the executor, we look for authority first to the provisions of the state's estates and trusts or probate code *statutes*, which usually delineate many executor's powers. If nothing pertinent is found, the executor may feel obliged to request permission from the *court*. For example, in the absence of explicit permission in the will, executors in many states must seek formal written permission to be able to sell real property. Thus, specifying powers explicitly in the will can offer the executor greater *flexibility* by minimizing unnecessary delays in probate. And enumerating powers in the will can reveal more to the survivors about the testator's *wishes*, especially with regard to the degree of court supervision originally envisioned by the testator.

---

3. See the Moore-Pennell paper cited at the end of Chapter 1.

Allocation of Death Taxes

Which beneficiaries should bear the burden of death taxes? All of them, or only some? If only some, which ones? If all, should the taxes be shared equally or in proportion to the amount bequeathed? A number of important considerations in determining how to allocate death taxes are examined next.

No clause in will usually means apportionment. In the absence of a provision in the will, both federal and state law determine which beneficiaries will share the cost of death taxes.

Federal law. Federal law controls the burden on a few types of assets. The Internal Revenue Code provides that the prorata FET on life insurance,[4] property subject to a general power of appointment,[5] QTIP property[6] (usually at the second death), and property included in the gross estate because of a retained interest[7] is payable out of those assets.

State law. Under state law, with regard to all assets owned by the decedent, the old common law rule provided that death taxes were paid from the residuary probate estate. However, most states have changed this rule by enacting a type of *equitable apportionment statute*, which spreads the tax burden more or less proportionately among all of the beneficiaries receiving the taxed assets. Thus, even recipients of nonprobate assets, such as property held by the decedent in joint ownership, would owe a portion of the tax. Of course, *charitable recipients* and most *spouses* would not ordinarily incur a tax burden, since their distributions are deducted before one arrives at the taxable estate.

Tax clause in will. The client can override these federal and state directives by expressly including a tax clause in the will.

Residuary tax clause. Most attorneys do this by routinely drafting wills containing a tax clause embracing the old common law rule: all taxes will be paid out of the residuary estate. The simple will in Exhibit 3-2 and the trust-will in Exhibit 3-3 each contain such a provision. Payment of taxes from the residue can speed up the probate process by making it unnecessary to obtain reimbursement from nonresiduary and nonprobate beneficiaries.

---

4. §2206.

5. §2207.

6. §2207A.

7. §2207B.

In addition, recipients of specific nonresiduary bequests of illiquid assets won't be forced to search for the required cash. And paying the taxes out of the residue may be especially helpful if the will specifically bequeaths certain assets over which the testator does not wish the *tax burden* to fall. For example, if the testator leaves only one relatively illiquid asset, such as a piano, to a particular beneficiary, should that person have to pay any transfer taxes attributable to it? Most clients would probably say no, unless that beneficiary is known to have considerable wealth, or at least access to a reasonable amount of discretionary liquid assets.

Problems with the residuary tax clause. Yet there are at least four situations where a residuary tax clause will conflict with the testator's wishes. First, the testator may specifically bequeath an asset such as a closely held business that comprises a very *large portion* of the entire estate. If the tax clause allocates the entire tax burden to the residue, the effect may be to radically reduce the total of net after-tax residuary gifts, or wipe them out entirely.

> EXAMPLE 17-1 Livingston's estate consists of a closely held business currently worth $800,000 and other assets also worth $800,000. He has two children: A, who works in the business, and B, who does not. Livingston would like to leave the business to A and the same amount of property (the other assets) to B. The attorney drafts a will bequeathing the business to A and the residue to B, and includes a conventional "boiler plate" residuary tax clause. At Livingston's death, B's after-tax share will be reduced to about $400,000, or one half of the amount passing to A.

Second, many clients view their *residuary legatees* as the primary "objects of their bounty;" such clients often want them to receive as much wealth as possible. An apportionment tax clause would more closely meet this objective.

A third consideration is the effect of the tax allocation upon a bypass plan that provides for determination of the amount of the *marital deduction by formula.* To minimize FET, such plans invariably incorporate an allocation clause placing the burden of the tax on the property that is subject to the estate tax. Which clause is chosen, of course, will then depend on whether the marital share comes from a specific bequest (residuary tax clause preferred), or from the residue (apportionment clause preferred).

Whatever the provisions of state law, the client would be well advised to consider including a desired tax clause in the will for greater certainty. Determining the best tax clause can be a difficult job, particularly when there are several beneficiaries. An undesired provision can mean unnecessary delay, or a pattern of property distribution radically different from that envisioned by the testator. Yet rarely will the courts override the provisions of a will or the applicable statute to prevent an undesired result. Consequently, the client should consider the alternatives carefully.

Lapse Problem and Survival Clauses

The phrase "If A survives me, I give her. . ." is a survival clause and is commonly included in wills and trusts instruments, partly to avoid the consequences of a lapse.

Effect of a lapse. A lapse occurs when a beneficiary named in a will fails to survive the testator. Each state's probate code contains sections which determine, in the absence of a provision in the will, to whom a lapsed testamentary bequest will pass. A very common type of *antilapse statute*, as it is called, provides that bequests to one of the testator's *predeceased blood relatives* will instead pass to that relative's *surviving issue*. The UPC limits the antilapse to predeceased to grandparents and descendants of grandparents.[8]

> EXAMPLE 17-2 Rudolph died. His will left his car to his *brother*, Randall, and the residue of his estate to his friend James. Randall had predeceased Rudolph. Due to the state's antilapse statute, the bequest of the car will pass to Randall's only son, Jeremy.

Antilapse statutes expressly apply only to wills, not living trust instruments or property held in joint tenancy. However, some courts have applied their antilapse statutes to living trust instruments by analogy. On the other hand, the interests of predeceased co-joint tenants are always cut off by their death; thus, the surviving cotenants will share a greater percentage of the property.

If the state has *no antilapse statute*, or if the particular statute does not apply, perhaps because the lapsed bequest was to a nonrelated beneficiary, or in a UPC state to a remote relative, then a lapsed specific bequest will ordinarily pass to the *residuary beneficiary*.

> EXAMPLE 17-3 In Example 17-2, if the car was left to Rudolph's predeceased *friend* Josef instead of Randall, the car will pass to James, the residuary beneficiary, because the state's antilapse statute applies only to relatives.

---

8. UPC §2-603.

These last two results are unfortunate if the testator actually wished, in the event the named beneficiary predeceased the testator, to leave the property to certain of the named beneficiary's survivors who are not blood relatives. An example might be a son- or daughter-in-law, such as the dearly loved ex-spouse of the testator's child who is raising the testator's grandchild.

> EXAMPLE 17-4 Grandpa, a widower, died recently, and in his will he left his entire estate to his son. Because the son predeceased Grandpa the property will pass to son's children, based on the state's antilapse statute. Nothing will pass directly to Mary, who is son's ex-spouse and will be raising the children alone. This result could easily have been avoided if Grandpa's will had explicitly named Mary to receive a portion of his property in the event that his son predeceased him.

If a *residuary gift lapses* in the absence of a specific antilapse statute provision, the property will pass by *intestate succession*.

> EXAMPLE 17-5 In Example 17-3, if James had also predeceased Rudolph, the residuary bequest will lapse, and the estate will pass in accordance with that state's intestacy laws.

Avoiding a lapse with a survival clause. A lapse can usually be avoided with a *survival clause* designating an alternate taker.

> EXAMPLE 17-6 Continuing the series of examples above, if Rudolph's will instead left the car to Isaac "in the event that Randall fails to survive me," and Isaac survives Rudolph, then Isaac, the alternate taker, will receive the car.

Survival period. A survival clause may require survival for some *period* beyond the testator's death. An example would be the phrase, "...if she survives me *by 30 days*..." Extending the survivorship requirement reduces the likelihood that bequeathed property will be subject to two successive probates in situations when the beneficiary dies shortly after the decedent.

> EXAMPLE 17-7 In Example 17-2, if Randall survived Rudolph by only one month, the car will still pass to Randall and also be subject to administration in his estate. If, instead, Rudolph's will bequeathed the car to Randall "if he survives me by six months, otherwise to Isaac," then Isaac will receive the car, which will be subject to administration only in Rudolph's estate.

FET and survival periods. Bypass planning also influences the decision whether or not to use a survival period. One rule of thumb used is to insert a survival period requirement in the wills or trusts of both spouses unless their estates are substantially unequal in amount. In that case use it only in the document of the less wealthy spouse. The basic rationale is twofold: first, to take advantage of both unified credits, where practical; second, to avoid unnecessarily loading up a wealthier S2's gross estate.

In a common accident, there may be an estate tax reason for providing that the *beneficiary* will always be presumed to have survived the testator. For example, to achieve *estate equalization* (see Chapter 11) in a common accident situation, disposition of property can be based on a stated assumption that the wealthier spouse (W) predeceased the less wealthy spouse (L). In that event, W's estate will receive a marital deduction, reducing the taxable estate, while L's gross estate will increase by the amount of the bequest. And to prevent property from passing to L's named beneficiaries, W's bequest can be structured to qualify as a QTIP transfer.[9]

> Example 17-8 While alive, both William, owner of $1 million in property, and his wife Mary, owner of $200,000 in property, executed simple wills leaving all their property to the other spouse, if he/she survived by four months, otherwise to the children of each of their prior marriages. Mary survived William by 36 days. Thus, all of William's $1 million estate, reduced by an FET of $153,000, passed outright to his children, and all of Mary's $200,000 estate (no FET) passed outright to her children. The entire FET could have been avoided had William's will been different in two ways: First, if his survival clause had not included a survival period; and second, if the will instead had passed $600,000 to a credit shelter bypass trust and $400,000 to a QTIP trust, with the remainders for both trust to his children.

Selecting length of survival period. How long should the survival period be? Making it at least several months in duration will provide for the multiple death event which, relatively speaking, probably occurs most frequently: death of the decedent and the intended beneficiary in a common accident. However, specifying too long a survival period can delay distribution of estate assets since the executor will be required to wait that long to determine whether or not the named beneficiary in fact survived that period. Further, as mentioned in Chapter 6, a marital bequest will not qualify for the marital deduction if it is contingent on the spouse's surviving the decedent by any period greater than six months.

Many planners use a survival period of about one month for tangible personal property and between four and six months for other property. The shorter period for tangible personal property reflects the usual testator's desire to permit the surviving beneficiary to be able to use such property

---

9. For greater detail, see the Clary-Anderson article cited at the end of the chapter.

almost immediately, if even for only a short while, and to avoid storage and other additional costs.

Selection of Trustee and Trustee's Powers

Below we consider the factors involved in selecting a suitable trustee, and in determining which trustee powers to include in the trust instrument. It should become clear that the factors are quite similar to those mentioned earlier, in the section dealing with selection of executor.

Selection. We saw that a good executor (and financial guardian) is characterized by longevity, skill in managing, familiarity, integrity, loyalty and impartiality. In general, these traits also apply to selecting a trustee, except that in the case of a trustee, greater weight is accorded to skill in ongoing financial management. Since the trustee's job can to be long term, the trustee's ability to manage and invest property over a long period becomes a major criterion.[10] As in the case of the executor, potential nominees include family members, friends, the family attorney, and a corporate fiduciary.

Family member, friend. Selecting a family member or friend to be trustee can minimize costs, maximize administrative speed, and may ensure a personal relationship with the survivors.

Disadvantage of family member as trustee. But selecting a family member to be trustee can also result in mismanagement, since few family members have much experience in maintaining, investing, and accounting for an investment portfolio, all critical responsibilities of the trustee. Thus, family members may feel compelled to hire professionals for advice. In addition, family conflicts can arise. For example, nominating the client's children of a former marriage to be trustees of a QTIP trust can create a difficult situation for the client's second and surviving spouse.

Selecting a trust beneficiary to be trustee can also cause problems of proper distribution. For example, in one case, the trustee, who was also a remainder beneficiary, was ordered to by the court to make additional distributions to the decedent-trustor's disabled son, under a trust which

---

10. For a brief examination of the history of the "prudent person rule" and its inconsistency with current trustee investment management practices in the face of inflation and modern portfolio theory, see the Cheris article cited at the end of the chapter. The Halbach paper describes how investment law *(Third Restatement of Trusts)* has responded to these significant factors.

allowed such distributions.[11] In this situation a conflict of interest resulted in a breach of fiduciary obligation that nearly frustrated the trustor's dispositive intent.

Finally, selecting as trustee a family member having general invasion powers may result in undesirable income, gift and estate tax consequences. First, under the grantor trust rules, the trustee will be taxed on the trust income.[12] Second, exercise of a general power by the trustee during the trustee's lifetime will constitute a taxable gift.[13] Third, the trust corpus will be includable in the trustee's gross estate at the trustee's death.[14] Tax problems can also arise for interested trustees having less sweeping powers.[15]

Attorney Selecting an attorney to be trustee can create the same minor risk of a will contest as in nominating an attorney to be executor. In addition, since management of the trust may be a long-term assignment, the client should determine whether the attorney has the time and expertise required to perform effectively. Finally, anticipating trusteeship, the attorney may be tempted to include unconventional *self-serving clauses* in the trust instrument and be subject to other conflicts of interest, similar to the problems described earlier in the selection of the attorney as executor.[16]

Corporate trustee. Selecting a corporate trustee, such as a bank trust department or a trust company, will increase the likelihood that an impartial, technically satisfactory job will be performed. The corporate trustee, however, can be excessively conservative in asset management and is often unable to establish a personal relationship with the beneficiaries.

Cotrustees. A common choice is a cotrusteeship of family member and

---

11. *Pollock v. Phillips* 41 S.E. 2d 242 (W. Va., 1991).

12. §678.

13. §2514.

14. §2041(a)(2).

15. For a general discussion of tax problems of "interested trustees," see the Adams article cited at the end of Chapter 8.

16. In *Marsman v. Nasca* 573 N.E. 2d 1025 (Mass. App. 1991, the court exonerated an attorney-trustee's "abuse of discretion," where a clause in the trust exculpated the trustee from liability except for willful neglect or fraud; for a contrary holding see, *First Alabama Bank of Huntsville v. Spraquins* 515 S. 2d 962 (Ala. 1987).

corporate trustee. It can combine the advantages of each: personal knowledge of the family situation and competent asset management. And naming the surviving spouse to be a cotrustee can be psychologically uplifting to that spouse.

Ordinarily, cotrusteeships do not save management fees, since the corporate trustee will probably charge its customary fee. There may be some situations where corporate trustees will turn down cotrustee arrangements, particularly when they anticipate that the other trustee may be difficult to accommodate. When cotrustees disagree, they may have to seek a resolution in court, unless the trust instrument authorizes a less formal method, such as giving the corporate trustee the final say.

Nominating an alternate trustee. As in nominating an executor, the client should always nominate a successor trustee and should consult with the proposed trustees to ensure that the job will be accepted. Many bank trust departments set minimum asset amounts, which creates the possibility that they may refuse to manage small trusts. Minimum amounts can range between $100,000 and $500,000, depending upon the bank and the ease with which the portfolio's assets can be managed.

Trustee's powers: three common options. The client has at least three commonly used options in deciding what trustee powers to confer in a trust document.[17]

No explicit powers. First, the client can specify no powers, relying entirely on implied powers, and on that state's statutory and case-law framework, which explicitly confers some powers to trustees. Many states have adopted the Uniform Trustees Powers Act, which codifies numerous trustee powers. This approach is often used for clients having relatively small estates and no assets requiring difficult administration, such as a closely held business.

Some explicit powers. The second approach is to rely on the state's laws in general but also explicitly grant in the trust instrument some other desirable powers not found in the statute, ones that may facilitate asset administration. This is the approach used in Exhibit 3-2, the living trust, and in Exhibit 3-3, the trust-will.

Many, many explicit powers. A third approach is not to rely at all on state law and instead draft a document that exhaustively includes all powers that the trustee should be permitted to have. The resulting independent tailor-made document eliminates certain risks, such as future legislative and judicial revision of the law, and the uncertain consequence of a change in the client's residence state. On the negative side, a custom-drafted form will

---

17. For a more detailed discussion, see the Hayes paper cited at the end of the chapter.

be a more complex document, more difficult to read and perhaps more prone to internal inconsistency.

Determining Age At Time of Outright Distribution From A Trust

Age. All estate planning trusts specify a time when the corpus will be distributed outright to the beneficiaries. Determining in advance the best time can be difficult for a client with minor children, because the client cannot accurately predict their rates of maturation.[18] A client may prefer to delay distribution of corpus to a later age, such as age 30 or 40. Others prefer staggered ages. For example, the client may specify that one third be distributed at age 21, half the balance at age 25, and the remainder at age 30. Other clients may prefer to delay distribution to beneficiaries until age 50 or so, by which time the beneficiaries will have fully established their own lives. Other clients, seeking an alternative to mandatory distribution and trust termination when a beneficiary reaches a certain age, simply give the beneficiary a power of withdrawal over the property. Thus, their trustee would be empowered to continue to manage the property indefinitely if the beneficiary became unable or unwilling to make a withdrawal request.

Finally, a few clients may prefer to leave the bulk of their wealth to charity. They may fear the potentially devastating impact the anticipation of inherited wealth can have on financially immature children. For example, a study by the National Bureau of Economic Research found that a single person inheriting more than $150,000 is four times as likely to quit working than one getting less than $25,000. Children of wealthier families may be prone to a malady one commentator had called "affluenza," characterized by the following symptoms: lack of connection between work and reward, inadequate self discipline, distorted view of money, lack of motivation, guilt, and low self esteem. Finally, some clients may feel their children simply do not deserve any inheritance.[19]

Single versus multiple trusts. For clients with more than one child, a separate trust can be established for each child, or a single trust can include all children. How much each child will receive may depend upon how many trusts are created.

Multiple trusts. Creating multiple trusts, i.e., a *separate trust* for each

---

18. For an interesting discussion of alternative distribution strategies for presently immature children, see the Gallo paper cited at the end of the chapter.

19. "How much sharper than a serpent's tooth it is to have a thankless child." *King Lear*, Act 1, Scene V.

child, adds flexibility but increases administration costs. In addition, separate trusts may be considered unfair to the younger children for the following reason. If the client lives, expenses in raising all children will ordinarily come from family property in general and not from separate shares reserved for each child. Thus, expenses to raise even the youngest child will come from what could be called the family "pot" of wealth. On the other hand, if the client dies leaving orphan minor children, and if a separate trust is immediately created for each child, the pot will likely be split before all expenses in raising the children have been incurred. Thus, each child's remaining expenses will be financed out of his or her own separate share, rather than from the pot. Consequently, the younger children will receive a relatively smaller final distribution upon reaching adulthood because living expenses over a longer period of time will have been charged only to their shares. A single trust can solve this problem.

Single pot trust. The name given by some attorneys to a type of single trust created for more than one child, one that retains the "pot" characteristic, is the pot trust or family pot trust. Under its usual terms, the trust remains undivided until the *youngest child reaches age 21*, the age at which parental obligations are commonly perceived to terminate. At that time, the assets are divided into *equal separate shares*, one for each child. The assets are distributed outright, or they are held for distribution at some older age.

The choice of the age at which the assets in a pot trust are divided into separate shares or separate trusts involves a *trade-off* between inequality and delay. The younger that age, the more *unequal* will be the total cumulative amounts distributed to the children, but the *sooner* will the older children be certain of the size of their shares. Conversely, the older the age at which the assets are divided into separate shares, the less the inequality, but the later the share amounts will be determined.

> EXAMPLE 17-9 Mrs. Hunsaker, a widow, is pondering the type of distribution clause for her trust. She has two children, Colleen, age 20, and Nancy, age 15. Colleen is a senior in college and is engaged to be married, and Nancy, still in high school, is headed for college. One alternative would split the trust into two equal shares immediately upon her death, with outright distribution to each child at age 21. Another alternative would delay dividing the assets into equal shares until Nancy reaches age 21, at which time both children would equal shares outright. If Mrs. Hunsaker dies just after the trust is executed, with the first alternative, Colleen will receive her distribution in less than one year and none of it will have been used to finance Nancy's living expenses. With the second alternative, Colleen will have to wait until age 26 to receive her distribution, and the entire corpus will have been available to meet Nancy's living expense, including most of her college education.

Delaying division of the trust assets probably better reflects the financial condition that would have resulted had the client not died: One pot of wealth would have been the source for both children's needs. For this reason, most attorneys recommend delaying the division. However, some attorneys recommend dividing the corpus of a pot trust into separate shares sooner, when the *oldest child reaches age 18*, rather than age 21, reasoning that parents would probably prefer that each child bear subsequent (perhaps very unequal) costs (e.g., college, graduate school) only out of his or her own share. This, of course, reflects a very different philosophy of family financial planning. The planner should determine which best suits the preferences of each client rather than using boiler plate changes.

Restrictions against Assignment

As mentioned in Chapter 3, the client may wish to include a *spendthrift clause*, insulating the trust from the claims of the beneficiaries' creditors and restricting beneficiaries from transferring their interests in trust income or principal prior to their receipt. Spendthrift clauses are legally recognized in the majority of American jurisdictions, even if the beneficiary is not a "spendthrift." And they can help a financially prudent beneficiary (e.g., a professional) by protecting trust assets from nonloan creditors. However, such clauses are not foolproof. Although they may deny a creditor the right to demand that the *trustee* directly hand a distribution over to it, they do not prevent the creditor from exercising the usual legal remedies (i.e., action in court) against a beneficiary *after* the beneficiary receives a distribution. In addition, all states will enforce a promise made by the beneficiary prior to a distribution that the beneficiary will hand it over to the creditor once it is received. Thus, while a spendthrift clause can discourage excessive spending, it cannot completely prevent the beneficiary from "spending" trust property prior to receiving it, as long as there are potential creditors around who are willing to risk having to seek payment from the beneficiary.

Several states, including California, have recently enacted exceptions to the general rule that spendthrift trust assets are not subject to the claims of beneficiaries creditors. Common exceptions apply to the following situations:

- revocable trusts, if the trustor is beneficiary,
- cases involving spousal and child support judgments,
- creditors that are government agencies.

In addition, California has established a procedure similar to wage garnishment for judgment creditors of up to 25 percent of amounts distributable in excess of support needs.

Spendthrift clauses work best in a discretionary trust, one in which the beneficiary has no legally enforceable right to income or principal.

Special Needs Trust. One interesting application of the spendthrift concept is a discretionary spendthrift trust used for the benefit of a *developmentally disabled child* after the parent's death. Called a *special needs trust*, it may not work in some states, where courts have ruled it in violation of public policy. It seeks to insulate trust assets from governmental claims, and, at the same time, keep the child eligible for public benefits, including Supplemental Security Income (SSI), Medicaid, and Social Security Disability Insurance (SSDI). The special needs trust provides for the health, safety and welfare of the beneficiary in ways not provided by any public agency, that no part of the corpus may be used to replace public benefits, and that in the event that the trust renders the beneficiary ineligible for public benefits, the trustee is authorized (but not required) to terminate the trust and distribute the corpus to a "precatory trustee," who is requested (but not required) to provide for the disabled person's basic living needs.[20] The word *precatory* originated from the word 'pray.' Precatory language is used in a will or trust when the writer wants to recommend a course of action but not impose an enforceable obligation on anyone.

Foreign trust. Clients owning substantial liquid assets and wishing to more completely protect them from *their own creditors* may consider creating a foreign "protection of assets" trust. Certain jurisdictions including the Bahamas, Bermuda and the Cayman Islands offer great protection from pre- and postjudgment remedies of future creditors. Drawbacks include setup costs in excess of $25,000, considerable reporting requirements, and ethical issues. However, at its best, such a trust will trigger no additional taxes.[21]

Perpetuities Savings Clause

Appendix 3A discusses the *rule against perpetuities*, which is a common law principle invalidating a trust dispositive clause if a contingent interest transferred might vest in a transferee beyond a life being plus 21 years. The reader is referred to that appendix for a discussion of ways in which the rule can be violated, as well as a description of savings clauses that can be used

---

20. For details, see the Ross article cited at the end of the chapter.

21. Many details are analyzed in the Bruce/Gray/Luria paper cited at the end of the chapter.

in wills and trusts to prevent the operation of the rule.

Trust Taxation: A Summary

Now that the text has covered all the major types of trusts in estate planning, it might help to summarize and compare the gift, estate and income taxation of these trusts. See Table 17-1.

Table 17-1 Summary of Trust Taxation

TRUST TYPE	TAXABLE GIFT?	IN ESTATE TAX BASE?	INCOME TAXABLE TO GRANTOR/ CLIENTS?
Revocable Living Trust	No, not a completed gift	Yes, in grantor's gross estate (§2038)	Yes, as a grantor trust (§676)
Bypass Trust	No, not effective until grantor's death.	S1: Yes, S2: No	No, taxable to trust or beneficiaries
Marital Trusts (QTIP trust, Pwr. of appt. trust, or Estate trust)	No, not effective until grantor's death (At that time, property probably includable in S1's gross estate)	S1: No, sheltered by marital deduction S2: Yes (QTIP and estate trust), or very likely (POA trust)	Yes; taxable to S2 if income in fact payable to S2 (Req'd. for QTIP & POA trusts; Not req'd. for estate trust)
Minor's Trusts (§2503(b), §2503(c), or Crummey)	Only to extent not sheltered by annual exclusion	Not unless taxable gift involved. If so, yes, as an adjusted taxable gift	No, taxable to trust or beneficiaries
Intentionally Defective Irrevocable Trust	Only to extent not sheltered by annual exclusion	Not unless taxable gift involved. If so, yes, as an adjusted taxable gift	Yes, by design, to reduce grantor's gross estate by amount of income tax paid
Irrevocable Life Insurance Trust	Only to extent not sheltered by annual exclusion	Not unless taxable gift involved. If so, yes, as an adjusted taxable gift	No, taxable to trust or beneficiaries
Grantor Retained Trust	Yes, value of remainder (does not qualify for annual exclusion)	Depends: Yes, if doesn't survive period; No, if does	Yes, as a mandatory distribution
Charitable Remainder Trust	No, completed gift, but deductible under §2522	No, includable in gross estate (§2036), but deductible (§2055)	Yes, as a mandatory distribution

In interpreting the comments, keep in mind that some of these trusts come into being under the terms of other trusts, often not until the client's death. Thus, the nature of a trust may change over time. For example, the bypass and marital trusts usually come into effect at the client's death under the terms of the client's revocable living trust instrument (or trust-will). Thus, the comments for the living trust above apply to tax effects during the client-grantor's lifetime or at his or her death, while the comments for the bypass and marital trusts refer to tax effects at, or after, the grantor's death.

PLANNING FOR NONTRADITIONAL RELATIONSHIPS

Recently, planners have been asked for advice from more and more *unmarried* clients involved in nontraditional, long term relationships with members of the same or opposite sex. These relationships present some unique planning challenges and can lead to a set of surprisingly different planning strategies. Two characteristics not applicable to married clients explain most of the differences. First, being unmarried, the partners *will not be entitled* to the advantages offered by law to married couples. Second, since unmarried partners usually do not have children in common, they usually have *totally different sets of surviving kin*. Thus, while they may have a strong desire to leave most or all property for the benefit of the partner *for life*, they will not want the partner to be able to control disposition of their property at or after the partner's death. Underlying strategies based on these characteristics are discussed next.

Greater Need To Avoid Intestacy

Unmarried partners are not included as heirs in intestate succession statutes, making written estate planning documents even more important. Intestacy will have the undesired effect of *disinheriting* the surviving partner, who is hardly ever a blood relative.

Less Shelter From FET May Dictate Larger Bypass

In theory, the largest combined estate size that unmarried partners can transfer to survivors, FET free, with a credit shelter bypass is $1,200,000, just as for married clients. However, *in fact*, the true maximum is usually less, to the extent that one of the partners owns less than $600,000. While the first $600,000 owned by a partner will be sheltered by the unified credit, any excess amount can not be sheltered by the marital deduction. Thus, deathtime planning can not "zero out" the FET for any first partner to die (P1) owning greater than $600,000. Since P1 will incur an FET whether the excess is left to the surviving partner (P2) or to the bypass, P1 may prefer to leave the *entire* estate to the bypass, in order to minimize P2's FET, and to ensure that the property will ultimately pass to P1's surviving kin.

As a partial solution, the partners may agree to arrange separate wills leaving everything to one another, and agreeing that at P2's death, property originating from P1 will pass to P1's surviving kin. But, short of executing a joint and mutual will, P1 has no way to prevent P2 from revising the instrument later on. So the surest plan requires use of bypass trusts to minimize P2's FET and to ensure that each will have selected his or her own remaindermen as the ultimate beneficiaries of their respective estates.

Greater Need for Life Insurance at First Death

Since P1 estates exceeding $600,000 will usually owe an FET, liquidity planning will often require life insurance on P1 as well as P2. The proceeds can still be kept out of both partner's gross estates with irrevocable life insurance trusts.

Lifetime Giving More Important

Inability to save as much FET on transfers at death may prompt unmarried partners to engage in greater gift planning. Although unmarried partners will not be able to utilize the gift tax marital deduction, they can still take advantage of one annual exclusion per donee per year. Thus, they can still undertake an ongoing program of lifetime giving to reduce their estate tax base. Careful planning should *avoid outright gifts* to the partner, however, to enable the donor, as a potential P1, to retain final dispositive control. Instead, the planner should encourage gifting *in trust*, with provisions granting a life estate in the income to the partner and the remainder to the trustor's surviving relatives. As future interests, however, the remainder interest portion of such gifts in trust will not qualify for the annual exclusion and will either use up the client's unified credit or result in a actual gift tax.

Joint Tenancies in Community Property States May Be More Attractive

Finally, in community property states, joint tenancies as a means of disposing of property of unmarried decedents may be more attractive, relative to the will and the trust. Only married couples can own community property. Lacking the income tax advantage of a full step-up in basis, a uniquely characteristic of community property, unmarried couples with smaller estates may choose joint tenancies as a simple form of co-ownership. From a tax basis point of view, joint tenancies will be no worse than any other form of ownership of property. Furthermore, if the first partner to die is the one who owned the property before it was transferred into joint tenancy, this form of ownership also provides a full step-up in basis since the entire value would be included in his or her estate. However, from a control point of view, joint tenancies may still not be desirable. It does not keep dispositive control in the hands of the original owner, whereas a trust would do so.

We turn next to the second major topic of the chapter: planning for the client's own incapacity.

PLANNING FOR THE CLIENT'S INCAPACITY

More and more, disability is preceding death as people live longer and longer. To cite just two examples of demographic data, consider a 1992 U.S. Census Bureau report that the number of Americans 65 and older grew by 22 percent in the 1980's, more than twice the growth rate for the nation as a whole. It also found that two thirds of Americans 75 and older consider themselves "healthy".

A client's disability creates the need for care by a surrogate decision maker. Since the client will usually have specific preferences regarding care, planning for incapacity while the client is physically and mentally fit increases the likelihood of more satisfying final years.

As in the case of minors, the law recognizes two types of care for incapacitated adults: care for the client's property and personal care for the client. The final two sections of this chapter deal with planning for each.

Planning for the Care of the Incapacitated Client's Property

Four techniques are available to care for the property of an incapacitated client: the guardianship or conservatorship, revocable living trust, durable power of attorney for property, and the special needs trust. Only the last two will be described in detail.

1. Guardianship or conservatorship of the client's property.
Similar to the guardianship of the estate of a minor, all states recognize a court-supervised arrangement to manage the property of an incapacitated client. Called a *guardianship* or a *conservatorship*, depending on the state, establishment of either normally requires a court hearing, and the appointee is ordinarily subject to continuing court supervision. The guardian or conservator is required to give periodic accountings to the court, and is typically required to obtain court permission before engaging in most property transactions. Most guardians and conservators have little or no discretionary authority. However, some states are reducing court involvement in guardianships and conservatorships in much the same way they are reducing court involvement for probate proceedings.[22]

For reasons similar to those for avoiding probate, many clients will plan to avoid the necessity of having a property guardian or conservator. Some clients, however, may prefer the protection offered from their closer court supervision. Clients owning larger estates, or those who cannot recommend a friend or relative to manage property, might prefer a court-administered alternative. Most clients will prefer one or both of the arrangements described next.

2. Revocable living trust. In planning for incapacity, the client could create a self-trusteed revocable living trust, funding it with family assets. The trust instrument could provide for a successor trustee when the client became unable to manage the trust's financial affairs. The successor trustee could be the spouse, an adult child, another relative, a trusted friend, or a corporate trustee. In comparison with a guardianship or conservatorship, a living trust offers the advantages of privacy, flexibility, and freedom from court appearances and accountings. On the other hand, since the trust is a private, noncourt-supervised arrangement, there exists a greater potential for *undiscovered fraud and mismanagement* by the successor trustee.

One additional disadvantage of the trust arrangement to handle incapacity is the possible requirement of a *formal legal determination* of the trustee-client's *incapacity* before a successor trustee can take over the job. Embarrassing litigation can develop between the trustor and a family member who is attempting to establish that the trustor is incompetent. However, this conflict can also arise if a guardianship or conservatorship is being established. The trust can contain a clause providing for a *private* determination of incapacity, in the same manner provided by the springing durable power of attorney for property, discussed next.

3. Durable power of attorney for property. Creation of a trust can be

---

22. For example, see California Probate Code §2590-95.

relatively expensive. Clients owning smaller estates may prefer to execute a simpler document, known as a durable power of attorney for property. Popularized by the Uniform Probate Code, the durable power of attorney for property has been recognized by the statutes of every state. The durable power of attorney for property is different from the durable power of attorney for health care, described in the next section. Since state laws vary, the reader is strongly urged to examine the law of his or her particular state.[23]

A power of attorney is a written document executed by one person, called the *principal*, authorizing another person, called the *attorney-in-fact* or the *agent*, to perform designated acts on behalf of the principal. A durable power of attorney for property (DPOA) creates an agency relationship that allows the agent to perform acts to protect the principal's property interests, even if the principal becomes incapacitated.

Durable versus nondurable powers of attorney. General powers of attorney can be either durable or nondurable. Nondurable powers of attorney are not practical alternatives for caring for the property of elderly clients because they become legally invalid at the onset of the client's incapacity, just when they are needed most. In one situation, an attorney-in-fact under a nondurable power of attorney gifted property after the principal became mentally incompetent and the IRS ruled that the gift was voidable under local law (by a court-appointed guardian or by the principal had he regained mental capacity), and therefore the gift was included in the principal's gross estate under §2038.[24]

The *durable* power of attorney was developed to overcome this deficiency. Thus, a DPOA is durable because it survives the client's incapacity. Exhibit 17-1 illustrates the common provisions of a DPOA. The italicized sentence makes it "durable."

---

23. For a description of some peculiarities in state law, see the Brown article cited at the end of the chapter.

24. R 8623004

EXHIBIT 17-1 Durable Power of Attorney (for property)

TO WHOM IT MAY CONCERN:

I, John Jones, a resident of Anytown, Anystate, in the county of Anycounty, do hereby constitute and appoint Aaron Agent, a resident of Anytown, Anystate, to be my attorney-in-fact, with full power to name and stead and on my behalf and with full power to substitute at any time or times for the purposes described below one or more attorneys and to revoke the appointment of my attorney so substituted and to do the following:

1. To manage my affairs; handle my investments; arrange for the investment, reinvestment, and disposition of funds; exercise all rights with respect to my investments; accept remittances of income and disburse the same, including authority to open bank accounts in my name and to endorse checks for deposit therein or in any bank where I may at any time have money on deposit and sign checks covering withdrawals therefrom.
2. To endorse and deliver certificates for transfer of bonds or other securities to be sold for my account and receive the proceeds from such sale.
3. To sign, execute, acknowledge, and deliver on my behalf any deed of transfer or conveyance covering personal property or real estate wherever situated (including transfers or conveyances to any trust established by me), any discharge or release of mortgage held by me on real estate or any other instrument in writing.
4. To negotiate and execute leases of any property, real or personal, which I may own, for terms that may extend beyond the duration of this power and to provide for the proper care and maintenance of such property and pay expenses incurred in connection therewith.
5. To subdivide, partition, improve, alter, repair, adjust boundaries of, manage, maintain, and otherwise deal with any real estate held as trust property, including power to demolish any building in whole or in part and to erect buildings.
6. To enter into a lease or arrangement for exploration and removal of minerals or other natural resources or to enter into a pooling or unitization agreement.
7. To hold securities in bearer form or in the name of a nominee or nominees and to hold real estate in the name of a nominee or nominees.
8. To continue or participate in the operation of any business or other enterprise.
9. To borrow money from time to time in my name and to give notes or other obligations therefore, and to deposit as collateral, pledge as security for the payment thereof, or mortgage any or all my securities or other property of whatever nature.
10. To have access to any and all safe deposit boxes of which I am now or may become possessed, and to remove therefrom any securities, papers, or other articles.

EXHIBIT 17-1 *continued*

11. To make all tax returns and pay all taxes required by law, including federal and state returns, and to file all claims for abatement, refund, or other papers relating thereto.
12. To demand, collect, sue for, receive, and receipt for any money, debts, or property of any kind, now or hereafter payable, due or deliverable to me; to pay or contest claims against me; to settle claims by compromise, arbitration, or otherwise; and to release claims.
13. To employ as investment counsel, custodians, brokers, accountants, appraisers, attorneys-at-law, or other agents such persons, firms, or organizations, including my said attorney and any firm of which my said attorney may be a member or employee, as deemed necessary or desirable, and to pay such persons, firms, or organizations such compensation as is deemed reasonable and to determine whether or not to act upon the advice of any such agent without liability for acting or failing to act thereon.
14. To expend and distribute income or principal of my estate for the support, education, care, or benefit of me and my dependents.
15. To make gifts to any one or more of my spouse and my descendants (if any) of whatever degree (including my said attorney who is a spouse or descendant of mine) in amounts not exceeding $10,000 annually with respect to any one of them and gifts to charity in amounts not exceeding 20 percent of my federal adjusted gross income in any one year.
16. To renounce and disclaim any interest otherwise passing to me by testate or intestate succession or by inter vivos transfer.
17. To exercise my rights to elect options and change beneficiaries under insurance and annuity policies and to surrender the policies for their cash value.

In general I give to my said attorney full power to act in the management and disposition of all my estate, affairs and property of every kind and wherever situate in such manner and with such authority as I myself might exercise if personally present.

This power of attorney shall be binding on me and my heirs, executors, and administrators and shall remain in force up to the time of the receipt of my attorney of a written revocation signed by me.

This power of attorney shall not be affected by my subsequent disability or incapacity.

EXHIBIT 17-1 *concluded*

IN WITNESS THEREOF, I have hereunto set my hand and seal on this day of March 19, 1999.

_____(Signature)_____

Executed in counterparts

STATE OF ANYSTATE

County of Anycounty

_____, 19_____

Then personally appeared the above named _____ and acknowledged the foregoing instrument to be his free act and deed,

Before me,

_____
Notary Public
My commission expires:

_____

This is a slightly modified version of the sample form contained in Charles M. Hamann. "Durable Powers of Attorney," *Trusts and Estates*, February 1983, pp. 30-31. Reprinted with permission.

This particular example of a DPOA form can be criticized for being simply a *unilateral authorizing instrument*, which means that the named attorney-in-fact would not be liable for failure to act. Some commentators recommend instead creating a *bilateral contract* between principal and attorney-in-fact, particularly if the latter is not the client's spouse, to eliminate this problem. This may require a signature by the attorney in fact, and the payment of some compensation.

Nonspringing versus springing DPOAs. There are two common types of DPOAs. The first type becomes effective as soon as it is executed. The second type, called a "springing" DPOA, becomes effective *at* the principal's incapacity. It will contain the following clause, in addition to those found in Exhibit 17-1:

> *This power of attorney shall become effective upon my disability or my incapacity. I shall be deemed disabled or incapacitated upon the election of my said attorney to accept the certificate of a physician which states that such physician has examined me and that I am incapacitated mentally or physically and am therefore incapable of attending to my business affairs.*[25]

Some attorneys recommend that, instead of a physician, a "trusted committee" of three of the client's trusted friends and relatives should be empowered to determine when the power of attorney becomes effective.

Springing powers are authorized by about two-fifths of the states.[26] Clients in states not authorizing springing powers have no choice but to execute a nonspringing DPOA while they are competent and then hope that their attorney-in-fact does not improperly act on their behalf prior to their incapacity. Delaying delivery of the document may help.

To be valid, of course, any DPOA must be *executed* prior to the principal's incapacity. To ensure competent execution, many advisers recommend the preparation of a DPOA for an older client at the time the will is being prepared.

Advantages of the DPOA. The DPOA has several advantages over the other devices designed to manage an incapacitated client's property. Compared to a guardianship or conservatorship, the DPOA is less expensive to create and to administer. The nonspringing type can avoid the necessity of a court-held incompetency proceeding, an event that can be painful and embarrassing to all parties, especially the client. Compared with the living trust, the DPOA is also less expensive to create and administer. Some clients who refuse to set up a trust may be willing to executing a DPOA, because of its relative simplicity. Yet a trust can continue after the client's death, whereas a DPOA, being based on agency law, must terminate when the principal dies. It may be durable but it is not that durable.

---

25. Reprinted with permission from Charles M. Hamann, "Durable Powers of Attorney," *Trusts & Estates*, February 1983, pp. 30-31.

26. Including AK, CA, DL, ID, KN, MA, MI, MT, NE, NJ, NY, NC, OK, TN, UT, VT, VA, WA, WI. Three state specifically prohibit it (CT, IL, SC).

However, the trust and the DPOA need not be considered alternatives; greater flexibility may result if a DPOA authorizes the attorney-in-fact to add newly acquired property (by gift, inheritance, etc) to the clients partially funded living trust, or to fund an existing unfunded revocable living trust (a "standby trust") with the client's assets, at the onset of incapacity. Upon funding, the assets could be managed by a skilled trustee. Thereafter, the attorney-in-fact may be permitted to perform other duties that were not given to the trustee, including establishing and funding other trusts, making gifts and disclaimers, and appearing at tax audits.[27]

Regarding the power of the attorney-in-fact to make gifts, one court has ruled that failure to explicitly include that power in the document will totally frustrate gift planning. In that case, the attorney-in-fact did make gifts before the principal's death. Relying on Virginia's narrow construction of powers of attorney law, the appellate court treated the gift as revocable at the time of the principal's death, resulting in inclusion of gifted assets in the gross estate under §2036(a) and §2038.[28] However, in a more recent Virginia case, the tax court allowed gifts by an attorney-in-fact because Virginia law authorizes attorneys-in-fact to make gifts "in accordance with the principal's personal history of making or joining in lifetime gifts."[29]

Drawbacks of the DPOA. The DPOA has at least two potential estate tax drawbacks for the attorney in-fact, either of which might subject the principal's property to inclusion in the *attorney-in-fact's* gross estate in the event the attorney-in fact dies first.[30] First, the attorney-in-fact may be deemed to have a general power of appointment over the principal's property. Eliminating this danger may require either prohibiting entirely the ability of the attorney-in-fact to make gifts to him or herself, etc., or limiting such gifts to an ascertainable standard, or to the greater of $5,000 or 5 percent of the value of the property.

One nontax drawback to the DPOA concerns its *acceptance.* Certain financial institutions may be unwilling to honor the DPOA if they cannot

---

27. For a discussion of a trust that expands the power of the *trustee* to make certain lifetime gifts and undertake other actions otherwise often exercisable by an attorney in fact, see the Blattmachr article cited at the end of Chapter 10.

28. *Estate of Casey v. Commissioner*, 948 F2d. 895 (1991). Also see LR 9231003.

29. *J. Ridenour Estate* 46 TCM 1850 (1992).

30. For a discussion of a potential §2036 problem involving spousal "cross powers," see the Brown article cited at the end of the chapter.

satisfy themselves that it is currently valid. The power, they reason, may already have been revoked by the principal or the principal may be dead. Due to their uncertainty about the validity of custom drafted DPOAs they may insist on the execution on their own form. The industry's increasing use of the DPOA should substantially lessen these concerns. The attorney can minimize acceptance problems with careful and specific custom-drafting of enumerated powers, and by having the client periodically re-execute the DPOA to prevent it from appearing outdated. Nevertheless, some institutions refuse to accept a DPOA, and some banks and the IRS will, but might require the use of their own forms.

Other helpful techniques to maximize acceptability include a provision in the document that empowers the attorney-in-fact to bring legal action against a recalcitrant third party and indemnifies the third party when it acts in reliance on the document and the agent's instructions. However, pursuing legal action can be expensive and time consuming. Finally, the clients themselves, while competent, can show the document to banks, insurance companies, health care providers, etc., to find out whether it will be accepted, and to stop dealing with those institutions that refuse. New York has recently adopted a statute making it unlawful to refuse to recognize the New York statutory form DPOA and indemnifying a bank when it does. California's statute permits the filing of an action to compel the honoring of a statutory durable power and specifies that a refusal is unreasonable if the sole reason for the refusal is that it's not on a form prescribed by the reluctant party.[31]

The second nontax drawback of the DPOA is that it can be *misused.* Lawyers will attest to situations where attorneys-in-fact, particularly the children of clients, have used the property in a manner clearly contrary to clients' best interests. Although such behavior is actionable, it is rarely challenged. Because the DPOA delegates very fundamental property rights, the client should first think long and hard about the possible consequences.

4. Special needs trust and other asset "spend-down" planning. A different kind of living trust may be capable of preserving assets owned by clients anticipating possible long-term disability.

The medical profession has been tremendously successful in prolonging the life of the seriously ill, often comes at great economic cost. Such patients often need *custodial care* for help with feeding, bathing, dressing and transportation. Later, they may need *skilled nursing care* provided in a licensed facility, and costing $3,000 per month or more. Their condition may finally require a lengthy period of *hospitalization,* costing far more.

---

31. CA Civil Code §2480.5.

Private and public insurance can help pay these costs, but often not entirely. Long-term care insurance has recently become available, but policies usually are expensive and contain significant restrictions and exclusions, so few people are willing to buy it. Federal Medicare insurance for patients over 65 will pay for up to 150 days of hospitalization, with sizable deductibles after the first 50 days. Medicare pays for little or no post-hospitalization nursing facility care. These limitations in private and public insurance raise the possibility that a client will totally deplete the wealth acquired over a lifetime, thereby preventing any significant amount going to the children.

To prevent this, some clients are turning to attorney who specialize in *elder law*. Many recommend "spending down" assets through the use of gifts and trusts. This action seeks to accomplish two goals. First, it strives to insulate the client's assets from the claims of health care providers and government agencies. Second, it attempts to impoverish the client sufficiently to qualify for certain types of federal and state assistance, including Supplemental Security Income, In-Home Supportive Services, In-Home Medical Care Services, and perhaps most importantly, Medicaid. Each state, in exchange for matching federal Medicaid grants, imposes federally influenced limits on both 1) assets (roughly $3,000 for spouses living together, and $70,000 if one spouse is in a nursing home, not counting the residence), and 2) income (income limit depends upon the actual cost of medical and custodial care).

Three common spending-down strategies will be compared. First, the client may wish to make *outright gifts* of property to children. However, outright gifts have the major drawback covered in earlier chapters: the client loses total control over the property. Second, the client could purchase a single premium annuity. Although distributions from the annuity do count for purposes of the income test, the overall value of the annuity does not count under the assets test. Finally, and perhaps most effective, the client could make substantial gifts to an irrevocable *special needs trust*, also called a *discretionary support trust*. Under this trust, the client-trustor retains the following powers and interests:

- While competent, the power to act as trustee.
- While *not* competent, or while completely disabled and subject to catastrophic health care costs, the right to invade principal on the basis of health, education, maintenance or support.
- The power to appoint an unlimited amount of trust property to family members other than the trustor.
- The power to change beneficiaries so as to reallocate the estate among the children, if desired.

In addition, a group of other persons, including children, advisors, and siblings (the more the better) are given a power to authorize the trustee to revest any trust property in the trustor. Any one of these persons may individually exercise this power.

The special needs trust will be incomplete for both FET and income tax purposes, and its assets will not be counted for purposes of eligibility under Medicaid. The trustee may also own the long-term health care insurance policy, if any, to further exclude payments from the income test. If the residence is in this grantor trust, it will qualify for the §121 one-time exclusion of $125,000 of gain, and for the §1034 rollover. In addition, all trust assets will obtain a basis step-up at the trustor's death. Under Medicaid rules, the client would be ineligible for public assistance for up to thirty six months (sixty months, in the case of certain transfers, including those from revocable trusts) after the date of the transfers into trust.[32] In addition, states may recover property after the beneficiary's death from the probate estate as well as other former assets of the beneficiary, including those conveyed to a survivor, heir or assign through joint tenancy, tenancy in common, survivorship, life estate and living trusts. Property in the estate of the surviving spouse is exempt.

Although the law prohibits nursing homes from charging patients greater than the amount paid under government assistance, the client's trust assets can be used to improve care by acquiring for the patient services not funded by public assistance. These could include an extra private nurse, physiotherapists, additional medication, or a paid companion who reads to the patient or takes the patient on special outings. However, even with these extras, wealthier clients will probably not be interested in spending down or in establishing a special needs trust. Most will want a higher overall quality of care, and may not like being regarded as a "welfare case."

Impoverishing a client owning sizable assets so as to qualify for public assistance funds is a controversial subject and raises ethical issues. Some planners will not recommend it, because they see it as taking unfair advantage of an imperfect system designed for truly needy people, and also encouraging children to treat Medicaid as if it were "their personal inheritance insurance." Others find no moral dilemma, and consider it no different from tax planning, such as when providing for a credit shelter bypass trust to minimize FET. Perhaps all planners might agree that clients should be encouraged to understand, at a minimum, other basic protective planning

---

32. The Omnibus Budget Reconciliation Act of 1993, besides increasing the period from thirty months, made several other restrictive changes, reflecting Congressional interest in discouraging spend down planning. (Amendments made to 42 USC §1396).

steps well in advance by purchasing an effective long-term care insurance policy[33] and by carefully saving for their future care.[34]

Planning for the Personal Care of the Incapacitated Client

Similar to the procedure for selecting the guardian of a minor child, the procedure for selecting the person who will care for an incapacitated adult is usually undertaken in the county probate court after a noticed hearing. Some states call this fiduciary a *guardian* or *committee*, while others use the name *conservator*. States define guardian, conservator, and committee differently. In some states, such as California, a conservator deals the person and the property of an adult unable to provide for personal needs or to manage financial resources. In other states, such as New York, a conservator concerns itself primarily with an "impaired" person's property, while a committee cares for both the person and the property of an "incompetent" person. The UPC parallels the New York terminology and, in addition, permits a guardian to be appointed to oversee the person and the property of an "incapacitated" person. In any case, the court chooses the party only after careful, formal consideration.

Selecting a personal care provider. Whom should the client recommend to provide personal care in the event of his or her incapacity? Ordinarily, the client has few choices.

Spouse, family members. The spouse is usually the best first choice. Next come other family members, especially adult children. However, the children may lead busy lives and may not be capable nor willing to do all the work required. This problem will be even more likely to arise for a client in an advanced stage of incapacity, such as at the onset of incontinence. Prior to this degree of impairment, the client may simply need home delivery of meals, other housekeeping services, or adult day care, all of which are often commercially available. While these services

---

33. For a discussion of long-term care insurance, see the Feldesman/Canning article cited at the end of the chapter. Four states (California, Connecticut, Indiana and New York) now provide for asset protection when Medicaid is applied for if a person purchases an approved long-term care policy.

34. For a further discussion of the use of special needs trusts and other transfer devices designed to provide benefits for an elderly disabled person and still qualify that person for state and federal aid, see the Schlesinger (1993 and 1986), Strauss, Barreira and Feldesman/Canning papers cited at the end of the chapter.

are often not inexpensive, some programs are government subsidized. Services can be arranged for a fee by a "private geriatric care manager," who is often a social worker or nurse. Helpful sources of information include: County and local departments for the aging, for referrals on services for elders; the National Association of Area Agencies on Aging ((800) 677-1116), which has an "elder care locator"; the National Association of Professional Geriatric Care Managers (602-881-8808); the National Academy of Elder Law Attorneys (602-881-4005); and the Children of Aging Parents, offering a clearing house of information including contacts for supports groups for adult children.

Nursing home. Older clients would be well advised to visit residential health care facilities for the elderly. Such facilities vary widely in cost, extent of services offered, and the degree of incapacity permitted. At one end of the spectrum is the traditional nursing home, which offers complete care, but is quite expensive and in general has a reputation, at worst, for offering "a life sentence to mental and physical imprisonment," where patients lose nearly all of their independence in a dehumanizing environment.

Assisted living. Other less structured facilities offer a new and increasingly popular style of housing called assisted living for elderly people without serious medical problems. Private apartments are provided, as well as meals, laundry, housekeeping, social activities and transportation, and regular visits by nurses. Such facilities usually cost considerably less than nursing homes, and offer the greatest degree of independence possible.[35]

Life care facility. Finally, one other type of organization called a life care facility offers seniors the right to occupy, for life, an apartment in a large residential health-care facility, which also provides, on the premises, all meals and round-the-clock nursing, medical, and hospital services. And many of them now permit the client or the client's estate to sell the apartment later on. Clients selling their personal residence to acquire a life care facility can more than likely enjoy the one time $125,000 exclusion on gain on sale under §121, but probably will not be able to roll over any excess gain under §1034, if the acquired interest is simply one for life.

Some figures from the U.S. Census Bureau regarding the elderly living in commercial facilities like the three described above plus long-term care rooms in hospital wards, and soldiers', fraternal or religious homes for the aged, may be helpful. In 1990, 1.8 million people lived in commercial facilities, with women outnumbering men almost 3 to 1. Residents 85 and older constituted 42 percent, up from 34 percent in 1980. Overall, only 5.1

---

35. Wall Street Journal articles on December 3 and 4, 1992. Both on page A1.

percent of the nation's elderly occupy these facilities, but the figure was 24.5 percent for those 85 and older. Only one in seven was married, and 61 percent were widowed. These figures suggest that a significant minority of elderly clients will reside in a commercial facility prior to death.

Delegation of health care decisions. Until recently, people have not had the ability to delegate the power to make *medical* decisions. Today, almost all states recognize an individual's ability either to delegate to some degree important medical decisions, or at least to state in writing what those decisions should be.

Cruzan case. The need to state medical choices clearly and in writing is dramatically illustrated by the 1990 U.S. Supreme Court decision, *Cruzan v. Missouri.*[36] A victim of an automobile accident seven years earlier, 32 year old Nancy Cruzan had remained in a persistent vegetative state, with functioning respiratory and circulatory systems, but little else. She was unable to swallow or recognize her relatives. After it became clear that there was no reasonable hope of any improvement in her condition, her family sought to let her die by withdrawing her feeding tube. The state of Missouri would not allow it, despite the fact that a year before the accident, Nancy had told a friend that "if sick or injured she would not wish to continue her life unless she could live at least halfway normally." On appeal, the U.S. Supreme Court affirmed, approving the Missouri requirement that the family would have to show "clear and convincing evidence" of Nancy's wishes to remove life sustaining equipment, something the jury determined that the Cruzans did not establish.

After the Supreme Court decision and just after the Cruzans requested a new hearing in the local court claiming new evidence that Nancy would not wish to live, the state attorney general withdrew as a party to the case, which meant that there was no longer anyone to oppose removal of Nancy's feeding tube. Nancy died at age 33 on December 26, 1990, twelve days after the tube was removed.

Based on the Supreme Court's ruling, it would appear that standards of proof such as Missouri's "clear and convincing evidence" may be difficult to meet without a written statement by the incapacitated person. Estate planning has two common written documents for this purpose: the durable power of attorney for health care and the living will.

Durable power of attorney for health care. Like the durable power of attorney for property (DPOA), the durable power of attorney for health care (DPOAHC) appoints a person as attorney-in-fact to make decisions on behalf of the principal. However, the documents are different in three im-

---

36. 110 S.Ct. 2841 (1990)

portant respects.

Types of decisions. First, of course, the DPOAHC concerns *medical*, not property decisions. Examples of medical decisions listed in this type of "advance directive" include the power to secure the placement in or removal from a medical facility, to withhold future medical treatment, to use or not use medication, to perform or not perform surgery, and the power to use or not use artificial life-sustaining methods, such as respiration, nourishment, and hydration. As one might expect, this last power is quite controversial, and some legal commentators have defended it ardently. Reflecting an increasingly popular dissatisfaction with the zealous use of artificial life-sustaining methods, Dubler, in the article cited at the end of the chapter, emphatically argues that rapid advances in medical technology combined with the implicit premise of medicine to "do everything" for the patient, has led some to conclude that "doing everything" might violate rather than support the rights of the patient, and "could condemn a body to endless non-sapient, nonrelational existence in a dehumanizing antiseptic setting," one actually not preferable to death.

Delegating a surrogate with the power to terminate life support can be helpful in situations where the physician in charge refuses to act. One study has shown that physicians are reluctant to terminate life support in cases where the patient would take a relatively long time to die, where the life support became necessary because of medical errors, and in cases where the patient has been on life support for a relatively long period of time.[37]

Springing power. Second, the DPOAHC differs from the DPOA in that the DPOAHC is always a springing power, whereas the DPOA can be non-springing. Thus the DPOAHC becomes effective only upon the principal's incapacity, that is, upon his or her inability to make health care decisions. The DPOAHC does not apply just to situations where the principal is terminally ill but to all situations where the principal is unable to give "informed consent" with respect to a particular medical decision.

Separate documents. Third, while it is possible to include the legal content of a DPOAHC within a DPOA document they are usually drafted as separate documents. They involving very different situations, different evolving law, and possibly different attorneys-in-fact. In addition, many attorneys prefer to use a preprinted state medical association form for health care because of its widespread acceptance by the medical profession. In contrast, a custom drafted form can generate decision making delay as, for example, when a hospital requires its own lawyers to carefully evaluate it. Appendix 17A shows an example of a statutory form of DPOAHC, that is,

---

37. *Lancet*, Sept. 11, 1993, p. 645.

a form produced in a statute from a state that also permits custom instruments.

Acceptance of the document. The DPOAHC is statutorily recognized in almost every state.[38] State law varies in terms of both the scope of the authority of the attorney in fact to act on behalf of the client and the protection afforded to health care providers who act on those instructions. Some states such as California have statutes permitting health care providers to *assume* that a DPOAHC is valid in absence of knowledge to the contrary. Offering some support, the American Medical Association has ruled that it is appropriate for doctors to withdraw life-supporting, artificial feeding systems from hopelessly comatose patients.

Drawback. One drawback of the DPOAHC concerns the fact that it is so powerful. It can place reluctant family members in the difficult position of having to make critical life or death decisions, ones they may regrettably relive in their minds over and over, long after the crisis has ended. Nevertheless, the durable power of attorney for health care has become one of the most popular estate planning devices.

Living will. The DPOAHC has become widely accepted in the United States. Before then, most states only recognized some variation of the living will, which typically addresses just one of the two features of the DPOAHC: it details those health care interventions that the person does or does not wish to be subjected to in situations when he or she is no longer capable of making those decisions.

Appendix 17B illustrates one example of a living will. The reader will notice that this particular one, reflecting the modern trend of about eight states, enables the signer to name another person, called a "proxy," to "act on my behalf" regarding these wishes. Living wills are recognized in the statutes of most states. Many attorneys in states where living wills are not yet officially recognized, nevertheless urge their clients to execute them, with the expectation that the courts will accept them if and when tested.

Disadvantages of living will. When compared to the DPOAHC, living wills have at least five limitations. First, a living will does not appoint a surrogate decision maker, which restricts its flexibility considerably, especially in view of the rapid advances in medical technology. Second, living wills are typically very brief, covering only a few possible outcomes, mostly in the area of life-sustaining treatment. No living will, no matter how detailed, can spell out all of the possible treatment decisions that may be needed. Third, most living will statutes apply only to terminal patients,

---

38. Several other states seem to recognize such a power to one degree or another. For a list, see the Collin (1991) article cited at the end of the chapter.

not those who are just incurably ill, such as a person in a persistent vegetative state, and many states require that death be "imminent." Fourth, the language of living wills is usually quite vague, failing to define important terms, leaving the physician and the family to disagree over proper care. Finally, a number of states' living will statutes provide that a physician is obligated to comply with the directives in a living will concerning withdrawal or withholding of life-sustaining procedures. In the event the physician chooses not to comply, he or she must transfer the patient to another physician.

Living wills can be very detailed. With regard to the second and fourth limitations, more and more attorneys are drafting quite specific living wills (and DPOAHCs, for that matter). For example, the client may be asked to enter preferences in writing in a matrix-table depicting alternative medical scenarios and procedures. The *rows* of the matrix might list ten to fifteen medical *procedures*, such as invasive diagnostic tests; CPR; pain medication; artificial nutrition and hydration; mechanical breathing, and the like. The *columns* of the matrix might list alternative physical *scenarios*, such as coma or persistent vegetative state with no chance of regaining awareness; irreversible brain damage or disease; irreversible brain damage or disease combined with terminal illness; coma with small chance of recovery and greater chance of surviving with brain damage, etc. Then, for each cell in the matrix-table, the client would insert one of several letters signifying a desired action, such as U = uncertain; N = do not want procedure; T = yes, try procedure but have it stopped if no clear improvement is shown; and Y = yes try procedure for as long as possible. The danger in documenting this detail is that the client may thoughtlessly and hastily fill in the blanks on a written instrument that may wind up being the only hard evidence available, thereby ruling out the possibility of an alternative choice which may reflect the careful contemplation of the client's sincere loved ones.

Miscellaneous factors. In some states, planners recommend that clients execute both a living will and a DPOAHC, particularly in states where DPOAHCs are not written to include the main characteristic of the living will. Finally, in their attempt at coordination, more and more states are adopting integrated statutes that deal with both types of advance directive.[39]

Several states, including Virginia, recognize a variation on the living will called the *directive to physicians*, giving instructions with regard to the use of life-sustaining treatment. The directive to physicians has been largely

---

39. For a discussion of post-drafting experience with the DPOAHC, see the West paper, cited at the end of the chapter.

rendered obsolete in most other states by the common acceptance of the DPOAHC.

Whatever documents are used, they should be updated periodically, for three reasons. First, state law may require it. Second, the client's wishes may have changed. And third, the planner should make sure the documents remain consistent with the rapidly changing law in this area.

This chapter has described miscellaneous lifetime estate planning techniques not covered earlier. Chapter 18 will examine tax planning techniques which can be employed on behalf of the client after the client's death.

QUESTIONS AND PROBLEMS

1. (*a*) Describe the attributes of an effective parental guardian, executor, and trustee. (*b*) Why are they different?

2. One of your clients asks you to describe the legal alternatives available to provide for her young son's financial care. Be sure to mention the advantages and disadvantages of each.

3. What factors will influence which beneficiaries a testator should choose to bear the burden of death taxes?

4. (*a*) What is a survival clause? (*b*) How does it overcome the consequences of lapse?

5. Cassie's will simply says, "I leave all my securities to John, and everything else to Mary." If John predeceases Cassie, analyze the possible recipients of the securities, using the alternative assumptions made in the text about the contents of the will and the influence of state law. Apply the law of your state, if possible.

6. Describe the family pot trust and the trade-off involved in determining the age of distribution to young adult beneficiaries.

7. Hancock and his wife died on January 1, 1978, the victims of an auto accident. They were survived by two children, Tiffany and Thomas, who had just turned age 19 and 17, respectively, on that very date. All of the Hancock's property, totaling $1 million, passed to a single pot trust, whose terms were identical to those found in the trust-will in Exhibit 3-3, except that instead of receiving their remainder distributions at age 21, each child received one half of the principal at age 25 and the balance at age 30. Over the years, the trustee made, in addition to mandatory distributions, the following discretionary principal distributions (all on January 1) for education expenses:

1979: $50,000 to Tiffany.
1981: $40,000 each to the children.
1983: $10,000 to Thomas.

a. If all assets (i.e., *principal*, consisting entirely of low dividend paying stock) in the trust appreciated exactly ten percent per year and all (dividend) *income* was distributed annually to the children, how much did each child receive, as the final, mandatory distribution of *principal*, and when did they receive it? (Assume no trustee fees or other expenses. Hint: Calculate chronologically the two share amounts at beginning and end of each year. Ignore all dividend income. Answers: Tiffany: $637,985.62; Thomas: $761,244.66. Value of trust assets: on 12/31/78-- $1,100,000; on 12/31/81-- $1,309,550).

b. Would Tiffany's final distribution have been more or less if the trust was instead divided into separate shares when the *oldest* child reached age 18 rather than 21? (General answer can be inferred without making specific recalculations).

8. You are the creditor of a deadbeat who is a beneficiary under a trust containing a spendthrift clause similar to the one in Exhibit 3-2. What ability, if any, do you have at getting at the trust assets?

9. Pat and Kris, lovers for many years, do not ever wish to get married. They have no children. Pat owns $700,000 and Kris owns $900,000 in property.
   a. Assuming Kris dies today and Pat survives by 10 years, calculate the total FET incurred at both deaths under the following plans:
      1. Simple wills, naming each other as contingent beneficiaries, leaving all property to the partner, if surviving.
      2. A *credit shelter bypass* using a will or a living trust, with the remaining share outright to Pat.
      3. A similar bypass, but in the amount of Kris' *total net property* after payment of the FET.
   b. Would your answers to part *a* change if Pat survived Kris by less than 10 years? Why or why not?
   c. How well can each of the plans listed in part *a* achieve both partner's desire to leave their property to their own relatives after the surviving partner dies? If none will succeed, recommend an alternative solution.
   d. How much can lifetime gifting help reduce FET in part *a*? Is it consistent with the client's goals?

10. What legal alternatives does a client have in property planning for his or her own incapacity? Describe the advantages and disadvantages of each.

11. Your 86-year-old mentally competent client wishes to plan for her incapacity but refuses to immediately transfer her assets to anyone. Is planning impossible, or does this refusal merely create a

particular problem?

12. Your friend says, "I just signed four estate planning documents at my estate planning attorney's office." Name and briefly describe the likely four.

13. An attorney jokingly tells a client: "Today you'll be signing two documents, one wealth and one for health. One gives someone the power to steal from you, while the other gives someone the power to kill you." (*a*) What two documents is she talking about? (*b*) Is there any truth to her cynicism?

14. Explain several reasons why you might urge a client to consider additional estate planning after each of the following events?
   a. marriage
   b. birth or adoption of a child
   c. divorce of client
   d. remarriage
   e. death, separation or divorce of any child
   f. family estate amount becomes medium sized
   g. retirement
   h. death of spouse
   i. death of a parent
   j. changes in tax laws
   k. a change in the value of the client's business
   l. a change in the client's state of residency

15. In view of your answers to the question immediately above, what do you think of mail-order type estate plans, or other marketing approaches for plans that render it difficult to revise the plans periodically?

RECOMMENDED READING

Anonymous. "Who Can Afford a Nursing Home?" *Consumer Reports*, May 1988, pp. 300-309 (includes ratings of nursing home insurance policies).

Adams, Frank T. "Estate Planning for the Elderly." *Trusts & Estates*, February 1986, pp. 37-40.

Adams, Roy M., and Carter, Howard. "Coping with a New Threat." (Increasing liability exposure to professional fiduciaries.) *Trusts & Estates*, October 1987, pp. 25-36.

*Alvarez, Edna R. "The Attorney as Fiduciary: Problems When You Say 'Yes.'" *Estate Planning, 1988*, California Continuing Education of the Bar. Also, paper presented at the 10th annual UCLA/CEB Estate Planning Institute, May 1988.

*_____. "Acting as Fiduciary." *California Lawyer*, October, 1988, pp. 80-81.

Baer, Susan T. "Avoiding Estate Depletion in the Face of Catastrophic Illness." *Pace Law Review* 47(1984), pp. 783-826.

*Barreira, Brian E., "Despite Medicaid Transfer Restrictions, The Home May Still Be Kept in the Family", *Estate Planning*, March 1990, pp 102-7.

Beckman, Gail M. "Changes Highlight Need for Making Special Provisions for Adopted or Illegitimate Children." *Estate Planning*, November 1985, pp. 352-55.

Berteau, John T. "Steps to Avoid Beneficiary Conflicts over Bequests of Tangible Personal Property." *Estate Planning*, November 1985, pp. 356-61.

Bienemann Jr, Charles E., "Liabilities of Fiduciaries: Guidelines for Strategic Planning and Self Protection," *Estate Planning*, Jan 1989 pp 26-31. (Focuses on executors and trustees)

Blake, John F. "Drafting a QTlP Trust Where Extended Medical Care for the Surviving Spouse Is Foreseeable." *Estate Planning*, July 1987, pp. 200-05.

Blattmachr, Douglas J., and Jonathan G. Blattmachr. "Estate Planning for Individuals with Short Life Expectancies." *Trusts & Estates*, August 1985, pp. 22-28.

*Brown, Kenneth R. "Options Available to the Estate Planner in Anticipating a Client's Disability," *Estate Planning*, September 1986, pp. 282-87.

*Bruce, Charles M., Stephen Gray & Edward M. Luria. "Exploring the Protection of Assets Trusts." *Trusts and Estates*, November, 1991, pp. 32-41.

*Cheris, Samuel D. "Making Responsible Investment Decisions in Light of the Evolving Prudent Person Rule." *Estate Planning*, November 1987, pp. 338-42.

*Clary, Duane A., and Kevin R. Anderson. "Anticipating the Possibility of Simultaneous Deaths in Light of Uniform Act's Presumptions." *Estate Planing*, September 1987, pp. 28084.

*Collin, Francis J. "Planning and Drafting Durable Powers of Attorney for Health Care." University of Miami 22nd Annual Estate Planning Institute, 1988.

*_____. "Health Care Powers of Attorney- Planning and Drafting After Cruzan," 1991 UCLA/CEB Estate Planning Institute.

Collin, Francis J., John J. Lombard, Albert L. Moses, and Harley J. Spliter. *Drafting the Durable Power of Attorney: A Systems Approach."* Colorado Springs: Shepard's/McGraw-Hill, 1987.

Davis, A. Kimbrough. "Proper Planning Can Reduce Estate Taxes in the Event of the Simultaneous Death of Spouses." *Taxation for Lawyers*, July, 1984, pp. 10-13.

*Dubler, Nancy N. "Health Care Decisions: Enforcing Autonomy and Delegating Authority." *Estate Planning for the Aging or Incapacitated Client 1986.* Practicing Law Institute.

Edwards, Mark B. "Long-Term Care for the Elderly: A Primer for the Estate Planner." University of Miami 22nd Estate Planning Institute, 1988.

*Feldesman, Walter & Joann Canning. "Long-Term Care Insurance Helps Preserve an Estate." *Estate Planning*, March, 1993, pp. 76-82.

French, Susan F. "Antilapse Statutes Are Blunt Instruments: A Blueprint For Reform," *Hastings Law Journal* 37, November, 1985, pp. 335-75.

Frolik, Lawrence A. "Discretionary Trusts for a Disabled Beneficiary: A Solution or A Trap for the Unwary?" *University of Pittsburgh Law Review* 46, no. 335 (1985), pp. 335-71.

Frolik, Lawrence A. & Melissa C. Brown. *Advising the Elderly or Disabled Client,* Boston: Warren, Gorham Lamont, 1992.

*Gallo, Jon J., and Eileen F. Gallo. "Incentive Estate Planning For the Postponed Child." *Estate Planning 1987*, California Continuing Education of the Bar.

Gamble, Richard H. "Estate Planning For the Unmarried Person. *Trusts & Estates*, April 1986, pp. 25-28.

Gentle III, Edgar C. "Lawyers as Executors and Trustees: Snakes and Ladders." *The Alabama Lawyer*, March 1987, pp. 94-5.

Gilman, Sheldon. "Trustee Selection: Corporate vs. Individual." *Trusts & Estates*, June 1984, pp. 29-36.

Goldberg, Irene V. "Supreme Court Case Shows When Living Wills Can be Used to Carry Out a Clients Wishes," *Estate Planning*, November, 1990, pp. 328-31

Granelli, L. F., Janet Wright; and John Schooling. "Treating Children Equally (An Estate Planning Challenge)." *Estate Planning, Trust & Probate News* (State Bar of California publication) 6 (Winter 1985), p. 1.

Haddleton, Russell E. "How to Provide for the Surviving Spouse and Children during Administration of an Estate." *Estate Planning*, January 1988, pp. 14-l8.

Halbach, Edward C., Jr. "Trust Investment Laws In The Third Restatement," *Iowa Law Review*, Vol. 77 (1992) pp. 1151-85.

_____, "Issues About Issue: Some Recurrent Class Gift Problems," *Missouri Law Review* 48 (1983), pp. 333-70.

*Hamann, Charles M. "Durable Powers of Attorney." *Trusts & Estates*, February 1983, pp. 28-32.

*_____, "More Durable Powers of Attorney." *Trusts and Estates*, August 1983, pp. 30-32.

*Hayes, Eric P., "Protecting the Fiduciary by Drafting in Anticipation of Administration", 1990 University of Miami Estate Planning Institute.

Hershberger, William S. "Fiduciary Investing in the 90's-- Restatement Third of Trusts: Panacea or Placebo?" *1993 University of Miami Estate Planning Institute.*

Horwood, Richard M. & Jeffrey A. Zaluda, "Planning Strategies When A Client's Death Is Imminent" *Estate Planning*, May, 1993, pp 168-74.

"Isn't It Time You Wrote a Will? Seven Out of Ten Americans Don't Have Wills. They Should." *Consumer Reports*, February 1985, pp. 103-8.

Kanner, James R. "Tax Apportionment Clauses that Carry Out a Clients' Intent." *Estate Planning*, May, 1992, pp. 150-56.

Kirkland, Richard I., JR. "Should You Leave It All to the Children?" *Fortune*, September 29, 1986, pp. 18-26.

Leimberg, Stephan R., and Charles K. Plotnick. "What a Probate Attorney Must Know about the Psychological Aspects of Death and Dying." *The Practical Lawyer*, October 1986, pp. 3846.

_____, "How to Review a will" *The Practical Lawyer*, Sept., 1988 pp 13-28

Levin, Joel A. "Sufficient Administrative Authority May Require Special Provisions beyond State Fiduciary Powers." *Estate Planning*, November 1984, pp. 336-41.

Lombard, John J. "Asset Management under a Durable Power of Attorney The Ideal Solution to Guardianships or Conservatorships." *Probate Notes* 9 (1983), pp. 189-212.

_____, "Planning for Disability: Durable Powers, Standby Trusts and Preserving Eligibility for Governmental Benefits." *1986 University of Miami Institute on Estate Planning*, chap. 16.

Lundergan, Barbara. "Elderly Clients Require Special Lifetime Planning." *Trusts & Estates*, February 1986, pp. 33-35.

Milani, Ken, and Claude D. Renshaw. "Tax Strategies Especially Designed for Disabled or Handicapped Individuals." *Taxation for Accountants*, October 1987, pp. 25~6.

Mirabello, Francis J. & Catherine M. Keating, "Estate Planning For The Nonresident Alien With United States Assets Or Family," *1994 University of Miami Estate Planning Institute.*

Moses, A. L., and Adele J. Pope. "Estate Planning, Disability, and the Durable Power of Attorney." *South Carolina Law Review* 30(1979), pp. 511-55.

Nadlman, Jay. "Spendthrift Trusts: Enforceability of Agreements to Pay Over On Receipt" *UMKC Law Review* 52, no. 1(1983), pp. 115-27.

Neuwirth, Gloria S. "Steps a Client Can Take to Plan for Future Medical Treatment Decisions." *Estate Planning*, January 1985, pp. 14-20.

Nordstron, Kenneth V. "Estate Planning for Unmarried Individuals," *CLU Journal*, September 1987, pp. 38-46.

Olsen, Rory R., and David C. Sharman. "Practical and Tax Considerations in Deciding Who Should Be a Trustee." *Estate Planning*, July 1981, pp.214-20.

Owens, Rodney J., and Raymond C. Jordan. "Estate Planning for Parents of Mentally Disabled Children." *Trusts & Estates*, September 1987, pp. 41-8.

Pennell, Jeffrey N. "Avoiding Tax Problems for Settlers and Trustees When an Individual Trustee Is Chosen." *Estate Planning*, September 1982, pp. 264-72.

_____, "Tax Payment Provisions and Equitable Appointment", *1990 UCLA/CEB Estate Planning Institute.* Complex, technical analysis. Appendix contains state-by-state summary of state tax payment laws.

_____. "Tax Payment Provisions And Equitable Apportionment: Drafting to Span Legal Voids." University of Miami 22nd annual Estate Planning Institute, 1988. A complex, exhaustive analysis of state laws, and document planning.

Pierson, Donald R. II. "Steps a Practitioner Can Take to Facilitate the Planning and Probate of a Client's Estate." *Estate Planning*, March 1987, pp. 88-95.

*Ross, Sterling L. "The Special-Needs Trust and Its Use in Estate Planning for Families with Disabled Children." *Estate Planning for the Aged or Incapacitated Client* 1986, Practising Law Institute.

Roush, Nancy S and Robert K. Kirkland. "Spendthrift Trusts Not Limited to Protection of Immature Dependents," *Estate Planning*, January, 1991, pp. 16-21.

*Schlesinger, Sanford J, Barbara J. Schneider & Lisa A. Schneider, "Medicaid Planning Ideas: What Works And What Doesn't," Estate Planning, November, 1993, pp. 331-38.

* _____, "Estate Planning for Elderly or Disabled Clients after the Tax Reform Act (Internal Revenue Code of 1986)." *New York University Institute on Federal Taxation*, 1986.

Seligmann, William A. "Distributions to Children in the Sprinkling Trust." *Trusts & Estates*, February 1975, pp. 78-80.

Simpson, Samuel S. "Living Wills: A Matter of Life and Death." *Trusts & Estates*, April 1986, pp. 10-20.

Solomon, Lewis D. "Planning Estates for the Forgotten Middle Class." *1982 University of Miami Institute on Estate Planning,* chap. 13, pp. 1-Il.

*Strauss, Peter J., "The Geri-Hat-Trick: Three Goals of Estate Planning For Senior Citizens: *1990 University of Miami Estate Planning Institute.*

_____, "Financing Long-Term Care In An Age Of Broken Promises," *1994 University of Miami Estate Planning Institute.*

Street, Kimbrough, "Practical Guidelines For Selecting An Individual Trustee," *Estate Planning*, September, 1993, pp 268-74.

Suter, Philip H. "Techniques to Apportion Estate Taxes Will Have to Be Reviewed to the New Tax Law." *Estate Planning*, March 1982, 96-l00.

Van Ess, Craig K. "Living Wills and Alternatives to Living Wills: A Proposal-- The Supreme Trust." *Valparaiso University Law Review*, Vol. 26 (1992), pp. 567-93.

Van Houten, Margaret D. "Divorce Negotiations Carry Substantial Estate Planning Implications." *Estate Planning*, November 1987, pp. 344-19.

Weir, George C. "Can Fiduciaries Avoid Liability Under Environmental Law?" *Estate Planning*, July, 1992, pp. 224-30.

*West, Suzanne F. "Practical Experience with Durable Powers of Attorney for Health Care." *Estate Planning* 1986, California Continuing Education of the Bar.

Wicker, William H. "Spendthrift Trusts Are an Excellent Way to Leave Money to Someone Who Can't Handle It." *Estate Planning*, Summer 1975, pp. 202-5.

Williams, John C. ". . . but Some Are More Equal than Others: Factors to Consider in Creating Trusts for Groups of Children or Grandchildren." *Trusts & Estates*, March 1975, pp. 140-44.

Durable Power of Attorney for Health Care*

*Reproduced with permission of the California Medical Association.

APPENDIX 17A

California Medical Association
DURABLE POWER OF ATTORNEY FOR HEALTH CARE DECISIONS
(California Civil Code Sections 2410- 2444)

WARNING TO PERSON EXECUTING THIS DOCUMENT

This is an important legal document. Before executing this document, you should know these important facts:

This document gives the person you designate as your agent (the attorney-in-fact) the power to make health care decisions for you. Your agent must act consistently with your desires as stated in this document or otherwise made known.

Except as you otherwise specify in this document, this document gives your agent power to consent to your doctor not giving treatment or stopping treatment necessary to keep you alive.

Notwithstanding this document, you have the right to make medical and other health care decisions for yourself so long as you can give informed consent with respect to the particular decision. In addition, no treatment may be given to you over your objection, and health care necessary to keep you alive may not be stopped or withheld if you object at the time.

This document gives your agent authority to consent, to refuse to consent, or to withdraw consent to any care, treatment, service, or procedure to maintain, diagnose, or treat a physical or mental condition. This power is subject to any statement of your desires and any limitations that you include in this document. You may state in this document any types of treatment that you do not desire. In addition, a court can take away the power of your agent to make health care decisions for you if your agent (1) authorizes anything that is illegal, (2) acts contrary to your known desires or (3) where your desires are not known, does anything that is clearly contrary to your best interests.

This power will exist for an indefinite period of time unless you limit its duration in this document.

You have the right to revoke the authority of your agent by notifying your agent or your treating doctor, hospital, or other health care provider orally or in writing of the revocation.

Your agent has the right to examine your medical records and to consent to their disclosure unless you limit this right in this document.

Unless you otherwise specify in this document, this document gives your agent the power after you die to (1) authorize an autopsy, (2) donate your body or parts thereof for transplant or therapeutic or educational or scientific purposes, and (3) direct the disposition of your remains.

If there is anything in this document that you do not understand, you should ask a lawyer to explain it to you.

1. CREATION OF DURABLE POWER OF ATTORNEY FOR HEALTH CARE

By this document I intend to create a durable power of attorney by appointing the person designated below to make health care decisions for me as allowed by Sections 2410 to 2444, inclusive, of the California Civil Code. This power of attorney shall not be affected by my subsequent incapacity. I hereby revoke any prior durable power of attorney for health care. I am a California resident who is at least 18 years old, of sound mind, and acting of my own free will.

2. APPOINTMENT OF HEALTH CARE AGENT

(Fill in below the name, address and telephone number of the person you wish to make health care decisions for you if you become incapacitated. You should make sure that this person agrees to accept this responsibility. The following may not serve as your agent: (1) your treating health care provider; (2) an operator of a community care facility or residential care facility for the elderly; or (3) an employee of your treating health care provider, a community care facility, or a residential care facility for the elderly, unless that employee is related to you by blood, marriage or adoption. If you are a conservatee under the Lanterman-Petris-Short Act (the law governing involuntary commitment to a mental health facility) and you wish to appoint your conservator as your agent, you must consult a lawyer, who must sign and attach a special declaration for this document to be valid.)

I, _____, hereby appoint:
                              (insert your name)

Name _____

Address _____

Work Telephone (_____) _____   Home Telephone (_____) _____

as my agent (attorney-in-fact) to make health care decisions for me as authorized in this document. I understand that this power of attorney will be effective for an indefinite period of time unless I revoke it or limit its duration below.

(Optional) This power of attorney shall expire on the following date: _____.

APPENDIX 17A *(continued)*

3. AUTHORITY OF AGENT

If I become incapable of giving informed consent to health care decisions, I grant my agent full power and authority to make those decisions for me, subject to any statements of desires or limitations set forth below. Unless I have limited my agent's authority in this document, that authority shall include the right to consent, refuse consent, or withdraw consent to any medical care, treatment, service, or procedure; to receive and to consent to the release of medical information; to authorize an autopsy to determine the cause of my death; to make a gift of all or part of my body; and to direct the disposition of my remains, subject to any instructions I have given in a written contract for funeral services, my will or by some other method. I understand that, by law, my agent may not consent to any of the following: commitment to a mental health treatment facility, convulsive treatment, psychosurgery, sterilization or abortion.

4. MEDICAL TREATMENT DESIRES AND LIMITATIONS (OPTIONAL)

(Your agent must make health care decisions that are consistent with your known desires. You can, but are not required to, state your desires about the kinds of medical care you do or do not want, including your desires concerning life-sustaining treatment. If you do not want your agent to have the authority to make certain decisions, you must write a statement to that effect in the space provided below; otherwise, your agent will have the broad powers to make health care decisions for you that are outlined in paragraph 3 above. In either case, it is important that you discuss your health care desires with the person you appoint as your agent.)

(Following are three general statements about withholding and removal of life-sustaining treatment. If, after carefully reading all of these statements, you agree with one of them, you may initial that statement. If you wish to add to one of the printed statements, or to write your own instead, you may do so in the space provided.)

> I do **not** want efforts made to prolong my life and I do **not** want life-sustaining treatment to be provided or continued: (1) if I am in an irreversible coma or persistent vegetative state; or (2) if I am terminally ill and the application of life-sustaining procedures would serve only to artificially delay the moment of my death; or (3) under any other circumstances where the burdens of the treatment outweigh the expected benefits. I want my agent to consider the relief of suffering and the quality as well as the extent of the possible extension of my life in making decisions concerning life-sustaining treatment.
>
> *If this statement reflects your desires, initial here:* _____

> I want efforts made to prolong my life and I want life-sustaining treatment to be provided **unless I am in a coma or persistent vegetative state** which my doctor reasonably believes to be irreversible. Once my doctor has concluded that I will remain unconscious for the rest of my life, I do not want life-sustaining treatment to be provided or continued.
>
> *If this statement reflects your desires, initial here:* _____

> I want efforts made to prolong my life and I want life-sustaining treatment to be provided **even if** I am in an irreversible coma or persistent vegetative state.
>
> *If this statement reflects your desires, initial here:* _____

Other or additional statements of medical treatment desires and limitations: _____

_____

(You may attach additional pages if you need more space to complete your statements. Each additional page must be dated and signed at the same time you date and sign this document.)

5. APPOINTMENT OF ALTERNATE AGENTS (OPTIONAL)

(You may appoint alternate agents to make health care decisions for you in case the person you appointed in Paragraph 2 is unable or unwilling to do so.)

If the person named as my agent in Paragraph 2 is not available or willing to make health care decisions for me as authorized in this document, I appoint the following persons to do so, listed in the order they should be asked:

First Alternate Agent: Name _____ Work Telephone (_____) _____

Address _____ Home Telephone (_____) _____

Second Alternate Agent: Name_____ Work Telephone (_____) _____

Address _____ Home Telephone (_____) _____

APPENDIX 17A *(continued)*

6. USE OF COPIES

I hereby authorize that photocopies of this document can be relied upon by my agent and others as though they were originals.

DATE AND SIGNATURE OF PRINCIPAL
(You must date and sign this power of attorney)

I sign my name to this Durable Power of Attorney for Health Care at _____, _____
(City)   (State)

on _____ . _____
(Date)   (Signature of Principal)

STATEMENT OF WITNESSES

(This power of attorney will not be valid for making health care decisions unless it is either (1) signed by two qualified adult witnesses who are personally known to you (or to whom you present evidence of your identity) and who are present when you sign or acknowledge your signature or (2) acknowledged before a notary public in California. If you elect to use witnesses rather than a notary public, the law provides that none of the following may be used: (1) the persons you have appointed as your agent and alternate agents, (2) a health care provider or an employee of a health care provider, or (3) an operator or employee of a community care facility or residential care facility for the elderly. Additionally, at least one of the witnesses cannot be related to you by blood, marriage or adoption, or be named in your will. IF YOU ARE A PATIENT IN A SKILLED NURSING FACILITY, ONE OF THE WITNESSES MUST BE A PATIENT ADVOCATE OR OMBUDSMAN.)

I declare under penalty of perjury under the laws of California that the person who signed or acknowledged this document is personally known to me to be the principal, or that the identity of the principal was proved to me by convincing evidence,* that the principal signed or acknowledged this durable power of attorney in my presence, that the principal appears to be of sound mind and under no duress, fraud, or undue influence, that I am not the person appointed as attorney in fact by this document, and that I am not a health care provider, an employee of a health care provider, the operator of a community care facility or a residential care facility for the elderly, nor an employee of an operator of a community care facility or residential care facility for the elderly.

Signature _____   Signature _____

Print name _____   Print name _____

Date _____   Date _____

Residence Address _____   Residence Address_____

_____   _____

(AT LEAST ONE OF THE ABOVE WITNESSES MUST ALSO SIGN THE FOLLOWING DECLARATION)

I further declare under penalty of perjury under the laws of California that I am not related to the principal by blood, marriage, or adoption, and, to the best of my knowledge I am not entitled to any part of the estate of the principal upon the death of the principal under a will now existing or by operation of law.

Signature: _____

---

*The law allows one or more of the following forms of identification as convincing evidence of identity: a California driver's license or identification card or U.S. passport that is current or has been issued within five years, or any of the following if the document is current or has been issued within five years, contains a photograph and description of the person named on it, is signed by the person, and bears a serial or other identifying number: a foreign passport that has been stamped by the U.S. Immigration and Naturalization Service; a driver's license issued by another state or by an authorized Canadian or Mexican agency; or an identification card issued by another state or by any branch of the U.S. armed forces. If the principal is a patient in a skilled nursing facility, a patient advocate or ombudsman may rely on the representations of family members or the administrator or staff of the facility as convincing evidence of identity if the patient advocate or ombudsman believes that the representations provide a reasonable basis for determining the identity of the principal.

APPENDIX 17A *(concluded)*

SPECIAL REQUIREMENT: STATEMENT OF PATIENT ADVOCATE OR OMBUDSMAN

(If you are a patient in a skilled nursing facility, a patient advocate or ombudsman must sign the Statement of Witnesses above __and__ must also sign the following declaration.)

I further declare under penalty of perjury under the laws of California that I am a patient advocate or ombudsman as designated by the State Department of Aging and am serving as a witness as required by subdivision (f) of Civil Code Section 2432.

Signature: _____   Address: _____

Print Name: _____   _____

Date: _____   _____

CERTIFICATE OF ACKNOWLEDGMENT OF NOTARY PUBLIC

(Acknowledgment before a notary public is __not__ required if you have elected to have two qualified witnesses sign above. If you are a patient in a skilled nursing facility, you __must__ have a patient advocate or ombudsman sign the Statement of Witnesses on page 3 __and__ the Statement of Patient Advocate or Ombudsman above)

State of California   )

)ss.

County of _____)

On this _____ day of _____, in the year _____,

before me, _____,
(here insert name of notary public)

personally appeared _____
(here insert name of principal)

personally known to me (or proved to me on the basis of satisfactory evidence) to be the person whose name is subscribed to this instrument, and acknowledged that he or she executed it. I declare under penalty of perjury that the person whose name is subscribed to this instrument appears to be of sound mind and under no duress, fraud, or undue influence.

NOTARY SEAL

_____
(Signature of Notary Public)

COPIES

YOUR AGENT MAY NEED THIS DOCUMENT IMMEDIATELY IN CASE OF AN EMERGENCY. YOU SHOULD KEEP THE COMPLETED ORIGINAL AND GIVE PHOTOCOPIES OF THE COMPLETED ORIGINAL TO (1) YOUR AGENT AND ALTERNATE AGENTS, (2) YOUR PERSONAL PHYSICIAN, AND (3) MEMBERS OF YOUR FAMILY AND ANY OTHER PERSONS WHO MIGHT BE CALLED IN THE EVENT OF A MEDICAL EMERGENCY. THE LAW PERMITS THAT PHOTOCOPIES OF THE COMPLETED DOCUMENT CAN BE RELIED UPON AS THOUGH THEY WERE ORIGINALS.

Additional forms can be purchased from: Sutter Publications, P.O. Box 7690, San Francisco, CA 94120-7690 • (415) 882-5175

Advance Directive:
Living Will and Health Care Proxy*

* Reprinted by permission of Choice in Dying (formerly Concern For Dying/Society for the Right to Die), 200 Varick St., New York, NY 10014.

APPENDIX 17B

ADVANCE DIRECTIVE
Living Will and Health Care Proxy

*D*eath is a part of life. It is a reality like birth, growth and aging. I am using this advance directive to convey my wishes about medical care to my doctors and other people looking after me at the end of my life. It is called an advance directive because it gives instructions in advance about what I want to happen to me in the future. It expresses my wishes about medical treatment that might keep me alive. I want this to be legally binding.

If I cannot make or communicate decisions about my medical care, those around me should rely on this document for instructions about measures that could keep me alive.

I do not want medical treatment (including feeding and water by tube) that will keep me alive if:
- I am unconscious and there is no reasonable prospect that I will ever be conscious again (even if I am not going to die soon in my medical condition), or
- I am near death from an illness or injury with no reasonable prospect of recovery.

I do want medicine and other care to make me more comfortable and to take care of pain and suffering. I want this even if the pain medicine makes me die sooner.

I want to give some extra instructions: *[Here list any special instructions, e.g., some people fear being kept alive after a debilitating stroke. If you have wishes about this, or any other conditions, please write them here.]*

The legal language in the box that follows is a health care proxy.
It gives another person the power to make medical decisions for me.

I name _____ , who lives at _____

_____ , phone number _____ ,

to make medical decisions for me if I cannot make them myself. This person is called a health care "surrogate," "agent," "proxy," or "attorney in fact." This power of attorney shall become effective when I become incapable of making or communicating decisions about my medical care. This means that this document stays legal when and if I lose the power to speak for myself, for instance, if I am in a coma or have Alzheimer's disease.

My health care proxy has power to tell others what my advance directive means. This person also has power to make decisions for me, based either on what I would have wanted, or, if this is not known, on what he or she thinks is best for me.

If my first choice health care proxy cannot or decides not to act for me, I name _____

_____ , address _____ ,

phone number _____ , as my second choice.

(over, please)

LWGEN

APPENDIX 17B *(concluded)*

I have discussed my wishes with my health care proxy, and with my second choice if I have chosen to appoint a second person. My proxy(ies) has(have) agreed to act for me.

I have thought about this advance directive carefully. I know what it means and want to sign it. I have chosen two witnesses, neither of whom is a member of my family, nor will inherit from me when I die. My witnesses are not the same people as those I named as my health care proxies. I understand that this form should be notarized if I use the box to name (a) health care proxy(ies).

Signature _____

Date _____

Address _____

Witness' signature _____

Witness' printed name _____

Address _____

Witness' signature _____

Witness' printed name _____

Address _____

Notary [to be used if proxy is appointed]_____

Drafted and Distributed by Choice In Dying, Inc.—the National Council for the right to Die. Choice In Dying is a National not-for-profit organization which works for the rights of patients at the end of life. In addition to this generic advance directive, Choice In Dying distributes advance directives that conform to each state's specific legal requirements and maintains a national Living Will Registry for completed documents.

CHOICE IN DYING INC.—
the national council for the right to die
(formerly Concern for Dying/Society for the Right to Die)
200 Varick Street, New York, NY 10014 (212) 366-5540

5/92

-18

Postmortem Tax Planning

OVERVIEW

The estate planning process does not end at the client's death. Assets must still be marshaled, preserved, and distributed by the decedent's representatives, a group that includes executors, trustees, accountants, attorneys, and survivors. In the transmission process, tax law often enables these aides to recommend and make choices. This chapter focuses on the tax elections available to them as parties dealing in the decedent's property. The technical detail in this chapter is testimony to the claim that estate administration after the client's death can involve complex tax issues requiring the expert advice of an estate planning attorney, not one conducting a general law practice.

The chapter will begin with an overview of the principles of postmortem tax compliance, better known as the preparation of tax returns. Next, it will survey those planning devices primarily designed to reduce income taxes, including estate expense elections, choice of tax year, and distribution-planning strategies. Finally, the chapter will present those planning devices primarily designed to save death taxes, including the alternate valuation date, the use of disclaimers, and the decision to make the QTIP election.

TAX RETURNS AFTER DEATH

Overview of Tax Compliance After Death

We already know that death of an individual may trigger estate and inheritance taxes. Transfer of a decedent's property is often not a transfer tax-free procedure. But can the work be done free of income tax? Will the death of an income-earning individual terminate the obligation to pay taxes on all income received thereafter? Of course, the answer to both questions is no, because income ordinarily subject to taxation will be received by survivors, estates, and trusts. If income ordinarily subject to taxation is being received, you can be sure that the Internal Revenue Code imposes a tax on that income to one or another recipient in the year received.

Since death can create or continue the obligation to pay transfer and income taxes, we must first study the nature of these tax obligations and their effects on the survivors. This section will introduce principles of postmortem federal tax *compliance*, that is, the completion of federal tax returns and the payment of federal taxes on income and on property in connection with the death of a decedent.

Several transfer tax and income tax returns will usually be filed after the client's death.

Transfer Taxes

With regard to transfer taxes, the decedent's representatives may be required to file a state estate or inheritance tax return, and a Form 706, federal estate tax return, which is due within nine months after date of death. As mentioned in Chapter 6, a federal estate tax return must be filed for decedents dying with a total gross estate plus adjusted taxable gifts equaling or exceeding $600,000, the amount of the exemption equivalent of the unified credit for the year of death. For example, the estate of a decedent who died this year having a gross estate of $555,000 and adjusted taxable gifts of $100,000 must file a return because their sum exceeds $600,000. Unfortunately, filing is required even though no FET will be due, as in the case where the entire estate is left to a surviving spouse.

One further point regarding the estate tax return: Since evidence of a step-up in basis is essentially derived from the information on Form 706, many tax practitioners will recommend filing this return for smaller estates in order to ensure that the death value of appreciated property will be recognized as its new basis. However, the IRS is not bound by such FET values in an income tax dispute.

Income Taxes

With regard to income taxes, the representatives may be required to file state returns, and the following two types of federal returns. First, the *decedent's final income tax return* will be reported on Form 1040, covering all income for the last tax year up to date of death. Second, if the decedent leaves a probate estate, one *estate fiduciary income tax return*, Form 1041, will be filed for each tax year of the estate's existence. The fiduciary return for the first year will report all income from the decedent's date of death to the end of the first tax year. When the estate is terminated, usually by final distribution, the last estate income tax return will be filed for a "short" year, from the beginning of the tax year to date of distribution. After estate termination, the beneficiaries will report income from distributed estate property on their own tax returns.

The following example summarizes these federal income tax rules and assumes that all taxpayers report taxes on a *calendar year* basis; that is, their tax year begins January 1 and ends December 31. Actually, an estate needn't use a calendar year. Planning with the use of a fiscal rather than calendar year will be discussed later in the chapter.

> EXAMPLE 18-1 Farley, a widower, died on May 12, 1990. In his will, Farley left 100 shares of Xerox stock outright to his son Jordan and the residue of his estate in trust for the benefit of his granddaughter Sheila. The date of final estate distribution to Jordan and the trust was February 25, 1992. The following postdeath tax returns were filed. All income earned by the decedent from January 1 through May 12, 1990, was reported by the executor on the decedent's final income tax return, Form 1040. All income earned by the estate between May 13 and December 31, 1990, was reported by the executor on the first estate income tax return, Form 1041. The executor filed a second Form 1041 return for all estate income for the entire year 1991 and a third for income earned during the period from January 1 to February 25, 1992. Jordan reported on his Form 1040 all income received on the stock after February 25, 1992. Trust property income, or DNI, earned after that date will be reported by the trust, on Form 1041, and by Sheila on her Form 1040, to the extent the income is actually distributed to her.

All capital gains income on trust property will be reported by the trust except in the trust's last year, when these gains will be "carried out" and reported by the beneficiaries. All nongrantor trusts must use a calendar tax year.

A *joint return* may be filed for a decedent and the surviving spouse for the year of death, covering income of the decedent to date of death and income of the spouse for the entire year.[1] In the alternative, returns may be filed for each spouse separately. In most situations, filing jointly will save total taxes in the same way it does when both spouses are alive. The greater the difference between the two spousal incomes, the greater the tax usually saved by filing jointly. The surviving spouse will also be permitted to enjoy the lower rates applicable to joint returns for *two years after the decedent's death*, provided that he or she (*a*) has not remarried and (*b*) maintains a home for one or more dependent children.[2]

Next, we turn to postmortem income tax planning ideas.

PLANNING DEVICES PRIMARILY DESIGNED TO SAVE INCOME TAXES

Some postmortem planning strategies are primarily undertaken to reduce the income tax bite. They include various expense elections, selection of probate estate tax year, and distribution planning. Before examining these techniques, let us survey three tax principles on which most of them will be based.

First, greater income tax can be saved when taxable income can be spread among more taxpaying entities. This idea was first mentioned and developed in Chapter 9. Proper predeath planning can result in the creation of *additional taxpaying entities* after the client's death. These tax entities can include the estate, several trusts (with at least one trust for each beneficiary), and the beneficiaries themselves. After death, proper timing of distributions among these entities can often save significant tax dollars, as we shall see.

A second tax principle on which postmortem income tax planning is based is the notion of the *conduit*, introduced in Chapter 8. The conduit principle prevents double taxation of estate or trust income. It is derived from the concept of distributable net income, or DNI, which is roughly equal to the estate or trust's fiduciary accounting income, and which constitutes the maximum amount of income taxable to the beneficiaries, as well as the maximum amount deductible by the estate or trust. The amount taxable to an estate or trust roughly equals its total income, including capital gains and losses, reduced by the distribution deduction, which roughly equals the lesser of the amount distributed or its DNI. Thus, a trust

---

1. §6013(a)(2).

2. §1(a)(2), §2(a)(1).

or estate that distributes all of its income will be taxed only on its capital gains. Consequently, under the conduit principle, DNI earned by an estate or trust which is distributed to the beneficiaries in the year earned will be taxed to the beneficiaries and not to the estate or trust, which simply acts as a conduit for delivering income from the source to the beneficiaries. Conversely, any DNI retained by the estate or trust will not be offset by a distribution deduction, which will make that DNI taxable to it rather than to the beneficiaries. Further, all capital gains are taxed to the estate or trust, except in the last taxable year.

A third tax principle on which postmortem income tax planning is based is that in the year in which an estate or trust makes its final distribution, all income, including capital gains, will be *carried out* to and taxable to the beneficiaries. Thus in its *termination year,* a trust or estate will have no taxable income.

These tax principles represent only the briefest summary of the principles of income taxation of estates and trusts detailed in Chapter 8. The reader is strongly urged to review that more comprehensive section before continuing.

Expense Elections Available to the Executor

During administration, the executor is able to make several informal elections with regard to estate expenses. We will refer to the executor's ability to make elections because the executor is the person having that legal authority. Of course, most executors rely on their attorney or accountant to apprise them of the tax alternatives. These include the medical expense election, the administration expense and losses election, and the election to waive the executor's commission. They are covered next.

Medical expense election. Any of the decedent's unreimbursed medical expenses which are unpaid at death may be deducted either on the decedent's final income tax return or on the federal estate tax return, but not on both.[3]

The choice of where to deduct unpaid medical expenses will depend on which alternative will yield the greater tax saving. The size of the tax saving will be a function of the marginal tax rate which, in turn, will be influenced by the size of the estate tax base. However, smaller estates may be unable to benefit from a deduction on either return. If deducted on the *income tax return*, only the excess of the medical expense amount over 7.5

---

3. §213; §2053

percent of adjusted gross income is deductible, and any remaining nondeductible amount may not be deducted on the FET return. With regard to the *estate tax return*, no estate tax may be due for smaller estates, even without the deduction, either because no estate tax return need be filed or because other deductions, including the marital deduction, may independently reduce the taxable estate to zero.

Administration expense and losses election. Expenses in administering the decedent's estate, including executor's commission, attorney's fees, and casualty losses, are deductible either on the federal estate tax return or on the estate income tax return, or partly on each.[4] However, double deductions are not allowed.

Again, the choice of where to deduct these items will usually turn on which return will produce the greater tax saving. And again, smaller estates may be unable to enjoy a deduction on either return. Casualty losses are deductible against income only to the extent that they exceed 10 percent of adjusted gross income. And there may be no FET to save in the case of a small estate, or any size estate for that matter, which will essentially pass to the surviving spouse. Larger estates not incorporating a 100 percent marital deduction often will be able to choose because they can save taxes on either return, but there may be situations, as in the next example, when the deduction can and should be divided between the two returns.

> EXAMPLE 18-2 Let's assume that Maggie, owning a gross estate of $5 million, will die later this year leaving everything to her husband, Earl. Expenses in administering Maggie's estate are expected to total $700,000. If the estate's marginal income tax rate exceeds the marginal FET rate, greater taxes would be saved by deducting the entire amount on Form 1041. On the other hand, if the marginal FET rate is higher, a greater tax saving would result if only $100,000, not the entire amount, is deducted on Form 706 and the rest is deducted on Form 1041. To see why, consider the effect of the expense outlay on the amount of the maximum marital deduction. Since the actual amount passing to Earl will be only $4.3 million, this amount will constitute the maximum allowable marital deduction. If the executor deducts all of the administration expenses on the estate income tax return, the estate will wind up incurring an FET, despite the fact that Maggie left her entire estate to her spouse, since the taxable estate of $700,000 will exceed $600,000, the exemption equivalent of the unified credit. Alternatively, if the executor deducts at least $100,000 of these expenses on the estate tax return, the FET will be zero since the taxable estate will have been reduced to the amount of the exemption equivalent. Since no more than $100,000 is needed to do this, the other $600,000 can be deducted on the income tax return.

---

4. Reg. 1.642 (g)-2.

Thus, if an amount is deductible on another return, it would be imprudent to deduct it on any FET return that can already shelter all taxable estate property with the unified credit or some other shield.

Election to waive executor's commission. The executor's commission, as a deductible administration expense, will be taxable as income to the executor. However, the executor may elect to waive (i.e., refuse) that commission. Waiver of the commission may be worthwhile if the executor is residuary beneficiary of the estate and if his or her personal marginal income tax rate exceeds the marginal tax rate for both the estate FET and the estate income tax. If the executor is not residuary beneficiary of the estate, a waiver of the commission will mean a complete forfeit of that amount. Thus, the nonresiduary executor will usually prefer to receive the commission, no matter the tax cost.

EXAMPLE 18-3 An estate has been left entirely to the decedent's *daughter*, who is the executor. The executor's commission will be $10,000. The estate's marginal FET rate is 41 percent and its marginal income tax rate is 28 percent. The daughter's marginal income tax rate is 31 percent. *Not waiving* the commission will lower the FET by $4,100 and raise daughter's income tax by $3,100, for a net tax saving of $1,000.

EXAMPLE 18-4 Facts similar to Example 18-3, except that decedent left his entire estate to his *spouse*, who is executor. Due to the unlimited marital deduction, the effective marginal FET rate is 0 percent. Regarding income tax rates, assuming that spouse's effective marginal rate is 31 percent, and the estate's marginal rate is 28 percent, *waiving* the commission will raise estate income tax by $2,800 and lower spouse's income tax by $3,100, for a net tax saving of $300.

EXAMPLE 18-5 Facts similar to Example 18-4, except that the entire estate has been left outright *to the decedent's children* of a former marriage. Waiving the executor's commission would mean totally forfeiting the receipt of that amount. As executor, spouse, not wishing to forfeit all cash flow from the estate, elects *not to waive* the commission. Instead of nothing, spouse will receive $6,900, after tax, from the estate.

Selection of Estate Taxable Year

The executor of a probate estate has considerable flexibility in choosing its taxable, or tax, year. Although all income tax years except the first and the last must be 12 months long, the executor can choose the estate's tax year to end on the last day of any month. If it ends on December 31, the estate is said to be on a *calendar year* with the first tax year running from date of death to December 31. All other tax years will then run from January 1 to

December 31, except for the year of final distribution of the estate assets, which will run for a "short year," from January 1 to date of distribution. Alternatively, if the estate's elected tax year ends on the last day of any month other than December, it is said to be on a *fiscal year*.

Whether an estate is on a calendar year or fiscal year, two basic income tax benefits are available to it. First, it can be made a separate taxpaying entity, capable of *splitting income* with the other tax entities involved in the estate distribution process. By lowering tax rates and by radically lowering bracket amounts for estates, tax reform since 1986 has reduced the tax saving benefit of splitting income.

Second, further tax saving can be realized in the first and last tax years of an estate's life, since both years are usually shorter than 12 months. The first tax year is shorter because date of death does not usually coincide with the last day of the tax year. The last tax year is shorter than 12 months because date of final distribution doesn't usually coincide with the last day of the tax year. A *short tax year* produces income tax savings because proportionately less income will ordinarily be taxed in those years, at proportionately lower rates.

In contrast to the tax benefits available to all estates, some benefits are available only to estates having a carefully selected fiscal year. In each of the next two examples, assume that the decedent died on March 10, 1991.

EXAMPLE 18-6 The estate of a decedent is planning the distribution of income to its beneficiary, the surviving spouse. It elects a fiscal year ending January 31. If the estate distributes income earned on March 15, 1992, to the spouse during the month of January, 1993, the spouse may not have to report the income until April, 1994, more than two full years after the income was initially received by the estate. This assumes that no quarterly estimated tax payments will have to be filed by the spouse.

EXAMPLE 18-7 An estate, which has a lower marginal income tax rate than its beneficiaries, expects to receive an income of $30,000 every three months starting in June 1992, until estate termination on November 30, 1994. To spread the income out over as many tax years as possible, the estate elects to have its fiscal year close just before the expected date of final distribution. Thus, it chooses a fiscal year ending September 30. Estate taxable income (DNI) for each year will be the following: first year, $60,000; second year, $120,000; third year up to September 30, 1994, $120,000. Thus, for each of the first three tax years, the estate will be taxed on all of this accumulated income, and DNI carried out to beneficiaries will be zero. In the final year, the beneficiaries will receive the after-tax accumulation, tax free. In contrast, more total tax would be owed if the estate elected a fiscal year that effectively prevented it from being a taxpaying entity in the third year. For example, had the estate elected a fiscal year ending November 30, the pattern of estate taxable income would be as follows: first year, $60,000; second and last estate taxable year ending November 30, 1991, $120,000. DNI to the beneficiaries would be $120,000.

The beneficiaries would receive tax free the after-tax accumulation on $180,000 of income, but the last year's $120,000 would constitute taxable DNI to them, not to the estate. In the last taxable year of an estate, DNI is totally carried out to the beneficiaries.

If the executor of an estate expects an unusually large income receipt shortly after the period of administration begins, he or she may wish to elect a year end which would give it a rather short first year, so that other taxable income received later will be taxed during the following year rather than lumped with the large receipt and taxed at a higher rate.

EXAMPLE 18-8 Decedent Malley was an accountant who died on May 19 owning, among other things, account receivables amounting to $50,000. The estate elects a fiscal year ending July 31 to include most of this income in the first tax year, while causing most other income to be taxed in the second and later years.

On the other hand, a relatively long first tax year would be desirable if a large deduction is expected within 6 to 12 months from date of death.

EXAMPLE 18-9 Combined with a large amount of early income, as in Example 18-8, the estate expects to make a large distribution to the beneficiaries in April of the following year. The estate instead elects a fiscal year closing on April 30, so that the deduction can be used to reduce estate taxable income.

Distribution Planning

Although federal tax reform since 1986 reduced income tax rates substantially for all tax entities, an estate or trust may be able to save some income tax for its beneficiaries by properly planning the amount and timing of beneficiary distributions. Much of distribution planning hinges on the existence of differentials in marginal tax rates, and thus one of the planner's tasks is to compare the tax rates of the various entities and allocate taxable income to those in lower brackets. In this section, we will consider situations where the beneficiaries are, alternatively, in a higher bracket and in a lower bracket in comparison with the distributing estate or trust. This section will also examine the income tax advantage of prolonging the estate's life.

Estate or trust in lower bracket than beneficiaries. When the estate or trust is in a lower income tax bracket than its beneficiaries, consideration should be given to distribution arrangements that will generate a greater taxable income to itself and a correspondingly lesser taxable income to its beneficiaries.

Accumulation of income. The most common device used accumulates income by reducing and delaying distributions of DNI. In some cases, excess accumulations will be subject to the *throwback rules*, which, as mentioned in Chapter 8, seek to prevent a trustee from delaying a distribution to a beneficiary in years when the beneficiaries' tax rate is high, only to distribute the income in later years when the rate is expected to be lower. The throwback rules require excess distributions to a beneficiary in later years to be taxed to the beneficiary as if they had been received in the years in which the trust actually received and accumulated them. However, the throwback rules do not apply to estates nor to any trust accumulations made for a beneficiary when under the age of 21.

> EXAMPLE 667-1 Jonathan died earlier this year, leaving his entire estate to his wife, Kathleen. The estate has earned some income this year but elects *not to distribute* it to Kathleen until next year. This year Kathleen, who has earned considerable income herself, is also recipient of a large lump-sum pension distribution from Jonathan's employer. Therefore, she is in the 31 percent marginal tax bracket. The estate, on the other hand, is subject to a 15 percent marginal tax rate, partly because the executor has elected a fiscal year that will give the estate a very short first taxable year. The accumulated income will be distributed to Kathleen in later years when her tax rate is likely to be lower. The throwback rules will not apply.

Nonapplication of the throwback rules to estates can constitute a reason not to avoid probate. Without probate, there is no taxpaying estate capable of accumulating income in one year and making an accumulation distribution in another. Since the probate-avoiding revocable living trust is usually subject to the throwback rules, it cannot usually exploit this tax strategy. With the lower rates brought about by tax reform, however, the decision to elect probate cannot rest solely on income tax savings. And the probate fees might substantially wipe out any tax saving.

Realization of a gain. Another way to benefit from the estate or trust having a lower tax rate than the beneficiaries is through the realization of a gain. If an estate asset has appreciated after death and is expected to be quickly sold upon receipt by the designated beneficiary, the executor of a lower-bracket estate should give consideration to *selling the asset* prior to distribution so that the estate can recognize the gain. The after-tax proceeds can be distributed to the beneficiary tax free, assuming all DNI has already been distributed. However, to be taxed to the estate, the sale will have to be made before its last taxable year so that the gain is not automatically "carried out" to the beneficiary.

Despite having a lower marginal tax rate, the executor of an estate may wish to distribute rather than sell the asset if the beneficiary has a *realized loss* that is presently unusable for lack of any offsetting gains. The beneficiary, who could sell the asset, then would not have to carry over an unused loss to future years.

Estate or trust in higher marginal tax bracket than beneficiaries. In cases where an estate or trust is subject to a higher marginal income tax rate than one or more of its beneficiaries, the executor or trustee may prefer to *distribute income* to them in the year the income is received, so that it is taxed at the beneficiaries lower rate. In addition, when the estate or trust's tax year overlaps those of the beneficiaries, the executor or trustee can time the distribution so that it is made in one of two years in which the beneficiaries' tax rate is lower.

> EXAMPLE 18-10 It is the month of November, and the beneficiary of an estate just lost his job as a law firm associate and expects to be unemployed for about six months. Instead of distributing $50,000 of income to him in late December, the executor distributes it early next January, during a year in which the beneficiary's taxable income is expected to be substantially lower. The estate has a fiscal year ending February 28, so the choice to distribute in either December or January has no effect on its own taxation; both months are in the same tax year, the year in which the income is received.

Tax planning of distributions from estates and trusts are subject to some other tax constraints, one of which is described next.

Unduly prolonging the estate life. By now, the reader is aware of several potential income tax advantages to having a probate estate. This will encourage some executors to delay closing their estates. Since termination of an estate by final distribution cuts off the tax benefits available to this separate taxpayer, tax planning would suggest undertaking this ploy by delaying the estate's date of final distribution. Unfortunately, the IRS has authority to treat an estate as *terminated* for tax purposes if it concludes that the estate's life had been "unduly" prolonged.[5]

How long can an estate usually be kept open without generating IRS disapproval? Some authorities believe that a reasonable life is about 3 to 4 years for an ordinary estate, and as long as 15 years for an estate which elects to defer payment of taxes under Section 6166.

The income tax benefit from prolonging an estate's life has been significantly curtailed in recent years due to tax reform's compression of income tax rates. The effective federal differential in rates, once as high as 55 percentage points not too long ago, is now approximately 18 percentage points.

---

5. Reg. §1.641(b)-3(a).

PLANNING DEVICES PRIMARILY DESIGNED
TO SAVE DEATH TAXES

We turn now to an examination of several postmortem tax planning strategies which have their greatest impact on death taxes. They include the alternate valuation date election, disclaimers, QTIP election, and several miscellaneous other techniques discussed briefly in Chapters 15 and 16.

Alternate Valuation Date Election

The size of the FET for an estate will, of course, often be a direct function of the value of its interests includable in the gross estate. An intelligent executor or estate adviser will try to keep valuation as low as possible. Often, conflicts with the IRS arise regarding the correct valuation of particular estate assets and deductions. While such conflicts make the entire subject of estate valuation seem quite subjective, there is one specific rule in this field that offers some objective certainty. The Code allows the executor the option to value estate assets and deductions as of either one of two different points in time.

Under Section 2032, the value of the assets included in the gross estate (and corresponding liabilities) may be determined as of date of death, *or* they may be determined as of the alternate valuation date (AVD), which is *six months after date of death*. This section was enacted after the Great Depression to limit the adverse tax and liquidity effects that radical changes in market values could have on an estate. For example, consider a hypothetical decedent who died in mid- to late 1929 owning a considerable amount of stock, which had to be included in the gross estate at high, precrash date-of-death values. Such an estate could have wound up owing, nine months after death, an FET that was considerably larger than its total current market value!

Under AVD rules, the executor may not pick and choose which assets to value at which of the two dates. If the election is made, *all* assets (and deductions) must be valued at the AVD. However, any assets sold or distributed after death and before the AVD must be valued as of that sale or distribution date.

Prior to 1984, the AVD election was permitted in situations where it *increased* the gross estate, thereby resulting in greater step-up in basis for assets owned at death. This strategy was attractive for estates completely sheltered by the unified credit and/or marital deduction. §2032© now permits the AVD election only if it reduces both the value of the gross estate and the FET (and GSTT, if any).

As implied above, if the AVD is elected, assets valued at that date will be so valued for purposes of step-up (or step-down) in income tax basis. Thus, with a smaller step-up (or greater step-down), a lower estate tax value will save FET but will risk a larger income tax in the future. Since the minimum marginal FET rate is 37 percent while the maximum marginal income tax rate on capital gains is 28 percent, the AVD election should lower net taxes by at least nine cents for every dollar of reduced valuation. In addition, if the inherited asset is not sold, the AVD advantage increases to at least 37 cents per dollar. Finally, even if the heir chooses to sell the asset, a time value of money savings will result to the extent that the income tax can be paid after the FET is due.[6]

Based on a survey of experienced estate planning attorneys conducted by this author, the alternate valuation date is being elected in the estate tax returns of approximately 11 percent of decedents.

Disclaimer Planning

A disclaimer is an unqualified refusal to accept a gift. We have already studied disclaimers in two earlier chapters. First, in Chapter 7, covering the federal gift tax, we examined the transfer tax aspects of disclaimers, including the requirements for a valid disclaimer. Second, in Chapter 12, surveying marital deduction and bypass planning, we saw how a disclaimer provision could be included in a bypass arrangement to add postmortem flexibility to the client's estate plan. That discussion also mentioned several disadvantages of the use of disclaimers. The purpose of the present discussion is to add additional detail to disclaimer planning, in the context of general postmortem planning.

Because of the requirement that the disclaiming donor can not have accepted any interest in the benefits, the client's survivors must be told as soon as possible not to accept the decedent's property or income if a disclaimer is anticipated. The following material describes three general situations where disclaimers can be effectively utilized. They include spousal disclaimers to reduce the marital deduction, disclaimers by a nonspouse to increase the size of the marital deduction, and disclaimers to correct defective or inefficient dispositive documents.

Spousal disclaimer to reduce the marital deduction. We have seen how a spousal disclaimer of a marital deduction bequest can add postmortem flexibility by enabling the surviving spouse to choose the amount of the

---

6. For a more detailed discussion of planning with the AVD election, see the Stikker article cited at the end of the chapter.

marital bequest to disclaim to the bypass share, thereby self-determining the amount of FET to defer to the second death. That section was described as Option 4, "100 percent marital deduction with disclaimer into bypass," in which the surviving spouse was bequeathed the entire amount of the decedent spouse's estate, subject to S2's ability to disclaim all or part of it in the event that a bypass eventually became desirable.

The marital deduction disclaimer can be used for any size estate but is probably most needed for certain rapidly appreciating *smaller estates*. For example, a plan for an estate that is currently too small to justify the use of a bypass could include a disclaimer provision, available in the event that the estate grew large enough to warrant a bypass distribution.

On the other hand, the disclaimer can also work well in *larger estates* in which S1 has under-utilized the million dollar GSTT exemption. The surviving spouse, at S1's death, may be able to disclaim assets being received outright *into* a GSTT exempt credit shelter bypass trust or QTIP trust.

Factors that may help the surviving spouse decide whether and how much to disclaim include S2's needs and his or her income tax bracket. First, the greater S2's perceived *need* for S1's assets to live comfortably, the less S2 will probably be willing to disclaim. This, in turn, will depend on the size of S2's estate. Of course, by disclaiming, S2 would not ordinarily be relinquishing all interests in the property, since the typical recipient bypass or QTIP trust provides for some invasion powers and for most or all income to be paid to S2. However, many S2s are still likely to react emotionally that by disclaiming, they are in reality making a complete relinquishment.

Second, S2's willingness to disclaim will also depend on his or her marginal *income tax rate*, since the higher S2's rate, the more desirable will be a disclaimer if it has the effect of redirecting taxable income to other beneficiaries.

For a further discussion of the benefits and drawbacks of providing for a spousal disclaimer into a bypass, see Chapter 12.

Disclaimer by a nonspouse to increase the marital deduction. A disclaimer can be used to raise a marital deduction that is subsequently found to be inadequate. For example, a client may have died with an estate plan that neither included a bypass nor took full use of the unlimited marital deduction. This can occur when a person dies intestate or dies owning a considerable amount of property in *joint tenancy* with someone other than a spouse. The nonspouse beneficiary may be encouraged to disclaim the interest so that it may qualify for the marital deduction by passing to the surviving spouse. However, problems in implementation may arise. First, only a *donee* of property held in joint tenancy may disclaim.[7] Thus, such a disclaimer will work only if the decedent was the original donor of the property. Second, courts may be unwilling to allow the guardian of a minor child (or unborn child) to disclaim rights to property, reasoning that full relinquishment of property is not in the child's best interest. However, since a disclaimer cannot be made by a person until he or she reaches age 21, a disclaimer that is delayed until the disclaimant reaches majority might be effective.

Third, until recently, the IRS had been taking the position that the disclaimer had to be made within nine months of the date the joint tenancy was *created*, rather than the date of death. Then, after losing in the courts, the Service acquiesced with regard to joint tenancies where state law gives the joint tenant the right to sever the joint tenancy or cause the property to be partitioned.[8] Thus, disclaimers of joint interests may not be valid in some states. For example, a qualified disclaimer is not permitted in states such as Arkansas where *tenancy by the entirety property* can not be partitioned by one spouse without the permission of the other.[9]

Disclaimers to correct defective and inefficient dispositive documents. Occasionally, wills and trusts are drafted erroneously. One always hopes that these mistakes will be discovered during the client's lifetime. If not, they can still often be corrected by disclaimer. For example, a disclaimer may also be used to refuse an undesirable bequest of a general power of appointment.

> EXAMPLE 2518-1 Barbara died seven months ago leaving a will that provides for a bypass trust for the benefit of her husband, Jake. The will gives Jake the right to invade the trust for reasons of "health or happiness." Since courts have consistently held that the term *happiness* does not constitute an ascertainable standard, Jake will be deemed to be the holder of a general power of appointment over the entire trust corpus, which will be includable in Jake's gross estate at his later death. Jake may be able to prevent this unfortunate result by properly disclaiming his power over the corpus.

---

7. Reg 25.2518-2(c)(4)(I).

8. IRS Administrative Documents, Feb. 22, 1990; LR 9106016; TAM 9208003.

9. LR 9208003.

A disclaimer can also be used to overcome an inefficient disposition, thereby increasing the size of a charitable contribution.

> EXAMPLE 2518-2 Sally, a widow, was 90 years old when she died six months ago. She left one surviving relative, her son Abbott, who is aged 73 and in failing health. Sally's will, paraphrased somewhat, reads, "All to Abbott, but if he does not survive me by 30 days, then all to the Girl Scouts of America." Abbott, who should be able to live for 30 days but is not likely to live more than six months, has no issue and would not mind leaving all of the property inherited from his mother to the Girl Scouts. To avoid taxation of the property in Sally's estate, Abbott could disclaim all interest in Sally's bequest. Consequently, the property would pass to the Girl Scouts without being subject to taxation in Sally's estate.

A disclaimer may be made with respect to an undivided *portion* of an interest, which the IRS defines as a fraction or percentage of each and every substantial interest owned by the disclaimant extending over the entire term of the disclaimant's interest.[10]

> EXAMPLE 2518-3 Lynn survived her husband, who bequeathed her 100 shares of stock outright and a life estate in $10,000 annual income in trust property. Lynn may disclaim fewer than 100 shares of the stock, and she may disclaim a life estate in less than $10,000 annually of the trust property. But she may not disclaim only a remainder interest in the stock, or only a term for years portion of her life estate, such as for the first five years of the income.

Two other common examples of disclaimers include one allowing a married couple to fully utilize their $2 million GSTT exemption, and a disclaimer by a wealthier child in favor of a sibling who is more in need.[11] These examples are merely illustrative of the many situations where post-mortem disclaimers can be used to alter estate dispositions to obtain more desirable results. Disclaimers are generally considered to be an extremely powerful estate planning tool. It should be noted that since the stakes can be quite high in this technical area of the law, the client is encouraged to seek competent counsel prior to attempting to make a qualified disclaimer.

---

10. Reg. 25.2518-3(b).

11. For an example of an unsuccessful disclaimer to correct a defect in a trust intended to achieve QTIP treatment, partly because the court felt that the disclaimer would amount to nearly a complete rewrite of the trust, see *Estate of Bennett*, 100 TC No. 5 (1993).

QTIP Election Planning

Overview. As mentioned in Chapter 6, property normally can qualify for the marital deduction only if it "passes" to the spouse. In other words, the spouse cannot ordinarily receive an interest that might terminate; the interest cannot be terminable. Over the years, however, the Code has carved out several exceptions to this rule. Up to 1982, the most commonly used marital trust designed to take advantage of an exception was the power of appointment trust, i.e., the one giving the spouse a life estate in the income and a general power of appointment over the corpus.[12] Since then, the QTIP trust, based on the QTIP election exception, effective in 1982, has become far more popular. It is found in §2056(b)(7) and provides that property subject to a terminable interest can qualify for the marital deduction if it meets the following two requirements for "qualified terminable interest property:"

1. The surviving spouse must be entitled to receive all income from the property for life, payable at least annually.
2. No person may have the power to appoint the property to anyone other than the surviving spouse.

Why might clients wish to bequeath only a terminable interest to their spouse? Why wouldn't clients always prefer to give marital deduction property to the spouse outright, or in trust with the spouse receiving a general power of appointment over the property? Why restrict the spouse's ability to control disposition of the property? There are several possible reasons, including the desire to protect the estate from the consequences of S2's immaturity or senility, and the goal of protecting assets from the surviving spouse's creditors. But perhaps the most common reason is a desire by S1 to absolutely *guarantee the ultimate disposition* to an intended remainder beneficiary.[13] The typical S1 choosing a QTIP arrangement has children of a former marriage and wishes to provide for the surviving spouse's income needs during lifetime, yet still absolutely ensure that his or her own children will eventually receive the property after the surviving spouse's death. Only a QTIP-type arrangement will do all this and still qualify the property for the marital deduction.

---

12. §2056(b)(5).

13. Word has it that the QTIP provisions were quickly passed in 1981 without debate because so many Congressmen and Senators were already on their second or third marriage!

Some planners also recommend the QTIP plan for clients still married to their first spouse to eliminate the risk that their surviving spouse might remarry and leave substantial property to the new spouse rather than the children. Others disagree, pointing out that most S2's either do not remarry or act prudently when they do.

From the above, it should be clear that a QTIP type of marital trust inherently conflicts with the goal of maximum *dispositive* flexibility through the use of surrogate decision makers. More specifically, this approach is in direct contrast with the less popular power of appointment trust, discussed in Chapter 12, that grants to S2 a general power of appointment over the trust property. A QTIP plan, on the other hand, usually allows no discretionary distributions by S2 to others, relying instead on the "dead hand" control and directives of the immutable S1 will or trust instrument. Commentators strongly recommend that the QTIP trusts of more trusting clients grant the surviving spouse a limited power of appointment to distribute, at death, principal to permissible appointees named in the instrument. This power will add additional flexibility, for example, by allowing a surrogate decision maker to take greater advantage of GSTT exemptions under changing circumstances.[14] Thus, while the effect of federal legislation was once to foster dispositive flexibility by requiring, as a condition for qualifying for the marital deduction, that the surviving spouse be granted a general power of appointment, its effect now is to discourage it by allowing a marital deduction for property over which the surviving spouse may have little or no control. However, in contrast to dispositive inflexibility, the QTIP plan can offer some additional *FET planning* flexibility by means of the actual QTIP election. This will be shown in the next three examples, presented shortly.

Making the Election. "QTIPable" property need not be included in the S1 marital deduction; to include it, an election must be made at S1's death.

Uniqueness of QTIP election. In contrast with the decision as to who will ultimately *receive* the property outright, the final decision whether to make that election to *include* QTIP property in the S1 marital deduction will not be up to the S1-transferor. And in contrast with the spousal disclaimer, that decision will not be up to S2. Instead, *S1's executor* will be required to make the choice on the S1 FET return.

Deferral versus equalization revisited. If the election is made, the QTIP property can qualify for the S1 marital deduction, and S1's taxable estate and FET will be reduced. However, at S2's death, the S2 date of-

---

14. For a discussion of this and other drafting techniques promoting flexibility, see the Gardner article cited at the end of the chapter.

death value of the qualifying property *must* be taxed as though it were includable in S2's gross estate.[15] The estate of S2 will receive reimbursement from the QTIP trust for the tax incurred by it.[16]

Thus, in considering the QTIP election, the S1 executor must choose one of the following two tax consequences: (1) making the election will defer the FET by reducing the S1 taxable estate and increasing the S2 taxable estate; and, alternatively, (2) not making the election will accelerate the FET by producing a larger S1 taxable estate, but can result in a smaller S2 taxable estate, via bypass.[17] The choice whether or not to make the election essentially boils down to a tax issue: whether to *defer or to equalize spousal* FET. The reader is directed back to Chapter 12 for an extended discussion of the factors influencing this decision.

As you study and review the present section, you might keep in mind that the S1 executor's QTIP election has nothing to do with determining who will receive the property; the trust terms decide that and, except for the possibility of disclaimer by a beneficiary, it is no longer subject to change by anyone.

> EXAMPLE 2056(b)(7)-1 Kenneth died three months ago. He is survived by his ex-wife, his second wife (S2), and D, E, and F, three adult children of the first marriage. There are no children from the second marriage. At his death, Kenneth owned $2 million in property. S2 owns $1 million in property, and she intends to leave it to X and Y, the children of *her* first marriage. Kenneth's will creates two trusts, trust B and trust A. Trust B is a bypass trust and will receive an amount equal to the exemption equivalent of the unified credit. Trust A will receive the residue of Kenneth's estate. The trustees of both trusts are required to pay all income monthly to S2 for her life. At S2's death, the amount of each corpus will pass outright in equal shares to Kenneth's three children. S2 is given a power to invade the corpus of trust B, subject to an ascertainable standard. S2 is given no power over the corpus of trust A. The property in trust A, which includes the decedent's residence, meets the requirements for qualified terminable interest property. As executor of Kenneth's estate, S2 *decides to elect* to include the value of this property in the S1 marital

---

15. §2044.

16. §2207(a).

17. However, the IRS and case law have ruled that the marital deduction will be disallowed in the case of a trust that is not to be funded if the QTIP election is not made, LR9104003; *Estate of Clayton*, 97 TC 327 (1991), or if failure to elect resulted in the property passing to a second trust that did not qualify for QTIP treatment. *J. Spencer Estate* TC CCH ¶12,908(M).

deduction. By so electing, S2 has made it certain that this QTIP property will be included in her gross estate at her death. During his lifetime, Kenneth created a plan which both ensures that the children of his first marriage will eventually receive all of his property, and preserves the marital deduction for his estate, as S1. Trust A is called the QTIP trust.

EXAMPLE 2056(b)(7)-2 Modifying the facts in the preceding example a bit, assume that S2, as executor of the S1 estate, *does not elect* to include the A trust property in the S1 marital deduction. The property will still pass to the children upon S2's death, but will neither be deductible from S1's gross estate nor be includable in S2's gross estate. By not electing, S2 has chosen not to defer the FET. *Both trusts*, not just the B trust, will *bypass* S2's estate. Both are called bypass trusts.

EXAMPLE 2056(b)(7)-3 Again modifying the facts in Example 2056(b)(7)-1 a bit, assume that S2, as executor of Kenneth's estate, makes a QTIP election as to only five fourteenths, or $500,000 of the trust A property. A partial bypass of the A trust property will result.

Tax law permits *partial QTIP elections* with regard to fractional asset shares.

EXAMPLE 2056(b)(7)-4 In all three examples above, Kenneth's three children, as named remainder beneficiaries, will be certain to receive the entire corpus of each trust at S2's death. Making or not making the QTIP election will not alter this result. However, it can influence the size of each remainder distribution to the extent that it influences the size of the total FET. Calculation of the contrasting results is the subject of Question 12 at the end of the chapter.

Disclaimers and QTIP elections can also frequently be used to remedy the problem illustrated in Example ERTA-1 in Chapter 1. In essence, they can partially raise the marital deduction for an S2 in spite of the forced application of the pre-1982 marital deduction rules for certain wills and trusts executed before September 12, 1981.[18]

Thus, as an alternative to the power of appointment marital trust described in Chapter 12, the QTIP election, while offering less dispositive flexibility to S2, does give S2 some greater flexibility in marital deduction and bypass planning, while enabling S1 to retain total dispositive control over the property.

QTIP Election Versus Disclaimer. The astute reader will observe that

---

18. For a further discussion of this and other postmortem strategies to salvage the marital deduction, see the Alvarez article cited at the end of the chapter.

the disclaimer and the QTlP election are *both* strategies that can enable a surrogate decision maker to decide on behalf of the deceased client whether or not to defer the FET. One advantage of the QTIP alternative over the disclaimer is the ability to delay the decision an additional six months. While a disclaimer must usually be made within 9 months after date of death, a QTIP election is made on the federal estate tax return which, when including an automatically granted 6-month extension to file, will be due 15 months after date of death. An advantage of the disclaimer over the QTIP election is that under the QTIP election, the spouse's right to income can not be made contingent upon the election being made.[19]

Perhaps the most fundamental difference between the disclaimer and the QTIP arrangement concerns the amount of control S2 is given over the assets involved. Often, it is the single deciding factor in making the choice. Thus, if the client wishes the spouse to have complete control, an outright transfer anticipating the possibility of a disclaimer will be preferred. If, on the other hand, minimal S2 control is desired, a transfer to a QTIP trust will be the better choice.

Other Postmortem Death Tax-Saving Devices

Three other postmortem tax elections often available to the estates of business owners include the §6166 election to pay the FET in installments, the §303 redemption of stock, and the §2032A special use valuation election. These elections were covered in some detail in Chapter 15 and will not be discussed further here.

This chapter has focused on postmortem planning techniques designed to reduce income and death taxes. They have been the subject of this last chapter because they represent, conceptually, the final phase of planning undertaken on behalf of a client.

---

19. LR861106.

QUESTIONS AND PROBLEMS

1. List the federal tax returns that may have to be filed during a period of administration of a decedent's property.

2. Maxie, a widower, died recently, leaving his $2 million gross estate to his brother Morey. Maxie spent the last six months in a hospital, paying $50,000 of the $80,000 hospital bill before he died. Marginal tax rates for the taxpaying entities are as follows: Maxie's final Form 1040, 31 percent; the Form 1041, 28 percent; the Form 706, 41 percent. How much in tax will Maxie's estate save if the allowable expense is deducted, alternatively, on
   a. The Form 706?
   b. The final Form 1040?
   c. The estate's Form 1041?
   On which return should the deduction be made?

3. Moose died recently, leaving his entire $2 million gross estate to his wife, Trixie, who is named executor. Assume that the only estate expense is the executor's commission of $100,000. Marginal tax rates for the taxpaying entities are: Trixie's Form 1040, 31 percent; the final Form 1040, 15 percent; the Form 1041, 28 percent; the Form 706, 41 percent.
   a. Should Trixie accept or waive the commission? Why?
   b. Where, if at all, should the estate deduct the commission? Why?
   c. Would your answers to parts *a* and *b* change if Moose owned a $200,000 estate, and Trixie's Form 1040 marginal rate was 28 percent?
   d. Would your answers to parts *a* and *b* probably change if Trixie, the executor, was Moose's cousin to whom Moose left nothing by will or otherwise? Assume a $2 million gross estate.

4. Describe the income tax advantages available to all estates and those advantages available only to estates having a carefully chosen fiscal year.

5. How can the executor of an estate or the trustee of a trust reduce income taxes by planning the distributions to beneficiaries if the beneficiaries marginal tax rates are:
   a. Higher than that of the estate or trust?
   b. Lower than that of the estate or trust?

6. What is the benefit of prolonging an estate's life, and what is the tax consequence if it is "unduly" prolonged?

7. Explain. What two conditions must be met before an estate can make the alternate valuation date election? What is the tax advantage? When are assets valued?

8. Give two specific examples where a disclaimer can reduce the FET.

9. (*a*) Can "qualified terminable interest property" wind up not being part of the S1 marital deduction? (*b*) If yes, should the QTIP arrangement be considered a bust?

10. Describe the unique contribution of a QTIP arrangement to estate planning.

11. (*a*) Can a QTIP arrangement and a disclaimer provision be alternative methods of achieving a common objective? Why or why not? (*b*) Which will place greater property rights in the hands of S2? Why?

12. In the manner similar to your calculations for questions 9 © and (*d*) of chapter 11, determine the amount passing to the children based on the facts presented in the following QTIP examples illustrated in this chapter.
    a. Example 2056(b)(7)-1. (QTIP election- credit shelter bypass. Answer is the same as for problem 9*c* in Chapter 11).
    b. Example 2056(b)(7)-2. (no QTIP election- 100 percent bypass).
    c. Example 2056(b)(7)-3. (partial QTIP election- bypass with estate equalization. Answer is the same as for problem 9*d* in Chapter 11).

13. Brunk owned three assets at his death. Their description and appraised values at date of death, six months after death and nine months after death, respectively, are as follows: Home and furnishings, $300,000, $320,000, $340,000; securities, $800,000, $700,000, $600,000; and an interest in a closely held business, $500,000, $400,000, $300,000. Brunk bequeathed all assets to his son, who, as executor, sold the home for $310,000 four months after Brunk died, and sold the business for $320,000 eight months after Brunk died. Assuming no deductions, calculate Brunk's taxable estate.

14. (This question requires the ability to calculate present values).

Assume that decedent, a widower, died owning only one asset, 10,000 shares of stock that she originally purchased for one dollar a share. The stock's total date of death value was $800,000 and its value six months after death was $750,000. Decedent's son stands to inherit all of the stock and he is considering selling it exactly 21 months from now. The FET will be paid exactly nine months from now, out of the son's own funds. Assume that the income tax on any capital gain, based on a combined marginal tax rate of 35 percent, will be paid on day of sale.

a. Calculate the FET saved if the alternate valuation date (AVD) is elected. You'll need to determine the marginal FET rate.

b. If son never sells the asset, how much combined income tax and FET will be saved if the AVD is elected?

c. If son does sell the asset and has a combined marginal income tax rate of 50 percent, how much total income tax and FET will be saved if the AVD is elected?

d. If the AVD is elected, at 10 percent, calculate both the present value of the reduced FET and the present value of the higher income tax, as of the FET due date (i.e. take present value back to a point that is 9 months after today.)

e. Compare the net difference between your two answers to part d with your answer to part c.

15. With regard to the QTIP election:

a. Who makes it?

b. If the election is made, will it influence either the ultimate disposition of the property, or taxation of the qualifying property, or both? Explain.

c. If the election is not made, how will the tax result change?

16. (The facts of this question derive from an actual situation). Dad died eight months ago. He and Mom operated a successful farm for 50 years. All of their assets, worth about $3 million, were held in joint tenancy. Ten years ago, the family lawyer drafted a revocable living trust, which essentially left one half of S1s estate to S2 and the balance to a bypass trust for the benefit of S2, as life income beneficiary, and for Mom and Dad's three children (all adults), as remaindermen. This trust was never funded. The lawyer also drafted a pour over will, which Dad never signed.

a. Describe the FET consequences of the current "plan."

b. Recommend postmortem planning to reduce FET.

RECOMMENDED READING

*Alvarez, Edna. "Post-Mortem Reconstruction of the Marital Deduction: QTlPs, Disclaimers and Other Tools." *22nd Annual Institute on Estate Planning 1991*, Practicing Law Institute.

Ascher, Mark L. "The Fiduciary Duty to Minimize Taxes." *Real Property, Probate & Trust Journal* 20 (1985), pp. 663-717.

Barnett, Bernard. "Estate and Trust Distributions in Kind after TRA '84." *Trusts & Estates*, October 1984, pp. 32-38.

Bettigole, Bruce J. "Post-Mortem Remedies Can Salvage the Problem of Underfunded and Overfunded Marital Bequests." *Estate Planning*, March 1985, pp. 66-71.

Deveraux, James F. "Understanding Grief and the Grieving Process." *Trusts & Estates*, August 1985, pp. 30-32.

Dirkes, George R. "Tax Planning After Death." *1991 Institute on Estate Planning*, Practicing Law Institute.

Edwards, Mark B., and David L. Thomas, "Post-Mortem Tax Planning: Income Tax Aspects-The Overlooked Opportunities." *Trusts & Estates*, January 1985, pp. 46-51.

Eggleston, Jon R. "Post-Mortem Election of Subchapter S Can Benefit Estate with Closely Held Stock." *Estate Planning*, March 1984, pp. 104-7.

Esterces, Howard M. "Post-Mortem Transfers of Pension Plans Offer Opportunities." *Taxation for Accountants*, Feb., 1993, pp. 80-87.

Eubank, J. Thomas "When the Estate Plan Must Be Made Final: An Overview of Decisions and Techniques Shortly after the Decedent's Death." *1983 Institute on Estate Planning*, Chap. 20, pp. 1-31.

Ferguson, Barbara B. "Disclaimers Can Adjust Tax Consequences to Reflect Post-Mortem Changed Circumstances." *Taxation for Accountants*, January 1985, pp. 30-36.

Fevurley, Keith R. "Planning Must Be Revised to Obtain Maximum Benefits of Special-Use Valuation." *Estate Planning*, January 1986, pp. 14-19.

Frimmer, Paul N. "Qualified Disclaimers." *Estate Planning*, 1987, California Continuing Education of the Bar.

Fullerton, Gregory L. "When Can a Fiduciary Disclaim Property on Behalf of another?" *Estate Planning*, September, 1990, pp. 272-77.

*Gardner, Harrison. "Designing Wills and Trust Instruments to Provide Maximum Flexibility." *Estate Planning*, May, 1991, pp. 138-42.

Geu, Thomas E. "Post-Mortem Recognition of Informal Family Partnerships." *Nebraska Law Review* 63(1984), pp. 314-14.

Harrison, Louis S. & John M. Janiga "A Taxpayer's Death Triggers Many Filing Requirements," *Taxation For Accountants*, March, 1993, pp. 137-44.

Hart, Lynn C, "The Disclaimer: A Gift to the Post-Mortem Planner", *1990 UCLA/CEB Estate Planning Institute.*

_____, "Advanced Issues In Disclaimer Planning: Sharpening An Old Tool," *1994 University of Miami Estate Planning Institute.*

Hastings, Dan T. "The Discriminate 'No'." (On the final Section 2518 Disclaimer Regulations), *Trust & Estates*, October 1986, pp. 39-46.

Kasner, Jerry A. *Post Mortem Tax Planning*, New York: Shephard's/McGraw Hill, 1982.

Kinskern, Douglas. "When Will Transferees and Executors Be Personally Liable for Estate and Gift Taxes?" *Estate Planning*, March 1987, pp. 106-11.

Kupferberg, Alan. "How to Meet the QTIP Requirement that All Income Must Be Payable to the Spouse," *Estate Planning*, July, 1990, pp. 202-06.

Mariani, Michael M. "Form 1041 vs. Form 706: Where to Deduct Administration Expenses." *Trust & Estates*, June 1984, pp. 37-40.

Mays, Jr. R. L. "How to Stay Flexible in Estate Tax Decisions." *Trusts & Estates*, December 1985, p. 32.

Moore, Malcolm A., "The Ever Expanding Use of Disclaimers in Estate Planning; An Update," *1990 University of Miami Estate Planning Institute.*

_____, "Partnerships in Estate Administration: A Proposed road Map Through the thicket," *1992 University of Miami Estate Planning Institute.*

Pena, Emma. "Internal Revenue Code Section 2518 Disclaimers and the 1981 Economic Recovery Tax Act: Continued Unequal Treatment of Taxpayers." *Santa Clara Law Review* 22(1982), pp. 1179-1204.

Peters, Jeffrey A. "Deferral Strategies Still Exist Despite New Calendar Year and Estimated Tax Requirements." *Estate Planning*, July 1987, pp. 194-99.

Popper, Richard J. A. "Post-Mortem Estate Planning Strategies For Owners of Closely Held Businesses," *Estate Planning*, July, 1990, pp. 208-14.

Raabe, William A. "Sec. 6166: Computing the Estate's Interest Deduction." *The Tax Adviser*, August 1984, pp. 458-65.

Rhine, David S., and John H. Lavelle. "Post-Mortem Adjustments Affecting Estate and Beneficiaries are Significant in Planning Wills." *Estate Planning*, July 1984, pp. 210-15.

Salzarulo, W. Peter. "When to Elect to Recognize Gain or Loss on Distributions of Estate or Trust Property." *Estate Planning*, January 1986, pp. 38-44.

Stikker, Thomas J. "Decline in Value of Estate's Assets Does Not Always Call for Use Of Alternate Valuation Date" *Estate Planning*, September, 1989, pp. 296-301.

Sumerford, Rees M. "Administration Expenses Offer Opportunities for Planning to Maximize the Available Tax Benefits." *Taxation for Accountants*, July 1984, pp. 26-31.

Uchtmann, D. L., and P. K. Zigterman. Disclaimers of Joint Tenancy Interests Revisited." *Creighton Law Review* 18(1985), pp. 333-56.

Womer-Benjamin, Ann H. "Post Mortem Strategies Extend Planning Prospects." *Estate Planning*, January, 1992, pp. 24-29.

Three Study Aids:
Estate Planning Cases With Study Questions;
CFP Estate Planning Outline Topics

OVERVIEW

This chapter features three study aids. The first two are hypothetical case studies, included for two primary reasons. First, estate planning is an intensely fact oriented and client oriented subject, and the more analysis of family situations studied, the better. Second, some readers may be preparing to take a final exam or a certification examination in estate planning, estate and gift tax, or financial planning. These questions should help in that preparation.

The first case is one actually used in at least one 1992 CFP comprehensive examination. It is included verbatim.[1] The reader will notice it to be quite general in orientation, testing several other financial planning subjects

---

1. Reprinted with permission of the International Board of Standards and Practices for the CFP (IBCFP).

besides estate planning, which is the subject matter of about only one third of the nineteen questions. This author has been told that the IBCFP will continue to use, in future exams, only cases that are similarly general in scope.

The second case is far more estate planning oriented, and can be used to better test one's knowledge of numerous technical issues in estate planning.

The third part of the chapter includes the complete, official, "four level" outline of estate planning "job knowledge requirements" of the certified financial planner (CFP): the list of topics upon which the CFP estate planning exam questions are based.

ONE: CFP COMPREHENSIVE EXAM CASE

Case Scenario And Multiple-Choice Questions

The following case scenario with multiple-choice questions appeared on IBCFP comprehensive CFP certification examinations. The correct answer to each question is indicated with an asterisk *(Editor's note: to encourage greater analysis, the answers have instead been placed on a separate page at the end of the case)*. The case has been approved for publication by the IBCFP's Board of Examiners. If you have a question about the technical content of the case, please address your question to the Board by *writing* to them at the IBCFP's address: 1660 Lincoln Street, Suite 3050, Denver, CO 80264.

Instructions: Read the information provided about William and Marilyn Mathews and choose the best answer to the multiple choice questions that follow.

WILLIAM AND MARILYN MATHEWS

Your clients, Bill and Marilyn Mathews, have asked you to help them with a number of issues facing them as Bill prepares to sell his business and formally retire. Marilyn will also retire, having worked as the company bookkeeper for twenty years. Negotiations for the sale of Bill's business, Calculator City, are almost concluded, pending resolution of a number of questions Bill raised installment payments for the business as well as a request from the proposed owner that Bill continue to provide consulting services.

Personal Information

	Age	Health	Occupation
William Mathews	65	Excellent	Business Owner
Marilyn Mathews	63	Excellent	Bookkeeper
John Mathews (son)	32	Excellent	Engineer
James Mathews (son)	30	Excellent	CPA
Grandchildren	3,4,5, and 7	Excellent	-

Neither son has any intention of becoming involved in the business. The Mathews file a joint tax return. Client and spouse have simple wills leaving all to each other.

Economic Environment

The current economic environment exhibits low real short-term rates, high real long-term rates, little economic growth, and high unemployment.

Client Objectives

1. Maintain current lifestyle, including frequent travel.

2. Revise estate plan to minimize taxes, take advantage of opportunities in various elections available in the Internal Revenue Code, and maximize amounts passing to children and grandchildren.

3. Review investment portfolio and make changes as necessary to reflect different priorities and risk tolerance levels during retirement. Initial indications are that the clients are willing to take normal investment risks, desirous of adequate current income, reasonable safety of principal, inflation protection, tax advantage, and some modest long term appreciation, in that order of priority.

4. Review and revise total risk management and insurance situation as necessary to provide adequate protection, and eliminate gaps and overlaps.

5. Determine the most advantageous method of taking distributions from the 401(k) accounts.

WILLIAM AND MARILYN MATHEWS
Statement of Financial Position
12/31/92

Assets		Liabilities	
Invested Assets			
Cash/Cash Equivalents	$8,000.	Auto Loan	$6,000.
Marketable Securities[1]	1,580,000.	Mortgage[2]	12,000.
Business Interest[3]	1,500,000.	Mortgage[4]	74,000.
Life Ins. Cash Value[5]	$60,000.		92,000.
Annuity	120,000.		
	$3,268,000.		
Use Assets			
Primary Residence	$188,000.		
Summer Home	126,000.		
Personal Property	60,000.		
Automobiles	26,000.	Net Worth	$3,951,000.
	$400,000.		
Retirement Plan Assets[6]			
IRA (H)	$27,000.		
IRA (W)	28,000.		
401(k) (H)	280,000.		
401(k) (W)	40,000.		
	$375,000.		
Total Assets	$4,043,000.	Total Liabilities and Net Worth	$4,043,000.

---

[1]See separate Investment Portfolio Supplement
[2]Principal residence; originally, 30 years @ 7%
[3]Business is to be sold for $1.5 million. Purchase price was $700,000 in 1982. Terms of sale include $300,000 down payment on July 1, 1993, with the balance to be paid over 120 months starting August 1, 1993, at 10% interest.
[4]Summer home; originally, 15 years @9%
[5]Face Amount: $200,000; Bill is insured, Marilyn is beneficiary.
[6]Spouse is beneficiary for IRA and 401(k). The IRAs are invested in a common stock growth mutual fund. The 401(k) plans are invested in 3-year Treasury notes.

WILLIAM AND MARILYN MATHEWS
Projected Monthly Cash Flow Statement
1/1/93 through 12/31/93

(Incomplete)

Cash Inflows

Social Security (H)	$820.
Social Security (W)	$410.
Installment Payments (120 pmts @ 10%)	?
Interest Income (tax-exempt)	$600.
Dividend Income	$540.
Interest Income (taxable)	?
Other Investment Income	?

Outflows

Savings and Investment	?
Mortgage (residence: PITI)	$600.
Mortgage (summer home: PITI)	$1,100.
Food	$300.
Utilities	$400.
Transportation (gas, oil, maintenance)	$200.
Car Payment	$600.
Clothing	$250.
Entertainment	$450.
Travel	$1,680.
Family Gifts	$1,666.
Charitable Gifts	$500.
Life Insurance	$300.
Hospitalization (Medigap/Medicare)	$100.
Automobile Insurance	$150.
Miscellaneous	?
Federal income Tax	$5,800.
State Income Tax	$900.
Other	?

WILLIAM AND MARILYN MATHEWS
INSURANCE AND ANNUITY INFORMATION

Person Insured/Owner	Bill
Type of Policy	Whole Life
Face Amount	$200,000
Dividend Option	Paid-Up Additions
Issue Date	2/13/77
Beneficiary	Marilyn
Current Cash Value	$60,000
Premium	$300 per month

Person Insured/Owner	Bill
Type of Policy	Single Premium Deferred Annuity
Fixed or Variable	Fixed
Current Value	$120,000
Current Interest Rate	6.5%
Issue Date	1/1/81
Purchase Price	$40,000

Homeowners Policy

Type	HO-3
Amount on Dwelling	$175,000
Personal Property Coverage	$87,500
Personal Liability	$100,000

Automobile Policy

Type	Personal Auto policy
Bodily Injury/Property Damage	$300,000 Combined Single Limit
Collision	$250 Deductible
Comprehensive	Full, with $100 Deductible
Uninsured Motorist	$300,000 Single Limit

**WILLIAM AND MARILYN MATHEWS
INVESTMENT PORTFOLIO SUPPLEMENT**

Common Stocks	**Fair Market Value**
AT&T	$30,000.
Bell South	10,000.
Bell Atlantic	9,000.
Ameritech	8,500.
NYNEX	7,000.
Pacific Telesis	8,000.
Southwestern Bell	8,000.
U.S. West	7,000.
Canon	22,000.
Comerica Bank	29,000.
Danko	7,000.
de Beers	8,000.
du Pont	29,000.
Disney	12,000.
Dow Chemical	9,000.
Detroit Edison	24,000.
General Motors	8,000.
GME	10,500.
D&T, Inc.[*]	25,000.
Common stock mutual fund (IRAs)	55,000.

Municipal Bonds	
Franklin Intermediate Tax Exempt Fund	$100,000.

Annuities and Insurance	
Cash value life insurance	$60,000.
Single Premium Deferred Annuity	120,000.

Bonds	
Treasury notes (401(k))	$320,000.
U.S. EE Savings Bonds	75,000.

Cash and Equivalents	
Cash	$8,000.
Cash equivalents, incl. Money Markets	134,000.
Treasury Securities (T-Bills)	1,000,000.

TOTAL	$2,143,000.

[*]Small Business Corporation (§1244 stock) solely owned by Bill and originally purchased for $76,000 in 1/1/87.

1. The tax treatment of the down payment made to Bill for the sale of his business is:

   a. not taxable as a return of basis.
   b. fully taxable as a capital gain.
   c. partially a return of basis and partially taxable as ordinary income.
   d. partially a return of basis, partially a capital gain, and partially ordinary income.
   e. partially a return of capital and partially a capital gain.

2. How much will Bill receive from the monthly installment payments during 1993 (rounded to the nearest dollar)?

   a. $ 79,290
   b. $ 95,149
   c. $190,297
   d. $379,290
   e. $395,149

3. The amount of interest income from the installment sale for the year ending 12/31/93 is approximately:

   a. $ 49,000
   b. $ 59,000
   c. $ 60,000
   d. $ 72,000
   e. $120,000

4. How will Bill's receipt of installment payments for the sale of his business affect his Social Security benefits?

   a. His Social Security benefits will be reduced because of his installment payments.
   b. His Social Security benefits will <u>not</u> be taxable because installment payments are <u>not</u> wages.
   c. Receipt of installment payments will increase the amount of Modified Adjusted Gross Income, causing some of the Social Security benefits to be taxable.
   d. Because Bill is 65, his Social Security benefits will be subject to the excess earnings test applied to the installment payments. Benefits will be reduced $1 for every $2 earned over the base amount.
   e. Because Bill is 65, his Social Security benefits will be subject to the excess earnings test applied to the Installment payments. Benefits will be reduced $1 for every $3 earned over the base amount.

5. Bill and Marilyn both have account balances in the 401(k) Plan, and they want to determine what options they can pursue.

   Which of the following statements described options available for Bill and Marilyn?

   (1) Bill can make an IRA Rollover with his account; Marilyn can elect 10-Year Special Averaging for hers.
   (2) Both Bill and Marilyn can make IRA Rollovers.
   (3) Bill can elect a partial rollover and use 5-Year Special Averaging on the balance; Marilyn can roll over her entire amount.
   (4) Both Bill and Marilyn can elect either 5-Year or 10-Year Special Averaging for their respective distributions.

   a. (1), (2) and (4) only
   b. (1) and (3) only
   c. (2) only
   d. (2) and (3) only
   e. (1), (2), (3) and (4)

6. The Mathews family is considering the purchase of a survivorship life insurance policy, payable on the second death of either Bill or Marilyn, for the primary purpose of providing liquidity for the payment of the federal estate tax. The ownership and beneficiary arrangements are being studied for the best overall result.

Which of the following options for ownership and beneficiary arrangements are viable?

(1) Bill and Marilyn can purchase the policy and retain ownership; the proceeds will <u>not</u> be includable in either estate because of the unlimited marital deduction.

(2) Bill and Marilyn can purchase the policy, the then transfer ownership to one or both of their sons, so that the proceeds avoid inclusion in either Bill's or Marilyn's estate <u>no</u> matter when death occurs because they do <u>not</u> have any incidents of ownership.

(3) Ownership can be vested immediately in an irrevocable life insurance trust, with appropriate "Crummey" provisions, to avoid inclusion of the proceeds in either estate.

(4) The Mathews family Revocable Living Trust can be the initial owner and beneficiary, in order to avoid estate taxes in either estate, because life insurance death proceeds retain their tax-free character in the trust.

a. (1), (3) and (4) only
b. (2) and (4) only
c. (3) only
d. (2) only
e. (1) and (4) only

7. If Bill decides to make a partial withdrawal from his Single Premium Deferred Annuity, what income tax result will ensue?

   a. The withdrawal will be taxed as long-term capital gain, subject to a maximum rate of 28%.
   b. The withdrawal will be subject to ordinary income tax, since their is <u>no</u> preference for long-term capital gain.
   c. The withdrawal will be taxed according to the annuity rules, so that a portion will be taxable as ordinary income and the balance will be a tax-free recovery of capital.
   d. The withdrawal will be tax-free up to Bill's cost basis, since FIFO treatment applies to this annuity.
   e. The withdrawal will be taxable on a LIFO basis to the extent of earnings in the contract.

8. Bill is contemplating selling his D&T, Inc. stock for the fair market value. Assuming he sold D&T on 12/31/92, the tax impact would be:

   a. a fully deductible capital loss of $51,000.
   b. a capital loss limited to $3,000 assuming no other investment transactions; carryover $48,000 long-term capital loss.
   c. an ordinary loss of $50,000 with a $1,000 loss carryover.
   d. an ordinary loss of $51,000.
   e. a short-term capital loss of $51,000 because of Section 1244 status.

9. In view of the combined estate values for Bill and Marilyn, which of the following estate planning techniques may be appropriate?

   (1) placing life insurance in an irrevocable trust
   (2) making use of annual gift tax exclusion
   (3) establishing a revocable living trust, using the unlimited marital deduction and the full unified credit.
   (4) arranging for a preferred stock recapitalization for Bill's business interest

   a. (2) and (3) only
   b. (1), (2) and (3) only
   c. (1), (3) and (4) only
   d. (1), (2) and (4) only
   e. (1), (2), (3) and (4)

10. The Mathews currently own a number of tax-advantaged financial instruments. Which of the following statements is/are true with respect to these various instruments?

    (1) Interest income and capital appreciation from the municipal bond fund is federally tax exempt.
    (2) An initial partial withdrawal from the single premium deferred annuity is fully taxable.
    (3) When redeemed, the return on the savings bonds is not subject to state income taxes.
    (4) The Treasury bills are federally taxed only upon maturity.

    a. (1), (2) and (3) only
    b. (2) and (4) only
    c. (3) only
    d. (3) and (4) only
    e. (1), (2), (3) and (4)

11. If Bill and Marilyn wish to limit the growth of their combined estate, which techniques may be advisable?

    (1) use of the annual gift tax exclusion and split gift election
    (2) current use of both unified credits
    (3) payment of tuition for grandchildren
    (4) payment of direct medical expenses for children and grandchildren

    a. (1) and (2) only
    b. (2), (3) and (4) only
    c. (1) only
    d. (1), (2) and (3) only
    e. (1), (2), (3) and (4)

12. Assume that Bill wants to take advantage of the $1,000,000 Generation Skipping Transfer Tax exemption, by giving his grandson this amount now. What is the amount of the gift tax, given that there have been <u>no</u> prior taxable gifts?

    a. $121,800
    b. $153,000
    c. $390,000
    d. $345,800
    e. $410,000

13. Assume Bill provides consulting services for the new owner and is properly classified as an independent contractor. Which statements properly describe Bill's ability to shelter current taxable income?

    (1) Bill may take a non-deductible IRA for $2,000
    (2) Bill may set up a profit-sharing Keogh
    (3) Bill can set up a money purchase plan.
    (4) Bill can set up a combined money purchase and profit-sharing plan, but his contributions will be limited to 20% of Schedule C income.

    a. (2) and (3) only
    b. (1), (2) and (3) only
    c. (2), (3) and (4) only
    d. (1), (2), (3) and (4)
    e. (1) and (3) only

14. In reviewing Bill and Marilyn's cash-flow projections as well as the investment portfolio supplement, you question the appropriateness of some of the holdings. Which combination of portfolio weaknesses best summarizes a valid critique of their investments?

    a. excessive liquidity, inadequate tax advantage, marginal equity diversification

    b. inadequate tax advantage, excessive growth orientation, marginal equity diversification

    c. excessive liquidity, excessive growth orientation, inadequate tax advantage

    d. excessive reliance on Treasury Bills, insufficient growth opportunities, inadequate current income

    e. insufficient growth opportunities, inadequate liquidity, excessive tax advantage

15. Assuming that Bill reaches agreement with the new owner as to the installment payments for the business interest, what are the estate tax ramifications if Bill dies at the end of the third year of the ten-year payout schedule?

    a. The remaining value of the installments is <u>not</u> includable in Bill's estate, because the payments continuing to Marilyn qualify for the marital deduction.

    b. Seventy percent of the original cash purchase price upon which the installments were based is includable in Bill's estate but qualifies for the marital deduction because payments will continue to Marilyn.

    c. The present value of the future income stream to Marilyn in included in Bill's estate, but the continuing payments qualify for the marital deduction.

    d. The present value of the future income stream to Marilyn is included in Bill's estate, but the continuing income payments do <u>not</u> qualify for the marital deduction because it is a terminable interest.

    e. Nothing is included in the estate because the installment payments are <u>not</u> guaranteed.

16. The inadequacies in their estate planning can be summarized as follows:

> (1) failure to take full advantage of each unified credit.
> (2) failure to avoid probate.
> (3) lack of proper documents to address the potential problem of incapacity.
> (4) failure to coordinate titling of assets with documentation.

a. (1) and (2) only
b. (1), (2) and (3) only
c. (2), (3) and (4) only
d. (2) and (4) only
e. (1), (2), (3) and (4)

Regarding questions 17 and 18 and given the current economic conditions, you recommend allocating the Mathews' investment funds into three asset categories: equity, debt, and cash.

17. Which of the following statements describe(s) action(s) that you would recommend in order to meet the Mathews' goals?

> (1) Because of the economic environment, the Mathews should immediately increase the proportion of equity investments to provide for growth for the estate.
> (2) This is the opportune time to lengthen the maturity of the fixed income proportion of the portfolio.
> (3) Because of the current economic scenario and their retired status, the Mathews should liquidate the equity portion of the portfolio.
> (4) The Mathews should gradually increase the equity proportion of the portfolio over the next 3 years to provide for growth in their estate.

a. (3) and (4) only
b. (1) and (2) only
c. (2) and (4) only
d. (4) only
e. (2), (3) and (4) only

18. In order to meet their goals, the Matthews should:

   (1) reduce cash level, expand fixed income securities,
   (2) expand fixed income securities.
   (3) increase cash level, decrease equities.
   (4) expand fixed income securities, decrease equities.

   a. (1) only
   b. (1) and (4) only
   c. (2) and (3) only
   d. (2), (3) and (4)
   e. none of the above

19. You are considering liquidating the individual equity holdings and moving this amount into equity mutual funds. The following alternative allocations have been proposed:

CHOICE A		CHOICE B	
Market index fund	40%	Growth fund	33%
Growth fund	20%	International equity fund	33%
Value-oriented fund	20%	Value-oriented fund	34%
International equity fund		20%	

CHOICE C		CHOICE D	
Market index fund	30%	Small company fund	25%
Gold stock fund	50%	Aggressive growth fund	45%
Equity-income fund	20%	Growth fund	30%

   a. Choice A is preferred because it includes multiple management styles and market diversification.
   b. Choice B is preferred because it employs both active and passive funds.
   c. Choice C is preferred because it best meets the Mathews' goals.
   d. Choice D is preferred because it maximizes growth while meeting the Mathews' goal.
   e. Do not liquidate the current portfolio.

ANSWERS TO CASE QUESTIONS

1. e
2. a
3. a
4. c
5. a
6. c
7. d
8. d
9. b
10. d
11. e
12. b
13. c
14. a
15. c
16. e
17. d
18. e
19. a

TWO: ESTATE PLANNING CASE

The author submitted this case and accompanying questions as a possible CFP examination case to the International Board of Standards and Practices for the CFP (IBCFP) in early 1992, by invitation. IBCFP chose not to use the case when it decided that future exam cases will be more integrated, i.e. will cover questions on a diversity of planning subjects, not just one, such as estate planning. Thus, from one perspective, this case is not representative of the CFP exam. However, from another, it is. Many of the same concepts (calculation of gross estate and FET, choice of trust type, etc) could be tested in a more general case; there simply wouldn't be as many estate planning questions in any one case.

Item answers are not included in the chapter. This will force the reader to take some time to evaluate the answers prior to their discussion in class.

Sheila and Jerry Briggs

"I knew I should have talked with you first, I just knew it"..., exclaimed Jerry Briggs in your office one day last week. "...but our family attorney sounded so convincing..." Jerry had just finished showing you a copy of the wills that the attorney had just prepared for him and his wife, Sheila. You, of course, know them to be standard `simple wills', each document simply leaving everything outright to the spouse, if surviving, otherwise outright in equal shares to the children of their current marriage. After examining the wills, you pointed out some planning omissions and mistakes, and recommended that Jerry and Sheila set up an appointment for next week to discuss and develop an overall financial plan, with the assistance of an attorney specializing in estate planning. They agreed, and before they left filled out a questionnaire about their financial situation and objectives.

Jerry and Sheila Briggs, age 67 and 62 respectively, have been happily married for nearly 38 years. They have two children, Bob, 36 and Gail, 34. Jerry also has a son, Steve, 46, from a former marriage to a woman who passed away long ago. While Sheila is in excellent health, the stress of Jerry's business has taken its toll. Jerry suffers from a heart condition, having experienced a mild attack three years ago.

Figure 1 depicts the Jerry and Sheila Briggs' financial statement. Jerry is a 50 percent stockholder in Gardens Unlimited, a rapidly growing mail order garden supply distributor. The sole co-owner is Craig Toft, an old college buddy. Sales last year were $23 million, making the firm's common stock worth approximately $1,800,000. The firm has a defined contribution profit sharing plan, and Jerry's account is currently worth $200,000. Sheila is named surviving beneficiary in this plan. Jerry thrives in his business environment, but because of his bad heart, realizes that he must slow down. Sheila entered the job market about 12 years ago, after Bob and Gail graduated college, and is presently enjoying work as a senior citizen's supervisor for the local recreation district. This year, Jerry will pay himself a salary of $90,000, and Sheila will earn $28,000. Their son Bob, a personal injury attorney for a large firm, has a wife, Mary, and two children, Chris and Cass. Bob has always been regarded by his parents as relatively mature and responsible. On the other hand, Gail, who is not married, has been a bit of a problem for her parents. She never finished college, and may now have a drug problem; for the past year she has acted confused at times, and has frequently asked Jerry for money. To date, Gail has received nearly $6,000 "to help pay the rent and other odds and ends".

The Briggs are living quite comfortably, but, considering their sizable income, have been strikingly unable to save much money. And currently, their monthly cash inflows just equal their outflows, with fixed outflows of $82,000 and variable outflows of $42,000.

As indicated in the accompanying financial statement, their principal asset is Jerry's interest in his company's stock. The profit sharing plan invests primarily in commercial real estate. Three years ago, just before he died, Sheila's father gave her one sixth of his interest in his closely held Uniform Company, which is a thriving industrial uniform supply distributor. Her dad's basis in this interest was $175,000 and its FMV at date of gift was $160,000. Sheila would have difficulty selling this stock, as there is no secondary market. At his death, Sheila's dad left her his 30 year high yield bond issued by Trigger Co.

Jerry has always handled the financial affairs for the family, and Sheila admits, quite frankly, to being terrified of being placed in the position of undertaking this role.

The Briggs live in a common law, non-community property state, having a "pickup" or "sponge" inheritance tax equal to the amount of the federal credit for state death taxes.

In your analysis, you have decided to make several simplifying assumptions. First, there will be no funeral or administrative expenses incurred at either Jerry's or Sheila's death. Second, there will be no future appreciation in asset values, unless otherwise specified.

Sheila and Jerry's objectives include the following:

- To plan for Jerry's complete withdrawal from the firm by age 70.
- To provide for adequate income during retirement.
- To incur no death taxes at the death of the first spouse.
- To minimize death taxes at the death of the second spouse.
- To ensure adequate liquidity at all times.
- To dispose of the Briggs family assets in the following manner:
  - At the death of the first spouse:
    - Each spouse leave all property for the benefit of the surviving spouse.
  - At the death of the surviving spouse:
    - Sheila would like all of her property to go equally to Bob and Gail.
    - Jerry would like approximately one half of his property to go to Steve and one quarter to Bob and Gail each.

JERRY AND SHEILA BRIGGS

Statement of Financial Condition
As of year end, last year

ASSETS[1]

Cash/Cash Equivalents		**Liabilities[2]**		
Checking account (JT)	$10,000.	Credit card balance (JT)	$5,000.
Money market account (JT)	100,000.	Auto note balance (JT)	13,000.
Total Cash/Cash Equivalents	$110,000.	Home mortgage bal. (JT)	32,000.

Invested Assets

		Total Liabilities	$50,000.
Uniform Co. Common Stock (W)	$150,000.		
Trigger Co. Bond (W)	50,000.		
Gardens Unlimited Common Stock (basis $50,000)(H)	900,000.		
Profit sharing plan benefits (H)	200,000.		
Total Invested assets	1,300,000.		

Use Assets		Net Worth	$1,800,000.
Personal residence (JT)	$280,000.		
Personal Property (JT)	100,000.		
Automobiles (JT)	60,000.		
Total Use Assets	$440,000.		
		TOTAL LIABILITIES	
TOTAL ASSETS	$1,850,000.	AND NET WORTH	$1,850,000.

1. Presented at fair market value.
2. Principal only.

JT means: for assets- owned by spouses in joint tenancy with right of survivorship.
            for liabilities- spouses are jointly liable
W means owned solely by wife Sheila
H means owned solely by husband Jerry

Questions

1. If Jerry were to predecease Sheila and die today, without further planning, what would be the size of his federal gross estate, for estate tax purposes?

   a. zero
   b. $1,175,000
   c. $1,375,000
   d. $1,800,000
   e. none of the above

2. If Jerry were to predecease Sheila and die today, without further planning, how much of his gross estate would pass under his present will?

   a. none of his gross estate
   b. $900,000
   c. $1,100,000
   d. $1,175,000
   e. all of his gross estate

3. In this question only, assume that Jerry died today, is survived by Sheila, and that Jerry's will bequeathed to Sheila the Uniform Co. common stock, shown in Figure 1. At Jerry's death the stock was worth $168,000. If Sheila sells this stock one year from today for $170,000, she will realize

   a. a loss of $2,000
   b. a loss of $7,000
   c. no gain or loss
   d. a gain of $8,000
   e. none of the above is correct

For all further questions, assume that the Jerry and Sheila each presently own one additional asset that is not shown on the financial statement in Figure 1: each was given a gift of a valuable painting from Jerry's dad. These paintings cause the value of Jerry's gross estate to now total $1,600,000 and Sheila's gross estate to now total $500,000.

4. If Jerry were to predecease Sheila and die today without further planning, what would be the amount of the federal estate tax due on behalf of Jerry, assuming that Jerry's gross estate equals $1,600,000?

   a. zero
   b. $396,750
   c. $408,000
   d. $589,550
   e. $600,800

5. If Jerry died today with a gross estate of $1,600,000, and Sheila died, still unmarried, in ten years, without further planning, how much of the Briggs family assets would the children receive in total, after payment of death taxes? Assume no further savings or asset appreciation, no gifting or consumption of presently owned assets, and that all $50,000 of debts are paid off over time entirely with disposable income, not principal, prior to Sheila's death.

   a. more than $1,000,000 but no more than $1,400,000
   b. more than $1,400,000 but no more than $1,500,000
   c. more than $1,500,000 but no more than $1,600,000
   d. more than $1,600,000 but no more than $1,700,000
   e. more than $1,700,000

6. Assuming that Jerry presently owns $1,600,000 in assets and Sheila owns $500,000, how much of the Briggs family estate would the children receive in total, after payment of death taxes, if Jerry were to die today with an estate plan incorporating a credit shelter bypass plan, i.e., the plan includes a bypass in the amount of the exemption equivalent of the unified credit? Again assume no further savings or asset appreciation, no gifting or consumption of presently owned assets, that Sheila dies, still unmarried, in 10 years, and that all $50,000 of debts are paid off over time entirely with disposable income, not principal, prior to Sheila's death.

   a. more than $1,000,000 but no more than $1,700,000
   b. more than $1,700,000 but no more than $1,800,000
   c. more than $1,800,000 but no more than $1,900,000
   d. more than $1,900,000 but no more than $2,000,000
   e. more than $2,000,000

7. In considering the amount of property passing to the bypass at the death of the first spouse, you are trying to determine the federal estate tax consequences of recommending a bypass of an amount not equal to the exemption equivalent of the unified credit. Assuming that the surviving spouse does not remarry and does not consume or make gifts of principal, which statement below is the most correct appraisal, in light of the Briggs' situation?

   a. When compared with a credit shelter bypass, a bypass of an amount smaller than the exemption equivalent would probably reduce the federal estate tax for the estate of the first spouse to die.
   b. When compared with a credit shelter bypass, a bypass of an amount smaller than the exemption equivalent would probably increase federal estate tax for the estate of the second spouse to die.
   c. When compared with a credit shelter bypass, a bypass of an amount smaller than the exemption equivalent would probably increase federal estate tax for the estates of both spouses.
   d. When compared with a credit shelter bypass, a bypass of an amount larger than the exemption equivalent would probably reduce federal estate tax for the estate of the first spouse to die.
   e. When compared with a credit shelter bypass, a bypass of an amount larger than the exemption equivalent would probably increase federal estate tax for the estate of the second spouse to die.

8. In planning for the initial funding of the marital and bypass shares with specific assets, efficient estate tax planning for the Briggs would recommend funding the marital share with assets that are _____ likely to appreciate, and funding the bypass share with assets that are _____ likely to appreciate. Please fill in the blanks, respectively.

    a. more, less
    b. more, more
    c. less, more
    d. less, less
    e. none of the above answers is true. Relative appreciation has little or no bearing on efficient estate tax planning for the Briggs.

9. In recommending a bypass for Jerry's plan, you are considering how to structure the marital deduction portion. Based on the facts, select the best disposition arrangement for Jerry, with regard to assets that qualify for the marital deduction.

    a. An outright bequest, partly because it is simple and tax effective.
    b. A power of appointment trust, partly because the limited power of appointment given to Sheila will ensure the preservation of trust assets for other beneficiaries.
    c. A bypass trust, partly to qualify bypass assets for the marital deduction.
    d. A QTIP trust, partly because of Steve.
    e. A charitable remainder unitrust (CRUT), partly because Jerry has a charitable motive and has been a member of the Uniform Denominational Church for many years.

10. For this question, assume that you recommend to the Briggs that Jerry's estate plan 1) contain a bypass, and 2) incorporate two trusts, a bypass trust and a QTIP trust. What type of control over these trusts would you want the instrument to grant to Sheila, as surviving spouse?

    a. A power of appointment over the principal of the bypass trust to invade for her benefit, subject to an ascertainable standard.
    b. A power of appointment over the principal of the bypass trust to invade for her benefit, not subject to an ascertainable standard.
    c. A power of appointment over the principal of the QTIP trust to invade for her benefit, not subject to an ascertainable standard.
    d. A power of appointment over the principal of the QTIP trust to invade for her benefit, subject to an ascertainable standard.
    e. A power of appointment over the principal of the QTIP trust, with only Sheila and the children as permissible appointees.

11. Regarding planning for the federal generation-skipping transfer tax (GST), which of the following best describes the Briggs' situation?

    a. The Briggs do not need any planning for the GST since no GST, as we presently know it, could possibly be incurred, whether or not the Briggs do any further death tax planning.
    b. The present arrangement will likely result in a GST at Sheila's death, if she survives Jerry.
    c. No planning for the Briggs can prevent an inevitable GST from being incurred.
    d. Based on the $1 million exemption, the Brigg's family assets are vulnerable to the GSTT on amounts in excess of $1 million, even with the most careful planning.
    e. None of the above is true.

12. In recommending a bypass estate plan for the Briggs, you intend to suggest that their estate planning attorney include certain clauses in the final principal dispositive instrument, whether it turns out to be a will or a living trust. Which clause would you <u>not</u> want to recommend?

   a. A perpetuities saving clause, to prevent a contingent gift from being ruled invalid because it vests too long after the decedent's death.
   b. A residuary clause.
   c. A survival clause, because of the danger of lapsation.
   d. A clause allocating death taxes, because the alternative, state and federal law (by default), may be inefficient and undesirable.
   e. You would recommend all of the above clauses for the Briggs.

13. In this question only, assume that five years have gone by, and that Jerry died of a second heart attack ten months ago. Sheila has not remarried. The Briggs never returned to your lawyer-associate's office to sign any documents, which means that no additional planning has been implemented. In administering the affairs of Jerry's estate, Sheila has permitted Steve to drive Jerry's sports car, which is currently worth $18,000. (Sheila doesn't know how to drive it, and has never tried). Sheila intends to let Steve have the car, in accordance with Jerry's deathbed statements. If Sheila writes a letter today "irrevocably and unqualifiedly" refusing to accept the bequest of the car, and transfers title of the car to Steve in two weeks,

   a. Steve will be legally entitled to at least part ownership in the car. Sheila will not have been considered to have made a "gross" or "taxable" gift to Steve because she will never have owned the car.
   b. Steve will be legally entitled to full ownership in the car. Sheila will have made a "gross" gift, but will not have been considered to have made a "taxable" gift to Steve because of the benefit of the annual exclusion and the unified credit.
   c. Steve will be legally entitled to full ownership in the car. Sheila will have been considered to have made a "taxable" gift because she will have owned the car.
   d. Steve will be legally entitled to full ownership in the car. Sheila will have been considered to have made a taxable gift because she will have owned the car and the gift is one of a future interest.
   e. Steve will not be legally entitled to any ownership interest in the car.

14. You are now attempting to decide whether to recommend that Jerry dispose of his assets with a will or with a living trust document. If you recommend a will, you intend to make sure that title to all assets in joint tenancy between Jerry and Sheila will be converted to equal tenants in common. The costs for the will alternative are: drafting- $2,000; probate administration costs- $20,000. The costs for the trust alternative are: drafting- $3,800; nonprobate administration costs at death- $14,000. Assuming no other relevant costs, a discount rate of 11 percent, that any drafting costs will be incurred today, and that all administration costs in connection with Jerry's death will be incurred exactly 12 years from today, which answer below summarizes within five dollars a present value cost analysis taking into account the time value of money?

   a. The net advantage of the living trust alternative over a will is equal to $5,000.
   b. The net advantage of the living trust alternative over the will is greater than zero but less than $5,000.
   c. The net advantage of the will over the living trust alternative is greater than zero but less than $5,000.
   d. The net advantage of the will over the living trust alternative is equal to $5,000.
   e. None of the answers above is correct

15. While in your office, Jerry and Sheila mentioned that their family attorney had made several questionable assertions regarding the selection of either joint tenancies (WROS), the will, or the living trust as the overall best type of dispositive instrument for them. Which of that attorney's comments, all listed below, is correct?

    a. He said taking title to all assets in joint tenancy will prevent a step-up in tax basis of some or all property at the first spouse's death, thereby making joint tenancies distinctly disadvantageous in comparison with the other instruments of transfer.
    b. He said that proper planning with a living trust can make will planning entirely unnecessary.
    c. He said that a will is capable of disposing of all of the Briggs' present assets, except those held currently in joint tenancy form.
    d. He said that if the Briggs execute a will, at either of their deaths the posting of notice to creditors in a legal newspaper will effectively insulate the decedent's estate from all known creditors who delay in filing claims beyond the creditor's period.
    e. None of the above statements is true.

16. Regarding lifetime gift planning, Jerry and Sheila ask you to explain the possible consequences of gifting the Gardens unlimited stock to their children. If they were to arrange a split gift of $300,000 of this stock this year, with each of their three children receiving shares worth $100,000, calculate the amount of Jerry's remaining unused unified credit that would be available for gifts in succeeding years. Assume neither parent has made any prior taxable gifts.
    Jerry's remaining unused unified credit will be:

    a. $108,400
    b. $115,200
    c. $157,000
    d. $163,000
    e. $192,800

17. What planning recommendations would be appropriate in connection with Gail's situation?

      1. In the event of both spouse's premature death, give an independent trustee of any trust created the discretionary power to sprinkle income and principal among beneficiaries.
      2. Provide for outright distribution of assets immediately at the death of the surviving spouse.
      3. Name Gail to be a surrogate decision maker during the remaining lifetime of the surviving spouse.
      4. Include a restriction against assignment in all trust documents.

    a. 1 only
    b. 1 and 4 only
    c. 2 and 3 only
    d. 3 and 4 only
    e. 1, 2, 3 and 4

18. You next turn to liquidity and life insurance planning for the Briggs. Based on the family situation, and assuming that the final plan will include a credit shelter bypass plan, which statement below represents the best analysis and recommendation for the Briggs?

    a. The Briggs should consider an irrevocable life insurance trust having the following characteristics: trustee is owner and beneficiary of policy.
    b. The Briggs should consider a irrevocable life insurance trust having the following characteristics: trustee is owner of policy and Bob and Gail are co-beneficiaries.
    c. The Briggs should consider a irrevocable life insurance trust having the following characteristics: Jerry and Sheila are owners of policy and trustee is beneficiary.
    d. The Briggs should consider a revocable life insurance trust having the following characteristics: trustee is owner and beneficiary of policy.
    e. No liquidity problems can be reasonably anticipated in the future, since all expected future debts can be promptly paid with available assets.

19. Continuing your planning for liquidity, you estimate that if Jerry were to die today, Sheila would need, among other funds, a cash lump sum of $122,000 exactly one year from today and an annual cash inflow of $43,000 per year for 24 years with the first inflow arriving in exactly four years. Ignoring other cash needs and other sources of liquidity, how much life insurance should the Briggs own to fund just these two needs? Assume a discount rate of 9 percent.

    a. $434,223.88
    b. $529,310.92
    c. $539,384.31
    d. $1,154,000.00
    e. None of above answers is within $10 of correct answer

20. In planning for Jerry's business interests, which of the following represents a preferred recommendation and correct analysis, given the facts?

    a. While still alive, Jerry's selling his entire interest in Gardens Unlimited sometime in the next two years for $900,000 would be attractive from the point of view of both income tax and the overall objectives of the family.
    b. An entity business buyout arrangement between Jerry and Craig funded with life insurance would be preferable to a cross purchase arrangement because it would mean fewer policies would be needed and because the surviving owner would incur less income tax if and when he finally sells the firm.
    c. Jerry should bequeath the stock to Sheila, either outright or in trust, to be able to obtain a step-up in basis.
    d. If Jerry and Craig immediately sell the business to a ABC Corp., a large mail order firm, in exchange for ABC stock, they will incur no immediate income tax liability and will be able to diversify their holdings free of income tax consequences.
    e. None of the above statements represents preferred recommendations or correct analysis.

21. In recommending planning for the Briggs' incapacity, which statement below is correct?

    a. A living trust can explicitly provide for expert management of Jerry's property in the event of his incapacity.

    b. A living trust can explicitly provide for Jerry's personal care in the event of his incapacity.

    c. A will can explicitly provide for expert management of Jerry's property in the event of his incapacity.

    d. A will can explicitly provide for Jerry's personal care in the event of his incapacity.

    e. More than one of the answers above is correct.

THREE: CFP ESTATE PLANNING OUTLINE TOPICS

In the process of developing the estate planning questions for the CFP comprehensive examination, the International Board of Standards and Practices for the Certified Planner (IBCFP) commissioned a panel of three academics (including this author) and three practitioners to develop a revised list of topics recommended for examination. The following outline is the result of that work.[2] An abbreviated, "two level" outline version of the estate planning topics, plus all other 146 topics tested on the examination, can be found in the IBCFP's *General Information Booklet*, a manual that describes the certification requirements for the CFP. [3]

The numbers in parentheses refer to ratings made by the panel. The first number describes relative importance: 1 = important, 2 = more important. The second number describes the target cognitive level: 1 = knowledge of facts/terms, 2 = comprehension/application, 3 = analysis/synthesis, 4 = evaluation.

I. FUNDAMENTALS OF ESTATE PLANNING

147. Estate planning overview (2,3)

  A. The meaning of "estate planning"
  B. Situations in which individuals need estate planning and consequences of integrated planning
  C. Steps in estate planning process
  D. The financial planner's role on the estate planning team

---

2. Reprinted with permission of the International Board of Standards and Practices for the CFP.

3. The *General Information Booklet*, revised annually, is available free from IBCFP, 1660 Lincoln Street (Suite 3050), Denver CO 80264. Telephone (303) 830-7543. FAX (303) 860-7388.

148. Estate planning pitfalls and weaknesses (1,2)

A. Weaknesses in a client's existing estate plan

1. Nonexistent or outdated will or trust provisions.

a. changes in objectives, family circumstances, major tax laws
b. guardian clause
c. simultaneious death clause
d. contingent beneficiaries clause
e. residuary clause
f. tax clause
g. clause to address the "disinheritance" of a child

2. Failure to accomplish current estate planning objectives.
3. Failure to consider the tax impact on the interested parties.

B. Common pitfalls to avoid during estate planning
1. Funeral instructions in the client's will
2. Rule against perpetuities
3. Precatory language
4. Possible ancillary probate
5. Attempting to "disinherit" a spouse/minor children

149. Methods for property transfer at death (2,2)

A. The probate process
B. Survivorship
C. Trust distributions
D. Beneficiary designations
E. Other methods including insurance

150. Estate planning documents (1,2)

A. Will
B. Trusts
C. Personal care documents
D. Marital agreements
E. Durable power of attorney for property
F. Business agreements

154. Valuation techniques and the Federal gross estate (1,2)

    A. Valuation of specific property interests

        1. Closely held business (Rev. Rul. 59-60) real estate
        2. Life insurance: decedent is owner and insured; decedent is owner and insured is another.
        3. Savings bonds
        4. Flower bonds
        5. Annuities: commercial, private
        6. Life estates, remainder interests, and reversionary interests
        7. Publicly traded stocks or bonds

    B. Valuation techniques

        1. Fair market value at date of death
        2. Fair market value on the alternate valuation date
        3. Techniques for reducing the fair market value

155. Federal estate tax deductions (1,2)

    A. Identification of items deductible from the gross estate to calculate the adjusted gross estate

        1. Certain funeral expenses
        2. Certain administrative expenses
        3. Certain debts and taxes
        4. Certain casualty and theft losses

    B. Identification of items deductible from the adjusted gross estate to calculate the taxable estate
        1. Charitable deduction
        2. Marital deduction
        3. ESOP deduction

156. Calculation of federal estate tax liability (1,2)

    A. Identification of the steps to calculate the total estate tax

        1. Gross estate
        2. Adjusted gross estate
        3. Taxable estate
        4. Tentative tax base
        5. Tentative tax
        6. Net estate tax after credits
        7. Total estate tax

    B. Additional factors affecting the estate tax calculation (e.g., lifetime gifts, property from prior decedent within 10 years, excess retirement accumulations, generation-shipping transfers, surtax on large estates).

157. Characteristics and tax aspects of property interests (1,3)

    A. Title forms

        1. Sole ownership
        2. Joint tenancy with right of survivorship (JTWROS)
        3. Tenancy by entirety
        4. Tenancy in common
        5. Community property

    B. Other interests

        1. Interest in trust
        2. Present/future interest
        3. Life estate
        4. Powers of appointment
        5. Expectancies

    C. Advantages and disadvantages of forms of property interests

D. Taxation aspects

1. Income tax
2. Federal gift tax
3. Federal estate tax

E. Recommendation and justification of the most appropriate form of property interests

158. Probate avoidance (1,2)

A. Advantages and disadvantages of probate
B. Techniques of avoiding probate

1. Joint tenancy
2. Revocable living trusts
3. Other techniques

C. Recommendation and justification of the most appropriate probate avoidance technique

159. Liquidity planning (2,4)

A. Sale of assets
B. Life insurance

1. Trusts/Crummey Power
2. Assignment of ownership rights
3. Life insurance trusts
4. Settlement options

C. Special techniques for closely-held business owners (e.g., §6166, §303, §2032A)
D. Other techniques (e.g., Flower bonds)

160. Powers of appointment (1,2)

A. General
B. Special
C. Federal gift and estate tax implications

III. TOOLS AND TECHNIQUES FOR GENERAL ESTATE PLANNING

161. Features of trusts (2,3)

A. Classification of trusts

1. Lifetime v. testamentary
2. Revocable v. irrevocable
3. Simple v. complex

B. Characteristics of selected trust provisions

1. Discretionary
2. Sprinkling (or spray)
3. Support
4. Sprendthrift
5. Standby
6. Pourover
7. Crummey power

162. Taxation of trusts and estates (2,2)

A. Income tax implications of trusts

1. Grantor trust rules
2. Conduit principle/DNI and distribution deduction
3. Trust sale of appreciated property
4. To grantor, trustee and/or beneficiary in specific situations

B. Federal gift tax implications of trusts

1. Basic principles
2. To grantor, trustee and/or beneficiary in specific situations

C. Federal estate tax implications of trusts

1. Basic principles
2. To grantor, trustee and/or beneficiary in specific situations

D. Income tax implications of estates

    1. Income in respect of a decedent (IRD)

E. Recommendation and justification of the most appropriate trust

163. Life insurance for estate planning (2,3)

A. Characteristics of life insurance
B. Advantages and disadvantages of specific life insurance techniques in estate planning
C. Life insurance trust
D. Ownership, beneficiary designation and settlement options
E. Income, gift and estate taxation of life insurance
F. Recommendation and justification of the most appropriate life insurance technique

164. Gifts (2,3)

A. Suitability of gifts for client and recipient
B. Legal techniques for gift-giving

    1. Outright gifts
    2. Custodial gifts
    3. Trusts

        a. minors
        b. others

165. Taxation of gifts (2,3)

A. Income taxation of lifetime transfers

    1. Basic and income shifting implications
    2. Lifetime gifting v. testamentary transfer for appreciated property and loss property
    3. Gifts to minors/"Kiddie Tax"
    4. Net gifts
    5. Testamentary transfer by donee to decent within one year of gift (reverse gift)

B. Federal gift taxation of lifetime transfers

1. Definition of gift for gift tax purposes
2. Gratuitous transfers not considered taxable for gift tax purposes

C. Federal estate taxation of lifetime transfers

1. Lifetime v. testamentary transfer of appreciated property
2. Retained interest
3. Three-year rule

D. Calculation and analysis of the effect of a lifetime gift program

166. Recommendation and justification of the most appropriate property to give as a gift (2,4)

A. The most appropriate property to give as a gift

1. Factors to consider about the recipient

   a. age
   b. maturity
   c. educational level
   d. interpersonal relationships
   e. motives, other

2. Appropriateness of specific types of property

   a. high-income producing property
   b. property with high appreciation potential
   c. highly appreciated property
   d. property likely to be sold by donee
   e. loss property
   f. stock in closely held corporation
   g. out-of-state property
   h. low gift tax value to high estate tax value property (e.g. insurance)
   I. depreciable income-producing property

3. Recommendation and justification of the most appropriate property to gift in a given client's situation

B. The most appropriate lifetime gift-giving technique

1. Selection based on the client's situation

a. net gift
b. reverse gift
c. outright gifts
d. Uniform Gifts to Minors Act
e. Uniform Transfers to Minors Act
f. Section 2503(b) trusts
g. Section 2503(c) trusts for minors
h. Crummey trusts

C. Justification of the lifetime gift-giving techniques selected for the client's situation

167. Marital deduction and bypass planning (2,3)

A. Characteristics of the marital deduction

1. Qualifying conditions
2. Terminable interests and exceptions
3. Types of qualifying marital transfers

a. outright bequest to spouse
b. power of appointment trust
c. qualified terminable interest (Q-TIP) trust
d. qualified domestic trust (non-citizen)
e. estate trust
f. joint tenancy with right of survivorship between spouses
g. life insurance with spouse as beneficiary

B. Recommendation and justification of property interests that qualify for the marital deduction

168. Federal estate tax implications of the marital deduction and bypass planning (2,2)

    A. Federal estate tax implications of using the marital deduction

        1. Decedent spouse
        2. Surviving spouse
        3. Other beneficiaries

    B. Calculation of Federal estate tax savings generated from modifying a client's estate plan to minimize tax

        1. Decedent's estate
        2. Decedent and surviving spouse's combined estate

169. Recommendation of the most appropriate marital or nonmarital transfer (2,3)

    A. Factors to consider in selecting the optimum mix of marital and nonmarital transfers

        1. Ages of both spouses/value of tax deferral
        2. Intra-family relationships, especially where there are children from a prior marriage
        3. Each spouse's mental and financial competency
        4. Amount of unused unifed credit
        5. Value of individual and combined estate
        6. Need for spousal income stream v. desire to accumulate income
        7. Desire to minimize estate taxes

    B. Selection of the most appropriate single or combination of marital and/or nonmarital transfers for a client's situation

        1. Outright bequest to surviving spouse
        2. Life estate to surviving spouse
        3. Family bypass trust
        4. General power olf appointment trust
        5. Qualified terminable interest property (Q-TIP) trust

            a. election by decedent's executor
            b. non-election by decedent's executor

6. Qualified domestic trust
7. Estate trust

C. Justification of the marital and nonmarital transfer techniques selected for the client's situation

IV. TOOLS AND TECHNIQUES FOR SPECIAL ESTATE PLANNING SITUATIONS

170. Estate planning for nontraditional relationships (1,2)

A. Children of another relationship
B. Cohabitation
C. Adoption
D. Same sex relationship
E. Communal relationships

171. Charitable transfers (1,2)

A. Considerations for transfer

1. Charitable intent
2. Financial opportunity

B. Requirements for a gift to qualify for a charitable deduction
C. Tax and nontax characteristics of specific forms of charitable transfers

1. Outright charitable gift
2. Charitable lead trust
3. Charitable remainder annuity (CRAT)
4. Charritable remainder unitrust (CRUT)
5. Charitable pooled-income fund
6. Charitable bargain sale
7. Charitable stock bailout
8. Charitable remainder in farm or personal residence

D. Charitable income tax deduction limitations

1. Maximum deduction/carryover rules
2. Types of charitable organizations

3. Deduction rules for gifts of specific types of property
   a. cash
   b. long-term capital gain property
   c. short-term capital gain (ordinary income) property
   d. inventory
   e. use-related tangible personal property
   f. use-unrelated tangible personal property
   g. rent-free occupancy
   h. future interest property
   i. life insurance
   j. works of artists and artisans
   k. time

E. Calculation of the maximum total and/or maximum current year income tax deduction for a client's situation
F. Recommendation and justification of the most appropriate property and form of charitable transfer

172. Intra-family business and property transfers (1,3)

A. Characteristics of intra-family transfers

1. Installment sale
2. Private annuity
3. Outright gift
4. Sale-leaseback
5. Gift-leaseback
6. Grantor retained income trust (GRIT) grantor lead trust)
7. Grantor annuity trust
8. Remainder interest transaction (RIT)
9. Split interest purchase (split)
10. Partnership capital freeze
11. Preferred stock recapitalization
12. Family partnership
13. Personal holding company
14. Buy-sell agreement

B. Federal income, gift and estate tax implications of intra-family transfers
C. Recommendation and justification of the most appropriate intra-family business and property transfer technique

173. Postmortem planning techniques (1,2)

A. Characteristics of postmortem estate planning techniques

1. Techniques to rearrange property disposition

   a. qualified disclaimer
   b. disclaimer trust
   c. election of homestead allowance
   d. election of exempt property award
   e. election against the will
   f. will contest
   g. family settlement agreement
   h. Q-TIP election

2. Special tax treatments and elections

   a. filing joint final (Form 1040) income tax return
   b. deduction of unreimbursed medical expenses election (Form 1040 or Form 706)
   c. deduction of estate administrative expenses election (Form 1040 or Form 706)
   d. "EE" or "HH" interest election
   e. Subchapter S election or revocation
   f. partnership asset basis election
   g. selection of a fiscal estate tax year
   h. election to split gift
   i. waiver of exectuor fees
   j. election to use alternate valuation date
   k. election of Section 2032A special use valuation
   l. election of Section 303 stock redemption
   m. election of Section 6166 installment payment of estate taxes
   n. assumption of estate tax liability by decendent's ESOP

B. Determination of whether a client qualifies for special tax treatment

1. Election of Section 2032A special use valuation
2. Election of Section 303 stock redemption
3. Election of Section 6166 installment payment of estate taxes

4. Assumption of estate tax liability by decedent's ESOP

C. Recommendation and justification of the most appropriate postmortem planning technique

174. Planning for incapacity (2,3)

A. Definition of incapacity
B. Care of client's dependents

1. Personal care, selection of guardian
2. Financial care
   a. selection of guardian, trust or custodianship

C. Personal care of incapacitated client

1. Guardian/conservator
2. Delegation of health care decision

   a. living will
   b. directive to doctor
   c. durable power of attorney for health care

D. Care of incapacitated client's property

1. Guardianship/conservatorship
2. Trust
3. Durable power of attorney for property

175. Special topics (1,2)

A. Divorce and estate planning
B. Selection of fiduciaries

1. Relationship
2. Location
3. Other

Tax and Valuation Tables

TABLE 1 Federal Individual Income Tax Rates: Married Individuals Filing Joint Returns and Surviving Spouses

Taxable Income		Base Amount	+	Percent	On Excess Over
Over	But Not Over				

1994

Over	But Not Over	Base Amount	Percent	On Excess Over
$ 0.	$ 38,000.	$ 0.00	15.0%	$ 0.
38,000.	91,850.	5,700.00	28.0	38,000.
91,850.	140,000.	20,778.00	31.0	91,850.
140,000.	250,000.	35,704.50	36.0	140,000.
250,000.	-	75,304.50	39.6	250,000.

1993

Over	But Not Over	Base Amount	Percent	On Excess Over
$ 0.	$ 36,900.	$ 0.00	15.0%	$ 0.
36,900.	89,150.	5,535.00	28.0	36,900.
89,150.	140,000.	20,165.00	31.0	89,150.
140,000.	250,000.	35,928.50	36.0	140,000.
250,000.	-	75,528.50	39.6	250,000.

1992

Over	But Not Over	Base Amount	Percent	On Excess Over
$ 0.	$ 35,800.	$ 0.00	15.0%	$ 0.
35,800.	86,500.	5,370.00	28.0	35,800.
86,500.	-	19,566.00	31.0	86,500.

1991

Over	But Not Over	Base Amount	Percent	On Excess Over
$ 0.	$ 34,000.	$ 0.00	15.0%	$ 0.
34,000.	82,150.	5,100.00	28.0	34,000.
82,150.	-	18,582.00	31.0	82,150.

1990*

Over	But Not Over	Base Amount	Percent	On Excess Over
$ 0.	$ 32,450.	$ 0.00	15.0%	$ 0.
32,450.	78,400.	4,867.50	28.0	32,450.
78,400.	162,770.	17,733.50	33.0	78,400.
162,770.	-	45,575.60	28.0	162,770.

*Rate brackets for 1990 assume two personal exemptions.

TABLE 2 Federal Individual Income Tax Rates: Unmarried Individuals (Other than Surviving Spouses And Heads of Households)

Taxable Income		Base Amount	+	Percent	On Excess Over
Over	**But Not Over**				
		1994			
$ 0.	$ 22,750.	$ 0.00		15.0%	$ 0.
22,750.	55,100.	3,412.50		28.0	22,750.
55,100.	115,000.	12,470.50		31.0	55,100.
115,000.	250,000.	31,039.50		36.0	115,000.
250,000.	-	79,639.50		39.6	250,000.
		1993			
$ 0.	$ 22,100.	$ 0.00		15.0%	$ 0.
22,100.	53,500.	3,315.00		28.0	22,100.
53,500.	115,000.	12,107.00		31.0	53,500.
115,000.	250,000.	31,172.00		36.0	115,000.
250,000.	-	79,772.00		39.6	250,000.
		1992			
$ 0.	$ 21,450.	$ 0.00		15.0%	$ 0.
21,450.	51,900.	3,217.50		28.0	21,450.
51,900.	-	11,743.50		31.0	51,900.
		1991			
$ 0.	$ 20,350.	$ 0.00		15.0%	$ 0.
20,350.	49,350.	3,052.50		28.0	20,350.
49,300.	-	11,158.50		31.0	49,300.
		1990			
$ 0.	$ 19,450.	$ 0.00		15.0%	$ 0.
19,450.	47,050.	2,917.50		28.0	19,450.
47,050.	97,620.	10,645.50		33.0	47,050.
97,620.	-	16,688.10		28.0	97,620.

TABLE 3 Federal Income Tax Rates: Estates and Trusts

Taxable Income		Base Amount	+	Percent	On Excess Over
Over	But Not Over				

1994

Over	But Not Over	Base Amount	+	Percent	On Excess Over
$ 0.	$ 1,500.	$ 0.00		15.0%	$ 0.
1,500.	3,600.	225.00		28.0	1,500.
3,600.	5,500.	813.00		31.0	3,600.
5,500.	7,500.	1402.00		36.0	5,500.
7,500.	-	2122.00		39.6	7,500.

1993

Over	But Not Over	Base Amount	+	Percent	On Excess Over
$ 0.	$ 1,500.	$ 0.00		15.0%	$ 0.
1,500.	3,500.	225.00		28.0	1,500.
3,500.	5,500.	785.00		31.0	3,500.
5,500.	7,500.	1405.00		36.0	5,500.
7,500.	-	2125.00		39.6	7,500.

1992

Over	But Not Over	Base Amount	+	Percent	On Excess Over
$ 0.	$ 3,600.	$ 0.00		15.0%	$ 0.
3,600.	10,900.	540.00		28.0	3,600.
10,900.	-	2,584.00		31.0	10,900.

1991

Over	But Not Over	Base Amount	+	Percent	On Excess Over
$ 0.	$ 3,450.	$ 0.00		15.0%	$ 0.
3,450.	10,350.	517.50		28.0	3,450.
10,350.	-	2,449.50		31.0	10,350.

1990

Over	But Not Over	Base Amount	+	Percent	On Excess Over
$ 0.	$ 5,450.	$ 0.00		15.0%	$ 0.
5,450.	14,150.	817.50		28.0	5,450
14,150.	28,320.	3,253.50		33.0	14,150.
28,320.	-	7,929.60		28.0	28,320.

TABLE 4 Federal Unified Transfer Tax Rates Since 1977

If the Amount is:		Tentative Tax		
Over	But Not Over	Base Amount	+ Percent	On Excess Over

All years after 1976-taxable amounts up to $2,500,000

Over	But Not Over	Base Amount	Percent	On Excess Over
$ 0.	$ 10,000.	$ 0.	18.0%	$ 0.
10,000.	20,000.	1,800.	20.0	10,000.
20,000.	40,000.	3,800.	22.0	20,000.
40,000.	60,000.	8,200.	24.0	40,000.
60,000.	80,000.	13,000.	26.0	60,000.
80,000.	100,000.	18,200.	28.0	80,000.
100,000.	150,000.	23,800.	30.0	100,000.
150,000.	250,000.	38,800.	32.0	150,000.
250,000.	500,000.	70,800.	34.0	250,000.
500,000.	750,000.	155,800.	37.0	500,000.
750,000.	1,000,000.	248,300.	39.0	750,000.
1,000,000.	1,250,000.	345,800.	41.0	1,000,000.
1,250,000.	1,500,000.	448,300.	43.0	1,250,000.
1,500,000.	2,000,000.	555,800.	45.0	1,500,000.
2,000,000.	2,500,000.	780,800.	49.0	2,000,000.

1977-1981

Over	But Not Over	Base Amount	Percent	On Excess Over
$2,500,000.	$3,000,000.	$1,025,800.	53.0%	$2,500,000.
3,000,000.	3,500,000.	1,290,800.	57.0	3,000,000.
3,500,000.	4,000,000.	1,575,800.	61.0	3,500,000.
4,000,000.	4,500,000.	1,880,800.	65.0	4,000,000.
4,500,000.	5,000,000.	2,205,800.	69.0	4,500,000.
5,000,000.	-	2,550,800.	70.0	5,000,000.

1982

Over	But Not Over	Base Amount	Percent	On Excess Over
$2,500,000.	$3,000,000.	$1,025,800.	53.0%	$2,500,000.
3,000,000.	3,500,000.	1,290,800.	57.0	3,000,000.
3,500,000.	4,000,000.	1,575,800.	61.0	3,500,000.
4,000,000.	-	1,880,800.	65.0	4,000,000.

1983

Over	But Not Over	Base Amount	Percent	On Excess Over
$2,500,000.	$3,000,000.	$1,025,800.	53.0%	$2,500,000.
3,000,000.	3,500,000.	1,290,800.	57.0	3,000,000.
3,500,000.	-	1,575,800.	60.0	3,500,000.

1984 and later

Over	But Not Over	Base Amount	Percent	On Excess Over
$2,500,000.	$3,000,000.	$1,025,800.	53.0%	$2,500,000.
3,000,000.	-	1,290,800.	55.0	3,000,000.

(Note: amounts between $10 million and $21,040,000 are subject to an additional 5% tax)

TABLE 5 Federal Unified Credit

Year	Amount of Credit	Exemption Equivalent
1977	$ 30,000.	$120,667.
1978	34,000.	134,000.
1979	38,000.	147,333.
1980	42,500.	161,563.
1981	47,000.	175,625.
1982	62,800.	225,000.
1983	79,300.	275,000.
1984	96,300.	325,000.
1985	121,800.	400,000.
1986	155,800.	500,000.
1987 and thereafter	192,800.	600,000.

TABLE 6 Maximum Credit against Federal Estate Tax for State Death Taxes

Adjusted Taxable Estate:*		Maximum Credit			
At Least	But Not Over	Base Amount	+	Percent	On Excess Over
$ 40,000.	$ 90,000.	$ 0.		.8%	$ 40,000.
90,000.	140,000.	400.		1.6	90,000.
140,000.	240,000.	1,200.		2.4	140,000.
240,000.	440,000.	3,600.		3.2	240,000.
440,000.	640,000.	10,000.		4.0	440,000.
640,000.	840,000.	18,000.		4.8	640,000.
840,000.	1,040,000.	27,600.		5.6	840,000.
1,040,000.	1,540,000.	38,800.		6.4	1,040,000.
1,540,000.	2,040,000.	70,800.		7.2	1,540,000.
2,040,000.	2,540,000.	106,800.		8.0	2,040,000.
2,540,000.	3,040,000.	146,800.		8.8	2,540,000.
3,040,000.	3,540,000.	190,800.		9.6	3,040,000.
3,540,000.	4,040,000.	238,800.		10.4	3,540,000.
4,040,000.	5,040,000.	290,800.		11.2	4,040,000.
5,040,000.	6,040,000.	402,800.		12.0	5,040,000.
6,040,000.	7,040,000.	522,800.		12.8	6,040,000.
7,040,000.	8,040,000.	650,800.		13.6	7,040,000.
8,040,000.	9,040,000.	786,800.		14.4	8,040,000.
9,040,000.	10,040,000.	930,800.		15.2	9,040,000.
10,040,000.	-	1,082,800.		16.0	10,040,000.

* Adjusted taxable estate is taxable estate less $60,000.

TABLE 7 Federal Estate Tax Rates For Decedents Dying prior to 1977

Taxable Estate (after exemption)		Estate Tax			
At Least	But Not Over	Base Amount	+	Percent	On Excess Over
$ 0.	$ 5,000.	$ 0.		3.0%	$ 0.
5,000.	10,000.	150.		7.0	5,000.
10,000.	20,000.	500.		11.0	10,000.
20,000.	30,000.	1,600.		14.0	20,000.
30,000.	40,000.	3,000.		18.0	30,000.
40,000.	50,000.	4,800.		22.0	40,000.
50,000.	60,000.	7,000.		25.0	50,000.
60,000.	100,000.	9,500.		28.0	60,000.
100,000.	250,000.	20,700.		30.0	100,000.
250,000.	500,000.	65,700.		32.0	250,000.
500,000.	750,000.	145,700.		35.0	500,000.
750,000.	1,000,000.	233,200.		37.0	750,000.
1,000,000.	1,250,000.	325,700.		39.0	1,000,000.
1,250,000.	1,500,000.	423,200.		42.0	1,250,000.
1,500,000.	2,000,000.	528,200.		45.0	1,500,000.
2,000,000.	2,500,000.	753,200.		49.0	2,000,000.
2,500,000.	3,000,000.	998,200.		53.0	2,500,000.
3,000,000.	3,500,000.	1,263,200.		56.0	3,000,000.
3,500,000.	4,000,000.	1,543,200.		59.0	3,500,000.
4,000,000.	5,000,000.	1,838,200.		63.0	4,000,000.
5,000,000.	6,000,000.	2,468,200.		67.0	5,000,000.
6,000,000.	7,000,000.	3,138,200.		70.0	6,000,000.
7,000,000.	8,000,000.	3,838,200.		73.0	7,000,000.
8,000,000.	10,000,000.	4,568,200.		76.0	8,000,000.
10,000,000.	-	6,088,200.		77.0	10,000,000.

TABLE 8 Federal Gift Tax for Gifts Made prior to January 1, 1977

Taxable Gifts		Gift Tax			
At Least	But Not Over	Base Amount	+	Percent	On Excess Over
$ 0.	$ 5,000.	$ 0.00		2.25%	$ 0.
5,000.	10,000.	112.50		5.25	5,000.
10,000.	20,000.	375.00		8.25	10,000.
20,000.	30,000.	1,200.00		10.50	20,000.
30,000.	40,000.	2,250.00		13.50	30,000.
40,000.	50,000.	3,600.00		16.50	40,000.
50,000.	60,000.	5,250.00		18.75	50,000.
60,000.	100,000.	7,125.00		21.00	60,000.
100,000.	250,000.	15,525.00		22.50	100,000.
250,000.	500,000.	49,275.00		24.00	250,000.
500,000.	750,000.	109,275.00		26.25	500,000.
750,000.	1,000,000.	174,900.00		27.75	750,000.
1,000,000.	1,250,000.	244,275.00		29.25	1,000,000.
1,250,000.	1,500,000.	317,400.00		31.50	1,250,000.
1,500,000.	2,000,000.	396,150.00		33.75	1,500,000.
2,000,000.	2,500,000.	564,900.00		36.75	2,000,000.
2,500,000.	3,000,000.	748,650.00		39.75	2,500,000.
3,000,000.	3,500,000.	947,400.00		42.00	3,000,000.
3,500,000.	4,000,000.	1,157,400.00		44.50	3,500,000.
4,000,000.	5,000,000.	1,378,650.00		47.25	4,000,000.
5,000,000.	6,000,000.	1,851,150.00		50.25	5,000,000.
6,000,000.	7,000,000.	2,353,650.00		52.50	6,000,000.
7,000,000.	8,000,000.	2,878,650.00		54.75	7,000,000.
8,000,000.	10,000,000.	3,426,150.00		57.00	8,000,000.
10,000,000.	-	4,566,150.00		57.75	10,000,000.

TABLE 9 IRS Table S for Present Worth of Annuities, Life Estates, and Remainders *(first of twelve pages)*

TABLE S(3.0)
SINGLE LIFE, 3.0 PERCENT, BASED ON LIFE TABLE 80CNSMT
SHOWING THE PRESENT WORTH OF AN ANNUITY, OF A LIFE ESTATE,
AND OF A REMAINDER INTEREST

AGE	ANNUITY	LIFE ESTATE	REMAINDER	AGE	ANNUITY	LIFE ESTATE	REMAINDER
(1)	(2)	(3)	(4)	(1)	(2)	(3)	(4)
0	28.7622	.86287	.13713	55	15.9842	.47952	.52048
1	28.9967	.86990	.13010	56	15.6090	.46827	.53173
2	28.8940	.86682	.13318	57	15.2311	.45693	.54307
3	28.7798	.86339	.13661	58	14.8507	.44552	.55448
4	28.6577	.85973	.14027	59	14.4685	.43405	.56595
5	28.5292	.85588	.14412	60	14.0854	.42256	.57744
6	28.3956	.85187	.14813	61	13.7022	.41107	.58893
7	28.2572	.84771	.15229	62	13.3196	.39959	.60041
8	28.1136	.84341	.15659	63	12.9379	.38814	.61186
9	27.9645	.83894	.16106	64	12.5569	.37671	.62329
10	27.8101	.83430	.16570	65	12.1758	.36527	.63473
11	27.6498	.82949	.17051	66	11.7941	.35382	.64618
12	27.4847	.82454	.17546	67	11.4120	.34236	.65764
13	27.3160	.81948	.18052	68	11.0298	.33089	.66911
14	27.1459	.81438	.18562	69	10.6490	.31947	.68053
15	26.9749	.80925	.19075	70	10.2706	.30812	.69188
16	26.8027	.80408	.19592	71	9.8960	.29688	.70312
17	26.6295	.79888	.20112	72	9.5252	.28576	.71424
18	26.4542	.79363	.20637	73	9.1580	.27474	.72526
19	26.2757	.78827	.21173	74	8.7935	.26381	.73619
20	26.0939	.78282	.21718	75	8.4310	.25293	.74707
21	25.9086	.77726	.22274	76	8.0702	.24210	.75790
22	25.7191	.77157	.22843	77	7.7120	.23136	.76864
23	25.5252	.76575	.23425	78	7.3577	.22073	.77927
24	25.3254	.75976	.24024	79	7.0097	.21029	.78971
25	25.1194	.75358	.24642	80	6.6699	.20010	.79990
26	24.9065	.74719	.25281	81	6.3408	.19023	.80977
27	24.6864	.74059	.25941	82	6.0236	.18071	.81929
28	24.4595	.73378	.26622	83	5.7192	.17157	.82843
29	24.2254	.72676	.27324	84	5.4266	.16280	.83720
30	23.9844	.71953	.28047	85	5.1450	.15435	.84565
31	23.7358	.71207	.28793	86	4.8760	.14628	.85372
32	23.4803	.70441	.29559	87	4.6220	.13866	.86134
33	23.2172	.69652	.30348	88	4.3816	.13145	.86855
34	22.9471	.68841	.31159	89	4.1506	.12452	.87548
35	22.6701	.68010	.31990	90	3.9270	.11781	.88219
36	22.3867	.67160	.32840	91	3.7134	.11140	.88860
37	22.0969	.66291	.33709	92	3.5142	.10542	.89458
38	21.8006	.65402	.34598	93	3.3307	.09992	.90008
39	21.4980	.64494	.35506	94	3.1642	.09493	.90507
40	21.1893	.63568	.36432	95	3.0148	.09044	.90956
41	20.8745	.62623	.37377	96	2.8826	.08648	.91352
42	20.5543	.61663	.38337	97	2.7630	.08289	.91711
43	20.2288	.60687	.39313	98	2.6554	.07966	.92034
44	19.8981	.59694	.40306	99	2.5560	.07668	.92332
45	19.5621	.58686	.41314	100	2.4636	.07391	.92609
46	19.2212	.57664	.42336	101	2.3750	.07125	.92875
47	18.8756	.56627	.43373	102	2.2827	.06848	.93152
48	18.5258	.55577	.44423	103	2.1850	.06555	.93445
49	18.1727	.54518	.45482	104	2.0766	.06230	.93770
50	17.8164	.53449	.46551	105	1.9446	.05834	.94166
51	17.4568	.52370	.47630	106	1.7607	.05282	.94718
52	17.0934	.51280	.48720	107	1.5040	.04512	.95488
53	16.7265	.50179	.49821	108	1.1045	.03314	.96686
54	16.3567	.49070	.50930	109	0.4854	.01456	.98544

TABLE 9 *Continued (second of 12 pages)*

TABLE S(4.0)
SINGLE LIFE, 4.0 PERCENT, BASED ON LIFE TABLE 80CNSMT
SHOWING THE PRESENT WORTH OF AN ANNUITY, OF A LIFE ESTATE,
AND OF A REMAINDER INTEREST

AGE	ANNUITY	LIFE ESTATE	REMAINDER	AGE	ANNUITY	LIFE ESTATE	REMAINDER
(1)	(2)	(3)	(4)	(1)	(2)	(3)	(4)
0	22.9703	.91881	.08119	55	14.2490	.56996	.43004
1	23.1876	.92750	.07250	56	13.9493	.55797	.44203
2	23.1371	.92548	.07452	57	13.6456	.54582	.45418
3	23.0779	.92312	.07688	58	13.3381	.53352	.46648
4	23.0127	.92051	.07949	59	13.0273	.52109	.47891
5	22.9427	.91771	.08229	60	12.7141	.50856	.49144
6	22.8690	.91476	.08524	61	12.3990	.49596	.50404
7	22.7915	.91166	.08834	62	12.0829	.48331	.51669
8	22.7103	.90841	.09159	63	11.7658	.47063	.52937
9	22.6248	.90499	.09501	64	11.4477	.45791	.54209
10	22.5352	.90141	.09859	65	11.1278	.44511	.55489
11	22.4410	.89764	.10236	66	10.8056	.43222	.56778
12	22.3431	.89372	.10628	67	10.4812	.41925	.58075
13	22.2424	.88969	.11031	68	10.1550	.40620	.59380
14	22.1406	.88562	.11438	69	9.8283	.39313	.60687
15	22.0381	.88152	.11848	70	9.5020	.38008	.61992
16	21.9350	.87740	.12260	71	9.1775	.36710	.63290
17	21.8310	.87324	.12676	72	8.8546	.35418	.64582
18	21.7256	.86902	.13098	73	8.5354	.34134	.65866
19	21.6176	.86470	.13530	74	8.2130	.32852	.67148
20	21.5071	.86028	.13972	75	7.8926	.31570	.68430
21	21.3928	.85575	.14425	76	7.5721	.30289	.69711
22	21.2772	.85109	.14891	77	7.2524	.29009	.70991
23	21.1569	.84628	.15372	78	6.9345	.27738	.72262
24	21.0320	.84128	.15872	79	6.6208	.26483	.73517
25	20.9018	.83607	.16393	80	6.3132	.25253	.74747
26	20.7659	.83064	.16936	81	6.0141	.24056	.75944
27	20.6240	.82496	.17504	82	5.7246	.22899	.77101
28	20.4763	.81905	.18095	83	5.4458	.21783	.78217
29	20.3225	.81290	.18710	84	5.1770	.20708	.79292
30	20.1625	.80650	.19350	85	4.9172	.19669	.80331
31	19.9960	.79984	.20016	86	4.6682	.18673	.81327
32	19.8233	.79293	.20707	87	4.4326	.17730	.82270
33	19.6438	.78575	.21425	88	4.2088	.16835	.83165
34	19.4580	.77832	.22168	89	3.9931	.15972	.84028
35	19.2658	.77063	.22937	90	3.7835	.15134	.84866
36	19.0677	.76271	.23729	91	3.5828	.14331	.85669
37	18.8634	.75454	.24546	92	3.3950	.13580	.86420
38	18.6530	.74612	.25388	93	3.2217	.12887	.87113
39	18.4365	.73746	.26254	94	3.0640	.12256	.87744
40	18.2139	.72856	.27144	95	2.9223	.11689	.88311
41	17.9853	.71941	.28059	96	2.7969	.11188	.88812
42	17.7512	.71005	.28995	97	2.6833	.10733	.89267
43	17.5115	.70046	.29954	98	2.5811	.10324	.89676
44	17.2663	.69065	.30935	99	2.4868	.09947	.90053
45	17.0155	.68062	.31938	100	2.3989	.09596	.90404
46	16.7594	.67038	.32962	101	2.3149	.09260	.90740
47	16.4979	.65992	.34008	102	2.2274	.08910	.91090
48	16.2317	.64927	.35073	103	2.1346	.08538	.91462
49	15.9613	.63845	.36155	104	2.0316	.08127	.91873
50	15.6868	.62747	.37253	105	1.9058	.07623	.92377
51	15.4081	.61632	.38368	106	1.7293	.06917	.93083
52	15.1247	.60499	.39501	107	1.4810	.05924	.94076
53	14.8368	.59347	.40653	108	1.0910	.04364	.95636
54	14.5449	.58180	.41820	109	0.4808	.01923	.98077

TABLE 9 *Continued (third of 12 pages)*

TABLE S(5.0)
SINGLE LIFE, 5.0 PERCENT, BASED ON LIFE TABLE 80CNSMT
SHOWING THE PRESENT WORTH OF AN ANNUITY, OF A LIFE ESTATE,
AND OF A REMAINDER INTEREST

AGE	ANNUITY	LIFE ESTATE	REMAINDER	AGE	ANNUITY	LIFE ESTATE	REMAINDER
(1)	(2)	(3)	(4)	(1)	(2)	(3)	(4)
0	18.9478	.94739	.05261	55	12.8034	.64017	.35983
1	19.1426	.95713	.04287	56	12.5614	.62807	.37193
2	19.1180	.95590	.04410	57	12.3148	.61574	.38426
3	19.0867	.95433	.04567	58	12.0637	.60318	.39682
4	19.0507	.95254	.04746	59	11.8085	.59042	.40958
5	19.0112	.95056	.04944	60	11.5500	.57750	.42250
6	18.9688	.94844	.05156	61	11.2887	.56444	.43556
7	18.9238	.94619	.05381	62	11.0252	.55126	.44874
8	18.8759	.94379	.05621	63	10.7597	.53799	.46201
9	18.8248	.94124	.05876	64	10.4921	.52460	.47540
10	18.7705	.93853	.06147	65	10.2216	.51108	.48892
11	18.7128	.93564	.06436	66	9.9477	.49738	.50262
12	18.6521	.93261	.06739	67	9.6705	.48352	.51648
13	18.5894	.92947	.07053	68	9.3903	.46951	.53049
14	18.5260	.92630	.07370	69	9.1083	.45541	.54459
15	18.4623	.92312	.07688	70	8.8253	.44126	.55874
16	18.3984	.91992	.08008	71	8.5425	.42713	.57287
17	18.3340	.91670	.08330	72	8.2600	.41300	.58700
18	18.2687	.91344	.08656	73	7.9777	.39888	.60112
19	18.2016	.91008	.08992	74	7.6947	.38473	.61527
20	18.1326	.90663	.09337	75	7.4103	.37052	.62948
21	18.0617	.90308	.09692	76	7.1245	.35623	.64377
22	17.9883	.89941	.10059	77	6.8379	.34189	.65811
23	17.9120	.89560	.10440	78	6.5516	.32758	.67242
24	17.8321	.89161	.10839	79	6.2679	.31340	.68660
25	17.7481	.88741	.11259	80	5.9885	.29942	.70058
26	17.6594	.88297	.11703	81	5.7157	.28578	.71422
27	17.5659	.87829	.12171	82	5.4508	.27254	.72746
28	17.4676	.87338	.12662	83	5.1947	.25974	.74026
29	17.3642	.86821	.13179	84	4.9470	.24735	.75265
30	17.2558	.86279	.13721	85	4.7068	.23534	.76466
31	17.1418	.85709	.14291	86	4.4758	.22379	.77621
32	17.0225	.85112	.14888	87	4.2566	.21283	.78717
33	16.8975	.84487	.15513	88	4.0479	.20240	.79760
34	16.7670	.83835	.16165	89	3.8461	.19231	.80769
35	16.6309	.83154	.16846	90	3.6494	.18247	.81753
36	16.4895	.82448	.17552	91	3.4604	.17302	.82698
37	16.3427	.81714	.18286	92	3.2831	.16415	.83585
38	16.1904	.80952	.19048	93	3.1191	.15595	.84405
39	16.0326	.80163	.19837	94	2.9696	.14848	.85152
40	15.8691	.79346	.20654	95	2.8351	.14175	.85825
41	15.7001	.78501	.21499	96	2.7159	.13580	.86420
42	15.5259	.77630	.22370	97	2.6079	.13039	.86961
43	15.3465	.76732	.23268	98	2.5107	.12553	.87447
44	15.1617	.75809	.24191	99	2.4209	.12105	.87895
45	14.9715	.74858	.25142	100	2.3374	.11687	.88313
46	14.7761	.73880	.26120	101	2.2576	.11288	.88712
47	14.5753	.72877	.27123	102	2.1744	.10872	.89128
48	14.3697	.71849	.28151	103	2.0863	.10431	.89569
49	14.1597	.70799	.29201	104	1.9884	.09942	.90058
50	13.9454	.69727	.30273	105	1.8684	.09342	.90658
51	13.7266	.68633	.31367	106	1.6989	.08494	.91506
52	13.5028	.67514	.32486	107	1.4587	.07293	.92707
53	13.2741	.66371	.33629	108	1.0778	.05389	.94611
54	13.0410	.65205	.34795	109	0.4762	.02381	.97619

TABLE 9 *Continued (fourth of 12 pages)*

TABLE S(6.0)
SINGLE LIFE, 6.0 PERCENT, BASED ON LIFE TABLE 80CNSMT
SHOWING THE PRESENT WORTH OF AN ANNUITY, OF A LIFE ESTATE,
AND OF A REMAINDER INTEREST

AGE	ANNUITY	LIFE ESTATE	REMAINDER	AGE	ANNUITY	LIFE ESTATE	REMAINDER
(1)	(2)	(3)	(4)	(1)	(2)	(3)	(4)
0	16.0427	.96256	.03744	55	11.5878	.69527	.30473
1	16.2159	.97295	.02705	56	11.3904	.68342	.31658
2	16.2044	.97227	.02773	57	11.1880	.67128	.32872
3	16.1875	.97125	.02875	58	10.9810	.65886	.34114
4	16.1670	.97002	.02998	59	10.7696	.64617	.35383
5	16.1438	.96863	.03137	60	10.5543	.63326	.36674
6	16.1185	.96711	.03289	61	10.3358	.62015	.37985
7	16.0912	.96547	.03453	62	10.1144	.60686	.39314
8	16.0617	.96370	.03630	63	9.8904	.59342	.40658
9	16.0298	.96179	.03821	64	9.6635	.57981	.42019
10	15.9954	.95973	.04027	65	9.4331	.56599	.43401
11	15.9583	.95750	.04250	66	9.1987	.55192	.44808
12	15.9190	.95514	.04486	67	8.9604	.53762	.46238
13	15.8782	.95269	.04731	68	8.7182	.52309	.47691
14	15.8370	.95022	.04978	69	8.4733	.50840	.49160
15	15.7958	.94775	.05225	70	8.2265	.49359	.50641
16	15.7547	.94528	.05472	71	7.9789	.47874	.52126
17	15.7135	.94281	.05719	72	7.7305	.46383	.53617
18	15.6718	.94031	.05969	73	7.4811	.44887	.55113
19	15.6289	.93774	.06226	74	7.2300	.43380	.56620
20	15.5847	.93508	.06492	75	6.9766	.41860	.58140
21	15.5392	.93235	.06765	76	6.7207	.40324	.59676
22	15.4919	.92951	.07049	77	6.4628	.38777	.61223
23	15.4425	.92655	.07345	78	6.2041	.37225	.62775
24	15.3902	.92341	.07659	79	5.9466	.35679	.64321
25	15.3348	.92009	.07991	80	5.6919	.34151	.65849
26	15.2757	.91654	.08346	81	5.4424	.32655	.67345
27	15.2127	.91276	.08724	82	5.1993	.31196	.68804
28	15.1458	.90875	.09125	83	4.9635	.29781	.70219
29	15.0748	.90449	.09551	84	4.7347	.28408	.71592
30	14.9997	.89998	.10002	85	4.5120	.27072	.72928
31	14.9199	.89520	.10480	86	4.2973	.25784	.74216
32	14.8358	.89015	.10985	87	4.0930	.24558	.75442
33	14.7469	.88481	.11519	88	3.8979	.23388	.76612
34	14.6533	.87920	.12080	89	3.7088	.22253	.77747
35	14.5550	.87330	.12670	90	3.5239	.21143	.78857
36	14.4521	.86713	.13287	91	3.3455	.20073	.79927
37	14.3445	.86067	.13933	92	3.1778	.19067	.80933
38	14.2322	.85393	.14607	93	3.0224	.18135	.81865
39	14.1150	.84690	.15310	94	2.8805	.17283	.82717
40	13.9928	.83957	.16043	95	2.7526	.16516	.83484
41	13.8657	.83194	.16806	96	2.6392	.15835	.84165
42	13.7338	.82403	.17597	97	2.5364	.15218	.84782
43	13.5973	.81584	.18416	98	2.4438	.14663	.85337
44	13.4558	.80735	.19265	99	2.3583	.14150	.85850
45	13.3093	.79856	.20144	100	2.2788	.13673	.86327
46	13.1579	.78947	.21053	101	2.2029	.13217	.86783
47	13.0015	.78009	.21991	102	2.1238	.12743	.87257
48	12.8405	.77043	.22957	103	2.0399	.12240	.87760
49	12.6752	.76051	.23949	104	1.9468	.11681	.88319
50	12.5056	.75034	.24966	105	1.8323	.10994	.89006
51	12.3317	.73990	.26010	106	1.6694	.10017	.89983
52	12.1528	.72917	.27083	107	1.4370	.08622	.91378
53	11.9690	.71814	.28186	108	1.0649	.06389	.93611
54	11.7807	.70684	.29316	109	0.4717	.02830	.97170

TABLE 9 *Continued (fifth of 12 pages)*

TABLE S(7.0)
SINGLE LIFE, 7.0 PERCENT, BASED ON LIFE TABLE 80CNSMT
SHOWING THE PRESENT WORTH OF AN ANNUITY, OF A LIFE ESTATE,
AND OF A REMAINDER INTEREST

AGE	ANNUITY	LIFE ESTATE	REMAINDER	AGE	ANNUITY	LIFE ESTATE	REMAINDER
(1)	(2)	(3)	(4)	(1)	(2)	(3)	(4)
0	13.8711	.97098	.02902	55	10.5567	.73897	.26103
1	14.0251	.98176	.01824	56	10.3940	.72758	.27242
2	14.0204	.98143	.01857	57	10.2264	.71585	.28415
3	14.0112	.98079	.01921	58	10.0541	.70379	.29621
4	13.9992	.97995	.02005	59	9.8773	.69141	.30859
5	13.9851	.97895	.02105	60	9.6966	.67876	.32124
6	13.9693	.97785	.02215	61	9.5123	.66586	.33414
7	13.9520	.97664	.02336	62	9.3248	.65274	.34726
8	13.9330	.97531	.02469	63	9.1344	.63940	.36060
9	13.9122	.97385	.02615	64	8.9407	.62585	.37415
10	13.8894	.97226	.02774	65	8.7431	.61202	.38798
11	13.8644	.97051	.02949	66	8.5413	.59789	.40211
12	13.8377	.96864	.03136	67	8.3350	.58345	.41655
13	13.8098	.96669	.03331	68	8.1244	.56871	.43129
14	13.7819	.96473	.03527	69	7.9107	.55375	.44625
15	13.7542	.96279	.03721	70	7.6943	.53860	.46140
16	13.7267	.96087	.03913	71	7.4763	.52334	.47666
17	13.6994	.95896	.04104	72	7.2568	.50797	.49203
18	13.6719	.95704	.04296	73	7.0356	.49249	.50751
19	13.6437	.95506	.04494	74	6.8119	.47683	.52317
20	13.6146	.95302	.04698	75	6.5851	.46096	.53904
21	13.5846	.95093	.04907	76	6.3550	.44485	.55515
22	13.5534	.94874	.05126	77	6.1222	.42856	.57144
23	13.5207	.94645	.05355	78	5.8876	.41213	.58787
24	13.4858	.94401	.05599	79	5.6531	.39572	.60428
25	13.4485	.94139	.05861	80	5.4203	.37942	.62058
26	13.4082	.93858	.06142	81	5.1915	.36341	.63659
27	13.3648	.93554	.06446	82	4.9678	.34774	.65226
28	13.3183	.93228	.06772	83	4.7501	.33251	.66749
29	13.2685	.92880	.07120	84	4.5382	.31767	.68233
30	13.2154	.92508	.07492	85	4.3313	.30319	.69681
31	13.1584	.92109	.07891	86	4.1313	.28919	.71081
32	13.0979	.91685	.08315	87	3.9404	.27583	.72417
33	13.0333	.91233	.08767	88	3.7578	.26305	.73695
34	12.9648	.90754	.09246	89	3.5803	.25062	.74938
35	12.8923	.90246	.09754	90	3.4060	.23842	.76158
36	12.8160	.89712	.10288	91	3.2375	.22663	.77337
37	12.7357	.89150	.10850	92	3.0787	.21551	.78449
38	12.6513	.88559	.11441	93	2.9313	.20519	.79481
39	12.5626	.87939	.12061	94	2.7964	.19575	.80425
40	12.4697	.87288	.12712	95	2.6746	.18722	.81278
41	12.3724	.86607	.13393	96	2.5666	.17966	.82034
42	12.2710	.85897	.14103	97	2.4685	.17279	.82721
43	12.1654	.85158	.14842	98	2.3801	.16661	.83339
44	12.0553	.84387	.15613	99	2.2986	.16090	.83910
45	11.9408	.83586	.16414	100	2.2229	.15560	.84440
46	11.8218	.82753	.17247	101	2.1506	.15054	.84946
47	11.6982	.81888	.18112	102	2.0753	.14527	.85473
48	11.5704	.80993	.19007	103	1.9954	.13968	.86032
49	11.4386	.80070	.19930	104	1.9068	.13347	.86653
50	11.3027	.79119	.20881	105	1.7974	.12582	.87418
51	11.1627	.78139	.21861	106	1.6409	.11486	.88514
52	11.0181	.77126	.22874	107	1.4158	.09911	.90089
53	10.8687	.76081	.23919	108	1.0522	.07366	.92634
54	10.7149	.75005	.24995	109	0.4673	.03271	.96729

TABLE 9 *Continued (sixth of 12 pages)*

TABLE S(8.0)
SINGLE LIFE, 8.0 PERCENT, BASED ON LIFE TABLE 80CNSMT
SHOWING THE PRESENT WORTH OF AN ANNUITY, OF A LIFE ESTATE,
AND OF A REMAINDER INTEREST

AGE	ANNUITY	LIFE ESTATE	REMAINDER	AGE	ANNUITY	LIFE ESTATE	REMAINDER
(1)	(2)	(3)	(4)	(1)	(2)	(3)	(4)
0	12.1984	.97587	.02413	55	9.6749	.77399	.22601
1	12.3360	.98688	.01312	56	9.5394	.76315	.23685
2	12.3348	.98679	.01321	57	9.3994	.75195	.24805
3	12.3299	.98639	.01361	58	9.2547	.74038	.25962
4	12.3227	.98582	.01418	59	9.1056	.72845	.27155
5	12.3137	.98510	.01490	60	8.9526	.71621	.28379
6	12.3035	.98428	.01572	61	8.7959	.70367	.29633
7	12.2921	.98336	.01664	62	8.6360	.69088	.30912
8	12.2793	.98234	.01766	63	8.4729	.67783	.32217
9	12.2650	.98120	.01880	64	8.3064	.66452	.33548
10	12.2492	.97994	.02006	65	8.1360	.65088	.34912
11	12.2316	.97853	.02147	66	7.9610	.63688	.36312
12	12.2126	.97701	.02299	67	7.7814	.62251	.37749
13	12.1927	.97542	.02458	68	7.5974	.60779	.39221
14	12.1729	.97383	.02617	69	7.4097	.59278	.40722
15	12.1534	.97227	.02773	70	7.2190	.57752	.42248
16	12.1343	.97074	.02926	71	7.0263	.56210	.43790
17	12.1156	.96925	.03075	72	6.8314	.54651	.45349
18	12.0969	.96775	.03225	73	6.6343	.53074	.46926
19	12.0778	.96622	.03378	74	6.4342	.51473	.48527
20	12.0581	.96465	.03535	75	6.2305	.49844	.50156
21	12.0379	.96303	.03697	76	6.0229	.48183	.51817
22	12.0168	.96135	.03865	77	5.8120	.46496	.53504
23	11.9947	.95958	.04042	78	5.5986	.44788	.55212
24	11.9709	.95767	.04233	79	5.3844	.43075	.56925
25	11.9452	.95562	.04438	80	5.1710	.41368	.58632
26	11.9172	.95338	.04662	81	4.9605	.39684	.60316
27	11.8867	.95094	.04906	82	4.7541	.38032	.61968
28	11.8537	.94830	.05170	83	4.5526	.36421	.63579
29	11.8180	.94544	.05456	84	4.3559	.34847	.65153
30	11.7796	.94237	.05763	85	4.1633	.33307	.66693
31	11.7381	.93905	.06095	86	3.9766	.31812	.68188
32	11.6936	.93549	.06451	87	3.7980	.30384	.69616
33	11.6458	.93166	.06834	88	3.6267	.29014	.70986
34	11.5947	.92757	.07243	89	3.4597	.27677	.72323
35	11.5402	.92321	.07679	90	3.2953	.26362	.73638
36	11.4825	.91860	.08140	91	3.1359	.25087	.74913
37	11.4214	.91372	.08628	92	2.9853	.23882	.76118
38	11.3569	.90855	.09145	93	2.8451	.22761	.77239
39	11.2887	.90310	.09690	94	2.7167	.21734	.78266
40	11.2168	.89734	.10266	95	2.6006	.20805	.79195
41	11.1411	.89129	.10871	96	2.4976	.19981	.80019
42	11.0618	.88495	.11505	97	2.4039	.19231	.80769
43	10.9789	.87831	.12169	98	2.3196	.18557	.81443
44	10.8920	.87136	.12864	99	2.2417	.17934	.82066
45	10.8011	.86409	.13591	100	2.1694	.17356	.82644
46	10.7063	.85650	.14350	101	2.1005	.16804	.83196
47	10.6073	.84859	.15141	102	2.0288	.16230	.83770
48	10.5045	.84036	.15964	103	1.9527	.15622	.84378
49	10.3980	.83184	.16816	104	1.8682	.14946	.85054
50	10.2879	.82303	.17697	105	1.7638	.14110	.85890
51	10.1739	.81391	.18609	106	1.6132	.12906	.87094
52	10.0556	.80444	.19556	107	1.3952	.11162	.88838
53	9.9328	.79463	.20537	108	1.0399	.08319	.91681
54	9.8060	.78448	.21552	109	0.4630	.03704	.96296

TABLE 9 *Continued (seventh of 12 pages)*

TABLE S(9.0)
SINGLE LIFE, 9.0 PERCENT, BASED ON LIFE TABLE 80CNSMT
SHOWING THE PRESENT WORTH OF AN ANNUITY, OF A LIFE ESTATE,
AND OF A REMAINDER INTEREST

AGE	ANNUITY	LIFE ESTATE	REMAINDER	AGE	ANNUITY	LIFE ESTATE	REMAINDER
(1)	(2)	(3)	(4)	(1)	(2)	(3)	(4)
0	10.8762	.97886	.02114	55	8.9148	.80233	.19767
1	11.0000	.99000	.01000	56	8.8011	.79209	.20791
2	11.0007	.99006	.00994	57	8.6829	.78146	.21854
3	10.9982	.98984	.01016	58	8.5604	.77044	.22956
4	10.9938	.98944	.01056	59	8.4337	.75903	.24097
5	10.9879	.98891	.01109	60	8.3031	.74728	.25272
6	10.9810	.98829	.01171	61	8.1689	.73520	.26480
7	10.9731	.98758	.01242	62	8.0315	.72283	.27717
8	10.9642	.98678	.01322	63	7.8909	.71018	.28982
9	10.9540	.98586	.01414	64	7.7469	.69722	.30278
10	10.9425	.98483	.01517	65	7.5988	.68390	.31610
11	10.9296	.98366	.01634	66	7.4463	.67017	.32983
12	10.9154	.98239	.01761	67	7.2891	.65602	.34398
13	10.9006	.98105	.01895	68	7.1273	.64146	.35854
14	10.8859	.97973	.02027	69	6.9618	.62656	.37344
15	10.8717	.97845	.02155	70	6.7929	.61136	.38864
16	10.8579	.97721	.02279	71	6.6216	.59595	.40405
17	10.8446	.97601	.02399	72	6.4479	.58031	.41969
18	10.8315	.97483	.02517	73	6.2715	.56444	.43556
19	10.8181	.97363	.02637	74	6.0918	.54827	.45173
20	10.8044	.97240	.02760	75	5.9082	.53174	.46826
21	10.7904	.97114	.02886	76	5.7203	.51483	.48517
22	10.7759	.96983	.03017	77	5.5286	.49757	.50243
23	10.7606	.96846	.03154	78	5.3338	.48004	.51996
24	10.7441	.96697	.03303	79	5.1376	.46238	.53762
25	10.7261	.96535	.03465	80	4.9414	.44473	.55527
26	10.7062	.96356	.03644	81	4.7473	.42726	.57274
27	10.6843	.96159	.03841	82	4.5563	.41007	.58993
28	10.6604	.95944	.04056	83	4.3695	.39325	.60675
29	10.6343	.95709	.04291	84	4.1865	.37679	.62321
30	10.6060	.95454	.04546	85	4.0068	.36062	.63938
31	10.5751	.95176	.04824	86	3.8321	.34489	.65511
32	10.5418	.94876	.05124	87	3.6647	.32982	.67018
33	10.5057	.94551	.05449	88	3.5038	.31534	.68466
34	10.4668	.94201	.05799	89	3.3464	.30118	.69882
35	10.4251	.93826	.06174	90	3.1911	.28720	.71280
36	10.3807	.93427	.06573	91	3.0401	.27360	.72640
37	10.3335	.93001	.06999	92	2.8970	.26073	.73927
38	10.2832	.92549	.07451	93	2.7637	.24873	.75127
39	10.2299	.92069	.07931	94	2.6413	.23771	.76229
40	10.1734	.91560	.08440	95	2.5304	.22774	.77226
41	10.1136	.91022	.08978	96	2.4320	.21888	.78112
42	10.0506	.90456	.09544	97	2.3425	.21083	.78917
43	9.9845	.89860	.10140	98	2.2619	.20357	.79643
44	9.9149	.89234	.10766	99	2.1875	.19687	.80313
45	9.8419	.88577	.11423	100	2.1184	.19066	.80934
46	9.7652	.87887	.12113	101	2.0527	.18474	.81526
47	9.6850	.87165	.12835	102	1.9842	.17858	.82142
48	9.6012	.86411	.13589	103	1.9116	.17205	.82795
49	9.5142	.85627	.14373	104	1.8310	.16479	.83521
50	9.4238	.84814	.15186	105	1.7312	.15581	.84419
51	9.3299	.83970	.16030	106	1.5864	.14277	.85723
52	9.2321	.83089	.16911	107	1.3752	.12377	.87623
53	9.1302	.82172	.17828	108	1.0278	.09251	.90749
54	9.0245	.81221	.18779	109	0.4587	.04128	.95872

TABLE 9 *Continued (eighth of 12 pages)*

TABLE S(10.0)
SINGLE LIFE, 10.0 PERCENT, BASED ON LIFE TABLE 80CNSMT
SHOWING THE PRESENT WORTH OF AN ANNUITY, OF A LIFE ESTATE,
AND OF A REMAINDER INTEREST

AGE	ANNUITY	LIFE ESTATE	REMAINDER	AGE	ANNUITY	LIFE ESTATE	REMAINDER
(1)	(2)	(3)	(4)	(1)	(2)	(3)	(4)
0	9.8078	.98078	.01922	55	8.2550	.82550	.17450
1	9.9199	.99199	.00801	56	8.1586	.81586	.18414
2	9.9216	.99216	.00784	57	8.0581	.80581	.19419
3	9.9205	.99205	.00795	58	7.9536	.79536	.20464
4	9.9178	.99178	.00822	59	7.8449	.78449	.21551
5	9.9138	.99138	.00862	60	7.7326	.77326	.22674
6	9.9090	.99090	.00910	61	7.6169	.76169	.23831
7	9.9034	.99034	.00966	62	7.4980	.74980	.25020
8	9.8969	.98969	.01031	63	7.3760	.73760	.26240
9	9.8893	.98893	.01107	64	7.2507	.72507	.27493
10	9.8806	.98806	.01194	65	7.1213	.71213	.28787
11	9.8707	.98707	.01293	66	6.9876	.69876	.30124
12	9.8598	.98598	.01402	67	6.8492	.68492	.31508
13	9.8483	.98483	.01517	68	6.7063	.67063	.32937
14	9.8370	.98370	.01630	69	6.5595	.65595	.34405
15	9.8262	.98262	.01738	70	6.4093	.64093	.35907
16	9.8158	.98158	.01842	71	6.2564	.62564	.37436
17	9.8060	.98060	.01940	72	6.1009	.61009	.38991
18	9.7965	.97965	.02035	73	5.9425	.59425	.40575
19	9.7869	.97869	.02131	74	5.7805	.57805	.42195
20	9.7771	.97771	.02229	75	5.6144	.56144	.43856
21	9.7672	.97672	.02328	76	5.4437	.54437	.45563
22	9.7570	.97570	.02430	77	5.2689	.52689	.47311
23	9.7462	.97462	.02538	78	5.0906	.50906	.49094
24	9.7345	.97345	.02655	79	4.9103	.49103	.50897
25	9.7216	.97216	.02784	80	4.7295	.47295	.52705
26	9.7072	.97072	.02928	81	4.5501	.45501	.54499
27	9.6912	.96912	.03088	82	4.3730	.43730	.56270
28	9.6736	.96736	.03264	83	4.1993	.41993	.58007
29	9.6542	.96542	.03458	84	4.0287	.40287	.59713
30	9.6329	.96329	.03671	85	3.8608	.38608	.61392
31	9.6095	.96095	.03905	86	3.6970	.36970	.63030
32	9.5840	.95840	.04160	87	3.5398	.35398	.64602
33	9.5562	.95562	.04438	88	3.3883	.33883	.66117
34	9.5262	.95262	.04738	89	3.2399	.32399	.67601
35	9.4937	.94937	.05063	90	3.0929	.30929	.69071
36	9.4589	.94589	.05411	91	2.9496	.29496	.70504
37	9.4217	.94217	.05783	92	2.8136	.28136	.71864
38	9.3820	.93820	.06180	93	2.6865	.26865	.73135
39	9.3396	.93396	.06604	94	2.5697	.25697	.74303
40	9.2945	.92945	.07055	95	2.4638	.24638	.75362
41	9.2465	.92465	.07535	96	2.3697	.23697	.76303
42	9.1959	.91959	.08041	97	2.2840	.22840	.77160
43	9.1424	.91424	.08576	98	2.2069	.22069	.77931
44	9.0859	.90859	.09141	99	2.1356	.21356	.78644
45	9.0264	.90264	.09736	100	2.0696	.20696	.79304
46	8.9637	.89637	.10363	101	2.0068	.20068	.79932
47	8.8978	.88978	.11022	102	1.9414	.19414	.80586
48	8.8287	.88287	.11713	103	1.8721	.18721	.81279
49	8.7567	.87567	.12433	104	1.7952	.17952	.82048
50	8.6818	.86818	.13182	105	1.6997	.16997	.83003
51	8.6037	.86037	.13963	106	1.5603	.15603	.84397
52	8.5220	.85220	.14780	107	1.3557	.13557	.86443
53	8.4365	.84365	.15635	108	1.0160	.10160	.89840
54	8.3476	.83476	.16524	109	0.4545	.04545	.95455

TABLE 9 *Continued (ninth of 12 pages)*

TABLE S(11.0)
SINGLE LIFE, 11.0 PERCENT, BASED ON LIFE TABLE 80CNSMT
SHOWING THE PRESENT WORTH OF AN ANNUITY, OF A LIFE ESTATE,
AND OF A REMAINDER INTEREST

AGE	ANNUITY	LIFE ESTATE	REMAINDER	AGE	ANNUITY	LIFE ESTATE	REMAINDER
(1)	(2)	(3)	(4)	(1)	(2)	(3)	(4)
0	8.9281	.98209	.01791	55	7.6783	.84461	.15539
1	9.0302	.99333	.00667	56	7.5959	.83555	.16445
2	9.0325	.99357	.00643	57	7.5098	.82608	.17392
3	9.0322	.99354	.00646	58	7.4198	.81618	.18382
4	9.0305	.99335	.00665	59	7.3260	.80586	.19414
5	9.0277	.99305	.00695	60	7.2288	.79517	.20483
6	9.0242	.99267	.00733	61	7.1283	.78411	.21589
7	9.0201	.99221	.00779	62	7.0247	.77272	.22728
8	9.0152	.99167	.00833	63	6.9182	.76100	.23900
9	9.0094	.99103	.00897	64	6.8084	.74893	.25107
10	9.0027	.99029	.00971	65	6.6948	.73643	.26357
11	8.9948	.98943	.01057	66	6.5769	.72346	.27654
12	8.9860	.98846	.01154	67	6.4545	.71000	.29000
13	8.9768	.98745	.01255	68	6.3276	.69604	.30396
14	8.9678	.98646	.01354	69	6.1969	.68165	.31835
15	8.9593	.98552	.01448	70	6.0626	.66689	.33311
16	8.9513	.98464	.01536	71	5.9256	.65182	.34818
17	8.9438	.98382	.01618	72	5.7858	.63644	.36356
18	8.9367	.98303	.01697	73	5.6430	.62073	.37927
19	8.9295	.98225	.01775	74	5.4965	.60462	.39538
20	8.9224	.98146	.01854	75	5.3457	.58802	.41198
21	8.9152	.98067	.01933	76	5.1902	.57092	.42908
22	8.9078	.97986	.02014	77	5.0303	.55333	.44667
23	8.9001	.97901	.02099	78	4.8666	.53532	.46468
24	8.8917	.97808	.02192	79	4.7006	.51706	.48294
25	8.8823	.97705	.02295	80	4.5335	.49868	.50132
26	8.8717	.97589	.02411	81	4.3672	.48039	.51961
27	8.8597	.97457	.02543	82	4.2026	.46229	.53771
28	8.8465	.97311	.02689	83	4.0408	.44449	.55551
29	8.8317	.97149	.02851	84	3.8815	.42696	.57304
30	8.8155	.96970	.03030	85	3.7242	.40966	.59034
31	8.7974	.96772	.03228	86	3.5704	.39275	.60725
32	8.7777	.96554	.03446	87	3.4225	.37648	.62352
33	8.7559	.96315	.03685	88	3.2797	.36077	.63923
34	8.7322	.96054	.03946	89	3.1395	.34534	.65466
35	8.7065	.95771	.04229	90	3.0002	.33002	.66998
36	8.6788	.95467	.04533	91	2.8640	.31504	.68496
37	8.6491	.95140	.04860	92	2.7345	.30080	.69920
38	8.6172	.94789	.05211	93	2.6133	.28746	.71254
39	8.5830	.94413	.05587	94	2.5017	.27519	.72481
40	8.5465	.94011	.05989	95	2.4004	.26405	.73595
41	8.5075	.93582	.06418	96	2.3103	.25414	.74586
42	8.4661	.93127	.06873	97	2.2283	.24511	.75489
43	8.4223	.92645	.07355	98	2.1544	.23698	.76302
44	8.3759	.92135	.07865	99	2.0861	.22947	.77053
45	8.3268	.91594	.08406	100	2.0229	.22252	.77748
46	8.2748	.91023	.08977	101	1.9628	.21591	.78409
47	8.2201	.90421	.09579	102	1.9003	.20903	.79097
48	8.1625	.89787	.10213	103	1.8341	.20175	.79825
49	8.1023	.89126	.10874	104	1.7606	.19367	.80633
50	8.0395	.88435	.11565	105	1.6693	.18362	.81638
51	7.9739	.87712	.12288	106	1.5350	.16885	.83115
52	7.9049	.86954	.13046	107	1.3367	.14703	.85297
53	7.8326	.86159	.13841	108	1.0045	.11050	.88950
54	7.7571	.85329	.14671	109	0.4505	.04955	.95045

TABLE 9 *Continued (tenth of 12 pages)*

TABLE S(12.0)
SINGLE LIFE, 12.0 PERCENT, BASED ON LIFE TABLE 80CNSMT
SHOWING THE PRESENT WORTH OF AN ANNUITY, OF A LIFE ESTATE,
AND OF A REMAINDER INTEREST

AGE	ANNUITY	LIFE ESTATE	REMAINDER	AGE	ANNUITY	LIFE ESTATE	REMAINDER
(1)	(2)	(3)	(4)	(1)	(2)	(3)	(4)
0	8.1918	.98302	.01698	55	7.1710	.86052	.13948
1	8.2855	.99426	.00574	56	7.1001	.85201	.14799
2	8.2880	.99456	.00544	57	7.0256	.84308	.15692
3	8.2882	.99459	.00541	58	6.9477	.83372	.16628
4	8.2872	.99446	.00554	59	6.8661	.82394	.17606
5	8.2852	.99422	.00578	60	6.7814	.81376	.18624
6	8.2826	.99392	.00608	61	6.6935	.80322	.19678
7	8.2795	.99354	.00646	62	6.6028	.79233	.20767
8	8.2757	.99308	.00692	63	6.5092	.78110	.21890
9	8.2711	.99253	.00747	64	6.4125	.76950	.23050
10	8.2657	.99188	.00812	65	6.3122	.75746	.24254
11	8.2593	.99111	.00889	66	6.2077	.74493	.25507
12	8.2521	.99025	.00975	67	6.0989	.73187	.26813
13	8.2445	.98933	.01067	68	5.9857	.71829	.28171
14	8.2371	.98845	.01155	69	5.8687	.70424	.29576
15	8.2301	.98762	.01238	70	5.7482	.68979	.31021
16	8.2237	.98685	.01315	71	5.6250	.67500	.32500
17	8.2179	.98614	.01386	72	5.4988	.65985	.34015
18	8.2123	.98548	.01452	73	5.3696	.64435	.35565
19	8.2069	.98483	.01517	74	5.2366	.62839	.37161
20	8.2015	.98418	.01582	75	5.0993	.61191	.38809
21	8.1962	.98354	.01646	76	4.9571	.59486	.40514
22	8.1908	.98289	.01711	77	4.8105	.57726	.42274
23	8.1851	.98222	.01778	78	4.6598	.55918	.44082
24	8.1790	.98147	.01853	79	4.5065	.54078	.45922
25	8.1720	.98064	.01936	80	4.3517	.52221	.47779
26	8.1641	.97969	.02031	81	4.1972	.50367	.49633
27	8.1550	.97860	.02140	82	4.0440	.48528	.51472
28	8.1449	.97738	.02262	83	3.8929	.46715	.53285
29	8.1335	.97602	.02398	84	3.7438	.44926	.55074
30	8.1208	.97450	.02550	85	3.5962	.43155	.56845
31	8.1067	.97280	.02720	86	3.4516	.41420	.58580
32	8.0911	.97093	.02907	87	3.3123	.39747	.60253
33	8.0738	.96885	.03115	88	3.1775	.38129	.61871
34	8.0548	.96658	.03342	89	3.0447	.36537	.63463
35	8.0341	.96409	.03591	90	2.9126	.34951	.65049
36	8.0118	.96141	.03859	91	2.7830	.33396	.66604
37	7.9877	.95852	.04148	92	2.6596	.31915	.68085
38	7.9617	.95540	.04460	93	2.5438	.30526	.69474
39	7.9337	.95205	.04795	94	2.4371	.29245	.70755
40	7.9037	.94845	.05155	95	2.3401	.28081	.71919
41	7.8716	.94459	.05541	96	2.2538	.27045	.72955
42	7.8374	.94048	.05952	97	2.1751	.26101	.73899
43	7.8010	.93613	.06387	98	2.1042	.25250	.74750
44	7.7624	.93149	.06851	99	2.0387	.24465	.75535
45	7.7214	.92657	.07343	100	1.9781	.23737	.76263
46	7.6779	.92135	.07865	101	1.9206	.23047	.76953
47	7.6319	.91583	.08417	102	1.8608	.22329	.77671
48	7.5834	.91001	.08999	103	1.7975	.21570	.78430
49	7.5326	.90391	.09609	104	1.7273	.20727	.79273
50	7.4794	.89753	.10247	105	1.6398	.19678	.80322
51	7.4237	.89085	.10915	106	1.5105	.18126	.81874
52	7.3651	.88381	.11619	107	1.3182	.15818	.84182
53	7.3033	.87640	.12360	108	0.9932	.11919	.88081
54	7.2387	.86864	.13136	109	0.4464	.05357	.94643

TABLE 9 *Continued (eleventh of 12 pages)*

TABLE S(13.0)
SINGLE LIFE, 13.0 PERCENT, BASED ON LIFE TABLE 80CNSMT
SHOWING THE PRESENT WORTH OF AN ANNUITY, OF A LIFE ESTATE,
AND OF A REMAINDER INTEREST

AGE	ANNUITY	LIFE ESTATE	REMAINDER	AGE	ANNUITY	LIFE ESTATE	REMAINDER
(1)	(2)	(3)	(4)	(1)	(2)	(3)	(4)
0	7.5670	.98370	.01630	55	6.7221	.87387	.12613
1	7.6534	.99494	.00506	56	6.6606	.86587	.13413
2	7.6559	.99527	.00473	57	6.5958	.85746	.14254
3	7.6565	.99535	.00465	58	6.5278	.84861	.15139
4	7.6559	.99527	.00473	59	6.4564	.83934	.16066
5	7.6545	.99508	.00492	60	6.3821	.82967	.17033
6	7.6525	.99483	.00517	61	6.3048	.81962	.18038
7	7.6501	.99451	.00549	62	6.2248	.80922	.19078
8	7.6471	.99412	.00588	63	6.1421	.79848	.20152
9	7.6434	.99364	.00636	64	6.0565	.78735	.21265
10	7.6389	.99306	.00694	65	5.9675	.77577	.22423
11	7.6336	.99236	.00764	66	5.8744	.76368	.23632
12	7.6275	.99157	.00843	67	5.7773	.75104	.24896
13	7.6210	.99073	.00927	68	5.6758	.73786	.26214
14	7.6148	.98993	.01007	69	5.5707	.72419	.27581
15	7.6090	.98918	.01082	70	5.4621	.71008	.28992
16	7.6038	.98849	.01151	71	5.3508	.69560	.30440
17	7.5990	.98787	.01213	72	5.2365	.68075	.31925
18	7.5946	.98730	.01270	73	5.1192	.66550	.33450
19	7.5904	.98675	.01325	74	4.9981	.64976	.35024
20	7.5862	.98621	.01379	75	4.8727	.63344	.36656
21	7.5822	.98568	.01432	76	4.7424	.61651	.38349
22	7.5781	.98515	.01485	77	4.6075	.59897	.40103
23	7.5740	.98461	.01539	78	4.4685	.58090	.41910
24	7.5693	.98401	.01599	79	4.3265	.56245	.43755
25	7.5641	.98334	.01666	80	4.1829	.54377	.45623
26	7.5581	.98255	.01745	81	4.0390	.52507	.47493
27	7.5511	.98164	.01836	82	3.8960	.50649	.49351
28	7.5432	.98062	.01938	83	3.7547	.48811	.51189
29	7.5343	.97946	.02054	84	3.6149	.46994	.53006
30	7.5243	.97816	.02184	85	3.4762	.45190	.54810
31	7.5130	.97669	.02331	86	3.3400	.43419	.56581
32	7.5005	.97506	.02494	87	3.2084	.41709	.58291
33	7.4865	.97325	.02675	88	3.0810	.40053	.59947
34	7.4711	.97125	.02875	89	2.9552	.38417	.61583
35	7.4542	.96905	.03095	90	2.8296	.36785	.63215
36	7.4360	.96667	.03333	91	2.7063	.35181	.64819
37	7.4161	.96409	.03591	92	2.5885	.33650	.66350
38	7.3947	.96131	.03869	93	2.4778	.32211	.67789
39	7.3715	.95830	.04170	94	2.3756	.30882	.69118
40	7.3466	.95505	.04495	95	2.2826	.29674	.70326
41	7.3197	.95156	.04844	96	2.1998	.28597	.71403
42	7.2911	.94784	.05216	97	2.1243	.27615	.72385
43	7.2606	.94388	.05612	98	2.0562	.26731	.73269
44	7.2282	.93966	.06034	99	1.9934	.25914	.74086
45	7.1935	.93516	.06484	100	1.9352	.25158	.74842
46	7.1568	.93038	.06962	101	1.8801	.24441	.75559
47	7.1177	.92530	.07470	102	1.8228	.23696	.76304
48	7.0764	.91994	.08006	103	1.7622	.22909	.77091
49	7.0331	.91430	.08570	104	1.6951	.22036	.77964
50	6.9877	.90840	.09160	105	1.6113	.20946	.79054
51	6.9400	.90220	.09780	106	1.4866	.19326	.80674
52	6.8896	.89565	.10435	107	1.3001	.16901	.83099
53	6.8365	.88874	.11126	108	0.9822	.12768	.87232
54	6.7807	.88149	.11851	109	0.4425	.05752	.94248

TABLE 9 *Concluded (last of 12 pages)*

TABLE S(14.0)
SINGLE LIFE, 14.0 PERCENT, BASED ON LIFE TABLE 80CNSMT
SHOWING THE PRESENT WORTH OF AN ANNUITY, OF A LIFE ESTATE,
AND OF A REMAINDER INTEREST

AGE	ANNUITY	LIFE ESTATE	REMAINDER	AGE	ANNUITY	LIFE ESTATE	REMAINDER
(1)	(2)	(3)	(4)	(1)	(2)	(3)	(4)
0	7.0303	.98424	.01576	55	6.3227	.88518	.11482
1	7.1104	.99546	.00454	56	6.2689	.87765	.12235
2	7.1129	.99581	.00419	57	6.2122	.86971	.13029
3	7.1137	.99592	.00408	58	6.1525	.86134	.13866
4	7.1134	.99588	.00412	59	6.0896	.85255	.14745
5	7.1124	.99573	.00427	60	6.0240	.84336	.15664
6	7.1109	.99552	.00448	61	5.9556	.83378	.16622
7	7.1089	.99525	.00475	62	5.8847	.82386	.17614
8	7.1065	.99491	.00509	63	5.8113	.81358	.18642
9	7.1034	.99448	.00552	64	5.7351	.80292	.19708
10	7.0997	.99396	.00604	65	5.6557	.79179	.20821
11	7.0951	.99332	.00668	66	5.5724	.78014	.21986
12	7.0899	.99259	.00741	67	5.4853	.76794	.23206
13	7.0843	.99181	.00819	68	5.3940	.75516	.24484
14	7.0790	.99106	.00894	69	5.2991	.74188	.25812
15	7.0741	.99037	.00963	70	5.2009	.72813	.27187
16	7.0696	.98975	.01025	71	5.1000	.71400	.28600
17	7.0657	.98919	.01081	72	4.9961	.69946	.30054
18	7.0621	.98870	.01130	73	4.8893	.68450	.31550
19	7.0587	.98822	.01178	74	4.7787	.66902	.33098
20	7.0554	.98776	.01224	75	4.6637	.65292	.34708
21	7.0523	.98732	.01268	76	4.5440	.63616	.36384
22	7.0492	.98688	.01312	77	4.4196	.61874	.38126
23	7.0460	.98645	.01355	78	4.2910	.60074	.39926
24	7.0426	.98596	.01404	79	4.1593	.58230	.41770
25	7.0386	.98540	.01460	80	4.0256	.56358	.43642
26	7.0339	.98475	.01525	81	3.8914	.54480	.45520
27	7.0285	.98399	.01601	82	3.7577	.52608	.47392
28	7.0222	.98311	.01689	83	3.6253	.50754	.49246
29	7.0151	.98212	.01788	84	3.4940	.48916	.51084
30	7.0071	.98100	.01900	85	3.3633	.47087	.52913
31	6.9980	.97972	.02028	86	3.2348	.45287	.54713
32	6.9878	.97830	.02170	87	3.1105	.43547	.56453
33	6.9764	.97669	.02331	88	2.9898	.41858	.58142
34	6.9637	.97492	.02508	89	2.8705	.40187	.59813
35	6.9497	.97296	.02704	90	2.7510	.38515	.61485
36	6.9346	.97084	.02916	91	2.6334	.36868	.63132
37	6.9180	.96853	.03147	92	2.5209	.35292	.64708
38	6.9001	.96602	.03398	93	2.4149	.33809	.66191
39	6.8807	,96330	.03670	94	2.3170	.32437	.67563
40	6.8597	.96036	.03964	95	2.2277	.31188	.68812
41	6.8371	.95719	.04281	96	2.1482	.30075	.69925
42	6.8129	.95380	.04620	97	2.0757	.29059	.70941
43	6.7870	.95019	.04981	98	2.0103	.28144	.71856
44	6.7594	.94632	.05368	99	1.9499	.27298	.72702
45	6.7299	.94219	.05781	100	1.8940	.26516	.73484
46	6.6985	.93779	.06221	101	1.8412	.25777	.74223
47	6.6650	.93310	.06690	102	1.7862	.25007	.74993
48	6.6296	.92814	.07186	103	1.7282	.24195	.75805
49	6.5923	.92292	.07708	104	1.6639	.23295	.76705
50	6.5532	.91744	.08256	105	1.5836	.22171	.77829
51	6.5120	.91168	.08832	106	1.4635	.20489	.79511
52	6.4684	.90558	.09442	107	1.2825	.17955	.82045
53	6.4223	.89912	.10088	108	0.9713	.13599	.86401
54	6.3738	.89233	.10767	109	0.4386	.06140	.93860

TABLE 10 IRS Table B for Present Worth of Annuities, Income Interests, and Remainders for a Term Certain (*first of twelve pages*)

TABLE B
SHOWING THE PRESENT WORTH OF AN ANNUITY, OF AN
INCOME INTEREST, AND OF A REMAINDER INTEREST
FOR A TERM CERTAIN

INTEREST RATE

	3.0%				3.2%		
(1)	(2)	(3)	(4)	(1)	(2)	(3)	(4)
YEARS	ANNUITY	INCOME INTEREST	REMAINDER	YEARS	ANNUITY	INCOME INTEREST	REMAINDER
1	0.9709	.029126	.970874	1	0.9690	.031008	.968992
2	1.9135	.057404	.942596	2	1.9079	.061054	.938946
3	2.8286	.084858	.915142	3	2.8178	.090169	.909831
4	3.7171	.111513	.888487	4	3.6994	.118380	.881620
5	4.5797	.137391	.862609	5	4.5537	.145717	.854283
6	5.4172	.162516	.837484	6	5.3815	.172207	.827793
7	6.2303	.186908	.813092	7	6.1836	.197875	.802125
8	7.0197	.210591	.789409	8	6.9608	.222747	.777253
9	7.7861	.233583	.766417	9	7.7140	.246848	.753152
10	8.5302	.255906	.744094	10	8.4438	.270201	.729799
11	9.2526	.277579	.722421	11	9.1510	.292831	.707169
12	9.9540	.298620	.701380	12	9.8362	.314759	.685241
13	10.6350	.319049	.680951	13	10.5002	.336006	.663994
14	11.2961	.338882	.661118	14	11.1436	.356595	.643405
15	11.9379	.358138	.641862	15	11.7671	.376546	.623454
16	12.5611	.376833	.623167	16	12.3712	.395878	.604122
17	13.1661	.394984	.605016	17	12.9566	.414610	.585390
18	13.7535	.412605	.587395	18	13.5238	.432762	.567238
19	14.3238	.429714	.570286	19	14.0735	.450351	.549649
20	14.8775	.446324	.553676	20	14.6061	.467394	.532606
21	15.4150	.462451	.537549	21	15.1222	.483909	.516091
22	15.9369	.478107	.521893	22	15.6222	.499912	.500088
23	16.4436	.493308	.506692	23	16.1068	.515418	.484582
24	16.9355	.508066	.491934	24	16.5764	.530444	.469556
25	17.4131	.522394	.477606	25	17.0314	.545004	.454996
26	17.8768	.536305	.463695	26	17.4723	.559112	.440888
27	18.3270	.549811	.450189	27	17.8995	.572783	.427217
28	18.7641	.562923	.437077	28	18.3134	.586030	.413970
29	19.1885	.575654	.424346	29	18.7146	.598867	.401133
30	19.6004	.588013	.411987	30	19.1033	.611305	.388695
31	20.0004	.600013	.399987	31	19.4799	.623357	.376643
32	20.3888	.611663	.388337	32	19.8449	.635036	.364964
33	20.7658	.622974	.377026	33	20.1985	.646353	.353647
34	21.1318	.633955	.366045	34	20.5412	.657319	.342681
35	21.4872	.644617	.355383	35	20.8733	.667945	.332055
36	21.8323	.654968	.345032	36	21.1950	.678241	.321759
37	22.1672	.665017	.334983	37	21.5068	.688218	.311782
38	22.4925	.674774	.325226	38	21.8089	.697886	.302114
39	22.8082	.684246	.315754	39	22.1017	.707253	.292747
40	23.1148	.693443	.306557	40	22.3853	.716331	.283669
41	23.4124	.702372	.297628	41	22.6602	.725127	.274873
42	23.7014	.711041	.288959	42	22.9266	.733650	.266350
43	23.9819	.719457	.280543	43	23.1847	.741909	.258091
44	24.2543	.727628	.272372	44	23.4347	.749912	.250088
45	24.5187	.735561	.264439	45	23.6771	.757666	.242334
46	24.7754	.743263	.256737	46	23.9119	.765181	.234819
47	25.0247	.750741	.249259	47	24.1394	.772462	.227538
48	25.2667	.758001	.241999	48	24.3599	.779517	.220483
49	25.5017	.765050	.234950	49	24.5736	.786354	.213646
50	25.7298	.771893	.228107	50	24.7806	.792979	.207021
51	25.9512	.778537	.221463	51	24.9812	.799398	.200602
52	26.1662	.784987	.215013	52	25.1756	.805618	.194382
53	26.3750	.791250	.208750	53	25.3639	.811645	.188355
54	26.5777	.797330	.202670	54	25.5464	.817486	.182514
55	26.7744	.803233	.196767	55	25.7233	.823145	.176855
56	26.9655	.808964	.191036	56	25.8947	.828629	.171371
57	27.1509	.814528	.185472	57	26.0607	.833943	.166057
58	27.3310	.819930	.180070	58	26.2216	.839092	.160908
59	27.5058	.825175	.174825	59	26.3775	.844081	.155919
60	27.6756	.830267	.169733	60	26.5286	.848916	.151084

TABLE 10 *Continued (second of 12 pages)*

TABLE B
SHOWING THE PRESENT WORTH OF AN ANNUITY, OF AN
INCOME INTEREST, AND OF A REMAINDER INTEREST
FOR A TERM CERTAIN

INTEREST RATE

	3.8%				4.0%		
(1)	(2)	(3)	(4)	(1)	(2)	(3)	(4)
YEARS	ANNUITY	INCOME INTEREST	REMAINDER	YEARS	ANNUITY	INCOME INTEREST	REMAINDER
1	0.9634	.036609	.963391	1	0.9615	.038462	.961538
2	1.8915	.071878	.928122	2	1.8861	.075444	.924556
3	2.7857	.105855	.894145	3	2.7751	.111004	.888996
4	3.6471	.138589	.861411	4	3.6299	.145196	.854804
5	4.4769	.170124	.829876	5	4.4518	.178073	.821927
6	5.2764	.200505	.799495	6	5.2421	.209685	.790315
7	6.0467	.229773	.770227	7	6.0021	.240082	.759918
8	6.7887	.257970	.742030	8	6.7327	.269310	.730690
9	7.5036	.285135	.714865	9	7.4353	.297413	.702587
10	8.1923	.311306	.688694	10	8.1109	.324436	.675564
11	8.8557	.336518	.663482	11	8.7605	.350419	.649581
12	9.4949	.360807	.639193	12	9.3851	.375403	.624597
13	10.1107	.384207	.615793	13	9.9856	.399426	.600574
14	10.7040	.406751	.593249	14	10.5631	.422525	.577475
15	11.2755	.428469	.571531	15	11.1184	.444735	.555265
16	11.8261	.449392	.550608	16	11.6523	.466092	.533908
17	12.3566	.469549	.530451	17	12.1657	.486627	.513373
18	12.8676	.488969	.511031	18	12.6593	.506372	.493628
19	13.3599	.507677	.492323	19	13.1339	.525358	.474642
20	13.8342	.525700	.474300	20	13.5903	.543613	.456387
21	14.2912	.543064	.456936	21	14.0292	.561166	.438834
22	14.7314	.559792	.440208	22	14.4511	.578045	.421955
23	15.1555	.575907	.424093	23	14.8568	.594274	.405726
24	15.5640	.591433	.408567	24	15.2470	.609879	.390121
25	15.9576	.606390	.393610	25	15.6221	.624883	.375117
26	16.3368	.620800	.379200	26	15.9828	.639311	.360689
27	16.7021	.634682	.365318	27	16.3296	.653183	.346817
28	17.0541	.648056	.351944	28	16.6631	.666523	.333477
29	17.3932	.660940	.339060	29	16.9837	.679349	.320651
30	17.7198	.673352	.326648	30	17.2920	.691681	.308319
31	18.0345	.685311	.314689	31	17.5885	.703540	.296460
32	18.3377	.696831	.303169	32	17.8736	.714942	.285058
33	18.6297	.707930	.292070	33	18.1476	.725906	.274094
34	18.9111	.718622	.281378	34	18.4112	.736448	.263552
35	19.1822	.728923	.271077	35	18.6646	.746585	.253415
36	19.4433	.738847	.261153	36	18.9083	.756331	.243669
37	19.6949	.748407	.251593	37	19.1426	.765703	.234297
38	19.9373	.757618	.242382	38	19.3679	.774715	.225285
39	20.1708	.766491	.233509	39	19.5845	.783379	.216621
40	20.3958	.775040	.224960	40	19.7928	.791711	.208289
41	20.6125	.783275	.216725	41	19.9931	.799722	.200278
42	20.8213	.791209	.208791	42	20.1856	.807425	.192575
43	21.0224	.798853	.201147	43	20.3708	.814832	.185168
44	21.2162	.806217	.193783	44	20.5488	.821954	.178046
45	21.4029	.813311	.186689	45	20.7200	.828802	.171198
46	21.5828	.820145	.179855	46	20.8847	.835386	.164614
47	21.7560	.826730	.173270	47	21.0429	.841717	.158283
48	21.9230	.833073	.166927	48	21.1951	.847805	.152195
49	22.0838	.839184	.160816	49	21.3415	.853659	.146341
50	22.2387	.845071	.154929	50	21.4822	.859287	.140713
51	22.3880	.850743	.149257	51	21.6175	.864699	.135301
52	22.5318	.856207	.143793	52	21.7476	.869903	.130097
53	22.6703	.861471	.138529	53	21.8727	.874907	.125093
54	22.8038	.866543	.133457	54	21.9930	.879718	.120282
55	22.9323	.871428	.128572	55	22.1086	.884344	.115656
56	23.0562	.876135	.123865	56	22.2198	.888793	.111207
57	23.1755	.880670	.119330	57	22.3267	.893070	.106930
58	23.2905	.885038	.114962	58	22.4296	.897183	.102817
59	23.4012	.889247	.110753	59	22.5284	.901137	.098863
60	23.5079	.893301	.106699	60	22.6235	.904940	.095060

TABLE 10 *Continued (third of 12 pages)*

TABLE B
SHOWING THE PRESENT WORTH OF AN ANNUITY, OF AN
INCOME INTEREST, AND OF A REMAINDER INTEREST
FOR A TERM CERTAIN

INTEREST RATE

	5.0%				5.2%		
(1)	(2)	(3)	(4)	(1)	(2)	(3)	(4)
		INCOME				INCOME	
YEARS	ANNUITY	INTEREST	REMAINDER	YEARS	ANNUITY	INTEREST	REMAINDER
1	0.9524	.047619	.952381	1	0.9506	.049430	.950570
2	1.8594	.092971	.907029	2	1.8542	.096416	.903584
3	2.7232	.136162	.863838	3	2.7131	.141080	.858920
4	3.5460	.177298	.822702	4	3.5295	.183536	.816464
5	4.3295	.216474	.783526	5	4.3056	.223894	.776106
6	5.0757	.253785	.746215	6	5.0434	.262256	.737744
7	5.7864	.289319	.710681	7	5.7447	.298723	.701277
8	6.4632	.323161	.676839	8	6.4113	.333387	.666613
9	7.1078	.355391	.644609	9	7.0449	.366337	.633663
10	7.7217	.386087	.613913	10	7.6473	.397659	.602341
11	8.3064	.415321	.584679	11	8.2199	.427432	.572568
12	8.8633	.443163	.556837	12	8.7641	.455734	.544266
13	9.3936	.469679	.530321	13	9.2815	.482637	.517363
14	9.8986	.494932	.505068	14	9.7733	.508210	.491790
15	10.3797	.518983	.481017	15	10.2408	.532519	.467481
16	10.8378	.541888	.458112	16	10.6851	.555626	.444374
17	11.2741	.563703	.436297	17	11.1075	.577592	.422408
18	11.6896	.584479	.415521	18	11.5091	.598471	.401529
19	12.0853	.604266	.395734	19	11.8907	.618319	.381681
20	12.4622	.623111	.376889	20	12.2536	.637185	.362815
21	12.8212	.641058	.358942	21	12.5984	.655119	.344881
22	13.1630	.658150	.341850	22	12.9263	.672166	.327834
23	13.4886	.674429	.325571	23	13.2379	.688371	.311629
24	13.7986	.689932	.310068	24	13.5341	.703775	.296225
25	14.0939	.704697	.295303	25	13.8157	.718417	.281583
26	14.3752	.718759	.281241	26	14.0834	.732336	.267664
27	14.6430	.732152	.267848	27	14.3378	.745566	.254434
28	14.8981	.744906	.255094	28	14.5797	.758143	.241857
29	15.1411	.757054	.242946	29	14.8096	.770098	.229902
30	15.3725	.768623	.231377	30	15.0281	.781462	.218538
31	15.5928	.779641	.220359	31	15.2358	.792264	.207736
32	15.8027	.790134	.209866	32	15.4333	.802532	.197468
33	16.0025	.800127	.199873	33	15.6210	.812293	.187707
34	16.1929	.809645	.190355	34	15.7994	.821571	.178429
35	16.3742	.818710	.181290	35	15.9691	.830391	.169609
36	16.5469	.827343	.172657	36	16.1303	.838775	.161225
37	16.7113	.835564	.164436	37	16.2835	.846744	.153256
38	16.8679	.843395	.156605	38	16.4292	.854319	.145681
39	17.0170	.850852	.149148	39	16.5677	.861520	.138480
40	17.1591	.857954	.142046	40	16.6993	.868365	.131635
41	17.2944	.864718	.135282	41	16.8245	.874872	.125128
42	17.4232	.871160	.128840	42	16.9434	.881057	.118943
43	17.5459	.877296	.122704	43	17.0565	.886936	.113064
44	17.6628	.883139	.116861	44	17.1639	.892525	.107475
45	17.7741	.888703	.111297	45	17.2661	.897837	.102163
46	17.8801	.894003	.105997	46	17.3632	.902887	.097113
47	17.9810	.899051	.100949	47	17.4555	.907688	.092312
48	18.0772	.903858	.096142	48	17.5433	.912251	.087749
49	18.1687	.908436	.091564	49	17.6267	.916588	.083412
50	18.2559	.912796	.087204	50	17.7060	.920711	.079289
51	18.3390	.916949	.083051	51	17.7814	.924630	.075370
52	18.4181	.920904	.079096	52	17.8530	.928356	.071644
53	18.4934	.924670	.075330	53	17.9211	.931897	.068103
54	18.5651	.928257	.071743	54	17.9858	.935263	.064737
55	18.6335	.931674	.068326	55	18.0474	.938463	.061537
56	18.6985	.934927	.065073	56	18.1059	.941505	.058495
57	18.7605	.938026	.061974	57	18.1615	.944396	.055604
58	18.8195	.940977	.059023	58	18.2143	.947145	.052855
59	18.8758	.943788	.056212	59	18.2646	.949757	.050243
60	18.9293	.946464	.053536	60	18.3123	.952241	.047759

TABLE 10 *Continued (fourth of 12 pages)*

TABLE B
SHOWING THE PRESENT WORTH OF AN ANNUITY, OF AN
INCOME INTEREST, AND OF A REMAINDER INTEREST
FOR A TERM CERTAIN

INTEREST RATE

	5.8%				6.0%		
(1)	(2)	(3)	(4)	(1)	(2)	(3)	(4)
YEARS	ANNUITY	INCOME INTEREST	REMAINDER	YEARS	ANNUITY	INCOME INTEREST	REMAINDER
1	0.9452	.054820	.945180	1	0.9434	.056604	.943396
2	1.8385	.106636	.893364	2	1.8334	.110004	.889996
3	2.6829	.155610	.844390	3	2.6730	.160381	.839619
4	3.4810	.201900	.798100	4	3.4651	.207906	.792094
5	4.2354	.245652	.754348	5	4.2124	.252742	.747258
6	4.9484	.287006	.712994	6	4.9173	.295039	.704961
7	5.6223	.326092	.673908	7	5.5824	.334943	.665057
8	6.2592	.363036	.636964	8	6.2098	.372588	.627412
9	6.8613	.397955	.602045	9	6.8017	.408102	.591898
10	7.4303	.430959	.569041	10	7.3601	.441605	.558395
11	7.9682	.462154	.537846	11	7.8869	.473212	.526788
12	8.4765	.491639	.508361	12	8.3838	.503031	.496969
13	8.9570	.519508	.480492	13	8.8527	.531161	.468839
14	9.4112	.545849	.454151	14	9.2950	.557699	.442301
15	9.8404	.570745	.429255	15	9.7122	.582735	.417265
16	10.2462	.594277	.405723	16	10.1059	.606354	.393646
17	10.6296	.616519	.383481	17	10.4773	.628636	.371364
18	10.9921	.637542	.362458	18	10.8276	.649656	.350344
19	11.3347	.657412	.342588	19	11.1581	.669487	.330513
20	11.6585	.676193	.323807	20	11.4699	.688195	.311805
21	11.9646	.693944	.306056	21	11.7641	.705845	.294155
22	12.2538	.710722	.289278	22	12.0416	.722495	.277505
23	12.5272	.726580	.273420	23	12.3034	.738203	.261797
24	12.7857	.741569	.258431	24	12.5504	.753021	.246979
25	13.0299	.755737	.244263	25	12.7834	.767001	.232999
26	13.2608	.769127	.230873	26	13.0032	.780190	.219810
27	13.4790	.781784	.218216	27	13.2105	.792632	.207368
28	13.6853	.793747	.206253	28	13.4062	.804370	.195630
29	13.8802	.805053	.194947	29	13.5907	.815443	.184557
30	14.0645	.815740	.184260	30	13.7648	.825890	.174110
31	14.2386	.825842	.174158	31	13.9291	.835745	.164255
32	14.4033	.835389	.164611	32	14.0840	.845043	.154957
33	14.5588	.844413	.155587	33	14.2302	.853814	.146186
34	14.7059	.852942	.147058	34	14.3681	.862088	.137912
35	14.8449	.861004	.138996	35	14.4982	.869895	.130105
36	14.9763	.868624	.131376	36	14.6210	.877259	.122741
37	15.1005	.875826	.124174	37	14.7368	.884207	.115793
38	15.2178	.882633	.117367	38	14.8460	.890761	.109239
39	15.3287	.889067	.110933	39	14.9491	.896944	.103056
40	15.4336	.895149	.104851	40	15.0463	.902778	.097222
41	15.5327	.900897	.099103	41	15.1380	.908281	.091719
42	15.6264	.906330	.093670	42	15.2245	.913473	.086527
43	15.7149	.911465	.088535	43	15.3062	.918370	.081630
44	15.7986	.916318	.083682	44	15.3832	.922991	.077009
45	15.8777	.920906	.079094	45	15.4558	.927350	.072650
46	15.9524	.925242	.074758	46	15.5244	.931462	.068538
47	16.0231	.929340	.070660	47	15.5890	.935342	.064658
48	16.0899	.933214	.066786	48	15.6500	.939002	.060998
49	16.1530	.936875	.063125	49	15.7076	.942454	.057546
50	16.2127	.940335	.059665	50	15.7619	.945712	.054288
51	16.2691	.943606	.056394	51	15.8131	.948785	.051215
52	16.3224	.946698	.053302	52	15.8614	.951684	.048316
53	16.3728	.949620	.050380	53	15.9070	.954418	.045582
54	16.4204	.952382	.047618	54	15.9500	.956999	.043001
55	16.4654	.954992	.045008	55	15.9905	.959433	.040567
56	16.5079	.957459	.042541	56	16.0288	.961729	.038271
57	16.5481	.959792	.040208	57	16.0649	.963895	.036105
58	16.5861	.961996	.038004	58	16.0990	.965939	.034061
59	16.6221	.964079	.035921	59	16.1311	.967867	.032133
60	16.6560	.966048	.033952	60	16.1614	.969686	.030314

TABLE 10 *Continued (fifth of 12 pages)*

TABLE B

**SHOWING THE PRESENT WORTH OF AN ANNUITY, OF AN
INCOME INTEREST, AND OF A REMAINDER INTEREST
FOR A TERM CERTAIN**

INTEREST RATE

		7.0%					7.2%		
(1)	(2)	(3)	(4)		(1)	(2)	(3)	(4)	
YEARS	ANNUITY	INCOME INTEREST	REMAINDER		YEARS	ANNUITY	INCOME INTEREST	REMAINDER	
1	0.9346	.065421	.934579		1	0.9328	.067164	.932836	
2	1.8080	.126561	.873439		2	1.8030	.129817	.870183	
3	2.6243	.183702	.816298		3	2.6148	.188262	.811738	
4	3.3872	.237105	.762895		4	3.3720	.242782	.757218	
5	4.1002	.287014	.712986		5	4.0783	.293640	.706360	
6	4.7665	.333658	.666342		6	4.7373	.341082	.658918	
7	5.3893	.377250	.622750		7	5.3519	.385338	.614662	
8	5.9713	.417991	.582009		8	5.9253	.426621	.573379	
9	6.5152	.456066	.543934		9	6.4602	.465132	.534868	
10	7.0236	.491651	.508349		10	6.9591	.501056	.498944	
11	7.4987	.524907	.475093		11	7.4245	.534567	.465433	
12	7.9427	.555988	.444012		12	7.8587	.565827	.434173	
13	8.3577	.585036	.414964		13	8.2637	.594988	.405012	
14	8.7455	.612183	.387817		14	8.6415	.622190	.377810	
15	9.1079	.637554	.362446		15	8.9940	.647566	.352434	
16	9.4466	.661265	.338735		16	9.3227	.671237	.328763	
17	9.7632	.683426	.316574		17	9.6294	.693318	.306682	
18	10.0591	.704136	.295864		18	9.9155	.713916	.286084	
19	10.3356	.723492	.276508		19	10.1824	.733130	.266870	
20	10.5940	.741581	.258419		20	10.4313	.751054	.248946	
21	10.8355	.758487	.241513		21	10.6635	.767775	.232225	
22	11.0612	.774287	.225713		22	10.8802	.783372	.216628	
23	11.2722	.789053	.210947		23	11.0822	.797922	.202078	
24	11.4693	.802853	.197147		24	11.2708	.811494	.188506	
25	11.6536	.815751	.184249		25	11.4466	.824155	.175845	
26	11.8258	.827805	.172195		26	11.6106	.835965	.164035	
27	11.9867	.839070	.160930		27	11.7636	.846983	.153017	
28	12.1371	.849598	.150402		28	11.9064	.857260	.142740	
29	12.2777	.859437	.140563		29	12.0395	.866847	.133153	
30	12.4090	.868633	.131367		30	12.1638	.875790	.124210	
31	12.5318	.877227	.122773		31	12.2796	.884132	.115868	
32	12.6466	.885259	.114741		32	12.3877	.891915	.108085	
33	12.7538	.892765	.107235		33	12.4885	.899174	.100826	
34	12.8540	.899781	.100219		34	12.5826	.905946	.094054	
35	12.9477	.906337	.093663		35	12.6703	.912263	.087737	
36	13.0352	.912465	.087535		36	12.7522	.918156	.081844	
37	13.1170	.918191	.081809		37	12.8285	.923653	.076347	
38	13.1935	.923543	.076457		38	12.8997	.928781	.071219	
39	13.2649	.928545	.071455		39	12.9662	.933564	.066436	
40	13.3317	.933220	.066780		40	13.0281	.938026	.061974	
41	13.3941	.937588	.062412		41	13.0860	.942189	.057811	
42	13.4524	.941671	.058329		42	13.1399	.946071	.053929	
43	13.5070	.945487	.054513		43	13.1902	.949693	.050307	
44	13.5579	.949054	.050946		44	13.2371	.953072	.046928	
45	13.6055	.952387	.047613		45	13.2809	.956224	.043776	
46	13.6500	.955501	.044499		46	13.3217	.959164	.040836	
47	13.6916	.958413	.041587		47	13.3598	.961907	.038093	
48	13.7305	.961133	.038867		48	13.3954	.964465	.035535	
49	13.7668	.963676	.036324		49	13.4285	.966852	.033148	
50	13.8007	.966052	.033948		50	13.4594	.969078	.030922	
51	13.8325	.968273	.031727		51	13.4883	.971155	.028845	
52	13.8621	.970349	.029651		52	13.5152	.973093	.026907	
53	13.8898	.972289	.027711		53	13.5403	.974900	.025100	
54	13.9157	.974101	.025899		54	13.5637	.976586	.023414	
55	13.9399	.975796	.024204		55	13.5855	.978158	.021842	
56	13.9626	.977379	.022621		56	13.6059	.979625	.020375	
57	13.9837	.978859	.021141		57	13.6249	.980994	.019006	
58	14.0035	.980242	.019758		58	13.6426	.982270	.017730	
59	14.0219	.981535	.018465		59	13.6592	.983461	.016539	
60	14.0392	.982743	.017257		60	13.6746	.984572	.015428	

TABLE 10 *Continued (sixth of 12 pages)*

TABLE B
**SHOWING THE PRESENT WORTH OF AN ANNUITY, OF AN
INCOME INTEREST, AND OF A REMAINDER INTEREST
FOR A TERM CERTAIN**

INTEREST RATE

	7.8%				8.0%		
(1)	(2)	(3)	(4)	(1)	(2)	(3)	(4)
		INCOME				INCOME	
YEARS	ANNUITY	INTEREST	REMAINDER	YEARS	ANNUITY	INTEREST	REMAINDER
1	0.9276	.072356	.927644	1	0.9259	.074074	.925926
2	1.7882	.139477	.860523	2	1.7833	.142661	.857339
3	2.5864	.201741	.798259	3	2.5771	.206168	.793832
4	3.3269	.259500	.740500	4	3.3121	.264970	.735030
5	4.0138	.313080	.686920	5	3.9927	.319417	.680503
6	4.6511	.362783	.637217	6	4.6229	.369830	.630170
7	5.2422	.408889	.591111	7	5.2064	.416510	.583490
8	5.7905	.451660	.548340	8	5.7466	.459731	.540269
9	6.2992	.491336	.508664	9	6.2469	.499751	.500249
10	6.7710	.528141	.471859	10	6.7101	.536807	.463193
11	7.2088	.562283	.437717	11	7.1390	.571117	.428883
12	7.6148	.593954	.406046	12	7.5361	.602886	.397114
13	7.9915	.623334	.376666	13	7.9038	.632302	.367698
14	8.3409	.650588	.349412	14	8.2242	.659539	.340461
15	8.6650	.675870	.324130	15	8.5595	.684758	.315242
16	8.9657	.699323	.300677	16	8.8514	.708110	.291890
17	9.2446	.721079	.278921	17	9.1216	.729731	.270269
18	9.5033	.741261	.258739	18	9.3719	.749751	.250249
19	9.7434	.759982	.240018	19	9.6036	.768288	.231712
20	9.9660	.777349	.222651	20	9.8181	.785452	.214548
21	10.1726	.793459	.206541	21	10.0168	.801344	.198656
22	10.3641	.808404	.191596	22	10.2007	.816059	.183941
23	10.5419	.822267	.177733	23	10.3711	.829685	.170315
24	10.7068	.835127	.164873	24	10.5288	.842301	.157699
25	10.8597	.847057	.152943	25	10.6748	.853982	.146018
26	11.0016	.858123	.141877	26	10.8100	.864798	.135202
27	11.1332	.868389	.131611	27	10.9352	.874813	.125187
28	11.2553	.877912	.122088	28	11.0511	.884086	.115914
29	11.3685	.886745	.113255	29	11.1584	.892672	.107328
30	11.4736	.894940	.105060	30	11.2578	.900623	.099377
31	11.5710	.902542	.097458	31	11.3498	.907984	.092016
32	11.6615	.909594	.090406	32	11.4350	.914800	.085200
33	11.7453	.916135	.083865	33	11.5139	.921111	.078889
34	11.8231	.922203	.077797	34	11.5869	.926955	.073045
35	11.8953	.927832	.072168	35	11.6546	.932365	.067635
36	11.9622	.933054	.066946	36	11.7172	.937375	.062625
37	12.0243	.937898	.062102	37	11.7752	.942014	.057986
38	12.0819	.942391	.057609	38	11.8289	.946310	.053690
39	12.1354	.946560	.053440	39	11.8786	.950287	.049713
40	12.1850	.950427	.049573	40	11.9246	.953969	.046031
41	12.2309	.954013	.045987	41	11.9672	.957379	.042621
42	12.2736	.957341	.042659	42	12.0067	.960536	.039464
43	12.3132	.960428	.039572	43	12.0432	.963459	.036541
44	12.3499	.963291	.036709	44	12.0771	.966166	.033834
45	12.3839	.965947	.034053	45	12.1084	.968672	.031328
46	12.4155	.968411	.031589	46	12.1374	.970993	.029007
47	12.4448	.970697	.029303	47	12.1643	.973141	.026859
48	12.4720	.972817	.027183	48	12.1891	.975131	.024869
49	12.4972	.974784	.025216	49	12.2122	.976973	.023027
50	12.5206	.976608	.023392	50	12.2335	.978679	.021321
51	12.5423	.978301	.021699	51	12.2532	.980258	.019742
52	12.5624	.979871	.020129	52	12.2715	.981720	.018280
53	12.5811	.981327	.018673	53	12.2884	.983075	.016925
54	12.5984	.982678	.017322	54	12.3041	.984328	.015672
55	12.6145	.983932	.016068	55	12.3186	.985489	.014511
56	12.6294	.985094	.014906	56	12.3321	.986564	.013436
57	12.6432	.986173	.013827	57	12.3445	.987559	.012441
58	12.6561	.987173	.012827	58	12.3560	.988481	.011519
59	12.6680	.988101	.011899	59	12.3667	.989334	.010666
60	12.6790	.988962	.011038	60	12.3766	.990124	.009876

TABLE 10 *Continued (seventh of 12 pages)*

TABLE B

**SHOWING THE PRESENT WORTH OF AN ANNUITY, OF AN
INCOME INTEREST, AND OF A REMAINDER INTEREST
FOR A TERM CERTAIN**

INTEREST RATE

	9.0%				9.2%		
(1)	(2)	(3)	(4)	(1)	(2)	(3)	(4)
		INCOME				INCOME	
YEARS	ANNUITY	INTEREST	REMAINDER	YEARS	ANNUITY	INTEREST	REMAINDER
1	0.9174	.082569	.917431	1	0.9158	.084249	.915751
2	1.7591	.158320	.841680	2	1.7544	.161400	.838600
3	2.5313	.227817	.772183	3	2.5223	.232052	.767948
4	3.2397	.291575	.708425	4	3.2255	.296750	.703250
5	3.8897	.350069	.649931	5	3.8696	.355999	.644001
6	4.4859	.403733	.596267	6	4.4593	.410255	.589745
7	5.0330	.452966	.547034	7	4.9994	.459941	.540059
8	5.5348	.498134	.501866	8	5.4939	.505440	.494560
9	5.9952	.539572	.460428	9	5.9468	.547106	.452894
10	6.4177	.577589	.422411	10	6.3615	.585262	.414738
11	6.8052	.612467	.387533	11	6.7413	.620203	.379797
12	7.1607	.644465	.355535	12	7.0891	.652201	.347799
13	7.4869	.673821	.326179	13	7.4076	.681503	.318497
14	7.7862	.700754	.299246	14	7.6993	.708336	.291664
15	8.0607	.725462	.274538	15	7.9664	.732908	.267092
16	8.3126	.748130	.251870	16	8.2110	.755411	.244589
17	8.5436	.768927	.231073	17	8.4350	.776017	.223983
18	8.7556	.788006	.211994	18	8.6401	.794887	.205113
19	8.9501	.805510	.194490	19	8.8279	.812168	.187832
20	9.1285	.821569	.178431	20	8.9999	.827993	.172007
21	9.2922	.836302	.163698	21	9.1574	.842484	.157516
22	9.4424	.849818	.150182	22	9.3017	.855755	.144245
23	9.5802	.862219	.137781	23	9.4338	.867907	.132093
24	9.7066	.873595	.126405	24	9.5547	.879036	.120964
25	9.8226	.884032	.115968	25	9.6655	.889227	.110773
26	9.9290	.893607	.106393	26	9.7670	.898559	.101441
27	10.0266	.902392	.097608	27	9.8598	.907106	.092894
28	10.1161	.910452	.089548	28	9.9449	.914932	.085068
29	10.1983	.917845	.082155	29	10.0228	.922099	.077901
30	10.2737	.924629	.075371	30	10.0942	.928662	.071338
31	10.3428	.930852	.069148	31	10.1595	.934672	.065328
32	10.4062	.936562	.063438	32	10.2193	.940176	.059824
33	10.4644	.941800	.058200	33	10.2741	.945216	.054784
34	10.5178	.946605	.053395	34	10.3243	.949832	.050168
35	10.5668	.951014	.048986	35	10.3702	.954058	.045942
36	10.6118	.955059	.044941	36	10.4123	.957929	.042071
37	10.6530	.958769	.041231	37	10.4508	.961473	.038527
38	10.6908	.962174	.037826	38	10.4861	.964719	.035281
39	10.7255	.965297	.034703	39	10.5184	.967691	.032309
40	10.7574	.968162	.031838	40	10.5480	.970413	.029587
41	10.7866	.970791	.029209	41	10.5751	.972906	.027094
42	10.8134	.973203	.026797	42	10.5999	.975189	.024811
43	10.8380	.975416	.024584	43	10.6226	.977279	.022721
44	10.8605	.977445	.022555	44	10.6434	.979193	.020807
45	10.8812	.979308	.020692	45	10.6625	.980946	.019054
46	10.9002	.981016	.018984	46	10.6799	.982551	.017449
47	10.9176	.982584	.017416	47	10.6959	.984022	.015978
48	10.9336	.984022	.015978	48	10.7105	.985368	.014632
49	10.9482	.985341	.014659	49	10.7239	.986600	.013400
50	10.9617	.986551	.013449	50	10.7362	.987729	.012271
51	10.9740	.987662	.012338	51	10.7474	.988763	.011237
52	10.9853	.988681	.011319	52	10.7577	.989710	.010290
53	10.9957	.989615	.010385	53	10.7671	.990577	.009423
54	11.0053	.990473	.009527	54	10.7758	.991371	.008629
55	11.0140	.991259	.008741	55	10.7837	.992098	.007902
56	11.0220	.991981	.008019	56	10.7909	.992763	.007237
57	11.0294	.992643	.007357	57	10.7975	.993373	.006627
58	11.0361	.993251	.006749	58	10.8036	.993931	.006069
59	11.0423	.993808	.006192	59	10.8092	.994443	.005557
60	11.0480	.994319	.005681	60	10.8142	.994911	.005089

TABLE 10 *Continued (eighth of 12 pages)*

TABLE B
SHOWING THE PRESENT WORTH OF AN ANNUITY, OF AN
INCOME INTEREST, AND OF A REMAINDER INTEREST
FOR A TERM CERTAIN

INTEREST RATE

	9.8%				10.0%		
(1)	(2)	(3)	(4)	(1)	(2)	(3)	(4)
		INCOME				INCOME	
YEARS	ANNUITY	INTEREST	REMAINDER	YEARS	ANNUITY	INTEREST	REMAINDER
1	0.9107	.089253	.910747	1	0.9091	.090909	.909091
2	1.7402	.170540	.829460	2	1.7355	.173554	.826446
3	2.4956	.244572	.755428	3	2.4869	.248685	.751315
4	3.1836	.311997	.688003	4	3.1699	.316987	.683013
5	3.8102	.373403	.626597	5	3.7908	.379079	.620921
6	4.3809	.429329	.570671	6	4.3553	.435526	.564474
7	4.9006	.480263	.519737	7	4.8684	.486842	.513158
8	5.3740	.526651	.473349	8	5.3349	.533493	.466507
9	5.8051	.568899	.431101	9	5.7590	.575902	.424098
10	6.1977	.607376	.392624	10	6.1446	.614457	.385543
11	6.5553	.642419	.357581	11	6.4951	.649506	.350494
12	6.8810	.674334	.325666	12	6.8137	.681369	.318631
13	7.1776	.703401	.296599	13	7.1034	.710336	.289664
14	7.4477	.729873	.270127	14	7.3667	.736669	.263331
15	7.6937	.753983	.246017	15	7.6061	.760608	.239392
16	7.9178	.775941	.224059	16	7.8237	.782371	.217629
17	8.1218	.795939	.204061	17	8.0216	.802155	.197845
18	8.3077	.814152	.185848	18	8.2014	.820141	.179859
19	8.4769	.830740	.169260	19	8.3649	.836492	.163508
20	8.6311	.845847	.154153	20	8.5136	.851356	.148644
21	8.7715	.859605	.140395	21	8.6487	.864869	.135131
22	8.8993	.872136	.127864	22	8.7715	.877154	.122846
23	9.0158	.883548	.116452	23	8.8832	.888322	.111678
24	9.1219	.893942	.106058	24	8.9847	.898474	.101526
25	9.2184	.903408	.096592	25	9.0770	.907704	.092296
26	9.3064	.912029	.087971	26	9.1609	.916095	.083905
27	9.3865	.919881	.080119	27	9.2372	.923722	.076278
28	9.4595	.927032	.072968	28	9.3066	.930657	.069343
29	9.5260	.933544	.066456	29	9.3696	.936961	.063039
30	9.5865	.939476	.060524	30	9.4269	.942691	.057309
31	9.6416	.944878	.055122	31	9.4790	.947901	.052099
32	9.6918	.949798	.050202	32	9.5264	.952638	.047362
33	9.7375	.954278	.045722	33	9.5694	.956943	.043057
34	9.7792	.958359	.041641	34	9.6086	.960857	.039143
35	9.8171	.962076	.037924	35	9.6442	.964416	.035584
36	9.8516	.965461	.034539	36	9.6765	.967651	.032349
37	9.8831	.968543	.031457	37	9.7059	.970592	.029408
38	9.9117	.971351	.028649	38	9.7327	.973265	.026735
39	9.9378	.973908	.026092	39	9.7570	.975696	.024304
40	9.9616	.976237	.023763	40	9.7791	.977905	.022095
41	9.9832	.978358	.021642	41	9.7991	.979914	.020086
42	10.0030	.980289	.019711	42	9.8174	.981740	.018260
43	10.0209	.982049	.017951	43	9.8340	.983400	.016600
44	10.0373	.983651	.016349	44	9.8491	.984909	.015091
45	10.0521	.985110	.014890	45	9.8628	.986281	.013719
46	10.0657	.986439	.013561	46	9.8753	.987528	.012472
47	10.0781	.987649	.012351	47	9.8866	.988662	.011338
48	10.0893	.988752	.011248	48	9.8969	.989693	.010307
49	10.0995	.989756	.010244	49	9.9063	.990630	.009370
50	10.1089	.990670	.009330	50	9.9148	.991481	.008519
51	10.1174	.991503	.008497	51	9.9226	.992256	.007744
52	10.1251	.992261	.007739	52	9.9296	.992960	.007040
53	10.1322	.992952	.007048	53	9.9360	.993600	.006400
54	10.1386	.993581	.006419	54	9.9418	.994182	.005818
55	10.1444	.994154	.005846	55	9.9471	.994711	.005289
56	10.1498	.994676	.005324	56	9.9519	.995191	.004809
57	10.1546	.995151	.004849	57	9.9563	.995629	.004371
58	10.1590	.995584	.004416	58	9.9603	.996026	.003974
59	10.1630	.995978	.004022	59	9.9639	.996387	.003613
60	10.1667	.996337	.003663	60	9.9672	.996716	.003284

TABLE 10 *Continued (ninth of 12 pages)*

TABLE B

SHOWING THE PRESENT WORTH OF AN ANNUITY, OF AN
INCOME INTEREST, AND OF A REMAINDER INTEREST
FOR A TERM CERTAIN

INTEREST RATE

(1)	(2)	(3)	(4)	(1)	(2)	(3)	(4)
		11.0%				11.2%	
YEARS	ANNUITY	INCOME INTEREST	REMAINDER	YEARS	ANNUITY	INCOME INTEREST	REMAINDER
1	0.9009	.099099	.900901	1	0.8993	.100719	.899281
2	1.7125	.188378	.811622	2	1.7080	.191294	.808706
3	2.4437	.268809	.731191	3	2.4352	.272747	.727253
4	3.1024	.341269	.658731	4	3.0892	.345995	.654005
5	3.6959	.406549	.593451	5	3.6774	.411866	.588134
6	4.2305	.465359	.534641	6	4.2063	.471103	.528897
7	4.7122	.518342	.481658	7	4.6819	.524373	.475627
8	5.1461	.566074	.433926	8	5.1096	.572278	.427722
9	5.5370	.609075	.390925	9	5.4943	.615358	.384642
10	5.8892	.647816	.352184	10	5.8402	.654099	.345901
11	6.2065	.682717	.317283	11	6.1512	.688938	.311062
12	6.4924	.714159	.285841	12	6.4310	.720268	.279732
13	6.7499	.742486	.257514	13	6.6825	.748442	.251558
14	6.9819	.768005	.231995	14	6.9087	.773779	.226221
15	7.1909	.790996	.209004	15	7.1122	.796564	.203436
16	7.3792	.811708	.188292	16	7.2951	.817054	.182946
17	7.5488	.830367	.169633	17	7.4596	.835480	.164520
18	7.7016	.847178	.152822	18	7.6076	.852050	.147950
19	7.8393	.862322	.137678	19	7.7406	.866952	.133048
20	7.9633	.875966	.124034	20	7.8603	.880352	.119648
21	8.0751	.888258	.111742	21	7.9679	.892403	.107597
22	8.1757	.899331	.100669	22	8.0646	.903240	.096760
23	8.2664	.909307	.090693	23	8.1517	.912986	.087014
24	8.3481	.918295	.081705	24	8.2299	.921750	.078250
25	8.4217	.926392	.073608	25	8.3003	.929631	.070369
26	8.4881	.933686	.066314	26	8.3636	.936719	.063281
27	8.5478	.940258	.059742	27	8.4205	.943092	.056908
28	8.6016	.946178	.053822	28	8.4716	.948824	.051176
29	8.6501	.951512	.048488	29	8.5177	.953978	.046022
30	8.6938	.956317	.043683	30	8.5591	.958614	.041386
31	8.7331	.960646	.039354	31	8.5963	.962782	.037218
32	8.7686	.964546	.035454	32	8.6297	.966531	.033469
33	8.8005	.968060	.031940	33	8.6598	.969902	.030098
34	8.8293	.971225	.028775	34	8.6869	.972933	.027067
35	8.8552	.974076	.025924	35	8.7112	.975659	.024341
36	8.8786	.976645	.023355	36	8.7331	.978111	.021889
37	8.8996	.978960	.021040	37	8.7528	.980316	.019684
38	8.9186	.981045	.018955	38	8.7705	.982298	.017702
39	8.9357	.982923	.017077	39	8.7864	.984081	.015919
40	8.9511	.984616	.015384	40	8.8008	.985684	.014316
41	8.9649	.986140	.013860	41	8.8136	.987126	.012874
42	8.9774	.987514	.012486	42	8.8252	.988423	.011577
43	8.9886	.988751	.011249	43	8.8356	.989589	.010411
44	8.9988	.989866	.010134	44	8.8450	.990638	.009362
45	9.0079	.990870	.009130	45	8.8534	.991581	.008419
46	9.0161	.991775	.008225	46	8.8610	.992429	.007571
47	9.0235	.992590	.007410	47	8.8678	.993191	.006809
48	9.0302	.993324	.006676	48	8.8739	.993877	.006123
49	9.0362	.993986	.006014	49	8.8794	.994494	.005506
50	9.0417	.994582	.005418	50	8.8844	.995048	.004952
51	9.0465	.995119	.004881	51	8.8888	.995547	.004453
52	9.0509	.995603	.004397	52	8.8928	.995995	.004005
53	9.0549	.996038	.003962	53	8.8964	.996399	.003601
54	9.0585	.996431	.003569	54	8.8997	.996762	.003238
55	9.0617	.996785	.003215	55	8.9026	.997088	.002912
56	9.0646	.997103	.002897	56	8.9052	.997381	.002619
57	9.0672	.997390	.002610	57	8.9075	.997645	.002355
58	9.0695	.997649	.002351	58	8.9097	.997882	.002118
59	9.0717	.997882	.002118	59	8.9116	.998095	.001905
60	9.0736	.998092	.001908	60	8.9133	.998287	.001713

TABLE 10 *Continued (tenth of 12 pages)*

TABLE B
SHOWING THE PRESENT WORTH OF AN ANNUITY, OF AN
INCOME INTEREST, AND OF A REMAINDER INTEREST
FOR A TERM CERTAIN

INTEREST RATE

	11.8%				12.0%		
(1)	(2)	(3)	(4)	(1)	(2)	(3)	(4)
		INCOME				INCOME	
YEARS	ANNUITY	INTEREST	REMAINDER	YEARS	ANNUITY	INTEREST	REMAINDER
1	0.8945	.105546	.894454	1	0.8929	.107143	.892857
2	1.6945	.199951	.800049	2	1.6901	.202806	.797194
3	2.4101	.284393	.715607	3	2.4018	.288220	.711780
4	3.0502	.359922	.640078	4	3.0373	.364482	.635518
5	3.6227	.427480	.572520	5	3.6048	.432573	.567427
6	4.1348	.487907	.512093	6	4.1114	.493369	.506631
7	4.5928	.541956	.458044	7	4.5638	.547651	.452349
8	5.0025	.590300	.409700	8	4.9676	.596117	.403883
9	5.3690	.633542	.366458	9	5.3282	.639390	.360610
10	5.6968	.672220	.327780	10	5.6502	.678027	.321973
11	5.9900	.706816	.293184	11	5.9377	.712524	.287476
12	6.2522	.737760	.262240	12	6.1944	.743325	.256675
13	6.4868	.765439	.234561	13	6.4235	.770826	.229174
14	6.6966	.790196	.209804	14	6.6282	.795380	.204620
15	6.8842	.812339	.187661	15	6.8109	.817304	.182696
16	7.0521	.832146	.167854	16	6.9740	.836878	.163122
17	7.2022	.849862	.150138	17	7.1196	.854356	.145644
18	7.3365	.865709	.134291	18	7.2497	.869960	.130040
19	7.4566	.879883	.120117	19	7.3658	.883893	.116107
20	7.5641	.892561	.107439	20	7.4694	.896333	.103667
21	7.6602	.903900	.096100	21	7.5620	.907440	.092560
22	7.7461	.914043	.085957	22	7.6446	.917357	.082643
23	7.8230	.923116	.076884	23	7.7184	.926212	.073788
24	7.8918	.931230	.068770	24	7.7843	.934118	.065882
25	7.9533	.938489	.061511	25	7.8431	.941177	.058823
26	8.0083	.944981	.055019	26	7.8957	.947479	.052521
27	8.0575	.950788	.049212	27	7.9426	.953106	.046894
28	8.1015	.955982	.044018	28	7.9844	.958131	.041869
29	8.1409	.960628	.039372	29	8.0218	.962617	.037383
30	8.1761	.964784	.035216	30	8.0552	.966622	.033378
31	8.2076	.968500	.031500	31	8.0850	.970198	.029802
32	8.2358	.971825	.028175	32	8.1116	.973391	.026609
33	8.2610	.974799	.025201	33	8.1354	.976242	.023758
34	8.2835	.977459	.022541	34	8.1566	.978788	.021212
35	8.3037	.979838	.020162	35	8.1755	.981060	.018940
36	8.3217	.981966	.018034	36	8.1924	.983090	.016910
37	8.3379	.983869	.016131	37	8.2075	.984902	.015098
38	8.3523	.985572	.014428	38	8.2210	.986519	.013481
39	8.3652	.987095	.012905	39	8.2330	.987964	.012036
40	8.3768	.988457	.011543	40	8.2438	.989253	.010747
41	8.3871	.989675	.010325	41	8.2534	.990405	.009595
42	8.3963	.990765	.009235	42	8.2619	.991433	.008567
43	8.4046	.991740	.008260	43	8.2696	.992351	.007649
44	8.4120	.992611	.007389	44	8.2764	.993170	.006830
45	8.4186	.993391	.006609	45	8.2825	.993902	.006098
46	8.4245	.994089	.005911	46	8.2880	.994555	.005445
47	8.4298	.994713	.005287	47	8.2928	.995139	.004861
48	8.4345	.995271	.004729	48	8.2972	.995660	.004340
49	8.4387	.995770	.004230	49	8.3010	.996125	.003875
50	8.4425	.996216	.003784	50	8.3045	.996540	.003460
51	8.4459	.996616	.003384	51	8.3076	.996911	.003089
52	8.4489	.996973	.003027	52	8.3103	.997242	.002758
53	8.4516	.997292	.002708	53	8.3128	.997537	.002463
54	8.4541	.997578	.002422	54	8.3150	.997801	.002199
55	8.4562	.997834	.002166	55	8.3170	.998037	.001963
56	8.4582	.998062	.001938	56	8.3187	.998247	.001753
57	8.4599	.998267	.001733	57	8.3203	.998435	.001565
58	8.4614	.998450	.001550	58	8.3217	.998602	.001398
59	8.4628	.998613	.001387	59	8.3229	.998752	.001248
60	8.4641	.998760	.001240	60	8.3240	.998886	.001114

TABLE 10 *Continued (eleventh of 12 pages)*

TABLE B
SHOWING THE PRESENT WORTH OF AN ANNUITY, OF AN
INCOME INTEREST, AND OF A REMAINDER INTEREST
FOR A TERM CERTAIN

INTEREST RATE

	13.0%				13.2%		
(1)	(2)	(3)	(4)	(1)	(2)	(3)	(4)
		INCOME				INCOME	
YEARS	ANNUITY	INTEREST	REMAINDER	YEARS	ANNUITY	INTEREST	REMAINDER
1	0.8850	.115044	.884956	1	0.8834	.116608	.883392
2	1.6681	.216853	.783147	2	1.6638	.219618	.780382
3	2.3612	.306950	.693050	3	2.3532	.310617	.689383
4	2.9745	.386681	.613319	4	2.9622	.391004	.608996
5	3.5172	.457240	.542760	5	3.5001	.462018	.537982
6	3.9975	.519681	.480319	6	3.9754	.524751	.475249
7	4.4226	.574939	.425061	7	4.3952	.580169	.419831
8	4.7988	.623840	.376160	8	4.7661	.629124	.370876
9	5.1317	.667115	.332885	9	5.0937	.672371	.327629
10	5.4262	.705412	.294588	10	5.3831	.710575	.289425
11	5.6869	.739302	.260698	11	5.6388	.744324	.255676
12	5.9176	.769294	.230706	12	5.8647	.774138	.225862
13	6.1218	.795835	.204165	13	6.0642	.800475	.199525
14	6.3025	.819323	.180677	14	6.2405	.823742	.176258
15	6.4624	.840109	.159891	15	6.3962	.844295	.155705
16	6.6039	.858504	.141496	16	6.5337	.862451	.137549
17	6.7291	.874782	.125218	17	6.6552	.878490	.121510
18	6.8399	.889188	.110812	18	6.7626	.892659	.107341
19	6.9380	.901936	.098064	19	6.8574	.905176	.094824
20	7.0248	.913218	.086782	20	6.9412	.916233	.083767
21	7.1016	.923202	.076798	21	7.0152	.926001	.073999
22	7.1695	.932037	.067963	22	7.0805	.934630	.065370
23	7.2297	.939856	.060144	23	7.1383	.942253	.057747
24	7.2829	.946775	.053225	24	7.1893	.948986	.051014
25	7.3300	.952898	.047102	25	7.2344	.954935	.045065
26	7.3717	.958317	.041683	26	7.2742	.960190	.039810
27	7.4086	.963112	.036888	27	7.3093	.964832	.035168
28	7.4412	.967356	.032644	28	7.3404	.968933	.031067
29	7.4701	.971111	.028889	29	7.3678	.972556	.027444
30	7.4957	.974435	.025565	30	7.3921	.975756	.024244
31	7.5183	.977376	.022624	31	7.4135	.978583	.021417
32	7.5383	.979979	.020021	32	7.4324	.981080	.018920
33	7.5560	.982282	.017718	33	7.4491	.983286	.016714
34	7.5717	.984320	.015680	34	7.4639	.985235	.014765
35	7.5856	.986124	.013876	35	7.4769	.986957	.013043
36	7.5979	.987721	.012279	36	7.4885	.988478	.011522
37	7.6087	.989133	.010867	37	7.4986	.989822	.010178
38	7.6183	.990383	.009617	38	7.5076	.991008	.008992
39	7.6268	.991490	.008510	39	7.5156	.992057	.007943
40	7.6344	.992469	.007531	40	7.5226	.992983	.007017
41	7.6410	.993335	.006665	41	7.5288	.993801	.006199
42	7.6469	.994102	.005898	42	7.5343	.994524	.005476
43	7.6522	.994781	.005219	43	7.5391	.995163	.004837
44	7.6568	.995381	.004619	44	7.5434	.995727	.004273
45	7.6609	.995912	.004088	45	7.5472	.996225	.003775
46	7.6645	.996383	.003617	46	7.5505	.996665	.003335
47	7.6677	.996799	.003201	47	7.5534	.997054	.002946
48	7.6705	.997167	.002833	48	7.5560	.997398	.002602
49	7.6730	.997493	.002507	49	7.5583	.997701	.002299
50	7.6752	.997781	.002219	50	7.5604	.997969	.002031
51	7.6772	.998037	.001963	51	7.5622	.998206	.001794
52	7.6789	.998263	.001737	52	7.5638	.998415	.001585
53	7.6805	.998462	.001538	53	7.5652	.998600	.001400
54	7.6818	.998639	.001361	54	7.5664	.998763	.001237
55	7.6830	.998796	.001204	55	7.5675	.998907	.001093
56	7.6841	.998934	.001066	56	7.5684	.999035	.000965
57	7.6851	.999057	.000943	57	7.5693	.999147	.000853
58	7.6859	.999165	.000835	58	7.5701	.999247	.000753
59	7.6866	.999261	.000739	59	7.5707	.999335	.000665
60	7.6873	.999346	.000654	60	7.5713	.999412	.000588

TABLE 10 *Concluded (last of 12 pages)*

TABLE B
SHOWING THE PRESENT WORTH OF AN ANNUITY, OF AN
INCOME INTEREST, AND OF A REMAINDER INTEREST
FOR A TERM CERTAIN

INTEREST RATE

	13.8%				14.0%		
(1)	(2)	(3)	(4)	(1)	(2)	(3)	(4)
YEARS	ANNUITY	INCOME INTEREST	REMAINDER	YEARS	ANNUITY	INCOME INTEREST	REMAINDER
1	0.8787	.121265	.878735	1	0.8772	.122807	.877193
2	1.6509	.227825	.772175	2	1.6467	.230532	.769468
3	2.3294	.321464	.678536	3	2.3216	.325028	.674972
4	2.9257	.403746	.596254	4	2.9137	.407920	.592080
5	3.4496	.476051	.523949	5	3.4331	.480631	.519369
6	3.9101	.539588	.460412	6	3.8887	.544413	.455587
7	4.3146	.595420	.404580	7	4.2883	.600363	.399637
8	4.6702	.644482	.355518	8	4.6389	.649441	.350559
9	4.9826	.687594	.312406	9	4.9464	.692492	.307508
10	5.2571	.725478	.274522	10	5.2161	.730256	.269744
11	5.4983	.758768	.241232	11	5.4527	.763383	.236617
12	5.7103	.788021	.211979	12	5.6603	.792441	.207559
13	5.8966	.813727	.186273	13	5.8424	.817931	.182069
14	6.0603	.836315	.163685	14	6.0021	.840290	.159710
15	6.2041	.856165	.143835	15	6.1422	.859904	.140096
16	6.3305	.873607	.126393	16	6.2651	.877108	.122892
17	6.4415	.888934	.111066	17	6.3729	.892200	.107800
18	6.5391	.902402	.097598	18	6.4674	.905439	.094561
19	6.6249	.914238	.085762	19	6.5504	.917052	.082948
20	6.7003	.924638	.075362	20	6.6231	.927238	.072762
21	6.7665	.933776	.066224	21	6.6870	.936174	.063826
22	6.8247	.941807	.058193	22	6.7429	.944012	.055988
23	6.8758	.948864	.051136	23	6.7921	.950888	.049112
24	6.9208	.955065	.044935	24	6.8351	.956919	.043081
25	6.9602	.960514	.039486	25	6.8729	.962210	.037790
26	6.9949	.965302	.034698	26	6.9061	.966851	.033149
27	7.0254	.969510	.030490	27	6.9352	.970922	.029078
28	7.0522	.973207	.026793	28	6.9607	.974493	.025507
29	7.0758	.976456	.023544	29	6.9830	.977625	.022375
30	7.0965	.979311	.020689	30	7.0027	.980373	.019627
31	7.1146	.981820	.018180	31	7.0199	.982783	.017217
32	7.1306	.984025	.015975	32	7.0350	.984898	.015102
33	7.1447	.985962	.014038	33	7.0482	.986752	.013248
34	7.1570	.987664	.012336	34	7.0599	.988379	.011621
35	7.1678	.989160	.010840	35	7.0700	.989806	.010194
36	7.1774	.990475	.009525	36	7.0790	.991058	.008942
37	7.1857	.991630	.008370	37	7.0868	.992156	.007844
38	7.1931	.992645	.007355	38	7.0937	.993120	.006880
39	7.1995	.993537	.006463	39	7.0997	.993965	.006035
40	7.2052	.994321	.005679	40	7.1050	.994706	.005294
41	7.2102	.995009	.004991	41	7.1097	.995356	.004644
42	7.2146	.995614	.004386	42	7.1138	.995926	.004074
43	7.2185	.996146	.003854	43	7.1173	.996427	.003573 ·
44	7.2218	.996614	.003386	44	7.1205	.996865	.003135
45	7.2248	.997024	.002976	45	7.1232	.997250	.002750
46	7.2274	.997385	.002615	46	7.1256	.997588	.002412
47	7.2297	.997702	.002298	47	7.1277	.997884	.002116
48	7.2317	.997981	.002019	48	7.1296	.998144	.001856
49	7.2335	.998226	.001774	49	7.1312	.998372	.001628
50	7.2351	.998441	.001559	50	7.1327	.998572	.001428
51	7.2364	.998630	.001370	51	7.1339	.998747	.001253
52	7.2377	.998796	.001204	52	7.1350	.998901	.001099
53	7.2387	.998942	.001058	53	7.1360	.999036	.000964
54	7.2396	.999070	.000930	54	7.1368	.999154	.000846
55	7.2405	.999183	.000817	55	7.1376	.999258	.000742
56	7.2412	.999282	.000718	56	7.1382	.999349	.000651
57	7.2418	.999369	.000631	57	7.1388	.999429	.000571
58	7.2424	.999446	.000554	58	7.1393	.999499	.000501
59	7.2428	.999513	.000487	59	7.1397	.999561	.000439
60	7.2433	.999572	.000428	60	7.1401	.999615	.000385

TABLE 11 IRS Table 80CNSMT - MORTALITY

TABLE 80CNSMT

Age x	l(x)	Age x	l(x)	Age x	l(x)
(1)	(2)	(1)	(2)	(1)	(2)
0	100000	37	95492	74	59279
1	98740	38	95317	75	56799
2	98648	39	95129	76	54239
3	98584	40	94926	77	51599
4	98535	41	94706	78	48878
5	98495	42	94465	79	46071
6	98459	43	94201	80	43180
7	98426	44	93913	81	40208
8	98396	45	93599	82	37172
9	98370	46	93256	83	34095
10	98347	47	92882	84	31012
11	98328	48	92472	85	27960
12	98309	49	92021	86	24961
13	98285	50	91526	87	22038
14	98248	51	90986	88	19235
15	98196	52	90402	89	16598
16	98129	53	89771	90	14154
17	98047	54	89087	91	11908
18	97953	55	88348	92	9863
19	97851	56	87551	93	8032
20	97741	57	86695	94	6424
21	97623	58	85776	95	5043
22	97499	59	84789	96	3884
23	97370	60	83726	97	2939
24	97240	61	82581	98	2185
25	97110	62	81348	99	1598
26	96982	63	80024	100	1150
27	96856	64	78609	101	815
28	96730	65	77107	102	570
29	96604	66	75520	103	393
30	96477	67	73846	104	267
31	96350	68	72082	105	179
32	96220	69	70218	106	119
33	96088	70	68248	107	78
34	95951	71	66165	108	51
35	95808	72	63972	109	33
36	95655	73	61673	110	0

U.S. GOVERNMENT PRINTING OFFICE : 1990 0 - 257-273

I.D. LINE (808)

TABLE 12 Present Value of $1 Lump Sum

Period		1%	2%	3%	4%	5%	6%	7%	8%	9%	10%	11%	12%
									Percent				
1	....	0.990	0.980	0.971	0.962	0.952	0.943	0.935	0.926	0.917	0.909	0.901	0.893
2	....	0.980	0.961	0.943	0.925	0.907	0.890	0.873	0.857	0.842	0.826	0.812	0.797
3	....	0.971	0.942	0.915	0.889	0.864	0.840	0.816	0.794	0.772	0.751	0.731	0.712
4	....	0.961	0.924	0.885	0.855	0.823	0.792	0.763	0.735	0.708	0.683	0.659	0.636
5	....	0.951	0.906	0.863	0.822	0.784	0.747	0.713	0.681	0.650	0.621	0.593	0.567
6	....	0.942	0.888	0.837	0.790	0.746	0.705	0.666	0.630	0.596	0.564	0.535	0.507
7	....	0.933	0.871	0.813	0.760	0.711	0.665	0.623	0.583	0.547	0.513	0.482	0.452
8	....	0.923	0.853	0.789	0.731	0.677	0.627	0.582	0.540	0.502	0.467	0.434	0.404
9	....	0.914	0.837	0.766	0.703	0.645	0.592	0.544	0.500	0.460	0.424	0.391	0.361
10	....	0.905	0.820	0.744	0.676	0.614	0.558	0.508	0.463	0.422	0.386	0.352	0.322
11	....	0.896	0.804	0.722	0.650	0.585	0.527	0.475	0.429	0.388	0.350	0.317	0.287
12	....	0.887	0.788	0.701	0.625	0.557	0.497	0.444	0.397	0.356	0.319	0.286	0.257
13	....	0.879	0.773	0.681	0.601	0.530	0.469	0.415	0.368	0.326	0.290	0.258	0.229
14	....	0.870	0.758	0.661	0.577	0.505	0.442	0.388	0.340	0.299	0.263	0.232	0.205
15	....	0.861	0.743	0.642	0.555	0.481	0.417	0.362	0.315	0.275	0.239	0.209	0.183
16	....	0.853	0.728	0.623	0.534	0.458	0.394	0.339	0.292	0.252	0.218	0.188	0.163
17	....	0.844	0.714	0.605	0.513	0.436	0.371	0.317	0.270	0.231	0.198	0.170	0.146
18	....	0.836	0.700	0.587	0.494	0.416	0.350	0.296	0.250	0.212	0.180	0.153	0.130
19	....	0.828	0.686	0.570	0.475	0.396	0.331	0.277	0.232	0.194	0.164	0.138	0.116
20	....	0.820	0.673	0.554	0.456	0.377	0.312	0.258	0.215	0.178	0.149	0.124	0.104
25	....	0.780	0.610	0.478	0.375	0.295	0.233	0.184	0.146	0.116	0.092	0.074	0.059
30	....	0.742	0.552	0.412	0.308	0.231	0.174	0.131	0.099	0.075	0.057	0.044	0.033
40	....	0.672	0.453	0.307	0.208	0.142	0.097	0.067	0.046	0.032	0.022	0.015	0.011
50	....	0.608	0.372	0.228	0.141	0.087	0.054	0.034	0.021	0.013	0.009	0.005	0.003

TABLE 12 (*concluded*)

Percent

Period	13%	14%	15%	16%	17%	18%	19%	20%	25%	30%	35%	40%	50%
1	0.885	0.877	0.870	0.862	0.855	0.847	0.840	0.833	0.800	0.769	0.741	0.714	0.667
2	0.783	0.769	0.756	0.743	0.731	0.718	0.706	0.694	0.640	0.592	0.5490	0.510	0.444
3	0.693	0.675	0.658	0.641	0.624	0.609	0.593	0.579	0.512	0.455	0.406	0.364	0.296
4	0.613	0.592	0.572	0.552	0.534	0.515	0.499	0.482	0.410	0.350	0.301	0.260	0.198
5	0.543	0.519	0.497	0.476	0.456	0.437	0.419	0.402	0.320	0.269	0.223	0.186	0.132
6	0.480	0.456	0.432	0.410	0.390	0.370	0.352	0.335	0.262	0.207	0.165	0.133	0.088
7	0.425	0.400	0.376	0.354	0.333	0.314	0.296	0.279	0.210	0.159	0.122	0.095	0.059
8	0.376	0.351	0.327	0.305	0.285	0.266	0.249	0.233	0.168	0.123	0.091	0.068	0.039
9	0.333	0.308	0.284	0.263	0.243	0.225	0.209	0.194	0.134	0.094	0.067	0.048	0.026
10	0.295	0.270	0.247	0.227	0.208	0.191	0.176	0.162	0.107	0.073	0.050	0.035	0.017
11	0.261	0.237	0.215	0.195	0.178	0.162	0.148	0.135	0.086	0.056	0.037	0.025	0.012
12	0.231	0.208	0.187	0.168	0.152	0.137	0.124	0.112	0.069	0.043	0.027	0.018	0.008
13	0.204	0.182	0.163	0.145	0.130	0.116	0.104	0.093	0.055	0.033	0.020	0.013	0.005
14	0.181	0.160	0.141	0.125	0.111	0.099	0.088	0.078	0.044	0.025	0.015	0.009	0.003
15	0.160	0.140	0.123	0.108	0.095	0.084	0.074	0.065	0.035	0.020	0.011	0.006	0.002
16	0.141	0.123	0.107	0.093	0.081	0.071	0.062	0.054	0.028	0.015	0.008	0.005	0.002
17	0.125	0.108	0.093	0.080	0.069	0.060	0.052	0.045	0.023	0.012	0.006	0.003	0.001
18	0.111	0.095	0.081	0.069	0.059	0.051	0.044	0.038	0.018	0.009	0.005	0.002	0.001
19	0.098	0.083	0.070	0.060	0.051	0.043	0.037	0.031	0.014	0.007	0.003	0.002	0.000
20	0.087	0.073	0.061	0.051	0.043	0.037	0.031	0.026	0.012	0.005	0.002	0.001	0.000
25	0.047	0.038	0.030	0.024	0.020	0.016	0.013	0.010	0.004	0.001	0.001	0.000	0.000
30	0.026	0.020	0.015	0.012	0.009	0.007	0.005	0.004	0.001	0.000	0.000	0.000	0.000
40	0.008	0.005	0.004	0.003	0.002	0.001	0.001	0.001	0.000	0.000	0.000	0.000	0.000
50	0.002	0.001	0.001	0.001	0.000	0.000	0.000	0.000	0.000	0.000	0.000	0.000	0.000

TABLE 13 Present Value of $1 Annuity

Period	Percent											
	1%	2%	3%	4%	5%	6%	7%	8%	9%	10%	11%	12%
1	0.990	0.980	0.971	0.962	0.952	0.943	0.935	0.926	0.917	0.909	0.901	0.893
2	1.970	1.942	1.913	1.886	1.859	1.833	1.808	1.783	1.759	1.736	1.713	1.690
3	2.941	2.884	2.829	2.775	2.723	2.673	2.624	2.577	2.531	2.487	2.444	2.402
4	3.902	3.808	3.717	3.630	3.546	3.465	3.387	3.312	3.240	3.170	3.102	3.037
5	4.853	4.716	4.580	4.452	4.329	4.212	4.100	3.993	3.890	3.791	3.696	3.605
6	5.795	5.601	5.417	5.242	5.076	4.917	4.767	4.623	4.486	4.355	4.231	4.111
7	6.728	6.472	6.230	6.002	5.786	5.582	5.389	5.206	5.033	4.868	4.712	4.564
8	7.652	7.325	7.020	6.733	6.463	6.210	5.971	5.747	5.535	5.335	5.416	4.968
9	8.566	8.162	7.786	7.435	7.108	6.802	6.515	6.247	5.995	5.759	5.537	5.328
10	9.471	8.983	8.530	8.111	7.722	7.360	7.024	6.710	6.418	6.145	5.889	5.650
11	10.368	9.787	9.253	8.760	8.306	7.887	7.499	7.139	6.805	6.495	6.207	5.938
12	11.255	10.575	9.954	9.385	8.863	8.384	7.943	7.536	7.161	6.814	6.492	6.194
13	12.134	11.348	10.635	9.986	9.394	8.853	8.358	7.904	7.487	7.103	6.750	6.424
14	13.004	12.106	11.296	10.563	9.899	9.295	8.745	8.244	7.786	7.367	6.982	6.628
15	13.865	12.849	11.939	11.118	10.380	9.712	9.108	8.559	8.061	7.606	7.191	6.811
16	14.718	13.578	12.561	11.652	10.838	10.106	9.447	8.851	8.313	7.824	7.379	6.974
17	15.562	14.292	13.166	12.166	11.274	10.477	9.763	9.122	8.544	8.022	7.549	7.102
18	16.398	14.992	13.754	12.659	11.690	10.828	10.059	9.372	8.756	8.201	7.702	7.250
19	17.226	15.678	14.324	13.134	12.085	11.158	10.336	9.604	8.950	8.365	7.839	7.366
20	18.046	16.351	14.877	13.590	12.462	11.470	10.594	9.818	9.129	8.514	7.963	7.469
25	22.023	19.523	17.413	15.622	14.094	12.783	11.654	10.675	9.823	9.077	8.422	7.843
30	25.808	22.396	19.600	17.292	15.372	13.765	12.409	11.258	10.274	9.427	8.694	8.055
40	32.835	27.355	23.115	19.793	17.159	15.046	13.332	11.925	10.757	9.779	8.951	8.244
50	39.196	31.424	25.730	21.482	18.256	15.762	13.801	12.233	10.962	9.915	9.042	8.304

TABLE 13 *(concluded)*

Percent

Period	13%	14%	15%	16%	17%	18%	19%	20%	25%	30%	35%	40%	50%
1	0.885	0.877	0.870	0.862	0.855	0.847	0.840	0.833	0.800	0.769	0.7410	0.714	0.667
2	1.668	1.647	1.626	1.605	1.585	1.566	1.547	1.528	1.440	1.361	1.289	1.224	1.111
3	2.361	2.322	2.283	2.246	2.210	2.174	2.140	2.106	1.952	1.816	1.696	1.589	1.407
4	2.974	2.914	2.855	2.798	2.743	2.690	2.639	2.589	2.362	2.166	1.997	1.849	1.605
5	3.517	3.433	3.352	3.274	3.199	3.127	3.058	2.991	2.689	2.436	2.220	2.035	1.737
6	3.998	3.889	3.784	3.685	3.589	3.498	3.410	3.326	2.951	2.643	2.385	2.168	1.824
7	4.423	4.288	4.160	4.039	3.922	3.812	3.706	3.605	3.161	2.802	2.508	2.263	1.883
8	4.799	4.639	4.487	4.344	4.207	4.078	3.954	3.837	3.329	2.925	2.598	2.331	1.922
9	5.132	4.946	4.772	4.607	4.451	4.303	4.163	4.031	3.463	3.019	2.665	2.379	1.948
10	5.426	5.216	5.019	4.833	4.659	4.494	4.339	4.192	3.571	3.092	2.715	2.414	1.965
11	5.687	5.453	5.234	5.029	4.836	4.656	4.486	4.327	3.656	3.147	2.752	2.438	1.977
12	5.918	5.660	5.421	5.197	4.988	4.793	4.611	4.439	3.725	3.190	2.779	2.456	1.985
13	6.122	5.842	5.583	5.342	5.118	4.910	4.715	4.533	3.780	3.223	2.799	2.469	1.990
14	6.302	6.002	5.724	5.468	5.229	5.008	4.802	4.611	3.824	3.249	2.814	2.478	1.993
15	6.462	6.142	5.847	5.575	5.324	5.092	4.876	4.675	3.859	3.268	2.825	2.484	1.995
16	6.604	6.265	5.954	5.668	5.405	5.162	4.938	4.730	3.887	3.283	2.834	2.489	1.997
17	6.729	6.373	6.047	5.749	5.475	5.222	4.988	4.775	3.910	3.295	2.840	2.492	1.998
18	6.840	6.467	6.128	5.818	5.534	5.273	5.033	4.812	3.928	3.304	2.844	2.494	1.999
19	6.938	6.550	6.198	5.877	5.584	5.316	5.070	4.843	3.942	3.311	2.848	2.496	1.999
20	7.025	6.623	6.259	5.929	5.628	5.353	5.101	4.870	3.954	3.316	2.850	2.497	1.999
25	7.330	6.873	6.464	6.097	5.766	5.467	5.195	4.948	3.985	3.329	2.856	2.499	2.000
30	7.496	7.003	6.566	6.177	5.829	5.517	5.235	4.979	3.995	3.332	2.857	2.500	2.000
40	7.634	7.105	6.642	6.233	5.871	5.548	5.258	4.997	3.999	3.333	2.857	2.500	2.000
50	7.675	7.133	6.661	6.246	5.880	5.554	5.262	4.999	4.000	3.333	2.857	2.500	2.000

Internal Revenue Code: Selected Edited Sections[*]

---

*Note: Omitted passages are marked with five asterisks (*****).

SECTIONS INCLUDED

CHAPTER 1J: SUBPART D: GRANTOR TRUST RULES

SEC. 671: TRUST INCOME, DEDUCTIONS, AND CREDITS ATTRIBUTABLE TO GRANTORS AND OTHERS AS SUBSTANTIAL OWNERS

Where it is specified in this subpart that the grantor or another person shall be treated as the owner of any portion of a trust, there shall then be included in computing the taxable income and credits of the grantor or the other person those items of income, deductions, and credits against tax of the trust which are attributable to that portion of the trust to the extent that such items would be taken into account under this chapter in computing taxable income or credits against the tax of an individual. Any remaining portion of the trust shall be subject to subparts A through D.

*****

SEC. 672: DEFINITIONS AND RULES

(a) ADVERSE PARTY.-For purposes of this subpart, the term "adverse party" means any person having a substantial beneficial interest in the trust which would be adversely affected by the exercise or nonexercise of the power which he possesses respecting the trust. A person having a general power of appointment over the trust property shall be deemed to have a beneficial interest in the trust.

(b) NONADVERSE PARTY.-For purposes of this subpart, the term "nonadverse party" means any person who is not an adverse party.

(c) RELATED OR SUBORDINATE PARTY.-For purposes of this subpart, the term "related or subordinate party" means any nonadverse party who is-

> (1) the grantor's spouse if living with the grantor;
>
> (2) any one of the following: The grantor's father, mother, issue, brother or sister, an employee of the grantor, a corporation or any employee of a corporation in which the stock holdings of the grantor and the trust are significant from the viewpoint of voting control; a subordinate employee of a corporation in which the grantor is an executive.

For purposes of sections 674 and 675, a related or subordinate party shall be presumed to be subservient to the grantor in respect of the exercise or nonexercise of the powers conferred on him unless such party is shown not to be subservient by a preponderance of the evidence.

(d) RULE WHERE POWER IS SUBJECT TO CONDITION PRECEDENT.- A person shall be considered to have a power described in this subpart even though the exercise of the power is subject to a precedent giving of notice or takes effect only on the expiration of a certain period after the exercise of the power.

(e) GRANTOR TREATED AS HOLDING ANY POWER OR INTEREST OF GRANTOR'S SPOUSE.-For purposes of this subpart. if a grantor's spouse is living with the grantor at the time of the creation of any power or interest held by such spouse. the grantor shall be treated as holding such power or interest.

SEC. 673: REVERSIONARY INTERESTS

(a) GENERAL RULE.-The grantor shall be treated as the owner of any portion of a trust in which he has a reversionary interest in either the corpus or the income therefrom, if, as of the inception of that portion of the trust, the value of such interest exceeds 5 percent of the value of such portion.

(b) REVERSIONARY INTEREST TAKING EFFECT AT DEATH OF MINOR LINEAL DESCENDANT BENEFICIARY.-In the case of any beneficiary who-

(1) is a lineal descendant of the grantor, and

(2) holds all of the present interests in any portion of a trust, the grantor shall not be treated under subsection (a) as the owner of such portion solely by reason of a reversionary interest in such portion which takes effect upon the death of such beneficiary before such beneficiary attains age 21.

SEC. 674: POWER TO CONTROL BENEFICIAL ENJOYMENT

(a) GENERAL RULE.-The grantor shall be treated as the owner of any portion of a trust in respect of which the beneficial enjoyment of the corpus or the income therefrom is subject to a power of disposition, exercisable by the grantor or a nonadverse party, or both, without the approval or consent of any adverse party.

(b) EXCEPTIONS FOR CERTAIN POWERS.-Subsection (a) shall not apply to the following powers regardless of by whom held:

(1) POWER TO APPLY INCOME TO SUPPORT OF A DEPENDENT.-A power described in section 677(b) to the extent that the grantor would not be subject to tax under that section.

(2) POWER AFFECTING BENEFICIAL ENJOYMENT ONLY AFTER OCCUR-RENCE OF EVENT.-A power, the exercise of which can only affect the beneficial enjoyment of the income for a period commencing after the occurrence of an event such that a grantor would not be treated as the owner under section 673 if the power were a reversionary interest, but the grantor may be treated as the owner after the occurrence of the event unless the power is relinquished.

(3) POWER EXERCISABLE ONLY BY WILL.-A power exercisable only by will, other than a power in the grantor to appoint by will the income of the trust where the income is accumulated for such disposition by the grantor or may be so accumulated in the discretion of the grantor or a nonadverse party, or both, without the approval or consent of any adverse party.

(4) POWER TO ALLOCATE AMONG CHARITABLE BENEFICIARIES.-A power to determine the beneficial enjoyment of the corpus or the income therefrom if the corpus or income is irrevocably payable for a purpose specified in section 170(c) (relating to definition of charitable contributions).

(5) POWER TO DISTRIBUTE CORPUS.-A power to distribute corpus either-

(A) to or for a beneficiary or beneficiaries or to or for a class of beneficiaries (whether or not income beneficiaries) provided that the power is limited by a reasonably definite standard which is set forth in the trust instrument: or

(B) to or for any current income beneficiary, provided that the distribution of corpus must be chargeable against the proportionate share of corpus held in trust for the payment of income to the beneficiary as if the corpus constituted a separate trust.

A power does not fall within the powers described in this paragraph if any person has a power to add to the beneficiary or beneficiaries or to a class of beneficiaries designated to receive the income or corpus, except where such action is to provide for after-born or after-adopted children.

    (6) POWER TO WITHHOLD INCOME TEMPORARILY.-A power to distribute or apply income to or for any current income beneficiary or to accumulate the income for him, provided that any accumulated income must ultimately be payable-

        (A) to the beneficiary from whom distribution or application is withheld, to his estate, or to his appointees (or persons named as alternate takers in default of appointment) provided that such beneficiary possesses a power of appointment which does not exclude from the class of possible appointees any person other than the beneficiary, his estate, his creditors, or the creditors of his estate, or

        (B) on termination of the trust, or in conjunction with a distribution of corpus which is augmented by such accumulated income, to the current income beneficiaries in shares which have been irrevocably specified in the trust instrument.

Accumulated income shall be considered so payable although it is provided that if any beneficiary does not survive a date of distribution which could reasonably have been expected to occur within the beneficiary's lifetime, the share of the deceased beneficiary is to be paid to his appointees or to one or more designated alternate takers (other than the grantor or the grantor's estate) whose shares have been irrevocably specified. A power does not fall within the powers described in this paragraph if any person has a power to add to the beneficiary or beneficiaries or to a class of beneficiaries designated to receive the income or corpus except where such action is to provide for after-born or after-adopted children.

    (7) POWER TO WITHHOLD INCOME DURING DISABILITY OF A BENEFICI-ARY.-A power exercisable only during-

        (A) the existence of a legal disability of any current income beneficiary, or

        (B) the period during which any income beneficiary shall be under the age of 21 years,

to distribute or apply income to or for such beneficiary or to accumulate and add the income to corpus. A power does not fall within the powers described in this paragraph if any person has a power to add to the beneficiary or beneficiaries or to a class of beneficiaries designated to receive the income or corpus, except where such action is to provide for after-born or after-adopted children.

    (8) POWER TO ALLOCATE BETWEEN CORPUS AND INCOME.-A power to allocate receipts and disbursements as between corpus and income. even though expressed in broad language.

(c) EXCEPTION FOR CERTAIN POWERS OF INDEPENDENT TRUSTEES.-Subsection (a) shall not apply to a power solely exercisable (without the approval or consent of any other person) by a trustee or trustees, none of whom is the grantor. and no more than half of whom are related or subordinate parties who are subservient to the wishes of the grantor-

    (1) to distribute, apportion, or accumulate income to or for a beneficiary or beneficiaries, or to, for, or within a class of beneficiaries; or

    (2) to pay out corpus to or for a beneficiary or beneficiaries or to or for a class of beneficiaries (whether or not income beneficiaries).

A power does not fall within the powers described in this subsection if any person has a power to add to the beneficiary or beneficiaries or to a class of beneficiaries designated to receive the income or corpus, except where such action is to provide for after-born or after-adopted children.

(d) POWER TO ALLOCATE INCOME IF LIMITED BY A STANDARD. Subsection (a) shall not apply to a power solely exercisable (without the approval or consent of any other person) by a trustee or trustees, none of whom is the grantor or spouse living with the grantor, to distribute, apportion, or accumulate income to or for a beneficiary or beneficiaries, or to, for, or within a class of beneficiaries, whether or not the conditions of paragraph (6) or (7) of subsection (b) are satisfied, if such power is limited by a reasonably definite external standard which is set forth in the trust instrument. A power does not fall within the powers described in this subsection if any person has a power to add to the beneficiary or beneficiaries or to a class of beneficiaries designated to receive the income or corpus except where such action is to provide for after-born or after-adopted children.

SEC. 675: ADMINISTRATIVE POWERS

The grantor shall be treated as the owner of any portion of a trust in respect of which-

(1) POWER TO DEAL FOR LESS THAN ADEQUATE AND FULL CONSIDERA-TION.-A power exercisable by the grantor or a nonadverse party, or both, without the approval or consent of any adverse party enables the grantor or any person to purchase, exchange, or otherwise deal with or dispose of the corpus or the income therefrom for less than an adequate consideration in money or money's worth.

(2) POWER TO BORROW WITHOUT ADEQUATE INTEREST OR SECURITY.-A power exercisable by the grantor or a nonadverse party, or both, enables the grantor to borrow the corpus or income, directly or indirectly, without adequate interest or without adequate security except where a trustee (other than the grantor) is authorized under a general lending power to make loans to any person without regard to interest or security.

(3) BORROWING OF THE TRUST FUNDS.-The grantor has directly or indirectly borrowed the corpus or income and has not completely repaid the loan, including any interest, before the beginning of the taxable year. The preceding sentence shall not apply to a loan which provides for adequate interest and adequate security, if such loan is made by a trustee other than the grantor and other than a related or subordinate trustee subservient to the grantor.

(4) GENERAL POWERS OF ADMINISTRATION.-A power of administration is exercisable in a nonfiduciary capacity by any person without the approval or consent of any person in a fiduciary capacity. For purposes of this paragraph, the term "power of administration" means any one or more of the following powers: (A) a power to vote or direct the voting of stock or other securities of a corporation in which the holdings of the grantor and the trust are significant from the viewpoint of voting control; (B) a power to control the investment of the trust funds either by directing investments or reinvestments, or by vetoing proposed investments or reinvestments, to the extent that the trust funds consist of stocks or securities of corporations in which the holdings of the grantor and the trust are significant from the viewpoint of voting control; or (C) a power to reacquire the trust corpus by substituting other property of an equivalent value.

SEC. 676: POWER TO REVOKE

(a) GENERAL RULE.-The grantor shall be treated as the owner of any portion of a trust, whether or not he is treated as such owner under any other provision of this part, where at any time the power to revest in the grantor title to such portion is exercisable by the grantor or a non-adverse party or both.

(b) POWER AFFECTING BENEFICIAL ENJOYMENT ONLY AFTER OCCURRENCE OF EVENT. Subsection (a) shall not apply to a power the exercise of which can only affect the beneficial enjoyment of the income for a period commencing after the occurrence of an event such that a grantor would not be treated as the owner under section 673 if the power were a reversionary interest. But the grantor may be treated as the owner after the occurrence of such event unless the power is relinquished.

SEC. 677: INCOME FOR BENEFIT OF GRANTOR

(a) GENERAL RULE.-The grantor shall be treated as the owner of any portion of a trust, whether or not he is treated as such owner under section 674, whose income without the approval or consent of any adverse party is, or, in the discretion of the grantor or a nonadverse party, or both, may be-

>   (1) distributed to the grantor or the grantor's spouse;
>
>   (2) held or accumulated for future distribution to the grantor or the grantor's spouse; or
>
>   (3) applied to the payment of premiums on policies of insurance on the life of the grantor or the grantor's spouse (except policies of insurance irrevocably payable for a purpose specified in section 170(c) (relating to definition of charitable contributions)).

This subsection shall not apply to a power the exercise of which can only affect the beneficial enjoyment of the income for a period commencing after *the occurrence of an event* such that the grantor would not be treated as the owner under section 673 if the power were a reversionary interest; but the grantor may be treated as the owner after *the occurrence of the event* unless the power is relinquished.

(b) OBLIGATIONS OF SUPPORT.-Income of a trust shall not be considered taxable to the grantor under subsection (a) or any other provision of this chapter merely because such income in the discretion of another person, the trustee, or the grantor acting as trustee or co-trustee, may be applied or distributed for the support or maintenance of a beneficiary (other than the grantor's spouse) whom the grantor is legally obligated to support or maintain, except to the extent that such income is so applied or distributed. In cases where the amounts so applied or distributed are paid out of corpus or out of other than income for the taxable year, such amounts shall be considered to be an amount paid or credited within the meaning of paragraph (2) of section 661(a) and shall be taxed to the grantor under section 662.

SEC. 678: PERSON OTHER THAN GRANTOR TREATED AS SUBSTANTIAL OWNER

(a) GENERAL RULE.-A person other than the grantor shall be treated as the owner of any portion of a trust with respect to which:
  (l) such person has a power exercisable solely by himself to vest the corpus or the income therefrom in himself, or
  (2) such person has previously partially released or otherwise modified such a power and after the release or modification retains such control as would, within the principles of sections 671 to 677, inclusive, subject a grantor of a trust to treatment as the owner thereof.

(b) EXCEPTION WHERE GRANTOR IS TAXABLE.-Subsection (a) shall not apply with respect to a power over income, as originally granted or thereafter modified, if the grantor of the trust or a transferor (to whom section 679 applies) is otherwise treated as the owner under the provisions of this subpart other than this section.

(c) OBLIGATIONS OF SUPPORT. Subsection (a) shall not apply to a power which enables such person, in the capacity of trustee or co-trustee, merely to apply the income of the trust to the support or maintenance of a person whom the holder of the power is obligated to support or maintain except to the extent that such income is so applied. In cases where the amounts so applied or distributed are paid out of corpus or out of other than income of the taxable year, such amounts shall be considered to be an amount paid or credited within the meaning of paragraph (2) of section 661(a) and shall be taxed to the holder of the power under section 662.

(d) EFFECT OF RENUNCIATION OR DISCLAIMER.-Subsection (a) shall not apply with respect to a power which has been renounced or disclaimed within a reasonable time after the holder of the power first became aware of its existence.

*****

CHAPTER 11: ESTATE TAX

Subchapter A: Citizens or Residents

SEC. 2001: IMPOSITION AND RATE OF TAX

(a) IMPOSITION.-A tax is hereby imposed on the transfer of the taxable estate of every decedent who is a citizen or resident of the United States.

(b) COMPUTATION OF TAX.-The tax imposed by this section shall be the amount equal to the excess (if any) of-

> (1) a tentative tax computed in accordance with the rate schedule set forth in subsection (c) on the sum of-
> > (A) the amount of the taxable estate, and
> > (B) the amount of the adjusted taxable gifts, over
>
> (2) the aggregate amount of tax which would have been payable under chapter 12 with respect to gifts made by the decedent after December 31, 1976, if the rate schedule set forth in subsection (c) (as in effect at the decedent's death) had been applicable at the time of such gifts.

For purposes of paragraph (1)(b), the term "adjusted taxable gifts" means the total amount of the taxable gifts (within the meaning of section 2053) made by the decedent after December 31, 1976, other than gifts which are includable in the gross estate of the decedent.

(c) RATE SCHEDULE

> (1) (Editor's note: Transfer tax rates will be found in Table 4 of Appendix A.)
> *****
> (2) PHASEOUT OF GRADUATED RATES AND UNIFIED CREDIT.--The tentative tax determined under paragraph (1) shall be increased by an amount equal to 5 percent of so much of the amount (with respect to which the tentative tax is to be computed) as exceeds $10,000,000 but does not exceed $21,040,000.

(d) ADJUSTMENT FOR GIFT TAX PAID BY SPOUSE.
*****
(e) COORDINATION OF SECTIONS 2513 AND 2035.

SEC. 2002: LIABILITY FOR PAYMENT

Except as provided in section 2210, the tax imposed by this chapter shall be paid by the executor.

SEC. 2031: DEFINITION OF GROSS ESTATE

(a) GENERAL.-The value of the gross estate of the decedent shall be determined by including to the extent provided for in this part, the value at the time of his death of all property, real or personal, tangible or intangible, wherever situated.

(b) VALUATION OF UNLISTED STOCK AND SECURITIES.-In the case of stock and securities of a corporation the value of which, by reason of their not being listed on an exchange and by reason of the absence of sales thereof, cannot be determined with reference to bid and asked prices or with reference to sales prices, the value thereof shall be determined by taking into consideration, in addition to all other factors, the value of stock or securities of corporations engaged in the same or similar line of business which are listed on an exchange.

(c) CROSS REFERENCE.

*****

SEC. 2032: ALTERNATE VALUATION

(a) GENERAL.-The value of the gross estate may be determined, if the executor so elects, by valuing all the property included in the gross estate as follows:

(1) In the case of property distributed, sold, exchanged, or otherwise disposed of, within six months after the decedent's death such property shall be valued as of the date of distribution, sale, exchange, or other disposition.

(2) In the case of property not distributed, sold, exchanged, or otherwise disposed of, within six months after the decedent's death such property shall be valued as of the date six months after the decedent's death.

(3) Any interest or estate which is affected by mere lapse of time shall be included as its value as of the time of death (instead of the later date) with adjustment for any difference in its value as of the later date not due to mere lapse of time.

(b) SPECIAL RULES.

*****

(c) ELECTION MUST DECREASE GROSS ESTATE AND ESTATE TAX.- No election may be made under this section with respect to an estate unless such election shall decrease-

(1) the value of the gross estate. and

(2) the amount of the tax imposed by this chapter (reduced by credits allowable against such tax).

(d) ELECTION.

(1) In General.-The election provided for in this section shall be made by the executor on the return of the tax imposed by this chapter. Such election, once made, shall be irrevocable.

(2) Exception.-No election may be made under this section if such return is filed more than 1 year after the time prescribed by law (including extensions) for filing such return.

SEC. 2033: PROPERTY IN WHICH THE DECEDENT HAD AN INTEREST

The value of the gross estate shall include the value of all property to the extent of the interest therein of the decedent at the time of his death.

SEC. 2034: DOWER OR CURTESY INTERESTS

The value of the gross estate shall include the value of all property to the extent of any interest therein of the surviving spouse, existing at the time of the decedent's death as dower or curtesy, or by virtue of a statute creating an estate in lieu of dower or curtesy.

SEC. 2035: ADJUSTMENTS FOR GIFTS MADE WITHIN 3 YEARS OF DECEDENT'S DEATH

(a) INCLUSION OF GIFTS MADE BY DECEDENT.-Except as provided for in subsection (b), the value of the gross estate shall include the value of all property to the extent of any interest therein of which the decedent has at any time made a transfer, by trust or otherwise, during the three-year period ending on the date of the decedent 's death.

(b) EXCEPTIONS.-Subsection (a) shall not apply-
    (1) to any bona fide sale for an adequate and full consideration in money or money's worth, and
    (2) to any gift to a donee made during a calendar year if the decedent was not required by section 6019 [other than by reason of section 6019(2)] to file any gift tax return for such year with respect to gifts to such donee. Paragraph (2) shall not apply to any transfer with respect to a life insurance policy.

(c) INCLUSION OF GIFT TAX ON CERTAIN GIFTS MADE DURING 3 YEARS BEFORE DECEDENT'S DEATH.-The amount of the gross estate (determined without regard to this subsection) shall be increased by the amount of any tax paid under chapter 12 by the decedent or his estate on any gift made by the decedent or his spouse made after December 31. 1976, and during the three-year period ending on the date of the decedent's death.

(d) DECEDENTS DYING AFTER 1981-
    (1) IN GENERAL.-Except as otherwise provided in this subsection (a) shall not apply to the estate of a decedent dying after December 31, 1981.
    (2) EXCEPTIONS FOR CERTAIN TRANSFERS. Paragraph 1 of this subsection and paragraph (2) of subsection (b) shall not apply to a transfer of an interest in property which is included in the value of the gross estate under section 2036, 2037, 2038, or 2042 or would have been included under any of such sections if such interest had been retained by the decedent.
    (3) THREE-YEAR RULE RETAINED FOR CERTAIN PURPOSES.- Paragraph (1) shall not apply for purposes of-
        (A) section 303(b) (relating to distributions in redemption of stock to pay death taxes),
        (B) section 2032A (relating to special valuation of certain farm, etc., real property), and
        (C) subchapter C of chapter 64 (relating to lien for taxes).
    (4) COORDINATION OF THREE-YEAR RULE WITH SECTION 6166(a)(1). An estate shall be treated as meeting the 35 percent of adjusted gross estate requirement of section 6166(a)(1) only if the estate meets such requirements both with and without the application of paragraph (1).

SEC. 2036: TRANSFERS WITH RETAINED LIFE ESTATE

(a) GENERAL RULE.-The value of the gross estate shall include the value of all property to the extent of any interest therein of which the decedent has at any time made a transfer (except in case of a bona fide sale for an adequate and full consideration in money or money's worth), by trust or otherwise, under which he has retained for his life or for any period not ascertainable without reference to his death or for any period which does not in fact end before his death-

    (1) the possession or enjoyment of, or the right to the income from, the property, or

    (2) the right, either alone or in conjunction with any person, to designate the persons who shall possess or enjoy the property or the income therefrom.

(b) VOTING RIGHTS

    (1) IN GENERAL, For purposes of subsection (a)(l), the retention of the right to vote (directly or indirectly) shares of stock of a controlled corporation shall be considered to be a retention of the enjoyment of transferred property.

    (2) CONTROLLED CORPORATION.
                *****

    (3) COORDINATION WITH SECTION 2035.
                *****

(c) LIMITATION ON APPLICATION OF GENERAL RULE.

(Editor's note: In 1990, the anti-freeze provisions of old §2036(c) were repealed retroactive to inception, and old §2036(d) was relabeled new §2036(c).)
*****

SEC. 2037: TRANSFERS TAKING EFFECT AT DEATH

(a) GENERAL RULE.-The value of the gross estate shall include the value of all property to the extent of any interest therein of which the decedent has at any time after September 7, 1916, made a transfer (except in case of a bona fide sale for an adequate and full consideration in money or money's worth), by trust or otherwise, if-

    (1) possession or enjoyment of the property can, through ownership of such interest, be obtained only by surviving the decedent, and

    (2) the decedent has retained a reversionary interest in the property (but in the case of a transfer made before October 8, 1949, only if such reversionary interest arose by the express terms of the instrument of transfer), and the value of such reversionary interest immediately before the death of the decedent exceeds 5 percent of the value of such property.

(b) SPECIAL RULES.
                *****

SEC. 2038: REVOCABLE TRANSFERS

(a) IN GENERAL.-The value of the gross estate shall include the value of all property-
  (1) Transfers after June 22, 1936- To the extent of any interest therein of which the decedent has at any time made a transfer (except in case of a bona fide sale for an adequate and full consideration in money or money's worth), by trust or otherwise, where the enjoyment thereof was subject at the date of his death to any change through the exercise of a power (in whatever capacity exercisable) by the decedent alone or by the decedent in conjunction with any other person (without regard to when or from what source the decedent acquired such power), to alter, amend, revoke, or terminate, or where such power is relinquished during the three-year period ending on the date of the decedent's death.
  (2) TRANSFERS ON OR BEFORE JUNE 22, l936.
  *****

(b) DATE OF EXISTENCE OF POWER.
  *****

SEC. 2039: ANNUITIES

(a) GENERAL.-The gross estate shall include the value of an annuity or other payment receivable by any beneficiary by reason of surviving the decedent under any form of contract or agreement entered into after March 3, 1931 (other than as insurance under policies on the life of the decedent), if, under such contract or agreement, an annuity or other payment was payable to the decedent, or the decedent possessed the right to receive such annuity or payment, either alone or in conjunction with another for his life or for any period not ascertainable without reference to his death or for any period which does not in fact end before his death.

(b) AMOUNT INCLUDABLE.
  *****

SEC. 2040: JOINT INTERESTS

(a) GENERAL RULE.-The value of the gross estate shall include the value of all property to the extent of the interest therein held as joint tenants with right of survivorship by the decedent and any other person, or as tenants by the entirety by the decedent and spouse, or deposited, with any person carrying on the banking business, in their joint names and payable to either or the survivor, except such part thereof as may be shown to have originally belonged to such other person and never to have been received or acquired by the latter from the decedent for less than an adequate or full consideration in money or money's worth; Provided, That where such property or any part thereof, or part of the consideration with which such property was acquired, is shown to have been at any time acquired by such other person from the decedent for less than an adequate and full consideration in money or money's worth, there shall be excepted only such part of the value of such property as is proportionate to the consideration furnished by such other person: Provided further, that where any property has been acquired by gift, bequest, devise, or inheritance, as a tenancy by the entirety by the decedent and spouse, then to the extent of one half of the value thereof, or, where so acquired by the decedent and any other person as joint tenants with right of survivorship and their interests are not otherwise specified or fixed by law, then to the extent of the value of a fractional part to be determined by dividing the value of the property by the number of joint tenants with right of survivorship.

(b) CERTAIN JOINT INTERESTS OF HUSBAND AND WIFE.-

(1) INTERESTS OF SPOUSE EXCLUDED FROM GROSS ESTATE,- Notwithstanding subsection (a), in the case of any qualified joint interest, the value included in the gross estate with respect to such interest by reason of this section is one half of the value of such qualified joint interest,

(2) QUALIFIED JOINT INTEREST DEFINED.-For purposes of paragraph (1), the term "qualified joint interest" means any interest in property held by the decedent and the decedent's spouse as-

(A) tenants by the entirety, or

(B) joint tenants with right of survivorship, but only if the decedent and the spouse of the decedent are the only joint tenants.

SECTION 2041: POWERS OF APPOINTMENT

(a) IN GENERAL.-The value of the gross estate shall include the value of all property.

(1) POWERS OF APPOINTMENT CREATED ON OR BEFORE OCTOBER 21, 1942.

*****

(2) POWERS CREATED AFTER OCTOBER 2l, 1942.-To the extent of any property with respect to which the decedent has at the time of his death a general power of appointment created after October 21, 1942, or with respect to which the decedent has at any time exercised or released such a power of appointment by a disposition which is of such a nature that if it were a transfer of property owned by the decedent, such property would be includable in the decedent's gross estate under section 2035 to 2038, inclusive. For purposes of this paragraph (2), the power of appointment shall be considered to exist on the date of the decedent's death even though the exercise of the power is subject to a precedent giving of notice or even though the exercise of the power takes effect only on the expiration of a stated period after its exercise, whether or not on or before the date of the decedent's death notice has been given or the power has been exercised.

(3) CREATION OF ANOTHER POWER IN CERTAIN CASES.

*****

(b) DEFINITIONS.-For purposes of subsection (a)-

(1) GENERAL POWER OF APPOINTMENT-The term "general power of appointment" means a power which is exercisable in favor of the decedent, his estate, his creditors, or the creditors of his estate: except that-

(A) A power to consume, invade, or appropriate property for the benefit of the decedent which is limited to an ascertainable standard relating to the health, education, support, or maintenance of the decedent shall not be deemed a general power of appointment.

(B) A power of appointment created on or before October 21, 1942, which is exercisable by the decedent only in conjunction with another person shall not be deemed a general power of appointment.

(C) In the case of a power of appointment created after October 21, 1942, which is exercisable by the decedent only in conjunction with another person-

      (i) If the power is not exercisable by the decedent except in conjunction with the creator of the power-such power shall not be deemed a general power of appointment.

     (ii) If the power is not exercisable by the decedent except in conjunction with a person having a substantial interest in the property, subject to the power, which is adverse to the exercise of the power in favor of the decedent-such power shall not be deemed a general power of appointment.

*****

    (iii)

*****

For purposes of clauses (ii) and (iii), a power shall be deemed to be exercisable in favor of a person if it is exercisable in favor of such a person, his estate, his creditors, or the creditors of his estate.

(2) LAPSE OF POWER-The lapse of a power of appointment created after October 21, 1942, during the life of the individual possessing the power shall be considered a release of such power. The preceding sentence shall apply with respect to the lapse of powers during any calendar year only to the extent that the property, which could have been appointed by exercise of such lapsed powers, exceeded in value, at the time of such lapse, the greater of the following amounts:

    (A) $5,000, or

    (B) 5 percent of the aggregate value, at the time of such lapse, of the assets out of which, or the proceeds of which, the exercise of the lapsed powers could have been satisfied.

(3) DATE OF CREATION OF SUCH POWER

*****

SEC. 2042: PROCEEDS OF LIFE INSURANCE

The value of the gross estate shall include the value of all property-

    (1) RECEIVABLE BY THE EXECUTOR.-To the extent of the amount receivable by the executor as insurance under policies on the life of the decedent.

    (2) RECEIVABLE BY OTHER BENEFICIARIES.-To the extent of the amount receivable by all other beneficiaries as insurance under policies on the life of the decedent with respect to which the decedent possessed at his death any of the incidents of ownership, exercisable either alone or in conjunction with any other person.

*****

SEC. 2043: TRANSFERS FOR INSUFFICIENT CONSIDERATION

(a) IN GENERAL.-If any one of the transfers, trusts, interests, rights, or powers enumerated and described in sections 2035 to 2038, inclusive, and section 2041 is made, created, exercised, or relinquished for a consideration in money or money's worth, but is not a bona fide sale for an adequate and full consideration in money or money's worth, there shall be included in the gross estate only the excess of the fair market value at the time of death of the property otherwise to be included on account of such transaction, over the value of the consideration received therefore by the decedent.

(b) MARITAL RIGHTS NOT TREATED AS CONSIDERATION.
*****

SEC. 2044: CERTAIN PROPERTY FOR WHICH MARITAL DEDUCTION WAS PREVIOUSLY ALLOWED.

(a) GENERAL RULE.--The value of the gross estate shall include the value of any property to which this section applies in which the decedent had a qualifying income interest for life.

(b) PROPERTY TO WHICH THIS SECTION APPLIES.-- This section applies to any property if-
  (1) a deduction was allowed with respect of the transfer of such property to the decedent--
    (A) under section 2056 by reason of subsection (b)(7) thereof, or
    (B) under section 2523 by reason of subsection (f) thereof, and
  (2) section 2519 (relating to dispositions of certain life estates) did not apply with respect to a disposition by the decedent of part or all such properties.

(c) PROPERTY TREATED AS HAVING PASSED FROM DECEDENT For purposes of this chapter and chapter 13, property includable of the gross estate of the decedent under subsection (a) shall be treated as property passing from the decedent.

SEC. 2051: DEFINITION OF TAXABLE ESTATE

For purposes of the tax imposed by section 2001, the value of the taxable estate shall be determined by deducting from the value of the gross estate the deductions provided for in this part.

SEC. 2053: EXPENSES, INDEBTEDNESS, AND TAXES

(a) GENERAL RULE.-- For purposes of the tax imposed by section 2001, the value of the taxable estate shall be determined by deducting from the value of the gross estate such amounts--
  (1) for funeral expenses
  (2) for administration expenses,
  (3) for claims against the estate, and
  (4) for unpaid mortgages on, or any indebtedness in respect of, property where the value of the decedent's interest therein, undiminished by such mortgage or indebtedness, is included in the value of the gross estate,
as are allowed by the laws of jurisdiction, whether within or without the United States, under which the estate is being administered.

(b) OTHER ADMINISTRATION EXPENSES.--Subject to the limitations in paragraph (1) of subsection (c), there shall be deducted in determining the taxable estate amounts representing expenses incurred in administering property not subject to claims which is included in the gross estate to the same extent such amounts would be allowable as a deduction under subsection (a) if such property were subject to claims, and such amounts are paid before the expiration of the period of limitation for assessment provided in section 6501.

(c) LIMITATIONS.--

    (1) LIMITATIONS APPLICABLE TO SUBSECTIONS (a) AND (b).--

        (A) CONSIDERATION FOR CLAIMS.--The deduction allowed by this section in the case of claims against the estate, unpaid mortgages, or any indebtedness shall, when founded on a promise or an agreement, be limited to the extent that they were contracted bona fide and for an adequate and full consideration in money or money's worth; except that in any case in which any such claim is founded on a promise or agreement of the decedent to make a contribution or gift to or for the use of any donee described in section 2055 for the purposes specified therein, the deduction for such claims shall not be so limited, but shall be limited to the extent that it would be allowable as a deduction under section 2055 if such promise or agreement constituted a bequest.

        (B) CERTAIN TAXES.--Any income taxes on income received after the death of the decedent, or property taxes not accrued before his death, or any estate, succession, legacy, or inheritances taxes, shall not be deductible under this section. This subparagraph shall not apply to any increase in the tax imposed by this chapter by reason of section 4980A(d).

        (C) CERTAIN CLAIMS BY REMAINDERMEN.--No deduction shall be allowed under this section for a claim against the estate by a remainderman relating to any property described in section 2044.

    (2) LIMITATIONS APPLICABLE ONLY TO SUBSECTION (a).--In the case of the amounts described in subsection (a), there shall be disallowed the amount by which the deductions specified exceed the value, at the time of the decedent's death, of property subject to claims, except to the extent that such deductions represent amounts paid before the date prescribed for the filing of the estate tax return. For purposes of this section, the term "property subject to claims" means property includable in the gross estate of the decedent which, or the avails of which, would under the applicable law, bear the burden of the payment of such deductions in the final adjustment and settlement of the estate, except that the value of the property shall be reduced by the amount of the deduction under section 2054 attributable to such property.

(d) CERTAIN STATE AND FOREIGN DEATH TAXES--

*****

SEC. 2054: LOSSES

For purposes of the tax imposed by section 2001, the value of the taxable estate shall be determined by deducting from the value of the gross estate losses incurred during the settlement of estates arising from fires, storms, shipwrecks, or other casualties, or from theft, when such losses are not compensated for by insurance or otherwise.

SEC. 2055: TRANSFERS FOR PUBLIC, CHARITABLE, AND RELIGIOUS USES

(a) IN GENERAL.-- For purposes of the tax imposed by section 2001, the value of the taxable estate shall be determined by deducting from the value of the gross estate the amount of all bequests, legacies, devises, or transfers--

(1) to or for the use of the United States, any state, any political subdivision thereof, or the District of Columbia, for exclusively public purposes;

(2) to or for the use of any corporation organized and operated exclusively for religious, charitable, scientific, literary, or educational purposes, including the encouragement of art, or to foster national or international amateur sports competition (but only if no part of its activities involve the provision of athletic facilities or equipment), and prevention of cruelty to children or animals, no part of the net earnings of which inures to the benefit of any private stockholder or individual, which is not disqualified for tax exemption under section 501 (c)(3) by reason of attempting to influence legislation, and which does not participate in, or intervene in (including the publishing or distributing of statements), any political campaign on behalf of(or in opposition to) any candidate for public office;

(3) to a trustee or trustees, or a fraternal society, order or association operating under the lodge system, but only if such contributions or gifts are to be used by such trustee or trustees, or by such fraternal society, order, or association, exclusively for religious, charitable, scientific, literary, or educational purposes, or for the prevention of cruelty to children or animals, such trust, fraternal society, order, or association would not be disqualified for tax exemption under section 501(c)(3) by reason of attempting to influence legislation, and such trustee or trustees, or such fraternal society, order or association, does not participate in, or intervene in (including the publishing or distributing of statements), any political campaign on behalf of (or in opposition to) any candidate for public office; or

(4) to or for the use of any veterans' organization incorporated by Act of Congress, or of its departments or local chapters or posts, no part of the net earnings of which inures to the benefit of any private shareholder or individual.

For purposes of this subsection, the complete termination before the date prescribed for the filing of the estate tax return of a power to consume, invade, or appropriate property for the benefit of an individual before such power has been exercised by reason of the death of such individual or for any other reason shall be considered and deemed to be a qualified disclaimer with the same full force and effect as though he had filed such qualified disclaimer. Rules similar to the rules of section 501(j) shall apply for purposes of paragraph (2).

(Subsections b through g are omitted)

SEC. 2056: BEQUESTS, ETC., TO SURVIVING SPOUSE

(a) ALLOWANCE OF MARITAL DEDUCTION.-For purposes of the tax imposed by section 2001, the value of the taxable estate shall, except as limited by subsection (b), be determined by deducting from the value of the gross estate an amount equal to the value of any interest in property which passes or has passed from the decedent to his surviving spouse, but only to the extent that such interest is included in determining the value of the gross estate.

(b) LIMITATION IN THE CASE OF LIFE ESTATE OR OTHER TERMINABLE INTEREST-

    (1) GENERAL RULE.-Where, on the lapse of time, on the occurrence of an event or contingency, or on the failure of an event on contingency to occur, an interest passing to the surviving spouse will terminate or fail, no deduction shall be allowed under this section with respect to such interest-

        (A) if an interest in such property passes or has passed (for less than an adequate and full consideration in money or money's worth) from the decedent to any person other than such surviving spouse (or the estate of such spouse); and

        (B) if by reason of such passing such person (or his heirs or assigns) may possess or enjoy any part of such property after such termination or failure of the interest so passing to the surviving spouse; and no deduction shall be allowed with respect to such interest [even if such deduction is not disallowed under subparagraphs (A) and (B)]-

        (C) if such interest is to be acquired for the surviving spouse. pursuant to directions of the decedent, by his executor or by the trustee of a trust.
        *****

    (2) INTEREST IN UNIDENTIFIED ASSETS.
        *****

    (3) INTEREST OF SPOUSE CONDITIONAL ON SURVIVAL FOR LIMITED PERIOD-For purposes of this subsection, an interest passing to the surviving spouse shall not be considered as an interest which will terminate or fail on the death of such spouse if-

        (A) such death will cause a termination or failure of such interest only if it occurs within a period not exceeding six months after the decedent's death, or only if it occurs as a result of a common disaster resulting in the death of the decedent and the surviving spouse, or only if it occurs in the case of either such event; and

        (B) such termination or failure does not in fact occur.

    (4) VALUATION OF INTEREST PASSING TO SURVIVING SPOUSE.
        *****

    (5) LIFE ESTATE WITH POWER OF APPOINTMENT IN SURVIVING SPOUSE-In the case of an interest in property passing from the decedent, if his surviving spouse is entitled for life to all the income from the entire interest, or all the income from a specific portion thereof, payable annually or at more frequent intervals. with power in the surviving spouse to appoint the entire interest, or such specific portion (exercisable in favor of such surviving spouse, or of the estate of such surviving spouse, or in favor of either, whether or not in each case the power is exercisable in favor of others), and with no power in any other person to appoint any part of the interest, or such specific portion, to any person other than the

surviving spouse-

(A) the interest or such portion thereof so passing shall, for purposes of subsection (a), be considered as passing to the surviving spouse, and

(B) no part of the interest so passing shall, for purposes of paragraph (I)(A), be considered as passing to any person other than the surviving spouse.

This paragraph shall apply only if such power in the surviving spouse to appoint the entire interest, or such specific portion thereof, whether exercisable by will or during life, is exercisable by such spouse alone and in all events.

(6) LIFE INSURANCE OR ANNUITY PAYMENTS WITH POWER OF AP-POINTMENT IN SURVIVING SPOUSE.

*****

(7) ELECTION WITH RESPECT TO LIFE ESTATE FOR SURVIVING SPOUSE-

(A) IN GENERAL.-In the case of qualified terminable interest property-

(I) for purposes of subsection (a), such property shall be treated as passing to the surviving spouse, and

(ii) for purposes of paragraph (1)(A), no part of such property shall be treated as passing to any person other than the surviving spouse.

(B) QUALIFIED TERMINABLE INTEREST PROPERTY DEFINED.-For purposes of this paragraph-

(I) IN GENERAL.-The term "qualified terminable interest property" means property-

(I) which passes from the decedent,

(II) in which the surviving spouse has a qualifying income interest for life, and

(III) to which an election under this paragraph applies.

(ii) Qualifying Income Interest For Life- The surviving spouse has a qualifying income interest for life if-

(I) the surviving spouse is entitled to all the income from the property, payable annually or at more frequent intervals, or has a usifruct interest for life in the property, and

(II) no person has a power to appoint any part of the property to any person other than the surviving spouse.

Subclause (II) shall not apply to a power exercisable only at or after the death of the surviving spouse. To the extent provided in regulations, an annuity shall be treated in a manner similar to an income interest in property (regardless of whether the property from which the annuity is payable can be separately identified).

(iii) PROPERTY INCLUDES INTEREST THEREIN.- The term "property" includes an interest in property.

(iv) SPECIFIC PORTION TREATED AS SEPARATE PROPERTY.- A specific portion of property shall be treated as separate property.

(v) ELECTION.-An election under this paragraph with respect to any property shall be made by the executor on the return of tax imposed by section 2001. Such an election, once made, shall be irrevocable.

(8) SPECIAL RULE FOR CHARITABLE REMAINDER TRUSTS.

*****

(9) DENIAL OF DOUBLE DEDUCTION.

*****

CHAPTER 11: ESTATE TAX, CONTINUED

Subchapter B: Nonresidents Not Citizens

SEC. 2101: TAX IMPOSED

(a) IMPOSITION.--Except as provided in section 2107, a tax is hereby imposed on the transfer of the taxable estate(determined as provided in section 2106) of every decedent nonresident not a citizen of the United States.

(b) COMPUTATION OF TAX.-- The tax imposed by this section shall be the amount equal to the excess (if any) of--

    (1) a tentative tax computed under section 2001 (c) on the sum of--

        A) amount of the taxable estate, and

        B) the amount of the taxable gifts, over

    (2) a tentative tax computed under section 2001 (c) on the amount of adjusted taxable gifts.

For purposes of the preceding sentence, there shall be appropriate adjustments in the application of section 2001 (c)(2) to reflect the difference between the amount of credit provided under section 2012(c) and the amount of credit provided under section 2010.

(c) ADJUSTMENTS FOR TAXABLE GIFTS.--

    1) ADJUSTED TAXABLE GIFTS DEFINED.--For purposes of this section, the term "adjustable taxable gifts" means the total amount of the taxable gifts (within the meaning of section 2503 as modified by section 2511) made by the decedent after December 31, 1976, other than gifts which are includable in the gross estate of the decedent.

    2) ADJUSTMENT FOR CERTAIN GIFT TAX.-- For purposes of this section, the rules of section 2001 (d) shall apply.

CHAPTER 12: GIFT TAX

SEC. 2501: IMPOSITION OF TAX

(a) TAXABLE TRANSFERS.--

    (1) GENERAL RULE.-- A tax, computed as provided in section 2502, is hereby imposed for each calendar year on the transfer of property by gift during such calendar year by any individual, resident or nonresident.

    (2) TRANSFERS OF INTANGIBLE PROPERTY.-- Except as provided in paragraph (3), paragraph (1) shall not apply to the transfer of intangible property by a nonresident not a citizen of the United States.

    (3) EXCEPTIONS--Paragraph (2) shall not apply in the case of a donor who at any time after March 8, 1965, and within the 10-year period ending with the date of transfer lost United States citizenship unless--

        (A) such donor's loss of United States citizenship resulted from the application of section 301(b), 350, or 355 of the Immigration and Nationality Act, as amended (8 U. S. C. 1401 (b), 1482, or 1487), or

        (B) such loss did not have for one of its principal purposes the avoidance of taxes under this subtitle or subtitle A.

    (4) BURDEN OF PROOF.-- If the Secretary establishes that it is reasonable to believe that an individual's loss of United States citizenship would, but for paragraph (3), result in the substantial reduction for the calendar year in the taxes on the transfer of property by gift, the burden of proving that such loss of citizenship did not have for one of its principal purposes the avoidance of taxes under this subtitle A shall be on such individual.

    (5) TRANSFERS TO POLITICAL ORGANIZATIONS.--Paragraph (1) shall not apply to the transfer of money or other property to a political organization (within the meaning of section 527(e)(1)) for the use of such organization.

(b) CERTAIN RESIDENTS OF POSSESSIONS CONSIDERED CITIZENS OF THE UNITED STATES.--A donor who is a citizen of the United States and a resident of a possession thereof shall, for the purposes of the taxes imposed by this chapter, be considered a "citizen" of the United States within the meaning of the term wherever used in this title unless he acquired his United States citizenship solely by reason of, 1) his being a citizen of such possession of the United States, or 2) his birth or residence within such possession of the United States.

(c) CERTAIN RESIDENTS OF POSSESSIONS CONSIDERED NONRESIDENTS NOT CITIZENS OF THE UNITED STATES.--A donor who is a citizen of the United States and a resident of a possession thereof shall, for purposes of the tax imposed by this chapter, be considered a "nonresident not a citizen of the United States" within the meaning of the term wherever used in this title, but only if such donor acquired his United States citizenship solely by reason of (1) his being a citizen of such possession of the United States, or (2) his birth or residence within such possession of the United States.

(d) CROSS REFERENCES.--

    (1) For increase in basis of property acquired by gift for gift tax paid, see section 1015(d).

    (2) For exclusion of transfers of property outside the United States

SEC. 2503: TAXABLE GIFTS

(a) GENERAL DEFINITION.-The term "taxable gifts" means the total amount of gifts made during the calendar year, less the deductions provided in subchapter C (section 2522 and following).

(b) EXCLUSIONS FROM GIFTS.-In the case of gifts (other than gifts of future interests in property) made to any person by the donor during the calendar year, the first $10,000 of such gifts to such person shall not, for purposes of subsection (a), be included in the total amount of gifts made during such year. Where there has been a transfer to any person of a present interest in property, the possibility that such interest may be diminished by the exercise of a power shall be disregarded in applying this subsection, if no part of such interest will at any time pass to any other person.

(c) TRANSFER FOR THE BENEFIT OF A MINOR.-No part of a gift to an individual who has not attained the age of 21 years on the date of such transfer shall be considered a gift of a future interest in property for purposes of subsection (b) if the property and the income therefrom-
>   (1) may be expended by, or for the benefit of, the donee before his attaining the age of 21 years, and
>   (2) will to the extent not so expended-
>   (A) pass to the donee on his attaining the age of 21 years, and
>   (B) in the event that the donee dies before attaining the age of 21 years, be payable to the estate of the donee or as he may appoint under a general power of appointment as defined in section 2514(c).

(d) Repealed.
(e) EXCLUSION FOR CERTAIN TRANSFERS FOR EDUCATIONAL EXPENSES OR MEDICAL EXPENSES.-
>   (1) IN GENERAL-Any qualified transfer shall not be treated as a transfer of property by gift for purposes of this chapter.
>   (2) QUALIFIED TRANSFER.-For purposes of this subsection, the term "qualified transfer" means any amount paid on behalf of an individual-
>   (A) as tuition to an educational organization described in section 170(b)(I)(A)(ii) for the education or training of such individual, or
>   (B) to any person who provides medical care [as defined in section 213(e)] with respect to such individual as payment for such medical care.

SEC. 2513: GIFT BY HUSBAND OR WIFE TO THIRD PARTY

(a) CONSIDERED AS MADE ONE-HALF BY EACH.--

    (1) IN GENERAL.--A gift made by one spouse to any person other than his spouse shall, for the purpose of this chapter, be considered made one-half by him and one-half by his spouse, but only if at the time of the gift each spouse is a citizen or resident of the United States. This paragraph shall not apply with respect to a gift of an interest in property if he creates in his spouse a general power of appointment, as defined in section 2514 (c), over such interest. For purposes of this section, an individual shall be considered as a spouse of another individual only if he is married to such individual at the time of the gift and does not remarry during the remainder of the calendar year.

    (2) CONSENT OF BOTH SPOUSES.--Paragraph (1) shall apply only if both spouses have signified (under the regulations provided for its subsection(b)) their consent to the application of paragraph (1) in the case of all such gifts made during the calendar year by either while married to the other.

(b) MANNER AND TIME OF SIGNIFYING CONSENT.--

    (1) MANNER.--A consent under this section shall be signified in such manner as is provided under regulations prescribed by the secretary.

    (2) TIME.--Such consent may be so signified after the close of the calendar year in which the gift was made, subject to the following limitations--

        (A) The consent may not be signified after the 15th of April following the close of such year, unless before the 15th day no return has been filed for such year by either spouse, in which case the consent may not be signified after a return for such year is filed by either spouse.

        (B) The consent may not be signified after a note of deficiency with respect to the tax for such year has been set to either spouse in accordance with section 6212(a).

(c) REVOCATION OF CONSENT.--Revocation of consent previously signified shall be made in such manner as is provided under regulations prescribed by the secretary, but the right to revoke a consent previously signified with respect to a calendar year-

    (1) shall not exist after the 15th day of April following the close of such year if the consent was signified on or before such 15th day; and

    (2) shall not exist if the consent was not signified until after such 15th day.

(d) JOINT AND SEVERAL LIABILITY FOR TAX.--If the consent required by subsection (a)(2) is signified with respect to a gift made in the calendar year, the liability with respect to the entire tax imposed by this chapter of each spouse for such year shall be joint and several.

SEC. 2514: POWERS OF APPOINTMENT

(a) POWERS CREATED ON OR BEFORE OCTOBER 21, 1942.-- An exercise of general power of appointment created on or before October 21, 1942, shall be deemed a transfer of property by the individual possessing such power; but the failure to exercise such a power or the complete release of such a power shall not be deemed an exercise thereof. If a general power of appointment created on or before October 21, 1942, has been partially released so that it is no longer a general power of appointment, the subsequent exercise of such power shall not be deemed to be the exercise of a general power of appointment if--

(1) such partial release occurred before November 1, 1951, or

(2) the donee of such power was under a legal disability to release such power on October 21, 1942, and such partial release occurred not later than six months after the termination of such legal disability.

(b) POWERS CREATED AFTER OCTOBER 21, 1942.-- The exercise or release of a general power of appointment created after October 21, 1942, shall be deemed a transfer of property by the individual possessing such power.

(c) DEFINITION OF GENERAL POWER OF APPOINTMENT.--For purposes of this section, the term "general power of appointment" means a power which is exercisable in favor of the individual possessing the power (hereafter in this subsection referred to as the "possessor"), his estate, his creditors, or the creditors of his estate; except that--

(1) A power to consume, invade, or appropriate property for the benefit of the possessor which is limited by an ascertainable standard relating to health, education, support, or maintenance of the possessor shall not be deemed a general power of appointment.

(2) A power of appointment created on or before October 21, 1942, which is exercisable by the possessor only in conjunction with another person shall not be deemed a general power of appointment.

(3) In the case of a power appointment created on or before October 21, 1942, which is exercisable by the possessor only in conjunction with another person--

(A) if the power is not exercisable by the possessor in conjunction with the creator of the power--such power shall not be deemed a general power of appointment;

(B) if the power is not exercisable by the possessor except in conjunction with a person having a substantial interest in the property subject to the power, which is adverse to exercise of the power in favor of the possessor-- property subject to the power, which is adverse to exercise of the power in favor of the possessor-- such power shall not be deemed a general power of appointment. For the purposes of this subparagraph a person who, after the death of the possessor, may be possessed of a power of appointment(with respect to the property subject to the possessors power) which he may exercise in his own favor shall be deemed as having interest in the property and such interest shall be deemed adverse to such exercise of the possessor's power;

(C) if (after the application of subparagraphs(A) and (B) the power is a general power of appointment and is exercisable in favor of such other person--such power shall be deemed a general power of appointment only in respect of a fractional part of the property subject to such power, such part to be determined by dividing the value of such property by the number of such persons(including the possessor) in favor of whom such power is exercisable.

For purposes of subparagraphs (B) and (C), a power shall be deemed to be exercisable in favor of a person if it is exercisable in favor of such person, his estate, his creditors, or the creditors of his estate.

(d) CREATION OF ANOTHER POWER IN CERTAIN CASES.-- If a power of appointment created after October 21, 1942, is exercised by creating another power of appointment which, under the applicable local law, can be validly exercised so as to postpone the vesting of any estate or interest in the property which was subject to the first power, or suspend the absolute ownership or power of alienation of such property, for a period ascertainable without regard to the date of the creation of this first power, such exercise of the first power shall, to the extent of the property subject to the second power, be deemed a transfer of property by the individual possessing such power.

(e) LAPSE OF POWER.--The lapse of a power of appointment created after October 21, 1942, during the life of the individual possessing the power shall be considered a release of such power. The rule of the preceding sentence shall apply with respect to the lapse of powers during any calendar year only to the extent that the property which could have been appointed by exercise of such lapsed powers exceeds in value the greater of the following amounts:

(1) $5,000, or

(2) 5 percent of the aggregate value of the assets out of which, or the proceeds of which, the exercise of the lapsed powers could be satisfied.

(f) DATE OF CREATION OF POWER.--For purposes of this section a power of appointment created by a will executed on or before October 21, 1942, shall be considered a power on or before such date if the person executing the will dies before July 1, 1949, without having republished such will, by codicil or otherwise, after October 21, 1942.

SEC. 2518: DISCLAIMERS

(a) GENERAL RULE.-- For purposes of this subtitle, if a person makes a qualified disclaimer with respect to any interest in property, this subtitle shall apply with respect to such interest as if the interest had never been transferred to such person.

(b) QUALIFIED DISCLAIMER DEFINED.-- For purposes of subsection (a), the term "qualified disclaimer" means an irrevocable and unqualified refusal by a person to accept an interest in property but only if--

(1) such refusal is in writing

(2) such writing is received by the transferor of the interest, his legal representative, or the holder of the legal title to which the interest relates not later than the date which is nine months after the later of--

(A) the date on which the transfer in such person is made, or

(B) the day on which such person attains age 21.

(3) such person has not accepted the interest or any benefits, and

(4) as a result of such refusal, the interest passes without any direction on the part of the person making the disclaimer and passes either--

(A) to the spouse of the decedent , or

(B) to a person other than the person making the disclaimer.

(c) OTHER RULES.--For purposes of subsection (a)--

(1) DISCLAIMER OF UNDIVIDED PORTION OF INTEREST.-- A disclaimer with respect to an undivided portion of an interest which meets the requirements of the preceding sentence shall be treated as a qualified disclaimer of such portion of the

interest.
(2) POWERS.-- A power with respect to property shall be treated as an interest in such property.
(3) CERTAIN TRANSFERS TREATED AS DISCLAIMERS.--A written transfer of the transferor's [*sic*] entire interest in the property--
   (A) which meets requirements similar to the requirements of paragraphs (2) and (3) of subsection(b), and
   (B) which is to a person or persons who would have received the property had the transferor *[sic]* made a qualified disclaimer (within the meaning of subsection (b)), shall be treated as a qualified disclaimer.

CHAPTER 13: GENERATION-SKIPPING TRANSFER TAX

SEC. 2601: TAX IMPOSED

A tax is hereby imposed on every generation-skipping transfer (within the meaning of subchapter B).

SEC. 2602: AMOUNT OF TAX

The amount of the tax imposed by section 2601 is--
   (1) the taxable amount (determined under subchapter C), multiplied by
   (2) the applicable rate (determined under subsection E).

SEC. 2603: LIABILITY FOR TAX

(a) PERSONAL LIABILITY.--
   (1) TAXABLE DISTRIBUTIONS.--In the case of a taxable distribution, the tax imposed by section 2601 shall be paid by the transferee.
   (2) TAXABLE TERMINATION.-- In the case of a taxable termination or a direct skip from a trust, the tax shall be paid by the trustee.
   (3) DIRECT SKIP.-- In the case of a direct skip (other than a direct skip from trust), the tax shall be paid by the transferor.
(b) SOURCE OF TAX.--Unless otherwise directed pursuant to the governing instrument by specific reference to the tax imposed by this chapter, the tax imposed by this chapter on a generation- skipping transfer shall be charged to the property constituting such transfer.
(c) CROSS REFERENCE.-- For provisions making estate and gift tax provisions with respect to transferee liability, liens, and related matters applicable to the tax imposed by section 2601, see section 2661.

SEC. 2611: GENERATION-SKIPPING TRANSFER DEFINED

(a) IN GENERAL.--For purposes of this chapter, the term "generation-skipping transfer," means--
   (1) a taxable distribution,
   (2) a taxable termination, and
   (3) a direct skip.
(b) CERTAIN TRANSFERS EXCLUDED.-- The term "generation-skipping transfer" does not include--
   (1) any transfer which, if made inter vivos by an individual, would not be treated as a taxable gift by reason of section 2503 (e) (relating to exclusion of certain

transfers for educational or medical expenses), and
   (2) any transfer to the extent--
     (A) the property transferred was subject to a prior tax imposed under this chapter,
     (B) the transferee in the prior transfer was assigned to the same generation as (or a lower generation than) the generation assignment of the transferee in this transfer, and
     (C) such transfers do not have the effect of avoiding tax under this chapter with respect to any transfer.

SEC. 2612: TAXABLE TERMINATION; TAXABLE DISTRIBUTION; DIRECT SKIP

(a) TAXABLE TERMINATION.--
   (1) GENERAL RULE.--For purposes of this chapter, the term "taxable termination" means the termination (by death, lapse of time, release of power, or otherwise) of an interest in property held in a trust unless--
     (A) immediately after such termination, a non-skip person has an interest in such property, or
     (B) at no time after such termination may a distribution (including distributions on termination) be made from such trust to a skip person.
   (2) CERTAIN PARTIAL TERMINATIONS TREATED AS TAXABLE.-- If, upon the termination of an interest in property held in trust by reason of the death of a lineal descendant of the transferor, a specified portion of the trust's assets are distributed to 1 or more skip persons (or 1 or more trusts for the exclusive benefit of such persons), such termination shall constitute a taxable termination with respect to such portion of the trust property.
(b) TAXABLE DISTRIBUTION.-- For purposes of this chapter the term "taxable distribution" means any distribution from a trust to a skip person (other than taxable termination or direct skip).
(c) DIRECT SKIP.-For purposes of this chapter--
   (1) IN GENERAL.--The term "direct skip" means a transfer subject to a tax imposed by chapter 11 or 12 of an interest in property to a skip person.
   (2) SPECIAL RULE FOR TRANSFERS TO GRANDCHILDREN.-- For purposes of determining whether any transfer is a direct skip, if--
     (A) an individual is a grandchild of the transferor or the transferor's spouse or former spouse) and
     (B) as of the time of the transfer, the parent of such individual who is a lineal descendant of the transferor (or the transferor's spouse or former spouse) is dead,
such individual shall be treated as if such individual were a child of the transferor and all of that grandchild's children shall be treated as if they were grandchildren of the transferor. In the case of lineal decedents below a grandchild, the preceding sentence may be reapplied. If any transfer of property to a trust would be a direct skip but for this paragraph, any generation assignment under this paragraph shall apply also for purposes of applying this chapter to transfers from the portion of the trust attributable to such property.
   (3) LOOK-THRU RULES NOT TO APPLY.--Solely for the purposes of determining whether any transfer to a trust is a direct skip, the rules of section 2651 (e)(2) shall not apply.

SEC. 2613: SKIP PERSON AND NON-SKIP PERSON DEFINED

(a) SKIP PERSON.-- For purposes of this chapter, the term "skip person" means--
  (1) a natural person assigned to a generation which is 2 or more generations below the generation assignment of the transferor, or
  (2) a trust--
      (A) if all intents in such trust are held by skip persons, or
      (B) if--
          (I) there is no holding an interest in such trust, and
          (ii) at no such time after the transfer may a distribution (including distributions on termination) be made from such trust to a non-skip person.
(b) NON-SKIP PERSON.--For purposes of this chapter, the term "non-skip person" means any person who is not a skip person.

SEC. 2631: GST EXEMPTION

(a) GENERAL RULE.--For purposes of determining the inclusion ratio, every individual shall be allowed a GST exemption of $1,000,000 which may be allocated by such individual (or his executor) to any property with respect to which such individual is the transferor.
(b) ALLOCATIONS IRREVOCABLE.--Any allocation under subsection (a), once made, shall be irrevocable.

SEC. 2641:APPLICABLE RATE

(a) GENERAL RULE.--For purposes of this chapter, the term "applicable rate" means, with respect to any generation-skipping transfer, the product of--
  (1) the maximum Federal estate tax rate, and
  (2) the inclusion ratio to the transfer.
(b) MAXIMUM FEDERAL ESTATE TAX RATE.--For purposes of subsection (a), the term "maximum Federal estate tax rate" means the maximum rate imposed by section 2001 on the estates decedents dying at the time of the taxable distribution, taxable termination, or direct skip, as the case may be.

SEC. 2642: INCLUSION RATIO

(a) INCLUSION RATIO DEFINED.--For purposes of this chapter--
  (1) IN GENERAL.--Except as provided in this section, the inclusion ratio with respect to any property transferred in a generation-skipping transfer shall be excess (if any) of 1 over--
      (A) except as provided in subparagraph (b), the applicable fraction determined for the trust from which such transfer is made, or
      (B) in the case of a direct skip, the applicable fraction determined for such skip.

(2) APPLICABLE FRACTION.--For purposes of paragraph (1), the applicable fraction is a fraction--

(A) the numerator of which is the amount of the GST exemption allocated to the trust (or in the case of a direct skip, allocated to the property transferred in such skip), and

(B) the denominator of which is--

(I) the value of the property transferred to the trust (or involved in the direct skip), reduced by

(ii) the sum of-

(I) any Federal tax or State death tax actually recovered from the trust attributable such property, and

(II) any charitable deduction allowed under section 2055 or 2522 with respect to such property.

(b) VALUATION RULES, ETC.

*****

(c) TREATMENT OF CERTAIN DIRECT SKIPS WHICH ARE NONTAXABLE GIFTS.

(1) IN GENERAL. In the case of a direct skip which is a nontaxable gift, the inclusion ratio shall be zero.

(2) EXCEPTION FOR CERTAIN TRANSFERS IN TRUST. Paragraph (1) shall not apply to any transfer to a trust for the benefit of an individual unless--

(A) during the life of such individual, no portion of the corpus or income of the trust may be distributed to (or for the benefit of) any person other than such individual, and

(B) if the trust does not terminate before the individual dies, the assets of such trust will be includable in the gross estate of such individual.

Rules similar to the rules of section 2652(c)(3) shall apply for purposes of subparagraph (A).

(3) NONTAXABLE GIFT. For purposes of this subsection, the term "nontaxable gift" means any transfer of property to the extent such transfer is not treated as a taxable gift by reason of--

(A) section 2503(b) (taking into account the application of section 2513), or

(B) section 2503(e)

(d) SPECIAL RULES WHERE MORE THAN ONE TRANSFER MADE TO TRUST.--

*****

(e) SPECIAL RULES FOR CHARITABLE LEAD ANNUITY TRUSTS.--

*****

(f) SPECIAL RULES FOR CERTAIN INTER VIVOS TRANSFERS.-- Except as provided in regulations--

(1) IN GENERAL. For purposes of determining the inclusion ratio, if--

(A) an individual makes an inter vivos transfer of property, and

(B) the value of such property would be includable in the gross estate of such individual under chapter 11 if such individual died immediately after making such transfer (other than by reason of section 2035),

any allocation of GST exemption to such property shall not be made before the close of the estate tax inclusion period (and the value of such property shall be determined under paragraph (2)). If such transfer is a direct skip, such skip shall be treated as occurring as of the close of the estate tax inclusion period.

(2) VALUATION. In the case of any property to which paragraph (1) applies, the

value of such property shall be--

    (A) if such property is includable in the gross estate of the transferor (other than by reason of section 2035), its value for purposes of chapter 11, or

    (B) if subparagraph (A) does not apply, its value as of the close of the estate tax inclusion period (or, if any allocation of GST exemption to such property is not made on a timely filed gift tax return for the calendar year in which such period ends, its value as of the time such allocation is filed with the Secretary).

  (3) ESTATE TAX INCLUSION PERIOD. For purposes of this subsection, the term "estate tax inclusion period" means any period after the transfer described in paragraph (1) during which the value of the property involved in such transfer would be includable in the gross estate of the transferor under chapter 11 if he died. Such period shall in no event extend beyond the earlier of--

    (A) the date on which there is a generation-skipping transfer with respect to such property, or

    (B) the date of the death of the transferor.

  (4) TREATMENT OF SPOUSE. Except as provided in regulations, any reference in this subsection to an individual or transferor shall be treated as including a reference to the spouse of such individual or transferor.

  (5) COORDINATION WITH SUBSECTION (d). Under regulations, appropriate adjustments shall be made in the application of subsection (d) to take into account the provisions of this subsection.

CHAPTER 14: SPECIAL VALUATION RULES

SEC. 2701. SPECIAL VALUATION RULES IN CASE OF CERTAIN INTERESTS IN CORPORATIONS OR PARTNERSHIPS.

(a) Valuation Rules.
    (1) IN GENERAL.--Solely for purposes of determining whether a transfer of an interest in a corporation or partnership to (or for the benefit of) a member of the transferor's family is a gift (and the value of such transfer), the value of any right--
        (A) which is described in subparagraph (A) or (B) of subsection (b)(1), and
        (B) which is with respect to any applicable retained interest that is held by the transferor or an applicable family member immediately after the transfer,
shall be determined under paragraph (3). This paragraph shall not apply to the transfer of any interest for which market quotations are readily available (as of the date of transfer) on an established securities market.
    (2) EXCEPTIONS FOR MARKETABLE RETAINED INTERESTS, ETC.-- Paragraph (1) shall not apply to any right with respect to an applicable retained interest if--
        (A) market quotations are readily available (as of the date of the transfer) for such interest on an established securities market,
        (B) such interest is of the same class as the transferred interest, or
        (C) such interest is proportionally the same as the transferred interest, without regard to nonlapsing differences in voting power (or, for a partnership, nonlapsing differences with respect to management and limitations on liability).
Subparagraph (c) shall not apply to any interest in a partnership if the transferor or an applicable family member has the right to alter the liability of the transferee of the transferred property. Except as provided by the secretary, any difference described in subparagraph (C) which lapses by reason of any Federal or State law shall be treated as a nonlapsing difference for purposes of such subparagraph.
    (3) VALUATION OF RIGHTS TO WHICH PARAGRAPH (1) APPLIES.--
        (A) IN GENERAL.--The value of any right described in paragraph (1), other than a distribution right which consists of a right to receive a qualified payment, shall be treated as being zero.
        (B) VALUATION OF QUALIFIED PAYMENTS.--If--
            (I) any applicable retained interest confers a distribution right which consists of the right to a qualified payment, and
            (ii) there are 1 or more liquidation, put, call, or conversion rights with respect to such interest,
the value of all such rights shall be determined as if each liquidation, put, call, or conversion right were exercised in the manner resulting in the lowest value being determined for all such rights.
    (4) MINIMUM VALUATION OF JUNIOR EQUITY.--
        (A) IN GENERAL.--In the case of a transfer described in paragraph (1) of a junior equity interest in a corporation or partnership, such interest shall in no event be valued at an amount less than the value which would be determined if the total value of all the junior equity interests in the entity were equal to 10 percent of the sum of--

(I) the total value of all of the equity interests in such entity, plus

(ii) the total amount of indebtedness of such entity to the transferor (or an applicable family member).

(B) DEFINITIONS.--For purposes of this paragraph--

(I) JUNIOR EQUITY INTEREST.--The term "junior equity interest" means common stock or, in the case of a partnership, any partnership interest under which the rights as to income and capital are junior to the rights of all other classes of equity interests.

(ii) EQUITY INTEREST.--The term "equity interest" means stock or any interest as a partner, as the case may be.

(b) APPLICABLE RETAINED INTERESTS.--For purposes of this section--

(1) IN GENERAL.--The term "applicable retained interest" means any interest in an entity with respect to which there is--

(A) a distribution right, but only if, immediately before the transfer described in subsection (a)(1), the transferor and applicable family members hold (after application of subsection (e)(3)) control of the entity, or

(B) a liquidation, put, call, or conversion right.

(2) CONTROL.--For purposes of paragraph (1)--

(A) CORPORATIONS.--In the case of a corporation, the term "control" means the holding of at least 50 percent (by vote or value) of the stock of the corporation.

(B) PARTNERSHIPS.--In the case of a partnership, the term "control" means--

(I) the holding of at least 50 percent of the capital or profits interests in the partnership, or

(ii) in the case of a limited partnership, the holding of any interest as a general partner.

(c) DISTRIBUTION AND OTHER RIGHTS; QUALIFIED PAYMENTS.--

For purposes of this section--

(1) DISTRIBUTION RIGHT.--

(A) IN GENERAL.--The term "distribution right" means--

(I) a right to distributions from a corporation with respect to its stock, and

(ii) a right to distributions from a partnership with respect to a partner's interest in the partnership.

(B) EXCEPTIONS.--The term "distribution right" does not include--

(I) a right to distributions with respect to any junior equity interest (as defined in subsection (a) (4)(B)(I));

(ii) any liquidation, put, call, or conversion right, or

(iii) any right to receive any guaranteed payment described in section 707(c) of a fixed amount.

(2) LIQUIDATION, ETC. RIGHTS.--

(A) IN GENERAL.--The term "liquidation, put, call, or conversion right" means any liquidation, put, call, or conversion right, or any similar right, the exercise or nonexercise of which affects the value of the transferred interest.

(B) EXCEPTION FOR FIXED RIGHTS.--

(I) IN GENERAL.--The term "liquidation, put call, or conversion right" does not include any right which must be exercised at a specific time and at a specific amount.

(ii) TREATMENT OF CERTAIN RIGHTS.--If a right is assumed to be exercised in a particular manner under subsection (a)(3)(B), such right shall be treated as so exercised for purposes of clause (I).

(C) EXCEPTION FOR CERTAIN RIGHTS TO CONVERT.--The term "liquidation, put, call, or conversion right" does not include any right which--

    (I) is a right to convert into a fixed number (or a fixed percentage) of shares of the same class of stock in a corporation as the transferred stock in such corporation under subsection (a)(1) (or stock which would be of the same class but for nonlapsing differences in voting power),

    (ii) is nonlapsing,

    (iii) is subject to proportionate adjustments for splits, combinations, reclassification, and similar changes in the capital stock, and

    (iv) is subject to adjustments similar to the adjustments under subsection (d) for accumulated but unpaid distributions.

A rule similar to the rule of the preceding sentence shall apply for partnerships.

(3) QUALIFIED PAYMENT.--

    (A) IN GENERAL.-- Except as otherwise provided in this paragraph, the term "qualified payment" means any dividend payable on a periodic basis under any cumulative preferred stock (or a comparable payment under any partnership interest) to the extent that such dividend (or comparable payment) is determined at a fixed rate.

    (B) TREATMENT OF VARIABLE RATE PAYMENTS.--For purposes of subparagraph (A), a payment shall be treated as fixed as to rate if such payment is determined at a rate which bears a fixed relationship to a specified market interest rate.

    (C) ELECTIONS.--

        (I) WAIVER OF QUALIFIED PAYMENT TREATMENT.--A transferor or applicable family member may elect with respect to payments under any interest specified in such election to treat such payments as payments which are not qualified payments.

        (ii) ELECTION TO HAVE INTEREST TREATED AS QUALIFIED PAYMENT.--A transferor or any applicable family member may elect to treat any distribution right as a qualified payment, to be paid in the amounts and at the times specified in such election. The preceding sentence shall apply only to the extent that the amounts and times so specified are not inconsistent with the underlying legal instrument giving rise to such right.

        (iii) ELECTIONS IRREVOCABLE.--Any election under this subparagraph with respect to an interest shall, once made, be irrevocable.

(d) TRANSFER TAX TREATMENT OF CUMULATIVE BUT UNPAID DISTRIBUTIONS.--

    (1) IN GENERAL.--If a taxable event occurs with respect to any distribution right to which subsection (a)(3)(B) applied; the following shall be increased by the amount determined under paragraph (2):

    (A) the taxable estate of the transferor in the case of a taxable event described in paragraph (3)(A)(I).

    (B) The taxable gifts of the transferor for the calendar year in which the taxable event occurs in the case of a taxable event described in paragraph (3)(A)(ii) or (iii).

    (2) AMOUNT OF INCREASE.--

    (A) IN GENERAL.--The amount of the increase determined under this paragraph shall be the excess (if any) of--

(I) the value of the qualified payments payable during the period beginning on the date of the transfer under subsection (a)(1) and ending on the taxable event determined as if--

  (I) all such payments were paid on the date payment was due, and

  (II) all such payments were reinvested by the transferor as of the date of payment at a yield equal to the discount rate used in determining the value of the applicable retained interest described in subsection (a)(1), over

(ii) the value of such payments paid during such period computed under clause (I) on the basis of the time when such payments were actually paid.

(B) LIMITATIONS ON AMOUNT OF INCREASE.--

(I) IN GENERAL.--The amount of the increase under subparagraph (A) shall not exceed the applicable percentage of the excess (if any) of--

  (I) the value (determined as of the date of the taxable event) of all equity interests in the entity which are junior to the applicable retained interest, over

  (II) the value of such interests (determined as of the date of the transfer to which subsection (a)(1) applied).

(ii) APPLICABLE PERCENTAGE.--For purposes of clause (I), the applicable percentage is the percentage determined by dividing--

  (I) the number of shares in the corporation held (as of the date of the taxable event) by the transferor which are applicable retained interests of the same class, by

  (II) the total number of shares in such corporation (as of such date) which are of the same class as the class described in subclause (I).

A similar percentage shall be determined in the case of interests in a partnership.

(iii) DEFINITION.--For purposes of this subparagraph, the term "equity interest" has the meaning given such term by subsection (a)(4)(B).

(C) GRACE PERIOD.--For purposes of subparagraph (A), any payment of any distribution during the 4-year period beginning on its due date shall be treated as having been made on such due date.

(3) TAXABLE EVENTS.--For purposes of this subsection--

(A) IN GENERAL.--The term "taxable event" means any of the following:

(I) The death of the transferor if the applicable retained interest conferring the distribution right is includable in the estate of the transferor.

(ii) The transfer of such applicable retained interest.

(iii) At the election of the taxpayer, the payment of any qualified payment after the period described in paragraph (2)(C), but only with respect to the period ending on the date of such payment.

(B) EXCEPTION WHERE SPOUSE IS TRANSFEREE.--

(I) DEATHTIME TRANSFERS.--Subparagraph (A)(I) shall not apply to any interest includable in the gross estate of the transferor if a deduction with respect to such interest is allowable under section 2056 or 2106(a)(3).

(ii) LIFETIME TRANSFERS.--A transfer to the spouse of the transferor shall not be treated as a taxable event under subparagraph (A)(ii) if such transfer does not result in a taxable gift by reason of--

> (I) any deduction allowed under section 2523, or
>
> (II) consideration for the transfer provided by the spouse.
>
> (iii) SPOUSE SUCCEEDS TO TREATMENT OF TRANSFEROR.--If an event is not treated as a taxable event by reason of this subparagraph, the transferee spouse or surviving spouse (as the case may be) shall be treated in the same manner as the transferor in applying this subsection with respect to the interest involved.

(4) SPECIAL RULES FOR APPLICABLE FAMILY MEMBERS.--

> (A) FAMILY MEMBER TREATED IN SAME MANNER AS TRANSFEROR.-- For purposes of this subsection, an applicable family member shall be treated in the same manner as the transferor with respect to any distribution right retained by such family member to which subsection (a)(3)(B) applied.
>
> (B) TRANSFER TO APPLICABLE FAMILY MEMBER.--In the case of a taxable event described in paragraph (3)(A)(ii) involving the transfer of an applicable retained interest to an applicable family member (other than the spouse of the transferor), the applicable family member shall be treated in the same manner as the transferor in applying this subsection to distributions accumulating with respect to such interest after such taxable event.

(5) TRANSFER TO INCLUDE TERMINATION.--For purposes of this subsection, any termination of an interest shall be treated as a transfer.

(e) OTHER DEFINITIONS AND RULES.--For purposes of this section--

(1) MEMBER OF THE FAMILY.--The term "member of the family" means, with respect to any transferor--

> (A) the transferor's spouse,
>
> (B) a lineal descendant of the transferor or the transferor's spouse, and
>
> (C) the spouse of any such descendant.

(2) APPLICABLE FAMILY MEMBER.--The term "applicable family member" means, with respect to any transferor--

> (A) the transferor's spouse,
>
> (B) an ancestor of the transferor or the transferor's spouse, and
>
> (C) the spouse of any such ancestor.

(3) ATTRIBUTION RULES.--

> (A) INDIRECT HOLDINGS AND TRANSFERS.--An individual shall be treated as holding any interest to the extent such interest is held indirectly by such individual through a corporation, partnership, trust, or other entity. If any individual is treated as holding any interest by reason of the preceding sentence, any transfer which results in such interest being treated as no longer held by such individual shall be treated as a transfer of such interest.
>
> (B) CONTROL.--For purposes of subsections (b)(1), an individual shall be treated as holding any interest held by the individual's brothers, sisters, or lineal descendants.

(4) EFFECT OF ADOPTION.--A relationship by legal adoption shall be treated as a relationship by blood.

(5) CERTAIN CHANGES TREATED AS TRANSFERS.--Except as provided in regulations, a contribution to capital or a redemption, recapitalization, or other change in the capital structure of a corporation or partnership shall be treated as a transfer of an interest in such entity to which this section applies if the taxpayer or an applicable family member--

(A) receives an applicable retained interest in such entity pursuant to such contribution to capital or such redemption, recapitalization, or other change, or

(B) under regulations otherwise holds, immediately after the transfer, an applicable retained interest in such entity.

This paragraph shall not apply to any transaction (other than a contribution to capital) if the interests in the entity held by the transferor, applicable family members, and members of the transferor's family before and after the transaction are substantially identical.

(6) ADJUSTMENTS.--Under regulations prescribed by the Secretary, if there is any subsequent transfer, or inclusion in the gross estate, of any applicable retained interest which was valued under the rules of subsection (a), appropriate adjustments shall be made for purposes of chapter 11, 12, or 13 to reflect the increase in the amount of any prior taxable gift made by the transferor or decedent by reason of such valuation.

(7) TREATMENT AS SEPARATE INTERESTS.--The Secretary may by regulation provide that any applicable retained interest shall be treated as 2 or more separate interests for purposes of this section.

SEC. 2702: SPECIAL VALUATION RULES IN CASE OF TRANSFERS OF INTERESTS IN TRUSTS

(a) VALUATION RULES.-

(1) IN GENERAL.- Solely for purposes of determining- whether a transfer of an interest in trust to (or for the benefit of) a member of the transferor's family is a gift (and the value of such transfer), the value of any interest in such trust retained by the transferor or any applicable family member (as defined in section 2701(e)(2)) shall be determined as provided in paragraph (2).

(2) VALUATION OF RETAINED INTERESTS.-

(A) IN GENERAL.- The value of any retained interest which is not a qualified interest shall be treated as being zero.

(B) VALUATION OF QUALIFIED INTEREST.- The value of any retained interest which is a qualified interest shall be determined under section 7520.

(3) EXCEPTIONS

(A) IN GENERAL.- This subsection shall not apply to any transfer-

(I) to the extent that such transfer is an incomplete transfer, or

(ii) if such transfer involves the transfer of an interest in trust all the property in which consists of a residence to be used as a personal residence by persons holding term interests in such trust.

(B) INCOMPLETE TRANSFER.- For purposes of subparagraph (A), the term "incomplete transfer" means any transfer which would not be treated as a gift whether of not consideration was received for such transfer.

(b) QUALIFIED INTEREST.- For purposes of this section, the term "qualified interest" means-

(1) any interest which consists of the right to receive fixed amounts payable not less frequently than annually,

(2) any interest which consists of the right to receive fixed amounts which are payable not less frequently than annually and are a fixed percentage of the fair market value of the property in the trust (determined annually), and

(3) any noncontingent remainder interest if all of the other interests in the trust consists of interests described in paragraph (1) or (2).

(c) CERTAIN PROPERTY TREATED AS HELD IN TRUST.- For purposes of this section-

    (1) IN GENERAL.- The transfer of an interest in property with respect to which there is 1 or more term interests shall be treated as a transfer of an interest in a trust.

    (2) JOINT PURCHASES.- If 2 or more members of the same family acquire interests in any property described in paragraph (1) in the same transaction (or a series of related transactions), the person (or persons) acquiring the term interests in such property shall be treated as having acquired the entire property and then transferred to the other persons the interests acquired by such other persons in the transaction (or series of transactions). Such transfer shall be treated as made in exchange for the consideration (if any) provided by such other persons for the acquisition of their interests in such property.

    (3) TERM INTEREST.- The term "term interest" means-

        (A) a life interest in property, or

        (B) an interest in property for a term of years.

    (4) VALUATION RULE FOR CERTAIN TERM INTERESTS.- If the nonexcercise of rights under a term interest in tangible property would not have a substantial effect on the valuation of the remainder interest in such property-

        (A) subparagraph (A) of subsection (a)(2) shall not apply to such term interest, and

        (B) the value of such term interest for purposes of applying subsection (a)(1) shall be the amount which the holder of a term interest establishes as the amount for which such interest could be sold to an unrelated third party.

(d) TREATMENT OF TRANSFERS OF INTEREST IN PORTION OF TRUST.- In the case of a transfer of an income or remainder interest with respect to a specified portion of the property in a trust, only such portion shall be taken into account in applying this section to such transfer.

(e) MEMBER OF THE FAMILY.- For purposes of this section, the term "member of the family" shall have the meaning given such term by section 2704(c)(2).

SEC. 2703 CERTAIN RIGHTS AND RESTRICTIONS DISREGARDED

(a) GENERAL RULE.- For purposes of this subtitle, the value of any property shall be determined without regard to-

    (1) any option, agreement, or other right to acquire or use the property at a price less than the fair market value of the property (without regard to such option, agreement, or right), or

    (2) any restriction on the right to sell or use such property.

(b) EXCEPTIONS.- Subsection (a) shall not apply to any option, agreement, right or restriction which meets each of the following requirements:

    (1) It is a bona fide business arrangement.

    (2) It is not a device to transfer such property to members of the decedent's family for less than full and adequate consideration in money or money's worth.

    (3) Its terms are comparable to similar arrangements entered into by persons in an arm's length transaction.

SEC. 2704 TREATMENT OF CERTAIN LAPSING RIGHTS AND RESTRICTIONS

(a) TREATMENT OF LAPSED VOTING OR LIQUIDATION RIGHTS.--

    (1) IN GENERAL.--For purposes of this subtitle, if--

        (A) there is a lapse of any voting or liquidation right in a corporation or partnership, and

        (B) the individual holding such right immediately before the lapse and members of such individual's family hold, both before and after the lapse, control of the entity,

such lapse shall be treated as a transfer by such individual by gift, or a transfer which is includable in the gross estate of the decedent, whichever is applicable, in the amount determined under paragraph (2).

    (2) AMOUNT OF TRANSFER.-- For purposes of paragraph (1), the amount determined under this paragraph is the excess (if any) of--

        (A) the value of all interests in the entity held by the individual described in paragraph (1) immediately before the lapse (determined as if the voting and liquidation rights were nonlapsing), over

        (B) the value of such interests immediately after the lapse.

    (3) SIMILAR RIGHTS.--The Secretary may by regulations apply this subsection to rights similar to voting and liquidation rights.

(b) CERTAIN RESTRICTIONS ON LIQUIDATION DISREGARDED.--

    (1) IN GENERAL.--For purposes of this subtitle, if--

        (A) there is a transfer of an interest in a corporation or partnership to (or for the benefit of) a member of the transferor's family, and

        (B) the transferor and members of the transferor's family hold, immediately before the transfer, control of the entity,

any applicable restriction shall be disregarded in determining the value of the transferred interest.

(2) APPLICABLE RESTRICTION.--For purposes of this subsection, the term "applicable restriction" means any restriction--

(A) which effectively limits the ability of the corporation or partnership to liquidate, and

(B) with respect to which either of the following applies:

(I) The restriction lapses, in whole or in part, after the transfer referred t to in paragraph (1).

(ii) The transferor or any member of the transferor's family, either alone of collectively, has the right after such transfer to remove, in whole or in part, the restriction.

(3) EXCEPTIONS.--The term "applicable restriction" shall not include--

(A) any commercially reasonable restriction which arises as part of any financing by the corporation or partnership with a person who is not related to the transferor or transferee, or a member of the family of either, or

(B) any restriction imposed, or required to be imposed, by any Federal or State law.

(4) OTHER RESTRICTIONS.--The secretary may by regulations provide that other restrictions shall be disregarded in determining the value of the transfer of any interest in a corporation or partnership to a member of the transferor's family if such restriction has the effect of reducing the value of the transferred interest for purposes of this subtitle but does not ultimately reduce the value of such interest to the transferee

CHAPTER 77: MISCELLANEOUS PROVISIONS

SEC 7520 VALUATION TABLES

(a) GENERAL RULE.- For purposes of this title, the value of any annuity, any interest for life or a term of years, or any remainder or reversionary interest shall be determined-

    (1) under tables prescribed by the Secretary, and

    (2) by using an interest rate (rounded to the nearest 2/10ths of 1 percent) equal to 120 percent of the Federal midterm rate in effect under section 1274(d)(1) for the month in which the valuation date falls.

If an income, estate, or gift tax charitable contribution is allowable for any part of the property transferred, the taxpayer may elect to use such Federal midterm rate for either of the two months preceding the month in which the valuation date falls for purposes of paragraph (2). In the case of transfers of more than 1 interest in the same property with respect to which the taxpayer may use the same rate under paragraph (2), the taxpayer shall use the same rate with respect to each such interest.

*****

Federal Estate Tax Return (Form 706)

Form **706**	**United States Estate (and Generation-Skipping Transfer) Tax Return**		OMB No. 1545-0015

Form **706**
(Rev. August 1993)
Department of the Treasury
Internal Revenue Service

United States Estate (and Generation-Skipping Transfer) Tax Return
Estate of a citizen or resident of the United States (see separate instructions). To be filed for decedents dying after October 8, 1990. For Paperwork Reduction Act Notice, see page 1 of the instructions.

OMB No. 1545-0015
Expires 12-31-95

Part 1.—Decedent and Executor

1a Decedent's first name and middle initial (and maiden name, if any)	1b Decedent's last name	2 Decedent's social security no.

3a Domicile at time of death (county and state, or foreign country)	3b Year domicile established	4 Date of birth	5 Date of death

6a Name of executor (see instructions)	6b Executor's address (number and street including apartment or suite no. or rural route; city, town, or post office; state; and ZIP code)

| 6c Executor's social security number (see instructions) | |

7a Name and location of court where will was probated or estate administered	7b Case number

8 If decedent died testate, check here ▶ ☐ and attach a certified copy of the will. | 9 If Form 4768 is attached, check here ▶ ☐

10 If Schedule R-1 is attached, check here ▶ ☐

Part 2.—Tax Computation

1	Total gross estate (from Part 5, Recapitulation, page 3, item 10)	1	
2	Total allowable deductions (from Part 5, Recapitulation, page 3, item 20)	2	
3	Taxable estate (subtract line 2 from line 1)	3	
4	Adjusted taxable gifts (total taxable gifts (within the meaning of section 2503) made by the decedent after December 31, 1976, other than gifts that are includible in decedent's gross estate (section 2001(b))	4	
5	Add lines 3 and 4	5	
6	Tentative tax on the amount on line 5 from Table A in the instructions	6	
7a	If line 5 exceeds $10,000,000, enter the lesser of line 5 or $21,040,000. If line 5 is $10,000,000 or less, skip lines 7a and 7b and enter -0- on line 7c . 7a		
b	Subtract $10,000,000 from line 7a 7b		
c	Enter 5% (.05) of line 7b	7c	
8	Total tentative tax (add lines 6 and 7c)	8	
9	Total gift tax payable with respect to gifts made by the decedent after December 31, 1976. Include gift taxes by the decedent's spouse for such spouse's share of split gifts (section 2513) only if the decedent was the donor of these gifts and they are includible in the decedent's gross estate (see instructions)	9	
10	Gross estate tax (subtract line 9 from line 8)	10	
11	Maximum unified credit against estate tax 11	192,800	00
12	Adjustment to unified credit. (This adjustment may not exceed $6,000. See page 6 of the instructions.) 12		
13	Allowable unified credit (subtract line 12 from line 11).	13	
14	Subtract line 13 from line 10 (but do not enter less than zero)	14	
15	Credit for state death taxes. Do not enter more than line 14. Compute the credit by using the amount on line 3 less $60,000. See Table B in the instructions and **attach credit evidence** (see instructions)	15	
16	Subtract line 15 from line 14	16	
17	Credit for Federal gift taxes on pre-1977 gifts (section 2012) (attach computation) 17		
18	Credit for foreign death taxes (from Schedule(s) P). (Attach Form(s) 706CE) 18		
19	Credit for tax on prior transfers (from Schedule Q) 19		
20	Total (add lines 17, 18, and 19)	20	
21	Net estate tax (subtract line 20 from line 16)	21	
22	Generation-skipping transfer taxes (from Schedule R, Part 2, line 10)	22	
23	Section 4980A increased estate tax (from Schedule S, Part I, line 17) (see instructions) . . .	23	
24	Total transfer taxes (add lines 21, 22, and 23)	24	
25	Prior payments. Explain in an attached statement 25		
26	United States Treasury bonds redeemed in payment of estate tax . 26		
27	Total (add lines 25 and 26).	27	
28	Balance due (or overpayment) (subtract line 27 from line 24).	28	

Under penalties of perjury, I declare that I have examined this return, including accompanying schedules and statements, and to the best of my knowledge and belief, it is true, correct, and complete. Declaration of preparer other than the executor is based on all information of which preparer has any knowledge.

Signature(s) of executor(s)	Date

Signature of preparer other than executor	Address (and ZIP code)	Date

Cat. No. 20548R

Form 706 (Rev. 8-93)

Estate of:

Part 3.—Elections by the Executor

Please check the "Yes" or "No" box for each question.

		Yes	No
1	Do you elect alternate valuation?		
2	Do you elect special use valuation? . . . . If "Yes," you must complete and attach Schedule A–1		
3	Do you elect to pay the taxes in installments as described in section 6166? . . . . If "Yes," you must attach the additional information described in the instructions.		
4	Do you elect to postpone the part of the taxes attributable to a reversionary or remainder interest as described in section 6163?		

Part 4.—General Information (Note: *Please attach the necessary supplemental documents.* **You must attach the death certificate.**)

Authorization to receive confidential tax information under Regulations section 601.504(b)(2)(i), to act as the estate's representative before the Internal Revenue Service, and to make written or oral presentations on behalf of the estate if return prepared by an attorney, accountant, or enrolled agent for the executor:

Name of representative (print or type)	State	Address (number, street, and room or suite no., city, state, and ZIP code)

I declare that I am the ☐ attorney/ ☐ certified public accountant/ ☐ enrolled agent (you must check the applicable box) for the executor and prepared this return for the executor. I am not under suspension or disbarment from practice before the Internal Revenue Service and am qualified to practice in the state shown above.

Signature	CAF number	Date	Telephone number

1 Death certificate number and issuing authority (attach a copy of the death certificate to this return).

2 Decedent's business or occupation. If retired, check here ▶ ☐ and state decedent's former business or occupation.

3 Marital status of the decedent at time of death:

  ☐ Married
  ☐ Widow or widower—Name, SSN, and date of death of deceased spouse ▶ ....

  ☐ Single
  ☐ Legally separated
  ☐ Divorced—Date divorce decree became final ▶

4a Surviving spouse's name	**4b** Social security number	**4c** Amount received (see instructions)

5 Individuals (other than the surviving spouse), trusts, or other estates who receive benefits from the estate (do not include charitable beneficiaries shown in Schedule O) (see instructions). For Privacy Act Notice (applicable to individual beneficiaries only), see the Instructions for Form 1040.

Name of individual, trust, or estate receiving $5,000 or more	Identifying number	Relationship to decedent	Amount (see instructions)

All unascertainable beneficiaries and those who receive less than $5,000 . . . . ▶

Total . . . .

(Continued on next page)

Form 706 (Rev. 8-93)

Part 4.—General Information (continued)

Please check the "Yes" or "No" box for each question.

		Yes	No
6	Does the gross estate contain any section 2044 property (qualified terminable interest property (QTIP) from a prior gift or estate) (see page 5 of the instructions)?		
7a	Have Federal gift tax returns ever been filed?		
	If "Yes," please attach copies of the returns, if available, and furnish the following information:		

7b Period(s) covered	7c Internal Revenue office(s) where filed

If you answer "Yes" to any of questions 8–16, you must attach additional information as described in the instructions.

		Yes	No
8a	Was there any insurance on the decedent's life that is not included on the return as part of the gross estate?		
b	Did the decedent own any insurance on the life of another that is not included in the gross estate?		
9	Did the decedent at the time of death own any property as a joint tenant with right of survivorship in which (a) one or more of the other joint tenants was someone other than the decedent's spouse, and (b) less than the full value of the property is included on the return as part of the gross estate? If "Yes," you must complete and attach Schedule E .		
10	Did the decedent, at the time of death, own any interest in a partnership or unincorporated business or any stock in an inactive or closely held corporation?		
11	Did the decedent make any transfer described in section 2035, 2036, 2037, or 2038 (see the instructions for Schedule G)? If "Yes," you must complete and attach Schedule G .		
12	Were there in existence at the time of the decedent's death:		
a	Any trusts created by the decedent during his or her lifetime?		
b	Any trusts not created by the decedent under which the decedent possessed any power, beneficial interest, or trusteeship?		
13	Did the decedent ever possess, exercise, or release any general power of appointment? If "Yes," you must complete and attach Schedule H		
14	Was the marital deduction computed under the transitional rule of Public Law 97-34, section 403(e)(3) (Economic Recovery Tax Act of 1981)? If "Yes," attach a separate computation of the marital deduction, enter the amount on item 18 of the Recapitulation, and note on item 18 "computation attached."		
15	Was the decedent, immediately before death, receiving an annuity described in the "General" paragraph of the instructions for Schedule I? If "Yes," you must complete and attach Schedule I .		
16	Did the decedent have a total "excess retirement accumulation" (as defined in section 4980A(d)) in qualified employer plans and individual retirement plans? If "Yes," you must complete and attach Schedule S		

Part 5.—Recapitulation

Item number	Gross estate	Alternate value	Value at date of death
1	Schedule A—Real Estate .		
2	Schedule B—Stocks and Bonds.		
3	Schedule C—Mortgages, Notes, and Cash		
4	Schedule D—Insurance on the Decedent's Life (attach Form(s) 712) .		
5	Schedule E—Jointly Owned Property (attach Form(s) 712 for life insurance) .		
6	Schedule F—Other Miscellaneous Property (attach Form(s) 712 for life insurance) .		
7	Schedule G—Transfers During Decedent's Life (attach Form(s) 712 for life insurance)		
8	Schedule H—Powers of Appointment .		
9	Schedule I—Annuities .		
10	Total gross estate (add items 1 through 9). Enter here and on line 1 of the Tax Computation .		

Item number	Deductions	Amount
11	Schedule J—Funeral Expenses and Expenses Incurred in Administering Property Subject to Claims .	
12	Schedule K—Debts of the Decedent .	
13	Schedule K—Mortgages and Liens .	
14	Total of items 11 through 13 .	
15	Allowable amount of deductions from item 14 (see the instructions for item 15 of the Recapitulation) .	
16	Schedule L—Net Losses During Administration .	
17	Schedule L—Expenses Incurred in Administering Property Not Subject to Claims .	
18	Schedule M—Bequests, etc., to Surviving Spouse .	
19	Schedule O—Charitable, Public, and Similar Gifts and Bequests .	
20	Total allowable deductions (add items 15 through 19). Enter here and on line 2 of the Tax Computation .	

Page 3

Form 706 (Rev. 8-93)

Estate of:

SCHEDULE A—Real Estate

(For jointly owned property that must be disclosed on Schedule E, see the instructions for Schedule E.)

(Real estate that is part of a sole proprietorship should be shown on Schedule F. Real estate that is included in the gross estate under section 2035, 2036, 2037, or 2038 should be shown on Schedule G. Real estate that is included in the gross estate under section 2041 should be shown on Schedule H.)

(If you elect section 2032A valuation, you must complete Schedule A and Schedule A-1.)

Item number	Description	Alternate valuation date	Alternate value	Value at date of death
1				
	Total from continuation schedule(s) (or additional sheet(s)) attached to this schedule . .			
	TOTAL. (Also enter on Part 5, Recapitulation, page 3, at item 1.)			

(If more space is needed, attach the continuation schedule from the end of this package or additional sheets of the same size.)

(See the instructions on the reverse side.)

Schedule A—Page 4

Form 706 (Rev. 8-93)

Instructions for Schedule A—Real Estate

If the total gross estate contains any real estate, you must complete Schedule A and file it with the return. On Schedule A list real estate the decedent owned or had contracted to purchase. Number each parcel in the left-hand column.

Describe the real estate in enough detail so that the IRS can easily locate it for inspection and valuation. For each parcel of real estate, report the area and, if the parcel is improved, describe the improvements. For city or town property, report the street and number, ward, subdivision, block and lot, etc. For rural property, report the township, range, landmarks, etc.

If any item of real estate is subject to a mortgage for which the decedent's estate is liable, that is, if the indebtedness may be charged against other property of the estate that is not subject to that mortgage, or if the decedent was personally liable for that mortgage, you must report the full value of the property in the value column.

Enter the amount of the mortgage under "Description" on this schedule. The unpaid amount of the mortgage may be deducted on Schedule K. If the decedent's estate is NOT liable for the amount of the mortgage, report only the value of the equity of redemption (or value of the property less the indebtedness) in the value column as part of the gross estate. Do not enter any amount less than zero. Do not deduct the amount of indebtedness on Schedule K.

Also list on Schedule A real property the decedent contracted to purchase. Report the full value of the property and not the equity in the value column. Deduct the unpaid part of the purchase price on Schedule K.

Report the value of real estate without reducing it for homestead or other exemption, or the value of dower, curtesy, or a statutory estate created instead of dower or curtesy.

Explain how the reported values were determined and attach copies of any appraisals.

Schedule A Examples

In this example, the alternate valuation is not adopted; the date of death is January 1, 1993.

Item number	Description	Alternate valuation date	Alternate value	Value at date of death
1	House and lot, 1921 William Street NW, Washington, DC (lot 6, square 481). Rent of $2,700 due at end of each quarter, February 1, May 1, August 1, and November 1. Value based on appraisal, copy of which is attached			108,000
	Rent due on item 1 for quarter ending November 1, 1992, but not collected at date of death			2,700
	Rent accrued on item 1 for November and December 1992			1,800
2	House and lot, 304 Jefferson Street, Alexandria, VA (lot 18, square 40). Rent of $600 payable monthly. Value based on appraisal, copy of which is attached			96,000
	Rent due on item 2 for December 1992, but not collected at date of death . . .			600

In this example, alternate valuation is adopted; the date of death is January 1, 1993.

Item number	Description	Alternate valuation date	Alternate value	Value at date of death
1	House and lot, 1921 William Street NW, Washington, DC (lot 6, square 481). Rent of $2,700 due at end of each quarter, February 1, May 1, August 1, and November 1. Value based on appraisal, copy of which is attached. Not disposed of within 6 months following death	7/1/93	90,000	108,000
	Rent due on item 1 for quarter ending November 1, 1992, but not collected until February 1, 1993	2/1/93	2,700	2,700
	Rent accrued on item 1 for November and December 1992, collected on February 1, 1993	2/1/93	1,800	1,800
2	House and lot, 304 Jefferson Street, Alexandria, VA (lot 18, square 40). Rent of $600 payable monthly. Value based on appraisal, copy of which is attached. Property exchanged for farm on May 1, 1993	5/1/93	90,000	96,000
	Rent due on item 2 for December 1992, but not collected until February 1, 1993 .	2/1/93	600	600

Schedule A—Page 5

Form 706 (Rev. 8-93)

Instructions for Schedule A-1.—Section 2032A Valuation

The election to value certain farm and closely held business property at its special use value is made by checking "Yes" to line 2 of Part 3, Elections by the Executor, Form 706. Schedule A-1 is used to report the additional information that must be submitted to support this election. In order to make a valid election, you must complete Schedule A-1 and attach all of the required statements and appraisals.

For definitions and additional information concerning special use valuation, see section 2032A and the related regulations.

Part 1.—Type of Election

Estate and GST Tax Elections.—If you elect special use valuation for the estate tax, you must also elect special use valuation for the GST tax and vice versa.

You must value each specific property interest at the same value for GST tax purposes that you value it at for estate tax purposes.

Protective Election.—To make the protective election described in the separate instructions for line 2 of Part 3, Elections by the Executor, you must check this box, enter the decedent's name and social security number in the spaces provided at the top of Schedule A-1, and complete line 1 and column A of lines 3 and 4 of Part 2. For purposes of the protective election, list on line 3 all of the real property that passes to the qualified heirs even though some of the property will be shown on line 2 when the additional notice of election is subsequently filed. You need not complete columns B–D of lines 3 and 4. You need not complete any other line entries on Schedule A-1. Completing Schedule A-1 as described above constitutes a Notice of Protective Election as described in Regulations section 20.2032A-8(b).

Part 2.—Notice of Election

Line 10.—Because the special use valuation election creates a potential tax liability for the recapture tax of section 2032A(c), you must list each person who receives an interest in the specially valued property on Schedule A-1. If there are more than eight persons who receive interests, use an additional sheet that follows the format of line 10. In the columns "Fair market value" and "Special use value," you should enter the total respective values of all the specially valued property interests received by each person.

GST Tax Savings

To compute the additional GST tax due upon disposition (or cessation of qualified use) of the property, each "skip person" (as defined in the instructions to Schedule R) who receives an interest in the specially valued property must know the total GST tax savings on all of the interests in specially valued property received. This total GST tax savings is the difference between the total GST tax that was imposed on all of the interests in specially valued property received by the skip person valued at their special use value and the total GST tax that would have been imposed on the same interests received by the skip person had they been valued at their fair market value.

Because the GST tax depends on the executor's allocation of the GST exemption and the grandchild exclusion, the skip person who receives the interests is unable to compute this GST tax savings. Therefore, for each skip person who receives an interest in specially valued property, you must attach worksheets showing the total GST tax savings attributable to all of that person's interests in specially valued property.

How To Compute the GST Tax Savings.—Before computing each skip person's GST tax savings, you must complete Schedules R and R-1 for the entire estate (using the special use values).

For each skip person, you must complete two Schedules R (Parts 2 and 3 only) as worksheets, one showing the interests in specially valued property received by the skip person at their special use value and one showing the same interests at their fair market value.

If the skip person received interests in specially valued property that were shown on Schedule R-1, show these interests on the Schedule R, Parts 2 and 3 worksheets, as appropriate. Do not use Schedule R-1 as a worksheet.

Completing the Special Use Value Worksheets.—On lines 2–4 and 6, enter -0-.

Completing the Fair Market Value Worksheets.—*Lines 2 and 3, fixed taxes and other charges.*—If valuing the interests at their fair market value (instead of special use value) causes any of these taxes and charges to increase, enter the increased amount (only) on these lines and attach an explanation of the increase. Otherwise, enter -0-.

Line 6—GST exemption.—If you completed line 10 of Schedule R, Part 1, enter on line 6 the amount shown for the skip person on the *line 10 special use allocation schedule* you attached to Schedule R. If you did not complete line 10 of Schedule R, Part 1, enter -0- on line 6.

Total GST Tax Savings.—For each skip person, subtract the tax amount on line 10, Part 2 of the special use value worksheet from the tax amount on line 10, Part 2 of the fair market value worksheet. This difference is the skip person's total GST tax savings.

Part 3.—Agreement to Special Valuation Under Section 2032A

The agreement to special valuation by persons with an interest in property is required under section 2032A(a)(1)(B) and (d)(2) and must be signed by all parties who have any interest in the property being valued based on its qualified use as of the date of the decedent's death.

An interest in property is an interest that, as of the date of the decedent's death, can be asserted under applicable local law so as to affect the disposition of the specially valued property by the estate. Any person who at the decedent's death has any such interest in the property, whether present or future, or vested or contingent, must enter into the agreement. Included are owners of remainder and executory interests; the holders of general or special powers of appointment; beneficiaries of a gift over in default of exercise of any such power; joint tenants and holders of similar undivided interests when the decedent held only a joint or undivided interest in the property or when only an undivided interest is specially valued; and trustees of trusts and representatives of other entities holding title to, or holding any interests in the property. An heir who has the power under local law to caveat (challenge) a will and thereby affect disposition of the property is not, however, considered to be a person with an interest in property under section 2032A solely by reason of that right. Likewise, creditors of an estate are not such persons solely by reason of their status as creditors.

If any person required to enter into the agreement either desires that an agent act for him or her or cannot legally bind himself or herself due to infancy or other incompetency, or due to death before the election under section 2032A is timely exercised, a representative authorized by local law to bind the person in an agreement of this nature may sign the agreement on his or her behalf.

The Internal Revenue Service will contact the agent designated in the agreement on all matters relating to continued qualification under section 2032A of the specially valued real property and on all matters relating to the special lien arising under section 6324B. It is the duty of the agent as attorney-in-fact for the parties with interests in the specially valued property to furnish the IRS with any requested information and to notify the IRS of any disposition or cessation of qualified use of any part of the property.

Schedule A-1—Page 6

Form 706 (Rev. 8-93)

Checklist for Section 2032A Election—*If you are going to make the special use valuation election on Schedule A-1, please use this checklist to ensure that you are providing everything necessary to make a valid election.*

To have a valid special use valuation election under section 2032A, you must file, in addition to the Federal estate tax return, **(a)** a notice of election (Schedule A-1, Part 2), and **(b)** a fully executed agreement (Schedule A-1, Part 3). You must include certain information in the notice of election. To ensure that the notice of election includes all of the information required for a valid election, use the following checklist. The checklist is for your use only. Do not file it with the return.

1. Does the notice of election include the decedent's name and social security number as they appear on the estate tax return?

2. Does the notice of election include the relevant qualified use of the property to be specially valued?

3. Does the notice of election describe the items of real property shown on the estate tax return that are to be specially valued and identify the property by the Form 706 schedule and item number?

4. Does the notice of election include the fair market value of the real property to be specially valued and also include its value based on the qualified use (determined without the adjustments provided in section 2032A(b)(3)(B))?

5. Does the notice of election include the adjusted value (as defined in section 2032A(b)(3)(B)) of **(a)** all real property that both passes from the decedent and is used in a qualified use, without regard to whether it is to be specially valued, and **(b)** all real property to be specially valued?

6. Does the notice of election include **(a)** the items of personal property shown on the estate tax return that pass from the decedent to a qualified heir and that are used in qualified use and **(b)** the total value of such personal property adjusted under section 2032A(b)(3)(B)?

7. Does the notice of election include the adjusted value of the gross estate? (See section 2032A(b)(3)(A).)

8. Does the notice of election include the method used to determine the special use value?

9. Does the notice of election include copies of written appraisals of the fair market value of the real property?

10. Does the notice of election include a statement that the decedent and/or a member of his or her family has owned all of the specially valued property for at least 5 years of the 8 years immediately preceding the date of the decedent's death?

11. Does the notice of election include a statement as to whether there were any periods during the 8-year period preceding the decedent's date of death during which the decedent or a member of his or her family **(a)** did not own the property to be specially valued, **(b)** use it in a qualified use, or **(c)** materially participate in the operation of the farm or other business? (See section 2032A(e)(6).)

12. Does the notice of election include, for each item of specially valued property, the name of every person taking an interest in that item of specially valued property and the following information about each such person: **(a)** the person's address, **(b)** the person's taxpayer identification number, **(c)** the person's relationship to the decedent, and **(d)** the value of the property interest passing to that person based on both fair market value and qualified use?

13. Does the notice of election include affidavits describing the activities constituting material participation and the identity of the material participants?

14. Does the notice of election include a legal description of each item of specially valued property?

(In the case of an election made for qualified woodlands, the information included in the notice of election must include the reason for entitlement to the woodlands election.)

Any election made under section 2032A will not be valid unless a properly executed agreement (Schedule A-1, Part 3) is filed with the estate tax return. To ensure that the agreement satisfies the requirements for a valid election, use the following checklist.

1. Has the agreement been signed by each and every qualified heir having an interest in the property being specially valued?

2. Has every qualified heir expressed consent to personal liability under section 2032A(c) in the event of an early disposition or early cessation of qualified use?

3. Is the agreement that is actually signed by the qualified heirs in a form that is binding on all of the qualified heirs having an interest in the specially valued property?

4. Does the agreement designate an agent to act for the parties to the agreement in all dealings with the IRS on matters arising under section 2032A?

5. Has the agreement been signed by the designated agent and does it give the address of the agent?

Form 706 (Rev. 8-93)

Estate of:	**Decedent's Social Security Number**

SCHEDULE A-1—Section 2032A Valuation

Part 1.—Type of Election (Before making an election, see the checklist on page 7.):

☐ **Protective election (Regulations section 20.2032A-8(b)).**—Complete Part 2, line 1, and column A of lines 3 and 4. (See instructions.)
☐ **Regular election.**—Complete all of Part 2 (including line 11, if applicable) and Part 3. (See instructions.)

Before completing Schedule A-1, see the checklist on page 7 for the information and documents that must be included to make a valid election.

The election is not valid unless the agreement (i.e., Part 3-Agreement to Special Valuation Under Section 2032A)—

● Is signed by each and every qualified heir with an interest in the specially valued property, and
● Is attached to this return when it is filed.

Part 2.—Notice of Election (Regulations section 20.2032A-8(a)(3))
Note: *All real property entered on lines 2 and 3 must also be entered on Schedules A, E, F, G, or H, as applicable.*

1 Qualified use—check one ▶ ☐ Farm used for farming, or
　　　　　　　　　　 ▶ ☐ Trade or business other than farming
2 Real property used in a qualified use, passing to qualified heirs, and to be specially valued on this Form 706.

A Schedule and item number from Form 706	B Full value (without section 2032A(b)(3)(B) adjustment)	C Adjusted value (with section 2032A(b)(3)(B) adjustment)	D Value based on qualified use (without section 2032A(b)(3)(B) adjustment)

Totals . . . .

Attach a legal description of all property listed on line 2.
Attach copies of appraisals showing the column B values for all property listed on line 2.

3 Real property used in a qualified use, passing to qualified heirs, but not specially valued on this Form 706.

A Schedule and item number from Form 706	B Full value (without section 2032A(b)(3)(B) adjustment)	C Adjusted value (with section 2032A(b)(3)(B) adjustment)	D Value based on qualified use (without section 2032A(b)(3)(B) adjustment)

Totals . . . .
If you checked "Regular election," you must attach copies of appraisals showing the column B values for all property listed on line 3.

(Continued on next page)   **Schedule A-1—Page 8**

Form 706 (Rev. 8-93)

4 Personal property used in a qualified use and passing to qualified heirs.

A Schedule and item number from Form 706	B Adjusted value (with section 2032A(b)(3)(B) adjustment)	A (continued) Schedule and item number from Form 706	B (continued) Adjusted value (with section 2032A(b)(3)(B) adjustment)
		"Subtotal" from Col. B, below left	....

Subtotal . . . .   **Total adjusted value** . . .

5 Enter the value of the total gross estate as adjusted under section 2032A(b)(3)(A). ▶ _____

6 Attach a description of the method used to determine the special value based on qualified use.

7 Did the decedent and/or a member of his or her family own all property listed on line 2 for at least 5 of the 8 years immediately preceding the date of the decedent's death? . . . . ☐ **Yes** ☐ **No**

8 Were there any periods during the 8-year period preceding the date of the decedent's death during which the decedent or a member of his or her family:

	Yes	No
a Did not own the property listed on line 2 above?		
b Did not use the property listed on line 2 above in a qualified use?		
c Did not materially participate in the operation of the farm or other business within the meaning of section 2032A(e)(6)?.		

If "Yes" to any of the above, you must attach a statement listing the periods. If applicable, describe whether the exceptions of sections 2032A(b)(4) or (5) are met.

9 Attach affidavits describing the activities constituting material participation and the identity and relationship to the decedent of the material participants.

10 Persons holding interests. Enter the requested information for each party who received any interest in the specially valued property. **(Each of the qualified heirs receiving an interest in the property must sign the agreement, and the agreement must be filed with this return.)**

	Name	Address
A		
B		
C		
D		
E		
F		
G		
H		

	Identifying number	Relationship to decedent	Fair market value	Special use value
A				
B				
C				
D				
E				
F				
G				
H				

You must attach a computation of the GST tax savings attributable to direct skips for each person listed above who is a skip person. (See instructions.)

11 **Woodlands election.**—Check here ▶ ☐ if you wish to make a woodlands election as described in section 2032A(e)(13). Enter the Schedule and item numbers from Form 706 of the property for which you are making this election ▶ ....
You must attach a statement explaining why you are entitled to make this election. The IRS may issue regulations that require more information to substantiate this election. You will be notified by the IRS if you must supply further information.

Schedule A-1—Page 9

Form 706 (Rev. 8-93)

Part 3.—Agreement to Special Valuation Under Section 2032A

Estate of:	Date of Death	Decedent's Social Security Number

There cannot be a valid election unless:

- The agreement is executed by each and every one of the qualified heirs, and
- The agreement is included with the estate tax return when the estate tax return is filed.

We (list all qualified heirs and other persons having an interest in the property required to sign this agreement)

_____

_____ ,

being all the qualified heirs and _____

_____ ,

being all other parties having interests in the property which is qualified real property and which is valued under section 2032A of the Internal Revenue Code, do hereby approve of the election made by _____ ,

Executor/Administrator of the estate of _____ ,

pursuant to section 2032A to value said property on the basis of the qualified use to which the property is devoted and do hereby enter into this agreement pursuant to section 2032A(d).

The undersigned agree and consent to the application of subsection (c) of section 2032A of the Code with respect to all the property described on line 2 of Part 2 of Schedule A-1 of Form 706, attached to this agreement. More specifically, the undersigned heirs expressly agree and consent to personal liability under subsection (c) of 2032A for the additional estate and GST taxes imposed by that subsection with respect to their respective interests in the above-described property in the event of certain early dispositions of the property or early cessation of the qualified use of the property. It is understood that if a qualified heir disposes of any interest in qualified real property to any member of his or her family, such member may thereafter be treated as the qualified heir with respect to such interest upon filing a Form 706-A and a new agreement.

The undersigned interested parties who are not qualified heirs consent to the collection of any additional estate and GST taxes imposed under section 2032A(c) of the Code from the specially valued property.

If there is a disposition of any interest which passes or has passed to him or her or if there is a cessation of the qualified use of any specially valued property which passes or passed to him or her, each of the undersigned heirs agrees to file a **Form 706-A**, United States Additional Estate Tax Return, and pay any additional estate and GST taxes due within 6 months of the disposition or cessation.

It is understood by all interested parties that this agreement is a condition precedent to the election of special use valuation under section 2032A of the Code and must be executed by every interested party even though that person may not have received the estate (or GST) tax benefits or be in possession of such property.

Each of the undersigned understands that by making this election, a lien will be created and recorded pursuant to section 6324B of the Code on the property referred to in this agreement for the adjusted tax differences with respect to the estate as defined in section 2032A(c)(2)(C).

As the interested parties, the undersigned designate the following individual as their agent for all dealings with the Internal Revenue Service concerning the continued qualification of the specially valued property under section 2032A of the Code and on all issues regarding the special lien under section 6324B. The agent is authorized to act for the parties with respect to all dealings with the Service on matters affecting the qualified real property described earlier. This authority includes the following:

- To receive confidential information on all matters relating to continued qualification under section 2032A of the specially valued real property and on all matters relating to the special lien arising under section 6324B.
- To furnish the Service with any requested information concerning the property.
- To notify the Service of any disposition or cessation of qualified use of any part of the property.
- To receive, but not to endorse and collect, checks in payment of any refund of Internal Revenue taxes, penalties, or interest.
- To execute waivers (including offers of waivers) of restrictions on assessment or collection of deficiencies in tax and waivers of notice of disallowance of a claim for credit or refund.
- To execute closing agreements under section 7121.

(continued on next page)

Schedule A-1—Page 10

Form 706 (Rev. 8-93)

Part 3.—Agreement to Special Valuation Under Section 2032A *(Continued)*

Estate of:	Date of Death	Decedent's Social Security Number

● Other acts (specify) ▶ _____

By signing this agreement, the agent agrees to provide the Service with any requested information concerning this property and to notify the Service of any disposition or cessation of the qualified use of any part of this property.

Name of Agent	Signature	Address

The property to which this agreement relates is listed in Form 706, United States Estate (and Generation-Skipping Transfer) Tax Return, and in the Notice of Election, along with its fair market value according to section 2031 of the Code and its special use value according to section 2032A. The name, address, social security number, and interest (including the value) of each of the undersigned in this property are as set forth in the attached Notice of Election.

IN WITNESS WHEREOF, the undersigned have hereunto set their hands at _____ ,

this _____ day of _____ .

SIGNATURES OF EACH OF THE QUALIFIED HEIRS:

Signature of qualified heir	Signature of qualified heir
Signature of qualified heir	Signature of qualified heir
Signature of qualified heir	Signature of qualified heir
Signature of qualified heir	Signature of qualified heir
Signature of qualified heir	Signature of qualified heir
Signature of qualified heir	Signature of qualified heir

Signatures of other interested parties

Signatures of other interested parties

Schedule A-1—Page 11

Form 706 (Rev. 8-93)

Estate of:

SCHEDULE B—Stocks and Bonds

(For jointly owned property that must be disclosed on Schedule E, see the instructions for Schedule E.)

Item number	Description including face amount of bonds or number of shares and par value where needed for identification. Give CUSIP number if available.	Unit value	Alternate valuation date	Alternate value	Value at date of death
1					

Total from continuation schedule(s) (or additional sheet(s)) attached to this schedule . .

TOTAL. (Also enter on Part 5, Recapitulation, page 3, at item 2.) . . . .

(If more space is needed, attach the continuation schedule from the end of this package or additional sheets of the same size.)

(The instructions to Schedule B are in the separate instructions.)

Schedule B—Page 12

Form 706 (Rev. 8-93)

Estate of:

SCHEDULE C—Mortgages, Notes, and Cash

(For jointly owned property that must be disclosed on Schedule E, see the instructions for Schedule E.)

Item number	Description	Alternate valuation date	Alternate value	Value at date of death
1				

Total from continuation schedule(s) (or additional sheet(s)) attached to this schedule .

TOTAL. (Also enter on Part 5, Recapitulation, page 3, at item 3.) . . . .

(If more space is needed, attach the continuation schedule from the end of this package or additional sheets of the same size.)
(See the instructions on the reverse side.)

Schedule C—Page 13

Form 706 (Rev. 8-93)

Instructions for Schedule C.— Mortgages, Notes, and Cash

If the total gross estate contains any mortgages, notes, or cash, you must complete Schedule C and file it with the return.

On Schedule C list mortgages and notes *payable to* the decedent at the time of death. (Mortgages and notes *payable by* the decedent should be listed (if deductible) on Schedule K.) Also list on Schedule C cash the decedent had at the date of death.

Group the items in the following categories and list the categories in the following order:

1. Mortgages.—List: (a) the face value and unpaid balance; (b) date of mortgage; (c) date of maturity; (d) name of maker; (e) property mortgaged; and (f) interest dates and rate of interest. For example: bond and mortgage of $50,000, unpaid balance $24,000; dated January 1, 1980; John Doe to Richard Roe; premises 22 Clinton Street, Newark, NJ; due January 1, 1993, interest payable at 10% a year January 1 and July 1.

2. Promissory notes.—Describe in the same way as mortgages.

3. Contract by the decedent to sell land.—List: (a) the name of the purchaser; (b) date of contract; (c) description of property; (d) sale price; (e) initial payment; (f) amounts of installment payment; (g) unpaid balance of principal; and (h) interest rate.

4. Cash in possession.—List separately from bank deposits.

5. Cash in banks, savings and loan associations, and other types of financial organizations.—List: (a) the name and address of each financial organization; (b) amount in each account; (c) serial number; and (d) nature of account, indicating whether checking, savings, time deposit, etc. If you obtain statements from the financial organizations, keep them for IRS inspection.

Form 706 (Rev. 8-93)

Estate of:

SCHEDULE D—Insurance on the Decedent's Life

You must list **all** policies on the life of the decedent and attach a Form 712 for each policy.

Item number	Description	Alternate valuation date	Alternate value	Value at date of death
1				

Total from continuation schedule(s) (or additional sheet(s)) attached to this schedule .

TOTAL. (Also enter on Part 5, Recapitulation, page 3, at item 4.) . . . .

(If more space is needed, attach the continuation schedule from the end of this package or additional sheets of the same size.)

(See the instructions on the reverse side.)

Schedule D—Page 15

357-328 O - 93 - 2

Instructions for Schedule D.—Insurance on the Decedent's Life

If there was any insurance on the decedent's life, whether or not included in the gross estate, you must complete Schedule D and file it with the return.

Insurance you must include on Schedule D.—Under section 2042 you must include in the gross estate:

- Insurance on the decedent's life receivable by or for the benefit of the estate; and
- Insurance on the decedent's life receivable by beneficiaries other than the estate, as described below.

The term "insurance" refers to life insurance of every description, including death benefits paid by fraternal beneficiary societies operating under the lodge system, and death benefits paid under no-fault automobile insurance policies if the no-fault insurer was unconditionally bound to pay the benefit in the event of the insured's death.

Insurance in favor of the estate.—Include on Schedule D the full amount of the proceeds of insurance on the life of the decedent receivable by the executor or otherwise payable to or for the benefit of the estate. Insurance in favor of the estate includes insurance used to pay the estate tax, and any other taxes, debts, or charges that are enforceable against the estate. The manner in which the policy is drawn is immaterial as long as there is an obligation, legally binding on the beneficiary, to use the proceeds to pay taxes, debts, or charges. You must include the full amount even though the premiums or other consideration may have been paid by a person other than the decedent.

Insurance receivable by beneficiaries other than the estate.—Include on Schedule D the proceeds of all insurance on the life of the decedent not receivable by or for the benefit of the decedent's estate if the decedent possessed at death any of the incidents of ownership, exercisable either alone or in conjunction with any person.

Incidents of ownership in a policy include:

- The right of the insured or estate to its economic benefits;
- The power to change the beneficiary;
- The power to surrender or cancel the policy;
- The power to assign the policy or to revoke an assignment;
- The power to pledge the policy for a loan;
- The power to obtain from the insurer a loan against the surrender value of the policy;
- A reversionary interest if the value of the reversionary interest was more than 5% of the value of the policy immediately before the decedent died. (An interest in an insurance policy is considered a reversionary interest if, for example, the proceeds become payable to the insured's estate or payable as the insured directs if the beneficiary dies before the insured.)

Life insurance not includible in the gross estate under section 2042 may be includible under some other section of the Code. For example, a life insurance policy could be transferred by the decedent in such a way that it would be includible in the gross estate under section 2036, 2037, or 2038. (See the instructions to Schedule G for a description of these sections.)

Completing the Schedule

You must list every policy of insurance on the life of the decedent, whether or not it is included in the gross estate.

Under "Description" list:

- Name of the insurance company and
- Number of the policy.

For every policy of life insurance listed on the schedule, you must request a statement on **Form 712,** Life Insurance Statement, from the company that issued the policy. Attach the Form 712 to the back of Schedule D.

If the policy proceeds are paid in one sum, enter the net proceeds received (from Form 712, line 24) in the value (and alternate value) columns of Schedule D. If the policy proceeds are not paid in one sum, enter the value of the proceeds as of the date of the decedent's death (from Form 712, line 25).

If part or all of the policy proceeds are not included in the gross estate, you must explain why they were not included.

Form 706 (Rev. 8-93)

Estate of:

SCHEDULE E—Jointly Owned Property
(If you elect section 2032A valuation, you must complete Schedule E and Schedule A-1.)

PART 1.—Qualified Joint Interests—Interests Held by the Decedent and His or Her Spouse as the Only Joint Tenants (Section 2040(b)(2))

Item number	Description For securities, give CUSIP number, if available.	Alternate valuation date	Alternate value	Value at date of death
	Total from continuation schedule(s) (or additional sheet(s)) attached to this schedule			
1a	Totals			
1b	Amounts included in gross estate (one-half of line 1a)			

PART 2.—All Other Joint Interests

2a State the name and address of each surviving co-tenant. If there are more than three surviving co-tenants, list the additional co-tenants on an attached sheet.

Name	Address (number and street, city, state, and ZIP code)
A.	
B.	
C.	

Item number	Enter letter for co-tenant	Description (including alternate valuation date if any) For securities, give CUSIP number, if available.	Percentage includible	Includible alternate value	Includible value at date of death
		Total from continuation schedule(s) (or additional sheet(s)) attached to this schedule			
2b		Total other joint interests			
3		**Total includible joint interests** (add lines 1b and 2b). Also enter on Part 5, Recapitulation, page 3, at item 5			

(If more space is needed, attach the continuation schedule from the end of this package or additional sheets of the same size.)
(See the instructions on the reverse side.)

Schedule E—Page 17

Instructions for Schedule E.—Jointly Owned Property

You must complete Schedule E and file it with the return if the decedent owned any joint property at the time of death, whether or not the decedent's interest is includible in the gross estate.

Enter on this schedule all property of whatever kind or character, whether real estate, personal property, or bank accounts, in which the decedent held at the time of death an interest either as a joint tenant with right to survivorship or as a tenant by the entirety.

Do not list on this schedule property that the decedent held as a tenant in common, but report the value of the interest on Schedule A if real estate, or on the appropriate schedule if personal property. Similarly, community property held by the decedent and spouse should be reported on the appropriate Schedules A through I. The decedent's interest in a partnership should not be entered on this schedule unless the partnership interest itself is jointly owned. Solely owned partnership interests should be reported on Schedule F, "Other Miscellaneous Property."

Part 1.—Qualified joint interests held by decedent and spouse.—Under section 2040(b)(2), a joint interest is a qualified joint interest if the decedent and the surviving spouse held the interest as:

- Tenants by the entirety, or
- Joint tenants with right of survivorship if the decedent and the decedent's spouse are the only joint tenants.

Interests that meet either of the two requirements above should be entered in Part 1. Joint interests that do not meet either of the two requirements above should be entered in Part 2.

Under "Description," describe the property as required in the instructions for Schedules A, B, C, and F for the type of property involved. For example, jointly held stocks and bonds should be described using the rules given in the instructions to Schedule B.

Under "Alternate value" and "Value at date of death," enter the full value of the property.

Note: *You cannot claim the special treatment under section 2040(b) for property held jointly by a decedent and a surviving spouse who is not a U.S. citizen. You must report these joint interests on Part 2 of Schedule E, not Part 1.*

Part 2.—Other joint interests.—All joint interests that were not entered in Part 1 must be entered in Part 2.

For each item of property, enter the appropriate letter A, B, C, etc., from line 2a to indicate the name and address of the surviving co-tenant.

Under "Description," describe the property as required in the instructions for Schedules A, B, C, and F for the type of property involved.

In the "Percentage includible" column, enter the percentage of the total value of the property that you intend to include in the gross estate.

Generally, you must include the full value of the jointly owned property in the gross estate. However, the full value should not be included if you can show that a part of the property originally belonged to the other tenant or tenants and was never received or acquired by the other tenant or tenants from the decedent for less than adequate and full consideration in money or money's worth, or unless you can show that any part of the property was acquired with consideration originally belonging to the surviving joint tenant or tenants. In this case, you may exclude from the value of the property an amount proportionate to the consideration furnished by the other tenant or tenants. Relinquishing or promising to relinquish dower, curtesy, or statutory estate created instead of dower or curtesy, or other marital rights in the decedent's property or estate is not consideration in money or money's worth. See the Schedule A instructions for the value to show for real property that is subject to a mortgage.

If the property was acquired by the decedent and another person or persons by gift, bequest, devise, or inheritance as joint tenants, and their interests are not otherwise specified by law, include only that part of the value of the property that is figured by dividing the full value of the property by the number of joint tenants.

If you believe that less than the full value of the entire property is includible in the gross estate for tax purposes, you must establish the right to include the smaller value by attaching proof of the extent, origin, and nature of the decedent's interest and the interest(s) of the decedent's co-tenant or co-tenants.

In the "Includible alternate value" and "Includible value at date of death" columns, you should enter only the values that you believe are includible in the gross estate.

Form 706 (Rev. 8-93)

Estate of:

SCHEDULE F—Other Miscellaneous Property Not Reportable Under Any Other Schedule
(For jointly owned property that must be disclosed on Schedule E, see the instructions for Schedule E.)
(If you elect section 2032A valuation, you must complete Schedule F and Schedule A-1.)

		Yes	No
1	Did the decedent at the time of death own any articles of artistic or collectible value in excess of $3,000 or any collections whose artistic or collectible value combined at date of death exceeded $10,000? . . . . If "Yes," submit full details on this schedule and attach appraisals.		
2	Has the decedent's estate, spouse, or any other person, received (or will receive) any bonus or award as a result of the decedent's employment or death? . . . . If "Yes," submit full details on this schedule.		
3	Did the decedent at the time of death have, or have access to, a safe deposit box? . . . . If "Yes," state location, and if held in joint names of decedent and another, state name and relationship of joint depositor.		

If any of the contents of the safe deposit box are omitted from the schedules in this return, explain fully why omitted.

Item number	Description For securities, give CUSIP number, if available.	Alternate valuation date	Alternate value	Value at date of death
1				
	Total from continuation schedule(s) (or additional sheet(s)) attached to this schedule. .			
	TOTAL. (Also enter on Part 5, Recapitulation, page 3, at item 6.)			

(If more space is needed, attach the continuation schedule from the end of this package or additional sheets of the same size.)
(See the instructions on the reverse side.)

Schedule F—Page 19

Form 706 (Rev. 8-93)

Instructions for Schedule F.—Other Miscellaneous Property

You must complete Schedule F and file it with the return.

On Schedule F list all items that must be included in the gross estate that are not reported on any other schedule, including:

- Debts due the decedent (other than notes and mortgages included on Schedule C)
- Interests in business
- Insurance on the life of another (obtain and attach **Form 712,** Life Insurance Statement, for each policy)

Note for single premium or paid-up policies: *In certain situations, for example where the surrender value of the policy exceeds its replacement cost, the true economic value of the policy will be greater than the amount shown on line 56 of Form 712. In these situations, you should report the full economic value of the policy on Schedule F. See Rev. Rul. 78-137, 1978-1 C.B. 280 for details.*

- Section 2044 property
- Claims (including the value of the decedent's interest in a claim for refund of income taxes or the amount of the refund actually received)
- Rights
- Royalties
- Leaseholds
- Judgments
- Reversionary or remainder interests
- Shares in trust funds (attach a copy of the trust instrument)
- Household goods and personal effects, including wearing apparel
- Farm products and growing crops
- Livestock
- Farm machinery
- Automobiles

If the decedent owned any interest in a partnership or unincorporated business, attach a statement of assets and liabilities for the valuation date and for the 5 years before the valuation date. Also attach statements of the net earnings for the same 5 years. You must account for goodwill in the valuation. In general, furnish the same information and follow the methods used to value close corporations. See the instructions for Schedule B.

All partnership interests should be reported on Schedule F unless the partnership interest, itself, is jointly owned. Jointly owned partnership interests should be reported on Schedule E.

If real estate is owned by the sole proprietorship, it should be reported on Schedule F and not on Schedule A. Describe the real estate with the same detail required for Schedule A.

Line 1.—If the decedent owned at the date of death articles with artistic or intrinsic value (e.g., jewelry, furs, silverware, books, statuary, vases, oriental rugs, coin or stamp collections), check the "Yes" box on line 1 and provide full details. If any one article is valued at more than $3,000, or any collection of similar articles is valued at more than $10,000, attach an appraisal by an expert under oath and the required statement regarding the appraiser's qualifications (see Regulations section 20.2031-6(b)).

Estate of:

SCHEDULE G—Transfers During Decedent's Life

(If you elect section 2032A valuation, you must complete Schedule G and Schedule A-1.)

Item number	Description For securities, give CUSIP number, if available.	Alternate valuation date	Alternate value	Value at date of death
A.	Gift tax paid by the decedent or the estate for all gifts made by the decedent or his or her spouse within 3 years before the decedent's death (section 2035(c))	X X X X X		
B.	Transfers includible under section 2035(a), 2036, 2037, or 2038:			
1				
	Total from continuation schedule(s) (or additional sheet(s)) attached to this schedule .			
	TOTAL. (Also enter on Part 5, Recapitulation, page 3, at item 7.)			

SCHEDULE H—Powers of Appointment

(Include "5 and 5 lapsing" powers (section 2041(b)(2)) held by the decedent.)

(If you elect section 2032A valuation, you must complete Schedule H and Schedule A-1.)

Item number	Description	Alternate valuation date	Alternate value	Value at date of death
1				
	Total from continuation schedule(s) (or additional sheet(s)) attached to this schedule .			
	TOTAL. (Also enter on Part 5, Recapitulation, page 3, at item 8.)			

(If more space is needed, attach the continuation schedule from the end of this package or additional sheets of the same size.)

(The instructions to Schedules G and H are in the separate instructions.)

Schedules G and H—Page 21

Form 706 (Rev. 8-93)

Estate of:

SCHEDULE I—Annuities

Note: *Generally, no exclusion is allowed for the estates of decedents dying after December 31, 1984 (see instructions).*

A Are you excluding from the decedent's gross estate the value of a lump-sum distribution described in section 2039(f)(2)? . . . .
If "Yes," you must attach the information required by the instructions.

Item number	Description Show the entire value of the annuity before any exclusions.	Alternate valuation date	Includible alternate value	Includible value at date of death
1				
	Total from continuation schedule(s) (or additional sheet(s)) attached to this schedule .			
	TOTAL. (Also enter on Part 5, Recapitulation, page 3, at item 9.).			

(If more space is needed, attach the continuation schedule from the end of this package or additional sheets of the same size.)

Schedule I—Page 22   (See instructions to Schedule I are in the separate instructions.)

Form 706 (Rev. 8-93)

Estate of:

SCHEDULE J—Funeral Expenses and Expenses Incurred in Administering Property Subject to Claims

Note: *Do not list on this schedule expenses of administering property not subject to claims. For those expenses, see the instructions for Schedule L.*

If executors' commissions, attorney fees, etc., are claimed and allowed as a deduction for estate tax purposes, they are not allowable as a deduction in computing the taxable income of the estate for Federal income tax purposes. They are allowable as an income tax deduction on Form 1041 if a waiver is filed to waive the deduction on Form 706 (see the Form 1041 instructions).

Item number	Description	Expense amount	Total Amount
1	**A. Funeral expenses:**		
	Total funeral expenses		....
	B. Administration expenses:		
1	Executors' commissions—amount estimated/agreed upon/paid. (Strike out the words that do not apply.)		....
2	Attorney fees—amount estimated/agreed upon/paid. (Strike out the words that do not apply.) . . .		....
3	Accountant fees—amount estimated/agreed upon/paid. (Strike out the words that do not apply.) . .		....
		Expense amount	
4	Miscellaneous expenses:		
	Total miscellaneous expenses from continuation schedule(s) (or additional sheet(s)) attached to this schedule		
	Total miscellaneous expenses		
	TOTAL. (Also enter on Part 5, Recapitulation, page 3, at item 11.)		

(If more space is needed, attach the continuation schedule from the end of this package or additional sheets of the same size.)
(See the instructions on the reverse side.)

Schedule J—Page 23

Form 706 (Rev. 8-93)

Instructions for Schedule J.—
Funeral Expenses and Expenses Incurred in Administering Property Subject to Claims

General.—You must complete and file Schedule J if you claim a deduction on item 11 of Part 5, Recapitulation.

On Schedule J, itemize funeral expenses and expenses incurred in administering property subject to claims. List the names and addresses of persons to whom the expenses are payable and describe the nature of the expense. **Do not list expenses incurred in administering property not subject to claims on this schedule. List them on Schedule L instead.**

Funeral Expenses.—Itemize funeral expenses on line A. Deduct from the expenses any amounts that were reimbursed, such as death benefits payable by the Social Security Administration and the Veterans Administration.

Executors' Commissions.—When you file the return, you may deduct commissions that have actually been paid to you or that you expect will be paid. You may not deduct commissions if none will be collected. If the amount of the commissions has not been fixed by decree of the proper court, the deduction will be allowed on the final examination of the return, provided that:

● The District Director is reasonably satisfied that the commissions claimed will be paid;

● The amount entered as a deduction is within the amount allowable by the laws of the jurisdiction where the estate is being administered;

● It is in accordance with the usually accepted practice in that jurisdiction for estates of similar size and character.

If you have not been paid the commissions claimed at the time of the final examination of the return, you must support the amount you deducted with an affidavit or statement signed under the penalties of perjury that the amount has been agreed upon and will be paid.

You may not deduct a bequest or devise made to you instead of commissions. If, however, the decedent fixed by will the compensation payable to you for services to be rendered in the administration of the estate, you may deduct this amount to the extent it is not more than the compensation allowable by the local law or practice.

Do not deduct on this schedule amounts paid as trustees' commissions whether received by you acting in the capacity of a trustee or by a separate trustee. If such amounts were paid in administering property not subject to claims, deduct them on Schedule L.

Note: *Executors' commissions are taxable income to the executors. Therefore, be sure to include them as income on your individual income tax return.*

Attorney Fees.—Enter the amount of attorney fees that have actually been paid or that you reasonably expect to be paid. If on the final examination of the return the fees claimed have not been awarded by the proper court and paid, the deduction will be allowed provided the District Director is reasonably satisfied that the amount claimed will be paid and that it does not exceed a reasonable payment for the services performed, taking into account the size and character of the estate and the local law and practice. If the fees claimed have not been paid at the time of final examination of the return, the amount deducted must be supported by an affidavit, or statement signed under the penalties of perjury, by the executor or the attorney stating that the amount has been agreed upon and will be paid.

Do not deduct attorney fees incidental to litigation incurred by the beneficiaries. These expenses are charged against the beneficiaries personally and are not administration expenses authorized by the Code.

Miscellaneous Expenses.—Miscellaneous administration expenses necessarily incurred in preserving and distributing the estate are deductible. These expenses include appraiser's and accountant's fees, certain court costs, and costs of storing or maintaining assets of the estate.

The expenses of selling assets are deductible only if the sale is necessary to pay the decedent's debts, the expenses of administration, or taxes, or to preserve the estate or carry out distribution.

Form 706 (Rev. 8-93)

Estate of:

SCHEDULE K—Debts of the Decedent, and Mortgages and Liens

Item number	Debts of the Decedent—Creditor and nature of claim, and allowable death taxes	Amount unpaid to date	Amount in contest	Amount claimed as a deduction
1				

Total from continuation schedule(s) (or additional sheet(s)) attached to this schedule . . . .

TOTAL. (Also enter on Part 5, Recapitulation, page 3, at item 12.) . . . .

Item number	Mortgages and Liens—Description	Amount
1		

Total from continuation schedule(s) (or additional sheet(s)) attached to this schedule . . . .

TOTAL. (Also enter on Part 5, Recapitulation, page 3, at item 13.) . . . .

(If more space is needed, attach the continuation schedule from the end of this package or additional sheets of the same size.)
(The instructions to Schedule K are in the separate instructions.)

Schedule K —Page 25

Form 706 (Rev. 8-93)

Estate of:

SCHEDULE L—Net Losses During Administration and Expenses Incurred in Administering Property Not Subject to Claims

Item number	Net losses during administration (Note: Do not deduct losses claimed on a Federal income tax return.)	Amount
1		
	Total from continuation schedule(s) (or additional sheet(s)) attached to this schedule	
	TOTAL. (Also enter on Part 5, Recapitulation, page 3, at item 16.)	

Item number	Expenses incurred in administering property not subject to claims (Indicate whether estimated, agreed upon, or paid.)	Amount
1		
	Total from continuation schedule(s) (or additional sheet(s)) attached to this schedule	
	TOTAL. (Also enter on Part 5, Recapitulation, page 3, at item 17.)	

(If more space is needed, attach the continuation schedule from the end of this package or additional sheets of the same size.)

Schedule L —Page 26   (The instructions to Schedule L are in the separate instructions.)

Form 706 (Rev. 8-93)

Estate of:

SCHEDULE M—Bequests, etc., to Surviving Spouse

Election To Deduct Qualified Terminable Interest Property Under Section 2056(b)(7).—If a trust (or other property) meets the requirements of qualified terminable interest property under section 2056(b)(7), and

   a. The trust or other property is listed on Schedule M, and

   b. The value of the trust (or other property) is entered in whole or in part as a deduction on Schedule M,

then unless the executor specifically identifies the trust (all or a fractional portion or percentage) or other property to be excluded from the election the executor shall be deemed to have made an election to have such trust (or other property) treated as qualified terminable interest property under section 2056(b)(7).

   If less than the entire value of the trust (or other property) that the executor has included in the gross estate is entered as a deduction on Schedule M, the executor shall be considered to have made an election only as to a fraction of the trust (or other property). The numerator of this fraction is equal to the amount of the trust (or other property) deducted on Schedule M. The denominator is equal to the total value of the trust (or other property).

Election To Deduct Qualified Domestic Trust Property Under Section 2056A.—If a trust meets the requirements of a qualified domestic trust under section 2056A(a) and this return is filed no later than 1 year after the time prescribed by law (including extensions) for filing the return, and

   a. The entire value of a trust or trust property is listed on Schedule M, and

   b. The entire value of the trust or trust property is entered as a deduction on Schedule M,

then unless the executor specifically identifies the trust to be excluded from the election, the executor shall be deemed to have made an election to have the entire trust treated as qualified domestic trust property.

		Yes	No
1	Did any property pass to the surviving spouse as a result of a qualified disclaimer?		
	If "Yes," attach a copy of the written disclaimer required by section 2518(b).		
2a	In what country was the surviving spouse born? _____		
b	What is the surviving spouse's date of birth? _____		
c	Is the surviving spouse a U.S. citizen?		
d	If the surviving spouse is a naturalized citizen, when did the surviving spouse acquire citizenship? _____		
e	If the surviving spouse is not a U.S. citizen, of what country is the surviving spouse a citizen? _____		
3	**Election out of QTIP Treatment of Annuities.**—Do you elect under section 2056(b)(7)(C)(ii) **not** to treat as qualified terminable interest property any joint and survivor annuities that are included in the gross estate and would otherwise be treated as qualified terminable interest property under section 2056(b)(7)(C)? (see instructions)		

Item number	Description of property interests passing to surviving spouse	Amount
1		
	Total from continuation schedule(s) (or additional sheet(s)) attached to this schedule	

4	**Total** amount of property interests listed on Schedule M	**4**	
5a	Federal estate taxes (including section 4980A taxes) payable out of property interests listed on Schedule M	**5a**	
b	Other death taxes payable out of property interests listed on Schedule M . . .	**5b**	
c	Federal and state GST taxes payable out of property interests listed on Schedule M	**5c**	
d	Add items a, b, and c	**5d**	
6	Net amount of property interests listed on Schedule M (subtract 5d from 4). Also enter on Part 5, Recapitulation, page 3, at item 18	**6**	

(If more space is needed, attach the continuation schedule from the end of this package or additional sheets of the same size.)

(See the instructions on the reverse side.)

Schedule M—Page 27

Form 706 (Rev. 8-93)

Examples of Listing of Property Interests on Schedule M

Item number	Description of property interests passing to surviving spouse	Amount
1	One-half the value of a house and lot, 256 South West Street, held by decedent and surviving spouse as joint tenants with right of survivorship under deed dated July 15, 1957 (Schedule E, Part I, item 1)	$ 32,500
2	Proceeds of Gibraltar Life Insurance Company policy No. 104729, payable in one sum to surviving spouse (Schedule D, item 3)	20,000
3	Cash bequest under Paragraph Six of will	100,000

Instructions for Schedule M.—Bequests, etc., to Surviving Spouse (Marital Deduction)

General

You must complete Schedule M and file it with the return if you claim a deduction on item 18 of Part 5, Recapitulation.

The marital deduction is authorized by section 2056 for certain property interests that pass from the decedent to the surviving spouse. You may claim the deduction only for property interests that are included in the decedent's gross estate (Schedules A through I).

Note: *The marital deduction is generally not allowed if the surviving spouse is not a U.S. citizen. The marital deduction is allowed for property passing to such a surviving spouse in a "qualified domestic trust" or if such property is transferred or irrevocably assigned to such a trust before the estate tax return is filed. The executor must elect qualified domestic trust status on this return. See the instructions on pages 27, 29, and 30 for details on the election.*

Property Interests That You May List on Schedule M

Generally, you may list on Schedule M all property interests that pass from the decedent to the surviving spouse and are included in the gross estate. However, you should not list any "Nondeductible terminable interests" (described below) on Schedule M unless you are making a QTIP election. The property for which you make this election must be included on Schedule M. See "Qualified Terminable Interest Property" on the following page.

For the rules on common disaster and survival for a limited period, see section 2056(b)(3).

You may list on Schedule M only those interests that the surviving spouse takes:

1. As the decedent's legatee, devisee, heir, or donee;

2. As the decedent's surviving tenant by the entirety or joint tenant;

3. As an appointee under the decedent's exercise of a power or as a taker in default at the decedent's nonexercise of a power;

4. As a beneficiary of insurance on the decedent's life;

5. As the surviving spouse taking under dower or curtesy (or similar statutory interest); and

6. As a transferee of a transfer made by the decedent at any time.

Property Interests That You May Not List on Schedule M

You should not list on Schedule M:

1. The value of any property that does not pass from the decedent to the surviving spouse.

2. Property interests that are not included in the decedent's gross estate.

3. The full value of a property interest for which a deduction was claimed on Schedules J through L. The value of the property interest should be reduced by the deductions claimed with respect to it.

4. The full value of a property interest that passes to the surviving spouse subject to a mortgage or other encumbrance or an obligation of the surviving spouse. Include on Schedule M only the net value of the interest after reducing it by the amount of the mortgage or other debt.

5. Nondeductible terminable interests (described below).

6. Any property interest disclaimed by the surviving spouse.

Terminable Interests

Certain interests in property passing from a decedent to a surviving spouse are referred to as *terminable interests*. These are interests that will terminate or fail after the passage of time, or on the occurrence or nonoccurrence of some contingency. Examples are: life estates, annuities, estates for terms of years, and patents.

The ownership of a bond, note, or other contractual obligation, which when discharged would not have the effect of an annuity for life or for a term, is not considered a terminable interest.

Nondeductible terminable interests.— A terminable interest is *nondeductible,* and should not be entered on Schedule M (unless you are making a QTIP election) if:

1. Another interest in the same property passed from the decedent to some other person for less than adequate and full consideration in money or money's worth; and

2. By reason of its passing, the other person or that person's heirs may enjoy part of the property after the termination of the surviving spouse's interest.

This rule applies even though the interest that passes from the decedent to a person other than the surviving spouse is not included in the gross estate, and regardless of when the interest passes. The rule also applies regardless of whether the surviving spouse's interest and the other person's interest pass from the decedent at the same time. Property interests that are considered to pass to a person other than the surviving spouse are any property interest that: **(a)** passes under a decedent's will or intestacy; **(b)** was transferred by a decedent during life; or **(c)** is held by or passed on to any person as a decedent's joint tenant, as appointee under a decedent's exercise of a power, as taker in default at a decedent's release or nonexercise of a power, or as a beneficiary of insurance in the decedent's life.

For example, a decedent devised real property to his wife for life, with remainder to his children. The life interest that passed to the wife does not qualify for the marital deduction because it will terminate at her death and the children will thereafter possess or enjoy the property.

However, if the decedent purchased a joint and survivor annuity for himself and his wife who survived him, the value of the survivor's annuity, to the extent that it is included in the gross estate, qualifies for the marital deduction because even though the interest will terminate on the wife's death, no one else will possess or enjoy any part of the property.

The marital deduction is not allowed for an interest that the decedent directed the executor or a trustee to convert, after death, into a terminable interest for the surviving spouse. The marital deduction is not allowed for such an interest even if there was no interest

Page 28

in the property passing to another person and even if the terminable interest would otherwise have been deductible under the exceptions described below for life estate and life insurance and annuity payments with powers of appointment. For more information, see Regulations sections 20.2056(b)-1(f) and 20.2056(b)-1(g), Example (7).

If any property interest passing from the decedent to the surviving spouse may be paid or otherwise satisfied out of any of a group of assets, the value of the property interest is, for the entry on Schedule M, reduced by the value of any asset or assets that, if passing from the decedent to the surviving spouse, would be nondeductible terminable interests. Examples of property interests that may be paid or otherwise satisfied out of any of a group of assets are a bequest of the residue of the decedent's estate, or of a share of the residue, and a cash legacy payable out of the general estate.

Example: A decedent bequeathed $100,000 to the surviving spouse. The general estate includes a term for years (valued at $10,000 in determining the value of the gross estate) in an office building, which interest was retained by the decedent under a deed of the building by gift to a son. Accordingly, the value of the specific bequest entered on Schedule M is $90,000.

Life Estate With Power of Appointment in the Surviving Spouse.—A property interest, whether or not in trust, will be treated as passing to the surviving spouse, and will not be treated as a nondeductible terminable interest if: **(a)** the surviving spouse is entitled for life to all of the income from the entire interest; **(b)** the income is payable annually or at more frequent intervals; **(c)** the surviving spouse has the power, exercisable in favor of the surviving spouse or of the estate of the surviving spouse, to appoint the entire interest; **(d)** the power is exercisable by the surviving spouse alone and (whether exercisable by will or during life) is exercisable by the surviving spouse in all events; and **(e)** no part of the entire interest is subject to a power in any other person to appoint any part to any person other than the surviving spouse (or the surviving spouse's legal representative or relative if the surviving spouse is disabled. See Rev. Rul. 85-35 1985-1 C.B. 328). If these five conditions are satisfied only for a specific portion of the entire interest, see the section 2056(b) regulations to determine the amount of the marital deduction.

Life Insurance, Endowment, or Annuity Payments, With Power of Appointment in Surviving Spouse.—A property interest consisting of the entire proceeds under a life insurance, endowment, or annuity contract is treated as passing from the decedent to the surviving spouse, and will not be treated as a nondeductible terminable interest if: **(a)** the surviving spouse is entitled to receive the proceeds in installments, or is entitled to interest on them, with all amounts payable during the life of the spouse, payable only to the surviving spouse; **(b)** the installment or interest payments are payable annually, or more frequently, beginning not later than 13 months after the decedent's death; **(c)** the surviving spouse has the power, exercisable in favor of the surviving spouse or of the estate of the surviving spouse, to appoint all amounts payable under the contract; **(d)** the power is exercisable by the surviving spouse alone and (whether exercisable by will or during life) is exercisable by the surviving spouse in all events; and **(e)** no part of the amount payable under the contract is subject to a power in any other person to appoint any part to any person other than the surviving spouse. If these five conditions are satisfied only for a specific portion of the proceeds, see the section 2056(b) regulations to determine the amount of the marital deduction.

Charitable Remainder Trusts.—An interest in a charitable remainder trust will **not** be treated as a nondeductible terminable interest if:

1. The interest in the trust passes from the decedent to the surviving spouse; and

2. The surviving spouse is the only beneficiary of the trust other than charitable organizations described in section 170(c).

A "charitable remainder trust" is either a charitable remainder annuity trust or a charitable remainder unitrust. (See section 664 for descriptions of these trusts.)

Election To Deduct Qualified Terminable Interests (QTIP)

You may elect to claim a marital deduction for qualified terminable interest property or property interests. You make the QTIP election simply by listing the qualified terminable interest property on Schedule M and deducting its value. You are presumed to have made the QTIP election if you list the property and deduct its value on Schedule M. If you make this election, the surviving spouse's gross estate will include the value of the "qualified terminable interest property." See the instructions for line 6 of General Information for more details. **The election is irrevocable.**

If you file a Form 706 in which you do not make this election, you may not file an amended return to make the election unless you file the amended return on or before the due date for filing the original Form 706.

The effect of the election is that the property (interest) will be treated as passing to the surviving spouse and will not be treated as a nondeductible terminable interest. All of the other marital deduction requirements must still be satisfied before you may make this election. For example, you may not make this election for property or property interests that are not included in the decedent's gross estate.

Qualified Terminable Interest Property is property (a) that passes from the decedent, and (b) in which the surviving spouse has a qualifying income interest for life.

The surviving spouse has a *qualifying income interest for life* if the surviving spouse is entitled to all of the income from the property payable annually or at more frequent intervals, or has a usufruct interest for life in the property, and during the surviving spouse's lifetime no person has a power to appoint any part of the property to any person other than the surviving spouse. An annuity is treated as an income interest regardless of whether the property from which the annuity is payable can be separately identified.

The QTIP election may be made for all or any part of a qualified terminable interest property. A partial election must relate to a fractional or percentile share of the property so that the elective part will reflect its proportionate share of the increase or decline in the whole of the property when applying sections 2044 or 2519. Thus, if the interest of the surviving spouse in a trust (or other property in which the spouse has a qualified life estate) is qualified terminable interest property, you may make an election for a part of the trust (or other property) only if the election relates to a defined fraction or percentage of the entire trust (or other property). The fraction or percentage may be defined by means of a formula.

Qualified Domestic Trust Election (QDOT)

The marital deduction is allowed for transfers to a surviving spouse who is not a U.S. citizen only if the property passes to the surviving spouse in a "qualified domestic trust" (QDOT) or if such property is transferred or irrevocably assigned to a QDOT before the decedent's estate tax return is filed.

A QDOT is any trust:

1. That requires at least one trustee to be either an individual who is a citizen of the United States or a domestic corporation;

2. That requires that no distribution of corpus from the trust can be made unless such a trustee has the right to withhold from the distribution the tax imposed on the QDOT;

3. That meets the requirements of any applicable regulations; and

4. For which the executor has made an election on the estate tax return of the decedent.

You make the QDOT election simply by listing the qualified domestic trust or the **entire value** of the trust property on Schedule M and deducting its value. You are presumed to have made the QDOT election if you list the trust or trust property and deduct its value on Schedule M. **Once made, the election is irrevocable.**

If an election is made to deduct qualified domestic trust property under section 2056A(d), the following information should be provided for each qualified domestic trust on an attachment to this schedule:

1. The name and address of every trustee;

2. A description of each transfer passing from the decedent that is the source of the property to be placed in trust; and

3. The employer identification number for the trust.

The election must be made for an entire QDOT trust. In listing a trust for which you are making a QDOT election, unless you specifically identify the trust as not subject to the election, the election will be considered made for the entire trust.

The determination of whether a trust qualifies as a QDOT will be made as of the date the decedent's Form 706 is filed. If, however, judicial proceedings are brought before the Form 706's due date (including extensions) to have the trust revised to meet the QDOT requirements, then the determination will not be made until the court-ordered changes to the trust are made.

Line 1

If property passes to the surviving spouse as the result of a qualified disclaimer, check "Yes" and attach a copy of the written disclaimer required by section 2518(b).

Line 3

Section 2056(b)(7) creates an automatic QTIP election for certain joint and survivor annuities that are includible in the estate under section 2039. To qualify, only the surviving spouse can have the right to receive payments before the death of the surviving spouse.

The executor can elect out of QTIP treatment, however, by checking the "Yes" box on line 3. Once made, the election is irrevocable. If there is more than one such joint and survivor annuity, you are not required to make the election for all of them.

If you make the election out of QTIP treatment by checking "Yes" on line 3, you cannot deduct the amount of the annuity on Schedule M. If you do not make the election out, you must list the joint and survivor annuities on Schedule M.

Listing Property Interest on Schedule M

List each property interest included in the gross estate that passes from the decedent to the surviving spouse and for which a marital deduction is claimed. This includes otherwise nondeductible terminable interest property for which you are making a QTIP election. Number each item in sequence and describe each item in detail. Describe the instrument (including any clause or paragraph number) or provision of law under which each item passed to the surviving spouse. If possible, show where each item appears (number and schedule) on Schedules A through I.

In listing otherwise nondeductible property for which you are making a QTIP election, unless you specifically identify a fractional portion of the trust or other property as not subject to the election, the election will be considered made for all of the trust or other property.

Enter the value of each interest before taking into account the Federal estate tax or any other death tax. The valuation dates used in determining the value of the gross estate apply also on Schedule M.

If Schedule M includes a bequest of the residue or a part of the residue of the decedent's estate, attach a copy of the computation showing how the value of the residue was determined. Include a statement showing:

● The value of all property that is included in the decedent's gross estate (Schedules A through I) but is not a part of the decedent's probate estate, such as lifetime transfers, jointly owned property that passed to the survivor on decedent's death, and the insurance payable to specific beneficiaries.

● The values of all specific and general legacies or devises, with reference to the applicable clause or paragraph of the decedent's will or codicil. (If legacies are made to each member of a class, for example, $1,000 to each of decedent's employees, only the number in each class and the total value of property received by them need be furnished.)

● The date of birth of all persons, the length of whose lives may affect the value of the residuary interest passing to the surviving spouse.

● Any other important information such as that relating to any claim to any part of the estate not arising under the will.

Lines 5a, b, and c.—The total of the values listed on Schedule M must be reduced by the amount of the Federal estate tax, the Federal GST tax, and the amount of state or other death and GST taxes paid out of the property interest involved. If you enter an amount for state or other death or GST taxes on lines 5b or 5c, identify the taxes and attach your computation of them. For additional information, see **Pub. 904,** Interrelated Computations for Estate and Gift Taxes.

Attachments.—If you list property interests passing by the decedent's will on Schedule M, attach a certified copy of the order admitting the will to probate. If, when you file the return, the court of probate jurisdiction has entered any decree interpreting the will or any of its provisions affecting any of the interests listed on Schedule M, or has entered any order of distribution, attach a copy of the decree or order. In addition, the District Director may request other evidence to support the marital deduction claimed.

Form 706 (Rev. 8-93)

Estate of:

SCHEDULE O—Charitable, Public, and Similar Gifts and Bequests

		Yes	No
1a If the transfer was made by will, has any action been instituted to have interpreted or to contest the will or any of its provisions affecting the charitable deductions claimed in this schedule? . . . . If "Yes," full details must be submitted with this schedule.			
b According to the information and belief of the person or persons filing this return, is any such action planned? If "Yes," full details must be submitted with this schedule.			
2 Did any property pass to charity as the result of a qualified disclaimer? . . . . If "Yes," attach a copy of the written disclaimer required by section 2518(b).			

Item number	Name and address of beneficiary	Character of institution	Amount
1			

Total from continuation schedule(s) (or additional sheet(s)) attached to this schedule . . . .

3 Total		**3**	
4a Federal estate tax (including section 4980A taxes) payable out of property interests listed above	**4a**		
b Other death taxes payable out of property interests listed above	**4b**		
c Federal and state GST taxes payable out of property interests listed above	**4c**		
d Add items a, b, and c		**4d**	
5 Net value of property interests listed above (subtract 4d from 3). Also enter on Part 5, Recapitulation, page 3, at item 19		**5**	

(If more space is needed, attach the continuation schedule from the end of this package or additional sheets of the same size.)
(The instructions to Schedule O are in the separate instructions.)

Schedule O—Page 31

Form 706 (Rev. 8-93)

Estate of:

SCHEDULE P—Credit for Foreign Death Taxes

List all foreign countries to which death taxes have been paid and for which a credit is claimed on this return.

If a credit is claimed for death taxes paid to more than one foreign country, compute the credit for taxes paid to one country on this sheet and attach a separate copy of Schedule P for each of the other countries.

The credit computed on this sheet is for the ....
(Name of death tax or taxes)

.... imposed in ....
(Name of country)

Credit is computed under the ....
(Insert title of treaty or "statute")

Citizenship (nationality) of decedent at time of death

(All amounts and values must be entered in United States money)

1	Total of estate, inheritance, legacy, and succession taxes imposed in the country named above attributable to property situated in that country, subjected to these taxes, and included in the gross estate (as defined by statute)	
2	Value of the gross estate (adjusted, if necessary, according to the instructions for item 2)	
3	Value of property situated in that country, subjected to death taxes imposed in that country, and included in the gross estate (adjusted, if necessary, according to the instructions for item 3)	
4	Tax imposed by section 2001 reduced by the total credits claimed under sections 2010, 2011, and 2012 (see instructions)	
5	Amount of Federal estate tax attributable to property specified at item 3. (Divide item 3 by item 2 and multiply the result by item 4.)	
6	Credit for death taxes imposed in the country named above (the smaller of item 1 or item 5). Also enter on line 18 of Part 2, Tax Computation	

SCHEDULE Q—Credit for Tax on Prior Transfers

Part 1.—Transferor Information

	Name of transferor	Social security number	IRS office where estate tax return was filed	Date of death
A				
B				
C				

Check here ▶ ☐ if section 2013(f) (special valuation of farm, etc., real property) adjustments to the computation of the credit were made (see instructions).

Part 2.—Computation of Credit (see instructions)

Item	Transferor			Total A, B, & C
	A	B	C	
1 Transferee's tax as apportioned (from worksheet, (line 7 ÷ line 8) × line 35 for each column) . .				
2 Transferor's tax (from each column of worksheet, line 20)				
3 Maximum amount before percentage requirement (for each column, enter amount from line 1 or 2, whichever is smaller)				
4 Percentage allowed (each column) (see instructions)	%	%	%	
5 Credit allowable (line 3 × line 4 for each column)				
6 TOTAL credit allowable (add columns A, B, and C of line 5. Enter here and on line 19 of Part 2, Tax Computation				

Schedules P and Q—Page 32   (The instructions to Schedules P and Q are in the separate instructions.)

Form 706 (Rev. 8-93)

SCHEDULE R—Generation-Skipping Transfer Tax

Note: *To avoid application of the deemed allocation rules, Form 706 and Schedule R should be filed to allocate the GST exemption to trusts that may later have taxable terminations or distributions under section 2612 even if the form is not required to be filed to report estate or GST tax.*

The GST tax is imposed on taxable transfers of interests in property located **outside the United States** *as well as property located inside the United States.*

Part 1.—GST Exemption Reconciliation (Section 2631) and Section 2652(a)(3) (Special QTIP) Election

Check box ▶ ☐ if you are making a section 2652(a)(3) (special QTIP) election (see instructions)

1 Maximum allowable GST exemption	**1**	$1,000,000
2 Total GST exemption allocated by the decedent against decedent's lifetime transfers	**2**	
3 Total GST exemption allocated by the executor, using Form 709, against decedent's lifetime transfers	**3**	
4 GST exemption allocated on line 6 of Schedule R, Part 2	**4**	
5 GST exemption allocated on line 6 of Schedule R, Part 3	**5**	
6 Total GST exemption allocated on line 4 of Schedule(s) R-1	**6**	
7 Total GST exemption allocated to intervivos transfers and direct skips (add lines 2–6)	**7**	
8 GST exemption available to allocate to trusts and section 2032A interests (subtract line 7 from line 1)	**8**	

9 Allocation of GST exemption to trusts (as defined for GST tax purposes):

A Name of trust	B Trust's EIN (if any)	C GST exemption allocated on lines 2–6, above (see instructions)	D Additional GST exemption allocated (see instructions)	E Trust's inclusion ratio (optional—see instructions)

9D Total. May not exceed line 8, above'	**9D**	
10 GST exemption available to allocate to section 2032A interests received by individual beneficiaries (subtract line 9D from line 8). You must attach special use allocation schedule (see instructions)	**10**	

(The instructions to Schedule R are in the separate instructions.)

Schedule R—Page 33

Form 706 (Rev. 8-93)

Estate of:

Part 2.—Direct Skips Where the Property Interests Transferred Bear the GST Tax on the Direct Skips

Name of skip person	Description of property interest transferred	Estate tax value

1	Total estate tax values of all property interests listed above	1	
2	Estate taxes, state death taxes, and other charges borne by the property interests listed above .	2	
3	GST taxes borne by the property interests listed above but imposed on direct skips other than those shown on this Part 2. (See instructions.)	3	
4	Total fixed taxes and other charges. (Add lines 2 and 3.)	4	
5	Total tentative maximum direct skips. (Subtract line 4 from line 1.)	5	
6	GST exemption allocated	6	
7	Subtract line 6 from line 5	7	
8	GST tax due. (Divide line 7 by 2.818182)	8	
9	Enter the amount from line 8 of Schedule R, Part 3	9	
10	**Total GST taxes payable by the estate.** (Add lines 8 and 9.) Enter here and on line 22 of the Tax Computation on page 1	10	

Schedule R—Page 34

Form 706 (Rev. 8-93)

Estate of:

Part 3.—Direct Skips Where the Property Interests Transferred Do Not Bear the GST Tax on the Direct Skips

Name of skip person	Description of property interest transferred	Estate tax value

1 Total estate tax values of all property interests listed above	**1**	
2 Estate taxes, state death taxes, and other charges borne by the property interests listed above.	**2**	
3 GST taxes borne by the property interests listed above but imposed on direct skips other than those shown on this Part 3. (See instructions.)	**3**	
4 Total fixed taxes and other charges. (Add lines 2 and 3.)	**4**	
5 Total tentative maximum direct skips. (Subtract line 4 from line 1.)	**5**	
6 GST exemption allocated	**6**	
7 Subtract line 6 from line 5	**7**	
8 GST tax due (multiply line 7 by .55). Enter here and on Schedule R, Part 2, line 9	**8**	

Schedule R—Page 35

SCHEDULE R-1 **(Form 706)** (August 1993) Department of the Treasury Internal Revenue Service	**Generation-Skipping Transfer Tax** Direct Skips From a Trust Payment Voucher	OMB No. 1545-0015 Expires 12-31-95

Executor: File one copy with Form 706 and send two copies to the fiduciary. Do not pay the tax shown. See the separate instructions.
Fiduciary: See instructions on following page. Pay the tax shown on line 6.

Name of trust		Trust's EIN
Name and title of fiduciary	Name of decedent	
Address of fiduciary (number and street)	Decedent's SSN	Service Center where Form 706 was filed
City, state, and ZIP code	Name of executor	
Address of executor (number and street)	City, state, and ZIP code	
Date of decedent's death	Filing due date of Schedule R, Form 706 (with extensions)	

Part 1.—Computation of the GST Tax on the Direct Skip

Description of property interests subject to the direct skip	Estate tax value

1	Total estate tax value of all property interests listed above	**1**
2	Estate taxes, state death taxes, and other charges borne by the property interests listed above .	**2**
3	Tentative maximum direct skip from trust. (Subtract line 2 from line 1.)	**3**
4	GST exemption allocated	**4**
5	Subtract line 4 from line 3	**5**
6	**GST tax due from fiduciary.** (Divide line 5 by 2.818182) **(See instructions if property will not bear the GST tax.)**	**6**

Under penalties of perjury, I declare that I have examined this return, including accompanying schedules and statements, and to the best of my knowledge and belief, it is true, correct, and complete.

Signature(s) of executor(s) _____ Date _____

_____ Date _____

Signature of fiduciary or officer representing fiduciary _____ Date _____

Schedule R-1 (Form 706)—Page 36

Form 706 (Rev. 8-93)

Instructions for Fiduciary

Purpose of Schedule R-1

Code section 2603(a)(2) provides that the Generation-Skipping Transfer (GST) tax imposed on a direct skip from a trust is to be paid by the trustee. Schedule R-1 (Form 706) serves as a payment voucher for the trustee to remit the GST tax to the IRS. See the instructions for Form 706 as to when a direct skip is from a trust.

How To Pay the GST Tax

The executor will compute the GST tax, complete Schedule R-1, and give you two copies. You should pay the GST tax using one copy and keep the other copy for your records.

The GST tax due is the amount shown on line 6. Make your check or money order for this amount payable to "Internal Revenue Service," write "GST tax" and the trust's EIN on it, and send it and one copy of the completed Schedule R-1 to the IRS Service Center where the Form 706 was filed, as shown on the front of the Schedule R-1.

When To Pay the GST Tax

The GST tax is due and payable 9 months after the decedent's date of death (entered by the executor on Schedule R-1). Interest will be charged on any GST taxes unpaid as of that date. However, you have an automatic extension of time to file Schedule R-1 and pay the GST tax due until 2 months after the due date (with extensions) for filing the decedent's Schedule R, Form 706. This Schedule R, Form 706 due date is entered by the executor on Schedule R-1. Thus, while interest will be due on unpaid GST taxes, no penalties will be charged if you file Schedule R-1 by this extended due date.

Signature

You, as fiduciary, must sign the Schedule R-1 in the space provided.

Form 706 (Rev. 8-93)

Estate of:

SCHEDULE S—Increased Estate Tax on Excess Retirement Accumulations

(Under section 4980A(d) of the Internal Revenue Code)

Part I   **Tax Computation**

1   Check this box if a section 4980A(d)(5) spousal election is being made. . . . . ▶ ☐
You must attach the statement described in the instructions.

2   Enter the name and employer identification number (EIN) of each qualified employer plan and individual retirement account in which the decedent had an interest at the time of death:

	Name	EIN
Plan #1		
Plan #2		
Plan #3		
IRA #1		
IRA #2		
IRA #3		

		A Plan #1	B Plan #2	C Plan #3	D All IRAs
3	Value of decedent's interest	▨	▨	▨	
4	Amounts rolled over after death	▨	▨	▨	
5	Total value (add lines 3 and 4)				▨
6	Amounts payable to certain alternate payees (see instructions)				▨
7	Decedent's investment in the contract under section 72(f)				▨
8	Excess life insurance amount				
9	Decedent's interest as a beneficiary				
10	Total reductions in value (add lines 6, 7, 8, and 9) . . .				
11	Net value of decedent's interest (subtract line 10 from line 5)				

12   Decedent's aggregate interest in all plans and IRAs (add columns A–D of line 11) . . . . . . ▶   **12**

13   Present value of hypothetical life annuity (from Part III, line 4) . . . . . | **13** |

14   Remaining unused grandfather amount (from Part II, line 4) . . . . . | **14** |

15   Enter the greater of line 13 or line 14 . . . . **15**

16   Excess retirement accumulation (subtract line 15 from line 12) **16**

17   Increased estate tax (multiply line 16 by 15%). Enter here and on line 23 of the Tax Computation on page 1 . . . . **17**

(The instructions to Schedule S are in the separate instructions.)

Schedule S —Page 38

Form 706 (Rev. 8-93)

Part II	**Grandfather Election**

1 Was a grandfather election made on a previously filed Form 5329? . . . . ▶   ☐ Yes ☐ No
If "Yes," complete lines 2–4 below. **You may not make or revoke the grandfather election after the due date (with extensions) for filing the decedent's 1988 income tax return.** If "No," enter -0- on line 4 and skip to Part III.

2 Initial grandfather amount . . . . | 2 |

3 Total amount previously recovered . . . . | 3 |

4 Remaining unused grandfather amount (subtract line 3 from line 2). Enter here and on Part I, line 14, on page 38 . . . . | 4 |

Part III	**Computation of Hypothetical Life Annuity**

1 Decedent's attained age at date of death (in whole years, rounded down) . . . . | 1 |

2 Applicable annual annuity amount (see instructions) . . . . -. . . . | 2 |

3 Present value multiplier (see instructions) . . . . | 3 |

4 Present value of hypothetical life annuity (multiply line 2 by line 3). Enter here and on Part I, line 13, on page 38 . . . . | 4 |

Form 706 (Rev. 8-93)   (Make copies of this schedule before completing it if you will need more than one schedule.)

Estate of:

CONTINUATION SCHEDULE

Continuation of Schedule _____

(Enter letter of schedule you are continuing.)

Item number	Description For securities, give CUSIP number, if available.	Unit value (Sch B, E, or G only)	Alternate valuation date	Alternate value	Value at date of death or amount deductible

TOTAL. (Carry forward to main schedule.) . . . .

See the instructions on the reverse side.   **Continuation Schedule—Page 40**

Form 706 (Rev. 8-93)

Instructions for Continuation Schedule

The Continuation Schedule on page 40 provides a uniform format for listing additional assets from Schedules A, B, C, D, E, F, G, H, and I and additional deductions from Schedules J, K, L, M, and O. Use the Continuation Schedule when you need to list more assets or deductions than you have room for on one of the main schedules.

Use a separate Continuation Schedule for each main schedule you are continuing. For each schedule of Form 706, you may use as many Continuation Schedules as needed to list all the assets or deductions to be reported. Do not combine assets or deductions from different schedules on one Continuation Schedule. Because there is only one Continuation Schedule in this package, you should make copies of the schedule before completing it if you expect to need more than one.

Enter the letter of the schedule you are continuing in the space provided at the top of the Continuation Schedule. Complete the rest of the Continuation Schedule as explained in the instructions for the schedule you are continuing. Use the *Unit value* column only if you are continuing Schedules B, E, or G. For all other schedules, you may use the space under the *Unit value* column to continue your description.

To continue Schedule E, Part 2, you should enter the *Percentage includible* in the *Alternate valuation date* column of the Continuation Schedule.

To continue Schedule J, you should use the *Alternate valuation date* and *Alternate value* columns of the Continuation Schedule as *Amount unpaid to date* and *Amount in contest* columns, respectively.

To continue Schedules J, L, and M, you should use the *Alternate valuation date* and *Alternate value* columns of the Continuation Schedule to continue your description of the deductions. You should enter the amount of each deduction in the *amount deductible* column of the Continuation Schedule.

To continue Schedule O, you should use the space under the *Alternate valuation date* and *Alternate value* columns of the Continuation Schedule to provide the *Character of institution* information required on Schedule O. You should enter the amount of each deduction in the *amount deductible* column of the Continuation Schedule.

Carry the total from the Continuation Schedule(s) forward to the appropriate line of the main schedule.

For sale by the U.S. Government Printing Office
Superintendent of Documents, Mail Stop: SSOP, Washington, DC 20402-9328

U.S. GOVERNMENT PRINTING OFFICE : 1993 O - 357-328

Federal Gift Tax Return (Form 709)

Form **709**	**United States Gift (and Generation-Skipping Transfer) Tax Return**		
(Rev. November 1991)	(Section 6019 of the Internal Revenue Code) (For gifts made after October 8, 1990, and before January 1, 1993)		OMB No. 1545-0020
Department of the Treasury Internal Revenue Service	**Calendar year 19** .... ▶ **See separate instructions. For Privacy Act Notice, see the Instructions for Form 1040.**		Expires 8-31-93

Part 1.—General Information

1 Donor's first name and middle initial	2 Donor's last name	3 Social security number
4 Address (number, street, and apartment number)		5 Legal residence (Domicile)
6 City, state, and ZIP code		7 Citizenship

		Yes	No
8	If the donor died during the year, check here ▶ ☐ and enter date of death ...., 19		
9	If you received an extension of time to file this Form 709, check here ▶ ☐ and attach the Form 4868, 2688, 2350, or extension letter		
10	Enter the total number of separate donees listed on Schedule A—count each person only once ▶ ☐		
11a	Have you (the donor) previously filed a Form 709 (or 709-A) for any other year? If the answer is "No," do not complete line 11b .		
11b	If the answer to line 11a is "Yes," has your address changed since you last filed Form 709 (or 709-A)?		
12	Gifts by husband or wife to third parties.—Do you consent to have the gifts (including generation-skipping transfers) made by you and by your spouse to third parties during the calendar year considered as made one-half by each of you? (See instructions.) (If the answer is "Yes," the following information must be furnished and your spouse must sign the consent shown below. If the answer is "No," skip lines 13–18 and go to Schedule A.)		
13	Name of consenting spouse	14 SSN	
15	Were you married to one another during the entire calendar year? (See instructions.)		
16	If the answer to 15 is "No," check whether ☐ married ☐ divorced or ☐ widowed, and give date (see instructions) ▶		
17	Will a gift tax return for this calendar year be filed by your spouse?		
18	**Consent of Spouse**—I consent to have the gifts (and generation-skipping transfers) made by me and by my spouse to third parties during the calendar year considered as made one-half by each of us. We are both aware of the joint and several liability for tax created by the execution of this consent.		

Consenting spouse's signature ▶   Date ▶

Part 2.—Tax Computation

1	Enter the amount from Schedule A, Part 3, line 15	1	
2	Enter the amount from Schedule B, line 3	2	
3	Total taxable gifts (add lines 1 and 2)	3	
4	Tax computed on amount on line 3 (see Table for Computing Tax in separate instructions). . .	4	
5	Tax computed on amount on line 2 (see Table for Computing Tax in separate instructions). . .	5	
6	Balance (subtract line 5 from line 4)	6	
7	Maximum unified credit (nonresident aliens, see instructions)	7	192,800 00
8	Enter the unified credit against tax allowable for all prior periods (from Sch. B, line 1, col. C) . .	8	
9	Balance (subtract line 8 from line 7)	9	
10	Enter 20% (.20) of the amount allowed as a specific exemption for gifts made after September 8, 1976, and before January 1, 1977 (see instructions)	10	
11	Balance (subtract line 10 from line 9)	11	
12	Unified credit (enter the smaller of line 6 or line 11)	12	
13	Credit for foreign gift taxes (see instructions)	13	
14	Total credits (add lines 12 and 13)	14	
15	Balance (subtract line 14 from line 6) (do not enter less than zero)	15	
16	Generation-skipping transfer taxes (from Schedule C, Part 3, col. H, total)	16	
17	Total tax (add lines 15 and 16)	17	
18	Gift and generation-skipping transfer taxes prepaid with extension of time to file	18	
19	If line 18 is less than line 17, enter BALANCE DUE (see instructions)	19	
20	If line 18 is greater than line 17, enter AMOUNT TO BE REFUNDED	20	

Under penalties of perjury, I declare that I have examined this return, including any accompanying schedules and statements, and to the best of my knowledge and belief it is true, correct, and complete. Declaration of preparer (other than donor) is based on all information of which preparer has any knowledge.

Donor's signature ▶   Date ▶

Preparer's signature
(other than donor) ▶   Date ▶

Preparer's address
(other than donor) ▶

For Paperwork Reduction Act Notice, see page 1 of the separate instructions for this form.   Cat. No. 16783M   Form **709** (Rev. 11-91)

Form 709 (Rev. 11-91)   Page **2**

SCHEDULE A   **Computation of Taxable Gifts**

Part 1.—Gifts Subject Only to Gift Tax. *Gifts less political organization, medical, and educational exclusions—see instructions*

A Item number	B Donee's name, relationship to donor (if any), and address and description of gift. If the gift was made by means of a trust, enter trust's identifying number below and attach a copy of the trust instrument. If the gift was securities, enter the CUSIP number(s), if available.	C Donor's adjusted basis of gift	D Date of gift	E Value at date of gift
1				

Part 2.—Gifts Which are Direct Skips and are Subject to Both Gift Tax and Generation-Skipping Transfer Tax. You must list the gifts in chronological order. *Gifts less political organization, medical, and educational exclusions—see instructions. (Also list here direct skips that are subject only to the GST tax at this time as the result of the termination of an "estate tax inclusion period." See instructions.)*

A Item number	B Donee's name, relationship to donor (if any), and address and description of gift. If the gift was made by means of a trust, enter trust's identifying number below and attach a copy of the trust instrument. If the gift was securities, enter the CUSIP number(s), if available.	C Donor's adjusted basis of gift	D Date of gift	E Value at date of gift
1				

Part 3.—Gift Tax Reconciliation

1	Total value of gifts of donor (add column E of Parts 1 and 2)	1	
2	One-half of items .... attributable to spouse (see instructions)	2	
3	Balance (subtract line 2 from line 1)	3	
4	Gifts of spouse to be included (from Schedule A, Part 3, line 2 of spouse's return—see instructions) . .	4	
	If any of the gifts included on this line are also subject to the generation-skipping transfer tax, check here ▶ ☐ and enter those gifts also on Schedule C, Part 1.		
5	Total gifts (add lines 3 and 4)	5	
6	Total annual exclusions for gifts listed on Schedule A (including line 4, above) (see instructions) . . .	6	
7	Total included amount of gifts (subtract line 6 from line 5)	7	

Deductions (see instructions)

8	Gifts of interests to spouse for which a marital deduction will be claimed, based on items ....of Schedule A	8		
9	Exclusions attributable to gifts on line 8	9		
10	Marital deduction—subtract line 9 from line 8	10		
11	Charitable deduction, based on items ....to ....less exclusions	11		
12	Total deductions—add lines 10 and 11		12	
13	Subtract line 12 from line 7		13	
14	Generation-skipping transfer taxes payable with this Form 709 (from Schedule C, Part 3, col. H, Total) .		14	
15	Taxable gifts (add lines 13 and 14). Enter here and on line 1 of the Tax Computation on page 1 . . .		15	

(If more space is needed, attach additional sheets of same size.)

Form 709 (Rev. 11-91)   Page **3**

SCHEDULE A   Computation of Taxable Gifts (continued)

16 Terminable Interest (QTIP) Marital Deduction. (See instructions.)

If a trust (or other property) meets the requirements of qualified terminable interest property under section 2523(f), and

 a. the trust (or other property) is listed on Schedule A, and

 b. the value of the trust (or other property) is entered in whole or in part as a deduction on line 8, Part 3 of Schedule A,

then the donor shall be deemed to have made an election to have such trust (or other property) treated as qualified terminable interest property under section 2523(f).

 If less than the entire value of the trust (or other property) that the donor has included in Part 1 of Schedule A is entered as a deduction on line 8, the donor shall be considered to have made an election only as to a fraction of the trust (or other property). The numerator of this fraction is equal to the amount of the trust (or other property) deducted on line 10 of Part 3. The denominator is equal to the total value of the trust (or other property) listed in Part 1 of Schedule A.

 If you make the QTIP election (see instructions for line 8 of Schedule A), the terminable interest property involved will be included in your spouse's gross estate upon his or her death (section 2044). If your spouse disposes (by gift or otherwise) of all or part of the qualifying life income interest, he or she will be considered to have made a transfer of the entire property that is subject to the gift tax (see Transfer of Certain Life Estates on page 3 of the instructions).

17 Election out of QTIP Treatment of Annuities

 ☐ ◀ Check here if you elect under section 2523(f)(6) **NOT** to treat as qualified terminable interest property any joint and survivor annuities that are reported on Schedule A and would otherwise be treated as qualified terminable interest property under section 2523(f). (See instructions.) Enter the item numbers (from Schedule A) for the annuities for which you are making this election ▶

SCHEDULE B   Gifts From Prior Periods

If you answered "Yes" on line 11a of Page 1, Part 1, see the instructions for completing Schedule B. If your answer is "No," skip to the Tax Computation on Page 1 (or Schedule C, if applicable).

A Calendar year or calendar quarter (see instructions)	B Internal Revenue office where prior return was filed	C Amount of unified credit against gift tax for periods after December 31, 1976	D Amount of specific exemption for prior periods ending before January 1, 1977	E Amount of taxable gifts

1 Totals for prior periods (without adjustment for reduced specific exemption)	**1**		
2 Amount, if any, by which total specific exemption, line 1, column D, is more than $30,000	**2**	
3 Total amount of taxable gifts for prior periods (add amount, column E, line 1, and amount, if any, on line 2) (Enter here and on line 2 of the Tax Computation on page 1.)	**3**	

(If more space is needed, attach additional sheets of same size.)

Form 709 (Rev. 11-91) Page **4**

| SCHEDULE C | Computation of Generation-Skipping Transfer Tax |

Note: *Inter vivos direct skips which are completely excluded by the GST exemption must still be fully reported (including value and exemptions claimed) on Schedule C.*

Part 1.—Generation-Skipping Transfers

A Item No. (from Schedule A, Part 2. col. A)	B Value (from Schedule A, Part 2. col. E)	C Split Gifts (enter ½ of col. B) (see instructions)	D Subtract col. C from col. B	E Nontaxable portion of transfer	F Net Transfer (subtract col. E from col. D)
1					
2					
3					
4					
5					
6					

	Split gifts from spouse's Form 709 (enter item number)	Value included from spouse's Form 709	Nontaxable portion of transfer	Net transfer (subtract col. E from col. D)
If you elected gift splitting and your spouse was required to file a separate Form 709 (see the instructions for "Split Gifts"), you must enter all of the gifts shown on Schedule A, Part 2, of your spouse's Form 709 here. In column C, enter the item number of each gift in the order it appears in column A of your spouse's Schedule A, Part 2. We have preprinted the prefix "S-" to distinguish your spouse's item numbers from your own when you complete column A of Schedule C, Part 3. In column D, for each gift, enter the amount reported in column C, Schedule C, Part 1, of your spouse's Form 709.	S- S- S- S- S- S- S- S- S-			

Part 2.—GST Exemption Reconciliation (Code section 2631) and Section 2652(a)(3) Election

Check box ▶ ☐ if you are making a section 2652(a)(3) (special QTIP) election (see instructions)

Enter the item numbers (from Schedule A) of the gifts for which you are making this election ▶ ....

1	Maximum allowable exemption	1	$1,000,000
2	Total exemption used for periods before filing this return	2	
3	Exemption available for this return (subtract line 2 from line 1)	3	
4	Exemption claimed on this return (from Part 3, col. C total, below)	4	
5	Exemption allocated to transfers not shown on Part 3, below. You must attach a Notice of Allocation. (See instructions.)	5	
6	Add lines 4 and 5	6	
7	Exemption available for future transfers (subtract line 6 from line 3)	7	

Part 3.—Tax Computation

A Item No. (from Schedule C, Part 1)	B Net transfer (from Schedule C, Part 1, col. F)	C GST Exemption Allocated	D Divide col. C by col. B	E Inclusion Ratio (subtract col. D from 1.000)	F Maximum Estate Tax Rate	G Applicable Rate (multiply col. E by col. F)	H Generation-Skipping Transfer Tax (multiply col. B by col. G)
1					55% (.55)		
2					55% (.55)		
3					55% (.55)		
4					55% (.55)		
5					55% (.55)		
6					55% (.55)		
					55% (.55)		
					55% (.55)		
					55% (.55)		
					55% (.55)		

| Total exemption claimed. Enter here and on line 4, Part 2, above. May not exceed line 3, Part 2, above . . . . . | | **Total generation-skipping transfer tax.** Enter here, on line 14 of Schedule A, Part 3, and on line 16 of the Tax Computation on page 1 . . . . | |

(If more space is needed, attach additional sheets of same size.)

★ U.S.GPO:1992-0-343-034/60164

Federal Individual Income Tax Return

(Form 1040)

Form **1040** Department of the Treasury—Internal Revenue Service
U.S. Individual Income Tax Return (O) **1993**

IRS Use Only—Do not write or staple in this space.

For the year Jan. 1–Dec. 31, 1993, or other tax year beginning _____ , 1993, ending _____ , 19 __ | OMB No. 1545-0074

Label

(See instructions on page 12.)

Use the IRS label. Otherwise, please print or type.

L A B E L   H E R E

Your first name and initial | Last name | Your social security number

If a joint return, spouse's first name and initial | Last name | Spouse's social security number

Home address (number and street). If you have a P.O. box, see page 12. | Apt. no.

City, town or post office, state, and ZIP code. If you have a foreign address, see page 12.

For Privacy Act and Paperwork Reduction Act Notice, see page 4.

Presidential Election Campaign

(See page 12.)

Yes | No | **Note:** *Checking "Yes" will not change your tax or reduce your refund.*

Do you want $3 to go to this fund? . . . .
If a joint return, does your spouse want $3 to go to this fund? . . . .

Filing Status

(See page 12.)

Check only one box.

1 ☐ Single
2 ☐ Married filing joint return (even if only one had income)
3 ☐ Married filing separate return. Enter spouse's social security no. above and full name here. ▶ _____
4 ☐ Head of household (with qualifying person). (See page 13.) If the qualifying person is a child but not your dependent, enter this child's name here. ▶ _____
5 ☐ Qualifying widow(er) with dependent child (year spouse died ▶ 19 __). (See page 13.)

Exemptions

(See page 13.)

If more than six dependents, see page 14.

6a ☐ **Yourself.** If your parent (or someone else) can claim you as a dependent on his or her tax return, **do not** check box 6a. But be sure to check the box on line 33b on page 2.

b ☐ **Spouse** . . . .

c **Dependents:**

(1) Name (first, initial, and last name)	(2) Check if under age 1	(3) If age 1 or older, dependent's social security number	(4) Dependent's relationship to you	(5) No. of months lived in your home in 1993

d If your child didn't live with you but is claimed as your dependent under a pre-1985 agreement, check here ▶ ☐
e Total number of exemptions claimed . . . .

No. of boxes checked on 6a and 6b

No. of your children on 6c who:
• lived with you _____
• didn't live with you due to divorce or separation (see page 15) _____

Dependents on 6c not entered above _____

Add numbers entered on lines above ▶

Income

Attach Copy B of your Forms W-2, W-2G, and 1099-R here.

If you did not get a W-2, see page 10.

If you are attaching a check or money order, put it on top of any Forms W-2, W-2G, or 1099-R.

7 Wages, salaries, tips, etc. Attach Form(s) W-2 . . . . | 7
8a **Taxable** interest income (see page 16). Attach Schedule B if over $400 . . . . . | 8a
b **Tax-exempt** interest (see page 17). DON'T include on line 8a | 8b |
9 Dividend income. Attach Schedule B if over $400 . . . . . . | 9
10 Taxable refunds, credits, or offsets of state and local income taxes (see page 17) . . | 10
11 Alimony received . . . . | 11
12 Business income or (loss). Attach Schedule C or C-EZ . . . . . . | 12
13 Capital gain or (loss). Attach Schedule D . . . . | 13
14 Capital gain distributions not reported on line 13 (see page 17) . . . . . | 14
15 Other gains or (losses). Attach Form 4797 . . . . | 15
16a Total IRA distributions . | 16a | b Taxable amount (see page 18) | 16b
17a Total pensions and annuities | 17a | b Taxable amount (see page 18) | 17b
18 Rental real estate, royalties, partnerships, S corporations, trusts, etc. Attach Schedule E | 18
19 Farm income or (loss). Attach Schedule F . . . . | 19
20 Unemployment compensation (see page 19) . . . . | 20
21a Social security benefits | 21a | b Taxable amount (see page 19) | 21b
22 Other income. List type and amount—see page 20 _____ | 22
23 Add the amounts in the far right column for lines 7 through 22. This is your **total income** ▶ | 23

Adjustments to Income

(See page 20.)

24a Your IRA deduction (see page 20) . . . . | 24a |
b Spouse's IRA deduction (see page 20) . . . . | 24b |
25 One-half of self-employment tax (see page 21) . . . | 25 |
26 Self-employed health insurance deduction (see page 22) | 26 |
27 Keogh retirement plan and self-employed SEP deduction | 27 |
28 Penalty on early withdrawal of savings . . . . . | 28 |
29 Alimony paid. Recipient's SSN ▶ _____ | 29 |
30 Add lines 24a through 29. These are your **total adjustments** . . . . ▶ | 30

Adjusted Gross Income

31 Subtract line 30 from line 23. This is your **adjusted gross income.** If this amount is less than $23,050 and a child lived with you, see page EIC-1 to find out if you can claim the "Earned Income Credit" on line 56 . . . . ▶ | 31

Cat. No. 11320B

Form **1040** (1993)

Form 1040 (1993)   Page **2**

Tax Computation

(See page 23.)

32 Amount from line 31 (adjusted gross income) . . . . | **32** |

33a Check if: ☐ **You** were 65 or older, ☐ Blind; ☐ **Spouse** was 65 or older, ☐ Blind.
Add the number of boxes checked above and enter the total here . . . ▶ **33a** |

b If your parent (or someone else) can claim you as a dependent, check here . ▶ **33b** ☐

c If you are married filing separately and your spouse itemizes deductions or
you are a dual-status alien, see page 24 and check here . . . . ▶ **33c** ☐

34 Enter the larger of your:
{ **Itemized deductions** from Schedule A, line 26, **OR**
Standard deduction shown below for your filing status. **But if you checked
any box on line 33a or b,** go to page 24 to find your standard deduction.
If you checked **box 33c,** your standard deduction is zero.
● Single—$3,700   ● Head of household—$5,450
● Married filing jointly or Qualifying widow(er)—$6,200
● Married filing separately—$3,100 } | **34** |

35 Subtract line 34 from line 32 . . . . | **35** |

36 If line 32 is $81,350 or less, multiply $2,350 by the total number of exemptions claimed on
line 6e. If line 32 is over $81,350, see the worksheet on page 25 for the amount to enter . | **36** |

If you want the IRS to figure your tax, see page 24.

37 **Taxable income.** Subtract line 36 from line 35. If line 36 is more than line 35, enter -0- | **37** |

38 Tax. Check if from **a** ☐ Tax Table, **b** ☐ Tax Rate Schedules, **c** ☐ Schedule D Tax Work-
sheet, or **d** ☐ Form 8615 (see page 25). Amount from Form(s) 8814 ▶ **e** _____ | **38** |

39 Additional taxes (see page 25). Check if from **a** ☐ Form 4970 **b** ☐ Form 4972 . . . | **39** |

40 Add lines 38 and 39 . . . . ▶ | **40** |

Credits

(See page 25.)

41 Credit for child and dependent care expenses. Attach Form 2441 | **41** |

42 Credit for the elderly or the disabled. Attach Schedule R . | **42** |

43 Foreign tax credit. Attach Form 1116 | **43** |

44 Other credits (see page 26). Check if from **a** ☐ Form 3800
b ☐ Form 8396 **c** ☐ Form 8801 **d** ☐ Form (specify) _____ | **44** |

45 Add lines 41 through 44 . . . . | **45** |

46 Subtract line 45 from line 40. If line 45 is more than line 40, enter -0- . . . . . . ▶ | **46** |

Other Taxes

47 Self-employment tax. Attach Schedule SE. Also, see line 25 . . . . | **47** |

48 Alternative minimum tax. Attach Form 6251 . . . . | **48** |

49 Recapture taxes (see page 26). Check if from **a** ☐ Form 4255 **b** ☐ Form 8611 **c** ☐ Form 8828 | **49** |

50 Social security and Medicare tax on tip income not reported to employer. Attach Form 4137 | **50** |

51 Tax on qualified retirement plans, including IRAs. If required, attach Form 5329 . . . . | **51** |

52 Advance earned income credit payments from Form W-2 . . . . | **52** |

53 Add lines 46 through 52. This is your **total tax** . . . . ▶ | **53** |

Payments

Attach Forms W-2, W-2G, and 1099-R on the front.

54 Federal income tax withheld. If any is from Form(s) 1099, check ▶ ☐ | **54** |

55 1993 estimated tax payments and amount applied from 1992 return . | **55** |

56 **Earned income credit.** Attach Schedule EIC . . . . . | **56** |

57 Amount paid with Form 4868 (extension request) . . . | **57** |

58a Excess social security, Medicare, and RRTA tax withheld (see page 28) . | **58a** |

b Deferral of additional 1993 taxes. Attach Form 8841 . . . . | **58b** |

59 Other payments (see page 28). Check if from **a** ☐ Form 2439
b ☐ Form 4136 . . . . | **59** |

60 Add lines 54 through 59. These are your **total payments** . . . . ▶ | **60** |

Refund or Amount You Owe

61 If line 60 is more than line 53, subtract line 53 from line 60. This is the amount you **OVERPAID**. ▶ | **61** |

62 Amount of line 61 you want **REFUNDED TO YOU** . . . . ▶ | **62** |

63 Amount of line 61 you want **APPLIED TO YOUR 1994 ESTIMATED TAX** ▶ | **63** |

64 If line 53 is more than line 60, subtract line 60 from line 53. This is the **AMOUNT YOU OWE**.
For details on how to pay, including what to write on your payment, see page 29 . . | **64** |

65 Estimated tax penalty (see page 29). Also include on line 64 | **65** |

Sign Here

Keep a copy of this return for your records.

Under penalties of perjury, I declare that I have examined this return and accompanying schedules and statements, and to the best of my knowledge and belief, they are true, correct, and complete. Declaration of preparer (other than taxpayer) is based on all information of which preparer has any knowledge.

| Your signature | Date | Your occupation |
| Spouse's signature. If a joint return, BOTH must sign. | Date | Spouse's occupation |

Paid Preparer's Use Only

Preparer's signature ▶	Date	Check if self-employed ☐	Preparer's social security no.
Firm's name (or yours if self-employed) and address ▶		E.I. No.	
		ZIP code	

✩U.S. Government Printing Office: 1993 -- 345-190

Federal Fiduciary Income Tax Return

(Form 1041)

Form **1041** Department of the Treasury—Internal Revenue Service
U.S. Fiduciary Income Tax Return 19**93**

| For the calendar year 1993 or fiscal year beginning | , 1993, and ending | , 19 | OMB No. 1545-0092 |

A Type of Entity | Name of estate or trust (grantor type trust, see instructions) | **C** Employer identification number

☐ Decedent's estate
☐ Simple trust
☐ Complex trust
☐ Grantor type trust
☐ Bankruptcy estate–Chpt. 7
☐ Bankruptcy estate–Chpt. 11
☐ Pooled income fund

D Date entity created

Name and title of fiduciary

E Nonexempt charitable and split-interest trusts, check applicable boxes (see instructions):

Number, street, and room or suite no. (If a P.O. box, see page 5 of instructions.)

B Number of Schedules K-1 attached (see instructions) . ▶

City, state, and ZIP code

☐ Described in section 4947(a)(1)
☐ Not a private foundation
☐ Described in section 4947(a)(2)

F Check applicable boxes: ☐ Initial return ☐ Final return ☐ Amended return
Change in Fiduciary's ▶ ☐ Name ☐ Address

G Pooled mortgage account (see instructions)
☐ Bought ☐ Sold Date:

Income

1	Interest income	1
2	Dividends	2
3	Business income or (loss) (attach Schedule C or C-EZ (Form 1040))	3
4	Capital gain or (loss) (attach Schedule D (Form 1041))	4
5	Rents, royalties, partnerships, other estates and trusts, etc. (attach Schedule E (Form 1040))	5
6	Farm income or (loss) (attach Schedule F (Form 1040))	6
7	Ordinary gain or (loss) (attach Form 4797)	7
8	Other income (state nature of income) _____	8
9	**Total** income (combine lines 1 through 8) . . . . ▶	9

Deductions

10	Interest. (Check if Form 4952 is attached ▶ ☐)	10
11	Taxes	11
12	Fiduciary fees	12
13	Charitable deduction (from Schedule A, line 7)	13
14	Attorney, accountant, and return preparer fees	14
15a	Other deductions NOT subject to the 2% floor (attach schedule)	15a
b	Allowable miscellaneous itemized deductions subject to the 2% floor	15b
16	**Total** (add lines 10 through 15b)	16
17	Adjusted total income or (loss) (subtract line 16 from line 9). Enter here and on Schedule B, line 1 ▶	17
18	Income distribution deduction (from Schedule B, line 17) (see instructions) (attach Schedules K-1 (Form 1041))	18
19	Estate tax deduction (including certain generation-skipping taxes) (attach computation) . . .	19
20	Exemption	20
21	**Total** deductions (add lines 18 through 20) . . . . ▶	21

Tax and Payments

22	Taxable income of fiduciary (subtract line 21 from line 17).	22
23	**Total** tax (from Schedule G, line 7)	23
24	Payments: a 1993 estimated tax payments and amount applied from 1992 return . . .	24a
b	Estimated tax payments allocated to beneficiaries (from Form 1041-T)	24b
c	Subtract line 24b from line 24a	24c
d	Tax paid with extension of time to file: ☐ Form 2758 ☐ Form 8736 ☐ Form 8800	24d
e	Federal income tax withheld	24e
	Credits: f Form 2439 _____ ; g Form 4136 _____ ; h Other _____ ; Total ▶	24i
25	**Total** payments (add lines 24c through 24e, and 24i) . . . . . ▶	25
26	**Penalty** for underpayment of estimated tax (see instructions)	26
27	**Tax Due.** If line 25 is smaller than the total of lines 23 and 26, enter amount owed . . .	27
28	**Overpayment.** If line 25 is larger than the total of lines 23 and 26, enter amount overpaid	28
29	Amount of line 28 to be: **a** Credited to 1994 estimated tax ▶ ; **b** Refunded ▶	29

Please Sign Here

Under penalties of perjury, I declare that I have examined this return, including accompanying schedules and statements, and to the best of my knowledge and belief, it is true, correct, and complete. Declaration of preparer (other than fiduciary) is based on all information of which preparer has any knowledge.

▶ Signature of fiduciary or officer representing fiduciary | Date | ▶ EIN of fiduciary (see instructions)

Paid Preparer's Use Only

Preparer's signature ▶	Date	Check if self-employed ▶ ☐	Preparer's social security no.
Firm's name (or yours if self-employed) and address ▶		E.I. No. ▶	
		ZIP code ▶	

For Paperwork Reduction Act Notice, see page 1 of the separate instructions. Cat. No. 11370H Form **1041** (1993)

Form 1041 (1993)   Page **2**

Schedule A   Charitable Deduction—Do not complete for a simple trust or a pooled income fund.

1	Amounts paid for charitable purposes from current year's gross income	1
2	Amounts permanently set aside for charitable purposes from current year's gross income . .	2
3	Add lines 1 and 2	3
4	Tax-exempt income allocable to charitable contribution (see instructions)	4
5	Subtract line 4 from line 3	5
6	Amounts paid or set aside for charitable purposes other than from the current year's income . .	6
7	**Total** (add lines 5 and 6). Enter here and on page 1, line 13	7

Schedule B   Income Distribution Deduction (see instructions)

1	Adjusted total income (from page 1, line 17) (see instructions).	1
2	Adjusted tax-exempt interest	2
3	Net gain shown on Schedule D (Form 1041), line 17, column (a). (see instructions)	3
4	Enter amount from Schedule A, line 6	4
5	Long-term capital gain included on Schedule A, line 3	5
6	Short-term capital gain included on Schedule A, line 3	6
7	If the amount on page 1, line 4, is a capital loss, enter here as a positive figure	7
8	If the amount on page 1, line 4, is a capital gain, enter here as a negative figure	8
9	Distributable net income (combine lines 1 through 8)	9
10	Accounting income for the tax year as determined under the governing instrument	10	
11	Income required to be distributed currently	11
12	Other amounts paid, credited, or otherwise required to be distributed	12
13	Total distributions (add lines 11 and 12). (If greater than line 10, see instructions.)	13
14	Enter the amount of tax-exempt income included on line 13	14
15	Tentative income distribution deduction (subtract line 14 from line 13)	15
16	Tentative income distribution deduction (subtract line 2 from line 9)	16
17	Income distribution deduction. Enter the smaller of line 15 or line 16 here and on page 1, line 18	17

Schedule G   Tax Computation (see instructions)

1	Tax: **a** ☐ Tax rate schedule or ☐ Schedule D (Form 1041) . .	1a	
	b Other taxes	1b	
	c Total (add lines 1a and 1b) . . . . ▶	1c
2a	Foreign tax credit (attach Form 1116)	2a	
b	Check: ☐ Nonconventional source fuel credit ☐ Form 8834 . .	2b	
c	General business credit. Enter here and check which forms are attached:		
	☐ Form 3800 or ☐ Form (specify) ▶	2c	
d	Credit for prior year minimum tax (attach Form 8801)	2d	
3	**Total** credits (add lines 2a through 2d) . . . . ▶	3
4	Subtract line 3 from line 1c	4
5	Recapture taxes. Check if from: ☐ Form 4255 ☐ Form 8611	5
6	Alternative minimum tax (from Schedule H, line 39)	6
7	**Total** tax (add lines 4 through 6). Enter here and on page 1, line 23 . . . . . . ▶	7

Other Information (see instructions)

		Yes	No
1	Did the estate or trust receive tax-exempt income? (If "Yes," attach a computation of the allocation of expenses.) Enter the amount of tax-exempt interest income and exempt-interest dividends ▶ $		
2	Did the estate or trust have any passive activity losses? (If "Yes," get **Form 8582,** Passive Activity Loss Limitations, to figure the allowable loss.)		
3	Did the estate or trust receive all or any part of the earnings (salary, wages, and other compensation) of any individual by reason of a contract assignment or similar arrangement?		
4	At any time during the tax year, did the estate or trust have an interest in or a signature or other authority over a bank, securities, or other financial account in a foreign country? (See the instructions for exceptions and filing requirements for Form TD F 90-22.1.) . . . . If "Yes," enter the name of the foreign country ▶		
5	Was the estate or trust the grantor of, or transferor to, a foreign trust which existed during the current tax year, whether or not the estate or trust has any beneficial interest in it? (If "Yes," you may have to file Form 3520, 3520-A, or 926.)		
6	Did the estate or trust receive, or pay, any seller-financed mortgage interest?		
7	If this entity has filed or is required to file **Form 8264,** Application for Registration of a Tax Shelter, check here . ▶ ☐		
8	If this is a complex trust making the section 663(b) election, check here . . . . ▶ ☐		
9	To make a section 643(e)(3) election, attach Schedule D (Form 1041), and check here . . . . . . ▶ ☐		
10	If the decedent's estate has been open for more than 2 years, check here . . . . ▶ ☐		

Schedule H | **Alternative Minimum Tax (see instructions)—To Be Completed by any Decedent's Estate, or Simple or Complex Trust**

Part I—Fiduciary's Share of Alternative Minimum Taxable Income

1	Adjusted total income or (loss) (from page 1, line 17)		**1**
2	Net operating loss deduction (Enter as a positive amount.)		**2**
3	Add lines 1 and 2		**3**
4a	Interest	**4a**	
b	Taxes	**4b**	
c	Miscellaneous itemized deductions (from page 1, line 15b) . . .	**4c**	
d	Refund of taxes	**4d** ( )	
e	Combine lines 4a through 4d		**4e**
5	Adjustments:		
a	Depreciation of property placed in service after 1986	**5a**	
b	Circulation and research and experimental expenditures paid or incurred after 1986	**5b**	
c	Mining exploration and development costs paid or incurred after 1986	**5c**	
d	Long-term contracts entered into after February 28, 1986	**5d**	
e	Pollution control facilities placed in service after 1986	**5e**	
f	Installment sales of certain property	**5f**	
g	Adjusted gain or loss (including incentive stock options)	**5g**	
h	Certain loss limitations	**5h**	
i	Tax shelter farm activities	**5i**	
j	Passive activities	**5j**	
k	Beneficiaries of other trusts or decedent's estates	**5k**	
l	Combine lines 5a through 5k		**5l**
6	Tax preference items:		
a	Tax-exempt interest from specified private activity bonds	**6a**	
b	Depletion	**6b**	
c	Combine lines 6a and 6b		**6c**
7	Other items of tax preference:		
a	Accelerated depreciation of real property placed in service before 1987	**7a**	
b	Accelerated depreciation of leased personal property placed in service before 1987	**7b**	
c	Intangible drilling costs	**7c**	
d	Combine lines 7a through 7c		**7d**
8	Add lines 3, 4e, 5l, 6c, and 7d		**8**
9	Alternative tax net operating loss deduction (see instructions for limitations)		**9**
10	Adjusted alternative minimum taxable income (subtract line 9 from line 8). Enter here and on line 13		**10**
	Note: *Complete Part II before proceeding with line 11.*		
11a	Income distribution deduction from line 27	**11a**	
b	Estate tax deduction (from page 1, line 19)	**11b**	
c	Add lines 11a and 11b		**11c**
12	Fiduciary's share of alternative minimum taxable income (subtract line 11c from line 10) . . .		**12**

Note: *If line 12 is more than $22,500, proceed to Part III. If line 12 is $22,500 or less, stop here, as you are not liable for the alternative minimum tax.*

(continued on page 4)

Part II—Income Distribution Deduction on a Minimum Tax Basis

13	Adjusted alternative minimum taxable income (from line 10)	13	
14	Adjusted tax-exempt interest (other than amounts included in line 6a)	14	
15	Net capital gain from Schedule D (Form 1041), line 17, column (a) (If a loss, enter -0-.)	15	
16	Capital gains allocable to corpus paid or set aside for charitable purposes (from Schedule A, line 6)	16	
17	Capital gains paid or permanently set aside for charitable purposes from current year's income (see instructions)	17	
18	Capital gains computed on a minimum tax basis included in line 10	18	( )
19	Capital losses computed on a minimum tax basis included in line 10 (Enter as a positive amount.)	19	
20	Distributable net alternative minimum taxable income (DNAMTI) (combine lines 13 through 19).	20	
21	Income required to be distributed currently (from Schedule B, line 11)	21	
22	Other amounts paid, credited, or otherwise required to be distributed (from Schedule B, line 12)	22	
23	Total distributions (add lines 21 and 22)	23	
24	Tax-exempt income included on line 23 (other than amounts included in line 6a)	24	
25	Tentative income distribution deduction on a minimum tax basis (subtract line 24 from line 23).	25	
26	Tentative income distribution deduction on a minimum tax basis (subtract line 14 from line 20).	26	
27	Income distribution deduction on a minimum tax basis. Enter the smaller of line 25 or line 26. Enter here and on line 11a	27	

Part III—Alternative Minimum Tax Computation

28	Enter amount from line 12 *(If at least $165,000, but not more than $175,000, skip lines 29a through 33. If more than $175,000, skip lines 29a through 34.)*		28	
29a	Exemption amount	29a	$22,500	
b	Phase-out of exemption amount	29b	$75,000	
30	Subtract line 29b from line 28 (If zero or less, enter -0-.)		30	
31	Multiply line 30 by 25% (.25)		31	
32	Subtract line 31 from line 29a (If zero or less, enter -0-.)		32	
33	Subtract line 32 from line 28		33	
34	Multiply line 33 by 26% (.26). *(If line 28 is at least $165,000, but not more than $175,000, multiply line 28 by 26% (.26).)* Enter the result here, and skip line 35.		34	
35	If line 28 is $175,000 or more, subtract $175,000 from line 28. Multiply the difference by 28% (.28). Add the result to $45,500 and enter the result here		35	
36	Alternative minimum tax foreign tax credit (see instructions)		36	
37	Tentative minimum tax (subtract line 36 from line 34 or 35, whichever applies)		37	
38a	Regular tax before credits (see instructions)	38a		
b	Section 644 tax (see instructions)	38b		
c	Add lines 38a and 38b		38c	
39	**Alternative minimum tax.** (subtract line 38c from line 37). (If zero or less, enter -0-.) Enter here and on Schedule G, line 6		39	

GLOSSARY

Abatement The legal process of reducing or eliminating the bequests of a decedent-testator who died owning insufficient assets to pay all bequests, debts and administration expenses.

Ademption The failure to fulfill a specific bequest in a will because the property bequeathed was sold, given away or lost before the testator's death.

Adjusted basis The amount subtracted from the amount realized to calculate gain or loss on sale or exchange of property.

Adjusted taxable gifts In federal estate tax (FET), the sum of post-1976 taxable gifts. It is added to the taxable estate on the federal estate tax return to arrive at the estate tax base.

Administrator A personal representative who was not nominated in the will.

Adverse party In the Internal Revenue Code, a person having a substantial interest in the property, subject to the power, which is adverse to exercise of the power in favor of the decedent.

After-born child A child who was born after the execution of a parent's will.

Alternate valuation date Under FET law, the date that is six months after date of death. Assets may be valued on this date or on date of death.

Annual exclusion Under the federal gift tax, a deduction, up to $10,000, from gross gifts for gifts by any donor to each donee in a given year.

Annual exclusion gift A gift of property worth no more than the annual gift tax exclusion.

Antilapse statute A state statutory provision that specifies, in the absence of a provision in the will, to whom a lapsed testamentary bequest will pass.

Appointee (of a power of appointment) The party or parties whom the holder of a power of appointment actually appoints.

Apportionment statute See Equitable apportionment statute.

Ascertainable standard Wording in a will or trust intentionally limiting the freedom of holder of a power of appointment over property. The most common words of limitation are, "health," "education," "support," and "maintenance," derived from Section 2041. Use of the words avoid FET taxation to the holder of the power as a general power of appointment.

Assignment Any type of passing of property in which the transferor gives up some kind of interest to the transferee. See transfer.

Assignment of income doctrine Under income tax law, a doctrine holding that earnings from services performed will always be taxable to the person performing those services.

Bargain sale The part-gift, part-sale of an asset for some amount less than what would be regarded full and adequate consideration. The difference between the consideration received by the client-donor and the value of the asset transferred constitutes a gift, for tax purposes.

Beneficial interest An interest that carries an economic benefit. Examples of beneficial interests in property include the temporary or permanent right to possess, consume, and pledge the property.

Beneficiary A person who is receiving or will receive a gift of a beneficial interest in property. See Donee.

Bequest A gift, by will, of personal property. Also called a legacy.

Blockage discount A valuation discount given to a large quantity of a stock listed on an exchange, or certain other property, if its sale all at one time could have a temporarily depressing effect on the market price.

Bond In probate, an agreement under which an insurance company guarantees that the personal representative will faithfully perform required probate duties.

Business buyout agreement An agreement between one or more owners of a closely held business and one or more other persons that obligates one or more of the parties to purchase the interest of one of the others upon the occurrence of specific future events, such as the latter's death and, often, the onset of his or her permanent disability.

Buyout agreement See Business buyout agreement.

Buy-sell agreement See Business buyout agreement.

Bypass An arrangement under which property owned by a decedent and intended for the lifetime benefit of the surviving spouse does not actually pass to the surviving spouse, thereby avoiding inclusion in the latter's gross estate.

Bypass trust A trust designed to contain property that bypasses the surviving spouse's estate. See Bypass.

Cash value life insurance policy A policy that accumulates economic value because the insurer charges a constant premium that is considerably higher than mortality costs requires during the earlier years. Part of this overpayment accumulates as a cash surrender value which, prior to the death of the insured, can be enjoyed by the owner, basically in one of two ways. First, at any time the owner can surrender the policy and receive this value in cash. Second, the owner can make a policy loan and borrow up to the amount of this value.

Charitable lead trust A trust under which the client donates an asset's income interest to charity, at the end of which the remainder interest passes to a private party, typically children or grandchildren for a specified term of years. The client (or the client's estate) will receive an income tax deduction for the value of the income interest.

Charitable remainder annuity trust (CRAT) A trust into which the client transfers assets in exchange for a fixed annuity income of at least 5 percent of the original value of the assets transferred into trust, payable at least annually, usually for life. The value of the remainder is deductible on the income tax return.

Charitable remainder unitrust (CRUT) A trust that is much like the charitable remainder annuity trust, except that the annual income depends on a fixed percentage of the current fair market value of the assets in the trust, determined annually.

Chose in action A claim or debt recoverable in a lawsuit.

Closely held business A firm privately owned by one or a few individuals who actively participate in its management.

Codicil A separate written document that amends or revokes a prior will. It is executed if the testator wishes to change or add to the will.

Collateral A relative who shares a common ancestor with a person but who is neither a descendant nor an ascendant of that person. Contrast with issue.

Committee See Guardian.

Community property In the eight states recognizing it, all property that has been acquired by the efforts of either spouse during their marriage while living in a community property state, except property acquired by only one of the spouses by gift, devise, bequest or inheritance, or, in most of the community property states, by the income therefrom. The eight states are: Arizona, California, Idaho, Louisiana, Nevada, New Mexico, Texas, and Washington. In addition, Wisconsin has recently adopted a form of community property known as "marital partnership property."

Completed gift A gift in which the donor has so parted with dominion and control (in an interest in property) as to leave him no power to change its disposition, whether for his own benefit or for the benefit of another. (Rev. Rul. 67-396, 1969-2 C.B. 351).

Complex trust A nongrantor trust which, in a given year, either (a) accumulates some fiduciary accounting income (FAI) (i.e., does not pay out all FAI, which it has received, to the beneficiaries) or (b) distributes principal.

Conduit principle In the income taxation of estates and trusts, the rule that fiduciary accounting income distributed to beneficiaries will be taxed to them, rather than to the estate or trust.

Consanguinity Degrees of blood relationship between a decedent and the decedent's relatives.

Conservator A court-appointed fiduciary responsible for the person or property of an elderly incompetent person, or both.

Consideration furnished test Under the federal estate tax, the proposition that includes in a decedent's gross estate the entire value of property held by the decedent in joint tenancy, reduced only by an amount attributable to that portion of the consideration in money or money's worth which can clearly be shown to have been furnished by the survivors.

Contingent interest A future interest that is not vested; that is, an interest whose possession and enjoyment are dependent on the happening of some future event, not on just the passage of time.

Corpus The property in a trust. Also called principal.

Creator The person who creates the trust and whose property usually winds up in it. Also called grantor, settlor, or trustor.

Credit shelter bypass A bypass of an amount approximately equal to $600,000, the exemption equivalent of the unified credit.

Crummey provision A general power clause found in some trusts that give one or more beneficiaries the right to withdraw, for a limited period of time each year, the lesser of the amount of the annual exclusion or the value of the gift property transferred into the trust. Allows the donor to claim an annual exclusion. Often found in trusts for minors and in irrevocable life insurance trusts.

Cumulative gift doctrine The requirement that all lifetime gifts be accumulated; that is, that prior taxable gifts be added to current taxable transfers to determine the estate or gift tax base.

Curtesy A surviving husband's life interest in a portion of the real property owned by his deceased wife.

Custodial gift A gift to a custodian for the benefit of a child, under the Uniform Gifts to Minors Act or the Uniform Transfers to Minors Act.

Death tax A tax levied on certain property owned or transferred by the decedent at death. Either an estate tax or an inheritance tax.

Decedent In estate planning nomenclature, the person who has died.

Deferral A term used in this text to mean delaying payment of the FET until the death of S2 by taking the marital deduction in the estate of S1.

Descendant *See* issue.

Devise A gift, by will, of real property.

Devisee A beneficiary, under a will, of a devise, i.e., a gift of real property.

Direct skip Under federal generation-skipping tax law, a transfer to a skip person that is subject to the gift tax or the estate tax.

Disclaimer An unqualified refusal to accept a gift. In estate planning, a valid disclaimer must meet the requirements of both local law and IRC Section 2518.

Distributable net income (DNI) An amount more or less equal to fiduciary accounting income (FAI) that acts as the measuring rod for estate and trust income taxation.

Distribution deduction In the income taxation of estates and trusts, an amount equal to the lesser of distributable net income or the amount actually distributed to beneficiaries.

Distribution planning Planning the amount and timing of beneficiary distributions from an estate or irrevocable trust, usually with the objective of reducing income tax.

DNI See Distributable net income.

Donee A person who is receiving or will receive a gift of a beneficial interest in property. See Beneficiary.

Donor A person making a gift.

Dower A surviving wife's life interest in a portion of the real property owned by her deceased husband.

Durable power of attorney A power of attorney that does not become legally invalid at the onset of the principal's incapacity.

Durable power of attorney for health care (DPOAHC) A durable power of attorney granting to the attorney-in-fact the power to make medical decisions on behalf of the principal.

Durable power of attorney for property A durable power of attorney granting to the attorney-in-fact the power to make decisions concerning the property of the principal.

Equalization A term used in this text to mean a plan of property disposition by the spouses so that the taxable estates (or estate tax bases) of the two are more or less equal.

Equitable apportionment statute A state statute that spreads the death tax burden more or less proportionately among all of the beneficiaries receiving the taxed assets.

Escheat The reversion of an intestate decedent's property to the state, because either the decedent left no next of kin, or all surviving relatives are considered under state law to be too remote for purposes of inheritance.

Estate A quantity of wealth or property. See also Net estate, Gross estate, and Probate estate.

Estate tax A federal or state tax on the decedent's right to transfer property.

Estate planning The study of the principles of planning for the use, conservation, and efficient transfer of an individual's wealth.

Estate tax base This author's name for the sum of the taxable estate plus adjusted taxable gifts on the federal estate tax return. It more or less represents the sum of deathtime gifts plus lifetime gifts, and constitutes the amount used to calculate the tentative estate tax.

Estate trust One type of marital trust under which the corpus is made payable to the estate of the surviving spouse at his or her death. Its unique feature is that during the surviving spouse's lifetime, some or all of the income can be made payable to someone else.

Execute To complete a document (i.e., to do what is necessary to render it valid).

Executor A personal representative who was nominated in the will.

Exemption equivalent (of the unified credit) In federal estate taxation, the amount by which the taxable amount can exceed zero and still be sheltered by the unified credit.

Exercise a power of appointment To invoke the power by appointing a permissible appointee.

FAI See Fiduciary accounting income.

FET Used in this text to mean the net federal estate tax.

Family limited partnership A limited partnership meeting the requirements of §704(e) for the benefit of family members, generally with parents as the general partners and children as the limited partners. Used to take advantage of lack of control discounts and lack of marketability discounts as the parents transfer limited partnership units to the children.

Family pot trust See Pot trust.

Fee simple interest The greatest interest that a person can have over property, corresponding to the layperson's usual notion of full ownership.

Fiduciary A person in a position of trust and confidence; one who has a legal duty to act for the benefit of another. Examples include executor, trustee, attorney-in-fact, and custodian.

Fiduciary accounting income (FAI) In the income taxation of estates and trusts, most sources of federal gross income, including cash dividends, interest, and rent (reduced by certain expenses) but not including stock dividends and capital gains.

Fiscal year An income tax year that ends on the last day of any month except December.

Flower bonds Certain issues of long-term U.S. Treasury bonds which, if owned by the decedent at death, can be used at par value to pay the federal estate tax.

Fractional interest discount A valuation discount for real property that is neither easily partitioned nor readily marketable.

Freezing the estate tax value Using estate planning transfer techniques to effectively ensure that the future value of certain appreciating property includable in the estate tax base will not be significantly higher than its current value.

Future interest A beneficial interest in property in which the right to possess or enjoy the property is delayed, either by a specific period of time or until the happening of a future event.

General bequest A gift payable out of the general assets of the estate, but not one that specifies one or more particular items.

General power of attorney A document executed by one person called the principal, authorizing another person called the attorney-in-fact, to perform designated acts on behalf of the principal.

Generation-skipping transfer tax (GSTT) A federal or state tax on certain property transfers to a skip person, that is, someone who is two generations or more younger than the donor.

Gift A completed lifetime or deathtime transfer of property by an individual in exchange for any amount that is less than full consideration.

Gift tax A tax on a completed lifetime transfer of property for less than full consideration.

Grantor The person who creates the trust and whose property usually ends up in it. Also called creator settlor, or trustor.

Grantor retained annuity trust (GRAT) A grantor retained trust that pays the grantor a fixed income for a specified period and meets all other requirements of IRC §2702.

Grantor retained trust (GRT) An irrevocable trust into which the client transfers appreciating property in exchange for the right to receive income for a period of years. Under most GRTs, distribution of corpus at the end of the period depends upon whether or not the client survived this period. If not, the corpus reverts to the client-grantor's estate. If the client did survive the period, the corpus passes to a younger-generation beneficiary.

Grantor retained unitrust (GRUT) A grantor retained trust that pays the grantor a fixed percentage of the trust's principal for a specified period and meets all other requirements of IRC §2702.

Grantor trust A living trust in which the trustor, also called the grantor, has retained sufficient interest in the trust to make the income received by the trust taxable to the grantor, not to the trust or its beneficiaries.

Grantor trust rules The federal income tax rules concerning grantor trusts. They are located in Internal Revenue Code Sections 671-78.

Gross estate An FET term indicating property owned by the decedent at death, property transferred by the decedent under which the decedent retained an interest or control, and certain amounts in connection with property transferred within three years of death.

Grossing up Inclusion in the gross estate of gift taxes paid on any gifts made within three years of death.

GSTT See Generation-skipping transfer tax.

Guardian A court-appointed fiduciary responsible for the person or property of a minor or, in some cases, an incompetent adult, or both. In some states, a guardian is called a committee.

Heir A beneficiary who will receive property that passes by intestacy.

Holder (of a power of appointment) The person who has received the power of appointment, i.e., the one who has the right to appoint designated property to a permissible appointee. Also called the donee of the power.

Holding period In income tax law, the length of time that property is held. It determines whether a gain is short term or long term. The current threshold is one year.

Holographic will A will, recognized in many states, that is usually required to be written entirely in the hand of the testator. It need not be witnessed.

Incidents of ownership Powers and interests over an insurance policy on decedent's life that would subject the proceeds to inclusion in the decedent's gross estate under Section 2042.

Income beneficiary The beneficiary of a trust who has a life estate or estate for years in the trust income.

Income shifting See Shifting income.

Income tax A tax levied on income earned by a taxpayer during a given year.

Incomplete Not complete, i.e., rescindable or amendable, made with total relinquishment of dominion and control.

Inherit To receive property by intestate succession.

Inheritance tax A state tax on the right of a beneficiary to receive property from a decedent.

Installment sale The sale of an asset in exchange for an installment note, in which the buyer agrees to make periodic payments of principal and interest, based on a fair market rate of interest.

Intangible personal property Personal property that is not in itself valuable, but derives its value from that which it represents.

Intentionally defective irrevocable trust An irrevocable trust funded with gift assets that is complete for estate tax and incomplete for gift tax. Its objective is to give the grantor greater asset control and reduce FET by a greater amount than an outright gift.

Inter vivos transfer A transfer made while the transferor is alive.

Inter vivos trust A trust taking effect during the life of the trustor. Also called a living trust.

Interest by the entirety An interest in property similar to a joint interest; however, it can be created only between husband and wife. And unlike joint tenancy, neither spouse may transfer the property without the consent of the other.

Interest for years An interest in property giving the transferee the right to possess it for a fixed period.

Interest-free loan A demand loan, having no interest charge, usually to a family member in a lower income tax bracket. TRA 86 virtually eliminated its use.

Interest in common An interest in property held by two or more persons, each having an equal undivided right to possess property. Unlike a joint interest, however, an interest in common may be owned in unequal percentages, and when one owner dies the remaining owners do not automatically succeed in ownership. Instead, the decedent's interest passes through his or her estate, by will, by some other document, or by the laws of intestate distribution.

Intestate Having died leaving probate property not disposed of by a valid will.

Instrument Any legal document.

Inventory and appraisement A probate document that delineates all probate assets at their fair market value.

Irrevocable Subject to no right to rescind or amend (the terms of a transfer of one or more interests in property).

Issue A person's direct offspring, including children, grandchildren, great-grandchildren, and the like. Also called descendants. Contrast with Collaterals.

Itemized deductions In federal income tax law, deductions from adjusted gross income that are specifically listed, and taken in lieu of the standard deduction.

Joint interest A form of equal, undivided ownership in property that, upon death of one owner, automatically passes to the surviving owner(s). Also called joint tenancy.

Joint tenancy See Joint interest.

Kiddie tax In federal income tax law, the taxation of the unearned income of a minor child at the parent's marginal income tax rate.

Lack of marketability discount A valuation discount given stock in a business arising from the lack of an established market making the stock more difficult to sell.

Lapse The result when a beneficiary named in a will fails to survive the testator. Also, a power of appointment is said to lapse if the holder does not exercise it within the permitted period.

Leasehold An interest in property entitling the lessee to possess and use the property for a specified time, usually in exchange for a fixed series of payments.

Legacy A gift, by will, of personal property. Also called a bequest.

Legatee A beneficiary, under a will, of a gift of personal property.

Letters testamentary A formal court document in probate indicating the court's authorization and empowerment of the estate's personal representative to deal legally with third parties.

Leveraging The process by which a given amount of exclusion, exemption, or credit can shelter a multiple of that amount from future transfer taxation.

Life estate An interest in property that ceases upon someone's death.

Life insurance policy A contract in which the insurance company agrees to pay a cash lump-sum amount (the face value or policy proceeds) to the person named in the policy to receive it (the beneficiary) upon the death of the subject of the insurance (the insured).

Limited liability companies A business organization in which the owners, called members, do not have personal liability for the contracts or the torts of the business, yet the organization is taxed like a partnership.

Living trust A trust taking effect during the lifetime of the trustor. Also called an inter vivos trust.

Living will A document detailing those health care interventions that a person does or does not want to be subjected to in situations when he or she is no longer capable of making those decisions.

Marital deduction In federal gift and estate taxation, the deduction for certain transfers to a spouse.

Marital trust A trust structured to receive property that will qualify for the marital deduction.

Minority discount A valuation discount given to an interest in a business that is not c controlling interest.

Net estate The net worth of a person; i.e., total assets minus total liabilities.

Omitted child See Omitted heir.

Omitted heir Any living spouse, child, or issue of any deceased child who is not provided for in a will.

Omitted spouse See Omitted heir.

Opportunity shifting The transfer of a rapidly appreciating wealth- or an income-producing opportunity to a family member before it is objectively ascertainable.

Outright transfer A transfer in which the transferee receives both legal interests and all beneficial interests, subject to no restrictions or conditions.

Partnership capital freeze Like a recapitalization, the reorganization of a partnership for the purpose of freezing the FET value of the client's partnership interest. Severely restricted by the Revenue Reconciliation Act of 1990.

Permissible appointee (of a power of appointment) A party whom the holder may appoint by exercising the power.

Per capita A scheme of distribution from a will or trust requiring that issue of a decedent of all degrees share equally.

Perfect unification The author's theoretical set of conditions in which an individual would be indifferent, from a total transfer tax planning point of view, between making lifetime and deathtime gifts. It helps identify the factors that make our current system imperfect, which serves as the basis for transfer tax planning.

Per stirpes A scheme of distribution from a will or trust requiring that certain issue of a decedent, as a group, inherit the share of an estate that their immediate ancestor would have inherited if he or she had been living.

Perpetuities saving clause A clause in a will or trust that prevents interests from being ruled invalid under the rule against perpetuities.

Personal exemption In federal income tax law, amounts deductible on behalf of the taxpayer, the spouse, and each dependent, in calculating taxable income.

Personal property All property except fee simple and life estates in land and its improvements.

Personal representative The person appointed by the probate court to represent and manage the estate. If nominated in the will, called an executor.

Pickup tax A state death tax set at least equal to the federal credit for state death taxes.

Pooled income fund An investment fund created and maintained by the target charity, which "pools" property from many similar contributors. This arrangement ordinarily provides that the charity will pay to the grantor an income for life and, if desired, for the life of the grantor's spouse, based on the rate of return actually earned by the fund as a whole. At their death, the property passes to the charity.

Pot trust A trust established for the benefit of minor children which typically remains undivided until the youngest child reaches age 21 (or age 18). At that time, the assets are divided into equal separate shares, one for each child. The assets are distributed outright, or they are held for distribution at some older age. Also called a Family pot trust.

Pour-over will A will that distributes, at the testator's death, probate assets to a trust that had been created during the testator's lifetime.

Power of appointment A power to name someone to receive a beneficial interest in property.

Power of appointment trust A marital trust that gives to the surviving spouse the right to receive all income from the property for life, payable at least annually. It also gives him or her a general power of appointment over the principal, exercisable alone and in all events, at death or during life.

Power of attorney A document executed by one person, called the principal, authorizing another person, called the attorney-in-fact, to perform designated acts on behalf of the principal.

Precatory language Language in a will that does not direct or command, but merely expresses a wish, hope or desire. Precatory language is not given recognition by the courts in probate.

Present interest An immediate right to possess or enjoy property.

Pretermitted heir See omitted heir.

Principal The property in a trust. Also called corpus.

Private annuity A transfer of property under which the seller receives an unsecured promise of a life annuity.

Probate The legal process of administering the estate of a decedent. It focuses on the will and the probate estate, that is, property which will be disposed of by, and only by, either the will or by the state laws of intestate succession. More narrowly and less commonly, probate is used to mean certifying or proving the validity of the will after the death of the testator.

Probate estate All of the decedent's property passing to others by means of the probate process. This includes all property owned by the decedent except joint tenancy interests. In addition, the probate estate does not include property transferred by the decedent before death to a trustee, life insurance proceeds on the decedent's life, and the decedent's interest in pension and profit sharing plans.

QTIP election An election by the executor of the estate of the first spouse to die to treat certain property as QTIP property, thereby qualifying it for the marital deduction.

QTIP trust A marital trust for which a federal estate tax election is made. It provides that the surviving spouse is entitled to all of the income from the trust property, payable at least annually. In addition, the trust cannot give anyone a power to appoint any of the property to anyone other than the surviving spouse. Its uniqueness lies in the fact that its property need not pass to or be controlled by the surviving spouse.

Real property Fee simple or life estate interests in land and any improvements.

Recapitalization A reorganization of a closely held corporation for the purpose of freezing the value of the client's interest in the firm. Severely restricted by enactment of Revenue Reconciliation Act of 1990.

Reciprocal wills Two wills for two different people that are virtually identical; each leaves all (or substantially all) property to the other if the latter survives, otherwise to third persons. Sometimes called mirror wills. Reciprocal wills are usually simple wills; more complex wills are invariably unique in structure.

Remainder In the context of trusts, the future interest right to the remaining trust assets at the termination of all other interests. More technically, the right to use, possess and enjoy property after a prior owner's interest ends, in a situation where both interests were created at the same time and in the same document.

Remainderman The beneficiary of a trust who will receive the remainder at the termination of all other interests.

Residuary bequest A gift of that part of the testator's estate not otherwise disposed of by the will.

Reversion A future interest in property that is retained by the transferor; it will become a present interest when all other interests created at the same time have ended.

Revocable Subject to the right to rescind or amend (the terms of a transfer of one or more interests in property).

Rule against perpetuities A common law principle invalidating a dispositive clause in a will or a trust if the contingent interest transferred may vest in the transferee too long after the client's death.

S1 The author's nomenclature for the first spouse to die.

S2 The author's nomenclature for the second spouse to die.

Sale A transfer of property under which each transferor receives an amount of consideration that is regarded equivalent in value.

Self-canceling installment note (SCIN) An installment note which provides that no further payments will be made after the seller's death.

Self-proved will A will containing a formal affidavit by witnesses stating that all formalities have been complied with. It eliminates the need for the witnesses to later testify in probate.

Separate property In community property states, all property that is not community property. That is, all property acquired by a person not during marriage, and all property acquired during a marriage by gift, devise, bequest or inheritance, or, in most community property states, income earned on property so acquired.

Settlor The person who creates the trust and whose property usually winds up in it. Also called creator, grantor, or trustor.

Shifting income In estate planning, saving income tax by enabling income otherwise taxable to the client to be taxable to a family member in a lower tax bracket.

Short-term trust An irrevocable trust that reverts to the grantor sometime after 10 years. TRA 86, in subjecting this trust to the grantor trust rules, virtually eliminated its further use.

Simple will A will prepared for a family having a small estate, one for whom death tax planning is not a significant concern.

Skip person In federal generation-skipping transfer tax law, a beneficiary who is at least two generations younger than the transferor.

Soakup tax See Pickup tax.

Special use valuation A provision in federal estate tax law (Section 2032A) that permits qualifying estates to value farm or other trade or business property at its present "qualified-use value" rather than at its "highest and best use" value.

Specific bequest A gift of a particular item of property which is capable of being identified and distinguished from all other property. Contrasted with general bequest and residuary bequest.

Spendthrift clause A clause in a trust that restricts the beneficiary from transferring any of his or her future interest in the corpus or income. For example, a typical spendthrift clause would not permit the beneficiary to pledge the interest as collateral against a loan.

Splitting a gift Treating a gift of the property owned by one spouse, on the federal gift tax return, as if it were made one half by each spouse.

Sponge tax See Pickup tax.

Spousal remainder trust An irrevocable trust providing for income for a period to a lower-income tax bracket family member, then remainder to the trustor's spouse. Future use of this trust was virtually eliminated by TRA 86, which subjected it to the grantor trust rules.

Springing durable power of attorney A durable power of attorney that becomes effective at the onset of the principal's incapacity.

Standard deduction In federal income tax law, a fixed amount that may be deducted from adjusted gross income. It may be used instead of specifically subtracting actual "itemized" deductions.

Standby trust An unfunded living trust whose principal financial management and control provisions do not come into effect until the grantor is determined to be incapacitated. At that point, the trust is usually funded by the grantor's attorney-in-fact, and, if the grantor had served as a trustee, management of the trust is taken over by a successor trustee.

Step-up in basis In income tax law, the upward adjustment in basis resulting from the acquisition of property from a decedent.

Surrogate decision makers Individuals capable of making decisions regarding a client's property and family at times when the client is unable, either due to incapacity or death. Examples include attorney-in-fact, trustee, and executor.

Survival clause A disposition provision in a will or trust naming an alternate taker of certain property if the donee fails to survive the donor.

Takers in default Persons who receive property subject to a power of appointment if the holder permits the power to lapse.

Tangible personal property Personal property which has value of its own.

Taxable estate In federal estate tax law, the gross estate reduced by total deductions.

Taxable distribution In federal generation-skipping transfer tax law, any distribution of property out of a trust to a skip person (other than a taxable termination or a direct skip).

Taxable gift In federal gift tax law, for a given year, total gross gifts reduced by total deductions and exclusions.

Taxable termination In federal generation-skipping transfer tax law, a termination of a nonskip person's interest in income or principal of a trust, with the result that skip persons become the only remaining trust beneficiaries.

Tax clause A provision in a will specifying which property bears the burden of paying taxes.

Tenancy by the entirety *See* interest by the entirety.

Terminable interest An interest which will terminate or fail on the lapse of time, on the occurrence of an event or contingency, or on the failure of an event or contingency to occur. Property otherwise qualifying for the marital deduction will not qualify if the interest passing to the spouse is terminable, unless it is QTIP property, or otherwise excepted.

Terminal value Used in this text to indicate the value of a cash value life insurance policy that is currently in force. Formally called the policy's interpolated terminal reserve value, its amount is nearly equal to its cash surrender value.

Term life insurance A type of life insurance policy that has no value prior to the death of the insured because the premium charged, which increases over time with increasing risk of death. Term insurance simply buys pure protection: if the insured dies during the policy term, the company will pay the face value; otherwise, it will pay nothing.

Testamentary capacity The mental ability required of a testator to validly execute a will.

Testamentary transfer A transfer at death by will.

Testamentary trust A trust established by a trust-will into which probate property is transferred at the testator's death.

Testate Dying with a valid will.

Testator The person who executes a will.

Throwback rules In the income taxation of trusts, rules that subject income accumulated by a trust in one year and distributed to a beneficiary in another year to possible additional taxation to that beneficiary.

TRA 86 Tax Reform Act of 1986.

Transfer Any type of passing of property in which the transferor gives up some kind of interest to the transferee. Sometimes called an assignment.

Trust A legal arrangement between trustor and trustee that divides legal and beneficial interests in property among two or more people.

Trust beneficiary A person who is named to enjoy a beneficial interest in the trust.

Trust-will A will disposing of some or all of the testator's probate property to a trust, the terms of which are described in the document. The trust usually takes effect at the testator's death.

Trustor The person who creates the trust and whose property usually winds up in it. Also called creator, grantor, or settlor.

Undue influence Influence by a confidante which has the effect of impeding the testator's free will. A will can be denied probate (or at least certain clauses will be disregarded) if it can be established that the testator, at execution, was subject to undue influence.

Unification of gift and estate taxes Partially successful efforts by Congress in 1976 to tax lifetime and deathtime transfers equally, so that an individual would be indifferent, from a total transfer tax planning point of view, between making lifetime and deathtime gifts.

Unified credit Presently $192,800, a reduction in the tentative gift tax and tentative estate tax.

Uniform Gifts to Minors Act Like the Uniform Transfers to Minors Act, a statute in many states permitting custodial gifts for the benefit of a minor.

Uniform Probate Code (UPC) A complete set of probate laws originally promulgated by legal scholars and practitioners and currently adopted in whole or in part by about two fifths of the states.

Uniform Simultaneous Death Act (USDA) A statute providing that when transfer of title to property depends on the order of deaths, and that when no sufficient evidence exists that two people died other than simultaneously, the property of each is disposed of as if each had survived the other.

Uniform Transfers to Minors Act See Uniform Gifts to Minors Act.

Vested interest A nonforfeitable future interest whose possession and enjoyment are delayed only by time and not dependent on the happening of any future event.

Wait-and-see statute A provision in some state statutes that can overcome the effect of the rule against perpetuities by finding an interest void only if its turns out, in fact, not to vest within the required period.

Will A written document disposing of a person's probate property at death.

Witnessed will A written will, recognized in all states, that must be signed by two or more witnesses who acknowledge, among other things, that the testator asked them to witness the will, that they in fact did witness the testator's signing, and that the testator is mentally competent to execute a will (in accordance with state law).

Index

Note: Items in **boldface** are defined in glossary.